Leeds United

A Complete Record

Leeds United

A Complete Record

Includes Leeds City 1904-1919

Martin Jarred & Malcolm Macdonald

The Breedon Books
Publishing Company
Derby

First published in Great Britain by
The Breedon Books Publishing Company Limited
Breedon House, 44 Friar Gate, Derby, DE1 1DA.
1996

ISBN 1 85983 061 7

Printed and bound by Butler & Tanner Ltd., Selwood Printing Works, Caxton Road, Frome, Somerset.

Colour separations by Colour Services, Wigston, Leicester.

Jackets printed by Lawrence-Allen, Weston-super-Mare, Avon.

Contents

Acknowledgments

The authors wish to acknowledge the help of the following:

David Barber (Football Association), Jim Bullions, Derby Central Library staff, Football League staff, Terry Frost, Tom Hindle, Douglas Lamming, Leeds City Reference Library staff, Isobel Macdonald, Gordon M. Readyhough, Roy Shoesmith, John Short, Bert Sproston, Keith Warsop, Willis Walker, Joe Waters, Richard Wells, Alex Wilson, Colin S. Jeffrey, Jim Creasy and the relatives of Bob Kane and George Wilson.

Introduction

THIS book has been compiled over a number of years using many different sources to arrive at what the authors firmly believe to be the most comprehensive and accurate record of Leeds United Football Club ever attempted.

Many hundreds of hours have been spent studying dusty, sometimes crumbling Edwardian newspapers and delving through Football League records at Lytham St Anne's.

Inevitably, the authors have found difficulties. Before 1925, for instance, the League kept no attendance records and before then we have had to rely on those widely reported in newspapers of the time. It should be said that even different editions of the same newspaper could disagree on the number of people watching a particular game.

The same applies to teams and scorers where goals were sometimes 'rushed through in a scrimmage'. Wartime games sometimes proved difficult and for a handful of matches the authors have had to piece together United's team, although there has been no doubt over the actual 11 who turned out, simply that some educated guesswork has very occasionally been needed to identify their actual positions.

With the advent of players being allocated individual numbers, the numbering of the players has been continued in the familiar 1-11 format in order to give readers and future historians a concept of the starting 11 and substitutes, let alone positions played. The actual numbers worn from 1993-94 are bracketed beside those players making an appearance in subsequent seasons. In addition the Premier League has, for the first time, determined officially who is the scorer of each goal. As a result two goals originally credited by the club to Lee Chapman in 1992-93 were subsequently credited as own-goals by the Premier League.

Nevertheless, we are happy that what follows is as accurate as anyone is ever likely to get and the areas of doubt, both for Leeds United and Leeds City, are minute compared with the overall content of the book.

This fourth edition carries an updated biographical section which includes *every* player to have appeared in first-class competitive football for each club.

Martin Jarred
Malcolm Macdonald
July 1996

The Leeds United Story

ONLY hours after the famous Leeds City auction, more than 1,000 of the club's shocked supporters turned up at the Salem Hall to try and salvage something from a disastrous day.

Leeds solicitor Alf Masser was elected to chair the meeting and a proposal that a professional club be formed was unanimously carried and a supporters' club formed. It was agreed that a seven-man committee should run the club. It comprised Masser, Joe Henry junior (son of the Lord Mayor of Leeds who had worked so hard to save City), Mark Barker, R.E.H. Ramsden, Charles Snape and former players Dick Ray and Charles Morgan.

Things gained momentum when the new club, called Leeds United, was invited to join the Midland League where they took over the place vacated by Leeds City Reserves. Yorkshire Amateurs, who now occupied Elland Road, graciously offered to make way for the newly-formed United.

Dick Ray was appointed manager and the committee chipped in with money to help meet the club's expenses. Advertisements asking for players were placed in the *Athletic News* and local newspapers.

All this activity was watched with great interest by Huddersfield Town's wealthy chairman, Mr Hilton Crowther. Disillusioned by the lack of support in Huddersfield, where the sports-loving public preferred to watch the local rugby team at Fartown rather than the Town, Crowther offered to take this team 'lock, stock and barrel' to play at Leeds.

Crowther proposed that Second Division Huddersfield would play all their remaining fixtures that season at Elland Road. His idea won the blessing of the Huddersfield players, and talks were opened with the United committee. Part of the debate centred on whether the club should be called Leeds United or Leeds Trinity. The Football League studied the proposals and gave Town until 31 December to find £25,000 to pay-off Crowther or move its operation to Elland Road.

Faced with the prospect of losing their town's soccer team, Huddersfield supporters stirred themselves and got behind the Town whose playing fortunes began to

Leeds United in 1920-21, their first season in the Football League. Back row (left to right): J.Baker, R.Murrell (trainer), E.Hart, W.Downes, Mr Barker (director), R.Rogerson, Mr H.Crowther (president), J.Walton. Front row: G.Mason, B.Duffield, T.Howarth, M.Ellson, B.Wood, J.Frew.

Tom Jennings charges West Ham goalkeeper Ted Hufton over his own line during an FA Cup-tie at Upton Park in January 1930, but United still lost 4-1.

improve. Attendances had increased at Huddersfield's Leeds Road ground but only £8,000 had been raised to pay off Crowther. Complicated legal problems also dogged the proposals and as Town continued to improve and their support swelled, the scheme eventually fell through.

Crowther, however, decided that his future still lay at Elland Road. He loaned United £35,000, to be repaid when Leeds won promotion to Division One, and gave the new club his full backing. He wasted no time in bringing Barnsley's successful manager, Arthur Fairclough, to Leeds and on 26 February 1920, Ray stepped down to become Fairclough's assistant.

Dick Murrell was recruited as trainer and Albert Stead as assistant trainer and groundsman. Crowther, now chairman of the Leeds United board, was supported by fellow directors Alf Masser, Mark Barker, Kaye Aspinall and William Platts.

On 31 May 1920, Leeds United were elected to the Football League. They polled 31 votes and stepped into the Second Division along with Cardiff City, who won 23 votes.

There was a touch of irony when the 1920-21 fixtures were published and United found their first-ever Football League match would be at Port Vale, the club who took over Leeds City's fixtures after their expulsion. United made little impact that season, particularly in attack and their ten away goals remain the worst tally in the club's history. Luckily, they had a strong defence with skipper Jim Baker and full-back Bert Duffield outstanding; and over the next few years they were to be supplemented by Ernie Hart who was destined to play for England.

United finished 14th in their first League season. Thereafter, they consolidated their position and by 1923-24 had brought together a blend of players good enough to win the Second Division title with 54 points. In attack, United now had the formidable trio of Jack Swan, Percy Whipp and Joe Richmond with winger Joe Harris their main supplier. United made a great start to the season with only two defeats in a 17-match sequence which included seven successive wins.

Adjustment to the demands of First Division football did not come easily and United finished 18th in their first season in the top flight. Strengthened by new men Tom Jennings and Willis Edwards, only a 4-1 home win against Spurs in the final match for 1925-26 ensured Leeds' safety as they limped to 19th place.

It proved third time unlucky for United in 1926-27, although they lost out only after a quite remarkable season. Tom Jennings ran riot with 35 League goals and overall United's tally was a club best of 69 – yet they were relegated with only 30 points. It must be said, however, that goals were plentiful around this time as defences were still coming to terms with the new offside law introduced the previous season.

United returned to Division One at the first attempt. Dick Ray had taken over as manager from Arthur Fairclough and again the emphasis was on attack. Jennings and Russell Wainscoat were joined up front by young Charlie Keetley and Jock White, a Scottish international signed from Hearts for £5,000. All four hit double figures as United set yet another club record with 98 League goals. They finished runners-up behind Manchester City who compounded Leeds' atrocious FA Cup record by beating them in that season's third round.

Back in Division One, United reached respectability despite a late-season slump when they picked up only one point out of a possible 12.

In 1929-30, Ray's men finished fifth – the club's best position before the Revie days – thanks to a major improvement in defence where the experienced Edwards and Hart had been joined by full-back Jack Milburn. There was now genuine belief in the United camp that they could mount a serious title challenge, yet they inexplicably slid into Division Two.

The defence was unreliable and the attack blew hot and cold, capable of brilliance in one match and infuriating inaccuracy the next. The team went into their final match needing to beat Derby County by at least a two-goal margin – praying that Blackpool lost at Maine Road.

United obtained their immediate objective with a 3-1 victory, but Blackpool fought back from behind to snatch a late draw and win the point which sent Leeds tumbling into the Second Division. The Seasiders had escaped despite a staggering total of 125 goals against, the highest total conceded by any club that managed to stay up. To compound United's anguish they could look back to their 7-3 win at Bloomfield Road that season – the only time Leeds have ever scored seven League goals away from home.

Once more United bounced back at the first time of asking. Some of the old guard like Jennings and Wainscoat had moved on and Leeds' strength now lay in their brilliant half-back line of Edwards, Hart and Wilf Copping. United finished second, two points behind Wolves, but could have finished with the same number of points as the champions had they not lost their final game, at home to Port Vale, who had to win to avoid relegation.

A 15-match unbeaten run early in 1931-32 guaranteed a promising return to Division One, followed by 14 games without defeat in 1932-33 and a respectable mid-table showing in 1933-34.

Billy Hampson succeeded Ray as manager and immediately opted for experience with men like Albert McInroy in goal and George Brown in attack, both former England internationals. No great improvement was forthcoming, however, and in 1936-37 the drop was narrowly avoided. Pitiful away form – only three points won on opponent's grounds – put Leeds in danger and they hauled themselves to safety only after the signing of the burly South African centre-forward, Gordon Hodgson, from Aston Villa.

Hodgson, a former Liverpool and England star, scored many of the goals which put Leeds up amongst the title challengers early the following season, but a dismal run beginning in February dashed their championship dreams. United also made a good start to the last full season before World War Two. In November 1938, they held third spot. Again they ran out of steam and slipped to a mid-table position.

When the League programme resumed for 1946-47, United relied on many of the men who had served them in the late-1930s but it soon became obvious that they were well past their best. United gained only 18 points – the equal lowest First Division total until Stoke's woeful 1984-85 season – and Leeds' final 17 fixtures brought 15 defeats and two draws. Only one point was secured away from home all season.

Predictably, rock-bottom United also struggled in Division Two, despite the appointment of Willis Edwards as manager. Again, Leeds suffered from travel sickness with only one away victory as they escaped relegation to the Third Division North by only two points.

To add to United's problems they had recorded financial losses for three successive seasons. New manager Major Frank Buckley boldy predicted better things and introduced a large number of young players, including a giant Welsh teenager called John Charles. But the team hit a new low with an embarrassing 3-1 home defeat by Newport County in the FA Cup.

United's Cup record was about the worst of any side in the top two divisions and they had failed to get beyond the fifth round since the club's formation. That changed in 1949-50 as United began to show signs of improvement. A magnificent fourth-round replay win at First Division Bolton caught the mood and huge crowds poured into Elland Road to see Buckley's boys. Victory over Cardiff took them to the quarter-finals for the first time and they came desperately close to grabbing a replay at mighty Arsenal.

As the Cup run gathered momentum, so United's League form improved dramatically and the highlight of the campaign was a dazzling show at Elland Road which ended Tottenham's 22-game unbeaten run. With the brilliant Charles in commanding form, United finished fifth and were highly fancied for promotion the following season.

Yet, although Leeds had the likes of Tommy Burden, Grenville Hair, George Meek and Ray Iggleden at their disposal, they continually missed out on promotion. Even when Charles smashed the club scoring record with 42 goals in 1953-54, United flattered to deceive and finished tenth.

Major Buckley had failed in his ambition to lead United back to Division One but in 1955-56, under the stewardship of Raich Carter, Leeds United returned to the top flight – the fourth time they had won promotion in a leap year.

With Charles in magnificent form in attack, young Jack Charlton improving at centre-half, and Harold Brook and Albert Nightingale proving key inside men, United owed their success to their form at Elland Road.

Their home record was stretched to 34 games without defeat until Blackburn Rovers popped up with a surprise win in March. United then unleashed a late run of six successive victories to come up on the rails and pinch promotion behind Sheffield Wednesday.

Charles continued his brilliance in the First Division but when he moved to the Italian giants Juventus for a British record fee in April 1957, United's fortunes began to wane.

The 1958-59 season was one of great change. Carter was surprisingly sacked, chief coach Bill Lambton was appointed in his place but lasted

Leeds United, Second Division runners-up in 1956. Back row (left to right): Charlton, Gibson, Dunn, Wood, Hair, Kerfoot. Front row: Williams, Hutchison, Charles, Vickers, Overfield. Insets Nightingale and Brook.

only a matter of months, and then Jack Taylor stepped into the hot seat. All this managerial chopping and changing had a profound effect on the team and in 1960 United were relegated again.

Taylor had a big clear-out that summer but United looked a very ordinary Second Division side when the directors appointed Don Revie as player-manager in March 1961 – a move which was ultimately to change the entire course of Leeds United's history. United were £100,000 in debt and Revie, like his immediate predecessors, found that he needed all his skills to keep United on an even keel. His first full season in charge saw them flirt with relegation to Division Three and only a 3-0 win at Newcastle in the final game of 1961-62 guaranteed them safety.

Revie had decided to build a young side around the veteran Scottish international inside-forward, Bobby Collins. Rookies like Norman Hunter, Paul Reaney, Gary Sprake and the tigerish Billy Bremner all shone as United managed fifth place and got past the FA Cup third round for the first time in a decade.

United kicked-off 1963-64 later than the rest when their first match of the season, at Northampton, was postponed due to a championship cricket match being staged at the County Ground. But they wasted no time in catching up and new winger Johnny Giles, from Manchester United, proved the vital piece of Revie's promotion-winning jigsaw. They reached the New Year with a run of 13 wins in 15 matches and the arrival of centre-forward Alan Peacock helped the drive towards the title.

Promotion was assured after victory at Swansea, the championship captured with a 2-0 win at Charlton in the final game of the season. United remained unbeaten at Elland Road and had lost only three games away from home, both club records, as was their final points tally of 63.

Revie's men based their achievements on a cast-iron defence, sheer hard work and ultra-efficiency. The same formula was used to take the First Division by storm in 1964-65 when the hitherto impossible dream of a League and Cup double lingered on until the dying moments of a dramatic season.

United were a physically hard, no-nonsense team and their style of play took them to the top of Division One for the first time in the club's history when they won 2-1 at home to Sunderland. United had extended their unbeaten League and Cup run to 25 games when they were beaten at home by their nearest rivals, Manchester United, on 17 April – a defeat which eventually cost them the title.

United gained revenge by winning their FA Cup semi-final against the Reds at the second time of asking with a dramatic 88th-minute header from Bremner. The fiery little Scot was also on target at Wembley against Liverpool, but United lost 2-1 after extra-time. It had been a memorable but cruelly frustrating season for Leeds – something to which they were to grow accustomed over the next ten years.

Armed with a new seven-year contract, Revie led his men on their first European quest and they turned in some brave performances in a Fairs Cup competition marred by violence on the field. With midfield general Bobby Collins ruled out with a broken thigh sustained in Turin, in United's first-ever European match, the Peacocks were involved in a bruising battle against Valencia.

Police were called on to the pitch as fighting erupted, referee Leo Horn sent off three players – Jack Charlton and two Spaniards – and took both teams to the dressing-rooms for an 11-minute cooling-off period. Fears of a blood bath in Spain did not materialise and United turned in a magnificent display to win with a Mike O'Grady goal.

Újpesti Dózsa were swept aside in the quarter-finals but although United won the toss for choice of ground advantage in their semi-final play-off against Real Zaragoza, the Spaniards made a breathtaking start with three goals in 13 minutes to clinch a place in the Final.

In the League, United maintained the high standards they had set the previous year, finishing runners-up again, this time six points behind champions, Liverpool.

The 1966-67 season saw United faced with a crippling injury list, but

United celebrate with the Fairs Cup after the second leg of the 1968 Final in Budapest.

the emergence of players like Peter Lorimer, Eddie Gray and Paul Madeley, saw them to fourth place and another season of European competition.

In the FA Cup, United lost their Villa Park semi-final against Chelsea in controversial fashion, and there was further disappointment in the Fairs Cup. United enjoyed a slice of luck when they won their fourth-round match against Bologna on the toss of a coloured disc, and there was no questioning their right to a Final place when a Rod Belfitt hat-trick killed off Kilmarnock. Against Dinamo Zagreb, however, United lacked the guile and penetration to break the Yugoslavians' tough defence and they lost 2-0 on aggregate.

In 1967-68, United played no less than 68 competitive games and at last won some tangible reward for their labours when a series of steady performances saw them through to the Football League Cup Final against Arsenal. The only goal of a disappointing game came from United's attacking left-back, Terry Cooper, and it gave Leeds United their first major trophy. One month later, despite having £100,000 centre-forward Mick Jones in their side, United failed to puncture Everton's defence in the FA Cup semi-final and a second Wembley appearance that season disappeared when John Morrissey scored a penalty for the Blues.

United, now with several fully-fledged internationals in their ranks, were again on the fringe of the title race, finishing fourth and in Europe they powered their way to the Fairs Cup Final, beating Scottish opposition, Hibs, Rangers and Dundee *en route*. The Final, against the Hungarian outfit, Ferencváros, was held over until the following season when a magnificent defensive display in Budapest meant that Jones' goal at Elland Road had been enough to win the trophy.

After coming near to the League championship so many times, United landed the prize in 1968-69 when they stormed through their League programme. Only two games were lost – at Maine Road and Turf Moor – and their 67 points was a record, most of them, the result of a 28-match unbeaten run. A draw with closest rivals, Liverpool, at Anfield on 28 April gave them the title; two days later, a Johnny Giles goal against Nottingham Forest at Elland Road, swept them to the new points record.

Surprise defeats in the FA Cup and the League Cup, and defeat by Újpesti Dózsa in the Fairs Cup, had cleared the way for United to concentrate on the League championship.

Revie strengthened his already powerful squad by signing the clinically efficient goalscoring talents of Leicester City's Allan Clarke in summer 1969. Clarke made his mark as United set off on a season which was to see them make a serious bid for what would have been a unique treble.

In the League, Leeds stretched their unbeaten run to 34 matches, breaking Burnley's 48-year old record. United's feat was eventually surpassed by Nottingham Forest who in 1978, extended it to 42 matches without defeat.

Everton, the side which finally ended Leeds' own great run, also proved to be the team who pipped them for the championship. by Easter, the strain of a long season had finally caught up with Leeds and a surprise win by Southampton at Elland Road helped Everton to the top of the table. On Easter Monday, United practically conceded defeat by fielding an entire reserve side at Derby who won 4-1. The move cost United a £5,000 FA fine.

Revie was anxious to spare his first-teamers' energy because they were still in contention for the European Cup and FA Cup. Leeds had blazed a trial to the European Cup semi-final, including a 10-0 thrashing of Lyn Oslo, and were favourites to beat Celtic and reach the Final. The Scots however, played brilliantly in both legs to end United's challenge.

The FA Cup now remained as the Peacocks' last chance of a trophy. After three energy-sapping semi-final battles against Manchester United, Leeds outplayed Chelsea for long periods on a heavy Wembley pitch but were held to a draw. In the replay at Old Trafford, United again had much of the territorial advantage but lost in extra-time.

Further disappointments followed in 1970-71 when United were again runners-up with 64 points, the most ever accumulated by a side finishing second under the two-points-for-a-win system. Arsenal pipped them with a fabulous late run which took the Gunners to the double.

Leeds, sensationally knocked out of the FA Cup by Colchester United, led the championship- race until a controversial home defeat at the hands of relegation-haunted West Brom. Arsenal assumed the lead and even though United beat them in the penultimate match of the season, the Gunners took the title with a last-gasp goal against North London rivals Spurs.

But Leeds did not finish the season empty-handed. For the second time they won the Fairs Cup, beating Juventus on the away-goals rule.

United had battled long and hard to rid themselves of the image of a dour side and, in 1971-72, they finally achieved more widespread appreciation with a series of breath-taking home performances. Forced to play their first four home games of the season on neutral grounds because of crowd trouble, they returned to Elland Road with a vengeance, dropping only two points in their remaining 17 home matches. The chanting of 'Super Leeds' came to the fore that season. Better away form would have surely ensured them the championship.

A string of fine FA Cup displays took Leeds to Wembley and the Centenary Final against Arsenal. United broke their duck with a 1-0 win which gave them the Cup for the first time, but there was little time for celebrations as, 48 hours later, Revie took his team to Wolverhampton in search of the League and Cup double, despite protestations to the Football League for rearranging the game so close to the Final. But Leeds failed at this last hurdle and so did Liverpool who were at Highbury the same night, leaving Derby County as champions for the first time and Leeds runners-up for the fifth time in eight seasons.

Twelve months later, United were back at Wembley in a bid to retain the FA Cup. Outside Wearside there were few prepared to back against them but Second Division Sunderland and Jim Montgomery in particular, gave a great display to cause one of the biggest Cup Final upsets of all time.

Eleven days later United's disappointment doubled when a scratch Leeds side went down to AC Milan by the only goal of a controversial European Cup-winners' Cup Final. In the League, Leeds were hindered by long-term injuries to Terry Cooper and Eddie Gray, and they did well to maintain their title challenge until they lost to the ultimate champions, Liverpool, towards the end of April.

Fittingly, Revie's last season at Elland Road ended with the club recapturing the championship. United began 1973-74 in blistering style with seven consecutive wins. They were untouchable and by Boxing Day had built up a nine-point lead. A temporary slump cast doubts over what had been a relentless pursuit of the title, but they recovered and were confirmed as champions without kicking a ball when nearest rivals, Liverpool, lost a midweek game at Anfield, against Arsenal.

United went into their final game, at Queen's Park Rangers, as champions and thousands of Leeds supporters poured into the capital to see United finish in style with a 1-0 win in front of Loftus Road's biggest-ever crowd.

In the FA Cup, United inexplicably lost a fifth-round replay at Elland Road against Bristol City, and in Europe they fielded sides with a fair sprinkling of reserves, yet did enough to eliminate Scottish challengers, Hibernian, after a penalty shoot-out, before falling to Vitória Setúbal of Portugal.

With Revie installed as England's new manager, the colourful Brian Clough took over at Elland Road, only to be dismissed within weeks amid allegations of 'player-power'. It was left to the quietly-mannered Jimmy Armfield to guide Leeds to a mid-table position after a dire start to the season.

United were generally below par in the League, struggled to beat non-League Wimbledon in the FA Cup, and were sent reeling out of the League Cup by lowly Chester, yet they gave some splendid performances in the European Cup. Two classic performances against Anderlecht clinched a semi-final meeting with Spanish giants Barcelona.

Taking a 2-1 lead to the vast Nou Camp Stadium, United went further ahead on aggregate through Peter Lorimer, then defended stoutly after centre-half Gordon McQueen had been sent off. Barcelona pulled a goal back but 'keeper David Stewart played magnificently and Leeds earned a place in the European Cup Final. Everything went wrong for Leeds in Paris where Bayern Munich scored twice on the break after United had controlled most of the match. To make matters worse, a section of Leeds' so-called supporters ran riot.

Manager Armfield, now assisted by coach Don Howe, carefully rebuilt Revie's marvellous Leeds team. United finished a creditable fifth in 1975-76, although they lost to inferior opposition in both FA and Football League Cups.

The following season, Leeds played some fine football to reach the FA Cup semi-finals but were outgunned by Manchester United at Hillsborough where two early defensive lapses cost Armfield's men dearly.

In 1977-78, Leeds again had the scent of Wembley in their nostrils, this time through the League Cup, but Brian Clough extracted revenge for his dismissal three years earlier, taking his Nottingham Forest side through against Leeds in the semi-finals.

Crowd trouble in the FA Cup match against Manchester City led to a ban on ties at Elland Road.

Impatient for success, Leeds relieved Armfield of his duties and after Jock Stein's brief spell in charge, appointed Jimmy Adamson as the new manager. Adamson made a useful start, taking United back into Europe after they finished fifth in the League. There was, however, bitter disappointment when Leeds allowed Southampton to come back from 2-0 down in the first leg of the League Cup semi-final. The Saints won 1-0 at The Dell to go through on aggregate.

United's promise failed to materialise and the following season they finished mid-table, crashed out of the FA Cup in the third round,

Wayne Entwistle, an £80,000 signing from Sunderland the previous October, has a shot at goal at Highbury, in January 1980. Leeds beat Arsenal 1-0, with Connor getting the only goal.

and made little impact in Europe. Worst of all was a humiliating 7-0 League Cup defeat at Highbury. Attendances at Elland Road slumped dramatically and demonstrations were mounted for Adamson's dismissal. In September 1980, the beleaguered Leeds boss lost his job.

New manager Allan Clarke tightened the defence as Leeds climbed to middle-of-the-table respectability. He paid West Brom £930,000 for winger Peter Barnes and there was the promise of better things on the Elland Road horizon. But Barnes and other investments failed to pay off for United, who found goalscoring a continual problem.

Veteran striker Frank Worthington did almost enough to ensure safety, but even when United came from behind to beat Brighton in an emotion-charged penultimate game at Elland Road, Leeds still needed a point from their final game, at West Brom, to stay up. They lost 2-0 and, to make matters worse, serious crowd disorder led to an FA inquiry. Clarke paid the price for failure and was replaced by Eddie Gray, who became player-manager.

United began their first Division Two campaign for 19 years well enough, but a loss of form in November prompted Gray to introduce a brood of promising youngsters. Leeds were back in the pack of clubs tucked in behind the leaders, but failure to win any of their last seven matches ruined any chance of a quick return to the First Division.

Relegation inevitably affected attendances and in an effort to cut their losses, Leeds sold expensive players who earned big money, for relatively small sums. Yet during 1982-83, United lost £1.5 million and were £2 million in debt.

The season had also seen the club's image blighted by crowd trouble at Grimsby, Chelsea and Derby, and during the home game against Newcastle. Such was United's predicament that chairman Manny Cussins warned that a heavy FA fine could force the club to call in the Receiver.

Gray's youth policy stemmed the tide and a profit of £196,000 was recorded, although his young team were eliminated from the FA Cup by Allan Clarke's Third Division Scunthorpe, and put out of the Milk Cup (the now-sponsored League Cup) by the rapidly-improving Oxford United. Perhaps Leeds' lowest ebb had already been reached when Chester City, the team that had knocked them out of the League Cup in 1974-75, and who were now bottom of Division Four, won a first-leg tie at Elland Road.

In 1984-85, United showed some signs of improvement and a splendid later run gave them a flicker of hope for promotion until defeat in the final game, at Birmingham when both sets of fans ran riot, dashed their First Division dreams.

A young man died at St Andrew's during the trouble – the game was played on the same day as the Valley Parade fire disaster – and United were later fined £5,000 for their fans' part in the affair. Moreover, it was ruled that all Leeds' 1985-86 matches must be all-ticket. There had been crowd violence involving Leeds followers at Oxford, Barnsley and Huddersfield in 1984-85 and there was genuine talk of closing the club down to avoid further trouble.

After a mediocre start to 1985-86, Gray was sacked and Billy Bremner appointed in his place, but United slipped closer still to the relegation zone before a frustrating season ended in safety, although the team's defensive record gave the fans real cause for concern.

In his first full season in charge, Bremner came within minutes of steering United to a famous double – promotion to Division One and a place in the FA Cup Final. This change also brought about a surge of support that was to serve Leeds well in the seasons ahead.

The 1986-87 season saw the introduction of the end-of-season Play-offs and United finished fourth to enter the sudden-death showdown.

Skipper Ian Snodin was sold to Everton midway through the season, for a United record of £840,000, and the cash used to strengthen the Leeds side. In the opening round of the Play-offs, United squeezed past Oldham to set up a dramatic finale with Charlton Athletic, who were fighting for their First Division lives.

United lost 1-0 in London but won the return leg at Elland Road by the same score to force a final game on a neutral ground, St Andrew's, Birmingham. Leeds snatched the lead in extra-time and clung on until seven minutes from the end when two goals in quick succession preserved the Valiants' first Division status and dashed United's promotion dreams.

That bitter disappointment came nearly two months after United's brave FA Cup adventure came to an equally dramatic end.

In the third round they were paired with GM Vauxhall Conference side, Telford United, but the police ruled that Telford's Buck's Head ground could not stage the match. A section of United's 'fans' had rioted in a League game at Bradford City earlier in the season – the first game at which an existing ticket-only system had been lifted by the authorities – and the police feared that it would be virtually impossible to police a game at Telford, given United's huge following.

Although the all-ticket scheme had been restored by the FA, the Telford game was switched to The Hawthorns, home of West Bromwich Albion, and kicked-off at noon on a Sunday, on a snow-covered pitch in front of a huge police presence.

FA Cup football on Sunday was something United were to get used to in their bid to reach Wembley. After beating the Telford minnows 2-1, they put out Swindon Town, by the same score, also on a Sunday.

Saturday afternoon Cup football returned in the fifth round when a partisan Elland Road crowd saw United knock out First Division Queen's Park Rangers with an excellent performance.

In another high-noon Sunday kick-off in the sixth round, Leeds won 2-0 at Wigan to clinch a place in the semi-finals against First Division Coventry City.

Again, the tie – United's first major semi-final since 1977 – was switched to a Sunday and a thrilling see-saw encounter finally tipped Coventry's way, 3-2, in a game which was watched by millions live on television.

United's exploits meant the Peacocks were installed as hot promotion favourites for 1987-88, but they struggled to recapture the high standards they had set the previous season and were never really in the promotion hunt.

When United began the 1988-89 campaign in disappointing style, Bremner, whose contract had been extended in 1987, was sacked in October 1988 and replaced by Howard Wilkinson, manager of Yorkshire rivals Sheffield Wednesday.

Leeds were 21st in Division Two when Wilkinson took charge, but by mid-February he had lifted them to sixth position without making any major signings.

Then, having fought their way into contention for a place in the end-of-season promotion Play-offs, they fell away badly in the closing weeks of the season and hopes of First Division football were dashed for another year.

Before the transfer deadline, Wilkinson swooped to recruit two big-money signings. Scottish international midfielder Gordon Strachan came from Manchester United for £300,000 and England Under-21 defender Chris Fairclough from Spurs for £500,000.

Wilkinson continued his team-building during the summer. The biggest surprise was the £600,000 signing of 'hard man' midfielder Vinny Jones from Wimbledon. Another expensive purchase was former Bradford City striker John Hendrie, who went to Elland Road from Newcastle United for £600,000. In July, former Sheffield Wednesday full-back Mel Sterland joined Leeds from Glasgow Rangers for £650,000.

Howard Wilkinson had thus shown Leeds United supporters that he was acutely aware of the need to strengthen the playing staff in order to mount another challenge for First Division football. United's fans therefore looked forward to the new season with great expectations.

Wilkinson's gamble paid off as big-spending Leeds swept to the top of the table in December and hung on to take the title on goal-difference from Yorkshire rivals, Sheffield United, with a club record 85 points.

The championship was sealed on the final day of the season when Leeds won 1-0 at Bournemouth, thanks to a goal from Lee Chapman, the £400,000 striker, who proved to be the final piece of Wilkinson's promotion jigsaw when he signed from Nottingham Forest in January.

But United's promotion celebrations were marred when ticketless hooligans fought running battles with police after unsuccessfully trying to gain entry to Bournemouth's tiny Dean Court ground.

Dorset police bitterly criticised the Football League for failing to switch the fixture, which was held on a Bank Holiday weekend. There were calls from various quarters to strip United of the title, but it is difficult to see what more Leeds could have done to prevent trouble.

Promotion meant United were back in the First Division after eight long seasons and the fans flocked to Elland Road to cheer their heroes every step of the way. The average attendance topped 28,000 at Elland Road as the big time returned to Leeds. This, coupled with the return to the First Division, prompted a doubling of season-ticket charges for 1990-91 with a promise of even more ambitious signings. The club record signing of £1m goalkeeper John Lukic in May indicated that the promise was to be kept and there was further transfer activity with the signings of West Brom's former England Under-23 defender, Chris Whyte, for an estimated £600,000 and Leicester City's £1 million-rated star Gary McAllister, a Scottish international who was in his country's World Cup squad for Italy, although he did not play.

Summer departures included John Hendrie, who linked up with Iain Baird at Middlesbrough in a £550,000 move. But that was overshadowed by the exit of fans' favourite Vinnie Jones, just a few weeks after the start of the season. Jones, unable to gain a regular place since the arrival of McAllister, joined up with his old Wimbledon boss, Dave Bassett, at Sheffield United in a £650,000 deal.

It didn't take long for Leeds to adapt to life at the top and they were being tipped as dark horses for the title until a 3-0 defeat at Liverpool on New Year's Day. Eventually Wilkinson's men finished fourth and also launched a three-pronged attack on the Cup front.

Leeds reached the Football League Cup semi-finals before losing out to Manchester United, slugged it out in four epic FA Cup games with Arsenal in the fourth round before giving second best to the Gunners and lost the Northern Area Final of the Zenith Data Systems Cup to Everton, 6-4 on aggregate.

It had been a tremendous season with Chapman finishing with 31 goals and taking his career tally beyond the 200 mark in senior football. Leeds-born David Batty also had a campaign to remember, his sparkling midfield displays earning him full England honours.

Gary Speed also established himself on the international scene with Wales while veteran Gordon Strachan not only regained his place in Scotland's team but was appointed skipper by Andy Roxburgh and was voted Footballer of the Year, following in the footsteps of Bobby Collins, Jack Charlton and Billy Bremner.

They were individual successes, but team glory was just around the corner, thanks to a bit of fine tuning by Wilkinson.

The first season back in Division One had seen Leeds lose £2.5m to add to the £3m loss from the Division Two championship-winning campaign, but the Leeds board had anticipated the loss and handed Wilkinson more cash to push his team to the pinnacle of English football.

In came Southampton's exciting young striker Rod Wallace for £1.6m, Chelsea's England left-back Tony Dorigo for £1.3m, Steve Hodge, another England man, arrived from Nottingham Forest for £900,000 while Wilkinson raided his old club, Sheffield Wednesday, for a couple of reserves, Jon Newsome and David Wetherall for a combined fee of £275,000.

Interest reached fever pitch with the Leeds public and United raked in a staggering £3.5m in season ticket sales. The 1991-92 title soon developed into a two-horse race between the two Uniteds of Leeds and Manchester. A superb 4-1 win at Aston Villa took Leeds to the top in November and the following month soccer fans were licking their lips at the prospect of three titanic clashes between Leeds and Manchester United at Elland Road – in the League, FA Cup and Football League Cup.

League honours were shared thanks to a late Sterland penalty that gave Wilkinson's men a 1-1 draw, but Alex Ferguson's Red Devils won 3-1 in the League Cup and 1-0 in the FA Cup. These Cup setbacks may have worked in Leeds' favour as far as the title race was concerned. While their cross-Pennine rivals became embroiled in a fixture tangle, Leeds were able to focus on the championship. As the finish line grew nearer, Leeds had the points in the bag, but Manchester had matches in hand.

Wilkinson added momentum to his side's challenging by signing French star Eric Cantona from Nimes from under the noses of his old club Sheffield Wednesday. Cantona helped Leeds' drive towards the tape while surprise defeats for Manchester United meant that Leeds would take the title if they won their last two matches.

In fact, the race didn't go down to the wire. In the penultimate match of the season, Leeds won 3-2 at Sheffield United, and hours later Manchester United lost 2-0 at Liverpool – the title went to Elland Road for the first time in 18 years.

Wilkinson, named Manager of the Year, now set his sights on European Cup glory but the 1992-93 season was to go horribly wrong for his champions.

With David Rocastle signed from Arsenal for £2m and former player Scott Sellars returning from Blackburn for £800,000, United's squad, with a fully-fit Cantona available, looked stronger than ever.

Cantona's hat-trick in a 4-3 Charity Shield success at Wembley confirmed his cult status, but United spluttered badly in the League, failing to win a single away match in the new-look Premier League, and flirted dangerously with relegation before scrambling to safety.

Early exits at the hands of Watford and Arsenal soon ended any interest in the FA Cup or League Cup and the biggest prize of them all, the European Cup, also slipped from United's grasp.

An Eric Cantona hat-trick helped win the Charity Shield for Leeds as they beat Liverpool 4-3 at Wembley.

John Lukic lifts the Football League championship trophy.

Only an error by the Stuttgart management over the foreign players ruling gave United another chance to beat the Germans, which they did, gloriously, in Barcelona. That set up the 'Battle of Britain' against Rangers with the victors going through to the money-spinning Euro-Leagues. Leeds grabbed an early lead at Ibrox through Gary McAllister, but lost 2-1 and were beaten by the same scoreline at Elland Road.

Behind the scenes a rift between Cantona and Wilkinson was growing and eventually the player joined arch rivals Manchester United in a £1.2m deal. The move angered Leeds fans, who watched in disbelief as the Frenchman inspired the Red Devils to successive League titles.

Wilkinson went back to the drawing board for the start of 1993-94. Chris Whyte joined Birmingham City and Lee Chapman went to Portsmouth, the latter's place in attack going to £2.7m Brian Deane from Sheffield United. Other departures during the season included Hodge to QPR and Rocastle to Manchester City in a swap deal which saw David White move to Leeds from Maine Road.

But the biggest shock was the selling of David Batty to Blackburn Rovers for £2.7m in October 1993 – a deal for which the Leeds board came in for considerable criticism. Despite all the upheaval, Wilkinson got his team back on track and they did well to finish fifth, losing only two of their last 15 League games.

He cleverly blooded several members of the squad that had won the FA Youth Cup the previous season, but the biggest success was Gary Kelly. The 18-year-old forward was converted to right-back in pre-season games, was thrown into the deep end for the opening match at Manchester City and finished the season an ever-present and a key member of the Republic of Ireland World Cup squad.

South African pair Lucas Radebe and Philomen Masinga were added in the summer, but the big capture was former England midfielder

Gary McAllister scores the first of his two goals against Port Vale in the FA Cup fifth-round tie at Vale Park in February 1996.

Ghanaian striker Tony Yeboah couldn't stop scoring when he first joined Leeds at the end of the 1994-95 season.

Carlton Palmer from Sheffield Wednesday for £2.6m.

Midway through the season there were two important developments for Leeds. Gordon Strachan, around whom Wilkinson had built the second great era in the club's history, opted to join Coventry City as number two to Ron Atkinson, whom he was earmarked to succeed as manager. As one hero departed, another arrived in the shape of Anthony Yeboah, the Ghanaian striker from Eintracht Frankfurt, who had a tremendous scoring pedigree in German football.

He rattled in a dozen goals in only 16 Premiership starts and triggered a tremendous late sprint which saw them lose just two League matches in the New Year to finish fifth and earn a place in the UEFA Cup.

Fittingly it was Yeboah who announced United's return to Europe in spectacular fashion when he scored a stunning hat-trick as Leeds won 3-0 in Monaco.

The second leg was lost 1-0 and in the next round Dutch masters PSV Eindhoven thrashed United 8-3 over two legs. But it was in domestic Cup competitions in which United made

Leeds United in 1995-96. Back row (left to right): David White, Brian Deane, Carlton Palmer, John Lukic, David Wetherall, Mark Beeney, Phil Masinga, Lucas Radebe, Paul Beesley. Middle row: Michael Hennigan (coach), Matthew Smithard, Mark Ford, Noel Whelan, Rob Bowman, Mark Tinkler, Andy Cousens, Kevin Sharp, Tony Dorigo, Nigel Worthington, David O'Leary, David Williams (coach), Geoff Ladley (physiotherapist). Front row: Rod Wallace, Tony Yeboah, Gary McAllister, Howard Wilkinson (manager), John Pemberton, Gary Speed, Gary Kelly.

their mark as they struggled to find any consistency in the Premiership. Thanks to some spirited away performances in the Coca-Cola Cup, they reached the Final of the competition for the first time since winning it in 1967. But their return to Wembley was a sour one as they crashed 3-0 to Aston Villa – just four days after losing by the same score at Liverpool in an FA Cup sixth-round replay.

With dreams of a Cup double in tatters, United fell apart in the final months of the season, suffering a club record-equalling seven successive League defeats, a new mark being avoided with a draw at Coventry in the final game of the season.

Many fans, disillusioned at the way United had failed to capitalise on their championship triumph of 1991-92, called for Wilkinson's head. But the board, who were considering offers for the club, stood by him and after the European championship, United were sold to media group Caspian, who reportedly gave Wilkinson £12 million to spend on rebuilding the side so that it would be capable of mounting another title challenge.

Memorable Matches

29 NOVEMBER 1913

Leeds City 8 Nottingham Forest 0

OPTIMISM was the watchword among City supporters at the start of 1913-14, as England amateur international winger Ivan Sharpe and rugged Northampton centre-half John Hampson were persuaded to join the Elland Road staff. Interest in the club's progress had increased to such an extent that £2,000-worth of season tickets were sold before the season started. Ace marksman Billy McLeod began in prime goalscoring form and enhanced his reputation with a sharp-shooting display against lowly Nottingham Forest as City scored their biggest-ever win.

Inside-right Arthur Price was switched to inside-left and had a sparkling game, scoring two goals and creating another in the opening half-hour. Forest 'keeper John Hanna did well to block an early Price pile-driver, but the alert McLeod followed up the rebound to score. Price then rattled in the second and third to put City in an impregnable position by half-time.

The floodgates opened early in the second half when Hampson headed in a Sharpe corner. McLeod added the fifth and Scottish international Jimmy Speirs the sixth, before McLeod completed the rout with two more goals to leave Forest floundering.

The *Leeds Mercury* football correspondent 'JRB' enthused: 'The City forwards were a brilliant lot, who displayed fire and resolution in their attack. they were supported by a trio of halves who did their work excellently, while Copeland and Affleck were a puissant pair of backs.'

The emphatic victory, played out before 14,000 fans who paid £370 for the privilege, pushed City into third place in Division Two and left struggling Forest anchored firmly at the bottom of the table.

Leeds City: Hogg; Copeland, Affleck, Law, J.Hampson, Foley, Bainbridge, Speirs, McLeod, Price, Sharpe.
Nottingham Forest: Hanna; Dudley, Gibson, Armstrong, Mercer, Needham, Firth, Bell, Jones, Derrick, Banks.
Referee: J.Butterfield (London) *Attendance: 14,000*

4 MAY 1918

Leeds City 2 Stoke 0

AS BRITAIN clashed with the Kaiser's troops across Europe, the FA kept the sporting home fires burning by organising a League championship based on Midland and Lancashire sections, with the section leaders playing off for the right to be called League champions.

Leeds City were the Midland champions and played the Lancashire champions, Stoke, in a two-legged Final in May 1918. Leeds had assembled a strong side with Billy Hibbert, the former Newcastle winger, and ex-Rochdale man Ernie Goodwin, operating on the flanks. A good crowd at Elland Road saw Leeds make a flying start when Goodwin picked up a loose Stoke clearance and put in a perfect centre for Hibbert to head in. Stoke responded with a spell of pressure and full-back Harold Millership headed a goal-bound shot off the line to preserve City's lead. Play quickly switched to the other end and Leeds went further ahead when centre-forward Jack Peart raced past a defender and scored with a fine drive.

Play had been frantic and furious, prompting 'Old Ebor' of the *Yorkshire Evening Post* to report: 'The pace of the first half had been exceptionally fast, and the players had neither spared themselves nor each other, though the play had not been by any means rough. It was now largely a case of stamina, though the Leeds City lead was formidable to say the least.'

More pressure from Stoke after the interval forced two outstanding saves from City goalkeeper Tom Hampson to thwart the Potters' dangerman, Arthur Bridgett. Stoke grew in confidence and in the final ten minutes play was exclusively in the Leeds half, but they held on to take their two-goal advantage to Staffordshire.

Leeds City: T.Hampson; Millership, W.Hampson, Hewison, Sherwin, Lamph, Goodwin, Cawley, Peart, Price, Hibbert.
Stoke: Peers; Milne, Twemlow, Jones, Parker, Turner, Harrison, Wittingham, Howell, Herbert, Bridgett.
Referee: J.A.Palmer (Notts) *Attendance: 15,000*

11 MAY 1918

Stoke 1 Leeds City 0

UNCHANGED Leeds had to put up a tremendous rearguard action to prevent Stoke from pegging back the two-goal lead they had built up at Elland Road. The Leeds goal had several narrow escapes and only some inspired goalkeeping by Tom Hampson in the early stages kept Stoke out.

Leeds were just starting to show the Victoria Ground crowd the best of their skills when, 15 minutes from half-time, disaster struck right-half Bob Hewison. 'Old Ebor' of the *Yorkshire Evening Post* reported: 'Hewison, in trying a shot at goal came to grief, apparently in collision with an opponent. After lying on the ground he had to be carried off helpless. The injury was to his right knee. His retirement, after half an hour's play, was a serious blow to the City, who at this point had been the better side.'

Arthur Price moved to half-back in the reshuffle and City were forced to play with four forwards. With ten minutes left and Leeds desperately hanging on by their fingertips, Stoke's inside-right Bob Wittingham was brought down in the penalty area and Charlie Parker scored to set up a grandstand finish.

Stoke kept plugging away for the equaliser but ten-man City were rewarded for their fighting spirit and prevented any further score to take the championship 2-1 on aggregate.

Leeds City had won their first-ever major trophy – although many record books do not acknowledge the fact because it was a wartime competition.

Gate receipts from both matches totalled about £913 and went towards the National Footballers' War Fund.

Stoke: Peers; Maddock, Twemlow, Jones, Parker, Smith, Harrison, Wittingham, Howell, Herbert, Tempest.
Leeds City: T.Hampson; Millership, W.Hampson, Hewison, Sherwin, Lamph, Goodwin, Cawley, Peart, Price, Hibbert.
Referee: J.T.Howcroft (Bolton) *Attendance: 15,000*

26 APRIL 1924

Leeds United 1 Nelson 0

THOUSANDS of supporters poured on to the Elland Road pitch at the final whistle to celebrate the victory which brought First Division football to the city of Leeds for the first time. Working

Leeds United, Second Division champions in 1923-24. Back row (left to right, players only): Shirwin, Duffield, Down, Armand, Menzies. Front row: Coates, Whipp, Richmond, Baker, Swan, Harris, Hart.

on a shoe-string budget, the management team of Arthur Fairclough and Bill Norman had skilfully pieced together the squad which won the 1923-4 Second Division title.

With Nelson struggling near the foot of the table, United's fans expected to be swept into Division One on a tidal wave of goals, but the floodgates never opened.

For much of the first half United's defence were left chasing shadows as the lively Nelson forwards pushed the ball around with considerable poise and skill. Just before the interval United came desperately close to falling behind as dependable full-back Bert Duffield headed off the line with goalkeeper Billy Down beaten.

Fired by some choice words from Fairclough during the break, Leeds came out and gradually grew in confidence. The *Yorkshire Post* reported: 'By sweeping passes, the Nelson goal was often in jeopardy, but good approach play was missed by faulty shooting from scoreable positions.'

Time ticked away, but the vital goal continued to elude United's front men. Then, with three minutes left, Joe Harris took a corner on the left and floated it over the packed penalty area to Walter Coates, who steadied himself before firing in the goal which sent United up to the First Division.

The fans stayed on at the end to celebrate with the players, hear speeches of congratulation and appeals for financial help – even in times of glory United's cash problems were never far away.

Leeds United: Down; Duffield, Menzies, Baker, Hart, Smith, Coates, Whipp, Richmond, Swan, Harris.

Nelson: Abbot; Liley, Rigg, Newnes, Braidwood, Wilson, Hood, Wolstenholme, Edleston, McCulloch, Humphries.

Referee: A.F.Kirby (Lostock Hall) *Attendance: 20,000*

14 JANUARY 1933

Newcastle United 0 Leeds United 3

FA CUP kings Newcastle, who had swept to success against Arsenal at Wembley seven months earlier, were expected to see off Leeds with little trouble in their first defence of the Cup. The previous month had seen newly-promoted Leeds crash 3-1 at St James' Park and there had been little in their recent form to suggest they could gain any reward from their third-round tie.

Leeds were soon under the hammer as Newcastle made their traditional thundering start. But with inside-left Billy Furness setting up some clever counter-attacks, Leeds took control and made the most of their possession by stunning the Cup holders with two goals from Arthur Hydes in three minutes midway through the first half.

With a two-goal lead under their belts, Leeds, responding to the intelligent promptings of Furness, played some superbly controlled football. Wingers Tom Cochrane and Johnny Mahon beat their opponents at will while the Newcastle attacks floundered on the redoubtable half-back line of Willis Edwards, Ernie Hart and Wilf Copping.

A third goal duly arrived in the 79th minute when a brilliant feint by Furness put Cochrane down the wing and his cross was met by Hydes who completed a memorable hat-trick.

Said the *Yorkshire Post*: 'Furness, for all-round cleverness and the tremendous amount of work he did was an outstanding figure. But the whole Leeds line was in wonderful form with ball-control and combination of a high order. Only a super display by Michael Burns prevented Leeds from piling up more goals, as Furness continued his brilliant scheming and the wingers Cochrane and Mahon ran the Newcastle defence ragged.'

Newcastle United: Burns; Nelson, Fairhurst, Bell, Betton, Murray, Cape, Boyd, Allen, McMenemy, Dryden.

Leeds United: Potts; G.Milburn, J.Milburn, Edwards, Hart, Copping, Mahon, Hydes, Keetley, Furness, Cochrane.

Referee: E.Pinkston (Warrington) *Attendance: 47,554*

7 APRIL 1934

Leeds United 8 Leicester City 0

FOR much of their 1933-34 First Division campaign United had to cope without injured star, right-half Willis Edwards. An experienced England international, Edwards had been out of action for three months before returning to Elland Road for a mid-table clash with FA Cup semi-finalists Leicester City.

The presence of Edwards inspired those around him as United turned in their best performance of the season to bury luckless Leicester under a landslide of goals. Billy Furness was in top form and winger Johnny Mahon provided a string of chances as the Leeds forwards peppered Sandy McLaren in the City goal.

The *Yorkshire Post* reported: 'Taking complete command, Leeds launched almost continual offensives to expose the mediocrity of the Leicester wing-halves, and the backs' unsteadiness. McLaren had a thankless task in goal. the shrewd scheming of Furness and the dashing wing play of Mahon were features of the Leeds attack... Leicester struggled gamely and sportingly after the interval but were outplayed to an astonishing degree.'

Goals by Mahon (2), Furness and Irish international Harry Duggan gave Leeds a four-goal lead at half-time, which they doubled with further efforts by Furness, Duggan and Joe Firth (2), to complete an unusual feat of four men scoring two goals for the same side in one match. It all added up to United's biggest League win in history.

Ironically, United's leading scorer that season, Arthur Hydes, did not play and missed out on the goal feast.

Leeds United: Moore; G.Milburn, J.Milburn, Edwards, Hart, Copping, Mahon, Firth, Duggan, Furness, Cochrane.

Leicester City: McLaren; Jones, Wood, Smith, Sharman, Ritchie, Maw, Paterson, Gardner, Lochhead, Liddle.

Referee: T.J.Bootham (Walsall) *Attendance: 11,871*

1 OCTOBER 1938

Leeds United 8 Leicester City 2

IN A desperate bid to pep up United's flagging attack manager Billy Hampson dropped regular wingers Arthur Buckley and Sammy Armes and drafted in two younger players, David Cochrane and John Hargreaves. The move paid instant dividends as the newcomers scored a goal apiece and produced a string of chances for big South African centre-forward Gordon Hodgson to blast his way into the record books with five goals – the best-ever haul by a player in a United shirt.

Gordon Hodgson, United's South African star who scored five goals against poor Leicester City to set a new record for a Leeds player.

Hodgson, a prolific scorer at Liverpool, was signed by United in March 1937 from Aston Villa and maintained his goal-getting form at Elland Road, excelling in the League game with Leicester.

United were helped on their way by a freak accident to City's goalkeeper Sandy McLaren – the man who had eight goals struck past him at Elland Road four years earlier. After half an hour the luckless 'keeper turned quickly, caught his studs in the ground and tore the tendons in an instep. He was replaced by centre-half Fred Sharman who was beaten within a minute of pulling on the green jersey. Full-back William Frame took over but fared no better as the burly Hodgson set his sights on goal.

United held a 3-0 half-time lead and continued to attack relentlessly, despite an injury to half-back James Makinson who hobbled off only when the game was safely won.

Hodgson, Cochrane and Hargreaves were joined on the score-sheet by full-back Jack Milburn who scored from the penalty-spot. City's consolation goals came from Stan Baines and Jack Bowers, but they were to gain revenue for their hiding by winning 2-0 at Filbert Street the following February.

Leeds United: Twomey; Milburn, Gadsby, Makinson, Holley, Browne, Cochrane, Thomson, Hodgson, Powell, Hargreaves.
Leicester City: McLaren; Frame, Reeday, Smith, Sharman, Grosvenor, Griffiths, Coutts, Bowers, Moralee, Baines.
Referee: E.Pinkston (Warrington) *Attendance: 15,001*

4 MARCH 1950

Arsenal 1 Leeds United 0

FA CUP fever gripped Leeds as United finally made an impression in the competition after years of failure. Manager Frank Buckley changed all that, adding pride and passion to United's vocabulary and sending fans flocking to Elland Road in their thousands.

Second Division Leeds had won easily at Carlisle, dispensed with Bolton Wanderers of the First Division and beat Cardiff before they drew a plum sixth-round tie at Highbury against the mighty Arsenal. The clamour for tickets was unprecedented and an estimated 150 coaches made the trip from West Yorkshire to roar on their heroes. Staff at the Highbury underground station had to call for more ticket collectors to cope with the mass of supporters and hours before the kick-off thousands were already queuing outside the ground.

Underdogs Leeds took the Highbury stage by storm, matching Arsenal stride for stride in a pulsating tie. Young Welsh star John Charles dominated the Gunners' centre-forward, Don Roper, full-backs Jimmy Dunn and Jack Milburn subdued their wingers and half-backs Jim McCabe and Tommy Burden prompted a series of intelligent United raids.

When the decisive goal came, however, it was scored by Arsenal in the 52nd minute when Reg Lewis toe-poked in a cross after brilliant left-wing run by Alex Forbes.

Leeds fought tooth and nail for a replay as Arsenal pulled eight men back to cope with the mounting United pressure. Goalkeeper George Swindin blocked a Frank Dudley header with his knees before Ray Iggleden grazed the bar with a two-yard shot in the dying minutes.

But Arsenal held out and went on to win the Cup, defeating Liverpool 2-0 at Wembley, leaving Leeds to reflect on what might have been.

Arsenal: Swindin; Scott, Barnes, Forbes, L.Compton, Mercer, Cox, Logie, Roper, Lewis, D.Compton.
Leeds United: Searson; Dunn, Milburn, McCabe, Charles, Burden, Cochrane, Iggleden, Browning, Dudley, Williams.
Referee: W.H.E.Evans (Liverpool) *Attendance 62,573*

28 APRIL 1956

Hull City 1 Leeds United 4

ANXIOUS for First Division action, United's multi-talented John Charles once asked for a transfer, sending the Leeds directors scurrying behind locked doors to discuss his request.

Manager Raich Carter pours John Charles a cup of champagne after United's win at Hull had gained promotion to the First Division in April 1956.

They rejected Charles' plea and told him the best way to get into the top flight was by playing for United.

Equally brilliant as centre-half or centre-forward, John Charles took the advice to heart. Manager Raich Carter switched him from defence to attack during the 1955-56 season and United's fortunes immediately began to rise, taking them to the brink of promotion, needing just one point from their final match.

That game was at Hull, scene of so many triumphs for Carter, who had been idolised during his days at Boothferry Park both as player and manager.

United clinched promotion with a big win, and it was that man Charles who sent them on their way with a thunderous left-foot shot in the sixth minute. Hull, already relegated, fought hard and drew level in the 13th minute when Tommy Martin knocked in a David Fraser pass.

The tension in United's play snapped in the 62nd minute when little George Meek was brought down and Charles smashed in the penalty, his 29th goal for the season. Leeds took command with some beautiful football and Harold Brook added further goals in the 78th and 80th minutes after Meek had created the openings.

Now the awesome power of the mighty Charles could be unleashed in soccer's toughest arena – the First Division of the Football League.

Hull City: Fisher; Harrison, Jensen, Davidson, Berry, Bulless, Stephens, Martin, Bradbury, Clarke, Fraser.
Leeds United: Wood; Dunn, Hair, Ripley, Charlton, Kerfoot, Meek, Charles, Brook, Nightingale, Overfield.
Referee: T.J.Wood (Bury) *Attendance: 31,123*

28 APRIL 1962

Newcastle United 0 Leeds United 3

DURING the early part of 1961-62 United, under new manager Don Revie, looked to have booked a one-way ticket to Division Three. His side seemed unable to shake the nasty habit of giving away sloppy goals and they looked certainties for relegation until a late-season run of eight games without defeat gave them some breathing space.

On the last Saturday of the season United travelled to St James' Park, Newcastle, still needing a precious point which would keep them up and send Bristol Rovers to the Third Division along with Brighton.

Facing a stiff Tyneside wind, Leeds controlled the ball skilfully on a hard surface and made a mockery of their lowly League placing. In pint-sized Bobby Collins, a vastly experienced player who Revie recruited from Everton, Leeds had a natural leader in midfield; defender Willie Bell played his heart out in the unaccustomed role of inside-forward; and coloured winger Albert Johanneson ran the Magpies ragged with his blistering speed and delicate ball-control.

Scottish youngster Billy Bremner, whose performances attracted scouts from bigger clubs to Elland Road, came close to scoring early on, but after 37 minutes Johanneson smashed the ball in off the crossbar from Billy McAdams' cross. McAdams, a big, strong Irishman, then hit a post with a header but had better luck in the 65th minute when he rose to head in Johanneson's cross after goalkeeper Dave Hollins fumbled.

Ten minutes later Leeds' passage to safety was guaranteed when Bremner's centre was deflected into the net by Newcastle right-back Bobby Keith.

Newcastle United: Hollins; Keith, Clish, Wright, Thompson, Turner, Day, Kerray, Thomas, Allchurch, Fell.
Leeds United: Younger; Hair, Mason, Goodwin, Charlton, Smith, Bremner, Collins, McAdams, Bell, Johanneson.
Referee: J.Kelly (Chorley) *Attendance: 21,708*

11 APRIL 1964

Swansea Town 0 Leeds United 3

VICTORY at the Vetch field would be enough to recapture the First Division status United lost in 1960 – and they achieved their target with a spectacular success.

Manager Don Revie, who had welded together a strong squad, created a major surprise by giving 19-year-old Terry Cooper his League debut on the left wing in place of the injured Albert Johanneson. Cooper, destined to become an international star of the 1970s after moving to full-back, supplied the 15th-minute cross which centre-forward Alan Peacock gleefully hammered in to set United on their way to victory.

Peacock, a £53,000 signing from Middlesbrough in February, added more weight to United's end-of-season promotion push, and struck again four minutes later after Johnny Giles flicked on a Bobby Collins corner. United, oozing confidence, were in full flow and a third goal came in the 34th minute when Cooper's corner was rifled in by Republic of Ireland international Giles via defender Roy Evans.

Revie, a superstitious character, had banned the purchase of champagne before the game just in case United were beaten, so after the match Leeds players and officials scoured Swansea's pubs to hunt down bottles of bubbly for the train journey back to Yorkshire.

In their remaining games United drew with Plymouth at Elland Road, then won 2-0 at Charlton, with a couple more goals from Peacock, to wrap up the Second Division title and embark on a golden era.

Swansea Town: Dwyer; R.Evans, Hughes, Johnson Purcell, Williams, Jones, Draper, Thomas, McLaughlin, B.Evans.
Leeds United: Sprake; Reaney, Bell, Bremner, Charlton, Hunter, Giles, Weston, Peacock, Collins, Cooper.
Referee: N.A.S.Matthews (Bicester) *Attendance: 14,321*

26 APRIL 1965

Birmingham City 3 Leeds United 3

PREDICTIONS that Leeds would struggle on their return to the First Division in 1964-65 proved wide of the mark as United made an impression with the skill, spirit and professionalism which were the hallmarks of their game. Throughout the winter they continued to accrue points and went into their final match against bottom club Birmingham as League leaders.

Snapping at their heels were talented Manchester United, just one point behind with a game in hand and the advantage of a better goal average. For Don Revie's men the equation was simple – they had to win at St Andrew's and hope Manchester United would slip up in their remaining two matches, against Arsenal and Aston Villa.

Nervous Leeds fell behind after four minutes when Dennis Thwaites scored past Gary Sprake. Minutes later City winger Alex Jackson left the field with a shoulder injury and with the age of the substitute still four months away, Leeds looked certain to benefit from their numerical advantage.

Birmingham kept off-form United at bay and astonishingly built up a three-goal cushion through Malcolm Beard and Geoff Vowden ten minutes after half-time with Leeds seeming throwing away an entire season's labour in embarrassing fashion.

United came back after 65 minutes when Johnny Giles scored from the penalty-spot and 11 minutes later Paul Reaney capitalised on a goalmouth scramble to further reduce the arrears.

With four minutes left Jack Charlton grabbed an equaliser, but Leeds were unable unable to conjure the miracle they needed in the dying seconds.

At Old Trafford, Manchester United won 3-1 and only a Villa landslide stood between them and the title. Leeds' tally of 61 points would have won them the championship on all but three occasions since World War Two.

Birmingham City: Schofield; Lynn, Green, Hennessey, Foster, Page, Jackson, Martin, Vowden, Beard, Thwaites.
Leeds United: Sprake; Reaney, Cooper, Bremner, Charlton, Hunter, Giles, Weston, Peacock, Collins, Johanneson.
Referee: L.Callaghan (Merthyr Tydfil) *Attendance: 16,638*

Roger Hunt (not in picture) heads Liverpool into an early lead in the 1965 FA Cup Final as Leeds defenders look on in dismay.

1 MAY 1965

Leeds United 1 Liverpool 2

ONLY five days after the League championship was snatched from under their noses United's players strode out at Wembley for their first-ever FA Cup Final appearance.

They had booked their place with a last-gasp goal from Billy Bremner in the replayed semi-final against Manchester United and now faced the mighty Reds of Liverpool, championship winners the previous season.

Prospects of a close contest were good, but Leeds froze on the occasion, leaving the more experienced Liverpool to dominate midfield. United's 34-year old veteran, Bobby Collins, struggled on a sodden surface and was unable to bring wingmen Giles and Johanneson into the game.

United toiled under strong pressure and only a series of fine saves by Gary Sprake enabled the game to go into extra-time for the first time since 1947.

The best soccer was telescoped into the extra period. Only three minutes had gone when full-back Gerry Byrne, who played for 85 minutes of the game with a broken collarbone, crossed the ball for Roger Hunt to dive in and head Liverpool into the lead. United, however, snatched an equaliser eight minutes later when firebrand Billy Bremner unleashed a shot which ripped into the Liverpool net.

With nine minutes remaining United found themselves behind again – and this time there was no way back. Ian Callaghan's superb cross eluded the United defence and Ian St John smacked in the header which took the FA Cup to Anfield for the first time.

Having missed the League title by 0.686 of a goal and the FA Cup in extra-time it had been double heartbreak for Leeds, a situation they would learn to live with during the next decade.

Leeds United: Sprake; Reaney, Bell, Bremner, Charlton, Hunter, Giles, Storrie, Peacock, Collins, Johanneson.

Liverpool: Lawrence; Lawler, Byrne, Strong, Yeats, Stevenson, Callaghan, Hunt, St John, Smith, Thompson.

Referee: W.Clements (West Bromwich) *Attendance: 100,000*

15 MARCH 1967

Leeds United 1 Sunderland 1

THE biggest-ever crowd to squeeze into Elland Road – 57,896 – saw arch-rivals United and Sunderland slug out another draw in this FA Cup fifth-round replay.

The clubs had been promoted together in 1964 and matches between the two were not for the faint-hearted. That was certainly the case during the 1-1 draw in the first match at Roker Park, but the replay saw most of the action off the pitch.

Thousands of supporters were locked out when the turnstiles shut 23 minutes before the kick-off with some fans, desperate to see the action, scrambling on to the Scratching Shed roof.

Leeds had been unable to make the match all-ticket because of the time factor and it was only ten minutes into the game that a 10ft crush barrier at the corner of Lowfields Road and the Scratching Shed collapsed. Fans, many shocked and dazed, suffering from crush injuries, spilled beyond the perimeter track and on to the pitch for safety.

Referee Ray Tinkler halted the match and a fleet of ambulances took 18 people to Leeds General Infirmary as United chairman Harry Reynolds appealed for calm on the public address system. After 15 minutes, United officials, police and Tinkler agreed that the match could continue with hundreds of people squatting near the touch-lines.

United fell behind in the 37th minute when Scottish forward John O'Hare, later to join United during Brian Clough's brief reign, latched on to George Herd's through ball and fired in a shot which looped off Gary Sprake's outstretched foot into the net.

United were level within a minute, winning a free-kick on the edge of the Sunderland box which Billy Bremner tapped to Johnny Giles, who sent a low shot scorching past Jimmy Montgomery. After that defences remained on top and even extra-time could not determine a victor, so the tie moved on to Boothferry Park, Hull, where United won a stormy game 2-1 with a controversial late Giles penalty after which two Sunderland men, George Herd and George Mulhall, were sent off. But it was soon to be United's turn to find out that the Cup fates can deal a cruel hand.

Leeds United: Sprake; Reaney, Bell, Bremner, Charlton, Hunter, Lorimer, Belfitt, Greenhoff, Giles, Johannesson(Cooper).
Sunderland: Montgomery; Irwin, Harvey, Todd, Kinnell, Baxter, Gauden, O'Hare, Martin, Herd, Mulhall.
Referee: R. Tinkler (Boston) *Attendance: 57,896*

29 APRIL 1967

Chelsea 1 Leeds United 0

CONTROVERSY raged for weeks about referee Ken Burns' decision to disallow a last-minute Peter Lorimer effort which would have put United level in a tense, close-fought FA Cup semi-final at Villa Park.

United, a goal down, thought they had squared the tie seven minutes from time when Terry Cooper raced on to Bremner's flick and his shot flew past Peter Bonetti, only to have a marginal offside decision go against him.

If that was a biter pill to swallow, worse medicine was to come. Only seconds remained when United won a free-kick on the edge of the Chelsea penalty area and Giles rolled the ball to substitute Lorimer, whose fierce shot zipped past the defensive wall, beyond Bonetti's reach and into the net for a breathtaking 'goal'. As the young Scot turned to celebrate, referee Burns was already ruling 'no goal' and ordered that the kick be retaken because the Chelsea defenders had not been ten yards from the ball when the kick was taken. Despite protests from the United players the official stood firm, the kick was retaken, and Chelsea cleared the ball to find themselves in the Final with London rivals Tottenham Hotspur.

Chelsea, who had eliminated Leeds from the fourth round of the FA Cup the previous season, won the game with a fine goal about which there could be no argument. Tricky winger Charlie Cooke skipped past a couple of United defenders before whipping over a cross for Tony Hateley to head powerfully past Sprake with only a minute of the first half remaining.

Hateley, a big-money signing from Aston Villa, was a constant aerial threat to a United defence lacking the dominance of centre-half Jack Charlton, while the Leeds attack collectively made little impression until Lorimer replaced Rod Belfitt.

Chelsea: Bonetti; A.Harris, McCreadie, Hollins, Hinton, R.Harris, Cooke, Baldwin, Hateley, Tambling, Boyle.
Leeds United: Sprake; Reaney, Bell, Bremner, Madeley, Hunter, Giles, Belfitt(Lorimer), Greenhoff, Gray, Cooper.
Referee: K.H.Burns (Dudley) *Attendance: 62,378*

Jack Charlton lends weight to the Leeds attack during the 1967 Fairs Cup Final first leg in Zagreb.

30 AUGUST 1967

Dinamo Zagreb 2 Leeds United 0

LEEDS, now an established First Division outfit, began to make a name for themselves in European competitions after qualifying for the Inter-Cities Fairs Cup. In their opening campaign United reached the semi-final, then in 1966-67 went one better to meet Yugoslavian team Dinamo Zagreb in a two-legged Final.

Injuries to Johnny Giles, Willie Bell, Paul Madeley and Albert Johanneson wrecked manager Don Revie's preparations and it became clear that United faced an uphill battle in the humid night air of Zagreb.

Leeds defended stoutly and tried to catch Dinamo on the break until the 39th minute when 18-year-old reserve winger Cercek raced into the penalty area to crash a header past Gary Sprake – although United claimed the teenager had unfairly barged Jack Charlton out of the way.

United came out of their defensive shell and shots by Mike O'Grady and Norman Hunter raised hopes of an equaliser, but the crucial second goal came in the 55th minute when brilliant work by skipper Slaven Zambata created the opening for Rora to score.

United had chosen their first European Final to surrender two goals on foreign soil for the first time and leave themselves an extremely difficult task in the second leg at Elland Road. Yet Eric Stanger of the *Yorkshire Post* was not too pessimistic: 'Leeds, in fact, ran harder and more often than in any game so far this season, while the defence, in which Charlton and Bremner kept a tight hold on the quick-raiding Zagreb attack, was seldom in difficulty'.

Dinamo had pulled back a three-goal deficit against Eintracht Frankfurt in their semi-final, so United were still in with a chance, albeit a slim one.

Dinamo Zagreb: Skoric; Grancanin, Brnic, Belin, Ramljak, Blaskovic, Cercek, Piric, Zambata, Gurmirtl, Rora.
Leeds United: Sprake; Reaney, Cooper, Bremner, Charlton, Hunter, Bates, Lorimer, Belfitt, Gray, O'Grady.
Referee: A.Perales (Spain) *Attendance: 40,000*

6 SEPTEMBER 1967

Leeds United 0 Dinamo Zagreb 0

DESPERATE to add punch to his toothless attack, manager Don Revie toyed with the idea of recalling former England centre-forward Alan Peacock to try and break through Zagreb's defensive iron curtain in the second leg of the Inter-Cities Fairs Cup Final at Elland Road.

United were finding goals hard to come by in domestic competition and the injury-prone Peacock was considered to worry the Slavs with his aerial power. Eventually Revie opted against the move but pulled a surprise by switching right-back Paul Reaney to the wing, bringing in experienced Willie Bell at the back.

For all their possession, persistence and pressure, Leeds could not force open a defence which was snapped tightly shut. They forced a dozen corners but were suffocated by a blanket ten-man defence. Jack Charlton added his height to the attack, Jimmy Greenhoff went close with a header and both Charlton and Rod Belfitt had attempts disallowed. Charlton had another effort cleared off the goal-line, Billy Bremner saw another goal-bound shot cleared from under the crossbar and goalkeeper Skoric pulled off a string of acrobatic saves as United threw everything at Dinamo.

At the other end Gary Sprake watched helplessly as his colleagues entrenched themselves in the Zagreb half, yet he was almost beaten himself when a rare Dinamo raid ended with a fierce shot shaking the Leeds crossbar.

FIFA president Sir Stanley Rous presented the trophy to Zagreb -- the first Yugoslavian side to win the competition – leaving United with the consolation of collecting record receipts of £20,177 from the game.

Leeds United: Sprake; Bell, Cooper, Bremner, Charlton, Hunter, Reaney, Belfitt, Greenhoff, Giles, O'Grady.

Dinamo Zagreb: Skoric; Grancanin, Brnic, Belin, Ramljak, Blaskovic, Cercek, Piric, Zambata, Gurmirtl, Rora.

Referee: A.Sbardella (Italy) *Attendance: 35,604*

7 OCTOBER 1967

Leeds United 7 Chelsea 0

ON THE eve of Chelsea's Division One game at Elland Road, their manager Tommy Docherty quit for 'personal reasons' within hours of being suspended by the FA over incidents on the London club's tour of Bermuda. Now the time was ripe for Leeds to take quick revenge against a shocked Chelsea team for that controversial FA Cup semi-final defeat five months earlier. Although the wise-cracking Docherty had hit the headlines, it was another Scot under impending suspension, Billy Bremner, who overshadowed events on the pitch. The fiery Leeds skipper was making his last appearance for United before starting a 28-day ban for being sent off against Fulham in September and was at his impish best as Leeds turned on a superb attacking display.

Eric Stanger of the *Yorkshire Post* reported: 'Bremner teased and tormented them with his astonishing dexterity of foot and his remarkable sense of balance so that he could turn and twist on the proverbial sixpence'.

It was Bremner's spectacular Brazilian-style bicycle-kick eight minutes from time which crowned a five-star Leeds performance.

Speedy winger Albert Johanneson, recalled to the side, opened the scoring and the rest came, in order, from Jimmy Greenhoff, Jack Charlton, Peter Lorimer, Eddie Gray, Marvin Hinton (own-goal) and the ubiquitous Bremner. Apart from the quality of Bremner's spectacular overhead kick, the goal earned a place in the record books – it is the first match in the Football League in which seven different players have scored for one side.

One name missing from the scorers was centre-forward Mick Jones, a recent £100,000 buy from Sheffield United. He left the field injured midway through the game and was replaced by substitute Terry Hibbitt.

Leeds United: Sprake; Reaney, Madeley, Bremner, Charlton, Hunter, Greenhoff, Lorimer, Jones(Hibbitt), Gray, Johanneson.

Chelsea: Bonetti; Thompson, Hinton, Harris, Butler, Hollins, Boyle, Cooke, Osgood, Baldwin, McCreadie.

Referee: K.Dagnall (Bolton) *Attendance: 40,460*

2 MARCH 1968

Arsenal 0 Leeds United 1

AT LAST, a dream came true for Leeds United – and in the case of Terry Cooper, literally true. For three successive nights before the League Cup Final against Arsenal at Wembley, the left-back dreamed he would score the winning goal. After 17 minutes of a hard-fought game he did just that.

Eddie Gray curled in a wicked corner which Arsenal centre-forward George Graham headed away from under the crossbar to the edge of the penalty area where Cooper moved up to smash

Billy Bremner's spectacular overhead kick – just one of the seven goals which demolished Chelsea in October 1967.

Terry Cooper scores his 17th-minute winner against Liverpool in the 1968 League Cup Final – just like he dreamt he would!

a terrific knee-high volley high in the Arsenal net. Having snatched a precious lead, United concentrated on the art of defence and Arsenal simply did not have the know-how to find a way past the likes of Paul Reaney, Norman Hunter and Jack Charlton.

Gary Sprake's only serious save of the match came when he turned a John Radford shot around the post late in the game. United, who had 'play-anywhere' star Paul Madeley at centre-forward in place of Cup-tied attacker Mick Jones, found goal chances scarce and were content to play a game of containment.

Although the match was disappointing as a spectacle, United had conquered a psychological barrier to win the first major trophy in the club's history.

Thousands of United supporters welcomed home their heroes as the League Cup was displayed on the steps of the Town Hall. So often United had failed at the final hurdle because their play had been riddled with anxiety, but now they had cast off the mantle of also-rans and were ready to make more room available for trophies in the Elland Road boardroom.

Arsenal: Furnell; Storey, McNab, McLintock, Simpson, Ure, Radford, Jenkins(Neill), Graham, Sammels, Armstrong.
Leeds United: Sprake; Reaney, Cooper, Bremner, Charlton, Hunter, Greenhoff, Lorimer, Madeley, Giles, Gray(Belfitt).
Referee: L.J.Hamer (Horwich) *Attendance: 97,887*

7 AUGUST 1968

Leeds United 1 Ferencváros 0

AFTER battling through to their second successive Inter-Cities Fairs Cup Final, this time United were intent on getting their name inscribed on the trophy.

Ferencváros coach, Dr Karoly Lahat, sent his powerful team out at Elland Road with the classic European battle orders to defend in depth and counter attack quickly. His men obeyed his instructions to the full stop, breaking United's rhythm with their hard tackling in a disjointed game of 45 free-kicks, and hitting back with swift breaks.

The Hungarians had the first chance to score when an error by Jack Charlton, who was not under pressure, let in Istvan Szoke, but the midfielder squandered the chance. United let an even easier chance go begging minutes later when goalkeeper Istvan Geczi mishit a free-kick straight to Mick Jones near the edge of the penalty area. Jones quickly fed the ball inside to Peter Lorimer but the Scots' shot was well saved by the grateful Geczi.

Lorimer made amends in the 40th minute by swinging in a corner for Charlton, standing virtually under the bar, to nod down for Jones to bundle the ball over the line, leaving the Hungarians complaining that Charlton had impeded the goalkeeper.

Ferencváros responded with some controlled football and their quick breaks almost brought success. First Florian Albert opened United's rearguard with Stoke putting the chance wide, then Gary Sprake pulled off the save of the match, with a twisting leap, to prevent Gyula Rakosi equalising.

Club officials hoped to have banked more money from the match. Televised live in the middle of the annual Leeds holidays, it attracted a mere 25,268 spectators.

Leeds United: Sprake; Reaney, Cooper, Bremner, Charlton, Hunter, Lorimer, Madeley, Jones(Belfitt), Giles(Greenhoff), Gray.
Ferencváros: Geczi; Novak, Pancsics, Havasi, Juhasz, Szucs, Stoke, Varga, Albert, Rakosi, Fenyvesi(Balint).
Referee: R.Scheuber (Switzerland) *Attendance: 25,268*

Mick Jones (dark shirt) forces the ball over the line for a priceless goal against Ferencváros in the first leg of the 1967-68 Fairs Cup Final.

11 SEPTEMBER 1968

Ferencváros 0 Leeds United 0

ON A NIGHT of immense tension, United were subjected to their most rigorous European examination in the white-hot atmosphere of the Nep Stadium, before emerging heroically to become the first British winners of the Inter-Cities Fairs Cup.

A human barrier of white shirts was strung around the penalty area to keep the Magyars at bay for virtually the entire 90 minutes. Ferencváros hopes of quickly wiping out United's slender advantage soon evaporated as the Leeds defence gave one of its greatest displays by throttling every promising attack the Hungarians could mount.

After 20 minutes it looked as though Gyula Rakosi must score, but Cooper produced an acrobatic overhead clearance on the line to keep United's advantage. When the Hungarians did find a way through United's ten-man defence, Sprake stood up extremely well to a barrage of testing shots and centres, pulling off one world-class save from Istvan Szoke which helped sap the home team's spirit.

United attacks were rare, but they almost snatched a goal in the 33rd minute when winger Mike O'Grady chipped in a free-kick which Mick Jones headed powerfully against the crossbar.

Leeds did not need that extra goal, but it would have gone a long way to soothing manager Don Revie's nerves, as he disclosed at the end of the game: "When we got into those final few minutes my heart nearly stopped beating. As the final whistle drew nearer every minute seemed like an hour."

Just as Dinamo Zagreb had frustrated Leeds the previous season, so United, learning quickly, had suffocated Ferencváros into submission to earn their first tangible reward in Europe.

Ferencváros: Geczi; Pancsics, Havasi, Juhasz, Szucs, Szoke (Kraba), Varga, Albert, Rakosi, Katona, Novak.
Leeds United: Sprake; Reaney, Cooper, Bremner, Charlton, Hunter, O'Grady, Lorimer, Jones, Madeley, Hibbitt(Bates).
Referee: G.Schulenberg (West Germany) *Attendance: 76,000*

28 APRIL 1969

Liverpool 0 Leeds United 0

UNITED strode into the Anfield arena on the threshold of their greatest achievement – the 1968-69 League championship. Only the power of nearest challenges Liverpool could deprive United of the vital point which would land the coveted crown.

The atmosphere appeared to crackle with anticipation as two soccer giants clashed on a Monday evening in April. The game quickly fell into the expected pattern with Liverpool throwing men forward frantically as Leeds relied upon the superb defence which had served them so valiantly throughout the season.

In a game of blurring speed, United, with Jack Charlton and Norman Hunter magnificent in the heart of the defence, denied Liverpool time and space. Such was United's efficiency that Gary Sprake had only one shot to deal with in the first half – an ambitious 35-yard drive by Ian Callaghan, to which United responded with a deflected Billy Bremner shot which almost beat the scrambling Tommy Lawrence.

One goal looked as though it might settle the game and the Merseysiders should have snatched it in the 35th minute when young striker Alun Evans wasted a good chance, but United closed ranks again. Callaghan forced Sprake into action in the 62nd minute with a curling shot and United had one more scare when Evans hooked a shot wide late in the game. Leeds fans howled for referee Dimond to blow the final whistle, yet with the last moments melting away seemingly in slow motion United's players remained clam amid the cauldron of noise.

Two nights later at Elland Road the new champions beat Nottingham Forest with a Johnny Giles goal to finish the season having beaten or equalled nine club records – most points (67), most home points (39), most wins (27), most home wins (18), fewest defeats (two, both away, another record), unbeaten at home, 26 goals conceded with only nine at home.

Liverpool: Lawrence; Lawler, Strong, Smith, Yeats, Hughes, Callaghan, Graham, Evans, St John, Thompson.
Leeds United: Sprake; Reaney, Cooper, Bremner, Charlton, Hunter, O'Grady, Madeley, Jones, Giles, Gray.
Referee: A.Dimond (Harlow) *Attendance: 53,750*

17 SEPTEMBER 1969

Leeds United 10 SK Lyn Oslo 0

NO CLUB made a more dramatic entry into the European Cup than United, who turned in a blockbusting performance to demolish the Norwegian champions and set up a new club record score.

With four seasons of Fairs Cup experience behind them, Leeds were rated one of the best prepared and equipped teams to carry the English flag in Europe's premier club competition, but no one was ready for the landslide which was to bury Lyn's team of students, teachers and clerks.

Lyn, who reached the quarter-finals of the European Cup-winners' Cup the previous season, were on the rack from the start. Just 35 seconds after the kick-off United swept into attack and the transfer-listed Mike O'Grady drove in a left-foot shot for what was believed to be the quickest goal in European Cup history.

Three minutes later Mick Jones powered in a header, then hooked a shot in for the third after nine minutes. Goals continued to fly past goalkeeper Sven Olsen, who had only arrived at the ground 35 minutes before kick-off.

The rout continued with goals from Allan Clarke after 19 minutes; Johnny Giles, 34th minute; Clarke, 47th minute; Giles, 51st minute; Jones (hat-trick), 61st minute, Billy Bremner completed the annihilation with goals in the 65th and 88th minutes, to equal the best-ever score by a British club in Europe.

United scored a further six goals without reply in Oslo to sink the Norwegians. For the poor amateurs of Lyn the misery dragged on and at the end of their season they were relegated.

Leeds United: Sprake; Reaney, Cooper, Bremner, Charlton, Hunter, Madeley, Clarke, Jones, Giles(Bates), O'Grady.
SK Lyn Oslo: S.Olsen; Rodvang, Ostvold, Morisbak, Kolle, Gulden, Boerrehaug, Christopherson, Berg, O.Olsen(Hovden), Austnes.
Referee: E.Smejkal (Czechoslovakia) *Attendance: 25,979*

24 JANUARY 1970

Sutton United 0 Leeds United 6

THE draw for the fourth round of the FA Cup handed United a trip to Gander Green Lane, home of Isthmian League side Sutton United. United were overwhelming favourites to swamp the minnows, but the ever-cautious Don Revie was taking nothing for granted and organised a practice match on East End Park WMC's Skelton Road ground as part of the build up to the tie. There was talk of switching the game to Leeds, but Sutton pressed ahead with their plans to stage the game and managed to squeeze 14,000 fans into the tiny arena. Those who expected to see one of the greatest giant-killing acts in the history of the competition were disappointed as Leeds turned on the style with Allan Clarke leading the way with four of the goals.

Leeds in action against Celtic under the Elland Road floodlights in April 1970, in one of two epic European Cup semi-finals against the Parkhead club.

He netted United's opener after 14 minutes by turning in a Norman Hunter cross, and tapped in the third from Peter Lorimer's pass just four minutes after Lorimer's 25-yard power shot slipped through the hands of goalkeeper Dave Roffey.

The match won, the game was a stroll for United in the second half with Clarke showing razor-sharp reactions to complete his hat-trick, knocking the ball home after his initial header came back off a post.

Clarke and Mick Jones let a Hunter cross runs through their legs for Lorimer to bundle in the fifth, and Clarke completed his great day when Lorimer's pass released him on a run from the halfway line to slot the ball coolly past Roffey.

Leeds were in total control and had four other efforts disallowed, but the way young centre-half John Faulkner kept Mick Jones off the scoresheet impressed Revie, who soon returned to Sutton to sign the tall defender. Sutton's Dario Gradi, an England amateur international, later became manager at Crewe, where he developed the likes of David Platt and Rob Jones into England internationals.

Sutton United: Roffey; Brookes, Clarke, Powell, Faulkner, Gradi, Mellows, Bladon, Drabwell, Pritchard, Howard.

Leeds United: Harvey; Reaney, Cooper, Bremner, Charlton, Hunter, Lorimer, Clarke, Jones, Giles, Madeley.

Referee: J. Finney (Hereford) *Attendance: 14,000*

1 APRIL 1970

Leeds United 0 Glasgow Celtic 1

BILLED as 'The Battle of Britain', United clashed with Scottish champions Celtic in two epic semi-finals in the 1970 European Cup. United had been locked in a titanic struggle all season with Everton in a desperate effort to cling on to their League championship crown and went into the first leg against Celtic with 52 games played in an already arduous season.

Manager Don Revie knew his men were mentally and physically fatigued in their hunt for a unique League championship, European Cup and FA Cup treble. The Division One title was moving towards Merseyside, but United had battled through to the FA Cup Final against Chelsea after three nerve-racking semi-final games with Manchester United, and now faced the pride of Scotland to go for the biggest prize of all – the European Cup.

It was Celtic, European Cup winners in 1967, who took a massive stride towards another Final by scoring after only 85 seconds when a high bouncing ball was cracked through the indecisive Leeds defence by inside-forward George Connelly, clipping Terry Cooper's leg on its way past a flat-footed Gary Sprake.

United visibly wilted. The strain of the season leadened their limbs and slowed their thinking, while confident Celtic were quicker and more imaginative, with the diminutive Jimmy Johnstone taking complete control of the match with a magical display of wing wizardry which had Cooper in knots.

United's only clear-cut chance came fairly late in the game when Eddie Gray danced through the Celtic defence and thumped in a shot which rattled the crossbar.

To add to the gloom, Everton beat West Bromwich Albion 2-0 on the same night to clinch the League title.

Leeds United: Sprake; Reaney, Cooper, Bremner(Bates), Charlton, Madeley, Lorimer, Clarke, Jones, Giles, Gray.

Glasgow Celtic: Williams; Hay, Gemmell, Murdoch, McNeill, Brogan, Johnstone, Connelly(Hughes), Wallace, Auld, Lennox.

Referee: M.Kitabdjian (France) *Attendance: 45,505*

4 APRIL 1970

Leeds United 2 Burnley I

WITH the League title gone, weary United were dealt another blow 24 hours after their European Cup semi-final home failure against Celtic – a fractured leg for right-back Paul Reaney in a meaningless 2-2 draw at West Ham. The injury cost him a place in United's FA Cup Final line-up against Chelsea and a trip to Mexico as part of England's World Cup squad.

Manager Don Revie sent out a patched-up side to face

Wembley, April 1970: Allan Clarke watches his header hit the Chelsea post but it rebounded out for Mick Jones to come running in to score. Leeds lost the Cup Final replay though.

Burnley on the Saturday before the FA Cup Final, lacking Reaney, Gary Sprake (bruised shoulder), Mick Jones (leg strain), Terry Cooper and Jack Charlton (shin injuries), Billy Bremner (concussion) and Norman Hunter (knee injury).

The game against the Clarets was United's ninth in 18 days, so with the Cup Final coming up, a shadow side on view, the extra cost of watching a game with nothing at stake and the Grand National on television, only 24,691 fans turned up at Elland Road - about 12,000 less than the average.

The stay-away fans not only missed a chance to see some of the blossoming young reserve talent, but two of the finest goals ever seen at Elland Road.

Both were scored by young Scottish international Eddie Gray, but both were entirely different in their execution.

After only ten minutes, Gray, wearing the unfamiliar number-six shirt, moved through the centre-circle towards the Kop and spotted Burnley goalkeeper Peter Mellor off his line and produced a stunning chip from 40 yards that floated over Mellor's head into the net.

Burnley drew level after 25 minutes when John Faulkner, the former Sutton United centre-half, making his debut, deflected a shot past David Harvey.

But the Leeds youngsters were not fazed and Gray produced a truly stunning winner on 71 minutes. He was hemmed in on the by-line to the left of the Burnley goal, but twisted and turned into the box where a posse of defenders were left trailing in his wake by his mesmerising ball skills before he thundered an angled shot past Mellor. It was an amazing solo effort and was the main topic of conversation the following day as fans queued for FA Cup Final tickets at Elland Road alongside touts from London who were offering £25 for £4 tickets - but they were worth just a fraction of the quality of Gray's magnificent goals against Burnley.

Leeds United: Harvey; Yorath, Peterson, Madeley, Faulkner, Gray, Lorimer, Bates, Johannesson, Galvin, Hibbitt.

Burnley: Mellor; Angus, Docherty, Waldron, Dobson, Todd, Casper, Bellamy(O'Neill), Probert, Thomas, Kindon.

Referee: J. Taylor (Wolverhampton) *Attendance: 24,691*

11 APRIL 1970

Chelsea 2 Leeds United 2

AGAINST Celtic in the European Cup semi-final, Leeds looked lethargic, but against Chelsea at Wembley, the spring was back in their stride and they produced football of the highest quality - yet still failed to return to Yorkshire with the FA Cup.

Wembley looked more like Blackpool beach, with masses of sand spread over the pitch in an effort to patch up the damage caused during the recent Horse of the Year Show at the stadium.

United, sensing the game was their last real chance of ending the season with a trophy, outplayed Chelsea for most of the match, yet could never convert their superiority into the goals that would put the game beyond the resilient Londoners' each.

Leeds scored first in the 21st minute with a curious goal. Gray took an inswinging corner on the right, Jack Charlton headed goalwards with little power, but the ball eluded two defenders and trickled gently over the line. Another freak goal 20 minutes later brought Chelsea level. Houseman cut in from the left, put in a rather weak, if hopeful, long-range shot, and Gary Sprake, mistiming his dive, allowed the ball to slither under his body.

Determined Leeds pushed forward and Gray rattled the crossbar with a tremendous shot near the end before United scored the goal they thought would lift the Cup. An Allan Clarke header hit the post in the 83rd minute and Mick Jones was there to smack in the rebound with a left-foot shot.

The trophy looked destined for Elland Road but, four minutes later, the usually solid Leeds defence was caught napping following a free-kick, when Ian Hutchinson headed in the second equaliser from Hollins' accurate centre.

With the game going into extra-time, and producing no further score, the draw – the first ever in a Wembley Final – had extended United's marathon season still further.

Chelsea: Bonetti; Webb, McCreadie, Hollins, Dempsey, Harris (Hinton), Baldwin, Houseman, Osgood, Hutchinson, Cooke.

Leeds United: Sprake; Madeley, Cooper, Bremner, Charlton, Hunter, Lorimer, Clarke, Jones, Giles, Gray.

Referee: E.Jennings (Stourbridge) *Attendance: 100,000*

15 APRIL 1970

Glasgow Celtic 2 Leeds United 1

IT SEEMED that all of Scotland wanted to see Celtic sweep aside the English champions in the European Cup semi-final return in Glasgow. To cater for the tremendous demand for tickets the tie was switched from Celtic Park to Hampden, with around 136,000 fans crammed in to make it the biggest attendance of any European Cup-tie.

After withstanding an early barrage of Celtic attacks, United hit back to silence the massive crowd. With 14 minutes gone, Norman Hunter received a throw-in from the right and rolled the ball forward to Billy Bremner who unleashed a fierce right-foot shot which flew past Evan Williams.

The goal clearly angered the Scots and they stormed frantically back into the attack, Paul Madeley and Terry Cooper making desperate clearances to keep rampant Celtic at bay. The inevitable goal came two minutes after half-time when John Hughes flung himself at Bertie Auld's corner and flicked the ball beyond Gary Sprake's reach.

United's hopes evaporated in the white-hot atmosphere when the heroic Sprake was carried off after a collision with Hughes. The first time replacement David Harvey touched the ball was to pick it out of the net.

Jimmy Johnstone, turning on his breathtaking skills, fed Bobby Murdoch whose 15-yard shot flashed past Harvey to seal Celtic's victory and wrap up a 3-1 aggregate score.

Celtic went on to lose 2-1 to Dutch masters Feyenoord in the Final, while Leeds had a little unresolved business with Chelsea before they could finally pull off their boots and put their feet up.

Glasgow Celtic: Williams; Hay, Gemmell, Murdoch, McNeill, Brogan, Johnstone, Connelly, Hughes, Auld, Lennox.

Leeds United: Sprake(Harvey); Madeley, Cooper, Bremner, Charlton, Hunter, Lorimer(Bates), Clarke, Jones, Giles, Gray.

Referee: G.Schulenberg (West Germany) *Attendance: 136,505 (some reports state 135,826)*

29 APRIL 1970

Chelsea 2 Leeds United 1

UNITED'S rematch with Chelsea at Old Trafford was the last throw of the dice for Don Revie's men to finish with something to show for their season's Herculean efforts. The replay was a more physical match than the Wembley encounter and although Chelsea were able to curb United's attacking flair, Leeds still looked the classier side.

United pushed forward and a desperate Eddie McCreadie cleared from Peter Lorimer before Leeds nosed in front with a superb 35th-minute goal. Allan Clarke beat three men in a mazy midfield run before sending Jones past McCreadie and Dempsey for the centre-forward to shoot a brilliant goal.

Some of the tackling became fierce, but United maintained their shape and rhythm and seemed to be moving relentlessly towards victory, when Chelsea illustrated their capacity for survival. Twelve minutes from time, Charlie Cooke clipped a perfect ball into the penalty area for Peter Osgood to torpedo a fine header past David Harvey and force extra-time.

The thunderous action continued with United still looking the better side, but, for the first time in 224 minutes of a sizzling Final, Chelsea moved in front.

Ian Hutchinson wound up one of his famous long throw-ins from the left, Dempsey flicked the ball on, and David Webb climbed to nod home from close-range at the far post.

United hammered away at the Blues in the final minutes, but Chelsea, with substitute Marvin Hinton on to reinforce their defence, clung on frantically to wrest the Cup from United's grasp.

Chelsea: Bonetti; Harris, McCreadie, Hollins, Dempsey, Webb, Baldwin, Cooke, Osgood(Hinton), Hutchinson, Houseman.

Leeds United: Harvey; Madeley, Cooper, Bremner, Charlton, Hunter, Lorimer, Clarke, Jones, Giles, Gray.

Referee: E.Jennings (Stourbridge) *Attendance: 62,078*

13 FEBRUARY 1971

Colchester United 3 Leeds United 2

THIS date will go down as one of the blackest days in Leeds' history as Fourth Division minnows Colchester United pulled off one of the greatest FA Cup shocks by knocking out star-studded United in the fourth round.

Leeds, without Billy Bremner and Eddie Gray, never looked comfortable on the tight compact Layer Road ground against opponents who fought for every ball. Quicker and more decisive, Colchester made life hard for the Leeds defence to the point of embarrassment.

Leading the U's attack was 34-year-old Ray Crawford, an England international during his days at Ipswich Town. He rolled back the years to give the Leeds back line an awful roasting and took just 18 minutes to set lowly Colchester on the way to a place in the record books. Gary Sprake came out to pick off a free-kick from the left, missed, and Crawford, with plenty of time and space, headed in easily.

Ten minutes later Crawford rose above Paul Reaney to win aerial possession and, as Sprake raced out to smother the danger, Crawford recovered to prod the ball over the line via an upright.

Colchester went even further ahead after half-time when Dave Simmons scored the third after another mix-up between Reaney and Sprake. United's fearsome defence was falling apart at the seams.

An hour had gone before Hunter threw Leeds a lifeline by heading in a corner and with Colchester tiring, United's confidence drifted back when Giles pulled another goal back.

With 17 minutes left for United to salvage a replay, a brilliant save by Graham Smith saw Colchester through for the shock of the round. Leeds had produced too little, too late.

Colchester United: Smith; Cram, Hall, Gilchrist, Garvey, Kurila, Lewis, Simmons, Mahon, Crawford, Gibbs.

Leeds United: Sprake; Reaney, Cooper, Bates, Charlton, Hunter, Lorimer, Clarke, Jones, Giles, Madeley.

Referee: D.Lyden (Birmingham) *Attendance: 16,000*

29 MAY 1971

Juventus 2 Leeds United 2

TORRENTIAL rain washed out the first attempt to play the first leg of the 1971 Inter-Cities Fairs Cup Final in Turin. Referee Lauren van Ravens had little option but to abandon the game after 53 minutes as huge pools of water made play impossible.

Three days later battle commenced in the Stadio Comunale with Juventus, the club which had once lured John Charles away from Leeds, the favourites with the bookmakers. The Italians looked a good bet early on when their multi-million lire forward line swept into action with a swift breakaway move form their own half. West German international Helmut Haller won possession and the ball was moved on by Anastasi and Causio for Roberto Bettega to finish clinically.

United responded with a lengthy spell of pressure in which both Jack Charlton and Johnny Giles went close before the equaliser came three minutes before the break. Peter Lorimer found Paul Madeley who cracked in a 35-yard shot which brushed defender Sandro Salvadore before entering the net. It was United's first goal in Italy, but within 12 minutes they were behind again to a superb 20-yard goal by Fabio Capello.

An unlikely hero emerged from United's ranks to snatch a second equaliser - substitute Mick Bates. Bates, one for the talented reserves on the fringe of a first-team place, was thrown into the action after an injury to Mick Jones. Terry Cooper overlapped on the left and his cross was mispunched by Piloni to the feet of Bates, who calmly beat defender Marchetti and drove the ball in from close-range for a priceless goal.

Juventus: Piloni; Spinosi, Marchetti, Furino, Morini, Salvadore, Haller, Causio, Anastasi (Novellini), Capello, Bettega.
Leeds United: Sprake; Reaney, Cooper, Bremner, Charlton, Hunter, Lorimer, Clarke, Jones(Bates), Giles, Madeley.
Referee: L.van Ravens (Holland) *Attendance: 45,000*

2 JUNE 1971

Leeds United 1 Juventus 1

WITH both sides playing out an action-packed 90 minutes, the outcome of the second leg of the 1971 Inter-Cities Fiars Cup Final was in doubt right up to the final whistle.

Elland Road fans believed their side could end their luckless run and clinch the trophy for the second time - optimism which seemed justified after only 12 minutes when the razor-sharp Allan Clarke whipped around like a spinning-top to crack a loose ball past Tancredi for a brilliant goal.

The celebrations lasted only seven minutes. A loose ball from Paul Madeley was picked up in midfield and fed to the quicksilver Pietro Anastasi, who justified his £440,000 price-tag by drawing Gary Sprake off his line and calmly slipping the ball past him for the equaliser.

The match finely balanced, Leeds carried the extra threats of Johnny Giles and overlapping full-back Terry Cooper.

Said Barry Foster of the *Yorkshire Post*: 'Giles gave the Italians plenty of problems from midfield and it was from his prompting that most of Leeds' attacking play developed. Juventus never really mastered the adventurous left-wing play of Cooper... one lost count of the number of times the Leeds full-back was brought down in full flight.'

The action continued to bubble and boil. Salvadore was booked for yet another foul on Cooper, Madeley left the field with a cut above an eye and Tancredi, recalled in place of Piloni, made an athletic stop to keep out a Mick Jones header.

With away goals now counting double, United were content to play out time as Juventus failed to make any impression in attack as the game wore on. Juventus coach Cestimir Vycpalek was naturally disappointed. His side had not lost a game, yet still failed to lift the trophy. On the other hand, United, who had lost in the second round but squeezed through on the away-goals rule, had finally enjoyed some luck.

United find themselves waterlogged in Turin in the 1970-71 Fairs Cup Final.

Leeds United: Sprake; Reaney, Cooper, Bremner, Charlton, Hunter, Lorimer, Clarke, Jones, Giles, Madeley(Bates).
Juventus: Tancredi; Spinosi, Marchetti, Furino, Morini, Salvadore, Haller, Causio, Anastasi, Capello, Bettega.
Referee: R.Glockner (East Germany) *Attendance: 42,483*

19 FEBRUARY 1972

Leeds United 5 Manchester United I

SINCE gaining promotion in 1964, Don Revie had always regarded Manchester United as the yardstick by which to measure his own team's progress.

In the mid-1960s, the men from Old Trafford held the upper hand, but the balance of power tilted east of the Pennines after the three block-busting FA Cup semi-final matches in 1970 and this match confirmed that Leeds had overhauled their arch rivals as a soccer super-power.

With Mick Jones back after a bout of 'flu to renew his lethal striking partnership with Allan Clarke, Leeds tore the visiting defence to shreds with some stunning attacking play.

Amazingly there was no score at half-time despite Jones (twice) and Jack Charlton going close, but it took only two minutes after the break for Revie's boys to unlock the Manchester defence.

Eddie Gray, tantalising and tormenting on the wing, saw his shot pushed on to a post but Jones was on hand to nudge the ball over the line.

Seven minutes later, Leeds produced another sweeping attack which saw Peter Lorimer's cross find Jones, whose shot was deftly flicked in by Clarke.

Leeds were pouring forward at every opportunity and even when Francis Burns pulled a goal back in the 57th minute, Leeds hit back instantly when Jones got on the end of Billy Bremner's cross to head into the ground and over Alex Stepney.

Jones completed his hat-trick six minutes later when he prodded the ball over the line after more excellent approach work by Gray and Lorimer.

Man-of-the-match Jones then turned provider, whipping in a

cross which Lorimer thrashed into the roof of the net to complete a five-goal storm in 27 minutes.

The victory had taken United's points tally to 450 since returning to the First Division seven and a half years earlier and must rank as one of the sweetest in the club's history, particularly as the opposition had been sitting on top of the table only a few weeks earlier.

Leeds United: Sprake; Madeley, Cooper, Bremner, Charlton, Hunter, Lorimer, Clarke, Jones, Giles, Gray.

Manchester United: Stepney; O'Neil, Dunne, Burns, James, Sadler, Morgan, Kidd(McIlroy), Charlton, Gowling, Best.

Referee: N.C. Burtenshaw (Gt Yarmouth) *Attendance: 45,394*

4 MARCH 1972

Leeds United 7 Southampton 0

UNITED'S critics had often branded them dour, defensive and downright dull in their quest for success, but in 1971-72 Leeds set the First Division alight with dazzling, fluent football that won thousands of new friends.

Emphasis was placed on attack and Leeds produced the sort of soccer that had the back pages of national newspapers dubbing them 'Super Leeds' and drawing comparisons with the legendary Real Madrid. Such acclaim gained credence in the eyes of millions of television viewers who turned in to see BBC's *Match of the Day* cameras capture the action at Elland Road. One of the televised games was against Southampton in the midst of United's purple patch when they delighted the viewing public with a scintillating performance.

None of the goals were particularly spectacular, but each one followed great sweeping movements around the pitch, which had the crowd roaring 'Ole' each time the ball was passed from one Leeds player to another.

United's magnificent seven came like this: 37th minute, brilliant inter-play between Mick Jones and Eddie Gray opened up the defence for Allan Clarke to crack in an angled drive; 42nd minute, Peter Lorimer drove Gray's superb through-pass beyond the luckless Eric Martin; 60th minute, Clarke's footwork took him round a defender before slotting in the third; 64th minute, Lorimer hit the fourth; 68th minute, Lorimer intercepted an ill-judged Roger Fry back-pass to complete his hat-trick; 73rd minutes, Jack Charlton arrived in the penalty area to head in Norman Hunter's cross; 78th minute, Jones celebrated his 300th league game by forcing the ball in from close range after Lorimer headed down a left wing Gray centre.

Leeds United: Sprake; Reaney, Madeley, Bremner, Charlton, Hunter, Lorimer, Clarke, Jones, Giles, Gray.

Southampton: Martin; McCarthy, Fry, Stokes, Gabriel, Steele, Paine(Byrne), Channon, Davies, O'Neill, Jenkins.

Referee: D.Corbett (Wolverhampton) *Attendance: 34,275*

6 MAY 1972

Arsenal 0 Leeds United 1

AT ABOUT 4.10pm on the first Saturday in May 1972, the forehead of slim striker Allan Clarke narrowed the ball past

Billy Bremner watches one of Leeds' seven goals against Southampton in March 1972.

Geoff Barnett's desperate dive and into the Arsenal net to take the FA Cup to Leeds for the first time.

The game began sensationally when full-back Bob McNab was cautioned in the first minute - the first player to be booked in a Wembley Final - and was later joined by Norman Hunter, Billy Bremner and Charlie George, although it was never a physical game.

After taking the lead, United opened up with some fine attacking moves with Clarke, who had rattled the crossbar with a first-half header, a constant menace and Bremner and Johnny Giles controlling the midfield.

Arsenal were restricted to a handful of chances - Paul Reaney kicked an Alan Ball shot off the line, David Harvey pulled off a

Arsenal goalkeeper Geoff Barnett cannot prevent a header from Allan Clarke (out of picture) entering the Gunners' net for the only goal of the 1972 FA Cup Final.

fine twisting save to keep out a deflected Frank McLintock shot and in the 75th minute Charlie George's shot hit the crossbar - but these were isolated incidents in a game mastered by Leeds.

United were dealt a painful blow in the 88th minute when Mick Jones dislocated an elbow and he was still receiving treatment when his colleagues climbed to the Royal box to receive their winners' medals from the Queen. Norman Hunter made a return journey after collecting the bandaged Jones and led him up the steps in a touching scene as Wembley was awash in a sea of white, old gold and blue.

Arsenal: Barnett; Rice, McNab, Storey, McLintock, Simpson, Armstrong, Ball, George, Radford(Kennedy), Graham.
Leeds United: Harvey; Reaney, Madeley, Bremner, Charlton, Hunter, Lorimer, Clarke, Jones, Giles, Gray.
Referee: D.Smith (Gloucester) *Attendance: 100,000*

8 MAY 1972

Wolverhampton Wanderers 2 Leeds United 1

WITH the FA Cup already in the bag, half of Yorkshire seemed to follow United from Wembley to Molineux for another historic night as Leeds went in search of the coveted League and Cup double. They needed at least a draw in this, their final match for the season, to lift the title.

A goal down, United found time slipping away when Welsh international Terry Yorath, substitute for the injured Allan Clarke, flicked the ball over the head of Wolves 'keeper Phil Parkes, only to see defender Gerry Taylor emerge from nowhere and head off the line.

Leeds claimed that Parkes had brought down Clarke, and that full-back Bernard Shaw handled shots from Clarke and Peter Lorimer in the penalty box, but the referee ignored their pleas.

It was Wolves, with little but pride to play for, who seized the initiative three minutes before half-time when United failed to clear a corner and Francis Munro cracked an angled drive past David Harvey.

United looked desperately for the equaliser, but the home side increased their lead with a fine goal after an hour when John Richards' pass opened up the heart of the United defence for striker Derek Dougan to run through and finish superbly.

Within minutes United's 'double' hopes were rekindled when Billy Bremner scurried on to Paul Madeley's long pass to thump the ball in from close range.

The frantic pace continued and although United came desperately close to snatching the crucial equaliser, Wolves clung on to deny Leeds their glory.

On the same night another of the title challengers, Liverpool, failed to beat Arsenal at Highbury, leaving Derby County, whose players were on holiday, champions for the first time in their history.

Wolverhampton Wanderers: Parkes; Shaw, Taylor, Hegan, Munro, McAlle, McCalliog, Hibbitt, Richards, Dougan, Wagstaffe.
Leeds United: Harvey; Reaney, Madeley, Bremner, Charlton, Hunter, Lorimer, Clarke(Yorath), Bates, Giles, Gray.
Referee: W.J.Gow (Swansea) *Attendance: 53,379*

5 MAY 1973

Leeds United 0 Sunderland 1

AS UNITED came clattering down in the 1973 FA Cup Final, the thud could be heard from John O'Groats to Land's End. Second Division Sunderland completely ripped up the form book to pull off one of the biggest upsets in a Wembley Final.

Sunderland had reached Wembley with a refreshing brand of soccer and, after weathering an early flurry of United attacks, began to play to their full potential. The Sunderland defence, centre-half Dave Watson in particular, closed down quickly on the off-form Allan Clarke, Mick Jones and Eddie Gray, and pieced together some promising moves of their own.

After 32 minutes, diminutive midfield man Bobby Kerr put in a cunning lob which David Harvey was forced to tip away for a corner. Billy Hughes curled the kick in from the right, beyond United's defensive cover, where Ian Porterfield cushioned the ball on his thigh before crashing in a superb knee-high, right-foot volley for the goal which was to win the Cup.

Yet the game is often remembered for the save that enabled the Wearsiders to hang on to the Cup rather than for the goal that won it.

Sunderland goalkeeper Jim Montgomery makes a brilliant save from Peter Lorimer in the 1973 FA Cup Final.

Midway through the second half Trevor Cherry linked up with his attack and put in a diving header which goalkeeper Jim Montgomery did well to parry. The ball ran loose to Peter Lorimer who hit the ball hard and true from close range, only for Montgomery to twist in the air and fling out his arms to tip the ball onto the underside of the crossbar for an amazing double save.

Montgomery's superb effort sapped United spirit and, although they pushed forward belatedly, anything less than victory would have been harsh on underdogs Sunderland.

Leeds United: Harvey; Reaney, Cherry, Bremner, Madeley, Hunter, Lorimer, Clarke, Jones, Giles, Gray(Yorath).

Sunderland: Montgomery; Malone, Guthrie, Horswill, Watson, Pitt, Kerr, Porterfield, Halom, Hughes, Tueart.

Referee: K.H.Burns (Stourbridge) *Attendance: 100,000*

16 MAY 1973

AC Milan 1 Leeds United 0

WITH the Wembley defeat by Sunderland still dogging them, rumours that Don Revie was to leave the club, the suspensions of Allan Clarke and Billy Bremner and an injury to Johnny Giles, it was a deflated and depleted Leeds United who prepared to contest the European Cup-winners' Cup Final in Salonika against the might of AC Milan.

Thunder and heavy rain greeted the teams as they stepped out into the new Kaftatzoglio Stadium in northern Greece. It was to prove an appropriate backcloth for an infamous match.

After only four minutes, the referee curiously penalised Paul Madeley for an infringement and Luciano Chiarugi saw his free-kick clip a United defender and brush one of his own forwards before hitting the base of a post and going in.

Once in front, the Italians retreated to their own penalty area and did not appear to mind how they stopped Leeds as referee Christos Michas ignored a succession of fouls, much to the anger of both the Leeds and Greek supporters in the crowd. Mick Jones and Peter Lorimer were both flattened in the penalty area, a Paul Reaney cross was blatantly handled by Romeo Benetti and a host of shots and headers all went desperately close.

United's frustration finally boiled over minutes from the end when Norman Hunter was hacked down from behind by Gianni Rivera and retaliated. In the confused mêlée which followed, Hunter and one of the Italians, Sogliano, were ordered off. It was a bitter end to a bitter season.

AC Milan: Vecchi; Sabadini, Zignoli, Anquilletti, Turone, Rosato(Dolci), Sogliano, Benetti, Bigon, Rivera, Chiarugi.

Leeds United: Harvey; Reaney, Cherry, Bates, Yorath, Hunter, Lorimer, Jordan, Jones, F.Gray(McQueen), Madeley.

Referee: C.Michas (Greece) *Attendance: 45,000*

9 APRIL 1975

Leeds United 2 Barcelona 1

DUTCH masters Johann Cruyff and Johann Neeskens were brought down to earth at a packed Elland Road as United edged closer to their first European Cup Final.

The pair had played in Holland's World Cup Final side beaten 2-1 by West Germany the previous year and were regarded as among the best midfield players on the planet. But it was Scottish skipper Billy Bremner and his partner Johnny Giles who controlled this nerve-tingling match, United's 60th game of the season.

It was Bremner who gave Leeds a flying start with a goal after only nine minutes. Giles played the ball up to Joe Jordan, whose header found Bremner in space. He took a few strides forward before driving the ball past Salvador Sadurni with an angled shot to become the first player to score against the Spanish side in the competition that season.

Leeds knew they would probably need a two-goal lead to take to the vast Nou Camp Stadium and headers by Allan Clarke and Gordon McQueen went close to give them that cushion.

With Paul Madeley keeping Cruyff quiet, the Spaniards were largely on the defensive but did produce some dangerous counter-attacks – and it was from one of these that they grabbed an equaliser.

In the 66th minute Cruyff slid the ball through to Juan Carlos Heredia, who was checked on the edge of the area by Paul Reaney, although Leeds were unhappy at the award of the free-kick against their full-back. Cruyff stood over the ball, bided his time and rolled it sideways for Juan Manuel Asensi to crack his shot unerringly beyond David Stewart.

It was a hammer blow for United, but 12 minutes later they regained the lead. Reaney surged down the right wing and crossed for Joe Jordan to head down in the box where Allan Clarke, six yards out, lashed in his 21st goal of the season.

United pushed hard for a third goal but with Barcelona killing time at every opportunity, they had to settle for a 2-1 lead to take to Spain.

In the second leg, Peter Lorimer's early goal gave United much-needed breathing space and, despite having McQueen sent off, they hung on for a 1-1 draw and a 3-2 aggregate win to reach their first European Cup Final.

Leeds United: Stewart; Reaney, F.Gray, Bremner, McQueen, Madeley, Yorath, Clarke, Jordan, Giles, E.Gray.

Barcelona: Sadurni; Costas(Rife), Marinho, Gallego, De a Cruz, Neeskens(Juan Carlos), Rexach, Migueli, Cruyff, Asensi, Heredi.

Referee: V. Loraux (Belgium) *Attendance: 50,393*

28 MAY 1975

Bayern Munich 2 Leeds United 0

UNITED reached new heights when they lifted the 1973-74 League championship, producing a brand of football which earned them another shot at the European Cup. This time they bettered their semi-final appearance in 1970.

This latest European venture was undertaken without the guidance of Don Revie who was by now England manager. Leeds' experienced squad were now led by the calm and influential Jimmy Armfield, who nursed the club through a difficult period after Revie's departure and Brian Clough's 44 days at Elland Road. Armfield extracted some excellent displays from his side during their route to the Final.

In Paris, luck deserted Untied in their hour of need. Playing well in the first half, they had two penalty appeals rejected and the game turned around dramatically in a matter of minutes midway through the second half. Peter Lorimer thundered a 66th-minute volley past Maier, only to have the effort disallowed because skipper Billy Bremner had strayed offside, although Leeds claimed that he was not interfering with play.

Both the mood and complexion of the match altered minutes later as Danish star Conny Tortensson slipped a neat through ball to Franz Roth who clipped it past the advancing Stewart. Seven minutes later Jupp Kapellmann cut the ball back from the by-line for goal-poacher Gerard Müller to steal in front of Paul Madeley, playing at centre-half for the suspended Gordon McQueen, and turn the ball in at the near post.

To complete a night of disaster for United, hordes of their supporters rioted inside and outside the ground – actions which cost Leeds a ban from European competition.

Peter Lorimer finds the net against Bayern Munich in the 1975 European Cup Final in Paris but the goal was disallowed because Bremner (right) was offside.

Bayern Munich: Maier; Durnberger, Andersson(Weiss), Schwarzenbeck, Beckenbauer, Roth, Tortensson, Zobel, Müller, Hoeness(Wunder), Kapellmann.
Leeds United: Stewart; Reaney, F.Gray, Bremner, Madeley, Hunter, Lorimer, Clarke, Jordan, Giles, Yorath(E.Gray).
Referee: M.Kitabdjian (France) *Attendance: 48,374*

27 OCTOBER 1982

Newcastle United 1 Leeds United 4

TRAILING to an Imre Varadi goal from the home leg, Leeds' hopes of progress in the League Cup, seemed to have vanished when they immediately went 1-0 down on Tyneside.

There were only 90 seconds on the referee's watch when Newcastle defender Jeff Clarke volleyed his side into a 2-0 aggregate lead and it seemed Leeds had only pride left to play for in their second-round tussle.

Both sides were in the Second Division, but it was the Magpies, inspired by former Liverpool and England star Kevin Keegan, who had made the brighter start to the League campaign so there were few who gave Leeds much hope of clawing their way back into the tie.

But, inspired by new player-manager Eddie Gray and the dazzling dribbling skills of Arthur Graham, Leeds always carried a threat down the left and hauled themselves back into contention on 32 minutes when Wes Saunders, under pressure from Aiden Butterworth, turned Graham's cross into his own net. Both sides produced some brilliant attacking soccer, but with Kenny Burns and Trevor Cherry rock-solid in the Leeds defence, it was the visiting United who started to carry the bigger threat and deservedly drew level on aggregate 20 minutes from the end.

Frank Gray, celebrating his 28th birthday, pushed the ball down the left for elder brother Eddie to curl over the perfect cross to the far post where Frank Worthington netted with a diving header.

Leeds went into extra-time with the edge of away goals counting double at the end of the extra period, but there was no question of Leeds going on the defensive.

During half-time of extra-time, player-manager Gray took himself off and brought on another striker, 19-year-old Terry Connor, who within seven minutes of his arrival slid the ball across to Butterworth, 20, to side foot Leeds ahead.

Connor then rounded off a superb Leeds comeback when more intricate passing around the Newcastle defence put him in the clear and he chipped a close-range shot over advancing goalkeeper, Kevin Carr, to give Leeds a remarkable 4-2 aggregate victory.

It had been a stirring Leeds fightback in their 75th tie in the competition, sponsored for the first time and played under the name of the Milk Cup, but hopes of an extended run were dashed in the next round when neighbours Huddersfield Town won 1-0 at Elland Road.

But for two hours at St James' Park, Leeds revived memories of some of the great Cup triumphs of the Don Revie era.

Varadi and Newcastle defender Peter Haddock were later both to play for Leeds.

Newcastle United: Carr; Anderson, Saunders, Martin, Clarke (Craggs), Haddock, Keegan, McCreery, Varadi, Wharton, Waddle.
Leeds United: Lukic; Cherry, E.Gray(Connor), Burns, Hart, Thomas, Hird, Butterworth, Worthington, F.Gray, Graham.
Referee: C. N. Seel(Carlisle) *Attendance: 24,948*

2 FEBRUARY 1983

Leeds United 1 Arsenal 1

RELEGATION in 1982 came as a big shock to United and their followers, but after disposing of lowly Preston in the third round of the FA Cup, United were given an early return to the big-time.

At Highbury, Leeds gave a solid team performance, took the lead through an own-goal by Peter Nicholas after 61 minutes, then immediately conceded their advantage to experienced striker Alan Sunderland and finally held on to take Arsenal's star-spangled side back to Elland Road.

On a heavy pitch, both sides traded attack for attack, but the defences held out without much difficulty and the game dragged on into extra-time. With the tacky, sanded surface sapping the energy from tired limbs, a second replay was looming as United built an attack on the left in the final minute.Striker Terry Connor did well to beat his marker before whipping a low cross into the penalty-box, where his young co-striker Aidan Butterworth had just enough strength to stab the ball home.

'Elland Road erupted when Butterworth's shot went in, despite a touch on the ball by Kenny Sansom, but tragedy struck United – and goalkeeper John Lukic in particular – seconds later, when Graham Rix took a 30-yard free-kick and sent the ball skidding into United's net at the near post', reported Don Warters of the *Yorkshire Evening Post.*

Referee John Hunting barely had time to restart the game before time ran out, and to add to United's agony, Arsenal won the toss for the right to stage the second replay. At Highbury they won 2-1 to progress into the fifth round.

Leeds United: Lukic; Aspin, E.Gray, Thomas, Hart, Dickinson, Hird, Butterworth, Connor, F.Gray, Graham.
Arsenal: Jennings; Hollins, Sansom, Robson, O'Leary, Nicholas, Talbot, Sunderland(Davis), Petrovic, Woodcock, Rix.
Referee: J.Hunting (Leicester) *Attendance: 24,410*

12 APRIL 1987

Coventry City 3 Leeds United 2

UNITED'S first appearance in a major semi-final for ten years produced a tremendous duel in the Sunday sunshine with the eventual FA Cup winners, Coventry City, at Hillsborough, Sheffield.

The game, televised live, kicked-off 15 minutes late because an estimated 6,000 fans were still waiting to get into the ground at 12.15pm, the scheduled starting time. The match proved well worth the wait.

United, who had eliminated Telford United, Swindon Town, Queen's Park Rangers and Wigan Athletic, made a blistering start, going a goal up after 14 minutes when David Rennie headed in Micky Adams' corner-kick. Only two brilliant saves by Coventry 'keeper Steve Ogrizovic prevented United from taking complete control and gradually the Sky Blues began to create chances.

With only 22 minutes between United and a Wembley appearance, the Leeds heroes were coping fairly easily with the Coventry attack when United skipper Brendan Ormsby made the error which was to tip the game City's way.

Instead of hoofing a misdirected through ball clear, he opted to guide it over the dead-ball line but was robbed by the persistent David Bennett whose cross was cracked in from 12 yards by substitute Micky Gynn.

Ten minutes later the United defence was opened up again and Keith Houchen rounded Mervyn Day in style to give City the lead. A pulsating match reached fever pitch seven minutes from normal time when substitute Keith Edwards headed in United's equaliser from Andy Ritchie's cross.

The pace inevitably dropped in the extra period, but it was Coventry who made most of the running and won the game in the 99th minute when Bennett shot home from close range after Day blocked a Houchen effort with his legs. United fought hard and it needed another marvellous Ogrizovic save to deny Edwards a late equaliser.

Underdogs Leeds had acquitted themselves superbly and their much-maligned supporters also made it a trouble-free game to remember, on a day when the club won back much of its self-respect.

Coventry City: Ogrizovic; Borrows, Downs, McGrath, Kilcline, Peake, Bennett, Phillips, Regis, Houchen, Pickering(Gynn).
Leeds United: Day; Aspin, Adams, Stiles(Haddock), Ashurst, Ormsby, Ritchie, Sheridan, Pearson(Edwards), Baird, Rennie.
Referee: R.G.Milford (Bristol) *Attendance: 51,372*

16 APRIL 1990

Leeds United 4 Sheffield United 0

YORKSHIRE's championship-chasing duo clashed head on in front of the biggest Second Division crowd of the season in the white-hot atmosphere of Elland Road on Easter Monday.

Pundits reckoned that the outcome of the battle would be crucial in the race for the title – and so it proved as Leeds strengthened their grip at the top of the table with an emphatic victory.

After a tense opening, Leeds skipper Gordon Strachan gave

Lee Chapman scores the second goal in the vital all-Yorkshire promotion battle against Sheffield United at Elland Road on Easter Monday 1990.

his side the lead after 18 minutes, from close range after Chris Kamara's shot had been blocked on the line by Paul Stancliffe.

Leeds continued to dominate but had to wait until 16 minutes from the end to kill off the Blades. Gary Speed powered down the left and his fierce, low centre was turned in at the far post by Lee Chapman.

Leeds began to turn on the style and in the 82nd minute went 3-0 up when Bobby Davison blocked Simon Tracey's clearance and was fouled by the young 'keeper as he scampered after the rebound. Ice-cool Strachan stepped up to chip the penalty wide of Tracey.

To seal a great afternoon for Leeds, Kamara broke up a last-minute Sheffield attack and sent Speed on a long run towards goal. The Welsh youngster drew Tracey before driving a diagonal shot into the net.

Leeds eventually went on to clinch the championship, with a club record 85 points, on goal-difference from the Blades and returned to Division One after an absence of eight years.

Leeds United: Day; Sterland, Beglin, Jones, Fairclough, McClelland, Strachan, Kamara, Chapman, Davison(Shutt), Speed.

Sheffield United: Tracey; Hill, Barnes, Booker, Stancliffe, Morris, Webster, Gannon(Wood), Whitehurst(Agana), Deane, Bryson.

Referee: A.Gunn (South Chailey, Sussex) *Attendance: 32,727*

13 APRIL 1991

Leeds United 4 Liverpool 5

ELLAND Road has witnessed many remarkable matches over the years but few could match this goal-feast for sheer excitement.

United's return to the First Division had seen them up among the front-runners for most of the season without ever winning enough games to challenge the likes of Arsenal and Liverpool at the top.

Second-placed Liverpool produced some mesmerising football in the first half as they powered into a four-goal lead with Paul Barnes the tormentor-in-chief.

Barnes' 11th-minute chip into the box was picked out Ray Houghton, who finished clinically. Six minutes later Ian Rush was brought down by John Lukic and Jan Molby slotted home the penalty kick. United just could not get hold of the ball and fell further behind when David Speedie forced home Barnes' 25th-minute cross at the far post; and that man Barnes played in Rush to make it 4-0 after just 27 minutes.

But the team spirit and determination which had been a key part in the Second Division championship success still remained and United produced a brave, if unrewarded, second-half fightback that brought the crowd to fever pitch.

Central striker Lee Chapman was the focal point of United's attack and his prowess in the air gave Liverpool an uncomfortable second 45 minutes.

United had little option to attack, but didn't get on the scoresheet until the 68th minute when Chapman poked the ball in from close range. Nine minutes later Carl Shutt got on the end of Gary Speed's long throw into the box and swivelled to shoot past Mike Hooper.

But within a minute Liverpool checked United's revival when Rush's back-heel sent Barnes towards goal and he beat Lukic with an angled shot.

Still United refused to die and Chapman headers in the 81st and 88th minutes completed the big striker's hat-trick inside 20 minutes and whipped the crowd into a frenzy. Controversially, he also had another header disallowed for a slight nudge on Hooper.

There was no questioning Liverpool's right to maximum points but with another five minutes at their disposal, Leeds might have won.

Both teams left the pitch to a thunderous ovation after the crowd had been royally entertained. Liverpool went on to finish runners-up behind Arsenal – the chinks in defence which showed at Elland Road probably costing them the title – while

Gordon Strachan chips the ball beyond John Barnes for Lee Chapman to score in the 5-4 defeat by Liverpool at Elland Road in April 1991.

Leeds finished a brilliant fourth on their return to the top flight.

Chapman completed the season with 31 goals in all competitions, the best return by any of the marksmen from the First Division.

Leeds United: Lukic; Sterland, Whitlow, Batty, Fairclough, Whyte, Strachan, Shutt, Chapman, McAllister, Speed.

Liverpool: Hooper; Hysen, Staunton, Nichol, Molby, Burrows, Beardsley, Houghton, Rush, Barnes, Speedie.

Referee: K Redfearn (Whitley Bay) *Attendance: 31,460*

12 JANUARY 1992

Sheffield Wednesday 1 Leeds United 6

AFTER such an impressive return to the First Division, United were tipped as title contenders by several pundits, particularly as the side had been strengthened by the arrival of England left-back Tony Dorigo from Chelsea and England Under-21 forward Rod Wallace from Southampton.

The championship race was developing into a two-horse affair between the Uniteds of Leeds and Manchester. The men from Old Trafford struck a psychological blow four days before the League game at Hillsborough by knocking Leeds out of the Rumbelows Cup.

But Leeds, despite the absence of inspirational skipper Gordon Strachan (injured) and David Batty (suspended), stormed back to the top of the First Division with a blistering attacking display televised live by Sky TV.

Wednesday had not lost at home for 14 matches, but Howard Wilkinson, back at Hillsborough for the first time since leaving the Owls to manage United, had a glorious return. To rub salt into Sheffield's wounds, the scoring feast was spearheaded by another Wednesday old boy, Lee Chapman, who netted the first hat-trick on away soil by a United player in 12 years.

It took Chapman just nine minutes to open his account,

forcing home Chris Fairclough's headed knock down.

After that United took total control with Rod Wallace and Tony Dorigo creating havoc down the left. It was no surprise when Dorigo thumped home a 25-yard free-kick on the half-hour to increase United's lead, but Wednesday briefly crept into the game via a controversial 37th-minute penalty.

Gordon Watson went down spectacularly in the box and referee Philip Don point to the spot. Up stepped former Leeds player John Sheridan, whose spot-kick was touched on to a post but came back for him to net the rebound.

Leeds were in no mood to feel sorry for themselves and two minutes before the interval Chapman headed in Gary Speed's superb left-wing cross to restore United's two-goal cushion. Chapman completed his hat-trick on 65 minutes when he nodded in from close range after a Speed header came back off the bar.

Four minutes later a towering header by substitute Mike Whitlow made it 5-1.

Leeds were in irresistible mood and Wallace wrapped up the scoring four minutes from the end when he cut through the Wednesday defence and clipped the ball past Chris Woods.

It was United's best away victory since their 7-3 thumping of Blackpool 56 years earlier, and although Leeds were knocked out of the FA Cup by Manchester United the week after their Hillsborough super-show, they were in position in the race for the championship.

Sheffield Wednesday: Woods; Nilsson, King, Palmer, Pearson (Harkes), Anderson, Watson, Sheridan, Bart-Williams, Jemson, Worthington(Williams).

Leeds United: Lukic; Sterland, Dorigo, Hodge(Davison), Fairclough, Whyte, Shutt(Whitlow), Wallace, Chapman, McAllister, Speed.

Referee: P.Don (Middlesex) *Attendance: 32,228*

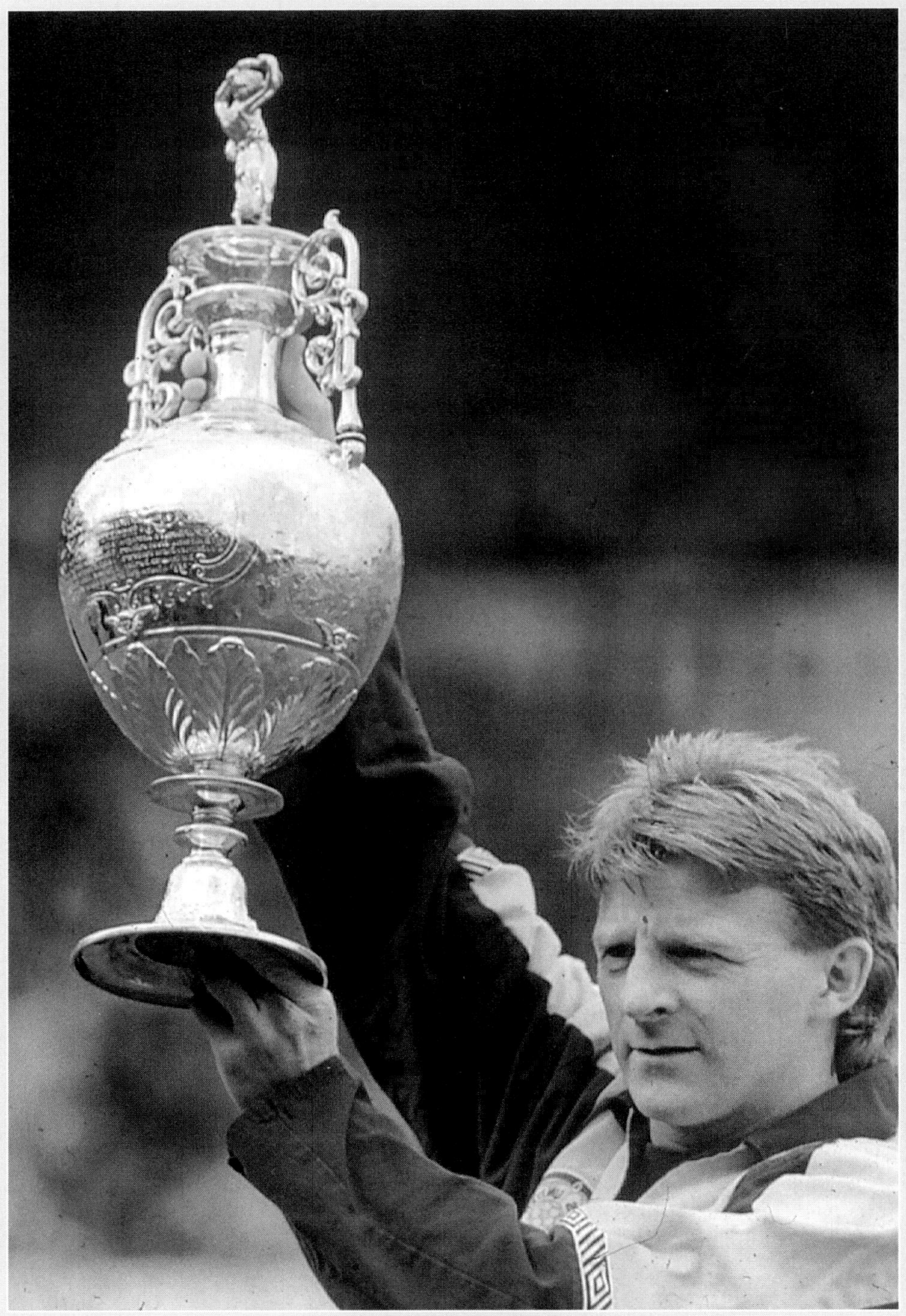

A week after their victory over Sheffield United, Gordon Strachan holds aloft the League championship trophy at Elland Road when they entertained Norwich City.

26 APRIL 1992

Sheffield United 2 Leeds United 3

CHAMPAGNE corks were popping after a truly extraordinary Sunday which ended with the League championship returning to Elland Road for the first time since 1973-74. Leeds kicked off at midday at Bramall Lane, knowing that victory would mean that Manchester United could not afford to lose their game at Liverpool later that afternoon, or the crown would almost certainly go to Howard Wilkinson's team. On a windswept afternoon, a bizarre match unfolded before the eyes of a 32,000 crowd swelled by a huge following from up the Ml.

Leeds were clearly nervous and had several uneasy moments in defence before veteran striker Alan Cork gobbled up a half-chance after 28 minutes to put the Blades in front. United came more into the game as the interval approached and they levelled on the stroke of half-time with a freak goal. A stretched Sheffield defence tried to hack the ball out of their area, but the clearance struck Gary Speed and bounced off Rod Wallace and into the net.

Blades' goalkeeper Mel Rees was injured in the mayhem and spent the whole of the second half in some discomfort.

Sheffield-born Jon Newsome powered in a header from Gary

Eric Cantona and Rod Wallace celebrate Brian Gayle's own-goal which virtually clinched the 1991-92 League championship for Leeds United.

McAllister's 65th-minute cross which the injured Rees was unable to reach. But Leeds' lead lasted only a few minutes as the Blades drew level with another strange goal when prolific Leeds marksman Lee Chapman turned a cross-shot from John Pemberton, later to join Leeds, into his own net.

But there was yet another twist in this strange game which was settled 13 minutes from the end. Blades' skipper Brian Gayle, struggling to clear in the blustery wind, miscued the ball high back into his own area. As Wallace and substitute Eric Cantona, sensing an opening, moved into pressure the home defence, Gayle could only head the ball over Rees, who had come out of his goal to try to clear the danger, for the winner.

Three hours later Manchester United kicked-off at Liverpool needing at least a draw to keep their title hopes alive, but goals by Ian Rush and Mark Walters condemned them to a 2-0 defeat and Leeds were League champions for the first time in 18 years.

The following Saturday, Leeds completed their League programme with a 1-0 home win against Norwich City, courtesy of a great Wallace solo goal after the championship trophy was presented to skipper Gordon Strachan.

Sheffield United: Rees; Pemberton, Cowan, Gannon(Bryson), Gayle, Beesley, Hodges, Rogers, Cork(Whitehouse), Deane, Bradshaw.

Leeds United: Lukic; Newsome, Dorigo, Batty, Fairclough, Whyte, Strachan(Shutt), Wallace, Chapman, McAllister(Cantona), Speed.

Referee: G Courtney (Spennymoor) *Attendance: 32,000*

8 AUGUST 1992

Leeds United 4 Liverpool 3

TO help Leeds in their push for the 1991-92 championship, manager Howard Wilkinson had snatched charismatic Frenchman Eric Cantona from under the noses of his old club Sheffield Wednesday.

Although used sparingly in the thrilling run-in, Cantona's class was obvious and, despite his reputation for being difficult to handle, he was seen as a key factor in United's title defence and European Cup campaign.

Cries of "Ooh-aah, Cantona," were echoing around Wembley after his hat-trick clinched a marvellous Charity Shield victory over Liverpool a week before the start of the season.

It was the first time, other than the Mercantile Credit appearance in the mid-1980s, that Leeds had played beneath the famous Twin Towers since 1975 when Liverpool beat them in a penalty competition.

Revenge was sweet for Leeds in a match full of attacking soccer. Liverpool played with only three outright defenders and United revelled in the extra space and up front had the match-winner in Cantona.

He fired Leeds into a 26th-minute lead with a shot that deflected past Bruce Grobbelaar off David Burrows, but the Reds were level eight minutes later when Ronnie Rosenthal's cross to the far post was headed in by Ian Rush.

Hat-trick hero Eric Cantona (left) and United's other goalscorer, Tony Dorigo, with the FA Charity Shield after Leeds' thrilling 4-3 win over Liverpool at Wembley in August 1992.

United recaptured the lead just before the break with another deflected goal. This time Tony Dorigo saw his left-foot shot clip Rosenthal before going in. Leeds looked dangerous in attack, but suspect in defence and Liverpool drew level in the second half with a well-placed snap shot from Dean Saunders.

However, United finished the stronger in the hot sun and Cantona blasted them back in front 13 minutes from the end with an excellent goal. Pulling away from his marker, he took the ball on his chest and drilled a fierce angled drive into the net.

The game was made safe two minutes from time when Grobbelaar misjudged a cross and Cantona headed in his hat-trick goal. Wilkinson, who opted not to play midfielder David Rocastle, the £2 million summer purchase from Arsenal, had sent on veteran Gordon Strachan, who scored an own-goal with virtually his first touch as the ball got stuck between his feet when he defended a corner on the right-hand post and saw the ball trickle over the line.

But there was no denying Cantona his Wembley glory and there was a nice touch at the end when skipper Gary McAllister invited Strachan to lift the Charity Shield and show it to United's delighted fans.

Leeds United: Lukic; Newsome(Strachan), Dorigo, Batty, Fairclough, Whyte, Cantona, Wallace, Chapman(Hodge), McAllister, Speed.

Liverpool: Grobbelaar; Tanner, Burrows, Marsh(Hutchison), Whelan, Wright, Saunders, Stewart, Rush, Rosenthal(Kozma), Walters.

Referee: D Elleray (Middlesex) *Attendance: 61,291*

30 SEPTEMBER 1992

Leeds United 4 VfB Stuttgart I

EUROPEAN Cup football returned to Elland Road for the first time since 1975 and in quite extraordinary fashion, too, as United came close to pulling off one of the greatest comebacks in the competition's illustrious history.

Leeds trailed 3-0 from the first leg in Stuttgart and hardly anyone gave them a prayer of overturning the deficit against the German champions.

But United were really pumped-up for action and a glance at the team-sheet showed manager Howard Wilkinson's intentions with attacking midfielder Scott Sellars playing at right-back. And when Gary Speed volleyed home from close range early on, the impossible seemed possible.

United were committed to all-out attack and went close to stretching.their lead several times before Stuttgart struck a hammer blow on 34 minutes when Andreas Buck cut in from the right to fire in their equaliser.

Within four minutes, though, United's faint hopes were lifted by a Gary McAllister penalty. And when Eric Cantona rattled the ball home from close range in 66 minutes, the great escape was on again.

The 20,457 crowd sounded more like 50,000 as Leeds stormed forward and the roof nearly blew off Elland Road when Lee Chapman's close-range header made it 4-1 on the night and 4-4 overall with ten minutes remaining. Panic-stricken Stuttgart sent on Adrian Knup and Jovo Simakic for striker Fritz Walter and midfield man Maurizio Gaudino to shore up their wilting defence. The Germans just held out, but Leeds won enormous praise for their courageous display which was laced with lashings of skill and determination.

The following day it transpired that Stuttgart had broken UEFA rules by using Swiss international Knup, which meant they had fielded too many foreign players during the game. The match was declared void, and Leeds awarded a 3-0 victory and the teams ordered to play-off in Barcelona for the right to go through to the next round and meet Scottish champions Rangers.

Nine days after that extraordinary night at Elland Road, United triumphed 2-1 in a near-deserted Nou Camp Stadium with substitute Carl Shutt, on the eve of his 31st birthday, netting the winner near the end.

Leeds United: Lukic; Sellars, Dorigo, Batty, Fairclough, Whyte, Strachan, Cantona, Chapman, McAllister, Speed.
VfB Stuttgart: Immel; Schaefer, Frontzeck, Dubajic, Struntz, Buchwald, Buck, Sverisson, Walter(Knup), Gaudino(Simakic), Kogl.
Referee: K.Mifton Meiste (Denmark) *Attendance: 20,457*

12 SEPTEMBER 1995

AS Monaco 0 Leeds United 3

UNITED fans had a new goal hero to cheer in Tony Yeboah, who scored a stunning hat-trick in Monaco to continue his sizzling start with Leeds.

Snapped up the previous January from Eintracht Frankfurt in Germany, the Ghanan star's goals had helped United put together a great late run to clinch a place in Europe.

The draw was not kind to United, pairing them with star-studded French champions Monaco, the previous season's European Cup semi-finalists, but they were simply brushed aside by Yeboah's superb finishing.

It took the star of Africa only three minutes to open the scoring when Monaco goalkeeper Fabien Piveteau collided with his central defender Lillian Thuram, dropped the ball and the alert Yeboah hooked it over his head into the empty net.

Monaco had plenty of possession, but United's defence was in determined mood and the French side, driven forward by Belgian midfield star Enzo Schifo, were unable to carve out too many chances.

Then Yeboah brought Leeds fans in the Stade Louis II to their feet with a stunning second goal. Receiving Gary McAllister's throw-in from the left, he turned superbly beyond his marker to create the space to curl a magnificent shot beyond the reach of Marc Delaroche, who had come on for the injured Piveteau at half-time.

Ten minutes from the end there was more misery for Delaroche when he was involved in a sickening collision with defender Basile Boli as the cunning Yeboah lobbed in his hat-trick goal.

Delaroche and Boli were both stretchered off after receiving prolonged attention and Monaco brought on outfield player Claude Puel goal for the final minutes.

Yeboah, who scored another stunning treble in United's 4-2 Premiership win at Wimbledon 11 days later, was hailed by manager Wilkinson.

"Words can't describe Tony Yeboah nor his importance to the team," purred the Leeds boss. "He's always been able to score straightforward goals, but increasingly he is scoring more difficult ones. That was a great result for us."

Unfortunately, United lost the home leg 1-0 and were outclassed by Dutch side PSV Eindhoven 8-3 on aggregate in the next round, so a European campaign which began so brightly was soon extinguished.

AS Monaco: Piveteau(Delaroche replaced by Puel); Valery, Di Meco, Boli, Thuram, Dumas, Dos Santos, Legwinski(Henry), Anderson, Schifo, Wreh.
Leeds United: Lukic; Kelly, Pemberton, Wetherall, Dorigo (Beesley), Whelan, McAllister, Palmer, Speed, Deane, Yeboah.
Referee: J.M.Garcia-Aranda Encinar (Spain) *Attendance: 12,500*

Tony Yeboah, who scored a magnificent hat-trick against AS Monaco in September 1995.

The Elland Road Story

TODAY'S Elland Road stadium, with its impressive facilities, is a lasting monument to Leeds United's triumphant years under Don Revie and Howard Wilkinson and is a far cry from the open grass field of Victorian times. Before the turn of the century the land, nestling at the foot of Beeston Hill on the main road to the neighbouring town of Elland, was owned by Bentley's Brewery. It was known as the Old Peacock Ground, named after a local pub standing opposite the playing field. It was from the pub that the club took its nickname of the Peacocks, after being known as the Citizens during the days of Leeds City.

The Old Peacock Ground was brought by Holbeck Rugby Club, for £1,100 in 1897, on condition that it remained a football ground for at least seven years and that the catering rights should be held by Bentley's. Despite problems of getting sufficient labour, Holbeck were able to build a new stand ready for the following season. Rugby was immensely popular in the West Riding, but it was not long before the ground, now known as Elland Road, hosted its first competitive soccer match.

On 23 April 1898, local soccer administrators were delighted when 3,400 people turned up to see Hunslet, forerunners of Leeds City, beat Harrogate 1-0 in the West Yorkshire Cup Final at Elland Road.

Soccer became a regular attraction at the ground during the 1902-03 season when Leeds League soccer side, Leeds Woodville, shared the ground with Holbeck. But it was not until Leeds City were formed that soccer really took root at Elland Road.

Holbeck became defunct in 1904 and put the ground on the market. The men behind Leeds City were anxious to have a ground good enough to support any future application to join the Football League and saw Elland Road as their ideal home. City officials gave instructions to sign the lease on 13 October 1904, for an annual rent of £75 with an option to buy for no more than £5,000 the following March. When the lease was finally signed, in November, the purchase figure was reduced to £4,500.

Two days after giving the all-clear to sign the lease, Leeds City played their first game on the Elland Road turf. City officials were determined to make it a red-letter day in the club's history. The 3,000 crowd were entertained by a local boys match, and a band, before Leeds City were beaten 2-0 by Hull City in a friendly.

After the sale went through, Leeds City directors set about improving the ground as the club prepared to move from the West Yorkshire League to the Football League. In August 1905, work began on an ambitious reconstruction scheme which ended with a £1,050 covered stand for 5,000 people being erected on the west side of the ground.

As soccer grabbed the imagination of the local footballing public, Elland Road pulled in some big early crowds – a 22,000-plus gate, bringing in receipts of £487, was recorded for the local derby with Bradford City on 30 December 1905.

Expansion continued in February 1906 as City bought 3,961 square yards of land on the Churwell and Geldard Road side of the ground, for £420, from the Monk's Bridge Iron Company.

Soccer's administrators were anxious to reward the effort that had been made in gaining a foothold in rugby-dominated West Yorkshire and selected Elland Road as the venue for an England trial match in 1906 and an amateur international against Ireland in 1909.

But the Football Association clearly acted in haste by choosing Elland Road for the 1910 FA Cup semi-final between Barnsley and Everton. It turned out to be a disaster because the ground was not big enough to cope with the thousands of fans who poured in to Leeds to see the big game. Although an estimated 36,000 got inside the ground, many could hardly see the pitch and thousands more were locked outside.

The gates were closed even before many of the excursion trains and coaches from Liverpool arrived in the city. Well before kick-off, thousands of disappointed spectators were forced to scramble up Beeston Hill or perch precariously on neighbouring roof-tops to get a fleeting glimpse of the action.

The *Athletic News* reported: 'It is clear that the Association and the clubs concerned lost considerably by allotting the match to a small ground constructed for Second Division football and not for events of national importance'.

Not surprisingly it was another 20 years before a much improved Elland Road was to host another FA Cup semi-final.

Financially, Leeds City had always found it hard to make ends meet and when the club fell into the hands of the Receiver in 1912, the Leeds Cricket, Football and Athletic Club offered to take over City's affairs and use Headingley as the soccer ground. On 14 August 1914, however, a Leeds syndicate of sportsmen announced that they had offered to run City, guaranteeing to put down £1,000 and pay an annual ground rent of £250 to keep City at Elland Road.

Despite the constant financial problem, manager Herbert Chapman was anxious to brighten the image of the ground and even arranged for a new flag to be flown from the masthead outside the main stand.

As World War One raged across Europe, Elland Road contributed to the war effort by being used for Army drilling and shooting practice.

After City disbanded, the future of Elland Road hung in the balance. There was even a scheme dreamed up in October 1919 to make use of the rich clay deposits below the top soil of the pitch and turn it into a brickyard – even today there is a deep well sunk in the corner of the Spion Kop and West Stand. But Elland Road was spared such an ignominious fate when local club, Yorkshire Amateurs, played several games there before newly-formed Leeds United moved in.

During the 1920s, more changes were made, including the covering of the Elland Road terrace with a wooden barrel-shaped roof which became known as the Scratching Shed. Along the whole length of the pitch on the Lowfields Road side was a stand built on a bank of terracing and opposite the Scratching Shed stood a huge open Spion Kop terrace which got its name, like many other Kops in England, after the hill in South Africa on which 322 British soldiers lost their lives during the Boer War.

During the 1920s, the Football Association considered the ground good enough to stage more England trial games, although on 19 February 1923, one had to be called off because the pitch was covered by six inches of snow.

Rugby briefly returned to the ground when Elland Road hosted the 1938 Rugby Championship Final between Leeds and Hunslet in front of a massive 54,112 crowd. However, even that figure failed to beat the official 56,796 attendance which saw United and Arsenal fight out a goalless draw on 27 December 1932 – a figure which remained a record at Elland Road for 35 years.

When neighbours Huddersfield Town's main stand was destroyed by fire in April 1950, the Town played Easter Saturday and Easter Tuesday fixtures at Elland Road, against Derby County and Newcastle United – the latter before a crowd of 37,700. United repeated the good neighbours act in 1985 when Bradford City played three home games at Leeds because Valley Parade was still closed after the tragic fire which swept through Bradford's main stand. Two months after the Valley Parade horror, the 1966 World Cup Final teams from England and West Germany met in a rematch at Elland Road and raised £46,000 for the Fire Disaster Fund. England won 6-4.

United can also testify to the destruction that fire can leave in its wake. During the early hours of Tuesday, 18 September 1956, a blaze swept through the West Stand with such ferocity that large sections of the pitch were scorched by the heat.

Fish and chip shop proprietor Arnold Price, whose premises were opposite the main gates, dashed barefoot and pyjama-clad to raise the alarm. But the fire spread so rapidly that the stand roof had already collapsed into the seating area before the fire brigade arrived.

With damage estimated at £100,000, United lost not only the stand, but all the club's kit, records, physiotherapy equipment, dressing-rooms, offices, directors'-rooms and press-box, leaving a charred skeleton of twisted, smouldering metal.

As the players helped clear up the rubble and wreckage during the week, it was clear that it would be impossible to salvage the 2,500-seater stand and, after a five-hour board meeting, the directors decided to launch an appeal to build a new stand with assistance from Leeds City Council.

For manager Raich Carter there was the more immediate problem of preparing for Saturday's home game with Aston Villa. The fire struck just as United had made a fine start to their return to the First Division and Carter was determined that the Villa match should go ahead as scheduled, in an effort to consolidate their position in the table.

He immediately ordered 40 pairs of boots for his players, giving them strict instructions that they should be worn as much as possible to break them in before the game. United's injured players were treated in the home of former trainer Arthur Campey, who had set up in private practice.

The fire-ravaged stand was cordoned-off and the Leeds and Villa players, together with the match officials, changed in the dressing-rooms of the Whitehall Printeries sports ground in Lowfields Road before boarding a coach which took them the short distance to the ground where they picked their way through the burnt-out shell of the stand to reach the pitch.

United's determination to play the game paid off. They won 1-0 with a John Charles goal and after the game not a single United player reported any blisters.

The public appeal raised £60,000 and at the start of the following season, the new £180,000 West Stand was unveiled. Tickets for the 4,000 seats cost 7s 6d each per game in those days and in front of the seated area was a large paddock capable of holding 6,000 standing spectators – although this was eventually replaced with seats in the successful 1970s. The new West Stand was christened in style with a 2-1 victory over Leicester City on 31 August 1957.

Two years later another fire hit Elland Road – also in the West Stand – but club secretary Cyril Williamson and several directors became fire-fighters to snuff out another potential disaster. After a home defeat by Preston Reserves in a Central League game, the small crowd were wandering home when flames were spotted in the stand behind the directors' box. Williamson and members of the board ran from the club's offices, armed themselves with hoses and put out the fire, thought to have been started by a carelessly dropped cigarette, before much damage could be done.

The West Stand was an impressive structure but the stadium really started to take shape when Don Revie steered United through their golden era. Cash poured into United's coffers as massive crowds turned up to see his successful teams and a lot of the money was pumped back into ground improvements.

It was during the Revie era that the attendance record at Elland Road was set – although the price had to be paid. After forcing a draw at Sunderland in the fifth round of the FA Cup, United brought the Rokerites to Elland Road for a thrilling battle, fought out in front of a record crowd of 57,892 on 15 March 1967.

There had not been sufficient time to make the replay all-ticket and at 7.07pm the gates were shut, locking thousands outside. Inside, the crowd – about 5,000 more than the usual all-ticket limit – were packed like sardines. During the game one of the steel and concrete crush barriers on Lowfields Road gave way under the pressure and amid the panic about 1,000 spectators poured on to the pitch, as police and ambulancemen moved in to tend the injured.

The match was held up as 32 people were ferried to hospital, but luckily no one was seriously hurt. Some people had also taken their lives into their hands by scrambling on top of the Scratching Shed roof to see the game which, after extra-time, ended 1-1.

With money in the bank, United's directors embarked on a massive improvement scheme to create a stadium worthy of the great sides Revie had assembled. At the end of April 1968, the huge banked terracing of the Spion Kop was stripped away in six days to make way for a new roofed Kop, also known as the Geldard End, costing £250,000. During the clearance work United entertained Dundee in a semi-final second-leg game in the Inter-Cities Fairs Cup. There was the unusual sight of the Kop behind the goal a vast sealed-off gaping emptiness. When the new Kop was completed, United had about 60 feet of space spare behind the goal, so it was turfed and the pitch moved 30 feet towards the Kop.

A further £200,000 was spent in 1970 in the corner linking the Kop and the West Stand and £200,000 was outlayed on the corner of Lowfields Road and the Kop.

Improvements continued in 1974 when the old Scratching Shed was dismantled and replaced by the impressive £500,000 South Stand on Elland Road itself. It held 3,500 seats, with a standing paddock at the front capable of holding a further 4,000 fans. But as United's performances on the pitch began to wane, so the building around it ceased. Plans to link the South Stand with Lowfields Road were scrapped because of lack of cash.

Although major construction stopped, cosmetic improvements continued. The South Stand was later made all-seater, and 16 executive boxes added at the top, each one complete with TV set, refrigerator and luxury seating, all linked to a box-holders' executive lounge and restaurant.

Other alterations and additions to the Elland Road scene during the late 1970s and early 1980s continued, including the installation of an 81ft by 5ft electronic scoreboard in the Kop.

Commercially the club took a major step forward on 30 September 1972, when the Leeds United Sports and Souvenir Shop, to which a well-stocked programme shop was later added, opened.

Hooliganism was to blight the club for many years, and there was a pitch invasion during United's crucial 2-1 home defeat against West Bromwich Albion on 17 April 1971, when referee Ray Tinkler was jostled by irate Leeds fans after allowing the visitors a goal which looked well offside.

Although United became the first club in the country to install a police compound to hold arrested thugs on the ground – in the extension below the link between the Kop and West Stand – crowd trouble continued. The West Brom incident saw United banned from playing at Elland Road for the first four games of the 1971-72 season, playing two games at Huddersfield, one at Hull and another at Sheffield Wednesday during their 'home' exile.

But the lesson was not heeded by the troublemakers. As United were knocked out of the FA Cup by Manchester City at Elland Road in 1978, mounted police went on the pitch and there was a 20-minute delay as missiles were cleared and hooligans arrested. United were banned from staging FA Cup home games for the next three seasons and when United came out of the hat first against West Brom in the fourth round the following year, the 'home' game had to be played at The Hawthorns. The ban was later lifted.

More missiles were thrown during Manchester City's League visit on 29 September 1979, so a section of the South Stand – from where objects were hurled – was closed for a period. Later in the same season the Kop was closed for two matches after more objects were thrown on the pitch against Nottingham Forest. The FA meted out the same punishment after Leeds and

The East Stand at Elland Road and (left) the Don Revie Stand with its name picked out in coloured seats.

Newcastle players were taken off the pitch on 30 October 1982, when ball-bearings were thrown.

During the two-match Kop closure in 1982 it was reckoned that United actually benefited financially because fans watched the next two home games from the more expensive seated area.

Over the years Elland Road has seen some memorable European nights under its floodlights as Revie's teams destroyed a succession of the best teams that the continent could provide.

Floodlit football first came to Elland Road on 9 November 1953, when Hibernian provided the opposition for the big switch-on of the £7,000 lights – said to be the most expensive in the country at the time. The game pulled in 31,500 spectators who saw two goals apiece from John Charles and manager Raich Carter as Leeds beat the Scottish side 4-1. It was the first of several Monday night games against teams from north of the border and in successive weeks, Dundee and Falkirk were the visitors to Elland Road.

Three new floodlights were put up in 1973 and a fourth, in the south-east corner, was erected four years later. At 260ft, the diamond-shaped lights were the highest in Europe, with 55 lamps on each pylon.

Record receipts at Elland Road, which stood for over a decade, were established on 10 April 1980, when the FA Cup semi-final replay between West Ham United and Everton brought in £146,483. The record for a game involving United at Elland Road is £322,644 from the FA Cup third-round game against Manchester United on 15 January 1992. The biggest European crowd at Leeds was achieved when Rangers were the visitors for the Fairs Cup quarter-final in 1968 when 50,498 fans were shoe-horned into the ground.

The first leg of the Rangers tie at Ibrox was covered by closed circuit TV and watched by 22,000 supporters at Elland Road. Television cameras were regular visitors to Elland Road during the Revie heyday, but the first match to be screened entirely live was on 4 January 1985, when FA Cup holders Everton began their defence with a convincing 2-0 win against Second Division Leeds. Coincidentally, the first visit by BBC *Match of the Day* cameras, on 20 March 1965, was also for a Leeds-Everton game. Leeds won the First Division match 4-1.

For many years the pitch was a churned-up muddy morass and in November 1969, United considered installing an experimental pitch cover made of treated nylon but the idea was later scrapped. The pitch was reseeded in the summer of 1970, making it one of the best in the country after United had called in experts from the Sports Turf Research Institute at Bingley.

Undersoil heating was later installed in an effort to keep the pitch in prime condition during the bitter West Yorkshire winters, thus reducing the number of games which had to be called off. Before the advent of the undersoil heating the pitch, which now measures 117 yards by 76 yards, was protected in winter by tons of straw and burning braziers.

Nothing, however, could save United the embarrassment of losing a youth international game to a local working mens' club pitch in 1964. On 14 March that year the England-Wales match, scheduled for Elland Road, was switched to the city's East End Park WMC ground after United's pitch was waterlogged.

In the big freeze of 1963, Leeds experimented with de-icing pellets which successfully cleared part of a rock-hard surface but the club decided against using them over the whole pitch. To obtain much-needed match practice, Leeds played a Saturday morning friendly against Bradford at Elland Road dog-track. They drew 2-2 with the Park Avenue club on a snow-covered pitch. The clubs' reserve teams also met in similar fashion.

Superstitious Revie was convinced that the bad luck his team seemed to suffer stemmed from a curse laid on the ground long before football had been played there, so in 1971 he called in a gypsy to lift that curse.

The pitch had improved so much that Rugby League was able to make a permanent return to Elland Road when New Hunslet's home at the nearby greyhound stadium was demolished. Apart from staging New Hunslet's games, Elland Road also became a venue for several key Rugby League games.

Two other sports to make their presence felt at Elland Road have been American Football and Gaelic Football. The Leeds

Aerial view of Elland Road which was one of the venues used for Euro 96.

Cougars, members of the British American Football League, switched from their base at Bramley Rugby League Club's McLaren Field to Elland Road in May 1986. However, they moved off the following year because extra work needed doing on the pitch. A Gaelic Football match between Dublin and Mayo, organised by the Yorkshire County Board of the Gaelic Athletic Association, was played at Elland Road in 1987.

The ground has even staged live rock concerts with music fans flocking to Elland Road to see the band Queen in 1982 and U2 five years later. Two weeks after U2's performance, Elland Road hosted a three-day Jehovah's Witnesses Convention which attracted 15,000 people. Boxing has also been held at Elland Road with Bradford's Frank Grant beating Herol 'Bomber' Graham and Henry Wharton (York) outpointing Fidel Castro Smith (Sheffield) in British title fights in 1991.

Exciting new plans to develop Elland Road and its surroundings as a major sporting complex were revealed in a major deal between United and Leeds City Council in the summer of 1985. United sold the ground to the council for £2.5 million and, in return, the council granted the club a 125-year lease and unveiled ambitious plans to improve the stadium and neighbouring sporting facilities.

In 1987 outline plans were designed by a Newcastle-based firm of architects and put forward by Baltic Consortium and W.H.White, developers. The estimated costs varied between £50 million and £75 million. The scheme included replacing the 1920s Lowfields Road stand with a new 7,500-seater stand, with a 2,000-seater indoor sports arena at the other side of the stand.

Plans for the stadium complex also included a shopping centre, ice rink, cricket hall, cinema, nightclub, café, restaurant, water park, leisure centre and shops. Other innovations included provision for a railway halt for visiting supporters, and an open-air car park on three levels.

Although that actual scheme did not get off the ground, it was not long before the Lowfields Road Stand was to provide an impressive new landmark on the city's skyline.

The 1988-89 season was totally overshadowed by the Hillsborough disaster which eventually claimed the lives of 96 people at the Liverpool-Nottingham Forest FA Cup semi-final. Inevitably, ground safety came under review and the Lord Justice Taylor Report pointed the way to all-seater stadiums and big reductions in ground capacities.

United cut the Elland Road capacity of 40,176 at the start of the 1989-90 season by 8,782, to comply with the interim Taylor Report, with the Kop bearing the brunt of virtually all of the reduction.

With United blazing a trail at the top of Division Two, huge crowds turned up at Elland Road and a restriction of 1,500 was put on visiting supporters to enable Leeds to house their own fans, even though it meant a loss of revenue to the home club.

Midway through the season, managing director Bill Fotherby announced that Elland Road could become all-seater and that a new Lowfields Road Stand, costing between £6m to £10m, would be built.

Within days of United celebrating their 1991-92 League title success, the bulldozers moved in to demolish the old Lowfields Road stand to make way for the £5.5 million East Stand – much of the cost coming via a successful bond scheme introduced by the club.

By January 1993, it was sufficiently completed for part of the upper section to be opened for the first time. The whole stand was ready, on schedule, for the start of the 1993-94 season. However, United's floodlights, once the tallest in Europe, were removed and new lighting installed on the facia of the stand itself. Its 51 metre cantilever roof is believed to be the largest in the world, beating a stand in Seattle, USA, by two and a half metres.

The 17,000 capacity stand houses 10,000 in the lower tier and 7,000 in the upper tier, making it one of the largest in Britain. It includes 25 executive boxes, shopping mall, restaurant and bars, plans for a club museum are in hand. The whole of the lower section was designated as the Family Stand, which was previously housed in the South Stand.

As a result of the work, Elland Road's capacity shot up to 43,000 from 30,937, but is now at 40,000 following the installation of seats in the Kop.

The East Stand was fully operational for the first time when Leeds beat West Ham 1-0 with a Gary Speed goal on 17 August 1993.

The final phase of making Elland Road all-seater began in summer 1994 when seats were installed in the Geldard End Kop at a cost of £1.1 million – around £400,000 coming from the Football Trust. Fans stood on the Kop for the last time on 3 May 1994 to witness a 2-2 draw with Sheffield Wednesday but late the following season it was renamed the Revie Stand and opened by Elsie Revie, widow of the late Don Revie.

The Leeds board had promised to make Elland Road one of the finest stadiums in the country and had delivered the goods.

When England was allocated the 1996 European Championships, Elland Road was named as one of the host grounds after rigorous inspections by UEFA officials.

As a trial run, England played a full international against Sweden at Elland Road on 8 June 1995 and 32,008 fans saw England hit back with two late goals to force a 3-3 draw. It was the first full England international held in England outside Wembley since a 1-1 draw with Poland at Goodison Park on 5 January 1966.

No Leeds player appeared but Harrogate-born John Scales who was a United junior under Eddie Gray came on as a substitute.

Two months earlier, Elland Road had staged its eighth FA Cup semi-final when Everton beat Tottenham 4-1 in front of a 38,226 crowd which paid record ground receipts of just over £1 million. In Group 'B' of the 1996 European championships, Elland Road staged the Spain v Bulgaria, France v Spain and Romania v Spain games.

Major Games Played at Elland Road

Full International
8 June 1995

England 3 Sweden 3
Sheringham, Platt, Anderton *Mild 2, K.Andersson*

England: T.Flowers (Blackburn Rovers), W.Barton (Newcastle United), G.Le Saux (Blackburn Rovers), D.Platt (Sampdoria), C.Cooper (Nottingham Forest), G.Pallister (Manchester United – sub J.Scales, Liverpool), D.Anderton (Tottenham Hotspur), P.Beardsley (Newcastle United – sub N.Barmby, Tottenham Hotspur), A.Shearer (Blackburn Rovers), J.Barnes (Liverpool – sub P.Gascoigne, Lazio), E.Sheringham (Tottenham Hotspur).
Sweden: T.Ravelli (IFK Gothenburg), G.Sundgren (AIK Stockholm), P.Kamark (IFK Gothenburg), N.Alexandersson (Halmstads), T.Lucic (Vastra Frolunda), J.Bjorkland (IFK Gothenburg), H.Mild (Servette), M.Erlingmark (IFK Gothenburg – sub O.Andersson, AIK Stockholm), N.Gudmundsson (IFK Gothenburg), K.Andersson (SM Caen – sub D.Lidman, AIK Stockholm), H.Larsson (Feynoord).
Attendance: 32,008 **Referee:** L.W.Mottram (Scotland)

European Championship Group 'B'
9 June 1996

Spain 1 Bulgaria 1
Alfonso *Stoitchkov (pen)*

Spain: A.Zubizarretta (Valencia), A.Belsue (Real Zaragosa), Aberlardo (Barcelona), Sergi (Barcelona), J.P Caminero (Atlético Madrid – sub Donato, Deportivo La Coruna), G.Amor (Barcelona – sub Alfonso, Real Betis), F.R.Hierro (Real Madrid), Luis Enrique (Real Madrid), J.Guerrero (Athletic Bilbao – sub J.E.Amavista Atlético Madrid), J.A.Pizzi (CD Tenerife).
Bulgaria: B.Mihailov (Reading), R.Kischischev (Neftochimik Burgas), P.Hubchev (SV Hamburg), T.Ivanov (Rapid Vienna), I.Kiriakov (Aberdeen – sub T.Tzvetanov, WaldhofMannheim), Y.Letchkov (SV Hamburg), Z.Yankov (KFC Uerdingen), K.Balakov (VfB Stuttgart), E.Kostandinov (Bayern Munich – sub I.Iordanov, Sporting Lisbon), H.Stoitchkov (Parma), L.Penev (Atlético Madrid - sub D.Borimov, 1860 Munich).
Attendance: 24,006 **Referee:** P.Ceccsarini (Italy)

---

15 June 1996

France 1 Spain 1
Djorkaeff *Caminero*

France: B.Lama (Paris St Germain), J.Angloma (Torino – sub A.Roche, Paris St Germain), L.Blanc (Auxerre), M.Desailly (AC Milan), B.Lizarazu (Bordeaux), C.Karembeu (Sampdoria), D.Deschamps (Juventus), V.Guerin (Paris St Germain – sub L.Thuram, Monaco), Y.Djorkaeff (Paris St Germain), Z.Zidane (Bordeaux), P.Loko (Paris St Germain – sub C.Dugarry, Bordeaux).
Spain: A.Zubizaretta (Valencia), J.Otero (Valencia – sub F.N.Kiko, Atlético Madrid), J.M.Lopez (Atlético Madrid), Aberlardo (Barcelona), Sergi (Barcelona), R.Alkorta (Real Madrid), F.R.Hierro (Real Madrid), J.E.Amavisca (Real Madrid), Luis Enrique (Real Madrid – sub J.Manjarin, Deportivo La Coruna), J.P.Caminero (Atlético Madrid), Alfonso (Real Betis – sub J.Salinas).
Attendance: 35,626 **Referee:** V.Zhuk (Bulgaria)

---

18 June 1996

Romania 1 Spain 2
Radiciou *Manjarin, Amor*

Romania: F.Prunea (Dinamo Bucharest), A.Dobos (Steaua Bucharest), D.Prodan (Steaua Bucharest – sub I.Lupescu, Bayer Leverkusen), T.Selymes (Cercle Bruges), D.Petescu (Chelsea), O.Stinga (UD Salamanca), G.Popescu (Barcelona), G.Hagi (Barcelona), C.Galaca (Steaua Bucharest), F.Raducioiu (Espanyol – sub I.Vladoiu, Steaua Bucharest), A.Ilie (Teaua Bucharest – sub D.Munteanu, Koln).
Spain: A.Zubizerreta (Valencia), J.M.Lopez (Atlético Madrid), Abelardo (Barcelona – sub G.Amor, Barcelona), R.Alkorta (Real Madrid), Sergi (Barcelona), M.Nadel (Barcelona), F.R.Hierro (Real Madrid), J.Manjarin (Deportivo La Coruna), F.N.Kiko (Atlético Madrid), J.E.Amavisca (Real Madrid) – sub J.Guerrero (Athletic Bilbao), J.A.Pizzi (CD Tenerife – sub Alfonso, Real Betis).
Attendance: 32,719 **Referee:** C.Cakar (Turkey)

England Trials
22 January 1906

The North 0 The South 2
Day, Woodward

The North: A.C.Robinson (Birmingham), R.Crompton (Blackburn Rovers), S.Rodway (Preston North End), B.Warren (Derby County), C.C.K.Veitch (Newcastle United), J.Bradley (Liverpool), R.Bond (Preston North End), A.Common (Middlesbrough), A.S.Brown (Sheffield United), J.W.Bache (Aston Villa), A.A.Gosnell (Newcastle United).
The South: J.Ashcroft (Woolwich Arsenal), A.G.Cross (Woolwich Arsenal), J.Riley (Brentford), A.Collins (Fulham), W.Bull (Tottenham Hotspur), A.E.Houlker (Southampton),

G.C.Vassall (Old Carthusians), S.H.Day (Old Malvernians), V.J.Woodward (Tottenham Hotspur), S.S.Harris (Old Westminsters), E.D.G.Wright (Cambridge University).
Attendance: 7,000 **Referee:** E.Case (Birkenhead)

19 February 1923
England v The North
Cancelled because of snow

21 January 1924
The North 5 The South 1
Bradford 2, Stephenson, Jack, Seymour *Haines*

The North: W.R.Sewell (Blackburn Rovers), W.Cresswell (Sunderland), S.J.Wadsworth (Huddersfield Town), F.W.Kean (Sheffield Wednesday), J.Seddon (Bolton Wanderers), P.Barton (Birmingham), S.Chedgzoy (Everton), D.B.N.Jack (Bolton Wanderers), J.A.Bradford (Birmingham), C.Stephenson (Huddersfield Town), G.S.Seymour (Newcastle United).
The South: B.Howard Baker (Corinthians), T.R.Parker (Southampton), A.G.Bower (Corinthians), B.Smith (Tottenham Hotspur), C.T.Ashton (Corinthians), T.Meehan (Chelsea), Dr J.A. Paterson (Arsenal), S.G.J.Earle (Clapton), W.P.Haines (Portsmouth), J.E.Elkes (Tottenham Hotspur), K.E.Hegan (Corinthians).
Attendance: 6,000 **Referee:** E.Farrar (Leeds)

Under 23 International
9 November 1961

England 7 Israel 1
Byrne 2, F.Hill 2, Farmer, S.Hill, Harris *Levy*

England: G.West (Blackpool), A.Kirkup (West Ham United), B.Jones (Middlesbrough), R.F.C.Moore (West Ham United), B.L.Labone (Everton), A.R.Deakin (Aston Villa), S.Hill (Blackpool), J.J.Byrne (Crystal Palace), T.Farmer (Wolverhampton Wanderers), F.Hill (Bolton Wanderers), G.Harris (Burnley).
Israel: H.Hodorov (sub Nusowski), Aharahov (sub Grundman), Tendler, Peterburg, Levokovitch, Tish, Menchel, Steimach, R.Rosenbaum, S.Levy, Young.
Attendance: 12,419 **Referee:** M.Askenaz (Israel)

7 April 1965
England 0 Czechoslovakia 0

England: W.J.Glazier (Coventry City), L.Badger (Sheffield United), R.A.Thomson (Wolverhampton Wanderers), T.Smith (Liverpool), V.Mobley (Sheffield Wednesday), H.A.Newton (Nottingham Forest), A.G.Murray (Chelsea), M.H.Chivers (Southampton), M.D.Jones (Sheffield United), A.J.Ball (Blackpool), G.Armstrong (Arsenal).
Czechoslovakia: Vencel (Slovan Bratislava), Camarada (Dukla Prague), Taborsky (Sparta CDK Prague), Migas (Dukla Slany), Knesl (Dukla Prague), Hrdlicka (Slovan Bratislava), Vesely (Slavia Prague), Strunc (Sparta Plzn), Gaborik (Slovan Bratislava), Rodr (Dukla Prague), Kabat (Dukla Prague).
Attendance: 8,533 **Referee:** A.Faucheux (France)

Inter-League
9 October 1957
Football League 3 League of Ireland 1
Parry 2, Broadbent *Nolan*

Football League: N.D.Sims (Aston Villa), J.C.Armfield (Blackpool), R.Moran (Liverpool), R.J.Barlow (West Bromwich Albion), J.Charlton (Leeds United), R.S.Pearce (Luton Town), A.Kaye (Barnsley), P.A.Broadbent (Wolverhampton W), R.A. E.Tindall (Chelsea), R.A.Parry (Bolton W), P.J.Hooper (Bristol Rovers).
League of Ireland: J.A.Kelly (Drumcondra), B.Fullam (Drumcondra), R.Nolan (Shamrock Rovers), T.Dunne (St Patrick's Athletic), S.Keogh (Shamrock Rovers), T.Rowe (Drumcondra), S.Pownhall (Drumcondra), N.Peyton (Shamrock Rovers), D.Leahy (Evergreen United), P.Ambrose (Shamrock Rovers), L.Tuohy (Shamrock Rovers).
Attendance: 13,000 **Referee:** J.H.Clough (Bolton)

Amateur Internationals
20 November 1909
England 4 Ireland 4
Jordan 2, Owen, Woodward *Robertson 2, McDonnell, Hooper*

England: R.G.Brener (Darlington), W.S.Corbett (Birmingham), A.E.Scothern (Oxford City), F.Fayers (Watford), F.W.Chapman (South Nottingham), J.E.Olley (Clapton), A.Berry (Fulham), V.J.Woodward (Chelmsford), W.C.Jordan (West Bromwich Albion), A.S.Owen (Leicester Fosse), E.W.Williams (Portsmouth).
Ireland: F.McKee (Cliftonville), P.McCann (Belfast Celtic), P.J.Thunder (Bohemians), J.Wright (Cliftonville), D.Martin (Cliftonville), L.Donnelly (Distillery), J.Wright (Distillery), J.Robertson (Cliftonville), J.McDonnell (Bohemians), Dr W.F.Hooper (Bohemians), F.Thompson (Cliftonville)
Attendance: 8,000 **Referee:** A.A.Jackson (Scotland)

16 March 1929
England 3 Scotland 1
Kail 2, C.Ashton *McLelland*

England: B.Howard Baker (Corinthians), F.J.Gregory (Millwall), E.H.Gates (London Corinthians), C.E.Glenister (Navy), A.H.Chadder (Corinthians), J.G.Knight (Casuals), L.Morrish (Dulwich Hamlet), E.Kail (Dulwich Hamlet), C.T.Ashton (Corinthians), A.G.Doggart (Corinthians), K.E.Hogan (Army).
Scotland: R.L.Small (St Bernmard's), W.O.Walker (Queen's Park), W.Wiseman (Queen's Park), J.McDonald (Queen's Park), R.Gillespie (Queen's Park), W.S.King (Queen's Park), I. McDonald (Murrayfield Amateurs), W.S.Chalmers (Queen's Park), D.McLelland (Queen's Park), J.R.Russell (Edinburgh University), W.G.Nicholson (Queen's Park).
Attendance: 15,571 **Referee:** G.D.Nunnery (Salop)

26 April 1958
England 1 France 1
Bradley *Chistobal (pen)*

England: M.J.Pinner (Pegasus), J.Dougall (Pegasus), J.H.Valentine (Loughborough College), R.Vowells (Corinthian Casuals), S.Prince (Walthamstow Avenue), H.Dodkins (Ilford), W.Bradley (Bishop Auckland), D.Bumpstead (Tooting and Mitcham), G.Mortimore (Woking), G.Hamm (Woking), A.M.Peel (Sheffield University).

France: R.Cesaire (VS Quevilly), B.Rodzik (Stade de Rheims), F.Phillipe (AS Brest), M.Christobal (St Etienne), G.Lelong (VS Quevilly), R.Monnet (Olympique Lyonnaise), R.Hauser (FC Mulhouse), M.Mouchel (AS Cherbourg), J.L.Bettenfield (AAJ Sainte Fountaine), J.Buron (Dieppe), M.Longle (SCO Angers).

Attendance: 6,000 **Referee:** H.Anderson (Denmark)

FA Amateur Cup Final
4 April 1914
Bishop Auckland 1 Northern Nomads 0
Kirby
Bishop Auckland: E.J.North, T.Roe, C.J.Rudd, F.Hopper,

A.M.Spence, T.Maddison, A.Appleby, D.Douglass, F.Kirby, T.Spence, T.Lunson
Northern Nomads: H.Peever, C.Barlow, H.N.Cunliffe, R.Gotobed, T.C.Porter, M.McKinnon, M.D.Davies, H.Douglass, A.Cruse, L.L.Boardman, G.O.Salt.
Attendance: 5,294 **Referee:** A.Warner (Notts)

FA Cup Semi-Finals
26 March 1910
Barnsley 0 Everton 0

Barnsley: F.C.Mearns, R.W.Downs, H.M.Ness, R.Glendenning, T.W.Boyle, G.Utley, W.Bartop, E.Gadsby, G.B.Lilcrop, Tufnell, T.Forman.
Everton: W.Scott, J.S.Maconnachie, R.Clifford, J.W.H.Makepeace, J.Taylor, V.Harris, G.H.Barlow, A.Young, B.C.Freeman, W.White, J.Sharp.
Attendance: 36,000 **Referee:** H.S.Bamlett (Gateshead)

---

22 March 1930
(Replay)
Arsenal 1 Hull City 0
Jack

Hull City attack the Arsenal goal during the FA Cup semi-final replay held at Elland Road in March 1930, when 46,200 spectators saw the Gunners win 1-0.

Arsenal: D.Lewis, T.R.Parker, E.A.Hapgood, A.Baker, W.C. Seddon, C.Jones, J.J.Williams, D.B.N.Jack, J.Lambert, A.James, C.S.Bastin
Hull City: F.W.Gibson, G.Goldsmith, M.Bell, T.Bleakley, J.A.Childs, A.W.Gowdy, P.Cartwright, R.W.Starling, B.R.Mills, J.Howieson, D.Duncan.
Attendance: 46,200 **Referee:** A.H.Kingscott (Long Eaton)

---

14 March 1931
Birmingham 2 Sunderland 0
Curtis 2

Birmingham: H.E.Hibbs, G.M.Liddell, E.Barkas, J.A.Cringan, G.R.Morrall, A.J.Leslie, G.R.Briggs, J.A.Crosbie, J.Bradford, J.Firth, E.R.Curtis.
Sunderland: R.Middleton, W.Murray, H.V.Shaw, A.G.Hastings, J.McDougall, A.Andrews, W.Eden, J.Devine, R.Gurney, J.Leonard, J.Connor.
Attendance: 43,572 **Referee:** A.E.Fogg (Bolton)

---

16 March 1935
West Bromwich Albion 1 Bolton Wanderers 1
W.G.Richardson *Walton*

West Bromwich Albion: H.F.Pearson, G.E.Shaw, H.F.Trentham, J.P.Murphy, W.Richardson, J.Edwards, A.R.Gale, J.H.Carter, W.G.Richardson, E.A.Sandford, W.E.Boyes.
Bolton Wanderers: R.Jones, R.Smith, A.E.Finney, H.A.Goslin, J.E.Atkinson, G.Taylor, G.T.Taylor, G.R.Eastham, G.Walton, R.W.Westwood, W.L.Cook.
Attendance: 49,605 **Referee:** R.Bowie (Northumberland)

---

29 March 1947
Charlton Athletic 4 Newcastle United 0
Dawson, Welsh 2, Hurst

Charlton Athletic: S.Bartram, E.J.Croker, J.T.T.Shreeve, W.H.Johnson, H.J.Phipps, C.Revell, G.Hurst, T.Dawson, W. Robinson, D.Welsh, C.Duffy.
Newcastle United: T.A.Swinburne, R.G.Cowell, R.Corbett, J.Harvey, F.Brennan, J.D.Wright, J.E.T.Milburn, R.T.F.Bentley, G.C.Stobbart, L.F.Shackleton, T.U.Pearson.
Attendance: 47,978

---

2 April 1952
Newcastle United 2 Blackburn Rovers 1
G.Robledo, Mitchell (pen) *Crossan*

Newcastle United: R.C.Simpson, G.G.Cowell, A.McMichael, J.Harvey, F.Brennan, E.O.Robledo, T.J.Walker, W.J.Foulkes, J.E.T.Milburn, G.O.Robledo, R.C.Mitchell
Blackburn Rovers: R.Elvey, D.Gray, W.Eckersley, J.J.Campbell, W.M.Kelly, R.Clayton, A.Glover, E.Crossan, E.Quigley, A.Nightingale, J.E.Whaton.
Attendance: 54,066 Referee: R.J.Leafe (Nottingham)

---

18 March 1961
Sheffield United 0 Leicester City 0

Sheffield United: A.Hodgkinson, G.C.Colwell, G.L.Shaw, B.Richardson, J.Shaw, G.T.Summers, W.Hodgson, W.Russell, D.J.Pace, K.F.Kettleborough, R.Simpson.
Leicester City: G.Banks, L.Chalmes, R.Norman, F.McLintock, J.A.King, C.H.Appleton, H.Riley, J.Walsh, K.Leek, K.Keymorth, G.F.Wills.
Attendance: 52,095 **Referee:** J.Finney (Hereford)

---

16 April 1980
Replay
Everton 1 West Ham United 2
Latchford *Devonshire, Lampard*
(after extra time)

Everton: M.J.Hodge, J.Gidman, J.A.Bailey, W.Wright, M.Lyons, K.Ratcliffe, A.E.King (sub I.Varadi), P.R.Eastoe, R.D.Latchford, R.A.Hartford, T.W.Ross.
West Ham United: P.Parkes, F.R.G.Lampard, P.Brush, R.S.M.Stewart, W.A.Bonds, A.E.Devonshire, P.K.Allen, S.J. Pearson, D.Cross, T.D.Brooking, G.A.Pike.
Attendance: 40,720 **Referee:** C.N.Seel (Carlisle)

---

9 April 1995
Everton 4 Tottenham Hotspur 1
Jackson, Stuart, Amokachi 2 *Klinsmann (pen)*

Everton: N.Southall, M.A.Jackson, G.I.Ablett, J.S.Parkinson, D.D.Watson, D.G.Unsworth, A.Limpar (sub D.Amokachi), B. Horne, G.C.Stuart, P.D.Rideout (sub D.Ferguson), A.G. Hinchliffe.
Tottenham Hotspur: I.Walker, D.B.Austin, S.Nethercott (sub A.W.Rosenthal), G.Popescu, C.Calderwood, G.V.Mabbutt, D.R.Anderton, N.Barmby, J.Klinsmann, E.P.Sheringham, D.Howells.
Attendance: 38,226 **Referee:** R.Hart (Darlington)

Wartime Representative Games
13 December 1941
FA XI 2 RAF 2
D.Compton (pen), Rowley *Dodds, Smith*

FA XI: R.T.Hesford (Huddersfield Town), L.Goldberg (Leeds United), A.Beattie (Preston North End), C.K.Willingham (Huddersfield Town), A.Young (Huddersfield Town), J.Mercer (Everton), R.J.E.Birkett (Newcastle United), W.J.Mannion (Middlesbrough), J.F.Rowley (Manchester United), J.Hagan (Sheffield United), D.C.S.Compton (Arsenal).
RAF: G.W.Marks (Arsenal), H.G.Turner (Charlton), E.A.Hapgood (Arsenal), F.C.Soo (Chelsea), T.G.Jones (Everton), G.D.Paterson (Glasgow Celtic), A.J.Kirchen (Arsenal), J.T.Smith (Crystal Palace), J.Dodds (Blackpool), L.Jones (Arsenal), W.H.Wrigglesworth (Manchester United).
Attendance: 13,000. Match in aid of RAF Benevolent Fund

---

21 February 1942
Northern Command 1 Southern Command 1
Robinson *Hamilton*

Northern Command: J.D.Harkess (Heart of Midlothian), E.Westwood (Manchester City), A.Beattie (Preston North End), K.Kirton (Stoke City), T.Holley (Leeds United), J.S.McInnes (Liverpool), A.Powell (Leeds United), J.Balmer (Liverpool), F.C.Steele (Stoke City), S.Robinson (Sheffield Wednesday), W.E.Boyes (Everton).
Southern Command: J.Lynch (Dundee), J.Carabine (Third Lanark), A.Winning (Clyde), M.Busby (Liverpool), A.Collier (Third Lanark), H.A.Betmead (Grimsby Town), R.Campbell (Falkirk), T.Walker (Heart of Midlothian), G.Hamilton (Heart of Midlothian), A.McCall (Aberdeen), J.Johnston (Motherwell).
Attendance: 8,500 In aid of Army Welfare Funds

---

26 December 1942
Army 3 RAF 1
Wescott 2, Hagan *Dodds*

Army: F.V.Swift (Manchester City), J.Carabine (Third Lanark), L.H.Compton (Arsenal), C.S.Britton (Everton), S.Cullis (Wolverhampton Wanderers), J.Mercer (Everton), R.J.E.Birkett (Newcastle United), J.Hagan (Sheffield United), D.Westcott (Wolverhampton Wanderers), G.H.Bremner (Arsenal), D.C.S.Compton (Arsenal).
RAF: G.W.Marks (Arsenal), R.Shankly (Preston North End), W.M.Hughes (Birmingham), F.C.Soo (Preston North End), B.Joy (Arsenal), G.D.Paterson (Celtic), S.Matthews (Stoke City), H.S.Carter (Sunderland), J.Dodds (Blackpool), R.A.J.Brown (Charlton Athletic), A.J.Kirchen (Arsenal).
Attendance: 20,000 **Referee:** H.Berry (Huddersfield)

Major Rugby League Games at Elland Road

Test Matches

9 November 1985	Great Britain	6	New Zealand	6	Att: 22,209
8 November 1986	Great Britain	4	Australia	34	Att: 30,808
10 November 1990	Great Britain	0	Australia	14	Att: 32,500
20 November 1994	Great Britain	4	Australia	23	Att: 39,468

Challenge Cup Final (Replay)

19 May 1982	Hull	18	Widnes	9	Att: 41,171

Challenge Cup semi-finals

2 April 1983	Hull	11	Castleford	7	Att: 26,031
24 March 1984	Wigan	14	York	8	Att: 17,156
23 March 1985	Wigan	18	Hull KR	11	Att: 19,275
29 March 1986	Hull KR	24	Leeds	24	Att: 23,866
3 April 1986 (R)	Hull KR	17	Leeds	0	Att: 32,485
1988 (R)	Halifax	4	Leeds	3	Att: 25,117
27 March 1993	Wigan	15	Bradford N	6	Att: 20,085
1 April 1995	Leeds	39	Featherstone	22	Att: 21,485

Championship Final

30 April 1938	Hunslet	8	Leeds	2	Att: 54,112

Premiership Final

11 May 1985	St Helens	36	Hull KR	16	Att: 15,518
18 May 1986	Warrington	38	Halifax	0	Att: 13,683

John Player/Regal Trophy Final

22 January 1983	Leeds	5	Wigan	15	Att: 19,553
11 January 1986	Wigan	11	Hull KR	8	Att: 17,573
23 January 1993	Wigan	15	Bradford	8	Att: 13,221

Major Rugby Union Games at Elland Road

Representative Match

10 November 1992	The North	3	South Africa	19	Att: 14,471

Attendance Figures at Elland Road

Seasonal League Attendance Figures

Leeds City

Year	Aggregate	Highest	Lowest	Average	Div	Pos
1905-06 e	189,585	22,000	2,000	9,978	2	6th
1906-07	192,500	20,000	3,000	10,131	2	10th
1907-08	213,000	35,000	4,000	11,210	2	12th
1908-09	215,000	20,000	4,500	11,513	2	12th
1909-10	133,500	12,000	2,000	7,026	2	17th
1910-11	179,200	18,000	5,000	9,431	2	11th
1911-12	146,500	15,000	3,000	7,710	2	19th
1912-13	254,000	20,000	6,000	13,368	2	6th
1913-14	305,000	30,000	8,000	16,052	2	4th
1914-15	130,000	12,000	4,000	6,842	2	15th

Leeds United

Year	Aggregate	Highest	Lowest	Average	Div	Pos
1920-21 a	339,958	25,000	10,000	16,188	2	14th
1921-22	286,540	20,540	5,000	13,644	2	8th
1922-23	274,000	27,000	4,000	13,047	2	7th
1923-24	317,639	25,000	8,000	15,125	2	1st
1924-25	483,022	41,800	15,000	23,001	1	18th
1925-26	449,029	29,501	12,186	21,382	1	19th
1926-27	433,980	48,590	10,997	20,666	1	21st
1927-28	458,536	48,470	12,752	21,835	2	2nd
1928-29	470,392	32,866	8,151	22,399	1	13th
1929-30	418,594	40,789	3,950	19,933	1	5th
1930-31	281,455	30,625	5,572	13,402	1	21st
1931-32	295,655	34,005	8,388	14,078	2	2nd
1932-33	359,381	56,796	7,971	17,113	1	8th
1933-34	323,988	33,192	6,092	15,428	1	9th
1934-35	313,170	29,477	7,408	14,912	1	18th
1935-36	412,562	38,733	10,509	19,645	1	11th
1936-37	382,337	30,647	11,752	18,220	1	19th
1937-38	446,379	37,020	10,512	21,256	1	9th
1938-39	405,480	34,158	12,006	19,308	1	13th
1946-47	546,830	37,884	14,097	26,039	1	22nd
1947-48	598,951	37,135	17,573	28,520	2	18th
1948-49	615,333	42,053	19,945	29,301	2	15th
1949-50	634,258	50,476	8,913	30,202	2	5th
1950-51	551,211	42,114	11,213	26,252	2	5th
1951-52	510,168	47,985	12,860	24,293	2	6th
1952-53	429,071	39,858	10,644	20,431	2	10th
1953-54	458,028	27,571	13,930	21,810	2	10th
1954-55	449,134	39,208	8,831	21,387	2	4th
1955-56	513,350	49,274	12,348	24,445	2	2nd
1956-57	585,616	47,216	20,905	32,648	1	8th
1957-58	523,330	39,401	17,600	24,920	1	17th
1958-59	523,015	48,574	11,257	24,905	1	15th
1959-60	459,413	36,037	8,557	21,876	1	21st
1960-61	282,235	22,146	6,975	13,439	2	14th
1961-62	285,479	21,482	7,967	13,594	2	19th
1962-63	424,511	28,501	11,314	20,214	2	5th
1963-64	628,963	41,167	21,108	29,950	2	1st
1964-65	787,164	52,368	27,339	37,484	1	2nd
1965-66	751,232	49,762	25,200	35,772	1	2nd
1966-67	739,553	45,092	23,052	35,216	1	4th
1967-68	771,399	51,818	25,760	36,733	1	4th
1968-69	773,201	48,145	24,229	36,819	1	1st
1969-70	726,745	46,770	22,932	34,606	1	2nd
1970-71	828,927	50,190	29,675	39,472	1	2nd
1971-72 b	665,853	46,565	30,942	39,167	1	2nd
1972-73 a	748,617	46,468	25,008	35,639	1	3rd
1973-74	812,739	47,058	26,778	38,701	1	1st
1974-75	730,834	50,084	25,832	34,801	1	9th
1975-76	661,732	45,139	22,799	31,511	1	5th
1976-77	641,185	48,708	16,891	30,056	1	10th
1977-78	610,737	45,560	16,531	29,082	1	9th
1978-79	580,236	41,324	20,121	27,630	1	5th
1979-80	482,847	39,779	15,541	22,922	1	11th
1980-81	448,665	39,206	14,333	21,364	1	9th
1981-82	464,558	33,689	16,385	22,121	1	20th
1982-83	336,184	26,570	8,741	16,008	2	8th
1983-84	325,560	30,806	8,278	15,502	2	10th
1984-85	318,552	25,547	10,644	15,171	2	7th
1985-86	278,575	21,104	9,641	13,265	2	14th
1986-87	369,823	24,839	12,014	17,610	2	4th
1987-88 c	446,253	36,004	13,217	20,284	2	7th
1988-89 d	501,567	33,325	13,280	21,807	2	10th
1989-90	648,380	32,727	21,694	28,190	2	1st
1990-91 e	550,265	31,460	25,684	28,961	1	4th
1991-92 a	619,349	32,673	26,582	29,493	1	1st
1992-93	587,729	34,166	25,797	27,897	Prem	17th
1993-94	724,594	41,127	28,717	34,504	Prem	5th
1994-95	691,729	39,426	27,246	32,939	Prem	5th
1995-96 e	619,942	39,801	26,077	32,629	Prem	13th

Note: a = 21matches
b = 17matches (4 games played at other venues in 1971-72 – 83,123 total)
c = 22 matches
d = 23 matches
e = 19 matches
f = 18 matches
g = 11 matches

Leeds City's four home games in 1919-20 (40,000 total) and Leeds United's 2 games in 1939-40 (21,828 total), have been excluded. The two Play-off matches (60,867 total) in 1986-87 have also been excluded.

Unofficial Seasons
(Leeds City in World War 1 and Leeds United in World War 2)

Year	Aggregate	Highest	Lowest	Average	Division	Pos
1915-16 f	87,000	10,000	1,000	4,833	Mid.Sect P & S	10/1st
1916-17	83,000	10,000	2,000	4,611	Mid.Sect P & S	1/7th
1917-18	95,000	15,000	1,000	5,278	Mid.Sect P & S	1/5th
1918-19	112,500	11,000	3,000	6,250	Mid.Sect P & S	4/3rd
1939-40 g	43,765	9,000	200	3,979	North East	5th
1940-41 b	57,900	5,000	1,500	3,406	North Region	15th
1941-42 f	51,700	6,000	1,500	2,872	Northern Sects.	26/NQ
1942-43 b	46,500	4,000	1,000	2,735	Northern Sects.	43/47
1943-44	98,700	15,000	2,000	5,806	Northern Sects.	27/35
1944-45 a	158,260	15,000	2,000	7,536	Northern Sects.	22/32
1945-46	252,284	22,219	7,339	12,014	Northern Sects.	22nd

Championship Play-off with Stoke included in 1917-18 figures.
League War Cup games in 1939-40 and 1940-41 included in figures for these seasons.

Aggregate League Attendance Figures for Elland Road

	Competition	Aggregate	Highest	Lowest	Average	Played
United	League (1920-96)	35,517,719	56,796	3,950	24,563	1,446
United	1939-40 Season	21,828				2
United	1986-87 Play Offs	60,867				2
United	(WW2)	709,109	22,219	200	5,812	122
Totals		**36,309,523**	**56,796**	**200**	**23,068**	**1,574**
City	League (1905-19)	1,958,285	35,000	2,000	10,307	190
City	(WW1)	377,500	15,000	1,000	5,243	72

Aggregate Cup Attendance Figures for Elland Road

	Competition	Aggregate	Highest	Lowest	Average	Played
United	FA Cup	3,005,331	57,892	1,500	33,392	90
United	League Cup	608,469	43,222	4,517	19,628	31
United	Full Members' Cup	56,712	13,387	2,274	6,301	9
United	Charity Shield	39,835				1
United	European Cup	344,816	50,393	20,012	34,482	10
United	Cup-winners' Cup	107,049	32,051	22,411	26,762	4
United	UEFA/Fairs Cup	1,037,875	50,498	13,682	29,654	35
Totals		**5,200,087**	**57,892**	**1,500**	**28,889**	**180**
City	FA Cup	173,950	31,471	1,000	14,496	12

NB Including Preliminary Round FA Cup-ties in 1904-05, 1905-06 and 1920-21.

Leeds Chairmen Etc.

UNITED'S first chairman, **Joe Henry junior**, was also the one who had the shortest reign in the club's history.

His father Joe Henry, of the well-known Holbeck engineering firm, had fought hard to save the old Leeds City club in his capacity as Lord Mayor of Leeds (See The Leeds City Scandal). Joe Henry junior was equally anxious to keep League football alive and kicking in Leeds and was a key figure at the public meeting on Friday, 17 October 1919, which agreed to form Leeds United out of the remnants of the disgraced Leeds City club.

The following day, Joe Henry junior, a keen sponsor of Leeds City was appointed United's chairman.

However, within a few weeks, West Yorkshire industrialist **Hilton Crowther** had switched his interests from neighbouring Huddersfield Town to the new club at Elland Road and in December 1919 was installed as United's new chairman.

Crowther was a director of Crowther Bros, a Milnsbridge woollen manufacturer and first became involved in football when he was asked by Huddersfield Town representatives in 1909 to provide financial support in Town's bid for election to the Football League.

Crowther and his brothers, Leonard, Stoner and Edgar, the latter a county golfer, all joined the Huddersfield board and made generous loans and donations to the Terriers.

But Hilton Crowther, dissatisfied with the lack of public support for Huddersfield football, switched his allegiance to Leeds United, who were glad to accept his promise of financial security.

Crowther was genuinely interested in expanding soccer in the region and in 1923 founded the Yorkshire Midweek League, being its president until it was disbanded in 1949.

The colourful Crowther, who was married to Mona Vivian, a London revue star of the 1920s, was the financial platform on which Leeds United were built. One examination of the club's accounts showed that Crowther had invested £54,000 in United – a huge sum in those days. In 1924 Crowther indicated that he wanted to be bought out by the club and stepped down as chairman. He remained on the Leeds board until his death in Blackpool on 23 March 1957. His 49 years as a director at both Leeds and Huddersfield, was only surpassed by Dick Parker, who, ironically, had joined the Huddersfield Town board during the turmoils of 1919 and remained on it until his death in 1974.

Crowther's replacement was **Sir Albert Braithwaite**, who went on to make a name for himself in politics.

A former pupil of Woodhouse Grove School, Bradford, and a graduate of Leeds University, he enjoyed a distinguished Army career with the West Yorkshire Regiment and Yorkshire Hussars, reaching the rank of major.

An engineer, he was director of Sir Lindsay Parkinson and Co Ltd and remained chairman of United until 1931, despite entering politics midway through his chairmanship. He was elected MP for the Buckrose Division of the East Riding of Yorkshire in 1926, serving his constituents until 1945 – the same year in which he was knighted. He was elected MP for West Harrow in April 1951 and the political world was stunned in October 1959 when he committed suicide in London, aged 66.

Towards the end of his chairmanship, Sir Albert found less and less time to devote to United's affairs. He often had to miss meetings and in his absence **Eric Clarke** took the chair.

It was fitting that Clarke, a Leeds City Alderman and noted solicitor, should be appointed United's new chairman in August 1931. He had joined the board in 1925, spent three years as chairman of the finance committee and was regarded as the most experienced man for the job.

Under Clarke's stewardship, United regained their place in Division One, but after only two years he stepped down in July 1933. The mantle of chairman was taken on by another Leeds City Alderman and solicitor, **Alf Masser**.

He was an original shareholder of the Leeds City club and had a spell as its vice-chairman. He left City during World War One, but after its demise returned to help get Leeds United off the ground, chairing the public meeting in Salem Hall the day after Leeds City's players were auctioned off.

Masser, a skilful advocate, successfully put the case for United's admission to the League to the Football League administrators in May 1920, but later stood down from the board, chiefly to concentrate on his legal business and his work for Leeds City Council.

A chairman of the Council's Parks Committee, Masser was instrumental in establishing municipal golf courses in the city and the introduction of Sunday games of the city's parks. He gave the City Council 40 years unbroken service.

The son of a commercial traveller, he was educated at Churwell College, Yorkshire College and Leeds University. A keen sportsman, he was a founder of Headingley Rugby Club, serving as both captain and secretary, and was secretary of Leeds Springfield Cricket Club. Masser was United's chairman between 1934 and 1937 and his sphere of influence went beyond Elland Road. He was a key figure in the Football League negotiations which obtained money for the game from the Football Pools companies in the 1930s. He also narrowly missed becoming the first United chairman to serve on the Football League Management Committee, just failing in elections in 1937 and 1939.

Masser made an enormous contribution to United's history and when he died, in October 1950, aged 73, he was still serving on the United board.

Former Football League referee **Ernest Pullan** was elected chairman in succession to Masser on 29 July 1937. He had been one of United's most active directors on the playing front and had actually acted as team manager for some weeks when Dick Ray quit in March 1935. Pullan had been chairman of United's finance committee, but as chairman during World War Two and the 1946-47 relegation season, he was in charge during difficult times for the club.

When Pullan resigned in 1948 he was succeeded by **Sam Bolton**, a motor haulage contractor who had gone a long way on the road to success.

Born and bred in Leeds, he was educated at Hunslet and joined Thomas Spence Ltd, a haulage company, and went on to become its managing director. During World War One he served with the Coldstream Guards before joining the Royal Flying Corps.

A football fanatic, he played for Rothwell White Rose in the Leeds League and watched Leeds City play as a 'bob-side' youngster and went on to have trials with them.

Bolton rose from United fan to United director in 1945, becoming chairman three years later. He remained as chairman for 14 years until December 1961, although he remained on the board until his death, at the age of 82 on 18 December 1976 when he was the club's vice-chairman.

Under his chairmanship he experienced the joys of promotion, the disappointment of relegation, the despairs of the 1957 West Stand fire and the sale of John Charles to Juventus for the then British record of £65,000. Bolton was acknowledged as one of the hardest working chairmen in the game. An FA Council life member, he was a member of the Football League Management Committee (1964-75), an England Under-23 selector and chairman of the FA Cup Committee being the man who pulled the numbered balls out of the famous velvet bag to make the FA Cup draw. His devotion to football did not prevent him from serving the people of Leeds in his capacity of City Councillor. He was the deputy Lord Mayor of Leeds in 1965-66 and in 1970 was appointed an honorary Alderman. He also found time for a regular round of golf and was a member of the South Leeds and Moortown Golf Clubs.

One of the men whom Bolton invited to join the board, in 1955, **Harry Reynolds**, took over the helm on 11 December 1961.

A typical Tyke, he was a self-made millionaire, who was managing director of H.L.Reynolds Engineers and Steel Erectors. He did much to help United build into a soccer superpower by persuading the board to appoint Don Revie as manager.

Revie had asked Reynolds to support his application for the vacant managerial job at Bournemouth. As Reynolds wrote down Revie's managerial virtues, he suddenly realised that Revie could do the job for Leeds, tore up his letter of support and got the rest of the United's directors to agree to Revie's appointment.

Later that year Reynolds became the new United chairman and soon pulled United's finances round from debts of £150,000 to a profit of £138,000 by the time he resigned in August 1967 because of ill health.

It was that sort of business acumen which marked Reynolds as a highly successful industrialist. His rise to the top of the financial ladder was rapid.

The son of Holbeck working-class parents, he worked as a flour boy with Leeds Co-op, a railway cleaner and a fireman before founding a steel stock holding company in Leeds and turning to metal dealing.

Rumoured to be a millionaire in the late 1950s, he lived at Hough Top, Bramley, went hunting with the Bramham Moor Hunt, played polo and became a familiar face at the captain's table on the liners Queen Mary and Queen Elizabeth.

His work for United took him to less glamorous places and would regularly visit tenement flats in Glasgow with Revie to recruit up-and-coming stars for Leeds.

The work he did for United saw him appointed as a life vice-president after his resignation. Suffering from arthritis, he travelled to London to see United win their first major trophy, the Football League Cup, in March 1968, but was unable to take his seat despite travelling by rail in a wheelchair and carrying crutches. Reynolds died in September 1974.

His successor, **Albert Morris**, had been a director since November 1961. Prior to becoming chairman in 1967 he had been the club's finance director for three years where his experience in business proved vital.

A director of Morris Wallpapers Ltd, he was the son of Alderman Hyman Morris, Lord Mayor of Leeds in 1941-42. The family were one of the most well-known Jewish families in Leeds and Albert Morris was president of the Leeds Jewish Board of Guardians and a founder member and former treasurer of the Leeds Jewish Housing Association.

Apart from his involvement with United he was a member of Yorkshire Amateurs FC and a former captain of Moor Allerton Golf Club, close to his home in Harrogate Road.

He died on 7 April 1968 in Leeds General Infirmary, only four weeks after United beat Arsenal 1-0 at Wembley to lift the Football League Cup.

After Morris' death, the club's vice-chairman **Percy Woodward** became the new chairman and it was during his reign at the top that United landed their first Division One championship. Woodward, who had supported United as a youngster from the terraces, was vice-president of Leeds Wanderers before joining the United board in 1946 with Harold Marjason. Within a year Woodward, who ran P.A.Woodward & Son Ltd, Packing Case Merchants & Manufacturers in Hillidge Road, Leeds 10, was appointed vice-chairman – a position he held for 20 years until his elevation to chairman.

Woodward's daughter, Jacqueline, married United reserve player Terry Duffy and his son, Brian, was also a part-time professional on United's books after the war. Brian Woodward later played first-team football at Hereford United and York City and from 1976 was also a United director until he resigned in protest over the sacking of manager Eddie Gray in October 1985.

Woodward senior was a well-known Leeds City councillor, serving the Beeston Ward for 15 years and was Lord Mayor of Leeds in 1961. He was chairman of South Leeds Conservative Association and president of West Hunslet Conservative Club for many years.

He remained as United's chairman until 1972 when he was suceeded by **Manny Cussins**, but continued as vice-chairman until the 1976 close season.

Cussins was named as chairman on 17 May 1972 and was in the boardroom hot-seat during a period of immense change at the club.

When he was appointed he announced £500,000 improvements to the ground and in his first full season Leeds won the Division One championship. But after the departure of Revie to take up the England job, Cussins was a central figure in the 44-day appointment and sacking of Brian Clough when he sided with the disgruntled players.

Jimmy Armfield, Jock Stein, Jimmy Adamson and Allan Clarke all came and went, but they could not add to United's collection of silverware and the club dropped back into Division Two and much of Cussins' time was spent trying to combat United's growing hooliganism problem. Cussins, a millionaire, found that restoring United to former glories was no easy task, but it was not for the want of trying, something which was apparent throughout his life.

A native of Hull, his appetite for work and financial success began when he was 13, pushing a handcart around to collect furniture to launch a new business. It certainly paid off. In 1954 he sold the Cussins Group for £1 million and began the John Peters chain of furniture shops which had expanded to over 100 retail outlets, a dozen clothing factories and a building business by 1975.

The John Peters Group changed its name to Waring and Gillow with Cussins remaining at the helm. He also was the head of Arncliffe Holdings, a residential property group he set up in 1971.

Cussins himself never admitted to being a rich man. "Rich men do not work," he said, adding that retirement only turned men into cabbages.

He was co-opted on to the board at Elland Road in November 1961 at the same time as Albert Morris. He was among United's most long-serving directors when he became chairman, holding the post until December 1983 when he stepped down in favour of relative newcomer London-born **Leslie Silver**, originally an Arsenal fan after being mesmerised by Alex James, watching at his first Highbury match in 1934 at the age of nine.

Cussins remained vice-chairman until his death in London on 5 October 1987, aged 82. Silver, like Cussins, was a highly successful businessman. He came out of the RAF as a warrant officer in 1947 and launched a paint firm called Kalon Paints with other members of his family, with £1,000 from his his wartime gratuity and other loans and developed it into a thriving business.

Silver became chairman of Silver Paint and Lacquer (Holdings) Ltd and his firm's Home Charm Paint became one of Britain's best-known names. A former president of the Oil and Colour Chemists' Association, he was awarded the OBE in June 1982 for services to export.

His company was highly regarded on the stockmarket and in 1991 when he wanted to sell 18.5 per cent of the shares he had no difficulty finding buyers. The sale brought him nearly £12 million, leaving his family interests with another £27 million worth of shares.

Six months after being honoured, Silver was elevated from vice-chairman to chairman of Leeds United. He had been on the board at Elland Road for a relatively short time, but was quick to tackle two of the club's major problems – hooliganism and finance.

The club introduced an identity card scheme to help root out troublemakers who were dragging the club's name down and introduced a system of all-ticket away games to curb the yob element and appointed a representative of the Supporters' Club, Eric Carlisle, to the board. Major steps were taken to reshape the image of Leeds United as a family club, while, at the same time, United were able to tap into the commercial potential of the broad base of fans. The sale of Elland Road to Leeds City Council for £2.5 million, generated much-needed cash and gradually the club's shaky finances got back on an even keel.

Silver was instrumental in appointing Howard Wilkinson as manager and the winning of the Second Division championship triggered a boom within the club. Season ticket sales rocketed as Leeds returned to the big time after Silver and Wilkinson gambled on the direct route back to the top – forking out big fees for quality players.

Although it plunged the club into the red, the gamble paid off, promotion was achieved, and the First Division championship triumph in 1991-92 saw more cash roll into the Elland Road coffers, enabling the old Lowfields Road stand to be demolished and replaced by the imposing South Stand, while the conversion of the old Kop to the Don Revie Stand made Elland Road into an all-seater stadium that was deemed fit to stage a full England international and host three games in the 1996 European Championships.

United were big business now and from the ranks of the boardroom, Bill Fotherby was appointed managing director and became instrumental in clinching the transfer of big-money players like Tomas Brolin and Tony Yeboah.

However, the need to spend big sums on players and ground improvements to keep Leeds near the top of the Premiership tree ate away at the club's finances and in March 1996 Silver told shareholders that the club expected to lose between £3.5 million and £4.5 million in the forthcoming year so the board were prepared to listen to offers for the club. The 71-year-old Leslie Silver announced on 9 April 1996 that he was to resign as chairman and was to be replaced by Bill Fotherby in an acting capacity, another of the three-man directorate with a 33 per cent holding in the club (Peter Gilman was the other). Fotherby was a member of the three-man team which spearheaded the commercial drive for the new Premier League in October 1991. He became the first-ever salaried director of the club when appointed commercial director in the 1990s. He received a salary of £244,098 in 1995.

Silver had suffered from heart problems and weeks before his resignation he and his wife Sheila were tied up during a robbery at their Leeds home, an incident which undoubtedly played a part in his decision to stand down.

There was much speculation about the future of the club throughout the summer, with London-based media group Caspian being installed as favourites, particularly as executive director Richard Thompson resigned his chairmanship at QPR.

United's financial advisors Rothchilds studied takeover bids for the club, which were also believed to include one from the Yorkshire-based Conrad Leisure Group, former United player Trevor Cherry being among Conrad's backers.

But in July, Caspian were named as United's new owners, the asking price reported as being between £30 million and £35 million.

Chris Akers, chairman of Caspian said: "We intend to maintain Leeds' position as one of the top Premier League teams. Leeds should be well placed to strengthen the first-team squad so that the club can continue to compete at the highest level, both domestically and in Europe, for the foreseeable future."

Since December 1961, the **Earl of Harewood** has been Leeds United's first president – an honour he still holds.

George Henry Hubert Lascelles, seventh Earl of Harewood, elder son of the sixth Earl and Princess Mary, daughter of King George V, first became a United follower in the 1930s. An Old Etonian, he was president of the Football Association from 1963 to 1972. After leaving Kings College, Cambridge, he became a captain in the Grenadier Guards and was wounded and captured in France. Following imprisonment at Spangenberg and Moosberg, he was sent to Colditz on the direct orders of Adolf Hitler.

A noted patron of the arts, he has been, at various times, director of the Royal Opera House, Covent Garden; artistic director of both the Edinburgh and Leeds Arts Festivals, managing director of the English National Opera, an Arts Council member, artistic advisor to the New Philharmonic Orchestra, governor of the BBC, president of the British Board of Film Censors and a former Chancellor of York University.

Leeds United Secretaries

When the club was first formed in 1904, the post of secretary was part of the manager's job. But as football expanded it became necessary for clubs to appoint a secretary to keep the club organised on a day-to-day footing and let the manager concentrate on matters on the field.

United's first full-time secretary was the bespectacled **C.Arthur Crowther** who was appointed in 1935 and held the position until he retired in 1958 shortly after the opening of the new West Stand. Crowther's assistant was **Harry Lunn**. Ironically most of his records and ledgers had been destroyed in the fire that had burnt down the old stand. Unfortunately, he did not enjoy a long retirement, dying shortly after ending his 23-year service with the club.

Succeeding Crowther was **Cyril Williamson**, who worked under the title of general manager-secretary soon after arriving at Elland Road. He turned to professional football quite late in life, joining Leeds from the Midland Electricity Board where he was an administrative official.

A Leicester man, he had a good background in football, having spent 17 years as secretary of Leicester and Rudland County FA.

A fine amateur centre-half, he was an FA councillor and chairman of the FA Youth International Selectors, travelling to 20 countries with the Under-18 national side. Ill health forced Williamson into early retirement in December 1967. **Keith Archer** followed Williamson on 9 March 1968, as general manager-secretary and in his first full season United won the 1968-69 championship. Archer was no stranger to Elland Road as his father, Frank, had spent over 50 years as one of the match day officials.

Archer, born on 9 October 1938, used to travel with the Intermediates on away trips and joined the club in May 1966 as assistant secretary, quickly stepping up to secretary. He gave up the secretary's job in 1982 but continued as general manager for a few more months before leaving the club in February 1984. **Mike Dooley** had worked as assistant secretary between August 1974 and July 1982 having previously been with Sheffield United. After a spell with Hull Rugby League club he returned to soccer administration with Scarborough. In September 1983 the post of chief executive was created to halt United's financial decline and **Terry Nash** became the first – and last – man to occupy the job. On 1 November 1985 a deal was concluded with Leeds City Council which saw Elland Road become community property and United's cash problems were back on a financial footing. Nash departed in February 1986.

Archer's replacement was **David Dowse**, who had been Grimsby Town's secretary since 1974. Dowse, born on 14 April 1957, was appointed at Leeds on 1 October 1982, staying at the club until August 1990 when the current company secretary **Nigel Pleasants**, the son of a former Ipswich Town reserve player, arrived from Cambridge United, where he had worked since 1989. Pleasants, born in 1948, joined his home club, Norwich City, in 1973 as assistant secretary; two years later he was on the short list for the Football League's deputy secretary's post. He became secretary at Carrow Road in 1979 but left after 15 years service. He was out of the game for 18 months and ran a pub in the suburbs of Norwich before his appointment at Cambridge in November 1989. A member of the management committee of the Football Administrators Association, he was involved in the discussions which set up the Premier League.

Another key figure in the current set-up at Elland Road is **Alan Roberts**, who was a goalkeeper on United's staff as a 17-year-old. Born on 12 February 1944, he started work with the club on a part-time basis in 1964, earning promotion to administration manager in 1986 and general manager five years later.

In September 1991 he was elected chairman of the Junior and Family Supporters Association and named North East Regional Director for the 1996 European Championships.

Assistant Managers, Trainers and Coaches

An essential part of the smooth running of any football club is the backroom staff and United has had more than its fair share of well known, and not so well known, names working behind the scenes.

One man was around before Leeds City even moved into Elland Road – **Albert Stead**. He was trainer and groundsman when the change from rugby to soccer was made in 1905 and worked at the ground until his retirement in 1945.

However, the most famous trainer in Leeds City's days was former Loughborough left-back **George Swift**, who worked under Gilbert Gillies when the club was first formed. He represented the Football League in his days with Loughborough and was later to have a spell in charge with Southampton.

It was not until the arrival of Herbert Chapman that the club got on a proper organised footing and one of the men on his staff, trainer **Dick Murrell,** served both City and United. He was a hard task master who would send players on endless laps around Elland Road and make them sweat off extra weight in Turkish Baths when they reported back for pre-season training.

Murrell, christened Aubrey John, but always called Dick, was a key part of the backroom staff assembled by United's first manager, Arthur Fairclough. Born in Grimsby, he played for Grimsby Town (1892-95), Grimsby All Stars, Newark, Wellingborough and Grimsby Town (1900-01) again, breaking a leg in a practice game in August 1901. He died in Leeds, aged 80, in 1951.

Bill Norman was Fairclough's assistant manager and arrived at Elland Road in June 1923 from Blackpool with his son-in-law, **Allan Ure**, who became Murrell's assistant. Norman was dubbed 'The Sergeant Major' when he had whipped the Barnsley team which won the 1912 FA Cup into shape. He spent nine years with Barnsley before becoming Huddersfield's trainer just before World War One broke out. At the end of the hostilities he became Blackpool's first full-time manager and together with Ure moulded them into one of the fittest sides around. Despite a promising start to his managerial career, including winning the Central League championship, Norman jumped at the chance to work under his old Barnsley mentor, Arthur Fairclough, at Leeds.

Norman helped prepare the team for promotion in 1924 but quit after relegation three years later and took charge at Hartlepool in August 1927. His toughness was legendary and according to one story demonstrated this during a bitter Hartlepool winter when one group of timid 'Pool players were complaining about the biting cold during a training session. Norman immediately put them to shame by stripping off and rolling naked in the snow. Such bravery didn't bring Hartlepool much success on the field and he left in April 1932 and resumed training at Barnsley.

Ure, born on 12 January, probably in 1892, only played reserve football at Blackpool but was their trainer for four years, earning a reputation as a top-class masseur and physiotherapist before joining Leeds with his father-in-law. Ure stayed at Leeds until 1928 when he returned to Blackpool and after training Barnsley was appointed Gillingham's manager in May 1937. His 12 months in charge was a disaster and the Gills were voted out of the Southern Section of the League in preference to Ipswich.

He was trainer to Millwall in 1938 and, after the war, Bradford Park Avenue, before acting as Halifax Town's physiotherapist and trainer for ten years until his retirement in 1962.

During the reign of Dick Ray, **Arthur Campey**, the successor to Murrell, became a familiar figure as he dashed on to the field in his fluttering white coat to attend to injured players. He made an unexpected return to United after the 1957 West Stand fire, helping fix players up with boots to replace ones which had gone up in smoke.

The colourful Campey was a hard act to follow but new trainer **Bob Roxburgh** proved more than an able replacement, giving 19 years service at Elland Road.

Born in Morpeth on 5 February 1896, Roxburgh played for Morpeth Comrades, joining Newcastle United in November 1920. A right-back, he was kept out of the team by veteran Billy Hampson, a future Leeds manager, so moved to Blackburn Rovers in May 1924 for £375. He totalled 128 appearances with the Ewood Park club before taking up a coaching appointment in Holland.

When Hampson was appointed as manager at Elland Road, he was instrumental in recruiting Roxburgh to the United staff. Roxburgh struck up a great rapport with the players and retired in November 1957 after 19 years on the training staff. He died, aged 78, on 20 November 1974.

After World War Two, training became more technical and United were able to boast several top names on their coaching staff in the late 1940s, including

England internationals **Willis Edwards**, **Gordon Hodgson** and **Ken Willingham**, all former United players. Edwards was assistant trainer to Roxburgh with responsibility for looking after the reserves, Hodgson was appointed to the coaching staff during wartime before moving on to Port Vale and Willingham had a few years as a Leeds coach after retiring in May 1948 as a player. He later was a coach at Halifax Town.

A fourth England international, **Sammy Weaver**, also worked behind the scenes at Leeds immediately after the war. He won three England caps at wing-half and was an assistant trainer at Elland Road between summer 1947 and June 1949.

A native of Pilsley, Derbyshire, he had turned out for United in wartime games after a distinguished playing career began with Sutton Junction, Sutton Town and Hull City, who he joined in March 1928. A £2,500 move took him to Newcastle United in November 1929 and he won a FA Cup winners' medal with the Magpies in 1932. Another big money move saw him go to Chelsea in August 1936 for just over £4,000 and after guesting for Leeds, finished his playing career with Stockport County.

Weaver left Elland Road to become Millwall's trainer, a job he held until January 1954 when he had a brief spell with non-League Bromley before being appointed coach at Mansfield, where he was manager between June 1958 and January 1960, starting a seven-year stint as assistant trainer the following month.

A sporting all-rounder, Weaver also played county cricket for Derbyshire and Somerset. He died, in Mansfield, on 15 April 1985, aged 74.

Fitness fanatic **Bill Lambton** was appointed United's trainer-coach by Raich Carter in November 1957 and introduced some novel training methods. He later had a three-month spell as United's manager.

Welsh international wing-half **Ivor Powell** joined the coaching staff in July 1956 and remained at Leeds until his appointment as Carlisle's manager in May 1960, a post he held for three years. He later managed Bath City, coached in Greece and returned to Bath, where he coached the university's soccer team.

Powell began his career with Bargoed in South Wales before having trials with Queen's Park Rangers but wasn't taken on. He remained in London to work and turned out for Barnet in the lsthmian League. In September 1937 QPR gave him a second chance and he made his League debut just before the war. He then joined the War Reserve Police before becoming a PT instructor in Blackpool, guesting for the Seasiders. At Bloomfield Road he became big pals with Stanley Matthews, who was best man at Powell's wedding. Capped eight times by Wales, Powell also made four wartime international appearances, the last coming at Wembley in September 1943 when he was substituted and replaced by Blackpool chum Stan Mortensen.

After being posted to India, he returned to football and won a Division Three South championship medal with QPR, then joined Aston Villa for £17,500, a record fee for a wing-half. Blighted by cartilage trouble he moved into player-management with Port Vale (August 1951) and Bradford City (May 1954), quitting as a player six months later, remaining as manager until February 1955.

He then ran a pub in the Manningham district of Bradford before United tempted him back to coaching.

The appointment of Don Revie as Leeds boss in March 1961 proved to be the turning point in the club's history and it was acknowledged that the strength of his support staff was a solid plank on which United were able to build their glory years.

Revie's able lieutenant was **Les Cocker**, a journeyman forward, who worked as a painter and decorator before becoming a professional footballer. His skills as a trainer became a Leeds legend after a modest career began with his native Stockport where he was born on 13 March 1924. He was in the Reconnaissance Regiment in France with the 53rd Division when he played his first wartime games for County, travelling up from his Army base in Dorset to play home games.

He turned professional in August 1947, joining Accrington Stanley six years later, scoring 48 League goals in 122 games for the Peel Park club, including hat-tricks in successive games in January 1955 against Barrow and Chesterfield. He was appointed Accrington's assistant trainer in May 1957, but was re-signed four months later because of an injury crisis.

In August 1959 Cocker went to Luton as assistant trainer-coach and arrived at Elland Road with the Hatters' coach, Syd Owen, in 1960.

A fully qualified FA coach, Cocker, studied anatomy and physiology and was highly regarded, earning promotion as trainer to the England Under-23 side in November 1961. Four weeks after Revie was appointed England manager, Cocker left Leeds to become England's trainer and Revie's assistant in July 1975. He had previously assisted England during the 1970 World Cup finals.

When Revie quit the England job for the Middle East, Cocker joined Doncaster Rovers as trainer-coach, linking up with former Leeds player Billy Bremner, who was in charge at Belle Vue. It was during one of Doncaster's training sessions that Cocker collapsed and died on 4 October 1977.

At Leeds, Cocker had whipped the Elland Road stars into shape, but it was his former Luton colleague **Syd Owen** who coached the players in the arts and skills of the game. Owen enjoyed a splendid soccer career culminating in three England caps, FA tours to Australia, South Africa, Rhodesia and West Indies, and an FA Cup Final appearance for Luton – his last-ever senior game.

Born in Birmingham on 29 September 1922, Owen represented Formans Road and South Birmingham Schools, worked as an engineer in his late teens and enlisted in the RAF in 1941, seeing service with his mobile radio unit in Egypt, Palestine, Sicily, Italy and Austria.

He played several representative matches for the RAF and the Central Meditteranean Forces against British Army of the Rhine before demobilisation in 1946. After a short time at Birmingham City he joined Luton in 1947. A highly mobile centre-half, he helped the Hatters to the 1959 FA Cup Final – the same year he was named Footballer of the Year. He was skipper in nine of his 12 years at Luton and had qualified as an FA coach in 1952. Soon after the Cup Final defeat against Nottingham Forest Owen was appointed Luton manager, a position he held until April 1960. Three months later he arrived at Elland Road as coach and worked daily honing the skills of the stars during Revie's glittering era.

He resigned in October 1975 because the club could not promise him a written contract, but returned, at Eddie Gray's invitation, to be chief scout in October 1982 after Ron Atkinson's arrival at Manchester United saw him lose a similar post at Old Trafford. **Maurice Lindley**, the former Everton centre-half, arrived at Leeds at the same time as Owen, as Revie's assistant manager and chief scout.

He was born in Keighley on 5 December 1915 and played for Keighley Schools, Keighley Town and Bradford City (as an amateur) before turning professional with Everton in March 1936, but actually made his name in wartime football with the RAF, regularly playing Combined Services and FA representative matches. He played one game for United as a guest in March 1944.

After the war he returned to Goodison

until 1951 when he was named Swindon's coach, stepping up to manager in 1953 and staying until May 1955. Brief spells at Barry Town and Crewe (1955-58) followed before he was named Newcastle's chief scout in 1956. Two years later he joined Leeds as trainer-coach, but the following year moved to Sheffield Wednesday in a similar capacity.

Lindley rejoined Leeds in July 1960 as cheif scout and proved a great ally to Revie, compiling meticulous dossiers sizing up the strengths and weaknesses of future opponents, particularly continental opposition.

After Revie's departure Lindley acted as caretaker manager no less than five times, but never sought the job on a full-time basis and was happy to work with a succession of managers, many of them ex-players.

When he left Elland Road in October 1981, Lindley held the title Chief Playing Staff Executive. He became chief scout, at the age of 66, at Bradford City on 5 March 1982, and took on the familiar mantle of caretaker manager after the dismissal of Terry Dolan and before the appointment of Terry Yorath in February 1988. He retired in 1991 and died at his home in Horsforth two years later, aged 78.

Revie's troops often embarked on long and strenuous seasons so the role of physiotherapist was crucial. Between 1959 and October 1981 it was held by ex-Army man **Bob English**.

Despite trials with Swindon in 1936 he didn't play full-time soccer and spent nearly 25 years with the Army Physical Training Corps, having joined up in 1933.

A preliminary FA coach, he spent a season as physiotherapist at QPR before joining Leeds, where, in the late 1970s, he became club kit convenor before becoming a victim of cost-cutting measures in October 1981.

Strength in depth was one of the features of Revie's backroom staff and York-born **Cyril Partridge** helped groom a string of youngsters into fully-fledged internationals in his role as second-team trainer.

Born on 12 October 1931, he was a relatively late developer in football terms, joining QPR as a winger in August 1954. He failed to make the first team and joined Rotherham three years later, making only a handful of League games.

Future manager **Brian Doyle** also helped Leeds out briefly as a coach in the 1960s. The Mancunian, born on 15 July 1930, began as a full-back with non-League Lostock Green before joining Stoke City in March 1951. He then played for Exeter City (April 1954) and Bristol Rovers (August 1957) until injury forced his retirement in 1959.

He coached Carlisle United and served as Workington's manager between July 1968 and 1969, was a coach at Blackpool in 1971 and was manager at Stockport between March 1972 and May 1974. He died, aged 62, on 22 December 1992.

After Revie and Cocker left, Brian Clough swept through Elland Road like a new broom. Although his assistant Peter Taylor remained at Brighton, trainer **Jimmy Gordon**, who had worked with Clough at Derby replaced the England-bound Les Cocker. Glaswegian Gordon had a great footballing pedigree. Born on 23 October 1915, he was schooled by Wishaw Juniors before joining Newcastle United as a polished wing-half in April 1935 for £50. Surprisingly overlooked by Scotland, he moved to Middlesbrough in November 1945 for £3,500, retiring ten years later to become assistant trainer at Ayresome Park. A qualified FA coach, he joined Blackburn as trainer in 1961, moving to Derby in summer 1969 to link up with Clough, with whom he had played at Middlesbrough.

After Clough's dramatic departure from Elland Road, Gordon worked for Rolls-Royce in Derby until Clough appointed him as Nottingham Forest's trainer in January 1975. He shared in all of Forest's memorable triumphs under Clough, who asked Gordon to lead Forest out at Wembley for one of their League Cup Finals. He retired in summer 1980. After the Clough turbulence, Leeds opted for the calm of mild-mannered Jimmy Armfield as manager and he brought in one of the most experienced coaches of the post-war era, **Don Howe**.

Wolverhampton-born Howe was a fine full-back with West Bromwich Albion and Arsenal, winning 23 England caps, several with Armfield, and went on to manage both clubs.

Born on 12 October 1935, he was rejected by Wolves and joined Albion as an amateur, turning professional in November 1952. In April 1964 a £45,000 transfer took him to Highbury, where a broken leg ended his career in March 1966, so he moved into coaching, playing a major part in shaping their double-winning side of 1970-71. He also coached the Gunners to three Wembley Cup Finals and a European Cup-winners' Cup Final.

Stepping into management at The Hawthorns in July 1971, he suffered relegation in 1973 and left in April 1975, being appointed manager of Turkish side Galatasary in May 1975. But when Armfield invited him to Leeds four months later, Howe jumped at the chance to re-enter the English game. In fact, Howe didn't stay long, returning to Arsenal as coach in August 1977, when he was also acting as Bobby Robson's assistant manager with England, and was manager of the Gunners between December 1983 and March 1986. After a spell in Saudi Arabia, Howe spent a few weeks on Bristol Rovers' coaching staff before joining Wimbledon in August 1987 as assistant to Bobby Gould and helped the Dons win the 1988 FA Cup.

Another move saw him in charge at QPR, after a period as assistant, returning to Wimbledon as coach in May 1991. He replaced Terry Butcher as manager at Coventry five months later and in May 1992 was joined by Gould as the pair worked together as joint managers. However, within a couple of months Howe, then suffering from heart problems, accepted an offer to become Chelsea's assistant. Later he was part of Terry Venables' England coaching set-up.

Howe's departure from Leeds left a big hole in Armfield's plans, but he plugged the gap by recruiting **Brian Green** in September 1977 to his coaching staff after Leeds old boy **Bobby Collins**, the youth coach, had temporarily helped with the seniors.

Although he only had moderate success as a centre-forward in the lower divisions with Rochdale, Southport, Barrow, Exeter and Chesterfield, and non-League Runcorn, New Brighton, Altrincham, Wisbech, Boston, Stalybridge, Ashton United and Glossop, Droylsden-born Green was highly-rated as a coach.

After playing in New South Wales, Australia, for the Prague club, and coaching in Kuwait, Green returned to his old club, Southport, as player-coach and took a lot of credit for their 1972-73 Division Four championship triumph.

He moved on to Chester, helping to plot United's dramatic defeat in the League Cup, before being appointed coach of the Australian national team. Back in England he became Rochdale's manager in June 1976 before his arrival at Leeds.

Subsequently, he has been assistant manager at Stockport and managed Norwegian club Bryne for several seasons. In the 1990s he was reported to be a hotel sales manager near Oldham.

After the brief 44-day reign of ex-Scotland boss Jock Stein, United turned to Jimmy Adamson as their manager in 1978 and he brought in a new backroom staff. His assistant was **Dave Merrington**, his former playing colleague at Burnley. Merrington, born in Newcastle on 26 January 1945, went to Bristol City after his Burnley days, but didn't play a first-team game there, then went into coaching and was Adamson's second in command at Sunderland prior to arriving at Leeds.

Supporting Merrington were coaches **Jimmy McAnearney**, the former Sheffield Wednesday, Plymouth, and Watford wing-half, and former Bradford City manager **Bryan Edwards**.

Dundee-born McAnearney had entered coaching with Rotherham under Tommy Docherty in May 1968, moving up to be manager between December 1968 and May 1973. He then spent two years on Sheffield Wednesday's coaching staff, acting as caretaker manager in 1975. McAnearney, whose brothers John and Tom also played League football, spent some time in industry before being appointed Scarborough's manager in 1981 and in the late 1980s was in charge at Hallam.

Edwards was born in Woodlesford, between Leeds and Wakefield, on 27 October 1930 and played for Oulton Youth Club before signing for Bolton in October 1947. An FA Cup winner in 1958, he played 518 games for Bolton before retiring to become Blackpool's assistant coach. After coaching and assisting at Plymouth, Edwards was in charge at Valley Parade between November 1971 and January 1975, then worked as Huddersfield's physiotherapist and coach until his arrival at Leeds where he ran the youth team. He returned to Bradford in July 1977, holding a variety of posts until November 1986.

After Adamson's dismissal, Merrington was out of football for six months and then worked for the probation service for three years. He joined Southampton in 1984, running the South East Counties League side and in 1990 was appointed youth-team manager, helping bring on the likes of Alan Shearer and Matthew Le Tissier. A lay preacher, he was appointed as manager of the Saints in succession to Alan Ball in July 1995.

Former United star Allan Clarke brought the nucleus of his Barnsley staff with him when he was appointed in charge at Leeds in September 1980.

His assistant was **Martin Wilkinson**, who had failed to make the grade as a youngster with Rotherham and was working as a sales rep before joining the Barnsley coaching staff. The 34-year-old Wilkinson was sacked from his £12,000 a year job as Clarke's right-hand man at Leeds in June 1982 as part of the club's economy drive, but within a fortnight was appointed Peterborough's manager, a position he held until February 1983 when he was relieved of his duties.

Wilkinson's departure from Leeds, after relegation from Division Two, spelled the end for Clarke, whose other key man, coach **Barry Murphy**, did stay on a bit longer. Murphy was a Barnsley stalwart, clocking up over 500 games as a full-back between July 1962 and April 1978 – including 177 consecutive League games – after going to Oakwell from South Shields. He was club captain and had a spell as player-coach.

Born in Consett on 10 February 1940, Murphy went straight into the Barnsley coaching staff after retiring and arrived at Leeds with Clarke on October 1980.

After Clarke's dismissal Murphy stayed at Elland Road for a while until becoming a sports development officer at Penistone Sports Centre in 1984.

Another of Clarke's men, chief scout **Tony Collins,** was a victim of United's financial pruning.

Born in Kensington, London on 19 March 1926, Collins played for Brentford as an amateur left winger before joining Sheffield Wednesday (November 1947), York City (July 1949), Watford (August 1950 and July 1957)), Norwich City (July 1953), Torquay United (July 1955), Crystal Palace (November 1957) and Rochdale (June 1959).

He became Rochdale's manager in June 1960 and steered them to the first Football League Cup Final in 1962, losing to Norwich in a two-legged Final. He quit in September 1967 and for five years worked at Bristol City as chief scout, before doing a similar job for Leeds between 1972 and 1976. He returned to Bristol City as assistant manager and, for 19 days, caretaker manager, leaving in October 1980 to join Leeds again.

After losing his job at Leeds in October 1981, he stayed on the scouting circuit, unearthing future stars for Manchester United, QPR, Newcastle and Millwall.

Clarke's successor, Eddie Gray, immediately named his former Leeds teammate and old friend **Jimmy Lumsden** as his assistant. The Gray-Lumsden partnership was supported by another former United player, **Peter Gunby**, who was on the coaching staff, and **Tony Fawthrop**, who spent a year as full-time chief scout for Gray.

Gunby was a Leeds loiner, born in the city on 20 November 1934 and signing for Leeds in September 1955 after completing his National Service. Gunby didn't make the first team and joined Bradford City in July 1956, where he played just three games, before going into non-League football after rejecting a move to QPR in 1958. He was player-manager at Harrogate Town for several years.

A qualified Army Physical Training Instructor, Gunby gained his FA coaching badge while working as an electrician. He was offered a part-time coaching post at Huddersfield in 1983 but soon moved to Leeds to work under Gray and was put in temporary command at Leeds when Gray was sacked in October 1985.

Also on the coaching staff at this time was **Keith Mincher**, a former schoolteacher who had a strong background in non-League football. He was one of several departures following the appointment of Billy Bremner and took over as Sheffield United's juniors' coach.

Bremner brought in his own management team based around **Dave Bentley** and **Dave Blakey**.

Bentley, born in Worksop on 30 May 1950, was Bremner's assistant. A former Rotherham United junior, he made 250 League appearances for the Millers from July 1967 before joining Chesterfield in June 1974. A battling midfielder, he also had a month on loan with Mansfield before joining Doncaster in August 1977. It was at Doncaster that he first forged his partnership with Bremner but despite helping to take Leeds close to an FA Cup Final and promotion in 1987, the pair, along with chief scout Blakey, were replaced in October 1988. Bentley then worked as Mansfield's Football in the Community Officer.

Blakey, born in Newburn in the North-East on 22 August 1929, was signed by Chesterfield in May 1947 from Chevington Juniors and amassed a club record 613 appearances for the Spireites up to his retirement in 1966.

Also on the Bremner coaching staff were former defensive lynchpin **Norman Hunter**, who had only been appointed eight months before Bremner's sacking, and **Alan McIvor**, a part-time assistant to the Northern Intermediate League side, who had joined Leeds after being physiotherapist at Doncaster Rovers for 11 years.

Bremner's replacement, Howard Wilkinson, kept on physiotherapist **Alan Sutton**, who, had taken over from **Geoff Ladley**, who had two spells with the club, the first in 1976 and then between 1982 and 1986.

Ladley, born on 24 June 1932, went into private practice and became a lecturer at Pinderfields Hospital, Wakefield, but returned to Elland Road for a third spell in January 1993 as physiotherapist with former Bradford City reserve player Sutton, who had previously served with Halifax RL and Halifax Town, becoming his assistant. Sutton was physiotherapist to United's 1991-92 League championship side. Ladley also worked with the England squad in the early 1970s. Wilkinson's second in command remains **Mick Hennigan**, previously the youth coach at Sheffield Wednesday.

Hailing from Thrybergh, outside Rotherham, Hennigan played as an amateur with the Millers before joining Wednesday in March 1961 and it was at Hillsborough where he first met Wilkinson as a young player.

Henningan never really made it as a player, contracts with Southampton (June 1962) and Brighton (July 1974) – where Wilkinson was also a player – furnished just seven appearances. However, he was supremely fit and coached in several countries before being appointed Sutton United's coach prior to joining Sheffield Wednesday's staff in 1984 where he was youth coach.

Hennigan, who will be 54 on 20 December 1996, was the natural choice to accompany Wilkinson when he arrived at Elland Road in October 1988.

Gunby, who had looked after the reserves and juniors since Allan Clarke's reign was kept on until retirement in 1995.

Wilkinson and Hennigan both believed that a productive youth policy should be at the heart of the club and appointed former United defender **Paul Hart** as director of youth coaching in summer 1992. The move soon paid dividends as United lifted the FA Youth Cup for the first time in 1993.

In January 1990, **Dick Bate** a man whose clubs mirrored that of Howard Wilkinson, was appointed reserve-team coach/youth development officer.

He was a team-mate of Wilkinson's at Boston United in the 1970s and although he featured in the reserves at Sheffield Wednesday and York City, didn't manage any Football League appearances and went to Alfreton Town in 1968, joining Boston three years later.

A physical education teacher, he played for Frickley Athletic for a couple of years, qualified as an FA staff coach and coached Sheffield United's youngsters between 1978 and 1980. FA North West Regional Coach between 1980 and 1985, he was assistant to the England youth team before spending two seasons as coach at Notts County.

He then spent just four months as Southend's manager until September 1987, was assistant manager at Lincoln and spent two years as national coach in Malaysia before linking up with Wilkinson at Elland Road between January 1990 and January 1992. After another spell in Malaysia, he became chief coach at Hereford, where he was later assistant manager.

Into Bate's shoes stepped **Eddie Beaglehole**, who was no stranger to Elland Road. He had been youth development officer at Leeds for several years – apart from a stint at Doncaster Rovers – working with Don Revie, Allan Clarke and Eddie Gray at Leeds and spent 17 years as team manager and English Schools FA coach to the national Under-18 side. His son Steve manages Doncaster Rovers and his other son, Andy, helps at the Leeds School of Excellence.

With Premiership football demanding larger squads, the coaching staff was bolstered by the return of former favourite **Eddie Gray** in summer 1995 to help with the development of youngsters and when Gordon Strachan announced his retirement in January 1995 he helped out with coaching and there was much talk of him becoming Wilkinson's eventual successor.

Strachan was quickly persuaded to become assistant to his old Manchester United mentor, Ron Atkinson, at Coventry City, where he resumed his playing career. Former Welsh international **David Williams** added his considerable wealth of coaching experience to United's cause in summer 1995 when he arrived from Everton where he had been assistant manager to Mike Walker.

Born in Cardiff on 11 March 1955, midfield man Williams attended Howardian High School and was spotted by Bristol Rovers playing for local club Clifton Athletic. Rovers signed him in December 1975 and he made over 350 League appearances for the Pirates, being at one time the youngest player-manager in the League. He moved to Norwich as a player in May 1985, becoming player-coach two years later and assistant manager in August 1988.

The holder of five Welsh caps, he took charge of the Welsh team as caretaker manager for a game against Yugoslavia after the dismissal of Mike England, for whom he had worked as assistant.

He moved to Bournemouth as assistant manager in July 1992 after seven years at Norwich and leapt at the chance to work with Walker again at Everton in February 1994. But when Walker left Goodison, Williams also departed and was installed at Elland Road.

Another newcomer to Leeds is former Rotherham reserve goalkeeper **John Bilton** who took over as Youth Development Officer from Beaglehole in October 1995. A former Worksop and Frickley player, he has acted as a part-time coach for many non-League sides before managing Sutton United, where Hennigan did some coaching. Bilton was also a coach and scout at Doncaster and spent 25 years as an electrical engineer with British Coal before joining a micro-electronics company.

Current chief scout is **Geoff Sleight** who was recruited in May 1994 and was instrumental in United signing South African duo Lucas Radebe and Philomen Musinga. Sleight has been associated with Howard Wilkinson for over 30 years. He played in 1960-61 with Wilkinson for Yorkshire and England Grammar Schools. Born in Royston on 20 June 1943, Sleight played just two games for Bolton in 1961 before going to Australia where he played for the Prague club and featured in World Cup qualifying rounds for that country. A full-back, he returned to England to play for Buxton, then Mossley, before becoming an FA coach and managed Frickley.

Shirt Sponsors

1982-83	RFW
1983-84	Systime
1984-85	WGK
1985-86	Lion Cabinets
1986-89	Burton
1989-91	Top Man
1991-92	*Yorkshire Evening Post*
1992-93	Admiral Sportswear
1993-96	Thistle Hotels
1996-	Packard-Bell

Badge/Motif

1905-06	None
1906-14	City Arms
1914-19	None
1920-35	None
1935-61	City Arms
1961-64-	None
1964-71	Owl
1971-73	LUFC
1973-79	LU Circle
1979-84	Peacock
1984-95	White Rose
1995-96	White Rose & LUFC

Leeds Managers

Gilbert Gillies
1905-1908

WHEN the post of manager of Leeds City was advertised, the sub-committee set up to run the club in its early days received over 100 applications. The man they selected for the job was Gilbert Gillies, a journalist, who became the club's first-ever manager on 16 March 1905. He had a three-year contract worth £156 a year.

As secretary-manager of Chesterfield, he had been instrumental in getting the Derbyshire club elected to the Football League in 1899 and his pedigree persuaded the founder-directors that he was the man for Elland Road.

City came top of the voting when they were elected to the Football League, but in his three years at the club as secretary-manager, Gillies did little more than consolidate the newcomers in the Second Division.

Together with trainer George Swift, a former Loughborough left-back who had represented the Football League in 1895 against the Irish League, Gillies attracted forwards of the calibre of Billy McLeod and Fred Croot and goalkeeper Harry Bromage to Leeds, but his team struggled to make much of an impact.

Scottish-born Gillies was a man of exceptional organisational ability and was not scared to experiment with his line-ups but he never achieved the ambitious high standards he sought for the club. When his contract expired it was not renewed and he immediately took the manager's job at neighbouring Bradford where he remained until February 1911. A former Football League referee, by 1914 he was out of full-time football and running a hotel in the Derbyshire town of Matlock.

Frank Scott-Walford
1908-1912

EXACTLY three years after Gillies' appointment. City approached Frank Scott-Walford, manager of Southern League side Brighton, and offered him the manager's job.

Born in 1868, a native of Perry Barr, Birmingham, Scott-Walford was an amateur goalkeeper on Tottenham's books before joining Isthmian League club London Caledonians. But his playing ability never matched his organisational skill and he went on to form the Enfield and District League and became a Southern League referee. He was also a keen cricketer and cyclist.

Scott-Walford became Brighton's manager in March 1905 but within two months, all but three of his playing staff had departed, leaving him with the awesome task of piecing together a new squad before the start of the next season. He managed to get his players together, but an FA Council meeting on 2 April 1906 reported that Scott-Walford was mainly responsible for irregularities in approaching other clubs' players before their contracts had expired and he was suspended from management from 16 April until 1 August.

Despite the ban, Leeds' directors felt he could do the job at Elland Road but, because Scott-Walford had two years of his contract still to run with Brighton, negotiations were protracted and on 26 March 1908 it was announced that he would be released by the southern club as soon as they could find a replacement.

Scott-Walford brought in many of his trusted Brighton players, like Jimmy Burnett, Davie Dougal, Dickie Joynes. Tom Rodger and Willie McDonald, yet none made a lasting impact. Even though Tom Morris, said to be the best defender in the Second Division, was introduced in the latter half of the campaign, no real improvement was achieved.

Scott-Walford later switched his attention to Ireland and brought a host of up-and-coming players to Elland Road, including Shelbourne pair Joe Enright and Joe Moran – both of whom won Irish caps at Leeds – and Derry Celtic inside-left Billy Gillespie.

Gillespie was about to sign for Linfield when Scott-Walford persuaded him to turn professional, but after a loss of form he moved from Elland Road to Sheffield United where he became a star.

Many of the Irish acquisitions failed to make the grade at Leeds and with little cash to spend on new players, Scott-Walford found difficulty in making an impression and at the end of the 1911-12 season City had to seek re-election. It came as no surprise when the manager stood down in May 1912. He was manager at Coventry from 1913 to 1915.

Herbert Chapman
1912-1919

HAD Herbert Chapman remained with Leeds after the illegal payments scandal led to City's expulsion from the Football League, then perhaps the club might have reached great heights in its early days. After his days at Leeds, Chapman, undoubtedly one of the greatest managers the game has ever seen, achieved remarkable successes at Huddersfield and Arsenal, setting both clubs on the road to a hat-trick of League championships.

Son of a coal-miner from Kiveton Park, Sheffield, Chapman, born on 19 January 1878, was a nomadic amateur inside-forward playing for Kiveton Park, Ashton North End, Stalybridge, Rochdale, Grimsby, Swindon, Sheppey United and Worksop between 1897 and 1901 as he pursued his career as a mining engineer, before turning professional with Northampton. His brother, Harry, played for Sheffield Wednesday and in May 1902 joined Sheffield United. In May 1903, a £300 move took him to Notts County before joining Tottenham in March 1905 after another year at Northampton. He was not a great player, but the Northampton directors recognised that he was a great tactician and thinker and brought him back to manage the Cobblers in 1907.

He steered Northampton to the 1908-09 Southern League title and that was sufficient for Leeds City to persuade him to join them in May 1912 as manager-secretary. After successfully canvassing for City's re-election to the Football League, he confidently predicted that he could take Leeds into Division One. The nearest he came was in his first season in charge when City missed promotion by two points. Despite the disappointment, the directors were pleased because gate receipts were well up and the club was able to record a £400 profit.

Chapman became heavily involved in the club's affairs and was particularly anxious to instill team spirit, organising team talks at which players were encouraged to speak their minds and introducing weekly golf sessions to encourage comradeship.

In 1914-15, city failed to live up to the promise of the previous season and once again they struggled financially. During World War One, Chapman worked at a local munitions factory and although he returned in 1916 he was suspended as investigations went on into illegal payments to wartime guest players.

Chapman quit on 16 December 1919 and became industrial manager of an oil and coke firm in Selby, claiming he had been harshly dealt with by the FA Commission because he was not in office when the payments were allegedly made. Only after his appeal was upheld did he move back into management – this time with Huddersfield in September 1921, where he embarked on an astonishing sequence of success, winning the Division One title in 1923-24 and 1924-25, and taking the FA Cup to Leeds Road in 1922.

Arsenal lured Chapman to London in June 1925 and he proved his triumphs were no fluke by steering the Gunners to the League championship in 1930-31 and 1932-33 and the FA Cup in 1930. He is also credited with inventing one of the game's most significant tactical developments – the 'stopper' centre-half.

After a scouting mission during the height of his powers, Chapman caught pneumonia and died on 6 January 1934 – 13 days short of his 65th birthday, leaving football to mourn the loss of one of its most popular and charismatic characters.

Arthur Fairclough 1920-1927

AFTER the trauma of City's dismissal from the Football League, the directors of the newly-formed Leeds United appointed former Huddersfield Town manager Arthur Fairclough to the managerial chair at Elland Road on 26 February 1920.

Born in Redbrook, Barnsley, in March 1873, Fairclough was player-secretary of a Barnsley junior side in 1891-92 but had to give up the game through ill health. Elected to Barnsley's committee in 1896, he became club secretary at Oakwell two years later as Barnsley entered the Football League for the first time.

In 1901 he gave up the secretary's job because of business commitments, but returned to football in July 1902 when he was elected to the Sheffield FA. Two years later he returned to Barnsley as manager-secretary and took his unfancied side to the 1910 FA Cup Final where they lost 2-0 to Newcastle after a replay. Two years later, Fairclough and Barnsley were back in the Final again, this time beating West Brom 1-0 after a scoreless first game.

Fairclough, who was also a Football League referee, was a football fanatic and in 1909, his weekly wage of £2 was less than his club trainer and most of his players.

In April 1912, he moved to Huddersfield and laid down the platform of the great side Herbert Chapman was to take to glittering success. When Huddersfield chairman J.Hilton Crowther switched his allegiance to Leeds, he persuaded Huddersfield manager Fairclough to join him at Elland Road and he resigned his secretary-manager post on 23 December 1919.

With his assistant and former City player, Dick Ray, Fairclough scoured the country for talent to make an impact on Division Two. When Ray left United in June 1923, Fairclough brought in Blackpool manager Dick Norman as his new assistant.

The Fairclough-Norman partnership had flourished in their days at Oakwell and it did not take long for the duo to work their magic at Leeds. In 1923-24 they took United into Division One for the first time in the club's short history.

After promotion, star players like Tom Jennings, Russell Wainscoat, Tom Townsley, Willis Edwards and Bobby Turnbull were brought to Leeds but, despite the injection of new blood, United found it tough going and relegation followed in 1926-27. Fairclough quit at the end of that season to make way for the return of Dick Ray, who inherited a side good enough to return to the First Division immediately.

Fairclough returned to Barnsley on 12 May 1929 as manager-secretary but resigned a year later. He was appointed a Barnsley director in 1935. Norman, his assistant at Leeds, went on to manage Hartlepools. Fairclough died in Sheffield on 18 March 1948.

Dick Ray 1927-1935

DICK Ray (see Leeds City Who's Who) served the Leeds clubs loyally as a player, captain and committee man, secretary and manager. Born at Newcastle-under-Lyme on 4 February 1876, he began his soccer career with Macclesfield in 1893, joining Burslem Port Vale the following year, then Manchester City, Stockport County and Chesterfield before signing for Leeds City for the club's inaugural season in the Football League.

A dependable left-back, he skippered Leeds before leaving in 1908. An all-round sportsman, he played cricket with Bradford League club, Laisterdyke. After hanging up his boots in 1912, Ray served in the RASC in World War One.

Following Leeds City's expulsion, he became a member of the original committee formed to get the new United on its feet and before Fairclough arrived, Ray ran the Midland League side on a shoe-string budget with considerable skill.

After a spell as Fairclough's assistant, Ray joined Doncaster Rovers as manager after they were elected to the Northern Section of the Third Division. At Doncaster he signed four Keetleys – Tom, Harry, Joe and Frank, all brothers of Charlie, who was to become one of United's greatest goalscorers.

On Fairclough's resignation in the 1927 close season, Ray was installed as manager-secretary at Elland Road, responsible for both team selection and playing policy. An outspoken character, he liked to do things his own way and achieved success in developing Bert Sproston, Bill Furness, Eric Stephenson, Wilf Copping, Arthur Hydes, Tom Cochrane, and George and Jimmy Milburn into outstanding performers in his eight years in charge.

With what was essentially Fairclough's team, Ray took Leeds back to Division One in 1928. Two seasons later Leeds achieved fifth position, their highest placing at that time, only to slither back to the Second Division the following year. Once again, however, they bounced straight back.

Ray's skill as a manager did not go unnoticed by the Football League administrators who appointed him the first-ever team manager of a Football League XI, for the 2-2 draw at Ibrox against the Scottish League in February 1934. He received a gold medal for this honour.

With Leeds failing to make an impression in Division One, Ray resigned his £1,000-a-year job on 5 March 1935 and succeeded Jack Peart as Bradford City manager the following month, leaving Valley Parade in February 1938 after the directors relieved him of team selection. At the age of 62 he became Millwall's chief scout but by 1940 he was out of full-time football running a garage business in Leeds and having an interest in billiard saloons. Ray, who established a solid foundation for subsequent Leeds managers to build upon, died in St James' Hospital, Leeds, on 28 December 1952.

Billy Hampson 1935-1947

UNITED's directors turned to another Leeds City old boy, Billy Hampson, to fill Dick Ray's shoes. A relatively late developer, he gave service to Rochdale, Bury and Norwich City at full-back before moving to Newcastle United in January 1914 for £1,250.

When Newcastle closed St James' Park during World War One, Hampson joined Leeds City as a guest, rejoining the Geordies after hostilities ceased. At Newcastle he was in the shadow of the legendary Bill McCracken, but when McCracken became Hull City's manager in February 1923, the veteran Hampson, born in Radcliffe on 26 August 1882, went on to win a regular first-team place and became the oldest FA Cup Finalist when he played right-back in the Geordies' 2-0 win over Aston Villa in 1924 at the age of 41 years and eight months. Hampson joined South Shields in September 1927 and when he finally hung up his boots in March 1930 he became boss at Carlisle where he discovered Bill Shankly and Bob Batey – the latter having a brief spell with United.

Carlisle did nothing noteworthy under Hampson's guidance and he had a spell at Ashington before taking the Leeds job. He consolidated United's status as a Division One club and trips to Ireland to sign Jim Twomey (Newry Town), David Cochrane (Portadown) and Bobby Brown (Derry City) paid off. All three went on to represent their country.

Hampson had plenty of experienced players at Elland Road but also brought on a fine crop of youngsters who were to win the Central League for the first and only time in 1936-37, but the war prevented them from reaching full football maturity.

Highly respected by the players as a manager and a gentleman, Hampson pinned faith in many of his loyal squad when peacetime football returned, but the long break in competitive football had taken its toll. Age caught up with several key players and United suffered their worst-ever season, finishing bottom of Division One with only six wins.

Hampson was made chief scout, but he held the post for only eight months before going freelance, later coaching Northumberland Schools. He died in Congleton, Cheshire, on 23 February 1966. He had two footballing brothers, Tom who played for Darlington and Walter for Charlton.

Willis Edwards 1947-1948

HAMPSON's resignation saw another former Leeds player, Willis Edwards, appointed manager. Edwards was one of the Elland Road legends (See Leeds United Who's Who) and when he retired he became assistant to trainer Bob Roxburgh with prime responsibility for the Central League side immediately after the war. He became manager in April 1947 with only a handful of games in United's nightmare season remaining and his clear priority was to build a side to win back United's Division One status as quickly as possible.

But the slide continued despite Edwards' efforts to sharpen his men's fitness and skills, and for much of the season they were haunted by the spectre of Third Division football. Eventually they finished 18th in Division Two and Edwards was moved back to assistant trainer in April 1948 after only a year as manager.

He remained one of the backroom staff for well over a decade, stretching his association with Leeds to 35 years. He died 27 September 1988 in Leeds, aged 85, having spent the last years of his working life employed in a jam factory.

Frank Buckley 1948-1953

NEW United chairman Sam Bolton, who once had a trial with Leeds City, announced one of the biggest names in football, Major Frank Buckley as the new manager in May 1948. Even though he was 64, United believed that Buckley's charisma and forceful style of management could bring Elland Road back to life.

A tough centre-half in his playing days, Buckley's first managerial job was at Norwich, prior to their League days, and after a spell as a commercial traveller, he was appointed boss at Blackpool on 6 October 1923. He joined Wolves in the summer of 1927 where he developed a superb youth policy, steering the Molineux side from the lower reaches of Division Two to Division One runners-up spot and FA Cup Finalists. In February 1944, he broke a contract for life to join Notts County for £4,000 a year. Within hours of his resignation from Meadow Lane in January 1946, he took charge at Hull City from where he joined Leeds.

Buckley was not afraid to experiment with training methods and at Elland Road soon installed a mechanical kicking machine into which footballs were loaded before it spat them out, one at a time, at different heights and speeds to improve heading, trapping, volleying and goalkeeping.

In an attempt to improve his footballers' balance and mobility, Buckley even introduced dancing sessions where the players paired up on the pitch and tripped the light fantastic to dance-music coming over the public-address system.

During his time at Wolves, Buckley had created a sensation by treating some of his players with monkey-gland extract which he believed would sharpen their thinking. He introduced a more advanced form of the treatment at Leeds where some players were injected while others took the tonic in a capsule. Nobody could say if it worked.

Despite his age, Buckley was remarkably fit and could do press-ups and high-kicking tricks in the dressing-room much to the embarrassment of some of the less nimble senior players.

On a more conventional note, Buckley organised and refereed practice games for younger players. An advocate of youth, he sold internationals Con Martin and Aubrey Powell to raise cash to wipe out a five-figure overdraft.

United continued to struggle and the club's abysmal FA Cup record continued with an embarrassing home defeat by Newport, putting Buckley under further pressure. He did not flinch from criticism, however, and in 1950 took Leeds to the FA Cup quarter-finals and unearthed a major star in John Charles. Despite the giant Welshman's influence on the side, United repeatedly missed out on promotion and in April 1953, Buckley left to become manager at Walsall, bowing out of the game two years later at the age of 72 and perhaps realising that his authoritarian approach was out of touch with the post-war game.

Born in Urmston, Manchester, on 9 November 1883, Franklin Charles Buckley had served with Aston Villa, Brighton, Manchester United, Manchester City, Birmingham, Derby County and Bradford City as a player before World War One, winning one England cap, against Ireland in 1914. He had fought in the Boer War, and in World War One joined the 17th Middlesex Regiment as an officer reaching the rank of Major in 1916. He commanded the 'Footballers' Battalion', made up of soccer professionals, and on his return to the game continued to be known as Major Buckley. He died, aged 84, on 22 December 1964 in Walsall.

Raich Carter 1953-1958

JUST as he had done at Hull five years earlier, former England inside-forward Horatio Carter took over the manager's job from Major Buckley.

Horatio Stratton Carter was born at Hendon, Sunderland on 21 December 1913. He made his mark as a schoolboy international in 1927 and played for Whitburn St Marys, Sunderland Forge and Esh Wiming before signing as an anmateur at Roker Park in November 1930 and professional on 31 November 1931. The silver-haired maestro of an inside-forward had a golden career with Sunderland and Derby County, becoming the only player to win FA Cup medals either side of World War Two. With Sunderland, he also won a League championship medal and was the youngest man ever to have skippered a First Division title-winning side. The former apprentice engineer gained 13 full England caps but reached his peak as a master tactician in his 16 Wartime and Victory internationals when he struck up marvellous partnership with the immortal Stanley Matthews. At Derby, he teamed up with the great Peter Doherty.

In 1948, Carter succeeded Major Buckley as Hull's player-manager and stretched his Football League goal haul to 218 in 451 games. Carter was quick to make an impact, buying and selling the star international Don Revie, and took the Tigers to the Division Three North title in 1949. He resigned in September 1951 and retired to run a confectionery shop in Hull. Hull sweet-talked him to play again when they faced relegation and he later moved to Ireland where he took Cork Athletic to the 1953 FA of Ireland Cup Final.

From Irish soccer, Carter arrived at Leeds with First Division football his top priority. Building his team around the brilliance of John Charles, Carter achieved that aim – the vital result being gained at his old stamping ground, Boothferry Park, on 28 April 1956, ending for Leeds nine fairly uneventful seasons in Division Two.

Charles was an awesome goalscoring weapon who kept United riding high, but glamour clubs were always sniffing after him and when the big Welshman finally succumbed

to the lure of the lire, United's form inevitably suffered. After slipping to 17th position, Leeds surprisingly dispensed with Carter's services when his five-year contract came up for renewal in May 1958.

Carter argued that United were in a much stronger position than when he joined them and that too much could not be expected after the sale of the mighty Charles, particularly as he claimed he was given less than half of the £65,000 Charles transfer fee to buy new players.

Carter re-emerged as manager of Mansfield in February 1960 and got them promoted from Division Four before being appointed Middlesbrough's manager, staying for just over three years and leaving the game in February 1966. Later he became a sports department manager of a large Hull store.

Had not football occupied such a large slice of his life, Carter might have become an outstanding cricketer. He played for Derbyshire in 1946 and for Durham in the Minor Counties championship. He died in Hull on 9 October 1994.

Bill Lambton 1958-1959

BILL Lambton stepped out of the Elland Road shadows to become United's fifth post-war manager – but it was to be a brief reign lasting only three months.

Born in Nottingham on 2 December 1914, he was a goalkeeper with local side Basford North End before joining Nottingham Forest. During World War Two, he went to Exeter City and had a short spell with Doncaster Rovers before concentrating on coaching.

A fitness fanatic, Lambton even helped keep British amateur boxers in trim when he was coaching in Denmark. On his return to England he coached Scunthorpe United and among his unorthodox training methods were trampolining sessions aimed at keeping players supple and fit.

Carter persuaded 38-year-old Lambton to join Leeds as trainer-coach in November 1957, taking over from Bob Roxburgh who had been trainer since the mid-1930s but had moved over to run the physiotherapy department. As Carter departed, Lambton was made acting manager, being officially appointed as manager on 9 December 1958.

Lambton's training methods did not win favour with the directors and he quit after only three months, yet during is short time he made a contribution which was to shape the destiny of Leeds United – he signed Don Revie and later made him skipper after Irish international Wilbur Cush quit the captaincy.

Lambton's next move earned him a place in the Football League record books for the shortest managerial spell. In April 1959, he spent three days as Scunthorpe's manager, although his appointment had been only verbal.

He was later in office at Chester (November 1961 to July 1963) before going out of football. Lambton died at his home in Sherwood, Nottingham, on 16 September 1976, aged 61.

Jack Taylor 1959-1961

FAVOURITE to gather up the managerial reins after Lambton's resignation was Arthur Turner, the Headington United and former Birmingham manager. He was on the brink of coming to Elland Road but was persuaded to stay at Headington, where, as Oxford United, he helped them gain admission to the Football League. After the unsettled period of managerial musical chairs, the United directors appointed Queen's Park Rangers manager Jack Taylor as Lambton's successor.

Barnsley-born Taylor played for local side Worborough Bridge before joining the Wolves groundstaff in 1931. Together with his brother Frank he formed a full-back partnership in Major Buckley's fine team of the late-1930s. Jack Taylor then played for Norwich, guested for Barnsley and Watford in wartime football, and joined Hull in July 1947.

He cut his managerial teeth at Southern League club Weymouth and did enough to prompt Queen's Park

Rangers to appoint him as the managerial replacement for former United player Dave Mangnall in June 1952. In nine years with the London club, Taylor proved a solid if unspectacular manager, often picking up useful players from the Leeds area. He was just the type United wanted to consolidate their position and he took on the job in May 1959. But within the year United were relegated with Taylor unable to plug a leaky defence, and the team showed little sign of being able to recapture their premier status.

Taylor resigned on 13 March 1961, even though he still had a year of his £2,000-per-annum contract to run. He drifted out of full-time football and died in his home town on 22 February 1978, one week after his 64th birthday.

Don Revie OBE 1961-1974

FOUR days after Jack Taylor's resignation Don Revie (see Leeds United Who's Who) was given the job of player-manager. The appointment followed inquiries by Chester and Bournemouth about Revie's availability. Director Harry Reynolds, soon to become chairman, drafted a letter recommending Revie to Bournemouth but then he realised he was just the man for Leeds. Reynolds tore up the letter and persuaded the rest of the board to agree to Revie's appointment.

Yet even they could not have dreamed that Revie would transform Leeds from a run-of-the-mill Second Division club to one of Europe's best in such a short time.

Born in Middlesbrough on 10 July 1927, Revie began his career with Leicester in 1944 and figured in four major transfer deals totalling almost £80,000 – a record at the time. Hull paid Leicester £20,000 for him in November 1949; Manchester City £25,000 in October 1951; Sunderland £22,000 in November 1956; and Leeds £12,000 in November 1958.

As a cultured inside-right he won six England caps, was Football of the Year in 1955 and won an FA Cup winners' medal with Manchester City the following year. He was the deep-lying centre-forward in City's 'Revie Plan' which was hailed as a tactical master-stroke in the mid-1950s, evolving from that of the Hungarian national team.

Revie made his Leeds debut on 29 November 1958 in a 3-2 win over Newcastle. Later he was made skipper, but handed the job to centre-half Freddie Goodwin after a string of poor results.

Revie's managerial career got off to a slow start and Leeds narrowly avoided relegation to the Third Division in 1962.

Patient Revie looked forward and developed the youth policy launched by Taylor and Lambton, nurturing a crop of youngsters who were to reap a golden harvest of success in the senior ranks. Gary Sprake, Paul Reaney and Norman Hunter were among those who made the breakthrough. Leeds powered their way to the Division Two title in 1964 under the leadership of midfield general Bobby Collins, an inspired Revie signing from Everton.

United made an immediate impact in Division One and in ten years at the top they won two League titles, the FA Cup, Football League Cup and the Fairs Cup twice, plus having a string of near-misses.

But Revie was more than the most successful manager in United's history. To the players he was the father of the Elland Road family, a man who made all reserves and juniors feel an important part of the club. An astute tactician, he surrounded himself with a fine backroom staff. There was trainer Les Cocker, the former Stockport and Accrington player, coach Syd Owen, the ex-Luton and England centre-half, and assistant manager Maurice Lindley, who spent 17 years as a player with Everton.

Revie had a knack of keeping his large squad of stars happy even though some of the reserves would have commanded first-team places at virtually any other club in the country. He was adept in the transfer market, picking up one of football's great bargains with the signing of Manchester United winger Johnny Giles, and his big-money signings Allan Clarke, Trevor Cherry and Mick Jones proved they were worth every penny.

During his reign at Elland Road, Revie was named Manager of the Year in 1969, 1970 and 1972, and was awarded the OBE in January 1970. After United's failure to beat Sunderland in the 1973 FA Cup Final, Everton looked set to lure Revie to Goodison Park, but he stayed and was rewarded with another League title.

The honeymoon could not go on indefinitely, however, and in July 1974, Revie ended 13 years at Leeds by becoming England's manager. With his track record he appeared the obvious choice to win England a place in the 1978 World Cup Finals.

Unable to recapture the club atmosphere at national level, however, Revie failed to set England firmly on the road to Argentina. In July 1977, he quit to take a lucrative job as coach to the United Arab

Emirates on a tax-free contract reputed to be worth £60,000 a year. Revie's move was bitterly criticised by the Football Association and the Press. The FA suspended the ex-Leeds boss from working in England until he was willing to face a charge of bringing the game into disrepute. Revie later won a High Court case against the FA and was granted an injunction quashing the ban, although many considered it a hollow victory when Justice Cantley criticised aspects of Revie's character. There had also been startling allegations in newspapers concerning matches involving Leeds when Revie was manager. Leaving the UAE coaching post in May 1980 he took over club side Al Nasr where he stayed for three years. In August 1984 he went to manage Al Al of Cairo but returned to Britain before Christmas.

Although he never returned to full-time football, Revie's court victory enabled him to take up a consultancy job at Elland Road and whatever his standing nationally, his place in United's folklore is guaranteed – near Elland Road there is even a road named after him and the new all-seater Geldard End Kop was renamed the Revie Stand in 1994. His influence remained in the game with his old players Terry Cooper, Jack Charlton, Norman Hunter, Johnny Giles, Trevor Cherry, Terry Yorath, Billy Bremner, Eddie Gray and Allan Clarke all making their mark in management – the last three each filling Revie's old seat at Leeds.

In 1988 Revie revealed he was suffering from motor-neurone disease, a muscle-wasting affliction for which there is no known cure. The illness confined the once hyperactive Revie to a wheelchair, but he still managed to visit Elland Road in April 1988 to renew old acquaintances at a joint testimonial game for John Charles and Bobby Collins. On 26 May 1989, however, Don Revie died at Murrayfield Hospital in Edinburgh.

Brian Clough 1974

WHOEVER replaced Don Revie as Leeds manager faced the awesome task of eventually breaking up the ageing United team. As Maurice Lindley took temporary charge once more, the board were left to ponder their choice. Early favourite was midfield man Johnny Giles who had been recommended by Revie, but Brighton boss Brian Clough emerged as the man for the job in July 1974.

Despite the outspoken Clough's impressive track record, he was a curious choice because of his past criticism of United's tactics. Like Revie, he hailed from Middlesbrough. Born on 21 March 1935, Clough was a prolific scorer with his home-town team and neighbouring Sunderland, winning two England caps in 1960 before injury cut short his brilliant career. His 251 League goals in 274 games is still the highest ratio since World War Two.

As a young manager he impressed at Hartlepools before going to Derby and steering them to the 1971-72 League championship with his assistant Peter Taylor. It was a remarkable feat, for Derby had been in the doldrums for years before Clough and Taylor rekindled their fire. After a row at Derby which stemmed from the club's embarrassment at Clough's outspoken remarks on television and in newspapers, he and Taylor moved to Brighton and it was there that Clough accepted a five-year contract reported to be worth £20,000 a year. His association with Brighton was brief and although Taylor remained at the Goldstone Ground, elevated to manager, Clough eagerly accepted the opportunity to replace Revie at Leeds. He arrived at Elland Road with trainer Jimmy Gordon and immediately began a new-broom approach. Sweeping changes began when he paid £250,000 to Nottingham Forest for Duncan McKenzie, and £125,000 to his old club, Derby County, for John McGovern and John O'Hare.

But early results were disappointing for United and amid rumours of an unhappy dressing-room atmosphere, Clough was sensationally sacked after only 44 days in office. Before a League Cup game against Huddersfield, chairman Manny Cussins met the players and detected a great deal of unrest and apprehension. The directors called a special board meeting and agreed to part company with their new manager.

Newspapers reported that 'player power' was behind Clough's dismissal, but Cussins said that the decision had been taken for the good for the club. Clough, who won much sympathy after the incident, commented: "I think it is a very sad day for Leeds and for football."

The players issued a statement

denying that they had forced Clough out. Suspended skipper Billy Bremner, assistant manager Maurice Lindley and chief coach Syd Owen picked the team for the next fixture at Burnley two days after Clough's departure. None of Clough's signings were in the squad.

Many people felt the board, having opted for Clough, should have stuck with him and his methods, others felt the directors had been big enough to admit they had made a mistake in approaching him in the first place. Whatever the view, it was a costly decision and Clough received an estimated £20,000 compensation.

In January 1975, he joined Nottingham Forest and, reunited with Peter Taylor, transformed an ailing Second Division side into League championship, League Cup and European Cup winners. O'Hare and McGovern, exiled at Elland Road after Clough's departure, shared in his glories at Forest, leaving Leeds to contemplate what might have been. Clough's success at Forest saw the City Ground virtually re-built, and although never offered the England job, he was invited by Wales to run their national side, although Forest would not release him to do the job on a part-time basis. He retired in May 1993 after Forest's shock Premier League relegation, amid much bad publicity. His son Nigel, who played under him for many years then moved to Liverpool.

Jimmy Armfield 1974-1978

AFTER the upheaval at Elland Road, a man with ability to soothe a troubled club was needed for the hottest of managerial jobs.

Despite the Clough affair, the club's stature ensured plenty of candidates and in Jimmy Armfield, United acquired a man with an excellent footballing brain and a calming influence. Quiet and unassuming, the pipe-smoking Armfield, aged 38, was relatively inexperienced on the managerial front, but had a long and distinguished playing career behind him.

Born in Blackpool on 21 September

1935, he played a record 568 League games for the Bloomfield Road club, was capped 43 times by England at right-back and skippered his country. His immaculate temperament earned him the nickname of 'Gentleman Jim' and in his first managerial post, at Bolton, he gained the Trotters the Third Division title in 1972-73.

The Leeds board deliberated at length before announcing Armfield's appointment and he proved a steadying hand on the tiller as he guided Leeds through troubled waters.

United's League form improved but the poor start meant they could not retain their title, so Armfield concentrated his players' efforts on the European Cup. In that first season, he made few changes to the playing staff and relied on the hunger of older Leeds stars to take United to their first European Cup Final with a string of outstanding performances.

Within a few months he had achieved what even Revie could not do, but luck deserted United in the Paris Final against Bayern Munich. After the riot by the hooligan element among United's support, Armfield's well-reasoned defence at the UEFA hearing helped cut United's European ban from four years to two.

He went about the inevitable break-up of Revie's ageing aces quietly and efficiently, releasing Terry Cooper, Johnny Giles, Billy Bremner, Norman Hunter and Terry Yorath, and bringing in the immensely popular Tony Currie from Sheffield United, Burnley duo Brian Flynn and Ray Hankin and skilful Scottish winger Arthur Graham from Aberdeen.

When Leeds reached the FA Cup semi-final in 1977 and the League Cup semi-final the following year, it appeared that Armfield had the basis of a side which needed only time to bring the great days back to Elland Road. But Leeds could not wait and with League performances far short of past efforts, and with Armfield's new-look team still some way from improving matters, the manager was dismissed.

Today, Armfield lends his vast experience of football to the roles of newspaper reporter and radio summariser.

Jock Stein CBE 1978

AFTER only one match of the 1978-79 season, Leeds appointed former Celtic supremo Jock Stein as manager. Stein was a big man both physically and in terms of football stature, an old adversary, and friend, of Don Revie. Yet Stein, one of Britain's greatest-ever managers, spent precious little time as Leeds boss.

Born in Lanarkshire on 5 October 1922, he was a rugged part-timer with Albion Rovers before turning professional at the late age of 27. He returned to his old job as a miner, this time in the South Wales coalfield, and played centre-half for Llanelli before joining Celtic in 1951. They wanted him to captain their reserves but he went on to skipper the League side before injury forced his retirement. As a player Stein led Celtic to their first Scottish League and Cup double in 40 years in 1954, before hanging up his boots the following year. He remained with Celtic as a coach until 1960 when he moved on to Dunfermline.

Stein managed the Pars, taking them to victory in the 1961 Scottish Cup, and then Hibernian before joining Celtic in 1965 to embark on an unprecedented run of success. In 1967, Celtic became the first British winners of the European Cup and at home were virtually unbeatable under Stein, with 10 League titles (nine in a row), eight Scottish Cups and six Scottish League Cups. In 1970, Stein was awarded the CBE but was out of the game for ten months when a serious motor accident in July 1975 was followed by a series of major operations and a heart attack.

At the age of 55, he was given the less taxing job of general manager and was offered a seat on the Celtic board as the directors paved the way for Billy McNeill to take over as manager. Stein, however, did not relish his new role and jumped at the chance to join Leeds on 21 August 1978, on a three-year contract reputed to be worth £85,000.

The appointment was a major coup for United but the big man never signed his contract and within weeks had replaced beleaguered Scotland boss, Ally McLeod. For Stein, who had been Scotland's caretaker boss briefly in the mid-1960s, it was a particularly happy return because his wife did not fancy living in the Leeds area. He had spent only 44 days at Elland Road, the same length of time as Brian Clough, and when he left, Leeds were in mid-table and had struggled to beat West Bromwich Albion in the League Cup.

Stein took Scotland to the 1982 World Cup Finals in Spain and steered them to the brink of the Mexico Finals four years later. On 10 September 1985, in the pandemonium which followed a nail-biting draw in Cardiff – essential to Scotland's World Cup progress – Stein collapsed and died, aged 62, having spent seven years rebuilding the passion and dignity of Scottish football.

Jimmy Adamson 1978-1980

FOLLOWING Jock Stein's shock departure from Leeds, United appointed Jimmy Adamson, a man once offered the England manager's job, to become the new chief at Elland Road. He took the post in October 1978, three weeks after Stein left. In the interim period, Maurice Lindley had been caretaker boss.

Born in Ashington in April 1929, Adamson was snapped up by the excellent Burnley scouting system from First Chevington, turning professional on New Year's Day 1947. He made the senior team in 1950-51 and within three years won an England 'B' cap. He also represented the Football League and although a full international cap eluded him, success at Turf Moor did not. He skippered Burnley's 1960 League championship side and two years later had his most memorable season, taking Burnley to the FA Cup Final, where they lost to Spurs, being named Footballer of the Year and gaining inclusion in the World Cup squad for

Chile where he was assistant to England manager Walter Winterbottom.

When Winterbottom resigned. Adamson refused the post because he felt he lacked managerial experience and instead the position was filled by Alf Ramsey. Adamson became a coach at Burnley when he retired, being appointed manager six years later. He took the Lancashire club back to Division One in 1973 but, disillusioned at continually having to sell talented youngsters, he quit in January 1976. In May, he spent a fortnight with Sparta Rotterdam but failed to settle and returned to England. Within a few months he took charge of struggling Sunderland, arriving too late to stop them sliding into Division Two.

At Leeds, Adamson made an immediate impact, taking United to fifth spot – the best since Revie's era – and a place in Europe, as well as to the League Cup semi-final. But that early promise failed to materialise. Talented players like top scorer John Hawley, Frank Gray and Tony Currie were sold, whilst Adamson's own signings were unsuccessful.

Alan Curtis (£370,000 from Swansea), Brian Greenhoff (£360,000 from Manchester United), Derek Parlane (£200,000 from Rangers), and Alex Sabella (£400,000 from Sheffield United) all failed to slot in, leaving the restless Leeds supporters impatient and angry. Mounted police broke up a demonstration after a dismal performance against Coventry in March 1980, before the lowest crowd at Elland Road for 17 years.

Pressure mounted on Adamson at the start of the following season. He appealed for calm, stating that demonstrations would only lower players' confidence, but in October 1980, he bowed to the inevitable and resigned, slipping out of full-time soccer.

Allan Clarke 1980-1982

DETERMINED to bring back former glories to Elland Road, the directors turned to a man who had shared in those halcyon days as a player – Allan Clarke (see Leeds United Who's Who).

As player-manager of Barnsley, Clarke had made an immediate impression, getting them out of the Fourth Division, preparing for a big push into the Second and generally revitalising interest in what had become a moribund club. Clarke was nothing if not confident, declaring that he was a winner as a player and wanted to be a winner as a manager.

His drive and ambitious approach prompted the Leeds board to bring him back to Elland Road on 16 September 1980 when United were just one place from the foot of Division One. Clarke concentrated on tightening up the United defence and although the attack netted only 39 League goals, they finished the season in a respectable ninth spot.

To boost his flagging attack, Clarke paid a club record fee of £930,000 to West Bromwich Albion for winger Peter Barnes, but the move proved unsuccessful for both the player and the Leeds club.

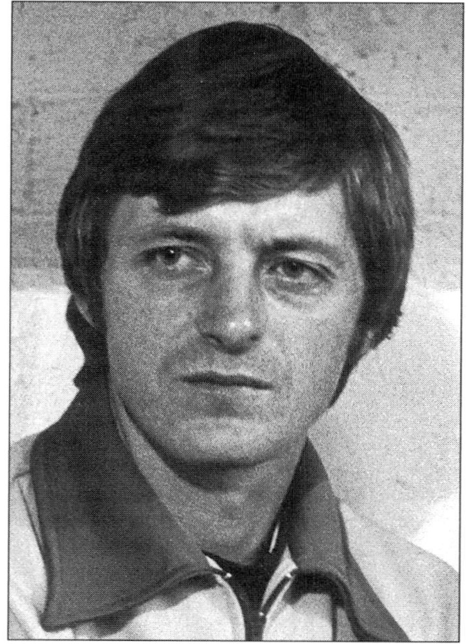

Again only 39 goals were scored, but this time the defence was not as reliable and First Division status was lost for the first time since 1964. Before Clarke had time to rebuild for the future, he found himself out of a job, together with his assistant Martin Wilkinson, before the new season began.

Scunthorpe United offered Clarke the way back to management and by one of those splendid football ironies, his Third Division side eliminated Leeds from the FA Cup the following season. But life at Scunthorpe was a struggle and Clarke rejoined Barnsley, taking over from another Leeds old boy, Bobby Collins, in July 1985. Martin Wilkinson later had a brief spell as manager of Peterborough United, whilst Clarke remained at Oakwell until midway through the 1989-90 season. In June 1990 he was appointed manager of Lincoln City, but left after five months following a string of poor results.

Eddie Gray MBE 1982-1985

IN JULY 1982, popular Scottish winger Eddie Gray (see Leeds United Who's Who) was named player-manager of the club he had served so loyally for nearly two decades. Gray had no managerial experience but during one of his lengthy spells of injury as a player, he had impressed when coaching the juniors.

A quiet family man, some thought he would struggle to adapt to the hard, frantic world of soccer management, but he carefully dismantled the existing team, at the same time ending his own playing career in May 1984. He brought back old favourite Peter Lorimer as skipper and blooded a batch of talented youngsters from the juniors and reserves, all of which helped check United's slide.

Gray, who received an MBE for his services to football, was unable to win back United's First Division place although they were promotion candidates for three successive seasons. Bookmakers reckoned that the team's rich promise would bear fruit in 1985-86 and installed them as promotion favourites. Indeed, Leeds looked a good bet, but the skilful squad lacked physical presence and lost out to less able but harder-tackling opponents.

United made a bad start and soon began to lack confidence, but with only one defeat in eight games they seemed to have turned the corner when 38-year-old Gray was sacked on 11 October 1985, along with his right-hand man Jimmy Lumsden. For Gray it ended a 22-year association with the club.

As coach Peter Gunby was put in temporary charge, chairman Leslie Silver paid tribute to Gray's work but said that 14th place in Division Two was not good enough. The board had voted 6-2 to end Gray's stewardship and one of the directors, Brain Woodward, a former United reserve, resigned in protest.

The repercussions went further still. Some senior players cried openly after being told of the sacking and Lorimer handed a statement to the board in which the players condemned the timing and handling of the announcement, although they pledged to continue to do their best for the club.

The day after the shock news, United beat Middlesbrough with a Lorimer penalty as Leeds fans demonstrated against Gray's dismissal, calling for Silver's resignation. The board, however, were adamant.

Gray, typically, showed no bitterness at the decision and bowed out quietly from the Elland Road scene, later joining his old teammate Davie Harvey as a player for non-League Whitby Town, to where Lorimer also moved.

It did not take long for a man of Gray's quality to get back into the full-time game and at the start of the 1986-87 season he was working as Middlesbrough's reserve and youth-team coach. In December 1986 he was appointed team manager at Rochdale but quickly stepped up the managerial ladder when he became Hull City's boss in June 1988. Sadly he was sacked by Hull in May 1989. The following September he became manager of Whitby Town but quit in May 1990 to concentrate on outside business interests. However, he rejoined the Leeds coaching staff in summer 1995. His son Stuart now plays for Celtic and nephew Andrew has sampled senior football at Leeds.

Billy Bremner 1985-1988

IN NOVEMBER 1978, Billy Bremner (see Leeds United Who's Who) effectively ended his brilliant playing career when he left Hull City to take over as manager of Doncaster Rovers – their 17th boss since World War Two. Bremner retained his playing registration and turned out for Rovers in emergencies.

With very little cash at his disposal, Bremner built his teams on the basis of hard-working players rather than expensive talent. Rovers had been languishing in Division Four for many years but, within two years of his appointment, Bremner took them to promotion when they finished third behind Southend and Lincoln.

Bad luck and crippling injuries saw Doncaster relegated in 1983 but they bounced back the following season as Division Four runners-up. Bremner had several good young players in his ranks, including Ian Snodin, a midfielder whom he sold to Leeds for £200,000 in May 1985. Within months, the pair linked up again when Bremner was appointed manager at Elland Road, succeeding the loyal Eddie Gray.

On the field, Bremner had led

Leeds to their greatest triumphs and now he aimed to do the same from the dug-out. United took time to adjust to the demands of his preferred style of play. He used a five-man defence in front of goalkeeper Mervyn Day, but a series of disappointing displays saw them slip briefly into the relegation zone before playing their way out of trouble.

The following season Bremner steered his beloved United to the brink of double glory They came within 20 minutes of reaching the 1987 FA Cup Final and ten minutes of gaining promotion to Division One. A late surge took Leeds into the promotion Play-offs but they fell at the final hurdle in a replay against battling Charlton on an emotion-charged night at St Andrew's, Birmingham, going down 2-1 to two late extra-time goals. United's FA Cup run was an unexpected bonus but again they came a cropper when glory beckoned, losing 3-2 to Coventry City after extra-time in one of the most thrilling semi-finals Hillsborough had ever staged.

Bremner's reward was an extended contract but in 1987-88 Leeds appeared to go backwards and failed to live up to their billing as promotion favourites. Poor results at the start of the next season saw Leeds lingering near the foot of the table and Bremner was axed in late September 1988. Coach Peter Gunby was put in charge until United found a replacement for Bremner, whose devotion to the club he served so well could not be doubted. In July 1989, Bremner returned to Doncaster as manager, a job he held until he was dismissed in November 1991.

Howard Wilkinson 1988-

FITNESS fanatic Howard Wilkinson was appointed United's manager on Monday, 10 October 1988 – the club's eighth boss in 14 years. One of the first things that Wilkinson tackled was to improve the fitness of players throughout the club and good early results were a reflection of Wilkinson's organisation and eye for detail.

United had lured Wilkinson away from First Division Sheffield Wednesday where a lack of spending power had prompted him to drop a division. Born in Sheffield on 13 November 1943, Wilkinson had a steady but unspectacular playing career. He signed amateur forms with Sheffield United as a youngster and represented England Grammar Schools. The young winger crossed the city to join Sheffield Wednesday in June 1962 and won England Youth honours the same year. In four years at Hillsborough he made 22 Football League appearances before moving to Brighton in July 1966.

In six seasons with the Seagulls he clocked up over 100 League appearances and first entered the coaching arena. In 1971 Wilkinson joined Northern Premier League club Boston United as player-coach, then as player-manager. He gained a degree in physical education at Sheffield University and taught for two years at his old school in Abbeydale, Sheffield. After becoming FA regional coach in Sheffield, he became manager of the England semi-professional side and then the England Under-21 side in November 1982 when Ron Greenwood was in charge of the national senior side.

In January 1980 Wilkinson had re-entered League football as coach to Notts County and played his part in getting them promoted to Division One in 1980-81 and later succeeded Jimmy Sirrel as manager at Meadow Lane. In June 1983 Wilkinson succeeded former Leeds favourite Jack Charlton as manager at Sheffield Wednesday and took them back to Division One in his first season in charge. The Owls were rarely out of the top half of the table under Wilkinson's guidance and had several good Cup runs without breaking through to the big time. Sensing that Leeds had greater potential, Wilkinson took the chance to move to Elland Road when he was offered the job by United's board.

In his first full season in charge, Wilkinson took Leeds United back to the top flight as Second Division champions. He believed that Leeds could take 'route one' back to the top by gambling on big-money players. With the full backing of the board, Wilkinson went on a big pre-season spending spree to sign the likes of Vinnie Jones, Mel Sterland and John Hendrie, later adding striker Lee Chapman to the pay-roll.

The risk paid off as Leeds, backed by big crowds at Elland Road, took the title with a club-record 85 points, on goal-difference from Sheffield United. That completed a promotion hat-trick for Wilkinson, but Leeds had provided him with his first championship. In the summer of 1990, Wilkinson was part of the England set-up, assessing likely opposition in the World Cup in Italy.

Leeds finished fourth in their first season back in the top flight and the following season won the League championship, pipping Manchester United in a nail-biting run-in. Wilkinson, named 1991-92 Manager of the Year, pulled off a major coup by signing skilful Frenchman Eric Cantona. When Leeds beat Liverpool 4-3 in the Charity Shield – Cantona getting a hat-trick– a good season looked in prospect for the champions. However, they failed to win an away game in the League in 1992-93 and suffered early exits from the European Cup, FA Cup and Football League Cup.

Cantona was controversially sold to Manchester United and was later followed by the sale of popular Leeds-born midfielder David Batty to Blackburn.

Wilkinson reshaped his side which finished fifth in 1993-94 and the purchase of Ghana's star striker Tony Yeboah enabled United to snatch a European place from under Newcastle's noses in the following season.

Wilkinson, chairman of the Managers' Association, signed a new contract to keep him at Elland Road until the turn of the century, although

in October 1995, the FA were given permission to speak to him with a view to him being interviewed for the post of technical director.

In 1995-96 he blooded several young players but also invested heavily, spending £4.2million, a club record, on Swedish international Tomas Brolin.

Although United reached the Final of the Coca-Cola Cup in 1996 they were outplayed by Aston Villa and Wilkinson was booed off the Wembley pitch after the 3-0 defeat. Speculation mounted over his future as United collapsed after that game in March, losing seven, winning one and drawing one of their last nine Premiership games.

After the resignation of Leslie Silver as chairman, the future of the club was clouded, but Wilkinson began his rebuilding programme immediately by snapping up veteran Welsh international goal-poacher Ian Rush from Liverpool.

When the Caspian takeover went through Wilkinson was given an estimated £12 million by the new owners to spend on players and within hours broke the British transfer record for a teenager by signing Charlton Athletic starlet Lee Bowyer for £2.6 million, adding youth to the valuable experience of Rush. The manager followed this with the £2.4 million capture of Crystal Palace goalkeeper Nigel Martyn.

Less popular news concerned the departure of two Elland Road favourites as Gary Speed joined Everton for £3.4 million. This was compounded by the £3 million sale to Coventry City in the summer of 1996 of Scottish international skipper Gary McAllister, who had been such a major influence in the Leeds side during recent seasons.

Leeds United Who's Who

This section contains biographies of every player who has made a first-team appearance for Leeds United. Each entry shows (where known) the player's position, date and place of birth, debut game, height, weight and appearance record. The year immediately following height and weight details are when those details were recorded.

ABEL, Robert C. *1931-1936*

Right-back. Born: Manchester, 28 April 1915.
Debut v Aston Villa (h) Division One, 20 April 1935, D 1-1.
Leeds picked up reserve defender Robert Abel from Manchester junior football in September 1931. Unable to dislodge Jack Milburn, he went to Bradford City in July 1936 but left for Stalybridge Celtic in May 1937.
League: App 1, Gls 0.

ADAMS, Micky R. *1987-1989*

Midfield/full-back. Born: Sheffield, 8 November 1961.
Debut v Blackburn Rovers (h) Division Two, 24 January 1987, D 0-0.
5ft 7in, 10st 10lb (1987).
Within ten weeks of joining Leeds from Coventry (£110,000) in January 1987, Adams played

against the Sky Blues in an FA Cup semi-final. He started as an apprentice with Gillingham, turned professional in November 1979 and won England Youth honours. Coventry bought him (£75,000) in July 1983. Leeds used him mostly at left-back before he was sold to Southampton in March 1989 for £250,000. He left Saints for Stoke City in March 1994, then went to Fulham (player-coach August 1994 and player-manager February 1996, when he became the League's youngest manager).
League: App 77/1, Gls 2; FA Cup: App 6, Gls 1; League Cup: App 4, Gls 0; Full Members' Cup: App 1, Gls 0.

ADDY, Mick *1962-1964*

Wing-half. Born: Knottingley, 20 February 1943.
Debut v Rotherham United (h) League Cup 2nd round, 15 December 1961, L 1-2.
5ft 10½in, 12st 2lb (1962).
After his apprenticeship, Addy turned professional in May 1962 but failed to make an impact at Elland Road and moved to Barnsley in June 1964. Despite cartilage trouble, he was a regular there until joining Corby Town on a free transfer in summer 1967.
League: App 2, Gls 0; League Cup: App 2, Gls 0.

AGANA, Tony *1992*

Winger. Born: Bromley, London, 2 October 1963.
Debut v Luton Town (a) Division One, 29 February 1992, W 2-0.
5ft 11in, 12st 2lb (1992)
Agana played two games on loan – one as a substitute – in United's League championship season of 1991-92. He was brought in for a few weeks from Notts County by Howard Wilkinson to strengthen the squad for the final run-in for the title. Agana returned to Meadow Lane and the Magpies were relegated at the end of the season. Agana also recruited Leicester City midfielder Ali Mauchlan on the same basis but the nearest he got to a game was as a non-playing substitute.
Agana started at non-League Weymouth where he won an England semi-professional cap against the Republic of Ireland before joining Watford in August 1987. He stayed only four months before a £40,000 transfer took him to Sheffield United where he forged a powerful attacking partnership with Brian Deane which pushed the Blades all the way to the Second Division title. Notts County shattered their transfer record, which had stood for ten years, to recruit Agana for £685,000 in November 1991.
League: App 1/1, Gls 0.

AINSLEY, George E. *1936-1947*

Centre-forward. Born: South Shields, 15 April 1915.
Debut v Sunderland (a) Division One, 19 December 1936, L 1-2.
6ft, 13st (1939).
Ainsley began with South Shields St Andrew's before joining Sunderland in April 1932. In August 1936, after only four appearances, a £2,500 transfer took him to Bolton, but in December that year he joined Leeds. In 1939 he toured South Africa with the FA and during the war guested for Blackpool, Southport, Liverpool and Bradford. In November 1947, he moved to Bradford and then became an FA staff coach, working in India, Israel and the USA. He managed Workington (July 1965-November 1966) and was national coach of the Libyan Olympic team before returning to England in 1970. He died in Seacroft, Leeds, in April 1985.
League: App 91, Gls 30; FA Cup: App 6, Gls 4.

AIZLEWOOD, Mark *1987-1989*

Midfield. Born: Newport, South Wales, 1 October 1959.
Debut v Sheffield United (a) Division Two, 7 February 1987, D 0-0.
6ft, 12st 8lb (1987).
Mark Aizlewood began his career with Cromwell FC in 1975 before becoming an apprentice with Newport County in 1975-6 and a full-time professional in October 1977. After joining Leeds in February 1987, defensive midfielder Aizlewood might have won promotion to Division One for the third time. He went up with Luton and Charlton before United signed him for £200,000 from Charlton. Ironically, United lost to Charlton in the last Play-off game of 1986-87. In October 1977, Aizlewood followed his elder brother, Steve, by joining Newport County, making his League debut as a 16-year-old schoolboy, after getting permission from his headmaster to play. He won Welsh Schoolboy and Under-23 honours before a £50,000 move to Luton. Another £50,000 deal took him to Charlton in November 1982 and he was their Player of the Year in 1984-85 and 1985-86. He had won ten full Welsh caps by the end of 1987-88. At the end of 1988-89 he was stripped of the captaincy and banned for 14 days for giving a rude gesture to the crowd after being barracked. It came as no surprise when he joined Bradford City in August 1989 for £200,000. He left Bradford the following August to join Bristol City for £125,000 before moving to Cardiff City in October 1993 where he was player-coach under Terry Yorath in 1994-95. At Cardiff he won the last of his 39 full Welsh caps. He is now a part-time professional with Merthyr Town. Aizlewood is a fine performer at baseball, cricket and golf.
League: App 70/5, Gls 3; FA Cup: App 1, Gls 0; League Cup: App 3, Gls 0; Full Members' Cup: App 2, Gls 1.

ALDERSON, Tom *1930-1932*

Centre-forward. Born: West Auckland, County Durham, Spring 1909.
Debut v West Ham United (h) Division One, 21 March 1931, W 3-0.
5ft 10½in, 12st 4lb. (1930).
Despite a two-goal debut against West Ham, Alderson did not prosper at Leeds. He played for West Auckland and had trials with Bradford City before joining Huddersfield in December 1929, from Cockfield. Leeds signed him in November 1930 and he went to Luton in May 1932. In June 1933 he joined Darlington and then Chester in June 1936. He returned to Darlington in February 1938.
League: App 4, Gls 2.

ALLAN, Jimmy *1925-1927*

Full-back. Born: Airdrie.
Debut v Bolton Wanderers (a) Division One, 7 September 1925, L 0-1.
5ft 8in, 11st 3lb (1926).
A contemporary observer described Allan as 'speedy with a dashing style' when he joined Leeds in June 1925 from Airdrie. He began with Ashfield and could play right or left-back, although he looked more comfortable in the latter position. In July 1928 he was transferred to Third Lanark.
League: App 70; Gls 0; FA Cup: App 4, Gls 0.

ALLEN, Jack W.A. *1922-1924*

Outside-left. Born: Newburn, Northumberland, 31 January 1903.
Debut v Fulham (a) Division Two, 22 March 1924, W 2-0.
5ft 10in, 12st 4lb (1933).
Leeds let Allen slip away to forge an excellent career elsewhere. United signed him in February 1922, from Prudhoe Castle, but in August 1924 he joined Brentford. He switched to centre-forward and newly-promoted Sheffield Wednesday signed him in March 1927. Allen won League championship medals with the Owls in 1928-29 and 1929-30 and after 85 goals in 114 games was sold to Newcastle in June

1931. He scored both goals in the Tynesiders' 1932 FA Cup Final win before being transferred to Bristol Rovers (£200), in November that year. He moved to Gateshead (£100) in August 1935 and retired the following year. A keen motorist and wireless enthusiast, he became a publican. He died on 19 November 1957, aged 54, at Burnopfield, County Durham, where he was a publican at the Travellers' Rest. His brother, Ralph, also played for Fulham, Brentford, Charlton, Reading and Torquay.
League: App 2, Gls 0.

ANDREWS, Ian E. *1988*

Goalkeeper. Born: Nottingham, 1 December 1964.
Debut v Crystal Palace (a) Division Two, 17 December 1988, D 0-0.
6ft 2in. 12st 2lb. (1988).
On-loan goalkeeper Andrews, distinguished himself in his only game for United by keeping a clean sheet during his month's loan spell from Celtic. He was an associate schoolboy with Nottingham Forest and an apprentice at Mansfield Town before signing for Leicester City and won an England Youth honours in September 1981. Loaned to Middlesbrough and Swindon Town in January 1984, he joined Celtic as an understudy to Republic of Ireland international Pat Bonner for £300,000 in July 1988. After his loan to Leeds in December 1988 – for a four-week spell when Mervyn Day was out of action. – he joined Southampton for £200,000 12 months later after another loan period. Unable to get a regular place at The Dell, he was loaned to Plymouth in August 1994 before finally establishing himself as first choice at Bournemouth, whom he joined for £20,000 in September 1994.
League: App 1, Gls 0.

ARINS, Tony F. *1980-1982*

Wing-half. Born: Chesterfield, 26 October 1958.
Debut (as sub) v Ipswich Town (a) Division One, 26 September 1981, L 1-2.
5ft 11in, 11st 8lb (1981).
Arins sampled 30 minutes of first-team action after coming on as substitute for Brian Greenhoff. He made his mark by being booked almost immediately. Arins joined Burnley as an apprentice and turned professional in July 1976. He was taken to Elland Road by his former Burnley boss, Jimmy Adamson, in May 1980, but joined Scunthorpe United on a free transfer in February 1982, having gone there on loan in November 1981. He was released in May that year.
League: App 0/1, Gls 0.

ARMAND, John E. *1922-1929*

Inside-forward. Born: Sabathu, India, 11 August 1898.
Debut v Manchester United (h) Division Two, 27 January 1923, L 0-1.
5ft 7in, 11st (1925).
Jack Armand – who was also known as 'Snowy' – was the first player from outside the British Isles to turn out for United. He played in an Army international against France in Belgium before joining West Stanley in August 1922. Leeds signed him in December 1922, along with his Stanley teammate Albert Bell. Although he was never a regular at Leeds, he commanded a £500 fee when transferred to Swansea in May 1929. He represented the Welsh League against the League of Ireland in 1930, scoring twice in a 6-1 win. He moved to Ashton National (for whom he scored 48 goals) in June 1931 and signed for Newport County in August 1932 and Scarborough in October 1933. In January 1934 he joined Denaby United. Armand died in Grimsby in summer 1974.
League: App 74, Gls 23; FA Cup; App: 5, Gls 1.

ARMES, Sammy *1936-1939*

Winger. Born: New Seaham, Sunderland, 30 March 1908.
Debut v Grimsby Town (h) Division One, 1 February 1936, L 1-2.
5ft 10in, 10st 4lb (1936).

United made two payments to sign Armes in October 1935. Although he was with non-League Wigan, his League registration was held by Blackpool. One report called him a 'sprinter marksman'. He began with Howden FC and Dawdon Colliery before turning professional with Carlisle in May 1930. He moved to Chester in June 1932 and scored nine goals in three successive home matches in 1933-34. Blackpool signed him in January 1934, but farmed him out before Leeds boss Billy Hampson, who was Armes' manager at Carlisle, resurrected his career. In February 1939 he joined Middlesbrough and was released by them in August 1946 having lost the latter years of his career to World War Two. He died in Sunderland on 27 August 1958.
League: App 79, Gls 8; FA Cup: App 3, Gls 1.

ARMITAGE, Len *1920-1925*

Centre-forward. Born: Sheffield, 20 October 1899.
Debut v South Shields (h) Division Two, 1 September 1920, L 1-2.
5ft 9½in, 11st 7lb (1923).
Armitage marked his Leeds debut by scoring their first goal in the Football League. He won an ESFA Shield medal while playing for Sheffield Boys in 1914 and turned out for Sheffield Forge and Rolling Mills, Walkley Amateurs and Wadsley Bridge before joining Sheffield Wednesday in 1914, being transferred to Leeds in June 1920. He left for Wigan Borough in summer 1923 and Stoke signed him in March 1924. He enjoyed his best days with them, winning a Division Three North medal in 1926-27 and touring South Africa with the FA in 1929. In summer 1931 he went to Rhyl before signing for Port Vale, as a defender, a year later. He died in Wortley, Sheffield, in the spring of 1972. His grandfather, Tom Armitage, was a Yorkshire cricketer who was in the first-ever England touring party to Australia.
League: App 48, Gls 11; FA Cup*: App 5, Gls 3.
*Includes one of United's preliminary round games in 1920-21.

ASHALL, Jimmy *1951-1961*

Full-back. Born: Temple Normanton, near Chesterfield, 13 December 1933.
Debut v Swansea Town (a) Division Two, 1 October 1955, D 1-1.
5ft 10in, 11st 6lb (1956).
Ashall signed for United as a 17-year-old after a month's trial. He was spotted in the Chesterfield & District Youth League with Hasland Old Boys and represented Doe Lea Valley. He turned professional in October 1951 but National Service with the Green Howards delayed his League debut. In June 1961 he moved to Weymouth.
League: App 89, Gls 0; FA Cup: App 2, Gls 0.

ASHURST, Jack *1986-1988*

Centre-half. Born: Coatbridge, Lanarkshire, 12 October 1954.
Debut v Blackburn Rovers (a) Division Two, 23 August 1986, L 1-2.
6ft, 12st 4lb. (1987).
Eyebrows were raised in July 1986 when Billy Bremner signed 31-year-old Ashurst for £35,000 from Carlisle United, who had just been relegated to Division Three. But he proved reliable and skippered the side in the absences of Snodin and Aizlewood. He joined Sunderland as an apprentice in 1969, turned professional in October 1971 and won a Division Two championship medal in 1975-76. He moved to Blackpool (£110,000) in 1979 and to Carlisle (£40,000) in August 1981. He was player-coach at Carlisle and made over 200 appearances for the Cumbrians. He joined Doncaster Rovers in October 1988 for £10,000. Released in the summer of 1990, he spent a brief period with Bridlington Town before rejoining Doncaster in November 1990. He played one game for Rochdale in August 1992 and later had a spell with North Shields.
League: App 93/1, Gls 1; FA Cup: App 6, Gls 0; League Cup: App 6, Gls 0; Full Members' Cup: App 3, Gls 0.

ASPIN, Neil *1982-1989*

Right-back. Born: Gateshead, 12 April 1965.
Debut v Ipswich Town (h) Division One, 20 February 1982, L 0-2.
6ft, 12st 3lb (1987).
Aspin was 16 and expecting to play in a Northern Intermediate League game when Allan Clarke told him he would be making his League debut. A product of Heathfield Senior High School, Gateshead, he won Durham County Schools honours and had England Schoolboy trials. He is popular at Elland Road with his never-say-die attitude and willingness to join the attack. He postponed his wedding to play for United when the date clashed

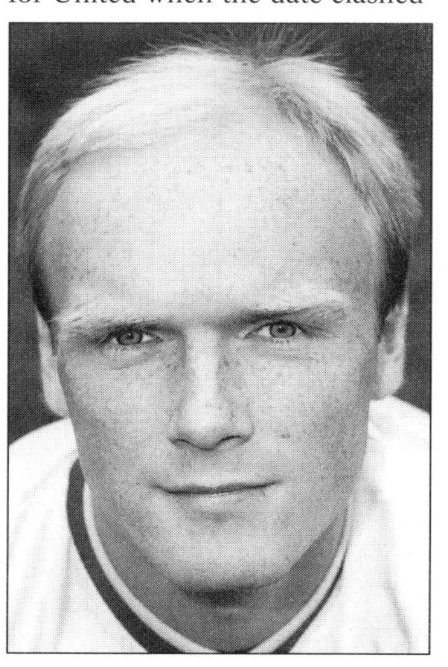

with the FA Cup semi-final in March 1987. In July 1989 he left Leeds for Port Vale in a £200,000 move. Aspin became a rock at the heart of the Valiants' defence and was a member of their side which beat Stockport County 2-1 in the 1993 Autoglass Trophy Final. Hopes of a Wembley double evaporated, however, when Vale lost 3-0 to West Brom in the Second Division Play-off Final a few weeks later.
League: App 208/4, Gls 5; FA Cup: App 17, Gls 0; League Cup: App 9, Gls 1; Full Members' Cup: App 6, Gls 0.

ATKINSON, Josh W. *1924-1928*

Wing-half. Born: Blackpool, 28 March 1902.
Debut v Huddersfield Town (a) Division One, 31 January 1925, L 0-1.
5ft 11in, 11st 4lb (1925)
Atkinson understudied Willis Edwards at Leeds. He started with Blackpool and in May 1924 signed for Leeds, where the assistant manager was Bill Norman, who had been his boss at Bloomfield Road. Atkinson went to Barnsley in July 1928 and joined Chester in June 1930 (£250) before going into non-League football. He died in Manchester in 1983.
League: App 52, Gls 0; FA Cup: App 1, Gls 0.

BAIRD, Hugh *1957-1958*

Centre-forward. Born: New Monkland, Calderhead, Lanarkshire, 14 March 1930.
Debut v Blackpool (a) Division One, 24 August 1957, L 0-3.
5ft 11½in, 11st 6½lb (1957).
Despite a brief spell at Leeds, Baird made his mark as a goalscorer. He began with Dalry Thistle and joined Airdrie in March 1951. In six seasons he netted 165 goals, including 37 to be top scorer in Scotland in 1954-55 as Airdrie won the 'B' Division championship. In 1956 he won his only cap, against Austria. Leeds bought him (£12,000) in June 1957 as successor to John Charles. He scored 20 League goals in 1957-58 but could not settle and joined Aberdeen (£11,000) in October 1958. He scored in the 1959 Scottish Cup Final, when they lost to St Mirren. In 1962 he moved to Brechin City and later played in the Highland League for Deveronvale and Rothes.
League: App 45, Gls 22.

BAIRD, Ian J. *1985-1987 & 1988-1990*

Forward. Born: Rotherham, 1 April 1964.
Debut v Portsmouth (a) Division Two, 12 March 1985, L 1-3.

6ft, 12st (1986).
A robust striker, Baird's aggression often got him into trouble with referees but he was United's top scorer in 1986-87. He moved to Hampshire as a youngster and played for Bitterne Saints, St Mary's College, Southampton, Southampton & Hampshire Schools and won England Schoolboy caps in 1978-79. He joined Saints as an apprentice in July 1980, turning professional in April 1982. After a handful of League games for Southampton and loan spells at Cardiff (November 1983) and Newcastle (December 1984), he moved to Leeds (£75,000) in March 1985. In June 1987 he joined newly-promoted Portsmouth to play First Division football, an FA tribunal setting the fee at £285,000. Hard-up Portsmouth sold him back to Leeds in February 1988 (£185,000). After Lee Chapman's arrival, Baird was sold to Middlesbrough in January 1990 for £500,000. He scored twice in 'Boro's 4-1 win over Newcastle on the final Saturday of the season. That result kept 'Boro up and helped Leeds beat off the challenge of Newcastle, enabling Baird to collect a Second Division championship medal, even though he was no longer a Leeds player. He left Middlesbrough to join Joe Jordan's Hearts in July 1991, for £400,000, but returned to England in July 1993 with Bristol City in a £295,000 deal. A further move took him to Plymouth Argyle in the summer of 1995.
League: App 165/2, Gls 50; FA Cup: App 8, Gls 6; League Cup: App 9, Gls 1; Full Members' Cup: App 8, Gls 0.

BAKER, Aaron *1927-1928*

Right-half. Born: Basford Green, Staffordshire, 1904.
Debut v Swansea Town (h) Division Two, 8 October 1927, W 5-0.
5ft 9in, 11st 4lb (1925).
Baker was the least known of a trio of brothers who played League football (qv). He joined Leeds from Ilkeston Town in October 1927 and went to Sheffield Wednesday in December 1927 but he failed to make the first team at Hillsborough and left for Luton Town in 1929-30, making one appearance for the Hatters. He died on 18 October 1963 at Broxtowe Estate, Nottingham, aged 59.
League: App 2, Gls 0.

BAKER, Jim W. *1920-1926*

Centre-half. Born: Basford Green, Staffordshire, 15 November 1891.
Debut v Port Vale (a) Division Two, 28 August 1920, L 0-2.
5ft 8½in, 11st 8lb (1925).
United's first skipper, Baker played 149 consecutive League and Cup games for Leeds. One of three brothers who played League football: Alf (Arsenal and England); and Aaron (qv) (Leeds). Nicknamed 'T'Owd War 'oss', he played for Portsmouth

and Hartlepools before joining Huddersfield (May 1914), where the manager was Arthur Fairclough, who later signed him for Leeds. His consistency and leadership were important platforms on which the new club was built. He skippered United to promotion in 1923-24 before going to Nelson in June 1926 and later playing for Colne Valley FC. Baker scouted for Leeds and served on the board (1959-61). He ran the Smyth's Arms in Whitehall Road, Leeds, then the Mexborough Arms in Chapeltown. He died on 13 December 1966, aged 75.
League: App 200, Gls 2; FA Cup: App 8, Gls 0.

BAKER, Lawrie H. *1923-1925*

Centre-half. Born: Sheffield, 18 November 1897.
Debut v Hull City (a) Division Two, 22 September 1923, W 2-1.
5ft 10in, 12st (1920).
Baker was mainly a reserve after being signed from Blackpool in May 1923. They were his first League club after he had played for Beighton FC and he broke into their first team in 1919-20. His manager was Bill Norman, who joined Leeds as assistant to Arthur Fairclough and recommended him. He moved to Barnsley in May 1925, joined Rochdale in summer 1929 and, like his brother Jim, he ended his career with Nelson in 1930-31. He died early in 1979.
League: App 11, Gls 0.

BALCOMBE, Steve W. *1979-1982*

Centre-forward. Born: Bangor, North Wales, 2 September 1961.
Debut v Aston Villa (h) Division One, 3 October 1981, D 1-1.
6ft 1in, 11st (1981).
Balcombe was brought up in Ireland and joined Home Farm (Dublin) after winning Republic of Ireland Schoolboy caps. He signed for Leeds in June 1978, turning professional in October 1979. He won Welsh Under-18 and Youth caps and scored a brilliant goal on his full Leeds debut. Despite winning a Welsh Under-23 cap, he was released by United and had trials with several continental clubs before rejoining Home Farm (September 1982). He went to Dundalk (August 1983) and from December spent five-months with Shamrock Rovers. Player-coach to Irish club Oaklands, he later played for Whitby Town under Eddie Gray. He combined part-time soccer in Ireland with work as an insurance salesman and is currently playing for Collingham and is landlord of the Crown Inn, Great Ouseburn, York.
League: App 1, Gls 1; League Cup: App 1, Gls 0.

BANNISTER, Eddie *1946-1949*

Full-back. Born: Leyland, near Preston, 2 June 1920.
Debut v Stoke City (a) Division One, 16 September 1946, L 2-5.
5ft 10in, 12st 8lb (1948).
One of the few men to play League football in spectacles, Bannister proved highly effective for Leeds. After trials with Preston he joined them from Leyland and Oaks Fold in May 1946, when he was demobbed from the Irish Guards, in which he had served as a regular soldier. He later played in contact lenses and once lost a lens and tackled Liverpool referee Bill Evans. Bannister moved to Barnsley in July 1950 and spent a season there. His father, Ernest, played for Preston and Manchester City before World War One.
League: App 44, Gls 1.

BARNES, Peter S. *1981-1982 & 1983-1984*

Outside-left. Born: Rugeley,

Manchester, 10 June 1957.
Debut v Swansea City (a) Division One, 30 August 1981, L 1-5.
5ft 10in, 11st (1981).
At £930,000, Peter Barnes is one of the most expensive players in United's history, but he never reproduced the form he showed at Manchester City, which earned him England caps. Son of Ken Barnes, the City wing-half and chief scout, Peter went to Maine Road from school, having played for Chorlton Parch Juniors, Chorlton GS, Whitehall, Gatley Rangers, Mane & Orst Boug (July 1972). He turned professional in August 1974 and won England Youth honours. His dazzling displays earned him Under-21 caps and in 1976 he enjoyed a magnificent year, scoring in City's League Cup Final win over Newcastle and being named Young Player of the Year. In November 1977 he won the first of 22 England caps. In July 1979 a surprise £650,000 transfer took him to West Brom. Allan Clarke signed him for Leeds in August 1981, but he was loaned to Spanish club, Real Betis, on a £130,000 option for one year, in August 1982. Twelve months later he was back at Leeds, who were now a Second Division club. In October 1984 he went to Coventry (£65,000), after a brief loan spell with Manchester United in May. He spent a season at Highfield Road, returning to Old Trafford permanently in July 1985 (£50,000). In January 1987 he rejoined Manchester City but was loaned to Bolton in October and to Port Vale just before Christmas, then joined Hull on a free transfer in March 1988. In November/December 1988 he was with Farense (Portugal) but played only one game as substitute. Barnes signed permanently for Bolton in January 1989 but left for Sunderland after a month. Just before the transfer deadline he moved to Stockport. He and Ken Barnes remain the only father-and-son combination who have each scored a Division One hat-trick since World War Two. Barnes played in Ireland in February 1990, with Drogheda on a match-to-match basis. His later clubs were Tampa Bay Rowdies (USA) from April to August 1990, then Northwich Victoria (August-October 1990), Wrexham (1991), Radcliffe Borough (1991), Mossley (close season 1991 to October 1991), Cliftonville (November 1992) and a short spell as Runcorn manager from January 1996 before resigning two months later. He also worked as a summariser for local radio, helped run the Manchester City social club at Maine Road and coached youngsters at City's Platt Lane training complex.
League: App 56/2, Gls 5; FA Cup: App 1, Gls 0; League Cup: App 5, Goals 1.

BARRITT, Ron *1951-1952*

Centre-forward. Born: Huddersfield, 15 April 1919.
Debut v Doncaster Rovers (a) Division Two, 25 August 1951, L 0-2.
5ft 9in, 12st (1951).
An engineer who made cutting tools, Barritt joined Leeds as a part-timer in April 1951 for a second try at a career in League soccer. He began with Wombwell before signing for Doncaster Rovers in January 1949 but, despite scoring within two minutes of his debut, he slipped back to non-League football with Rickley Colliery in summer 1950. Leeds paid £500 for him but in July 1952 he was transferred to York City.
League: App 6, Gls 1.

BATES, Mick J. *1964-1976*

Midfield. born: Doncaster, 19 September 1947.
Debut v Burnley (a) Division One, 3 September 1966, D 1-1.
5ft 7in, 10st 7lb (1975).

A neat, compact player, Bates provided vital cover for Billy Bremner and Johnny Giles in the great Leeds sides of the 1960s and 1970s. A Yorkshire Schools player who had trials for England, Bates signed in September 1964, after serving his apprenticeship. He could have commanded a regular First Division place elsewhere but stayed loyal, to Leeds. Although not a noted goalscorer, the one he netted in the 2-2 draw with Juventus in the first leg of the 1971 Inter-Cities Cup Final in Turin was priceless as Leeds went on to lift the trophy on away goals. He was transferred to Walsall (£25,000 in June 1976 and was appointed captain. Two years later, a £20,000 move took him to Bradford City. He went to Doncaster Rovers in June 1980 and later played for Bentley Victoria, alongside Rod Belfitt.
League: App 106/15, Gls 4; FA Cup: App 10/4, Gls 1; League Cup: App 9/8, Gls 1; Europe: App 26 /9, Gls 3.

BATEY, Bob *1946-1947*

Wing-half. Born: Haltwhistle, near Greenhead, Northumberland, 18 October 1912.
Debut v Preston North End (a) Division One, 31 August 1946, L 2-3.
5ft 9in, 11st 2lb (1946).
Batey's League debut for Leeds was against one of his former clubs, Preston, after he won an FA Cup winners' medal with them in 1938. He played for Greenhead South Tyne Rangers, then signed amateur forms for Carlisle United in September 1931, turned professional the following September and moved to Preston in March 1934, enjoying his best days at Deepdale before the war. He guested for Leeds in wartime games and joined them full-time in April 1946. A free transfer took him to Southport in June 1947 in the following close season he was appointed player-coach of North Eastern League club, Annfield Plain. He later worked for Leyland Motors, playing for their works team from 1949, and then became player-coach of Chorley FC. Bob Batey died in a Chorley hospital on 29 November 1988 after suffering a series of heart attacks.
League: App 8, Gls 0.

BATTY, David *1985-1993*

Midfield. Born: Leeds, 2 December 1968.
Debut v Swindon Town (h) Division Two, 21 November 1987, W 4-2.
5ft 6in, 10st 5lb (1987).

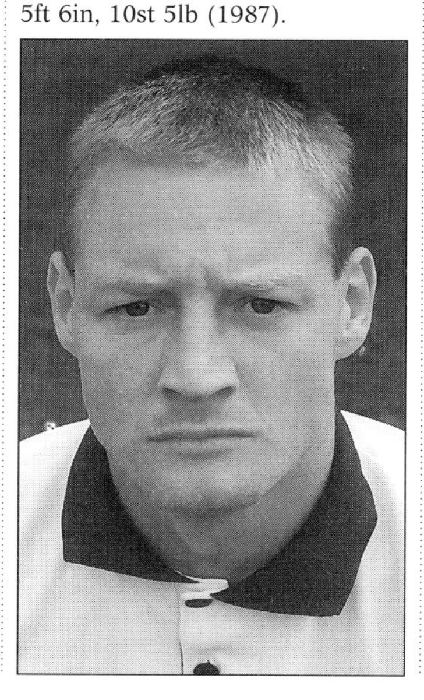

Batty was 18 when he made his debut and impressed with his tackling and speed, going on to be capped by England Under-21 despite only half a season of League experience. Educated at Allerton Grange School, Leeds, he represented the city at every schoolboy level, played for West Yorkshire Schools Under-15 and had England trials. From local side Tingley Athletic he signed apprentice forms in July 1985 and was tipped for a first-team place at the start of 1987-88, but a fractured ankle delayed his debut. He clinched a regular place and earned a call to an England Under-20 training squad in March 1988, going on to win Under-21 caps. Batty progressed during United's 1989-90 Second Division championship campaign to win England 'B' honours. A superb ball-winner and passer, he became an established England midfielder under Graham Taylor. He left Leeds in a surprise £2.75 million transfer to Blackburn Rovers in October 1993 and finished the season as their player of the year. The following campaign Batty collected a Premership medal with the Ewood Park club to go with the League championship medal he had won with Leeds in 1991-92. He missed a big part of 1995-96 through injury before Kevin Keegan bought him for Newcastle in February 1996, but in the final run-in the Geordies faltered and Batty missed out on a third championship medal in the top flight.
League: App 201/10, Gls 4; FA Cup: App 12, Gls 0; League Cup: App 17, Gls 0; Europe: App 4, Gls 0; Charity Shield: App 1, Gls 0; Full Members' Cup: App 12, Gls 0.

BEENEY Mark R. *1993-*

Goalkeeper. Born: Pembury, Kent, 30 December 1967.
Debut v Coventry City (a) Premiership, 8 May 1993, D 3-3.
6ft 4in, 14st 7lb (1995).
United gained special permission from the FA for Beeney to make his debut in the final match of the 1992-93 season. Signed from Brighton for £350,000 the previous month, he was ineligible to play until the start of the following season, but with nothing at stake for either Coventry or United, the FA agreed that he could play instead of John Lukic. Beeney proved a reliable deputy for Lukic and enjoyed a couple of lengthy runs in the side when the United first-choice lost form, but was never able to cement a regular first-team slot, although in June 1996 he signed a new two-year contract with Leeds. He started as an apprentice with Gillingham,

turning professional in August 1985 but after only a handful of games joined non-League Maidstone United in January 1987 and was ever-present as they won the GM Vauxhall

Conference title and promotion to the Football League. After two months on loan at Aldershot, in March-April 1989, he returned to Maidstone where his sparkling form gained him a £30,000 move to Brighton. A big goalkeeper, he has proved meticulous in his preparation and even keeps a video of penalties so he knows what to expect when he faces a spot-kick. His pastimes are golf and cricket.
League: Apps 33, Gls 0; FA Cup: App 4, Gls 0; League Cup: App 3, Gls 0.

BEESLEY, Paul *1995-*

Central defender. Born: Liverpool, 21 July 1965.
Debut (as sub) v West Ham United (a) Premiership, 19 August 1995, W 2-1.
6ft 1in 11st 5lb (1995)
The only Leeds signing in the summer of 1995, the experienced Beesley was recruited from Sheffield United as cover for United's central defence. A Merseysider, he began with non-League Marine, joining Wigan Athletic in September 1984 and playing against Leeds in the FA Cup sixth round at Springfield Park in 1987. Both Wigan and Leyton Orient broke their transfer records when he moved to Brisbane Road for £175,000 in October 1989. Orient soon reaped a handsome profit as Sheffield United snapped him up for £365,000 in July 1990. The Blades' player of the year in 1993, he has played both in central defence and at full-back for Leeds.
League: Apps 8/2, Gls 0; FA Cup: App 4, Gls 0; League Cup: App 4/1, Gls 0; Europe: App 2/2, Gls 0.

BEGLIN, Jim M. *1989-1990*

Left-back. Born: Dublin, 29 July 1963.
Debut v Newcastle United (a) Division Two, 19 August 1989 L 2-5.
5ft 11ins; 11st (1989).
Leeds boss Howard Wilkinson resurrected Beglin's career after it was cruelly shattered in his Liverpool days, when he broke a leg in a 1987 derby game against Everton. His United debut was his first senior game in two and a half years since that incident. Further injuries at Leeds disrupted his progress, but a month's loan spell at Plymouth (December 1989) helped him back to full fitness and at the end of the Division Two championship campaign he was in possession of the No.3 slot. He began his career with Shamrock Rovers, joining Liverpool in May 1983. He broke into the Anfield first team 18 months later and went on to collect 15 Republic of Ireland caps, featuring in the 1986 Liverpool double-winning side and the ill-fated Hysel European Cup Final against Juventus in 1985. He joined Leeds on a free transfer and was pushing strongly for a place in the Republic's World Cup squad. In the end he missed out and ended up covering the tournament on Irish radio. In October 1990 he was loaned out to Blackburn Rovers in an effort to recapture his fitness. A couple of months later he played his final game for Leeds, a 2-1 success at Molineux in the ZDS Cup before a troublesome knee injury finally ended his professional career. He still does a lot of radio work.
League: App 18/1, Gls 0; Full Members' Cup: App 1, Gls 0.

BELFITT, Rod M. *1963-1971*

Forward. Born: Doncaster, 30 October 1945.
Debut v Huddersfield Town (h) League Cup 2nd round, 23 September 1964, W 3-2.
5ft 10½in. 11st 6½lb (1970).
An intelligent front runner, Belfitt served his apprenticeship as a draughtsman and played for Doncaster United and Retford Town before Leeds signed him in July 1963. He provided excellent cover as United battled on several fronts and his greatest triumph came in the 1967 Inter-Cities Fairs Cup semi-final first leg against Kilmarnock, when he netted a hat-trick. A £55,000 transfer to Ipswich in November 1971 saw the start of a nomadic career in which he moved to Everton (November 1972 for £80,000), Sunderland (October 1973, £70,000), Fulham (loan, November 1974) and Huddersfield Town (February 1975). He later played for Worksop Town, Frickley Athletic and Bentley Victoria and now works as a draughtsman.
League: App 57/19, Gls 17; FA Cup: App 6/1, Gls 3; League Cup: App 17/2, Gls 5; Europe: App 24/2, Gls 8.

BELL, Albert *1922-1925*

Right-back. Born: Sunderland, 8 February 1898.
Debut v Southampton (a) Division Two, 1 March 1924, W 1-0.
5ft 10in, 11st 12lb (1922).
Leeds pipped Sheffield Wednesday and Stoke to Bell's signature in December 1922, when he and John Armand joined the Elland Road playing staff from West Stanley, after Bell had earlier played for Annfield Plain. Armand was fairly successful but Bell managed only one senior game before going to Accrington Stanley in May 1925. In August 1927 he was transferred to Durham City. He died in Annfield Plain in autumn 1973, aged 75.
League: App 1, Gls 0.

BELL, Tom *1922-1925*

Left-back. Born: Usworth, near Gateshead, 11 April 1899.
Debut v Bury (a) Division Two, 25 December 1922, D1-1
5ft 7in, 11st 2lb (1922).
Bell developed into a fine player after United released him in June 1925. He signed from Birtley in March 1922 and left for Southend, where he became the club captain. Portsmouth signed him in March 1928 and the following year he was in their side which lost to Bolton in the FA Cup Final. In May 1930 he joined Carlisle, then moved to Burton Town (August 1931) and Usworth Colliery (October 1931).
League: App 1, Gls 0.

BELL, Willie J. *1960-1967*

Left-back. Born: Johnstone, Lanarkshire, 3 September 1937.
Debut v Leyton Orient (h) Division Two, 7 September 1960, L 1-3.
5ft 10in, 11st 8lb (1963).
Bell was a run-of-the-mill left-half when he arrived at Elland Road in July 1960, from Queen's Park, but was successfully converted into one of the best full-backs United ever had. He succeeded Grenville Hair and was an important part of the defence in the early 1960s. Bell joined Queen's Park from Neilston Juniors in 1957. He rejected an offer from Stoke City, completed an engineering apprenticeship and won two Scottish Amateur Caps before taking his chance

with Leeds. Bell won a Division Two championship medal in 1963-64 and appeared in the 1965 FA Cup Final. He was capped twice by Scotland and in September 1967 joined Leicester (£45,000), then Brighton in July 1969. He coached at Birmingham City under Freddie Goodwin, before becoming manager there (October 1975-September 1977). In October 1977 he took over as Lincoln manager, leaving in October 1978 to join a religious sect in the USA called the Campus Crusade for Christ. He coached at Liberty Baptist College, Virginia.
League: App 204, Gls 15; FA Cup; App 24, Gls 1; League Cup: App 15, Gls 1; Europe: App 17, Gls 1.

BENNETT, Willie *1928-1933*

Inside-forward. Born: Manchester.
Debut v Bradford (h) Division Two, 26 December 1931, W 3-2.
5ft 8in, 10st (1930).
United plucked Bennett from Winsford United in November 1928. He was a consistent scorer with the Reserves and rarely let the side down when he got a first-team chance. Southport signed him in July 1933 but he was released in August 1934 and joined Rossendale. He spent three seasons there before a broken leg effectively ended his career in 1937-38. Bennett also played with Upton Colliery in the 1930s.
League: App 10, Gls 4; FA Cup: App 1, Gls 0.

BEST, Jerry *1920*

Outside-left. Born: Mickley, Northumberland, 23 January 1901.
Debut v Port Vale (a) Division Two, 28 August 1920, L 0-2.
5ft 10in, 10st 7lb (1920).
A member of a big Northumberland footballing family. Best appeared in United's first-ever League game. He joined

Newcastle United from Mickley Colliery Welfare in December 1919 and Leeds paid £100 for him in July 1920 after they remembered him playing as a wartime guest for Huddersfield Town. He was soon ousted by Basil Wood and then played in the USA with River Fall FC before re-entering the Football League in August 1931 with Clapton Orient. He joined Darlington in 1933 and had his final season with Hull City whom he joined in October 1936. Best, whose brother Robert played for Sunderland and Wolves, died in Darlington early in 1975.
League: App 11, Gls 1.

BLAKE, Noel L. *1988-1990*

Centre-half. Born: Kingston, Jamaica, 12 January 1962.
Debut v Oxford United (h) Division Two, 27 August 1988, D 1-1.
6ft, 13st 5lb (1988).
Centre-half Noel Blake was snapped up on a free transfer from Portsmouth in summer 1988. The first West Indian-born player to turn out for Leeds, Blake was a non-contract player with Walsall after starting with Sutton Coldfield. He moved to Aston Villa in August 1979 and made his League debut the following April. Opportunities at Villa Park were few and far between and he started a month's loan with Shrewsbury Town in March 1982 before joining Birmingham City the following September for £55,000. He went straight into City's first team and was a consistent performer until a £150,000 transfer to Portsmouth. At Fratton Park he was Player of the Year in successive seasons, helping them reach promotion to Division One in 1986-87. Leeds reaped a handsome profit when they sold Blake to Stoke City for £175,000 in February 1990. He spent a month on loan to Bradford City (February-March 1991) before joining them permanently in the summer of 1992. In December 1993 he signed for Dundee before a long haul took him to Exeter City for the start of the 1995-96 season.
League: App 51, Gls 4; FA Cup: App 2, Gls 0; League Cup: App 4/1, Gls 0; Full Members' Cup: App 4, Gls 0.

BLUNT, Jason J. *1995-*

Midfield. Born: Penzance, 16 August 1977.
Debut (as sub) v Middlesbrough (h) Premiership, 30 March 1996, L 0-1.
5ft 8in, 10st 10lb (1996).
Howard Wilkinson blooded a batch of youngsters the week after the Coca-Cola Cup Final debacle against Aston Villa and 18-year-old Cornishman Blunt found himself on the bench against Middlesbrough. He came on at half-time when Lucas Radebe went in goal because of an injury to John Lukic, United's young team going down 1-0. Blunt won a full place in the following match, against Southampton.
League: Apps:2/1, Gls 0.

BOARDMAN, Billy *1920-1922*

Centre-forward. Born: Urmston, Manchester, 14 October 1895.
Debut v Stoke (a) Division Two, 6 November 1920, L 0-4.
5ft 10in, 11st 4lb (1920).
A free-scoring reserve forward recruited from Eccles in October 1920, Boardman managed few senior matches before going to Doncaster Rovers in January 1922. He netted over 50 goals for Rovers in less than 100 appearances, including 35 in 1922-23, before going to Crewe in August 1927. He once played for the Manchester League v the Irish League. He died in Manchester in 1968.
League: App 4, Gls 0.

BOWMAN Rob *1992-*

Defender. Born: Durham 21 November 1975.
Debut (as sub) v Wimbledon (a) Premiership, 6 February 1993, L 0-1.
6ft 1in, 11st 121b (1995).
Bowman came from nowhere to make his Premiership debut, aged just 17 years 77 days, after hardly any reserve-team football, coming off the bench at Wimbledon to replace David Rocastle. Two days later he made his full debut against leaders Manchester United in front of 34,166 fans at Elland Road, keeping England winger Lee Sharpe quiet in a goalless draw. Bowman figured in a couple more senior games that season but made his mark against Manchester United again at the end of the campaign, playing in both legs of the FA Youth Cup Final which saw Leeds' young guns gain a 4-1 aggregate victory. To cap a superb season, Bowman also featured in the England Under-18 side which won the European Youth championship. Bowman earned himself a professional contract, but did not play in the first team for a couple of seasons until he was surprisingly called up to play against PSV Eindhoven in the UEFA Cup at the end of October 1995. He had enjoyed a fine schoolboy career. He was a member of Manchester United's Soccer School of Excellence as a 13 and 14-year-old, then had a similar spell with Newcastle United before Leeds signed him as a schoolboy in December 1989. He then became a YTS player before signing as a professional in November 1992. He had captained Durham District Under-16s as well as Durham City Juniors and represented Durham in the triple-jump. His father played for Durham City.
League: Apps: 4/3, Gls 0; League Cup: App 0/1, Gls 0; Europe: App 1, Gls 0.

BREMNER, Billy J. *1959-1976*

Midfield. Born: Stirling, 9 December 1942.
Debut v Chelsea (a) Division One, 23 January 1960, W 3-1.
5ft 5½in, 9st 13lb (1974).
The core of Don Revie's great Leeds sides was the midfield blend of Billy Bremner's commitment and Johnny Giles' skill. Bremner, though, was also skilful and his passing, leadership, never-say die attitude and eye for goal made him one of the game's great midfielders. He played for St Modan's High School and Gowanhill Juniors (Stirling) and, after being rejected by Arsenal and Chelsea for being 'too small', he joined Leeds in December 1959. In his early days he often brushed with football's authorities but gradually matured and collected many honours. He won the first of 54 Scottish caps

in May 1965, adding to Schoolboy and Under-23 honours, and is United's most capped player. He is the most successful skipper in the club's history, leading United to two League championships, an FA Cup win and two Inter-Cities Fairs Cup triumphs. He won the 1970 Football of the Year award as United narrowly missed a unique treble of League, FA Cup and European Cup. Bremner moved to Hull City in September 1976 (£35,000) and ended his playing career after joining Doncaster Rovers in November 1978, where he played a handful of games. He led Doncaster to promotion from Division Four on two occasions and returned to Elland Road as manager in October 1985 (see Leeds Managers) He currently lives in the Doncaster area and his son, Billy, is a notable amateur golfer.
League: App 586/1, Gls 90; FA Cup: App 69, Gls 6; League Cup: App 38, Gls 3; Europe: App 77, Gls 16; Charity Shield: App 2, Gls 0.

BROCK, John B.E. *1920-1921*

Winger. Born: Edinburgh.
Debut v Sheffield Wednesday (h) Division Two, 16 October 1920, W 2-0.
5ft 9in, 11st 6lb (1920).
Brock opted to join Leeds instead of Hearts after both clubs sought his services from Edinburgh City. He signed in October 1920, after trials in United's Midland League side. He was released in May 1921.
League: App 6, Gls 0.

BROCKIE, Vince *1988-1989*

Right-back. Born: Greenock, 2 February 1969.
Debut v Crystal Palace (h) Division Two, 2 May 1988, W 1-0.
5ft 8in, 10st (1988).
Brockie attended Linworth High School (Paisley) and appeared for Paisley & District Schoolboys in the Scottish Amateur League. He was on Morton's books as a schoolboy and signed apprentice forms for Leeds in July 1985, turning professional in July 1987. After a two-month trial at Doncaster he was sold to Rovers for £15,000 in March 1989. Released by Doncaster in the summer of 1991, he joined first Goole Town and then Guiseley.
League: App 2, Gls 0.

BROLIN, Tomas *1995-*

Forward/midfield Born: Hudiksvall, Sweden, 29 November 1969.
Debut (as sub) v Newcastle United (a) 25 November 1995, Premiership, L 1-2.
At £4.5 million, Brolin is the most expensive player ever to pull on a United shirt. Yet despite the size of the fee paid to Italian club Parma, the multi-capped Swedish international struggled to make an impact in his early months with Leeds as he fought to adapt to the rigours of the English game and an ankle injury sustained the previous season. He started with GIF Sundsvall in his native Sweden and after three years moved on to IFK Norrkoping, hitting the national headlines with a debut hat-trick. The Under-21 striker was soon elevated to full

international status, making his full debut in a 4-2 win over Wales, scoring twice. Two more goals in his next international, a 6-0 thumping of Scandinavian rivals Finland confirmed that Sweden had a major star. He became one of the leading lights of the 1990 World Cup, scoring a brilliant goal in Sweden's opening game against Brazil. Sweden lost all their opening three games, but Brolin had left his mark and Parma, newly-promoted from Serie 'B', signed the blond-haired 20-year-old. He soon established himself among the top echelons of the Italian game as Parma won the Italian Cup in 1992 and the European Cup-winners' Cup the following year with a 3-1 win over Antwerp in the Wembley Final. Parma lost that trophy to Arsenal in the Final the following year, although Brolin did not play against the Gunners, and also missed out when Parma lost to Italian rivals Juventus in the Final on the UEFA Cup in May 1995 because he suffered an ankle injury in a World Cup qualifier against Hungary. Coupled with his success in Italy has been his progress with Sweden, for whom he has now scored 27 goals in 47 games. He was joint top scorer with three goals in four games in the 1992 European Championships, including the strike which knocked out England. Two years later, in a new midfield role, he helped Sweden to third place in the World Cup finals in America, but injury has kept him off the international stage and he knows that he needs to establish himself with Leeds to make an impact on the 1998 World Cup. Most of the time he found himself warming the substitutes' bench and after failing to make the starting line-up for the Coca-Cola Cup Final, he said that he might be better off with another club.
League: App 17/2, Gls 4; FA Cup: App 1/1, Gls 0; League Cup: App 2/2, Gls 0.

BROOK, Harold *1954-1958.*

Forward. Born: Sheffield, 15 October 1921.
Debut v Hull City (a) Division Two, 21 August 1954, W 209.
5ft 9½in, 10st 12lb (1947).
Brook was approaching 33 when he joined United, yet still managed to score nearly 50 goals for Leeds. He led the Division Two promotion-winning attack of 1955-56 and celebrated United's return to the First Division with a 21-minute hat-trick against Everton on the opening day of the following season. He played for Sheffield Schools, then junior clubs Woodburn Alliance, Hallam and Fulwood before making his senior debut in wartime football for Sheffield United in April 1941, turning professional two years later. He appeared in virtually all the forward positions, at wing-half and full-back for the Blades, enjoyed a spell as skipper and was the regular penalty-taker. He had 89 League goals to his credit when they transfer-listed him, thinking his best days were over. In July 1954, Leeds signed him for a bargain £600. He left for Lincoln in March 1958 and ended his career there. After retiring he ran a newsagent's shop in Meadowcroft, Sheffield, and coached Yorkshire League side Sheffield FC in the 1960s.
League: App 102, Gls 46; FA Cup: App 4, Gls 1.

BROWN, George *1935-1936*

Centre-forward. Born: Mickley, Northumberland, 22 June 1903.
Debut v Chelsea (a) Division One, 14 September 1935, L 0-1.
5ft 9in, 10st 7lb (1935).
'Mickley' Brown was one of the biggest names in soccer when he led Huddersfield's attack during their dominance of the 1920s. A pit boy on strike when the Terriers signed him from Mickley in May 1921, he proved an inspired purchase, scoring 142 League goals in eight years to set a Huddersfield aggregate record which he shares with Jimmy Glazzard. His 35 League goals in 1925-26 – Town's third successive championship-winning season – equalled their club record for a season. He led their attack in the 1928 FA Cup Final and moved to Aston Villa (£5,000) in August 1929, adding another England cap to the eight he collected at Huddersfield. He signed for Burnley in October 1934 and joined Leeds, aged 32, in September 1935. He was top scorer (18 goals) in 1935-36, before being appointed Darlington player-manager in October 1936, a position he held for two years. Cousin of Manchester United and England player, Joe Spence, Brown's spell at Leeds was brief but he made an immense contribution to English soccer over a 15-year period. He later ran a pub in Aston and died on 10 June 1948.
League: App 37, Gls 19; FA Cup: App 4, Gls 2.

BROWN, Tony J. *1983-1985*

Centre-half. Born: Bradford, 17 September 1958.
Debut v Leicester City (h) Division Two, 2 May 1983, D 2-2.
6ft 2in, 12st 10lb (1984).
Brown was a late starter in League football, being 24 when he was signed by Eddie Gray in March 1983, from Northern Counties East League side, Thackley. He failed to establish himself and when Andy Linighan was signed, Brown found himself out of the first team. He had a loan spell with Doncaster Rovers before moving to Belle Vue permanently in March 1985. He became Rovers' skipper and was a consistent and reliable defender for them until he went to Scunthorpe in August 1987. He joined Rochdale in August 1989.
League: App 24, Gls 1.

BROWN, Vic C. *1928-1933*

Right-back. Born: Bedford, 26 July 1903.
Debut v Leicester City (h) Division One, 18 February 1931, L 1-3.
5ft 11in, 12st (1928).
The remarkable consistency of brothers George and Jack Milburn gave Vic Brown little chance to show what he could do after signing from Bedford Town in August 1929. After leaving for Coventry in June 1933 his talents finally began to emerge and he skippered Coventry to the Division Three South championship in 1935-36. After rejecting terms to stay for a seventh season, Brown joined Chester in June 1939, after approaches from Bristol Rovers, Northampton Town, Walsall, Lincoln City and Accrington Stanley. He had a spell in Holland with Haarlem before rejoining Coventry as a member of the coaching staff. During World War Two he guested for New Brighton and Wrexham. He died in 1971.
League: App 1, Gls 0.

BROWNE, Bobby J. *1935-1947*

Wing-half. Born: Londonderry, 9 February 1932.
Debut v Aston Villa (h) Division One, 26 October 1935, W 4-2.
5ft 8in, 10st 10lb (1935).
Former Leeds City, Sheffield United and Irish international star Billy Gillespie helped launch Browne's career. He played part-time soccer in Ireland while working as a joiner, beginning with junior clubs, Maleven and Clooney Rovers, before joining Derry City where Gillespie was manager. He twice represented the Irish League against the Football League before joining Leeds (£1,500) in October 1935 and won six Northern Ireland caps as a United player. An Army PT Staff Sergeant, he played for Derry City, when a wartime posting took him back to Ulster, and guested for Watford whilst stationed at Colchester. In August 1947 he joined York City and two years later became player-manager at Yorkshire League club, Thorne Colliery, becoming coach at Halifax Town in August 1954. He had a brief spell as Halifax manager, taking over from former Leeds teammate, Gerry Henry.
League: App 110, Gls 0; FA Cup: App 4, Gls 0.

BROWNING, Len J. *1946-1951*

Centre-forward. Born: Leeds, 30 March 1928.
Debut v Charlton Athletic (a) Division One, 25 September 1946, L 0-5.
6ft 2½in, 11st 8lb (1948).
A pupil of Leeds Modern School, Browning represented England Youth Clubs against Wales and against the Air Training Corps (at Wembley on his 18th birthday) before joining Leeds' nursery side, Headingley Rangers. He joined the United groundstaff in August 1946 and, after a hat-trick for the Reserves, soon made his debut as a precocious 18-year-old. It was almost two years before he appeared again, as he learnt his trade in the Central League. Although he was leading scorer in 1948-49 and 1950-51, he was transfer-listed and joined Sheffield United (£12,000) in November 1951. He won a Second Division championship medal with the Blades in 1952-53, but quit League football in October 1953 because of tuberculosis. He played for East End Park in the Yorkshire League before a broken leg ended his playing days altogether. Browning's other great sporting love was table tennis and he and his wife, Mollie, played for Leeds Victoria, even when he was a Sheffield player. He later worked as a technician at All Saints' College, Horsforth.
League: App 97, Gls 42; FA Cup: App 8, Gls 4.

BUCK, Teddy *1927-1929*

Wing-half. Born: Dipton, County Durham, 29 October 1904.
5ft 9½in, 12st (1928).
Buck learnt his soccer with West Stanley in the North Eastern League before joining Leeds in May 1927. He made all his appearances in 1928-29, as cover for Willis Edwards and then George Reed, and spent most of his time in the Reserves. He enjoyed better days at Grimsby Town, whom he joined in December 1929 (£2,000), making 354 appearances for them, many after switching to left-back, and winning a Second Division championship medal in 1933-34. In 1945 he joined Grimsby's coaching staff.
League: App 8, Gls 0.

BUCKLEY, Arthur *1936-1939*

Outside-left. Born: Greenfield, near Oldham, April 1913.
Debut v Birmingham City (a) Division One, 10 October 1936, L 1-2.
5ft 10in, 11st 4lb (1936).
Yet another player whose career ended during World War Two, Buckley was a winger of considerable promise. He began with Greenfield before signing amateur forms for Oldham Athletic in March 1932, turning professional a fortnight after his 19th birthday. Leeds paid £2,500 for him in October 1936 and he proved a sound investment, providing plenty of crosses for centre-forward Gordon Hodgson to convert into goals.
League: App 83, Gls 20; FA Cup: App 3, Gls 1.

BUCKLEY, John W. *1986-1987*

Winger. Born: East Kilbride, Lanarkshire, 10 May 1962.
Debut (as sub) v Huddersfield Town (a) Division Two, 6 September 1986, D 1-1.
5ft 9in, 10st 7lb (1986).
In June 19865, Billy Bremner went back to Doncaster Rovers to buy Buckley for £35,000. The winger began with Queen's Park, then had a spell at Celtic, but did not make an impact until he joined Partick Thistle. He scored on his Scottish League debut in April 1983 and a string of fine performances had many clubs chasing him. Bremner signed him for Doncaster in July 1984 and he did well at Belle Vue but could not recapture his form at Leeds. After two months' loan to Leicester City (March 1987) and Doncaster Rovers (October 1987), he was sold to Rotherham United (£30,000) in November 1987. In October 1990 he returned to Scotland in a £45,000 move to Partick Thistle, went to Scunthorpe United the following August for £40,000 and rejoined Rotherham for £20,000 in February 1993. In his only his second full start back at Millmoor he fractured his skull against Plymouth. For a time the injury was life threatening and brought a premature end to his career. He attempted a comeback with Northern Counties East League club Hatfield Main in 1995-96 but collapsed during a game against Maltby MW and was advised to give up football.
League: App 6/4, Gls 1; FA Cup: App 0/1, Gls 0; Full Members' Cup: App 1, Gls 0.

BULLIONS, Jim L. *1947-1950*

Wing-half. Born: Dennyloanhead, Stirlingshire, 12 March 1924.
Debut v Chesterfield (a) Division Two, 29 November 1947, L 0-3.
5ft 11in, 11st 10lb (1945).
Bullions, the youngest member of Derby County's 1946 FA Cup winning side, served Leeds as a ball-winning wing-half. An amateur with Chesterfield, he turned down Blackpool to begin work as a Derbyshire miner. He played for Clowne FC before Derby signed him in October 1944 and joined Leeds in November 1947. He recalls the unusual training sessions masterminded by Major Buckley, including dancing lessons on the pitch while music blasted out from the Elland Road public address system. He moved to Shrewsbury in September 1950 and made over 100 appearances for them as they established themselves in the League. He then played for Worksop Town, Matlock Town, Gresley Rovers, and Sutton Town before starting a nine-year spell as Alfreton Town's manager in September 1960. In April 1996, the 50th anniversary of Derby County's only FA Cup win, Bullions was one of only two members of that team still alive. The other was Reg Harrison, who was the second-youngest member of the Wembley team.
League: App 35, Gls 0; FA Cup: App 2, Gls 0.

BURBANKS, W.Eddie *1953-1954*

Winger. Born: Bentley, near Doncaster, 1 April 1913.
Debut v Notts County (h) Division Two, 19 August 1953, W 6-0.
5ft 8in, 10st 7lb (1953).
Burbanks earned his place in United's history as the oldest man to play for the club. He began with Doncaster YMCA, Thorne and Denaby United before Sunderland signed him in February 1935 (£750). He scored in Sunderland's 1937 FA Cup Final victory and was a veteran when he joined Hull in June 1948. Under Raich Carter he helped Hull win the Third Division North championship and it was Carter who signed him for Leeds in July 1953. The move did not pay off and Burbanks retired in 1954. He guested for Doncaster Rovers, Chesterfield and Blackpool in World War Two. His last game for Leeds was as captain against Hull on 24 April 1954 – three weeks after his 41st birthday. He ran a sweet shop in Hull for 23 years until his retirement in November 1979. He died in Hull on 26 July 1983.
League: App 13, Gls 1.

BURDEN, Tommy D. *1948-1955*

Wing-half. Born: Andover, 21 February 1924.
Debut v Sheffield Wednesday (a) Division Two, 11 September 1948, L 1-3.

5ft 8½in, 11st 5lb (1951).
United's skipper for four seasons, Burden led by example and was a natural choice as captain. He played for Somerset County Boys and was recommended to Wolves, then managed by Major Frank Buckley, by his headmaster. He was only 16 when he played for Wolves in wartime football. He served with the Rifle Brigade and Royal Fusiliers and despite being wounded in the D-Day landings, completed a PT course at Loughborough College. Burden was with Chester when Major Buckley, now Leeds' boss, signed him again in July 1948. He continued to live in his beloved West Country but his commitment to United could not be questioned. After over 250 appearances he finally asked to move nearer home and joined Bristol City in October 1954 (£1,500 plus £500 a year for three years). At Ashton Gate he won a Third Division South championship medal, his only tangible reward for a dedicated career. He later worked as a senior executive with Clark's Shoes in Street, Somerset.
League: App 243, Gls 13; FA Cup: App 16, gls 0.

BURGIN, Ted *1958-1961*

Goalkeeper. Born: Stannington, Sheffield, 29 April 1927.
Debut v Leicester City (a) Division One, 31 January 1959, W 1-0.
5ft 9in, 11st 7lb (1959).
An acrobatic goalkeeper, Burgin might have won a full England cap, had he not suffered badly from injuries during his career. He was playing for Lincolnshire side Alford Town when he wrote to Sheffield United for a trial and the Blades signed him on professional forms in March 1949. He went to Australia with the FA in 1951, won England 'B' honours and was in the 1954 World Cup squad as Gil Merrick's deputy. Future England 'keeper Alan Hodgkinson emerged at Bramall Lane and after another FA tour, to South Africa in 1956, Burgin joined Doncaster Rovers in December 1957. Three months later he signed for Leeds and moved to Rochdale in January 1961, playing for them in the 1962 League Cup Final. After over 200 games for the Spotland club, he became player-manager at Glossop in July 1966. He later served Oswestry, Wellington Town and Burton. Albion and worked for Rochdale Council before retiring to live on the Fylde Coast. A fully-qualified FA coach, he is the younger brother of former Yorkshire cricketer, Edwin Burgin.
League: App 58; Gls 0; League Cup: App 1, Gls 0.

BURNS, Kenny *1981-1984*

Defender. Born: Glasgow, 23 September 1953.
Debut v West Bromwich Albion (h) Division One, 17 October 1981, W 3-1.
5ft 10½in, 11st (1981).
Burns shot to stardom as a striker with Birmingham, then became a fine defender with Forest before joining Leeds (£400,000) in October 1981. He was on Rangers' books before Birmingham signed him in July 1971 and won Scottish Youth, Under-23 and the first of 20 full caps at St Andrew's. A free-scoring but inconsistent striker, he excelled after moving into defence. Brian Clough signed him for Forest in July 1977 (£150,000) and Burns, the core of a team which swept to domestic and European glory, was Footballer of the Year in 1978. A lucrative contract lured him to Leeds, where he was also used in midfield, but he could not stop United sliding into Division Two. He was loaned to Derby in March 1983 and signed permanently for the Rams in February 1984. In February 1985 he went on loan to Notts County and moved to Barnsley in August 1985. He joined former Forest and Scotland colleague, John Robertson, at Sutton Town and in summer 1986 had trials with Swedish club, IF Elfsborg. After a spell as manager of Sutton Town, he joined GM Vauxhall Conference club, Stafford Rangers in the 1988 close season, then had spells with Gainsborough Trinity and Grantham. He later ran a pub in Marchington, near Uttoxeter.
League: App 54/2, Gls 2; FA Cup: App 3, Gls 0; League Cup: App 7, Gls 2.

BUTLER, Walter J. *1920-1921*

Inside-forward. Born: Leeds.

Debut v Stockport County (h) Division Two, 19 February 1921, L 0-2.
Butler won a stack of medals in local football before joining newly-formed United from Leeds Steelworks in August 1920. He netted a hat-trick against his old club the following month, when United fielded a reserve side in an FA Cup game. In summer 1921 he moved to Doncaster Rovers, playing regularly in their Midland League side in 1921-22. In summer 1922 he joined Goole Town.
League: App 1, Gls 0; FA Cup*: App 2, Gls 3.
*These were United's preliminary round games in 1920-21.

BUTTERWORTH, Aiden J. *1980-1984*

Forward. Born: Leeds, 7 November 1961.
Debut (as sub) v Coventry City (h) Division One, 4 April 1981, W 3-0.
5ft 8in, 11st (1982).
Tadcaster Grammar School pupil Butterworth represented England Schools alongside Steve Moran (Southampton, Leicester and Reading). Leeds recruited Butterworth in May 1980 and he broke into the first team with a flurry of goals. In summer 1984 he announced that he was disillusioned with professional football and wanted to go to college to pursue a different career (August 1984). He returned to the League scene with Doncaster before joining Guiseley in 1987.
League: App 54/10, Gls 15; FA Cup: App 6, Gls 1; League Cup: App 4, Gls 1.

BUTTERWORTH, Frank C. *1942-1946*

Centre-half. Born: Barking, London.
Debut v Middlesbrough (h) FA Cup 3rd round (1st leg), 5 January 1946, D 4-4.
6ft, 12st (1946).
Butterworth made 108 wartime appearances for United and also guested for Watford. His peacetime appearances in United's colours were in the two legs of the 1945-46 FA Cup. An amateur with Isthmian League Barnet, he signed for Leeds in 1942, after starring in a pre-season practice match.
FA Cup: App 2, Gls 0.

CALDWELL, Terry *1959-1961*

Full-back. Born: Sharlston, near Wakefield, 5 December 1938.
Debut v Blackpool (h) League Cup 2nd round, 28 September 1960, D 0-0.
5ft 8in, 11st 13½lb (1960).
Caldwell was a teenage prodigy on Huddersfield's groundstaff and won England Youth caps before United signed him in December 1959. His Leeds debut came in the club's first-ever League Cup game but he could not dislodge Grenville Hair and was transferred to Carlisle United in July 1961. He won a Third Division championship medal in 1964-65 and made 340 League appearances before going to Barrow in July 1970 to finish his professional career.
League: App 20, Gls 0; League Cup: App 2, Gls 0.

CAMERON, Bobby *1959-1962*

Inside-forward/right-half. Born: Greenock, 23 November 1932.
Debut v Luton Town (a) Division One, 29 August 1959, W 1-0.
5ft 7in, 11st 11lb (1960).
Scottish Schoolboy international Bobby Cameron spent three years at Elland Road after giving great service to Queen's Park Rangers. He joined the Londoners from junior side, Port Glasgow, in June 1950 and scored over 50 goals in more than 250 League matches. He joined Leeds in July 1959, but found himself in a struggling side. After going to Gravesend & Northfleet in July 1962, he returned to League football in October 1963 with Southend United. He later emigrated to Australia.
League: App 58, Gls 9; FA Cup: App 2, Gls 0; League Cup: App 4, Gls 2.

CANTONA Eric D.P. *1992*

Forward. Born: 24 May 1966, Paris, France.
Debut (as sub) v Oldham Athletic (a) Division One, 8 February 1992, L 0-2.
6ft 2in, 13st 11lb (1992).
Hailed as a hero, fiery French star Eric Cantona's shock departure to arch rivals Manchester United stunned Leeds fans, many of whom turned their adulation to spite. Cantona spent just nine months at Elland Road, arriving in time to add impetus to the charge to the League championship and started the following campaign in grand style with a hat-trick in the 4-3 Charity Shield success over Liverpool. In the League another treble against Tottenham soon followed and the "Ooh-ah, Cantona" love affair with Leeds looked likely to blossom. But the relationship turned sour when the Gallic star and manager Howard Wilkinson failed to see eye to eye and the mercurial Frenchman went to Old Trafford for £1.2 million in November 1992. Controversy was nothing new to Cantona and it was to surface at Manchester where he became an idol. He went to Grande Bastide Secondary School in Mazargue and played for youth side Caillols before joining Nice juniors, signing for Auxerre in May 1981 as a 15-year-old. He did his French National Service with Joinville Batallion at Fontainbleau in Paris and played with the French Army XI. On his return to Auxerre, with whom he made his French League debut against Nancy on 22 October 1983, Cantona, a French Youth and Under-21 international, was loaned to Martigues in September 1985 before signing a professional contract with Auxerre in June

1986. He made his full international debut against West Germany in Berlin, but the following year proved a black one for Cantona. He was transferred to Marseille in June for £2.2 million and, two months later, a verbal blast at national team manager Henri Michel earned him a year's ban from international football. After a loan spell at Bordeaux he moved to Montpellier in July 1989, winning a French Cup winners' medal the following year after a 2-1 triumph over Matra Racing. But a scuffle with a team-mate in the dressing-room heralded Cantona's departure to Nimes in the close season of 1991 for £1 million, but his contract was cancelled there in December 1991 after he threw a ball at a referee and stormed off the pitch. After his disciplinary hearing he announced his retirement from football, but surfaced at Sheffield Wednesday in January 1992, for trials, but Wilkinson snatched Cantona away from the Owls, signing him on loan from Nimes the following month. After the title was wrapped up Wilkinson concluded a £900,000 deal only to sell him to Manchester United, whom Leeds had pipped to the title, three months later. A gifted player, his delightful weighted passes, thunderous shooting and all-round vision were major reasons behind the Reds' League success in 1992-93 and the double triumph the following season when he coolly stroked home two penalties in the 4-0 thumping of Chelsea in the FA Cup Final; he capped the season by being named PFA Player of the Year. But trouble was lurking round the corner and on 25 January 1995 he attacked a spectator with a 'kung-fu' style kick after being ordered off against Crystal Palace at Selhurst Park. Suspended by Manchester United for the rest of the season, he was also fined £20,000 by his club, while the French FA stripped him of his country's captaincy. An initial two-week jail sentence was reduced on appeal to community service while the football authorities imposed a worldwide ban on him, causing him to miss the start of the 1995-96 campaign. But his belated return, against Liverpool, brought the inevitable Cantona goal and after the New Year he was back to his brilliant best as the Reds clawed away the lead of Newcastle United. In the final run-in, a Cantona-inspired Manchester United clinched the Premiership title and he completed his rehabilitation by being named as the 1996 Footballer of the Year.
League: App 18/10, Gls 9; League Cup: App 1, Gls 0; Europe: App 5, Gls 2; Charity Shield: App 1, Gls 3.

CARLING, Terry *1956-1962*

Goalkeeper. Born: Otley, 26 February 1939.
Debut v Chesterfield (a) League Cup 3rd round, 23 November 1960, W 4-0.
5ft 9in, 12st (1956).
Carling had few opportunities at Leeds after he joined them in November 1956, from local club Dawsons PE. He moved to Lincoln City in July 1962, to Walsall in June 1964, then Chester in December 1966 before going to Macclesfield Town. He later worked as a milkman in Chester.
League: App 5, Gls 0; League Cup: App 1, Gls 0.

CARR, Jimmy P. *1935-1938*

Centre-forward. Born: Sedgefield, County Durham, January 1913.
Debut v Portsmouth (h) Division One, 21 March 1936, W 1-0.
5ft 9in, 11st 6lb. (1935).
A West Ham representative was rushing north, hoping to sign Carr, when Leeds manager Billy Hampson arranged to meet the Spennymoor player at Darlington, where the deal was completed. In his first spell with Spennymoor, Carr had signed for Arsenal on a railway station platform in January 1934, as he waited for a train to Norwich. He

returned to Spennymoor on a free transfer in May 1935 and Leeds snapped him up four months later. It proved another unsuccessful move and he transferred to York City in January 1938. He also failed to settle there and at the end of the season returned to Spennymoor yet again.
League: App 2, Gls 0.

CASEY, Terry D. *1960-1962*

Half-back. Born: Swansea, 5 September 1943.
Debut v Rotherham United (a) League Cup 4th round, 12 December 1961, D 1-1.
5ft 7in, 11st 3lb (1961).
Casey joined United's groundstaff and was signed in October 1960. He made his first-team debut at the age of 17, in place of the injured Eric Smith, but soon faded from the scene.
League: App 3, Gls 0; League Cup: App 1, Gls 0.

CASEY, Tom *1949-1950*

Wing-half. Born: Camber, Bangor, Northern Ireland, 11 March 1930.
Debut v Preston North End (a) Division Two, 27 August 1949, D 1-1.
5ft 8½in, 11st 4lb (1950).
Tom Casey was given his first chance by Leeds before winning Irish caps with Newcastle and Portsmouth. He attended Camber School, Second Argyle School (Belfast) and played for Belfast YMCA and East Belfast before joining Bangor. He won Youth caps in 1948 and in May 1949 was one of three Bangor youngsters who joined Leeds. He moved to Bournemouth in August 1950 and Newcastle signed him in August 1952 (£7,500). With Newcastle he won the first of 12 full caps and played in their 1955 FA Cup winning side. In July 1958, just after he had played in the World Cup finals for Northern Ireland, he joined Portsmouth, then went to Bristol City (March 1959). He was player-manager at Gloucester City, joined Swansea (trainer-coach) in October 1966 and in summer 1967 became Distillery's manager. He was later trainer-coach at Everton, Coventry's chief coach (July 1972) and manager of Grimsby (February 1975-November 1976). Grimsby sacked him on the day he moved into his newly-purchased house.
League: App 4, Gls 0.

CASWELL, Brian L. *1985-1988*

Left-back. Born: Wednesbury, near Birmingham, 14 February 1956.
Debut v Carlisle United (a) Division Two, 23 November 1985, W 2-1.
5ft 10in, 10st 7lb (1987).
Caswell arrived at Leeds with a reputation as one of the best full-backs in the lower divisions, but a string of injuries prevented him from reaching his best form. He began as an apprentice with Walsall in June 1969, turned professional in September 1973 and, after 400 League appearances, was signed by Billy Bremner for Doncaster in August 1985 (£20,000). Bremner paid a further £10,000 to take him to Leeds in November 1985 but, after injury and loss of form, Caswell was loaned to Wolves in January 1987. More injury problems kept him out of the first team when he returned to Leeds and he retired in March 1988. In 1990 he was a member of the Birmingham City coaching staff.
League: App 9, Gls 0.

CHADWICK, Wilf *1925-1926*

Inside-forward. Born: Bury, 7 October 1900.
Debut v Sheffield United (a) Division One, 21 November 1925, L 0-2.
5ft 10in, 11st 7lb (1926).
Great things were expected of Chadwick when he joined Leeds in November 1925, but he failed to recapture the goalscoring touch he had shown with Everton. Rejected by Bury, he drifted into non-League soccer with Nelson (November 1920) and Rossendale before Everton signed him (£350) in February 1922. He was their leading scorer (28 League goals) in 1923-24, the best return in Division One that season, but then lost form and his place. Leeds gambled on him but it was a dazzling performance against Wolves Reserves which prompted the Midlanders to sign him in September 1926. He netted 44 goals in 97 games for them before joining Stoke in summer 1929 for £250. He left in October 1930, for a brief spell at Halifax (£100) where he ended his League career. He died in Bury in 1975.
League: App 16, Gls 3.

CHANDLER, Jeff G. *1979-1981*

Midfield/winger. Born: Hammersmith, London, 19 June 1959.
Debut (as sub) v Manchester City (h) Division One, 29 September 1979, L 1-2.
5ft 6½in, 10st 1lb (1979).
Chandler's displays on the left side of midfield made him an effective player. He began at Blackpool in August 1976, after serving his apprenticeship, and arrived at Leeds in September 1979 (£100,000) at a time of great upheaval. with United he won two Republic of Ireland caps, through parental qualification, but did not find life easy at Elland Road and was sold to Bolton in October 1981 (£40,000). After over 150 League appearances for Bolton, he joined Derby County in July 1985 and played his part in the Rams' 1986-87 Second Division championship campaign, although he was at Mansfield Town on loan in November 1986. He rejoined Bolton in August 1987 but was injured within a few weeks. He had a spell with Cardiff City during 1989-90.
League: App 21/5, Gls 2; FA Cup: App 1, Gls 0; League Cup: App 1, Gls 0.

CHAPMAN, Lee R. *1990-1993 & 1996*

Forward. Born: Lincoln, 5 December 1959.
Debut v Blackburn Rovers (a) Division Two, 13 January 1990, W 2-1.
6ft 3in, 13st (1989).
Chapman scored the only goal at Bournemouth which clinched the 1990 Second Division title for Leeds. A powerful man in the air, he joined the large ex-Sheffield Wednesday contingent at Elland Road when he linked up with former boss, Howard Wilkinson, in a £400,000 move from Nottingham Forest in January 1990. Feeding off some great crosses, particularly from full-back Mel Sterland on the right, Chapman's goal tally continued to mount and two goals against his old club, Forest, in the final game of 1990-91 took his seasonal tally to 31 – the best by a striker in the First Division – and his career total to 200. The arrival of Brian Deane heralded the departure of Chapman to Portsmouth in August 1993 for £250,000, but after only five games he was back in the top flight with West Ham for a similar fee. Now past his prime, Chapman was loaned to Southend in January 1995, scored on his only appearance and was hastily recalled to West Ham to be sold for a cut-price £70,000 to Ipswich. He failed to capture the fans' hearts at Portman Road but rejoined Leeds on loan in January 1996 as Howard Wilkinson found his attack badly affected by injuries, suspensions and international calls. Chapman lined up against his old club, West Ham, and had a big part to play in the opening goal of a 2-0 win, but minutes later was sent off. The following week he played in a 5-0 thrashing at Liverpool, was substituted and, after serving his suspension, returned to Ipswich. He joined Swansea City in March 1996. Chapman, whose father, Roy, played for Aston Villa and Port Vale, began his professional career with Stoke

City in June 1978 and showed enough early promise to win an England Under-21 cap. He was loaned to Plymouth as a youngster in December 1978 but, after establishing himself at Stoke, his career faltered after two big-money moves to Arsenal (£500,000 August 1982), then Sunderland (£100,000 (December 1983). Wilkinson got the best out of Chapman when he signed him for Sheffield Wednesday in August 1984. He netted 69 goals in 149 appearances for the Owls before trying his luck in France with Niort (July 1988) in a £240,000 deal. But the move was a disaster and in October he joined Nottingham Forest for £300,000. He played in both Forest's 1989 Littlewoods Cup and Zenith Data Systems Cup successes at Wembley. Chapman, who is married to actress Lesley Ash, netted a hat-trick against Leeds for Stoke at Elland Road in 1980-81.
League: App 135/4, Gls 62; FA Cup: App 11, Gls 4; League Cup: App 15, Gls 10; Europe: App 5, Gls 1; Charity Shield: App 1 Gls 0; Full Members' Cup: App 4, Gls 3.

CHARLES, W. John *1949-1957 & 1962*

Centre-half/centre-forward. Born: Swansea, 27 December 1931.
Debut v Blackburn Rovers (a) Division Two, 23 April 1949, D 0-0.
6ft 1½in, 13st 12lb (1957).
John Charles was the greatest Leeds United player outside the Revie era and he made an enormous impact after being signed on his 16th birthday, by Major Buckley. within three months he had made his League debut and at 18 years and 71 days old he became the youngest-ever Welsh international player when he won the first of 38 full caps. Despite his awesome physique, he earned the tag, 'Gentle Giant'. As a centre-half virtually nobody could beat him

in the air and when he switched to attack, he responded magnificently. In 1953-54 he scored 42 League goals to set a new United seasonal record. Pressure to sell Charles for vast sums was enormous and the board finally gave way when Juventus offered a world record £65,000 in May 1957. Critics said that Charles would struggle in ultra-defensive Italian football but he became an idol there. He won three Italian championship medals, an Italian Cup medal, played for the Italian League and was Italy's Footballer of the Year.

He enhanced his reputation still further as Wales reached the quarter-finals of the 1958 World Cup. After 108 goals for Juventus, he returned to Leeds in August 1962, in a £53,000 transfer. Charles was not the same player that the fans of the 1950s had worshipped and, after only 11 League games, United reaped a quick profit when Roma made a £70,000 bid in October 1962. In August 1963, Charles, nearing his 32nd birthday, joined Cardiff and was still good enough to play for Wales. In 1966 he became Hereford United's player-manager and helped lay some of the foundations of their successful bid for League status. After spells on the Swansea coaching staff and as manager of Merthyr, he returned to Yorkshire to become a publican. In 1987 he was technical director to Hamilton Steelers in the Canadian Soccer League. Alas, Charles fell on hard times but enjoyed a joint benefit with Bobby Collins when Leeds played Everton in April 1988. He ran a pub, then a toy shop and children's clothes shop. His brother, Mel Charles (Swansea, Arsenal and Cardiff) and nephew Jeremy (Swansea, Queen's Park Rangers and Oxford) also played for Wales.

League: App 308, Gls 153; FA Cup: App 19, gls 4.

CHARLTON, Jack *1952-1973*

Centre-half. Born: Ashington, 8 May 1935.
Debut v Doncaster Rovers (h) Division Two, 25 April 1953, D 1-1.
6ft 1½in, 12st 13lb (1971).

'Big Jack' was part of the Elland Road scene for 21 years. A native of Ashington, he attended Hurst Park Modern School, represented East Northumberland Schools and played for Ashington YMCA and Ashington Welfare before joining Leeds as an amateur in 1950, turning professional in May 1952. His uncles, George, Jim and Jack Milburn, all starred with United and it was Jim who recommended the gangling Jack Charlton to Leeds. After National Service with the Royal Horse Guards he occupied the centre-half spot vacated by John Charles, who had switched to attack. In October 1957 he played for the Football League against the League of Ireland. International honours looked likely but his career reached a plateau as he found himself in a struggling United team. He had a brief spell as captain – he gave it up because of his superstition of coming on to the pitch last. With Norman Hunter alongside, Charlton, a supreme header of the ball and excellent tackler, developed into the best centre-half in England. He won a belated first cap in 1965 against Scotland when his brother Bobby, a household name with Manchester United, was in the side. The brothers played vital roles in England's 1966 World Cup success and Jack won 34 full caps altogether, represented the Football League six times and was Footballer of the Year in 1967. He figured in United's early successes under Revie and won an FA Cup winners' medal in 1972, two days before his 37th birthday. The following year he became Middlesbrough manager and was named as Manager of the Year in his first season as 'Boro swept to the Second Division title by a record points margin in 1973-74. In October 1977 he took over as manager of Sheffield Wednesday and revived their flagging fortunes before quitting in May 1983. A brief spell as Newcastle's boss was followed by his appointment as the Republic of Ireland's manager. The first Englishman to hold the post, he steered them to the European championship Finals in 1988, where his side pulled off a famous victory over England. Charlton finished runner-up in *World Soccer* magazine's Manager of the Year poll. To prove that rare Irish success was no fluke, in 1990 he led the Republic to the World Cup finals for the first time. They reached the quarter-final before losing to hosts, Italy. Such deeds earned Jack the Freedom of Dublin. He retired in January 1996 after the Irish just failed to qualify for that year's European Championships in England.

League: App 629, Gls 70; FA Cup: App 52, Gls 7; League Cup: App 35, Gls 7; Europe: App 56, Gls 10; Charity Shield: App 1, Gls 1.

CHERRY, Trevor J. *1972-1982*

Defender/midfield. Born: Huddersfield, 23 February 1948.
Debut v Chelsea (a) Division One, 12 August 1972, L 0-4.
5ft 10in, 11st 6lb (1977).
Trevor Cherry was picked up from Huddersfield Town and groomed into an England regular after being the only non-international in Leeds' first-team squad. He skippered Leeds and captained England against

Australia in 1980. Cherry attended Newsham County Secondary Modern School and played for Huddersfield YMCA before signing professional forms with Huddersfield in July 1965. He captained the Terriers from left-half when they won the Second Division title in 1969-70. Leeds bought him in June 1972 (£100,000) and although he signed as a central defender, his ability to play at full-back and in Midfield made him a valued first-teamer. He won 27 England caps but was also one of the few England players to be sent off, in Buenos Aires in June 1977, when he lost two teeth after being punched by an Argentinian player. Cherry won a League championship medal in only his second season with Leeds, when he replaced the injured Terry Cooper at left-back. After Leeds dropped into Division Two, Cherry joined Bradford City as player-manager in December 1982 and led them into Division Two for the first time since 1937, with Terry Yorath as his assistant. Cherry was surprisingly axed in January 1987. Since then he has become a director of a sports promotions firm called SLP Consulting and also does some local radio sports work. He is now an associate director with Huddersfield Town.

League: App 393/6, Gls 24; FA Cup: App 28/1, Gls 1; League Cup: App 35, Gls 4; Europe: App 20/1, Gls 2; Charity Shield: App 1, Gls 1.

CHISHOLM, Ken McT. *1948-1949*

Inside-forward. Born: Glasgow, 12 April 1925.
Debut v Fulham (h) Division Two, 17 January 1948, L 0-1.
5ft 11in, 12st (1949).
Chisholm, a former RAF fighter pilot, came desperately close to winning full international honours for Scotland. His career took off with Queen's Park, whom he joined in February 1941 and with whom he won a Scottish Victory cap against Ireland in 1945, and after a spell at Partick Thistle (for whom he signed in the 1946 close season) he joined Leeds in January 1948. An exchange deal involving Ray Iggleden saw him move to Leicester City in December 1948 and he was in the Leicester team which lost the 1949 FA Cup Final. In March 1950 he went to Coventry, followed by Cardiff (March 1952), Sunderland (December 1953, £15,000) and Workington (June 1956, £10,000). He ended his League career with 132 goals in 328 games and became Glentoran's player-manager in January 1958. In September 1958 he joined Spennymoor and later played for

Los Angeles Kickers. Chisholm was one of the players involved in the Sunderland illegal payments scandal of the 1950s. He was suspended *sine die* for refusing to answer the investigating committee's questions. Subsequently he admitted receiving illegal payments and forfeited his benefit qualification terms. During the war he guested for Leicester, Chelsea, Manchester City, Portsmouth and Bradford PA. He died in Chester-le-Street on 30 April 1990.
League: App 40, Gls 17.

CLARK, James R. *1924-1925*

Winger. Born: Washington, County Durham, c.1902.
Debut v Notts County (a) Division One, 1 September 1924, L 0-1.
5ft 9in. 11st (1924).
Clark was infuriatingly inconsistent during his brief stay at Elland Road. He possessed blistering pace, but too often let himself down with sloppy ball-control. He began with Annfield Plain and joined Newcastle United in December 1921, after they paid £350 to Jarrow for his services. He welcomed a £300 transfer to Leeds in May 1924 but again failed to make his mark and went to Swindon Town in June 1925. In December 1926 he joined Morton, then Ashington in March 1927.
League: App 3, Gls 0.

CLARK, Wallace *1921-1923*

Winger. Born: Jarrow, County Durham, 14 July 1896.
Debut v Port Vale (h) Division Two, 27 August 1921, W 2-1.
5ft 7in, 11st 10lb (1922).
Like Jimmy Clark, Wallace was a Geordie winger who could play on either flank. Middlesbrough signed him from Durham City in May 1919 and he joined Leeds in May 1921. His form was mixed and he was allowed to go to Birmingham in March 1923. He held a first-team place until injured and moved to Coventry in October 1924. He was released at the end of 1924-25, for Boston United. He later played for Barrow (cs 1926), Torquay (July 1927), Connah's Quay and Shotton. He died in Jarrow on 20 November 1975.
League: App 13, Gls 0.

CLARKE, Allan J. *1969-1978*

Forward. Born: Short Heath, near Willenhall, 31 July 1946.
Debut v Manchester City (h) Charity Shield, 2 August 1969, W 2-1.
6ft, 11st 1lb (1972).
'Sniffer' Clarke's instinctive nose for goals won scores of games for United. Sometimes he was criticised for a lack of work-rate, but when it came to goal-poaching he was devastating. His partnership with Mick Jones was one that few club sides have bettered. He came from a footballing family – brothers Wayne, Frank, Derek and Kelvin played League soccer – but Allan was the pick of the crop. He represented Birmingham Schools and South East Staffordshire Boys before joining Walsall as an apprentice in 1961, turning professional in August 1963. He began knocking in goals and joined First Division Fulham in March 1966. Despite playing in a struggling side, he scored 45 goals in only 85 League games before going to Leicester City (£150,000) in June 1968. After Leicester lost the 1969 FA Cup

Final and were relegated, Leeds paid a then British record fee of £165,000 in June 1969 for Clarke. Top scorer in four of his seasons with Leeds, Clarke scored the most famous goal in United's history – a powerful diving header which beat Arsenal in the 1972 FA Cup Final. He won 19 England caps, six at Under-23 level and represented the Football League twice. After over 150 goals in nine years with Leeds, he joined Barnsley as player-manager in June 1978, getting them promoted from Division Four. He was appointed Leeds manager in September 1980 (see Leeds Managers). He now lives in Scunthorpe and was working as a representative for a firm which makes ventilating extractors.
League: App 270/3, Gls 110; FA Cup: App 43/2, gls 25; League Cup: App 13, Gls 2; Europe: App 33, Gls 14; Charity Shield: App 2, Gls 0.

CLARKE, J.Harry *1947*

Centre-forward. Born: Broomhill, Northumberland, 27 March 1921.
Debut v Wolverhampton Wanderers (h) Division One, 22 February 1947, L 0-1.
5ft 6½in, 10st 2lb (1946).
In an effort to boost their flagging attack, United paid £4,000 for free-scoring Darlington centre-forward Clarke. But the deal misfired and in 14 appearances he managed only one goal and was never on the winning side. He began with Goole Town, then joined Rotherham in 1938, playing for the Millers during the war. In 1946 he went to Darlington and his eye for goal suggested he could be the man to answer United's problems. He returned to Darlington in November 1947 and began scoring again. In November 1949 he went to Hartlepools, then joined Stockton, before going back to Darlington for a third spell in September 1952.
League: App 14, Gls 1.

COATES, Walter A. *1921-1925*

Outside-right. Born: Burnhope, near Annfield Plain, County Durham, *c.*1899.
Debut v Clapton Orient (h) Division Two, 24 September 1921, W 2-0.
5ft 8in, 11st 6lb (1921).
Coates scored the goal which beat Nelson in the penultimate game of 1923-24 and guaranteed Leeds United the Second Division title. It was a rare moment of glory for the popular winger, who was in and out of the senor side in his four years at Elland Road. He starred in wartime football with the Army and Sacriston United before joining Fulham in August 1919. Fulham allowed him to drift back to Leadgate Park in the North Eastern League in July 1920 but Leeds monitored his progress and in 1921 gave him a second chance. The championship season was undoubtedly his best but he found himself out of his depth in Division One and was transferred to Newport County in July 1925, moving to Hartlepools in August 1928.
League: App 47, Gls 3; FA Cup: App 3, Gls 1.

COCHRANE, David *1937-1950*

Outside-right. Born: Portadown, 14 August 1920.
Debut v Derby County (h) Division One, 26 March 1938, L 0-2.
5ft 4in, 10st (1938).
Teenage starlet Cochrane, one of Northern Ireland's youngest-ever professionals, was the first Leeds United winger to win full international honours. A player of blistering pace and tantalising ball-control, he learnt well from his father who had been an inside-right with Linfield. Cochrane junior was playing for Portadown Reserves at 15 and turned professional five days after his 16th birthday. He was only 17 when he scored 14 Irish League and Cup goals in 13 games and that persuaded United to sign him for £2,000 after Portadown's Gold Cup semi-final replay with Derry City in January 1937. At first he was used sparingly, but the Irish selectors soon gave him his debut, against England at Old Trafford when he was only 18 years and three months old. The war restricted him to 12 caps and during the hostilities he played for Portadown and Shamrock Rovers, before Linfield, where he won a Cup winners' medal in 1945. He made eight appearances for the Northern Ireland Regional League before playing for Shamrock Rovers once again, making four appearances for the League of Ireland. He returned to Leeds on the resumption of peacetime football and remained first choice until he retired in October 1950.
League: App 175, Goals 28; FA Cup: App 10, Gls 4.

COCHRANE, Tom *1928-1936*

Outside-left. Born: Newcastle upon Tyne, 7 October 1908.
Debut v Manchester City (h) Division One, 20 October 1928, W 4-1.
5ft 8½in, 11st 4lb (1933).
Once he had won over United's fickle fans, Cochrane played with the confidence of a world-beater. He began with St Peter's Albion in the Tyneside League and had trials with Hull City and Sheffield Wednesday. Also present at those games was Doncaster manager, Dick Ray, who, after taking over at Leeds, persuaded Cochrane to turn professional in August 1928. Cochrane was inconsistent in those early days and was subjected to some barracking from Leeds fans who preferred to see popular Tom Mitchell in the left wing. Cochrane won over his critics and his partnership with Billy Furness was one of the keys to United's Division Two promotion success in 1931-32. He moved to Middlesbrough in October 1936 and in May 1939 joined Bradford, retiring after a few wartime games at Park Avenue. He died in Cleveland in 1976.
League: App 244, Gls 23; FA Cup: App 15, Gls 4.

COLLINS, Bobby Y. *1962-1967*

Inside-forward. Born: Govanhill, Glasgow, 16 February 1931.
Debut v Swansea Town (h) Division Two, 10 March 1962, W 2-0.
5ft 4in, 10st 3lb (1963).
Small in stature, but huge in

standing amongst United's galaxy of greats, Bobby Collins was the platform on which manager Don Revie launched his great sides. Revie paid £25,000 to Everton in March 1962 for the 31-year-old former Scottish international, who went on to lift a mediocre club out of the depths of Division Two to one of the most respected in Europe. He captained Leeds to the Second Division title in 1963-64 and the following season was voted Footballer of the Year as Leeds came close to League and Cup double. He was recalled to the Scottish side after an absence of six years an added three more caps to the 28 he had won with Everton and Celtic. He joined Celtic in April 1948, after playing for Polmadie Street School in

Glasgow, Polmadie Hawthorns and Glasgow Pollok. In ten years at Parkhead he won a Scottish League championship medal in 1954, Scottish Cup winners' medals in 1951 and 1955, Scottish League Cup winners' medals in 1957 and 1958, turned out for the Scottish League representative side 16 times and was one of the few players to score a hat-trick of penalties, against Aberdeen in September 1953. He was sold to Everton in September 1958 (£23,000) and when he moved to Leeds it seemed as though his career was nearly over. But he nurtured a talented brood of young players who went on to grab glory for Leeds. Collins broke a thigh in United's first European tie (2nd leg), in Turin, but recovered well. He left on a free transfer to Bury and embarked on a journey which took in Morton (April 1969), Ringwood City (Melbourne) as player-coach in summer 1971, followed by a move to another Australian club, Hakoah, as coach in October 1971. He had a spell with Shamrock Rovers, followed by Oldham Athletic (player-coach September 1972, assistant manager January 1973), Huddersfield Town (manager July 1974-December 1975), Leeds United (youth coach 1976), Hull City (coach July 1977, manager October 1977-February 1978), Blackpool (coach March to May 1978), Barnsley (youth coach 1980, manager cs 1984-June 1985). He has always been held in affection at Elland Road and shared a testimonial with John Charles in April 1988, when Collins was managing Northern Counties East League side, Guiseley. He left the game to work in the wholesale fashion business and then worked as a chauffeur at Leeds University garage.
League: App 149, Gls 24; FA Cup: App 13, Gls 1; League Cup: App 2, Gls 1; Europe: App 3, Gls 0.

CONNOR, Terry F. *1979-1983*

Forward. Born: Leeds, 9 November 1962.
Debut (as sub) v West Bromwich Albion (h) Division One, 17 November 1979, W 1-0.
5ft 7in, 10st (1982).
Precocious 17-year-old Connor made a name for himself by coming on as substitute on his debut and netting the only goal of the game. It was a fairy-tale start for the lively forward, who had starred for Foxwood School and Leeds City Boys, and he continued the happy knack of scoring early in his career with Leeds. He was capped by England Youth in 1980-81 but lost form in a struggling Leeds team and, after a temporary spell in midfield, was traded for Brighton's Andy Ritchie in March 1983. Connor became a big favourite with the Seagulls and won an Under-21 cap as an over-age player in 1986. He returned to Division One in June 1987, when he joined Portsmouth for £200,000. He left Pompey for Swansea City in a £150,000 deal in August 1990 before teaming up with ex-Leeds players Mark Aizlewood, David Rennie and Mark Gavin at Bristol City 13 months later in a £190,000 transfer. Connor was loaned back to Swansea in November 1992, then had a spell in the GM Vauxhall Conference with Yeovil from January 1994 before being appointed Football in the Community Officer at Bristol Rovers.
League: App 83/13, Gls 19; FA Cup: App 6, Gls 2; League Cup: App 4/2, Gls 1; Full Members' Cup: App 1, Gls 0.

COOPE, Dick *1920-1921*

Right-back. Born: Bradford.
Debut v Boothtown (h) FA Cup Extra preliminary round, 11 September 1920, W 5-2.
5ft 9in, 11st 10lb (1920).
Did not play in the Football League. He joined United in July 1920 from Laisterdyke and left for Denaby United, then moved on to Frickley Colliery in the summer of 1924.
FA Cup*: App 2, Gls 0.
*He played only in both of United's preliminary round games in 1920-21.

COOPER, George F. *1920-1921*

Half-back.
Debut v Boothtown (h) FA Cup Extra preliminary round, 11 September 1920, W 5-2.
6ft, 11st 10lb (1920).
Did not play in the Football League. He joined United from Kimberworth Old Boys in August 1920.
FA Cup*. App 2, Gls 0.
*He played only in both of United's preliminary round games in 1920-21.

COOPER, Terry *1961-1975*

Left-back. Born: Brotherton, near Castleford, 12 July 1944.
Debut v Swansea Town (a) Division Two, 11 April 1964, W 3-0.
5ft 7½in, 10st 9lb (1970).
Terry Cooper was a pacey left winger when he made a surprise debut on the day Leeds gained promotion to Division One in 1964, but he later switched to full-back with devastating effect and became a master of the attacking overlap. He attended Brotherton School and played for Wath Wanderers, the Wolves' nursery team. He had trials with Wolves, but was playing for Ferrybridge Amateurs when he joined Leeds as an apprentice in May 1961, turning professional in July 1962. He eventually displaced Willie Bell, putting his experience as a winger to good effect with breathtaking runs

adding weight to United's attack. His goals were relatively rare, but he scored against Arsenal in the 1968 League Cup Final to give Leeds their first major trophy. Two years later he won the first of 20 England caps and played in the 1970 World Cup. He broke a leg at Stoke in 1972 but fought back to earn an England recall from Don Revie in November 1974, although he limped off after only 23 minutes against Portugal. The following March, Cooper joined Middlesbrough (£50,000) and made over 100 League appearances for them before going to Bristol City (£20,000) in July 1978. He became player-coach at Bristol Rovers in August 1979 and assisted Doncaster for a brief spell under Billy Bremner. In May 1982 he returned to Bristol City as player-manager and became Britain's first player-director. He helped bail City out of deep financial trouble and steered them to victory in the 1986 Freight/Rover Trophy, but failure to push City into the Division Three promotion frame saw him axed in March 1988 and replaced by his assistant, Joe Jordan. Cooper's son, Mark, who overcame the bone disease osteomyelitis, was signed by Bristol City in September 1987. Cooper senior was appointed Exeter's manager in May 1988 and took them to the Fourth Division title in 1989-90. That success saw him named as Birmingham manager in August 1991 and he became a director at St Andrew's but left the Blues in November 1993, rejoining Exeter as manager in January 1994 before ill-health prompted him to quit in June 1995. His son, Mark, is also back at Exeter, having joined them from Bristol City, then following his father to Birmingham before spells with Fulham, Huddersfield (loan) and Wycombe.
League: App 240/10, Gls 7; FA Cup: App 30/1, Gls 0; League Cup; App 21, Gls 2; Europe: App 48, Gls 2.

COPPING, Wilf *1930-1934 & 1939-1942*

Left-half. Born: Barnsley, 17 August 1909.
Debut v Portsmouth (h) Division One, 30 August 1930, D 2-2.
5ft 7in, 10st 3lb (1934).
'Iron Man' Wilf Copping could put opponents off, even before the kick-off. He rarely shaved before a game and his stubble chin added to the menace of a man renowned for bone-jarring tackles. The destructive side of his game brought him fame but he was scrupulously fair, made excellent use of the ball and was a long-throw expert. A pupil of Houghton Council School,

Copping played for Dearne Valley Old Boys and was signed by Leeds from Middlecliffe Rovers in March 1929. He was ever-present in his first season and became part of Leeds' formidable Edwards-Hart-Copping half-back line, all of them England players. Copping won his first cap in May 1933 and in June 1934, Arsenal

signed him for £6,000. With the Gunners he won two League championship medals and an FA Cup winners' medal before returning to Leeds in March 1939. He won 20 England caps, seven with Leeds and represented the Football League twice. During the war he played a few games for Leeds – when on leave from the Army in which he served as a Company Sergeant-Major Instructor in North Africa – scattered over three seasons, before retiring in 1942. He was trainer to the Army XI in Düsseldorf in 1945, then coached Royal Beerschot (Antwerp) and the Belgian national team, became trainer at Southend United (summer 1946), Bristol City (July 1954), and Coventry (November 1956-May 1959). A keen wireless enthusiast, he worked at Ford's at Dagenham and later lived at Prittlewell, near Southend, where he died in June 1980.
League: App 174, Gls 4; FA Cup: App 9, Gls 0.

COUTTS, TOM *1927-1928*

Right-back. Born: Birtley, County Durham.
Debut: v Grimsby Town (a) Division Two, 22 October 1927, L 2-3.
5ft 8in, 11st 4lb (1928).
Coutts played for Saltwell Villa and Ashington before Leeds signed him from Dunstan Atlas Villa (Tyneside League) in January 1927. His only League appearance was in United's 1927-28 promotion season and he went to Southampton in August 1928. He did not make a first-team appearance for the Saints and was transfer-listed (£100) at the end of 1928-29. He spent ten seasons with Newport (Isle of Wight). Mild mannered off the pitch, he had a quick temper on the field and was sent off on numerous occasions, once leaving the pitch to punch a spectator. He lived in Botley, near Southampton, until his death in the early 1980s.
League: App 1, Gls 0.

COUZENS, Andy *1993-*

Midfield/Defender. Born: Shipley, 4 June 1975.
Debut (as sub) v Coventry City (h), Premiership, 18 March 1995, W 3-1.
5ft 9in 11st 6lb (1995)
A member of the 1993 FA Youth Cup-winning squad, Couzens made his debut as a substitute for Lucas Radebe in a Premiership victory over Coventry after leading the Reserves to third place in the Pontin's Central League the previous season. His breakthrough was quickly followed by a call up for the England Under-21s for the annual Toulon summer tournament in France. His versatility gave manager Howard Wilkinson more options during the fragmented 1995-96 campaign as the youngster was used in midfield and defence. He represented Yorkshire at badminton for five years as a teenager and was Bradford Under-16 and Under-18 tennis champion. He went to school at Salts.
League: App 10/8, Gls 0; League Cup: App 1/1, Gls 1; Europe: App 0/2, Gls 0.

COYNE, Cyril *1944-1946*

Wing-half. Born: Barnsley, 2 May 1924.
Debut v Middlesbrough (h) FA Cup 3rd round (1st leg), 5 January 1946, D 4-4.
5ft 8in, 10st 8lb (1946).
Coyne made over 50 wartime appearances for United – and some as a York City guest – but never played League soccer for Leeds, who signed him from Barnsley Main in October 1944. He played in both legs of their 1945-46 FA Cup-tie, then dropped out of favour and went to Stalybridge Celtic (Cheshire League). He finally made his League debut after signing for Halifax Town in June 1951, when his old Leeds wartime colleague, Gerry Henry, was in charge. He died in Leeds just before Christmas 1981. FA Cup: App 2, Gls 0.

CROWE, Chris *1956-1960*

Winger. Born: Newcastle upon Tyne, 11 June 1939.
Debut v Burnley (a) Division Two, 20 October 1956, D 0-0.
5ft 7½in, 11st 11lb (1957).
Crowe had the distinction of playing for Scotland Schoolboys and the full England team. He moved to Edinburgh with his family before joining Leeds as an amateur in October 1954. He won eight England Youth caps and turned professional in June 1956. Crowe was allowed to go to Blackburn Rovers in March 1960 (£25,000) and it was not until he joined Wolves (£28,000) in February 1962 that he reached his peak, winning a full cap against France in 1963 to add to four Under-23 appearances. In August 1964, Nottingham Forest signed him (£30,000), when Crowe was still only 25 and he stayed at the City Ground until January 1967 before moving to Bristol City for £15,000. He signed for Auburn FC (Australia) in May 1969 but returned to England in September that year to join Walsall. He ran a pub in Leeds and a newsagents in Bristol before coming out of retirement to play for Bath City in February 1971.
League: App 95, Gls 27; FA Cup: App 3, Gls 0.

CURRIE, Tony W. *1976-1979*

Midfield. Born: Edgware, London, 1 January 1950.
Debut v West Bromwich Albion (h) Division One, 21 August 1976, D 2-2.
5ft 11in, 12st 9lb (1977).
Tony Currie was the nearest thing Leeds had to fill the vacuum created by the departure of the Bremner-Giles combination. His delicate skills and passing ability saw him win 11 of his 17 England caps while a Leeds player. He attended Childs Hill Junior School and Whitefield Secondary Modern School (Cricklewood) and represented Hendon Boys before signing amateur forms with QPR, while working for a building company. He was rejected by Chelsea after a brief spell as an apprentice, but was picked up by Watford in May 1967 and won England Youth honours. After only 17 appearances for Watford, Sheffield United signed him (£35,000) and he was soon pushing for full England recognition, although the Blades were not then a fashionable club. He played for the Football League and England Under-23s and won his first full cap in 1972. Sheffield United eventually succumbed to a £240,000 bid by Leeds and Currie maintained his star status at Elland Road, adding consistency to his talents. For two seasons he was a regular in the England squad, but could not add domestic honours. His wife became unsettled and he

returned to London to join QPR (£400,000), helping them to the 1982 FA Cup Final before injuries checked his progress. After two months with Toronto Nationals (Canada) he spent a month with Chesham United before joining Southend, then Torquay as a non-contract player. In October 1984 he signed for Tranmere, but was released before making a senior appearance. He later played for Dunstable, Hendon and Goole Town. In February 1988 he became full-time community organiser at Sheffield United.
League: App 102, Gls 11; FA Cup: App 9, Gls 0; League Cup: App 13, Gls 5.

CURTIS, Alan T. *1979-1980*

Forward. Born: Ton Pentre, near Pontypridd, 16 April 1954.
Debut v Bristol City (a) Division One, 18 August 1979, D 2-2.
5ft 11in, 12st 7½lb (1979).
Despite a two-goal debut for Leeds, Curtis' time with United was blighted by injury and loss of form. He built his reputation as Swansea surged out of the lower divisions and in May 1979, Leeds paid £400,000 for him, a record for a Third Division player. He first joined Swansea in July 1972 and in December 1980, Leeds cut their losses and sold him back to the Swans (£165,000). A regular for Wales, he moved to Southampton in November 1983 (£85,000), was loaned to Stoke City in February 1986 and joined Cardiff in summer 1987, on a free transfer. One of the most expensive flops in United's history – he suffered a bad knee injury while at Elland Road – he nevertheless played 35 times for the full Welsh side, winning six of his caps as a Leeds player. He is a nephew of Roy Paul, the former Manchester City and Wales star. In October 1989, Curtis returned to his old stomping ground at Swansea, with Cardiff receiving a

nominal fee. He announced his retirement at the end of 1989-90 and joined Barry Town as player-coach in the summer of 1990, then signed for Haverford West County in July 1991. He now works as a financial consultant with a life assurance company and is Swansea City's Football in the Community Officer.
League: App 28, Gls 5; FA Cup: App 1, Gls 0; League Cup: App 2, Gls 0; Europe: App 4, Gls 1.

CUSH, Wilbur W. *1957-1960*

Half-back/inside-forward. Born: Lurgan, Northern Ireland, 10 June 1928.
Debut v Manchester City (h) Division One, 16 November 1957, L 2-4.
5ft 5in, 11st 7lb (1957).
Cush was already an Irish international and Ulster's Footballer of the Year when Leeds snapped him up for £7,000 from Glenavon in November 1957. He was developed at Carrisk School, Lurgan Boys' Club and Shankhill YMCA before signing for Glenavon in 1947. They were one of the 'Cinderella' clubs of Irish football but, inspired by Cush, they swept to their first-ever Irish League and Cup wins. Appointed United's captain, he was a member of Northern Ireland's 1958 World Cup squad. In June 1960 he moved to Portadown and in November 1966 rejoined Glenavon, later becoming their trainer-coach. He was capped 26 times between 1951 and 1962, played for the Irish League and won Irish Gold Cup winners' medals (1954 and 1956), an Ulster Cup winners' medal (1955), an Irish Cup winners' medal (1957) and an Irish League championship medal (1952). Cush died in July 1981, aged 53.
League: App 87, Gls 9; FA Cup: App 3, Gls 0.

DANIELS, John F. *1933-1935*

Goalkeeper. Born: Bramley, Leeds, 1906.
Debut v Chelsea (a) Division One, 16 March 1935, L 1-7.
5ft 10in, 11st 10lb (1935).
Although Daniels' only peacetime appearance for Leeds was a disaster – they lost 7-I at Stamford Bridge – he gave United distinguished service during the war. He joined Stockport County as an amateur in August 1932 and they blooded him as an 18-year-old in their 'A' team, but he was released and joined Manchester North End, then Ashton National. Leeds signed him in October 1933, on amateur forms, and he turned professional the following April but within three months of the Chelsea debacle he rejoined Stockport and established himself as first choice. He left for Accrington Stanley in July 1938 and injured his hand in one match against Gateshead, prompting him to come out of goal to play on the wing. A move to Tranmere Rovers in June 1939 followed and during the war he made 121 appearances for Leeds as a guest. An excellent cricketer, he was also an FA coach. In the 1950s he was games mater at Boston Spa Special School.
League: App 1, Gls 0.

DANSKIN, Bob *1929-1932*

Centre-half. Born: Scotswood, near Newcastle, 28 May 1908.
Debut v Derby County (h) Division One, May 1931, W 3-1.
5ft 8in, 11st 7lb (1938).
Danskin, a regular Methodist church-goer who liked a round of golf, began with Throckley (East Tyne League) before joining Leeds from Wallsend United in May 1929. He found it impossible to dislodge the consistent Ernie Hart and a £2,000 move in December 1932 took him to Bradford. He made 506 League and wartime appearances for the Park Avenue club before retiring in 1947. He later bred pigs and dairy cattle and also figured on the post-war Bradford staff as a coach. He died in September 1985, in Newcastle.
League: App 5, Gls 1; FA Cup: App 1, Gls 0.

DARK, Alf J. *1920-1923*

Half-back/centre-half. Born: Bristol, 21 August 1893.
Debut v Leicester City (a) Division One, 28 October 1922, L 1-2.
6ft, 12st (1922).
Originally an inside-right, Dark was among United's earliest signings, joining them from Newcastle in May 1921. He failed to get into Newcastle's first team after joining them from Wallsend in 1920 and did not get a chance at Leeds until the 1922-23 season, at a relatively old age. Transferred to Port Vale in June 1923, he returned to Yorkshire the following summer when Halifax pipped Chesterfield for his signature. He left Halifax in summer 1928 for a spell with Barrow. He died on 3 August 1964.
League: App 3, Gls 0.

DAVEY, Nigel G. *1964-1974*

Full-back. Born: Garforth, 20 June 1946.
Debut v West Bromwich Albion (h) League Cup 3rd round, 13 October 1965, L 2-4.
5ft 9in, 10st 10lb (1970).
Fate conspired against Davey when the chance of an extended run in Don Revie's team eventually came his way. On the same day Terry Cooper broke his leg at Stoke in April 1972, Davey fractured his leg in a Reserve game against West Brom. Spotted playing for Great Preston Juniors, he joined Leeds as an apprentice in February 1964 and moved to Rotherham in July 1974, but was released without making a senior appearance.
League: App 13/1, Gls 0; FA Cup: App 1, Gls 0; League Cup: App 2, Gls 0; Europe: App 4/2, Gls 0.

DAVIES, Byron *1952-1956*

Half-back. Born: Llanelli, 5 February 1932.
Debut v Luton Town (h) Division Two, 19 April 1954, W 2-1.
5ft 11in, 12st (1956).
Davies, a product of Camarthenshire League football, joined Lanelli at the start of 1951-52 and soon attracted Leeds, who signed him in May 1952. He looked promising in the Reserves but could not bridge the gap to the Football League and in June 1956, after National Service, he moved Newport County on the recommendation of former Leeds and Newport player, Harry Duggan, but did not appear in Newport's senior side.
League: App 1, Gls 0.

DAVISON, Bobby *1987-1992*

Forward. Born: South Shields, 17 July 1959.
Debut v Swindon Town (h) Division Two, 21 November 1987, W 4-2.
5ft 8in, 11st 8lb (1987).
Davison, a proven goalscorer, signed from Derby County in November 1987 (£350,000) to add firepower to United's understrength attack. Derby's top scorer for four successive seasons, he started his Leeds career with a flurry of goals. A former shipyard worker, he began with Seaham Red Star before joining Huddersfield Town in July 1980. Transferred to Halifax Town in August 1981 (£20,000), his performances there persuaded Second Division Derby to buy him in November 1982 (£80,000). The Rams were relegated but Davison's goals helped them back from Third to First Division in successive seasons and altogether he scored 83 goals in just over 200 League appearances for them. Despite injury he still maintained a decent strike rate during the Second Division championship season. He found goals harder to come by in the First Division and after being loaned to his old club Derby (September 1991) and Sheffield United (March 1992), he joined Leicester City for £50,000 in August 1992. Sheffield United boss Dave Bassett had been impressed with Davison during his brief stay at Bramall Lane and snapped him up on a free transfer in November 1993, but he remained with the Blades for only 11 months, moving on to Rotherham where he briefly formed a striking partnership with former Leeds man lmre Varadi. Davison spent a month on loan with Hull City during 1995-96 and returned to Halifax Town in the 1996 close season.
League: App 79/12, Gls 31; FA Cup: App 2/4, Gls 1; League Cup: App 4, Gls 1; Full Members' Cup: App 7/2, Gls 3.

DAWSON, Bobby *1953-1955*

Right-back. Born: South Shields, 31 January 1935.
Debut v Hull City (a) Division Two 24 April 1954 D 1-1.
5ft 10in, 11st 4lb (1957).
Dawson worked as an electrician at Harton Colliery before joining Leeds from South Shields in November 1953. He had earlier played for Bolden School and the Durham County Amateur League and had an unsuccessful trial with Manchester City when he was 16. He could not dislodge veteran Jimmy Dunn at Leeds and his only appearance came when Dunn was injured. In November 1955 he signed for Gateshead and made over 100 League appearances in the lower divisions.
League: App 1, Gls 0.

DAY, Mervyn R. *1985-1993*

Goalkeeper. Born: Chelmsford, Essex, 26 June 1955.
Debut v Oldham Athletic (a) Division Two, 2 February 1985, D 1-1.
6ft 2in, 15st 1lb (1987).
Hailed as a future England goalkeeper, after a breathtaking start to his career, Day never quite fulfilled that early promise, although he enjoyed a successful 'second career' at Leeds. He excelled as an all-round sportsman at King Edward VI Grammar School (Chelmsford) before joining West Ham in March 1973. He broke into the first team five months later and a series of brilliant displays made him a favourite for full England honours. But, after becoming the youngest FA Cup Final goalkeeper in 1975 – the same year he was named Young Player of the Year – and winning Youth and Under-23 caps, he lost form and was transferred to Orient in July 1979 (£100,000). Aston Villa signed him for £15,000, as cover for Nigel Spink, before Eddie Gray took him to Leeds for £30,000 in February 1985. Day

did well and was a key figure in United's run to the 1987 FA Cup semi-final. He passed his 600th League appearance on his way to a Second Division championship medal in 1989-90. John Lukic's arrival for £1 million saw Day pushed to the sidelines, spending his last season at Elland Road as a player-coach. He joined Carlisle United, on a free transfer, as player-coach in July 1993 after loan spells at Luton Town (March 1992) and Sheffield United (May 1992). The Cumbrians stormed to the Division Three title in 1994-95 and were beaten 1-0 by a sudden death goal by Birmingham City in the Auto Windscreens Final at Wembley the same season. Day stepped up as manager at Carlisle in February 1996 when Mick Wadsworth was appointed to the staff at Norwich. Day's son, Richard, a midfielder with Yorkshire Amateurs and Leeds City Boys, signed associate schoolboy forms with United in April 1994.
League: App 232, Gls 0; FA Cup: 11, Gls 0; League Cup: App 14, Gls 0, Full Members' Cup: App 11, Gls0

DE MANGE, Ken J.P.P. *1987-1988*

Midfield. Born: Dublin, 3 September 1964.
Debut v Manchester City (h) Division Two, 26 September 1987, W 2-0.
5ft 9in, 11st 10lb.
De Mange marked his Leeds debut with an eighth-minute goal following his £65,000 transfer from Liverpool, but that was his only strike in a brief career at Elland Road. He represented Dublin Schools and Republic of Ireland Youth, winning the Irish Young Player of the Year award as a 17-year-old with Home Farm. He signed a three-year contract for Liverpool but never got a League game, although he won a full cap as substitute against Brazil in Dublin in May 1987. He was also capped at Under-21 level the previous year. In January, he spent a month on loan to Scunthorpe and when he joined Leeds in September, looked to have the makings of a fine player before moving to Hull City in March 1988 in a surprise £65,000 deal. In and out of the side at Hull, he was loaned to Cardiff twice, in November 1990 and the following March, before returning to play in his native Ireland with Limerick in summer 1992. Twelve months later he moved north to Ards, returning to the Republic in November 1993 to play for Bohemians, leaving for Dundalk on a free transfer the following October.

DEANE, Brian *1993-*

Striker. Born: Leeds, 7 February 1968.
Debut v Manchester City (a) Premiership, 14 August 1993, D 1-1.
6ft 3in, 12st lb (1996)
Although a club record signing when he arrived at Elland Road for £2.7 million, Deane had played for Leeds' youth team in 1984 after starring with Leeds City Boys. He was not taken on, but instead joined Doncaster Rovers as an apprentice in December 1985. A traditional

target-man striker, he proved highly popular at Rovers and his powerful displays saw him move up to Sheffield United in July 1988 for £30,000. In his first season at Bramall Lane he struck up a devastating partnership with Tony Agana and they netted 46 goals between them as the Blades earned promotion to Division Two. He was top scorer the following season, when Sheffield United finished runners-up to Leeds in Division Two, and went on the England tour of Australasia, earning two caps against New Zealand. A third followed against Spain to add to his three 'B' international caps. Despite scoring a last-minute equaliser on his United debut, Deane struggled to live down his big price tag and it was onIy when Tony Yeboah arrived that he really got a new lease of life, playing on the left side of the attack. He was voted the Supporters' Player of the Year in 1994-95.
League: App 104/6, Gls 27; FA Cup: App 9/3, Gls 3; League Cup: App 8/3 Gls 2; Europe: App 3, Gls 0.

DEPEAR, E.Roly *1948-1949*

Centre-half. Born: Spalding, 10 December 1923.
Debut v Leicester City (h) Division Two, 18 December 1948, W 3-1.
6ft 3in, 14st (1950).
Depear, who had served as a Royal Marine commando in World War Two, was Major Frank Buckley's first signing for Leeds when he joined them from Boston United in May 1948. United paid £500 plus an agreement for a further £300 if he made ten or more appearances. They also agreed to meet Boston in the Mather Cup, a Lincolnshire charity competition. In the event Leeds did not have to find the extra money and the player was transferred to Newport in an exchange deal involving winger Harold Williams in June 1949. Depear was valued at £8,000 and Williams at £12,000, so Leeds paid Newport £4,000. Depear signed for Shrewsbury in July 1950 and skippered the Shrews before moving on to Bangor City in July 1952, serving them as player-manager until 1955.
League: App 4, Gls 0; FA Cup: App 1, Gls 0.

DICKINSON, Martin J. *1980-1986*

Defender. Born: Leeds, 14 March 1963.
Debut v Middlesbrough (h) Div One, 2 April 1980, W 2-0.
5ft 10in, 11st (1985).
Dickinson, who made his First Division debut only three weeks after his 17th birthday, starred with Foxwood School, Leeds City Boys and Yorkshire Boys before joining the Elland Road staff. He did not turn professional until May 1980 and went on to play a useful role in defence, also figuring as a ball-winning midfielder. In February 1986, he was sold to West Brom (£40,000) on the day centre-half Brendan Ormsby joined Leeds from Aston Villa. Dickinson moved to Sheffield United in July 1988, but his progress was checked by injuries sustained in a car crash. Finally, he was forced to give up the game.
League: App 100/2; Gls 2; FA Cup: App 6, Gls 0; League Cup: App 10, Gls 0.

DOIG, Russell *1986-1988*

Winger. Born: Millport, Isle of Cumbrae, 17 January 1964.
Debut (as sub) v Derby County (h) Division Two, 29 November 1986, W 2-0.
5ft 8in, 10st 9lb (1986).
A Scottish Schoolboy international, Doig was spotted by St Mirren scout Jack Gilmour but did not make their first team and moved to East Stirlingshire in summer 1983. After 109 appearances for them, he joined Leeds in July 1986 (£15,000). Unable to claim a regular first-team place, he spent a month on loan with Peterborough in October 1986, then joined Hartlepool (£10,000) in March 1988. Released by Hartlepool in summer 1990 he later played for Halifax Town, Harrogate Town, Nuneaton Borough and Farsley Celtic and was believed to be working as a taxi driver in the Leeds area.
League: App 3/3, Gls 0; FA Cup: App 1, Gls 0; League Cup: App 1/2, Gls 0.

DONNELLY, John *1983-1985*

Midfield. Born: Glasgow, 8 March 1961.
Debut v Blackburn Rovers (h) Division Two, 5 March 1983, W 2-1.
5ft 10½in, 11st 6lb (1983).
Leeds offered Donnelly his second chance in League football when he became Eddie Gray's first signing in March 1983. Rejected as an apprentice by Notts County, he played for Motherwell and then Dumbarton before United bought him for £10,000, plus £5,000 for each League game up to 15 appearances. He went straight into the first team but inconsistency cost him a place and he was loaned to Partick Thistle in November 1984, joining them permanently the following March. He signed for Dunfermline in June 1986 and helped them win promotion to the Scottish Premier Division in his first season. On 19 April 1988, Dunfermline announced they had sacked him for breach of contract after he failed to turn up to play or train.
League: App 36/4, Gls 4; FA Cup: App 1, Gls 0; League Cup: App 3, Gls 0.

DORIGO, Tony *1991-*

Left back. Born: Melbourne, Australia, 31 December 1965.
Debut v Nottingham Forest (h) Division One, 20 August 1991, W 1-0.
5ft 10in, 10st 10lb (1996).
Instant control and acceleration marks Australian-born left-back Tony Dorigo as the best Leeds player in the position since Terry Cooper. Player of the Year in United's 1991-92 League championship season, he has

suffered badly through knee and hamstring injuries in the last two seasons which has also seen him fall in the international pecking order. His family moved from Australia to Birmingham and he had trials with Aston Villa as a youngster and was taken on as an apprentice in 1981, turning professional in January 1982. He won 11 Under-21 caps at Villa Park before a £475,000 move took him to Chelsea in July 1987.

In four years at Stamford Bridge, he won six full caps, helped the Blues to the 1988-89 Second Division championship and scored the winner in the 1990 Zenith Data Systems Final at Wembley against Middlesbrough. The holder of seven 'B' international caps, he was signed by Howard Wilkinson in May 1991 for £1.3 million and was a scorer when champions Leeds beat Liverpool 4-3 in the FA Charity Shield in 1992. He continued to make progress on the international front under Graham Taylor, but did not figure in a Terry Venables team after his last two seasons were blighted by injury.
League: App 153, Gls 5; FA Cup: App 12, Gls 0; League Cup: App 10/1, Gls 0; Europe: App 7, Gls 0; Charity Shield: App 1, Gls 1; Full Members' Cup: App 1, Gls 0.

DOWN, Billy *1920-1925*

Goalkeeper. Born: Ryehope, near Sunderland, 22 January 1898.
Debut v Port Vale (a) Division Two, 28 August 1920, L 0-2.
5ft 9in, 11st 7lb (1922).
Down kept goal in United's first Football League fixture and was ever-present in their debut season. He signed from Ashington in July 1920 and, despite losing his place to Fred Whalley in 1921-22, battled back to recapture the position for most of United's 1923-24 Division Two championship-winning campaign. In September 1925 he moved to Doncaster Rovers before joining Burnley in September 1927, on a

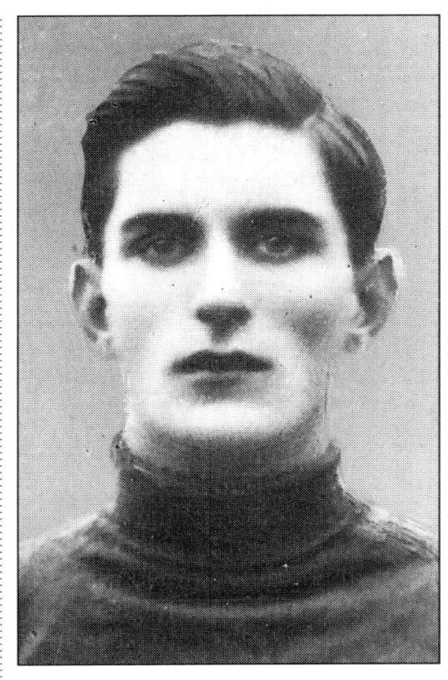

month's trial. He was first choice at Turf Moor until November 1929, when he suffered a haemorrhage of his left kidney after a collision in a game against Blackburn Rovers. He collapsed on the way home and was seriously ill in hospital. He never played for Burnley again, but. after a brief spell with Torqau United, joined Wigan Borough for an equally brief trial in December 1930. During World War One he was in the mine-sweeping service. He died in Northumberland in spring 1977.
League: App 96 Gls 0; FA Cup: App 5, Gls 0.

DUDLEY, Frank E. *1949-1951*

Inside-forward. Born: Southend, 9 May 1925.
Debut v West Ham United (a) Division Two, 22 August 1949, L 1-3.
5ft 11in, 10st 12lb (1950).
As a 15-year-old, Dudley was only 5ft 4in tall and had no ambitions to be a footballer, but when he shot up another six inches he joined his native Southend as an amateur triallist in September 1945, turning professional the following month. His versatility proved a great asset and in August 1949 he joined Leeds and was top scorer in his first full season, when he filled all the forward positions. Known for his fierce shooting, he moved to Southampton in February 1951 and to Cardiff City (September 1953) and Brentford (December 1953). He signed terms which made him a Southampton player on a Leeds-London train which saw Ernie Stevenson join Leeds as part of the deal. He achieved a remarkable record in 1953-54, when his first three League goals were for different clubs in different divisions: Southampton (Third South), Cardiff (First) and Brentford (Second). When he retired, he had 118 League goals to his credit. He qualified as a coach in 1952 and after retiring from the professional game in July 1958, joined Folkestone for a couple of seasons before returning to Southend to run their youth team between 1961 and 1965. He worked as a local government officer in the resort until retirement in 1985.
League: App 64, Gls 23; FA Cup: App 7, Gls 4.

DUFFIELD, Albert ('Bert') *1920-1925*

Right-back. Born: Owston Ferry, Lincolnshire, 3 March 1894.
Debut v Port Vale (a) Division Two, 28 August 1920, L 0-2.
5ft 7½in, 11st 10lb (1922).
Ever-present in their first League season, Duffield was one of the unsung heroes of United's early years. He spent two seasons with Gainsborough Trinity before World War One, served as a bombardier in France during the war and was wounded. He joined

Midland League Castleford Town and caught the eye when he scored four goals as a stand-in centre-forward against Notts County Reserves. But it was for his defensive work that Leeds wanted him when they signed him in July 1920. He struck up a fine partnership with Jimmy Frew and after helping United win promotion to Division One for the first time, he joined Bradford in November 1925, retiring three years later to go into the licensed trade. He worked as a greengrocer at Elland Road greyhound stadium and ran a poultry farm at Rawcliffe, near Goole, where he coached the village team. He died in Beeston, Leeds, aged 87, on 27 September 1981.
League: App 203, Gls 0; FA Cup; App 8, Gls 0.

DUGGAN, Harry A. *1925-1936*

Outside-right. Born: Dublin, 8 June 1903.
Debut v Aston Villa (h) Division One, 15 September 1926, W 3-1.
5ft 7in, 9st 13lb (1928).
Duggan worked as a stonemason on leaving school and played for Dublin junior club, Richmond United, for whom he scored 49 goals in 1924-25. Leeds signed the talented 19-year-old in May 1925. He developed as Bobby Turnbull's understudy and was described by one contemporary reported as 'a livewire, enterprising and enthusiastic individual who did not stand idle or wait for things to turn up'. He won eight caps for Northern Ireland and four for the Republic between 1926 and 1935. In October 1936 he moved to Newport County and skippered them to the Third Division South title in 1938-39, before retiring the following year. He was an ARP warden in the war and returned to Leeds to work for a firm of glass merchants. He died in Leeds in September 1968.
League: App 187, Gls 45; FA Cup: App 9, Gls 4.

DUNDERDALE, W.Len *1939-1946*

Centre-forward. Born: Willingham-by-Stow, near Gainsborough, 6 February 1915.
Debut v Blackpool (h) Division One, 25 March 1939, W 1-0.
6ft 1in, 13st 6lb (1938).
Dunderdale was one of many players whose career were ruined by World War Two. He began with Goole Town before joining Sheffield Wednesday in 1934, then Walsall, where he once hit seven goals in a Reserve game. He left the Saddlers in May 1938 for Watford (£1,000) and Watford set a club record when they sold him to Leeds for £3,750 in March 1939. However, United got little value from their new investment. He played only a few wartime games for Leeds and guested for Lincoln, Mansfield and Grimsby before rejoining Watford in April 1946. He later played at Margate and joined Sittingbourne in 1948-49. A Watford scout, Dunderdale was later coach to Berkhampstead Town, leader of Berkhampstead YMCA and coach to loan club Sun Sports. He retired to live in Sturton-by-Stow and died in February 1989.
League: App 4, Gls 0.

DUNN, Jimmy *1947-1959*

Right-back. Born: Rutherglen, 23 October 1922.
Debut v Cardiff City (a) Division Two, 1 November 1947, D 0-0.
5ft 8in, 11st 9lb (1951).
Consistent Jimmy Dunn was manifestly unlucky not to win a full Scotland cap. In 11 years at Elland Road he barely put a foot wrong and, although he was often tipped for full honours, he never received an international call. He served with the Royal

Marines in World War Two and played in the Services Cup final at Home Park, Plymouth. He then took a labouring job and played for the Scottish junior club Rutherglen Glencairn. Several clubs were on his trail and although Arbroath were favourites to sign him, they were beaten by Leeds in June 1947. Dunn became a permanent fixture at right-back, including four seasons when he was ever-present, and played a key role in United's 1955-56 promotion season. He left for Darlington in July 1959, but a knee injury cut short his career. He assisted Scarborough and later worked as a driver's mate and for the Post Office. A regular spectator at Elland Road, he retired from work in 1987.
League: App 422, Gls 1; FA Cup: App 21, Gls 0.

DUTHOIT, Jack *1945-1946*

Full-back. Born: Beeston, Leeds, 4 November 1918.
Debut v Middlesbrough (h) FA Cup 3rd round (1st leg), 5 January 1946, D 4-4.
5ft 10in, 11st 10lb (1949).
Duthoit was signed from West Riding Amateur League club, Carlton United in April 1945 and made 21 wartime appearances for Leeds, plus both legs of the 1945-46 FA Cup. He worked as an electrical engineer and played as an amateur. Leeds did not reckon he would be up to first Division standard and he moved to York in May 1946, finishing his career in 1949. He did not play in United's League side. After York he joined Boston United in June 1950.
FA Cup: App 2, Gls 0.

DUXBURY, Tom *1924-1926*

Wing-half. Born: Accrington.
Debut v Notts County (a) Division One, 1 September 1924, L 0-1.
5ft 7in, 11st 8lb (1922).
Duxbury had already played in an FA Cup Final when he joined Leeds from Preston in June 1924 (£300). He was a member of the North End team which lost to Huddersfield in the controversial 1922 Final. Duxbury began his career at Accrington, but sprang to prominence at Preston, whom he joined in December 1919. He made 52 League appearances for the Deepdale club before joining Leeds, but his time at Elland Road was not successful. In 1926 he was with non-League Fleetwood.
League: App 3, Gls 0.

EDWARDS, Keith *1986-1987*

Forward. Born: Stockton-on-Tees, 16 July 1957.
Debut v Blackburn Rovers (a) Div Two, 23 August 1986, L 1-2.
5ft 8in, 10st 3lb (1987).
Leeds paid £125,000 to Sheffield United for Keith Edwards, who had trials at Elland Road as a youngster. He arrived at Leeds in July 1986 but, after a disappointing start to the season, lost form and his place. A late flurry of Edwards' goals contributed to United's push in the 1986-87 promotion Play-offs, but in September 1987 he moved to Aberdeen (£60,000), linking up with his old Blades boss, Ian Porterfield. Edwards played for Roseworth School and Stockton Boys and also had trials with Wolves and Orient and a spell with Middlesbrough juniors before signing for Sheffield United in October 1975, initially on a three-month trial. He joined Hull City (£55,000) in August 1978 and maintained an excellent striking rate before returning to Bramall Lane (£75,000) in September 1981. He spearheaded the Blades to the Fourth Division title that season and netted 119 goals in his second spell at Bramall Lane, taking his tally to 206 with Leeds. He returned to Hull in March 1988 (£50,000). He moved from Hull in September 1989, to Stockport County for £60,000. In April the following year he joined yet another Yorkshire club, Huddersfield Town, on loan. His move to Huddersfield was made permanent in August 1990, for £25,000, and a hat-trick against Bolton in the third game of the season suggested he had lost none of his scoring instinct. But within a couple of months was out of the team and was loaned to Plymouth in December before returning to Huddersfield where he scored the last of his 256 League goals. He then became a lorry driver based in Sheffield.
League: App 29/14, Gls 8; FA Cup: App 2/3 Gls 1; League Cup: App 2, Gls 0; Full Members' Cup: App 1, Gls 0.

EDWARDS, M.Keith *1969-1972.*

Defender. Born: Neath, 26 September 1952.
Debut (as sub) v Huddersfield Town (a) Division One, 25 September 1971, L 1-2.
5ft 11in, 12st 3lb (1971).
Welsh Schoolboy and Youth international Keith Edwards has the shortest career of any United player. It lasted 19 minutes, when he came on as substitute for Paul Reaney at Leeds Road. It was the sum total of his Football League experience. In July 1972, after completing his apprenticeship, he went to Swansea a for a three-month trial, but he did not make their first team.
League: App 0/1, Gls 0.

EDWARDS, Neil R. *1989-1991*

Goalkeeper. Born: Aberdare, 5 December 1970.
Debut v Barnsley (a) Zenith Data Systems Cup, 28 November 1989, W 2-1.
5ft 8in, 11st 2lb (1989).
Welsh Youth, Under-15, Under-18 international and Mid-Glamorgan Schools goalkeeper who got his first-team chance in a Zenith Data Systems Cup-tie at Oakwell after a rare injury to Mervyn Day. That remained his only Leeds appearance, although he had two loan spells with Huddersfield and one with Irish club Shelbourne before rejecting a contract at Blackpool to join Stockport County on loan. After three impressive games, he joined County permanently for £10,000 in September 1991. He played at Wembley three times in 12 months with County, finishing on the losing side each time. In 1992 they were beaten 1-0 by Stoke City in the Autoglass Cup Final, eight days later he was in the Stockport side beaten 2-1 by Peterborough in the Division Three Play-off Final, and in 1993 Edwards featured in another Autoglass Cup Final when Stockport were beaten 2-1 by Port Vale.
Full Members' Cup: App 1, Gls 0.

EDWARDS, Walter *1949*

Winger. Born: Mansfield Woodhouse, 26 June 1924.
Debut v Grimsby Town (a) Division Two, 26 March 1949, L 1-5.
5ft 9½in, 11st (1947).
Edwards played Army football when he served in the REME in Palestine. He joined Mansfield Town from Woodhouse as an amateur in August 1947, signing professional forms three months later. He represented Nottinghamshire in the Northern Counties Amateur championship and Leeds signed him in March 1949. He was released in August the same year and joined Leicester. He did not make the first team there and in September 1950 signed for Rochdale, where he also failed to make a League appearance.
League: App 2, Gls 0.

EDWARDS, Willis *1925-1939*

Right-half. Born: Newton, near Alfreton, 28 April 1903.
Debut v Newcastle United (a) Division One, 21 March 1925, L 1-4.
5ft 8in, 11st 9lb (1930).
Former Sheffield United and England player Ernest 'Nudger' Needham went to see young Edwards, who was earning rave reviews with Chesterfield. 'Too small', Needham told the Blades

but, ironically, Edwards grew considerably taller than Needham and went on to play for England. He worked as a Derbyshire miner and starred with local club, Newton Rangers. On his way for a trail with Blackburn Rovers, he was intercepted by Chesterfield who promptly signed him on for 30s (£1.50) a week. He made his debut in 1919 against Grimsby, when he was 17, and Leeds signed him in March 1925 (£1,500). He developed into the finest wing-half of his day. His splendid ball control, incisive passing and supreme heading ability earned him 16 England caps, 11 appearances for the Football League and 444 games for Leeds in a marvellous career which stretched into World War Two, when he played for United in emergencies. He became assistant to trainer Bob Roxburgh, with responsibility for the Reserves. In April 1947, Edwards replaced Billy Hampson as United's manager (see Leeds Managers). He died in September 1988, aged 85.
League: App 417, Gls 6; FA Cup: App 27, Gls 0.

ELI, Roger *1982-1985*

Midfield. Born: Bradford, 11 September 1965.
Debut (as sub) v Wimbledon (h) Division Two, 1 December 1984, W 5-2.
5ft 11in, 11st 3lb (1987).
A product of Hanson Upper School, Bradford, Eli represented Bradford Schools, won Yorkshire County honours, had England Schools trials and was an associate schoolboy with Nottingham Forest before joining Leeds in June 1982. He went to Wolves in January 1985, but struggled with injuries and moved to Cambridge United for the start of 1987-88, on a non-contract

basis. He joined Crewe as a non-contract player in September 1987, was released at the end of the season and joined Pontefract Collieries for a few weeks before linking up with York City on a non-contract basis in November 1988. The following month he tried his luck at Bury, again as a non-contract player, before dropping into the GM Vauxhall Conference with Northwich Victoria. In July 1989 he joined Burnley where he proved a very useful all-rounder able to play in midfield or defence until a succession of injuries prompted his release. After playing in China with Fushan, he tried to re-establish his career at Scarborough where he had trials before the start of the 1994-95 season. Scunthorpe United took him on in February 1995, but two months later he teamed up with Partick Thistle.
League: App 1/1, Gls 0.

ELLAM, Roy *1972-1974*

Centre-half. Born: Hemsworth, 13 January 1943.
Debut v Chelsea (a) Division One, 12 August 1972, L 0-4.
6ft, 12st 6lb (1973).
Don Revie signed Ellam as a possible replacement for Jack Charlton, but a return to form by the veteran Charlton and the emergence of Gordon McQueen left him in the cold. He played for South Elmsall Boys, was rejected after trials with QPR and joined Bradford City as an amateur in August 1959 from Robin Hood Athletic. Turning professional in May 1960, he gave the Paraders distinguished service before moving to Huddersfield Town in January 1966, where he formed a fine partnership with Trevor Cherry. Ellam collected a Division Two championship medal in 1969-70 and soon afterwards Cherry joined Leeds. Ellam signed in August 1972 (£35,000) but rejoined Huddersfield in July 1974. Nine months later he was given a free transfer and went to play in the NASL. He later joined Mossley and then Gainsborough Trinity, whom he managed for a spell. After retiring from the game, Ellam became landlord of the Nelson Inn, Thornton Lees, near Huddersfield.
League: App: 9/2, Gls 0; FA Cup: App 2, Gls 0; League Cup: App 2, Gls 0; Europe: App 6, Gls 0.

ELLSON, Merton F. *1920-1922*

Inside-right. Born: Thrapston, Northamptonshire, 10 July 1893.
Debut v South Shields (h) Division Two, 1 September 1920, L 1-2.
5ft 10in, 11st 6lb (1922).
A schoolmaster, Ellson – known as 'Matt' – joined Leeds in July 1920, from Frickley Colliery. He quickly established himself but the arrival of experienced Jim

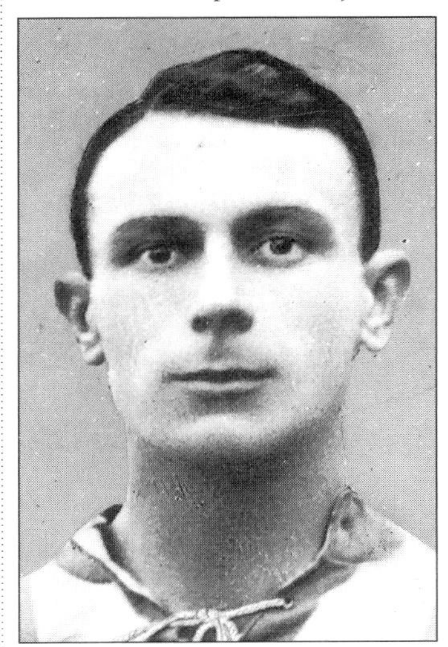

Moore, coupled with an ankle injury sustained on the way to a friendly at Brodsworth in May 1922, forced him out of first-team action. He rejoined Frickley in May 1922, but was given another chance in the Football League by Halifax Town.
League: App 37, Gls 8.

ENTWISTLE, Wayne P. *1979-1980*

Centre-forward. Born: Bury, 6 August 1958.
Debut v Tottenham Hotspur (h) Division One, 20 October 1979, L 1-2.
5ft 11in, 11st 5lb.
An England Youth international, Entwistle joined Bury in August 1976 and was transferred to Sunderland (£30,000) in November 1977. Jimmy Adamson signed him for Leeds in October 1979 (£80,000), but 13 months and two goals later he was released on a free transfer to Blackpool. He then moved around the lower divisions: Crewe (loan, March 1982), Wimbledon (free transfer, July 1982), Grays Athletic, Bury (August 1983), Carlisle United (July 1985), Bolton Wanderers (October 1985), Burnley (loan, August 1986-September 1986), Stockport County (October 1986) and Wigan Athletic (cs 1988). After a brief spell at Hartlepool at the start of the 1989-90 season he joined Altrincham.
League: App 7/4, Gls 2; FA Cup: App 0/1, Gls 0.

FAIRCLOUGH, Chris H. *1989-1995*

Defender. Born: Nottingham, 12 April 1964.
Debut v Portsmouth (h) Division Two, 25 March 1989, W 1-0.
5ft 11in, 11st 2lb (1989).
Leeds recruited Fairclough on loan just before the 1989 March transfer deadline, from Spurs, with an agreement to pay the London club £500,000 at the end of the 1988-89 season to make the move permanent. After playing for Parkhead Academicals, Fairclough joined Nottingham Forest as an apprentice in October 1981. He won the first of seven England Under-21 caps in 1985 and moved to Spurs in August 1987 for £387,000, a fee fixed by a Football League tribunal. He was voted Supporters' Player of the Year at the end of the Second Division title-winning season. Fairclough prefers to be called Chris, although his first name is Courtney. One of the stars of the 1991-92 League championship-winning side, he was later deployed as a defensive midfielder after David Batty's departure to Blackburn. His six years at Elland Road came to an end in July 1995 when he signed for Premiership newcomers Bolton Wanderers in a £1 million deal.
League: App 187/6, Gls 21; FA Cup: App 14/1, Gls 0; League Cup: App 17/2, Gls 2; Europe: App 5, Gls 0; Charity Shield: App 1, Gls 0; Full Members' Cup: App 8, Gls 0.

FAULKNER, John G. *1970-1972*

Centre-half. Born: Orpington, Surrey, 10 March 1948.
Debut v Burnley (h) Division One, 4 April 1970, W 2-1.
6ft, 12st 3lb (1971).
Although United thrashed Sutton United 6-0 in the FA Cup in January 1970, the non-Leaguers' Faulkner caught Don Revie's eye. He did well against Mick Jones and within a few weeks joined Leeds. However, both his League appearances were undistinguished. He scored an own goal on his debut and fractured his kneecap against Manchester City a fortnight later. He managed two European appearances, both against Leirse SK in the 1971-72 UEFA Cup. In March 1972 he moved to Luton Town and made 209 League appearances for the Hatters, playing a key role in the squad which won promotion to Division One in 1973-74. He played in the NASL (1978-81). In 1984 he became manager of Barton Rovers and later rejoined Luton as a coach. He then joined the Norwich coaching staff, resigning in January 1996.
League: App 2, Gls 0; Europe: App 2, Gls 0.

FEARNLEY, Harry L. *1941-1949*

Goalkeeper. Born: Morley, 27 May 1923.
Debut v Huddersfield Town (h) Division One, 5 October 1946, W 5-0.
Fearnley began as an amateur with Bradford but never made the first team at Park Avenue before he joined Leeds in 1941, aged 17. A commando during the war, he made ten wartime appearances for United and was kept on when normal League football resumed. He never established himself and moved to Halifax in January 1949. Six months later he was at Newport County (where he supplemented his income with a window cleaning round), then played for Selby Town before moving to Rochdale in July 1955. He played once for the 'Dale before being released in September 1955 to join Winsford United.
League: App 28, Gls 0; FA Cup: App 1, Gls 0.

FELL, John W. *1925-1927*

Outside-left. Born: Quebec, County Durham, 14 May 1902.
Debut v Manchester United (a) Division One, 13 February 1926, L 1-2.
5ft 6in, 10st 9lb (1925).
'Jackie' Fell enjoyed a productive career with several clubs in North-East amateur soccer before turning professional with Leeds. He played for Durham Schools before working at Hamsteels Colliery, Quebec, County Durham, combining pit life with playing for Tow Law Town. He joined Durham City in July 1921, Crook Town in the summer of 1924 and joined Leeds as an amateur in May 1925, becoming a professional in September that year. Mostly a reserve at Leeds, he transferred, in July 1927, to Southend United, where he broke a leg, returning to the North-East with Hartlepools United in May 1928, followed by Connah's Quay and Shotton (July 1929), Southport (July 1930), returning to Connah's Quay and Shotton in November 1930. Fell went back to pit work, at Blackhall Colliery, where he was secretary of the football team for 12 years, and he later trained the side, having finished his top class amateur playing career in the early 1930s with West Stanley, then Hamsteels. He retired in 1967 and died in Hartlepool on 14 January 1979.
League: App 13, Gls 1.

FIDLER, Frank *1951-1952*

Forward. Born: Middleton, near Manchester, 16 August 1924.
Debut v Blackburn Rovers (a) Division Two, 27 October 1951, W 3-2.
6ft 1in, 12st 12lb (1951).
Fidler had useful scoring rate at Leeds before John Charles switched to centre-forward. He enjoyed a good career as an amateur with Manchester United during World War Two but was

released to Witton Albion. He scored 179 goals for Witton in only three seasons and, after winning a Cheshire League championship medal, joined Wrexham in May 1950. Leeds signed him in October 1951 and he made his League debut 12 hours later. He moved to Bournemouth in December 1952 and was released in May 1955 after scoring 32 League goals for them.
League: App 22, Gls 8; FA Cup: App 1, Gls 0.

FINLAY, John *1951-1952*

Outside-right. Born: Glasgow, 1 July 1925.
Debut v Doncaster Rovers (a) Division Two, 25 August 1951, L 0-2.
5ft 8½in, 10st 10lb (1951).
Finlay played in five divisions in three Leagues in a two-and-a-half-year spell. He began in the Scottish League with Clyde before, in March 1951, becoming the last professional signed by New Brighton before they dropped out of Division Three North. Three months later, Second Division Leeds signed Finlay and Bill Heggie for a joint fee of £6,000. Neither was a success, full-back Heggie moving to Wrexham without ever making the Leeds senior team, while Finlay managed only three games before going to Southern League Yeovil Town. in 1952 He then signed for Walsall (Division Three South) in August 1953, leaving them in June 1954.
League: App 1, Gls 0.

FIRM, Neil J *1976-1982*

Centre-half. Born: Bradford, 12 January 1958.
Debut v Manchester City (a) Division One, 16 February 1980, D 1-1.
6ft 3in, 13st 9lb (1982).
Firm came up through United's junior ranks before turning professional in January 1976. He was effective in the air but sometimes lacked control on the ground. He was loaned to Oldham in March 1982, before joining Peterborough United in August that year. He did a good job for Peterborough until a prolonged knee injury forced him out of full-time soccer in January 1986. He joined Ramsay Town and ran a pub.
League: App 11/1, Gls 0.

FIRTH, Joe *1927-1935*

Half-back/inside-forward. Born: Glasshoughton, 27 March 1909.
Debut v Birmingham City (h) Division One, 4 May 1929, L 0-1.
5ft 9in, 10st 12lb (1930).
South Yorkshire miner Firth was picked up as a youngster in July 1927. He eventually became a regular in 1931-32, playing a key role at inside-right in United's promotion campaign. Despite a useful goalscoring record over the next few seasons, he struggled to retain his place in Division One and moved to Southend in June 1935. He joined York City in June 1938, moved to Rochdale in December that year and retired during the war. He died in 1983.
League: App 72, Gls 25; FA Cup: App 3, Gls 0.

FITZGERALD, Peter J. *1960-1961*

Centre-forward. Born: Waterford, Ireland, 17 June 1937.
Debut v Liverpool (a) Division Two, 20 August 1960, L 0-2.
5ft 10in, 11st 7lb (1960).
Despite making little impression for United, Fitzgerald won all his five Republic of Ireland apps during his stay at Leeds. He won an FA of Ireland Cup runners-up medal with Waterford in 1959 before joining St Patrick's Athletic. He linked up with Northern Ireland international John Crossan at Dutch club, Sparta Rotterdam, before Leeds paid £7,000 for him in August 1960. He moved to Chester in July 1961 and in 1963 returned to Waterford. He made four appearances for the League of Ireland XI.
League: App 8, Gls 0.

FLYNN, Brian *1977-1982*

Midfield. Born: Port Talbot, 12 October 1955.
Debut v Norwich City (h) Division One, 5 November 1977, D 2-2.
5ft 3½in, 9st (1978).
Flynn was one of United's smallest footballers but his appetite for work was remarkable and his midfield partnership with Tony Currie was he best of the post-Revie era. He also won 66 Welsh caps and skippered his country. He played for Neath and Wales Schools and trained with Cardiff City before joining Burnley in 1970, turning

professional in October 1972. At Turf Moor he won Under-23 honours and became established on the full international scene, scoring an international goal before netting his first in the League. He joined Leeds in November 1977 (£175,000) and won 32 caps whilst at Elland Road. Neat control, hard work and passing ability put him among the best midfielders of his day. He was loaned to Burnley in March 1982, rejoining them permanently eight months later (£60,000). He then played for Cardiff City (£15,000, November 1984), Doncaster Rovers (November 1985), Bury (July 1986), Limerick (coach, January 1987), Doncaster (non-contract, August 1987), Wrexham (February 1988). He continued to play for Wrexham until 1993 as player-manager. Earlier Flynn had been appointed caretaker manager at Wrexham in November 1989 and was later given the job on a permanent basis. After Wrexham finished bottom of the Football League under his stewardship in 1990, he rebuilt the side and steered them to promotion in 1992-93. At one time he was linked with the Welsh manager's job, but remains at Wrexham.
League: App 152/2, Gls 11; FA Cup: App 6/1, Gls 0; League Cup: App 12, Gls 0; Europe: App 4, Gls 0.

FLYNN, Peter *1953-1956*

Inside-right. Born: Glasgow, 11 October 1934.
Debut v Fulham (h) Division Two, 23 January 1954, L 1-2.
5ft 7in, 9st 9lb (1953).
Flynn joined Leeds as a 17-year-old from Scottish club Petershill in October 1953. Despite being a highly-rated member of the juniors, he made only one appearance before going to Bradford in June 1957. He gave Park Avenue seven years' service, helping them win promotion to Division Three in 1960-61. Altogether he made 130 League appearances (plus one as substitute) for them.
League: App 1, Gls 0.

FORD, Mark *1993-*

Midfield. Born: Pontefract, 10 October 1975.
Debut (as sub) v Swindon Town (a) Premiership, 7 May 1994, W 5-0.
5ft 8in, 10st 8lb (1995).
Hard-tackling England Under-18 midfielder Ford looked like a player in the David Batty mould when he broke into the side during the 1995-96 season on a more regular basis. Handed his debut in the final game of the 1993-94 season, he failed to make the senior side the following campaign and it looked as though the skipper of United's successful FA Youth Cup winning side could be on the way out of Elland Road. But the former Youth international made a solid contribution to United's run to the Coca-Cola Cup Final, earning a place in the starting line-up against Aston Villa. However, bookings piled up and suspension forced him out of the team towards the end of the season. As a youngster he represented York and North Yorkshire Boys, joining United's professionals in March 1993 after coming through the juniors.
League: App 12/1, Gls 0; FA Cup App 5, Gls 0; League Cup: 4, Gls 0; Europe: 0/1, Gls 0.

FORREST, J. Bobby *1952-1957*

Inside-forward. Born: Rossington, near Doncaster, 13 May 1931.
Debut v Nottingham Forest (a) Division Two, 4 April 1953, L 1-2.
5ft 10in, 10st 5lb (1957).
Forrest went to Rossington Modern School and played for Rossington YC and Rossington Colliery. One day he went to watch a match at Retford Town with a friend. The home side were two players short and asked the youngsters to play. Forrest signed for the club and his strong displays attracted Leeds. He signed (£500) just before Christmas 1952 and his non-stop running made him a favourite at Elland Road before he was transferred to Notts County in February 1957. At County he formed a devastating partnership with Hateley and Astle and skippered their 1959-60 Fourth Division promotion side. In July 1962 he joined Weymouth.
League: App 119, Gls 36; FA Cup: App 2, Gls 1.

FORRESTER, Jamie M. *1992-1995*

Striker. Born: Bradford, 1 November 1974.
Debut (as sub) v Nottingham Forest (a) Premiership, 21 March 1993.
5ft 7in, 10st (1995).
A spectacular overhead kick goal in the 1993 FA Youth Cup Final second leg against Manchester United in front of 31,037 fans at Elland Road earmarked razor-sharp striker Jamie Forrester as a star of the future. But the diminutive front man, who also featured in the England side that won the Under-18 European championship the same year, couldn't establish himself in the Premiership and after loan spells with Southend United (September 1994) and Grimsby Town (March-May 1995), he returned to Leeds in the summer,

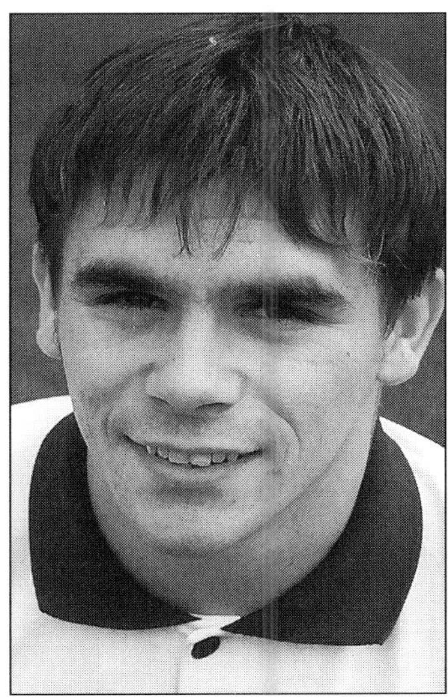

rejoining the Mariners on a free transfer in October 1995. His only senior goals both came in a 3-1 FA Cup win over Crewe in January 1994. Bradford-born, he started with Blackpool Rangers, then Poulton le Fylde where he teamed up with Kevin Sharp and the pair went to the FA National School of Excellence before spending some time in France as a teenagers, joining United from Auxerre in October 1992 for £120,000.
League: App 7/2, Gls 0; FA Cup: App 1/1, Gls 2

FOWLER, Alan *1927-1934*

Centre-forward. Born: Rothwell, near Leeds, 20 November 1911.
Debut v Birmingham (a) Division One, 11 February 1933, L 1-3.
5ft 6in, 10st 6lb (1928).
Fowler played for Rothwell Schools and joined United's groundstaff from Whitehall printers in November 1927. He was loaned back to his old club, and to Brodsworth Main, but United knew they had a potential star. A former Schoolboy international, he understudied the likes of Tom Jennings, Charlie Keetley and Arthur Hydes and maintained a good scoring rate in the senior side. In May 1934 he went to Swindon Town, hoping for regular League football. and his tricky dribbling and accurate shooting brought him plenty of goals. He died on 10 July 1944, serving as a sergeant with the Dorset Regiment. There is a plaque dedicated to him on the North Stand at the County Ground.
League: App 15, Gls 8.

FRANCIS, Cliff T. *1935-1938*

Inside-left. Born: Methyr Tydfil, 28 December 1915.
Debut v Arsenal (h) Division One, 9 April 1938, L 0-1.
Francis joined Leeds from Aberawan in October 1935 and went to Swindon Town in June 1938. World War Two interrupted his career and after a few games for Swindon in 1945-46, he retired.
League: App 1, Gls 0.

FRANCIS, Gerry *1957-1961*

Outside-right. Born: Johannesburg, South Africa, 6 December 1933.
Debut v Everton (h) Division One, 10 October 1959, D 3-3.
5ft 8in, 10st 7lb (1959).
Francis, a shoe repairer, came to England from South Africa in 1956-57, hoping to achieve soccer fame. Leeds tried him out as an amateur before signing him as a professional in July 1957. United's first coloured player, he had played for City & Suburban in Johannesburg. He was at Leeds during a period of considerable change, when United struggled to find a settled side. He moved to York City in October 1961, leaving Bootham Crescent the following summer to play for Tonbridge. He later became a postman.
League: App 46, Gls 9; FA Cup: App 1, Gls 0; League Cup: App 3, Gls 0.

FREW, Jimmy H. *1920-1924*

Left-back. Born: Kinghorn, Fife, 1892.
Debut v Port Vale (h) Division Two, 4 September 1920, W 3-1.
5ft 9in, 11st 4lb (1920).
Frew formed a fine full-back partnership with Bert Duffield in United's early years. He came to prominence in May 1913, joining Hearts from Newcastle City. He made his Scottish League debut, against Celtic, the following year. When war broke out, Frew enlisted in the 1st Lowland, Edinburgh Royal Garrison Artillery, as a farrier, rising to the rank of sergeant. He played in a 'Grand Military International' at Goodison Park in May 1916 when England beat Scotland 4-3, and signed for Leeds (£200) in June 1920. He joined Bradford City in June 1924, but his playing days were brought to a premature end in December 1926, through injury. He became chief coach to the West Riding FA and ran a sports outfitters in Harehills, Leeds, which was the official supplier to Leeds United for many years. He died in Leeds in April 1967, aged 75.
League: App 96, Gls 0; FA Cup: App 3, Gls 0.

FROST, Desmond *1949-1951*

Centre-forward. Born: Congleton, Cheshire, 3 August 1931.
Debut v Southampton (a) Division Two, 17 September 1949, L 1-2.
5ft 10½in, 12st (1950).
Frost played for Congleton amateur side, Civil Defence Messengers, then served with the Northamptonshire Regiment and the RASC, representing England against Scotland in a services international in Singapore. After demob he joined Congleton Town before signing for Leeds in April 1949. His hat-trick for the Reserves against Blackpool in January 1951 prompted watching Halifax Town officials to sign him. He had spells with Rochdale (November 1953) and Crewe (September 1954).
League: App 10, Gls 2.

FULLAM, Bob *1923-1924*

Inside-left. Born: Ringstead, Dublin *c*.1897.
Debut v Stoke (a) Division Two, 25 August 1923, D 1-1.
5ft 9in, 12st (1923).
Fullam scored the Republic of Ireland's first-ever international goal, in a 2-1 defeat by Italy at Lansdowne Road in April 1927. He worked as a docker in Dublin while playing for St Brendan's North End. He joined Shelbourne in 1917-18 and won an Irish FA Cup medal with them in 1920. Joining Shamrock Rovers in 1921, he became their captain and scored a club record 27 League goals when they won the 1922-23 Irish championship. With teammate, John Joe Flood, he joined Leeds in May 1923. Flood did not make the first team and, although Fullam did, he struggled in the Football League and rejoined Shamrock in 1924. Flood also returned to Shamrock and went on to win five Irish caps. Fullam managed two caps, played six times for the League for Ireland and won a stack of domestic honours before spending 1927-28 in the USA with Detroit club, Holly Carburettors. He returned to Shamrock in 1929 to take his championship medal tally to three. Fullam died in London in 1974.
League: App 7, Gls 2.

FURNESS, Billy I. *1928-1937*

Inside-left. Born: New Washington, County Durham, 8 June 1909.
Debut v Middlesbrough (h) Division One, 30 November 1929, L 1-2.
5ft 6in, 10st 6in (1930).
Billy Furness was plucked out of non-League football and matured into an England player. Leeds spotted him playing for Usworth Colliery in the North Eastern League Second Division. Earlier, he had played for Washington Colliery, where he worked as a clerk. His boundless energy and skill caught their eye and the £50 they paid Usworth in August 1928 was a bargain. He quickly became a regular and with his Geordie mate, Tom Cochrane, formed a left-sided attack as good as any at that time. Furness was capped in May 1933 and went to Hungary and Czechoslovakia with England in 1934, although he did not play on tour. He continued his fine form for United right up until signing for Norwich City – the club against whom he had broken his collarbone two years earlier – for £2,700, in June 1937. He proved as popular with the Canaries as he had with Leeds and after the war played a handful of games for them before retiring to become their trainer-coach. He was later rewarded with a testimonial. He died on 29 August 1980, aged 71.
League: App 243, Gls 62; FA Cup: App 14, Gls 4.

GADSBY, Ken J. *1934-1948*

Left-back. Born: Chesterfield, 3 July 1916.
Debut v Everton (a) Division One, 3 March 1937, L 1-7.
5ft 9in, 11st 10lb (1938).
Ken Gadsby was being tipped as a future England player when World War Two broke out. He signed from Middlecliffe Rovers – the club which produced Wilf Copping – in October 1934. He waited three years for what turned out to be a nightmare League debut, but when a regular first-team chance came, he took it confidently. He toured South Africa with the FA in 1939 an played fairly regularly for Leeds during the war. He guested for Sheffield United in the 1943 League (North) Cup Final and had a few games with Yeovil in 1945-46. He picked up his career with Leeds after the war, but was past his best and moved to King's Lynn in summer 1948. His father, Ernest, was a member of Barnsley's 1910 FA Cup Final side against Newcastle.
League: App 81, Gls 0; FA Cup: App 6, Gls 0.

GALVIN, Chris J. *1968-1973*

Winger. Born: Huddersfield, 24 November 1951.
Debut (as sub) v Ferencváros (a) European Cup 2nd round (2nd leg), 26 November 1969, W 3-0.
5ft 10in, 10st 7lb (1972).
English Youth international Galvin acted as cover for Leeds' all-star attack. He turned professional in November 1968, after serving his apprenticeship, but found it difficult to make his presence felt. In July 1973 he moved to Hull City (£25,000) where he made over 100 League appearances. Loaned to York City for four months, starting in December 1976, he signed for Stockport County in April 1979. In 1981 he went to manage Taun Wan FC, Hong Kong. His younger brother, Tony, a Republic of Ireland international, won FA Cup winners' medals with Spurs in 1981 and 1982 before joining Sheffield Wednesday, and later Swindon.
League: App 6/1, Gls 1; FA Cup: App 0/2, Gls 0; League Cup: App 1, Gls 0; Europe: App 4/2, Gls 1.

GASCOIGNE, Thomas C. *1921-1924*

Right-half. Born: Scotswood, Newcastle upon Tyne, 4 November 1899.
Debut v Notts County (h) Division Two, 10 December 1921, D 1-1.
5ft 9in, 11st (1922).
Gascoigne, signed from Scotswood in May 1921 and was effective cover for Harry Sherwin. Anxious for more first-team opportunities, he moved to Doncaster Rovers in summer 1924 and became their captain. He left in March 1926 for Bradford City and ran a business in Bradford. In September 1927 he joined Tranmere Rovers.
League: App 20, Gls 0.

GAVIN, Mark W. *1980-1985*

Outside-left. Born: Baillieston, near Glasgow, 10 December 1963.
Debut (as sub) v Cambridge United (h) Division Two, 2 October 1982, W 2-1.
5ft 8in, 10st 7lb (1985).
Within a few weeks, Gavin was released by one Leeds manager, then re-signed by his successor. He played for High Tunstall School (Hartlepool), Cleveland and Durham Boys and had Scottish Youth trials. He joined Leeds in May 1980 but in summer 1982 was freed by Allan Clarke. After Clarke was dismissed, Eddie Gray re-signed Gavin, but the player did not live up to his early promise and, after a seven-match loan spell with Hartlepool, he joined Carlisle United in July 1985. He moved to Bolton in March 1986 and rejoined his old mentor, Gray, at Rochdale in July 1987. He was transferred to Hearts in February 1988 (£30,000) then joined Bristol City in October 1988 for £30,000. He shone at Ashton Gate and a £100,000 move, which included a player-exchange with Wayne Allison, took him to Watford in August 1990, but Gavin never really settled and returned to Bristol City in December 1991 for £60,000, moving on to Exeter City in February 1994.
League: App 20/20; Gls 3; League Cup: App 4/1, Gls 1.

GIBSON, Archie *1951-1960*

Right-half. Born: Daılly, near Girvan, 30 December 1933.
Debut v Birmingham City (a) Division Two, 2 March 1955, L 0-2.
5ft 8in, 10st (1956).
A former apprentice joiner, Gibson built a fine career at

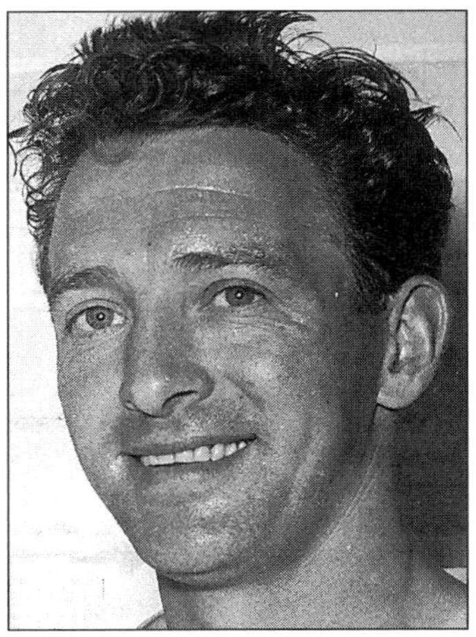

Elland Road in the 1950s, based on sheer hard work. He attended Girvan High School before joining Coylston Juventiles, an Ayrshire club. Leeds spotted him playing in a Scottish Juvenile Cup semi-final at Falkirk and signed him in May 1951. During National Service with the RAC, Gibson was based at Catterick and played for Northern Command. He switched from inside-forward to right-half and broke into United's first team. He held a regular place until July 1960. United had been relegated from Division One and Gibson was one of the victims of the clearout. He was transferred to Scunthorpe and played 134 League games for the Iron before going to Barnsley in September 1964, but did not make a League appearance for the Oakwell club.
League: App 169, Gls 5; FA Cup: App 5, Gls 0.

GILES, M.John *1963-1975*

Midfield. Born: Cabra, Dublin, 6 January 1940.
Debut v Bury (h) Division Two, 31 August 1963, W 3-0.
5ft 7in, 10st (1973).
It was said that Johnny Giles could place a football on a sixpence from 50 yards with either foot. He was a master of the passing art and with Billy Bremner crafted a partnership which became the envy of football. Giles' early career spanned Brunswick Street School, St Colombus FC, Dublin and Republic of Ireland Schools, Dublin City FC, The Leprechauns, Stella Maris and Home Farm, leaving the latter for Manchester United in November 1957. He was a right winger at Old Trafford and won his first

cap aged 18 years 361 days – the youngest Eire international at the time. Altogether his international career spanned 19 years and 60 caps, partially covering a spell when he managed the Irish side between 1973 and 1980. He won an FA Cup winners' medal in 1963, before a surprise £33,000 transfer the following August took him to Second Division Leeds. Once Giles took over Bobby Collins' role as midfield general, his career took off and Leeds' glory years began in earnest. He was the complete midfielder and no slouch when it came to scoring goals – particularly from the penalty-spot. Revie suggested that Giles would be the ideal man to take over as manager but in June 1975, after the European Cup Final, he joined West Brom as player-manager. Giles immediately steered Albion back to Division One, but left in May 1977. He was player-manager at Shamrock Rovers, winning an FA of Ireland Cup winners' medal in 1978. He had a stint in the NASL with Philadelphia Fury and was a highly-successful coach with Vancouver Whitecaps. From February 1984 to September 1985 he had a second spell in charge at West Brom. Giles also proved to be a successful businessman and then went into journalism, penning a column for the *Daily Express* and working for Irish television.
League: App 380/3, Gls 88; FA Cup: App 61, Gls 15; League Cup: App 19, Gls 1; Europe: App 61/1, Gls 11; Charity Shield: App 2, Gls 0.

GOLDBERG, Les *1934-1947*

Right-back. Born: Leeds, 3 January 1918.
Debut v Sunderland (h) Division One, 4 December 1937, W 4-3.
5ft 9in, 11st (1946).
Goldberg is one of the few players to change his name from Goldberg to Gaunt – by deed poll. He trained at Elland Road and won England Schoolboy caps before joining the Leeds groundstaff in 1934, turning professional the following year. During the war he guested for Arsenal and saw service in India. He left Leeds in March 1947, for Reading where he changed his name in 1948. Injury forced him to quit in 1950 and he later managed Metropolitan League side Newbury Town. He returned to Reading in 1969 as an administrative and technical assistant, and later ran a menswear business and scouted for Reading and Oxford.
League: App 33, Gls 0.

GOLDTHORPE, Ernie H. *1920-1922*

Centre-forward. Born: Middleton, Leeds, 8 June 1898.
Debut v Port Vale (a) Division Two, 28 August 1920, L 0-2.
5ft 9½in, 11st 7lb (1920).
Bad injuries prevented Goldthorpe from fulfilling his potential he showed as a youngster. Son of Walter Goldthorpe, a well-known Northern Rugby player, he played for Yorkshire Schools against Lancashire at Bury before joining the Army as a teenager, serving with the Guards. Based in London, he spent some time training with Spurs but joined Bradford City when he left the Army in June 1919. Leeds signed him in June 1920 but he was troubled by a serious knee injury and in March 1922 rejoined Bradford City. Six months later he went to Manchester United on a free transfer and showed flashes of his true form, including four goals in a match against Notts County. He moved to Rotherham United in October 1925, after dislocating a collar-bone with United, but eventually drifted out of football to look after his farming interests.
League: App 6,Gls 2.

GOODWIN, Freddie *1960-1964*

Centre-half. Born: Heywood, Lancashire, 28 June 1933.
Debut v Manchester City (h)

Division One, 19 March 1960, W 4-3.
6ft 1½in, 13st 4lb (1960).
Freddie Goodwin's career with Leeds was ended by the triple fracture of a leg in an FA Cup game against Cardiff in January 1964. It was the worst of a succession of injuries which plagued the popular defender following his £10,000 move from Manchester United. He turned professional at Old Trafford in October 1953, after shining at Chorlton County Secondary School. His chance came after the 1958 Munich Air Disaster and he played in the side which lost that year's FA Cup Final. He joined Leeds in March 1960 and partnered Jack Charlton in defence, often at right-half, although he was better known as a centre-half. He became Scunthorpe United's player-manager in November 1964 and in November 1966 joined New York Generals, returning to England in October 1968 to manage Brighton. In May 1970 he went to Birmingham and steered them to Division One in 1972. He stayed at St Andrew's until September 1975 and returned o the USA the following year, as manager-coach of Minnesota Kicks. During the 1980s he recruited players for the American Indoor League. Goodwin played in 11 first-class cricket matches for Lancashire, taking 27 wickets.
League: App 107, Gls 2, FA Cup: App 4, Gls 0; League Cup: App 9, Gls 0.

GRAHAM, Arthur *1977-1983*

Outside-left. Born: Castlemilk, Glasgow, 26 October 1952.
Debut v Newcastle United (a) Division One, 20 August 1977, L 2-3.
5ft 8in, 11st 10lb (1980).
After only a handful of Scottish League appearances, Arthur Graham won a Scottish FA Cup medal for Aberdeen against Celtic in 1970, when he was 17. He began with junior club, Cambuslang Rangers, before joining Aberdeen in 1969-70. He played 230 League games for Aberdeen and added three Scottish Under-23 caps, a Scottish League XI appearance and a 1977 and within months won the first of ten Scottish caps. A direct winger, he netted three hat-tricks for Leeds, including a quick-fire effort at Birmingham in January 1978. After United slumped, he stayed one more season before a surprise £50,000 transfer to Manchester United in August 1983. Graham revitalised his career and there was speculation about a Scotland recall until he lost his place to Danish international Jesper

Olsen. He joined Trevor Cherry at Bradford City in June 1985 and took over as reserve and junior coach when he retired in February 1987. Graham was temporarily in charge when Terry Dolan was sacked in January 1989, until Terry Yorath joined City a month later. In February 1990, Graham was promoted to assistant manager and first-team coach at Bradford when Yorath was sacked. Graham's brother, Tommy, played for Motherwell, Aston Villa, Barnsley Halifax Town, Doncaster Rovers, Scunthorpe United and Scarborough. Arthur Graham now lives in Halifax where he works as a physiotherapist.
League: App 222/1, Gls 37; FA Cup: App 12, Gls 3; League Cup: App 22, Gls 4; Europe: App 3, Gls 3.

GRAINGER, Colin *1960-1961*

Outside-left. Born: Wakefield, 10 June 1933.
Debut v Liverpool (a) Division Two, 20 August 1960, L 0-2.
5ft 9½in, 10st 12lb (1959).
Grainger, the 'singing winger', was a well-known crooner on the Northern pub and club circuit, but also played to thousands on Saturday afternoons for a string of clubs, including Leeds. He learnt his soccer at Ryehill Junior and South Hindley Secondary Modern Schools in the South Elmsall area before joining Wrexham's groundstaff in 1949, turning professional in October 1950. In July 1953 he joined Sheffield United (£2,500) and it was there that he won the first of seven England caps, netting twice on his debut in a 4-2 win over Brazil at Wembley. Sunderland signed him in February 1957 (£7,000) and made a handsome profit when they sold him to Leeds (£15,000) in August 1960. Grainger could not hit peak form at Leeds and within 14 months was at Port Vale. In August 1964 he moved to Doncaster Rovers, then to Macclesfield Town in summer 1966. He played for the Football League three times.
League: App 33, Gls 5; FA Cup: App 1, Gls 0; League Cup: App 3, Gls 1.

GRAINGER, Dennis *1945-1947*

Outside-left. Born: Royston, near Barnsley, 5 March 1920.
Debut v Middlesbrough (h) FA Cup 3rd round (1st leg), 5 January 1946, D 4-4.
Dennis Grainger arranged a trial for his cousin, Colin, when he was on Wrexham's books. The Graingers had a great pedigree in professional soccer – Colin played for England, Dennis was a regular on the League circuit and his brother, Jack, was with Southport and Barnsley and guested for Leeds during the war; their cousin, Eddie Holliday, played for Middlesbrough, Sheffield Wednesday and England. Dennis began with South Kirby, then Southport (October 1938), and joined Leeds in October 1945 (£1,000). He figured in both legs of the 1945-46 FA Cup and made a two-goal League debut for United against Preston in their opening Division One game after the war. He moved to Wrexham in December 1947 and was transferred to Oldham Athletic in June, leaving prior to 1952-53 to join Bangor City.
League: App 37, Gls 5; FA Cup: App 3, Gls 1.

GRAVER, Fred *1924-1925*

Inside-right. Born: Craghead, County Durham, 8 September 1897.
Debt v Notts County (a) Division One, 1 September 1924, L 0-1.
5ft 9in, 12st (1922).
Graver moved quickly round the soccer circuit after leaving Burnhope Institute to join Darlington in 1920-21. In August 1921 he was with North Eastern League club Shildon and Grimsby signed him in May 1922. He returned to North Eastern League football with West Stanley in May 1923 and, after scoring 41 goals for them, joined Leeds in May 1924. He moved to Southend United in May 1925 and enjoyed a fairly productive spell at Roots Hall before signing for Wallsend in 1926. His son, Andy, holds Lincoln City's aggregate League goalscoring record with 144 goals in two spells. Fred Graver died in 1950.
League: App 3, Gls 0.

GRAY, Andrew D. *1994-*

Winger. Born Harrogate, 15 November 1977.
Debut (as sub) v Notts County (h) League Cup, 19 September 1995, D 0-0.
5ft 11in, 11st (1996).
Remarkably, Andy Gray's fourth start for United came as an 18-year-old in the 1996 Coca-Cola Cup Final against Aston Villa at Wembley, where he was United's star performer. His first taste of senior action had come in the same competition the previous September, but he only re-emerged in the senior ranks the following February to stake a late claim to a place in the Final. The son of Frank Gray, he is a winger more in the mould of his uncle, Eddie, and joined United on associate schoolboy forms in April 1993 after starring for John Fisher, Harrogate and North Yorkshire Schools.
League: Apps 12/2, Gls 0; FA Cup: App 0/2, Gls 0; League Cup: App 1/1, Gls 0.

GRAY, Eddie *1965-1984*

Outside-left/left-back. Born: Holyrood, Glasgow, 17 January 1948.
Debut v Sheffield Wednesday (h) Division One, 1 January 1966, W 3-0.
5ft 11in, 12st 7lb (1979).
It seems remarkable that Eddie Gray won only 12 Scotland caps, but his career was interrupted by a succession of injuries which would have prompted a lesser man to quit the game long before he did. Gray could confuse a full-back simply by dropping one of his hunched shoulders and feinting to go one way and dribbling off in the other. A Schoolboy international he representated Glasgow Schools

and signed for United in January 1965, after being discovered by Leeds scout John Barr. A gifted and graceful player, he made his League debut a year later and after winning two Under-23 caps, won his full international spurs against England at Wembley in 1969. The following year he gave a virtuoso performance in the FA Cup Final against Chelsea. After establishing himself as one of Scotland's most exciting post-war players, he ran into injury problems that threatened to end his career. Written-off by some, but encouraged by Leeds boss Jimmy Armfield, he fought his way back to full health and during his rehabilitation coached the juniors at Leeds. Although he had lost some of his speed, he staged a remarkable comeback in January 1974 when his ball skills were still very much in evidence. Gray was still playing when he was appointed United's manager in succession to Allan Clarke in July 1982 and dropped to left-back before retiring from playing in May 1984. (see Leeds Managers).EddieGray rejoined Leeds as a coach in March 1995. His son, Stuart, has played for Celtic, and had a loan spell at Bournemouth. Eddie's nephew, Andy, broke into the Leeds team in 1995-96.

League: App 441/13, Gls 52; FA Cup: App 46/1, Gls 5; League Cup: App 33/2, Gls 6; Europe: App 39/2, Gls 5; Charity Shield: App 2, Gls 1.

GRAY, Frank T *1971-1979 & 1981-1985*

Midfield/left-back. Born: Castlemilk, Glasgow, 27 October 1954.

Debut (as sub) v Leicester City (a) Division One, 10 February 1973, L 0-2.

5ft 9½in, 11st 10lb (1973).

Although not as gifted as his elder brother Eddie, Frank Gray won 32 caps for Scotland in a career which saw him avoid

major injury. His career in his early days followed that of his brother's – Glasgow Schools representative and Schoolboy international. A former Parkhead ball-boy, he went to Leeds in summer 1970, after United signed him in the face of competition from about 30 other clubs. He turned professional in November 1971 and scored on his full debut to emulate another feat of Eddie's. He also played on the left, but in a deeper midfield role, and won five Scottish Under-23 caps. Later, he switched to left-back and often played in the same Leeds team as his elder brother, providing United with a very solid left side. Leeds banked a then club record £500,000 when he moved to Nottingham Forest in July 1979. Under Brian Clough, Gray enjoyed his best years, climaxing in a European Cup winners' medal in 1980 to go with the loser's one he got with Leeds in 1975. He returned to Leeds in a £300,000 deal in May 1981 and was Scotland's left-back in the 1982 World Cup in Spain. Gray was a United regular until July 1985 when he sought a break from Leeds and was transferred by his brother to Sunderland for £100,000, helping them out of Division Three in 1987-88. He was freed by Sunderland in April 1989 and was appointed player-assistant manager at Darlington, helping to steer them back to the Fourth Division as champions of the GM Vauxhall Conference in 1990. He remained at Feethams until February 1992, later scouting for Blackburn and Sheffield Wednesday, before taking over as Harrogate Town's manager in December 1993, resigning the following June to take charge of Al Mananmah in Bahrain. In 1995-96, his son, Andy, became the latest of the Gray clan to play for Leeds.

League: App 327/5, Gls 27; FA Cup: App 27/1, Gls 3; League Cup: App 30/1, Gls 4; Europe: App 12/2, Gls 1.

GRAYSON, Simon N. *1986-1992*

Midfield. Born: Ripon, North Yorkshire, 16 December 1969.

Debut v Huddersfield Town (a) Division Two, 15 September 1987, D 0-0.

5ft 11in, 11st 7lb (1987).

Grayson made his League debut as a 17-year-old when United were hit by a crop of injuries in 1987-88. A Bedale School pupil, he represented North Yorkshire Schools before joining Leeds as an apprentice in 1986. He played at Wembley in only his fourth game for Leeds, in the Mercantile Credit Centenary competition in April 1988. Unable to force his way into the first team on a regular basis, he joined Leicester City for £50,000 in March 1992, on the same day Ali Mauchlen made the opposite journey on a loan spell. Mauchlen didn't get a first-team outing and returned to Filbert Street where Grayson featured in the Foxes side beaten 1-0 by Blackburn at Wembley in the 1992 Division One Play-offs. Grayson returned to Wembley two years later as Leicester's skipper and Player of the Year and led his side to Play-off glory over Derby County. Cricketing brother Paul, now at Essex, also had trials at Elland Road. His father, Adrian, was once on York City's books.

League: App 2, Gls 0; Full Members' Cup: App 1/1, Gls 0.

GREEN, Harry *1930-1934*

Outside-right. Born: Sheffield, 1908.

Debut v Sunderland (a) Division One, 7 February 1931, L 0-4.

5ft 5in, 10st 4lb (1934).

Green, a Sheffield steelworker, forged his career as a professional footballer at the second attempt. He joined Oldham Athletic in November 1928, but they did not think he would make the grade and released him the following summer. He drifted back to non-League soccer with Mexborough, but Leeds gave him another crack at League football in April 1930. The presence of internationals Bobby Turnbull and Harry Duggan kept him in the shadows, so he moved to Bristol City in May 1934. In June 1935, he signed for York City and was ever-present in his first season with them. In March 1937 he joined Frickley Colliery.

League: App 19, Gls 4.

GREENHOFF, Brian *1979-1983*

Full-back/midfield. Born: Barnsley, 24 April 1953.

Debut v Arsenal (h) League Cup 2nd round (1st leg), 29 August 1979, D 1-1.

5ft 10in, 12st 2lb (1979).

Brian Greenhoff was a ball-boy at Wembley when he saw brother Jimmy win a 1968 League Cup winners' medal for Leeds. Brian later played in an FA Cup Final and trod the Wembley turf as an England player. The Greenhoffs' father was a professional and Brian pre-dated Jimmy at Old Trafford by six years, signing for Manchester United in June 1970. His versatility made him an important member of the Old Trafford set up and, after Under-23 honours, he won his first England cap against Wales in 1976. He played in two FA Cup

Finals for Manchester United, gaining a winners' medal in 1977, and was non-playing substitute in the 1979 Final. In the late-1970s he was an England regular and it needed a £350,000 fee to take him to Leeds in August 1979. With Leeds he made one more England appearance, taking his total of full caps to 18, but his stay at Elland Road was disrupted by injuries and, after a loan period, he joined brother Jimmy at Rochdale in December 1983, retiring in 1984 to run a shop in that town. He now helps Chadderton FC and works as a sales representative for a sports goods wholesaler.

League: App 68/4, Gls 1, FA Cup: App 1, Gls 0; League Cup: App 5, Gls 0.

GREENHOFF, Jimmy *1963-1968*

Forward. Born: Barnsley, 19 June 1946.

Debut v Swansea Town (h) League Cup 3rd round, 22 October 1963, W 2-9.

5ft 10in, 11st 2lb (1968).

Jimmy Greenhoff was transferred in the middle of a Cup Final, leaving Leeds for Birmingham City (£70,000) in August 1968, between the first and second legs of the Inter-Cities Fairs Cup Final against Ferencváros, having come on as substitute in the first leg. He was in the Barnsley side which won the 1960-61 English Schools Trophy and, after representing Yorkshire Schools, joined Leeds after his apprenticeship in August 1963. He made a valuable contribution to the side which established itself as a First Division force in the mid-1960s. A £100,000-transfer from Birmingham to Stoke City saw him help the Potters lift the League Cup in 1972. He went to Manchester United (£200,000) in November 1976 and played alongside brother Brian. His experience helped nurture a crop of exciting young players and he won an FA Cup winners' medal in 1977, when he deflected home the winning goal. Despite a series of good performances at top level, he never won a full England cap, although he appeared in four at Under-23 level with Birmingham and played for the Football League with Stoke. In December 1980 he went to Crewe, where he had a spell as manager, replacing his old Stoke boss Tony Waddington, before going to Canada for a second season with Toronto Blizzard. In August 1981 he joined Port Vale, then went to Rochdale as player-manager in March 1983. He left Spotland in March 1984 and returned to Vale as player-coach. He later coached youngsters at holiday camps and now runs his own insurance

business in the Stoke area.
League: App 88/6, Gls 21; FA Cup: App 10/1, Gls 2; League Cup: App 12, Gls 4; Europe: App 18/1, Gls 6.

GRIBBEN, Bill H. *1928*

Centre-half. Born: Glasgow, 28 October 1906.
Debut v Blackburn Rovers (a) Division One, 8 December 1928, W 1-0.
Gribben rose from obscurity to deputise for Ernie Hart in 1928-29, after signing from Beeston Parish Church in August 1928. His debut, against the FA Cup holders, came on the same day as George McNestry's first appearance. He joined Harrogate in 1929 and played for the Yorkshire League XI v Leeds.
League: App 3, Gls 0.

HADDOCK, Peter M. *1986-1991*

Midfield/defender. Born: Newcastle upon Tyne, 9 December 1961.
Debut v Blackburn Rovers (a) Division Two, 23 August 1986, L 1-2.
5ft 11in, 11st 5lb (1986).
Haddock suffered badly from injuries after his £45,000 transfer to Leeds from Newcastle United in June 1986, but his versatility meant that he was a valuable squad member. A former pupil of Cramlington High School, he joined Newcastle as an apprentice in June 1978, turning professional in December 1979. He made his debut for Newcastle at Queen's Park Rangers in September 1981, despite not being on the team coach which left for the game. He had to be rushed down to London on the morning of the game when the Geordies' regular left-back went down with illness. After that he made 57 appearances, plus seven on loan to Burnley in March 1986, before moving to Leeds. He was one of the club's most consistent performers during the 1989-90 Second Division title success. A knee injury sustained in the Rumbelows Cup semi-final second leg against Manchester United in February 1991 ended his career prematurely and he now sells insurance.
League: App 106/12, Gls 1; FA Cup: App 6/2, Gls 0; League Cup: App 9/2, Gls: 0; Full Members' Cup: 9/1, Gls 0.

HAIR, K.Grenville A. *1948-1964*

Left-back. Born: Burton upon Trent, 16 November 1931.
Debut v Leicester City (h) Division Two, 31 March 1931, W 3-1.
5ft 9in, 11st 2lb (1962).
Had Grenville Hair been with a more fashionable club in the

1950s, then he would surely have been a serious candidate for an England cap. He was a masterful full-back, quick into the tackle and an excellent passer of the ball. He went to Burton Technical High School, where he was an athletics champion. Major Frank Buckley signed him from Burton & District League club, Newhall United, in November 1948. Hair did his National Service with the 12th Royal Lancers at Barnard Castle in North Yorkshire, playing alongside John Charles when they won the Northern Command Trophy. Hair, who also excelled at basketball and tennis, achieved remarkable consistency after he became a Leeds first-team regular. He had deserved reputation as a fine clubman and sportsman and was rewarded with trips with FA touring teams to the West Indies in 1955, Nigeria and Ghana in 1958 and New Zealand in 1960. He played at Leeds well into his 30s before becoming player-manager of Wellington Town in May 1964. In February 1967 he was appointed trainer at Bradford City, taking over as manager the following year. He had been in the Valley Parade hot-seat for only a few weeks when he collapsed and died on 7 March 1968, whilst supervising a City training session.
League: App 443, Gls 1; FA Cup: App 21, Gls 1; League Cup: App 10, Gls 0.

HALLETT, Tom *1956-1963*

Half-back. Born: Glenneath, near Swansea, 10 April 1939.
Debut v Blackburn Rovers (a) League Cup 3rd round, 17 October 1962, L 0-4.
5ft 11¼in, 12st 10lb (1962).
Hallett, a Welsh Schoolboy international, joined the groundstaff in June 1954, after playing for Glenneath Secondary Modern and Neath Grammar Schools. He turned professional in April 1956 but did not play for Leeds in the League. He joined Swindon Town in July 1963 and Bradford City (£1,200) in June 1966, for whom he made 177 League appearances before being released in June 1971.
League Cup: App 1, Gls 0.

HAMPSON, Tom *1934-1939*

Wing-half. Born: Salford, 1916.
Debut v Chelsea (a) Division One, 27 December 1938, D 2-2.
5ft 8½in, 10st 12lb (1938).
Hampson joined Leeds as a teenager from Droylesden in November 1934 and was transferred to Oldham Athletic in August 1939. He did not get into their first team in the truncated 1939-40 season, but turned out 81 times in wartime football. After demob he suffered a bad knee injury and had to retire. He became a plumber and died on 18 October 1947, aged 31, after a fall in which he fractured his skull.
League: App 2, Gls 0.

HAMPTON, Peter J. *1971-1980*

Full-back. Born: Oldham, 12 September 1954.
Debut v Southampton (a) Division One, 28 April 1972, L 1-3.
5ft 7½in, 11st 2lb (1979).
Hampton, a Bishop Auckland

Grammar School boy and Durham County Schools player, was recruited in September 1971. He won England Youth caps and enjoyed a good run in 1976-77, when Frank Gray switched to midfield. Transferred to Stoke City (£175,000) in August 1980, he made over 150 appearances before going to Burnley on a free transfer in May 1984. After another century of first-team games he moved on another 'free' to Rochdale in August 1987, becoming Carlisle's player-physiotherapist in December that year and now also coaches at Brunton Park. His father was president of Crook Town FC.
League: App 63/5, Gls 2; FA Cup: App 5, Gls 1; League Cup: App 5/1, Gls 0; Europe: App 3/1, Gls 0.

HAMSON, Gary *1979-1986*

Midfield/full-back. Born: Nottingham, 24 August 1959.
Debut (as sub) v Ipswich Town (h) Division One, 6 October 1979, W 2-1.
5ft 8in, 11st (1986).
Hamson was capable of filling a variety of roles. He had trials with Derby County before joining Sheffield United, turning professional in November 1976. The following February he was selected for England Youth against Wales but the match was called off and he never got another chance. Leeds signed him in July 1979 (£140,000). An aggressive player, he received a nine-match ban – a record under the penalty points system at the time – in February 1981. A bad knee injury in the last game of 1981-82 kept him sidelined for a long period, but he fought his way back into the first team before going to Bristol City on a free transfer in July 1986. In December that year he went to Port Vale (£5,000) and was forced to retire prematurely in March 1988 because of a recurring ankle injury.
League: App 126/8, Gls 3; FA Cup: App 10/1, Gls 1; League Cup: App 4, Gls 0; Full Members' Cup: App 1, Gls 0; Europe: App 1/1, Gls 0.

HANKIN, Ray *1976-1980*

Forward. Born: Wallsend, near Newcastle upon Tyne, 2 February 1956.
Debut v Everton (a) Division One, 6 November 1976, W 2-0.
6ft 2in, 14st (1979).
Hankin won three England Under-23 caps and Youth caps at his first club, Burnley, whom he joined in February 1973. A £172,000 transfer took him to Leeds in September 1976, but injury restricted him to four matches in his first season before he came back as a fearsome spearhead the following campaign when he topped 20 League goals. In March 1980 he joined Vancouver Whitecaps and won an NASL North-West Division winners' medal in 1981. In November that year Arsenal were prepared to pay £400,000 for his scoring talents but, although he signed on a trial basis, he was released in January 1982 without a senior appearance. After a brief spell at Shamrock Rovers he returned to Vancouver, then joined Middlesbrough in September 1982 (£80,000). He continued with Peterborough (September

1983), Wolves (March 1985), Whitby Town (1986), Blue Star (December 1986). He worked in a mental hospital near Middlesbrough whilst playing for Guisborough Town (cs 1987). He was appointed manager of Northallerton Town in March 1989. He now works as Newcastle United's Football in the Community officer.
League: App 82/1, Gls 32; FA Cup: App 1, Gls 0; League Cup: App 15, Gls 3; Europe: App 4, Gls 1.

HARGEAVES, Jack *1934-1945*

Outside-left. Born: Rotherham, 1 May 1915.
Debut v Sheffield Wednesday (a) Division One, 29 February 1936, L 0-3.
5ft 9in, 10st 2lb (1938).
Hargreaves played for Bristol City after he was sent by the RAF to work at an aircraft factory near the city during the war and eventually joined them in August 1945. He moved to Reading in April 1947 and wound up his career with Southern League Yeovil in summer 1948. Hargreaves signed for Leeds in August 1934, after impressing in Sheffield junior football. He competed with Arthur Buckley for the Leeds left-wing place in the years immediately before the war. Hargreaves died in 1978.
League: App 46, Gls 10; FA Cup: App 2, Gls 1.

HARLE, David *1985-1986*

Midfield. Born: Denaby, near Doncaster, 15 August 1963.
Debut v Oldham Athletic (h) Division Two, 1 January 1986, W 3-1.
5ft 9in, 10st 7lb (1986).
Harle was twice signed and then released by Billy Bremner. An England Youth international, he joined Doncaster in November 1980, after serving his apprenticeship, but was given a free transfer to Exeter in July 1982. Bremner re-signed Harle for Doncaster in September 1983 – and when Bremner became Leeds' manager, he signed Harle yet again (£5,000) just before Christmas 1985. Within three months, however, the player began a loan spell with Bristol City before joining them permanently in June 1986 (£10,000). In November 1986 he joined Scunthorpe, his fourth club in a year. In March 1989, Harle went to Peterborough United (£15,000) and joined Doncaster for a third time (£13,000) in March 1990. In 1991-92 he joined Stafford Rangers on loan.
League: App 3, Gls 0.

HARRIS, Carl S. *1973-1982*

Outside-right. Born: Neath, 3 November 1956.
Debut (as sub) v Ipswich Town (h) Division One, 19 April 1975, W 2-1.
5ft 9in, 11st 1lb (1979).
Leeds persisted in their pursuit of Harris and were rewarded by moulding him into an international player. He represented Neath Schools and Wales Schoolboys and was rejected by Burnley before joining Leeds. Within days he was homesick and left to get a job in

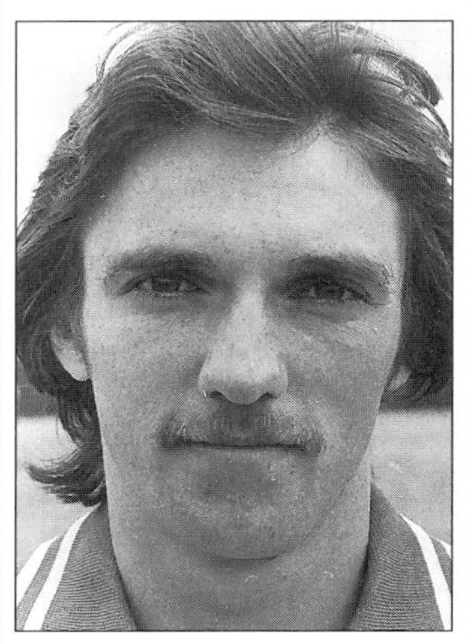

a factory in Wales. Leeds persuaded him to return and he signed in November 1973. He made a scoring debut and became the regular substitute, even though he was first capped by Wales against England in March 1976, adding to Under-23 and Youth honours. In 1980-81 he was United's top scorer and an established international with 24 caps, but after Leeds were relegated he was transferred to Charlton (£100,000 in July 1982. He maintained his form at The Valley but was unable to add more caps. After struggling with injuries he returned to Leeds, for an unsuccessful trial in the Central League, eventually joining Bury in December 1985. In July 1987 he had trials with Swansea and Cardiff, then after further trials with Airdrie, joined Rochdale in January 1988 then Exeter City in December 1988. In summer 1989 he was given a free transfer by Exeter and was appointed player-manager at Abacus Welsh League club Briton Ferry, later becoming the club's general manager.
League: App 123/30, Gls 26; FA Cup: App 5, Gls 2; League Cup: App 7/7, Gls 1; Europe: App 1/3, Gls 0.

HARRIS, Joe *1922-1925*

Outside-left. Born: Glasgow, 5 November 1891.
Debut v Blackpool (h) Division

Two, 26 August 1922, D 1-1.
5ft 10in, 11st 10lb (1922).
Joe Harris was a mainstay of United's 1923-24 Division Two championship-winning side, laying on goals for Jack Swan and Joe Richmond. He began his League career with Burnley in September 1910 after starring with Vale of Clyde and Ashfield in Scottish junior football. He left Turf Moor for Bristol City in summer 1912 and made over 200 appearances for them and also played a good deal of Army representative football. He was suspended for 12 months and Bristol City fined £50 after he was paid whilst on amateur forms. Harris was awarded a £600 benefit at Bristol before joining Leeds in July 1922. An ever-present in United's first-ever Division One campaign, he moved to Fulham in October 1925, retiring in 1928. His brother, Neil, played for Newcastle and Scotland; nephew, John, played for Chelsea and later managed Sheffield United. Joe Harris, who played a total of 428 League games, died in summer 1966.
League: App 126, Gls 14; FA Cup: App 8, Gls 0.

HARRISON, Peter *1948-1952*

Outside-left. Born: Sleaford, Lincolnshire, 25 October 1949, L 1-2.
5ft 6in, 9st 2lb (1951).
Harrison had balance, skill and speed and enjoyed a scoring debut for United, but an inclination to hang on to the ball probably restricted his appearances. He played for a works side, Aveling and Barford, then signed as an amateur under Major Frank Buckley at Notts County, then joined Peterborough from where he was recruited by Leeds in August 1948, turning professional five months later. He played Army representative football when serving in the RAOC in Germany and held a regular place at Elland Road until he moved to Bournemouth in August 1952. After 172 appearances for the Cherries he went to Reading (June 1957), Southport (July 1959), Macclesfield (1962) and Runcorn (1963). After his playing days were over he moved to Cardiff and was trainer and youth team coach at Ninian Park He and John Charles were best man at each other's wedding.
League: App 54, Gls 9; FA Cup: App 2, Gls 0.

HARRISON, Ralph *1949*

Outside-left. Born: Clayton-le-Moors, near Blackburn, 18 December 1926.
Debut v Tottenham Hotspur (a) Division Two, 10 September 1949, L 0-2.
5ft 11½in, 11st 8lb (1949).
During the late-1940s, United had two left wingers called Harrison on their books, although they were not related. Curiously, Ralph, who joined Leeds in January 1949 from Great Harwood, played only two games in the 1949-50 season before his place on the wing was immediately taken by Peter Harrison. Ralph worked for the National Coal Board, saw service with the Royal Navy in Ceylon during World War Two and on demob joined Harwood St Hubert's and then Great Harwood. His only Football League experience was with Leeds.
League: App 2, Gls 0.

HART, Ernie A. *1920-1936*

Centre-half. Born: Overseal, near Burton upon Trent, 3 January 1902.
Debut v Stockport County (h) Division Two, 19 February 1921, L 0-2.
5ft 11in, 13st (1933).
Burly ex-miner Ernie Hart proved to be a tower of strength in United's defence. He went to Overseal School, played for Overseal Juniors and was signed by Leeds from Doncaster minor club, Woodlands Wesleyans, in 1920, when United were formed. His storming displays in the Reserves soon saw him promoted to the first team – making his debut at 19. A defender with a penchant for attack, he won a Second Division championship medal in 1923-24, captained Leeds, played for England eight times, represented the Football League twice and toured South Africa with the FA in 1929. He was known as a hard but fair performer. He fell foul of a referee's wrath only once, but it could have cost him England honours. He was sent off by Bradford referee J.E.Mellor in the

1933 West Riding Cup Final against Huddersfield. Hart was banned for a month for swearing at a referee – his only misdemeanour in all his years at Elland Road – and, apart from losing £32 in wages, was axed by the FA from the England tour to Italy and Switzerland. It was tough punishment which a player of Hart's calibre barely deserved.

He left for Mansfield in August 1936 and in July 1938 was appointed manager at Tunbridge Wells. He also scouted for Coventry. Hart went into business as a haulage contractor and bus-service operator at Adwick-le-Street, near Doncaster. He was a scout for Leeds until his death on 21 July 1954, aged 52.
League: App 447, gls 14; FA Cup*: App 25, Gls 1.
*Includes both of United's preliminary round games in 1920-21.

HART, Paul A. *1978-1983*

Centre-half. Born: Manchester, 4 May 1953.
Debut v Liverpool (a) Division One, 11 March 1978, L 0-1.
6ft 2in, 12st 8lb (1979).
Paul Hart, son of former Manchester City star Johnny Hart, was a commanding stopper for Leeds and often tipped for England honours, although that recognition never came his way. He played for Manchester Boys before joining Stockport County in September 1970, making his debut a fortnight before he signed professional forms. He moved to Blackpool (£25,000) in June 1973 and proved skilful enough to warrant a few games in midfield. Leeds turned to Hart in their search for a replacement for Gordon McQueen and paid Blackpool £300,000 in March 1978. His early days were marred by a flurry of own-goals and errors before he settled at the core of the Leeds defence. In summer 1983 a £40,000 move took him to Nottingham Forest and he went to Sheffield Wednesday in summer 1985. He left for Birmingham in December 1986 but broke a leg on his only appearance for the Blues, on New Year's Day 1987. He joined Notts County as player-coach in June 1987 (£15,000) before becoming Chesterfield's manager in 1989. His reign at Chesterfield ended in January 1991 and he

joined Grantham as a player before being appointed to the Nottingham Forest coaching staff in June 1991. The following summer he returned to Leeds to supervise United's youth development work and enjoyed a super first year in charge as the FA Youth Cup was won for the first time in the club's history.
League: App 191, Gls 16; A Cup: App 11, Gls 1; League Cup: App 17, Gls 1; Europe: App 4, Gls 2.
Utility player. Born Drogheda, 31 August 1977.

HARTE, Ian P. *1994-*

Debut (as sub) v Reading (h) League Cup, 10 January 1996, W 2-1.
When 18-year-old Ian Harte came on for his Leeds debut in the Coca-Cola Cup against Reading it completed an amazing family double as his uncle, Gary Kelly, himself only 21, was already on the pitch. The uncle and nephew helped United to a narrow 2-1 success to take Leeds a further step down the road to Wembley. Harte, who played for St Kevin's Boys in Drogheda, was on the verge of leaving Leeds two months into his two-year apprenticeship. He had played in a variety of positions for the juniors and reserves and later in the season sampled some Premiership action. At the end of the campaign he was included in the full Republic of Ireland international squad for their summer tour.
League: App 2/2, Gls 0; League Cup: App 0/1, Gls 0.

HARVEY, David *1965-1980 & 1983-1985*

Goalkeeper. Born: Leeds, 7 February 1948.
Debut v West Bromwich Albion (h) League Cup 3rd round, 13 October 1965, L 2-4.
5ft 11in, 12st 3lb (1972).
Had Don Revie brought Harvey into the team earlier, then Leeds might have won more trophies – that was an adnmission Revie was to make in later years. It is a great testimony to a 'keeper whose patience was rewarded with honours for Leeds and Scotland. Harvey was educated at Foxwood and Secroft Grange Schools (Leeds) and worked at a shoe factory before signing as a professional in February 1965

after a couple of years as an apprentice. Sprake's brilliance kept him in the Reserves and he made about 200 Central League games before winning a regular first-team place in 1971-72, when he played in United's 1972 FA Cup winning side. His career took off and he was capped by Scotland – qualifying because his father was Scottish – in November 1972; was rated the best 'keeper in the 1974 World Cup and finished with 16 caps. Harvey was set for a long run in the Leeds goal, but a bad car accident in February 1975 saw him temporarily lose his place to David Stewart. Although he won back his place, Harvey joined Vancouver Whitecaps in the NASL (£40,000), returning briefly in December that year before going back to Vancouver via Irish side, Drogheda, in 1980-81. He left Canada for Leeds again in March 1983, aged 35, and remained a first-team regular until going on loan to Partick Thistle in February 1985. His tally of United first-team appearances is remarkable when it is considered how many games he also played for the Reserves. He appeared a few times for Bradford City before going to Whitby Town as player-manager in May 1985, a post he held until the summer 1986. In 1987 he was with Harrogate Town and signed for Carlisle on a non-contract basis in 1987-88. He came out of football and had a variety of occupations including running a pub, delivering fruit and vegetables to hotels in the Harrogate area, being a postman in Knaresborough and, finally, moving to a farmhouse and smallholding on the island of Sanday in the Orkneys.
League: App 350, Gls 0; FA Cup: App 31, Gls 0; League Cup: App 38, Gls 0; Europe: App 25/2, gls 0; Charity Shield: App 1, Gls 0.

HASTIE, J.Ken A. *1952*

Inside-forward. Born: Cape Town, South Africa, 6 September 1928.
Debut v Birmingham City (a) Division Town, 17 September 1952, D 2-2.
5ft 10in, 11st 12lb (1952).
United must have thought they had unearthed a diamond when South African-born Hastie made a two-goal debut at St Andrew's, but he never reached his full potential and slipped quietly out of the game. A printer by trade, he caught the eye in 1951 when he gave an excellent display at full-back for the South Africans against Newcastle United. Leeds signed him from his South African club, Clyde Athletic, in August 1952. A versatile player, he switched to a forward role after the 1951 tour and, after only one Reserve game for Leeds, was thrown in at the deep end.
League: App 4, Gls 2.

HAWKINS, Dennis R. *1964-1968*

Forward. Born: Swansea, 22 October 1947.
Debut v West Bromwich Albion (h) League Cup 3rd round, 13 October 1965, L 2-4.
5ft 7in, 10st 12lb (1970).
Such was United's strength in the early 1960s that Hawkins won his first Welsh Under-23 cap before making his League debut. He joined Leeds in October 1964, after serving his apprenticeship, and won Welsh Schoolboy caps. He made his senior bow in an experimental Leeds side and, with little opportunity to show what he could do, he left in October 1968 for Shrewsbury where he took his Welsh Under-23 appearances to six. He went on loan to Chester (September 1970) and Workington (March 1972) before going to Newport County (May 1972), later playing for Telford (1973) and Nuneaton. In 1988 he was manager of Tadcaster Albion, the Northern Counties East League club.
League: App 2, Gls 0; League Cup: App 2, Gls 0.

HAWKSBY, John F. *1959-1964*

Inside-forward. Born: York, 12 June 1942.
Debut v Rotherham United (h) Division Two, 27 August 1960, W 2-0.
5ft 9in, 10st 10lb (1962).
Hawksby was an outstanding prospect who played for Yorkshire Schools and England Youth in 1959, signing for Leeds in June that year. He soon pushed for a first-team place and made a sensational start when he went into the senior side at 18, for the injured Don Revie, and scored in each of his first two games. He could not sustain that sort of form, however, and in August 1964 went to Lincoln before joining York in March 1966 and King's Lynn in July 1988. In his four years at Lincoln and York, he was in sides that had to apply re-election each season. He had an extended non-League career, joining Cambridge City in summer 1970 from Kings Lynn, then joined Kettering Town in August 1972 before a £4,000 move to Dunstable in July 1974 and subsequent games with Stevenage, Rushden Town and Desborough Town.
League: App 37, Gls 2; FA Cup: App 1, Gls 0; League Cup: App 7, Gls 0.

HAWLEY, John E. *1978-1979*

Forward. Born: Withernsea, East Yorkshire, 8 May 1954.
Debut v Arsenal (a) Division One, 19 August 1978, D 2-2.
6ft, 13st 5lb (1978).
Hawley proved a consistent marksman in his one season at Elland Road. He played East Riding junior football before joining Hull City as an amateur in April 1972, when he was helping to run the family antique business in Beverley. He did not go full-time until August 1976 and was scoring regularly for the Tigers when Leeds bought him (£81,000) in May 1978. United made a handsome profit when he was sold by Jimmy Adamson in September 1979 (£200,000) to Sunderland, where he scored a debut hat-trick. He joined Arsenal (£50,000, in September 1981), Orient (loan, October 1982), Hull City (loan, November 1982), Happy Valley FC in Hong Kong (1983), Bradford City (August 1983) and Scunthorpe (July 1985). He is now back in Beverley working for the family antique and furniture restoration business.
League: App 30/3, Gls 16; FA Cup: App 3, Gls 0; League Cup: App 6, Gls 1.

HEATON, Billy H. *1937-1949*

Outside-left. Born: Holbeck, Leeds, 26 August 1918.
Debut v Liverpool (a) Division One, 28 September 1946, L 0-2.
5ft 6in, 10st (1948).
A product of Ingram Road School, Holbeck, not far from Elland Road, Heaton played for Leeds City Boys and Yorkshire Schools before joining United from Whitkirk in December 1937. He won amateur international and FA XI honours at Leeds after serving in India during World War Two. A £7,000 transfer took himn to Southampton in February 1949. He left Southampton in summer 1949 after he refused to move down south and opted to play for Stalybridge Celtic in September 1949 while the Saints held on to his reglstration until he joined Rochdale in November 1950, but after only four games he retired to work for a Leeds slating and roofing company. He died in Leeds on 16 January 1990.
League: App 59, Gls 6; FA Cup: App 1, Gls 0.

HENDERSON, John S.P. *1955-1956*

Inside-forward. Born: Glasgow, 13 October 1923.
Debut v Plymouth Argyle (a) Division Two, 19 March 1955, L 1-3.
5ft 6in, 11st 4lb (1956).
'Jock' Henderson wrapped up his career with Leeds after giving good service to clubs in England and Scotland. He began with Falkirk in 1940 and played in their side which lost the 1948 Scottish League Cup Final to East Fife. In September 1948 he joined Third Lanark, then signed for Rotherham in November 1953. He joined Leeds just before the transfer deadline in March 1955, adding considerable experience to United's promotion drive. Although they missed out that season, Henderson was in the team at the start of the following campaign when United did go up. He spent three seasons in the Southern League with Weymouth, three years at Trowbridge and two at Frome Town. In 1972 he was manager at Devizes and later coached Calne Town in Wiltshire while working for the South Western Gas Board. During his playing days he was noted for his tattooed forearms.
League: App 15, Gls 4.

HENDERSON, Tommy W. *1959 & 1962-1965*

Outside-right. Born: Larkhall, Lanarkshire, 25 July 1943.
Debut v Grimsby Town (a) Division Two, 10 November 1962, D 1-1.
5ft 4in, 11st (1963).
Scottish Schoolboy international Henderson had two spells with Leeds. He was snapped up from school in 1959, but was released because of homesickness and returned to play for Hearts and St Mirren, apeparing in the 1962 Scottish Cup Final for the latter against Rangers. Leeds kept tabs on him and were successful at getting him to return to Elland Road in November 1962 in a £1,500 transfer. He was a first-teamer until Don Revie purchased Johnny Giles, when Henderson moved to Bury in June 1965. Swindon acquired him in January 1966, but he joined Stockport six months later and helped County win the Fourth Division title in his only season at Egdeley Park. In October 1967 he moved to Altrincham.
League: App 24, Gls 2; FA Cup: App 6, Gls 0; League Cup: App 4, Gls 0.

HENDRIE, John G. *1989-1990*

Winger-Striker. Born: Lennoxtown, Lanarkshire, 24 October 1963.
Debut v Newcastle United (a) Division Town, 19 August 1989 L 2-5.
5ft 7in, 11st 4lb (1989).
Lightning-quick winger Hendrie was finally caught by Leeds boss Howard Wilkinson after weeks of trying to sign him from Newcastle United. He eventually arrived at Elland Road in June 1989 after a £600,000 deal was agreed. Scottish Youth international Hendrie joined Coventry City as an apprentice in June 1980, turning full-time the following May. Unable to command a regular place with Coventry, he was loaned to Hereford United (January 1984) before joining Bradford City in June 1984 on a free transfer. A key figure in City's 1984-85 Division Three championship-winning side, he helped the Paraders to the brink of Division One before a £500,000 move took him to Newcastle United in June 1988. Injuries restricted his appearances for Leeds – something which never happened to him at Bradford, where he missed only one of a possible 130 League games. In June 1990, Hendrie joined Middlesbrough for £550,000. He gained promotion to Division One with Boro in 1991-92 and was top scorer in their Division One championship season in 1994-95.
League: App 22/5, Gls 5; FA Cup: App 1, Gls 0; League Cup: App 1, Gls 0; Full Members' Cup: app 2, Gls 0.

HENRY, Gerry R. *1937-1947*

Inside-forward. Born: Hemsowrth, 5 October 1920.
Debut v Manchester United (a) Division One, 7 April 1939, D 0-0.
5ft 5in, 11st 4lb (1946).
Henry played for Yorkshire schools in 1934 and joined Leeds as a 17-year-old from local junior side, Outwood Stormcocks. He made 186 wartime appearances and scored 94 goals for United – both club records – and guested for Doncaster. He left for Bradford in November 1947 and played for Sheffield Wednesday (February 1950) and Halifax Town (December 1951). Shortly after he arrived at Shay he was appointed player-coach, then had a spell as player-manager until 1954.
League: App 44, Gls 4; FA Cup: App 3, Gls 1.

HIBBITT, Terry A. *1964-1971*

Midfield. Born: Bradford, 1 December 1947.
Debut (as sub) v Nottingham Forest (a) Division One, 19 February 1966, W 4-1.
5ft 6½in, 9st 10lb (1970).
Few players have made such a dramatic entry into League football as Terry Hibbitt. Coming on as substitute, he scored for Leeds with his first touch of the ball at the City Ground. Hibbitt signed from school and became a professional in December 1964. He was a member of the excellent shadow squad, used as cover to the international stars in the early part of Revie's reign. After a £30,000 transfer took him to Newcastle in August 1971, he starred with the Geordies for four seasons and played in their side which reached the 1974 FA Cup Final. A £100,000 move took him to Birmingham in September 1975, but he returned to Newcastle in May 1978, in an exchange deal involving winger Stewart Barrowclough. A persistent knee injury forced him to give up League football and he ran a newsagent's business. He played for Gateshead and between May 1986 and October 1986 was their player-coach. His younger brother, Kenny, an England Under-23 international, gave sterling service to Bradford, Wolves, Coventry and Bristol Rovers. Terry Hibbitt died, in Newcastle, aged 47, from cancer on 5 August 1994.
League: App 32/15, Gls 9; FA Cup: App 1, Gls 0; League Cup: App 5, Gls 0; Europe: App 8/2, Gls 2.

HILAIRE, Vince M. *1988-1990*

Winger. Born: Forest Hill, London, 10 October 1959.
Debut v Oxford United (h) Division Two, 27 August 1988, D 1-1.
5ft 6in, 10st (1988).
Tricky winger Vince Hilaire cost United £190,000 in summer 1988 – a fee settled by tribunal after

Leeds had offered £70,000 for a player Portsmouth valued at £270,000. Hilaire kicked off his career as an apprentice with Crystal Palace, turning professional on October 1976. An England Youth international, he was often tipped as a future full international but the nearest he got was nine Under-21 caps and an England 'B' appearance. He clocked up over 250 League games for Palace before a move to Luton Town in July 1984, but six months later he moved to Portsmouth for £100,000 in November 1984. Hilaire was a key member of the Pompey team which won promotion from Division Two in 1986-87. Unable to make much impression with Leeds during 1989-90, he had loan spells with Stoke City (November) and Charlton Athletic (April). Eventually he joined Stoke in November 1990, moving to Exeter City the following September. He then joined Waterlooville as player-coach, resigning in 1994 and joined Bognor Regis in November of that year.
League: App 42/2, Gls 6; FA Cup: App 2, Gls 0; League Cup: App 3, Gls 1; Full Members' Cup: App 2, Gls 0.

HILL, George *1920*

Winger. Born: Dronfield, near Sheffield.
Debut v South Shields (a) Division Two, 8 September 1920, L 0-3.
5ft 9in, 11st (1920).
Hill featured in United's first League season. He was recruited from Rotherham Town in July 1920, having joined them from Birmingham in September 1919. He left United in May 1921.
League: App 7, Gls 0; FA Cup*: App 1, Gls 0.
*this was one of United's preliminary round games in 1920-21.

HILTON, Joe *1948-1950*

Centre-forward. Born: Bromborough, Cheshire, 20 July 1931.
Debut v Swansea Town (h) Division Two, 3 September 1949, L 1-2.
5ft 11in, 11st 10lb (1950).
Although Hilton figured mostly at centre-forward in United's Reserves, 'A' and junior teams his only senior appearance was at inside-left. He signed as a youngster from a Doncaster junior club in September 1948, after being offered trials by Sunderland and Sheffield Wednesday. He was farmed out to Scarborough in April 1949, before going to Chester in August 1950 and later playing for New Brighton.
League: App 1, Gls 0.

HINDLE, Tom *1943-1948*

Inside-forward. Born: Keighley, 22 February 1921.
Debut v Stoke City (a) Division One, 16 September 1946, L 2-5.
5ft 8in, 11st (1946).
A product of Ingnow Council School (Keighley) Hindle captained Keighley Boys and had trials with Bradford before joining Leeds. During World War Two he worked for an engineering firm and joined United on a permanent basis from Keighley Town in September 1943. He played nearly 100 wartime games and was in the side when peacetime football resumed in 1946. In February 1949 he went to York City in an exchange deal involving Billy Rudd. He later had spells with Halifax Town (September 1952) and Rochdale (March 1952), before going to Lancashire Combination clubs Wigan (cs 1952) and Nelson in 1955. During the war his brother played for East Fife. He is now retired and living in Keighley.
League: App 43, Gls 2; FA Cup: App 3, Gls 0.

HIRD, Kevin *1979-1984*

Midfield/defender. Born: Colne, 11 February 1952.
Debut v Norwich City (h) Division One, 3 March 1979, D 2-2.
5ft 7in, 10st 6lb (1979).
When Leeds signed Hird from Blackburn Rovers for £357,000, it made him the most expensive

full-back in the British game at the time. As it turned out Hird spent much of his days at Elland Road as a midfielder, where his forays down the right owed much to his skilful dribbling. A Burnley fan, he was picked up by Blackburn from school in February 1973 and built a big reputation as an attacking full-back. At Leeds he netted some spectacular goals and took on the responsibility of penalty taker. Known as 'Jasper' to the fans, he was a bit of an enigma, capable of both mind-boggling skills and basic errors, but he never gave anything less than 100 per cent for Leeds. He moved to Burnley in August 1984 and scored 16 League goals in his first season with the Clarets. He stayed at Turf Moor until 1986, when he gave up full-time football and began work in a timber merchant's and also played for North West Counties League club, Colne Dynamoes. He joined Colne in summer 1986 and in September 1991 joined Barnoldswick United after Colne folded.
League: App 165/16, Gls 19; FA Cup: App 6/2, Gls 2; League Cup: App 7/1, Gls 0; Europe: App 3, Gls 0.

HODGE, Stephen B. *1991-1994*

Midfield. Born: Nottingham, 25 October 1962.
Debut (as sub) v Sheffield Wednesday (h) Division One, 24 August 1991, D 1-l.
5ft 8in, 10st 3lb (1993).
Former England international midfielder Steve Hodge made an instant impact with Leeds, coming on as a substitute on his debut and scoring a point-saving goal against Sheffield Wednesday. Indeed, he made only a dozen starts during that 1991-92 championship season after signing from Nottingham Forest for £900,000 and during his injury-blighted time at Elland Road didn't really command a regular place. A native of Nottingham, he represented that city and his county at schoolboy level, then played for Notts County Boys before joining Nottingham Forest as an apprentice in May 1978, turning professional in October 1980. A midfield man with an eye for goals, he gained the first of his eight England Under-21 caps against Greece in March 1983. A surprise £450,000 move took him to Aston Villa and his skillful forays down the left earned him a full England debut in March 1986, against the USSR, and he was a member of the World Cup team that year. He was captain at Villa, but accepted the chance to join Tottenham Hotspur in a £650,000 deal in December and played in their side which lost to Coventry in the 1987 FA Cup Final. He continued to pick up England caps, but became unsettled when Terry Venables took over from David Pleat at White Hart Lane and returned to Forest, for £575,000, in August 1988. Back in familiar surroundings, he rediscovered his best form, helping Brian Clough's side to win the 1989 Wembley Finals of both the Simod and

Littlewoods Cup, the latter being won the following year when Hodge played in the 1-0 Final win over Oldham. He regained his place in the England squad and was a member of the 1990 World Cup party, but injuries and the emergence of Irish star Roy Keane saw Hodge on the sidelines at his club, although he did appear as substutute for Forest in the 1991 FA Cup Final against Tottenham, having played his last League game for the Reds the previous week against Leeds. He was unable to add to his tally of 24 international caps at Leeds and after struggling with injury and a loss of form was loaned to Derby County in August 1994 before joining QPR for £300,000 two months later. Unable to make an impression as Rangers struggled in the Premiership, he moved to Watford in December 1995.
League: App 28/26, Gls 10; FA Cup: App 2/1, Gls 0; League Cup: App 4/3, Gls 0; Europe: 0/2, Gls 0. Charity Shield: 0/1.

HODGKINSON, Eddie *1946-1948*

Right-half. Born: Ilkeston, 27 November 1920.
Debut v Everton (a) Division One, 26 May 1947, L 1-2.
5ft 8in, 11st 8lb (1948).
Keep-fit fanatic Hodgkinson was signed from junior football in December 1946 and made his debut in the last match of that season. During his days at Elland Road he ran a youth club in Mansfield. He moved to Halifax in July 1948 after the Shaymen beat Mansfield, Stockport and Bournemouth to his signature.
League: App 2, Gls 0.

HODGSON, Gordon *1937-1939*

Centre-forward. Born: Johannesburg, South Africa, 16 April 1904.
Debut v Everton (a) Division One, 3 March 1937, L 1-7.
6ft, 12st 7lb (1928).
South African boilermaker Gordon Hodgson ran United's

attack in the years leading up to World War Two. He was a month short of his 34th birthday when he joined Leeds from Aston Villa in March 1937 (£1,500) but he led the attack with zest and vigour. He even turned out for Leeds in wartime football and

helped to coach the younger players at the club between 1942 and October 1946. He played for Rustenburg (1921), Pretorian (1922-23) and Transvaal (1924-25) and arrived in England in 1925 with the South African team, netting 15 goals on their tour. Liverpool signed him in November 1925 and he scored a remarkable tally of 233 goals in 258 League games to earn a place in Liverpool's hall of fame. Such talent brought him three full England caps, four Amateur apps and three Football League XI appearances. He joined Aston Villa in January 1936 (£3,000) but within four months became a Leeds player. He remains the only United player to score five goals in a game – against Leicester City in October 1938. Hodgson, who managed Port Vale from 1946 until his death at Stoke on 14 June 1951, was also a fast bowler with Lancashire CCC.
League: App 82, Gls 51; FA Cup: App 4, Gls 2.

HODGSON, John P. *1944-1948*

Goalkeeper. Born: Dawdon, County Durham, 10 May 1922.
Debut v Middlesbrough (h) FA Cup 3rd round (1st leg), 5 January 1946, D 4-4.
5ft 11½in, 11st 8lb (1945).
During wartime football United fielded some fine goalkeepers and Hodgson proved to be among the safest. He signed from North-East club Murton Colliery in 1944 and, despite being on the receiving end of an 8-1 defeat at York in his first match in February that year, he showed considerable promise. In the first season after the war he and Harry Fearnley battled it out for a first-team place before both lost out to Jim Twomey. He moved to Middlesbrough in March 1948 but made only 13 League appearances in eight seasons there.
League: App 20, Gls 0; FA Cup: App 2, Gls 0.

HOLLEY, Tom *1936-1949*

Centre-half. Born: Wolverhampton, 15 November 1913.
Debut v Stoke City (a) Division One, 5 September 1936, L 1-2.
6ft 2in, 13st (1938).
Tom Holley looked a born centre-half and gave Leeds excellent service either side of the war. His father, George, played for Sunderland (where he won ten England caps) and Wolves. Tom was a schoolboy star in Wolverhampton but it was his

father's other club, Sunderland, who took him on as a youngster. Holley never made the first team at Sunderland and moved to Barnsley where his father was the trainer. He soon established himself at Oakwell before joining Leeds (£3,750) in July 1936. He succeeded Bob Kane as United's centre-half, went on to become the skipper and proved an outstanding clubman. During the war he played 104 times for Leeds, guested for Fulham and saw active service in India. Both he and United colleague George Ainsley were selected by the FA for a ten-strong party to coach in Norway in summer 1946. Holley retired three summers later and went into journalism. He proved to be a highly knowledgeable soccer writer for both the *Yorkshire Evening Post* in Leeds and the *Sunday People* before retiring to live in Majorca. He returned to Yorkshire in 1989 and died in October 1992.
League: App 164, Gls 1; FA Cup: App 5, Gls 0.

HORNBY, Cyril F. *1929-1936*

Half-back/inside-forward. Born: West Bromwich, 25 April 1907.
Debut v Leicester City (a) Division One, 11 October 1930, L 0-4.
5ft 11in, 11st 4lb (1930).
A robust and willing worker, Hornby found his versatility made him a key player at Elland Road in the 1930s. Primarily a left-half, he could fill a variety of roles and established himself as a solid First Division all-rounder. Originally he was an inside-left with Birmingham League club, Oakengates Town, from whom he joined Leeds in May 1929. Although he took time to find his feet, he had made a valuable contribution before joining Sunderland in February 1936. He rejoined Oakengates Town as player-manager in July 1937.
League: App 88, Gls 5; FA Cup: App 1, Gls 0.

HOWARTH, J.Tommy *1921-1922*

Centre-forward. Born: Bury, 15 April 1890.
Debut v Bury (a) Division Two, 12 March 1921, D 1-1.
5ft 8in, 12st (1922).
Howarth, an all-action player with something of a short temper, was United's leading scorer in

their second League season. He began with Bury before joining Bristol City in January 1914 and scored all City's goals on their way to the 1920 FA Cup semi-final. He joined Leeds in March 1921 (£1,750 with Howarth receiving £460) and scored on his debut, against one of his old clubs. In November 1922 he signed for Bristol Rovers for £500 and became manager of Welsh League side, Lovells Athletic, in May 1923 for £750, becoming player-manager three months later. He died in Rochdale on 20 September 1969. His son, Sid, played for Swansea Town, Merthyr Town, Aston Villa and Walsall.
League: App 45, Gls 19; FA Cup: App 1, Gls 0.

HUDSON, Billy A. *1951-1952*

Outside-right. Born: Swansea, 10 March 1925.
Debut v Cardiff City (h) Division Two, 12 September 1951, W 2-1.
5ft 7½in, 10st 9lb (1951).
Hudson made his League debut after only one Central League appearance but generally struggled to get into Leeds' side. After coming out of the forces he joined Pembroke Dock to whom he was recommended by his uncle, Albert Hudson, a former Fulham, Llanelly and Pembroke player. He soon impressed and, despite being rejected by Manchester City after trials, won a Welsh Amateur cap in 1951 and within a few weeks was a Leeds player. He left for Sheffield United in May 1952 and joined Mansfield Town in May 1954, being released on a free transfer a year later.
League: App 4, Gls 0.

HUGHES, Charlie *1950-1952*

Outside-left. Born: Manchester, 17 April 1927.
Debut v Barnsley (h) Division Two, 16 September 1950, D 2-2.
5ft 6½in, 9st 9lb (1950).
Hughes, a former Manchester United junior, was pitched into Leeds' first team within a day of signing from non-League football. He began at Old Trafford in September 1946, but could not get into the first team and went to Altrincham in August 1950. After only six games for the Cheshire League club, he joined Leeds the following month. Although he was a left winger, he played some games at left-back as cover for Grenville Hair in 1951-52, before fading from the scene.
League: App 21, Gls 2; FA Cup: App 2, Gls 0.

HUGHES, Phil A. *1983-1985*

Goalkeeper. Born: Manchester, 19 November 1964.
Debut v Cardiff City (h) Division Two, 10 September 1983, W 1-0.
5ft 11in, 12st 7lb (1985).
Leeds were quick to move for Hughes when he was released by Manchester United in January 1983, after serving his apprenticeship. A Northern Ireland Youth international, qualifying via parentage, he was unable to budge veteran David Harvey and went on a free transfer to Bury in June 1985. A member of the 1986 Northern Ireland World Cup squad, he was one of several young 'keepers earmarked as a possible successor to Pat Jennings in the Irish team. He made his full

debut against England at Wembley in April 1987, but a shoulder injury cost him his place at Bury and in November 1987 he moved to Wigan Athletic (£35,000). Released on a free transfer, he joined Scarborough in October 1991, initially on a three-month contract, but left the Seasiders towards the end of the 1991-92 season. He later played for Guiseley for a couple of seasons before moving to Pontefract Colliers. He won three international caps.
League: App 6, Gls 0; FA Cup: App 1, Gls 0.

HUMPHREYS, Alan *1960-1961*

Goalkeeper. Born: Chester, 18 October 1939.
Debut v Fulham (a) Division One, 27 February 1960, L 0-5.
5ft 11½in, 11st 5lb (1960).
At Overleigh School, Chester, Alan Humphreys was a star centre-half but later developed into an outstanding goalkeeper with Lache Youth Club. Shrewsbury Town signed him in October 1956 and he quickly built himself a reputation as one of the best 'keepers in the lower divisions, earning a call as reserve for the England Under-23 squad. Leeds snapped him up in February 1960, but he never fulfilled his potential at Elland Road and went to Gravesend & Northfleet in July 1962 before re-emerging with good effect at Mansfield in January 1964 and Chesterfield in July 1968. He later worked as commercial manager for Derbyshire CCC.
League: App 40, Gls 0; FA Cup: App 1, Gls 0; League Cup: App 3, Gls 0.

HUMPHRIES, Billy M. *1958-1959*

Outside-right. Born: Belfast, 8 June 1936.
Debut v Arsenal (h) Division One, 27 September 1958, W 2-1.
5ft 4½in, 9st 12lb.
Leeds were the first club to recognise the talent of Billy Humphries, but unfortunately did not reap the rewards of his skills. At school he was a rugby scrum-half, but also shone as a soccer player and joined Glentoran as an amateur while working as a clerical officer with the Belfast Transport department. His career took off when he joined Ards and Leeds beat Blackpool to his signature in September 1958 (£5,000). The 22-year-old did not settle at Leeds and returned to Ards in November 1959. In 1962 he won the first of 14 Irish caps. Coventry bought him in April 1962 and he made over 100 League appearances for them before a £14,000 transfer to Swansea, where he made another 100-plus appearances. In summer 1968 he returned to Ireland for his third, and longest, spell with Ards. Humphries was manger of Bangor from 1983 to April 1985. He represented the Irish League 12 times and won a Third Division champion ship medal with Coventry in 1963-64.
League: App 25, Gls 2; FA Cup: App 1, Gls 0.

HUNTER, Norman *1960-1976*

Defender. Born: Eighton Banks, County Durham, 24 October 1943.
Debut v Swansea Town (a) Division Two, 5 September 1962, W 2-0.
5ft 11½in, 12st 8lb (1973).
Norman 'Bites Yer Legs' Hunter was one of the fiercest competitors to pull on a Leeds United jersey. The United defender, renowned for his tackling, relished the awesome reputation that often disguised the fact that he was an excellent footballer. He joined the Leeds groundstaff as a youngster in November 1960 after playing for Birtley Secondary Modern School, Birtley juniors and Chester-le-Street. The former electrical fitter turned professional in April 1961 and made quick progress thought the ranks and never looked back after his first-team debut at

Swansea early in 1962-63. He won three England Under-23 caps and these were followed by 28 full international appearances. He was the first England player to be capped as substitute when he played against Spain just a few weeks after his full debut against West Germany in September 1966. Hunter also turned out for the Football League six times and only the presence of England captain Bobby Moore stopped him from earning more international honours. He was remarkably consistent, playing in five ever-present seasons and featured in all United's Cup Finals from 1965 to 1975, finishing with two League championship medals, an FA Cup winners' medal, League Cup winners; medal and two Inter-Cities Fairs Cup winners' medals and a Second Division championship medal to add to the honour of being voted the PFA's first-ever Player of the Year in 1973. His glorious reign at Leeds ended when he went to Bristol City in October 1976 and he became a firm favourite at Ashton Gate, making over 100 League appearances. In June 1979 he was appointed player-coach at Barnsley under Allan Clarke. When Clarke left for Leeds, Hunter took over at Oakwell in September 1980 and steered them into Division Two. He was surprisingly axed in February 1984 and had a spell as assistant manager at West Bromwich Albion before going to Rotherham United as manager in June 1985. He was dismissed in December 1987 and joined the coaching staff at Leeds in February 1988 but lost his job in October that year when Howard Wilkinson became manager. Hunter became assistant to Terry Yorath at Bradford in February 1989, but was axed 12 months later. He is now a summariser for BBC Radio Leeds.
League: App 540, Gls 18; FA Cup: App 65/1, Gls 1; League Cup: App 39, Gls 1; Europe: App 78/1, Gls 1; Charity Shield: App 2, Gls 0.

HUTCHINSON, George H. *1955-1957*

Forward. Born: Allerton Bywater, near Castleford, 31 October 1929.
Debut v Doncaster Rovers (h) Division Two, 3 December 1955, W 3-0.
5ft 8in, 10st 2lb (1955).
Hutchinson joined Huddersfield Town as an amateur in December 1946, turned professional in January 1947 and had his first taste of League football with the Terriers as a teenager before leaving in March 1958 for Sheffield United, in an exchange deal involving Albert Nightingale, who also became a Leeds player. Hutchinson was a regular at Bramall Lane before joining Spurs in June 1955. After a stint with Guildford (July 1954) he signed for Leeds in August 1955. He started with a flurry of goals – including one on his debut – but moved to Halifax Town in July 1957 where he ended his League career.
League: App 11, Gls 5.

HYDES, Arthur J.E. *1930-1938*

Centre-forward. Born: Barnsley, 24 November 1911.
Debut v Blackburn Rovers (a) Division One, 17 January 1931, L 1-3.
5ft 8½in, 10st 6lb (1930).
Former toffee factory worker Hydes proved a handful for many a defender during his days with Leeds. The spikey-haired forward played for Central School, Barnsley, and spent a month on trial with Southport at the start of 1929-30. He was not kept on by the Lancashire club and returned to the Barnsley area to play for Ardsley recreation, the club from whom he was signed by Leeds in May 1930. He made a scoring League debut and quickly developed into a player of pace and aggression. He was United's top scorer for three successive seasons from 1933 to 1936 when he notched 54 League goals in only 88 League games – easily his best period at Elland Road. Injuries checked his progress and he went to Newport County in May 1938. During the war he guested for York and Exeter, joining the latter permanently in February 1946. Leg and knee injuries forced him to give up the professional game the following season. He died in June 1990.
League: App 127, Gls 74; FA Cup: App 10, Gls 8.

IGGLEDEN, Ray *1948-1954*

Inside-forward. Born: Hull, 17 March 1925.
Debut v Luton Town (a) Division Two, 1 January 1949, D 0-0.
6ft, 11st 10lb (1951).
Horatio Iggleden – always known as Ray – was a player of considerable class. Born in Hull, he played for Constable Street Old Boys in that city but it was Leicester City who signed him during the war, when he guested for Grimsby and also served as an RAF pilot. Leicester took him on as an amateur in July 1941 and as a professional in March 1942. An exchange deal involving another footballing pilot, Ken Chisholm, saw Iggleden move from Leicester to Leeds in late December 1948. He was an excellent acquisition, capable of playing in either inside position, but proved particularly effective on the left in tandem with Welsh international winger Harold Williams. Iggleden was United's top scorer in 1951-52 and hit a hat-trick against his old club, Leicester, in January 1954. In July 1955 he moved to Exeter City, returning to Yorkshire the following summer to play Midland League football for Goole Town.
League: App 169, Gls 47; FA Cup: App 12, Gls 3.

INGHAM, Tony *1947-1950*

Half-back. Born: Harrogate, 18 February 1947.

Debut v West Bromwich Albion (a) Division Two, 4 October 1947, L 2-3.
5ft 11in, 11st 5lb (1950).
Crisp-tackling Ingham was given his first break in League football by Leeds before going on to become a loyal servant with QPR. He joined United's staff in April 1947, from Harrogate Town, and played as a half-back until a highly-successful conversion to full-back. He joined QPR in June 1950 (£5,000) and proved a real bargain. He made a record number of appearances for Rangers (514 League, 30 FA Cup and four League Cup games) and represented the Third Division South against the North in 1958. After retiring, he had a spell as Rangers' trainer, then became the club's commercial manager and later worked in the pools office at Loftus Road where he is now a director.
League: App 3, Gls 0.

IRWIN, Dennis J. *1982-1986*

Right-back. Born: Cork, Republic of Ireland, 31 October 1965.
Debut v Scunthorpe (a) FA Cup 3rd round (2nd replay) 16 January 1984, L 204.
5ft 8in, 11st (1983).
Irwin was developed at Turners Cross College (Cork) and represented Ireland Schools. He joined Leeds in February 1982 and captained both the Northern Intermediate League and Central League sides before breaking into the senior ranks. He won Irish Youth and Under-21 honours before moving to Oldham Athletic in a £60,000 deal in May 1986. His headed own-goal which gave Newcastle a 1-0 home win in 1984-85 completed a unique double as the Geordies had won the League game on the opening day of the season with an own-goal by Martin Dickinson – both Irwin and Dickinson wore the number-six shirt. He played in Oldham's 1990 Littlewoods Cup Final team which lost to Nottingham Forest, and was chosen for the Republic of Ireland 'B' team. In June 1990 he was transferred to Manchester United for £650,000. Remarkably consistent, he collected the first of his full Eire caps against Morocco in September 1991 and featured in the 1994 World Cup after establishing himself as a regular in Jack Charlton's side. He was also firmly entrenched at Old Trafford where his cool, unflappable style made him the only member of the squad to play in all matches in the 1993-94 double-winning campaign. He also won a Premiership winners' medal in 1992-93, a European Cup-winners' Cup medal in 1991, FA Cup winners' medal in 1995, League Cup winners' medal in

1992 – after being a loser the previous year to Sheffield Wednesday – and added a second Premiership and FA Cup double to his collection in 1996. He ranks as one of the best defenders allowed to leave Elland Road.
League: App 72, Gls 1; FA Cup: App 3, Gls 0; League Cup: App 5, Gls 0; Full Members' Cup: App 2, Gls 0.

JACKLIN, Harold *1920-1922*

Goalkeeper. Born: Chesterfield, 8 March 1902.
Debut v Boothtown (h) FA Cup extra preliminary round, 11 September 1920, W 5-2.
5ft 11in, 11st 4lb (1925).
Jacklin was recruited for United's first season in the League, but his only senior appearances – apart from FA Cup preliminary round outings – came in 1921-22. A product of Sheffield junior football, he joined Blackpool in 1919 and won a Central League winners' medal with them before joining Leeds in August 1920. He was Billy Down's understudy until moving to Doncaster Rovers in summer 1922 and played in the Midland League for a season before Rovers were re-elected to Division Three North. He remained at Doncaster until summer 1926. Jacklin died in 1967. League: App 3, Gls 0; FA Cup*: App 2, Gls 0.
*These were United's preliminary round games in 1920-21.

JACKSON, Billy *1925-1927*

Outside-left. Born: Farnworth, Lancashire, 15 July 1902.
Debut v Bolton Wanderers (a) Division One, 7 September 1925, L 0-1.
5ft 8in, 11st 3lb (1925).
Jackson was United's first-choice left winger for most of 1925-26, until he was forced out by the brilliance of Tom Mitchell. Jackson began his career with Leyland before joining Altricham in 1922, then Darwen in the summer of 1923 before being transferred to, Sunderland in May 1924, becoming a Leeds player 12 months later. He left for West Ham in May 1927, but as chiefly confined to reserve-team football and moved to Chelsea in February 1928. Again he found himself in the Reserves and moved to Leicester City (May 1931), Ashford Town (1932 loan), Bristol Rovers (May 1932), Cardiff (May 1934) and Watford (January 1935). He later played for Chorley (1935) and Netherfield (1936). He died in November 1974. His brother, Robert, was on Bury's books.
League: App 38, Gls 2; FA Cup: App 1, Gls 0.

JACKSON, Matthew *1995-*

Defender. Born: Leeds, 30 September 1977.
Debut (as sub) v Middlesbrough (h) Premiership, 30 March 1996, L 0-1.
Trainee professional Matt Jackson earned his Premiership debut in the wake of United's disastrous 3-0 Coca-Cola Cup Final defeat against Aston Villa. The 18-year-old came off the bench the following week against Middlesbrough, late in the game for John Pemberton.
League: App 0/1, Gls 0.

JENNINGS, Tom H.O. *1925-1931*

Centre-forward. Born: Strathaven, Lanarkshire, 8 March 1902.
Debut v Sheffield United (h) Division One, 14 March 1925, D 1-1.
5ft 8in, 12st (1925).
Before John Charles, Tom Jennings held Leeds' records for aggregate League goals (112) and the seasonal best of 35. He played for Strathaven Academy, won a Scottish Juvenile Cup-winners' medal with Cadzow St Annes and was rejected by Spurs after trials. He joined Raith Rovers in January 1921 and was a member of the team shipwrecked en route to the Canary Islands. He soon established a reputation in their free-scoring attack, which also included Alex James and Jimmy McClelland, who netted all five Middlesbrough goals against Leeds in the FA Cup in 1926. Jennings joined Leeds in March 1925. In 1925-26 he was ever-present an the following season scored 35 goals – including three successive hat-tricks, a feat equalled only by Gilbert Allsopp in 1939 and Liverpool's Jack Balmer in 1947. Despite Jennings' deadly marksmanship, United were relegated that season. He continued to score at a tremendous rate and would have increased his total but for bouts of blood poisoning which sidelined him. After 112 goals in 167 League games he went to Chester in June 1931, scoring 31 times in his first season. He later managed Bangor City and Third Lanark. Despite his record, Jennings was never capped by Scotland, although he played in a trial, scoring for the Anglo-Scots in a 1-1 draw what the Home-Scots in March 1928. He died on 2 July 1973, aged 71. His brother, Charlie, was also on Raith's books.
League: App 167, Gls 112; FA Cup: App 7, Gls 5.

JOBSON, Richard *1995-*

Defender. Born: Hull, 9 May 1963.
Debut v Chelsea (h) Premiership, 18 November 1995, W 1-0.
6ft lin, 13st 5lb (1995).
Jobson, a £1 million signing from Oldham Athletic in November 1995, managed only a dozen appearances before injury ruled him out for the rest of the season. Howard Wilkinson had tried to sign the England 'B' defender 14 months earlier but the deal had fallen through because the player had an ankle problem. Although a native of Hull, he was brought up in the Derby area and after trials as a 15-year-old at Birmingham City played part-time with Burton Albion while studying for a civil engineering degree at Nottingham University. When Watford came in with a £22,000 offer for former English Universities player Jobson, in November 1982, he cut short his studies to become a professional footballer and helped them to runners-up spot behind Liverpool in Division One in his first full season. A £40,000 transfer saw him join his native Hull in February 1985 and he amassed over 200 League appearances for the Tigers, helping them to promotion from Division Three before a £460,000 move to Oldham Athletic where he gained a Second Division championship medal in 1991. England manager Graham Taylor, the man who had sold him at Watford, called him up for the full England squad for the European championship qualifier against Norway and although he never won a full cap, he made a couple of starts for England 'B'.
League: App 12, Gls 1; FA Cup: App 1, Gls 0.

JOHANNESON, Albert *1961-1970*

Outside-left. Born: Johnanesburg, South Africa, 13 March 1940.
Debut v Swansea Town (h) Division Two, 8 April 1961, D 2-2.
5ft 7in, 10st 3lb (1969).
Albert Johanneson was the first

coloured player to appear in an FA Cup Final at Wembley, for Leeds against Liverpool in 1965. He had great speed, neat ball skills and an eye for goal. The 'Black Flash' was recommended to Leeds by a teacher after Johanneson starred with

Germiston Coloured School and Germiston Colliers. He arrived on a three-month trial and was signed in April 1961, making his debut the same month. He was United's joint leading scorer when they swept to the Second Division title in 1964 and he continued to cause havoc for defences in Division One. Injuries and the emergence of Eddie Gray effectively ended his career at Leeds and at the age of 30 he moved to York City in July 1970. He moved back to South Africa for a spell of coaching but returned to Leeds where he fell under the influence of drink and drifted through life as a lonely and broken man. Friends made efforts to get Johanneson to beat the bottle and a dinner was held at Elland Road in his honour, but he was unable to win his personal battle and was found dead in his high-rise flat in Leeds on 29 September 1995, although it is thought he had died several days earlier.
League: App 170/2, Gls 48; FA Cup: App 14, Gls 5; League Cup: App 8, Gls 6; Europe: App 5/1, Gls 8.

JOHNSON, Bill *1923-1931*

Goalkeeper. Born: Sheffield.
Debut v Southampton (a) Division Two, 1 March 1924, W 1-0.
5ft 11in, 11st (1925).
Johnson spent eight seasons at Elland Road, despite long spells of reserve-team football. A product of Sheffield junior football, he spent two seasons with Midland League Wombwell before joining Leeds in May 1923 and making his debut in their Second Division championship-winning season. In November 1924 his career was checked when he ruptured a kidney against Sheffield United. He went to Chester with Tom Jennings in June 1931, moving on to Crewe in September 1933 after a brief spell with Bangor City.
League: App 72, Gls 0; FA Cup: App 1, Gls 0.

JOHNSON, Rod *1962-1968*

Centre-forward. Born: Leeds, 8 January 1945.
Debut v Swansea Town (a) Division Two, 8 September 1962, W 2-0.
5ft 9in, 10st 12lb (1963).
Johnson enjoyed a scoring debut at the age of 17 – he was also carried off – when Don Revie picked a crop of promising youngsters. The others, Sprake, Reaney and Hunter, became household names but Johnson's impact was made in the lower divisions. A pupil of Cow Close School, Leeds, he was rejected by Reading after trials before joining United and winning England Youth honours. He moved to Doncaster (£5,000) in March 1968, playing a significant role in their Fourth Division championship success the following season. He went to Rotherham United (December 1970) and Bradford City (£9,000, December 1972). He skippered City and was also player-coach. In 1976 he played in the NASL with Chicago Sting. After returning to England he worked as an insurance salesman and played for Gainsborough Trinity (July 1979) and Garforth (September 1982), the latter as coach.
League: App 18/4, Gls 4; FA Cup: App 1, Gls 1; League Cup: App 6/1, Gls 1.

JONES, Alf *1960-1962*

Right-back. Born: Liverpool, 2 March 1937.
Debut v Liverpool (a) Division Two, 20 August 1960, L 0-2.
5ft 8in, 12st 6lb (1960).
Alf Jones signed from Marine in April 1960 and turned professional on the day he completed his National Service with the RAMC at Crookham, after playing as an amateur in United's North Midlands Combination League side. He could play on either flank but most of his senior outings were at right-back. He was transferred to Lincoln City in June 1962 (£4,000). He remained at Sincil Bank until summer 1967 when he joined Wigan Athletic, moving to Horwich RMI the following year, combining playing with working in a car factory.
League: App 25, Gls 0; FA Cup: App 1, Gls 0; League Cup: App 3, Gls 0.

JONES, Mick D. *1967-1975*

Centre-forward. Born: Worksop, 24 April 1945.
Debut v Leicester City (h) Division One, 23 September 1967, W 3-2.
5ft 10in, 11st 9lb (1969).
Three England caps were scant reward for all the effort Mick Jones put into the game – particularly with Leeds. His partnership with Allan Clarke was a deadly formation yet was never tried at international level. The pair's contrasting styles –

Jones' aggressive non-stop strong running and Clarke's delicate skills – proved an outstanding attacking combination. Jones' father kept goal for Worksop, but his son soon developed the knack of scoring goals and once hit 14 in a game for Priory Primary School. He played for Worksop Boys and Rotherham Boys and began work in a cycle factory while playing for Dinnington Miners' Welfare. He signed for Sheffield United in 1962, was capped at Under-23 level, then played twice for the full England team in 1965 but was instantly discarded. He became Leeds' first-ever £100,000 player in September 1967 and the signing of Clarke, two years later, gave Jones the perfect partner. Jones won League championship medals in 1968-69 and 1973-74, an FA Cup winners' medal in 1972 (when he was injured and was led up to the Royal Box with his arm in a sling) and Inter-Cities Fairs Cup winners' medals in 1969 and 1971. He also earned an England recall in 1970. Later in his career Jones struggled with injuries and a serious knee injury ended his career in October 1975. He later ran a sports shop and now lives in Worksop and sells sportswear in Nottingham.
League: App 216/4, Gls 77; FA Cup: App 36, Gls 12; League Cup: App 13/1, Gls 5; Europe: App 42, Gls 17; Charity Shield: App 1, Gls 0.

JONES, Vinnie *1989-1990*

Midfield. Born: Watford, 5 January 1965.
Debut (as sub) v Middlesbrough (h) 23 August 1989 W 2-1.
5ft 11in, 11st 10lb (1989).
Jones arrived at Elland Road in June 1989 for £600,000 from Wimbledon and became a Leeds cult figure overnight. Notoriety seemed to follow the former hod-

carrier from the day he joined the professional ranks with Wimbledon. GM Vauxhall Conference side Wealdstone first spotted his potential as a ball-winning midfielder in parks football. He joined Wimbledon in November 1986 and in his early career with the Dons was sent off three times – including a friendly on the Isle of Wight. Dubbed 'Psycho' by the media, Jones arrived at Leeds with his bad-boy image in one of the most talked about transfers of the season. He certainly cleaned up his act at Leeds, where his enormous throw-ins were a regular source of goals during the 1989-90 campaign when he added a Division Two championship medal to the FA Cup winners' medal he got with Wimbledon in 1988. The arrival of Gary McAllister from Leicester saw Jones lose his first team place and in September 1990 he left Leeds after 15 happy months to join Sheffield United for £700,000. The following August he returned to London as a £575,000 Chelsea

player before seeing his League career come full circle by rejoining Wimbledon in September 1992, for £700,000. Always controversial he continued to incur the wrath of referees and was even ordered off at international level. He qualified to play for Wales through his grandparents and was dismissed in only his fourth international against Georgia.
League: App 44/2, Gls 5; FA Cup: App 1, Gls 0; League Cup: App 2, Gls 0; Full Members' Cup: App 4, Gls 0

JORDAN, Joe *1970-1978*

Centre-forward. Born: Carluke, Lanarkshire, 15 December 1951.
Debut (as sub) v Arsenal (a) Division One, 11 September 1971, L 0-2.
5ft 11¼in, 11st 3lb (1973).
Joe 'Jaws' Jordan toothless grin became a regular feature of the League circuit – usually after the muscular Scot had buried the ball in the back of the net. Jordan proved an excellent successor to Mick Jones as the focal point of the Leeds attack where his aggression and energy made him a constant threat. He worked in an architect's office and was rejected after trial with West Brom. He played for junior side Blantyre Victoria before being picked up by Morton in October 1968. He played only a handful of games for the Greenock club before he was recommended to Leeds by old favourite, Bobby Collins, and United signed the

18-year-old for a bargain £15,000 in October 1970. Jordan endured long spells as substitute, but United transformed him into an unselfish inspirational leader. He won his first Scottish cap, as sub against England in 1973 and the following year scored the goal which took Scotland to the 1974 World Cup Finals. Jordan, who won 52 full caps and one at Under-23 level, won a League championship medal with Leeds before going to Manchester United for a then record fee of £350,000 in January 1978. In July 1981 a £325,000 transfer took him to AC Milan and, following a spell with Verona, he signed for Southampton (£100,000) in August 1984. In summer 1986 he joined Bristol City and helped them to the 1987 Freight/Rover Trophy Final. Jordan became Terry Cooper's assistant at Bristol. He was appointed caretaker manager when Cooper was dismissed in March 1988 and then took over on a permanent basis as player-manager, steering them to the 1988-89 Littlewoods Cup semi-final. The following season he led City to promotion from the Third Division with a side containing ex-Leeds players Ronnie Sinclair, Bob Taylor, David Rennie and Mark Gavin. He acted as Scotland's public relations officer in the 1990 World Cup in Italy. In September 1990 he was appointed manager of Hearts, who were runners-up to Rangers in 1991-92, but unable to capitalise on that platform he had a spell as assistant manager at Celtic (June 1993) before going to Stoke City as manager in November 1993, but endured a torrid time there and 12 months later was named as Bristol City's boss again.
League: App 139/30, Gls 35; FA Cup: App 16/3, Gls 4; League Cup: App 9/1, Gls 3; Europe: App 18/4, Gls 6; Charity Shield: App 1, Gls 0.

KAMARA, Chris *1990-1991*

Midfield. Born: Middlesbrough, 25 December 1957.
Debut v Hull City (h) Division Two, 10 February 1990, W 4-3.
6ft 1in, 12st (1989).
Experienced midfielder Kamara proved a useful asset after being signed towards the end of the 1990 Division Two title race He began as an apprentice at Portsmouth, turning professional in January 1976. A £20,000 move took him to Swindon in August 1977, returning to Pompey in August 1981 for £50,000. But he left Fratton Park again after only three months to join Brentford in a player-exchange deal involving striker David Crown. In August 1985 he joined Swindon for a second time, then moved to Stoke City in July 1988. Kamara, with a reputation of being a hard man, joined Leeds in January 1990 for £150,000. The former dockyard apprentice was extremely popular in his short stay at Leeds and joined Luton Town for £150,000 in November 1991. Loan spells at Sheffield United (December 1992) and Middlesbrough (February 1993) were followed by a permanent move to Sheffield United on a free transfer in June 1993. He returned to West Yorkshire in July 1994 as assistant manager with Bradford City, where he was appointed manager in March 1996 and within two months led them out at Wembley in the Division Two play-off Final against Notts County.
League: Apps 15/5, Gls 1; League Cup: Apps 1/2, Gls 0; Full Members' Cup: App 1, Gls 0.

KANE, Bob *1935-1947*

Centre-half. Born: Cambuslang, Lanarkshire, 17 July 1911.
Debut v Huddersfield Town (a) Division One, 8 February 1936, W 2-1.
5ft 11½in, 11st 10lb (1946).
'Bertie' Kane was one of the few players to turn out for United either side of the war. He began with Rutherglen Rosebank and was provisionally signed by Celtic in 1934-35, although he remained with Scottish Central League side, St Rochs, from whom he joined Leeds in August 1935. Groomed as a successor to Jock McDougall, he found himself instead having to contest the centre-half position with Tom Holley. He played wartime football with Leeds and Hibernian and served with the Royal Artilley in Gibraltar and at Finnarts Bay, near Stranraer. After the war he added one more League outing to his total before retiring in May 1947. He returned to Cambuslang to work in the Hoover factory, then a steelworks. He died in January 1985, aged 73.
League: App 58, Gls 0; FA Cup: App 3, Gls 0.

KEETLEY, Charlie F. *1927-1934*

Centre-forward. Born: Derby, 10 March 1906.
Debut v South Shields (h) Division Two, 31 December 1927, W 3-0.
5ft 9in, 12st (1930).
Former Rolls-Royce worker Charlie Keetley was the youngest of a set of Derbyshire brothers who played League football between the wars. He had ten brothers and a sister and nine of the brothers – not Charlie – played for the same Victoria Ironworks team. Charlie scored 80 goals for Alvaston & Boulton in 1926-27 to secure a place in the Derby & District League squad which toured Ireland. Leeds signed him in July 1927 and he learnt a lot from Tom Jennings, putting it to good use in the Reserves, for whom he scored seven goals in a Central League match against Bolton. Keetley made a scoring League debut and finished the 1927-28 promotion season with 18 goals in only 16 League games. He topped the United scoring charts for three season and was reserve for the Football League against the Irish League in September 1932. He joined Bradford City in October 1934 and went to Reading in June 1935. Charlie died in 1979. Of his brothers, Frank, Harold, Joe and Tom all played for Doncaster (Frank also played for Derby), Albert played for Burton United, Jack assisted Hull City and Arthur turned out for Spurs.
League: App 160, Gls 108; FA Cup: App 9, Gls 2.

KELLY, Dominic *1935-1938*

Centre-half. Born: Sandbach, Cheshire, 23 June 1917.
Debut v Bolton Wanderers (a) Division One, 2 April 1938, D 0-0.
6ft 1in, 13st (1938).
Dominic Kelly was one of three men named Kelly who played for Leeds in the 1930s and was a brother of John 'Mick' Kelly. Noted for his excellent heading ability, Dominic signed from Sandbach Ramblers in September 1935. He played four times for Leeds in 1937-38, but could not dislodge Tom Holley and was transferred to Newcastle United in November 1938 (£1,165). The war ended his League days, but he enjoyed a fine career in Army football.
League: App 4, Gls 0.

KELLY, Gary *1991-*

Right-back. Born Drogheda, Ireland, 9 July 1974.
Debut (as sub) v Scunthorpe United (h), League Cup, 8 October 1991, W 3-0.
5ft 8in, 10st 12lb (1995).
From struggling reserve-team front man to World Cup full-back – that was the remarkable rise of Gary Kelly in 1993-94. The youngest of a family of 13, he was signed in July 1991 from Home Farm, the Dublin club that

has produced so many Irish stars over the years, Johnny Giles among them. He was a striker in the juniors when he was pitched into first-team action as a 17-year-old substitute winger in a League Cup tie against Scunthorpe, having had only 15 minutes of reserve- team football under his belt. Apart from brief sub appearances, he did not re-emerge until the start of the 1993-94 season when Howard Wilkinson fielded him at right-back on the opening day at Manchester City. With Mel Sterland out of the picture Kelly made the No 2 shirt his own with a series of superb displays, his blinding speed and tenacity making his a daunting opponent for any winger. He matured so rapidly that Jack Charlton awarded him his first full Eire cap against Russia in March 1994 and within months was on his way to the World Cup finals in the United States. Ever-present for two successive seasons, he has still to score for Leeds, but has found the mark at international level, netting in a 2-0 win in Germany.
League: Apps 118/2, Gls 0; FA Cup: App 12, Gls 0; League Cup: App 12/1, Gls 0; Europe: App 4, Gls 0.

KELLY, Jack *1935-1938*

Centre-forward. Born: Hetton-le-Hole, near Sunderland, 2 March 1913.
Debut v West Bromwich Albion (h) Division One, 20 February 1935, W 4-1.
5ft 8in, 11st 8lb (1934).
Part-time magician Jack Kelly was the best-known of Leeds' three Kellys of the 1930s. He started with Hetton Juniors and was recommended to Burnley by Jack Hill, the former England centre-half. Kelly, who worked as a butcher, joined Burnley as an amateur in October 1930 and turned professional the following month. He moved to Newcastle in April 1933 but a £1,150 transfer took him to Leeds in February 1935. A proven Central League marksman, he formed a useful partnership with the experienced George Brown before going to Birmingham in January 1938, then Bury in May 1939. He retired to live in Hetton-le-Hole.
League: App 59, Gls 17; FA Cup: App 5, Gls 1.

KELLY, John 'Mick' *1934-35*

Centre-forward. Born: Sandbach, Cheshire, *c.*1913.
Debut v Stoke City (h) Division One, 3 September 1934, W 4-2.
5ft 10½in, 12st (1933).
'Mick' was added to John Kelly's name to distinguish him from his colleague Jack Kelly. 'Mick' Kelly signed from Accrington Stanley in summer 1933 with a reputation as a free-scoring leader. He netted over 50 Yorkshire Midweek League and Central League goals for Leeds but first-team chances were few and after a proposed move to York City fell through, he joined Barnsley in October 1935. He left Barnsley for Bedford Town in 1935-36. During the war he served with the Irish Guards.
League: App 4, Gls 0.

KEMP, John J. *1957-1959*

Outside-left. Born: Clydebank, 11 April 1934.
Debut v Manchester City (h) Division One, 21 February 1959, L 0-4.
5ft 6in, 9st 9½lb (1957).
Kemp made his name with Clyde before joining United in December 1957. His stay at Leeds was not the most successful, for he broke a bone in a foot and made his only senior appearance in a disastrous home defeat. He went to Barrow in March 1959 and played 170 League games for them before ending his League career with Crewe in December 1963.
League: App 1, Gls 0.

KENNEDY, David *1968-1971*

Centre-half. Born: Sunderland, 30 November, 1950.
Debut v Derby County (a) Division One, 30 March 1970, L 1-4.
6ft ½in, 12st (1970).
Kennedy made a scoring debut for Leeds in the infamous match at the Baseball Ground on Easter Monday 1970, when United fielded a reserve side and were fined £5,000. He was an apprentice who signed in May 1968 and moved to Lincoln in July 1971, but played only a few games for the Imps.
League before leaving Sincil Bank in September1972.
App 2, Gls 1; Europe: App 1, Gls 0.

KERFOOT, Eric *1949-1959*

Wing-half. Born: Ashton-under-Lyne, 31 July 1924.
Debut v Queen's Park Rangers (a) Division Two, 17 December 1949, D 1-1.
5ft 9in, 10st 6lb (1951).
Eric Kerfoot switched from non-League to Second Division football like a duck to water. He was 25 when he signed from Stalybridge Celtic in December 1949, having built a reputation as one of the best wing-halves on the non-League scene. After Bradford City failed with a £2,000 bid, Leeds improved on that and rarely has £3,000 been better spent. He made his senior bow after only one Central League appearance and became one of the most consistent players United have ever had, figuring in four ever-present seasons, including the 1955-56 promotion campaign. He was appointed skipper and his drive and enthusiasm rubbed off on those around him. He left for Chesterfield in July 1959, but was among 23 professionals not retained by the Spireites the following summer after they had a poor season.
League: App 336, Gls 9; FA Cup: App 13, Gls 12.

KERR, Dylan *1989-1993*

Midfield. Born: Valletta, Malta, 14 January 1967.
Debut (as sub) v Brighton & HA (h) Division Two, 15 April 1989, W 1-0.
5ft 11in, 12st 5lb (1989).
Joined Leeds as a non-contract player in December 1988 after playing in South Africa with Arcadia Shepherds. Although born in Malta he learned his soccer at Maple Road School, Mexborough, South Yorkshire. His left foot was seen to good effect in several appearances and Malta were informed of his availability for the national side. Loaned to Doncaster Rovers (August 1991) and Blackpool (December 1991), he was sold to Reading in July 1993 for £75,000, gaining a Division Two championship medal in 1993-94.
League: App 6/7, Gls 0; FA Cup: App 0/1, Gls 0; League Cup: Apps 2, Gls 0; Full Members' Cup: Apps 0/4, Gls 0.

KERSLAKE, David *1993*

Right-back. Born: Stepney, London, 19 June 1966.
Debut v Manchester City (h) Premiership, 13 March 1993, W 1-0.
5ft 8in, 11st (1993).
With right-back Mel Sterland facing a lengthy lay-off because of injury, Leeds turned to former England Under-21 international David Kerslake from Swindon to fill the vacancy. However, injury curtailed his season and he was released after only six months at Elland Road, United taking a £50,000 loss as he joined Tottenham for £450,000. He started with Queen's Park Rangers as an amateur, signing schoolboy forms in June 1982. He had played for East London, Inner London, London District and England Schools at Under-15 and Under-16 level when a winger. He turned professional in June 1983 and Youth and England Under -19 internationals followed before his Under-21 cap against Turkey in 1985. A

£110,000 move to Swindon Town in November 1989 saw him play under current England boss Glenn Hoddle, but he gave up the chance to feature in the Division One promotion Play-offs to join Leeds for £500,000.
League: Apps 8, Gls 0.

KEWELL, Harry *1995-*

Left-back/Midfield. Born: Sydney, Australia, 22 September 1978.
Debut v Middlesbrough (h) Premiership, 30 March 1996, L 0-1.
Seventeen-year-old Kewell started the 1995-96 season as a trainee professional in the Northern Intermediate League and finished it as a full international. He made his senior debut against Middlesbrough the week after United's Coca-Cola Cup Final defeat at Wembley when he appeared on the left side of midfield. Three weeks later he lined up for the full Australian team in Chile with only two Premiership appearances under his belt.
League: Apps 2, Gls 0

KILFORD, John D. *1959-1961*

Full-back. Born: Derby, 18 November 1938.
Debut v Portsmouth (h) Division Two, 28 February 1959, D 1-1
5ft 10½in, 12st 6lb (1961).
Kilford was ordained into the church after his playing days ended. Educated at Stainsby House School, Smalley, near Derby, he worked at a Burton brewery and played for Derby Corinthians. He was signed by Notts County as an amateur, turning professional in July 1957. He joined Leeds in February 1959 and skippered the Reserves. In 1962 he moved to Southern League Tonbridge, joining ex-Leeds players Gerry Francis and Alan Shackleton. After working as a wages clerk in an estate agency he went to Oak Hill

Theology College in 1973. His last known parish was in Penge, South London, near Selhurst Park.
League: App 21, Gls 0; League Cup: App 2, Gls 0.

KIRBY, Dennis *1942-1950*

Left-half. Born: Holbeck, Leeds, 8 November 1924.
Debut v West Bromwich Albion (a) Division Two, 4 October 1947, L 2-3.
Kirby played in a few wartime games after joining Leeds in September 1942. He made eight League appearances in 1947-48 and was farmed out to Midland League Shrewsbury and Scarborough (October 1948). He joined Halifax in August 1950 but did not make the first team.
League: App 8, Gls 0.

KIRK, Roy *1948-1953*

Wing-half. Born: Shuttlewood, Derbyshire, 11 June 1929.
Debut v Blackburn Rovers (a) Division Two, 10 February 1951, L 1-2.
5ft 9½in, 11st 9½lb (1951).
Kirk was spotted playing for Bolsover Colliery and signed in October 1948. He played at centre-half, centre-forward, right-half and outside-right after being blooded in the Yorkshire Midweek League. In March 1953, a £10,000 transfer took him to Coventry City where he made 329 League appearances in eight seasons before joining Southern League Cambridge United. He became manager at Cambridge, helping to lay the foundations of the club which Bill Leivers got into the Football League. Kirk became Cambridge City's manager in 1967. At Coventry he had the unwanted distinction of scoring two own-goals in a match, in a 2-2 home draw against Leyton Orient in 20 September 1954. He died in 1983.
League: App 34, Gls 1; FA Cup: App 5, Gls 3.

KIRKPATRICK, Jim *1924-1927*

Left-back. Born: Annan, Dumfrieshire, *c.*1903.
Debut v Cardiff City (h) Division One, 14 November 1925, W 1-0.
5ft 7in, 11st (1924).
Kirkpatrick began with Annan before joining Queen of the South. He joined North Eastern League side, Workington, in 1921-22 and Leeds signed him in May 1924. He proved a capable deputy to Bill Menzies before going to Watford in June 1927. His elder brother, John, was a forward with Workington and Accrington Stanley.
League: App 10, Gls 0.

LAMBERT, Jack *1924-1927*

Centre-forward. Born: Greasborough, near Rotherham, 25 May 1902.
Debut v Leicester City (a) Division Two, 8 September 1923, L 0-2.
5ft 9in, 12st 6lb (1928).
Lambert was a goalscoring talent whom Leeds let slip through their fingers. He joined Methley Perseverance and, after Army football, had trials with Sheffield Wednesday. Leeds signed him in November 1922, but he was 'poached' by Rotherham County and scored in his only game for them. The League ordered him to return to Leeds and County were heavily fined. In December 1924, though, he went to Doncaster Rovers and in June 1926, Arsenal paid £2,000 to sign him. Never guaranteed a regular place in Arsenal's star-studded line-up, he nevertheless scored 95 goals in 146 games, including 32 when Arsenal won the League championship in 1930-31. He scored one of the goals in their 1930 FA Cup Final win over Huddersfield and also played in the 1932 Final. He joined Fulham in October 1933 (£2,500) before becoming Margate's player-manager. Just before the war he returned to Arsenal as a coach but in December 1940, aged 36, he died in North London as a result of injuries sustained in a road accident.
League: App 1, Gls 0.

LAMPH, Tommy *1921-1922*

Right-half. Born: Gateshead, Spring 1893.
Debut v Clapton Orient (a) Division Two, 26 February 1921, L 0-1.
5ft 9½in, 11st (1921).
Along with Ivan Sharpe, Tommy Lamph is one of the two players who turned out for both Leeds United and Leeds City. Lamph began his career with Pelaw United before joining Spennymoor and represented the North Eastern League against the Southern and Central Leagues. He joined City in May 1914 and made a handful of appearances before the club was wound up. He was one of the players auctioned off at the Metropole Hotel on 12 October 1919, when Manchester City acquired his services for £800. He stayed at Maine Road for only a few months before joining Derby County in March 1920, returning to Leeds to play for United in February 1921. Ill health kept him out of prolonged action and he died, aged 32 on 24 February 1926, after retiring from the game prematurely in summer 1922.
League: App 6, Gls 0.

LANGLEY, E.Jim *1951-1953*

Left-back. Born: Kilburn, London, 7 February 1929.
Debut v Bury (a) Division Two, 28 August 1952, D 2-2.
5ft 9½in, 11st 5lb (1957).
Langley, a future England full-back, was given his League debut by Leeds as a left winger. A product of Evelyns Yiewsley Senior School, Kilburn, he played as an amateur for Yiewsley, Hounslow, Uxbridge and Hayes before joining Brentford in 1946. He returned to non-League soccer with Guildford City and signed professional forms in 1949, after Army service. Leeds signed him in June 1952 and although he made a scoring debut, it was as a full-back that he made his name after joining Brighton in July 1953. Despite being a Third Division player, he won England 'B' caps and played for the Football League before a £12,000 transfer took him to Fulham in February 1957. There he formed an outstanding partnership with George Cohen. Both played for England with Langley making three appearances. After 323 League outings for Fulham he joined QPR in July 1965 and helped them to a League Cup and Third Division championship double in 1967, when he was 37. In September 1967 he was appointed manager of Hillingdon Borough and led them out at Wembley in the 1971 FA Challenge Trophy Final. In August 1971 he became trainer-coach at Crystal Palace. He is currently steward at West Drayton British Legion Club in Middlesex.
League: App 9, Gls 3.

LAWSON, F.Ian A. *1962-1966*

Centre-forward. Born: Onslow, County Durham, 24 March 1939.
Debut v Huddersfield Town (a) Division Two, 3 March 1962, L 1-2.
5ft 11in, 11st 8lb (1963).
Lawson, an England Youth international, made a sensational start by scoring four goals on his debut for Burnley against Chesterfield in a 7-0 FA Cup win in 1957, when he was 17. He joined Burnley from Pelton School in March 1956 but the strength of their squad saw him manage only eight games when they won the League championship in 1959-60. Leeds signed him (£20,000) in March 1962 and he became a valued member of the squad which won the Second Division title in 1963-64. In June 1966 he moved to Crystal Palace (£9,000) and was the first Palace player to be substituted. He later had spells with Port Vale (August 1966) and Barnsley (August 1967) but did not make a senior appearance for the latter.
League: App 44, Gls 17; FA Cup: App 3, Gls 1; League Cup: App 4, Gls 3.

LETHERAN, Glan *1973-1977*

Goalkeeper. Born: Llanelli, 1 May 1956.
Debut (as sub) v Hibernian (a) UEFA Cup 2nd round (2nd leg), 7 November 1973, D 0-0 (W 5-4 on penalties).
6ft 1½in, 12st 4lb (1977).
Letheran became an instant Leeds hero after a match-winning debut in a UEFA Cup-tie. With David Harvey injured, Leeds went to Hibernian, after a goalless first leg, with reserve John Shaw as first choice and youth-team 'keeper Letheran on the bench. Shaw was injured and Letheran came on to keep a clean sheet before surviving a penalty shoot-out as Leeds squeezed through 5-4. A Welsh Youth international, he joined Leeds in May 1973 but, although he won two Under-21 caps, he could not get a regular place and after loan spells at Scunthorpe (August 1976) and Notts County (September 1977) was transferred to Chesterfield in December 1977. He joined Swansea in September 1979 and had spells with Oxford City and Scarborough and appeared in the 1984 FA Challenge Trophy Final at Wembley for Bangor City against Northwich.
League: App 1, Gls 0; Europe: App 0/1, Gls 0.

LIDDELL, Gary *1971-1977*

Forward. Born: Bannockburn, Stirlingshire, 27 August 1954.
Debut (as sub) v Birmingham City (a) Division One, 30 April 1973, L 1-2.
5ft 9in, 9st 11½lb (1975).
Liddell joined Leeds straight from school – the same one attended by Billy Bremner – and turned professional in September 1971 after completing his apprenticeship. He showed his best form after joining Grimsby in March 1977. He joined Hearts in February 1981 before linking up with Doncaster Rovers, managed by Billy Bremner, in March 1992, leaving in summer 1993. His son Andy is a striker with Barnsley.
League: App 2/1, Gls 0; League Cup: App 1, Gls 0; Europe: App 1/1, Gls 1.

LINIGHAN, Andy *1984-1986*

Centre-half. Born: Hartlepool, 18 June 1962.
Debut v Notts County (a) Division Two, 25 August 1984, W 2-1.
6ft 4in, 13st (1985).

Linighan is one of the tallest outfield players to play for Leeds. He joined Hartlepool United from Smith's Dock in September 1980 and Leeds paid £20,000 for him in May 1984. His brother, David, also a Hartlepool player, had trials with Leeds in March 1985 before joining Shrewsbury, then Ipswich. A third brother, Brian, is on the books of Sheffield Wednesday. His father, Brian, played for Darlington and an uncle, Michael, also turned out for Darlington. Andy was ever-present in his first season but moved to Oldham in January 1986 (£55,000) and was soon joined by Leeds contemporaries Dennis Irwin, Tommy Wright and Andy Ritchie. The Latics reaped a useful profit when they sold Linighan to Norwich (£300,000) in March 1988 after a proposed move to Crystal Palace fell through. He showed continuing improvement and was rewarded by selection for England 'B'. Linighan was transferred to Arsenal for £1.3 million in July 1990. He sometimes struggled to make headway at Highbury because of the presence of England duo Tony Adams and Steve Bould, but became the toast of the North Bank when he netted the Gunners' late FA Cup Final replay extra-time winner against Sheffield Wednesday in 1993, Arsenal triumphing 2-1 after the first meeting finished 1-1.
League: App 66, Gls 3; FA Cup: App 2, Gls 0; League Cup: App 6, Gls 1; Full Members' Cup: App 2, Gls 0.

LOMAS, Albert *1948-1949*

Goalkeeper. Born: Tyldesley, near Bolton, 14 October 1924.
Debut v West Bromwich Albion (h) Division Two, 2 October 1948, L 1-3.
Lomas came from Bolton Wanderers (amateur) junior football in September 1948 and within weeks was plunged into the first team. He was released to Mossley the following year but had other chances in League football, with Rochdale (May 1950) and Chesterfield (July) 1951.
League: App 1, Gls 0.

LONGDEN, Eric *1929-1930*

Inside-right. Born: Goldthorpe, near Rotherham, 18 May 1904.
Debut v Sheffield United (a) Division One, 1 April 1929, D 1-1
5ft 11½in, 12st 4lb (1930).
Longden was amongst the most powerful tacklers of his day and a player who could occupy several positions. He began with Goldthorpe United in South Yorkshire before joining Doncaster Rovers in March 1926. He signed for Leeds in January 1929, but the emergence of Billy Furness saw him move to Hull City in October 1930. After going to Blackpool in January 1931 he returned to Hull in December 1932 and won a Third Division North medal that season. He retired in April 1935. A skilled ukulele player, he died, aged 79, in Blackpool on 7 September 1983.
League: App 28, Gls 7.

LORIMER, Peter P. *1962-1979 & 1983-1986*

Forward/midfield. Born: Dundee, 14 December 1946.
Debut v Southampton (h) Division Two, 29 September 1962, D 1-1.
5ft 10in, 11st 2lb (1970).
Peter Lorimer, possessor of one of the hardest shots in the game, is the only player to have netted over 200 goals for Leeds. He is also the club's youngest debutant, making his bow when he was 15 years, 289 days old. He once scored 176 goals in a season for

Stobswell School, Dundee, and represented Dundee Schools. Don Revie was in such a hurry to sign him that he was stopped for speeding on his way north. Lorimer signed in May 1962 and won Scottish Amateur caps on a tour of Kenya before turning professional in December 1963. He recovered from a fractured leg to establish himself. He won Under-23 caps and made his full international debut in November 1969. Lorimer won 22 caps and was a key figure in Scotland's 1974 World Cup campaign. His thunderous shooting helped Leeds reap a rich harvest of honours before a £25,000 move took him to Toronto Blizzard in March 1979. He returned to England that September to sparkle in York City's ranks, going back to Canada in March 1980 as player-coach with Vancouver Whitecaps. He was 37 when he rejoined Leeds in December 1983 and was older than his manager Eddie Gray. He played a key role in midfield and overhauled John Charles' League aggregate of goals before moving to Whitby Town in December 1985. He had a brief spell as player-coach in Israel with Hapoel Haifa before returning to Leeds to run the Commercial Hotel, near Leeds city centre.
League: App 503/22, Gls 168; FA Cup: App 56/3, Gls 20; League Cup: App 41/1, Gls 19; Europe: App 74/1, Gls 30; Charity Shield: App 1/1, Gls 0; Full Members' Cup: App 2, Gls 1.

LUKIC, John *1978-1983 & 1990-1996*

Goalkeeper. Born: Chesterfield, 11 December 1960.
Debut v Valletta (h) UEFA Cup 1st round (2nd leg), 3 October 1979, W 3-0.
6ft 4in, 13st 7lb (1982).
John Lukic ousted David Harvey and beat off the challenges of youngsters Henry Smith and Dave Seaman to make his name at Leeds. United's tallest-ever 'keeper, he was spotted in Derbyshire schools football and

signed in December 1978 after serving his apprenticeship. He learnt from Harvey and when he replaced him at Brighton in October 1979, went on to make a club record 146 successive League games. His run ended when he asked for a transfer and was promptly dropped. Arsenal were attracted by his ability in the air and marvellous reflexes and in July 1983, a £125,000 transfer took him to Highbury. Lukic, who won England Youth and Under-21 honours with United, left Leeds because he wanted success at domestic and international level. He never made a full international appearance but won a League Cup winners' medal in 1987 and appeared in the 1988 Final. Christened Jovan, he was always known as John in the football world. Lukic was a key figure as Arsenal won the 1988-89 First Division title and became United's most expensive signing when he returned to Elland Road for £1 million in May 1990. He proved a worthwhile investment in his second spell at Leeds and had a magnificent season as United won the League title in 1991-92, but in recent seasons he seemed to lose form and finding his first-team place under increasing threat from Mark Beeney, rejoined Arsenal on a free transfer in July 1996.
League: Apps: 335, Gls 0; FA Cup: App 28, Gls 0; League Cup: App 32, Gls 0; Europe: App 12, Gls 0; Full Members' Cup: App 5, Gls 0; Charity Shield: App 1, Gls 0.

LUMSDEN, Jimmy *1964-1970*

Inside-forward. Born: Glasgow, 7 November 1947.
Debut v Sheffield Wednesday (h) Division One, 15 May 1967, W 1-0.
5ft 5in, 12st 7lb (1970).
Lumsden was best known as assistant manager to Eddie Gray. From Kinning Park, he played for Glasgow Schools and had trials for Scotland before turning professional with Leeds in November 1964. Opportunities were rare but he did not move until September 1970, when he joined Southend. He signed for Morton in 1971 and was ever-present in 1971-72. In December 1972 he joined St Mirren, then played for Cork Hibernians before rejoining Morton in 1973. In summer 1975 he joined Clydebank and won a Scottish League Division Two medal in his first season and promotion to the Premier Division the following year. He was Celtic's youth-team manager and when his great friend Eddie Gray was appointed manager at Leeds, Lumsden became his assistant in July 1982. The pair were dismissed in October 1985 but linked up again at Rochdale in December 1986. Two weeks before Christmas 1987 Lumsden was made redundant as part of a cost-cutting exercise and later assisted Joe Jordan at Bristol City. When Jordan left for Hearts in September 1990, Lumsden took over as manager at Ashton Gate, but after a poor run of results was sacked in February 1992.
League: App 3/1, Gls 0.

LYDON, G.Micky *1954-1955*

Outside-left. Born: Sunderland, 5 November 1933.
Debut v Bury (h) Division Two, 15 January 1955, W 1-0.
5ft 8½in, 10st 7½lb (1957).
Lydon enjoyed an outstanding schoolboy career before arriving at Leeds via Sunderland. He went to school at St Bennet's and represented Sunderland Boys and Durham County Boys before

winning two England Youth caps in 1949. He joined Sunderland as a 17-year-old from Durham Junior League club, Hylton Juniors, in December 1950. Anxious for first-team football, he moved to Leeds in June 1954 but, unable to make an impression there, he signed for Gateshead in November 1955 and made over 100 League appearances for them.
League: App 4, Gls 1.

LYON, Jack *1920-1921*

Inside-left. Born: Prescot, Lancashire, 3 November 1893.
Debut v Port Vale (a) Division Two, 28 August 1920, L 0-2.
5ft 9in, 11st 10lb (1920).

Lyon played for Prescot before joining Hull City in October 1913. United signed him for £300 in July 1920 but, despite holding a regular place in their first League season, he returned to Prescot in 1921. In August that year he joined New Brighton and in August 1924 moved to Mold, winning a Welsh League championship medal in 1924-25. He rejoined Prescot in 1926-27. His elder brother, Sam, played for Prescot, Hull and Burnley. Younger brother James played for Derby and Wrexham.
League: App 33, Gls 3.

McADAM, David F. *1948-1950*

Half-back. Born: Hereford, 3 April 1923.
Debut v Tottenham Hotspur (a) Division Two, 13 September 1948, D 2-2.
5ft 9½in, 10st 4lb (1949).
McAdam was plucked from non-League football by Major Frank Buckley and enjoyed a brief spell with Leeds. He attended Abingdon Council School, Berkshire, and went into the Army in 1941, serving with the 1st Battalion, Wiltshire Regiment, in India, Burma and the North-West Frontier. He played at battalion level and on demob in September 1946 worked at the Branston Ordnance Depot near Burton upon Trent. He joined Stapenhill WMC and was spotted by Major Buckley. Within months he was in the first team but moved to Wrexham in May 1950. After a year there, he spent ten years with Burton Albion before joining Matlock for four years, helping run the Reserves before returning to Stapenhill.
League: App 24, Gls 0.

McADAMS, Billy J. *1961-1962*

Centre-forward. Born: Belfast, 20 January 1931.
Debut v Charlton Athletic (a) Division Two, 16 December 1961, L 1-3.
5ft 9½in, 11st 7lb (1959).
Billy McAdams had a seven-month stay at Elland Road during his distinguished career. A product of Grosvenor Secondary School, Belfast, he worked as an apprentice heating engineer and played for Bainbridge Town and Glenavon before turning down Burnley after trials. His performances for Irish League side Distillery prompted Manchester City to sign him in December 1953 and he was a regular marksman until a £15,000 transfer to Bolton Wanderers in September 1960. He missed an FA Cup Final with City because of a slipped disc and was told he would not play again, but he fought back well enough to establish himself in the Northern Ireland side. As a Bolton player he scored a hat-trick for the Irish against West Germany in a World Cup qualifying game but still ended up on the losing side. In December 1961 his former City teammate, Don Revie signed him for Leeds to boost a struggling attack. Although he gained his 15th and final cap with United, he was soon on the move, joining Brentford (£8,000) in July 1962. He won a Fourth Division medal with the Bees in 1962-63 and joined QPR (£5,000) in September 1964 and Barrow for a similar fee in July 1966 before going to non-League Netherfield.
League: App 11, Gls 3; FA Cup: App 2, Gls 1.

McALLISTER, Gary *1990-1996*

Midfield. Born: Motherwell, Lanarkshire, 25 December 1964.
Debut v Everton (a) Division One, 25 August 1990, W 3-2.
5ft 10in (1996).
Midfield architect Gary McAllister proved the most consistent Leeds player in his six seasons at Elland Road, and as articulate off the field as on it. When United won the Second Division championship, Howard Wilkinson invested £1 million in the rising Leicester City star, suggesting a change of emphasis as Leeds sought to add skill to the muscular aspects of their game. McAllister dovetailed superbly with Gordon Strachan, David Batty and Gary Speed, and the all-star international midfield quartet were magnificent as

Leeds won the 1991-92 title. McAllister succeeded Strachan as both captain of club and country and rarely missed a match in his time at Elland Road. He led Scotland's assault on the 1996 European Championships but will not want to dwell on the competition after missing a penalty which would have drawn Scotland level against England at Wembley. Born on Christmas Day 1964, he started with Fir Park Boys' Club before joining the professional ranks with his native Motherwell in 1981. There was constant speculation in Scotland about his future because of his great vision and passing accuracy and in August 1985 he headed for Leicester City with teammate Ali Mauchlen (later to have a few weeks on loan with Leeds) in a £250,000 deal. He made his debut for Scotland 'B' against France in April 1987. It was clear that he was destined for greater things, but he rejected a proposed £1.15 million move to Nottingham Forest because he was unimpressed by Brian Clough's blunt approach. With Forest out of the picture and McAllister out of contract, Leeds swooped and a transfer tribunal set the fee at £1 million. He arrived with three full caps to his credit but is now rapidly approaching the 50-mark and rated among Europe's top midfielders. The possessor of a wide variety of skills, he has proved a deadly exponent at free-kicks and penalties, always looks comfortable in possession, packs a powerful shot and proved an intelligent ambassador for the club before his sale to Coventry for £3 million in July 1996.
League: App 230/1, Gls 31; FA Cup: App 24, Gls 6; League Cup: App 26, Gls 4; Full Members' Cup: App 4, Gls 1; Europe: App 9, Gls 0; Charity Shield: App 1, Gls 0.

McCABE, Jim J. *1948-1954*

Half-back. Born: Draperstown near Derry, 17 September 1918.
Debut v Bradford (a) Division Two, 13 March 1948, L 1-3.
5ft 10in, 11st 10lb (1951).
McCabe filled various positions but his best was wing-half. He played for Billingham Synthonia Juniors an South Bank East End before Middlesbrough signed him in May 1937. After wartime service with the Green Howards, in France and the Middle East, he resumed his career at Ayresome Park and joined Leeds in March 1948. United paid £10,000 and transferred goalkeeper John Hodgson in part-exchange. Within months of joining Leeds, McCabe won the first of six Irish caps. He moved to Peterborough United in May 1954.
League: App 152, Gls 0; FA Cup: App 9, Gls 0.

McCALL, Andy *1952-1955*

Inside-forward. Born: Hamilton, Lanarkshire, 15 March 1925.
Debut v Huddersfield Town (a) Division Two, 23 August 1952, L 0-1.
5ft 6in, 9st 6lb (1954).
McCall, a pupil of Woodside School, Hamilton, played for Bent Royal Oak PSA in the Hamilton & District League before joining the Royal Navy as a 17-year-old. He enlisted in the Army at 20 and served with the KOSB. On returning to civilian life he joined Blantyre Celtic and won a Scottish Junior cap against Ireland. Blackpool signed him in April 1947 and he played at inside-forward between Matthews and Mortensen before a £15,000 transfer took him to West Brom in January 1951. He joined Leeds in August 1952 and later played for Lovells Athletic, then joined Halifax in July 1956 and made over 100 League outings for them. His son, Scotland, Rangers and Everton midfielder Stuart, played for Bradford City and Andy was among those who received treatment for burns as a result of the Valley Parade fire in May 1986.
League: App 62, Gls 8; FA Cup: App 2, Gls 0.

McCLELLAND, John *1989-1992*

Centre-half. Born: Belfast, 7 December 1955.
Debut v Newcastle United (a) Division Two, 19 August 1989 L 2-5.
6ft 2in, 13st 5lb (1989).
Multi-capped Northern Ireland

international John McClelland joined Leeds from Watford for £110,000 in June 1989 but managed only three appearances in their Division Two campaign because of injury. He began his career with Portadown in Ireland before trying his luck in the Football League with Cardiff City (February 1974). But League football had come too early for young McClelland and he signed for non-League Bangor City in the 1975 close season. Mansfield gave him a second chance at League football in May 1978. His career took off in a big way when he joined Rangers for £90,000 in May 1981. A £225,000 move took him to Watford in November 1984. He played in Northern Ireland's 1982 and 1986 World Cup finals teams and represented the Football League v the Rest of the World at Wembley in August 1987. Leeds loaned McClelland back to Watford in January 1990, for a month. Despite injury he still won another Northern Ireland cap to add to the 52 he gained in his pre-Leeds days. When he did play in the Leeds first team he rarely put a foot wrong, using his great experience to good effect against forwards much younger and quicker than himself. Loaned to Notts County in March 1992, he joined St Johnstone that summer as player-coach, later being elevated to player-manager, a position he held until November 1993. After losing his job with the Saints he turned out briefly for Carrick Rangers but soon moved back to Scotland with Arbroath. He then linked up with Wycombe Wanderers in February 1994 before joining Yeovil Town in the GM Vauxhall Conference the following month. In March 1996 he was appointed assistant to Chris Kamera at Bradford City after playing in the Northern Counties East League with Farsley Celtic.
League: App 22/2, Gls 0; FA Cup: App 2, Gls 0; League Cup: App 2/1, Gls 0;

McCLUSKEY, George M.C. *1983-1986*

Forward. Born: Hamilton, Lanarkshire, 19 September 1957.
Debut v Newcastle United (h) Division Two, 27 August 1983, L 0-1.
5ft 11in, 12st (1985).
McCluskey found it difficult to adapt to the English game after a successful time in Scottish football with Celtic. He played for St Catherine's Secondary School, Uddingston, Holy Cross, Hamilton, and won five Scottish Schoolboy caps and four Youth caps. He was with Celtic Boys' Club before signing for Celtic and made his senior debut in 1977-78. He scored Celtic's winner against Rangers in the 1980 Scottish Cup Final, won Scottish League championship medals in the following two seasons and was a member of Scotland's World Cup party in 1982 but never won a full cap, although he did represent the Under-21 side seven times. He joined Leeds for £161,000 in August 1983 but, despite his natural ability, he lacked consistency at Elland Road and in June 1986, signed for Hibernian. He left Hibs for Hamilton Academical in September 1989 for £35,000. Freed in May 1992, he joined Kilmarnock a couple of months later and was appointed player-coach in August 1994, but two months later was transferred to Clyde.
League: App 57/16, Gls 16; A Cup: App 4, Gls 0; League Cup: App 5/3, Gls 1; Full Members' Cup: App 1, Gls 0.

McCOLE, John *1959-1961*

Centre-forward. Born: Glasgow, 18 September 1936.
Debut v West Bromwich Albion (a) Division One, 19 September 1959, L 0-3.
5ft 10½in, 11st 9lb (1960).
McCole is the only Leeds player to have scored four goals in a League Cup-tie, achieving the feat against Brentford in September 1961. He maintained an excellent scoring record at Leeds, but his 22 League goals in 1959-60 were not enough to save United from relegation to Division Two. He started with Vale of Leven before moving to Falkirk. Bradford City signed him in September 1958 and he netted 32 goals in his first season, which prompted Leeds to buy him for £10,000 in September 1959. Despite his excellent record, McCole was allowed to go back to Bradford in October 1961, after spending the summer in the USA with New York Rangers, a side formed by British players. In December 1962 he took his talents to Rotherham United, where a broken leg in 1963 ruled him out for a year, then had a spell with Shelbourne before joining Newport County in October 1964 and Cork Hibernians in February 1965.
League: App 78, Gls 45; FA Cup: App 2, Gls 1; League Cup: App 5, Gls 7.

McCONNELL, Peter *1954-1962*

Half-back/inside-forward. Born: Reddish, near Stockport, 3 March 1937.
Debut v Bolton Wanderers (h) Division One, 20 December 1958, L 3-4.
5ft 9in, 11st 9lb (1961).
As a 15-year-old trialist with Leeds, McConnell was running the line in a first team v reserves game when one of the players was injured and he came on to show what he could do. The promise he displayed as a youngster at Elland Road finally bore fruit at Carlisle United. A pupil of North Reddish Primary School and Stockport Grammar School, he represented Stockport and Cheshire Schools before joining Leeds, turning professional in March 1954. He left in August 1962 for Carlisle, whose manager was Ivor Powell, the former Leeds trainer. McConnell made some 300 senior appearances for Carlisle, skippered the side and won a Third Division medal in 1964-65 before going to Bradford City in July 1969. A qualified FA coach, he joined Scarborough as player-coach in the 1971 close season and then became a licensee.
League: App 48, Gls 4; FA Cup: App 2, Gls 0; League Cup: App 3, Gls 1.

McDONALD, Bobby W. *1987-1988*

Left-back. Born: Aberdeen, 13 April 1955.
Debut v Sheffield United (a) Division Two, 7 February 1987, D 0-0.
5ft 10in, 12st 1lb (1987).
McDonald was a defender of great control and positional sense who also had a happy knack of scoring goals. He played for King Street Sports Club in Aberdeen before joining Aston Villa in 1971, turning professional in September 1972. A Scottish Youth international, he played in the 1972 Little World Cup when Frank Gray and Kenny Burns were among his contemporaries. After helping Villa win promotion to Division One in 1974-75 and picking up a 1975 League Cup-winners' medal, a £40,000 transfer in August 1976 took him to Coventry City where he made 161 consecutive appearances. Manchester City signed him (£270,000) in October 1980. He went to Oxford in September 1983 and won a Third Division medal in his first season followed by a Second Division medal in 1984-85. He went to Leeds on a month's loan in February 1987 before joining in a £25,000 deal to help United's push towards the Play-offs. Injury cost him his place the following season and he was loaned to Wolves for a few matches in February 1988. Granted a free transfer in May 1988, he joined VS Rugby during the 1988 close season. He later played for Burton Albion, joining the Brewers in summer 1989, and then moved around the non-League scene with some regularity, joining Nuneaton Borough (September 1989), Worcester City (October 1990), Sutton Coldfield Town (January 1991), Armitage Town (cs 1991) and Redditch United (cs 1992)..
League: App 23, Gls 1; League Cup: App 1, Gls 0.

McDOUGALL, Jock *1934-1937*

Centre-half. Born: Port Glasgow, 21 September 1901.
Debut v Leicester City (a) Division One, 24 November 1934, L 0-1.
5ft 11in, 12st 4lb (1925).
Although approaching the veteran stage when he joined Leeds, Scottish international Jock McDougall was still able to give First Division forwards a tough time. He worked as a marine engineer on Clydeside and played for Kilmacolm Amateurs, then Port Glasgow Juniors before signing for Airdrie in November 1921. He won a full cap against Northern Ireland in 1926, represented the Scottish League twice and picked up a Scottish Cup winners' medal in 1924. He joined Sunderland (£4,500) in May 1929 and captained them. In November 1934, Leeds beat Plymouth to sign the 33-year-old for £6,000 bid. He skippered Leeds before retiring in summer 1937. He worked at the Port of Glasgow Golf Club as a greenkeeper and died on 26 September 1973, five days after his 72nd birthday. He was an older brother of Jimmy McDougall, the Partick Thistle, Liverpool and Scotland player.
League: App 52, Gls 0; FA Cup: App 7, Gls 1.

McGEE, Jock *1920-1922*

Full-back. Born: Rothesay, Isle of Bute, *c.*1902.
Debut v Boothtown (h) FA Cup Extra preliminary round, 11 September 1920, W 5-2.
5ft 11in, 12st 6lb (1920).
Did not play in the Football League for United. Signed from Harrogate, he was a member of a family who worked on the Grantley Estate, near Ripon. In March 1922 he joined Hull City, but a broken leg against Wolves in an FA Cup-tie effectively ended his career.
FA Cup*: App 1, Gls 0.
*He played in one of United's preliminary round games in 1920-21.

McGHIE, Billy L. *1976-1979*

Forward. Born: Lanark, 19 January 1958.
Debut v Ipswich Town (h) Division One, 16 April 1977, W 2-1.
5ft 9in, 11st 8lb (1977).
McGhie was preparing to travel to Bury for a reserve game when he received his first-team call-up

and he scored after 19 minutes of his first game. He had lived in Doncaster since he was four years old and worked his way through United's junior ranks before signing professional forms in January 1976. He left for York City on a free transfer in December 1979, staying at Bootham Crescent until his contract was cancelled in November 1981.
League: App 2, Gls 1.

McGINLEY, Billy D. *1972-1974*

Midfield. Born: Dumfries, 12 November 1954.
Debut (as sub) v Birmingham City (a) Division One, 30 April 1973, L 1-2.
5ft 5½in, 9st 10lb (1972).
Although his Football League experience at Leeds lasted only 50 minutes as substitute for Roy Ellam – McGinley made some impression at his other clubs. After serving his apprenticeship in the juniors, he turned professional with Leeds in January 1972 but moved to Huddersfield in September 1974. He had spells at Bradford City (June 1975) and Crewe (August 1977).
League: App 0/1, Gls 0; Europe: App 0/1, Gls 0.

McGOLDRICK, John *1983-1985*

Right-back. Born: Coatbridge, Lanarkshire, 23 September 1963.
Debut v Chester City (h) Milk Cup 2nd round (1st leg), 5 October 1983, L 0-1.
5ft 11in, 10st 7lb (1983).
McGoldrick was unlucky enough to make his Leeds debut on one of the most humiliating nights in the club's history – when they lost to bottom-of-the-Fourth Division Chester in the Milk Cup. He played for Celtic Boys' Club before being recruited by Celtic. He did not make the first team at Parkhead and was signed by Leeds on a free transfer in June 1983. Another free transfer, in July 1985, took him to Motherwell but a persistent knee injury, first incurred at Parkhead, led to his premature retirement soon afterwards.
League: App 7, Gls 0; FA Cup: App 3, Gls 0; League Cup: App 2, Gls 0.

McGOVERN, John P. *1974-1975*

Midfield. Born: Montrose, 28 October 1949.
Debut v Birmingham City (h) Division One, 24 August 1974, W 1-0.
5ft 10in, 10st 13lb (1974).
McGovern endured a miserable seven months at Leeds after joining United during Brian Clough's brief but turbulent reign, but went on to achieve glory with Clough at Nottingham Forest. He attended a rugby-playing school but soon showed an aptitude for soccer and was taken on as a professional by Hartlepools United, where Clough was manager, in May 1967. Clough took him to Derby in September 1968 (£7,500) and the Rams won the Second Division title that season, so McGovern played in all four divisions inside 18 months – and he was still only 19. He played a key role in Derby's League championship success in 1971-72 and went to Leeds in August 1974. The fee of £125,000 also included Derby striker John O'Hare. McGovern enjoyed seven years of success at Forest which included European Cup winners' medals (1979 and 1980), a League championship medal (1977-78), and League Cup winners' medals (1978 and 1979). In July 1982 he joined Bolton as player-manager but was dismissed in January 1985. He played for Horwich RMI and later moved to Tenerife. He was appointed manager of Chorley in March 1990. In March 1992 he was named as Peter Shilton's assistant at Plymouth, but quit after a bust-up with his former Forest colleague. In September 1994, McGovern became joint manager (with Archie Gemmill, another ex-teammate) of Rotherham United and steered them to victory over Shrewsbury Town in the 1996 Auto Windscreen Shield Final at Wembley.
League: App 4, Gls 0.

McGREGOR, John R. *1985*

Midfield/defender. Born: Airdrie, 5 January 1963.
Debut v Portsmouth (h) Division Two, 2 November 1985, W 2-1.
5ft 11in, 12st (1986).
Despite being bought and sold by Liverpool, McGregor's only taste of League football was during a month's loan with Leeds. He was educated at Airdrie Academy and joined Queen's Park from school before Liverpool paid a big fee for him in summer 1982. He never made a senior appearance for the Reds and in April 1984 began a loan spell with St Mirren, where he sustained a bad knee injury. He returned to Anfield and after a long stint back in the Reserves, and his brief period at Elland Road, was sold to Rangers (£70,000) in summer 1987, winning a Scottish League Cup winners' medal in his first season to add to a string of Central League winners' medals gained at Anfield. A bad knee injury during 1987-88 ended his career. He is now the reserve-team coach at Ibrox.
League: App 5, Gls 0.

McGUGAN, John H. *1960-1961*

Centre-half. Born: Airdrie, 12 June 1939.
Debut v Ipswich Town (h) Division Two, 1 October 1960, L 2-5.
5ft 10½in, 11st 11½lb (1960).
Because of injury 'Jackie' McGugan was restricted to one senior game during his six months with Leeds. He began with Pollok before joining St Mirren in 1956 and quickly rose through their ranks to win Scottish Under-23 caps and a Scottish Cup winners' medal in 1959. He asked St Mirren for a transfer when he lost his first-team place and, although Rangers were keen to sign him, he joined Leeds (£15,000) in August 1960 after touring Austria, Hungary and Turkey with the Scottish squad, although he did not win a full cap. He left Leeds for Tranmere in February 1961 for £12,000, easily a record for the Birkenhead club at the time. He later played for Cambridge City and ran a pub in Cambridge.
League: App 1, Gls 0.

McINROY, Albert *1935-1937*

Goalkeeper. Born: Walton-le-Dale, near Preston, 23 April 1901.
Debut v Stoke City (a) Division One, 31 August 1935, L 1-3.
5ft 11in, 13st.
Although already at the veteran stage, McInroy turned in some highly-agile performances during his time with Leeds. At St Thomas High School in Preston he was an outside-left but after leaving school and getting a job as a packer at the Preston Co-operative Society he played in goal for local sides Upper Walton and Coppul Central. He signed amateur forms with Preston North End in 1921-22 but after a few reserve games he went to High Walton United, then Leyland Motors in November 1922. He signed for Sunderland in May 1923 and quickly established himself, going on to win a full England cap in October 1926 against Northern Ireland. In October 1929 he was transferred to Newcastle (£2,750) and won an FA Cup winners' medal in 1932. He returned to Roker in May 1934 and joined Leeds in June 1935, staying until June 1937 when he went to Gateshead. A well-known dressing-room comedian, he later played for Stockton and junior clubs in the North-East before taking a pub in Houghton-le-Spring. He died on 7 January 1985, aged 83.
League: App 67, Gls 0; FA Cup: App 4, Gls 0.

McKENNA, Frank *1956-1958*

Centre-forward. Born: Blaydon, near Newcastle upon Tyne, 8 January 1933.
Debut v Newcastle United (a) Division One, 3 November 1956, W 3-2.
5ft 9in, 11st 10lb (1956).
McKenna, an outstanding amateur, enjoyed a two-goal debut for Leeds against Newcastle United – the club nearest his home. A joiner by trade, he played for North Shields before joining Bishop Auckland, one for the most powerful clubs in the Northern League. With Bishops he won three England Amateur caps, an FA Amateur Cup medal in 1956 and played for Great Britain in an Olympic preliminary round game against Bulgaria. He turned professional with Leeds in July 1956 and, although he began in fine goalscoring form, he struggled to hold down a regular place and joined Carlisle in February 1958, later playing for Hartlepools United (July 1959), North Shields (cs 1960) and Gateshead (cs 1962).
League: App 6, Gls 4.

McKENZIE, Duncan *1974-1976*

Forward. Born: Grimsby, 10 June 1950.
Debut (as sub) v Liverpool (Wembley) Charity Shield, 10 August 1974, D 1-1 (Liverpool won 6-5 on penalties).
5ft 8in, 11st 3lb (1975).
Dazzling showman forward Duncan McKenzie became one of the most popular players ever at Elland Road with his highly-individual skills which brought him some stunning and spectacular goals. He learnt the game at Old Clee Junior School in Grimsby and played for Notre Dame and Old Clee before joining Nottingham Forest, where he turned professional in July 1968. After two loan spells with Mansfield (March 1970 and February 1973) he won a regular place at Forest. During his brief reign as Leeds boss, Brian Clough spent £240,000 in August 1974 to bring Mckenzie to Elland Road. Clough was soon forced to depart, but McKenzie stayed to become an idol of the Leeds fans who loved his style. Despite finishing top scorer in 1975-76, he was sold to Anderlecht in summer 1976 (£200,000). After netting 16 goals in 30 games for the Belgian club, a £200,000 move took him to Everton in December 1976. He went to Chelsea in September 1978 (£165,000) and Blackburn in March 1979 (£80,000) before playing in the NASL with Tulsa Roughnecks. After a spell in Warrington Sunday League

football he went to Hong Kong in March 1983 and later helped run a football community programme in Liverpool. He is also a noted after-dinner speaker and has written on football for national newspapers and worked as a summariser on radio.
League: App 64/2, Gls 27; FA Cup: App 6/3, Gls 2; League Cup: App 5, Gls 1; Europe: App 1, Gls 0; Charity Shield: App 0/1, Gls 0.

McMORRAN, Eddie J. *1949-1950*

Inside-forward. Born: Larne, 2 September 1923.
Debut v Sheffield Wednesday (h) Division One, 22 January 1949, D 1-1.
5ft 11½in, 13st (1949).
One-time blacksmith Eddie McMorran forged a top-class soccer career, including a short stay at Elland Road. He won Irish Schools honours when at Larne School, later playing for Ballyclare and Larne Olympic. He rose to prominence when he joined Belfast Celtic and in 1945-46 scored 60 goals. Soon after the war he won an Irish Cup winners' medal and a full cap against England. Manchester City signed him (£7,000) in July 1947 but his career seemed to lose its way and he joined Leeds in January 1949. Again he could not reproduce the great form he had shown in Ireland and a £10,000 transfer took him to Barnsley in July 1950. He won back his place in the Irish international side before transferring to Doncaster Rovers (£8,000) in February 1953. By the time he moved to Crewe in November 1957 he had won his 15th and last full cap. He joined Frickley Colliery in summer 1958 and was appointed coach to Dodsworth Miners' Welfare in August 1960. He died in Larne on 27 January 1984, aged 60.
League: App 38, Gls 6; FA Cup: App 2, Gls 0.

McNAB, Neil *1982*

Midfield. Born: Greenock, 4 June 1957.
Debut v Shrewsbury Town (h) Division Two, 18 December 1982, D 1-1.
5ft 7in, 10st 10lb (1982).
McNab made his appearances for Leeds during a loan spell and although they wanted to sign him, they could not afford the £65,000 fee demanded by Brighton. Instead he went to Manchester City and became a key figure for them. A Scottish Schoolboy and Youth international, he broke into Morton's first team when he was 16 and Tottenham signed him in February 1974. He won an Under-21 cap at Spurs but moved to Bolton in November 1978. In February 1981 he was transferred to Brighton (£220,000) and made 105 League appearances for them before joining Manchester City in July 1983. He was loaned to Portsmouth in March 1983, but did not make the first team. After helping Manchester City to promotion to the First Division in 1988-89, McNab joined Tranmere Rovers in January 1990, for £125,000 and won a Leyland Daf Cup winners' medal at Wembley. He did much to establish Tranmere as one of the leading teams in Division One after they won promotion via the Play-offs in 1991. In February 1992 he was loaned to Huddersfield Town for a couple of months and left Prenton Park in summer 1993 to play for Derry City. After a stint with Witton Albion he joined Manchester City's coaching staff.
League: App 5, Gls 0; FA Cup: App 1, Gls 0.

McNEISH, Sam *1951*

Forward. Born: Bo'ness, West Lothian, 4 August 1930.
Debut v Manchester City (a) Division Two, 4 March 1951, L 1-4.
5ft 10in, 10st 9lb (1951).
McNeish signed from Linlithgow Rose in February 1951. During his National Service he played for the Royal Scots against the Royal Lancers in Berlin's Olympic Stadium. Leeds was his only League club.
League: App 1, Gls 0.

McNESTRY, George *1928-1929*

Outside-right. Born: Chopwell, County Durham, 7 January 1908.
Debut v Blackburn Rovers (a) Division One, 8 December 1928, W 1-0.
5ft 9in, 12st (1928).
McNestry played for seven League clubs in ten years. A product of Durham amateur football he joined Bradford in 1926 and Doncaster Rovers in summer 1927. Leeds signed him in November 1928 and he joined Sunderland in November 1929. He played for Luton (August 1930), Bristol Rovers (May 1932) an Coventry City (June 1935). At Coventry he won a Third Division South medal in 1936, to add to the one he had gained with the Pirates a year earlier, before being forced to quit because of a knee injury. At Coventry he was a consistent goalscorer and was granted a £500 benefit.
League: App 3, Gls 0.

McNIVEN, David S. *1972-1978*

Forward. Born: Stonehouse, Lanarkshire, 9 September 1955.
Debut v Notts County (h) League Cup 3rd round, 8 October 1975, L 0-1.
5ft 6in, 11st 4lb (1977).
McNiven earned the nickname 'Supersub' after scoring vital goals after coming on for Leeds. A Scottish Schoolboy international, he was a prolific scorer in the juniors and turned professional in September 1972. He won three Under-21 caps at Leeds – two as a substitute. A £25,000 transfer took him to Bradford City in February 1978 and he enjoyed a productive five-year spell before going to Blackpool in February 1983. He left the Seasiders on a free transfer in May 1984 and had a spell with Portland Timbers and Pittsburgh Spirit in the NASL before going to Halifax Town in March 1985. In the 1985 close season he joined Morecambe where he worked as a milkman. His father, Tom, the former Third Lanark player, was Hibernian's physiotherapist and Scotland's physio therapist for the 1974, 1978 and 1982 World Cups. His son, Scott, is with Oldham Athletic.
League: App 15/7, Gls 6; League Cup: App 1, Gls 0.

McQUEEN, Gordon *1972-1978*

Centre-half. Born: Kilbirnie, Ayrshire, 26 June 1952.
Debut Derby County (a) Division One, 3 March 1973, W 3-2.
6ft 3½in, 13st (1977).
At school Gordon McQueen was a goalkeeper, following in the footsteps of his father, Tom, who kept goal for Hibernian, Berwick Rangers, East Fife and Accrington Stanley. Gordon switched to the wing before settling at centre-half where his aerial power made him a

formidable opponent. He had unsuccessful trials with Liverpool and Rangers before joining St Mirren from Largs Thistle in 1970. Leeds, looking for a successor to Jack Charlton, signed him (£30,000) in September 1972. He developed into an outstanding central defender who was first-choice during Leeds United's 1973-74 championship season. In June 1974 he won his first Scottish cap, in Brussels in a 2-1 defeat by Belgium, and it cost a then British record fee of £495,000 to take him to Manchester United in February 1978. For the Old Trafford club he won an FA Cup winners' medal in 1983 and took his haul of full international appearances to 30 – a figure that he would surely have increased had it not been for a spate of injuries at Manchester and a bad Achilles tendon injury at Leeds in 1975-76. In August 1985 he was appointed player-coach at Seiko FC (Hong Kong). He took over as manager of Airdrieonians in June 1987 but resigned in May 1989 because the majority of their players would not play full-time on the contracts offered. McQueen then ran a greetings card shop in Paisley and in June 1989 coached St Mirren and was a match analyser for Scottish Television before re-entering the English game as reserve-team coach at Middlesbrough in July 1994 under his former Manchester United colleague Bryan Robson.
League: App 140, Gls 15; FA Cup; App 13, Gls 1; League Cup: App 5, Gls 0; Europe: App 12/1, Gls 3; Charity Shield: App 1, Gls 0.

MADELEY, Paul E. *1962-1980*

Defender/midfield. Born: Beeston, Leeds, 20 September 1944.
Debut v Manchester City (h) Division Two, 11 January 1964, W 1-0.
6ft, 12st 13lb (1974).
Paul Madeley played in every position except goal in a 17-year career at Elland Road. Born

barely a goal-kick from the ground, he attended Cross Flatts Park Junior School and Parkside Secondary School and played for the Middleton Parkside Youth team along-side Paul Reaney,

Rod Johnson and Kevin Hector. An England Schools international, he began work in an insurance broker's office and played in the Yorkshire League with Farsley Celtic. He was asked for trials by Leeds and signed in May 1962. Originally he was groomed as Jack Charlton's successor before Don Revie realised he was a versatile performer and in one season Madeley played in nine positions. Ignored at Under-23 level, he played for the Football League, then turned down the chance to go to Mexico for the 1970 World Cup. He was omitted from the original squad but called up when Paul Reaney broke a leg. Madeley felt he would not survive when the squad was slimmed down, so opted not to go. Sir Alf Ramsey bore no grudge and Madeley won the first of 24 caps in 1971. In a team noted for its 'hard men', Madeley's attitude was exemplary and he was cautioned only twice in over 700 appearances which brought him two League championship medals, an FA Cup winners' medal, League Cup winners' medal and two Inter-Cities Fairs Cup winners' medals. He retired in 1980 and opened a sports shop in Leeds, as well as keeping an interest in the successful family home décor business which was sold in a multi-million pound deal in December 1987. His elder brother, John, was chairman of Halifax Town in 1987-88.
League: App 528/8, Gls 25; FA Cup: App 64/3, Gls 2; League Cup: App 49/2, Gls 3; Europe: App 70/1, Gls 4; Charity Shield: App 1, Gls 0.

MAGUIRE, Peter J. *1986-1989*

Forward. Born: Holmfirth, 11 September 1969.
Debut v Crystal Palace (h) Division Two, 2 May 1988, W 1-0.
5ft 9in, 11st 4lb (1988).
Maguire joined Leeds in July 1986 on the Youth Training Scheme and made enough progress for United to offer him a contract in July 1988. Playing in a Northern Intermediate League game against Sheffield United, his prompt action may have helped save the life of an opponent when Scott Exton swallowed his tongue after a collision. Maguire provided the first vital medical attention and Exton recovered following an overnight stay in hospital. In April 1989 he began a four-month loan with Swedish Club, IFK Osby. In September the same year he began a month's loan with Huddersfield Town, joining the Terriers for £10,000 when the loan period was completed. He did not establish himself at Leeds Road and was loaned to Stockport County in August 1990 and at the end of the season was released and joined Emley.
League: App 1, Gls 0.

MAHON, Johnny *1929-1935*

Outside-right. Born: Gillingham, 8 December 1911.
Debut v Plymouth Argyle (a) Division Two, 30 January 1932, L 2-3.
5ft 8in, 10st 13lb (1935).
Mahon served Leeds both as a player and a coach. His father, James, had a long association with Gillingham and represented the Southern League against the Football League in 1910. Young Mahon played for New Brompton Excelsior, Doncaster Grammar School and Doncaster Rovers Reserves before joining Leeds in June 1929. His father and uncle had also played for Rovers. Mahon could play on either wing, but his career took off only after leaving Leeds for West Brom in September 1935. He moved to Huddersfield Town in September 1938 and, despite breaking a leg on his debut, recovered to tour South Africa with the FA in 1939. During the war he played for Huddersfield and guested for QPR, going on to coach in Denmark (with IF Elsborg, 1947-50), Sweden (IFK Gothenberg, 1950-54) and Malaya before rejoining Leeds as a coach. He ran a youth club in the Dewsbury Road area at that time. He was also coach to York City and joined Hull City as trainer in 1953-54 before retiring.
League: App 78, Gls 20; FA Cup: App 6, Gls 3.

MAKINSON, James *1935-1944*

Right-half. Born: Aspull, near Wigan, 25 January 1913.
Debut v West Bromwich Albion (a) Division One, 19 February 1936, L 2-3.
5ft 9in, 10st 10lb (1935).
Makinson lost his best playing years to the war. He signed from Lancashire Combination club, Clitheroe, in November 1935. He made 103 wartime appearances for Leeds and in September 1943 was discharged from the Navy with an injured shoulder. He had a special support made for the shoulder and was able to play a few more wartime games before retiring in 1944. He died in 1979.
League: App 68, Gls 0; FA Cup: App 2, Gls 0.

MANGNALL, Dave *1927-1929*

Centre-forward. Born: Wigan, 21 September 1905.
Debut v Burnley (h) Division One, 28 September 1929, W 3-0.
5ft 10in, 11st 4lb (1933).
Despite scoring ten goals for Leeds in a Northern Midweek League game against Stockport, in a 13-0 win on 25 September 1929, Mangnall was transferred two months later. A coal miner, he had unsuccessful trials with Huddersfield Town, Doncaster Rovers and trials with Huddersfield Town, Doncaster Rovers and Rotherham United before Leeds signed him from Maltby Colliery in November 1927. Four days after his ten-goal feat he was given his League debut, but after scoring six times in nine consecutive appearances he was allowed to join Huddersfield Town in December 1929. He finished 1931-32 with 33 League goals but injuries interrupted his progress and he joined Birmingham in February 1934. He went to West Ham in March 1935 and joined Millwall in summer 1936, leading their attack when the Lions reached the FA Cup semi-final and won the Third Division South championship the following year. He moved to QPR in 1939, guesting for Millwall in wartime soccer when he was a member of the Civil Defence. He moved into management in 1944, taking QPR to the Third Division South title in 1947-48. In June 1952 he was replaced by Jack Taylor, later to become Leeds' manager. Mangnall died in Penzance on 10 April 1962, aged 56.
League: App 9, Gls 6.

MANN, Jimmy A. *1969-1974*

Forward. Born: Goole, 15 December 1952.
Debut (as sub) v Derby County (h) League Cup 2nd round replay, 27 September 1971, W 2-0.
5ft 6in, 11st 11lb (1973).
Mann played for Yorkshire Schoolboys before joining Leeds as an apprentice and turning professional in December 1969. A free transfer took him to Bristol City in May 1974 and he became a key player there, chiefly as a midfielder, helping them win promotion to Division One in 1975-76. As City hit deep financial trouble he was one of eight players who agreed to have their contracts cancelled to help save the club. With over 200 League games to his name, he was signed for Barnsley in February 1982 by Norman Hunter. In December that year he joined Scunthorpe on a non-contact basis and in February 1983 went to Doncaster Rovers on a free transfer.
League: App 2, Gls 0; League Cup: App 0/1, Gls 0; Europe: App 2, Gls 0.

MARSDEN, Jack *1948-1959*

Centre-half. Born: Leeds, 17 December 1931.
Debut v Lincoln City (h) Division Two, 14 March 1953, W 2-1.
5ft 11½in, 11st 12lb (1951).
Marsden, a former French polisher, was a devoted clubman for Leeds for over a decade, acting as stand-in for John Charles, then Jack Charlton he joined Leeds from Leeds Red Triangle League side, Osmondthorpe YMCA, in August 1948 and turned professional in 1950. Awarded a joint benefit with goalkeeper John Scott in 1956, he joined Barrow with winger John Kemp in March 1959 and had spells with Carlisle United (September 1960) and Doncaster Rovers (July 1964).
League: App 71, Gls 0; FA Cup: App 4, Gls 0.

MARSH, Cliff *1948-1949*

Inside-forward. Born: Atherton, near Manchester 29 December 1920.
Debut v West Bromwich Albion (h) Division Two, 2 October 1948, L 1-3.
Marsh was picked up by Leeds from Winsford United in the Cheshire League in September 1948 for £300 and made a scoring debut. He was with Tyldesley United before joining Winsford and arrived at Leeds three months after rejecting terms from Grimsby Town. He left Elland Road in May 1949 for Bournemouth. Marsh, a noted trumpet player, left Bournemouth for Yeovil Town in June 1952.
League: App 4, Gls 1; FA Cup: App 1, Gls 0.

MARTIN, Con J. *1946-1948*

Left-half/centre-half. Born: Dublin, 20 March 1923.
Debut v Sheffield United (a) Division One, 4 January 1947, L 2-6.
5ft 9¼in, 11st 6½lb (1948).
The versatility of dual Irish international Cornelius Martin was legendary, for he played in every position at senior level, including goalkeeping appearances for the Republic of Ireland and Aston Villa. He spent four years with Drumcondra before joining Glentoran, where he won his first cap. He joined Leeds in December 1946 (£8,000) but hard-up United sold him to Aston Villa in October 1948 (£10,000), the cash being used to rebuild the Leeds side. He enjoyed his best days at Villa, staying until July 1956 when he joined Watford. He later worked as an insurance agent. Martin finished with 30 Republic of Ireland caps and six Northern Ireland appearances. That total was surpassed by his son, Mick, who played in 51 Eire internationals with Bohemians, Manchester United and

Newcastle United. His grandson, Alan, is on associate schoolboy forms with Leeds.
League: App 47, Gls 1; FA Cup: App 2, Gls 0.

MARTIN, Geoff *1960-1961*

Outside-left. Born: New Tupton, Derbyshire, 9 March 1940.
Debut v Chesterfield (a) League Cup 2nd round, 23 November 1960, W 4-0.
5ft 9in, 11st 7lb (1960).
Martin's one senior appearance for Leeds was against his old club, Chesterfield. He began with Parkhouse Colliery before joining Chesterfield in October 1958, but played only in their juniors before going to Leeds on a free transfer in May 1960. He went to Darlington in July 1961 and broke into the first team, establishing himself with Carlisle (May 1962), Workington (December 1962, £3,000), Grimsby Town (November 1966, £7,000) and Chesterfield (July 1968, £3,000). He won a Fourth Division championship medal with the Spireites in 1969-70.
League Cup: App 1, Gls 0.

MARTIN, John *1924-1926*

Outside-left. Born: Gateshead, 1904.
Debut v West Ham United (a) Division One, 7 March 1925, D 0-0.
5ft 9½in, 11st 7lb (1924).
Jack Martin, as he was always known, made his name in North-East non-League soccer with Hebburn Colliery before joining Darlington in summer 1920. Leeds signed him in July 1924, for £250, but he was never a regular and went to Accrington Stanley in June 1926, later having a spell with Connah's Quay (August 1928) before joining Bury in May 1929. He later signed for Reading (June 1930) before ending his career at Doncaster Rovers (August 1931-May 1932).
League: App 2, Gls 0.

MASINGA, Philomen R. *1994-1996*

Forward. Born: Johannesburg, South Africa, 28 June 1969.
Debut (as sub) v West Ham United (a) Premiership, 20 August 1994, D 0-0.
6ft 2in, 12st 7lb (1995).
Masinga and fellow South African international Lucas Radebe were the surprise signings of summer 1994 after being spotted by Leeds scout Geoff Sleight playing for the national side against Zambia. Striker Masinga completed his move to Leeds in August 1994 for £250,000 from Mamelodi Sundowns, whom he helped to the South African title the previous season with 18 goals. He was on the wanted list of several European clubs, including Bobby Robson's Porto, and quickly showed his poaching talents at Leeds, scoring a nine-minute extra-time hat-trick after coming on as substitute against Walsall in an FA Cup replay. His first season at Leeds saw him progress, but he was only used sparingly in his second year, although he collected an African Nations Cup winners' medal when the competition was staged in his native South Africa. Tall and leggy, he has showed good ball skills, but his individual style did not always fit in with United's system. In July 1996 he was having talks with Swiss club Gallen with a view to a £500,000 move after he was unable to get his work permit renewed to stay with Leeds.
League: App 20/11, Gls 5; FA Cup: App 3/2, Gls 4; League Cup: App 3, Gls 2.

MASON, Bobby *1922-1927*

Centre-half. Born near Whitburn, near Sunderland.
Debut v Stoke (a) Division Two, 25 August 1923, D 1-1.
5ft 10in, 12st (1925).
Mason was overshadowed by Ernie Hart, for whom he proved a reliable deputy at Leeds. He was signed from Whitburn in March 1922 and began 1923-24 as first choice but lost out to Hart and joined Bristol Rovers in July 1927. In summer 1928 he was transferred to Hartlepools United where he replaced ex-Leeds player, Billy Poyntz, as captain. Later he played for West Stanley.
League: App 15, Gls 0.

MASON, Cliff E. *1962-1964*

Full-back. Born: York, 27 November 1929.
Debut v Swansea Town (h) Division Two, 10 March 1962, W 2-0.
5ft 10in, 11st 9lb (1962).
Rejected by York City, Mason joined Sunderland as a part-timer in January 1950. In July 1952 he signed for Darlington but enjoyed his best form after moving to Sheffield United in August 1955. He captained the Blades in Division One before a £10,000 transfer took him to Leeds in March 1962, in an effort to stabilise the Peacocks' leaky defence. He moved to Scunthorpe in February 1964 and after unsuccessfully applying for the post of Doncaster Rovers' player-manager, joined Chesterfield in July 1964, on a part-time basis while working as a printer.
League: App 31, Gls 0, League Cup: App 2, Gls 0.

MASON, George *1920-1924*

Outside-right. Born: Church Gresley, near Burton upon Trent, 16 September 1896.
Debut v Port Vale (a) Division Two, 28 August 1920, L 0-2.
5ft 8in, 11st (1922).

George Mason was United's first-choice right winger in their initial season in the Football League. He was signed from Frickley Colliery in July 1920 but was eventually edged out by Alan Noble and in June 1923 went to Swindon Town. They released him in May 1924, after only one appearance.
League: App 65, Gls 5; FA Cup: App 1, Gls 0.

MAYBURY Alan *1995-*

Utility player. Born: Dublin, 8 August 1978.
Debut v Aston Villa (a) Premiership, 3 February 1996, L 0-3.
Seventeen-year-old Irish-born first-year trainee Alan Maybury was the surprise choice in midfield for the Premiership tussle at Aston Villa when Leeds were decimated by injuries and suspension. At home in Dublin he played for St Kevin's and captained the Irish Under-15s and 16s before arriving at Elland Road in summer 1995. He did not make the best of starts at Leeds, suffering from homesickness and breaking his arm, but he gained a place in the Reserves where he played in a variety of positions. He has appeared for the Republic of Ireland's Under-21 team.
League: App 1, Gls 0.

MAYERS, Derek *1961-1962*

Outside-right. Born: Liverpool, 24 January 1935.
Debut v Charlton Athletic (h) Division Two, 19 August 1961, W 1-9.
5ft 8in, 10st 5lb (1961).
Mayers was signed by Don Revie from Preston in June 1961. He joined Everton as a youngster, turning professional in August 1953. He left Goodison in May 1957 for Preston, where he enjoyed the best football of his career. In his first season at Deepdale, Preston finished runners-up to Wolves. When they were relegated he joined Leeds, but moved to Bury in July 1962, then Wrexham in October 1963. He left Wrexham in summer 1964.
League: App 20, Gls 5; FA Cup: App 2, Gls 0; League Cup: App 2, Gls 0.

MEARS, Frank *1924-1928*

Centre-forward. Born: Manchester.
Debut v Bury (h) Division One, 31 October 1925, L 2-3.
5ft 10in, 12st (1928).
Mears was an understudy to Tom Jennings at Leeds. He sprang to prominence as an amateur with Stalybridge Celtic before joining United in April 1924. His chances were limited but he showed good form in the Reserves and was transferred to Barnsley in May 1928. The move made him Arthur Fairclough's first signing in his second spell at Oakwell. Fairclough had originally signed Mears for Leeds.
League: App 2, Gls 0; FA Cup: App 1, Gls 0.

MEEK, George *1952-1960*

Winger. Born: Glasgow, 15 February 1934.
Debut v Sheffield United (a) Division Two, 11 October 1952, L 1-2.
5ft 3in, 10st 7lb (1959).
George Meek proved an elusive customer during his days at Leeds. He possessed boundless

energy and proved a great winger on either flank. After playing for Thorniewood United, he began his senior career with Hamilton Academical, making a scoring

debut against Kilmarnock in December 1951. The following August he became a Leeds player. In 1954 he was called up for National Service with the Royal Armoured Corps and spent a season on loan with Walsall. He played for the Army against a Scottish XI at Ibrox in January 1955. On his return to Leeds he played his part in United's promotion to Division One in 1956 and remained at Elland Road until August 1960 when he was sold to Leicester City (£7,000). He returned to Walsall in July 1961 and gave them three years excellent service before playing for several non-League clubs, eventually ending his days with Rushall Olympic. In 1992 he was working as a postman in Walsall.
League: App 195, Gls 19; FA Cup: App 4, Gls 0.

MELROSE, Jim *1987-1988*

Forward. Born: Glasgow, 7 October 1958.
Debut v Manchester City (h) Division Two, 26 September 1987, W 2-0.
5ft 9in, 10st (1987).
Melrose scored a last-minute winner against Leeds which helped Charlton scrape through the Play-offs at the end of the dramatic 1986-87 season. But within months of condemning United to more Second Division football, he joined Leeds for £50,000. His brief stay at Elland Road was not a particularly happy one and he joined Shrewsbury (£45,000) in March 1988, following a month on loan. At Shrewsbury he received a fractured cheekbone in an on-field assault by another former Leeds player, Chris Kamara, then at Swindon, which saw Kamara become the first professional player to be prosecuted for such an act, for which he received a £1,000 fine. A Scottish Schools international (he went to Whitehill School, Glasgow), Melrose began with Eastercraigs and Sighthill Amateurs, before joining Partick Thistle in 1975, making his Scottish League debut as a 16-year-old. He won eight Under-21 caps and made one appearance for the Scottish League before moving to Leicester (£25,000) in July 1980. In September 1982 he was involved in a player-exchange with Coventry's Tom English, scoring a hat-trick on his home debut, but a £100,000 transfer in March 1983 took him to Celtic. The move did not prove particularly successful and after a loan spell with Wolves he joined Manchester City in November 1984 (£40,000), then Charlton in March 1986 (£45,000), helping the latter two clubs win promotion to Division One. He became a Leeds player in September 1987 but was mainly confined to the Reserves. In August 1990 he left Shrewsbury for Macclesfield Town, moving to Curzon Ashton two months later after a trial with St Mirren. In 1992 he went to Halesowen Harriers and later managed Cheshire side, Bollington Athletic.
League: App 3/1, Gls 0; FA Cup: App 0/1, Gls 0; League Cup: App 0/1, Gls 0.

MENZIES, Bill J. *1922-1934*

Left-back. Born: Bucksburn, near Aberdeen, 10 July 1901.
Debut v Oldham Athletic (a) Division Two, 25 December 1923, D 2-2.
5ft 8in, 11st (1925).
Menzies was one of the unlikeliest looking footballers to play for Leeds – but certainly one of the most effective. He was physically frail and used brain rather than brawn to establish himself. He joined Leeds from Mugiemoss in March 1922, after a month's trial, and, after a fine display on his debut went on to help United into Division One for first time in their history. He was virtually unchallenged at left-back for six years. He was one of the unsung heroes of United's early days, relying on skill and a remarkable sense of positioning rather than 'big foot' tactics. His last senior game for Leeds came in the final match of 1931-32. He joined Goole Town in September 1933 and retired in 1934. Menzies became a coach with the West Riding FA. He died on 3 January 1970, aged 69.
League: App 248, Gls 1; FA Cup: App 10, Gls 1.

MILBURN, George W. *1928-1937*

Right-back. Born: Ashington, 24 June 1910.
Debut v Sheffield Wednesday (h) Division One, 17 November 1928, L 0-2.
5ft 10in, 13lb (1935).
George Milburn was one of three brothers – all full-backs – who gave great service to Leeds. A fourth brother, Stan, played for Chesterfield, Leicester City and Rochdale, cousin Jackie Milburn was a legend with Newcastle and England and their nephews were Bobby and Jack Charlton. George was a centre-half with Ashington when he moved to Leeds in March 1928. He was converted to full-back and soon dropped into the consistent groove that was a hallmark of the Milburns. He partnered brother Jack regularly – they were both ever-present in 1932-33 – and George held his place until the emergence of Bert Sproston. George took his relegation to the Reserves in good grace and in 1936-37 captained United to their only Central League championship. He moved to Chesterfield in May 1937 and during World War Two guested for Leeds and Yeovil Town. At Chesterfield he linked up with brother Stan and went on to become one of the few players to score a hat-trick of penalties in League football – against Sheffield Wednesday on 7 June 1947. His hat-trick of spot-kicks came in the 56th, 64th and 77th minutes and saw the Spireites come from behind to beat the Owls 4-2. He retired the same year and became Chesterfield's assistant manager. He died in spring 1980.
League: App 157, Gls 1; FA Cup: App 9, Gls 0.

MILBURN, Jack *1927-1939*

Left-back. Born: Ashington, 18 March 1908.
Debut v Everton (h) Division One, 16 September 1929, W 2-1.
5ft 10in, 12st 2lb (1935).
Jack Milburn was the oldest of the Milburn clan at Leeds. Although christened John, fans knew him as Jack. An ex-miner, he began with Spen Black & White before signing for Leeds in November 1928. He started at Elland Road as a right-back but generally played on the left when he partnered brother George. Jack had a kick like a mule and was appointed United's penalty taker – a job he relished. In 1935-36 he scored from the spot nine times in League matches, a club record. He was rarely out of the side for ten years and enjoyed three seasons as an ever-present. He guested for United in 64 wartime games and recovered quickly from a broken leg sustained against Barnsley in August 1943. He also guested for Bradford City and Darlington. In February 1939, a £2,000 transfer took him to Norwich City but in October 1946 he signed for Bradford City as player-coach, aged 38. In January 1947 he became their first player-manager, keeping the job until July 1948. At his peak he was tipped for England honours, but the nearest he got was when he toured Czechoslovakia and Hungary in the 1934 close season but did not get a game. He died in Leeds on 21 August 1979, aged 71.
League: App 386, gls 28; FA Cup: App 22, Gls 2.

MILBURN, Jim *1935-1952*

Full-back. Born: Ashington, 21 September 1919.
Debut v Sheffield United (h) Division One, 2 September 1939, L 0-1.
5ft 6¼in, 11st 1½lb (1951).
'Iron Man' Jim Milburn was the youngest of the famous Leeds brothers. His career followed that of George and he played for Ashington before joining Leeds in November 1935. He did not get a first-team chance until the final match of the aborted 1939-40 season and had to wait seven years for his next League game. He played 52 times for Leeds in wartime football, served in India, was wounded in Belgium in 1944 and also served with the Civil Defence. In 1946-47 he made up for lost time with a series of stirring defensive displays. Although he was more slightly built than his brothers, his tackling was probably fiercer. Like Jack, he enjoyed taking penalties and, when Leeds struggled for goals, he played a number of games at centre-forward. When he left Leeds for Bradford in June 1952 it severed a 24-year link between United and the three Milburns. Jim continued to turn in high-qualify displays with the Park Avenue club until retiring in the mid-1950s.
League: App 208, Gls 15; FA Cup: App 12, Gls 2.

MILLER E. George *1950-1952*

Inside-right. Born: South Africa, 17 October 1927.
Debut v Doncaster Rovers (a) Division Two, 16 December 1950, D 4-4.
5ft 6¼in, 10st 3½lb (1951).
A friend of Major Frank Buckley recommended Miller to United. He signed from Arcadia FC (Western Province) in November 1950 and within weeks he had to acclimatise to snowbound pitches. In January 1952, a move to Preston fell through and two months later he went to Workington, but managed only 11 appearances before being released.
League: App 13, Gls 1; FA Cup: App 1, Gls 0.

MILLS, Don *1951-1952*

Inside-forward. Born: Bramley, near Rotherham, 17 August 1928.
Debut v Rotherham United (a) Division Two, 29 September 1951, L 2-4.
5ft 10in, 10st 5lb (1957).
Mills had a lengthy League career which included 15 months with Leeds. He was only 17 when he turned professional with QPR in October 1945, being signed by Dave Mangnall, the former Leeds player. He spent four months on loan with Torquay, beginning in March 1949, and proved so popular that the fans tried to buy him. Eventually Cardiff City bought him (£12,500) in February 1951 and in September

1951 he joined Leeds (£12,000). Torquay finally signed him in December 1952 and he stayed at Plainmoor for 20 years, retiring as a player in 1962. He is generally regarded as Torquay's greatest-ever player and remained as a coach and scout at Plaimoor until the 1970s. He later became a traffic warden in Torquay and died in February 1994.
League: App 34, Gls 9; FA Cup: App 3, Gls 1.

MILLS, Fred *1934-1939*

Wing-half. Born: Hanley, summer 1911.
Debut v Middlesbrough (h) Division One, 25 August 1934, L 2-4.
5ft 8½in, 11st 4lb (1938).
Mills made a two-goal League debut for Leeds as a centre-forward but was generally at wing-half. He learnt his soccer at East Woodvale School in Hanley, began work at a local pottery firm and played for Middleport before joining Port Vale in summer 1932. He soon established himself in the first team and moved to Leeds in June 1934. With Vale he began as an inside-right but was later converted to wing-half. He broke a leg playing for Leeds at Leicester in November 1934 and missed the entire 1935-36 season. He made a comeback in October 1936 and was in and out of the first team up to World War Two, when he retired.
League: App 67, Gls 2; FA Cup: App 3, Gls 0.

MITCHELL, Ron G. *1958-1959*

Right-back. Born: Morecambe, 13 February 1935.
Debut v Preston North End (h) Division One, 17 January 1959, L 1-3.
5ft 10½in, 12st 7lb (1959).
Mitchell followed the same path as Blackpool and England centre-forward Ray Charnley early in his career. Both went to Greaves School in Lancaster, played for Lancaster Schools and were juniors on Preston's books, then turned out for Bolton-le-Sands and Morecambe before going their separate ways. Mitchell joined United from Lancashire Combination club, Morecambe, in November 1958 (£1,000 deal, plus £1,500 if he played six senior games). Mitchell, who was converted from wing-half to full-back, soon faded from the scene, however.
League: App 4, Gls 0.

MITCHELL, Tom W. *1926-1931*

Outside-let. Born: Spennymoor, 30 September 1899.
Debut v Sunderland (h) Division One, 6 November 1926, D 2-2.
5ft 9in, 11st 6lb (1930).
Tom Mitchell was one of the most popular players at Leeds in the inter-war years. He played little football at school, but was talked into playing for Durham area junior club, Parkside United. Newcastle United took him on in 1920 but he spent most of his time there in the Reserves and he jumped at the chance to join Leeds, who paid £785 in November 1926. His pace and skill were two factors behind United's 1927-28 promotion season, when he played in every game. He continued to delight the crowds until he joined York City in September 1931. For several summers he coached in Norway and before the end of the war he was an RAF pilot stationed in Norway and was married in Oslo Cathedral. On demob he returned to York, where he had been manager since 1946. He later became a York City director and soccer coach to Yorkshire schools. He also excelled at tennis, ran a sports shop in Whitley Bay in his Newcastle days and later took a pub in Leeds.
League: App 142, Gls 19; FA Cup: App 10, Gls 2.

MOLLATT, Ron V. *1950-1955*

Wing-half. Born: Edwinstowe, Nottinghamshire, 24 March 1932.
Debut v Southampton (a) Division Two, 8 September 1951, D 0-0.
5ft 11in, 11st 7lb (1957).
Mollatt enjoyed a fine career as a junior before and during his time at Leeds. A Nottinghamshire Schools player, he played for Thoresby Colliery in the North Notts League. He joined Leeds in February 1950 and played for the West Riding Youth team and had England trials. After completing his National Service with the 12th Lancers, he joined York City in July 1955 and made over 100 League appearances before going to Bradford City in July 1960. He then combined work as a painter and decorator with involvement in local Yorkshire soccer, including managing Northern Counties East League sides Bridlington, Tadcaster Albion and York Railway Institute (November 1982 to May 1989. He was last known to be working at a brewery in Tadcaster and scouting for Barnsley.
League: App 17, gls 0.

MOORE, Bill R. *1924-1925*

Goalkeeper. Born: Sunderland, summer 1903.
Debut v Newcastle United (h) Division One, 15 November 1924, D 1-1.
5ft 9½in, 12st 7lb (1925).
Bill Moore, no relation to his goalkeeping namesake Stan, was one of the most colourful characters on United's books. He took up goalkeeping at school and also practised at a Sunderland fairground when he took time off his work as a shipyard carpenter. He played for Limited Yard Apprentices and was offered professional terms by Blackburn, but he rejected them as he wanted to continue his apprenticeship. After he became a qualified carpenter, Leeds signed him from Seaham Colliery in March 1924. He was also a pianist in a dance band. Although popular at Leeds, his chances were few and in June 1925 he moved to Southend, giving them ten years excellent service. He died in 1968.
League: App 6, Gls 0.

MOORE, Jim *1921-1922*

Inside-forward. Born: Boldon, near Felling-on-Tyne, County Durham, 1 September 1891.
Debut v Port Vale (h) Division Two, 27 August 1921, W 2-1.
5ft 8in, 10st 8lb (1922).
Veteran Jim Moore joined Leeds for their second season in the League, after making his name at Barnsley and Southampton. He began with Bolden Colliery, then played for Ardsley Nelson before joining Barnsley in August 1911. The following year he won an FA Cup winners' medal with the Oakwell club. He was known as 'The Player That Never Smiles'. During World War One he worked in a boatyard on Cowes on the Isle of Wight and guested for Southampton. He joined the Saints in May 1919 and was their first-ever player to be sent off in a League game when he was dismissed against Grimsby in December 1920. He signed for Leeds in May 1921 but was released in June 1922 to join Brighton. He then played for Halifax Town (summer 1923), QPR (cs 1924) and Crewe (July 1925). In 1926 he left Crewe and in March the following year went to Holland to coach NAC Breda. He later ran a pub in Barnsley, and also had a greengrocer's business, and after World War Two he was a director of Barnsley FC.
League: App 27, Gls 4; FA Cup: App 1, Gls 0.

MOORE, Stan *1931-1935*

Goalkeeper. Born: Worksop, 13 December 1912.
Debut v Barnsley (a) Division Two, 16 January 1932, W 2-0.
5ft 9½in, 11st 5lb (1931).
Former pit boy Stan Moore played in junior football before joining Worksop Town. A great display for Worksop against Leeds in a pre-season friendly clinched a move to Elland Road in August 1931. Competition for the goalkeeping job was fierce, but he soon forced his way into the side and was ever-present in 1933-34. He broke a leg at Huddersfield in February 1935, lost his place and was put on the transfer list. Swansea signed him in June 1935 and he was their regular 'keeper until he retired during World War Two. He died in Leeds late in 1983.
League: App 78, Gls 0; FA Cup: App 5, Gls 0.

MORTON, Norman *1945-1947*

Centre-forward. Born: Barnsley, 22 May 1925.
Debut v Luton Town (a) Division Two, 27 December 1947, L 1-6.
Morton made only two senior appearances for Leeds – and United were beaten 6-1 on both occasions. During World War Two he was on Sunderland's books but joined Leeds from Woolley Colliery in December 1945 and scored in the final game of 1944-45, at Chesterfield. He died in 1977.
League: App 1, Gls 0.

MOSS, Jack *1949-1950*

Inside-right. Born: Blackrod, near Bolton, 1 September 1923.
Debut v Lincoln City (a) Division Two, 5 February 1949, D 0-0.
5ft 6in, 10st 13lb (1950).
Leeds struck an unusual deal when Moss moved to Halifax in June 1951. A few weeks earlier Halifax had paid a substantial fee for his Leeds teammate Desmond Frost. That left little cash in the Shaymen's coffers, so United waived the fee for Moss. He began with Bury in wartime football, joined Rochdale in January 1947 and went to Leeds in January 1949. He was an accomplished Leeds League cricketer.
League: App 23, Gls 2.

MUMBY, Peter *1987-1989*

Forward. Born: Bradford, 22 February 1969.
Debut v Huddersfield Town (a) Division Two, 15 September 1987, D 0-0.
5ft 9in, 11st 8lb (1986).
A member of the well-known Rugby League family, Mumby opted for soccer. He represented Bradford Boys at Rugby League and looked set to follow in the footsteps of his illustrious brother, Keith, who played for Bradford Northern and Great Britain. Another brother, Colin, played RL for Halifax. Peter was a skilful soccer player at Rhodesway Upper School and played for Bradford and Yorkshire Schools, signing schoolboy forms for United in

November 1983. Only a few weeks after turning professional he made his League debut. He spent two months on loan to Shamrock Rovers in 1989. He was recalled by United to appear as substitute in the second to last game v Oldham (h). His father once had trials with Hull City. He joined Burnley in July 1989, playing in the same side as Roger Eli. In recent seasons he has appeared for Bradford Park Avenue and for Fields FC, a West Yorkshire League club.
League: App 3/3, Gls 0; League Cup: App 0/2, Gls 1.

MURRAY, Tommy *1960-1961*

Outside-right. Born: Bellshill, near Airdrie, 14 January 1933.
Debut v Southampton (a) Division Two, 3 September 1960, W 4-2.
5ft 7in, 11st (1960).
Murray was signed after proving a skilful performer in Scottish League football. A Scottish Junior international, he played for Dalry Thistle Juniors before joining Falkirk in 1955 via Army football. He won a Scottish FA Cup winners' medal in 1957, but when Falkirk were relegated in 1958-59 he joined Queen of the South. He left the Dumfries club for Leeds (£3,000) in August 1960 but never hit top form at Elland Road and United sold him to Tranmere (£3,000) in March 1961. His time at Prenton Park was disrupted by injuries.
League: App 7, Gls 2.

MUSGROVE, Robert *1920-1921*

Right-half. Born: Silksworth, near Sunderland, July 1893.
Debut v Port Vale (a) Division Two, 28 August 1920, L 0-2.
5ft 9in, 11st 4lb (1921).
Musgrove was among the best players in the North-East in the period immediately after World War One. He captained England Schools against Wales in 1907 and made his name with Durham City before joining Leeds in July 1920, in time for United's first season in the League. He was easily recognised because of his premature baldness. He returned to Durham City in July 1921 and enjoyed a long stay at the club, which included a spell as player-manager. He died in November 1934, aged 41.
League: App 36, Gls 2.

NEAL, Tom W. *1931-1936*

Left-half. Born: New Washington, near Gateshead, 28 November 1910.
Debut v Burnley (h) Division Two, 2 April 1932, W 3-1.
5ft 9½in, 9st 13lb (1934).
Neal, a former miner, joined Leeds in February 1931 from North-East side Usworth Colliery, the club which produced Billy Furness. He was used as cover for Wilf Copping, Cyril Hornby and Bobby Browne in his five years at Leeds. He moved to Hull City in May 1936, but never made the Tigers' first team. He suffered badly from severe head pains in the 1936 close season, was admitted to Newcastle Infirmary and never played senior football again.
League: App 20, Gls 0, FA Cup: App 3, Gls 0.

NEWSOME, Jon *1991-1994*

Central defender. Born: Sheffield, 6 September 1970.
Debut (as sub) v Wimbledon (a) Premiership, 2 November 1991, D 0-0.
6ft 2lb; 13st 11lb(1994).
Central defenders Jon Newsome and David Wetherall joined Leeds from Howard Wilkinson's

old club, Sheffield Wednesday, in June 1991 for a combined fee of £275,000. Many were surprised at the size of the fee for two youngsters because Newsome had made only half a dozen League starts for the Owls and Wetherall had no senior experience. But it proved money well spent as Newsome, who joined Wednesday in July 1989, broke into the senior side at Elland Road as the race for the 1991-92 League championship reached its climax. He scored one of the goals in United's 3-2 triumph at Sheffield United on the day Leeds won the title, but the following season his form dipped and in June 1994 Leeds reaped a big profit when Newsome was sold to Norwich City for £1 million. He was appointed skipper at Carrow Road, but could not prevent the Canaries being relegated in his first season. In March 1996 he returned to the Premiership with his first club, Sheffield Wednesday, for £1.2 million. He is a well- known dressing-room mimic and practical joker.
League: App 62/14, Gls 3; FA Cup: Apps 3/1, Gls 0; League Cup: App 3, Gls 0; European: App 3, Gls 0; Charity Shield: App 1, Gls 0; Full Members' Cup: App 1, Gls 0.

NIGHTINGALE, Albert *1952-1956*

Inside-forward. Born: Thrybergh, near Rotherham, 10 November 1923.
Debut v Sheffield United (a) Division Two, 11 October 1952, L 1-2.
5ft 8in, 10st 3lb (1954).
Albert Nightingale was among the best inside-forwards of his day. His stamina-sapping runs into opposition territory and his sense of fun on the field made him a big favourite with Elland Roaders. He starred in local football in the Rotherham area before joining Sheffield United during wartime. He also guested for Grimsby Town, Doncaster Rovers and Rotherham United. When Nightingale was transfer-listed at his own request, Leeds were in the running to sign him, but he joined Huddersfield Town in March 1948. When he left Huddersfield in October 1951, Leeds were again in the race to sign him, this time losing out to Blackburn Rovers who succeeded with a £12,000 bid. He made his debut only two hours after signing for Rovers, but in October 1952 was on his travels again – this time to Elland Road after the Peacocks made a £10,000 offer. He marked his League debut for Leeds with a goal and became an excellent inside-forward, particularly alongside John Charles. Nightingale's career was brought to an abrupt end when he received a bad knee injury in the opening game of 1956-57 against Everton. It proved to be his final League game and after retiring from football he worked as a greenkeeper. His nephew, Lawrence Morgan, was a full-back with Huddersfield, Rotherham and Darlington from 1949 to 1964.
League: App 130, Gls 48; FA Cup: App 5, Gls 0.

NIMMO, Willie R. *1956-1958*

Goalkeeper. Born: Forth, Lanarkshire, 11 January 1934.
Debut v Bolton Wanderers (a) Division One, 1 February 1958, W 2-0.
5ft 11in, 11st (1957).
Nimmo kept a clean sheet in his only senior appearance for Leeds after signing from Alloa Athletic in February 1956. He looked set for the top when he was playing in the Hearts 'A' team in the East of Scotland League when he was only 16. But a serious injury prompted Hearts to release him and he teamed up with Edinburgh Thistle before joining Alloa in summer 1955. He went to Leeds for £1,250, but moved to Doncaster Rovers in exchange for Ted Burgin in March 1958. Nimmo played 182 League games for Rovers before going to Mansfield in July 1962, although he did not appear in the Stags' League team.
League: App 1, Gls 0.

NOBLE, Alan H. *1922-1925*

Outside-right. Born: Southampton, 19 June 1900.
Debut v West Ham United (h) Division Two, 4 November 1922, W 3-1.
5ft 8in, 11st (1925).
Noble played in exactly half of United's games during their 1923-24 Division Two championship campaign after establishing himself in the team the previous season. He began as an amateur with Bournemouth and joined Leeds in May 1922, making his debut on the same day as Percy Whipp. He was transferred to Brentford in May 1925 and the Bees successfully converted him to right-half before allowing him to go to Millwall in May 1927. He died on 1 April 1973, in Southampton.
League: App 60, Gls 4; FA Cup: App 3, Gls 0.

NOTEMAN, Kevin S. *1987-1989*

Forward. Born: Preston, 15 October 1969.
Debut v Sheffield United (h) Simod Cup 1st round, 25 November 1987, W 3-0.
5ft 9in, 11st 2lb (1988).
Leeds City boys' representative Kevin Noteman joined United from Primrose Hill High School on the YTS scheme in 1987 and made his debut as an apprentice. His brothers Wayne and Ian, became well known on the Yorkshire non-League soccer circuit. In November 1989 he joined Doncaster Rovers for £10,000. In March 1992 he signed for Mansfield Town for £25,000 in time for their promotion to Division Three. He was a member of the Stags' team which knocked Leeds out of the League Cup in 1994-95.
League: App 0/1, Gls 0; Full Members' Cup: App 1, Gls 1.

O'BRIEN, George *1957-1959*

Inside-forward. Born: Dunfermline, 22 November 1935.
Debut v Newcastle United (h) Division One, 16 March 1957, D 0-0.
5ft 6in, 10st 11lb (1958).
O'Brien served Leeds for a couple of seasons before forging a highly-effective partnership with England international Terry Paine at Southampton. He began with

Fife club, Blairhall Colliery, before joining Dunfermline in 1952, winning promotion with them to the Scottish League First Division in 1954-55. In March 1957 he joined Leeds, but it was not until he was sold to Southampton (£10,000) in July 1959 that he showed his true value. He spent seven years with the Saints as they rose from Division Three to Division One and his powerful shooting brought him 154 goals in 243 League games. In March 1966 he went to Orient in exchange for David Webb, later to score Chelsea's 1970 FA Cup Final winner against Leeds, but nine months later became an Aldershot player. After turning down a one-year contract he left the Shots in 1968. After leaving football he ran a pub, then moved to Edinburgh where he was a sub-postmaster before returning to Southampton to run another pub, the Star and Garter in Freemantle. His son played for Dunfermline between 1979 and 1981.
League: App 44, Gls 6.

O'DOHERTY, Eugene F.J. *1920-1922*

Inside-forward. Born: Ballaghaderreen, Ireland, *c.*1896.
Debut v Boothtown (h) FA Cup Extra preliminary round, 11 September 1920, W 5-2.
5ft 8in, 11st 7lb (1920).
Did not play in the Football League for United. He was signed from Blackpool in August 1920 for £250. O'Doherty spent the 1921-22 season on United's books, but played for Ashton National, scoring 30 goals. In May 1922 he was transferred to Halifax. He later returned to Blackpool and had a spell at Walsall, who he joined in 1923.
FA Cup*: App 2, Gls 4.
*He played only in both of United's preliminary round games in 1920-21.

O'DONNELL, Chris *1989-1991*

Centre-half. Born: Newcastle upon Tyne, 26 May 1968.
Debut (as sub) v Hull City (h) Division Two, 10 February 1990 W 4-3.
5ft 9in, 12st (1989).
Stocky red-haired defender O'Donnell was snapped up on a free transfer from Ipswich Town in July 1989. He had joined Ipswich as a trainee in 1986 and had a spell on loan with Northampton Town in January 1988. His only first-team action for Leeds came as a substitute replacement for Jim Beglin. He joined Exeter City in summer 1991, but made only a couple of League appearances before switching to non-League Gateshead the following year.
League: App 0/1, Gls 0.

O'GRADY, Harry *1932-1933*

Inside-forward. Born: Tunstall, Staffordshire, 16 March 1907.
Debut v Wolverhampton Wanderers (h) Division One, 29 October 1932, W 3-2.
5ft 11in, 11st (1932).
O'Grady numbered Leeds among his eight League clubs. He began in Sunday Schools football in Staffordshire before spells with Nantwich and Witton Albion. Port Vale secured his services in November 1929 but after one game he joined Southampton in August 1931. He had pre-season trials with Leeds, using the name of 'Cousins' and was signed by Dick Ray in August 1932. Two months later he made a scoring debut but in May 1933 became a Burnley player. Successive moves took him to Bury (May 1934), Millwall (June 1935), Carlisle (August 1936), Accrington Stanley (May 1937) and Tunbridge Wells Rangers (October 1938).
League: App 8, Gls 2, FA Cup: App 1, Gls 0.

O'GRADY, Mike *1965-1969*

Winger. Born: Leeds, 11 October 1942.
Debut v Northampton Town (h) Division One, 16 October 1965, W 6-1.
5ft 9½in, 11st 2lb (1968).
Leeds had to pay dearly after letting the talents of Mike O'Grady slip through their fingers. Although he went to Corpus Christi School, it was United's West Riding rivals, Huddersfield Town, who signed him. He turned professional in October 1959 and after only 16 League and Cup matches won the first of three England Under-23 caps. Although Huddersfield were an unfashionable side, O'Grady continued to grab the headlines and scored twice on his full England debut in Belfast in October 1962 – and was promptly dropped. Don Revie had to pay Town £30,000 in October 1965 to bring him to his home-town club. Although he fared badly with injuries at Elland Road, he earned an England recall – over six years after his first cap – and scored in a 5-0 win over France in March 1969. It was his second and last England appearance, but he ended the season with a League championship medal. As Eddie Gray and Peter Lorimer began to establish themselves, O'Grady was transferred to Wolves in September 1969. Injuries took their toll on O'Grady at Molineux and after a spell on loan with Birmingham City in February 1972, he joined Rotherham in November that same year and ended his professional career with them. He then worked in Yorkshire TV's studio in Leeds for 18 years and also ran the Royal Oak pub in Aberford.
League: App 90/1, Gls 12; FA Cup: App 5, Gls 1; League Cup: App 5, Gls 0; Europe: App 20, Gls 3.

O'HARE, John *1974-1975*

Forward. Born: Renton, near Dumbarton, 24 September 1946.
Debut v Birmingham City (h) Division One, 24 August 1974, W 1-0.
5ft 8½in, 11st 7lb (1974).
Scottish international O'Hare had a short period at Leeds under the brief, turbulent reign of Brian Clough, who bought him for £50,000, in a deal involving John McGovern, from his old club, Derby County, in August 1974. O'Hare played for St Patrick's School (Dumbarton) and Drumchapel Amateurs before signing amateur forms for Sunderland in 1962. He turned professional in October 1963 and was helped by Clough, who was Sunderland's youth coach. O'Hare was Clough's first signing for Derby (£22,000) in August 1967. The player collected 13 full Scottish caps, three at Under-23 level, a League championship medal (1971-72) and a Second Division medal (1968-69) in seven years at Derby. After Leeds, he went to Clough's Nottingham Forest with McGovern in February 1975 (£60,000). That opened another chapter of glory as O'Hare won a European Cup medal (1980), another League championship medal (1977-78) and a League Cup winners' medal (1978). He was loaned to Dallas Tornado (NASL) in 1977 and left the professional game in summer 1981. He was later with Belper Town, Derby Carriage & Wagon FC and Ockbrook FC. He became manager of Central Midlands League side, Stanton, in March 1988. After leaving full-time football he ran a pub near Derby, worked for International Combustion in the city and then as a stock controller at Toyota's European plant on the outskirts of Derby.
League: App 6, Gls 1; League Cup; App 1, Gls 0.

O'LEARY, David A. *1993-1995*

Central defender. Born: Stoke Newington, London, 2 May 1958.
Debut v Manchester City (a) Premiership, 14 August 1993, D 1-1.
6ft 2in, 12st 6lb (1993).
Looking for experience to assist young central defenders David Wetherall and Jon Newsome, Leeds boss Howard Wilkinson opted for Arsenal legend David O'Leary on a three-year contract. The holder of 68 Republic of Ireland caps, he had spent 20 years at Highbury amassing a club record 558 League appearances. Although born in London he went to school in Dublin at St Kevin's, Glasnevin, and captained the Irish Schools side. He played for Shelbourne Juniors and had unsuccessful trials with Manchester United before joining Arsenal as an apprentice in June 1973. An Irish Youth international, he was at the heart of many of Arsenal's victorious teams, winning League championship medals in 1988-89 and 1990-91, FA Cup winners' medals in 1979 and 1992 and League Cup winners' medals in 1987 and 1992. Regarded as one of the best defenders in Europe, he was deceptively quick, supreme in the air and a wonderful distributor of the ball. He made his Republic of Ireland debut against England in a 1-1 draw at Wembley in September 1976 and was a member of the 1990 World Cup squad, earning national hero status when his spot-kick against Romania in a penalty competition put Jack Charlton's side into the quarter-finals for the first time in their history. He remained with Arsenal until he was given a free transfer and joined Leeds in July 1993, aged 35. His class was obvious on his debut, but it was not long before his ageing limbs ran into injury problems and he was forced to give up the game in 1995 with Achilles tendon trouble. When Jack Charlton stood down as Ireland's manager, O'Leary was among those suggested as a possible successor before the appointment of Mick McCarthy. O'Leary's younger brother, Pierce, played for Shamrock Rovers, Celtic, Vancouver Whitecaps and Philadelphia Fury, winning seven full Irish caps. He skippered Celtic when they met Arsenal at Highbury in August 1986 in his brother's testimonial game.
League: App 10, Gls 0.

O'NEILL, Jimmy J. *1969-1974*

Full-back. Born: Belfast, 24 February 1952.
Debut (as sub) v Strömgodset Drammen (h) UEFA Cup 1st round (2nd leg), 3 October 1973, W 6-1.
5ft 9½in, 12st 2lb (1973).
Like many of his contemporaries at Elland Road, O'Neill found it virtually impossible to prise his way into the first team because of the club's array of international talent. His brief moments of United senior action came as substitute. He joined Leeds from school and signed professional terms in May 1967. A free transfer took him to Chesterfield

in July 1974 and he made nearly 450 League appearances for the Spireites in a 12-year career in which he won an Anglo-Scottish Cup winners' medal (1981) and a Fourth Division medal (1984-85). At Chesterfield he was also known as Sean O'Neill. In 1985 he joined a local side, Staveley Works, and in July 1993 was appointed assistant manager of Dundee United.
League: App 0/1, Gls 0; Europe: App 0/2, Gls 0.

ORMSBY, Brendan T.C. *1986-1990*

Centre-half. Born: Birmingham, 1 October 1960.
Debut v Huddersfield Town (h) Division Two, 8 March 1986, W 2-0.
5ft 11in, 11st 9½lb (1986).
In 1986-87, inspirational captain Brendan Ormsby led Leeds to the FA Cup semi-final and the promotion Play-offs. He joined Aston Villa from school with eight England Schoolboy caps to his name. He turned professional in October 1978 and captained England Youth the following year. He broke an ankle and missed the whole of Villa's 1980-81 championship season but played three times in their European Cup-winning campaign in 1981-82. He made over 100 League appearances for Villa before joining Leeds in March 1986 (£65,000). He made a scoring debut but in the final Play-off against Charlton he severely damaged a cartilage. His injury was so serious that he did not get back into the Leeds first team for nearly two years – the final game of 1988-89, at Shrewsbury. However, it was not a lasting comeback and in January 1990 he was loaned to Shrewsbury for a month. He eventually resurrected his career with Doncaster Rovers in July 1990, often playing alongside his old Leeds partner, Jack Ashurst, under Billy Bremner's managership. He then joined Scarborough in summer 1992, for a year, before working a further year as player-coach of Waterford United until April 1994. More recently he has been playing in the Northern Counties East League with Farsley Celtic, where he was made assistant manager in November 1994.
League: App 51, Gls 6; FA Cup: App 4, Gls 1; League Cup: App 1, Gls 0; Full Members' Cup: App 1, Gls 0.

OVERFIELD, Jack *1953-1960*

Winger. Born: Leeds, 14 May 1932.
Debut v Nottingham Forest (h) Division Two, 8 October 1955, W 3-1.
5ft 10in, 10st 12lb (1957).
Jack Overfield was rejected by Sheffield United and Bolton Wanderers before making his mark in League football with Leeds. He attended Victoria Road School, Leeds, and played for

Ashley Road Methodists. After his double rejection he appeared in the Yorkshire League with Yorkshire Amateurs before becoming a Leeds United player in May 1953. During his National Service he played in several important representative matches of the RAF and on demob soon established himself in United's 1955-56 promotion side. He celebrated United's return to Division One with a goal against Everton after only two minutes on the opening day of the season, in Leeds' 5-1 triumph, but failed to score again that season, despite being ever-present. He was transferred to Sunderland in August 1960, joined Peterborough, briefly, in February 1963 and finished his League career with Bradford City in July 1964, being released the following summer.
League: App 159, Gls 20; FA Cup: App 4, Gls 0.

PALMER, Carlton L. *1994-*

Midfield/defender. Born: Rowley Regis, near Oldbury, 5 December 1965. Debut v West Ham United (a) Premiership, 20 August 1994, D 0-0.
6ft 2in, 11st 10lb (1995).
Leggy midfielder Carlton Palmer, a former England player, was also deployed in central defence by Howard Wilkinson after arriving at Elland Road from Sheffield Wednesday for £2.6 million. He proved a useful man-marker, but played the bulk of his games in midfield where his energetic long-striding style saw him score some last-minute winners which helped United some with a late surge in 1994-95 to clinch a European place. He played for Whiteheath, St Michael's, Oldbury, Rowley Regis & District Schools, Newton Albion, Netherton and Dudley Town before joining West Brom on YTS forms in July 1983, turning professional in October 1984. He soon made rapid strides at The Hawthorns, skippering England Under-21s, with whom he gained four caps. He joined his old boss, Ron Atkinson, at Sheffield Wednesday in February 1989 for £750,000. While he was at Hillsborough he forced his way into Graham Taylor's England side, making 17 appearances and five for England 'B'. He led Sheffield Wednesday to the FA Cup Final in 1993 when they lost in extra-time to Arsenal, for whom Andy Linighan headed the winner.
League: App 74, Gls 5; FA Cup: App 9, Gls 1; League Cup: App 10, Gls 0; Europe: App 4, Gls 1.

PARKER, Neil *1975-1981*

Left-back. Born: Blackburn, 19 October 1957.
Debut (as sub) v Liverpool (a) Division One, 11 March 1978, L 0-1.
5ft 6in, 10st 3lb (1978).
Parker's brief contribution was a 45-minute appearance as substitute for Peter Hampton. He joined Leeds as an apprentice and signed professional forms in October 1975. He went to Scarborough on a free transfer in July 1981, after the two sides played a pre-season friendly behind closed doors at Leeds. After Scarborough he played for Harrogate Town.
League: App 0/1, Gls 0.

PARKINSON, Keith J. *1973-1981*

Centre-half. Born: Preston, 28 January 1956.
Debut (as sub) v Middlesbrough (h) Division One, 21 February 1976, L 0-2.
6ft 1in, 12st 6lb (1981).
Parkinson was confined to the reserve and junior sides during much of his time at Leeds. A wholehearted type, he signed professional forms in February 1973 after serving his apprenticeship. He had to cope with a bout of injuries and, after spending a month to loan to Hull City in November 1981, joined Doncaster Rovers on a free transfer as a non-contract player in December 1982.
League: App 25/6, Gls 0; FA Cup: App 1, Gls 0; League Cup: App 4, Gls 0; Europe: App 2, Gls 0.

PARLANE, Derek J. *1980-1983*

Centre-forward. Born: Helensburgh, Dunbartonshire, 5 May 1953.
Debut v Southampton (h) Division One, 8 March 1980, W 2-0.
6ft, 11st 10lb (1981).
Parlane won a clutch of international and domestic honours in Scottish football before joining Leeds. He began as an amateur midfielder with Queen's Park before leaving in April 1970 to join Rangers – the club his father, Jimmy, had played for just after World War Two. He made a dramatic debut with a goal against Bayern Munich in the home semi-final of the European Cup-winners' Cup in 1972. He soon became an established star at Ibrox with his scoring ability, particularly headed goals, bringing him a dozen Scottish full caps, five at Under-23 level, one at Under-21 and two Scottish League XI appearances. In Scotland he won two League championship medals, three Cup winners' medals and two League Cup winners' medals before being sold to Leeds (£160,000) in March 1980. Although he scored on his debut, goals did not come easily and he spent nine months on loan to Hong Kong club, Bulova, ending in June 1983. Only when he joined Manchester City on a free transfer in August 1983 did he recapture his scoring form. In January 1985 he started a four-month spell with Swansea City before going to Hong Kong with North Shore FC. He joined Racing Jet (Belgium), then Rochdale in December 1986. A financial crisis saw Rochdale boss Eddie Gray release his former Leeds colleague. Parlane joined another Leeds old boy, Gordon McQueen, at Airdrie in January 1988. In summer that year he joined Macclesfield Town on a free transfer, then Curzon Ashton. Parlane is now a director of Macclesfield Town and works as a sportswear agent in the North-West and lives in Wilmslow.
League: App 45/5, Gls 10; FA Cup: App 2, Gls 0; League Cup: App 1, Gls 0.

PARRY, Bill *1937-1939*

Left-half. Born: Denaby, near Doncaster, *c.*1917.
Debut v Chelsea (h) Division One, 26 December 1938, D 1-1.
5ft 9in, 12st (1939).
Parry was released by Leeds just before World War Two when they had a surplus of good defenders. He played in the Midland League as a 16-year-old with Mexborogh, joining Denaby United in summer 1936 and moving to Frickley the following summer. He signed for Leeds in October 1937. Reading showed interest in him, but he signed for Southern League Chelmsford City in June 1939.
League: App 6, Gls 0; FA Cup: App 2, Gls 0.

PEACOCK, Alan *1964-1967*

Centre-forward. Born: Middlesbrough, 29 October 1937.
Debut v Norwich City (a)

Division Two, 8 February 1964, D 2-2.
6ft 1in, 11st 9lb (1963).
Alan Peacock was one of English soccer's best headers of a ball in the post-war era. A product of Lawson Secondary School, Middlesbrough, he joined Middlesbrough as a youngster, won England Youth honours and turned professional in November 1954. He formed a prolific spearhead with Brian Clough,

scoring 126 League goals in 218 apperances, and was an England international when Leeds paid out £53,000 for him in Feburary 1964. His goals lifted Leeds into Division One in 1964. A member of the 1965 FA Cup Final side, he added two more England appearances when a Leeds player to take his total to six caps – a number that could have been substantially increased, but for a succession of injuries. He went to Plymouth Argyle in October 1967 but was forced to retire in March 1968. He later ran a newsagent's business in Middlesbrough.
League: App 54, Gls 27; FA Cup: App 6, Gls 2; League Cup: App 2, Gls 1; Europe: App 3, Gls 1.

PEARSON, John S. *1987-1991*

Forward. Born: Sheffield, 1 September 1963.
Debut v Blackburn Rovers (h) Division Two, 24 January 1987, D 0-0.
6ft 2in, 13st 1lb (1987).
Pearson was captured from Charlton Athletic in January 1987 (£72,000) and faced his former colleagues in the end-of-season Play-offs. Although it took him 15 games to open his account for Leeds, his aerial ability created chances for others. He joined Sheffield Wednesday in 1979 from Wisewood School, turned professional in May 1981, scoring on his debut for them, and won England Youth honours in 1981 and 1982. He was often used as substitute by Wednesday. In May 1985 he was sold to Charlton (£100,000) and finished as their top scorer in his first season as the Valiants won promotion to Division One. He lost form at Leeds in 1987-88 but rejected a possible move to Shrewsbury in November 1987. He had to be content with largely reserve-team football and was loaned to Rotherham United in October 1992 before joining Barnsley for £135,000. Injury meant that he did not do himself justice and he went on loan to Hull City in January 1993 before joining Carlisle United on a free transfer in August that year. A qualified coach, he then had spells at Mansfield Town (November 1994) and Cardiff City (February 1995) before succumbing to a neck injury and giving up full-time football. He turned down a move to Chester City and spent a month on loan to Merthyr Town before joining Unibond League club Chorley in September 1995, combining playing with a job as an insurance salesman. He holds the record for the number of substitute appearances for Leeds.
League: App 55/48, Gls 12; FA Cup: App 5/5, Gls 0; League Cup: App 5/4, Gls 0; Full Members' Cup: App 2/3, Gls 0.

PEMBERTON, John M. *1993-*

Defender. Born: Oldham, 18 November 1964.
Debut v Tottenham Hotspur (a) Premiership, 20 November 1993, D 1-1.
5ft 11in, 11st 9lb (1993).
Aggressive, pacey defender John Pemberton was brought in to bolster United's squad midway through the 1993-94 season from Sheffield United. A fee of £250,000, plus £1,000 for each of his first 50 games, was agreed for the Blades skipper who had over 250 League games under his belt. He was playing for Manchester area side Chadderton and Oldham Boys with David Platt before turning professional with Rochdale in September 1984, but after only one League game was

given a free transfer. Crewe manager Dario Gradi, the master moulder of future stars, gave him a chance to restart his career at Gresty Road in March 1985. Like teammates Platt and Geoff Thomas, both future England internationals, Pemberton went on to better things, joining Crystal Palace in March 1988 for £80,000. He helped Palace win promotion to Division One the following season and figured in the Eagles' side beaten by Manchester United in the 1990 FA Cup Final. Within three months of that Wembley game he left Selhurst Park to join Dave Bassett's Sheffield United for £300,000 to play in the top flight after the Bramall Lane side had been pipped to promotion by Leeds in 1989-90. Mainly a central defender, he was also used as left-back cover at Leeds and even scored a hat-trick for the Reserves against Middlesbrough as an emergency centre-forward.
League: App 44/9, Gls 0; FA Cup: App 5/1, Gls 0; League Cup: App 3, Gls 0; Europe: App 4, Gls 0.

PETERSON, Paul W. *1969-1971*

Left-back. Born: Luton, 22 December 1949.
Debut v Derby County (a) Division One, 30 March 1970, L 1-4.
5ft 6in, 10st 6½lb (1970).
Peterson joined Leeds from school, served his apprenticeship and signed professional terms on his 17th birthday in December 1969. He went on a free transfer to Swindon in June 1971 and made one appearance for them before going into non-League soccer. He was later coach and assistant manager at Stevenage Borough, where he worked with Derek Montgomery, with whom he played in United's junior sides in the late 1960s.
League: App 3/1, Gls 0.

PEYTON, Noel *1958-1963*

Inside-forward. Born: Dublin, 4 December 1935.
Debut v Bolton Wanderers (a) Division One, 1 February 1958, W 2-0.
5ft 5in, 10st (1958).
Eire international Peyton was in and out of the Leeds team during his stay at Elland Road. He was with Shamrock Rovers for five years prior to joining Leeds (£5,000) in January 1958. At Rovers he won plenty of domestic honours and made his full Republic of Ireland debut against World Cup holders, West Germany, in Dublin in November 1956, when the Irish recorded a famous victory. He won five more caps at Leeds before a £4,000 transfer to York in July 1963. In May 1965 he became player-manager of Barnstaple Town, then played for St Patrick's Athletic. Approaching the veteran stage, he played for the League of Ireland against the Italian League, adding to the five League of Ireland appearances he made when at Shamrock.
League: App 105, Gls 17; FA Cup: App 3, Gls 1; League Cup: App 9, Gls 2.

PHELAN, Terry *1983-1986*

Left-back. Born: Manchester, 16 March 1967.
Debut v Shrewsbury Town (a) Division Two, 7 September 1985, W 3-1.
5ft 8in, 10st (1986).
A product of Cathedral High School, Manchester, Phelan represented Salford and Greater Manchester Schools but qualified to play for the Republic of Ireland because his mother was Irish. He joined Leeds from school in 1983 and won Under-21 and Youth honours before turning professional in August 1984. He was freed in May 1986 and joined Swansea and, after an excellent season with the Swans, signed for First Division Wimbledon (£100,000) in July 1987. At Plough Lane he joined John Scales, a former Leeds junior who played alongside Phelan at Elland Road. Phelan played in Wimbledon's 1988 FA Cup winning side and Scales, who joined the Dons via Bristol Rovers, came on as a substitute. Scales went on to play for Liverpool and England, while Phelan made his mark with the Republic in the 1992 World Cup as a pacey left-back. By this time he was in the £2.5 million class, signing for Manchester City in August 1992. He later moved to Chelsea in another big-money deal.
League: App 12/2, Gls 0; League Cup: App 3, Gls 0; Full Members' Cup: App 2, Gls 0.

POTTS, Jimmy F. *1926-1934*

Goalkeeper. Born: Ashington, 25 February 1899.
Debut v Huddersfield Town (a) Division One, 27 February 1926, L 1-3.
6ft 1in, 12st (1930).
Jimmy Potts was probably United's best goalkeeper of the inter-war period. Brother-in-law of the Milburns, he played for Blyth Spartans and worked as a coal-hewer at Ashington Colliery before he joined Leeds United as a professional in February 1926, making his League debut within two days of signing. He became firmly established at Elland Road, using his marvellous physique to dominate his penalty-area. He

was eventually replaced by the younger Stan Moore and in May 1934, at the age of 35, moved to Port Vale for a couple of seasons, during which he hardly missed a game.
League: App 247, Gls 0; FA Cup: App 15, Gls 0.

POTTS, Joe *1921-1923*

Right-back. Born: Newcastle upon Tyne, 25 February 1899.
Debut v Crystal Palace (h) Division Two, 17 December 1921, D 0-0.
5ft 11in, 12st 4lb (1922).
Potts was noted for his strong tackling during a lengthy career with Ashington before he left for Hull City in March 1912. In summer 1914 he went to Portsmouth but the war prevented him from making much progress with Pompey. He joined Leeds in June 1921 but found it difficult to dislodge Jimmy Frew and moved to Chesterfield in June 1923. He was an ever-present in his first season with the Spireites before moving to Bradford Park Avenue in 1925.
League: App 10, Gls 0.

POWELL, Aubrey *1935-1948*

Inside-forward. Born: Cynlais, near Pontardawe, 19 April 1918.
Debut v Middlesbrough (h) Division One, 25 December 1936, W 5-0.
5ft 5in, 10st 2lb (1938).
Despite being written off by doctors after breaking a leg in United's game at Preston on 20 March 1937, Powell fought back to give Leeds stout service and collect full Welsh honours. United spotted him playing as an amateur with Swansea Town (he had earlier been with Cwm Wanderers) and signed him in November 1935. He made an immediate impact on his debut but, three months later, was told he would never play again because of a fractured leg. He battled back and formed a highly-effecitve partnership with David Cochrane until the outbreak of war. He played 126 times for Leeds in wartime games and for Wales in wartime internationals, winning his first official cap in October 1946. During the war he served in Belgium. Hard-up Leeds sold him to Everton (£10,000) in June 1948. He joined Birmingham City in August 1950 before going to Wellington Town, where he retired in 1952. He later worked as a representative for a Leeds confectionary company.
League: App 114, Gls 5; FA Cup: App 5, Gls 0.

POWELL, Sam *1921-1925*

Centre-forward. Born: Holmes, near Rotherham, 25 May 1899.
Debut v Cardiff City (h) Division Two, 29 March 1921, L 1-2.
5ft 9in, 11st (1922).
Powell was sold to Sheffield Wednesday to help raise cash to sign Russell Wainscoat from Middlesbrough in March 1925. United signed Powell from Thornhill in January 1921 and he spent most of his time in the Reserves. It was a familiar story at Hillsborough where he managed only 25 League games in four seasons. He joined Stafford in 1930, but returned to Wednesday to spend 30 years as one of the backroom staff, including seven as the reserve-team trainer, before being appointed first-team trainer in 1937. He retired in 1959 and died in Sheffield on 21 June 1961, aged 62.
League: App 28, Gls 7.

POYNTZ, Bill I. *1921-1923*

Inside-forward. Born: Tylerstown, Glamorgan, 18 March 1921.
Debut v Stoke (a) Division Two, 29 October 1921, L 0-3.
5ft 11in, 11st 10lb (1921).
Welshman Bill Poyntz achieved the unwanted distinction of becoming the first United player to be sent off when he was dismissed against Bury on 18 February 1922. He soon made up for that blemish by getting married on the morning of the match against Leicester City the following week and promptly scored a hat-trick. Leeds signed him from Llanelli in the 1921 close season and he had already played in a Welsh international trial. In November 1923 he went to Doncaster Rovers and embarked on a lengthy jounrey around the soccer circuit with Northampton Town (May 1924), Bradford (cs 1925), Crewe Alexandra (December 1926) and Hartlepools United (cs 1927). He was signed at Hartlepools by Bill Norman, one-time assistant to Arthur Fairclough at Leeds, and was made centre-half and skipper. On leaving Hartlepools he was coach at Bury, then spent nine years on the training staff at Leeds after gaining qualification as a physiotherapist at Leeds General Hospital. Before the war he was the trainer with Newport County. Poyntz died on 5 April 1966, aged 72.
League: App 29, Gls 7.

PRICE, Arthur *1945-1946*

Half-back. Born: Rowlands Gill, County Durham, 12 January 1921.
Debut v Middlesbrough (a) FA Cup 3rd round (2nd leg), 9 January 1946, L 2-7.
5ft 6in, 10st 8lb (1946).
Leeds beat Newcastle in a race to sign Arthur Price from North Durham League side, Consett. He

worked as a maintenance engineer in Hebburn-on-Tyne and opted to play for Leeds as an amateur, signing in September 1945. He held down a fairly regular place in the 1945-46 wartime season and played in six of the opening eight games of 1946-47 before losing his place to Gerry Henry and leaving Elland Road.
League: App 6, Gls 0; FA Cup: App 1, Gls 0.

RADEBE, Lucas *1994-*

Midfield/defender. Born: Johannesburg, South Africa, 12 April 1969.
Debut (as sub) v Sheffield Wednesday (a) 26 September 1994, Premiership, D 1-1.
6ft lin, 11st 9lb (1995).
Versatile South African international Lucas Radebe has played in midfield, all the back positions and even in goal in a matter of weeks for United. Just for good measure he won an African Nations Cup winners' medal and played in the Coca-Cola Cup Final against Aston Villa in an astonishing 1995-96 season. His goalkeeping exploits emerged the week after that Wembley Final when Leeds were trailing 1-0 to Middlesbrough at Elland Road. Goalkeeper John Lukic did not reappear because he had taken a bang on the head, so with no 'keeper on the bench, Howard Wilkinson turned to Radebe, who kept a clean sheet. Weeks later he came off the bench at Old Trafford after only 16 minutes when Mark Beeney was sent off and kept Premiership champions Manchester United at bay until late in the game when Roy Keane scored the only goal. One of 14 children, Soweto-born Radebe in fact started his career as a goalkeeper, representing Bophuthatswana in the Homeland Games in 1990. He was playing for ICL Birds in the Bopsol League when his side had a crisis in central defence and he moved from between the sticks. He did well, kept his position and was signed by Kaiser Chiefs in April 1990, a move soon followed by his first international cap. A member of the Chiefs' 1992 double-winning side, he was runner-up in the South African Player of the Year awards the following year and arrived at Elland Road with countryman Phil Masinga for £250,000 in August 1994.
League: App 19/6, Gls 0; FA Cup: App 4/2, Gls 0; League Cup: App 1/3, Gls 0.

REANEY, Paul *1961-1978*

Full-back. Born: Fulham, 22 October 1944.
Debut v Swansea Town (a) Division Two, 8 September 1962, W 2-0.
5ft 10in, 11st 3lb (1971).
Only Jack Charlton and Billy Bremner have played more games for Leeds United than Paul Reaney. He was only a few weeks old when his family left London for Leeds, where he attended Cross Green School and played for Middleton Parkside Juniors. He was an apprentice motor mechanic when he joined Leeds'

groundstaff in October 1961. Reaney's League debut followed less than a year later and he shared in the glory days under Revie. He collected two League championship medals, an FA Cup winners' medal, League Cup winners' medal. Inter-Cities Fairs Cup medals and a Second Division championship medal in 17 years at Elland Road. He won three full England caps and five at Under-23 level. Virtually ever-present at Leeds, he was dubbed 'Speedy' for his quickness to overlap into attack and knock in teasing centres for his forwards. He was also rated as one of the top markers of his day. A broken

leg at West Ham towards the end of 1969-70 forced Reaney out of England's World Cup squad for Mexico. He made an excellent recovery and gave United eight more seasons' solid service before joining Bradford City on a free transfer in June 1978. In 1980 he joined Newcastle UB United (New South Wales) and was named Australia's Player of the Year. He returned to England and now lives in Knaresborough and runs coaching courses at schools and holiday camps.
League: App 549/8, Gls 6; FA Cup: App 72/1, Gls 3; League Cup: App 39, Gls 0; Europe: App 74/3, Gls 0; Charity Shield: App 2, Gls 0.

REED, George *1924-1931*

Left-half. Born: Altofts, near Wakefield, 7 February 1904.
Debut v Sunderland (h) Division One, 6 April 1926, L 0-2.
5ft 8in, 11st 2lb (1930).
Reed cost only a signing-on fee when he joined Leeds from Altofts in October 1924. He broke into the first team halfway through 1926-27 and missed only eight League games in the next three and a half seasons. He was quick, sharp in the tackle and a good passer of the ball. In April 1930 he shared a benefit game against Manchester United, with Harry Roberts, and then joined Roberts at Plymouth Argyle in May 1931. He stayed at Home Park until the 1934 close season, when he joined Crystal Palace. Later he was reserve-team trainer at Palace, had a spell at Clapton Orient, playing only once, in April 1936, and then returned to Plymouth as trainer.
League: App 141, Gls 2; FA Cup: App 9, Gls 1.

RENNIE, David *1986-1989*

Defender/midfield. Born: Edinburgh, 29 August 1964.
Debut v Charlton Athletic (a) Division Two, 18 January 1986, L 0-4.
5ft 11¼in, 11st 12lb (1986).
Rennie played in the heart of defence or as a ball-winning midfielder and even turned out at full-back for Leeds. Winner of 20 Scottish Youth caps, he played in Scotland's UEFA Youth championship-winning team of 1982. He joined Leicester from school and turned professional in May 1982, but was largely confined to the Reserves until his £50,000 transfer to Leeds in January 1986. In August 1989 he joined Bristol City for £200,000 and in February 1992 moved to Birmingham City. Blues' boss Terry Cooper swapped him for Coventry City winger David Smith in April 1993 and Rennie went on to skipper the Sky Blues in the Pemiership, although he did return to St Andrew's in February 1996, on a month's loan.
League: App 95/6, Gls 5; FA Cup: App 7, Gls 1; League Cup: App 7, Gls 0; Full Members' Cup: App 4, Gls 1.

REVIE, Don G. *1958-1961*

Inside-right. Born: Middlesbrough, 10 July 1927.
Debut v Newcastle United (h) Division One, 29 November 1958, W 3-2.
5ft 11in, 12st 9lb (1959).
Don Revie's remarkable achievements as Leeds United's manager have overshadowed his greatness as a player. He learnt his soccer at Archibald Road School, Middlesbrough, Newport Boys' Club and Middlesbrough Swifts before joining Leicester City in 1944. He was sold to Hull City in November 1949 (£20,000), then a £25,000 transfer in October 1951 took him to Manchester City. At Maine Road he was the centre-piece of what became known as the 'Revie Plan' of the deep-lying centre-forward. He masterminded City's 1956 FA Cup Final triumph against Birmingham, which made up for finishing on the losing side the year before against Newcastle and missing Leicester's 1949 Final against Wolves with a nose haemorrhage. Revie won six England caps with Manchester City before another big fee – £22,000 – took him to Sunderland in November 1956. He joined Leeds as a player in November 1958 (£12,000) and enjoyed a brief spell as captain before being appointed player-manager in March 1961, retiring from playing in the 1963 close season (see Leeds Managers). Revie, who was Footballer of the Year in 1955, also won one England 'B' cap and made two appearances for the Football League representative side, had a street named after him off Elland Road. In 1987 it was revealed that he was suffering from motor-neurone disease, a muscle wasting illness for which there is no known cure and from which he died in May 1989. The former Geldard End Kop at Elland Road, now all-seater, is known as the Revie Stand and was officially opened by his widow, Elsie, in October 1994.
League: App 76, Gls 11; FA Cup: App 1, Gls 0; League Cup: App 3, Gls 1.

RICHMOND, Joe *1922-1926*

Centre-forward. Born: Leasingthorpe, near Durham, spring 1897.
Debut v Wolverhampton Wanderers (a) Division Two, 9 December 1922, W 1-0.
5ft 11in, 11st 10lb (1925).
Although he was fairly inexperienced, Joe Richmond led United's 1923-24 promotion side with panache and vigour. A Durham Schools representative player he played for Sittingbourne before serving with the Royal Flying Corps as a flight-sergeant in World War One, winning the French Medal Militaire. In March 1922 he signed for Shildon from where he joined Leeds in December 1922. He moved to Barnsley in February 1926 but in July that year went to Norwich, where he made a successful transition to left-back before retiring in 1930. After World War Two he coached Letchworth Town and then became a publican, running the Quebec Tavern and the Beaufort Arms in Norwich. He died in Norwich on 6 March 1953.
League: App 56, Gls 19; FA Cup: App 4, Gls 0.

RILEY, Valentine *1924-1928*

Inside-forward. Born: Hebburn, near South Shields, *c.*1904.
Debut v Bolton Wanderers (a) FA Cup 4th round replay, 2 February 1927, L 0-3.
5ft 8in, 11st (1928).
Riley's only senior appearance for Leeds came when Bobby Turnbull and Albert Sissons were unable to play. He joined United in November 1924 from Wood Skinners, Hebburn, although he had earlier been on Middlesbrough's books (although he didn't appear for their first team) and Washington Colliery. In August 1928 he joined Newport County, via Annfield Plain, where he was converted to half-back. He left Newport in August 1931, for West Stanley, but 12 months later joined Southampton. He failed to make the senior team at The Dell and returned to the North-East with Jarrow.
FA Cup: App 1, Gls 0.

RIPLEY, S.Keith *1952-1958*

Wing-half. Born: Normanton, near Wakefield, 29 March 1935.
Debut v Stoke City (h) Division Two, 8 September 1954, L 0-1.
6ft 1in, 11st 2lb (1957).
Leeds had to beat off stiff competition from Blackpool and West Brom before capturing Ripley. He starred as a centre-half at Normanton Secondary School, but was a wing-half when he joined Leeds from Altofts YMCA in April 1952. He did his National Service with the Royal Signals and played for the Army against a Scotland XI at Ibrox Park in 1955. He was also selected against an Irish FA XI at Highbury in December 1954, but the match was called off. On demob he returned to Leeds before moving to Norwich in August 1958. Within three months he was sold to Mansfield (£4,000). In July 1960 he joined Peterborough and won a Fourth Division championship medal in his first season. In August 1962 he was transferred to Doncaster Rovers and played 123 League matches there before retiring in 1966.
League: App 67, Gls 15; FA Cup: App 2, Gls 0.

RITCHIE, Andy T. *1983-1987*

Forward. Born: Manchester, 28 November 1960.
Debut v Crystal Palace (h) Division Two, 26 March 1983, W 2-1.
5ft 9½in, 11st 11lb (1984).
Leeds remembered Andy Ritchie after he scored a hat-trick against them for Manchester United in March 1979. He attended Moseley Grammar School, played for Manchester and Stockport Boys and won eight England Schools caps under skipper Brendan Ormsby. Ritchie played for Whiteside in Sunday League

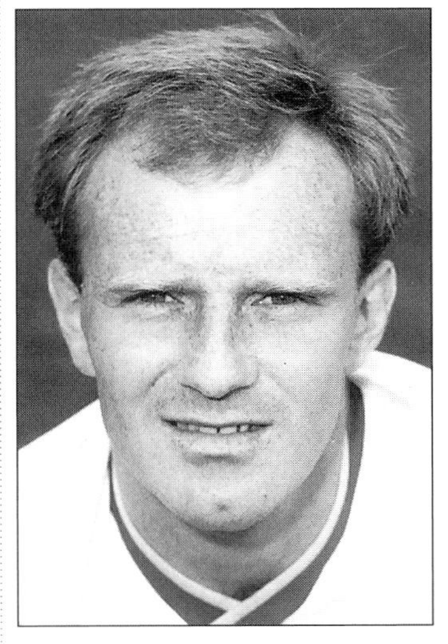

soccer, joined Manchester United as a youngster and turned professional in December 1977. He looked to have a big future at Old Trafford, but was sold to Brighton (£500,000) in October 1980. He won an Under-21 cap against Poland a couple of years later, then a swap deal with Terry Connor in March 1983 took him to Leeds. He was a hard-working, skilful player rather than an instinctive goalscorer, although he netted six goals in a Central League game at Blundell Park in September 1984. Much of his time at Leeds was spent in dispute over his contract and for over a year he was on a weekly contract before moving to Oldham Athletic (£50,000) in August 1987. He proved a bargain-buy, scoring a stack of goals for the Latics and helping

them reach the League Cup Final and the FA Cup semi-final in 1990 and win the championship of the old Second Division in 1991. Then, after struggling with injuries, he joined Scarborough in summer 1995.
League: App 129/10, Gls 40; FA Cup: App 9, Gls 1; League Cup: App 11, Gls 3.

ROBERTS, Harry *1925-1930*

Right-back. Born: Crofton, near Wakefield, 27 June 1904.
Debut v Bury (a) Division One, 13 March 1926, W 2-0.
5ft 7in, 11st 9lb (1930).
Like Bert Duffield, his predecessor at right-back, Roberts was signed from Midland League Castleford Town. He was 20 when he joined Leeds in February 1925 and broke into the first team on a regular basis in 1926-27. He moved to Plymouth Argyle in November 1930 and made 248 appearances for Argyle, where he earned a reputation as a firm tackler and deadly penalty-taker. An £820 transfer took him to Bristol Rovers in September 1937 and he was immediately appointed club captain. In August 1939 he returned to Yorkshire to play for Frickley Colliery and during the war he went back to Plymouth, where he had been dubbed 'the Rock of Gibralter' in his playing days, and later ran a stall in the local market. He died in Plymouth Naval Hospital on 18 May 1968. He was a keen golfer and bowls player.
League: App 84, Gls 2; FA Cup: App 3, Gls 0.

ROBINSON, David *1926-1928*

Left-back. Born: Dumfries or Longtown.
Debut v Blackburn Rovers (h) Division One, 9 October 1926, W 4-1.
5ft 7in, 11st 6lb (1928).
Early in his career it looked as though Robinson would not make the grade. He began as a winger with Workington and was rejected by Aston Villa after trials. He signed for Carlisle, who converted him to full-back before Leeds took him on via Solway Star in May 1926. He moved to Southend United in May 1928 and at last found his niche, making over 300 appearances for the Shrimpers, despite a bad injury in February 1933. After he retired he was appointed Southend's groundsman. He also ran a newsagents and tobacconists in the resort.
League: App 5, Gls 0.

ROBINSON, Ronnie *1985-1987*

Left-back. Born: Sunderland, 22 October 1966.
Debut v Carlisle United (a) Division Two, 23 November 1985, W 2-1.
5ft 9in, 11st (1986).
Robinson was picked up on a free transfer from Ipswich Town in November 1985. A Sunderland and Wearside Schools representative, he played for Vaux Breweries before going to Ipswich as an apprentice but did not make the first team at Portman Road. In February 1987 he joined Doncaster Rovers (£5,000) and switched to a central defensive position. In March 1989 he and Doncaster starlet Paul Raven joined West Bromwich Albion in a £200,000 package deal. Robinson then moved to Rotherham United in August 1989, for £40,000. A free transfer took him to Peterborough United in December 1991 and the Posh banked a tidy profit when they sold him to Exeter City in July 1993 for £25,000. Loaned to Huddersfield in January 1994, he had trials at Scarborough in 1995-96.
League: App 27, Gls 0.

ROBSON, Cuthbert *1924-1926*

Outside-right. Born: High Wheatley, County Durham, 19 October 1900.
Debut v West Bromwich Albion (a) Division One, 11 October 1924, L 1-3.
5ft 7in, 11st (1925).
'Cud' Robson was among the most popular players in North-East amateur football before returning professional with Leeds. He began with Thornley Albion, then Cockfield Albion from where he joined Leeds in July 1924. He made 17 successive appearances in United's first-ever season in Division One and scored on his debut, but a knee injury saw him lose his place. With newcomer Bobby Turnbull occupying the right-wing slot, Robson moved to Southend United in May 1926. In the following close season he joined Hartlepools United. From Hartlepools he went to Connah's Quay, re-entering League football with Bristol City in 1930, and finishing his career with Chester, who he joined in October 1931. He died in Durham East in October 1972.
League: App 17, Gls 4.

ROBSON, William *1921-1924*

Inside-right. Born: Shildon, County Durham.
Debut v Coventry City (a) Division Two, 18 March 1922, L 0-1.
5ft 7in, 11st 7lb (1924).
One of the many Robsons who came out of the amateur soccer breeding grounds of the North-East to play League football, Bill Robson joined Leeds in December 1921. He and Walter Coates represented the Yorkshire Midweek League in March 1923. Robson played for Ashington after leaving Leeds in 1924.
League: App 10, Gls 0; FA Cup: App 1, Gls 0.

ROCASTLE, David *1992-1993*

Midfield. Born: Lewisham, 2 May 1967.
Debut v VfB Stuttgart (a) European Cup 1st Rd, 1st leg, 16 September 1992, L 0-3.
5ft 9in, 11st 1lb (1993).
David 'Rocky' Rocastle's 16-month stay at Elland Road must rank as the most curious in the club's recent history. In July 1992 the elegant England midfield man became Leeds' most expensive signing when he left his first club, Arsenal, for £2 million to join the new champions. But he could not even get on the bench at the start of the season and that seemed to set the tone for a miserable spell with the club when he did not see eye to eye with manager Howard Wilkinson. He did feature in the European Cup, but did not start a League game until November when he sparkled in a 3-0 win against his old club. His rise to the top was rapid, joining the Gunners from Roger Manwoods School in London as an apprentice in August 1983, turning professional on New Year's Eve the following year. He won League championship medals at Highbury in 1988-89 and 1990-91 and a League Cup winners' medal in 1987. His skilful forays down the right earned him 14 caps at both full and Under-21 level, plus two more for England 'B'. After losing his way with Arsenal, Leeds seemed the perfect opportunity to rebuild his career, but it proved an unproductive time with United as Rocastle started only 17 League games. He left for Manchester City in December 1993, with David White going in the opposite direction in a deal the clubs estimated at £2 million. Maine Road did not solve Rocastle's problems and in August 1994 he was transferred for £1.25 million to Chelsea where his career remains in limbo because of injury.
League: App 17/8, Gls 2; FA Cup: App 0/3, Gls 0; League Cup: App 0/3, Gls 0; Europe: App 2/1, Gls 0.

RODGERSON, Ralph *1921-1923*

Left-back. Born: Sunderland.
Debut v Nottingham Forest (h) Division Two, 23 April 1921, D 2-2.
5ft 9in, 12st (1921).
Rodgerson's experience served Leeds well in their early days. He began with Pallion Institute, a local Sunderland side. In March 1913 he joined Huddersfield Town from Burnley and made his debut for the Terriers the following season. He played for Town after the war before moving to Leeds in March 1921. In October 1922 he returned to the North-East for a spell in the Wearside League, although Leeds retained his registration. In January 1923 he went to Dundee.
League: App 27, Gls 0; FA Cup: App 1, Gls 0.

ROPER, Harry *1929-1935*

Inside-forward. Born: Romiley, near Stockport, 13 April 1910.
Debut v Blackpool (a) Division One, 29 August 1932, L 1-2.
5ft 10in, 10st (1930).
Roper, a former warehouse clerk, signed from New Mills in August 1929. He had to wait three years for his League debut and marked it with a goal. It was only the second game of the season, but he was not picked again that term. He was bedevilled by cartilage problems and in May 1935 moved to Cardiff City, then joined Stockport County in October 1937. He died on 16 April 1983, three days after his 73rd birthday.
League: App 18, Gls 3.

ROSS, Bobby A. *1950-1954*

Full-back. Born: Wishaw, Lanarkshire, 25 May 1927.
Debut v Sheffield United (h) Division Two, 6 October 1951, W 3-1.
5ft 8in, 10st 9½lb (1951).
Ross made all his appearances in 1951-52. He was signed from North Eastern League club, Workington, for £500 in July 1950. Shortly afterwards he was joined by Workington goalkeeper John Scott. With Jimmy Dunn and Jim Milburn at Elland Road, Ross had little chance and after the emergence of Grenville Hair, he was transferred to Stockport County in June 1954.
League: App 5, Gls 0.

RUDD, Jimmy J. *1949*

Outside-left. Born: Hull, 25 October 1919.
Debut v Bury (h) Division Two, 12 February 1949, L 0-1.
5ft 6in, 10st (1949).
Rudd played for Dublin side, Fearons, in the Leinster League, then Tenure Athletic, another Dublin team, from whom he joined Manchester City in 1938. After one game for City he was picked for Ireland against England at the age of 18, but City refused to release him, saying he was not ready for international football. During the war (when

he was stationed in North Yorkshire with the Durham Light Infantry) he guested for York City and, after two post-war appearances for Manchester City, was released in March 1947 and joined York. In February 1949 he was involved in an exchange deal with Tom Hindle and became a Leeds player, only to move to Rotherham United in October that year. For Rotherham he once scored two goals direct from corners, against Wrexham in August 1950, and was a member of their 1950-51 Third Division (North) championship side. He played for Scunthorpe (October 1951), Workington (September 1952), Northwich Victoria (1953) and Stafford Rangers. Later he was a match-day steward at Maine Road. After ending his playing days he worked for Kellogs as a cooker operator and was a TGWU general secretary for 21 years, then a kitchen porter at Manchester Royal Infirmary. He died on 13 December 1985, aged 66. His nephew, Billy Rudd, played for Birmingham City, York City, Grimsby Town, Rochdale and Bury between 1959 and 1976.
League: App 18, Gls 1.

RUSSELL, David P. *1925-1926*

Goalkeeper. Born: Crossgates, near Dunfermline, 30 November 1902.
Debut v Huddersfield Town (a) Division One, 31 January 1925, L 0-2
5ft 10in, 11st 5lb (1925).
Despite having little senior experience, Russell was thrown in at the deep end to make his debut in a West Riding derby only days after arriving at Leeds. He had an outstanding career with Hearts of Blath in Scottish junior football, culminating in a Scottish junior international appearance in 1922-23. He later played for Kilsyth Rangers before joining Doncaster Rovers, where he understudied ex-Leeds 'keeper Harold Jacklin. Signed from Rovers in exchange for Jack Lambert in January 1925, he was transferred to Watford in August 1926, but was released after one season.
League: App 9, Gls 0.

SABELLA, Alex *1980-1982*

Midfield. Born: Buenos Aires, Argentina, 5 November 1954.
Debut v Aston Villa (h) Division One, 16 August 1980, L 1-2.
5ft 8in, 10st 13lb (1981).
Sabella found it difficult to bring his delicate skills to the surface in the hurly-burly of First Division football. He developed at River Plate, one of Argentina' top clubs, and signed for Sheffield United for £160,000 in July 1978. He was not an international but a string of virtuoso performances at Bramall Lane induced Leeds to sign him (£400,000) in May 1980. He found himself in a side battling against relegation, and in January 1982 returned to Argentina to Estudiantes (£120,000). There he hit his best form and won four Argentinian caps. He had a spell with Gremio of Porto Alegre (Brazil) in 1986-87, returning to Argentina in summer 1987 to play for Ferro Carril Oeste. Named Alejandro, English fans knew him as Alex. He went into coaching and at one stage was involved in his country's national set-up.
League: App 22/1, Gls 2; FA Cup: App 2, Gls 0; League Cup: App 2, Gls 0.

SAVAGE, Reg *1931-1939*

Goalkeeper. Born: Eccles, 5 July 1912.
Debut v Blackburn Rovers (a) Division One, 1 September 1934, D 1-1.
5ft 11½in, 11st (1931).
Savage succeeded ex-international Albert McInroy, but was eventually ousted, by another international, Jim Twomey. He began with Taylor Brothers (Lancashire) before going to Stalybridge Celtic, from where he joined Leeds in February 1931. With Twomey well established, Savage moved to Queen of the South in July 1939. When war broke out he assisted Nottingham Forest and Blackpool, winning a League Cup (North) winners' medal and a Cup-winners' medal in 1943 with the latter. He joined Forest in 1946, then moved to Accrington Stanley in August 1947.
League: App 79, Gls 0; FA Cup: App 5, Gls 0.

SCAIFE, George *1936-1939*

Full-back. Born: Bradford, early 1915.
Debut v Arsenal (h) Division One, 11 March 1939, W 4-2.
Scaife played all his senior games for Leeds in the last full season before the war. He was signed in August 1936 and turned professional in May 1937. An experienced amateur player, he played mostly at left-back in the Reserves. During the war he guested for Millwall.
League: App 9, Gls 0.

SCOTT, John A. *1950-1956*

Goalkeeper. Born: Crosby, near Whitehaven, 18 July 1928.
Debut v Manchester City (h) Division Two, 4 November 1950, D 1-1.
5ft 11in, 11st 2½lb (1951).
A former blacksmith at Birkby Colliery in Cumberland, Scott rarely played football at school and it was only when some pals asked him to go in goal during a 'kick about' that he was bitten by the soccer bug. He played for Crosby, then spent two and a half years at Workington. When Major Buckley was manager at Hull he invited Scott for trials at Boothferry Park but the youngster was not taken on. When Buckley became manager at Leeds he decided to have another look at Scott and signed him from Workington in May 1950. Ever-present in 1953-54, Scott was a very dependable 'keeper. He was also a noted golfer. He returned to Workington in summer 1956.
League: App 111, Gls 0; FA Cup: App 3, Gls 0.

SEARSON, Harry V. *1949-1952*

Goalkeeper. Born: Mansfield, 3 June 1924.
Debut v Carlisle United (a) FA Cup 3rd round, 7 January 1949, W 5-2.
6ft 1in, 12st 7lb (1949).
'Polly' Searson earned a reputation for long kicking and an ability to gather high centres during his days with Leeds. He was educated at High Oakham School and played for Mansfield and Nottinghamshire Schools and North Notts League side, Bilsthorpe Colliery (in 1941) before serving with the Fleet Air Arm in India. In 1942 he joined Sheffield Wednesday as an amateur, turning professional in August 1946. He returned to Mansfield in June 1947 and was transferred to Leeds (£2,000) in January 1949. During his time at Elland Road he was football coach to Hunslet Boys' Club and a noted club cricketer. When John Scott established himself, Searson asked for a transfer and moved to York City in November 1952, staying until 1954, when he joined Corby Town that summer. He is one of the few post-war players to play on his wedding day.
League: App 104, Gls 0; FA Cup: App 12, Gls 0.

SELLARS, Scott *1983-1986 & 1992-1993*

Midfield. Born: Sheffield, 27 November 1965.
Debut v Shrewsbury Town (a) Division Two, 7 May 1983, D 0-0.
5ft 6in, 10st (1986).
Early performances with Leeds United suggested that Sellars had a big future in the game. He was one of a number of talented youngsters encouraged to play open football by Leeds manager Eddie Gray, but struggled with some of the more physical aspects of the game. A pupil of Hindle House, Sheffield, he joined Leeds as an apprentice and turned professional in July 1983, three months after he made his League debut as a 17-year-old. After asking for a transfer he was sold to Blackburn Rovers (£20,000) in July 1986 and won a Full Members' Cup winners' medal at Wembley in 1987. In 1987-88 he was capped by England Under-21 against Scotland, France and Sweden. In 1991-92 he featured in Blackburn's Second Division promotion campaign but before he could help establish Rovers as a force in the Premiership he returned to Leeds for £800,000 in July 1992. He always seemed to struggle with injuries in his second spell at Elland Road and found himself on the fringes of the action. In March 1993 he joined Newcastle United for £700,000 and quickly returned to the Premiership as Kevin Keegan's Magpies swept to the First Division title. Competition at big-spending Newcastle was hot and in December 1995 Sellars was on the move again, this time going to Bolton for £720,000, but he could not prevent the Trotters from crashing out of the Premiership.
League: App 78/5, Gls 12; FA Cup: App 4, Gls 0; League Cup: App 5/1, Gls 1; Full Members' Cup: App 2, Gls 1; Europe: App 1, Gls 0.

SHACKLETON, Alan *1958-1959*

Centre-forward. Born: Padiham, near Burnley, 3 February 1934.
Debut v Manchester United (h) Division One, 1 November 1958, L 1-2.
5ft 11in, 11st 5lb (1959).
Shackleton was spotted by Leeds playing for Burnley in a Lancashire Senior Cup-tie against Accrington Stanley. He spent a year as an amateur on Bolton's books before joining Burnley in May 1954. He joined Leeds in October 1958 (£8,000) and maintained a good scoring rate – including a hat-trick in his fourth game – before going to Everton in September 1959. His career then drifted as he joined Nelson in summer 1960 and returned to the Football League after a £1,200 move to Oldham in August 1961. He was released in June 1962 and later joined Southern League Tonbridge.
League: App 30, Gls 16; FA Cup: App 1, Gls 1.

SHARP, Kevin *1992-1995*

Full back/midfield. Born: Ontario, Canada, 19 September 1974.
Debut v Crystal Palace (h) Premiership, 17 April 1993, D 0-0.

5ft 9in, 11st 11lb (1995).
Yet another from the FA Youth Cup-winning crop, blond bomber Sharp proved an effective left-sided player in either midfield or defence, acting as cover for Tony Dorigo in the latter role.

Although born in Canada, he was only 18 months old when his family returned to England where his father, Frank, once had trials with Tranmere Rovers when playing for Flint Town. Young Kevin was pigeon-toed as a youngster and later had to wear special shoes to correct a problem with the development of his knees, but it did not prevent him shining as a young footballer. He started with Poulton le Fylde in the Blackpool League before joining Blackpool Town. He then went on to the FA National School of Excellence for a couple of years. Together with Jamie Forrester he joined Auxerre in France and the pair cost Leeds £120,000 in September 1992 when Howard Wilkinson spotted their potential. An England Under-15, 16, 17 and 18 international, Sharp looked to have a promising future at Elland Road, but slipped down the pecking order and in December 1995 moved to Wigan for £50,000 with a clause giving United a further £25,000 after the 21-year-old makes 20 more appearances and another £25,000 after 40 games. In addition, United will receive 25 per cent of any profit if Wigan sell him on.
League: App 11/6, Gls 0;
Europe: App 0/1, Gls 0.

SHARPE, Ivan G. *1920-1922*

Winger. Born: St Albans, Hertfordshire, 15 June 1889.
Debut v Coventry City (h) Division Two, 1 December 1920, W 4-0.
5ft 6in, 10st 2lb (1913).
Famous sports journalist and author Ivan Sharpe was also one of England's greatest amateur players. A winger of great skill, he took his footballing talents wherever his journalistic career went. The son of a cobbler, he began at St Albans Abbey, then had spells with Watford and Glossop, winning the first of 12 amateur caps with the latter. In 1911 he joined Derby County, winning a Second Division championship medal in his first season and the following year won an Olympic soccer gold medal in Stockholm with great Britain. He played in a full international trial at Blackburn in 1912. In June 1913 he went to Leeds City, followed by a spell at Brighton. He also turned out for Nottingham Forest and Luton Town as an amateur. After World War One he played for Glossop, but returned to Elland Road with United in November 1920 – thus becoming the first man to play for both United and City. Tommy Lamph is the only other player to appear for both clubs. Sharpe retired in summer 1923 and went on to further his journalistic career. His soccer moves are reflected in the newspapers he worked for, starting with the *Herts Observer and St Albans Times*, *Glossop Chronicle*, *Yorkshire Evening News* (Leeds) and the *Sunday Chronicle*, whom he joined in 1922. In 1924 he became editor of *Athletic News* and was later editor of the *Sunday Chronicle*. Sharpe died in Southport on 9 February 1968, aged 78.
League: App 1, Gls 0.

SHAW, John *1971-1974*

Goalkeeper. Born: Stirling, 4 February 1954.
Debut v Lierse SK (h) UEFA Cup 1st round (1st leg), 29 September 1971, L 0-4.
6ft 1in, 13st 7lb (1971).
Shaw's only appearances for Leeds were in European ties – and he was substituted in both. With United holding a 2-0 first-leg lead in their first round UEFA Cup-tie against Belgium side Lierse SK, manager Revie fielded a string of reserves in the return leg. Leeds crashed 4-0 and Shaw was replaced by Gary Sprake during the game. Two years later Shaw figured in a dramatic match at Hibernian, keeping a clean sheet until he was injured and replaced by Glan Lethan. Shaw joined Leeds as an apprentice and turned professional in February 1971. He left for Bristol City on a free transfer in May 1984 and gave the Bristol club tremendous service, making 295 appearances, despite having to wait two years for his debut. He moved to Exeter City in the 1985 close season. during he later part of his career he suffered severe hair loss through a nervous complaint.
Europe: App 2, Gls 0.

SHERIDAN, John *1982-1989*

Midfield. Born: Manchester, 1 October 1964.
Debut v Middlesbrough (h) Division Two, 20 November 1982, D 0-0.
5ft 9in, 10st 8lb (1986).
Discarded by Manchester City, Sheridan went on to become a major influence in the Leeds midfield as they strove to recapture Division One status in the 1980s. He attended St Mary's School in Manchester and joined City on schoolboy forms but when he was released Leeds signed him in March 1982. Within six months he had made his League debut, his vision and

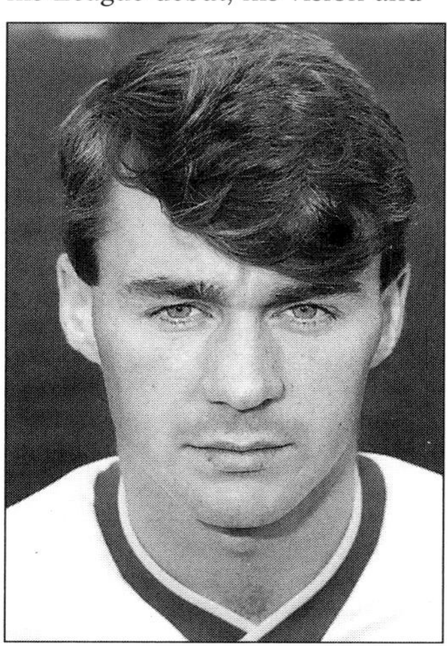

skill hallmarking him as a player for the future. He recovered well from a broken leg sustained at Barnsley in October 1983, to become United's most valuable playing asset, being particularly lethal from free-kicks and penalties. He played for the Republic of Ireland, through parental qualification, at Youth, Under-21 and Under-23 levels, before winning his first full cap in March 1988 and was a member of Jack Charlton's Irish squad for the European championships later that year. Leeds banked £650,000 when Sheridan was sold to Nottingham Forest in August 1989. Despite the big fee, Brian Clough did not give Sheridan his League debut and four months later, sold him to Sheffield Wednesday for £500,000. Sheridan was a member of the Republic of Ireland squads for the 1990 and 1994 World Cup. He scored the only goal of the 1991 League Cup Final when the Owls caused a big upset by beating Manchester United at Wembley. In February 1996 he went to Birmingham City on loan, playing against Leeds in a League Cup semi-final. Sheridan's brother, Darren, had a brief spell on United's books as a junior in 1984 and eventually became a Barnsley player after starring with non-League Winsford United.
League: App 230/5, Gls 48; FA Cup: App 11/1, Gls 1; League Cup: App 14, Gls 3, Full Members' Cup: App 6, Gls 0.

SHERWIN, Harry *1921-1925*

Right-half. Born: Walsall, late 1893.
Debut v Port Vale (h) Division Two, 27 August 1921, W 2-1.
5ft 8in, 11st 4lb (1925).
Sherwin was the first choice right-half during United's 1923-24 Division Two championship season. He played for Darlaston before joining Sunderland in December 1913. During World War One he spent the 1915-16

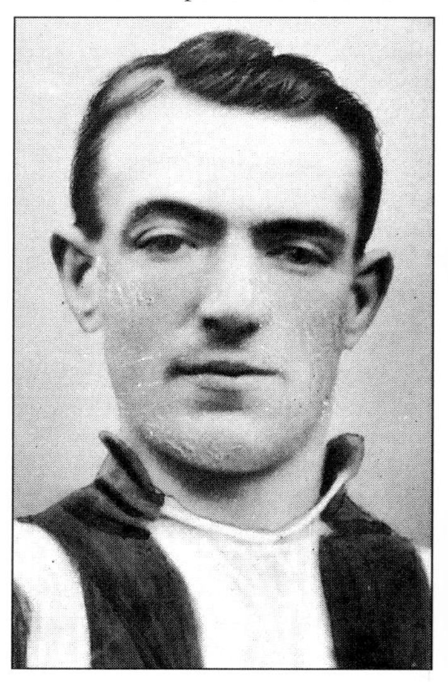

season with Sunderland Rovers, then made 91 wartime appearances as a guest with Leeds City, including the rarity of being a wartime ever-present in 1917-18. After hostilities ceased he returned to Roker Park, but joined United in May 1921. He was also a useful centre-half. In March 1925 he moved to Barnsley, with Leeds teammate Lawrie Baker. Sherwin died in Leeds on 8 January 1953.
League: App 98, Gls 2; FA Cup: App 9, Gls 0.

SHORT, John D. *1937-1948*

Inside-left. Born: Gateshead, 25 January 1921.
Debut v Preston North End (a) Division One, 31 August 1946, L 2-3.
5ft 10in, 12st (1953).
Short emerged during wartime football and went on to enjoy a lengthy and productive career. Leeds signed him from Gateshead junior club, St Hilda's, in February 1937 and his 36 goals in 58 wartime matches for United confirmed his pedigree. He was also a wartime guest at Newcastle

United and Hartlepools United and made his League debut for Leeds on the opening day of 1946-47. Transferred to Millwall in November 1948 (£4,000), he was appointed trainer-coach at The Den in November 1955 and retired with 243 League appearances for Millwall to his name. In June 1960 he became Huddersfield Town's coach and the following year occupied a similar post with Sheffield United, where he was appointed assistant manager to John Harris in August 1969. He was later chief scout and youth-team manager for the Blades before becoming physiotherapist at Gillingham in January 1978 and physio at Chesterfield in October 1981. In summer 1983 he was appointed trainer at Notts County, retiring in 1984.
League: App 60, Gls 18; FA Cup: App 3, Gls 1.

SHUTT, Carl S. *1989-1993*

Forward. Born: Sheffield, 10 October 1961.
Debut v Bournemouth (h) Division Two, 1 April 1989, W 3-0.
5ft 10in, 11st 10lb (1989).
Shutt quickly repaid a large slice of his £50,000 transfer fee by scoring a hat-trick on his debut for Leeds. He began in the Football League at the fairly advanced age of 23, when he joined Sheffield Wednesday from Spalding United (who were managed by Mick Hennigan when he joined them in May 1985). He maintained a good scoring record with the Owls before moving to Bristol City in October 1987. He joined Leeds in a player-exchange deal. Leeds received £200,000 for Bob Taylor and paid £50,000 for Shutt. He proved an excellent back-up striker for United and his finest hour came in Barcelona's Nou Camp Stadium when his late goal clinched United's 2-1 victory over Stuttgart in the infamous replayed European Cup game. His best season was 1990-91 when he forged a useful partnership with Lee Chapman after a loan spell in Sweden with Malmo in August 1990. He joined Birmingham City in November 1993, for £50,000, after two months on loan with the Blues, but when Barry Fry took over from Terry Cooper at St Andrew's, Shutt was loaned to Manchester City in December and started the following season on loan at Bradford City, joining the Paraders in a £75,000 transfer in September 1994. He went to the same school as Mel Sterland.
League: App 46/38, Gls 17, FA Cup: App 10, Gls 1; League Cup: App 6/2, Gls 2; Europe: App 0/2, Gls 1; Full Members' Cup: App 4/3, Gls 3.

SIBBALD, Bobby L. *1965-1969*

Full-back. Born: Hebburn, County Durham, 25 January 1948.
Debut (as sub) v Everton (a) Division One, 4 February 1967, L 0-2.
5ft 7in, 10st 3lb (1966).
Sibbald did not make much impression at Elland Road but rubbed shoulders with some of football's all-time greats in the NASL. He played for Jarrow, Felling and Hebburn Boys and was an apprentice at Leeds, signing for United in January 1965. He went to York City in February 1969. In July 1971 he joined Southport on a two-month trial before signing permanently. It proved an excellent move as he made 240 League appearances before teaming up with Los Angeles Aztecs in 1975, playing in the same side as Johann Cruyff and George Best. In 1980 he was appointed assistant coach to the Aztecs. He is reported still to be living in America, having enjoyed a big win on a US lottery.
League: App 1/1, Gls 0.

SIMMONDS R.Lyndon *1983-1987*

Forward. Born: Pontypool, Gwent, 11 November 1966.
Debut (as sub) v Blackburn Rovers (h) Division Two, 6 April 1985, D 0-0.
5ft 4in, 9st 10lb (1986).
A product of Blackwood Comprehensive School, Ebbw Vale, Simmonds played for Gwent and South Wales Schools. He was turned down by Arsenal after trials and was briefly on Cardiff City's books before joining Leeds as an apprentice, turning professional in July 1983. A prolific scorer in United's juniors and Reserves, he won five Welsh Youth caps and 11 at Schoolboy level. In October 1986 he began two months' loan at Swansea and in February 1987 went to Rochdale for the rest of the season, when Eddie Gray was in charge. Remarkably, he finished as top scorer and helped prevent relegation to the GM Vauxhall Conference. In May 1987 he joined Rochdale on a permanent basis (£4,000) and partnered another Leeds old boy, Derek Parlane in attack. Injury brought his career at Spotland to a premature end and he retired in 1987.
League: App 6/3, Gls 3; Full Members' Cup: App 1/1, Gls 0.

SINCLAIR, Ronnie M. *1986-1989*

Goalkeeper. Born: Stirling, 19 November 1964.
Debut v Blackburn Rovers (a) Division Two, 23 August 1986, L 1-2.
5ft 10in, 11st 9lb (1987).
A Scottish Schoolboy and Youth international, Sinclair was deputy to Mervyn Day in the 1980s. He went to Nottingham Forest from school and was signed as a professional in October 1982. He did not get a first-team break at the City Ground, but was loaned to Wrexham in March 1984, playing in the Welsh Cup Final that year against Shrewsbury Town. He was also loaned to Derby County (November 1984), Sheffield United (August 1985) and Leeds (March 1986). He impressed at Leeds and was signed on a free transfer in June 1986. However, his chances were few and in March 1987 he was loaned to Halifax Town for four games. He returned to Halifax Town for four games. He returned to Halifax in 1988-89 for another brief loan spell. Sinclair moved to Bristol City in September 1989. Yet another loan period followed (at Walsall in September 1991), but he enjoyed his longest spell of first-team football at Stoke City, whom he joined in November 1991 for £25,000. He featured in the Potters' 1992-93 Second Division championship-winning team before going on loan to Bradford City in August 1994 and then forcing his way back into Stoke's first team midway through that season. He was released by Stoke at the end of 1995-96.
League: App 8, Gls 0; League Cup: App 1, 0.

SISSONS, Albert E. *1925-1928*

Outside-right. Born: Kiveton Park, Sheffield, 5 July 1903.
Debut v Bury (h) Division One, 31 October 1925, L 2-3.
5ft 11in, 11st 12lb (1926).
Sissons made a name for himself in Sheffield junior football before arriving at Elland Road in October 1925. He began with Kiveton Park, where several clubs took an interest in his progress and Arsenal took him on trial. Doncaster Rovers signed him in July 1923 but a couple of years later he became a Leeds player. After making a useful contribution as understudy to Bobby Turnbull he moved to Southport in July 1928. He went to Northampton Town in July 1929 for a season before returning to the Sheffield area to play for Worksop Town. After football he worked as a male nurse at Winson Green Hospital in Birmingham, and died in that city on 4 October 1975, aged 72, after an overdose of aspirin when suffering from pneumonia, an inquest recording a verdict of misadventure. His son, Graham, played for Birmingham City, Peterborough United and Walsall after World War Two, and a cousin, Bill Sissons, was Lincoln City's goalkeeper in the 1920s.
League: App 30, Gls 1; A Cup: App 1, Gls 0.

SMELT, Alf *1920-1921*

Left-back. Born: Rotherham.
Debut v Leeds Steelworks (h) FA Cup preliminary round, 25 September 1920, W 7-0.
5ft 8in, 12st 3lb (1920).
Smelt played in one full League game after turning out in United's team which demolished Leeds Steelworks in the 1920-21 season. He was signed from Mexborough Town in the Midland League in July 1920. His younger brothers, Len and Tom, had more successful careers. Full-back Len was a member of Burnley's League championship-winning side of 1920-21; Tom was a centre-forward with Accrington Stanley, Exeter City, Chesterfield, Manchester City, Oldham Athletic, Crewe Alexandra, Scunthorpe United and Rotherham United. The Rotherham-born J.Smelt, who played for Leeds City during World War One, is believed to be a member of this family.
League: App 1, Gls 0; FA Cup*: App 1, Gls 0.
*This was one of United's preliminary round games in 1920-21.

SMITH, J.Barry *1951-1956*

Born: South Kirkby, near Hemsworth, 15 March 1934.
Debut v Fulham (h) Division Two, 13 September 1952, W 2-0.
5ft 10in, 12st 3lb (1951).
Barry Smith signed for Leeds as a 17-year-old from Farsley Celtic and marked his League debut with a goal. He played for Shipley St Walburga's School and Bradford Boys, Bradford United and the West Riding Youth team before joining Bradford's groundstaff and played in their Northern Intermediate League side before moving to Farsley. He joined Leeds in October 1951 and gave up his job as an apprentice plumber. He did his National Service with the Royal Artillery in Oswestry before being transferred to Bradford for a second time in May 1955. After 38 goals in a couple of seasons with the Avenue he was sold to Wrexham in June 1957. He played for Stockport County (July 1958), Headington United (October 1959), Oldham (loan, August 1960), Southport (August 1961) and Accrington Stanley (October 1961).
League: App 2, Gls 1.

SMITH, J.Eric *1960-1964*

Right-half. Born: Glasgow, 29 July 1934.
Debut v Liverpool (a) Division

Two, 20 August 1960, L 0-2.
5ft 5in, 11st 5½lb (1963).
Scottish international Eric Smith suffered badly from injuries during his time at Leeds. He began with St Andrew's Juveniles and Pollok in 1951, then Glasgow Benburb before joining Celtic in 1953 and became a regular at Parkhead, winning a Scottish Cup-winners' medal in 1956. He was capped twice in 1959 and signed for Leeds in June 1960 (£10,000). It was anticipated that his experience and grit would stiffen United's defence, but that idea was scuppered when he broke a leg in his first season with Leeds. In June 1964 he went to Morton, retiring in 1966 for a spell as coach with the Greenock club. He was manager for a short time in 1972, after spending some time in Cyprus as coach to Pezoporikos Larnaca. Shortly after recommending one of his young Morton players – Joe Jordan – to Leeds, he was appointed manager of Hamilton Academical in 1972, and he held that job until April 1978, when he became manager of Sharjah FC in the United Arab Emirates. Between June 1982 and May 1983 he was assistant manager to Don Revie at Al Nasr, becoming manager of Al Shaab the following year. He returned to Cyprus to coach Pezoporikos in the 1980s, and died of a heart attack on holiday in Dubai on 12 June 1991, when he was still coach of Pezoporikos.
League: App 65, Gls 3; FA Cup: App 4, Gls 0.

SMITH, Len *1922-1926*

Left-half. Born: Birmingham.
Debut v Derby County (a) Division Two, 28 April 1923, W 1-0.
5ft 10in, 12st 6lb (1925).
Len Smith was born 100 yards from Villa Park but was not picked up by Aston Villa. Instead he joined non-League Redditch and had trials with Leeds towards the end of 1921-22, signing for United in May 1922. He moved to Bristol Rovers in June 1926, but in March 1928 cancelled his contract to take up a commercial appointment. He re-emerged in June 1929 with Merthyr Town, for the Welsh club's last-ever season in the Football League. In May 1930 he joined Wolves, moving to Evesham Town in summer 1931 and Witley Wanderers in September 1932.
League: App 32, Gls 0; FA Cup: App 1, Gls 0.

SNODIN, Glynn *1987*

Full-back. Born: Rotherham, 14 February 1960.
Debut v Barnsley (a) Division Two, 16 August 1987, D 1-1.
5ft 6in, 9st 6lb (1987).
Glynn Snodin followed in the footsteps of his brother, Ian, in moving from Doncaster to Leeds to play for Billy Bremner. Glynn was taken on at Doncaster as a 16-year-old apprentice, turning professional in October 1977. He appeared for Rovers over 300 times, including six seasons playing alongside his brother. Within weeks the brotherly partnership was split, with Ian going to Leeds in May 1985 and Glynn transferring to Sheffield Wednesday (£135,000) the following month. In July 1987 he stepped out of the First Division to join Leeds in a £150,000 deal. A player with a terrific shot, he was a full-back and midfield player at Leeds. Glandular fever, a virus illness and injury all disrupted his career for a couple of seasons but he refused to give in to those problems and attempted comebacks on loan at Oldham (August 1991) and Rotherham United (February 1992) before leaving Leeds on a free transfer to Hearts in March 1992. He clinched his move to Boundary Park with only 60 seconds to spare after his car broke down and he needed two lifts and a mile-long run to sign in time to make his debut for the Latics. He returned to English football with Barnsley in July 1993 and in 1995-96 he was playing for Gainsborough Trinity.
League: App 83/11, Gls 10; FA Cup: App 5/2, Gls 0; League Cup: App 5/1, Gls 2; Full Members' Cup: App 6, Gls 0.

SNODIN, Ian *1985-1987*

Midfield. Born: Thrybergh, near Rotherham, 15 August 1963.
Debut v Fulham (a) Division Two, 17 August 1985, L 1-2.
5ft 7in, 8st 11½lb (1987).
United received a club record fee of £800,000 when they sold Ian Snodin to Everton in January 1986. Like his brother, Glynn, he joined Doncaster Rovers, in August 1980, as a teenager and was capped for England Youth in 1981 and 1982. Although he was with an unfashionable club, Snodin's displays won him four Under-23 caps in 1985. In May that year he joined Leeds (£250,000) and succeeded Peter Lorimer as captain. His boss at Rovers was Billy Bremner, and Bremner sold him again in January 1986, this time to Everton, as Leeds banked a healthy profit. He added impetus to Everton's midfield and just qualified to win a League championship medal in 1986-87. He later switched to right-back and only injury prevented him from being capped by England in Albania in 1989. He did play for

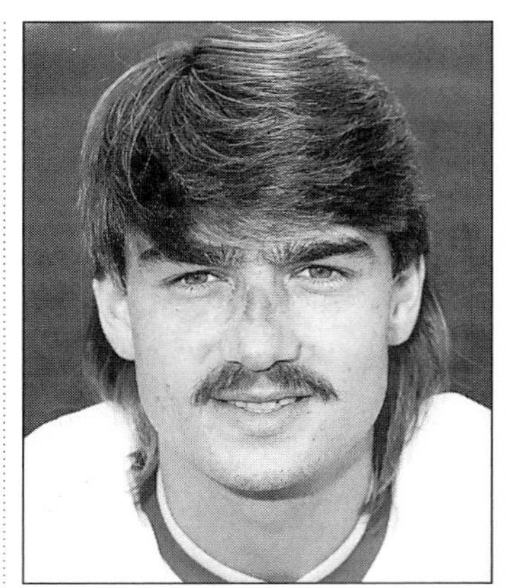

England 'B' but injuries continued to blight him and after going to Sunderland on loan (October 1994) he went to Oldham Athletic, where he was sent off on his debut in January 1995.
League: App 51, Gls 6; FA Cup: App 1, Gls 0; League Cup: App 3, Gls 2.

SPEAK, George *1923-1925*

Left-back. Born: Blackburn, 7 November 1890.
Debut v Stoke (a) Division Two, 25 August 1923, D 1-1.
5ft 8½in, 11st 7lb (1922).
Speak finished his distinguished career by winning a Division Two championship medal with Leeds in 1923-24. A rugged fearless character noted for his powerful clearance kicking, he began with Clitheroe Central, then Darwen, before having trials with Liverpool. In May 1911 he joined Grimsby Town and won his League spurs with them before going to Gainsborough Trinity in July 1913 and West Ham United in May 1914. During World War One he guested for Preston and signed for them in March 1919. He was sold to Leeds for £250 in August 1923 and stayed with United until he retired in summer 1925. He died in Blackburn on 10 March 1953, aged 62.
League: App 28, Gls 0; FA Cup: App 4, Gls 0.

SPEED, Gary A. *1987-1996*

Forward. Born: Mancot, North Wales, 8 September 1969.
Debut v Oldham Athletic (h) Division Two, 6 May 1989, D 0-0.
6ft, 12st (1989).
Speed joined Leeds straight from Hawarden Grammar School in 1987. A Welsh Youth international, he got his first-team chance after scoring in 12 consecutive Northern Intermediate League games. With only one full senior appearance to his name, Speed was called up for Wales in October 1989, as a late replacement to the squad for a World Cup qualifier at Wrexham. On that occasion he sat out the game on the substitutes' bench but he made a big impact as Leeds raced to the Second Division title the following season and on 19 and 20 May turned out for Wales Under-21 against Poland and then for the full side against Costa Rica. That was the start of a long international career which has seen him win 34 caps to date. For Leeds he had a truly tremendous League championship-winning season in 1991-92 when his forays down

the left and his ability in the air brought him, and others, plenty of goals. He was always one of the first names on Howard Wilkinson's team-sheet and a £3.4 million bid from Everton for the talented Welshman was turned down in March 1996, but under three months later the deal did go through, enabling Speed to join the side he had supported as a youngster when he played for Manchester City's nursery side, Blue Star, until he was 15.
League: App 231/16, Gls 39; FA Cup: App 21/1, Gls 5; League Cup: App 25, Gls 11; Europe: App 9, Gls 2; Charity Shield: App 1, Gls 0; Full Members' Cup: App 4/3, Gls 0.

SPRAKE, Gary *1962-1973*

Goalkeeper. Born: Winchwen, near Swansea, 3 April 1945.
Debut v Southampton (a) Division Two, 17 March 1962, L 1-4.
6ft, 13st 3lb (1971).
Gary Spake, then a 16-year-old apprentice, made his League debut in place of Tommy Younger, who had fallen ill. Sprake, who used to live near the great Welsh goalkeeper, Jack Kelsey, won Welsh Schools caps and turned professional in May 1962. He became Wales' youngest-ever 'keeper at 18 years 7 months and 17 days when he played against Scotland in November 1963. He won 37 Welsh caps – 32 of them as a Leeds player – and five at Under-23 level. An acrobatic player,

although prone to lapses in concentration, he was ever-present in United's 1968-69 championship side and also won a League Cup winners' medal,

two Inter-Cities Fairs Cup medals and a Division Two championship medal. After making more appearances than any other Leeds goalie, he was transferred to Birmingham in October 1973 (£100,000) but was soon forced to retire through illness. Currently he lives in Solihull and is a training officer with Birmingham City Council.
League: App 380, Gls 0; FA Cup: App 45, Gls 0; League Cup: App 22, Gls 0; Europe: App 57/2, Gls 0; Charity Shield: App 1, Gls 0.

SPROSTON, Bert *1933-1938*

Right-back. Born: Elworth, near Sandbach, 22 June 1914.
Debut v Chelsea (a) Division One, 23 December 1934, D 1-1.
5ft 7½in, 11st 10lb (1938).
Elegant right-back Bert Sproston emerged from non-League football to be one of England's most cultured defenders of the

1930s. He was rejected by Huddersfield Town after trials and went to Sandbach Ramblers, where he ousted his brother from the first team. Leeds signed Sproston as a 17-year-old from Sandbach in May 1933. Seven months later he made his League debut and established himself the following season. He won his first England cap in 1936 and had eight England appearances to his name when hard-up Leeds sold him to Spurs (near-record £9,500) in June 1938. Sproston did not settle in London and in November, only six months after going to the capital, he moved to Manchester City in another £9,500 deal – this one being a bit more unusual. He travelled to Manchester with his Spurs' teammates on a Friday, the deal was completed that night and he turned out against his old team the following day. During the war Sproston guested for Port Vale and Millwall and saw active service with the Army in India. He returned to City after the war and won a Second Division championship medal with them in 1946-47, to add to his 11 England caps, two wartime international appearances and Football League representative honours. In August 1950 he joined Ashton United and in July 1951 was appointed trainer at Bolton and later scouted for the Burnden Park club.
League: App 130, Gls 1; FA Cup: App 10, Gls 0.

STACEY, Alex *1927-1933*

Right-half. Born: London, *c.*1908.
Debut v Oldham Athletic (a) Division Two, 10 March 1928, W 1-0.
5ft 8in, 10st 12lb (1930).
Stacey was a sturdily-built replacement for the classy Willis Edwards. A product of Grove House Lads Club in Manchester, he played for Northwich Victoria before going to New Mills. He joined Leeds in October 1927 and stepped into the breach when Edwards was out of action with cartilage trouble. Because of his loyalty, he was granted a benefit but, after being the backbone of United's Central League side for over six years, he was transferred to Sheffield United in November 1933. A broken leg the following April effectively ended his playing career. His last senior game for the Blades was in January 1937 and he was not retained at the end of that season. He died in summer 1993.
League: App 51, Gls 0.

STEPHENSON, J.Eric *1933-1944*

Inside-left. Born: Bexleyheath, Kent, September 1914.
Debut v Portsmouth (h) Division One, 2 March 1935, W 3-1.
5ft 6½in, 10st 2lb (1938).
Eric Stephenson was tragically cut down in his prime during World War Two, after promising to be one of the big stars of the English game. He was an outstanding prospect at Tom Hood School in Leytonstone before moving to Leeds with his parents. He played for Outwood Stormcocks and Harrogate but trained at Elland Road and signed amateur forms, then turned professional in September 1934. He rose rapidly through the ranks and won two full England caps before the war. He played for Leeds for a couple of wartime seasons, but went on to become a major in the Ghurka Rifles in Burma, where he died on active service on 8 September 1944. During 1946-47, Leeds played Celtic in benefit game for Stephenson's widow. During the 1930s he was a lieutenant in the 30th Leeds Company Boys' Brigade.
League: App 111, Gls 21; FA Cup: App 4, Gls 1.

STERLAND, Mel *1989-1994*

Right-back. Born: Sheffield, 1 October 1961.
Debut v Newcastle United (a) Division Two, 19 August 1989, L 2-5.
5ft 10in, 12st 10lb (1989).
Attacking right-back Mel Sterland joined Leeds for £600,000 in July 1989 to link up with his old boss, Howard Wilkinson. He had joined Sheffield Wednesday in June 1978, straight from Waltheof School, turning professional in October 1979. He enjoyed his best spell at Hillsborough under Wilkinson and played a key role in Wednesday's promotion to Division One in 1984. The holder of seven England Under-21 caps, he also played for England 'B' and won a full cap against Saudi Arabia in November 1988. Wednesday sold Sterland to Rangers for a club record £800,000 in March 1989 and he stayed just long enough at Ibrox to win a Scottish League championship medal. Dubbed 'Zico' by Leeds fans because of his ability to score spectacular goals, his dynamic runs down the right and booming crosses brought a stack of goals for Lee Chapman as Leeds swept to the Second Division title and then the League championship in the space of three years. Sterland also contributed his fair share of goals, many of them thunderous free-kicks, but injuries took their toll, forcing him to give up the League game. In summer 1994 he was appointed player-manager of Boston United, a post he held until May 1996.
League: App 111/3, Gls 16; FA Cup: App 10, Gls 1; League Cup: App 13, Gls 1; Full Members' Cup: App 9, Gls 2.

STEVENSON, W.Byron *1973-1982*

Midfield/defender. Born Llanelli, 7 September 1956.
Debut v Sheffield United (a) Division One, 1 April 1975, D 1-1.
6ft 1in, 11st (1977).
Stevenson was recruited as a youngster and turned professional in September 1973. Initially he was earmarked as a replacement for Norman Hunter but found himself filling a variety of defensive positions. He won three Welsh Under-21 caps and made 15 appearances for the full side. A moment of madness in Izmir against Turkey in November 1979 certainly cost him several Welsh caps. He was sent off for violent conduct and was banned by UEFA from the European game for over four years, although the sentence was later reduced. In March 1982, Leeds found themselves in desperate need of a striker as they fought against relegation, so Stevenson was traded for Birmingham City forward Frank Worthington. At Birmingham, Stevenson resumed his international career before going to Bristol Rovers in July 1985. In 1988 he was assisting Garforth in the Northern Counties East League and running the Angel Hotel at nearby Rothwell. He later ran the Golden Lion in Pudsey.
League: App 88/7, Gls 4; FA Cup: App 5, Gls 0; League Cup: App 7/1, Gls 1; Europe: App 2, Gls 0.

STEVENSON, Ernie *1951-1952*

Inside-left. Born: Rotherham, 28 December 1923.
Debut v Sheffield United (h) Division Two, 3 February 1951, W 1-0.
5ft 6in, 10st 6lb (1951).
Like so many of his contemporaries, Ernie Stevenson's career was severely disrupted by the war. After playing for Wath Wanderers, Wolves' nursery side, he was a junior at Molineux during the war and played in the first leg of the League North Cup in 1942 and the War Cup-winners' Cup the following year. In October 1948 he went to Cardiff and in February 1950 joined Southampton, but the following February became a Leeds player when he was signed by his old Wolves boss, Major Frank Buckley, in a straight swap for Frank Dudley. In July 1952 he left for Wisbech Town (£1,000). He died in St Helens on 15 October 1970.
League: App 16, Gls 5.

STEWART, David S. *1973-1978*

Goalkeeper. Born: Glasgow, 11 March 1947.
Debut v Wolverhampton Wanderers (h) FA Cup 3rd round replay, 9 January 1974, W 1-0.
6ft 1½in, 12st (1977).
David Stewart, a marvellous reflex goalkeeper, played in United's 1974 European Cup Final side after a long and patient wait as understudy to David Harvey. Stewart played for local Glasgow sides, Wellshot, Shettleston Violet and Kilsyth Rangers, winning a Scottish Junior Cup medal with the latter in 1967. He worked as an upholsterer and carpet fitter in those days and joined Ayr United in the 1967 close season as a part-timer. Some excellent displays saw him capped at Scottish Under-23 level and a £30,000 move took him to Leeds in October 1973. Although he had to play second fiddle to Harvey most of the time, Stewart was good enough to win a full Scottish cap in 1978, giving Leeds two Scottish international 'keepers on their books. He marked his only full international with a penalty save. Harvey won back his Leeds place and Stewart was sold to West Bromwich Albion (£70,000) in November 1978. Swansea paid £60,000 for him in February 1980 and he won a 1981 Welsh Cup medal. In July 1982 he moved to Royden FC (Hong Kong). He later worked as a goldsmith in Swansea.
League: App 55, Gls 0; FA Cup: App 8, Gls 0; League Cup: App 6, Gls 0; Europe: App 5, Gls 0.

STEWART, J.Gordon *1951-1952*

Inside-forward. Born: Durban, South Africa, 7 August 1927.
Debut v West Ham United (h) Division Two, 26 January 1952, W 3-1.
5ft 7in, 10st (1952).
Leeds scouts Willis Edwards and Frank Taylor spotted Stewart playing for South Africa against a touring Wolves side when they were on the look-out for talent in that country. United signed him from Parkhill FC and he sailed aboard the liner Caernarfon Castle to England in October 1951. Also on board was another inside-forward called Skene but he was not taken on by Leeds after trials. Within three months of his arrival, Stewart made his first-team debut but he was largely confined to the Reserves and returned to South Africa in 1953 and worked as an engineering representative. He died as a result of a car crash in Northern Natal in December 1980.
League: App 9, Gls 2; FA Cup: App 2, Gls 0.

STILES, John C. *1984-1989*

Midfield. Born: Manchester, 6 May 1964.
Debut v Middlesbrough (a) Division Two, 2 March 1985, D 0-0.
5ft 9½in, 10st 12lb (1986).
John Stiles certainly had a hard family act to follow in football. His father Nobby, the Manchester United wing-half, was one of England's 1966 World Cup heroes and his uncle, Johnny Giles, had been a legend at Elland Road. It was Giles who gave his nephew his first break by signing him for Shamrock Rovers. Stiles played alongside his cousin, Johnny's son Michael, at Shamrock in 1981-82. Stiles then tried his luck in the NASL with Vancouver Whitecaps before joining Leeds in April 1984. A gritty midfielder he enjoyed good form in United's progress to the 1987 FA Cup semi-final but struggled with injuries the following two seasons. He was transferred to Doncaster Rovers for £40,000 in August 1989. He was a regular at Belle Vue for a couple of seasons, but lost his place through injury, was loaned to Rochdale in March 1992 and after playing in Ireland joined Gainsborough Trinity.
League: App 51/16, Gls 2; FA Cup: App 5, Gls 1; League Cup: App 4/2, Gls 0; Full Members' Cup: App 1/2, Gls 0.

STORRIE, Jim *1962-1967*

Centre-forward. Born: Kirkintilloch, Lanarkshire, 31 March 1940.
Debut v Stoke City (a) Division Two, 18 August 1962, W 1-0.
5ft 8½in, 11st 4lb (1963).
Storrie's goals helped United establish themselves as a force to be reckoned with on their return to Division One in 1964-65. He began in Scottish junior football with Kilsyth Rangers, then joined Airdrie in December 1957 where he was a prolific scorer. Leeds bought him (£15,650) in June 1962 and he marked his debut with the winning goal on the opening day of the following season. He finished 1962-63 with 25 League goals, played his part in United's promotion drive the following season and was top scorer when they returned to Division One. In February 1967 he signed for Aberdeen and missed a penalty in that year's Scottish Cup Final, when Celtic won 2-0. In December 1967 he joined Rotherham United and moved to Portsmouth in December 1969. He began a loan spell with Aldershot in February 1972 before joining St Mirren as player-coach in October the same year. Storrie was later player-manager of Waterloovile, coach at Airdrie and manager of St Johnstone. His father-in-law, Tony Weldon, played for Airdrie, Everton, Hull City, West Ham United, Lovells Athletic and Rochdale.
League: App 123/3, Gls 58; FA Cup: App 12, Gls 3; League Cup: App 8, Gls 5; Europe: App 10, Gls 1.

STRACHAN, Gordon D. *1989-1995*

Midfield. Born: Edinburgh, 9 February 1957.
Debut v Portsmouth (h) Division Two, 25 March 1989, W 1-0.
5ft 6in, 10st 3lb (1989).
Scottish international Strachan was signed by Leeds for £300,000 from Manchester United, just before the transfer deadline in March 1989. He enjoyed a top-level career on both sides of the border, winning a host of honours. A pupil at Craigroyston School, he represented Edinburgh Schools before joining Dundee as a schoolboy in October 1971 and was transferred to Aberdeen

(£50,000) in November 1977. At Pittodrie he won two Scottish League championship medals (1980 and 1984), a hat-trick of Scottish Cup winners' medals (1982 to 1984) and a European Cup-winners' Cup medal (1983). He also played in the 1979 Scottish League Cup Final and was Scottish Player of the Year in 1979-80. A £500,000 transfer took him to Old Trafford in August 1984 and he won an FA Cup-winners' medal the following year. He won his first Scottish cap in May 1980 against Northern Ireland and was a prominent figure in Scotland's World Cup campaigns of 1982 and 1986. His form at Leeds was good enough to earn him an international recall in October 1989 and he was the inspirational skipper of United's Second Division title-winning team. Anyone who felt that Strachan would lack pace back at the top level was woefully wide of the mark as he was named Footballer of the Year in 1991, led Leeds to the League championship the following season, and was awarded the OBE in New Year 1993. Despite several other contenders for his place on the right of United's midfield, Strachan outlasted them all with great skill and dedication. His much-publicised diet of seawood pills and bananas helped, but he was a model professional who was being strongly tipped to take over from Howard Wilkinson as the next man in charge at Elland Road. After retiring from international football, with 50 caps to his credit, Strachan started to play less club games because of a back injury and in October 1994 announced he was going to quit at the end of the season. He actually decided to call it a day the following January and concentrated on coaching matters at Leeds, but within two months his old boss at Old Trafford, Ron Atkinson, lured him to Coventry in March 1995 with the promise that the copper-haired Scot would be his successor at Highfield Road. It was an offer Strachan could not refuse and before the end of the season he had his boots on again, also playing in 1995-96 as Coventry just avoided relegation. His son, Gavin, signed associate schoolboy forms with Leeds in December 1994 and was part of the 1995-96 YTS intake.
League: App 188/9, Gls 37; FA Cup: App 14, Gls 2; League Cup: App 18, Gls 3; Europe: App 5, Gls 1; Charity Shield: App 0/1, Gls 0; Full Members' Cup: App 9, Gls 2.

STRANDLI, Frank *1993-1994*

Forward. Born: Norway, 16 May 1972.
Debut (as sub) v Middlesbrough (h) 30 January 1993, Premiership, W 3-0.
6ft 1in, 13st 13lb (1994).
Just minutes after coming on for Rod Wallace, international striker Frank Strandli opened the scoring against Middlesbrough, but it was to prove a false start for the big Norwegian. He had arrived at Elland Road just days earlier in a £250,000 transfer from 1K Start, but he struggled to adapt to the pace of the English game and his career at both domestic and international level dipped. It had all looked so promising for a player who had first trained with Leeds in 1991 and had been a fully paid-up member of the Leeds United Supporters' Club. He was capped by Norway as a 17-year-old against Bermuda. Leeds wanted him to come to England in

October 1992, but he had to complete his National Service with the Norwegian Army and his move was delayed because of difficulties in getting a work permit. He did get half a game in Leeds colours in a friendly against AC Milan in December, a month after collecting his sixth Norwegian cap against China. However, it all turned sour at Leeds and, suffering from homesickness, he failed to start a Premiership game in 1993-94 and in November 1994 was transferred to SK Brann for an undisclosed fee after spending six months on loan with the Norwegian club.
League: App 5/9, Gls 2; FA Cup: 1 App, Gls 0; League Cup: Apps 0/1, Gls 0.

STUART, George E. *1920-1921*

Wing-half. Born: East Wemyss, Fife.
Debut v Boothtown (h) FA Cup Extra preliminary round, 11 September 1920, W 5-2.
5ft 7in, 11st 7lb (1920).
Stuart was signed from Dundee in July 1920, for United's first campaign in the Football League. He played in both FA Cup preliminary ties that season and made his sole League appearance on the same day Ernie Hart made his debut at centre-half.
League: App 1, Gls 0; FA Cup*: App 2, Gls 0.
*These were United's preliminary round games in 1920-21.

SUTHERLAND, Harry R. *1938-1947*

Centre-forward. Born: Salford, 30 July 1915.
Debut v Wolverhampton Wanderers (a) Division One, 18 February 1939, L 1-4.
Sutherland joined Leeds from Sedgeley Park in July 1938 with a big goalscoring reputation. A two-goal debut in the Reserves clinched him a professional contract and he also scored on his League debut. He looked to have the makings of a good player but the war disrupted his career. He turned out for Leeds, Southport, Rochdale, Accrington Stanley, Doncaster and Chesterfield in wartime before resuming his career at Elland Road. In May 1947 he was transferred to Exeter City, then went to Bournemouth in July 1948 but failed to get into their first team and was given a free transfer in May 1949.
League: App 3, Gls 1.

SWAN, Jack *1921-1925*

Forward. Born: Easington, County Durham, 10 July 1893.
Debut v Hull City (a) Division Two, 19 November 1921, L 0-1.
5ft 10in, 11st 7lb (1922).

Swan was United's top scorer in their 1923-24 Division Two championship-winning season. He began with Seaham Harbour before joining Huddersfield Town in October 1919, and played in Town's 1920 FA Cup Final side which lost to Aston Villa. After losing his place to England international Clem Stephenson, who guested for Leeds in World War One, Swan joined Leeds in November 1921. His thunderbolt shooting – he was noted for his left foot – served Leeds well until he moved to Watford in September 1925. He joined QPR (February 1927), Thames (July 1928), and Lovells Athletic (October 1929). In 1986 he was living in Hendon and it was believed that no one still alive had played in an earlier FA Cup Final.
League: App 108, Gls 47; FA Cup: App 8, Gls 3.

SWAN, Peter H. *1985-1989*

Defender/forward. Born: Leeds, 28 September 1966.
Debut (as sub) v Manchester City (a) Full Members' Cup, 14 October 1985, L 1-6.
6ft, 11st 12lb (1987).
Although primarily a defender, Swan contributed some useful goals when used as a target man in attack, where he made good use of his physique. A pupil of Middleton Park School, he represented Yorkshire at Under-15 and Under-18 levels and played for Yorkshire Amateurs. After serving his apprenticeship he signed for Leeds in August 1984. He was sold to Hull City for £200,000 in March 1989, a club record fee for the Tigers. Port Vale paid £300,000 for Swan in August 1991 and he played at Wembley in 1993 in Vale's Autoglass Trophy Final side which beat Stockport County 2-1. Eight days later he returned to Wembley as Vale tackled West Brom in the Second Division Play-off Final, but suffered the indignity of being sent off as Albion won 3-0. In July 1994 he was signed by Plymouth for £300,000 and midway through the following season he moved to Burnley.
League: App 43/6, Gls 11; FA Cup: App 3, Gls 0; League Cup: App 3, Gls 2; Full Members' Cup: App 1/2, Gls 0.

SWINBURNE, Trevor *1985-1986*

Goalkeeper. Born: East Rainton, County Durham, 20 June 1953.
Debut v Grimsby Town (h) Division Two, 19 October 1985, D 1-1.
6ft, 14st 7lb (1985).
Swinburne was a veteran when he signed for Leeds in the 1985 close season as cover for Mervyn Day. He played for Lambton and Hetton Boys before joining Sunderland as an apprentice in July 1968, turning professional in June 1970. He made only ten appearances for Sunderland in seven seasons and was on loan to Sheffield United in December 1976. He moved to Carlisle in May 1977 and was an automatic choice, making 248 League appearances before going to Brentford in August 1983. Leeds signed him from the Bees and, after a loan period with Doncaster (September 1985) he joined Lincoln City in February 1986 on a free transfer. He retired in May 1987 and became a prison officer in Leicestershire. His father, Tom, played in goal for Newcastle United before and after the war and won an England wartime cap in 1940. Trevor's elder brother, Alan, was also on Newcastle's books and made four appearances in goal for Oldham Athletic.
League: App 2, Gls 0.

TAYLOR, Frank J. *1949-1950*

Outside-left. Born: Magherafelt, Co Londonderry, 2 January 1923.
Debut v Preston North End (h) Division Two, 24 December 1949, W 3-1.
5ft 6in, 11st (1950).
Taylor, an Irish junior international, signed from Bangor in July 1949. He worked as a draughtsman in Ireland.
League: App 3, Gls 0.

TAYLOR, J. Bob *1985-1989*

Forward. Born: Easington, County Durham, 3 February 1967.
Debut v Millwall (h) Division Two, 12 April 1986, W 3-1.
5ft 10in, 11st 2lb (1986).
Dick Malone, the manager of Northern Ireland side Horden Colliery Welfare, recommended his teenage centre-forward, Bob Taylor, to United's chief scout Dave Blakey. Malone, who was a member of Sunderland's 1973 FA Cup winning side against Leeds in 1973, reckoned that local council worker Taylor had the ability to score goals at League level. Taylor, who captained his district schools team, went to Leeds for trials in December 1985 and netted a hat-trick in his first game for United's juniors. He was signed and the following season was leading scorer for the Reserves. He left for Bristol City just before the transfer deadline in 1989, in an exchange deal involving Carl Shutt. He was an instant success at Ashton Gate, finishing City's promotion season as the Third Division's top scorer. He quickly scored 50 goals for City, triggering a £300,000 move to West Bromwich in January 1992. At The Hawthorns he proved equally prolific, scoring 30 League goals in 1992-93 when the Baggies swept into Division One via a Wembley Play-off.
League: App 34/9, Gls 9; FA Cup: App 1, Gls 0; League Cup: App 5/1, Gls 3; Full Members' Cup: App 3/1, Gls 1.

TAYLOR, J.Brian *1951-1953*

Goalkeeper. Born: Rossington, near Doncaster, 7 October 1931.
Debut v Birmingham City (a) Division Two, 22 August 1951, D 1-1.
5ft 10in, 11st 3lb (1951).
Leeds called back Taylor from National Service at York to make his League debut and he went on to make 11 consecutive appearances that season. He began as an amateur on Sheffield Wednesday's books, then joined Doncaster Rovers in March 1949. He went out of League Football during a spell with Worksop Town but Leeds, anxious to strengthen their squad, signed him in March 1951. In the 1953 close season he went to King's Lynn before moving to Bradford in June 1954.
League: App 11, Gls 0.

THOM, Jack *1924-1927*

Centre-forward. Born: Hurlford, Ayrshire, 18 May 1899.
Debut v Notts County (a) Division One, 1 September 1924, L 0-1.
5ft 8in, 12st (1924).
Thom was given little chance to show what he could do at Leeds but went on to enjoy a fair amount of success with other clubs. He began as a 17-year-old with Hurlford Thistle and, after unsuccessful trials with Birmingham, signed for Nottingham Forest in August 1922. He failed to get into the first team and was released in summer 1923, joining North Eastern League club, Workington, where he scored 30 goals in his first season. Leeds signed him

(£430) in May 1924 and he was transferred to Bristol Rovers in June 1927 (£175). In August 1928 he returned to Workington, then joined Aldershot in June 1930 and scored nearly 100 goals for them before joining Guildford in the 1933 close season. Later he returned to Aldershot as reserve-team trainer and was also a gateman at the Recreation Ground.
League: App 7, Gls 3.

THOMAS, D. Gwyn *1975-1984*

Midfield. Born: Swansea, 26 September 1957.
Debut (as sub) v Wolverhampton Wanderers (a) Division One, 26 April 1975, D 1-1.
5ft 8in, 11st (1982).
A prolific goalscorer at junior and reserve level, Thomas was converted to a hustling midfielder. He won Welsh

Schoolboy honours before joining Leeds in July 1975, after serving his apprenticeship, and he later won three Under-21 caps. After being converted to midfield he earned full international call-up but was injured playing prior to the game and had to pull out. In March 1984 he was sold to Barnsley (£40,000) and became a permanent fixture in their midfield until he broke a leg in 1989. Thomas fought back from that injury and joined Hull City in March 1990, for £25,000. In August 1991 he moved to Carlisle United, his final League club.
League: App 79/10, Gls 3; FA Cup: App 4/1, Gls 0; League Cup: App 9, Gls 0.

THOMAS, Mickey *1989-1990*

Midfield. Born: Mochdre, New Colwyn Bay, 7 July 1954.
Debut v Newcastle United (a) Division Two, 19 August 1989, L 2-5.
5ft 6in, 10st 7lb (1989).
Leeds United became Thomas' tenth Football League club when he joined the Elland Road payroll for £10,000 in June 1989. However, injury and illness restricted his first-team appearances to a minimum and he joined Stoke City on loan just before the 1990 March transfer deadline. After starring for Clwydand Conwy and North Wales Schools, Thomas began his long Football League career with Wrexham as an amateur, turning professional in April 1972. His bustling style earned rave reviews and he was soon in demand in a series of big-money moves in a career that saw him win 51 full Welsh caps and honours at Under-23 and 21 level. His travels took him to Manchester United (November 1978) £300,000; Everton (August 1981) £450,000; Brighton (November 1981) £400,000; Stoke City (August 1982) £200,000; Chelsea (January 1984) £75,000; West Bromwich Albion (September 1985); Derby County (March 1986); on loan to Wichita (cs 1986) in the American Indoor Soccer League; Shrewsbury Town (cs 1988) then Leeds, for a fee fixed at a tribunal. With only three League appearances for Leeds to his name, he joined Stoke on a permanent basis in August 1990, returning to his first club, Wrexham, in August 1991 at the age of 37. His fearsome free-kick helped Wrexham to a sensational FA Cup victory over Arsenal in January 1992 but later that year he made the headlines for the wrong reasons when he was the victim of a stabbling in a domestic incident; the following year he was jailed for his part in a counterfeit money racket. On his return to civilian life in July 1993 he linked up with Conway United but did not stay long and became manager of Portmadog.
League: App 3, Gls 0.

THOMPSON, Nigel D. *1984-1988*

Defender/midfield. Born: Leeds, 1 March 1967.
Debut v Swansea City (a) Division Two, 7 May 1984, D 2-2.
5ft 7in, 10st 12lb (1986).
Thompson, a left-sided midfielder or full-back, joined Leeds from Lawnswood School after playing for Leeds City Boys and West Yorkshire Boys and was a member of England's Under-18 squad. In August 1986 he began a spell on loan at Rochdale before joining Chesterfield in March 1988 (£10,000). A bad knee injury saw his League career ended during the 1989-90 season. He then played for Colne Dynamoes, Gainsborough Trinity, Alfreton Town and Goole Town.
League: App 6/1, Gls 0; League Cup: App 2, Gls 0; Full Members' Cup: 1/1, Gls 0.

THOMPSON, Robert *1920-1921*

Centre-forward. Born: Eldon, near Bishop, Auckland.
Debut v Port Vale (a) Division Two, 28 August 1920, L 0-2.
6ft, 12st (1920).
Thompson earned himself a place in United's record books by scoring the club's first-ever League hat-trick, on 11 December 1920, against Notts County at Elland Road. He also finished as top scorer in United's first League season. He was the fastest player on Leeds books in 1920, having won the famous Powderhall Sprint (now the Skol Sprint) in Edinburgh. Preston North End were the first League side to take him on, but he returned to the North-East in August 1919 to play for Durham City, from where he joined Leeds in July 1920. After Leeds bought Tommy Howarth, Thompson found himself on the sidelines and went to Ashington in May 1921. He later played for Luton Town (June 1922), Pontypridd (cs 1923, scoring 51 goals for them), Accrington Stanley (cs 1924), Bury (May 1925), Hartlepools United (December 1926) and Goole Town (January 1927). In February 1924 he represented the Welsh League against the Irish Free State.
League: App 23, Gls 11; FA Cup* App 2, Gls 1.
*These were United's preliminary round games in 1920-21.

THOMSON, John *1924-1939*

Inside-right. Born: Loanhead, near Edinburgh, 14 April 1916.
Debut v Everton (h) Division One, 17 October 1936, W 3-0.
Thomson was picked up by Leeds as an 18-year-old from Loanhead Steelworks in September 1934. He made a scoring debut and looked set for a long run in the first team. But the purchase of George Ainsley pushed him out of the limelight and he moved to Grimsby Town in February 1939. He had not made a senior appearance for the Mariners when war broke out. After the war he joined Hereford United before moving back north to join York City in November 1948.
League: App 41, Gls 11.

THORNTON, Richard G. *1925-1928*

Goalkeeper. Born: Bearpark, County Durham.
Debut v Burnley (a) Division One, 26 December 1925, L 3-6.
5ft 10in, 11st 4lb (1925).
Thornton's only League appearance for Leeds was a disaster. On Boxing Day 1925 he let in six goals against Burnley – all of them coming in the first half. He was a noted 'keeper in the North-East amateur scene, having played for Esh Winning before joining Leeds from Bearpark in May 1925. He left Elland Road for Accrington Stanley in 1929 and then joined York City (cs 1931) and Bridlington Town (1933), moving on to Leyland Motors in 1936 and Selby Town in August 1937.
League: App 1, Gls 0.

TILLOTSON, Arthur *1920*

Left-back. Born: Hunslet Leeds, spring 1903.
Debut v Port Vale (a) Division Two, 28 August 1920, L 0-2.
5ft 10in, 11st 10lb (1920).
Together with full-back partner Bert Duffield, Arthur Tillotson was signed from Midland League side Castleford Town in July 1920 for United's first season in the Football League. Arthur went on to become a fine servant at Elland Road, but Tillotson played only in the Peacocks' opening two games and returned to Castleford in September. His brother, Joe, also played for Castleford.
League: App 2, Gls 0.

TINKLER, Mark *1993-*

Midfield. Born: Bishop Auckland, 24 October 1974.
Debut v Sheffield United (a) 6 April 1993, Division One, L 1-2.
5ft 10in, 13st 3lb (1995).
Another of the 1993 FA Youth Cup winning side, he excelled in

central defence in the Final games against Manchester United, but has played virtually all his senior football in midfield. An England Schools and Youth player, he was a member of the Under-18 squad which won the European championship. He joined Leeds from school and did not land a senior contract until July 1993, after he made his senior debut, as an 18-year-old, in David Batty's No.4 shirt at Sheffield United. A broken ankle playing in a reserve game the following season put his career on hold, but he showed signs of getting back into the first-team picture during 1995-96.

League: App 13/9, Gls 0; League Cup: App 1, Gls 0; Europe: App 0/1, Gls 0.

TONER, Jim *1954-1955*

Outside-right. Born: Shettleston, Glasgow, 23 August 1924.
Debut v Hull City (a) Division Two, 21 August 1954, W 2-0.
5ft 6in, 11st 12lb (1954).
Toner enjoyed a fairly productive career in Scottish football before trying his luck with Leeds. He attended St Mungo's Academy (Glasgow) and won a Scottish Junior Cup winners' medal with Fauldhouse United before joining Dundee. With the Dens Park club he won Scottish League Cup winners' medals in 1952 and 1953. He first caught Major Buckley's eye but was signed by Buckley's successor, Raich Carter, in June 1954, after Leeds beat off competition from Hull City, Toner was a noted golfer.
Leaguer: App 7, Gls 1.

TOWNSLEY, Tom *1925-1931*

Centre-half. Born: Polmont, Stirlingshire, 28 April 1898.
Debut v Burnley (h) Division One, 25 December 1925, D 2-2.
5ft 11in, 11st 2lb (1930).
Scottish international Tom Townsley was successfully converted from centre-half to right-back during his stay at Elland Road. The switch served a

dual purpose, plugging a problem position at full-back and accommodating Ernie Hart at centre-half. He began with junior side, Laurieston Villa, then Cowie Wanderers before joining Falkirk in 1919. A dominating and mobile pivot, he played for Scotland once, against Wales in October 1925, and turned out for the Scottish League representative side four times. He joined Leeds (£5,000) in December 1925 and missed only four games in the next three and a half seasons. In October 1931 he went back to Falkirk and played until 1933. Five years later he was appointed manager of Peterhead and ran the side until well after the war. He died, aged 77, on 10 April 1976.
League: App 159, Gls 2; FA Cup: App 8, Gls 0.

TRAINOR, John *1935-1938*

Centre-forward. Born: Norham-on-Tweed.
Debut v Stoke City (h) Division One, 2 January 1937, W 2-1.
5ft 10in, 13st (1935).
Trainor eventually opted for a life in professional soccer after starring as an athlete and Rugby Union player at school. a Northumberland Schools soccer player, he played rugby for Berwick in 1933, then soccer for Berwick Rangers and Duns in the East of Scotland League. In 1934-35 he joined Ashington when Billy Hampson was the manager. When Hampson was appointed manager of Leeds he went back to Ashington in December 1935 to sign the powerful centre-forward. Trainor, a cousin of Charlie Napier, the Celtic, Derby, Sheffield Wednesday and Scottish international forward, was transferred to Southend in May 1938.
League: App 3, Gls 0; FA Cup: App 1, Gls 0.

TURNBULL, Bobby *1925-1932*

Outside-right. Born: South Bank, near Middlesbrough, 17 December 1895.
Debut v Notts County (a) Division One, 29 August 1925, L 0-1.
5ft 10in, 11st 7lb (1925).
Bobby Turnbull delighted United's fans for over six seasons with his dazzling footwork. He started with South Bank East End and Middlesbrough were hot favourites to sign him on. However, they lost their quarry in extraordinary circumstances. Bradford arrived in Middlesbrough to play a benefit match for the relatives of 'Boro full-back Donald McLeod, who died in World War One. Park Avenue were a man short and Turnbull was persuaded to turn out for them. He gave a great display and was signed by Bradford straight after the match. He scored five times in a sensational wartime debut against Barnsley on New Year's Day 1918 and was capped by England against Ireland in October 1919 and toured South Africa with an FA squad the following year. Leeds signed him in May 1925 and he sparkled consistently on the right flank into his mid-30s. He moved to Rhyl in September 1932, retiring the following year. He later returned to Teesside to work for Dorman, Long & Company. He died at Middlesbrough, aged 56, on 19 March 1952.
League: App 204, Gls 45; FA Cup: App 11, Gls 1.

TURNER, Charlie J. *1933-1935*

Centre-half. Born: Manchester, *c.*1911.
Debut v Middlesbrough (h) Division One, 28 August 1933, W 5-2.
5ft 10½in, 11st (1933).
Turner spent two seasons at Leeds as deputy to England international Ernie Hart. He represented Eccles Schools, playing in the same side as United 'keeper Reg Savage, and played for Lancashire Combination side, Atherton, then Manchester Central, before going to Stalybridge Celtic. He was signed by Leeds as a 21-year-old from Stalybridge in May 1933 and proved to be a reliable reserve. He moved to Southend United in June 1935.
League: App 13, Gls 0.

TURNER, Chris R. *1989*

Goalkeeper. Born: Sheffield 15 September 1958.
Debut v Watford (h) Division Two, 18 November 1989, W 2-1.
6ft, 12st 4lb (1984).
Former England Youth international Turner helped Leeds out on loan when regular 'keeper Mervyn Day was injured. An apprentice with Sheffield Wednesday, he turned professional with the Owls in August 1976. After a loan period at Lincoln City (October 1978) he joined Sunderland in July 1979, for £80,000, and helped them reach the 1985 Milk Cup Final. He moved to Manchester United in a £275,000 deal in August 1985 and rejoined Sheffield Wednesday in September 1988, for £175,000. He won a League Cup winners' medal with the Owls, against Manchester United, and helped them back into Division One. In October 1991, he went to Leyton Orient where he became assistant manager.
League: App 2, Gls 0.

TURNER, John A.K. *1935-1937*

Outside-right. Born: Worksop.
Debut v Aston Villa (a) Division One, 14 March 1936, D 3-3.
5ft 6in, 10st 7lb (1935).
Turner was signed by Leeds in October 1935 after a successful trial in a Yorkshire Midweek League game, when he scored against Mansfield under the pseudonym 'A Newman'. Ironically he had been recommended to Mansfield when he was a youngster on Worksop's books. He joined Leeds from Retford-based North Notts League club, Northern Rubber Works. He eventually joined Mansfield in December 1937 and went on to Bristol City in June 1939, playing in all three League games before League football was shut down.
League: App 14, Gls 0.

TWOMEY, Jim F. *1937-1939*

Goalkeeper. Born: Newry, Northern Ireland, 13 April 1914.
Debut v Blackpool (a) Division One, 19 March 1938, L 2-5.
5ft 11in, 12st 2lb (1937).
Twomey had the distinction of winning his first cap while still a reserve at Leeds. As a youngster he was a skilful boxer and Gaelic footballer but decided to further his soccer career and made his debut for Newry Town when he was only 15. He played twice for the Irish League and it was a brilliant display against the Football League at Blackpool in October 1937 that triggered off a stampede to sign him. Billy Hampson won the race and Twomey was persuaded to give up his job as a woodworking machinist to join Leeds in December 1937. In March 1938 he played for United Reserves at Blackpool on the 12th, kept a clean sheet against Wales on his full international debut on the 16th and made his League debut for Leeds on the 19th. His only other international cap came in a 7-0 thrashing by England. During the war he returned to Newry, although he played a few games for Leeds and returned to Elland Road when peacetime soccer resumed. In August 1949 he went to Halifax Town where he later became trainer-coach. He also did some part-time scouting for Leeds and worked in an office while living in Beeston, near Elland Road. Twomey did a great deal of charity work with the Leeds United Ex-Players Association before his death on 9 November 1984.
League: App 109, Gls 0; FA Cup: App 2, Gls 0.

TYRER, Arthur S. *1950-1954*

Outside-left. Born: Manchester, 25 February 1931.
Debut v Southampton (a) Division Two, 8 September 1951, D 0-0.
6ft, 11st 10½lb (1951).
Tyrer worked as a plumber before turning professional with Leeds in September 1950. He played in the Cheshire League with Mossley and earned himself the reputation of being an accurate crosser of the ball and a man with a fierce shot. He was in and out of the side at Leeds and in July 1954 went to Peterborough, moving to Shrewsbury in June 1955. His best days were

undoubtably at Aldershot, whom he joined in June 1956, and he made 235 League appearances for them until going to Fleet FC in 1964.
League: App 39, Gls 4, FA Cup: App 3, Gls 0.

UNDERWOOD, Ben R. *1928-1929*

Left-half. Born: Alfreton, 30 September 1901.
Debut v Birmingham City (h) Division One, 4 May 1929, L 0-1.
5ft 10in, 11st 8lb (1928).
Underwood was kept in the shadows by George Reed and Wilf Copping during his three seasons at Elland Road. He began with Derby County but, after failing to make the Rams' first team, played for New Hucknall (1920) and Sutton Town (1924) before joining Doncaster Rovers in June 1926. He held a regular place, for two seasons prior to joining Leeds in May 1928. He moved to Coventry in the 1931 close season an stayed there until 1933. He died, aged 56, on 9 March 1958.
League: app 6, Gls 0.

VARADI, Imre *1990-1993*

Born: Paddington, London, 8 July 1959.
Debut v Hull City (h) Division Two, 10 February 1990, W 4-3.
5ft 8in, 11st 11lb (1989).
Injuries to Bobby Davison and Carl Shutt prompted Howard Wilkinson to dip into the transfer market to sign the experienced Varadi to help keep United's Division Two championship bandwagon rolling. It was the third time that Varadi had been signed by Wilkinson and his £50,000 move from Sheffield Wednesday in February 1990 saw him link up with other ex-Owls in Lee Chapman, Mel Sterland, Carl Shutt, Glynn Snodin and John Pearson. Varadi was snapped up by Sheffield United in April 1978, from Letchworth Garden City, and flitted around the top divisions with Everton (March 1979) £80,000; Newcastle United (August 1981) £125,000; Sheffield Wednesday (August 1983) £150,000; West Bromwich Albion (July 1985) £285,000; Manchester City (October 1986); Sheffield Wednesday (September 1988) before arriving at Leeds. Most of his time at Elland Road was spent in the Reserves and after loans to Luton Town (March 1992) and Oxford United (January 1993) he joined Rotherham United on a free transfer in March 1993. He top-scored for the Millers the following season, but the season after that he was effectively replaced by Bobby Davison. After playing a couple of games for Mansfield Town at the start of 1995-96 he was appointed player-coach, by Mel Sterland, of Boston United in September 1995. That lasted only a matter of weeks as he re-entered League football with Scunthorpe United. Varadi now has over 100 League goals to his credit.
League: App 21/5, Gls 5; League Cup: App 1, Gls 0; Full Members' Cup: App 1/1, Gls 1.

VICKERS, Peter *1951-1956*

Forward. Born: Kilnhurst, near Doncaster, 6 March 1934.
Debut v Queen's Park Rangers (h) Division Two, 17 March 1951, D 2-2.
5ft 9in, 10st (1951).
Big things were expected of Vickers after a sparkling career as a schoolboy footballer, when he captained Rotherham, represented Yorkshire and won England honours. He joined the Leeds groundstaff as a 14-year-old and, only eight days after turning professional, made his League debut. During National Service in Germany with the Royal Armoured Corps he became an Army international. He was only 18 when he played for the Central League XI against champions Wolves Reserves in September 1952 and a promising future looked on the cards. However, after demob he did not progress as well as the Leeds management hoped and after spells with March Town and King's Lynn (July 1956), he re-emerged with Lincoln City in August 1959, but did not make the first team and went to Wisbech Town. He made a fleeting comeback in League football with Northampton Town in February 1960.
League: App 20, Gls 4; FA Cup: App 1, Gls 0.

WAINSCOAT, W.Russell *1925-1931*

Inside-left. Born: East Retford, 28 July 1898.
Debut v Newcastle United (a) Division One, 21 March 1925, L 1-4.
5ft 10½in, 12st (1922).
Russell Wainscoat made a dream debut in the Football League, scoring a hat-trick for Barnsley against Fulham on 6 March 1920. Later in his career he displayed his sharp-shooting touch with Leeds United over a six-year period. He began with his local side, Maltby Main, before joining Barnsley in March 1920. He left Oakwell in December 1923 for Middlesbrough (£4,000) and Leeds paid £2,000 for him in March 1925. He was selected for the FA tour of Canada in 1926 and in a game against Thunder Bay he scored five goals. Despite sustaining a broken nose and triple fracture of his arm, he maintained a high standard of performance with Leeds and was rewarded with an England cap against Scotland in April 1929.

He left Leeds for Hull City in October 1931 and won a Third Division North championship medal in 1932-33. After retiring in 1934 he held a variety of jobs including that of railway clerk, licensee, ran a shoe shop, confectioner's and a drapery store. Wainscoat was a fine cricketer and played for Barnsley in the Yorkshire Council. He died in July 1967 in Worthing.
League: App 215, Gls 87; FA Cup: App 11, Gls 6.

WAKEFIELD, Albert J. *1942-1949*

Centre-forward. Born: Pudsey, 19 November 1921.
Debut v Southampton (a) Division Two, 30 August 1947, W 2-1.
5ft 9in, 11st (1947).
Had Wakefield not returned to Leeds after World War Two he might have made a name for himself in Italian soccer. He was serving in Italy and after the war he turned down offers from some Italian clubs and opted to return to United. He joined Leeds in October 1942, from Stanningley Works, and enjoyed a belated League debut at the age of 25 with a goal against Southampton, finishing as top scorer that season with 21 goals. In August 1949 he was transferred to Southend United as Frank Dudley went in the opposite direction. Wakefield scored over 50 League goals for Southend before going to Clacton in July 1953.
League: App 49, Gls 23; FA Cup: App 1, Gls 0.

WALLACE, Ray M. *1991-1994*

Utility player. Born: Lewisham, 2 October 1969.
Debut v Nottingham Forest (h) Premiership, 5 December 1992,

L 1-4.
5ft 6in, 10st 2lb (1992).
Marginally youngest of the three Wallace brothers from Southampton, Ray accompanied Rod to Elland Road more as a psychological ploy by manager Howard Wilkinson than for his footballing skills. Ray was rated at £100,000 – a fraction of the £1.6 million on Rod's head – when the twins arrived at Elland Road in June 1991. Wilkinson believed the presence of Ray would help Rod settle at his new club. Although he had not figured in a senior game for the Saints in 20 months, Ray was no novice. Joining Southampton in July 1986 as a trainee, he turned professional in April 1988 and the following year won the first of his four England Under-21 caps. All three Wallaces, the twins and elder brother Danny, later to play for Manchester United and England, made history in October 1989 when they played together in a match against Sheffield Wednesday. At Leeds, Ray operated in midfield or defence but was confined to the shadows as his twin enjoyed the spotlight. Predictably, loans (to Swansea City in March 1992 and to Reading in March 1994) followed before he joined Stoke City in summer 1995. After initially enjoying a run in the Potters' first team he went to Hull City on loan in December 1994 for a couple of months. Back at Stoke he regained a starting place and helped them to the Division One Play-offs in 1995-96.
League: App 5/2, Gls 0.

WALLACE, Rod S. *1991-*

Forward. Born: Lewisham, 2 October 1969.
Debut v Nottingham Forest (h) Premiership, 20 August 1991, W 1-0.
5ft 7in, 10st 1lb (1992).
On his day, little Hot Rod's darting runs can slice open any Premiership defence and he

enjoyed a superb 1991-92 League championship campaign when his busy feet complemented the raw power of Lee Chapman. In September 1992 he was called up for an England trip to Spain, but injury prevented him from going and after that his confidence seemed to dip, taking his form with it. His partnership with Brian Deane failed to come up with the goals and towards the end of 1995-96 a return to Southampton looked on the cards, but Rod could not agree personal terms. His start at Southampton in 1986 mirrored that of twin Ray, but he was quickly being tipped for the top after some dazzling displays for the Saints and 11 Under-21 caps and a couple of England 'B' appearances followed. He netted 45 goals in 101 League starts for Southampton, and Leeds won the race to sign him, a tribunal setting the £1.6 million fee in July 1991. His 'Goal of the Season' winner against Tottenham Hotspur in April 1994 ranks as one of the greatest solo goals ever seen at Elland Road, when he cut a swathe through a posse of defenders at pace and curled in a wonderful shot from just inside the penalty area. Many believe his speed made him a better prospect as a winger rather than an out-and-out striker where competition at Elland Road became intense as Liverpool and Wales star Ian Rush signed in May 1996 to team up with Tony Yeboah.
League: App 141/18, Gls 40; FA Cup: App 8/5, Gls 1; League Cup: App 11/1, Gls 3; Europe: App 0/3, Gls 0; Charity Shield: App 1, Gls 0; Full Members' Cup: App 01/1, Gls 1.

WALTON, Jimmy *1920-1923*

Left-half. Born: Sacriston, County Durham, 3 December 1904.
Debut v Port Vale (a) Division Two, 28 August 1920, L 0-2./
5ft 9in, 11st 7lb (1920).
Walton missed only one game in United's first season in the Football League. He began with Cleator Moor before joining West Stanley in August 1919. Leeds recruited him from the North-East amateur club in July 1920. When skipper Jim Baker switched to left-half, Walton found his way to the first team barred and after a few games at inside-forward he went to Bristol Rovers in August 1923. He was a regular with Rovers until a disagreement with the club which resulted in a £125 transfer to Brentford in November 1924. The Bees released him at the end of the 1925-26 season and he wound up his League career with a couple of games for Hartlepools United in November 1926. He died on 20 November 1982.
League; App 69, Gls 4; FA Cup: App 2, Gls 0.

WATERHOUSE, Fred *1920-1921*

Winger. Born: Horsforth.
Debut v Boothtown (h) FA Cup Extra preliminary round, 11 September 1920, W 5-2.
5ft 8in, 12st (1920).
Waterhouse began with Huddersfield Town as an amateur, joining Leeds in August 1920. He did not play in the Football League for United.
FA Cup*: App 2, Gls 1.
*He played only in both of United's preliminary round games in 1920-21.

WATSON, Andy *1983-1984*

Midfield. Born: Aberdeen, 3 September 1959.
Debut v Newcastle United (h) Division Two, 27 August 1983, L 0-1.
5ft 10in, 11st 10lb (1983).
Watson pushed himself to the brink of full Scottish international honours before an 18-month period with Leeds. He began with junior side, Sunnyside, before joining Aberdeen where he won Scottish Youth honours and broke into the first team in 1977-78. His progress continued with four Under-23 caps and he was soon tipped for full honours. He won a Scottish Cup winners' medal in 1983, after coming on as a substitute against Rangers, and was s substitute in Aberdeen's European Cup-winners' Cup success the same year. Leeds bought him (£60,000) in June 1983, but he found it difficult to adapt to the pace of the English game and returned to Scotland in December 1984 with Hearts. In summer 1987 he moved to Hibernian where he linked up with another ex-Leeds player, George McCluskey. He left in May 1989.
League: App 37/1, Gls 7; FA Cup: App 1, Gls 0; League Cup: 4, Gls 0.

WEBB, Bobby *1951-1955*

Forward. Born: Altofts, near Castleford, 29 November 1933.
Debut v Brentford (h) Division Two, 6 March 1954, W 4-0.
5ft 5½in, 8st 11in (1951).
Webb was spotted in junior football by County FA coach Jimmy Frew, the former Leeds defender, who advised him to switch from full-back to inside-forward. The youngster, who was working as a miner, took Frew's advice and signed professional forms for Leeds in April 1951. He had earlier played for Normanton Boys, West Riding Boys, Silkstone Rovers and Whitwood Technical. Webb did his National Service with the KOYLI in Germany and was transferred to Walsall in March 1955. In July that year he joined Bradford City as a part-timer and made 208 appearances for them before going to Torquay United in July 19062. His career was brought to a premature end by a broken leg in 1964.
League: App 3, Gls 0.

WESTON, Don P. *1962-1965*

Centre-forward. Born: Mansfield, 6 March 1936.
Debut v Stoke City (h) Division Two, 15 December 1962, W 3-1.
5ft 7¼in, 11st 6lb (1963).
Weston made the best possible start to his career with Leeds by scoring a debut hat-trick and he went on to be joint top scorer with Albert Johanneson as United swept to the Second Division championship. After representing East Derbyshire Boys, he was spotted by Wrexham while playing for the 31st Training Regiment Royal Artillery (North Wales) and signed in June 1959. They sold him to Birmingham City (£15,000) in January 1960 and in December that year he joined Rotherham (£10,000). He played in the Millers' 1961 League Cup Final side which lost to Aston Villa. He joined Leeds in December 1962 but, after promotion, he found life harder in the First Division and was transferred to Huddersfield Town in October 1965. He returned to Wrexham in December 1966, then moved to Chester in August 1968 and later played for Altrincham and Bethesda.
League: App 68, Gls 24; FA Cup: App 7, Gls 1; League Cup: App 3, Gls 1.

WETHERALL, David *1991-*

Central defender. Born: Sheffield, 14 March 1971.
Debut (as sub) v Arsenal (h) Division One, 3 September 1991, D 2-2.
6ft 3in, 13st 12lb (1996).
Wetherall was still a student when he tasted tasted senior football for the first time. After winning a place on the bench at Old Trafford the previous week, the big defender came on towards the end of the next home game against Arsenal. It was his only slice of action in the title campaign, but Leeds fans had seen a glimpse of the future. Howard Wilkinson saw potential in Wetherall's play at England Schools level, where he was captain, and signed him in July 1989 for Sheffield Wednesday. He had played for Sheffield Boys and after a 14-month lay-off with a knee injury turned out for Middlewood Rovers before joining Wednesday where he won three England Under-19 caps and featured in the British Universities side which won a bronze medal in the World Student Games in Sheffield. With Wednesday pondering over the

future of Wetherall and fellow young defender Jon Newsome, Wilkinson pounced for his new club, Leeds, by signing the pair for £250,000. It was to prove a wise double investment as Newsome was sold on a few years later for £1 million to Norwich, and Wetherall became a regular in the heart of the United defence. After completing his chemistry degree at Sheffield, Wetherall was able to concentrate fully on football and enjoyed a fine 1994-95 Premiership season.
League: App 116/2, Gls 9; FA Cup: App 13/2, Gls 3; League Cup: App 13, Gls 0; Europe: App 4, Gls 0.

WHALLEY, Fred H. *1921-1924*

Goalkeeper. Born: Bolton, 9 October 1898.
Debut v Port Vale (h) Division Two, 27 August 1921, W 2-1.
6ft, 12st (1922).
Whalley thought nothing of chatting to the fans behind his goal when the action was at the other end of the pitch. His antics made him extremely popular at Leeds but beneath the comic exterior was a dedicated professional who excelled at his job. A product of Preston Schools and Army football, Whalley enlisted in the North Lancashire Regiment at 15 and saw active service in France before signing for Preston North End in June 1919. The following summer he joined Grimsby and became a Leeds player in May 1921. After losing his place to Billy Down he went to Fulham in March 1924, retiring in 1926 to return to Preston where he became a policeman. He died at Eccles, near Manchester, on 25 April 1976.
League: App 87, Gls 0; FA Cup: App 4, Gls 0.

WHARTON, C.Norman *1939*

Goalkeeper. Born: Askham-in-Furness, 28 July 1903.
Debut v Charlton Athletic (a) Division One, 30 August 1939, L 0-1.
6ft 1in, 12st 4lb (1928).
Veteran Norman Wharton ended a distinguished career with a couple of appearances for Leeds in the truncated 1939-40 season. He was not the most agile of 'keepers, but one of the bravest and most consistent. an electrician by trade, Wharton joined his local club, Barrow, in 1920 and went to Preston for a couple of seasons before returning to Barrow in 1927. He was transferred to Sheffield United in the 1928 close season (£250). In July 1931 he became a Norwich City player, then joined Doncaster Rovers in May 1935 and York City in summer 1936. He arrived at Leeds in August 1939, when he was 36-years-old, and retired in the war. He won a Third Division South championship medal with Norwich in 1933-34 when he was ever-present. After football he went back to working as an electrician. A keen pianist, Wharton died, aged 57, on 13 July 1961, in his home town where his seven brothers had all be good rugby players.
League: App 2, Gls 0.

WHEATLEY, Tom *1953*

Goalkeeper. Born: Hebburn, County Durham, 1 June 1929.
Debut v Swansea Town (h) Division Two, 2 September 1953, W 3-2.
5ft 11½in, 10st 10lb (1953).
Wheatley's six successive appearances came as deputy to John Scott. He signed in April 1953, from Northern Alliance club Amble. He had been at Amble two and a half years and had trials with Leeds and Lincoln in 1952-53.
League: App 6, Gls 0.

WHELAN, Noel *1993-1995*

Forward. Born: Leeds, 30 December 1974.
Debut v Sheffield United (a) Premiership, 4 May 1993, D 2-2.
6ft 2in, 11st 3lb (1995).
One of the surprises of the 1995-96 Premiership season was the sale of 21-year-old Whelan to Coventry City for £2 million. United, in need of cash, believed they had received an offer they could not refuse for their talented England Under-21 striker. The one-time ball-boy at Elland Road was signed after leaving school and turned professional in March 1993, quickly showing his skill on the ball. An England Youth international, he helped in the European Youth championship-winning squad of 1993 and the Leeds side which won the FA Youth Cup the same year when he scored one of the goals in the first leg of the Final at

Manchester United. He continued to progress and netted the only goal of the game against the Republic of Ireland on his Under-21 debut at Newcastle. Whelan looked poised for a long run in Premiership football, but a throat virus and the arrival of star striker Tony Yeboah pushed him out of the first-team picture. When he did get back in the team, goals did not come so readily but as soon as he went to Coventry, in December 1995, the goals started to flow. United stand to cash in on a 15 per cent sell-on clause should the Sky Blues transfer Whelan.
League: App 27/20, Gls 7; FA Cup: App 2, Gls 0; League Cup: App 3/2, Gls 1; Europe: App 3, Gls 0.

WHIPP, Percy L. *1922-1927*

Inside-forward. Born: Glasgow, 28 June 1897.
Debut v West Ham United (h) Division One, 4 November 1922, W 3-1.

5ft 9½in, 11st 12lb.
Percy Whipp soon made himself at home with a debut hat-trick, although when he signed the previous day from Sunderland (£750) he admitted he had never been to Leeds before. Dubbed 'The Arch General' by Leeds supporters, Whipp was a player of rare cunning. He started in junior football with West London Old Boys and first drew attention when he gave a star performance for a Hammersmith League XI against Fulham Reserves. His first professional club was the Welsh outfit, Ton Pentre, in the 1920 close-season. The following summer he joined Clapton Orient and in June 1922 signed for Sunderland where he was understudy to Charlie Buchan. used by United as an inside-right, he was an excellent servant at Elland Road for five seasons before rejoining Orient in June 1927. In May 1929 he went to Brentford, but after injuring his right wrist, he was given a free transfer and joined Swindon in May 1930. He left for Bath City in August 1931.
League: App 145, Gls 44; FA Cup: App 9, Gls 3.

WHITE, David *1993-1996*

Midfield/winger. Born: Manchester, 30 September 1967.
Debut v Queen's Park Rangers (h) Premiership, 29 December 1993, D 1-1.
6ft 1in, 12st 9lb (1993).

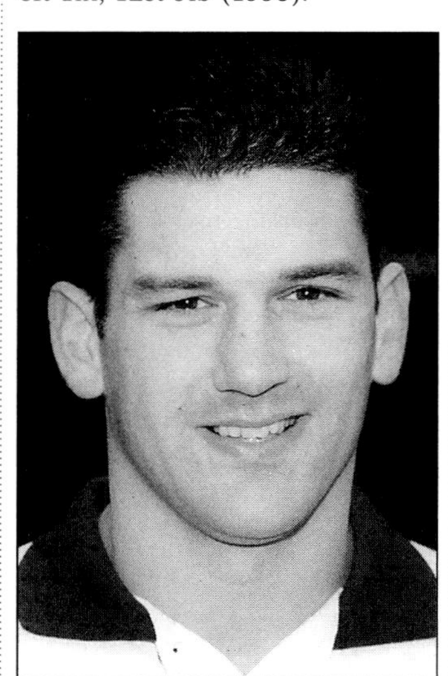

Out went the unhappy David Rocastle and in came David White as United and Manchester City traded right-sided midfield players in a deal that saw the players valued at £2 million apiece. But like Rocastle, White struggled with injury and the burden of replacing the inspirational Gordon Strachan. He never really nailed down a regular first-team place because of ankle trouble and many of his better performances in Leeds colours were as substitute with his powerful, direct running providing goals late in games against tiring teams. After only one Premiership start in 1995-96, White was sold to Sheffield United for £500,000 in January 1996. His Elland Road form was a far cry from the dynamic displays he produced at Manchester City, the team he joined in November 1985 after serving his apprenticeship and playing for Salford Boys He made one England appearance, against Spain in 1992, two for England 'B', six at Under-21 level and had an outing for the Youth side in a Maine Road career that brought him over a century of goals, including four against Aston Villa in a 5-1 triumph in April 1991.
League: App 28/14, Gls 9; FA Cup: App 6, Gls 2; League Cup: App 2, Gls 0; Europe: App 1/1, Gls 0.

WHITE, John *1927-1930*

Inside-forward. Born: Coatbridge, Lanarkshire, 27 August 1897, L 0-1.
Debut v Arsenal (a) Division One, 12 February 1927, L 0-1.
5ft 8½in, 11st 7lb (1927).
When Leeds signed Scottish international John White from Hearts in February 1927 (£5,600) he became one of the most expensive players of his day. He began with Bedley Juniors and joined Albion Rovers in 1920, playing in their losing Scottish Cup Final side in his first season. Two years later he was capped by Scotland against Wales and a £2,700 transfer to Hearts in May 1922 saw him fulfil his vast potential. He was top scorer at Hearts for five consecutive seasons, scoring 102 goals including four goals a game in three successive matches in 1925-26. He was Scotland's top scorer in 1922-23 with 30 goals. Curiously, he won only one more cap, although he played for the Scottish League four times. He took a season to adjust to the English game and United could have reaped a quick profit when Sheffield United put in a £6,000 bid in November 1927. They rejected the offer and White repaid them with a rich vein of form. At the age of 33 he returned to Hearts (£2,350) in August 1930 and on to Margate in 1934. He was one of four brothers who played professional football, including Willie White, who played for Hearts and the Scottish League. He was brother-in-law of Andy Anderson (Hearts and Scotland). White died, aged 88, in February 1986.
League: App 102, Gls 36; FA Cup: App 6, Gls 2.

WHITLOW, Mike L. *1988-1992*

Midfield/full-back. Born: Davenham, 13 January 1968.
Debut v Shrewsbury Town (h) Simod Cup 1st round, 9 November 1988, W 3-1.
5ft 11in, 12st 1lb (1989).
After joining them from Rudland Youth Club in 1985, Whitlow was rejected by Bolton Wanderers without making a League appearance. He drifted into non-League football. He was working as a labourer during his time with HFS Loans Northern Premier League club, Witton Albion. Whitlow and Albion right-back Neil Parsley caught the eye of Sheffield Wednesday boss Howard Wilkinson in 1988-89. Both players looked set to join the Owls, when Wilkinson succeeded Billy Bremner at Leeds. Wednesday did not follow up their interest but Wilkinson was quick to pay £30,000 to bring both players to Elland Road in November 1988. Seventeen days after his debut in the Simod Cup. Whitlow played his first game in the Football League – in midfield after just half a reserve game in that position. He made good progress in 1989-90 and was tipped for England Under-21 honours. He did not quite maintain that kind of progress, however, and was transferred to Leicester City in March 1992 for £250,000, just a couple of weeks after Simon Grayson joined the Foxes. He arrived at Filbert Street in time to appear in the First Division Play-offs, when Leicester were edged out by Blackburn, suffered the same fate the following year against Swindon, but was a Wembley winner against Derby in 1994. After a season of Premiership football he made his fourth Play-off Final appearance in five years, against Crystal Palace in 1996.
League: App 62/15, Gls 4; FA Cup: App 0/4, Gls 0; League Cup: App 4/1, Gls 0; Full Members' Cup: App 9, Gls 0.

WHYTE, Chris A. *1990-1993*

Central defender. Born: Islington, 2 September 1961.
Debut v Everton (a) Division One, 25 August 1990, W 3-2.
6ft 1in, 11st 10lb (1993).
Dependable defender Chris Whyte played a major part in establishing United back in the big time after the Second Division championship had been won in 1989-90. His days at Leeds were the best of his career where his skilful use of the ball at the back made him one of the most efficient members of the side which won the First Division title. He had learnt his trade at Arsenal, having played on their doorstep for Highbury Grove, Islington and Inner London Schools. He went to the Gunners in August 1977, turning professional in September 1978. Although he won four England Under-21 caps in 1982, it was not easy breaking into the Arsenal first team where David O'Leary was the king in central defence. Whyte spent two months on loan at Crystal Palace (August 1984) and in 1986 went to the United States to play indoor football with Los Angeles Lazers, returning two years later to play for West Bromwich Albion in August 1988. The Baggies' Player of the Year in 1989, he was snapped up by Leeds for £400,000 and proved a rock-solid investment. But as he started to approach his mid-30s at Leeds, a new breed of defenders like David Wetherall and Jon Newsome were coming through, so Whyte was sold to Birmingham City for £250,000 in August 1993. At St Andrew's he won a Division Two championship medal in 1994-95 and the following season played against Leeds in the Coca-Cola Cup semi-final after being recalled from a loan spell with West Ham, scoring an own-goal winner for Leeds in the first leg. Shortly afterwards he moved on to Charlton Athletic.
League: App 113, Gls 5; FA Cup: App 8, Gls 0; League Cup: App 14/1, Gls 1; Europe: App 5, Gls 0; Charity Shield: App 1, Gls 0; Full Members' Cup: App 5, Gls 0.

WHYTE, David *1977-1979*

Midfield. Born: Dunfermline, 2 March 1959.
Debut (as sub) v Aston Villa (a) Division One, 7 May 1977, L 1-2.
5ft 9in, 11st 5lb (1978).
Dunfermline Schools representative Whyte served his apprenticeship at Leeds, turning professional in 1977. After a brief flirtation with first-team football he went to Hibernian in July 1979 on a free transfer with another former Leeds junior, David Reid. Whyte later joined Bradford City as a non-contract player before going to Barnsley in November 1980. He did not play in the first team at either Bradford City or Barnsley. He now works as a fireman and plays for Harrogate Railway Athletic.
League: App 1/1, Gls 0.

WILCOCKSON, E.Stan *1934-1935*

Inside-forward/left-half. Born: Poplar, London, 11 May 1905.
Debut v Arsenal (h) Division One, 8 September 1934, D 1-1.
5ft 11in, 11st 5lb (1935).
Wilcockson spent one season with Leeds as a utility player. He began with Crittal Athletic, then went to Crystal Palace in June 1930, breaking into the first team in January 1932. Five months later he was back in non-League football with Dartford, but in June 1933 joined York City. Leeds recruited him in June 1934, but he left in August 1935, for Swindon, and gave them good service before signing for Tunbridge Wells Rangers in May 1939. During the 1950s he spent some time coaching West Ham's youth team. He died on 3 March 1965, aged 59, in Dartford.
League: App 4, Gls 0.

WILKINS, George *1949*

Inside-forward. Born: Hackney, London, 27 October 1917.
Debut v Southampton (a) Division Two, 9 September 1949, L 1-2.
Wilkins, the father of England intentional Ray Wilkins, began with Hayes and joined Brentford during the war, playing for the Bees at Wembley in the 1942 London Cup Final when they beat Portsmouth. He also played against Wolves in the Cup-winners' Cup match the same year. In February 1947 he joined Bradford, but ten months later was transferred to Nottingham Forest (£7,500). He became a Leeds player in September 1949 but soon ended his career. Two other sons, Graham and Dean, also played League football. Graham made over 100 appearances for Chelsea and Dean was on QPR's books.
League: App 3, Gls 0.

WILKINSON, Charlie E. *1928-1933*

Left-back. Born: Medomsley, County Durham, 7 April 1907.
Debut v Preston North End (a) Division Two, 26 March 1932, D 0-0.
5ft 10in, 11st 4lb (1930).
Former Durham miner Wilkinson played for Wallsend before being signed from Consett in September 1928, after a month's trial. Unable to make much impression at Leeds, he moved to Sheffield United in October 1933 and played in the Blades' 1936 FA Cup Final side which lost to Arsenal. In June 1938 he went to Southampton but was injured after only three games, underwent a cartilage operation and lost his place. He moved to Bournemouth at the start of 1939-40 and was a player-coach at Dean Court. He died in the third quarter of 1975 at Medomsley.
League: App 3, Gls 0.

WILLIAMS, Andy *1988-1991*

Midfield. Born: Birmingham, 29 July 1962.
Debut (as sub) v West Bromwich Albion (h) Division Two, 12 November 1988, W 2-1.
6ft, 11st 9lb (1988).
Williams, was Howard Wilkinson's first signing for Leeds. A former Dudley Town player, he was a relatively late-starter in League football, joining Coventry City from Solihull Borough and making his debut in Division One when he came on as substitute against Liverpool in November 1985, aged 23. In October 1986, he was transferred to Rotherham United and was a regular at Millmoor until his £170,000 move to Elland Road in November 1988. Another injury victim in 1989-90, he lost a stone in weight in December after an abcess in his groin became infected. Loaned to Port Vale in 1991, to recapture some fitness, he joined Notts County a couple of months later for £115,000 after an initial loan period. Huddersfield Town took him on loan in September 1993 before he returned to Rotherham, where he played in midfield, supplying scoring passes for Imre Varadi. Hull City had him on loan in 1995-96.
League: App 25/21, Gls 3; FA Cup: App 3, Gls 0, League Cup: App 3/3, Gls 0; Full Members' Cup: App 5/2, Gls 2.

WILLIAMS, Gary *1987-1990*

Full-back/midfield. Born: Wolverhampton, 17 June 1960.
Debut v Barnsley (a) Division Two, 16 August 1987, D 1-1.
5ft 9in, 11st 1lb (1987).
After making 240 League appearances for Aston Villa without a goal, Williams took a further 19 League matches with Leeds to open his account against Bradford City. Having broken his duck he went on to score two more League goals in the next six games. He joined Villa from school, turned professional in June 1978, won a League championship medal in 1980-81 and a European Cup winners' medal the following year. He held a fairly regular slot at right-back, apart from a loan spell with Walsall starting in March 1980, but was released when Villa were relegated in 1987 and joined Leeds (£230,000) in July. His only goals at Villa were in the League Cup. He left Leeds for Watford in January 1990, on a free transfer, and after a season at Vicarage Road he joined Bradford City in December 1991.
League: 39, Gls 3; FA Cup: App 1/1, Gls 0; League Cup: App 4, Gls 0.

WILLIAMS, Harold T. *1949-1957*

Winger. Born: Briton Ferry,

Glamorgan, 17 June 1924.
Debut v Queen's Park Rangers (h) Division Two, 20 August 1949, D 1-1.
5ft 4in, 8st 11lb (1953).
Harold Williams first came to Leeds' attention when he roasted United in an FA Cup-tie as a Newport County player. The Welsh minnows pulled off a shock 3-1 win, inspired by Williams who had been up in the early hours of the day to complete his milk round before travelling to Leeds. As a boy he was rejected by Swansea after trials, but he made wartime guest appearances for Belfast Celtic and Cliftonville. When he was demobbed from the Royal Navy, where he served on destroyers, he signed for Briton Ferry Athletic and joined Newport in November 1946. Major Buckley paid £12,000 for him in July 1949. The winger with the size 5½ boots could dribble with both feet and was therefore employed on either wing. He already had two Welsh caps when he joined Leeds and added a couple more during his stay at Elland Road. He fought back from a broken leg sustained in a game against Everton in 1952 to reclaim his first-team place. In March 1957 he returned to Newport, but left Somerton Park after only three months to join Bradford where his career ended after a succession of injuries. He moved into the licensed trade, running the Railway pub at Beeston, near Elland Road, and a pub in Gildersome before retiring in 1986.
League: App 211, Gls 32; FA Cup: App 17, Gls 3.

WILLIAMS, John *1948-1950*

Right-back. Born: Doncaster, 14 April 1920.
Debut v West Ham United (h) Division Two, 26 December 1948, L 1-3.
Williams, a part-time footballer who also sold insurance, made his only Football League appearance in United's colours when Jimmy Dunn was switched to left-half. Williams had joined Leeds from Midland League club Denaby United only a few days earlier. He returned to Denaby in August 1950.
League: App 1, Gls 0.

WILLIAMSON, Brian W. *1962-1966*

Goalkeeper. Born: Blyth, Northumberland, 6 October 1939.
Debut Grimsby Town (h) Division Two, 30 March 1963, W 3-0.
6ft 1in, 12st 1lb (1963).
Williamson began at Seaton Delaval before joining Gateshead in October 1958. When they were voted out of the Football League he joined Crewe in July 1960, moving to Leeds in December 1962. After serving under Sprake he went to Nottingham Forest in February 1966 where he found himself kept out of the side by Peter Grummitt. He went to Leicester on loan in August 1967, then joined Fulham (£10,000) in December 1968. He retired in September 1969 and began work as a security guard. Between June 1965 and February 1966, Leeds had two 'keepers called B.Williamson on their books. The least well-known, Bobby, went to Rochdale in July 1966, having previously been with St Mirren and Rochdale, He did not get into the Leeds first team.
League: App 5, Gls 0; FA Cup: App 1, Gls 0; League Cup: App 2, Gls 0.

WILLINGHAM, C. Ken *1947-1948*

Right-half. Born: Sheffield, 1 December 1912.
Debut v Arsenal (h) Division One, 22 March 1947, D 1-1.
5ft 7½in, 10st 7lb (1947).
Vastly experienced England defender Ken Willingham ended his professional career with Leeds. As a youngster he was an outstanding athlete, representing England Schools after becoming Sheffield half-mile schools champion. He played soccer for Yorkshire Schools six times, once as captain, and then played for Ecclesfield before joining Worksop Town as a 16-year-old. He went to Huddersfield Town as a member of the groundstaff and turned professional in November 1931. Willingham became one of Huddersfield's all-time greats, winning 12 England caps, representing the Football League six times and playing in the side which lost to Preston in the 1938 FA Cup Final. He ended a 14-year association with Huddersfield when he joined Sunderland in December 1945. In March 1947 he became a Leeds player, retiring in May the following year. He spent some time on the coaching staff at Elland Road and was later coach at Halifax Town. He became a publican after finishing with football and died in May 1975, aged 62.
League: App 35, Gls 0; FA Cup: App 1, Gls 0.

WILLIS, J. George *1953-1954*

Outside-left. Born: Shotton, County Durham, 5 July 1937.
Debut v Birmingham City (a) Division Two, 3 October 1953, D 3-3.
5ft 8in, 10st 5lb (1953).
Willis joined Leeds from Evenwood Town in March 1953 and made all his appearances in 1953-54. He completed his National Service with the 7th Battalion Royal Signals before returning to the North-East in November 1954 as a Hartlepools United player. Towards the end of 1958-59 he joined Blyth Spartans, then had spells with Horden Colliery welfare in 1961 and Eppleton Colliery Welfare in 1963.
League: App 3, Gls 0.

WILSON, George M. *1929-1930*

Inside-right. Born: Kilmarnock, 23 May 1905.
Debut v Arsenal (a) Division One, 27 April 1929, L 0-1.
5ft 10½in, 11st 7lb (1930).
Wilson appeared in United's final three games of 1928-29. He began with a junior club in Portobello before signing for Clydebank in August 1927 and Alloa Athletic three months later. He then went to Huddersfield Town, where he played one game, in March 1928. He became a Leeds player in March 1929 and was transferred to Chesterfield in June 1930. When he gave up playing he began work for an engineering firm in Huddersfield, which left him with severe tinnitus (a continual buzzing in the ears), when he retired. Wilson, who had worked as a miner before becoming a professional footballer, died on 22 May 1984, aged 78.
League: App 3, Gls 0.

WILSON, James *1928-1929*

Goalkeeper. Born: Garforth, *c.*1909.
Debut v Bury (a) Division One, 1 January 1929, D 2-2.
6ft 1in, 12st (1930).
Wilson signed from Rothwell Amateurs in March 1928, after a fine performance in a reserve game against Doncaster Rovers. His brief chance at Leeds was effectively ended when he was on the receiving end of an 8-2 thrashing at West Ham in February 1929. That was his final senior game for Leeds and he moved to Shirebrook in August 1930.
League: App 3, Gls 0, FA Cup: App 1, Gls 0.

WINDLE, Billy *1947-1948*

Outside-left. Born: Maltby, 9 July 1920.
Debut v Millwall (h) Division Two, 22 November 1947, W 2-1.
5ft 3in, 10st (1948).
Windle was an experienced Midland League player with Denaby United when he joined Leeds for a small fee in October 1947. Previously he had been on Hull City's books and played for Goole Town. Billy Heaton and Tom Hindle generally kept him out of the Leeds senior side, so he moved on to Lincoln in February 1948. He went to Chester in October 1951 and later played or Rhyl.
League: App 2, Gls 0.

WOOD, Basil M. *1920-1922*

Outside-left. Born: Wortley, near Sheffield, 9 November 1900.

Debut v Fulham (h) Division Two, 25 December 1920, D 0-0.
5ft 7in, 11st 6lb (1921).
Wood broke into United's team shortly after signing from Crook Town in November 1920. He held down a regular place with Leeds before being transferred to Sheffield Wednesday in June 1922, but failed to make a League appearance with the Owls. He died in Harrogate on 8 June 1979.
League: App 56, Gls 2.

WOOD, Roy L. *1952-1960*

Goalkeeper. Born: Wallasey, Merseyside, 16 October 1930.
Debut v Derby County (h) Division Two, 24 October 1953, W 3-1.
6ft 2in, 12st 8lb (1953).
In the mid-1950s, Roy Wood was a permanent fixture for Leeds. He was a good all-round athlete who excelled at soccer and hockey and was also reckoned to be one of the best wicketkeepers in the Leeds & District League during his days at Elland Road. He went to St George's School, Wallasey, and joined West Cheshire League side, Harrowby, as a teenager. During the war he served in the RAF in the Far East and played representative football. He joined New Brighton as an amateur but, after failing to make their senior ranks, left for Lancashire Combination club, Clitheroe. Leeds signed him in May 1952 and he proved a worthy successor to John Scott. After being transfer-listed in 1959 he decided to retire and became a betting-shop manager. He was

also a member of the PFA management committee which negotiated the abolition of the maximum wage for players.
League: App 196, Gls 0; FA Cup: App 7, Gls 0.

WORSLEY, Bert *1932-1935*

Outside-right. Born: Stockport, 20 September 1911.
Debut v Stoke City (a) Division One, 27 August 1934, L 1-8.
5ft 7in, 10st 7lb (1934).
Worsley was unlucky enough to make his debut in the worst defeat in United's history. He began his career at Altrincham and spent some time on Bolton's books as an amateur before playing for Cheshire League side, Manchester North End, from where he joined Leeds in August 1932. He moved to Fulham in June 1935 and figured in their successful run to the FA Cup semi-finals in 1936. He struggled with a crop of injuries at Craven Cottage and retired prematurely. He died, aged 69, in Denton, near Manchester, on 25 June 1971.
League: App 3, Gls 0.

WORTHINGTON, Frank S. *1982*

Forward. Born: Halifax, 23 November 1948.
Debut v Manchester City (h) Division One, 10 March 1982, L 0-1.
5ft 11in, 11st 8lb (1982).
Worthington, one of the game's most colourful characters, counted Leeds amongst his 11 League clubs. He joined Huddersfield as an apprentice in April 1964 and turned professional in November 1966. His goals were an essential ingredient of Town's Second Division title success in 1969-70 before he joined Leicester City (£80,000) in August 1972. He won eight full England caps at Leicester to add to two at Under-23 level. Bolton paid £87,000 for him in September 1977 and sold him (£150,000) to Birmingham in November 1979. Leeds wanted him for their understrength attack and traded Byron Stevenson for him in March 1982. Worthington provided goals, but it was not enough to prevent Leeds being relegated to Division Two. He was sold to Sunderland (£50,000) in December 1982 and in June 1983 signed for Southampton and played in the First Division when he was 35. In May 1984 he joined Brighton for a season, on a free transfer, and was appointed player-manager at Tranmere in the 1985 close season. He was relieved of his position the following summer but re-emerged as a player with Preston in March 1987. In November that year he signed for Stockport – his 11th club – with well over 200 League goals to his credit. In 1988 he played in South Africa with Capetown Spurs before returning to England for a brief spell with Chorley (October 1988) and joined Stalybridge Celtic (December 1988). Worthington's nomadic career then saw him at Galway United (February 1989), Weymouth (September 1989), Radcliffe Borough (November 1989), then Guiseley where he combined playing with a job on Preston North End's coaching staff. Worthington played for Guiseley in the 1990 FA Vase semi-final. His travels later took him to Hinckley Town as player-coach in 1991, Cemaes Bay, and in August 1991 he became Halifax Town's player-coach, appearing in their reserve side at the age of 43. In December 1993 he was appointed to Swindon's coaching staff. His nephew, Gary, has played for Wigan and Darlington.
League: App 32, Gls 14; League Cup: App 3, Gls 1.

WORTHINGTON, Nigel *1994-1996*

Defender. Born: Ballymena, Northern Ireland, 4 November 1961.
Debut v West Ham United (a) Premiership, 20 August 1994, D 0-0.
5ft 11in, 12st 8lb (1995).
After rejecting new terms from Sheffield Wednesday, Nigel Worthington opted to join his old boss Howard Wilkinson at Leeds – the third time Wilkinson had signed the Northern Ireland international. A tribunal fixed the fee at £325,000 after the deal went through in July 1994 and Worthington was used as cover at left-back and the left side of midfield but became the boo-boys' target in his second season when, at the age of 34, the speed required to fit into United's game plan seemed to have deserted him. He was freed at the end of the campaign, becoming an applicant for the vacant

managerial position at Blackpool. Wilkinson first spotted Worthington playing for his native Ballymena, where he was Young Footballer of the Year, and signed him for Notts County in July 1981 for £100,000, a couple of months after he collected an Irish Cup winners' medal after a 1-0 win over Glenavon. Shortly after Wilkinson joined Sheffield Wednesday he persuaded County to part with Northern Ireland Youth international Worthington for £125,000 in February 1984. Rarely has money been better spent as Worthington proved one of the Owls' most consistent performers over the next ten years, becoming a regular member of his national team and playing in Wednesday's League Cup triumph over Manchester United at Wembley in 1991. At Leeds he pushed his international appearances through the 60-cap barrier and in his final season often wore the skipper's armband for Northern Ireland.
League: App 33/10, Gls 1; FA Cup: App 6/1, Gls 0; League Cup: App 4/1, Gls 0.

WRIGHT, Barrie *1962-1964*

Left-back. Born: Bradford, 6 November 1945.
Debut v Preston North End (h) Division Two, 13 April 1963, W 4-1.
5ft 8½in, 11st 1½lb (1962).
Wright, who captained England Schools seven times, joined Leeds' groundstaff and turned professional on his 17th birthday in 1962. Capped at Youth level two years later, he was appointed skipper of United's Central League side and looked certain to make the top grade. However, he struggled and left in 1964 to play for New York Generals, then coached by former Leeds centre-half Freddie Goodwin. When the Generals folded, he teamed-up with Goodwin again at Brighton in January 1969. He then had a spell on loan with Hartlepool in September 1970, but quit full-time soccer soon afterwards at the age of 25. He began work as a warehouseman and played for Bradford and Gainsborough Trinity in the Northern Premier League and also had a spell with Thackley.
League: App 5, Gls 0; League Cup: App 3, Gls 0.

WRIGHT, Ronnie W. *1959-1960*

Inside-left. Born: Falkirk, 16 December 1940.
Debut v Blackpool (h) League Cup 2nd round, 28 September 1960, D 0-0.
5ft 7in, 10st 4½lb (1961).
Wright made his Leeds debut in the club's first-ever League Cup-tie. He was signed from junior side, Shettleston Rovers, in June 1959. St Johnstone scouts saw him score a hat-trick in a United 'A' team game and he was allowed to join the Scottish club in November 1960.
League: App 1, Gls 0; League Cup: App 1, Gls 0.

WRIGHT, Tommy E. *1982-1987*

Forward. Born: Dunfermline, 10 January 1966.
Debut v Fulham (h) Division Two, 16 April 1983, D 3-3.
5ft 9in, 11st (1984).
Scottish Youth international Tommy Wright made an enterprising start to his Leeds career with a flurry of goals – including one in a memorable debut game. A product of St Columba's School, Dunfermline, he went to Elland Road in January 1982 after being recommended by United's top scout in Scotland, John Barr. Injury forced him out of action, and, after losing his place, he was sold to Oldham Athletic in October 1986 (£80,000). He found a new lease of life at Boundary Park, playing alongside several old Leeds teammates and won an Under-21 cap in 1987. In August 1989, the Latics sold Wright to Leicester City for £300,000. Top scorer in his final season at Filbert Street, he went to Middlesbrough in July 1994, for £650,000, where injuries and loss of form meant that he did not do himself justice and accepted a move to Bradford City in July 1995, where Carl Shutt was one of his playing partners up front. He is a member of a well-known sporting family. Father Thomas was a Scottish international forward, who played for Sunderland, Partick Thistle, East Fife and Oldham Athletic. His uncle, Jackie Sinclair, played for Dunfermline Athletic, Leicester City, Newcastle United, Sheffield

Wednesday, Chesterfield and Stenhousemuir; and brother Barry is a National Hunt jockey.
League: App 73/8, Gls 24; FA Cup: App 4, Gls 3; League Cup: App 3/3, Gls 1; Full Members' Cup: App 0/1, Gls 0.

YEBOAH, Tony *1995-*

Striker. Born: Kumasi, Ghana, 6 June 1966.
Debut (as sub) v Queen's Park Rangers (h) Premiership, 24 January 1995, W 4-0.
5ft 11in, 13st 13lb (1995).
Few strikers in the modern game have made such an explosive impact as African star Tony Yeboah. Outside the Bundesliga, few fans had heard of the Ghananian's goal power but it did not take long for him to take English football by storm with a

series of spectacular goals. Howard Wilkinson shattered the club's transfer record and paid German side Eintracht Frankfurt £3.4 million in what proved to be a major coup. Yeboah arrived in Leeds in January 1995, after scoring 68 goals in 123 Bundesliga games, and soon picked up the pace with Leeds, his 13 goals from 16 starts including a hat-trick against Ipswich as United came up on the rails to snatch a UEFA Cup spot. He did not disappoint in Europe either, his spectacular hat-trick in Monte Carlo destroying Monaco, while the Premiership treble he notched at Wimbledon included a blistering shot which was bettered by a match-winning volley at Elland Road that beat Liverpool and earned him the Goal of the Season award. At last Leeds seemed to have a player of genuine star quality to replace Eric Cantona. But the goals dried up and after missing several games because of his involvement in the African Nations Cup finals he returned to Leeds to find himself without a regular playing partner and often up front on his own. A knee injury ruled him out for the last two months of the 1995-96 season in which he finished as the club's Player of the Year. Despite rumours of Yeboah being unhappy with developments at Leeds, he has vowed to honour his contract and see his playing days out with United before returning to Ghana where he started his career with Kumasi Corner Stones. He was then spotted by German Second Division side Saarbrucken in 1988, playing for Okwawu United, and it was his exploits with Frankfurt which earned him star status and second place in the 1993 African Footballer of the Year award.
League: App 38/2, Gls 24; FA Cup: App 6/2, Gls 2; League Cup: App 7, Gls 3; Europe: App 4, Gls 3.

YORATH, Terry C. *1967-1976*

Midfield. Born: Cardiff, 27 March 1950.
Debut v Burnley (a) Division One, 11 May 1968, L 0-3.
5ft 10in, 10st 12lb (1975).
Aggressive, hard-tackling Terry Yorath, emerged from the shadows at Elland Road to enjoy an international career which brought him 59 caps for Wales. Yorath's entry into soccer was quite by accident. He was more noted at school for his ability as a Rugby Union scrum-half and had trials for Cardiff Schools at the handling game. One day he went to watch his soccer-playing brother play for Cardiff Boys against Rhondda Valley. The Cardiff lads were a player short and Yorath was pressed into service and did so well that he went on to win four Welsh Schools caps at soccer. After turning down the two Bristol clubs and his native Cardiff, Yorath joined Leeds. He turned professional in April 1967 and went on to win seven Under-23 caps. He only had one Football League appearance under his belt when he won his first full cap in 1969. He waited patiently in the Reserves and was converted from a rugged defender to an effective ball-winning midfielder. He proved a fine clubman and, although he lacked basic speed, his assets were not always appreciated by some of the more vociferous United fans. He had 28 full Welsh appearances to his name when he left Leeds for Coventry City in August 1976 (£125,000). Coventry sold him to Spurs in August 1979 (£300,000) and he went to Bradford City as player-coach in December 1982 after a spell in Canada with Vancouver Whitecaps. He helped Trevor Cherry build the Paraders into one of the most improved sides in the country. In May

1986, Yorath was appointed manager of Swansea City an in April 1988 began a successful trial for the vacant Welsh managerial position. In February 1989, Yorath walked out on Swansea to become Bradford City's new manager. The move sparked off a tremendous row between the two clubs over compensation and the Swans tried to block Yorath's path to Valley Parade with legal action. Things did not work out at Bradford. however, and he left in March 1990, returning to his old job at Swansea within days. He was Swansea's manager until March 1991 and the following year suffered personal tragedy when his 15-year-old son, Daniel, collapsed and died of an undiagnosed heart condition. After his departure from Swansea he was made full-time manager of Wales, having run the side on a part-time basis since 1988, and he took them close to qualification for the 1992 European Championships but his contract was not renewed in December 1993. He is currently working in Beirut as the Lebanese national team coach. His daughter has represented Wales at gymnastics in the Commonwealth Games.
League: App 121/21, Gls 10; FA Cup: App 14/3, Gls 1, League Cup: App 10/1, Gls 0; Europe: App 20/7, Gls1.

YOUNGER, Tommy *1961-1962*

Goalkeeper. Born: Edinburgh, 10 April 1930.
Debut v Preston North End (a) Division Two, 30 September 1961, L 1-2.
6ft 1in, 14st 11lb (1957).
Veteran Scottish international goalkeeper Tommy Younger played out the autumn of his career at Elland Road. He began at Scottish junior club, Hutchinson Vale, then joined Hibernian in 1948. He did his National Service with the BAOR and flew home from Germany each weekend to play for Hibs. He won the first of 24 full Scottish caps at Easter Road, was picked for the Scottish League three times and won Scottish League championship medals in 1951 and 1952. A £9,000 move took him to Liverpool in June 1956 and he went on to captain Scotland's 1958 World Cup squad. In June 1959 he was appointed player-manager of Falkirk but quit because of back trouble in February 1960, returning to a playing role with Stoke City the following month. Younger was 31 when Leeds signed him in September 1961. He finally retired in October 1962 and did some scouting for Leeds until being appointed coach to Toronto City in Canada. In October 1969 he returned to Scotland as public relations officer at Hibernian, where he also became a director. Younger, who was a partner in a vending machine business, was president of the Scottish FA at the time of his death on 13 January 1984, aged 53.
League: App 37, Gls 0; FA Cup: App 2, Gls 0; League Cup: App 3, Gls 0.

Leeds United's First Season: 1919-20

AFTER United's formation they were invited by the Midland League secretary, Mr J.Nicholson, to enter the Midland League – a lifeline they were quick to seize.

United were voted into the Midland League on 31 October, effectively taking over the place vacated by Leeds City Reserves. New players were hurriedly recruited and among those signed during the season was Ernie Hart, a future United captain and England player.

United's first-ever game was a friendly against Yorkshire Amateurs with whom they shared Elland Road that season. After the demise of Leeds City, Amateurs rented the ground.

The week after the opening game, United began their belated Midland League campaign with a goalless draw against Barnsley Reserves. Sometimes, friendlies were played on the same day as League fixtures, with United fielding their weaker team to fulfil their Midland League obligations. Newcastle City were not connected with Newcastle United and were an amateur side from Tyneside. United did not play in any Cup competitions.

Midland League 1919-20

Date	Venue	Opponent	Score
22 Nov	(h)	Barnsley	0-0
29 Nov	(h)	Rotherham Town	2-2
6 Dec	(h)	Worksop Town	3-4
13 Dec	(a)	Sheffield United Reserves	0-4
20 Dec	(h)	Lincoln City Reserves	2-0
25 Dec	(h)	Halifax Town	3-3
1 Jan	(a)	Barnsley Reserves	1-2
3 Jan	(a)	Lincoln City Reserves	0-4
10 Jan	(a)	Chesterfield Mun	3-4
17 Jan	(h)	Sheffield Wednesday Reserves	1-0
24 Jan	(a)	Castleford Town	0-0
31 Jan	(h)	Hull City Reserves	1-0
5 Feb	(a)	Hull City Reserves	1-2
7 Feb	(a)	Mexborough Town	0-2
14 Feb	(a)	Halifax Town	0-0
21 Feb	(h)	Castleford Town	6-0
23 Feb	(a)	Sheffield Wednesday Reserves	2-5
28 Feb	(a)	Notts County Reserves	1-1
11 Mar	(a)	Rotherham Town	1-3
6 Mar	(h)	Notts County Reserves	2-0
13 Mar	(h)	Rotherham County Reserves	3-3
20 Mar	(a)	Rotherham County Reserves	1-0
24 Mar	(h)	Grimsby Town Reserves	1-1
27 Mar	(a)	Worksop Town	0-2
3 Apr	(a*)	Silverwood Colliery	4-1
5 Apr	(a)	Gainsborough Trinity	1-2
6 Apr	(a)	Grimsby Town Reserves	2-0
8 Apr	(a)	Scunthorpe United	2-3
14 Apr	(h)	Silverwood Colliery	3-1
17 Apr	(h)	Sheffield United Reserves	1-2
21 Apr	(h)	Mexborough Town	4-2
24 Apr	(h)	Chesterfield Mun	0-2
28 Apr	(h)	Scunthorpe United	0-0
1 May	(h)	Gainsborough Trinity	6-0

** at Millmoor, Rotherham.*

Record

P	*W*	*D*	*L*	*F*	*A*	*Pts*	*Pos*
34	11	9	14	57	55	31	12th

Midland League 1919-20 Final Table

	P	*W*	*D*	*L*	*F*	*A*	*Pts*
Chesterfield Municipal	34	24	5	5	78	35	53
Sheffield U Res	34	20	11	3	73	28	51
Scunthorpe U	34	18	7	9	71	39	43
Worksop T	34	20	3	11	71	52	43
Mexborough T	34	18	6	10	60	45	42
Sheffield W Res	34	16	6	12	50	44	38
Rotherham T	34	14	8	12	83	71	36
Castleford T	34	14	8	12	53	46	36
Hull C Res	34	16	2	16	74	59	34
Grimsby T Res	34	14	5	15	66	64	33
Rotherham Co Res	34	13	5	16	60	57	31
Leeds U	34	11	9	14	57	55	31
Notts Co Res	34	10	11	13	50	56	31
Halifax T	34	13	4	17	52	70	30
Lincoln C Res	34	8	7	19	43	83	23
Barnsley Res	34	6	9	19	46	72	21
Silverwood Colliery	34	6	7	21	38	89	19
Gainsborough Trinity	34	7	3	24	37	95	17

Friendlies

Date	Venue	Opponent	Score
15 Nov	(h)	Yorkshire Amateurs	5-2
26 Dec	(a)	Scarborough	1-1
27 Dec	(h)	Bradford	3-2
28 Feb	(h)	Crewe Alexandra	0-5
27 Mar	(h)	Yorkshire Amateurs	3-1
2 Apr	(h)	Bradford City	1-0
3 Apr	(h)	Newcastle City	5-0
5 Apr	(h)	Bradford	1-3
6 Apr	(h)	Rotherham Amateurs	3-0
10 Apr	(h)	Halifax Town	1-1

Leeds United's

Record Against Other League Clubs 1920-21 to 1995-96

Leeds United have played 74 clubs in the Football League since 1920-21. Below is their record against each club. Some clubs changed their names (eg Small Heath became Birmingham then Birmingham City) and some clubs modified their titles (eg Leicester Fosse became Leicester City). In all cases the current name used by each club covers all games under previous names. Does not include the abandoned season of 1939-40 or Play-offs in 1986-87.

		HOME					*AWAY*				
	P	W	D	L	F	A	W	D	L	F	A
AFC BOURNEMOUTH	6	3	0	0	9	2	1	2	0	1	0
ARSENAL	84	23	11	8	78	47	11	10	21	46	73
ASTON VILLA	64	16	10	6	56	31	7	10	15	40	55
BARNSLEY	42	10	6	5	37	21	5	7	9	24	30
BIRMINGHAM CITY	76	20	12	6	56	23	6	11	21	35	71
BLACKBURN R	70	18	10	7	62	38	11	10	14	49	55
BLACKPOOL	36	9	7	2	36	17	5	4	9	25	34
BOLTON WANDERERS	40	11	5	4	47	33	3	4	13	18	44
BRADFORD	10	4	1	0	12	4	2	1	2	5	8
BRADFORD CITY	16	5	3	0	12	6	3	3	2	6	7
BRENTFORD	24	7	3	2	23	11	3	5	4	16	20
BRIGHTON & HA	22	8	2	1	21	11	3	3	5	10	14
BRISTOL CITY	20	5	2	3	13	10	4	4	2	10	7
BRISTOL ROVERS	10	2	3	0	8	5	0	2	3	7	18
BURNLEY	42	12	5	4	46	27	8	5	8	29	34
BURY	42	13	3	5	38	18	5	7	9	31	39
CAMBRIDGE UNITED	4	2	0	0	5	2	0	2	0	2	2
CARDIFF CITY	30	9	5	1	24	5	1	4	10	7	22
CARLISLE UNITED	10	3	2	0	10	3	2	2	1	8	7
CHARLTON ATHLETIC	28	9	2	3	23	11	6	1	7	13	24
CHELSEA	74	24	9	4	79	29	10	10	17	42	67
CHESTERFIELD	10	3	2	0	9	3	0	1	4	3	11
COVENTRY CITY	60	22	7	1	62	18	11	8	11	36	41
CRYSTAL PALACE	40	13	4	3	37	14	3	9	8	14	24
DERBY COUNTY	72	23	7	6	62	29	11	9	16	48	65
DONCASTER ROVERS	14	4	3	0	11	3	2	3	2	7	10
EVERTON	88	32	9	3	92	40	11	12	21	43	73
FULHAM	40	10	6	4	32	17	8	3	9	33	32
GRIMSBY TOWN	38	12	5	2	34	11	4	5	10	21	35
HUDDERSFIELD T	52	11	8	7	38	29	5	7	14	22	42
HULL CITY	34	11	4	2	35	15	6	2	9	19	23
IPSWICH TOWN	46	14	6	3	45	27	8	6	9	31	34
LEICESTER CITY	86	25	11	7	100	51	11	15	17	64	82
LEYTON ORIENT	16	5	2	1	12	5	3	1	4	7	10
LINCOLN CITY	12	5	0	1	20	7	1	3	2	5	8
LIVERPOOL	84	16	12	14	60	53	5	10	27	24	76
LUTON TOWN	36	9	5	4	29	19	3	8	7	19	27
MANCHESTER CITY	88	23	8	13	70	53	11	8	25	42	81

		HOME					*AWAY*				
	P	W	D	L	F	A	W	D	L	F	A
MANCHESTER UNITED	76	13	13	12	54	45	8	15	15	32	54
MIDDLESBROUGH	64	18	6	8	72	36	6	10	16	32	56
MILLWALL	10	3	0	2	8	5	1	1	3	6	10
NELSON	2	1	0	0	1	0	0	0	1	1	3
NEWCASTLE UNITED	704	20	9	6	67	27	9	5	21	42	68
NORTHAMPTON TOWN	4	1	1	0	6	1	1	0	1	4	2
NORWICH CITY	36	10	4	4	27	21	4	4	10	24	38
NOTTINGHAM FOREST	66	16	10	7	51	31	6	13	14	37	45
NOTTS COUNTY	32	12	3	1	40	7	5	3	8	20	25
OLDHAM ATHLETIC	30	10	4	1	30	6	2	7	6	20	28
OXFORD UNITED	6	2	1	0	4	2	1	0	2	8	10
PLYMOUTH ARGYLE	32	10	5	1	36	14	3	4	9	20	31
PORTSMOUTH	46	15	5	3	42	21	5	8	10	30	48
PORT VALE	18	6	2	1	17	6	6	1	2	9	7
PRESTON NORTH END	36	7	3	8	31	30	3	4	11	16	38
QUEEN'S PARK RANGERS	36	7	5	6	33	23	5	5	8	18	23
READING	6	2	1	0	9	4	2	0	1	3	2
ROTHERHAM UNITED	26	8	1	4	29	18	5	1	7	20	23
SCUNTHORPE UNITED	8	2	1	1	5	6	2	0	2	6	5
SHEFFIELD UNITED	64	17	9	6	62	32	8	11	13	44	49
SHEFFIELD WEDNESDAY	68	18	11	5	64	36	9	7	18	42	65
SHREWSBURY TOWN	14	4	2	1	11	6	3	2	2	12	12
SOUTHAMPTON	64	19	9	4	59	27	14	7	11	53	45
SOUTH SHIELDS	10	2	1	2	6	4	3	0	2	8	6
STOCKPORT COUNTY	6	2	0	1	6	2	0	1	2	3	6
STOKE CITY	78	25	9	5	74	27	12	7	20	54	90
SUNDERLAND	68	18	10	6	62	40	9	6	19	39	60
SWANSEA CITY	30	11	3	1	41	15	4	3	8	25	32
SWINDON TOWN	10	3	2	0	11	2	1	2	1	11	6
TOTTENHAM HOTSPUR	72	16	12	8	56	39	6	11	19	41	65
WALSALL	6	3	0	0	8	1	1	2	0	5	2
WATFORD	4	1	0	1	2	2	0	1	1	1	2
WEST BROMWICH ALBION	70	18	9	8	61	37	12	5	18	43	58
WEST HAM UNITED	80	26	9	5	89	45	10	13	17	53	75
WIMBLEDON	16	6	2	0	23	6	3	3	2	10	6
WOLVERHAMPTON W	70	21	8	6	59	28	9	9	17	36	59
TOTALS	2900	824	370	256	2699	1400	378	388	684	1690	2459

1920-21

Manager: Arthur Fairclough

No.	Date	Opponent	Result	Scorers	Att	Down	Duffield	Tillotson	Musgrove	Baker	Walton	Mason	Goldthorpe	Thompson	Lyon	Best	Ellson	Armitage	Frew	Hill	Brock	Boardman	Sharpe	Wood	Smelt	Hart	Stuart	Butler	Lamph	Howarth	Powell	Rodgerson	Jacklin	Coope	McGee	Cooper	Waterhouse
1	Aug 28	(a) Port Vale	L 0-2		15,000	1	2	3	4	5	6	7	8	9	10	11																					
2	Sep 1	(h) South Shields	L 1-2	Armitage	16,958	1	2	3	4	5	6	7			10	11	8	9																			
3	4	(h) Port Vale	W 3-1	Best, Ellson 2	15,000	1	2		4	5	6	7			10	11	8	9	3																		
4	8	(a) South Shields	L 0-3		15,000	1	2		4	5	6		9		10	11	8		3	7																	
5	11	(a) Leicester C	D 1-1	Ellson	16,000	1	2		4	5	6		9		10	11	8		3	7																	
6	18	(h) Leicester C	W 3-1	Ellson, Goldthorpe 2 (1 pen)	11,000	1	2		4	5	6	7	9		10	11	8		3																		
7	25	(a) Blackpool	L 0-1		8,000	1	2		4	5	6	7	9		10	11	8		3																		
8	Oct 2	(h) Blackpool	W 2-0	Walton, Mason	10,000	1	2		4	5	6	7	9		10	11	8		3																		
9	9	(a) Sheffield W	L 0-2		20,000	1	2		4	5	6	7			10	11	8	9	3																		
10	16	(h) Sheffield W	W 2-0	Thompson, Ellson	15,000	1	2		4	5	6	7		9	10		8		3		11																
11	23	(a) Hull C	W 1-0	Thompson	10,000	1	2		4	5	6	7		9	10	11	8		3																		
12	30	(h) Hull C	D 1-1	Ellson	20,000	1	2		4	5	6	7			10	11	8	9	3																		
13	Nov 6	(a) Stoke	L 0-4		10,000	1	2		4	5	6	7			10		8	9	3			11															
14	13	(h) Stoke	D 0-0		15,000	1	2		4	5	6	7		9	10		8		3			11															
15	27	(a) Coventry C	D 1-1	Lyon	18,000	1	2		4	5	6	7		9	10		8		3	11																	
16	Dec 1	(h) Coventry C	W 4-0	Thompson 2, Ellson, Mason	10,000	1	2		4	5	6	7		9	10		8		3				11														
17	4	(a) Notts C	W 2-1	Lyon 2	14,000	1	2		4	5	6	7		9	10		8		3	11																	
18	11	(h) Notts C	W 3-0	Thompson 3	12,000	1	2		4	5	6	7		9	10		8		3	11																	
19	18	(a) Birmingham	L 0-1		20,000	1	2		4	5	6	7		9	10		8		3	11																	
20	25	(h) Fulham	D 0-0		25,000	1	2		4	5	6	7		9	10		8		3					11													
21	27	(a) Fulham	L 0-1		30,000	1	2		4	5	6	7		9	10		8		3	11																	
22	Jan 1	(h) Birmingham	W 1-0	Baker (pen)	24,000	1	2		4	5	6	7		9	10		8		3					11													
23	8	(h) Rotherham C	W 1-0	Ellson	18,000	1	2		4	5	6	7		9	10		8		3					11													
24	15	(a) Wolves	L 0-3		20,000	1	2		4	5	6	7		9	10		8		3					11													
25	22	(h) Wolves	W 3-0	Thompson 2, Lyon	14,000	1	2		4	5	6	7		9	10		8		3					11													
26	29	(h) West Ham U	L 1-2	Thompson	15,000	1	2		4	5	6			9	10		8		3		7			11													
27	Feb 5	(a) West Ham U	L 0-3		23,000	1	2		4	5	6			9	10				3		7	8		11													
28	12	(a) Stockport C	L 1-3	Thompson	9,000	1	2		4	5	6			9	10						7	8		11	3												
29	19	(h) Stockport C	L 0-2		20,000	1	2			4		7		9			8		3					11		5	6	10									
30	26	(a) Clapton O	L 0-1		17,000	1	2		8	5	6	7		9			10		3					11					4								
31	Mar 5	(h) Clapton O	W 2-1	Musgrove, Baker (pen)	18,000	1	2		8	5	6	7		9			10		3					11					4								
32	12	(a) Bury	D 1-1	Howarth	10,000	1	2		8	5	6			7			10		3					11					4	9							
33	19	(h) Bury	W 1-0	Musgrove	16,000	1	2		8	5	6			7			10		3					11					4	9							
34	26	(h) Bristol C	L 0-1		20,000	1	2			5	6	7					10		3		8			11					4	9							
35	28	(a) Cardiff C	L 0-1		30,000	1	2			5	6	7					10		3		8			11					4	9							
36	29	(h) Cardiff C	L 1-2	Howarth	20,000	1	2		4	5	6	7			10				3					11						9	8						
37	Apr 2	(a) Bristol C	D 0-0		24,000	1	2		4	3	6	7			10									11		5				9	8						
38	9	(h) Barnsley	D 0-0		13,000	1	2		4	5	6	7			10		8		3					11						9							
39	16	(a) Barnsley	D 1-1	Howarth	12,000	1	2		4	5	6	7			10		8		3					11						9							
40	23	(h) Nottingham F	D 1-1	Howarth	12,000	1	2			5	6	7			10		8							11		4				9		3					
41	30	(a) Nottingham F	L 0-1		8,000	1	8			4	6	7					10		2					11		5				9		3					
42	May 7	(a) Rotherham C	W 2-0	Howarth 2 (1 pen)	10,000	1	2			4	6	7						8						11		5				9	10	3					
FINAL LEAGUE POSITION: 14th in Division Two					Appearances	42	42	2	36	42	41	35	6	23	33	11	36	6	36	7	6	4	1	22	1	5	1	1	6	11	3	3					
					Goals				2	2	1	3	2	11	3	1	8	1												6							

FA Cup

No.	Date	Opponent	Result	Scorers	Att	Down	Duffield	Tillotson	Musgrove	Baker	Walton	Mason	Goldthorpe	Thompson	Lyon	Best	Ellson	Armitage	Frew	Hill	Brock	Boardman	Sharpe	Wood	Smelt	Hart	Stuart	Butler	Lamph	Howarth	Powell	Rodgerson	Jacklin	Coope	McGee	Cooper	Waterhouse
Q1	Sep 11	(h) Boothtown	W 5-2	Armitage 2, O'Doherty 3	1,500									11				9								5	4	10					1	2	3	6	7
Q2	25	(h*) Leeds Steelworks	W 7-0	Butler 3, Thompson, Hart, O'Doherty, Waterhouse	3,000									9						11					3	5	4	10					1	2		6	7
*Leeds Steelworks drawn at home but surrendered the advantage.					Appearances									2				1		1					1	2	2	2					2	2	1	2	2
Leeds United then withdrew from the competition.					Goals									1				2								1		3									1

O'Doherty played number-8 in Matches Q1 & Q2 and scored four goals.

1921-22

Manager: Arthur Fairclough

No	Date	Opponent	Result	Scorers	Att	Whalley	Duffield	Rodgerson	Baker	Sherwin	Walton	Clark	Armitage	Howarth	Moore	Wood	Hart	Mason	Coates	Frew	Poyntz	Swan	Down	Jacklin	Gascoigne	Ellson	Potts	Powell	Robson
1	Aug 27	(h) Port Vale	W 2-1	Howarth, Walton	18,000	1	2	3	4	5	6	7	8	9	10	11													
2	29	(a) Bristol C	D 0-0		16,000	1	2	3	4	5	6	7	8	9	10	11													
3	Sep 3	(a) Port Vale	W 1-0	Howarth	18,000	1	2	3	4	5	6	7	8	9	10	11													
4	5	(h) Bristol C	W 3-0	Howarth 2, Moore	18,000	1	2	3	4		6		8	9	10	11	5	7											
5	10	(h) Blackpool	D 0-0		18,000	1	2	3	4		6		8	9	10	11	5	7											
6	17	(a) Blackpool	W 3-1	Howarth, Wood, Mason	15,000	1	2	3	4		6		8	9	10	11	5	7											
7	24	(h) Clapton O	W 2-0	Wood, Howarth	20,000	1	2	3	4		6		8	9	10	11	5		7										
8	Oct 1	(a) Clapton O	L 2-4	Howarth (pen), Moore	20,000	1		3	4		6		8	9	10	11	5		7	2									
9	8	(h) South Shields	D 0-0		20,000	1	2	3	4		6		8	9	10	11	5		7										
10	15	(a) South Shields	W 1-0	Howarth	15,000	1	2	3	4		6		8	9	10	11	5		7										
11	22	(h) Stoke	L 1-2	Howarth	10,000	1	2	3	4		6		8	9	10	11	5		7										
12	29	(a) Stoke	L 0-3		15,000	1	2	3	6	4			8		10	11	5	7			9								
13	Nov 5	(h) Bradford	W 3-0	Howarth (pen), Armitage, Mason	18,000	1	2		6	4			8	9	10	11	5	7		3									
14	12	(a) Bradford	W 1-0	Howarth	20,000	1	2		6	4			8	9	10	11	5	7		3									
15	19	(a) Hull C	L 0-1		12,800	1	2		6	4				9	8	11	5	7		3		10							
16	26	(h) Hull C	L 0-2		20,000	1		3	6	4			8	9	10	11	5	7		2									
17	Dec 3	(a) Notts C	L 1-4	Howarth	12,000		2		6	4			8	9	10	11	5	7		3			1						
18	10	(h) Notts C	D 1-1	Moore	16,000		2		6	5				9	8	11		7		3				1	4	10			
19	17	(h) Crystal P	D 0-0		10,000		2		5		6	11			8			7			9			1	4		3	10	
20	24	(a) Crystal P	W 2-1	Swan, Moore	10,000		2	3	5		6			9	8	11		7				10		1	4				
21	26	(h) Sheffield W	D 1-1	Swan	20,540	1	2	3	5		6			9	8	11		7				10			4				
22	27	(a) Sheffield W	L 1-2	Howarth	25,000	1		3	6				8	9		11	5	7		2		10			4				
23	31	(h) Rotherham C	L 0-2		12,000	1	2	3	5					9	8	11		7		6		10			4				
24	Jan 14	(a) Rotherham C	L 0-1		6,000	1	2	3	5	4	6		8	9		11		7				10							
25	21	(h) West Ham U	D 0-0		7,000	1	2	3	5	4	6			9		11			7		8	10							
26	28	(a) West Ham U	D 1-1	Armitage	20,000	1	2	3	6	4			9			11	5		7		8	10							
27	Feb 4	(h) Bury	W 2-0	Armitage, Poyntz	5,000	1	2	3	6	4			9			11	5		7		8	10							
28	11	(a) Bury	L 1-2	Armitage	10,000	1	2	3	6	4			9			11	5		7		8	10							
29	20	(h) Leicester C	W 3-0	Poyntz 3	5,000	1		3	6	4			9		11		5		7	2	8	10							
30	25	(a) Leicester C	D 0-0		14,000	1	2		6	4			9		10	11	5		7	3	8								
31	Mar 4	(h) Derby C	W 2-1	Swan 2	12,000	1	2		6	4			9	8	11		5		7	3		10							
32	11	(a) Derby C	L 0-2		9,000	1	2		6	4				9	8	11	5		7	3		10							
33	18	(a) Coventry C	L 0-1		15,000	1	2		6		4			9		11	5		7	3		10							8
34	25	(h) Coventry C	W 5-2	Armitage 2, Swan 3	10,000	1	2		6	4			9			11	5		7	3		10							8
35	Apr 1	(a) Barnsley	D 2-2	Swan, Armitage	12,660	1	2		6	4		11	9				5		7	3	8	10							
36	8	(h) Barnsley	W 4-0	Swan 2, Gittins (og), Poyntz	10,000	1	2		6	4		11	9				5		7	3	8	10							
37	14	(h) Fulham	W 2-0	Poyntz, Coates	20,000	1	2		6	4		11	9				5		7	3	8	10							
38	15	(a) Wolves	D 0-0		10,000	1	2		6	4		11	9				5		7	3	8	10							
39	17	(a) Fulham	W 1-0	Armitage	20,000	1	2		6	4		11	9				5		7	3	8	10							
40	22	(h) Wolves	D 0-0		7,0000	1	2		6	4		11	9			7	5			3	8	10							
41	29	(a) Nottingham F	L 0-1		16,000	1		2	6	4				9	8	11	5	7		3		10							
42	May 6	(h) Nottingham F	D 0-0		10,000	1	2		6	4				9		11	5			3	8							10	7
FINAL LEAGUE POSITION: 8th in Division Two					Appearances	38	37	24	42	28	17	10	31	28	27	34	32	17	20	23	15	22	1	3	6	1	1	2	3
					Goals						1		8	13	4	2		2	1		6	10							

1 own-goal

FA Cup

No	Date	Opponent	Result	Scorers	Att	Whalley	Duffield	Rodgerson	Baker	Sherwin	Walton	Clark	Armitage	Howarth	Moore	Wood	Hart	Mason	Coates	Frew	Poyntz	Swan	Down	Jacklin	Gascoigne	Ellson	Potts	Powell	Robson
1	Jan 7	(a) Swindon T	L 1-2	Swan	16,000	1	2	3	5	4	6		8	9	11			7				10							
					Appearances	1	1	1	1	1	1		1	1	1			1				1							
					Goals																	1							

1922-23

Manager: Arthur Fairclough

No	Date	Opponent	Result	Scorers	Att	Whalley	Duffield	Frew	Sherwin	Hart	Baker	Mason	Poyntz	Howarth	Swan	Harris	Robson	Armitage	Walton	Powell	Gascoigne	Clark	Potts	Dark	Noble	Whipp	Richmond	Bell T	Armand	Coates	Smith
1	Aug 26	(h) Blackpool	D 1-1	Swan	18,000	1	2	3	4	5	6	7	8	9	10	11															
2	28	(a) Southampton	W 1-0	Swan	16,000	1	2	3	4	5	6	7	8	9	10	11															
3	Sep 2	(a) Blackpool	L 0-1		15,000	1	2	3	4	5	6	7	8	9	10	11															
4	4	(h) Southampton	W 1-0	Harris	6,000	1	2	3	4	5	6	7		9		11	8	10													
5	9	(h) Stockport C	W 2-0	Walton, Armitage	12,000	1	2	3	4	5	6	7				11		9	8	10											
6	16	(a) Stockport C	L 1-2	Armitage	14,000	1	2	3		5	6	7				11		9	8	10	4										
7	23	(h) Bradford C	W 1-0	Harris	20,000	1	2	3	4	5	6	7	8		10	11		9													
8	30	(a) Bradford C	W 2-0	Swan, Harris	22,000	1	2	3	4	5	6	7	8		10	11		9													
9	Oct 7	(a) Clapton O	L 0-3		14,000	1	2	3	4	5	6	7	8		10			9				11									
10	14	(h) Clapton O	D 0-0		15,000	1	2			5	6	7	8	9	10	11					4		3								
11	21	(h) Leicester C	D 0-0		12,000	1	2		4	5	6	7	8	9	10	11							3								
12	28	(a) Leicester C	L 1-2	Harris	20,000	1	2		4	5	6	7	9		10	11							3	8							
13	Nov 4	(h) West Ham U	W 3-1	Whipp 3 (1 pen)	12,000	1	2		4	5	6		9		10	11							3		7	8					
14	11	(a) West Ham U	D 0-0		14,000	1	2		4	5	6		9		10	11							3		7	8					
15	18	(h) South Shields	L 0-1		12,000	1	2		4	5	6		9		10	11							3		7	8					
16	25	(a) South Shields	W 2-0	Whipp, Poyntz	18,000	1	2		4	5	6		9			11			10				3		7	8					
17	Dec 2	(h) Wolves	W 1-0	Walton	14,000	1	2		4	5	6		9			11			10				3		7	8					
18	9	(a) Wolves	W 1-0	Hart	16,000	1	2	3	4	5	6					11			10						7	8	9				
19	16	(a) Coventry C	W 2-1	Richmond 2	12,000	1	2	3	4	5	6								10			11			7	8	9				
20	23	(h) Coventry C	W 1-0	Whipp	10,000	1	2	3	4	5	6								10			11			7	8	9				
21	25	(a) Bury	D 1-1	Whipp	20,000	1	2		4	5	6					11		9	10						7	8		3			
22	26	(h) Bury	D 0-0		27,000	1	2	3	4	5	6	7				11			10							8	9				
23	30	(a) Port Vale	W 2-1	Whipp 2	8,000	1	2	3	4	5	6					11		9	10						7	8					
24	Jan 6	(h) Port Vale	W 2-1	Whipp 2	15,000	1	2	3	4	5	6					11		9	10						7	8					
25	20	(a) Manchester U	D 0-0		25,000	1	2	3		5	6				10	11		9			4				7	8					
26	27	(h) Manchester U	L 0-1		25,000	1	2	3	4	5	6				10	11									7	8			9		
27	Feb 10	(a) Barnsley	L 0-1		11,000	1	2	3		5	6				10	11		9			4				7	8					
28	17	(h) Sheffield W	D 0-0		14,000	1	2	3		5	6					11					4				7	8	9		10		
29	24	(h) Barnsley	D 1-1	Swan	8,000	1	2	3		5	6				10	11					4				7	8			9		
30	Mar 3	(h) Hull C	D 2-2	Swan 2	12,000	1	2	3	4		5				10	11					6				7	8			9		
31	10	(a) Hull C	L 1-3	Swan	14,000	1	2	3		5	6				9	11					4				7	8			10		
32	17	(a) Crystal P	L 0-1		15,000	1	2	3		5	6				10	11					4				7	8			9		
33	19	(a) Sheffield W	L 1-3	Powell	11,000	1	2	3		5	6					11	8			9	4				7				10		
34	24	(h) Crystal P	W 4-1	Whipp, Swan, Powell, Sherwin	8,000	1	2	3	4	5	6				10	11				9					7	8					
35	30	(h) Rotherham C	W 2-0	Powell, Whipp	12,000	1	2	3	4	5	6				10	11				9					7	8					
36	31	(a) Fulham	L 0-3		16,000	1	2	3		5	6				10	11				9	4					8				7	
37	Apr 2	(a) Rotherham C	L 1-3	Harris (pen)	10,000	1		3		5	6				10	11				9			2	4	7	8					
38	7	(h) Fulham	D 1-1	Whipp	10,000	1	2	3		5	6					11	8			9				4	7	10					
39	14	(a) Notts C	L 0-1		10,000	1	2	3	4	5	6					11	8			9					7	10					
40	21	(h) Notts C	W 3-0	Whipp 2, Powell	8,000	1	2	3	4	5	6					11	8			9					7	10					
41	28	(a) Derby C	W 1-0	Noble	5,000	1	2	3		5	6					11	8			9					7	10					4
42	May 5	(h) Derby C	W 1-0	Powell (pen)	4,000	1	2	3		5	6					11	8			9					7	10					4
FINAL LEAGUE POSITION: 7th in Division Two					Appearances	42	41	33	28	41	42	13	14	6	23	39	7	11	11	12	11	3	9	3	28	29	5	1	7	1	2
					Goals				1	1			1		8	5		2	2	5					1	15	2				

FA Cup

Rd	Date	Opponent	Result	Scorers	Att	Whalley	Duffield	Frew	Sherwin	Hart	Baker	Mason	Poyntz	Howarth	Swan	Harris	Robson	Armitage	Walton	Powell	Gascoigne	Clark	Potts	Dark	Noble	Whipp	Richmond	Bell T	Armand	Coates	Smith
1	Jan 13	(a) Portsmouth	D 0-0		26,046	1	2	3	4	5	6					11		9	10						7	8					
R	17	(h) Portsmouth	W 3-1	Whipp, Armitage, Swan	21,240	1	2	3	4	5	6				10	11		9							7	8					
2	Feb 3	(a) Bolton W	L 1-3	Swan	43,389	1	2	3	4	5	6				10	11		9							7	8					
					Appearances	3	3	3	3	3	3				2	3		3	1						3	3					
					Goals										2			1								1					

1923-24

Manager: Arthur Fairclough

No	Date	Opponent	Result	Scorers	Att	Whalley	Duffield	Speak	Sherwin	Mason	Baker JW	Noble	Whipp	Richmond	Fullam	Harris	Powell	Frew	Lambert	Swan	Down	Baker LH	Gascoigne	Coates	Hart	Armand	Menzies	Johnson	Bell A	Smith	Allen
1	Aug 25	(a) Stoke	D 1-1	Noble	12,000	1	2	3	4	5	6	7	8	9	10	11															
2	27	(h) Crystal P	W 3-0	Fullam, Noble, Whipp	10,000	1	2	3	4	5	6	7	8	9	10	11															
3	Sep 1	(h) Stoke	D 0-0		12,900	1	2	3	4	5	6	7	8		10	11	9														
4	5	(a) Crystal P	D 1-1	Whipp	8,000	1	2	3	4	5	6	7	8	9	10	11															
5	8	(a) Leicester C	L 0-2		18,000	1	2		4	5	6	7	10			11	9	3	8												
6	15	(h) Leicester C	L 1-2	Swan	15,000	1	2	3	4	5	6	7	8	9		11				10											
7	22	(a) Hull C	W 2-1	Swan 2	11,500		2	3	4		6	7	8	9		11				10	1	5									
8	29	(h) Hull C	W 5-2	Richmond 3, Swan, Harris	12,000		2	3	4		6	7	8	9		11				10	1	5									
9	Oct 6	(a) Clapton O	W 1-0	Richmond	25,000		2	3			6	7	8	9		11				10	1	5	4								
10	13	(h) Clapton O	W 1-0	Harris	15,000		2	3			6		8	9		11				10	1	5	4	7							
11	20	(a) Port Vale	W 1-0	Richmond	10,000		2	3	4		6		8	9		11				10	1			7	5						
12	27	(h) Port Vale	W 3-0	Swan 2, Richmond	12,000		2		4		6		8	9		11		3		10	1			7	5						
13	Nov 3	(h) Bradford C	W 1-0	Whipp	17,000		2		4		6		8	9		11		3		10	1			7	5						
14	10	(a) Bradford C	D 0-0		25,000		2	3	4		6		8	9		11				10	1			7	5						
15	17	(h) Barnsley	W 3-1	Swan 2, Whipp	12,000		2	3	4		6		8	9		11				10	1			7	5						
16	24	(a) Barnsley	W 3-1	Harris, Richmond 2	12,000		2	3	4		6		8	9		11				10	1			7	5						
17	Dec 1	(h) Manchester U	D 0-0		20,000		2	3	4		6		8	9		11				10	1			7	5						
18	8	(a) Manchester U	L 1-3	Whipp	30,000		2	3	4		6		8	9		11				10	1			7	5						
19	15	(h) Bury	L 1-2	Whipp (pen)	17,000		2	3	4		6		8	9		11				10	1			7	5						
20	22	(a) Bury	L 0-3		10,000		2	3		4		7				11	9			10	1	6			5	8					
21	25	(a) Oldham A	D 2-2	Richmond 2	17,000		2		4			7		9		11				10	1	6			5	8	3				
22	26	(h) Oldham A	W 5-0	Swan 2, Richmond, Whipp 2	12,000		2	3			4	7	8	9						10	1	6			5	11					
23	Jan 5	(a) South Shields	L 0-2		10,000		2	3			4	7	8	9		11				10	1	6			5						
24	19	(a) Sheffield W	D 0-0		18,000		2		4	5			8	9		11				10	1	6				7	3				
25	26	(h) Sheffield W	W 1-0	Swan	15,000		2		4		6	7	8			11	9			10	1				5		3				
26	Feb 9	(h) Coventry C	W 3-1	Armand, Richmond, Harris	11,239		2			5	6			9		11		3		10	1		4	7		8					
27	16	(a) Bristol C	W 1-0	Swan	14,000		2		4		6		8	9		11				10	1			7	5		3				
28	27	(h) South Shields	W 2-1	Whipp, Armand	8,000	1	2		4		6	7	8			11				10					5	9	3				
29	Mar 1	(a) Southampton	W 1-0	Hart	8,000				4		6	7	8			11				10					5	9	3	1	2		
30	8	(h) Southampton	W 3-0	Shelley (og), Swan, Harris	15,000		2	3	4		6	7	8	9		11				10	1				5						
31	10	(a) Coventry C	L 1-2	Sherwin	6,000		2		4		6	7	8	9		11				10	1				5		3				
32	15	(h) Fulham	W 3-0	Swan 2, Coates	18,000		2		4		6		8	9		11				10				7	5		3	1			
33	19	(a) Bristol C	D 0-0		8,000		2		4		6		8	9		11				10	1			7	5		3				
34	22	(a) Fulham	W 2-0	Fullam, Whipp	17,000		2	3		5			8		10	7				9	1	4								6	11
35	29	(h) Blackpool	D 0-0		25,000		2				4		8		10	7				9	1				5		3			6	11
36	Apr 5	(a) Blackpool	D 1-1	Richmond	14,000		2				4	7	8	9		11				10	1				5		3			6	
37	12	(h) Derby C	D 1-1	Whipp	20,000				4		2	7	8	9		11				10	1				5		3			6	
38	18	(a) Stockport C	D 1-1	Richmond	15,000			3			4	7	8	9		11				10	1				5		2			6	
39	19	(a) Derby C	L 0-2		21,622			3	4				8	9	10	11								7	5		2	1		6	
40	21	(h) Stockport C	W 4-0	Swan 2, Richmond, Harris	22,500		2				4		8	9		11				10	1			7	5		3			6	
41	26	(h) Nelson	W 1-0	Coates	20,000		2				4		8	9		11				10	1			7	5		3			6	
42	May 3	(a) Nelson	L 1-3	Swan	10,000		2		4				8	9		11				10	1			7	5		3			6	
FINAL LEAGUE POSITION: 1st in Division Two					Appearances	7	38	23	30	10	36	21	39	34	7	41	4	4	1	36	32	10	3	18	29	7	17	3	1	9	2
					Goals				1			2	11	15	2	6				18				2	1	2					

1 own-goal

FA Cup

No	Date	Opponent	Result	Scorers	Att	Whalley	Duffield	Speak	Sherwin	Mason	Baker JW	Noble	Whipp	Richmond	Fullam	Harris	Powell	Frew	Lambert	Swan	Down	Baker LH	Gascoigne	Coates	Hart	Armand	Menzies	Johnson	Bell A	Smith	Allen
1	Jan 12	(h) Stoke	W 1-0	Whipp	26,574		2	3	4		6		8	9		11				10	1				5	7					
2	Feb 2	(a) West Ham U	D 1-1	Coates	30,123		2	3	4		6		8	9		11				10	1			7	5						
R	6	(h) West Ham U	W 1-0	Whipp	31,071		2	3	4		6		8	9		11				10	1			7	5						
3	23	(a) Aston Villa	L 0-3		51,238		2		4		6		8	9		11				10	1			7	5		3				
					Appearances		4	3	4		4		4	4		4				4	4			3	4	1	1				
					Goals								2											1							

1924-25

Manager: Arthur Fairclough

	Date		Opponent	Result	Scorers	Att	Down	Duffield	Menzies	Sherwin	Hart	Baker JW	Noble	Whipp	Richmond	Swan	Harris	Duxbury	Thom	Graver	Clark	Coates	Johnson	Speak	Robson	Smith	Moore	Armand	Mason	Baker LH	Powell	Russell	Atkinson	Martin	Jennings	Edwards	Wainscoat
1	Aug	30	(h) Sunderland	D 1-1	Swan	33,722	1	2	3	4	5	6	7	8	9	10	11																				
2	Sep	1	(a) Notts C	L 0-1		16,000	1	2	3		5	6				10	7	4	8	9	11																
3		6	(a) Cardiff C	L 0-3		30,000	1	2	3		5	6		8	9	10	11	4				7															
4		10	(h) Notts C	D 1-1	Swan	18,000	1	2	3	4	5	6		8	9	10	11					7															
5		13	(h) Preston NE	W 4-0	Swan 2, Thom, Harris	20,000	1	2	3	4	5	6		8		10	11		9			7															
6		17	(h) Everton	W 1-0	Thom	22,000	1	2	3	4	5	6		8		10	11		9			7															
7		20	(a) Burnley	D 1-1	Thom	23,000	1	2	3	4	5	6		8		10	11		9			7															
8		27	(h) Huddersfield T	D 1-1	Swan	41,800	1	2	3	4	5	6		8		10	11		9			7															
9	Oct	4	(h) Birmingham	L 0-1		24,000		2	3	4	5	6		8		10	11		9			7	1														
10		11	(a) West Brom A	L 1-3	Robson	21,332		2			5	6		8	9	10	11	4					1	3	7												
11		18	(h) Tottenham H	W 1-0	Whipp	23,000		2	3	4	5	6		8		10	11		9				1		7												
12		25	(a) Blackburn R	W 3-2	Robson 2, Swan	20,000		2	3		5	4		8	9	10	11						1		7	6											
13	Nov	1	(h) West Ham U	W 2-1	Richmond (pen), Swan	17,000		2	3		5	4		8	9	10	11						1		7	6											
14		8	(a) Sheffield U	D 1-1	Swan	30,000		2	3		5	4		8	9	10	11						1		7	6											
15		15	(h) Newcastle U	D 1-1	Whipp	30,000		2	3		5	4		8	9	10	11								7	6	1										
16		22	(a) Liverpool	L 0-1		20,000		2	3		5	4		8	9	10	11								7	6	1										
17		29	(h) Nottingham F	D 1-1	Robson	20,000	1	2	3	4	5			8	9	10	11								7	6											
18	Dec	6	(a) Bury	L 0-1		15,000	1	2	3		5	4	7	8	9	10	11									6											
19		13	(h) Manchester C	L 0-3		15,000	1	2	3		5	4		8		10	11								7	6		9									
20		20	(a) Arsenal	L 1-6	Whipp	30,000	1	2	3		5	6		9		10	11								7			8	4								
21		25	(h) Aston Villa	W 6-0	Whipp 3, Swan 2, Hart	24,000		2	3	4	5			9		10	11								7	6	1	8									
22		26	(a) Aston Villa	L 1-2	Swan	50,000			2			4				10	11							3	7	6	1	8		5	9						
23		27	(a) Sunderland	L 1-2	Richmond	18,000		2		4	5				9	10	11			8				3	7	6	1										
24	Jan	3	(h) Cardiff C	D 0-0		19,000		2	3	4	5			8	9	10	11								7	6	1										
25		17	(a) Preston NE	W 4-1	Whipp 2, Powell 2	15,000	1	2	3		5	4		8	9		11								7	6					10						
26		24	(h) Burnley	L 0-2		15,000	1	2	3			4		8	9		11								7	6			5		10						
27		31	(a) Huddersfield T	L 0-2		12,000		2	3		5	4		8		10	11					7									9	1	6				
28	Feb	7	(a) Birmingham	D 0-0		20,000			2		5	4	7	8			11			9				3							10	1	6				
29		14	(h) West Brom A	L 0-1		18,500	1		2		5	4	7	8		9	11							3							10		6				
30		28	(h) Blackburn R	D 1-1	Noble	17,000	1	2	3		5	4	7	9		10	11											8					6				
31	Mar	7	(a) West Ham U	D 0-0		15,000	1	2	3			6	4		9		7				10							8	5					11			
32		9	(a) Tottenham H	L 1-2	Armand	12,000	1	2	3			6	4		9		7				10							8	5					11			
33		14	(h) Sheffield U	D 1-1	Harris	25,000	1	2	3			4	7				11									6		8	5		10				9		
34		21	(a) Newcastle U	L 1-4	Wainscoat	15,000	1	2	3		5						11								7			8					6		9		
35		28	(h) Liverpool	W 4-1	Wainscoat, Armand, Harris, Jennings	25,000		2	3		5			7			11											8				1	6		9	4	10
36	Apr	4	(a) Nottingham F	L 0-4		5,000		2	3		5			7			11											8				1	6		9	4	10
37		10	(a) Bolton W	L 0-1		25,000		2	3		5			7			11											8				1	6		9	4	10
38		11	(h) Bury	W 1-0	Jennings	25,000		2	3		5		7	8			11															1	6		9	4	10
39		14	(h) Bolton W	W 2-1	Wainscoat, Jennings	30,000		2	3		5		7	8			11															1	6		9	4	10
40		18	(a) Manchester C	L 2-4	Wainscoat, Whipp	14,000		2	3		5		7	8			11															1	6		9	4	10
41		25	(h) Arsenal	W 1-0	Whipp	20,000		2	3		5			8			11											7				1	6		9	4	10
42	May	2	(a) Everton	L 0-1		10,000	1	2	3		5			8			11											7					6		9	4	10
FINAL LEAGUE POSITION: 18th in Division One						Appearances	21	39	40	12	37	29	11	35	17	27	42	3	7	3	3	8	6	5	17	15	6	14	5	1	7	9	13	2	10	9	9
						Goals					1		1	10	2	11	3		3						4			2			2				3		4

FA Cup

	Date		Opponent	Result	Scorers	Att	Down	Duffield	Menzies	Sherwin	Hart	Baker JW	Noble	Whipp	Richmond	Swan	Harris	Duxbury	Thom	Graver	Clark	Coates	Johnson	Speak	Robson	Smith	Moore	Armand	Mason	Baker LH	Powell	Russell	Atkinson	Martin	Jennings	Edwards	Wainscoat
1	Jan	10	(a) Liverpool	L 0-3		39,000	1		2	4	5			9		10	11							3	7	6		8									
						Appearances	1		1	1	1			1		1	1							1	1	1		1									
						Goals																															

1925-26

Manager: Arthur Fairclough

No	Date	Opponent	Result	Scorers	Att	Johnson	Duffield	Menzies	Edwards	Hart	Atkinson	Turnbull	Whipp	Jennings	Wainscoat	Harris	Allan	Baker	Jackson	Smith	Armand	Sissons	Mears	Kirkpatrick	Chadwick	Townsley	Thornton	Fell	Potts	Roberts	Reed
1	Aug 29	(a) Notts C	L 0-1		18,155	1	2	3	4	5	6	7	8	9	10	11															
2	31	(h) Bolton W	W 2-1	Jennings, Harris	24,188	1	2	3	4	5	6	7	8	9	10	11															
3	Sep 5	(h) Aston Villa	D 2-2	Jennings 2	29,501	1	2	3	4	5	6	7	8	9	10	11															
4	7	(a) Bolton W	L 0-1		23,343	1		3	4	5			8	9	10	7	2	6	11												
5	12	(a) Leicester C	W 3-1	Jennings, Turnbull 2	23,592	1	2	3	4	5		7	8	9	10			6	11												
6	16	(h) Newcastle U	W 2-0	Jennings, Jackson	21,291	1	2	3	4	5		7	8	9	10			6	11												
7	19	(h) West Ham U	W 5-2	Whipp, Jennings 2, Wainscoat 2	16,433	1		3	4	5		7	8	9	10		2		11	6											
8	26	(a) Arsenal	L 1-4	Wainscoat	32,531	1		3	4	5		7	8	9	10		2		11	6											
9	Oct 3	(h) Manchester U	W 2-0	Jennings, Wainscoat	26,265	1		3	4	5		7	8	9	10		2	6	11												
10	10	(a) Liverpool	D 1-1	Wainscoat	30,088	1		3	4	5		7	8	9	10		2	6	11												
11	17	(h) Huddersfield T	L 0-4		33,008	1	2	3	4	5			8	9	10			6	11		7										
12	24	(a) Everton	L 2-4	Jennings, Wainscoat	28,660	1		3	4	5		7		9	10		2	6	11		8										
13	31	(h) Bury	L 2-3	Hart, Jackson	15,008	1		3	4	5	6			9			2		11		8	7	10								
14	Nov 7	(a) Blackburn R	D 2-2	Hart, Jennings	9,190	1		3	4	5	6	10	8	9			2		11			7									
15	14	(h) Cardiff C	W 1-0	Turnbull	19,360	1			4	5	6	10	8	9			2		11			7		3							
16	21	(a) Sheffield U	L 0-2		22,327	1			4	5	6	11	8	9			2					7		3	10						
17	28	(h) West Brom A	L 0-1		14,774	1			4	5	6	7	8	9			2		11					3	10						
18	Dec 5	(a) Birmingham	L 1-2	Jennings	13,435	1			4	5	6	7	8	9			2		11					3	10						
19	12	(h) Manchester C	L 3-4	Armand 2 (1 pen), Chadwick	18,762	1		3	4	5	6	7		9			2		11		8				10						
20	19	(a) Tottenham H	L 2-3	Armand 2 (1 pen)	19,200	1			4		5	7	8	9			2		11	6	10			3							
21	25	(h) Burnley	D 2-2	Turnbull, Whipp	23,325	1			4		6	7	8	9			2		11		10			3		5					
22	26	(a) Burnley	L 3-6	Whipp, Armand, Jennings	22,207				4		2	7	8	9					11	6	10			3		5	1				
23	Jan 1	(a) Sunderland	W 3-1	Armand (pen), Townsley, Jennings	29,527	1		3	4		6	7	8	9			2		11		10					5					
24	2	(h) Notts C	W 2-1	Armand (pen), Whipp	14,615	1		3	4		6	7	8	9			2		11		10					5					
25	23	(h) Leicester C	W 1-0	Chadwick	19,569	1		3	4	5	6	7		9			2		11		8				10						
26	30	(a) West Ham U	L 2-4	Jennings 2	17,246	1		3	4		6	7		9	10		2		11						8	5					
27	Feb 3	(a) Aston Villa	L 1-3	Jennings	11,573	1		3	4		6	7		9	10		2		11						8	5					
28	6	(h) Arsenal	W 4-2	Jennings 3, Chadwick	26,239	1		3	4		6	7		9	10		2		11						8	5					
29	13	(a) Manchester U	L 1-2	Jennings	29,584	1		3	4		6	7		9	10		2								8	5		11			
30	20	(h) Liverpool	D 1-1	Jennings	24,158	1		3	4			7		9	10		2		11	6	8					5					
31	27	(a) Huddersfield T	L 1-3	Wainscoat	26,248			3	4				8	9	10		2	6	11			7				5			1		
32	Mar 6	(h) Everton	D 1-1	Wainscoat	18,163			3	4				8	9	10		2	6	11			7				5			1		
33	13	(a) Bury	W 2-0	Armand, Jennings	15,226			6		5		7		9	10		3				8					4		11	1	2	
34	20	(h) Blackburn R	W 2-1	Fell, Armand	22,419			3	4	5		7		9	10		2				8					6		11	1		
35	27	(a) Cardiff C	D 0-0		18,300			3	4	5		7		9	10		2				8					6		11	1		
36	Apr 3	(h) Sheffield U	W 2-0	Jennings, Turnbull	26,262			3	4	5		7		9	10		2				8					6		11	1		
37	5	(a) Newcastle U	L 0-3		16,666			3	4	5		7		9	10		2				8					6		11	1		
38	6	(h) Sunderland	L 0-2		27,345			3	4			7		9	10		2				11				8	5			1		6
39	10	(a) West Brom A	L 0-3		11,358			3	4	5		7	8	9			2								10	6		11	1		
40	17	(h) Birmingham	D 0-0		12,186			3			4	7	8	9			2		11	6					10	5			1		
41	27	(a) Manchester C	L 1-2	Jennings	43,475			3	4		6	7	8	9			2		11						10	5			1		
42	May 1	(h) Tottenham H	W 4-1	Turnbull, Jennings 2, Whipp	16,158			3	4		6	7	8	9			2		11						10	5			1		
FINAL LEAGUE POSITION: 19th in Division One					Appearances	29	6	35	40	26	23	37	27	42	25	4	35	9	30	6	17	6	1	7	14	21	1	7	12	1	1
					Goals					2		6	5	26	8	1			2		9				3	1		1			

FA Cup

Rd	Date	Opponent	Result	Scorers	Att	Johnson	Duffield	Menzies	Edwards	Hart	Atkinson	Turnbull	Whipp	Jennings	Wainscoat	Harris	Allan	Baker	Jackson	Smith	Armand	Sissons	Mears	Kirkpatrick	Chadwick	Townsley	Thornton	Fell	Potts	Roberts	Reed
3	Jan 9	(a) Middlesbrough	L 1-5	Armand (pen)	29,000	1		3	4		6	7	8	9			2		11		10						5				
					Appearances	1			1		1	1	1	1			1		1		1						1				
					Goals																1										

1926-27

Manager: Arthur Fairclough

No	Date	Opponent	Result	Scorers	Att	Potts	Allan	Menzies	Edwards	Townsley	Atkinson	Turnbull	Chadwick	Jennings	Wainscoat	Jackson	Hart	Sissons	Whipp	Fell	Armand	Kirkpatrick	Roberts	Duggan	Robinson	Mitchell	Reed	White	Mears
1	Aug 28	(h) Bolton W	L 2-5	Wainscoat, Turnbull	23,699	1	2	3	4	5	6	7	8	9	10	11													
2	30	(h) Cardiff C	D 0-0		14,242	1	2	3	4	5	6	7	8	9	10	11													
3	Sep 4	(a) Manchester U	D 2-2	Jennings, Wainscoat (pen)	26,338	1	2	3	4	6				9	10	11	5	7	8										
4	6	(a) Cardiff C	L 1-3	Whipp	13,653	1	2	3	4	6				9	10		5	7	8	11									
5	11	(h) Derby C	W 1-0	Jennings	17,411	1	2	3	4	6				9			5	7	8	11	10								
6	15	(h) Aston Villa	W 3-1	Armand, Jennings, Sissons	13,792	1	2	6	4	5				9				7	8	11	10	3							
7	18	(a) Sheffield U	L 0-1		19,940	1	2	6	4	5		11		9				7	8		10	3							
8	25	(h) Arsenal	W 4-1	Jennings 3, Wainscoat	20,544	1	2	6	4	5		11		9	10			7			8	3							
9	Oct 2	(a) Liverpool	W 4-2	Jennings 4	30,942	1	3	6	4	5				9				7	8	11			2	10					
10	9	(h) Blackburn R	W 4-1	Jennings 4	16,304	1		6		5	4	11		9	10			7					2	8	3				
11	16	(a) Leicester C	L 2-3	Jennings 2 (1 pen)	27,753	1	3	6	4	5		11		9	10			7					2	8					
12	23	(h) Everton	L 1-3	Jennings	24,867	1	3	6	4	5		11		9	10			7					2	8					
13	30	(a) Huddersfield T	L 1-4	Jennings	29,679	1	3	6	4	5		7		9	10					11			2	8					
14	Nov 6	(h) Sunderland	D 2-2	Jennings, Duggan	15,667	1	3	6	4	5		7		9	10								2	8		11			
15	13	(a) West Brom A	W 4-2	Mitchell 2, Whipp, Armand	10,269	1		3	4	5	6			9				7	8		10		2			11			
16	20	(h) Bury	W 4-1	Jennings 3, Mitchell	18,332	1		3	4	5	6			9				7	8		10		2			11			
17	27	(a) Birmingham	L 0-2		19,707	1		3		5	6			9			4	7	8		10		2			11			
18	Dec 4	(h) Tottenham H	D 1-1	Armand	24,470	1		3	4	5	6			9				7	8		10		2			11			
19	11	(a) West Ham U	L 2-3	Armand, Menzies	20,924	1		3	4	5	6			9				7	8		10		2			11			
20	18	(h) Sheffield W	W 4-1	Edwards, Jennings, Mitchell, Whipp	20,722	1		3	4	5		7		9					8		10		2			11	6		
21	27	(h) Newcastle U	L 1-2	Jennings	48,590	1		3	4	5		7		9					8		10		2			11	6		
22	28	(a) Aston Villa	L 1-5	Armand	43,963	1	3		4	5		7		9					8		10		2			11	6		
23	Jan 1	(a) Newcastle U	L 0-1		51,343	1	3		4	5		7		9					8		10		2			11	6		
24	15	(a) Bolton W	L 0-3		19,149	1	3		4	5		7		9							10		2	8		11	6		
25	22	(h) Manchester U	L 2-3	Jennings 2 (1 pen)	16,816	1		3	4	5				9				7			10		2	8		11	6		
26	Feb 5	(h) Sheffield U	D 1-1	Jennings	18,348	1		3	4	5		7		9	10						8		2			11	6		
27	12	(a) Arsenal	L 0-1		25,961	1		3		4		7		9	10		5						2			11	6	8	
28	19	(a) Derby C	L 0-1		14,597	1		3	4	5		7		9	10								2			11	6	8	
29	23	(h) Liverpool	D 0-0		13,776	1			4	5	6	7		9						11	10		2		3			8	
30	26	(a) Blackburn R	L 1-4	White	16,149	1			4	5		7									10		2		3	11	6	8	9
31	Mar 5	(h) Leicester C	D 1-1	Jennings	21,420	1			4	5		7		9	10								2		3	11	6	8	
32	12	(a) Everton	L 1-2	Jennings	57,440	1		3	4	5		7		9	10								2			11	6	8	
33	19	(h) Huddersfield T	D 1-1	Turnbull	36,364	1		3		5	4	7		9	10								2			11	6	8	
34	26	(a) Sunderland	L 2-6	Wainscoat 2	12,288	1		3	4	5		7		9	10								2			11	6	8	
35	Apr 2	(h) West Brom A	W 3-1	Jennings 2, Wainscoat	20,176	1	3			5	4	7		9	10	11							2				6	8	
36	9	(a) Bury	L 2-4	Wainscoat, Jennings	12,489	1	3		4	5		7		9	10	11							2				6	8	
37	15	(a) Burnley	L 2-3	Turnbull, Jennings	21,099	1	3		4	5		7		9	10	11							2				6	8	
38	16	(h) Birmingham	W 2-1	Turnbull, Jennings	18,703	1	3		4	5		7		9	10	11							2				6	8	
39	19	(h) Burnley	L 0-2		18,740	1		3	4	5		7		9	10	11							2				6	8	
40	23	(a) Tottenham H	L 1-4	Jennings	17,745	1		3	4	5		7		9	10								2			11	6	8	
41	30	(h) West Ham U	W 6-3	Turnbull, White, Wainscoat 4	10,997	1	3		4	5		7		9	10								2			11	6	8	
42	May 7	(a) Sheffield W	L 0-1		12,027	1	3		4	5		7		9	10								2			11	6	8	
FINAL LEAGUE POSITION: 21st in Division One					Appearances	42	22	30	37	42	11	31	2	41	25	8	5	16	15	6	18	3	34	8	4	23	22	16	1
					Goals			1	1			5		35	11			1	3		5			1		4		2	

FA Cup

Rd	Date	Opponent	Result	Scorers	Att	Potts	Allan	Menzies	Edwards	Townsley	Atkinson	Turnbull	Chadwick	Jennings	Wainscoat	Jackson	Hart	Sissons	Whipp	Fell	Armand	Kirkpatrick	Roberts	Duggan	Robinson	Mitchell	Reed	White	Mears
3	Jan 8	(h) Sunderland	W 3-2	Jennings 2 (1 pen), Duggan	31,000	1		3	4	5		7		9							10		2	8		11	6		
4	29	(h) Bolton W	D 0-0		42,694	1		3	4	5				9	8			7			10		2			11	6		
R	Feb 2	(a) Bolton W	L 0-3		46,686	1	2		4	5				9	10								3			11	6	8	7
					Appearances	3	1	2	3	3		1		3	2			1			2		3	1		3	3	1	1
					Goals									2										1					

1927-28

Manager: Dick Ray

No	Date	Opponent	Result	Scorers	Att	Potts	Roberts	Menzies	Edwards	Townsley	Reed	Turnbull	White	Jennings	Wainscoat	Mitchell	Hart	Sissons	Allan	Baker	Coutts	Atkinson	Keetley	Robinson	Johnson	Stacey	Armand
1	Aug 27	(a) South Shields	W 5-1	Wainscoat, Mitchell, White 2, Jennings	9,826	1	2	3	4	5	6	7	8	9	10	11											
2	29	(h) Barnsley	D 2-2	White, Jennings	21,219	1	2	3	4	5	6	7	8	9	10	11											
3	Sep 3	(h) Southampton	W 2-0	Wainscoat 2	19,479	1		3	4	2	6	7	8	9	10	11	5										
4	10	(h) Nottingham F	W 4-0	Turnbull, Jennings, Wainscoat, Mitchell	19,478	1		3	4	2	6	7	8	9	10	11	5										
5	17	(a) Manchester C	L 1-2	Jennings	40,931	1		3	4	2	6	7	8	9	10	11	5										
6	24	(h) Hull C	W 2-0	Jennings, Wainscoat	21,943	1		3	4	2	6		8	9	10	11	5	7									
7	26	(a) Barnsley	L 1-2	Mitchell	13,038	1	2	3	4	5	6	7	8	9	10	11											
8	Oct 1	(a) Preston NE	L 1-5	White	16,966	1	2		4	5	6	7	8	9	10	11			3								
9	8	(h) Swansea T	W 5-0	Jennings 2 (1 pen), Turnbull, White 2	18,697	1	2			5	6	7	8	9	10	11			3	4							
10	15	(a) Fulham	D 1-1	White	16,704	1	2			5	6	7	8	9	10	11			3	4							
11	22	(a) Grimsby T	L 2-3	Jennings, Wainscoat	11,909	1	2			5	6	7	8	9	10	11			3		4						
12	29	(h) Oldham A	W 1-0	Mitchell	17,615	1		3		5	6	7	8	9	10	11			2			4					
13	Nov 5	(a) Notts C	D 2-2	Jennings 2	9,866	1		3		5	6	7	8	9	10	11			2			4					
14	12	(h) Reading	W 6-2	Wainscoat, Turnbull 2, White 2, Jennings	17,257	1		3		5	6	7	8	9	10	11			2			4					
15	19	(a) Blackpool	W 2-0	Mitchell 2	9,008	1		3		5	6	7	8	9	10	11			2			4					
16	26	(h) West Brom A	L 1-2	Townsley	23,690	1		3		5	6	7	8	9	10	11			2			4					
17	Dec 3	(a) Clapton O	L 1-2	Mitchell	12,838	1			4	2	6	7	8	9	10	11	5		3								
18	10	(h) Chelsea	W 5-0	Jennings 4, White	22,059	1			4	2	6	7	8	9	10	11	5		3								
19	17	(a) Bristol C	W 2-1	Wainscoat, White	18,326	1			4	2	6	7	8	9	10	11	5		3								
20	24	(h) Stoke C	W 5-1	Jennings 2, White, Turnbull, Hart	12,889	1		3	4	2	6	7	8	9	10	11	5										
21	26	(a) Port Vale	W 2-1	Wainscoat, White	18,869	1		3	4	2	6	7	8	9	10	11	5										
22	27	(h) Port Vale	W 3-0	Wainscoat, Jennings 2	32,275	1		3	4	2	6	7	8	9	10	11	5										
23	31	(h) South Shields	W 3-0	Turnbull, Wainscoat, Keetley	12,752	1		3	4	2	6	7	8		10	11	5						9				
24	Jan 7	(a) Southampton	W 4-1	White 2, Wainscoat, Keetley	13,966	1		3	4	2	6		8		10	11	5	7					9				
25	21	(a) Nottingham F	D 2-2	White, Keetley	13,133	1		3	4	2	6		8		10	11	5	7					9				
26	28	(h) Bristol C	W 3-2	Keetley 3	15,534	1			4	2	6	7	8		10	11	5						9	3			
27	Feb 4	(a) Hull C	L 1-3	Jennings	12,502	1			4	2	6		8	9	10	11	5	7	3								
28	11	(h) Preston NE	L 2-4	Wainscoat 2	24,276			3	4	2	6		8		10	11	5	7					9		1		
29	18	(a) Swansea T	D 1-1	Jennings	13,444			3	4	2	6		8	9	10	11	5	7							1		
30	25	(h) Fulham	W 2-1	White, Wainscoat	17,358			3	4	2	6		8	9	10	11	5	7							1		
31	Mar 3	(h) Grimsby T	D 0-0		23,567			3	4	2	6		8	9	10	11	5	7							1		
32	10	(a) Oldham A	W 1-0	Keetley	22,029	1		3		2	6	7	8		10	11	5						9			4	
33	17	(h) Notts C	W 6-0	Keetley 3, Turnbull, Armand, White	17,643	1		3	4	2	6	7	8			11	5						9				10
34	24	(a) Reading	W 1-0	Keetley	13,098	1		3	4	2	6	7	8		10	11	5						9				
35	31	(h) Blackpool	W 4-0	Wainscoat 2, Mitchell, Armand	19,630	1		3		2	6	7			10	11	5						9			4	8
36	Apr 7	(a) West Brom A	W 1-0	Turnbull	23,644	1		3	4	2	6	7	8		10	11	5						9				
37	9	(a) Wolves	D 0-0		25,251	1		3	4	2	6	7	8		10	11	5						9				
38	10	(h) Wolves	W 3-0	Keetley 2, White	29,821	1		3	4	2	6	7	8		10	11	5						9				
39	14	(h) Clapton O	W 4-0	Keetley 3, White	22,884	1		3	4	2	6	7	8		10	11	5						9				
40	21	(a) Chelsea	W 3-2	Keetley 2, White	47,562	1		3	4	2	6	7	8		10	11	5						9				
41	25	(h) Manchester C	L 0-1		48,470	1		3	4	2	6	7	8		10	11	5						9				
42	May 5	(a) Stoke C	L 1-5	Wainscoat	12,401	1		3	4	2	6	7	8		10	11	5						9				
FINAL LEAGUE POSITION: 2nd in Division Two					Appearances	38	7	33	32	42	42	34	41	26	41	42	30	8	13	2	1	5	16	1	4	2	2
					Goals					1		8	21	21	18	8	1						18				2

FA Cup

Rd	Date	Opponent	Result	Scorers	Att	Potts	Roberts	Menzies	Edwards	Townsley	Reed	Turnbull	White	Jennings	Wainscoat	Mitchell	Hart	Sissons	Allan	Baker	Coutts	Atkinson	Keetley	Robinson	Johnson	Stacey	Armand
3	Jan 14	(a) Manchester C	L 0-1		50,473	1		3	4	2	6	7	8	9	10	11	5										
					Appearances	1		1	1	1	1	1	1	1	1	1	1										
					Goals																						

1928-29

Manager: Dick Ray

No	Date	Opponent	Result	Scorers	Att	Potts	Townsley	Menzies	Edwards	Hart	Reed	Turnbull	Armand	Keetley	Wainscoat	Mitchell	Roberts	Jennings	Buck	White	Cochrane	Milburn GW	Stacey	Gribben	McNestry	Wilson J	Longden	Wilson GM	Underwood	Firth
1	Aug 25	(h) Aston Villa	W 4-1	Keetley 3, Wainscoat	26,588	1	2	3	4	5	6	7	8	9	10	11														
2	27	(h) Bury	W 3-1	Armand, Wainscoat 2	18,354	1	2	3	4	5	6	7	8	9	10	11														
3	Sep 1	(a) Leicester C	D 4-4	Keetley 2, Turnbull, Armand	27,507	1	2	3	4	5	6	7	8	9	10	11														
4	8	(h) Manchester U	W 3-2	Wainscoat, Keetley, Armand	28,723	1	2	3	4	5	6	7	8	9	10	11														
5	15	(a) Huddersfield T	L 1-6	Wainscoat (pen)	39,869	1	4	3		5	6	7	8		10	11	2	9												
6	22	(a) Liverpool	D 1-1	Wainscoat	37,417	1	2	3		5	6	7			10	11		9	4	8										
7	29	(h) West Ham U	W 4-1	Jennings 2, Wainscoat, White	29,423	1	2	3	4	5	6	7			10	11		9		8										
8	Oct 6	(a) Newcastle U	L 2-3	Wainscoat, Jennings	39,166	1	2	3	4	5	6	7			10	11		9		8										
9	13	(h) Burnley	W 2-1	White, Jennings	29,565	1	2	3	4	5	6	7			10	11		9		8										
10	20	(h) Manchester C	W 4-1	White 3, Wainscoat	32,866	1	2	3	4	5		7			10			9	6	8	11									
11	27	(a) Everton	W 1-0	Wainscoat	41,504	1	2	3	4	5	6	7			10			9		8	11									
12	Nov 3	(h) Portsmouth	W 3-2	Wainscoat, Jennings, White	29,022	1	2	3	4	5	6	7			10			9		8	11									
13	10	(a) Bolton W	L 1-4	Turnbull	16,308	1	2	3	4	5	6	7	10					9		8	11									
14	17	(h) Sheffield W	L 0-2		25,519	1	5	3			6	7	10					9	4	8	11	2								
15	24	(a) Derby C	W 4-3	White, Keetley, Mitchell, Wainscoat	16,601	1	2	3	4	5	6	7		9	10	11				8										
16	Dec 1	(h) Sunderland	L 0-3		30,082	1	2	3	4	5	6	7		9	10	11				8										
17	8	(a) Blackburn R	W 1-0	Keetley	17,333	1	2	3			6			9	10	11				8			4	5	7					
18	15	(h) Arsenal	D 1-1	Keetley	20,293	1	2	3			6	7		9	10	11				8			4	5						
19	22	(a) Birmingham	L 1-5	Turnbull	16,057	1	2	3		5	6	7		9	10	11				8			4							
20	25	(h) Cardiff C	W 3-0	Keetley, White, Hart	28,188	1	2	3		5	6	7		9	10	11				8			4							
21	26	(a) Cardiff C	L 1-2	Turnbull	20,409	1	2	3		5	6	7		9	10	11			4	8										
22	29	(a) Aston Villa	L 0-1		31,565	1	2	3		5	6	7		9	10				4	8	11									
23	Jan 1	(a) Bury	D 2-2	Turnbull, Wainscoat	21,696		2	3		5	6	7		9	10				4	8	11					1				
24	5	(h) Leicester C	W 4-3	Keetley 3, Turnbull	18,870	1	2	3		5	6	7		9	10	11			4	8										
25	19	(a) Manchester U	W 2-1	Keetley, Hart	21,995	1	2	3	4	5	6	7		9	10					8	11									
26	Feb 2	(h) Liverpool	D 2-2	Done (og), Jennings	18,780		2	3	4	5	6	7		8	10			9			11					1				
27	9	(a) West Ham U	L 2-8	Wainscoat, Jennings	18,055		2		4	5	6	7		8	10	11	3	9								1				
28	16	(h) Newcastle U	D 0-0		16,036	1	2		4	5	6	7	11	8	10			9				3								
29	23	(a) Burnley	L 0-5		13,506	1	5	3	4		6	7		8	10	11		9				2								
30	Mar 2	(a) Manchester C	L 0-3		33,921	1	2	3	4		6	7	8	9	10	11								5						
31	9	(h) Everton	W 3-1	Keetley 3	22,459	1	2	3	4	5	6	7		9	10	11				8										
32	16	(a) Portsmouth	W 2-0	Mitchell, Wainscoat	17,700	1	2	3	4	5	6	7		9	10	11				8										
33	30	(a) Sheffield W	L 2-4	Wainscoat, Keetley	30,655	1	2	3	4	5	6	7		9	10	11				8										
34	Apr 1	(a) Sheffield U	D 1-1	Keetley	20,400	1			4					9	10		2		6	8	11	3			7		5			
35	2	(h) Sheffield U	W 2-0	Jennings, White	20,119	1		3	4	5	6	7			10	11	2	9		8										
36	6	(h) Derby C	D 1-1	Mitchell	19,985	1		3	4	5	6	7		9	10	11	2			8										
37	13	(a) Sunderland	L 1-2	Keetley	12,208	1	2	3		5	6	7		9		11				8			4				10			
38	20	(h) Blackburn R	L 0-1		17,201	1	2	3	4	5	6	7		9	10	11				8										
39	27	(a) Arsenal	L 0-1		21,465	1	2	3	4	5	6	7		9	10	11												8		
40	29	(h) Bolton W	D 2-2	Wainscoat 2	12,877	1	2	3	4	5	6	7			10	11		9										8		
41	May 1	(h) Huddersfield T	L 1-2	Jennings	17,291	1	2	3	4	5	6	7			10	11		9										8		
42	4	(h) Birmingham	L 0-1		8,151	1								9	10		2				11	3	4		7		5		6	8
FINAL LEAGUE POSITION: 13th in Division One					Appearances	39	38	38	29	35	39	39	9	29	39	30	6	17	8	28	11	5	6	3	3	3	3	3	1	1
					Goals					2		6	3	20	18	3		9		9										

1 own-goal

FA Cup

Rd	Date	Opponent	Result	Scorers	Att	Potts	Townsley	Menzies	Edwards	Hart	Reed	Turnbull	Armand	Keetley	Wainscoat	Mitchell	Roberts	Jennings	Buck	White	Cochrane	Milburn GW	Stacey	Gribben	McNestry	Wilson J	Longden	Wilson GM	Underwood	Firth
3	Jan 12	(a) Exeter C	D 2-2	Keetley, Menzies	13,500	1	2	3	4	5	6	7		9	10	11				8										
R	16	(h) Exeter C	W 5-1	Lowton (og), Wainscoat, Reed, Cochrane, Keetley	23,000	1	2	3	4	5	6	7		9	10					8	11									
4	26	(a) Huddersfield T	L 0-3		53,700		2	3	4	5	6	7		9	10					8	11					1				
					Appearances	2	3	3	3	3	3	3		3	3	1				3	2					1				
					Goals			1			1			2	1						1									

1 own-goal

1929-30

Manager: Dick Ray

No	Date	Opponents	Result	Scorers	Att	Potts	Roberts	Menzies	Edwards	Hart	Underwood	Turnbull	Longden	Jennings	Wainscoat	Mitchell	Johnson	Reed	White	Milburn J	Mangnall	Stacey	Townsley	Furness	Keetley	Duggan	Cochrane	Firth	Milburn GW
1	Aug 31	(a) Arsenal	L 0-4		41,855	1	2	3	4	5	6	7	8	9	10	11													
2	Sep 7	(h) Aston Villa	W 4-1	Roberts 2 (2 pens), Longden, Jennings	23,649		2	3	4	5	6	7	8	9	10	11	1												
3	11	(a) Everton	D 1-1	Turnbull	24,098		2	3	4	5	6	7	8	9	10	11	1												
4	14	(a) Huddersfield T	L 0-1		28,287		2	3	4	5		7	8		10	11	1	6	9										
5	16	(h) Everton	W 2-1	Wainscoat, Jennings	16,667		2		4	5		7		9	10	11	1	6	8	3									
6	21	(a) Sheffield W	W 2-1	Turnbull, Wainscoat	21,353		2		4	5		7		9	10	11	1	6	8	3									
7	23	(h) Portsmouth	W 1-0	White	14,027		2		4	5		7		9	10	11	1	6	8	3									
8	28	(h) Burnley	W 3-0	Wainscoat, Hart, White	26,676		2		4	5		7			10	11	1	6	8	3	9								
9	Oct 5	(a) Sunderland	W 4-1	Mangnall 2, Wainscoat, Turnbull	23,503		2		4	5		7			10	11	1	6	8	3	9								
10	12	(h) Bolton W	W 2-1	Turnbull, Mangnall	29,749		2		4	5		7			10	11	1	6	8	3	9								
11	19	(h) Birmingham	W 1-0	Turnbull	20,067		2					7			10	11	1	6	8	3	9	4	5						
12	26	(a) Leicester C	D 2-2	Mitchell, Mangnall	27,242		2		4	5		7			10	11	1	6	8	3	9								
13	Nov 2	(h) Grimsby T	W 6-0	White, Wainscoat 2, Turnbull, Mangnall, Reed	24,013		2					7			10	11	1	6	8	3	9	4	5						
14	9	(a) Sheffield U	L 2-3	Turnbull, Mangnall	25,359		2		4	5		7			10	11	1	6	8	3	9								
15	16	(h) West Ham U	L 1-3	Wainscoat	18,582		2		4	5		7			10	11	1	6	8	3	9								
16	23	(a) Liverpool	L 0-1		30,643		2		4	5		7			10	11	1	6	8	3	9								
17	30	(h) Middlesbrough	L 1-2	Reed	19,508	1	2		4	5		7		9		11		6	8	3				10					
18	Dec 7	(a) Blackburn R	L 1-2	Mitchell	13,504	1	2		4	5		7	8	9	10	11		6		3									
19	14	(h) Newcastle U	W 5-2	Wainscoat, Longden 2, Jennings 2	21,097	1	2		4	5		7	8	9	10	11		6		3									
20	21	(a) Manchester U	L 1-3	Longden	15,054	1	2		4	5		7	8	9	10	11		6		3									
21	25	(h) Derby C	W 2-1	Longden, Wainscoat	25,360	1	2		4	5		7	8		10	11		6		3					9				
22	26	(a) Derby C	L 0-3		30,307	1	2				6	7	8	9	10	11				3		4	5						
23	28	(h) Arsenal	W 2-0	Jennings 2	29,167	1	2		4			7		9	10	11		6	8	3			5						
24	Jan 4	(a) Aston Villa	W 4-3	Jennings 2, White, Wainscoat	32,476	1	2		4	5		7		9	10	11		6	8	3									
25	18	(h) Huddersfield T	L 0-1		40,789	1	2		4	5		7		9	10	11		6	8	3									
26	Feb 1	(a) Burnley	W 3-0	Duggan, Jennings 2	12,505	1		3	4				8	9	10			6		2			5			7	11		
27	8	(h) Sunderland	W 5-0	Cochrane, Wainscoat 2, Jennings, Longden	22,377	1		3	4				8	9	10			6		2			5			7	11		
28	15	(a) Bolton W	L 2-4	Jennings, Duggan	18,104	1		3	4				8	9	10			6		2			5			7	11		
29	22	(a) Birmingham	L 0-1		17,703			3	4	5		7	8	9	10	11	1	6		2									
30	Mar 1	(h) Leicester C	L 1-2	Jennings	18,486		2		4			7		9		11	1	6		3			5	10				8	
31	8	(a) Grimsby T	W 2-1	Firth, Jennings	16,591		2		4			7	5	9	10	11	1	6		3								8	
32	15	(h) Sheffield U	D 2-2	Turnbull, Wainscoat	7,569		2		4			7	5	9	10		1	6		3							11	8	
33	22	(a) West Ham U	L 0-3		18,351		2		4			7	8	9	10		1	6		3			5				11		
34	29	(h) Liverpool	D 1-1	Wainscoat	14,178			3	4			7	5	9	10		1	6		2				8			11		
35	Apr 5	(a) Middlesbrough	D 1-1	Keetley	14,136			3	4	5			8		10	7	1	6		2					9		11		
36	9	(h) Sheffield W	W 3-0	Keetley 3	3,950			3	4	5			8		10	11	1	6		2					9	7			
37	12	(h) Blackburn R	W 4-2	Longden, Keetley, Hart, Mitchell	15,451			3	4	5			8		10	11	1	6		2					9	7			
38	19	(a) Newcastle U	L 1-2	Keetley	23,066			3	4	5			8		10	11	1	6		2					9	7			
39	21	(a) Manchester C	L 1-4	Keetley	23,578			3	4	5		7	8		10	11	1	6		2					9				
40	22	(h) Manchester C	W 3-2	Turnbull, Keetley, Wainscoat	16,636	1	2		4	5		7			10			6		3					9		11	8	
41	26	(h) Manchester U	W 3-1	Keetley 2, Firth	10,596	1	2		4	5		7			10			6		3					9		11	8	
42	May 3	(a) Portsmouth	D 0-0		13,925	1			4	5		7	6		10					3					9		11	8	2
FINAL LEAGUE POSITION: 5th in Division One					Appearances	16	31	14	39	30	4	35	23	23	40	33	26	37	17	38	9	3	9	3	9	6	10	6	1
					Goals		2			2		9	7	14	15	3		2	4		6				10	2	1	2	

FA Cup

Rd	Date	Opponents	Result	Scorers	Att	Potts	Roberts	Menzies	Edwards	Hart	Underwood	Turnbull	Longden	Jennings	Wainscoat	Mitchell	Johnson	Reed	White	Milburn J	Mangnall	Stacey	Townsley	Furness	Keetley	Duggan	Cochrane	Firth	Milburn GW
3	Jan 11	(h) Crystal P	W 8-1	Wainscoat 3, White 2, Jennings 2, Turnbull	31,418	1	2		4	5		7		9	10	11		6	8	3									
4	25	(a) West Ham U	L 1-4	Jennings	31,000	1	2		4	5		7		9	10	11		6	8	3									
					Appearances	2	2		2	2		2		2	2	2		2	2	2									
					Goals							1		3	3				2										

1930-31

Manager: Dick Ray

No	Date		Opponent	Result	Scorers	Att	Johnson	Roberts	Milburn J	Edwards	Hart	Copping	Turnbull	Longden	Keetley	Wainscoat	Cochrane	Mitchell	Potts	Milburn GW	Duggan	Firth	Jennings	Furness	Townsley	Hornby	Underwood	Hydes	Green	Brown	Menzies	Alderson	Danskin
1	Aug	30 (h)	Portsmouth	D 2-2	Turnbull, Keetley	15,900	1	2	3	4	5	6	7	8	9	10	11																
2	Sep	3 (a)	Derby C	L 1-4	Wainscoat	13,924	1	2	3	4	5	6	7	8	9	10		11															
3		6 (a)	Arsenal	L 1-3	Furness	40,828			3	4	5	6					11		1	2	7	8	9	10									
4		8 (h)	Manchester C	W 4-2	Cochrane, Keetley 3 (1 pen)	12,295			3	4		6			9		11		1	2	7	8		10	5								
5		13 (h)	Blackburn R	W 4-2	Keetley, Duggan, Furness, Wainscoat	11,837			3	4		6			9	10	11		1	2	7			8	5								
6		17 (a)	Manchester C	L 0-1		17,051			3	4		6			9	10	11		1	2	7			8	5								
7		20 (a)	Blackpool	W 7-3	Furness 2, Keetley 2 (1 pen), Cochrane 2, Turnbull	25,473			3	4	5	6	7		9	10	11		1	2				8									
8		27 (h)	Huddersfield T	L 1-2	Wainscoat	30,625			3	4	5	6	7		9	10	11		1	2				8									
9	Oct	4 (h)	Sunderland	L 0-3		16,378			3	4	5	6	7		9	10	11		1					8	2								
10		11 (a)	Leicester C	L 0-4		19,405			3	4	5	6			9			11	1	2	7			10		8							
11		18 (a)	Liverpool	L 0-2		25,637			3	4	5	6			9			11	1		7			10	2	8							
12		25 (h)	Middlesbrough	W 7-0	Mitchell, Duggan 2, Wainscoat 2, Jennings 2	18,116		2	3	4	5	6				10		11	1		7		9	8									
13	Nov	1 (a)	Newcastle U	L 1-4	Jennings	13,534		2	3	4	5	6				10		11	1		7		9	8									
14		8 (h)	Sheffield W	L 2-3	Jennings, Hart	22,040		2	3	4	5	6				10	11		1		7		9	8									
15		15 (a)	West Ham U	D 1-1	Wainscoat	16,612	1		3	4	5	6				10	11			2	7		9	8									
16		22 (h)	Chelsea	L 2-3	Wainscoat, Duggan	13,602	1		3	4	5	6				10	11			2	7		9	8									
17		29 (a)	Grimsby T	L 0-2		6,783			3	4	5	6	7		9	10	11		1	2				8									
18	Dec	6 (h)	Bolton W	W 3-1	Turnbull	7,595			3	4	5	6	7		9	10		11	1	2				8									
19		13 (a)	Aston Villa	L 3-4	Turnbull, Keetley 2	26,272			3	4	5	6	7		9	10		11	1	2				8									
20		20 (h)	Manchester U	W 5-0	Wainscoat, Turnbull 3, Furness	11,282			3	4	5	6	7		9	10		11	1	2				8									
21		25 (a)	Birmingham	W 1-0	Furness	24,991			3	4	5	6	7		9	10		11	1	2				8									
22		26 (h)	Birmingham	W 3-1	Keetley, Furness 2	12,381			3	4	5	6	7		9	10		11	1	2				8									
23		27 (a)	Portsmouth	D 1-1	Keetley	18,530			3			6	7		9		11		1	2				8	5	10	4						
24	Jan	1 (a)	Manchester U	D 0-0		9,875			3	4	5	6	7			10		11	1	2			9	8									
25		17 (a)	Blackburn R	L 1-3	Hydes	11,975			3	4	5	6	7			10		11	1	2				8				9					
26		28 (h)	Blackpool	D 2-2	Hart, Turnbull	7,750			3	4	5	6	7		9	10		11	1	2				8									
27		31 (a)	Huddersfield T	L 0-3		13,044			3		5	6	7		9	10		11	1	2				8		4							
28	Feb	7 (a)	Sunderland	L 0-4		25,765			3	4	5	6			9		11		1	2				8		10			7				
29		18 (h)	Leicester C	L 1-3	Duggan	5,572			3	4		6				10	11		1		7				5	8		9		2			
30		21 (h)	Liverpool	L 1-2	Wainscoat	15,570			2	4	5	6	7			10	11		1				9	8							3		
31		28 (a)	Middlesbrough	L 0-5		15,707			2	4	5	6			9		11		1					10		8			7		3		
32	Mar	7 (h)	Newcastle U	W 1-0	Turnbull (pen)	6,845			2	4	5	6	7		9		11		1					10		8					3		
33		11 (h)	Arsenal	L 1-2	Turnbull (pen)	12,212			2	4	5	6	7		9	10	11		1							8					3		
34		14 (a)	Sheffield W	L 1-2	Wainscoat	14,562			2	4	5	6	7		9	10	11		1					8							3		
35		21 (h)	West Ham U	W 3-0	Turnbull (pen), Alderson 2	11,611			2	4	5	6	7			10	11		1					8							3	9	
36		28 (a)	Chelsea	L 0-1		25,446			2	4	5	6	7			10	11		1					8							3	9	
37	Apr	4 (h)	Grimsby T	D 0-0		14,951			2	4	5	6	7			10	11		1					8							3	9	
38		6 (a)	Sheffield U	D 1-1	Copping	12,948			2	4	5	6	7		9	10	11		1					8							3		
39		7 (h)	Sheffield U	W 4-0	Keetley 2, Thorpe (og), Wainscoat	13,315			2	4	5	6	7		9	10	11		1												3	8	
40		11 (a)	Bolton W	L 0-2		15,438			2	4	5	6	7		9	10	11		1					8							3		
41		18 (h)	Aston Villa	L 0-2		10,388			2	4	5	6	7		9	10	11		1					8							3		
42	May	2 (h)	Derby C	W 3-1	Keetley 2, Green	11,190				4		6			9		11		1	2				10		8			7		3		5
FINAL LEAGUE POSITION: 21st in Division One						Appearances	4	5	41	40	36	42	27	2	29	33	28	14	38	22	12	2	8	37	7	10	1	2	3	1	13	4	1
						Goals					2	1	11		16	12	3	1			5		4	8				1	1			2	

1 own-goal

FA Cup

Rd	Date		Opponent	Result	Scorers	Att	Johnson	Roberts	Milburn J	Edwards	Hart	Copping	Turnbull	Longden	Keetley	Wainscoat	Cochrane	Mitchell	Potts	Milburn GW	Duggan	Firth	Jennings	Furness	Townsley	Hornby	Underwood	Hydes	Green	Brown	Menzies	Alderson	Danskin
3	Jan	10 (h)	Huddersfield T	W 2-0	Hydes, Furness	41,103			3	4	5	6	7			10	11		1	2				8				9					
4		24 (h)	Newcastle U	W 4-1	Furness, Wainscoat 2, Mitchell	40,261			3	4	5	6	7		9	10	11		1	2				8									
5	Feb	14 (a)	Exeter C	L 1-3	Mitchell	19,130			3	4	5	6	7			10	11		1	2				8				9					
						Appearances			3	3	3	3	3		1	3	3		3	3				3				2					
						Goals										2	2							2				1					

1931-32

Manager: Dick Ray

No	Date	Opponent	Result	Scorers	Att	Potts	Milburn J	Menzies	Edwards	Hart	Copping	Green	Firth	Keetley	Wainscoat	Cochrane	Stacey	Danskin	Milburn GW	Hydes	Furness	Duggan	Turnbull	Hornby	Bennett	Moore	Mahon	Wilkinson	Neal
1	Aug 29	(a) Swansea T	W 2-0	Firth, Green	16,175	1	2	3	4	5	6	7	8	9	10	11													
2	31	(a) Port Vale	W 2-1	Wainscoat, Green	16,874	1	2	3			6	7	8	9	10	11	4	5											
3	Sep 5	(h) Barnsley	L 0-1		13,078	1	2	3	4	5	6	7	8	9	10	11													
4	7	(h) Millwall	L 0-1		8,388	1	3		4		6	7	8			11		5	2	9	10								
5	12	(a) Notts C	D 1-1	Cochrane	12,630	1	3		4	5	6		8	9		11			2		10	7							
6	14	(a) Millwall	W 3-2	Keetley, Furness, Cochrane	11,844	1	3		4	5	6		8	9		11			2		10	7							
7	19	(h) Plymouth A	D 0-0		10,782	1	2	3	4	5	6		8	9		11					10	7							
8	26	(a) Bristol C	W 2-0	Furness, Keetley	9,157	1	2	3	4	5	6		8	9		11					10	7							
9	Oct 3	(h) Oldham A	W 5-0	Keetley 3, Cochrane 2	12,336	1	2	3	4	5	6		8	9		11					10	7							
10	10	(a) Bury	W 4-1	Firth, Duggan, Hart, Keetley	16,353	1	2	3	4	5	6		8	9		11					10	7							
11	17	(h) Wolves	W 2-1	Furness, Keetley	13,825	1	2	3		5	6		8	9		11	4				10	7							
12	24	(a) Charlton A	W 1-0	Furness	11,303	1	2	3	4	5	6		8	9		11					10	7							
13	31	(h) Stoke C	W 2-0	Cochrane, Furness	15,524	1	2	3	4	5	6		8	9		11					10	7							
14	Nov 7	(a) Manchester U	W 5-2	Duggan, Firth 2, Keetley, Furness	9,512	1	2	3		5	6		8	9		11	4				10	7							
15	14	(h) Preston NE	W 4-1	Firth 2, Furness, Keetley	15,439	1	2	3	4	5	6		8	9		11					10	7							
16	21	(a) Burnley	W 5-0	Cochrane 2, Furness, Firth 2	12,767	1	2	3	4	5	6		8	9		11					10	7							
17	28	(h) Chesterfield	D 3-3	Keetley 2, Furness	13,483	1	2	3	4	5	6		8	9		11					10		7						
18	Dec 5	(a) Nottingham F	D 3-3	Keetley 2, Furness	12,214	1	2	3	4	5	6		8	9		11					10	7							
19	12	(h) Tottenham H	W 1-0	Green	15,689	1	2	3	4	5	6	7	8	9		11					10								
20	19	(a) Southampton	L 1-2	Duggan	11,736	1	2	3	4	5	6		8	9		11					10	7							
21	25	(a) Bradford	L 0-3		32,421	1	3			5	6		8			11	4		2	9	10	7							
22	26	(h) Bradford	W 3-2	Duggan, Keetley 2	34,005	1	2	3		5	6		8	9		11						7		4	10				
23	Jan 2	(h) Swansea T	W 3-2	Keetley, Firth, Danskin	12,885	1	3		4		6		8	9		11		5	2			7			10				
24	16	(a) Barnsley	W 2-0	Keetley, Firth	9,136		3		4	5	6		8	9		11			2			7			10	1			
25	23	(h) Notts C	D 2-2	Keetley 2	14,562		3		4	5	6		8	9		11			2	10		7				1			
26	30	(a) Plymouth A	L 2-3	Firth, Hydes	28,426		3			5	6	7	8	9					2	10				4		1	11		
27	Feb 6	(h) Bristol C	W 1-0	Firth	10,677		2	3		5	6		8	9		11				10		7		4		1			
28	13	(a) Oldham A	L 1-2	Keetley	6,496		2	3		5	6		8	9		11						7		4	10	1			
29	20	(h) Bury	W 1-0	Firth	13,748		2	3		5	6		8	9		11						7		4	10	1			
30	27	(a) Wolves	D 1-1	Cochrane	34,520		3			5	6			9		11	4		2			7		8	10	1			
31	Mar 5	(h) Charlton A	W 2-0	Firth, Keetley	11,092		3			5	6		8	9		11	4		2			7			10	1			
32	12	(a) Stoke C	W 4-3	Bennett 2, Keetley, Hornby	17,981		3		4	5	6			9		11			2			7		8	10	1			
33	19	(h) Manchester U	L 1-4	Bennett	13,644		3			5	6			9		11	4		2			7		8	10	1			
34	26	(a) Preston NE	D 0-0		12,151	1	2		4	5	6			9		11					10	7		8				3	
35	28	(a) Bradford C	L 1-4	Bennett	22,354	1	2			5	6			9		11	4					7		8	10			3	
36	29	(h) Bradford C	D 1-1	Hydes	18,277	1	2	3	4	5	6					10				9		7		8			11		
37	Apr 2	(h) Burnley	W 3-1	Cochrane, Furness, Hydes	13,037	1	2	3	4	5		7				11				9	10	8							6
38	9	(a) Chesterfield	D 1-1	Duggan	11,992	1	2	3		5		7		9		11	4				10	8							6
39	16	(h) Nottingham F	D 1-1	J.Milburn (pen)	12,195	1	2	3	4	5	6	7		9		11					10	8							
40	23	(a) Tottenham H	L 1-3	Furness	17,285	1	2	3	4	5	6		8			11				9	10	7							
41	30	(h) Southampton	W 1-0	Keetley	13,401	1	2	3	4	5	6		8	9		11					10	7							
42	May 7	(h) Port Vale	L 0-2		9,588	1	2	3	4		6		8	9		11		5			10	7							
FINAL LEAGUE POSITION: 2nd in Division Two					Appearances	32	42	28	28	38	40	9	33	37	3	41	9	4	12	8	25	35	1	11	10	10	2	2	2
					Goals		1			1		3	14	23	1	9		1		3	12	5		1	4				

FA Cup

Rd	Date	Opponent	Result	Scorers	Att	Potts	Milburn J	Menzies	Edwards	Hart	Copping	Green	Firth	Keetley	Wainscoat	Cochrane	Stacey	Danskin	Milburn GW	Hydes	Furness	Duggan	Turnbull	Hornby	Bennett	Moore	Mahon	Wilkinson	Neal
3	Jan 9	(a) Queen's Park R	L 1-3	J.Milburn (pen)	41,097		2	3	4		6		8	9		11		5				7			10	1			
					Appearances		1	1	1		1		1	1		1		1				1			1	1			
					Goals		1																						

1932-33

Manager: Dick Ray

No	Month	Match	Result	Scorers	Att	Potts	Milburn GW	Milburn J	Edwards	Hart	Copping	Green	Firth	Hydes	Furness	Mahon	Stacey	Roper	Cochrane	Keetley	Duggan	O'Grady	Neal	Hornby	Fowler	Moore
1	Aug	27 (h) Derby C	L 0-2		16,344	1	2	3	4	5	6	7	8	9	10	11										
2		29 (a) Blackpool	L 1-2	Roper	20,313	1	2	3		5	6	7		9	10		4	8	11							
3	Sep	3 (a) Blackburn R	D 1-1	Cochrane	13,010	1	2	3		5	6	7	8		10		4		11	9						
4		5 (h) Blackpool	W 3-1	Keetley, Copping, Furness	9,171	1	2	3		5	6			8	10		4		11	9	7					
5		10 (h) Huddersfield T	D 1-1	Keetley	23,882	1	2	3		5	6			8	10		4		11	9	7					
6		17 (h) Sheffield W	W 3-2	Keetley 2, Duggan	17,977	1	2	3		5	6			8	10		4		11	9	7					
7		24 (a) West Brom A	W 1-0	Keetley	26,497	1	2	3		5	6			8	10		4		11	9	7					
8	Oct	1 (h) Birmingham	D 1-1	Duggan	14,193	1	2	3		5	6	7		8	10		4		11		9					
9		8 (a) Sunderland	D 0-0		9,651	1	2	3		5	6			8	10		4		11	9	7					
10		15 (h) Manchester C	W 2-1	Hydes, J.Milburn (pen)	16,898	1	2	3		5	6			8	10		4		11	9	7					
11		22 (a) Sheffield U	D 0-0		13,842	1	2	3		5	6			8	10		4		11	9	7					
12		29 (h) Wolves	W 2-0	O'Grady, Hydes	11,486	1	2	3		5	6			9	10		4		11		7	8				
13	Nov	5 (a) Liverpool	W 1-0	Duggan	25,464	1	2	3		5	6			9	10		4		11		7	8				
14		12 (h) Leicester C	D 1-1	Hydes	12,426	1	2	3		5	6			9	10		4		11		7	8				
15		19 (a) Portsmouth	D 3-3	J.Milburn (pen), Furness, Cochrane	17,579	1	2	3		5	6			9	10		4		11		7	8				
16		26 (h) Chelsea	W 2-0	Hydes 2	19,709	1	2	3		5	6			9	10		4		11		7	8				
17	Dec	3 (a) Newcastle U	L 1-3	Hydes	20,965	1	2	3		5	6	7		8	10		4		11	9						
18		10 (h) Aston Villa	D 1-1	Hydes	23,794	1	2	3	4	5	6			8	10	7			11	9						
19		17 (a) Middlesbrough	W 1-0	Keetley	9,341	1	2	3		5	6			8	10	7	4		11	9						
20		24 (h) Bolton W	W 4-3	Hydes 2, Keetley, Furness	15,804	1	2	3		5	6			8	10	7	4		11	9						
21		26 (a) Arsenal	W 2-1	Keetley 2	55,876	1	2	3		5	6			8	10	7	4		11	9						
22		27 (h) Arsenal	D 0-0		56,796	1	2	3	4	5	6			8	10				11	9	7					
23		31 (a) Derby C	L 1-5	Keetley	13,375	1	2	3	4	5	6			8	10	7			11	9						
24	Jan	7 (h) Blackburn R	W 3-1	Furness, Keetley, Mahon	14,043	1	2	3	4	5	6			8	10	7			11	9						
25		21 (a) Huddersfield T	D 2-2	O'Grady, Furness	18,619	1	2	3	4	5	6				10	7			11	9		8				
26	Feb	4 (h) West Brom A	D 1-1	Hydes	19,696	1	2	3	4	5				9	10	7			11			8	6			
27		8 (a) Sheffield W	L 0-2		9,585	1	2	3	4					9	10	7			11			8	6	5		
28		11 (a) Birmingham	L 1-2	Hydes	22,157	1	2	3	4	5				8	10	7			11				6		9	
29		22 (h) Sunderland	L 2-3	Hydes, Duggan	7,971	1	2	3	4	5	6		8	9	10				11		7					
30	Mar	4 (h) Sheffield U	L 1-3	Hydes	13,448	1	2	3	4	5	6		8	9	10				11		7					
31		11 (a) Wolves	D 3-3	Keetley 3	24,901		2	3	4	5	6			8	10				11	9	7					1
32		18 (h) Liverpool	W 5-0	Bradshaw (og), Mahon 2, Hydes, Duggan	12,268		2	3	4	5	6			8	10	11				9	7					1
33		25 (a) Leicester C	L 1-3	Furness	13,669		2	3	4	5	6			8	10	11				9	7					1
34	Apr	1 (h) Portsmouth	L 0-1		9,839		2	3	4		6		8		10	11				9	7			5		1
35		5 (a) Manchester C	D 0-0		16,789		2	3	4	5	6			8	10	11				9	7					1
36		8 (a) Chelsea	L 0-6		31,095		2	3	4	5	6			8	10	11				9	7					1
37		15 (h) Newcastle U	W 6-1	Fowler 2, Mahon 2, Copping, Hydes	14,967		2	3	4	5	6			8	10	11					7				9	1
38		17 (a) Everton	W 1-0	Hydes	21,265		2	3	4	5	6			8	10	11					7				9	1
39		18 (h) Everton	W 1-0	Duggan	19,663		2	3	4	5	6			8	10	11					7				9	1
40		22 (a) Aston Villa	D 0-0		21,238		2	3	4	5	6			8	10	11					7				9	1
41		29 (h) Middlesbrough	L 0-1		9,006		2	3	4	5	6			8	10	11					7				9	1
42	May	6 (a) Bolton W	L 0-5		10,048		2	3	4		6			8	10	11				9	7			5		1
FINAL LEAGUE POSITION: 8th in Division One					Appearances	30	42	42	23	39	39	5	5	39	42	22	19	1	30	24	28	8	3	3	6	12
					Goals			2			2			16	6	5		1	2	14	6	2			2	

1 own-goal

FA Cup

Rd	Month	Match	Result	Scorers	Att	Potts	Milburn GW	Milburn J	Edwards	Hart	Copping	Green	Firth	Hydes	Furness	Mahon	Stacey	Roper	Cochrane	Keetley	Duggan	O'Grady	Neal	Hornby	Fowler	Moore
3	Jan	14 (a) Newcastle U	W 3-0	Hydes 3	47,554	1	2	3	4	5	6			8	10	7			11	9						
4		28 (a) Tranmere R	D 0-0		20,000	1	2	3	4	5	6			8	10	7			11	9						
R	Feb	1 (h) Tranmere R	W 4-0	J.Milburn (pen), Mahon, Cochrane, Hydes	25,000	1	2	3	4	5	6			9	10	7			11			8				
5		18 (a) Everton	L 0-2		58,073	1	2	3	4	5	6			8	10				11	9	7					
					Appearances	4	4	4	4	4	4			4	4	3			4	3	1	1				
					Goals			1						4		1			1							

1933-34

Manager: Dick Ray

No	Date	Opponent	Result	Scorers	Att	Moore	Milburn GW	Milburn J	Stacey	Edwards	Copping	Duggan	Roper	Hydes	Furness	Cochrane	Wilkinson	Turner	Hart	Fowler	Neal	Green	Keetley	Hornby	Sproston	Firth	Mahon
1	Aug 26	(a) Blackburn R	L 2-4	Hydes, Cochrane	10,130	1	2	3	4	5	6	7	8	9	10	11											
2	28	(h) Middlesbrough	W 5-2	Hydes 4, Roper	10,896	1	2		4		6	7	8	9	10	11	3	5									
3	Sep 2	(h) Newcastle U	W 3-0	J.Milburn (pen), Cochrane, Hydes	17,721	1	2	3	4		6	7	8	9	10	11		5									
4	9	(a) Huddersfield T	D 0-0		18,976	1	2	3	4		6	7	8	9	10	11		5									
5	16	(a) Derby C	L 1-3	Hydes	16,584	1	2	3	4		6	7	8	9	10	11		5									
6	23	(h) West Brom A	W 3-0	Hydes 2, G.Shaw (og)	17,364	1	2	3	4		6	7	8	9	10	11			5								
7	30	(a) Birmingham	L 0-4		21,566	1	2	3	4		6	7	8	9	10	11			5								
8	Oct 7	(h) Sheffield W	W 2-1	Fowler 2	16,165	1	2	3	4		6	7	8		10	11			5	9							
9	14	(a) Manchester C	W 1-0	Fowler	22,413	1	2	3	4				8		10	11			5	9	6	7					
10	21	(h) Portsmouth	W 1-0	Fowler	18,255	1	2	3	4		6	7	8		10	11			5	9							
11	28	(a) Sunderland	L 2-4	Fowler, Keetley	14,578	1	2	3	4		6	7			10	11			5	9			8				
12	Nov 4	(h) Aston Villa	L 2-4	Hornby, Furness (pen)	20,148	1	2	3	4		6	7			10	11			5	9				8			
13	11	(a) Liverpool	L 3-4	Hydes, Fowler, Duggan	26,181	1	2	3		4	6	7		8	10	11			5	9							
14	18	(h) Tottenham H	D 0-0		19,681	1	2	3		4	6	7		8	10	11			5	9							
15	25	(a) Leicester C	D 2-2	Duggan, Hydes	14,022	1	2	3		4	6	7		9	10	11			5				8				
16	Dec 2	(h) Stoke C	W 2-0	Keetley, Hydes	12,601	1	2	3		4	6	7		9	10	11			5				8				
17	9	(a) Sheffield U	L 1-2	Furness	11,113	1	2	3		4	6	7		9	10	11			5				8				
18	16	(h) Wolves	D 3-3	Keetley 2, Duggan	11,013	1	2	3		4	6	7		9	10	11			5				8				
19	23	(a) Chelsea	D 1-1	Keetley	18,157	1		3		4	6	7		9	10	11			5				8		2		
20	25	(h) Arsenal	L 0-1		33,192	1		3		4	6	7		9	10	11			5				8		2		
21	26	(a) Arsenal	L 0-2		22,817	1		3			6	7		9	10	11		5						4	2	8	
22	30	(h) Blackburn R	W 4-0	Hydes 3, Furness	10,722	1		3			6	7		9	10	11			5					4	2	8	
23	Jan 1	(a) Middlesbrough	L 1-2	Hydes	16,071	1		3			6	7		9	10	11			5					4	2	8	
24	6	(a) Newcastle U	L 0-2		21,587	1	2	3			6	7		9	10	11			5					4		8	
25	20	(h) Huddersfield T	D 1-1	J.Milburn (pen)	24,957	1	2	3			6		8		10			5		9		7		4			11
26	31	(h) Derby C	L 0-2		11,790	1	2	3			6		8		10	11		5		9				4			7
27	Feb 3	(a) West Brom A	W 3-0	Roper, Mahon 2	13,343	1	2	3			6		8		10	11			5				9	4			7
28	10	(h) Birmingham	W 1-0	Furness	14,753	1	2	3					8		10	11			5				9	4		6	7
29	24	(h) Manchester C	W 3-1	Firth, Mahon, Furness	15,761	1	2	3			6				10	11			5				9	4		8	7
30	26	(a) Sheffield W	W 2-0	Firth, Keetley	6,546	1	2	3			6				10	11			5				9	4		8	7
31	Mar 7	(a) Portsmouth	L 1-2	Copping	10,568	1	2	3			6				10	11			5				9	4		8	7
32	10	(h) Sunderland	W 3-1	Cochrane, Duggan, Furness	7,333	1	2	3			6	9			10	11			5					4		8	7
33	24	(h) Liverpool	W 5-1	Mahon, Firth 2, Duggan 2	12,907	1	2	3			6	9			10	11			5					4		8	7
34	30	(h) Everton	D 2-2	Duggan 2	19,951	1	2	3			6	9			10	11			5					4		8	7
35	31	(a) Tottenham H	L 1-5	Keetley	29,574	1	2	3			6	9				11			5				10	4		8	7
36	Apr 2	(a) Everton	L 0-2		25,624	1	2	3			6	9			10	11			5				8	4			7
37	7	(h) Leicester C	W 8-0	Duggan 2, Mahon 2, Furness 2, Firth 2	11,871	1	2	3		4	6	9			10	11			5							8	7
38	14	(a) Stoke C	W 2-1	Duggan, Firth	16,262	1	2	3		4		9			10	11		5						6		8	7
39	21	(h) Sheffield U	D 1-1	Holmes (og)	10,815	1	2	3		4	6	9			10	11			5							8	7
40	28	(a) Wolves	L 0-2		5,571	1	2	3		4	6	9			10	11			5							8	7
41	30	(a) Aston Villa	L 0-3		9,849	1	2	3		4	6				10	11			5				9			8	7
42	May 5	(h) Chelsea	W 3-1	Mahon, Firth, Cochrane	6,092	1	2	3		4		9			10	11			5					6		8	7
Final League Position: 9th in Division One					Appearances	42	37	41	12	15	38	33	14	19	41	41	1	8	33	9	1	2	15	19	5	18	18
					Goals			2			1	11	2	16	8	4				6			7	1		8	7

2 own-goals

FA Cup

Rd	Date	Opponent	Result	Scorers	Att	Moore	Milburn GW	Milburn J	Stacey	Edwards	Copping	Duggan	Roper	Hydes	Furness	Cochrane	Wilkinson	Turner	Hart	Fowler	Neal	Green	Keetley	Hornby	Sproston	Firth	Mahon
3	Jan 13	(h) Preston NE	L 0-1		29,158	1	2	3			6	7			10	11			5				9	4		8	
					Appearances	1	1	1			1	1			1	1			1				1	1		1	
					Goals																						

1934-35

Manager: Dick Ray until March 1935 then Billy Hampson

No	Date	Match	Result	Scorers	Att	Moore	Milburn GW	Milburn J	Edwards	Hart	Hornby	Duggan	Firth	Mills	Furness	Cochrane	Worsley	Savage	Keetley	Neal	Mahon	Kelly JM	Sproston	Wilcockson	Roper	Hydes	Turner	McDougall	Kelly J	Stephenson	Daniels	Abel
1	Aug 25	(h) Middlesbrough	L 2-4	Mills 2	15,949	1	2	3	4	5	6	7	8	9	10	11																
2	27	(a) Stoke C	L 1-8	Hornby	24,568	1	2	3	4	5	6		8	9	10	11	7															
3	Sep 1	(a) Blackburn R	D 1-1	J.Milburn (pen)	12,316		2	3		5	6		8	4	10	11	7	1	9													
4	3	(h) Stoke C	W 4-2	Cochrane, Mahon, Furness, Duggan	8,932		2	3		5		9		4	10	11		1		6	7	8										
5	8	(h) Arsenal	D 1-1	Furness	29,447			3		5		9		4	10	11		1		6	7		2	8								
6	15	(a) Portsmouth	D 0-0		17,470			3		5		9		4	10	11		1		6	7		2	8								
7	22	(h) Liverpool	L 0-3		10,877			3		5	6	9		4	10	11		1			7		2	8								
8	29	(h) Huddersfield T	W 2-0	Duggan 2	12,298			3		5	8	9		4	10	11		1		6	7		2									
9	Oct 6	(a) West Brom A	L 3-6	J.Milburn (pen), Duggan, Mahon	15,843			3		5	8	9		4	10	11		1		6	7		2									
10	13	(h) Sheffield W	D 0-0		16,860			3		5		9		4	10	11		1		6	7		2		8							
11	20	(h) Everton	W 2-0	Hydes, Furness	16,731			3		5	6			4	10	11		1			7		2		8	9						
12	27	(a) Grimsby T	L 2-3	Hydes 2	10,940			3		5	6	8		4	10	11		1			7		2			9						
13	Nov 3	(h) Chelsea	W 5-2	McAulay (og), Furness, Hydes 2, Mahon	13,295			3		5	6	8		4	10	11		1			7		2			9						
14	10	(a) Wolves	W 2-1	J.Milburn (pen), Mahon	13,602			3			6	8		4	10	11		1			7		2			9	5					
15	17	(h) Sunderland	L 2-4	Duggan, Furness	24,141			3			6	8		4	10	11		1			7		2			9	5					
16	24	(a) Leicester C	L 0-1		12,785	1		3				8		4	10	11					7		2	6		9		5				
17	Dec 1	(h) Derby C	W 4-2	Furness 2, Hydes 2	16,565	1		3	4		6	8			10	11					7		2			9		5				
18	8	(a) Aston Villa	D 1-1	Hydes	31,682	1		3	4		6	8			10	11					7		2			9	5					
19	15	(h) Preston NE	D 3-3	Hornby, Duggan 2	13,342	1		3	4		6	8			10	11					7		2			9	5					
20	22	(a) Tottenham H	D 1-1	Furness	23,662	1		3	4		6	8			10	11					7		2			9	5					
21	25	(h) Manchester C	L 1-2	J.Milburn (pen)	24,810	1		3	4		6	8			10	11					7		2			9		5				
22	26	(a) Manchester C	L 0-3		51,387	1		3	4		6	8			10	11					7	9	2					5				
23	29	(a) Middlesbrough	D 3-3	Hydes 2, Mahon	15,615	1		3	4			8			10	11				6	7		2			9		5				
24	Jan 5	(h) Blackburn R	W 5-1	Hydes 3, Firth, Furness	13,832	1		3	4				8		10	11				6	7		2			9		5				
25	19	(a) Arsenal	L 0-3		37,026	1		3	4	5			8		10	11				6	7		2			9						
26	Feb 2	(a) Liverpool	L 2-4	Hydes 2	21,201	1	2	3	4	5	6		8			11					7				10	9						
27	9	(a) Huddersfield T	L 1-3	Mahon	18,413	1	2	3	4	5	6	8	10			11					7								9			
28	20	(h) West Brom A	W 4-1	J.Milburn (pen), Mahon 2, Duggan	7,408		2	3	4	5	6	7				10		1			11					9			8			
29	23	(a) Sheffield W	L 0-1		19,591		2	3	4	5	6	7				10		1			11					9			8			
30	Mar 2	(h) Portsmouth	W 3-1	Hydes 2, G.W.Milburn	13,450		2	3	4	5	6	7						1			11					9			8	10		
31	6	(a) Everton	D 4-4	Hydes 2, Stephenson 2	10,441			3	4	5	6					11	7	1					2			9			8	10		
32	9	(h) Grimsby T	W 3-1	Hodgson (og), Hydes, J.Milburn (pen)	15,458		2	3	4		6	7				11		1								9		5	8	10		
33	16	(a) Chelsea	L 1-7	J.Kelly	35,698		2	3	4	5	6	7			10	11										9			8		1	
34	23	(h) Wolves	D 1-1	Hornby	9,001		2	3	4	5	6	7				11		1								9			8	10		
35	30	(a) Sunderland	L 0-3		19,118			3	4		6	7			10	11		1					2			9		5	8			
36	Apr 6	(h) Leicester C	L 0-2		12,086			3	4		6	7			10	11		1					2			9		5	8			
37	13	(a) Derby C	W 2-1	Furness 2	11,041		2	3	4	5	6	8			10	11		1			7					9						
38	19	(h) Birmingham	D 1-1	Furness	14,786		2	3	4	5	6	8			10	11		1			7					9						
39	20	(h) Aston Villa	D 1-1	Furness	16,234				4		6	8			10	11		1			7		2			9		5				3
40	22	(a) Birmingham	L 1-3	Furness	18,008		2	3	4	9	6	7			10	11		1								8		5				
41	27	(a) Preston NE	W 2-0	Duggan, Hydes	11,758		2	3	4	5	6	8			10	11		1			7					9						
42	May 4	(h) Tottenham H	W 4-3	Furness 2, Hydes, Hart	7,668		2	3	4	5	6	8			10	11		1			7					9						
FINAL LEAGUE POSITION: 18th in Division One					Appearances	14	17	41	28	27	34	35	7	16	34	41	3	27	1	9	32	2	25	4	3	30	5	11	10	4	1	1
					Goals		1	6		1	3	9	1	2	16	1					8					22			1	2		

2 own-goals

FA Cup

Rd	Date	Match	Result	Scorers	Att	Moore	Milburn GW	Milburn J	Edwards	Hart	Hornby	Duggan	Firth	Mills	Furness	Cochrane	Worsley	Savage	Keetley	Neal	Mahon	Kelly JM	Sproston	Wilcockson	Roper	Hydes	Turner	McDougall	Kelly J	Stephenson	Daniels	Abel
3	Jan 12	(h) Bradford	W 4-1	Hydes 2, Furness, Mahon	35,444	1		3	4			8			10	11				6	7		2			9		5				
4	26	(a) Norwich C	D 3-3	Mahon, Duggan, Cochrane	13,710	1		3		4		8			10	11				6	7		2			9		5				
R	30	(h) Norwich C	L 1-2	Hydes	27,269	1		3	4				8			11				6	7		2			9		5	10			
					Appearances	3		3	2	1		2	1		2	3				3	3		3			3		3	1			
					Goals							1			1	1					2					3						

1935-36

Manager: Billy Hampson

No	Date	Opponents	Result	Scorers	Att	McInroy	Milburn GW	Milburn J	Edwards	Hart	Hornby	Duggan	Kelly J	Hydes	Furness	Cochrane	Sproston	McDougall	Stephenson	Savage	Neal	Mahon	Kelly JM	Brown	Browne	Armes	Kane	Makinson	Hargreaves	Turner	Carr
1	Aug 31	(a) Stoke C	L 1-3	J.Milburn	22,552	1	2	3	4	5	6	7	8	9	10	11															
2	Sep 4	(h) Birmingham	D 0-0		13,271	1		3	4		6	7		9	10	11	2	5	8												
3	7	(h) Blackburn R	L 1-4	Hydes	14,514	1		3	4	5	6	7		9	10	11	2		8												
4	11	(a) Birmingham	L 0-2		14,298			3	4			8				11	2	5	10	1	6	7	8								
5	14	(a) Chelsea	L 0-1		35,720	1		3	4		6					11	2	5	10			7	9	8							
6	18	(h) Arsenal	D 1-1	J.Kelly	24,283	1		3	4		6		9			11	2	5	10			7		8							
7	21	(h) Liverpool	W 1-0	J.Milburn (pen)	17,931	1		3	4		6		9			11	2	5	10			7		8							
8	28	(a) Grimsby T	W 1-0	J.Kelly	11,236	1		3	4		6	7	9			11	2	5	10					8							
9	Oct 5	(h) Huddersfield T	D 2-2	J.Milburn (pen), Brown	33,224	1		3	4		6	7	9			11	2	5	10					8							
10	12	(h) West Brom A	D 1-1	J.Milburn (pen)	21,657	1		3	4		6	7	9		10	11	2	5						8							
11	19	(a) Middlesbrough	D 1-1	J.Milburn (pen)	12,256	1		3	4		6	7	9		10	11	2	5						8							
12	26	(h) Aston Villa	W 4-2	Brown 2, J.Kelly 2	19,358	1		3	4			7	9		10	11	2	5						8	6						
13	Nov 2	(a) Wolves	L 0-3		22,243	1		3	4			7	9		10	11	2	5						8	6						
14	9	(h) Sheffield W	W 7-2	J.Kelly, Cochrane, Duggan 3, Edwards, J.Milburn (pen)	19,897	1		3	4			7	9		10	11	2	5						8	6						
15	16	(a) Portsmouth	D 2-2	Duggan, Furness	15,120	1		3	4			7	9		10	11	2	5						8	6						
16	23	(h) Bolton W	W 5-2	Duggan, Brown 2, J.Kelly, Furness	22,973	1		3	4			7	9		10	11	2	5						8	6						
17	30	(a) Brentford	D 2-2	Cochrane, Brown	23,914	1		3	4			7	9		10	11	2	5						8	6						
18	Dec 7	(h) Derby C	W 1-0	Brown	21,331	1		3	4			7	9		10	11	2	5						8	6						
19	14	(a) Everton	D 0-0		28,901	1		3	4			7		9	10	11	2	5						8	6						
20	21	(h) Preston NE	L 0-1		17,749	1		3	4			7	9		10	11	2	5						8	6						
21	26	(a) Sunderland	L 1-2	J.Milburn (pen)	25,296	1		3	4			7	9		10	11	2	5						8	6						
22	28	(h) Stoke C	W 4-1	Brown 2, J.Kelly, J.Milburn (pen)	18,621	1		3	4			7	9		10	11	2	5						8	6						
23	Jan 4	(a) Blackburn R	W 3-0	Duggan, Brown, J.Kelly	13,110	1		3	4			7	9		10	11	2	5						8	6						
24	18	(h) Chelsea	W 2-0	Brown, Furness	18,999	1		3	4			7	9		10	11	2	5						8	6						
25	Feb 1	(h) Grimsby T	L 1-2	Hodgson (og)	24,212	1		3	4	5	6		9		10	11	2							8		7					
26	8	(a) Huddersfield T	W 2-1	J.Kelly, Brown	20,862	1		3	4				9		10	11	2							8	6	7	5				
27	19	(a) West Brom A	L 2-3	Furness, Stephenson	7,939	1		3					9		8	11	2		10						6	7	5	4			
28	22	(h) Middlesbrough	L 0-1		21,055	1		3					9		10	11	2				6			8		7	5	4			
29	29	(a) Sheffield W	L 0-3		6,316	1		3	4				9		10		2	5						8	6	7			11		
30	Mar 7	(h) Brentford	L 1-2	Brown	10,509	1		3	4				9				2	5	10		6			8		7			11		
31	14	(a) Aston Villa	D 3-3	Furness, Brown, J.Kelly	37,382	1	2	3	4				9		10	11		5						8	6					7	
32	18	(a) Liverpool	L 1-2	Brown	16,210	1		3	4				9		10	11	2	5			6			8						7	
33	21	(h) Portsmouth	W 1-0	J.Milburn (pen)	13,031	1		3	4			7			10	11	2							8	6		5				9
34	28	(a) Bolton W	L 0-3		21,289	1		3	4			7			10	11	2							8	6		5				9
35	Apr 4	(h) Wolves	W 2-0	Hydes, J.Kelly	10,754	1		3	4			7	9	8	10	11	2								6		5				
36	10	(a) Manchester C	W 3-1	Hydes 2, J.Kelly	17,175	1		3	4			7	9	8	10	11	2				6						5				
37	11	(a) Derby C	L 1-2	J.Kelly	15,585	1		3		6			9	8		11	2	5						10				4		7	
38	13	(h) Manchester C	D 1-1	Furness	38,773	1		3	4			7	9	8	10	11	2								6		5				
39	18	(h) Everton	W 3-1	J.Kelly, Brown 2	13,738	1		3	4			7	9		10	11	2							8	6		5				
40	22	(h) Sunderland	W 3-0	Brown (pen), J.Kelly, Cochrane	16,682	1	3		4			7	9		10	11	2	5						8	6						
41	25	(a) Preston NE	L 0-5		10,927	1	3		4			7		9	10	11	2							8	6		5				
42	May 2	(a) Arsenal	D 2-2	Furness (pen), Hydes	25,920	1	3		4				9	8	10	11	2	5							6	7					
					Appearances	41	5	39	39	4	11	29	34	10	34	40	40	29	10	1	5	4	2	33	25	7	10	3	2	3	2
					Goals			9	1			6	15	5	7	3			1					18							

FINAL LEAGUE POSITION: 11th in Division One

1 own-goal

FA Cup

Rd	Date	Opponents	Result	Scorers	Att	McInroy	Milburn GW	Milburn J	Edwards	Hart	Hornby	Duggan	Kelly J	Hydes	Furness	Cochrane	Sproston	McDougall	Stephenson	Savage	Neal	Mahon	Kelly JM	Brown	Browne	Armes	Kane	Makinson	Hargreaves	Turner	Carr
3	Jan 11	(a) Wolves	D 1-1	McDougall	39,176	1		3	4			7	9		10	11	2	5						8	6						
R	15	(h) Wolves	W 3-1	J.Kelly, Cochrane, Duggan	35,637	1		3	4			7	9		10	11	2	5						8	6						
4	28	(h) Bury	W 3-2	Brown 2, Duggan	19,633	1		3	4			7	9		10	11	2	5						8	6						
5	Feb 15	(a) Sheffield U	L 1-3	Furness	68,287	1		3	4				9		10	11	2	5						8	6	7					
					Appearances	4		4	4			3	4		4	4	4	4						4	4	1					
					Goals							2	1		1	1		1						2							

1936-37

Manager: Billy Hampson

	Date	Opponent	Result	Scorers	Att	McInroy	Sproston	Milburn J	Edwards	McDougall	Browne	Duggan	Brown	Kelly J	Furness	Cochrane	Milburn GW	Armes	Stephenson	Hargreaves	Kane	Holley	Hydes	Buckley	Mills	Turner	Thomson	Ainsley	Powell	Savage	Makinson	Trainor	Gadsby	Hodgson
1	Aug 29	(h) Chelsea	L 2-3	J.Milburn 2 (1 pen)	19,379	1	2	3	4	5	6	7	8	9	10	11																		
2	Sep 2	(a) Manchester C	L 0-4		24,726	1		3	4	5	6			9	8		2	7	10	11														
3	5	(a) Stoke C	L 1-2	Stephenson	19,193	1		3	4					9	8		2	7	10	11	5	6												
4	9	(h) Manchester C	D 1-1	Hargreaves	13,933	1		3			6			9	8		2	7	10	11	5	4												
5	12	(h) Charlton A	W 2-0	Edwards, Brown	13,789	1		3	4		6		9		8		2	7	10	11	5													
6	16	(a) Portsmouth	L 0-3		12,222	1		3	4		6		9		8		2	7	10	11	5													
7	19	(a) Grimsby T	L 1-4	Betmead (og)	11,217	1		3	4				9		8		2	7	10	11	5	6												
8	26	(h) Liverpool	W 2-0	Furness, Hargreaves	16,861	1		3	4		6			9	8		2	7	10	11	5													
9	Oct 3	(a) Huddersfield T	L 0-3		18,654	1	2	3	4		6			9	8	11		7	10		5													
10	10	(a) Birmingham	L 1-2	Hydes	23,833	1	2	3	4	5	6				10			7	8				9	11										
11	17	(h) Everton	W 3-0	Thomson, Stephenson, Hydes	16,861	1		3	4	5							2		10				9	11	6	7	8							
12	24	(a) Bolton W	L 1-2	Thomson	20,411	1	2	3	4	5									10				9	11	6	7	8							
13	31	(h) Brentford	W 3-1	Armes, Stephenson, Hydes	21,498	1	2	3	4	5								7	10				9	11	6		8							
14	Nov 7	(a) Arsenal	L 1-4	Thomson	32,535	1	2	3	4	5								7	10				9	11	6		8							
15	14	(h) Preston NE	W 1-0	Hydes	15,651	1	2	3	4	5								7	10				9	11	6		8							
16	21	(a) Sheffield W	W 2-1	Hydes 2	18,411	1	2	3	4	5								7	10				9	11	6		8							
17	28	(h) Manchester U	W 2-1	Stephenson, Thomson	17,610	1	2	3	4	5								7	10				9	11	6		8							
18	Dec 5	(a) Derby C	L 3-5	Buckley 2, Hydes	15,557	1	2	3	4	5								7	10				9	11	6		8							
19	19	(a) Sunderland	L 1-2	Ainsley	23,633	1	2	3	4	5					10								9	11	6	7		8						
20	25	(h) Middlesbrough	W 5-0	Hydes, Ross (og), Ainsley 2, Buckley	30,647		2	3							10						5		9	11	6			8	7	1	4			
21	26	(a) Chelsea	L 1-2	Hydes	27,761		2	3							10						5		9	11	6			8	7	1	4			
22	28	(a) Middlesbrough	L 2-4	Hydes, Powell	14,191		2		4						10		3				5		9	11	6			8	7	1				
23	Jan 2	(h) Stoke C	W 2-1	Buckley, Ainsley	13,506		2		4						10		3				5			11	6			8	7	1		9		
24	9	(a) Charlton A	L 0-1		26,760		2										3				5		10	11	6			8	7	1	4	9		
25	23	(h) Grimsby T	W 2-0	Hydes, Furness	11,752	1	2	3	4						10			7			5		9	11	6			8						
26	30	(a) Liverpool	L 0-3		11,252	1	2	3	4		6				10			7			5		9	11				8						
27	Feb 6	(h) Huddersfield T	W 2-1	Edwards, Mountford (og)	28,930	1	2	3	4						10						5		9	11	6			8	7					
28	13	(h) Birmingham	L 0-2		13,674	1	2	3	4						10					11	5		9		6			8	7					
29	27	(h) Bolton W	D 2-2	Edwards, Furness	15,090	1	2	3	4					9	10			7			5			11	6			8						
30	Mar 3	(a) Everton	L 1-7	Hodgson	17,064	1	2		4						10							5		11	6			8	7				3	9
31	6	(a) Brentford	L 1-4	Powell	16,588	1		3	4					8	10		2					5		11	6				7					9
32	13	(h) Arsenal	L 3-4	Thomson, Hodgson, Buckley	25,148			3	4						10		2				5			11	6		8		7	1				9
33	20	(a) Preston NE	L 0-1		18,050			3	4						10		2				5			11	6		8		7	1				9
34	27	(h) Sheffield W	D 1-1	Ainsley	20,776			3	4		6				10		2				5			11	7			8		1				9
35	29	(a) West Brom A	L 0-3		31,247			3			6						2		10		5			11	4	7	8			1				9
36	30	(h) West Brom A	W 3-1	Hodgson 2, Stephenson	16,016			3	4		6								10		5			11	2	7	8			1				9
37	Apr 3	(a) Manchester U	D 0-0		34,429			3	4		6								10		5			11	2	7	8			1				9
38	10	(h) Derby C	W 2-0	Stephenson, Hodgson	20,228			3	4		6								10		5			11	2	7	8			1				9
39	17	(a) Wolves	L 0-3		13,688			3	4										10		5	6		11	2	7	8			1				9
40	21	(h) Wolves	L 0-1		14,220		2	3	4												5		8	11	6	7	10			1				9
41	24	(h) Sunderland	W 3-0	Furness, Hodgson, J.Milburn (pen)	22,234			3			6			8	10			7		11	5				2					1	4			9
42	May 1	(h) Portsmouth	W 3-1	Furness, Kelly, J.Milburn (pen)	15,034			3			6			8	10			7		11		5			2					1	4			9
FINAL LEAGUE POSITION: 19th in Division One					Appearances	26	23	38	35	12	16	1	4	10	27	2	16	20	22	10	27	7	19	30	31	9	16	13	11	16	5	2	1	13
					Goals			4	3				1	1	5			1	6	2			11	5			5	5	2					6

3 own-goals

FA Cup

Rd	Date	Opponent	Result	Scorers	Att	McInroy	Sproston	Milburn J	Edwards	McDougall	Browne	Duggan	Brown	Kelly J	Furness	Cochrane	Milburn GW	Armes	Stephenson	Hargreaves	Kane	Holley	Hydes	Buckley	Mills	Turner	Thomson	Ainsley	Powell	Savage	Makinson	Trainor	Gadsby	Hodgson
3	Jan 16	(a) Chelsea	L 0-4		34,589		2		4								3				5		10	11	6			8	7	1		9		
					Appearances		1		1								1				1		1	1	1			1	1	1		1		
					Goals																													

1937-38

Manager: Billy Hampson

No	Date	Opponent	Result	Scorers	Att	Savage	Sproston	Milburn, Jack	Makinson	Holley	Browne	Armes	Ainsley	Hodgson	Stephenson	Buckley	Kelly J	Mills	Thomson	Edwards	Turner	Kane	Goldberg	Trainor	Hargreaves	Twomey	Cochrane	Kelly D	Francis
1	Aug 28 (a)	Charlton A	D 1-1	Hodgson	30,979	1	2	3	4	5	6	7	8	9	10	11													
2	Sep 1 (h)	Chelsea	W 2-0	Armes, Barber (og)	18,858	1	2	3	4	5	6	7	8	9	10	11													
3	4 (h)	Preston NE	D 0-0		22,513	1	2	3	4	5	6	7	8	9	10	11													
4	8 (a)	Chelsea	L 1-4	Hodgson	17,300	1	2	3	4	5	6	7	8	9	10	11													
5	11 (a)	Grimsby T	D 1-1	Hodgson	9,328	1	2	3	4	5	6	7	8	9	10	11													
6	15 (h)	Portsmouth	W 3-1	Hodgson 2, Ainsley	12,579	1	2	3	4	5	6	7	8	9	10	11													
7	18 (h)	Huddersfield T	W 2-1	Milburn (pen), Armes	33,200	1	2	3	4	5	6	7	8	9	10	11													
8	25 (h)	Liverpool	W 2-0	Armes, Ainsley	21,477	1	2	3	4	5	6	7	8	9	10	11													
9	Oct 2 (a)	West Brom A	L 1-2	Milburn (pen)	25,609	1	2	3	4	5	6	7	8		10	11	9												
10	9 (h)	Birmingham	W 1-0	Ainsley	20,698	1	2	3	4	5	6	7	8		10	11	9												
11	16 (a)	Everton	D 1-1	Armes	26,035	1	2	3	4	5		7	8			11	9	6	10										
12	23 (h)	Wolves	L 1-2	Buckley	13,304	1		3	4	5		7	8			11	9	2	10	4									
13	30 (a)	Leicester C	W 4-2	Hodgson 2, Milburn (pen), Buckley	18,833	1	2	3	4	5	6		8	9	10	11					7								
14	Nov 6 (h)	Blackpool	D 1-1	Buckley	18,438	1	2	3	4	5	6			9	10	11	8				7								
15	13 (a)	Derby C	D 2-2	Thomson, Hodgson	15,966	1	2	3	4	5	6	7		9	10	11			8										
16	20 (h)	Bolton W	D 1-1	Hodgson	23,687	1		3	4		6	7		9	10	11		2	8			5							
17	27 (a)	Arsenal	L 1-4	Stephenson	34,350	1	2	3	4	5		7		9	10	11		6	8										
18	Dec 4 (h)	Sunderland	W 4-3	Stephenson 3, Hodgson	15,349	1		3	4			7		9	10	11		6	8			5	2						
19	11 (a)	Brentford	D 1-1	Hodgson	18,184	1		3	4			7		9	10	11		6	8			5	2						
20	18 (h)	Manchester C	W 2-1	Stephenson, Buckley	22,144	1	2	3	4			7		9	10	11		6	8			5							
21	25 (h)	Middlesbrough	W 5-3	Hodgson 2, Buckley, Stephenson, Thomson	37,020	1	2	3	4			7		9	10	11		6	8			5							
22	27 (a)	Middlesbrough	L 0-2		34,640	1	2	3	4			7			10			6	8			5		9	11				
23	Jan 1 (h)	Charlton A	D 2-2	Stephenson, Buckley	26,433	1	2	3	4			7		9	10	11		6	8			5							
24	15 (a)	Preston NE	L 1-3	Thomson	14,032	1	2	3	4		6	7	8	9		11			10			5							
25	26 (h)	Grimsby T	D 1-1	Buckley	10,512	1	2	3	4			7	8	9	10	11		6				5							
26	29 (a)	Huddersfield T	W 3-0	Armes, Buckley, Thomson	16,677	1	2	3	4	5	6	7		9	10	11			8										
27	Feb 5 (a)	Liverpool	D 1-1	Hodgson	34,468	1	2	3	4	5	6	7		9	10				8						11				
28	12 (h)	West Brom A	W 1-0	Hodgson	21,819	1	2	3	4	5	6	7		9	10	11			8										
29	19 (a)	Birmingham	L 2-3	Hodgson, Thomson	20,403	1	2	3	4	5	6	7		9	10				8						11				
30	26 (h)	Everton	D 4-4	Hodgson 4	23,497	1	2	3	4	5	6	7		9	10				8						11				
31	Mar 5 (a)	Wolves	D 1-1	Sproston	38,849	1	2	3	4	5	6	7		9	10				8						11				
32	12 (h)	Leicester C	L 0-2		19,839	1	2	3	4		6	7	9		10				8			5			11				
33	19 (a)	Blackpool	L 2-5	Ainsley, Hodgson	18,029		2	3	4	5	6	7	8	9	10										11	1			
34	26 (h)	Derby C	L 0-2		19,911		2	3	4	5			8	9	10	11		6								1	7		
35	Apr 2 (a)	Bolton W	D 0-0		18,492		2	3			6	7	8	9	10	11				4						1		5	
36	9 (h)	Arsenal	L 0-1		29,365			3			6	7	8	9		11				4			2			1		5	10
37	16 (a)	Sunderland	D 0-0		21,450		2	3	4		6	7	8	9	10	11						5				1			
38	18 (a)	Stoke C	W 1-0	Mould (og)	25,114		2	3	4		6	7	8	9	10	11						5				1			
39	19 (h)	Stoke C	W 2-1	Ainsley, Stephenson	17,896		2	3	4		6	7	8	9	10	11						5				1			
40	23 (h)	Brentford	W 4-0	Hodgson 3, Ainsley	17,840		2	3	4		6	7	8	9	10	11						5				1			
41	30 (a)	Manchester C	L 2-6	Hodgson, Buckley	26,732		2	3	4		6	7	8	9	10	11										1		5	
42	May 7 (a)	Portsmouth	L 0-4		29,571		2	3	4		6	7	8	9	10	11										1		5	
FINAL LEAGUE POSITION: 9th in Division One					Appearances	32	37	42	40	24	31	39	26	36	38	35	5	12	19	3	2	14	3	1	7	10	1	4	1
					Goals		1	3				5	6	25	8	9			5										

2 own-goals

FA Cup

Rd	Date	Opponent	Result	Scorers	Att	Savage	Sproston	Milburn, Jack	Makinson	Holley	Browne	Armes	Ainsley	Hodgson	Stephenson	Buckley	Kelly J	Mills	Thomson	Edwards	Turner	Kane	Goldberg	Trainor	Hargreaves	Twomey	Cochrane	Kelly D	Francis
3	Jan 8 (h)	Chester	W 3-1	Armes, Buckley, Ainsley	37,155	1	2	3	4			7	8	9	10	11		6				5							
4	22 (a)	Charlton A	L 1-2	Hodgson	50,516	1	2	3	4			7	8	9	10	11		6				5							
Leeds United also played in the League Jubilee Fund Matches (See *Invitation Tournaments*)					Appearances	2	2	2	2			2	2	2	2	2		2				2							
					Goals							1		1		2													

1938-39

Manager: Billy Hampson

No.	Date	Opponent	Result	Scorers	Att.	Twomey	Milburn, Jack	Gadsby	Makinson	Holley	Browne	Armes	Ainsley	Hodgson	Stephenson	Buckley	Goldberg	Edwards	Kane	Cochrane	Thomson	Powell	Hargreaves	Mills	Parry	Hampson	Savage	Sutherland	Copping	Scaife	Dunderdale	Henry
1	Aug 27	(h) Preston NE	W 2-1	Hodgson, Buckley	19,255	1	2	3	4	5	6	7	8	9	10	11																
2	31	(h) Birmingham	W 2-0	Ainsley, Buckley	13,578	1	2	3	4	5	6	7	8	9	10	11																
3	Sep 3	(a) Charlton A	L 0-2		30,383	1	2	3	4	5	6	7	8	9	10	11																
4	5	(a) Stoke C	D 1-1	Hodgson	16,052	1	3		6				8	9	10	11	2	4	5	7												
5	10	(h) Bolton W	L 1-2	Hodgson	20,381	1	3		4		6	7	8	9	10	11	2		5													
6	17	(a) Huddersfield T	W 1-0	Hodgson	19,793	1	2	3	4	5	6	7		9	10	11					8											
7	24	(a) Liverpool	L 0-3		32,197	1	2	3	4	5	6	7		9		11					8	10										
8	Oct 1	(h) Leicester C	W 8-2	Hodgson 5, Cochrane, Milburn (pen), Hargreaves	15,001	1	2	3	4	5	6			9						7	8	10	11									
9	8	(a) Middlesbrough	W 2-1	Armes, Hodgson	23,009	1	2	3		5		7		9				4			8	10	11	6								
10	15	(h) Wolves	W 1-0	Thomson	25,860	1	2	3		5				9				4		7	8	10	11	6								
11	22	(a) Everton	L 0-4		30,747	1	2	3		5				9				4		7	8	10	11	6								
12	29	(h) Portsmouth	D 2-2	Ainsley, Rowe (og)	18,055	1	2	3		5	6	7	9		10	11		4				8										
13	Nov 5	(a) Arsenal	W 3-2	Stephenson 2, Buckley	39,092	1	2	3		5	6		9		10	11		4		7		8										
14	12	(h) Brentford	W 3-2	Hodgson 2, Buckley	22,555	1	2	3		5	6		8	9	10	11		4		7												
15	19	(a) Blackpool	W 2-1	Hodgson, Hargreaves	16,612	1	2	3		5	6	7		9	10			4				8	11									
16	26	(h) Derby C	L 1-4	Buckley	34,158	1	2	3		5	6			9	10	11		4		7		8										
17	Dec 3	(a) Grimsby T	L 2-3	Armes, Powell	11,202	1	2	3		5	6	7		9	10	11		4				8										
18	10	(h) Sunderland	D 3-3	Ainsley, Hargreaves, Powell	20,853	1	2	3		5			9		10			4		7		8	11	6								
19	17	(a) Aston Villa	L 1-2	Hargreaves	28,990	1	2	3		5	6		8	9	10			4		7			11									
20	24	(a) Preston NE	L 0-2		18,424	1	2	3		5	6		8	9	10			4		7			11									
21	26	(h) Chelsea	D 1-1	Edwards	27,586	1		3		5			9		10		2	4		7		8	11		6							
22	27	(a) Chelsea	D 2-2	Hodgson, Stephenson	32,692	1		3		5		7		9	10		2					8	11		6	4						
23	31	(h) Charlton A	W 2-1	Hodgson, Cochrane	18,774	1		3		5				9	10		2	4		7		8	11		6							
24	Jan 14	(a) Bolton W	D 2-2	Hodgson, Goslin (og)	14,893		2	3	4	5		7	8	9	10								11		6		1					
25	28	(h) Liverpool	D 1-1	Hodgson	13,679	1		3		5		7		9	10		2	4				8	11	6								
26	Feb 4	(a) Leicester C	L 0-2		12,618	1		3		5			8	9	10		2	4		7			11		6							
27	11	(h) Middlesbrough	L 0-1		18,273	1	2	3						9	10				5	7		8	11	4	6							
28	18	(a) Wolves	L 1-4	Sutherland	31,977	1		3							10		2		5	7		8	11	4		6		9				
29	25	(h) Everton	L 1-2	Ainsley	21,728			3	4				8		10		2		5	7			11	6			1	9				
30	Mar 8	(a) Portsmouth	L 0-2		14,469	1		3	4	5			8		10		2			7			11					9	6			
31	11	(h) Arsenal	W 4-2	Stephenson (pen), Powell, Hodgson, Hargreaves	22,160	1		3	4	5				9	10					7		8	11						6	2		
32	18	(a) Brentford	W 1-0	Hargreaves	21,480	1			4	5				9	10		2			7		8	11						6	3		
33	25	(h) Blackpool	W 1-0	Cochrane	21,818	1			4	5					10		2			7		8	11						6	3	9	
34	Apr 1	(a) Derby C	L 0-1		11,278	1				5					10		2	4		7		8	11						6	3	9	
35	7	(a) Manchester U	D 0-0		35,564	1		3	4	5			8		10								11						6	2	9	7
36	8	(h) Grimsby T	L 0-1		19,700			3		5			8	9				4		7		10	11				1		6	2		
37	10	(h) Manchester U	W 3-1	Ainsley, Hodgson, Buckley	13,771	1		3	4	5			10	9		11				7		8							6	2		
38	15	(a) Sunderland	L 1-2	Ainsley	10,913	1		3	4	5	6		10	9		11	2			7		8										
39	19	(h) Huddersfield T	W 2-1	Hodgson, Powell	12,006	1		3	4	5				9	10	11	2			7		8							6			
40	22	(h) Aston Villa	W 2-0	Hargreaves 2	14,241	1		3	4	5				9	10					7		8	11						6	2		
41	29	(a) Birmingham	L 0-4		12,522	1		3	4	5				9	10					7		8	11						6	2		
42	May 6	(h) Stoke C	D 0-0		12,048	1		3		5				9	10	11	2	4				8							6			7
FINAL LEAGUE POSITION: 13th in Division One					Appearances	39	22	37	20	37	16	13	20	32	34	16	16	20	5	27	6	28	26	8	6	2	3	3	12	9	3	2
					Goals		1					2	6	20	4	6		1		3	1	4	8					1				

2 own-goals

FA Cup

No.	Date	Opponent	Result	Scorers	Att.	Twomey	Milburn, Jack	Gadsby	Makinson	Holley	Browne	Armes	Ainsley	Hodgson	Stephenson	Buckley	Goldberg	Edwards	Kane	Cochrane	Thomson	Powell	Hargreaves	Mills	Parry	Hampson	Savage	Sutherland	Copping	Scaife	Dunderdale	Henry
3	Jan 17	(h) Bournemouth	W 3-1	Stephenson, Hargreaves, Cochrane	10,114		2	3		5				9	10			4		7		8	11		6		1					
4	21	(h) Huddersfield T	L 2-4	Hodgson, Cochrane	43,702		2	3		5				9	10			4		7		8	11		6		1					
					Appearances		2	2		2				2	2			2		2		2	2		2		2					
					Goals									1	1					2			1									

1939-40

Manager: Billy Hampson

No	Month	Day	Opponent	Result	Scorers	Att	Swindin	Goldberg	Gadsby	Makinson	Holley	Thompson	Henry	Powell	Hodgson	McGraw	Brown	Browne	Hargreaves	Milburn, Jim	Stephenson	Copping	Cochrane	Edwards	Lee	Stephens JW	Milburn, Jack	Short	Stephens A	Buckley	Murgatroyd	Saxon	Ainsley
1	Oct	28	(h) Bradford C	W 3-0	Hodgson 2, Brown	3,000	1	2	3	4	5	6	7	8	9	10	11																
2	Nov	4	(a) Hull C	W 3-0	Powell, Hodgson, McGraw	3,000	1	2	3	4	5	6	7	8	9	10	11																
3		11	(a) Darlington	W 3-1	McGraw, Hodgson, Brown	5,727	1	2	3	4	5	6	7	8	9	10	11																
4		18	(h) Hartlepools U	W 2-1	Holley, Hodgson	4,000	1	2	3	4	5		7		9	8	11	6	10														
5		25	(a) York C	D 1-1	Henry	4,000	1	2	3	4	5	6	7	8	9	10	11																
6	Dec	2	(h) Huddersfield T	D 0-0		4,000	1	2		4		5	7	8	9		11	6		3	10												
7		9	(a) Bradford	L 1-3	Hodgson (pen)	4,000	1	2	3	4		5	7	8	9	10		6	11														
8		23	(h) Middlesbrough	W 3-1	Cochrane, Powell, Henry	5,000	1	2	3	4	5		9	8			11				10	6	7										
9	Jan	6	(a) Newcastle U	L 0-3		6,000	1	2	3		5	9		8		10	11					6	7	4									
10	Mar	9	(h) Darlington	W 3-2	Cochrane, Stephenson (pen), Henry	4,000		2	3	4	5	6	11	8							10		7		1	4							
11		16	(a) Hartlepools U	L 1-2	Stephens JW	1,500			3	4	5	6	11								10		7		1	9	2	8					
12		23	(h) York C	W 3-1	Short 2, Powell	3,000		2	3	4	5			7					11		10	6			1	9		8					
13		30	(a) Huddersfield T	L 1-2	Short	5,833			3	4	5	6		8					11				7		1	9	2	10					
14	Apr	6	(h) Bradford	W 5-2	Powell, McGraw, A.Stephens, Cochrane 2	3,000		2	3	4	5	6		8		10							7		1				9	11			
15		13	(a) Middlesbrough	D 1-1	A.Stephens	1,000			3		5	6	11			10							7	4	1		2	8	9				
16	May	25	(a) Halifax T	L 2-3	Henry 2	600				4		6	9		5	10			11				7		1		3	8			2		
17	Jun	1	(h) Hull C	W 3-1	Henry, Cochrane 2	500				4		6	9		5	10			11				7		1		2	8			3		
18		8	(h) Newcastle U	L 1-3	Cochrane	200				4		6	9		5	10							7		1		2	8			3	11	
			FINAL LEAGUE POSITION: 5th in Regional League North-East Division			Appearances	9	12	14	16	13	15	14	12	10	12	8	3	6	1	5	3	10	2	9	4	6	7	2	1	3	1	
			The matches against Bradford City (a) and Halifax Town (h) were not played			Goals					1		6	4	6	3	2				1		7			1		3	2				

League War Cup

No	Month	Day	Opponent	Result	Scorers	Att	Swindin	Goldberg	Gadsby	Makinson	Holley	Thompson	Henry	Powell	Hodgson	McGraw	Brown	Browne	Hargreaves	Milburn, Jim	Stephenson	Copping	Cochrane	Edwards	Lee	Stephens JW	Milburn, Jack	Short	Stephens A	Buckley	Murgatroyd	Saxon	Ainsley
19	Apr	20	(h) Sheffield W	W 6-3	Thompson, A.Stephens 3, Hargreaves 2	8,065		2	3	4	5	6		8					11		10		7		1				9				
20		27	(a) Sheffield W	L 2-3	Powell, Hodgson	9,506		2	3	4	5	6		7	9				11		10				1				8				
21	May	4	(a) Sunderland	D 0-0		11,226		2	3		5	6							11		10		7	4	1				9				8
22		11	(h) Sunderland	L 0-1		9,000			3	6		5	8		9	10			11				7	4	1		2						
						Appearances		3	4	3	3	4	1	2	2	1			4		3		3	2	4		1		3				1
						Goals						1		1	1				2										3				

The following matches were in the aborted Football League programme of this season.

Aug 26 v Preston North End (h) 0-0
Twomey; Goldberg, Gadsby, Browne, Holley, Copping, Cochrane, Ainsley, Dunderdale, Stephenson, Hargreaves.
Att: 20,491
Aug 30 v Charlton Athletic (h) 0-1
Wharton; Goldberg, Gadsby, Browne, Holley, Copping, Cochrane, Powell, Ainsley, Stephenson, Buckley.
Att: 12,049
Sep 2 v Sheffield United (h) 0-1
Wharton; Jim Milburn, Gadsby, Browne, Kane, Copping, Cochrane, Powell, Hodgson, Stephenson, Buckley.
Att: 9,779

Leeds United were bottom of Division One when the competition was abandoned.

1940-41

Manager: Billy Hampson

No	Date	Opponent	Result	Scorers	Att	Lee	Milburn, Jim	Gadsby	Makinson	Holley	Thompson	Henry	Powell	Sutherland	Stephenson	Houldershaw R	Milburn, Jack	Short	Hodgson G	Hargreaves	Stacey	Edwards	Baird	McTavish	Goslin	Howitt	McGraw	Heaton	Townsend	Mahon	Ainsley	Hodgson J	Dempsey	Farrage	Copping	Daniels	Baker
1	Aug 31	(h) Bradford C	D 2-2	Stephenson, Sutherland	3,000	1	2	3	4	5	6	7	8	9	10	11																					
2	Sep 7	(a) Newcastle U	L 0-1		4,000	1		3	4	5	6	7		9	10	11	2	8																			
3	14	(h) Huddersfield T	W 5-2	Short 2, Hodgson, Young (og), Powell	3,000	1		3	6		5		7		10		2	8	9	11	4																
4	21	(h) Manchester C	D 0-0		5,000	1		3	6		5		7		10		2	9				4	8	11													
5	28	(a) Everton	L 1-5	Baird	3,000	1		3	4	5	6	7			10		2		9	11			8														
6	Oct 5	(a) Huddersfield T	D 1-1	Jack Milburn (pen)	3,368	1		3	6	5					10		2	8	9	11					4	7											
7	12	(a) Rotherham U	D 0-0		4,208	1		3	6	5					10	11	2		9			4				7	8										
8	19	(a) Bradford C	W 6-3	Hodgson 3, Powell 2, Short	3,000	1			6	2	5		7		10	11	3	8	9			4															
9	Nov 2	(a) Barnsley	L 0-3		1,244	1		3	6	5					10		2	8				4				7	9	11									
10	9	(h) Middlesbrough	W 2-1	Townsend, Stephenson	2,000	1		3	6	5			7		10		2	8				4						11	9								
11	16	(h) Bradford C	W 6-0	Jack Milburn (pen), Mahon, Stephenson, Townsend 2, Hodgson	2,500	1		3	6	5					10		2		8			4				7			9	11							
12	23	(h) Hull C	W 3-2	Townsend 2, Mahon	3,000	1		3	6	5	4				10		2		8			7							9	11							
13	30	(h) Newcastle U	W 3-2	Townsend 2, Stephenson	3,000	1		3	6	5					10		2	7	8	11		4							9								
14	Dec 7	(h) Burnley	D 1-1	Hargreaves	3,000	1		3	6	5	4				10		2		9	11		7					8										
15	14	(a) Chesterfield	L 0-3		1,000			3	6	5	4						2	8		11		7							9		10	1					
16	21	(a) Halifax T	D 2-2	McGraw, Townsend	3,000	1		3	6	5	4						2		8			7					10		9				11				
17	25	(h) Bradford	W 2-1	Hodgson, Townsend	4,500	1		3	6	5			7				2		8								10		9				4	11			
18	28	(h) Chesterifeld	L 1-2	Short	4,000	1		3	6	5							2	10	8										9	7			4	11			
19	Jan 4	(a) Chesterfield*	W 4-2	Townsend 2, Henry, Stephenson	2,000	1		3	6	5		7	8		10		2								4				9	11							
20	11	(h) Chesterfield*	L 2-3	Lee 2	5,000	1		3	6			7			10		2		8						4				9	11					5		
21	18	(a) Hull C	L 1-4	McGraw	1,500			3	4			9	8				2										10			11					6	1	5
22	Mar 22	(h) Sheffield W	W 3-2	Hargreaves, Makinson, Burditt	1,500	1			5			7			10		2			11		4					3		8						6		
23	29	(a) Rochdale	W 3-2	Burditt, Ainsley, Makinson	800		2		6			7			10				5	11		4									8				3	1	
24	Apr 5	(a) Doncaster R	W 4-1	Henry, Edwards, Hargreaves 2	4,000		2	3	4			8			10				5	11		7													6	1	
25	12	(a) Manchester C	D 1-1	Hargreaves	3,000		2	3	4				8		10				5	11											7				6	1	
26	14	(h) Bury	D 2-2	Henry, Hargreaves	2,400		3		4	5		8	10							11		7													6	1	
27	26	(h) Sheffield U	W 2-0	Hargreaves, Burditt	2,000		2		6	5		7	8		10					11															3	1	
28	May 3	(a) Newcastle U	L 2-3	Short 2	2,000		2		6	5		9			10			8	7	11							4									1	
29	10	(h) Huddersfield T*	W 1-0	Powell	4,000		2		6	5		7	8		10					11		4													3	1	
30	17	(a) Middlesbrough*	L 2-3	Jim Milburn (pen), Short	3,000		2	3	4			7	8					11									10								6	1	
					Appearances	20	9	23	30	21	10	14	13	2	23	4	21	12	17	14	1	16	2	1	3	4	9	2	11	6	3	1	3	2	10	9	1
					Goals	2	1		2			3	4	1	5		2	7	6	7		1	1				2		11	2	1						

FINAL LEAGUE POSITION: 15th in North Regional League

1 own-goal

Matches marked thus * were also in the West Riding Cup and counted towards the final League position which was decided on goal average only. United's average of 1.148 gave them 15th place in a table of 36 clubs.

Brown played number-7 in Match 21; Burditt played number-9 in Matches 22-27 & 29-30 and scored three goals; Goldberg played number-2 in Match 26; Jackett played number-4 in Match 27; Spike played number-3 in Match 28; Meens played number- 5 in Match 30.

League War Cup

No	Date	Opponent	Result	Scorers	Att	Lee	Milburn, Jim	Gadsby	Makinson	Holley	Thompson	Henry	Powell	Sutherland	Stephenson	Houldershaw R	Milburn, Jack	Short	Hodgson G	Hargreaves	Stacey	Edwards	Baird	McTavish	Goslin	Howitt	McGraw	Heaton	Townsend	Mahon	Ainsley	Hodgson J	Dempsey	Farrage	Copping	Daniels	Baker
31	Feb 15	(a) Halifax T	W 3-2	Townsend 3	4,000	1		3	4	5		7			10		2	8											9					11	6		
32	Mar 1	(h) Halifax T	D 2-2	Hodgson, Edwards	5,000	1		3	4	5					10		2		9	11		7					8								6		
33	8	(a) Middlesbrough	L 0-2		9,000	1			6	5		7			10		2		8	11		4													3		
34	15	(h) Middlesbrough	D 2-2	Henry, Jack Milburn	5,000	1			6	5		7	8		10		2		9	11		4													3		
					Appearances	4		2	4	4		3	1		4		4		4	3		3					1		1					1	4		
					Goals							1					1		1			1							3								

Burditt played number-9 in Match 33.

1941-42

Manager: Billy Hampson

							Lee	Goldberg	Murgatroyd	Stanton	Holley	Makinson	Livingstone	Powell	Henry	Litchfield	Hargreaves	Fowler	Short	Copping	Stephenson	McGraw	Adam	Daniels	Haddow	Milburn, Jim	Knight	Spike	Shanks	Gadsby	Milburn, Jack	Bush	Ramsden	Ainsley	McClure	Vickers	Eastham	Warburton
1	Aug 30	(h)	York C	W 2-0	Henry 2	3,000	1	2	3	4	5	6	7	8	9	10	11																					
2	Sep 6	(a)	York C	L 0-1		4,000	1		3	4	5	6	7	8	9	10	11	2																				
3	13	(a)	Gateshead	L 2-3	Henry, Short	4,000	1		3	4		6		8	9	10	11	2	7																			
4	20	(h)	Gateshead	W 5-1	Henry 2, Short 2, Hargreaves	2,500	1				5	4		8	9	10	11	2	7	6																		
5	27	(h)	Sunderland	L 1-2	Short	3,000	1				5	4		8	9		11	2	7	6	10																	
6	Oct 4	(a)	Sunderland	L 1-6	Stephenson	10,000	1				5	4		8	9		11	2	7		10	3																
7	11	(a)	Bradford	L 0-6		3,000	1	2			5	4		8	9	10		3		6			11															
8	18	(h)	Bradford	W 4-0	Hargreaves, Henry, Adam, Powell	2,000					5	6		8	9		10	2					11	1	4													
9	25	(a)	Chesterfield	L 0-3		1,500					5	6		8	9		7			3	10		11	1	4	2												
10	Nov 1	(h)	Chesterfield	D 2-2	Henry, Hargreaves	3,000					5	4		8	9		7			3	10		11	1		2	6											
11	8	(h)	Middlesbrough	L 2-3	Hargreaves 2	2,000					5	4		8	9	7	10			2				1			6											
12	15	(a)	Middlesbrough	W 2-1	Powell, Hargreaves	4,000						4		8	9	7	10	2					11	1				3	5									
13	22	(a)	Newcastle U	L 2-4	Hargreaves, Shanks (pen)	4,500						6		7	9		10		8				11	1	4			2	5	3								
14	29	(h)	Newcastle U	W 5-2	Hargreaves, Henry 4	3,000						4		8	9	7	10	3		6			11	1				2	5									
15	Dec 6	(h)	Bradford C	W 4-2	Gregory (og), Henry, Powell, Lichfield	1,500	11					6		8	9	7		3					10	1	4			2	5									
16	13	(a)	Bradford C	L 0-5		2,000						6		8	9	7		3					11	1	4		10	2	5									
17	20	(a)	Huddersfield T	L 2-4	Henry 2	2,063						4		8	9	2		3					10	1	6				5									
18	25	(h)	Huddersfield T	W 2-1	Henry, McGraw	6,000					5	4		8	9	7						10	11	1		2	6											
FINAL LEAGUE POSITION: 26th in Football League Northern Section (First Championship)						Appearances	8	2	3	3	11	18	2	18	18	12	13	12	5	7	4	2	11	11	6	3	4	5	6	1								
						Goals								3	15	1	8		4		1	1	1						1									

Bratley played number-5 in Match 3; Brown played number-3 in Matches 4 & 5; Maddison played number-6 in Match 6; Ramsley played number-7 in Matches 7 & 8; Keeping played number-3 in Matches 8 & 11; Heaton played number-11 in Matches 11 & 17; Harvey played number- 6 in Match 12; Spink played number- 7 in Match 17; Watson played number-3 in Match 18.

1 own-goal

							Lee	Goldberg	Murgatroyd	Stanton	Holley	Makinson	Livingstone	Powell	Henry	Litchfield	Hargreaves	Fowler	Short	Copping	Stephenson	McGraw	Adam	Daniels	Haddow	Milburn, Jim	Knight	Spike	Shanks	Gadsby	Milburn, Jack	Bush	Ramsden	Ainsley	McClure	Vickers	Eastham	Warburton
19	Dec 27	(a)	Rotherham U†	L 1-3	Powell	3,606					5	4		8	9	7		2		3		10	11	1			6											
20	Jan 3	(h)	Lincoln C†	W 5-1	Henry 3, Turner, Jack Milburn (pen)	3,000					5	4		7	9		11			6				1						3	2							
21	10	(a)	Rochdale†	L 0-2		2,000					5	4		8	9	10				6			11	1		2												
22	17	(h)	Rochdale†	W 5-0	Knight 2, Adam, Henry 2	3,000					5	6		8	9			3					11	1		4	10				2							
23	Feb 14	(h)	Barnsley†	W 3-2	Adam 2, Henry	2,500					5	4		8	9					6			11	1		2	10			3								
24	21	(a)	Blackburn R†	L 0-1		1,000						6			9								11	1		4	10			3		5	2	8				
25	28	(h)	Blackburn R	L 0-1		5,200						5		8	9		7					3	11	1			10							4	2			
26	Mar 14	(h)	Doncaster R†	W 6-1	Knight, Ainsley, Henry 4	3,000								7	9							11		1			6			2		5	3	8		4	10	
27	21	(a)	Barnsley†	L 2-3	Powell, Harper (og)	4,500					3	4		7	9		11							1			6					5	2	8			10	
28	28	(a)	Doncaster R†	L 0-1		1,225						5		8	9		7					2	11	1									3	4		6	10	
29	Apr 4	(h)	Sheffield W	L 1-2	McGraw	3,000						4		8			11					10		1		5					2		3			6		7
30	6	(a)	Halifax T*	L 1-6	Asquith	2,000					5	4		8			11					10		1		2										6		
31	11	(h)	Halifax T*	W 3-1	Henry, Holley, Ainsley	2,000					5	4			9								11	1		2	10						3	8		6		7
32	18	(a)	Huddersfield T*	L 1-5	Henry	1,636					5	6		8	9	10							11	1		3					2		7					
33	25	(a)	Middlesbrough*	W 3-2	Adam, Hepplewhite (og), Jim Milburn (pen)	2,500					5				7							10	11	1		6						4	3	8	2			
34	May 2	(h)	Chesterfield*	W 1-0	Henry	2,000					5	6		7	9							3	11	1		4								8				
35	9	(h)	Middlesbrough*	L 1-2	Adam	2,000		2				4			9				10				11	1		3	6							8	5			
FINAL LEAGUE POSITION: Failed to qualify in Football League Northern Section (Second Championship)						Appearances		1			11	15		13	15	3	6	2	1	4		8	12	17		11	9			4	4	4	8	9	3	5	3	2
						Goals					1			2	13							1	5			1	3				1			2				

Matches marked thus † were in the League War Cup Qualifying Competition. Matches marked thus * were in the Combined Counties Cup. All Cup games counted towards the League.

The First Championship consisted of 38 teams. The Second Championship provided a table of 22 whilst a further 29 teams - Leeds amongst them - failed to qualify because they had played fewer than 18 games.

Taylor played number-7 in Matches 22-24; Asquith played number-9 in Matches 29 & 30, scoring once; Bratley played number-4 in Match 32; Turner played number-10 in Match 20 and number-3 in Match 21, scoring once; W.Williams played number-8 in Match 20; R.Sellar played number-7 in Match 21; Attwell played number-6 in Match 25; Scaife played number-3 in Match 30; J.Wesley played number-7 in Match 30; J.Shafto played number-9 in Match 33; Kidd played number-2 in Match 34; Clarke played number-10 in Match 34; Burton played number-7 in Match 35.

2 own-goals

1942-43

Manager: Billy Hampson

No	Date	Opponent	Result	Scorers	Att	Daniels	Fowler	Gadsby	McInnes	Powell	Henry	Eastham	Patterson	Holley	Knight	Butterworth	Short	Rutherford	Milburn, Jack	McGraw	Brown	Wakefield	Milburn, Jim	Poxon	Moss	Limbert	Houldershaw R	Warren	Ainsley	Fallaize	Harper	Vickers	Bush	Taylor	Jones	Kinghorn	Goldberg
1	Aug 29	(h) Middlesbrough	L 0-1		3,000	1	2	3	6	7	9	10	11																			4	5	8			
2	Sep 5	(a) Middlesbrough	L 0-2		3,500	1	3		4	7	9	10	11	5	6																		2	8			
3	12	(a) Gateshead	L 1-3	Short	3,000	1	3		4	8	9	7			6	5	10																		2	11	
4	19	(h) Gateshead	L 1-2	Powell	3,000	1				8	9		10	5	6	4		7																	3	11	2
5	26	(a) Newcastle U	W 5-3	Wakefield, Short 2, Rutherford, Brown	6,000	1				8				5	6	4	10	7	2	3	11	9															
6	Oct 3	(h) Newcastle U	L 1-7	Powell	3,000	1				8	7			5						3		9															
7	10	(h) Doncaster R	W 6-0	Powell 2, Short 2, Rutherford, Wakefield	3,000	1				8				5	6	4	10	7	2		11	9	3														
8	17	(a) Doncaster R	D 2-2	Hargreaves, Henry (pen)	2,000	1				8	10					5		7		3		9	2	4	6												
9	24	(h) Sunderland	L 1-2	Wakefield	4,000	1		3		8	10			5		4		7			11	9	2														
10	31	(a) Sunderland	L 1-4	Powell	3,000	1		3		8	7			5		4	10		2			9				6	11										
11	Nov 7	(h) Bradford	D 1-1	Powell	3,000	1				8	10			5								9	2	4	6		11										
12	14	(a) Bradford	L 0-1		4,465	1				8	7			5		4				3		9		10	6		11										
13	21	(h) York C	W 2-1	Henry, R.Houldershaw	4,000	1				8	10				6				2				3		4		11	5	9								
14	28	(a) York C	L 1-3	Wakefield	5,000	1				8	7				6					3		9	2				11	5	10								
15	Dec 5	(h) Halifax T	D 1-1	Wakefield	1,000	1				8					6	4		7		3		9					11		10								
16	12	(a) Haliax T	L 1-5	Fallaize	4,000	1				8					6	4		7		3									10	9							
17	19	(a) Huddersfield T	L 1-4	Henry	2,286	1				8	9				6	4		7		2									10								
18	25	(h) Huddersfield T	D 3-3	Wakefield 2, Henry	4,000	1		3		8	9				6					2		10		6			11		4		7						
					Appearances	18	3	4	3	18	14	3	3	9	11	11	4	8	4	9	3	11	6	4	4	1	7	2	6	1	1	1	2	2	2	2	1
					Goals					6	4						5	2			1	7					1			1							

FINAL LEAGUE POSITION: 43rd in Football League Northern Section (First Championship)

Scaife played number- 2 in Match 6; Kirby played number- 4 in Match 6; Clutterbuck played number-6 in Match 6; O'Farrell played number- 10 in Match 6; Tindall played number- 11 in Match 6; Hargreaves played number-11 in Match 8, scoring once; H.Robbins played number-6 in Match 9; Simpson played number-3 in Match 11 and number-2 in Match 12; Marshall played number-7 in Match 11; Anson played number-7 in Match 13; Campbell played number-4 in Match 14; Harston played number-2 in Matches 15 & 16; Sturrock played number-5 in Matches 15 & 16; H.Houldershaw played number-11 in Matches 16 & 17; D'Arcy played number-3 in Match 17; Woofinden played number-5 in Match 17.

No	Date	Opponent	Result	Scorers	Att	Daniels	Fowler	Gadsby	McInnes	Powell	Henry	Eastham	Patterson	Holley	Knight	Butterworth	Short	Rutherford	Milburn, Jack	McGraw	Brown	Wakefield	Milburn, Jim	Poxon	Moss	Limbert	Houldershaw R	Warren	Ainsley	Fallaize	Harper	Rhodes	Argue	Harris	Binns	Smith	Boyes
19	Dec 26	(a) Barnsley†	L 1-2	Rutherford	6,000	1		2		8	9				6			7		3		10	5			4	11										
20	Jan 2	(h) Barnsley†	L 1-3	Powell	2,000	1				8	7				6	5				3		9			4		11		10								
21	9	(h) Huddersfield T†	L 2-4	Powell, R.Houldershaw	1,000	1				8					6	5		7	2	3		9			4		11		10								
22	16	(a) Huddersfield T†	L 1-4	Powell	1,179	1				8	10				6	2		7		3		9					11	5	4								
23	23	(a) Newcastle U†	L 0-9		7,000	1				7	9				6	5	8	11		3								4	10								
24	30	(h) Newcastle U†	W 7-2	Powell 4, Henry, Ainsley 2	2,000	1				8	7				6	5		11		10									9								
25	Feb 6	(a) Bradford†	L 1-2	Henry	4,500	1				8	7				6	5		11		3		9			4				10								
26	13	(h) Bradford†	D 2-2	Rutherford, Henry	3,000	1				8	7				6	5		11				10								9							
27	20	(a) Bradford C†	L 0-1		4,287	1				8	7			5	6	4		11		3		10						2		9							
28	27	(h) Bradford C†	L 1-5	Rutherford	3,000	1				8	7				6	5		11	2	3		10										4	9				
29	Mar 6	(h) Middlesbrough*	W 3-2	Wakefield 2, R.Houldershaw	2,000	1		3			9				6			7				10	2				11					4	8				
30	13	(a) Middlesbrough*	W 3-2	Lawn, Henry 2	2,500	1		3		8	7				6							10	2		5		11					4					
31	20	(h) Newcastle U	L 1-3	Short	2,500	1					7					5	8	11		3						6								2			
32	27	(a) Newcastle U	W 5-4	Short, Powell 2, Rutherford, Williams	8,000	1				10					6	5	8	7										4						3			
33	Apr 3	(h) Bradford*	W 2-0	Smith, Jim Milburn	3,000					8	9				6								3								5	4	10		1	7	11
34	10	(a) Bradford*	L 2-5	Argue, Powell	3,908					8					6		10											2			5		9		1	7	11
					Appearances	14		3		14	13			1	15	11	4	12	2	10		10	4		4	2	6	5	6	2	2	4	4	2	2	2	2
					Goals					10	5						2	4				2	1				2		2				1			1	

FINAL LEAGUE POSITION: 47th in Football League Northern Section (Second Championship)

Matches marked thus † were in the League War Cup Qualifying Competition. Matches marked thus * were in the Combined Counties Cup. All Cup games counted towards the League.

The First Championship consisted of 48 teams. The Second Championship provided a table of 54. In the League Cup 32 teams qualified for the knock-out competition. Leeds were amongst the 22 non-qualifiers.

Match 19 abandoned after 66 minutes but the result stood.

Bedford played number-2 in Match 20; Whittle played number-2 in Match 23; Wilcox played number-2 in Matches 24 & 25; Dunn played number-3 in Match 24; Wheeler played number-4 in Match 24; W.H.Jones played number-2 in Match 26 and number-3 in Match 34; Wilkinson played number-3 in Match 26; Edwards played number-4 in Match 26; Hick played number-5 in Match 29; Lawn played number-9 in Matches 30 & 31, scoring once; Dainty played number-4 in Match 31; Wildon played number-10 in Match 31; Taylor played number-2 in Matches 32 & 33; T.Williams played number-9 in Match 32, scoring once; Pyke played number-11 in Match 32; Bokas played number-4 in Match 34.

1943-44

Manager: Billy Hampson

No	Date	Opponent	Result	Scorers	Att	Daniels	Gadsby	Stokes	Butterworth	Knight	Henry	Powell	Poland	Wilcocks	Makinson	Boyes	McGraw	Hindle	Milburn, Jim	Short	Challinor	Kirton	Ward	Holley	Kirby	Mahon	Galley	Goldberg	Tatton	Dorling	Glover	Rodgers	Ainsley	Wakefield	Paton	Tremelling	Wright
1	Aug 28	(a) Sunderland	L 1-7	Wakefield	4,000	1	2	3	4	6	7	8																			5	9	10	11			
2	Sep 4	(h) Sunderland	L 1-5	Tremmelling	4,000		3			6		8	1	2	4	11																7			5	9	10
3	11	(h) Bradford C	L 1-5	Boyes (pen)	2,000	1			5	6	7				4	11	3																				10
4	18	(a) Bradford C	D 3-3	Henry 2, Boyes (pen)	6,000		3		5		9	8	1		4	11	6																				10
5	25	(h) Middlesbrough	W 3-0	Stevens, Jameson, Henry	3,000	1	3		5		7			2		11	4	10																			
6	Oct 2	(a) Middlesbrough	D 3-3	Powell, Henry, Short	3,000	1		3	5	6	9	7			4	11		10	2	8																	
7	9	(h) Gateshead	W 5-2	Henry, Tremmelling 3, Boyes	3,000	1		3	5		7				6	11	2	10		8																9	
8	16	(a) Gateshead	W 4-3	Short, Henry, Powell 2	3,000				5		9	7	1		6	11	2	10		8																	
9	23	(a) Doncaster R	D 3-3	Knight 2, Henry	8,264				5	9	7		1			11	8	10			3	4	6														
10	30	(h) Doncaster R	D 2-2	Henry (pen), Fallaize	5,000	1		3	4		9				6			10						5													
11	Nov 6	(a) Bradford	L 1-6	Henry	5,301			3	5		9	7	1		6	11		10																			
12	13	(h) Bradford	D 2-2	Henry, Hindle	6,000				5		8		1			11		10	2		3	6			4	7											
13	20	(a) York C	W 3-1	Henry 2, Knight	4,708				5	9	7	8	1			11	3	10	2						6		4										
14	27	(h) York C	W 1-0	Knight	4,000	1			5	9	7	8				11		10			3				6			2									
15	Dec 4	(a) Halifax T	L 1-2	Brown	3,000	1			5		7				6		2	10			3								11								
16	11	(h) Halifax T	W 4-0	Knight, Boyes, Dorling, Hindle (pen)	4,000		2		5	9	7	8	1			11	3	10									4			6							
17	18	(h Huddersfield T	L 0-3		5,000		2		5	9	7	8	1			11		10			3	6					4										
18	25	(a) Huddersfield T	L 0-3		7,792	1	3			6		8			5	11		10	2			4															
					Appearances	9	7	5	16	10	16	11	9	2	10	15	9	14	4	3	5	4	1	1	3	1	3	1	1	1	1	2	1	1	1	2	3
					Goals					5	12	3				4		2		2										1				1		4	

FINAL LEAGUE POSITION: 27th in Football League Northern Section (First Championship)

Hirst played number-2 in Match 3; Padgett played number-8 in Match 3; Lawn played number-9 in Match 3; Fallaize played number-7 in Match 4 and number-8 in Match 10, scoring once; Attwell played number-6 in Match 5; Stevens played number-8 in Match 5, scoring once; Jameson played number-9 in Match 5, scoring once; Rhodes played number-4 in Matches 7 & 8; O'Neill played number-3 in Match 8; Jones played number-2 in Matches 4, 9 & 10.

No	Date	Opponent	Result	Scorers	Att	Daniels	Gadsby	Stokes	Butterworth	Knight	Henry	Powell	Poland	Wilcocks	Makinson	Boyes	McGraw	Hindle	Milburn, Jim	Short	Challinor	Kirton	Ward	Holley	Kirby	Mahon	Galley	Goldberg	Tatton	Dorling	Antonio	Milburn, Jack	Davies	Rosier	Milburn G	Yeomanson	Davie
19	Dec 26	(a) Bradford+	L 1-2	Powell	13,186	1	3		5	6	7	8				11		10	2			4															
20	Jan 1	(h) Bradford+	W 3-1	Hindle, Powell, Antonio	7,200	1	2		5	6	9	7				11		10			3									4	8						
21	8	(h) Barnsley+	W 2-0	Antonio, Henry	7,000	1			5	6	9	7				11		10	2		3									4	8						
22	15	(a) Barnsley+	L 2-3	Henry 2	4,347	1				6	9	7			5	11	10				3									4	8	2					
23	22	(a) Huddersfield T†	L 1-4	Hindle	1,810				5	6	9	7	1			11	3	10													8		4				
24	29	(h) Huddersfield T†	W 2-0	Boyes, Antonio	8,000	1			4		9	7			6	11		10			3			5				2			8						
25	Feb 5	(a) Bradford C†	D 3-3	Antonio 2, Boyes	4,800	1			6		9				4	11	3	10						5							8	2					
26	12	(h) Bradford C†	W 2-0	Hindle, Boyes	8,000	1			5		8				4	11		10			3		6			7						2		9			
27	19	(h) York C+	W 2-1	Mahon, Henry	7,000	1			5		7						2	10			3		4			11					8		6	9			
28	26	(a) York C+	L 1-8	Knight	5,176				5	9						11	2	10			3					7					8		4				
29	Mar 4	(a) Sheffield U‡	L 1-3	Boyes	12,000	1			5		9	7				11		10									4				8	3	6		2		
30	11	(h) Sheffield U‡	W 1-0	Davies	15,000	1			4		9	7				11	3	10													8		6		2		
31	18	(a) Derby C	D 2-2	Curry 2	6,000	1					7				4		3		5							11								9	2		
32	Apr 1	(a) Chesterfield*	W 3-1	Davie 2, Gadsby	1,000	1	3		5	10	7	8				11																2	6			4	9
33	8	(h) Chesterfield*	W 1-0	Steele	4,500	1			5		7									8	3		6					2	11							4	9
34	10	(a) Rotherham U	L 3-5	Tatton, Powell, Short	8,000	1			5		7	10					3			8								2	11							4	9
35	15	(h) Halifax T*	D 2-2	Tatton, Davie	6,000	1			5	10	7	8			6		3												11							4	9
36	22	(a) Halifax T*	L 2-5	Steele, Davie	4,000	1			5		7				4	11					3	6							10							2	8
					Appearances	16	3		16	8	17	11	1		7	13	9	11	3	2	9	2	3	2		4	1	3	4	3	10	5	6	3	3	5	5
					Goals		1			1	4	3				4		3		1						1			2		5		1				4

FINAL LEAGUE POSITION: 35th in Football League Northern Section (Second Championship)

Matches marked thus * were in the Combined Counties Cup. Matches marked thus † were in the League War Cup Qualifying Competition. Matches marked thus ‡ were in the League War Cup knock-out competition which was on a two-legged basis. All Cup matches also counted towards the League.

The First Championship consisted of 50 teams; the Second Championship also provided a final table of 50 teams. Leeds were amongst the 32 qualifiers from the League War Cup's initial stages but were eliminated on aggregate in the first round of the knock-out stage.

Thompson played number-7 in Match 10, number-4 in Match 11 and number-2 in Match 23; H.Houldershaw played number-11 in Match 10; Bowen played number-2 in Match 11; Sharp played number-8 in Match 11; Jordan played number-9 in Match 12; Walker played number-4 in Matches 14 & 15; J.M.Brown played number-8 in Match 15, scoring once; McKellar played number-9 in Match 15; Moule played number-7 in Matches 18 & 25; Dewis played number-9 in Matches 18 & 19; J.Hodgson played number-1 in Match 28; Corbett played number-6 in Match 28; Lindley played number-5 in Match 30; Goodburn played number-6 in Match 31; Dutchman played number-8 in Match 31; Curry played n umber 10 in Match 31, scoring twice; Steele played number-10 in Match 33 and number-9 in Match 36, scoring twice; Farrell played number-6 in Match 34; C.E.Williams played number-2 in Match 35.

1944-45

Manager: Billy Hampson

No	Date	Opponent	Result	Scorers	Att	Daniels	Milburn, Jack	Gadsby	Yeomanson	Butterworth	Knight	Mahon	Henry	Sutherland	Hindle	Weaver	Pickering	Kirby	Short	Ainsley	Burbanks	Coyne	McGraw	Byrom	Campbell	Moule	Paton	Dunderdale	Bokas	Houndershaw R	Shotton	Twomey	Normanton	Fearnley	Duthoit	Crookes	Ruecroft
1	Aug 26	(a) Bradford	L 3-4	Jack Milburn (pen), Henry, Sutherland	8,416	1	2	3	4	5	6	7	8	9	10																						
2	Sep 2	(h) Bradford	D 3-3	Jack Milburn (pen), Yeomanson, Sutherland	6,000	1	2	3	4	5	6		8	9	10																						
3	9	(h) Sunderland	L 0-1		8,000	1			2	5	4	11	7	9	10	6	3																				
4	16	(a) Sunderland	L 1-5	Mahon	8,000			2		5		11	7		10		3	4	8	9																	
5	23	(a) Middlesbrough	L 2-3	Ainsley 2	4,500			3	2	5	4	7			10	6			8	9	11																
6	30	(h) Middlesbrough	W 4-2	Mahon 2, Hindle, Coyne	8,000	1			2	5	4	7			10	6				9	11	8															
7	Oct 7	(h) Hull C	W 5-2	Coyne 2, Mahon, Hindle, Henry	8,000	1			2	5		11	7		10	6		4		9		8	3														
8	14	(a) Hull C	D 0-0		5,000	1		3	2	5		7			10	6		4		9	11	8															
9	21	(h) Newcastle U	W 2-1	Coyne 2	8,000	1				5			7		10			4		9	11	8	2														
10	28	(a) Newcastle U	W 4-2	Hindle, Mahon, Short, Ainsley	25,000	1				5		11	7		10	6		4		9		8	2														
11	Nov 4	(a) Bradford C	W 6-2	Hindle 2, Ainsley 3, Coyne	6,657	1				5		11	7		10	6				9		8	3	2													
12	11	(h) Bradford C	W 4-1	Ainsley 3, Hindle	8,760	1				5	6	11	7		10					9		8		2	3												
13	18	(h) Hartlepools U	W 6-2	Short 3, Hindle 2, Ainsley	9,000	1	2			5		11	7		10				8	9			3	4	6												
14	25	(a) Hartlepools U	L 0-3		4,940	1	3		2	5		11	7		10	6			9			8		4													
15	Dec 2	(a) Huddersfield T	L 2-4	Henry, Moule	7,880	1				5		11	9		10	6						8	3		4	7											
16	9	(h) Huddersfield T	L 2-3	Henry, Moule	14,000	1				5	4	10	9			6					11	8	3		2	7											
17	16	(h) York C	W 3-1	Henry 3	5,000	1	2			5	4		9		10						11	8	3		6	7											
18	23	(a) York C	W 6-3	Hindle 3, Short 2, Moule	4,871	1		3	2		4				10	6			9		11	8			5	7											
FINAL LEAGUE APPEARANCE: 22nd in Football League Northern Section (First Championship)					Appearances	16	5	6	9	17	9	14	14	3	17	11	2	5	5	10	7	12	8	4	6	4											
					Goals		2		1			5	7	2	11				6	10		6				3											

Calverley played number-11 in Matches 1 & 2; Sharples played number-7 in Match 2; Dutchman played number- 8 in Match 3; Hodgson played number-1 in Matches 4 & 5; Howe played number- 6 in Match 4 and Match 9; Hardaker played number-3 in Matches 6 & 9; James played number-3 in Match 10; Booth played number-4 in Match 11 & 12; Birch played number-2 in Match 15.

No	Date	Opponent	Result	Scorers	Att	Daniels	Milburn, Jack	Gadsby	Yeomanson	Butterworth	Knight	Mahon	Henry	Sutherland	Hindle	Weaver	Pickering	Kirby	Short	Ainsley	Burbanks	Coyne	McGraw	Byrom	Campbell	Moule	Paton	Dunderdale	Bokas	Houndershaw R	Shotton	Twomey	Normanton	Fearnley	Duthoit	Crookes	Ruecroft
19	Dec 26	(h) Bradford C†	W 9-1	Hindle 3, Short 2, Henry, Mahon, Burbanks, Weaver(pen)	3,500	1		3	2	5	4	7	9		10	6			8		11																
20	30	(a) Bradford C†	L 2-6	Mahon, Henry	7,672	1		3	2	5	4	11	9		10	6						8				7											
21	Jan 6	(h) Barnsley†	L 0-1		12,000	1			2	5		7	9		10	6						8	3				11										
22	13	(a) Barnsley†	L 0-5		6,989	1			3	5		7	8		10	6											11	9									
23	20	(a) York C†	W 5-0	Moule, Dunderdale 2, Hindle 2	1,000	1			3	5					10	6			8							7	11	9	4								
24	27	(h) York C†	W 4-3	Moule, Henry, Hindle, Burbanks	6,000	1	2	3		5			8		10						11				6	7		9	4								
25	Feb 3	(h) Hull C†	W 6-1	Coyne, Hindle 2, Henry 2, Weaver (pen)	8,000	1	2			5		7	9		10	6						8	3		4					11							
26	10	(a) Hull C†	D 1-1	Campbell	4,000	1	2			5		7	9		10							8	3		6				4	11							
27	17	(a) Bradford†	L 2-5	Hindle, Henry	10,198	1	3			5		7	9		10							8	4		6					11	2						
28	24	(h) Bradford†	L 0-2		15,000	1	3			5		7	9		10							8			6				4	11	2						
29	Mar 3	(h) Sheffield W	W 4-3	Henry 3, Hindle	7,000		2	3		5			9		10							8			6	7				11		1					
30	10	(h) Preston NE	W 3-1	Hindle 2, Coyne	8,500		2			5			9		10	6					11	8			4		7				3	1					
31	17	(a) Sheffield W	D 1-1	Henry	7,000					5			9		10	6						8			4	7					3	1					
32	24	(h) Grimsby T	D 1-1	Knight	7,000				2	5	11		9		10	6						8			4	7					3	1					
33	Apr 2	(h) Chesterfield	L 0-2		6,500	1				5	4				10	6			8		11				2	7							9				
34	9	(a) Grimsby T	L 0-3		6,000		2			5	4		8		10						11	6				7		9				1					
35	14	(h) Hull C	W 6-2	Henry 2, Hindle 2, Coyne, Moule	2,000			3		5	4		9		10	6						8				7								1	2	11	
36	21	(a) Barnsley	W 3-1	Knight 2, Hartson (og)	3,380					5	9				10	6						7			3	11								1	2		
37	28	(h) Barnsley	L 1-3	Moule	4,000					5			9		10	4						8			3	7								1	2	11	
38	May 5	(a) Sheffield U	L 0-6		4,000		5				4				10	6						8	3			7							9	1	2	11	
39	12	(h) Sheffield U	W 4-1	Jim Milburn, Hindle, Ward, Henry	4,000			3			11		7		10	6						8			4									1			5
40	21	(a) Chesterfield	L 1-6	Morton	4,000			3			4					6			10			8												1			5
FINAL LEAGUE POSITION: 32nd in Football League Northern Section (Second Championship)					Appearances	11	9	7	6	19	10	8	17		21	16			4		5	17	5		13	12	4	4	4	5	5	5	2	6	4	3	2
					Goals						3	2	13		15	2			2		2	3			1	4		2									

1 own-goal

Matches marked thus † were in the League War Cup Qualifying Competition which also counted towards the League and in which Leeds failed to finish in the top 32 to qualify for the knock-out competition.
The First Championship consisted of 54 teams and the Second Championship 60.

Gleave played number-4 in Matches 21 & 22; Goldberg played number-2 in Matches 22 & 23; Glover played number-4 in Match 29; Harper played number-2 in Match 31; Hargreaves played number-11 in Match 31; Forde played number-3 in Matches 33 & 34; Bean played number-4 in Match 36; Powell played number-8 in Match 36; Cherry played number-6 in Match 37; Jim Milburn played number-2 in Match 39, scoring once; Ward played number-9 in Match 39, scoring once; Hulbert played number-2 in Match 40; Downing played number-7 in Match 40; Morton played number-9 in Match 40, scoring once; J.W.Stephens played number-11 in Match 40.

1945-46

Manager: Billy Hampson

No	Date	Opponent	Result	Scorers	Att	Milburn, Jack	Duffy	Butterworth	Coyne	Henry	Stephens JW	Hindle	Duthoit	Jones S	Moule	Short	Hodgson	Powell	Grainger	Hudson	Laidman	Chew	Gadsby	Dutchman	Price	Ainsley	McGraw	Holley	Barton	Heaton	Browne	Smith	Fearnley	Milburn, Jim	Knight	Goldberg	Batey
1	Aug 25	(a) Chesterfield	L 1-3	Hindle	7,229	2	4	5	6	7	9	10																									
2	Sep 1	(h) Chesterfield	L 1-3	Short	7,339		4	5	6		9	10	2	3	7	8																					
3	8	(h) Barnsley	L 1-2	Powell	8,561	2	4	5	6		9	10		3		8	1	7	11																		
4	13	(a) Stoke C	L 1-2	Hindle	6,882		4	5	6		8	10		3			1		7	2																	
5	15	(a) Barnsley	L 2-3	Henry, Hindle	10,055	2	4	5	6	7		10		3		8	1		11																		
6	22	(a) Everton	W 2-0	Grainger, Henry	19,711		4	5	6	9		10		3			1		7	2	8	11															
7	29	(h) Everton	L 2-3	Short, Hindle	13,541		4	5	6	9		10		3		7	1			2	8	11															
8	Oct 6	(h) Bolton W	W 2-1	Grainger, Hindle	11,836		4	5	6			10		3			1		7	2		8															
9	13	(a) Bolton W	L 0-6		17,770		4	5	6	9	8			2			1		7			10	3														
10	20	(h) Preston NE	W 2-1	Dutchman, Henry	11,782		4		6	9				2	7		1		11			10	3	8													
11	27	(a) Preston NE	L 2-8	Chew, Henry	12,344		4	5	6	9				3			1		7	2	8	10															
12	Nov 3	(h) Burnley	L 1-2	Ainsley	11,387		4	5	6			10		2		8	1								7	9											
13	10	(a) Burnley	W 3-2	Ainsley, Henry, Short	6,925		4	5	6	7		10				8	1		11	2						9											
14	17	(h) Manchester U	D 3-3	Ainsley, Short, Henry	12,013		4	5	6	7		10				8	1		11	2						9											
15	24	(a) Manchester U	L 1-6	Whalley (og)	21,312		4			7		10	2			8	1		11							9	3	5	6								
16	Dec 1	(h) Sunderland	W 4-2	Ainsley, Grainger, Stelling (og), Dutchman	9,509			4		7		10	2				1		11					8		9	3	5	6								
17	8	(a) Sunderland	L 1-5	Grainger	10,106			4		7	10		2				1		11					8		9	3	5	6								
18	15	(h) Sheffield U	L 2-4	J.W.Stephens, Henry	10,401			4	6	7	10		2			8	1		11				3			9		5									
19	22	(a) Sheffield U	L 2-6	Ainsley, Grainger	14,926			4	6	7		10	2				1	8	11				3			9		5									
20	25	(h) Middlesbrough	W 1-0	Grainger	12,217				6	7		10	2				1	8	11				3		4	9		5									
21	26	(a) Middlesbrough	L 1-4	Ainsley	23,019							10	2			8	1	7	11				3		4	9		5	6								
22	29	(h) Stoke C	D 0-0		22,219			4	6			10	2			8	1	7								9		5		11							
23	Jan 12	(h) Blackpool	L 1-2	Ainsley	14,372					8		10	2				1		7						4	9		5		11	6						
24	19	(a) Blackpool	L 2-4	Ainsley 2	8,734					7	8	10	2				1								4	9		5		11	6	3					
25	26	(a) Grimsby T	L 2-3	Ainsley, Henry	10,105				6	8		10	2				1		7						4	9		5		11		3					
26	Feb 2	(h) Liverpool	W 3-0	Henry 2 (1 pen), Ainsley	11,881				6	8		10	2				1		7						4	9		5		11		3					
27	9	(h) Bury	D 3-3	Hindle 2, Ainsley (pen)	13,474				6		8	10	2				1		7						4	9		5		11		3					
28	16	(a) Bury	L 1-3	Grainger	8,623				6	8		10	2				1		7						4	9		5		11		3					
29	23	(a) Blackburn R	D 0-0		6,048					8	9	10	2		7		1								4			5		11	6	3					
30	Mar 2	(h) Blackburn R	L 1-4	Ainsley (pen)	10,752					7	8	10	2				1		11						4	9		5			6	3					
31	9	(h) Grimsby T	D 2-2	Henry, Heaton	8,000				6	8		10					1		7						4	9	3	5		11		2					
32	16	(a) Bradford	L 4-9	Ainsley 2, McGraw, Grainger	11,302				6	8		10					1		7							9	3	5		11		2					
33	23	(a) Manchester C	L 1-5	Heaton	20,000					8		10							7						4	9		5		11		2	1	3	6		
34	30	(h) Manchester C	L 1-3	Price	10,000					8		10					1		7						4	9		5		11		2		3	6		
35	Apr 6	(h) Newcastle U	L 0-3		14,000					7		10					1	8	11							9		5						3		2	6
36	10	(a) Liverpool	D 1-1	Grainger	10,620												1	8	7						4	9		5		11				3	10	2	6
37	13	(a) Newcastle U	D 1-1	Ainsley	25,000												1	8	7						4	9		5		11				3	10	2	6
38	20	(h) Huddersfield T	W 3-2	Briggs (og), Powell, Heaton	15,000												1	8	7						4	9		5		11				3	10	2	6
39	22	(h) Sheffield W	L 0-1		14,000					9								8	7						4			5		11			1	3	10	2	6
40	23	(a) Sheffield W	L 0-2		14,000					9		10						8	7						4			5		11			1	3		2	6
41	27	(a) Huddersfield T	L 2-3	Ainsley 2	4,622							10					1	8	7						4	9		5		11				2			6
42	May 1	(h) Bradford	W 3-2	Hindle, Ainsley 2	10,000					8		10							7						4	9		5		11			1	3		2	6
					Appearances	3	15	18	24	30	11	33	17	11	3	11	36	12	35	7	3	6	6	3	21	28	5	28	4	19	4	11	4	10	6	7	8
					Goals					11	1	8				4		2	9			1		2	1	20	1			3							

FINAL LEAGUE POSITION: 22nd in Football League Northern Section (22 teams)

3 own-goals

Parker played number-1 in Matches 1 & 2; Oliver played number-3 in Match 1; Blair played number-8 in Match 1; Glackin played number-11 in Match 1; Crookes played number-11 in Match 2; Iceton played number-9 in Matches 4 & 5; E.Jones played number-11 in Match 4; A.Stephens played number-9 in Match 8; Burbanks played number-11 in Matches 8 & 12; Buckley played number-11 in Match 9; Alberry played number-5 in Match 10. Walker played number-11 in Match 11; Westlake played number-3 in Match 12; Skidmore played number-3 in Matches 13 & 14; Laking played number-3 in Match 22; Pope played number-3 in Match 23; Collier played number-4 in Matches 32 & 35; Pogson played number-3 in Match 41.

FA Cup

Rd	Date	Opponent	Result	Scorers	Att	Milburn, Jack	Duffy	Butterworth	Coyne	Henry	Stephens JW	Hindle	Duthoit	Jones S	Moule	Short	Hodgson	Powell	Grainger	Hudson	Laidman	Chew	Gadsby	Dutchman	Price	Ainsley	McGraw	Holley	Barton	Heaton	Browne	Smith	Fearnley	Milburn, Jim	Knight	Goldberg	Batey
3	Jan 5	(h) Middlesbrough	D 4-4	Henry, Ainsley, Hardwick (og), Short	18,000			4	6	7		10	2			8	1		11				3			9		5									
	9	(a) Middlesbrough	L 2-7	Grainger, Ainsley	23,878			5	4	7		10	2			8	1		11				3		6	9											
		Leeds lost 11-6 on aggregate.			Appearances			2	2	2		2	2			2	2		2				2		1	2		1									
					Goals					1						1			1							2											

1 own-goal

1946-47

Manager: Billy Hampson

						Hodgson	Goldberg	Milburn, Jim	Price	Holley	Batey	Cochrane	Powell	Henry	Short	Grainger	Ainsley	Bannister	Hindle	Kane	Browne	Browning	Heaton	Fearnley	Twomey	Gadsby	Martin	Clarke	Willingham	Hodgkinson
1	Aug 31	(a) Preston NE	L 2-3	Grainger 2	25,311	1	2	3	4	5	6	7	8	9	10	11														
2	Sep 4	(h) Charlton A	L 0-2		22,857	1	2	3	4	5	6	7	8	9	10	11														
3	7	(h) Sheffield U	D 2-2	Powell, Henry	28,543	1	2	3	4	5	6	7	8	9	10	11														
4	14	(a) Chelsea	L 0-3		57,184	1	2	3	4	5	6	7	8		10	11	9													
5	16	(a) Stoke C	L 2-5	Ainsley 2	21,141	1		3	4		6	7	8			11	9	2	10	5										
6	21	(h) Bolton W	W 4-0	Cochrane, Ainsley, Short 2	25,739	1		3			5	7	8	4	10	11	9	2			6									
7	25	(a) Charlton A	L 0-5		16,488	1		3			5	7	8	4	10	11		2			6	9								
8	28	(a) Liverpool	L 0-2		51,042	1		3	6	5			8	4	9	7		2	10				11							
9	Oct 5	(h) Huddersfield T	W 5-0	Ainsley 3, Powell, Short	30,622			3		5		7	8	4	10	11	9	2			6			1						
10	12	(h) Grimsby T	W 1-0	Powell	28,877			3		5		7	8	4	10	11	9	2			6			1						
11	19	(a) Wolves	L 0-1		40,113			3		5		7		4	8	11	9	2	10		6			1						
12	26	(h) Blackburn R	L 0-1		28,683			3		5	6	7	8	4	10	11	9	2						1						
13	Nov 2	(a) Portsmouth	L 1-4	Ainsley	25,984			3		5		7	8	4	10	11	9	2			6			1						
14	9	(h) Everton	W 2-1	Powell, Short	22,992			3		5		7	8	4	10	11	9	2			6			1						
15	16	(a) Arsenal	L 2-4	Ainsley 2	36,377			3		5		7	8	4	10	11	9	2			6			1						
16	23	(h) Blackpool	W 4-2	Powell 2, Ainsley, Grainger	25,829		2			5		7	8	4	10	11	9				6				1	3				
17	30	(a) Brentford	D 1-1	Cochrane	20,352		2			5		7	8	4	10	11	9						6		1	3				
18	Dec 7	(h) Sunderland	D 1-1	Cochrane	25,784		2			5		7	8	4	10	11	9				6				1	3				
19	14	(a) Aston Villa	L 1-2	Powell	29,410		2			5		7	8	4	10	11	9				6				1	3				
20	21	(h) Derby C	L 1-2	Henry (pen)	21,320		2			5		7		4	8		9		10		6		11		1	3				
21	25	(h) Middlesbrough	D 3-3	Milburn, Short, Cochrane	28,742		2	4		5		7	8		10	11	9				6				1	3				
22	26	(a) Middlesbrough	L 0-3		45,336		2	4		5		7			8	11	9		10		6			1		3				
23	28	(h) Preston NE	L 0-3		33,433			2		5		7	8		9	11		4	10		6			1		3				
24	Jan 4	(a) Sheffield U	L 2-6	Cochrane, Ainsley	31,947		2	4		5		7	8		10	11	9				6				1		3			
25	18	(h) Chelsea	W 2-1	Henry (pen), Cochrane	37,884	1		2		5		7	8	4	10	11	9	3									6			
26	Feb 1	(h) Liverpool	L 1-2	Grainger	25,430	1		2		5		7	8	4	10	11	9	3									6			
27	3	(a) Bolton W	L 0-2		6,278	1		2		5		7	8	4	10	11	9	3			6									
28	22	(h) Wolves	L 0-1		30,313	1		2		5		7	8	4	10	11		3									6	9		
29	Mar 1	(a) Blackburn R	L 0-1		28,371	1		2		5		7		4		11	8	3	10								6	9		
30	22	(h) Arsenal	D 1-1	Grainger	32,190	1		2		5		7	8	10		11		3									6	9	4	
31	29	(a) Blackpool	L 0-3		14,501	1		2		5		7		4		11	8	3	10								6	9		
32	Apr 5	(h) Brentford	L 1-2	Henry (pen)	23,962	1		2		5		7		10			8	3					11				6	9	4	
33	7	(a) Manchester U	L 1-3	Cochrane	41,912	1		2		5		7		6			8	3	10				11					9	4	
34	8	(h) Manchester U	L 0-2		15,528	1		2		5		7		6			8	3	10				11					9	4	
35	12	(a) Sunderland	L 0-1		30,429	1		2		5		7	8	6					10				11			3		9	4	
36	19	(h) Aston Villa	D 1-1	Clarke	22,291			2		5		7	8	10							6		11		1	3		9	4	
37	26	(a) Derby C	L 1-2	Powell	10,994			2		5		7	8	10							6		11		1	3		9	4	
38	May 3	(h) Stoke C	L 1-2	Short	21,714			2		5			8	6	10	7							11		1	3		9	4	
39	10	(a) Huddersfield T	L 0-1		20,596			2		5		7	8	6	10								11		1	3		9	4	
40	17	(a) Grimsby T	L 1-4	Short	10,795			2		5		7	8	6	10								11		1	3		9	4	
41	24	(h) Portsmouth	L 0-1		14,097			2		5			8	6	10	7	9						11		1	3			4	
42	26	(a) Everton	L 1-4	Powell	21,001					5			7	6	10		9	2					11		1	3		8		4
FINAL LEAGUE POSITION: 22nd in Division One					Appearances	19	12	36	6	39	8	38	34	36	32	32	28	23	11	1	19	1	14	9	14	16	8	14	11	1
					Goals			1				7	9	4	7	5	11											1		

FA Cup

						Hodgson	Goldberg	Milburn, Jim	Price	Holley	Batey	Cochrane	Powell	Henry	Short	Grainger	Ainsley	Bannister	Hindle	Kane	Browne	Browning	Heaton	Fearnley	Twomey	Gadsby	Martin	Clarke	Willingham	Hodgkinson
3	Jan 11	(a) West Brom A	L 1-2	Ainsley	31,007			2		5		7	8	4	10	11	9								1	3	6			
					Appearances			1		1		1	1	1	1	1	1								1	1	1			
					Goals												1													

1947-48

Manager: Willis Edwards

	Date	Opponent	Result	Scorers	Att	Twomey	Milburn	Gadsby	Henry	Holley	Martin	Cochrane	Powell	Ainsley	Short	Heaton	Wakefield	Hindle	Willingham	Ingham	Kirby	Grainger	Dunn	Hodgkinson	Windle	Bullions	Morton	Bannister	Chisholm	Hodgson	McCabe	Fearnley
1	Aug 23	(h) Leicester C	W 3-1	Short, Ainsley 2	26,519	1	2	3	4	5	6	7	8	9	10	11																
2	27	(a) Barnsley	L 0-3		23,440	1	2	3	4	5	6	7	8	9	10	11																
3	30	(a) Southampton	W 2-1	Smith (og), Wakefield	21,023	1	2	3	4	5	6	7			8	11	9	10														
4	Sep 3	(h) Barnsley	W 4-1	Wakefield 2, Short, Cochrane	36,501	1	2	3	4	5	6	7	8		10	11	9															
5	6	(a) Fulham	L 2-3	Short, Wakefield	26,247	1	2	3	4	5	6	7	8		10	11	9															
6	10	(h) Plymouth A	W 5-0	Short, Powell 3, Heaton (pen)	29,396	1	2	3		5	6	7	8		10	11	9		4													
7	13	(h) Coventry C	W 2-1	Powell 2	30,462	1	2	3		5	6	7	8		10	11	9		4													
8	17	(a) Plymouth A	L 0-1		21,126	1	2	3		5	6	7	8		10	11	9		4													
9	20	(a) Newcastle U	L 2-4	Wakefield, Cochrane	57,275	1	2	3		5	6	7	8		10	11	9		4													
10	27	(h) Birmingham C	L 0-1		37,135	1	2	3		5	6	7			8	11	9	10	4													
11	Oct 4	(a) West Brom A	L 2-3	Heaton, Wakefield	30,479	1	2	3					8		10	11	9		4	5	6	7										
12	11	(h) Doncaster R	D 0-0		34,775	1	2	3		5	6	7	8		10	11	9		4													
13	18	(a) Nottingham F	L 0-1		22,380	1	2	3		5	10	7			8	11	9		4		6											
14	25	(h) Bradford	W 2-0	Wakefield 2	31,532	1	2	3			5	7	8			10	9		4		6	11										
15	Nov 1	(a) Cardiff C	D 0-0		36,851	1		3			5	7	8			10	9		4		6	11	2									
16	8	(h) Sheffield W	D 2-2	Wakefield 2	32,547	1		3			5	7	8			10	9		4		6	11	2									
17	15	(a) Tottenham H	L 1-3	Cochrane (pen)	41,563	1		3	4		5	7	8			10	9				6	11	2									
18	22	(h) Millwall	W 2-1	Powell 2	24,160	1	3			5	6	7	8			10	9						2	4	11							
19	29	(a) Chesterfield	L 0-3		15,501	1	3			5	6	7	8		10	11	9						2			4						
20	Dec 6	(h) West Ham U	W 2-1	Short, Martin	21,866	1		3		5	6	7	8		10	11	9						2			4						
21	13	(a) Bury	D 1-1	Wakefield	13,104	1		3		5	10		7		8	11	9				6		2			4						
22	20	(a) Leicester C	L 0-2		22,252	1		3		5	6	7	8		10	11	9						2			4						
23	26	(h) Luton T	L 0-2		28,597	1	2			5	6	7	8				9	10					2		11	4						
24	27	(a) Luton T	L 1-6	Cochrane	16,964	1	2	3		5	10	7	8					11			6					4	9					
25	Jan 3	(h) Southampton	D 0-0		23,794	1	2	3			5	7	8			10	9	11	6							4						
26	17	(h) Fulham	L 0-1		29,640	1	2				5	7	8				9	11	6							4		3	10			
27	24	(h) Newcastle U	W 3-1	Cochrane, Wakefield 2	30,367	1	2				5	7	8				9	11	6							4		3	10			
28	31	(a) Coventry C	W 2-1	Wakefield 2	22,269	1	2				5	7	8				9	11	6							4		3	10			
29	Feb 14	(a) Birmingham C	L 1-5	Chisholm	39,955	1	2				5	7	8				9	11	6							4		3	10			
30	21	(h) West Brom A	W 3-1	Hindle, Pemberton (og), Chisholm	22,333		2				5	7	8				9	11	6							4		3	10	1		
31	28	(a) Doncaster R	L 0-3		26,569	1	2				5	7	8				9	11	6							4		3	10			
32	Mar 6	(h) Nottingham F	D 2-2	Powell, Wakefield	27,018	1	2				5	7	8				9	11	6							4		3	10			
33	13	(a) Bradford	L 1-3	Powell	21,060	1	2	3			5	7	8				9	11								4			10		6	
34	20	(h) Cardiff C	W 4-0	Chisholm 2, Powell, Short	34,276	1	2				3	7	8		9			11	6							4			10		5	
35	26	(a) Brentford	L 0-3		30,538	1	2				3		8		9		7	11	6							4			10		5	
36	27	(a) Sheffield W	L 1-3	Short	38,736	1					3		8		9		7	11	6				2			4			10		5	
37	29	(h) Brentford	D 1-1	Bannister (pen)	26,775							7	8		9			11	6				2			4		3	10		5	1
38	Apr 3	(h) Tottenham H	L 1-3	Wakefield	24,891		2	3				7	8				9	11	6							4			10		5	1
39	10	(a) Millwall	D 1-1	Chisholm	21,426		3			5		7	8				9	11					2			4			10		6	1
40	17	(h) Chesterfield	W 3-0	Hindle, Chisholm, Wakefield	28,794		3			5		7	8				9	11					2			4			10		6	1
41	24	(a) West Ham U	L 1-2	Chisholm	13,594		3			5		7	8				9	11					2			4			10		6	1
42	May 1	(h) Bury	W 5-1	Wakefield 3, Cochrane 2	17,573		3			5		7	8			11	9						2			4			10		6	1
FINAL LEAGUE POSITION: 18th in Division Two					Appearances	35	34	24	6	23	35	38	39	2	21	24	37	21	24	1	8	5	15	1	2	24	1	8	17	1	10	6
					Goals						1	7	10	2	7	2	21	2										1	1			

2 own-goals

FA Cup

	Date	Opponent	Result	Scorers	Att	Twomey	Milburn	Gadsby	Henry	Holley	Martin	Cochrane	Powell	Ainsley	Short	Heaton	Wakefield	Hindle	Willingham	Ingham	Kirby	Grainger	Dunn	Hodgkinson	Windle	Bullions	Morton	Bannister	Chisholm	Hodgson	McCabe	Fearnley
3	Jan 10	(a) Blackpool	L 0-4		28,500	1	2	3		9	5	7	8				10	11	6							4						
					Appearances	1	1	1		1	1	1	1				1	1	1							1						
					Goals																											

1948-49

Manager: Frank Buckley

No	Month	Day	Opponent	Result	Scorers	Att	Twomey	Dunn	Milburn	Bullions	Holley	McCabe	Hindle	Short	Wakefield	Chisholm	Heaton	Martin	Cochrane	Burden	McAdam	Lomas	Marsh	Fearnley	Browning	Depear	Williams J	Iggleden	Searson	McMorran	Moss	Rudd	Edwards	Bannister	Ingham	Charles
1	Aug	21	(a) Leicester C	L 2-6	Chisholm, Short	34,937	1	2	3	4	5	6	7	8	9	10	11																			
2		25	(h) Brentford	D 0-0		26,625	1	2	3	4	5	6	7	8	9	10	11																			
3		28	(h) Luton T	W 2-0	Chisholm 2	25,463	1	2	3	4	5	6	7	8	9	10	11																			
4	Sep	1	(a) Brentford	W 3-1	Milburn (pen), Short, Chisholm	19,212	1	2	3		5	4	11	8	9	10		6	7																	
5		4	(h) Coventry C	W 4-1	Chisholm 2, Short 2	29,557	1	2	3		5	4	11	8	9	10		6	7																	
6		8	(h) Tottenham H	D 0-0		37,640	1	2	3		5	4	11	8	9	10		6	7																	
7		11	(a) Sheffield W	L 1-3	Cochrane	31,735	1	2	3		5	4	11	9		10		6	7	8																
8		13	(a) Tottenham H	D 2-2	Milburn, Cochrane	33,793	1	2	3		5	4	11		9	10			7	8	6															
9		18	(h) Lincoln C	W 3-1	Wakefield, Milburn (pen), Cochrane	33,963	1	2	3		5	4	11		9	10			7	8	6															
10		25	(a) Chesterfield	L 1-3	Wakefield	15,150	1	2	3		5	4	11		9	10			7	8	6															
11	Oct	2	(h) West Brom A	L 1-3	Marsh	33,706		2	3		5	4				10	11		7	9	6	1	8													
12		9	(a) Bradford	D 1-1	Chisholm	25,587		2	3		5	4	7		9	10	11			8	6			1												
13		16	(h) Southampton	D 1-1	Cochrane	34,959		2	3		5	4			9	10	11		7	8	6			1												
14		23	(a) Barnsley	D 1-1	Browning	26,010		2	3		5	4				10	11		7	8	6			1	9											
15		30	(h) Grimsby T	W 6-3	Burden 2, Milburn (pen), Heaton, Chisholm, Browning	33,581		2	3		5	4				10	11		7	8	6			1	9											
16	Nov	6	(a) Nottingham F	D 0-0		24,237		2	3		5	4				10	11		7	8	6			1	9											
17		13	(h) Fulham	D 1-1	Browning	26,240		2	3		5	4				10	11		7	8	6			1	9											
18		20	(a) Plymouth A	L 1-2	Heaton	24,752		2	3		5	4				10	11		7	8	6			1	9											
19	Dec	4	(a) Cardiff C	L 1-2	Browning	31,973		2	3		5	4				10	11		7	8	6			1	9											
20		11	(h) Queen's Park R	L 1-2	Burden	26,420		2	3		5	4			9	10	11		7	8	6			1												
21		18	(h) Leicester C	W 3-1	Heaton 2, Chisholm	22,600		2	3			6				10	11		7	8	4			1	9	5										
22		25	(a) West Ham U	L 2-3	Holley, Browning	20,660		2	3		5	6				10	11		7	8	4			1	9											
23		26	(h) West Ham U	L 1-3	Chisholm	32,577		6	3							10	11		7	8	4			1	9	5	2									
24	Jan	1	(a) Luton T	D 0-0		15,310		2	3	4							11		7		6		10	1	9	5		8								
25		15	(a) Coventry C	L 1-4	Browning	23,670		2	3			4					11		7	10	6				9	5		8	1							
26		22	(h) Sheffield W	D 1-1	Cochrane	42,053		2	3		5	4					11		7	8	6							10	1	9						
27		29	(h) Blackburn R	W 1-0	McMorran	32,963		2	3		5	4					11		7	8	6							10	1	9						
28	Feb	5	(a) Lincoln C	D 0-0		18,060		2	3		5	4					11		7	6								10	1	9	8					
29		12	(h) Bury	L 0-1		27,063		2	3		5	4							7	6								9	1	11	8	10				
30		19	(h) Chesterfield	W 1-0	Browning	29,362		2	3		5	4							7	6					8			10	1	9		11				
31	Mar	5	(h) Bradford	W 4-2	Browning 2, Iggleden, Cochrane	22,477		2	3		5	4							7	6					9			10	1	8		11				
32		12	(a) Southampton	L 1-2	Webber (og)	25,736		2	3	4	5								7	6			8		9			10	1			11				
33		19	(h) Barnsley	W 4-1	Moss, McMorran, Browning 2	29,701		2	3	4	5								7	6					9				1	8	10	11				
34		26	(a) Grimsby T	L 1-5	Browning	15,848		2	3	6	5									4					9			8	1		10	11	7			
35	Apr	2	(h) Nottingham F	W 1-0	Iggleden	23,932		2	3	4	5	8							7	6					9			10	1			11				
36		6	(a) West Brom A	L 0-1		28,662			3		5	4							7	6					9			8	1		10		11	2		
37		9	(a) Fulham	L 0-1		23,961			3			5							7	6					9			11	1	8	10			2	4	
38		16	(h) Plymouth A	W 1-0	Browning	24,326		2	3	4		5							7	6					9			10	1	8		11				
39		18	(a) Bury	L 1-3	McMorran	15,305		2	3	4		5							7	6					9			10	1	8		11				
40		23	(a) Blackburn R	D 0-0		18,873			3			4							7	6					9			10	1	8		11		2		5
41		30	(h) Cardiff C	D 0-0		19,945			3			4							7	6					9				1	8	10	11		2		5
42	May	7	(a) Queen's Park R	L 0-2		16,730			3			4							7	6			8		9				1		10	11		2		5
FINAL LEAGUE POSITION: 15th in Division Two						Appearances	10	37	42	10	32	37	11	7	12	23	21	4	37	35	20	1	4	13	24	4	1	16	18	12	8	12	2	5	1	3
						Goals			4		1			4	2	10	4		6	3			1		13			2		3	1					

1 own-goal

FA Cup

Rd	Month	Day	Opponent	Result	Scorers	Att	Twomey	Dunn	Milburn	Bullions	Holley	McCabe	Hindle	Short	Wakefield	Chisholm	Heaton	Martin	Cochrane	Burden	McAdam	Lomas	Marsh	Fearnley	Browning	Depear	Williams J	Iggleden	Searson	McMorran	Moss	Rudd	Edwards	Bannister	Ingham	Charles
3	Jan	8	(h) Newport C	L 1-3	Browning	31,500		2	3	4		6					11		7	8			10	1	9	5										
						Appearances		1	1	1		1					1		1	1			1	1	1	1										
						Goals																			1											

1949-50

Manager: Frank Buckley

No	Date	Opponent	Result	Scorers	Att	Searson	Dunn	Milburn	McCabe	Charles	Burden	Williams HT	McMorran	Browning	Moss	Rudd	Dudley	Casey	Cochrane	Hilton	McAdam	Harrison P	Harrison R	Ingham	Iggleden	Frost	Wilkins	Bannister	Bullions	Kerfoot	Taylor
1	Aug 20 (h)	Queen's Park R	D 1-1	Milburn (pen)	31,589	1	2	3	4	5	6	7	8	9	10	11															
2	22 (a)	West Ham U	L 1-3	Rudd	24,728	1	2	3	4	5	6	7	8	9		11	10														
3	27 (a)	Preston NE	D 1-1	Burden	31,378	1	2	3	4	5	8	11			10		9	6	7												
4	31 (h)	West Ham U	D 2-2	Cochrane, Dudley	29,732	1	2	3	4	5	8				10	11	9	6	7												
5	Sep 3 (h)	Swansea T	L 1-2	Dudley	29,767	1	2	3	4	5	8					11	9	6	7	10											
6	5 (a)	Sheffield U	W 1-0	Browning	22,126	1	2	3		5	4			8	10	11	9		7		6										
7	10 (a)	Tottenham H	L 0-2		48,274	1	2	3		5	4			9	10		8		7		6	11									
8	14 (h)	Sheffield U	L 0-1		23,199	1	2	3		5	4			9			8		7			11		6	10						
9	17 (a)	Southampton	L 1-2	P.Harrison	23,214	1	2	3		5	4						9		7		6		11			8	10				
10	24 (h)	Coventry C	D 3-3	McMorran, Dudley, Cochrane	22,590	1	2	3		5	6		8				9		7		4		11				10				
11	Oct 1 (a)	Luton T	L 0-1		15,291	1	2	3	4	5	6	7	8			11	9										10				
12	8 (h)	Cardiff C	W 2-0	Dudley, Browning	25,523	1	2		4	5	6	11	8	9			10		7									3			
13	15 (a)	Blackburn R	W 1-0	Dudley	22,038	1	2		4	5	6	11	8	9			10		7									3			
14	22 (h)	Brentford	W 1-0	Dudley	27,342	1	2		4	5	6	11	8	9			10		7									3			
15	29 (a)	Hull C	L 0-1		47,638	1	2		4	5	6	11	8	9			10		7									3			
16	Nov 5 (h)	Sheffield W	D 1-1	Williams	33,733	1	2		4	5	6	11	8	9			10		7									3			
17	12 (a)	Plymouth A	W 2-1	Frost, Charles (pen)	21,923	1	2		4	5	6		8	9			11		7							10		3			
18	19 (h)	Chesterfield	D 0-0		24,409	1	2	3	4	5	6		8	9			11		7							10					
19	26 (a)	Bradford	W 2-1	Dudley, Frost	18,401	1	2	3	4	5	6	11	8				10		7							9					
20	Dec 3 (h)	Leicester C	D 1-1	P.Harrison	26,768	1	2	3	4	5	6	11	8				10						7			9					
21	10 (a)	Bury	L 0-2		13,381	1	2	3		5	6	7	8	9			11									10			4		
22	17 (a)	Queen's Park R	D 1-1	Dudley	13,256	1	2	3		5	6	11	8	9			10						7							4	
23	24 (h)	Preston NE	W 3-1	Browning, Dudley, Quigley (og)	41,303	1	2	3		5	6	7	8	9			10													4	11
24	26 (a)	Barnsley	D 1-1	Milburn	27,017	1	2	3		5	6	7		9			10								8					4	11
25	27 (h)	Barnsley	W 1-0	Williams	47,817	1	2	3		5	6	11	8	9			10		7											4	
26	31 (a)	Swansea T	W 2-1	Williams, Browning	23,192	1	2	3		5	6	11	8	9			10		7											4	
27	Jan 14 (h)	Tottenham H	W 3-0	Cochrane 2, Iggleden	50,476	1	2	3		5	6	11		9			10		7						8					4	
28	21 (h)	Southampton	W 1-0	Williams	38,646	1	2	3		5	6	11		9			10		7						8					4	
29	Feb 4 (a)	Coventry C	W 4-0	Williams 2, Iggleden, Browning	22,990	1	2	3	4	5	6	11		9			10		7						8						
30	18 (h)	Luton T	W 2-1	Browning, Iggleden	37,263	1	2	3	4	5	6	11		9			10		7						8						
31	25 (a)	Cardiff C	L 0-1		28,423	1	2	3	4	5	6	11		9			10		7						8						
32	Mar 11 (a)	Brentford	D 0-0		22,231	1	2	3	4	5	6	11	8	9			7								10						
33	18 (h)	Hull C	W 3-0	Williams, McMorran, Milburn (pen)	49,465	1	2	3	4	5	6	11	8	9			7								10						
34	25 (a)	Sheffield W	L 2-5	Browning, Williams	50,485	1	2	3	4	5	6	11	8	9					7						10						
35	Apr 1 (h)	Bradford	D 0-0		31,062	1	2	3	4	5	6	11		9			10		7						8						
36	7 (a)	Grimsby T	L 0-2		22,511	1	2	3	4	5	6	7		9				11							8	10					
37	8 (a)	Leicester C	D 1-1	McMorran	33,881	1		3	4	5	6		10	9											8	7		2			11
38	10 (h)	Grimsby T	W 1-0	Milburn (pen)	17,991	1		3	4	5	6	7	9				11								8	10		2			
39	15 (h)	Plymouth A	D 1-1	Williams	24,132	1	2	3	4	5	6	11	9				10		7						8						
40	22 (a)	Chesterfield	I 1-3	Dudley	11,346	1	2	3	4	5	6	11			10		9		7						8						
41	26 (h)	Blackburn R	W 2-1	Dunn, Williams	12,538	1	2	3		5	6	11	8		10		9		7											4	
42	29 (h)	Bury	W 4-1	Dudley 2, Moss, Cochrane	8,913	1	2	3		5	6	11	8		10		9		7											4	
					Appearances	42	40	36	27	42	42	32	26	29	8	6	38	4	29	1	4	2	4	1	16	9	3	8	1	9	3
					Goals		1	4		1	1	10	3	7	1	1	12		5				2		3	2					

FINAL LEAGUE POSITION: 5th in Division Two

1 own-goal

FA Cup

Rd	Date	Opponent	Result	Scorers	Att	Searson	Dunn	Milburn	McCabe	Charles	Burden	Williams HT	McMorran	Browning	Moss	Rudd	Dudley	Casey	Cochrane	Hilton	McAdam	Harrison P	Harrison R	Ingham	Iggleden	Frost	Wilkins	Bannister	Bullions	Kerfoot	Taylor
3	Jan 7 (a)	Carlisle U	W 5-2	Browning, Dudley 2, Williams, Cochrane	22,832	1	2	3	4	5	6	11	8	9			10		7												
4	28 (h)	Bolton W	D 1-1	Williams	51,488	1	2	3	4	5	6	11	8	9			10		7												
R	Feb 1 (a)	Bolton W	W3-2*	Dudley 2, Browning	29,440	1	2	3	4	5	6	11		9			10		7						8						
5	11 (h)	Cardiff C	W 3-1	Williams, Cochrane, Iggleden	53,099	1	2	3	4	5	6	11		9			10		7						8						
6	Mar 4 (a)	Arsenal	L 0-1		62,273	1	2	3	4	5	6	11		9			10		7						8						
					Appearances	5	5	5	5	5	5	5	2	5			5		5						3						
					Goals							3		2			4		2						1						

*After extra-time

1950-51

Manager: Frank Buckley

No	Month	Date	Venue	Opponents	Result	Scorers	Att	Searson	Dunn	Milburn	Kerfoot	Charles	Burden	Cochrane	Iggleden	Browning	Dudley	Williams	Moss	McCabe	Harrison P	Frost	Hughes	Scott	Miller	Stevenson	Kirk	Vickers	McNeish	Hair
1	Aug	19	(h)	Doncaster R	W 3-1	Dudley 2, Browning	40,208	1	2	3	4	5	6	7	8	9	10	11												
2		21	(a)	Coventry C	L 0-1		30,213	1	2	3	4	5	6	7		9	10	11	8											
3		26	(a)	Brentford	W 2-1	Williams, Burden	20,381	1	2	3	4		6			9	10	11	8	5	7									
4		30	(h)	Coventry C	W 1-0	Browning	28,938	1	2	3	4		6			9	10	11		5	7	8								
5	Sep	2	(h)	Blackburn R	L 0-1		32,799	1	2	3	4	5	8			9	10	11		6	7									
6		7	(a)	Swansea T	L 2-4	Dudley, Browning	19,501	1	2	3	4	5	6			9	10	11	8		7									
7		9	(a)	Southampton	L 0-2		25,806	1	2	3	4	5	6			9	10	11	8		7									
8		16	(h)	Barnsley	D 2-2	Browning, Williams	37,633	1	2	3	4	5	6		8	9	10	7					11							
9		23	(a)	Sheffield U	D 2-2	Dudley, Hughes	28,872	1	2	3	4	5	6		8	9	10	7					11							
10		30	(h)	Luton T	W 2-1	Dudley, Browning	21,209	1	2	3	4	5	6		8	9	10				7		11							
11	Oct	7	(h)	Bury	D 1-1	Williams	28,859	1	2	3	4	5	6		8	9	10	7					11							
12		14	(a)	Preston NE	L 0-2		35,578	1	2	3	4	5	6		8		9	7	10				11							
13		21	(h)	Chesterfield	W 2-0	Browning, Iggleden	23,032	1	2	3	4	5	6		8	9	11		10		7									
14		28	(a)	Queen's Park R	L 0-3		15,935	1	2	3	4	5	6		8	9	11	7	10											
15	Nov	4	(h)	Manchester C	D 1-1	Dudley	30,764		2	3	6	5	8			9	10			4	7		11	1						
16		11	(a)	Leicester C	W 5-1	Burden, Dudley 3, Williams	26,573		2	3	6	5	8			9	10	11		4	7			1						
17		18	(h)	Notts C	L 0-1		29,728		2	3	6	5	8			9	10	11		4	7			1						
18		25	(a)	Grimsby T	D 2-2	Browning 2	15,561		2	3	6	5	10		8	9	7	11		4				1						
19	Dec	2	(h)	Birmingham C	W 3-0	Milburn, Browning, Burden	23,355		2	3	6	5	8		10	9	11	7		4				1						
20		9	(a)	Cardiff C	L 0-1		23,716		2	3	6	5	8		10	9	11	7		4				1						
21		16	(a)	Doncaster R	D 4-4	Harrison 2, Dudley, Browning	16,745	1	2	3		5	6			9	10	11		4	7				8					
22		23	(h)	Brentford	W 1-0	Dudley	19,839		2	3		5	6			9	10	11		4	7			1	8					
23		25	(a)	West Ham U	L 1-3	Harrison	19,519		2	3		5	6			9	10	11		4	7			1	8					
24		26	(h)	West Ham U	W 2-0	Browning 2	33,162	1	2	3		5	6			9	10	11		4	7				8					
25	Jan	13	(h)	Southampton	W 5-3	Williams, Browning 3, Burden	29,253	1	2	3		5	6			9	10	11		4	7				8					
26		20	(a)	Barnsley	W 2-1	Milburn (pen), Glover (og)	21,967	1	2	3		5	6			9	10	11		4	7				8					
27	Feb	3	(h)	Sheffield U	W 1-0	Browning	28,438		2	3	6	5			8	9		11		4	7			1		10				
28		10	(a)	Blackburn R	L 1-2	Harrison	25,496		2	3			6		8	9		11		4	7			1		10	5			
29		17	(a)	Luton T	W 3-2	Iggleden, Stevenson, Browning	13,323		2	3			6		8	9				4	7		11	1		10	5			
30		24	(a)	Bury	W 1-0	Stevenson	13,517		2	3	6	5			8	9				4	7		11	1		10				
31	Mar	3	(h)	Preston NE	L 0-3		42,114		2	3		5	6		8	9		7		4			11	1		10				
32		10	(a)	Chesterfield	L 0-1		9,856		2	3		5	6			9		11		4	7			1	8	10				
33		17	(h)	Queen's Park R	D 2-2	Milburn, Browning	18,094		2	3	4	5	6			9		7					11	1	8			10		
34		23	(a)	Hull C	L 0-2		46,701		2	3	4	5	6			9					7		11	1	8			10		
35		24	(a)	Manchester C	L 1-4	Harrison	35,149		2	3	6	9	8					11		4	7			1			5		10	
36		26	(h)	Hull C	W 3-0	Charles 2, Stevenson	27,887	1	2	3	4	9	6		8			11			7					10	5			
37		31	(h)	Leicester C	W 2-1	Burden 2	14,397	1		2	6		9		8			11		4	7					10	5			3
38	Apr	7	(a)	Notts C	D 0-0		23,466	1		2	6	5	9		8			11		4	7					10				3
39		14	(h)	Grimsby T	W 1-0	Charles	15,524	1	2	3	6	9			8			11		4	7					10	5			
40		21	(a)	Birmingham C	W 1-0	Stevenson	23,809	1	2	3	6		9		8			11		4	7					10	5			
41		28	(h)	Cardiff C	W 2-0	Iggleden, Hollyman (og)	14,765	1	2	3	6		9		8			11		4	7					10	5			
42	May	5	(h)	Swansea T	W 2-0	Iggleden, Browning	11,213	1	2	3			6		8	9		11		4	7					10	5			
FINAL LEAGUE POSITION: 5th in Division Two							Appearances	25	40	42	31	34	39	2	23	34	26	36	7	28	30	1	11	17	9	13	9	2	1	2
							Goals			3		3	6		4	19	11	5			5		1			4				

2 own-goals

FA Cup

Rd	Month	Date	Venue	Opponents	Result	Scorers	Att	Searson	Dunn	Milburn	Kerfoot	Charles	Burden	Cochrane	Iggleden	Browning	Dudley	Williams	Moss	McCabe	Harrison P	Frost	Hughes	Scott	Miller	Stevenson	Kirk	Vickers	McNeish	Hair
3	Jan	6	(h)	Middlesbrough	W 1-0	Browning	45,583	1	2	3		5	6			9	10	11		4	7				8					
4		27	(a)	Manchester U	L 0-4		55,434	1	2	3		5	6		8	9	10	11		4	7									
							Appearances	2	2	2		2	2		1	2	2	2		2	2				1					
							Goals									1														

Leeds United also played in the Festival of Britain Matches (See *Invitation Tournaments*).

1951-52

Manager: Frank Buckley

	Date	Opponent	Result	Scorers	Att	Scott	Dunn	Milburn	McCabe	Kirk	Burden	Williams	Iggleden	Browning	Stevenson	Hughes	Taylor	Harrison	Finlay	Barritt	Miller	Kerfoot	Mollatt	Tyrer	Hudson	Mills	Ross	Searson	Hair	Fidler	Charles	Stewart
1	Aug 18	(h) Brentford	D 1-1	Browning	20,268	1	2	3	4	5	6	7	8	9	10	11																
2	22	(a) Birmingham C	D 1-1	Stevenson	17,081		2	3	4	5	6	11	8	9	10		1	7														
3	25	(a) Doncaster R	L 0-2		22,222		2	3	4	5	6		8		10		1	11	7	9												
4	29	(h) Birmingham C	D 1-1	Iggleden	15,098		2	3	4	5	6	11	8				1	7		9	10											
5	Sep 1	(h) Everton	L 1-2	Miller	16,873		2	3	5	9	6	11	8				1	7			10	4										
6	8	(a) Southampton	D 0-0		19,682		2	3		5	6	7	8	9		10	1						4	11								
7	12	(h) Cardiff C	W 2-1	Hughes, Milburn	12,860		2	3		5	6		8	9		10	1						4	11	7							
8	15	(h) Sheffield W	W 3-2	Browning 2, Tyrer	20,016		2	3		5	6		8	9		10	1						4	11	7							
9	22	(a) West Ham U	L 0-2		19,464		2	3		5	6		8	9		10	1						4	11	7							
10	29	(a) Rotherham U	L 2-4	Iggleden 2	21,352		2	3		5	6	7	8	9			1					4		11		10						
11	Oct 6	(h) Sheffield U	W 3-1	Iggleden 2, Mills	26,915		2			5	6	11	10	9			1	7				4				8	3					
12	13	(a) Barnsley	L 1-3	Iggleden	15,565		2			5	6	11	10	9			1	7				4				8	3					
13	20	(h) Hull C	W 2-0	Iggleden, Harrison	24,656					5	6	11	10					7		9		4				8	2	1	3			
14	27	(a) Blackburn R	W 3-2	Harrison, Fidler, Iggleden	20,631					5	6	11	10					7				4				8	2	1	3	9		
15	Nov 3	(h) Queen's Park R	W 3-0	Iggleden, Fidler, Williams	22,875					5	6	11	10					7				4				8	2	1	3	9		
16	10	(a) Notts C	W 2-1	Fidler, Kerfoot	25,307		2			5	6	11	10					7				4				8		1	3	9		
17	17	(h) Luton T	D 1-1	Iggleden	27,405		2			5	6	11	10					7				4				8		1	3	9		
18	24	(a) Bury	W 2-1	Fidler, Iggleden	11,836		2			5	6	11	10					7				4				8		1	3	9		
19	Dec 1	(h) Swansea T	D 1-1	Mills	26,235		2				6	11	10					7				4				8		1	3	9	5	
20	8	(a) Coventry C	L 2-4	Williams, Kerfoot	14,621		2			4		11	10					7				6				8		1	3	9	5	
21	15	(a) Brentford	L 1-2	Mills	17,957		2		4			11	10					7				6				8		1	3	9	5	
22	22	(h) Doncaster R	D 0-0		21,793		2				6	11	10					7				4				8		1	3	9	5	
23	25	(a) Leicester C	W 2-1	Iggleden, Mills	24,498		2				6	11	10					7				4				8		1	3	9	5	
24	26	(h) Leicester C	W 2-1	Fidler 2	29,422		2				6	11						7			10	4				8		1	3	9	5	
25	29	(a) Everton	L 0-2		37,616		2				6	11	10					7				4				8		1	3	9	5	
26	Jan 5	(h) Southampton	D 1-1	Fidler	25,319		2				6	11	10					7				4				8		1	3	9	5	
27	19	(a) Sheffield W	W 2-1	Iggleden 2	42,354		2			7	6	11	10							9	8	4						1	3		5	
28	26	(h) West Ham U	W 3-1	Milburn, Kirk, Iggleden	32,297		2	9		7	6	11	10									4						1	3		5	8
29	Feb 9	(h) Rotherham U	W 3-0	Stewart, Milburn, Iggleden	47,985		2	9		7	6	11	10									4						1	3		5	8
30	16	(a) Sheffield U	L 0-3		36,265		2	9		7	6	11	10									4						1	3		5	8
31	Mar 1	(h) Barnsley	W 1-0	Mills	32,221		2			9	6	7	10			11						4				8		1	3		5	
32	8	(a) Hull C	L 2-3	Stewart, Williams	28,767	1	2	9		5	6	11	10					7				4							3			8
33	15	(h) Blackburn R	W 1-0	Iggleden	29,226	1	2		5		6	11	10			3		7				4								9		8
34	22	(a) Queen's Park R	D 0-0		15,195	1	2				6		10			3		7				4			11					9	5	8
35	29	(h) Notts C	W 1-0	Barritt	12,867	1	2		5		6	11	10			3		7		9		4				8						
36	Apr 5	(a) Luton T	L 1-2	Iggleden	11,460	1	2				6	11	10					7		9		4				8			3		5	
37	11	(a) Nottingham F	D 1-1	Williams	28,808	1	2		5		6	11	10					7				4				8			3		9	
38	12	(h) Bury	W 2-1	Mills 2	23,004	1	2		5		6	11	10					7				4				8			3		9	
39	14	(h) Nottingham F	D 0-0		26,511	1	2		5		6	11	10					7				4							3		9	8
40	19	(a) Swansea T	L 1-4	Williams	18,206	1		9	5		6	11	10			3		7				4				8			2			
41	26	(h) Coventry C	W 3-1	Dorman (og), Kerfoot, Fidler	16,322	1		2	5		6	11	10					7				4				8			3	9		
42	May 3	(a) Cardiff C	L 1-3	Iggleden	45,925	1		2	5		6	11	10					7				4				8			3	9		
FINAL LEAGUE POSITION: 6th in Division Two					Appearances	12	36	17	14	25	40	37	41	9	3	10	11	31	1	6	4	34	4	5	4	25	5	19	27	17	18	7
					Goals			3		1		5	19	3	1	1		2		1	1	3		1		7				8		2

1 own-goal

FA Cup

	Date	Opponent	Result	Scorers	Att	Scott	Dunn	Milburn	McCabe	Kirk	Burden	Williams	Iggleden	Browning	Stevenson	Hughes	Taylor	Harrison	Finlay	Barritt	Miller	Kerfoot	Mollatt	Tyrer	Hudson	Mills	Ross	Searson	Hair	Fidler	Charles	Stewart
3	Jan 12	(a) Rochdale	W 2-0	Kirk 2	21,475		2			7	6	11	10									4				8		1	3	9	5	
4	Feb 2	(h) Bradford	W 2-0	Milburn, Iggleden	50,645		2	9		7	6	11	10									4						1	3		5	8
5	23	(h) Chelsea	D 1-1	Milburn	52,328		2	9		7	6	11	10									4				8		1	3		5	
R	27	(a) Chelsea	D 1-1*	Kirk	60,851		2			9	6	7	10			11						4						1	3		5	8
2R	Mar 3	(n†) Chelsea	L 1-5	Mills	30,504		2			9	6	7	10			11						4				8		1	3		5	
*After extra-time. †Played at Villa Park, Birmingham.					Appearances		5	2		5	5	5	5			2						5				3		5	5	1	5	2
					Goals			2		3			1													1						

1952-53

Manager: Frank Buckley

No	Month	Day	Venue	Opponent	Result	Scorers	Attendance	Scott	Dunn	Hair	Kerfoot	Charles	Burden	Williams	Iggleden	Mills	McCall	Tyrer	Fidler	Langley	Smith	Hastie	Stewart	McCabe	Meek	Nightingale	Mollatt	Marsden	Forrest	Charlton
1	Aug	23	(a)	Huddersfield T	L 0-1		35,230	1	2	3	4	5	6	7	8	9	10	11												
2		28	(a)	Bury	D 2-2	Iggleden, Langley	12,274	1	2	3	4	5	6	7	10		8		9	11										
3		30	(h)	Plymouth A	D 1-1	Rundle (og)	25,067	1	2	3	4	5	6	7	10		8		9	11										
4	Sep	3	(h)	Bury	W 2-0	Iggleden, Langley	14,623	1	2	3	4	5	6	7	10		8		9	11										
5		6	(a)	Rotherham U	L 1-3	Iggleden	14,900	1	2	3	4	5	6	7	10		8		9	11										
6		10	(h)	Birmingham C	L 0-1		14,133	1	2	3	4	5	6	7	10	8			9	11										
7		13	(h)	Fulham	W 2-0	Smith, Mills	18,371	1	2	3	4	5	6	7	10	8		11			9									
8		17	(a)	Birmingham C	D 2-2	Hastie 2	18,371	1	2	3	4	5	6	7	10	8		11				9								
9		20	(a)	West Ham U	D 2-2	Iggleden, Tyrer	22,437	1	2	3	4	5	6	7	10	8		11				9								
10		24	(h)	Southampton	D 1-1	Iggleden	13,299	1	2	3	4	5	6	7	10	8		11				9								
11		27	(h)	Leicester C	L 0-1		19,724	1	2	3	4	5	6	7	10	8		11			9									
12	Oct	4	(a)	Notts C	L 2-3	Iggleden, Southwell (og)	22,836	1	2	3	4	5	6	7	10			11				9	8							
13		11	(a)	Sheffield U	L 1-2	Nightingale	33,683	1	2	3	4	9	6	11	10									5	7	8				
14		18	(h)	Barnsley	W 4-1	Nightingale 2, Charles, Mills	22,155	1	2	3	4	9	6	7		8		11						5		10				
15		25	(a)	Lincoln C	D 1-1	Charles	15,491	1	2	3	4	9	6	7		8		11						5		10				
16	Nov	1	(h)	Hull C	W 3-1	Charles 3	25,538	1	2	3	4	9	6	11	10									5	7	8				
17		8	(a)	Blackburn R	D 1-1	Charles	22,510	1	2	3	4	9	6	11	8									5	7	10				
18		22	(a)	Everton	D 2-2	Charles 2	28,664	1	2	3	4	9	6	11	10									5	7	8				
19		29	(h)	Brentford	W 3-2	Charles 3	16,077	1	2	3	4	9	6		10			11						5	7	8				
20	Dec	6	(a)	Doncaster R	D 0-0		15,744	1	2	3	4	9	6		10			11						5	7	8				
21		13	(h)	Swansea T	W 5-1	Charles 2 (1 pen), Nightingale, Iggleden 2	21,065	1	2	3	4	9	6		10			11						5	7	8				
22		20	(h)	Huddersfield T	W 2-1	Iggleden, Charles	34,365	1	2	3	4	9	6		10			11						5	7	8				
23		26	(a)	Luton T	L 0-2		19,480	1	2	3	4	9	6		10			11						5	7	8				
24		27	(h)	Luton T	D 2-2	Charles, Langley	31,634	1	2	3	4	9	6		10					11				5	7	8				
25	Jan	3	(a)	Plymouth A	W 1-0	Iggleden	27,149	1	2	3	4	9	6		10			11						5	7	8				
26		17	(h)	Rotherham U	W 4-0	Charles 3, Nightingale	24,048	1	2	3	4	9	6		10			11						5	7	8				
27		24	(a)	Fulham	L 1-2	Tyrer	21,210	1	2	3	4	9	6		10			11						5	7	8				
28	Feb	7	(h)	West Ham U	W 3-2	Iggleden, Charles 2	17,680	1	2	3	4	9	6		10			11						5	7	8				
29		14	(a)	Leicester C	D 3-3	Meek, Charles 2	21,754	1	2	3	4	9	6		10		8	11						5	7					
30		21	(h)	Notts C	W 3-1	Burden, Iggleden, McCall	22,922	1	2		4	9	6		10		8	11		3				5	7					
31		28	(h)	Sheffield U	L 0-3		39,858	1	2		4	9	6		10		8	11		3				5	7					
32	Mar	7	(a)	Barnsley	D 2-2	Charles, McCall	11,536	1	2	3		9	4		10		8			11				5	7		6			
33		14	(h)	Lincoln C	W 2-1	Meek 2	18,293	1	2	3		9	6		10		7								11	8	4	5		
34		21	(a)	Hull C	L 0-1		25,387	1	2	3		9	6		10		7								11	8	4	5		
35		28	(h)	Blackburn R	L 0-3		10,644	1	2	3	4	9	6		7								10		11	8		5		
36	Apr	4	(a)	Nottingham F	L 1-2	Nightingale	18,734	1	2	3	4		6		10		7								11	8		5	9	
37		6	(a)	Southampton	D 2-2	Nightingale 2	17,704	1	2	3	4		6		10		7								11	8		5	9	
38		11	(h)	Everton	W 2-0	Forrest, Meek	15,363	1	2	3	4	8	6				7								11	10		5	9	
39		16	(a)	Swansea T	L 2-3	Meek, Charles	21,262	1	2	3	4	9	6				7								11	8		5	10	
40		18	(a)	Brentford	D 3-3	Charles 2, Forrest	12,783	1	2	3	4	8	6		7									5	11	10			9	
41		22	(h)	Nottingham F	W 2-1	Burden, Kerfoot	11,497	1	2	3	4	8	6		7									5	11	10			9	
42		25	(h)	Doncaster R	D 1-1	Kerfoot	12,715	1	2	3	4	9	6		10		7								11	8				5
FINAL LEAGUE POSITION: 10th in Division Two							Appearances	42	42	40	39	40	42	18	38	9	16	21	5	9	2	4	2	22	28	26	3	7	6	1
							Goals				2	26	2		12	2	2	2		3	1	2			5	8			2	

2 own-goals

FA Cup

Round	Month	Day	Venue	Opponent	Result	Scorers	Attendance	Scott	Dunn	Hair	Kerfoot	Charles	Burden	Williams	Iggleden	Mills	McCall	Tyrer	Fidler	Langley	Smith	Hastie	Stewart	McCabe	Meek	Nightingale	Mollatt	Marsden	Forrest	Charlton
3	Jan	10	(a)	Brentford	L 1-2	Charles	22,650	1	2	3	4	9	6		10			11						5	7	8				
							Appearances	1	1	1	1	1	1		1			1						1	1	1				
							Goals					1																		

1953-54

Manager: Raich Carter

No	Month	Date	Opponent	Result	Scorers	Att	Scott	Dunn	Hair	Kerfoot	McCabe	Burden	Williams	Nightingale	Charles	Iggleden	Burbanks	Wheatley	McCall	Mollatt	Marsden	Willis	Forrest	Wood	Tyrer	Flynn	Webb	Davies	Dawson
1	Aug	19 (h)	Notts C	W 6-0	Charles 4, Williams, Nightingale	18,432	1	2	3	4	5	6	7	8	9	10	11												
2		22 (h)	Rotherham U	W 4-2	Charles 3, Nightingale	24,309	1	2	3	4	5	6	7	8	9	10	11												
3		27 (a)	Swansea T	L 3-4	Charles, Nightingale, Burbanks	26,408	1	2	3	4	11	6	7	8	5	10	9												
4		29 (a)	Leicester C	L 0-5		21,984	1	2	3	4	5	6	7	8	9	10	11												
5	Sep	2 (h)	Swansea T	W 3-2	Nightingale, Charles 2	20,949		2	3	4	5	6	11	8	9	10	7	1											
6		5 (h)	Stoke C	D 1-1	Charles	27,571		2	3	4	5	6	7	8	9	10	11	1											
7		7 (a)	Plymouth A	D 1-1	Charles	20,356		2	3	4	5	6	7	8	9		11	1	10										
8		12 (a)	Fulham	W 3-1	Charles 2, Williams	26,044		2	3	4	5	6	7	8	9		11	1	10										
9		16 (h)	Plymouth A	D 1-1	Williams	20,621		2	3	4	5	6	7	8	9		11	1	10										
10		19 (h)	West Ham U	L 1-2	Charles	28,635		2	3	4	5	6	7	8	9		11	1	10										
11		26 (a)	Lincoln C	L 0-2		17,979	1	2	3	4	5		7	8	9		11		10	6									
12	Oct	3 (a)	Birmingham C	D 3-3	Charles, Iggleden, Kerfoot	26,434	1	2	3	4		8		7	9	10				6	5	11							
13		10 (h)	Bristol R	D 3-3	Forrest 3	19,386	1	2	3	4	5	8		7		10				6		11	9						
14		17 (a)	Brentford	L 1-2	Charles	18,329	1	2	3	4	5	10		7	9					6		11	8						
15		24 (h)	Derby C	W 3-1	Charles 2, Nightingale	26,430		2	3	4		6	7	8	9	10					5			1	11				
16		31 (a)	Blackburn R	D 2-2	Williams, Nightingale	25,272		2	3	4		6	7	8	9	10					5			1	11				
17	Nov	7 (h)	Doncaster R	W 3-1	Nightingale 3	26,830		2	3	4		6	7	8	9	10					5			1	11				
18		14 (a)	Bury	D 4-4	Charles 3, Nightingale	11,915		2	3	4		6	7	8	9	10					5			1	11				
19		21 (h)	Oldham A	W 2-1	Forrest, Nightingale	26,747		2	3	4		6	7	8		10					5		9	1	11				
20		28 (a)	Everton	L 1-2	Charles	55,970		2	3	4		6	7	8	9	10					5			1	11				
21	Dec	5 (h)	Hull C	D 0-0		21,070		2	3	4		6	7	8	9	10					5			1	11				
22		12 (a)	Notts C	L 0-2		17,552		2	3	4		6	7	8	9	10					5			1	11				
23		19 (a)	Rotherham U	W 4-2	Charles 3 (1 pen), Iggleden	13,145		2	3	4		6	7	8	9	10					5			1	11				
24		25 (a)	Nottingham F	L 2-5	Nightingale, Charles	19,725		2	3	4		6	7	8	9	10					5			1	11				
25		26 (h)	Nottingham F	L 0-2		22,135	1	2	3	4		6	7	8	9	10	11				5								
26	Jan	2 (h)	Leicester C	W 7-1	Inggleden 3, Williams, Charles, Nightingale, Tyrer	21,532	1	2	3	4		6	7	8	9	10					5				11				
27		16 (a)	Stoke C	L 0-4		26,794	1	2	3	4		6	7		9	10			8		5				11				
28		23 (h)	Fulham	L 1-2	Charles	20,170	1	2	3	4		6	7		9	10					5				11	8			
29	Feb	6 (a)	West Ham U	L 2-5	Iggleden, McCall	15,585	1	2	3	4	4	6	11		9	10			7		5								
30		13 (h)	Lincoln C	W 5-2	Charles 3, Iggleden, Nightingale	15,325	1	2	3	8		6	11	8	9	10			7		5								
31		20 (h)	Birmingham C	D 1-1	Burden	22,803	1	2	3	4		6	11	8	9	10			7		5								
32		27 (a)	Bristol R	D 1-1	Nightingale	26,846	1	2	3	4		6	11	8	9	10			7		5								
33	Mar	6 (h)	Brentford	W 4-0	Charles 2, Nightingale, Williams	16,501	1	2	3	4		6	11	8	9				7		5						10		
34		13 (a)	Derby C	W 2-0	Forrest 2	12,773	1	2	3	4		6	11	8					7		5		9				10		
35		20 (h)	Blackburn R	W 3-2	McCall, Nightingale, Charles (pen)	24,915	1	2	3	4		6	11	8	9				7		5		10						
36		27 (a)	Oldham A	L 2-4	Williams, Charles	18,067	1	2	3	4		6	11	8	9				7		5		10						
37	Apr	3 (h)	Everton	W 3-1	Williams, Forrest, Kerfoot	22,581	1	2	3	4		6	11	8	9	7					5		10						
38		10 (a)	Doncaster R	D 0-0		12,472	1	2	3	4		6	11	8	9	7					5		10						
39		17 (a)	Luton T	D 1-1	Charles	16,129	1	2	3	4		6	11	8	9				7		5		10						
40		16 (h)	Bury	L 3-4	Charles 2 (1 pen), Forrest	17,156	1	2	3	4		6		8	9	11			7		5		10						
41		19 (h)	Luton T	W 2-1	Charles 2 (1 pen)	13,930	1	2	3	4		6	11	8	9	10			7									5	
42		24 (a)	Hull C	D 1-1	Charles	18,619	1		3	4				8	9	10	11		7	6	5								2
FINAL LEAGUE POSITION: 10th in Division Two						Appearances	26	41	42	42	14	40	37	39	39	31	13	6	18	5	28	3	10	10	13	1	2	1	1
						Goals				2		1	8	17	42	7	1		2				8		1				

FA Cup

Rd	Month	Date	Opponent	Result	Scorers	Att	Scott	Dunn	Hair	Kerfoot	McCabe	Burden	Williams	Nightingale	Charles	Iggleden	Burbanks	Wheatley	McCall	Mollatt	Marsden	Willis	Forrest	Wood	Tyrer	Flynn	Webb	Davies	Dawson
3	Jan	9 (h)	Tottenham H	D 3-3	Iggleden, Charles, Ramsey (og)	41,465	1	2	3	4		6	7	8	9	10					5				11				
R		13 (a)	Tottenham H	L 0-1		35,023	1	2	3	4		6	7	8	9	10					5				11				
						Appearances	2	2	2	2		2	2	2	2	2					2				2				
						Goals									1	1													

1 own-goal

1954-55

Manager: Raich Carter

							Scott	Dunn	Hair	Kerfoot	Marsden	Burden	Toner	Nightingale	Charles	Brook	McCall	Williams	Charlton	Vickers	Forrest	Ripley	Wood	Mollatt	Iggleden	Lydon	Gibson	Webb	Meek	Henderson
1	Aug	21 (a)	Hull C	W 2-0	Brook, Charles	32,071	1	2	3	4	5	6	7	8	9	10	11													
2		25 (h)	Rotherham U	L 2-4	Charles 2	25,021	1	2	3	4	5	6	10	8	9		11	7												
3		28 (h)	Lincoln C	L 2-3	Toner, Vickers	22,326	1	2	3	4		6	7	8	9			11	5	10										
4		30 (a)	Rotherham U	L 0-3		17,799	1	2	3	4	5	6		8	9		11	7		10										
5	Sep	4 (a)	Bury	L 3-5	McCall, Charles, May (og)	15,357	1	2	3	4	5	6	7		9		11			10	8									
6		8 (h)	Stoke C	L 0-1		20,295	1	2	3	6				7	5	8	11			10	9	4								
7		11 (h)	Swansea T	W 5-2	Nightingale 3, Kerfoot, Brook	20,040	1	2	3	6				8	5	10	11	7			9	4								
8		13 (a)	Stoke C	W 1-0	Forrest	19,311	1	2	3	6				8	5	10	11	7			9	4								
9		18 (h)	Nottingham F	D 1-1	Forrest	22,402	1	2	3	6				8	5	10	11	7			9	4								
10		25 (a)	Ipswich T	W 2-1	Williams, Nightingale	16,716	1	2	3	6	5			8		10	11	7			9	4								
11	Oct	2 (h)	Birmingham C	W 1-0	Forrest	21,200	1	2	3	6				8	5	10	11	7			9	4								
12		9 (a)	Derby C	W 4-2	Brook 2, McCall 2	20,214	1	2	3	6				8	5	10	11	7			9	4								
13		16 (h)	West Ham U	W 2-1	Ripley, Forrest	21,074	1	2	3	6	5			8		10	11	7			9	4								
14		23 (a)	Bristol R	L 1-5	Brook	24,568	1	2	3	6	5			8	9	10	11	7				4								
15		30 (h)	Plymouth A	W 3-2	Williams, Nightingale, McCall	20,613		2	3	6				8	5	10	11	7			9	4	1							
16	Nov	6 (a)	Port Vale	W 1-0	Nightingale	16,062		2	3	6				8	5	10	11	7			9	4	1							
17		13 (h)	Doncaster R	W 1-0	Ripley	15,757		2	3	4				8	5	10	11	7			9	6	1							
18		20 (a)	Notts C	W 2-1	Nightingale 2	14,519		2	3	6				8	5	10	11	7			9	4	1							
19		27 (h)	Liverpool	D 2-2	Forrest, Charles (pen)	22,263		2	3	6				8	5	10	11	7			9	4	1							
20	Dec	4 (a)	Blackburn R	W 2-1	Nightingale 2	26,187		2	3	6				8	5	10	11	7			9	4	1							
21		11 (h)	Fulham	D 1-1	Charles	30,714		2	3	6			7	8	5		11			10	9	4	1							
22		18 (h)	Hull C	W 3-0	Brook, Nightingale, Forrest	23,991		2	3	6				8	5	10	11	7			9	4	1							
23		25 (h)	Middlesbrough	D 1-1	Forrest	26,344		2	3					8	5	10	11	7			9	4	1	6						
24		27 (a)	Middlesbrough	L 0-1		45,271		2	3					8	5	10	11	7			9	4	1	6						
25	Jan	1 (a)	Lincoln C	L 0-2		12,231		2	3					8	5	10	11	7			9	4	1	6						
26		15 (h)	Bury	W 1-0	Lydon	8,954		2	3	6			7		5	10					9		1	4	8	11				
27		22 (a)	Swansea T	L 0-2		19,637		2	3	6			7		5	10					9		1	4	8	11				
28	Feb	5 (a)	Nottingham F	D 1-1	Charles	14,074		2	3	6					5	10	11	7		8	9	4	1							
29		12 (h)	Ipswich T	W 4-1	Brook 2, Vickers 2	12,038		2	3	6				8	5	9	11	7		10		4	1							
30		26 (h)	Derby C	W 1-0	Charles (pen)	16,994		2	3	6				8	5	9		7				4	1		10	11				
31	Mar	2 (a)	Birmingham C	L 0-2		10,774		2	3	6				8	5	9		7					1		10	11	4			
32		5 (a)	West Ham U	L 1-2	Forrest	19,664		2	3	6				8	5	9	11				10		1				4	7		
33		12 (h)	Bristol R	W 2-0	Brook, Forrest	16,922		2	3	6				8	5	9	7				10		1				4		11	
34		19 (a)	Plymouth A	L 1-3	Brook	19,968		2	3	6				8	5	9		7					1				4		11	10
35		26 (h)	Port Vale	W 3-0	Henderson, Ripley, Charles (pen)	8,831		2	3	6				7	5	9						8	1				4		11	10
36	Apr	2 (a)	Doncaster R	W 1-0	Brook	12,740		2	3	6				7	5	9						8	1				4		11	10
37		8 (a)	Luton T	D 0-0		25,775		2	3	6				8	5	9		7					1				4		11	10
38		9 (h)	Notts C	W 2-0	Brook, Nightingale	24,564		2	3	6				8	5	9		7					1				4		11	10
39		11 (h)	Luton T	W 4-0	Brook, Charles 2 (2 pens), Henderson	29,583		2	3	6				8	5	9		7					1				4		11	10
40		16 (a)	Liverpool	D 2-2	Meek, Brook	34,950		2	3	6				8	5	9		7					1				4		11	10
41		23 (h)	Blackburn R	W 2-0	Brook 2	39,208		2	3	6				8	5	9		7					1				4		11	10
42		30 (a)	Fulham	W 3-1	Smith (og), Henderson, Nightingale	21,400		2	3	6				8	5	9		7					1				4		11	10
FINAL LEAGUE POSITION: 4th in Division Two						Appearances	14	42	42	39	7	5	7	38	40	37	28	32	1	7	25	25	28	5	4	4	12	1	10	9
						Goals				1			1	13	11	16	4	2		3	9	3				1			1	3

2 own-goals

FA Cup

							Scott	Dunn	Hair	Kerfoot	Marsden	Burden	Toner	Nightingale	Charles	Brook	McCall	Williams	Charlton	Vickers	Forrest	Ripley	Wood	Mollatt	Iggleden	Lydon	Gibson	Webb	Meek	Henderson
3	Jan	8 (h)	Torquay U	D 2-2	Kerfoot, Charles	28,150		2	3	6	5			8	9	10	11	7				4	1							
R		12 (a)	Torquay U	L 0-4		12,000		2	3	6	5			8	9	10	11	7				4	1							
						Appearances		2	2	2	2			2	2	2	2	2				2	2							
						Goals				1					1															

1955-56

Manager: Raich Carter

No	Month	Date	Opponent	Result	Scorers	Att	Wood	Dunn	Hair	Gibson	Charles	Kerfoot	Williams	Nightingale	Brook	Henderson	Meek	Ripley	Forrest	Charlton	Ashall	Marsden	Overfield	Vickers	Hutchinson
1	Aug	20	(a) Barnsley	L 1-2	Brook	19,341	1	2	3	4	5	6	7	8	9	10	11								
2		22	(h) Bury	W 1-0	Henderson	19,722	1	2	3	4	5	6	7	8	9	10	11								
3		27	(h) Middlesbrough	W 2-0	Nightingale, Brook	22,535	1	2	3	4	5	6	7	8	9	10	11								
4		30	(a) Bury	L 0-1		11,674	1	2	3	4	5	6	7	8	9	10	11								
5	Sep	3	(a) Bristol C	W 1-0	Forrest	31,060	1	2	3	4	5	6	7		9		11	8	10						
6		5	(h) Hull C	W 1-0	Ripley	17,524	1	2	3	4	5	6		7	9		11	8	10						
7		10	(h) West Ham U	D 3-3	Ripley, Nightingale, Meek	21,855	1	2	3	4	5	6	7	10	9		11	8							
8		17	(a) Port Vale	L 0-2		21,348	1	2	3	4	5	6	7	10	9		11	8							
9		24	(h) Rotherham U	W 4-1	Nightingale, Ripley 3	23,763	1	2	3		4	6	7	10	9		11	8		5					
10	Oct	1	(a) Swansea T	D 1-1	Brook	29,477	1	2			4	6	11	7	9	10		8		5	3				
11		8	(h) Nottingham F	W 3-0	Ripley, Brook, Charles	21,272	1	2			4	6		10	9		7	8		5		3	11		
12		15	(a) Sheffield W	L 0-4		27,640	1	2			4	6		10	9		7	8		5		3	11		
13		22	(h) Lincoln C	W 1-0	Overfield	17,378	1	2	3			6		8	9	8	7	4	10	5			11		
14		29	(a) Bristol R	L 1-4	Brook	24,575	1	2	3		9	6			10		7	4		5			11		
15	Nov	5	(h) Stoke C	W 1-0	Charles	21,261	1	2	3		9	6		8			7	4	10	5			11		
16		12	(a) Plymouth A	L 3-4	Robertson (og), Williams, Charles	19,122	1	2	3		9	6	7	8				4	10	5			11		
17		19	(h) Liverpool	W 4-2	Overfield, Charles 2, Brook	22,596	1	2	3		9	6	7		8			4		5			11	10	
18		26	(a) Leicester C	L 2-5	Charles 2 (2 pens)	30,196	1	2	3		9	6	7					4	8	5			11	10	
19	Dec	3	(h) Doncaster R	W 3-0	Hutchinson, Charles, Overfield	21,769	1	2	3		9	6	7	4						5			11	10	8
20		10	(a) Blackburn R	W 3-2	Overfield, Charles 2 (1 pen)	18,898	1	2	3	4	9	6	7							5			11	10	8
21		17	(h) Barnsley	W 3-1	Hutchinson 2, Williams	23,493	1	2	3	4	9	6	7							5			11	10	8
22		24	(a) Middlesbrough	L 3-5	Hutchinson, Charles, Vickers	19,416	1	2	3	4	9	6	11							5			7	8	10
23		26	(h) Notts C	W 1-0	Brook	24,869	1	2	3	4	9	6			8					5			11	10	7
24		27	(a) Notts C	L 1-2	Charles	23,910	1	2	3	4	9	6			8					5			11	10	7
25		31	(h) Bristol C	W 2-1	Hutchinson, Brook	31,751	1	2	3	4	9	6			8					5			11	10	7
26	Jan	14	(a) West Ham U	D 1-1	Charles	20,000	1	2	3	4	9	6			8					5			11	10	7
27		21	(h) Port Vale	D 1-1	Brook	23,680	1	2		4	9	6			10					5	3		11	8	7
28	Feb	11	(h) Swansea T	D 2-2	Charles (pen), Nightingale	20,089	1	2		4	9	6		8			7	10		5	3		11		
29		25	(h) Sheffield W	W 2-1	Charles, Forrest	43,268	1	2		4	8	6		10			7		9	5	3		11		
30		28	(a) Liverpool	L 0-1		21,068	1	2		4	8	6		10			7		9	5	3		11		
31	Mar	3	(a) Lincoln C	D 1-1	Charles (pen)	13,713	1	2		4	8	6			10		11		9	5	3				7
32		10	(h) Blackburn R	L 1-2	Charles	28,380	1	2	3	4	8	6			10				9	5			11		7
33		17	(a) Stoke C	L 1-2	Brook	22,784	1	2	3	4	8	6	7		10				9	5			11		
34		24	(h) Plymouth A	W 4-2	Brook, Nightingale, Charles 2	12,348	1	2	3	4	8	6	7	10	9		11			5					
35		30	(a) Fulham	W 2-1	Brook, Charles	25,459	1	2	3	4	8	6	7	10	9					5			11		
36		31	(a) Nottingham F	L 0-2		19,448	1	2	3	4	8	6			9		7		10	5			11		
37	Apr	2	(h) Fulham	W 6-1	Charles 3, Nightingale 2, Brook	20,115	1	2	3	4	8	6		10	9		7			5			11		
38		7	(h) Leicester C	W 4-0	Overfield, Brook, Charles 2 (1 pen)	26,408	1	2	3	4	8	6		10	9		7			5			11		
39		14	(a) Doncaster R	W 2-1	Charles, Nightingale	18,404	1	2	3		8	6		10	9		7	4		5			11		
40		21	(h) Bristol R	W 2-1	Charles, Overfield	49,274	1	2	3		8	6		10	9		7	4		5			11		
41		23	(a) Rotherham U	W 2-0	Nightingale 2	20,013	1	2	3		8	6		10	9		7	4		5			11		
42		28	(a) Hull C	W 4-1	Charles 2 (1 pen), Brook 2	31,123	1	2	3		8	6		10	9		7	4		5			11		
FINAL LEAGUE POSITION: 2nd in Division Two						Appearances	42	42	34	27	41	42	19	26	32	6	26	19	12	34	6	2	30	11	11
						Goals					29		2	10	16	1	1	6	2				6	1	5

1 own-goal

FA Cup

Rd	Month	Date	Opponent	Result	Scorers	Att	Wood	Dunn	Hair	Gibson	Charles	Kerfoot	Williams	Nightingale	Brook	Henderson	Meek	Ripley	Forrest	Charlton	Ashall	Marsden	Overfield	Vickers	Hutchinson
3	Jan	7	(h) Cardiff C	L 1-2	Brook	40,000	1	2	3	4	5	6	7		8					9			11	10	
						Appearances	1	1	1	1	1	1	1		1					1			1	1	
						Goals									1										

1956-57

Manager: Raich Carter

	Date		Opponents	Result	Scorers	Att	Wood	Dunn	Hair	Gibson	Charlton	Kerfoot	Meek	Charles	Brook	Nightingale	Overfield	Ripley	Forrest	Marsden	Crowe	McKenna	O'Brien
1	Aug	18	(h) Everton	W 5-1	Overfield, Charles, Brook 3	31,379	1	2	3	4	5	6	7	8	9	10	11						
2		23	(a) Charlton A	W 2-1	Charles 2	23,299	1	2	3	4	5	6	7	8	9		11	10					
3		25	(a) Tottenham H	L 1-5	Ripley	51,212	1	2	3	4	5	6	7	8	9		11	10					
4		29	(h) Charlton A	W 4-0	Forrest 2, Charles, Brook	34,444	1	2	3		5	6	7	8	9		11	4	10				
5	Sep	1	(h) Chelsea	D 0-0		38,679	1	2	3		5	6	7	8	9		11	4	10				
6		5	(a) Manchester C	L 0-1		34,185	1	2	3	4	5	6	7	8	9		11		10				
7		8	(h) Bolton W	W 3-2	Meek, Charles, Brook	40,010	1	2	3	4		6	7	8	9		11		10	5			
8		12	(h) Manchester C	W 2-0	Charles, Brook	35,068	1	2	3	4		6	7	8	9		11		10	5			
9		15	(a) Wolves	W 2-1	Charles 2	40,824	1	2	3	4		6	7	8	9		11		10	5			
10		22	(h) Aston Villa	W 1-0	Charles	35,388	1	2	3	4		6	7	8	9		11		10	5			
11		29	(a) Luton T	D 2-2	Charles 2	20,949	1	2	3	4		6	7	8	9		11		10	5			
12	Oct	6	(a) Cardiff C	L 1-4	Forrest	38,333	1	2	3	4		6	7	8			11	9	10	5			
13		13	(h) Birmingham C	D 1-1	Ripley	34,460	1	2	3	4		6	7	8			11	10	9	5			
14		20	(a) Burnley	D 0-0		26,440	1	2	3	4	5	6	7				11	10	9		8		
15		27	(h) Preston NE	L 1-2	Wilson (og)	36,571	1	2	3	4	5	6	7				11	10	9		8		
16	Nov	3	(a) Newcastle U	W 3-2	McKenna 2, Charles	49,034	1	2	3	4	5	6	7	8			11		10			9	
17		10	(h) Sheffield W	W 3-1	Charles 3	31,857	1	2	3	4	5	6	7	8			11		10			9	
18		17	(a) Manchester U	L 2-3	McKenna, Charles (pen)	52,401	1	2	3	4	5	6	7	8			11		10			9	
19		24	(h) Arsenal	D 3-3	Charles 2, Forrest	39,113	1	2	3	4	5	6	7	8			11		10			9	
20	Dec	1	(a) West Brom A	D 0-0		29,000	1	2	3	4	5	6	7	8	9		11		10				
21		8	(h) Portsmouth	W 4-1	Charles 2, Ripley 2	29,866	1	2	3	4	5	6	7	8			11	9	10				
22		15	(a) Everton	L 1-2	Ripley	33,765	1	2	3	4	5	6	7	8			11	9	10				
23		25	(a) Blackpool	D 1-1	Brook	20,517	1	2	3	4	5	6	7	8	9		11		10				
24		26	(h) Blackpool	W 5-0	Brook 3, Charles 2	22,689	1	2	3	4	5	6	7	8	9		11		10				
25		29	(a) Chelsea	D 1-1	Armstrong (og)	43,860	1	2	3	4	5	6	7	8	9		11		10				
26	Jan	12	(a) Bolton W	L 3-5	Charles 2, Meek	25,705	1	2	3	4		6	7	8	9		11			5	10		
27		19	(h) Wolves	D 0-0		32,910	1	2	3	4		6	7	8	9		11	10		5			
28	Feb	2	(a) Aston Villa	D 1-1	Forrest	39,432	1	2	3	4		6	7	8	9		11			5	10		
29		9	(h) Luton T	L 1-2	Charles	25,646	1	2	3	4		6	7	8			11		9	5	10		
30		16	(h) Cardiff C	W 3-0	McKenna, Charles, Forrest	21,695	1	2	3	4		6		8	9		11		10	5		7	
31		23	(a) Preston NE	L 0-3		14,036	1	2	3	4		6		8	9		11			5	10	7	
32	Mar	2	(h) Tottenham H	D 1-1	Charles	33,895	1	2	3	4		6	7	8	9		11		10	5			
33		9	(a) Portsmouth	W 5-2	Charles 2, Crowe 2, Meek	23,596	1	2	3	4		6	7	9	10		11			5	8		
34		11	(h) Burnley	D 1-1	Charles	31,956	1	2	3	4		6	7	9			11		10	5	8		
35		16	(h) Newcastle U	D 0-0		32,541	1	2	3	4		6	7	9	10		11			5			8
36		26	(a) Sheffield W	W 3-2	Charles 3	33,205	1	2	3	4	5	6	7	9			11				8		10
37		30	(h) Manchester U	L 1-2	Charles	47,216	1	2	3	4	5	6	7	9			11				8		10
38	Apr	6	(a) Arsenal	L 0-1		40,388	1	2	3	4	5	6	7	9			11				8		10
39		13	(h) West Brom A	D 0-0		20,905	1	2	3	4		6	7	9			11			5	8		10
40		19	(a) Sunderland	L 0-2		56,551	1	2	3	4		6	7	9	8		11			5			10
41		20	(a) Birmingham C	L 2-6	Charles 2	30,642	1	2	3	4		6	7	9			11			5	8		10
42		22	(h) Sunderland	W 3-1	Charles 2, Brook	29,328	1	2	3	4		6	7	9	8		11			5			10
FINAL LEAGUE POSITION: 8th in Division One						Appearances	42	42	42	40	21	42	40	40	24	1	42	11	27	21	13	6	8
						Goals							3	38	11		1	5	6		2	4	

2 own-goals

FA Cup

Round	Date		Opponents	Result	Scorers	Att	Wood	Dunn	Hair	Gibson	Charlton	Kerfoot	Meek	Charles	Brook	Nightingale	Overfield	Ripley	Forrest	Marsden	Crowe	McKenna	O'Brien
3	Jan	5	(h) Cardiff C	L 1-2	Charles	34,237	1	2	3	4	5	6	7	8	9		11		10				
						Appearances	1	1	1	1	1	1	1	1	1		1		1				
						Goals								1									

1957-58

Manager: Raich Carter

No	Date	Opponent	Result	Scorers	Att	Wood	Dunn	Hair	Gibson	Charlton	Kerfoot	Crowe	O'Brien	Baird	Meek	Overfield	Forrest	Ripley	Brook	Marsden	Ashall	Cush	Francis	Nimmo	Peyton
1	Aug 24	(a) Blackpool	L 0-3		26,700	1	2	3	4	5	6	7	8	9	10	11									
2	26	(a) Aston Villa	L 0-2		25,693	1	2	3	4	5	6		8	9	7	11	10								
3	31	(h) Leicester C	W 2-1	Baird (pen), Overfield	26,660	1	2	3	4	5	6		8	9	7	11	10								
4	Sep 4	(h) Aston Villa	W 4-0	Baird 2, O'Brien, Brook	22,685	1	2	3		5	6		8	9	7	11		4	10						
5	7	(a) Manchester U	L 0-5		50,842	1	2	3			6		8	9	7	11		4	10	5					
6	11	(h) Luton T	L 0-2		21,972	1	2			3	6		8	9	7	11		4	10	5					
7	14	(h) Nottingham F	L 1-2	Overfield	25,566	1	2		4	5	6			9	7	11	8		10		3				
8	18	(a) Luton T	D 1-1	Overfield	16,887	1	2		4	5	6			9	7	11	8		10		3				
9	21	(h) Bolton W	W 2-1	Meek, Baird	18,379	1			4	5	2	8		9	7	11	10	6			3				
10	25	(h) Sunderland	W 2-1	Baird, Gibson	17,600	1			4	5	6	8		9	7	11	10			2	3				
11	28	(a) Arsenal	L 1-2	Brook	39,538	1			4	5	2			9	7	11	10	6	8		3				
12	Oct 5	(h) Wolves	D 1-1	Baird	28,635	1			4	5	2	8		9	7	11	10	6			3				
13	12	(a) Portsmouth	W 2-1	Baird, Brook	23,534	1			4	5	2		8	9	7	11		6	10		3				
14	19	(h) West Brom A	D 1-1	Forrest	24,614	1		2		5	4			9	7	11	8	6	10		3				
15	26	(a) Tottenham H	L 0-2		33,860	1		2		5	4		8	9	7	11		6	10		3				
16	Nov 2	(h) Preston NE	L 2-3	Baird 2 (2 pens)	23,832	1	2	3	4	5	6		10	9	7	11		8							
17	9	(a) Sheffield W	L 2-3	Ripley, Forrest	21,469	1	2	3	4	5	6	7		8	11		10	9							
18	16	(h) Manchester C	L 2-4	Kerfoot, Baird	23,855	1	2	3		5	4	7		9	11		10	8				6			
19	23	(a) Burnley	L 1-3	Baird (pen)	24,144	1	2	3	8	5	4	10		9	7	11						6			
20	30	(h) Birmingham C	D 1-1	Cush	21,358	1	2	3	4	5	6	10		9	11							8	7		
21	Dec 7	(a) Chelsea	L 1-2	Baird	17,038	1	2	3	4	5	6	10		9	7	11						8			
22	14	(h) Newcastle U	W 3-0	Forrest, Crowe, Overfield	23,363	1	2	3	4	5	6	10			7	11	9					8			
23	21	(h) Blackpool	W 2-1	Cush, Forrest	32,411	1	2	3	4	5	6	10			7	11	9					8			
24	26	(a) Sunderland	L 1-2	Crowe	34,875	1	2	3	4	5	6	10			7	11	9					8			
25	28	(a) Leicester C	L 0-3		31,747	1	2	3	4	5	6	7		9		11	10					8			
26	Jan 11	(h) Manchester U	D 1-1	Baird	39,401	1	2	3	4	5	6			9	7	11	10					8			
27	18	(a) Nottingham F	D 1-1	Baird	23,368	1	2	3	4	5	6			9	7	11	10					8			
28	Feb 1	(a) Bolton W	W 2-0	Forrest, Cush	18,558		2	3		5	6			9	7	11	10					4		1	8
29	19	(a) Wolves	L 2-3	Peyton, Forrest	35,527	1	2	3		5	6			9	7	11	10					4			8
30	22	(h) Portsmouth	W 2-0	Baird 2	26,713	1	2	3		5	6			9	7	11	10					4			8
31	Mar 8	(h) Tottenham H	L 1-2	Baird	23,429	1	2	3		5	6			9	7	11	10					4			8
32	12	(a) West Brom A	L 0-1		16,412	1	2	3		5	6		10	9	7	11						4			8
33	15	(a) Preston NE	L 0-3		21,353	1	2	3		5	6			9	7	11	10					4			8
34	19	(h) Arsenal	W 2-0	Meek, Peyton	25,948	1	2	3		5	6	7	10	9	11							4			8
35	22	(h) Burnley	W 1-0	Meek	24,994	1	2	3		5	6	7	10	9	11							4			8
36	29	(a) Manchester C	L 0-1		21,962	1	2	3	4	5	6	7	10	9	11										8
37	Apr 4	(a) Everton	W 1-0	Baird	32,679	1	2	3	4	5	6	7	8	9		11	10								
38	5	(h) Sheffield W	D 2-2	Meek, Baird	26,212	1	2	3	4		6		10	9	7	11				5					8
39	7	(h) Everton	W 1-0	Forrest	25,188	1	2	3		5	6		10	9	7	11	8					4			
40	12	(a) Birmingham C	D 1-1	O'Brien	23,112	1	2	3		5	6	8	10	9	7	11						4			
41	19	(h) Chelsea	D 0-0		20,515	1	2	3		5	6	8	10	9	7	11						4			
42	26	(a) Newcastle U	W 2-1	Baird, O'Brien	32,594	1	2	3	4	5	6		10	9	7	11									8
FINAL LEAGUE POSITION: 17th in Division One					Appearances	41	35	34	25	40	42	19	19	39	40	36	24	12	9	4	9	21	1	1	11
					Goals				1		1	2	3	20	4	4	7	1	3			3			2

FA Cup

Rd	Date	Opponent	Result	Scorers	Att	Wood	Dunn	Hair	Gibson	Charlton	Kerfoot	Crowe	O'Brien	Baird	Meek	Overfield	Forrest	Ripley	Brook	Marsden	Ashall	Cush	Francis	Nimmo	Peyton
3	Jan 4	(h) Cardiff C	L 1-2	Forrest	30,374	1	2	3	4	5	6	10			7	11	9					8			
					Appearances	1	1	1	1	1	1	1			1	1	1					1			
					Goals												1								

1958-59

Manager: Bill Lambton

No	Date	Opponent	Result	Scorers	Att	Wood	Dunn	Hair	Gibson	Charlton	Cush	Crowe	Peyton	Forrest	O'Brien	Overfield	Ashall	Baird	Kerfoot	Meek	Marsden	Humphries	Shackleton	Revie	McConnell	Mitchell	Burgin	Kemp	Kilford
1	Aug 23	(a) Bolton W	L 0-4		25,922	1	2	3	4	5	6	7	8	9	10	11													
2	26	(h) Luton T	D 1-1	Crowe (pen)	25,498	1	2	3	4	5	6	7	8	9	10	11													
3	30	(h) Burnley	D 1-1	Forrest	22,739	1		3	4	5	6	7	8	10		11	2	9											
4	Sep 3	(a) Luton T	D 1-1	Baird	13,497	1		3	4	5	10			8		11	2	9	6	7									
5	6	(a) Preston NE	W 2-1	Baird (pen), Overfield	22,765	1		3	4	5	10			8		11	2	9	6	7									
6	10	(h) Birmingham C	D 0-0		25,228	1		3	4	5	10			8		11	2	9	6	7									
7	13	(h) Leicester C	D 1-1	Meek	23,487	1		3	4	5	10			8		11	2	9	6	7									
8	17	(a) Birmingham C	L 1-4	Forrest	24,068	1		3	4		6	8		9	10	11	2			7	5								
9	20	(a) Everton	L 2-3	Cush, Crowe	31,105	1		3	4		6	8		9	10	11	2			7	5								
10	27	(h) Arsenal	W 2-1	Crowe (pen), Overfield	33,961	1		3	6	5	4	8	10	9		11	2					7							
11	Oct 4	(a) Manchester C	L 1-2	Leivers (og)	31,989	1		3	4	5		8	10		6	11	2	9				7							
12	11	(a) Portsmsouth	L 0-2		22,570	1		3	4	5	8	10		9	6	11	2					7							
13	18	(h) Aston Villa	D 0-0		21,088	1		3	6	5	4	8		9	10	11	2					7							
14	25	(a) Tottenham H	W 3-2	Cush, O'Brien, Overfield	38,691	1		3	6	5	4	8		9	10	11	2					7							
15	Nov 1	(h) Manchester U	L 1-2	Shackleton	48,574	1		3	6	5	4	8			10	11	2					7	9						
16	8	(a) Chelsea	L 0-2		33,357	1		3	6	5	4	8			10	11	2			7			9						
17	15	(h) Blackpool	D 1-1	Crowe	29,252	1		3	6	5	4	8		10		11	2					7	9						
18	22	(a) Blackburn R	W 4-2	Shackleton 3, Humphries	28,727	1		3	6	5	4	8		10		11	2					7	9						
19	29	(h) Newcastle U	W 3-2	Overfield, Crowe, Scott (og)	23,732	1		3	6	5	4	8				11	2					7	9	10					
20	Dec 6	(a) West Ham U	W 3-2	Crowe (pen), Overfield, Bond (og)	22,022	1		3	6	5	4	8				11	2					7	9	10					
21	13	(h) Nottingham F	W 1-0	Crowe	26,341	1		3	6	5	4	8				11	2					7	9	10					
22	20	(h) Bolton W	L 3-4	Crowe (pen), Gibson, Shackleton	28,534	1	3		6	5		8				11	2					7	9	10	4				
23	26	(a) West Brom A	W 2-1	Humphries, Crowe (pen)	34,878	1		3	6	5	4	8				11	2					7	9	10					
24	27	(h) West Brom A	L 0-1		44,929	1		3	6	5	4	8				11	2					7	9	10					
25	Jan 3	(a) Burnley	L 1-3	Shackleton	26,013	1		3	6	5	4	8				11	2					7	9	10					
26	17	(h) Preston NE	L 1-3	Revie	22,043	1		3	6	5	4			10						11		7	9	8		2			
27	31	(a) Leicester C	W 1-0	Shackleton	23,376			3		5	4	8				11			6			7	9	10		2	1		
28	Feb 7	(h) Everton	W 1-0	Shackleton	18,200			3		5	4	8				11			6			7	9	10		2	1		
29	14	(a) Wolves	L 2-6	Shackleton, Overfield	26,790			3		5	6				10	11			4			7	9	8		2	1		
30	21	(h) Manchester C	L 0-4		18,515			3	6	5	4	8					2					7	9	10			1	11	
31	24	(a) Arsenal	L 0-1		30,034			3	6	5	4	8				11	2					7	9	10			1		
32	28	(h) Portsmouth	D 1-1	Cush	14,900				6	5	8				10		2			11		7	9	4			1		3
33	Mar 7	(a) Aston Villa	L 1-2	Overfield	27,631		2			5	10	8			6	11	3		4	7			9				1		
34	14	(h) Tottenham H	W 3-1	Crowe, Shackleton, Overfield	17,010		2			5	10	8				11	3		6	7			9	4			1		
35	21	(a) Manchester U	L 0-4		45,473		2			5	10	8				11	3		6	7			9	4			1		
36	28	(h) Chelsea	W 4-0	O'Brien 2, Shackleton, Crowe	16,676			3	4	5		8			10	11	2		6	7			9				1		
37	31	(h) Wolves	L 1-3	Crowe	35,819			3	4	5		8			10	11	2		6	7			9				1		
38	Apr 4	(a) Blackpool	L 0-3		14,089			3		5		8			10	11	2		6			7	9		4		1		
39	11	(h) Blackburn R	W 2-1	Shackleton, Charlton	15,232		2	3		5	8	7							6	11			9	10	4		1		
40	18	(a) Newcastle U	D 2-2	Revie, Peyton	19,321		2	3			5	7	10						6	11			9	8	4		1		
41	22	(a) Nottingham F	W 3-0	Shackleton 3	18,650		2	3		5		7	10						6	11			9	8	4		1		
42	25	(h) West Ham U	W 1-0	Shackleton	11,257		2	3		5	6	7	10							11			9	8	4		1		
FINAL LEAGUE POSITION: 15th in Division One					Appearances	26	10	37	31	39	36	35	8	15	17	35	32	6	16	18	2	23	28	20	6	4	16	1	1
					Goals				1	1	3	12	1	2	3	8		2		1		2	16	2					

3 own-goals

FA Cup

Rd	Date	Opponent	Result	Scorers	Att	Wood	Dunn	Hair	Gibson	Charlton	Cush	Crowe	Peyton	Forrest	O'Brien	Overfield	Ashall	Baird	Kerfoot	Meek	Marsden	Humphries	Shackleton	Revie	McConnell	Mitchell	Burgin	Kemp	Kilford
3	Jan 10	(a) Luton T	L 1-5	Shackleton	18,354	1		3	6	5	4	8				11	2					7	9	10					
					Appearances	1		1	1	1	1	1				1	1					1	1	1					
					Goals																		1						

1959-60

Manager: Jack Taylor

No.	Month	Date	Opponent	Result	Scorers	Att	Burgin	Ashall	Hair	McConnell	Charlton	Cush	Humries	Revie	Shackleton	Crowe	Meek	Overfield	Cameron	Kilford	Gibson	Peyton	McCole	Wood	Francis	Caldwell	Bremner	Humphreys	Goodwin
1	Aug	22	(h) Burnley	L 2-3	Charlton, Cush (pen)	20,233	1	2	3	4	5	6	7	8	9	10	11												
2		26	(a) Leicester C	L 2-3	Crowe, Cush	24,790	1	2	3	4	5	6		8	9	10	7	11											
3		29	(a) Luton T	W 1-0	Revie	15,822	1	2	3	4	5	6		9		10	7	11	8										
4	Sep	2	(h) Leicester C	D 1-1	Crowe	18,384	1	2	3	4	5	6		9		10	7	11	8										
5		5	(a) West Ham U	W 2-1	Crowe 2 (1 pen)	27,777	1	2	3	4	5	6		9		10	7	11	8										
6		9	(a) Manchester U	L 0-6		48,619	1	2	3		5	6		4			8	11	9			10			7				
7		12	(h) Chelsea	W 2-1	Crowe 2	17,011	1	2			5	6		9		10	7	11	8	3	4								
8		16	(h) Manchester U	D 2-2	Cush, Crowe	34,048	1	2			5	6		9		10	7	11		3	4	8							
9		19	(a) West Brom A	L 0-3		26,364	1	2	3		5	6				10	7	11	8		4		9						
10		26	(h) Newcastle U	L 2-3	McCole, Revie	28,306		2	3		5	6	7	8		10		11			4		9	1					
11	Oct	3	(a) Birmingham C	L 0-2		25,301		2	3		5			8		7		11	6		4	10	9	1					
12		10	(h) Everton	D 3-3	Crowe (pen), Francis, McCole	19,122		2	3		5	6				10		11	8		4		9	1	7				
13		17	(a) Blackpool	D 3-3	McCole 2, Francis	22,301	1	2	3		5	6		8		10		11			4		9		7				
14		24	(h) Blackburn R	L 0-1		17,159	1	2	3		5	6		8		10		11			4		9		7				
15		31	(a) Bolton W	D 1-1	McCole	20,183	1	2	3		5			8		11			4		6	10	9		7				
16	Nov	7	(h) Arsenal	W 3-2	Peyton 2, McCole	21,617	1	2	3		5			8		11			4		6	10	9		7				
17		14	(a) Wolves	L 2-4	Crowe, Peyton	21,546	1	2	3	6	5			8		7	11		4			10	9						
18		21	(h) Sheffield W	L 1-3	McCole	21,260	1	2	3		5	6		8		7			4			10	9		11				
19		28	(a) Nottingham F	L 1-4	Revie	21,366	1	2	3	4	5			8		7	11		10		6		9						
20	Dec	5	(h) Fulham	L 1-4	McCole	18,846	1		3		5	4		8		10	7	11			6		9			2			
21		12	(a) Manchester C	D 3-3	Revie, Crowe, Gibson	19,715	1		3		5	4		8		10	7	11			6		9			2			
22		19	(a) Burnley	W 1-0	Overfield	17,398	1		3		5	4				10	7	11	8		6		9			2			
23		26	(h) Tottenham H	L 2-4	McCole 2	36,037	1		3		5	4				10	7		8		6		9		11	2			
24		28	(a) Tottenham H	W 4-1	McCole 2, Cameron, Meek	54,170	1	2	3		5	4				7	11		8		6	10	9						
25	Jan	2	(h) Luton T	D 1-1	McCole	19,921	1	2	3		5	4				7	11		8		6	10	9						
26		16	(h) West Ham U	W 3-0	Crowe, McCole, Meek	15,284		2	3		5	4		8		7	11				6	10	9	1					
27		23	(a) Chelsea	W 3-1	McCole 2, Peyton	18,963		2	3		5	4		8			11				6	10	9	1			7		
28	Feb	6	(h) West Brom A	L 1-4	McCole (pen)	23,729		2	3		5	4		8			11				6	10	9	1			7		
29		13	(a) Newcastle U	L 1-2	Revie	16,148		2	3		5	4		8		7	11				6	10	9	1					
30		27	(a) Fulham	L 0-5		23,355		2	3		5	4		8		7	11				6	10	9					1	
31	Mar	5	(h) Blackpool	L 2-4	McCole, Meek	23,127		2			5	4		8		10	11			3	6		9				7	1	
32		9	(h) Birmingham C	D 3-3	Revie 2, Bremner	8,557		2		4		5		8			11			3	6	10	9				7	1	
33		19	(h) Manchester C	W 4-3	McCole 2 (2 pens), Bremner, Peyton	32,545	1	2	3		5			8			11				4	10	9				7		6
34		26	(a) Arsenal	D 1-1	Gibson	19,597	1	2	3		5			8			11				4	10	9				7		6
35	Apr	2	(h) Wolves	L 0-3		29,492	1	2	3		5	9		8			11				4	10					7		6
36		9	(a) Sheffield W	L 0-1		27,073	1	2	3		5			8			11		10		4		9				7		6
37		16	(h) Bolton W	W 1-0	Charlton	19,272	1	2			5			8			11		10		4		9			3	7		6
38		18	(a) Preston NE	D 1-1	Gibson	15,879	1	2			5	10		8			11				4		9		7	3			6
39		19	(h) Preston NE	W 2-1	Charlton, Francis	23,764	1	2			5	10		8			11				4		9		7	3			6
40		23	(a) Everton	L 0-1		37,885	1	2			5			8			11		10		4		9			3	7		6
41		27	(h) Blackburn R	L 2-3	Meek, McCole	19,295	1	2			5			8			11				4	10	9		7	3			6
42		30	(h) Nottingham F	W 1-0	McCole (pen)	11,699	1	2			5								8		4	10	9		11	3	7		6
FINAL LEAGUE POSITION: 21st in Division One						Appearances	32	38	32	8	41	30	2	35	2	28	33	16	21	4	34	20	33	7	12	10	11	3	10
						Goals					3	3		7		11	4	1	1		3	5	22		3		2		

FA Cup

Round	Month	Date	Opponent	Result	Scorers	Att	Burgin	Ashall	Hair	McConnell	Charlton	Cush	Humries	Revie	Shackleton	Crowe	Meek	Overfield	Cameron	Kilford	Gibson	Peyton	McCole	Wood	Francis	Caldwell	Bremner	Humphreys	Goodwin
3	Jan	9	(a) Aston Villa	L 1-2	McCole	43,421		2	3		5	4				7	11		8		6	10	9	1					
						Appearances		1	1		1	1				1	1		1		1	1	1	1					
						Goals																	1						

1960-61

Manager: Jack Taylor until March 1961 then Don Revie

	Date	Opponent	Result	Scorers	Att	Burgin	Ashall	Jones	Smith	Charlton	Goodwin	Bremner	Revie	McCole	Fitzgerald	Grainger	Hair	Francis	Peyton	Cameron	Hawksby	Murray	Bell	Humphreys	Caldwell	McGugan	Wright	McConnell	Kilford	Carling	Johanneson	Martin
1	Aug 20	(a) Liverpool	L 0-2		43,041	1	2	3	4	5	6	7	8	9	10	11																
2	24	(h) Bristol R	D 1-1	McCole	11,330	1		2	4	5	6		8	9		11	3	7	10													
3	27	(h) Rotherham U	W 2-0	Hawksby, McCole	16,480	1		2		5	6			9		11	3	7	10	4	8											
4	29	(a) Bristol R	D 4-4	Hawksby, Grainger, Peyton, McCole	18,864	1		2		5	6			9		11	3	7	10	4	8											
5	Sep 3	(a) Southampton	W 4-2	Grainger, Cameron, Francis, McCole	21,862	1	2			5	6			9		11	3	7	10	4		8										
6	7	(h) Leyton O	L 1-3	Cameron	17,363	1	2			5		6	7	8		11	3		10	4			6									
7	10	(h) Huddersfield T	L 1-4	Cameron (pen)	22,146		2			5	6		8	9		11	3		10	4		7		1								
8	14	(a) Leyton O	W 1-0	Revie	8,505	1				5	6		8	9		11	3		10	4		7			2							
9	17	(h) Middlesbrough	D 4-4	Stonehouse (og), Goodwin, Cameron (pen), McCole	17,799	1				5	6			9		11	3	7	10	4	8				2							
10	24	(a) Brighton & HA	L 1-2	McCole	16,276	1				5	6		8	9		11	3	7	10	4					2							
11	Oct 1	(h) Ipswich T	L 2-5	McCole 2	13,502	1				5	6		8	9		11	3	7		4						2	10					
12	8	(a) Sunderland	W 3-2	Peyton, Francis, McCole	22,296					5	6		8	9		11	3	7	10	4				1	2							
13	15	(h) Plymouth A	W 2-1	Grainger, Francis	12,229					5	6		8	9		11	3	7	10	4				1	2							
14	22	(a) Norwich C	L 2-3	Bremner 2	18,970					5		8			9	11	3	7	10	4			6	1	2							
15	29	(h) Charlton A	W 1-0	Grainger	14,014					5	6	8			9	11	3	7	10	4				1	2							
16	Nov 5	(a) Sheffield U	L 2-3	Cameron (pen), Francis	17,565					5	6	8		9		11	3	7	10	4				1	2							
17	12	(h) Stoke C	L 0-1		13,486					5	6	8	10		9	11	3	7		4				1	2							
18	19	(a) Swansea T	L 2-3	McCole, Cameron	11,140					5	6	8		9		11	3	7		4	10			1	2							
19	Dec 3	(a) Lincoln C	W 3-2	McCole, Bremner, Peyton	5,678			2		5	6	8		9		11	3	7	10	4				1								
20	10	(h) Portsmouth	D 0-0		9,421			2		5	6	8		9		11	3		10	4		7		1								
21	17	(h) Liverpool	D 2-2	Murray, Bremner	11,929			2		5	6	10	4	9		11	3			8		7		1								
22	24	(a) Derby C	W 3-2	McCole, Bremner 2	15,185			2		5	6	10	4	9		11	3	8				7		1								
23	27	(h) Derby C	D 3-3	McCole, Murray, Charlton	18,517			2		5	6	10	4	9		11	3	8				7		1								
24	31	(a) Rotherham U	W 3-1	McCole, Lambert (og), Waterhouse (og)	12,557			2	4	5	6	10		9		11	3	7		8				1								
25	Jan 14	(h) Southampton	W 3-0	Cameron, Francis 2	14,039			2		5	6	10	8	9		11	3	7		4				1								
26	21	(a) Huddersfield T	W 1-0	McCole	18,938			2	8	5	6	10		9		11	3	7		4				1								
27	Feb 4	(a) Middlesbrough	L 0-3		16,593			2	8	5	6	10		9		11	3	7		4				1								
28	10	(h) Brighton & HA	W 3-2	McCole, Charlton, Goodwin	12,598			2	8	5	6	10		9		11	3	7		4				1								
29	18	(a) Ipswich T	L 0-4		13,125			2	8	5	6	10		9			3	7		4	11			1								
30	25	(h) Sunderland	L 2-4	Smith, Bremner	15,136			2	8	5	6	10		9		11	3	7		4				1								
31	Mar 4	(a) Plymouth A	L 1-3	Grainger	14,878			2	8	5	6	10		9		11	3	7		4				1								
32	8	(h) Luton T	L 1-2	Cameron (pen)	9,995			2		5	8			9		11	3	7	10	4				1				6				
33	11	(h) Norwich C	W 1-0	Smith	11,294			2	8	5		10		9	7			11		4				1				6	3			
34	18	(a) Portsmouth	L 1-3	Charlton	16,230			2		9	5	10			8	11		7		4				1				6	3			
35	25	(h) Sheffield U	L 1-2	Shaw (og)	13,688				4	9	5	8		10		11	2	7						1				6	3			
36	Apr 1	(a) Luton T	D 1-1	Bremner	11,137				4	9	5	8		10			2	7			11							6	3	1		
37	3	(a) Scunthorpe U	L 2-3	Charlton 2 (1 pen)	8,725				4	9	5	8			7		2		10		11							6	3	1		
38	8	(h) Swansea T	D 2-2	Charlton 2	11,862				4	9	5	8			7		2		10					1				6	3		11	
39	15	(a) Stoke C	D 0-0		7,130				4	5		7		9			2	8	10					1				6	3		11	
40	22	(h) Lincoln C	W 7-0	McCole 2(1 pen), Bell, Peyton, McConnell, Bremner, Drysdale(og)	8,432				4	5		7		9			2		10				6	1				8	3		11	
41	25	(h) Scunthorpe U	D 2-2	McCole 2	6,975				4	5		7		9			2		10				6					8	3	1	11	
42	29	(a) Charlton A	L 0-2		9,081				4	9	5	7					2		10				6					8	3	1	11	
FINAL LEAGUE POSITION: 14th in Division Two					Appearances	10	4	20	18	41	36	31	14	35	8	33	39	31	23	30	7	7	5	28	10	1	1	11	10	4	5	
					Goals				2	7	2	9	1	20		5		6	4	8	2	2	1					1				

5 own-goals

FACup

	Date	Opponent	Result	Scorers	Att	Burgin	Ashall	Jones	Smith	Charlton	Goodwin	Bremner	Revie	McCole	Fitzgerald	Grainger	Hair	Francis	Peyton	Cameron	Hawksby	Murray	Bell	Humphreys	Caldwell	McGugan	Wright	McConnell	Kilford	Carling	Johanneson	Martin
3	Jan 7	(a) Sheffield W	L 0-2		34,821			2	4	5	6	10		9		11	3	7		8				1								
					Appearances			1	1	1	1	1		1		1	1	1		1				1								
					Goals																											

League Cup

	Date	Opponent	Result	Scorers	Att	Burgin	Ashall	Jones	Smith	Charlton	Goodwin	Bremner	Revie	McCole	Fitzgerald	Grainger	Hair	Francis	Peyton	Cameron	Hawksby	Murray	Bell	Humphreys	Caldwell	McGugan	Wright	McConnell	Kilford	Carling	Johanneson	Martin
2	Sep 28	(h) Blackpool	D 0-0		13,064	1				5	6		8	9		11	3	7		4					2		10					
R	Oct 5	(a) Blackpool	W3-1*	Revie, Grainger, McCole	9,614					5	6		8	9		11	3	7	10	4				1	2							
3	Nov 23	(a) Chesterfield	W 4-0	McCole, Cameron (pen), Bremner, Peyton	2,021			2		5	6	7	8	9			3		10	4										1		11
4	Dec 5	(a) Southampton	L 4-5	Peyton, McCole, Charlton, Cameron (pen)	13,448			2		5	6	8		9		11	3	7	10	4				1								
				*After extra-time	Appearances	1		2		4	4	2	3	4		3	4	3	3	4				2	2		1			1		1
					Goals					1		1	1	3		1			2	2												

1961-62

Manager: Don Revie

No	Date	Opponent	Result	Scorers	Att	Humphreys	Smith	Hair	Cameron	Charlton	Goodwin	Mayers	Bremner	McCole	Peyton	Johanneson	McConnell	Carling	Francis	Revie	Bell	Hawksby	Younger	Jones	Kilford	McAdams	Casey	Lawson	Mason	Collins	Sprake	Addy
1	Aug 19	(h) Charlton A	W 1-0	Bremner	12,916	1	2	3	4	5	6	7	8	9	10	11																
2	22	(a) Brighton & HA	W 3-1	Peyton, Bremner, Mayers	22,744	1	2	3		5	6	7	8	9	10	11	4															
3	26	(a) Liverpool	L 0-5		42,450	1	2	3		5	6	7	8	9	10	11	4															
4	30	(h) Brighton & HA	D 1-1	Bremner	12,642		2	3	4	5	6		9		10	11	8	1	7													
5	Sep 2	(h) Rotherham U	L 1-3	McCole	12,610	1	2	3	4	5	6		8	9	10	11			7													
6	6	(a) Norwich C	L 0-2		26,860	1	2	3		5	6	7	8	9	10	11				4												
7	9	(a) Sunderland	L 1-2	McCole	30,737	1	2	3			5	7	8	9	10	11				4	6											
8	16	(h) Stoke C	W 3-1	McCole, Peyton, Bremner	9,578	1	4	2		5	6	7	8	9	10						3	11										
9	20	(h) Norwich C	L 0-1		10,948	1	4	2		5	6	7	8	9	10						3	11										
10	23	(a) Bristol R	L 0-4		13,676	1	4	2		5	6	7		9	10				8		3	11										
11	30	(h) Preston NE	L 1-2	Charlton	9,360		4			5	6	7		9	10				8		3	11	1	2								
12	Oct 7	(a) Plymouth A	D 1-1	McConnell	10,144		4	3		9	5		8		7		10				6	11	1	2								
13	14	(h) Huddersfield T	W 1-0	Charlton	19,162		4	2		9	5		8		7		10				6	11	1		3							
14	21	(a) Swansea T	L 1-2	McConnell	11,091		4	2		9	5				7		10			8	6	11	1		3							
15	28	(h) Southampton	D 1-1	McConnell	10,145		4	2		9	5		7		11		10			8	6		1		3							
16	Nov 4	(a) Luton T	L 2-3	Revie, Bremner (pen)	10,341		4	2		9	5		7		11		10			8	6		1		3							
17	11	(h) Leyton O	D 0-0		7,967		4	2			5	7	8		10		6			9	3	11	1									
18	18	(a) Middlesbrough	W 3-1	Mayers, Bremner, Charlton	10,758		4	2		9	5	7	8		10		6				3	11	1									
19	25	(h) Walsall	W 4-1	Charlton 2, Bremner (pen), Peyton	10,999		4	2		9	5	7	8		10		6				3	11	1									
20	Dec 2	(a) Derby C	D 3-3	Peyton, Mayers, Bell	16,408			2		9	5	7	8		10		4				6	11	1		3							
21	16	(a) Charlton A	L 1-3	Bremner (pen)	9,459		4	2			5	7	8		10		6				3	11	1			9						
22	23	(h) Liverpool	W 1-0	Bremner	17,214		4	2		9	5	11	7		10		6				3		1			8						
23	26	(h) Scunthorpe U	L 1-4	Charlton	19,481		4	2		9	5	11	7		10		6				3		1			8						
24	Jan 12	(a) Rotherham U	L 1-2	McAdams	6,207		2				5	7	8		10		6					11	1		3	9	4					
25	20	(h) Sunderland	W 1-0	Smith	17,763		8				5		7		10		6				3	11	1	2		9	4					
26	27	(h) Newcastle U	L 0-1		17,120		8				5		7		10	11	6				3		1	2		9	4					
27	Feb 3	(a) Stoke C	L 1-2	Peyton	21,935		4	2		9	5		7		10		6				3	11	1			8						
28	10	(h) Bristol R	D 0-0		9,108		4	2		9	5	7	8		10		6				3	11	1									
29	20	(a) Scunthorpe U	L 1-2	Mayers (pen)	9,186		4	2		9	5	7	8		10		6				3	11	1									
30	24	(h) Plymouth A	L 2-3	Charlton, Mayers	8,554		6	2	4	9	5	7	8				10				3	11	1									
31	Mar 3	(a) Huddersfield T	L 1-2	Charlton	16,799		6	3	4	9	5		7		11					8			1	2				10				
32	10	(h) Swansea T	W 2-0	Collins, McAdams	17,314		6	2	4		5		7									11	1			9		10	3	8		
33	17	(a) Southampton	L 1-4	Lawson	11,924		6	2	4		5		7									11				9		10	3	8	1	
34	24	(h) Luton T	W 2-1	Bremner 2	13,078		6	2		5	4		7		10							11	1					9	3	8		
35	31	(a) Leyton O	D 0-0		13,290		6	2		5	4		7		10							11	1					9	3	8		
36	Apr 7	(h) Middlesbrough	W 2-0	Hair, Gates (og)	16,116		6	2		5	4		7		10							11	1					9	3	8		
37	9	(a) Preston NE	D 1-1	Cunningham (og)	10,492		6	2		5			7		10		4					11	1					9	3	8		
38	14	(a) Walsall	D 1-1	Johanneson	9,005		6	2		5	4		7		10	11							1					9	3	8		
39	20	(a) Bury	D 1-1	Charlton	11,313		6	2		5	4		7		10	11							1					9	3	8		
40	21	(h) Derby C	D 0-0		11,922		6	2		5	4		7		10	11							1					9	3	8		
41	24	(h) Bury	D 0-0		21,482		6	2		5	4		7			11							1			9		10	3	8		
42	28	(a) Newcastle U	W 3-0	Johanneson, McAdams, Keith (og)	21,708		6	2		5	4		7			11						10	1			9			3	8		
FINAL LEAGUE POSITION: 19th in Division Two					Appearance	9	41	38	7	34	41	20	39	10	37	13	23	1	4	7	23	25	31	5	6	11	3	11	11	11	1	
					Goals		1	1		9		5	11	3	5	2	3			1	1					3		1		1		

3 own-goals

FA Cup

Round	Date	Opponent	Result	Scorers	Att	Humphreys	Smith	Hair	Cameron	Charlton	Goodwin	Mayers	Bremner	McCole	Peyton	Johanneson	McConnell	Carling	Francis	Revie	Bell	Hawksby	Younger	Jones	Kilford	McAdams	Casey	Lawson	Mason	Collins	Sprake	Addy
3	Jan 6	(h) Derby C	D 2-2	Charlton, Peyton	27,089		4	2		9	5	11	7		10		6				3		1			8						
R	10	(a) Derby C	L 1-3	McAdams	28,168		4	2		9	5	11	7		10		6				3		1			8						
					Appearances		2	2		2	2	2	2		2		2				2		2			2						
					Goals					1					1											1						

League Cup

Round	Date	Opponent	Result	Scorers	Att	Humphreys	Smith	Hair	Cameron	Charlton	Goodwin	Mayers	Bremner	McCole	Peyton	Johanneson	McConnell	Carling	Francis	Revie	Bell	Hawksby	Younger	Jones	Kilford	McAdams	Casey	Lawson	Mason	Collins	Sprake	Addy
2	Sep 13	(h) Brentford	W 4-1	McCole 4	4,517	1	4	2		5	6	7	8	9	10						3	11										
3	Oct 4	(h) Huddersfield T	W 3-2	Bremner (pen), Charlton, McConnell	10,023		4	2		9	5		8		7		10				6	11	1		3							
4	Dec 12	(a) Rotherham U	D 1-1	Charlton	10,899			2		9	5	7	8		10		6				3	11	1				4					
R	Jan 15	(h) Rotherham U	L 1-2	Johanneson (pen)	6,385		4				5		7		8	11	6					10	1	2	3							9
					Appearances	1	3	3		3	4	2	4	1	4	1	3				3	4	3	1	2		1					1
					Goals					2			1	4		1	1															

1962-63

Manager: Don Revie

No	Date	Opponent	Result	Scorers	Att	Younger	Hair	Mason	Goodwin	Charlton	Smith	Bremner	Storrie	Charles	Collins	Johanneson	Bell	Lawson	Hawksby	Sprake	Reaney	Hunter	Peyton	Johnson	Addy	Lorimer	Henderson	Weston	Williamson	Wright	Greenhoff	Hallett
1	Aug 18 (a)	Stoke C	W 1-0	Storrie	27,118	1	2	3	4	5	6	7	8	9	10	11																
2	22 (h)	Rotherham U	L 3-4	Storrie, Charles, Johanneson	14,119	1	2	3	4	5	6	7	8	9	10	11																
3	25 (h)	Sunderland	W 1-0	Bremner	17,753	1	2	3	4	5		7	8	9	10	11	6															
4	28 (a)	Rotherham U	L 1-2	Charles	19,508	1	2	3		5		4	8	9	10		6	7	11													
5	Sep 1 (a)	Huddersfield T	D 1-1	Charles	34,946	1	2	3		5	4	7	8	9	10	11	6															
6	5 (h)	Bury	L 1-2	Bremner	28,313	1	2	3		5	4	7	8	9	10	11	6															
7	8 (a)	Swansea T	W 2-0	Johnson, Bremner	17,696			3		5	4	8			10	11				1	2	6	7	9								
8	15 (h)	Chelsea	W 2-0	Johanneson 2	27,520			3		5	4	8		9	10	11				1	2	6	7									
9	18 (a)	Bury	L 1-3	Storrie	18,876			3		5		4	8	9	10	11				1	2	6	7									
10	22 (a)	Luton T	D 2-2	Storrie, Collins	8,958			3		5		8	9		10	11				1	2	6		7	4							
11	29 (h)	Southampton	D 1-1	Storrie	25,408			3		5			8	9	10	11				1	2	6			4	7						
12	Oct 6 (h)	Middlesbrough	L 2-3	Hunter, Bremner	28,222		3	7		5		8	9	4	10	11				1	2	6										
13	13 (a)	Derby C	D 0-0		14,246			3		5			8	9	10	11	4		7	1	2	6										
14	20 (h)	Newcastle U	W 1-0	Johanneson	23,386			3		5					10	11	4		7	1	2	6	8	9								
15	27 (a)	Walsall	D 1-1	Johanneson	7,353			3		5			8		10	11	4		7	1	2	6		9								
16	Nov 3 (h)	Norwich C	W 3-0	Storrie, Bell, Johanneson	15,919			3	5			8	9		10	11	4		7	1	2	6										
17	10 (a)	Grimsby T	D 1-1	Storrie	9,183			3	5			8	9		10	11	4			1	2	6					7					
18	17 (h)	Plymouth A	W 6-1	Johanneson, Storrie 3, Collins, Bremner	15,301		2	3		5		8	9		10	11	4			1		6					7					
19	24 (a)	Preston NE	I 1-4	Bell	13,145			3		5		8	9		10	11	4			1	2	6					7					
20	Dec 1 (h)	Portsmouth	D 3-3	Storrie, Collins, Johanneson	15,519			3		5		8	9		10	11	4			1	2	6					7					
21	8 (a)	Cardiff C	D 0-0		11,334		3			5			9		10	11	4			1	2	6	8				7					
22	15 (h)	Stoke C	W 3-1	Weston 3	19,331		3			5			9		10	11	4			1	2	6					7	8				
23	22 (a)	Sunderland	L 1-2	Bremner	40,252		3			5		10	9			11	4			1	2	6					7	8				
24	Mar 2 (h)	Derby C	W 3-1	Weston, Storrie, Charlton (pen)	22,912		3			5			9		10	11	4			1	2	6					7	8				
25	9 (a)	Newcastle U	D 1-1	Storrie	29,570		3			5			9		10	11	4			1	2	6					7	8				
26	13 (h)	Walsall	W 3-0	Johanneson, Storrie 2	17,077		3			5			9		10	11	4			1	2	6					7	8				
27	23 (a)	Norwich C	L 2-3	Collins, Johanneson	26,154		3			5		8	9		10	11	4			1	2	6						7				
28	30 (h)	Grimsby T	W 3-0	Bremner, Collins 2	13,938		3			5		8	9		10	11	4				2	6						7	1			
29	Apr 3 (h)	Scunthorpe U	W 1-0	Bremner	15,783		3			5		8	9		10	11	4				2	6						7	1			
30	6 (a)	Plymouth A	L 1-3	Storrie	8,992		3			5		8	9		10	11	4				2	6						7	1			
31	13 (h)	Preston NE	W 4-1	Bremner 2, Storrie, Collins	16,016					5		8	9		10	11	4			1	2	6					7			3		
32	15 (a)	Charlton A	W 2-1	Charlton, Hunter	13,538					5		8	9		10	11	4			1	2	6					7			3		
33	16 (h)	Charlton A	W 4-1	Weston, Henderson, Johanneson, Storrie	24,646					5			9		10	11	4			1	2	6					7	8		3		
34	20 (a)	Portsmouth	L 0-3		7,773		3			5			9		10	11	4			1	2	6	8				7					
35	23 (a)	Scunthorpe U	W 2-0	Lawson 2	7,794		3		5				9		10	11	4	8		1	2	6					7					
36	27 (h)	Cardiff C	W 3-0	Storrie 3	19,752		3		5				9		10	11	4	8		1	2	6					7					
37	30 (a)	Chelsea	D 2-2	Lawson 2	24,387		3			5			9		10	11	4	8		1	2	6					7					
38	May 4 (h)	Luton T	W 3-0	Storrie 2, Weston	23,781		3			5			9		10	11	4			1	2	6					7	8				
39	6 (a)	Middlesbrough	L 1-2	Johanneson	17,365				4	5			9		10	11	3			1	2	6					7	8				
40	11 (h)	Huddersfield T	L 0-1		28,501		3			5					10	11	4	9		1	2	6					7	8				
41	15 (a)	Southampton	L 1-3	Weston	11,619		3			5		8	9		10	11				1	2	6						7			4	
42	18 (h)	Swansea T	W 5-0	Storrie 2, Lawson, Collins, Johanneson	11,314		3			5			9		10	11		8		1	2	6						7			4	
FINAL LEAGUE POSITION: 5th in Division Two					Appearances	6	26	20	8	38	6	24	38	11	41	41	32	6	5	33	35	36	6	4	2	1	20	15	3	3	2	
					Goals					2		10	25	3	8	13	2	5				2		1			1	7				

FA Cup

Rd	Date	Opponent	Result	Scorers	Att	Younger	Hair	Mason	Goodwin	Charlton	Smith	Bremner	Storrie	Charles	Collins	Johanneson	Bell	Lawson	Hawksby	Sprake	Reaney	Hunter	Peyton	Johnson	Addy	Lorimer	Henderson	Weston	Williamson	Wright	Greenhoff	Hallett
3	Mar 6 (h)	Stoke C	W 3-1	Collins, Reaney, Hair	36,873		3			5			9		10	11	4			1	2	6					7	8				
4	16 (a)	Middlesbrough	W 2-0	Storrie, Johanneson	39,672		3			5			9		10	11	4			1	2	6					7	8				
5	19 (a)	Nottingham F	L 0-3		36,392		3			5			9		10	11	4			1	2	6					7	8				
					Appearances		3			3			3		3	3	3			3	3	3					3	3				
					Goals		1						1		1	1					1											

League Cup

Rd	Date	Opponent	Result	Scorers	Att	Younger	Hair	Mason	Goodwin	Charlton	Smith	Bremner	Storrie	Charles	Collins	Johanneson	Bell	Lawson	Hawksby	Sprake	Reaney	Hunter	Peyton	Johnson	Addy	Lorimer	Henderson	Weston	Williamson	Wright	Greenhoff	Hallett
2	Sep 26 (h)	Crystal P	W 2-1	Charlton, Storrie	7,274		2	3		5			8					9	11	1		6	10	7	4							
3	Oct 17 (a)	Blackburn R	L 0-4		7,680			3					8				4	9	11	1	2	6	10	7								5
					Appearances		1	2		1			2				1	2	2	2	1	2	2	2	1							1
					Goals					1			1																			

1963-64

Manager: Don Revie

No	Date	Venue/Opponent	Result	Scorers	Att	Sprake	Reaney	Bell	Bremner	Charlton	Hunter	Weston	Lawson	Storrie	Collins	Johanneson	Giles	Hair	Henderson	Goodwin	Wright	Madeley	Williamson	Peacock	Greenhoff	Cooper	Hawksby	Smith	Lorimer
1	Aug 28	(h) Rotherham U	W 1-0	Weston	22,517	1	2	3	4	5	6	7	8	9	10	11													
2	31	(h) Bury	W 3-0	Collins, Storrie, Johanneson	26,041	1	2	3	4	5	6	8		9	10	11	7												
3	Sep 3	(a) Rotherham U	D 2-2	Charlton, Johanneson	14,178	1	2	3	4	5	6	8		9	10	11	7												
4	7	(a) Manchester C	L 2-3	Johanneson, Lawson	29,186	1	2	3	4	5	6	8	10	9		11	7												
5	11	(h) Portsmouth	W 3-1	Storrie, Weston, Bremner	24,926	1	2		4	5	6	8		9	10	11	7	3											
6	14	(h) Swindon T	D 0-0		33,301	1	2		4	5	6	8		9	10	11	7	3											
7	18	(a) Portsmouth	D 1-1	Henderson	12,569	1	2		4	5	6	8		9	10		7	3	11										
8	21	(a) Cardiff C	D 0-0		16,117	1	2		4	5	6	8		9	10		7	3	11										
9	28	(h) Norwich C	W 4-2	Weston 2, Johanneson, Collins (pen)	22,804	1	2		4		6	8		9	10	11	7	3		5									
10	Oct 1	(a) Northampton T	W 3-0	Lawson, Weston, Collins	15,079	1	2	3	4		6	9	8		10	11	7			5									
11	5	(a) Scunthorpe U	W 1-0	Lawson	10,793	1	2	3	4		6	9	8		10	11	7			5									
12	9	(h) Middlesbrough	W 2-0	Hunter, Collins	36,919	1	2	3	4	5	6	9	8		10	11	7												
13	12	(a) Huddersfield T	W 2-0	Giles, Weston	31,220	1	2	3	4	5	6	9	8		10	11	7												
14	19	(h) Derby C	D 2-2	Charlton, Weston	29,864	1	2	3	4	5	6	9	8		10	11	7												
15	26	(a) Southampton	W 4-1	Lawson 2, Giles, Johanneson	18,036	1	2	3	4	5	6	9	8		10	11	7												
16	Nov 2	(h) Charlton A	D 1-1	Charlton	32,344	1	2	3	4	5	6	9	8		10	11	7												
17	9	(a) Grimsby T	W 2-0	Lawson, Weston	12,194	1	2	3	4		6	9	8		10	11	7			5									
18	16	(h) Preston NE	D 1-1	Johanneson	33,841	1	2	3	4		6		8	9	10	11	7			5									
19	23	(a) Leyton O	W 2-0	Collins, Johanneson	12,072	1		3	4		6	9	8		10	11	7			5	2								
20	30	(h) Swansea T	W 2-1	Johanneson, Bell	21,870	1	2	3	4		6	9	8		10	11	7			5									
21	Dec 7	(a) Plymouth A	W 1-0	Johanneson	9,918	1	2	3	4		6	8		9	10	11	7			5									
22	14	(h) Northampton T	D 0-0		21,108	1	2	3	4		6	8		9	10	11	7			5									
23	21	(a) Bury	W 2-1	Lawson, Weston	7,453	1	2	3	4		6	8	9		10	11	7			5									
24	26	(h) Sunderland	D 1-1	Lawson	41,167	1	2	3	4		6	8	9		10	11	7			5									
25	28	(a) Sunderland	L 0-2		55,046	1	2	3	4		6	7	9	8	10		11			5									
26	Jan 11	(h) Manchester C	W 1-0	Weston	33,737	1	2	3	4		6	8	9		10	11	7					5							
27	18	(a) Swindon T	D 2-2	Giles, Hunter	19,015		2	3	4		6	8	9		10	11	7					5	1						
28	Feb 1	(h) Cardiff C	D 1-1	Johanneson	28,039	1	2	5	4		6	8	9		10	11	7				3								
29	8	(a) Norwich C	D 2-2	Weston, Peacock	20,843	1	2	3	4		6	8			10	11	7					5		9					
30	15	(h) Scunthorpe U	W 1-0	Johanneson	28,868	1	2		4		6	8			10	11	7	3				5		9					
31	22	(h) Huddersfield T	D 1-1	Storrie	36,439	1	2		4	5	6			8	10	11	7	3						9					
32	Mar 3	(a) Preston NE	L 0-2		35,612	1	2	4		5	6			8	10	11	7	3						9					
33	7	(h) Southampton	W 3-1	Lawson, Collins, Johanneson	24,077	1	2	3		5	6	7	8		10	11								9	4				
34	14	(a) Middlesbrough	W 3-1	Lawson, Peacock, Giles	15,986	1	2	3		5	6		8		10	11	7							9	4				
35	21	(h) Grimsby T	W 3-1	Lawson, Bremner, Peacock	25,351	1	2	3	4	5	6		8		10	11	7							9					
36	27	(a) Newcastle U	W 1-0	Giles	55,038	1	2	3	4	5	6		8		10	11	7							9					
37	28	(a) Derby C	D 1-1	Peacock	16,757	1	2	3	4	5	6		8		10	11	7							9					
38	30	(h) Newcastle U	W 2-1	Weston, Johanneson	40,105	1	2	3	4	5	6	8			10	11	7							9					
39	Apr 4	(h) Leyton O	W 2-1	Giles, Weston	30,920	1	2	3	4	5	6	8			10	11	7							9					
40	11	(a) Swansea T	W 3-0	Peacock 2, Giles	14,321	1	2	3	4	5	6	8			10		7							9		11			
41	18	(h) Plymouth A	D 1-1	Bell	34,725	1	2	3	4	5	6	8			10	11	7							9					
42	25	(a) Charlton A	W 2-0	Peacock 2	21,323	1	2	3	4	5	6	8			10		7							9		11			
FINAL LEAGUE POSITION: 1st in Division Two					Appearances	41	41	35	39	25	42	35	24	15	41	37	40	8	2	12	2	4	1	14	2	2			
					Goals			2	3	3	2	13	11	3	6	13	7		1					8					

FA Cup

Rd	Date	Venue/Opponent	Result	Scorers	Att	Sprake	Reaney	Bell	Bremner	Charlton	Hunter	Weston	Lawson	Storrie	Collins	Johanneson	Giles	Hair	Henderson	Goodwin	Wright	Madeley	Williamson	Peacock	Greenhoff	Cooper	Hawksby	Smith	Lorimer
3	Jan 4	(a) Cardiff C	W 1-0	Bremner	13,932	1	2	3	4		6	8	9			11	10		7	5									
4	25	(h) Everton	D 1-1	Lawson	48,826	1	2	3	4		6		9		10	11	8		7			5							
R	28	(a) Everton	L 0-2		66,167	1	2	3	4		6		9		10		8		7			5					11		
					Appearances	3	3	3	3		3	1	3		2	2	3		3	1		2					1		
					Goals				1				1																

League Cup

Rd	Date	Venue/Opponent	Result	Scorers	Att	Sprake	Reaney	Bell	Bremner	Charlton	Hunter	Weston	Lawson	Storrie	Collins	Johanneson	Giles	Hair	Henderson	Goodwin	Wright	Madeley	Williamson	Peacock	Greenhoff	Cooper	Hawksby	Smith	Lorimer
2	Sep 25	(h) Mansfield T	W 5-1	Lawson 2, Johanneson 2, Bell	9,843	1	2	4		5	6	9	8		10	11		3	7										
3	Oct 22	(h) Swansea T	W 2-0	Lawson, Storrie	10,748	1	2	3	6	5			10	9		11	7								4				8
4	Nov 27	(a) Manchester C	L 1-3	Weston	10,769	1		3			6	8		9			10	2	7	5							11	4	
					Appearances	3	2	3	1	2	2	2	2	2	1	2	2	2	2	1					1		1	1	1
					Goals			1				1	3	1		2													

1964-65

Manager: Don Revie

		Match	Result	Scorers	Att	Sprake	Reaney	Bell	Bremner	Charlton	Hunter	Giles	Weston	Storrie	Collins	Johanneson	Lawson	Cooper	Greenhoff	Henderson	Belfitt	Madeley	Williamson	Johnson	Peacock	Lorimer	Wright
1	Aug	22 (a) Aston Villa	W 2-1	Johanneson, Charlton	28,000	1		3	4	5	6	7	8	9	10	11											
2		26 (h) Liverpool	W 4-2	Yeats (og), Weston, Bremner, Giles	36,005	1	2	3	4	5	6	7	8	9	10	11											
3		29 (h) Wolves	W 3-2	Storrie 2, Charlton	34,538	1	2	3	4	5	6	7	8	9		11	10										
4	Sep	2 (a) Liverpool	L 1-2	Collins	52,548	1	2	3	4	5	6	7	8	9	10	11											
5		5 (a) Sunderland	D 3-3	Storrie, Bell, Johanneson	48,858	1	2	3	4	5	6	7		9	10	11	8										
6		7 (a) Blackpool	L 0-4		26,310	1	2		4	5	6	7		9	10	11	8	3									
7		12 (h) Leicester C	W 3-2	Bremner 2 (1 pen), Johanneson	32,300	1	2		8	5	6	7		9	10	11		3	4								
8		16 (h) Blackpool	W 3-0	Collins 2, Hunter	35,973	1	2		4	5	6	7	8	9	10	11		3		7	9						
9		19 (a) Chelsea	L 0-2		38,006	1	2	3	8	5	6	7		9	10	11			4								
10		26 (h) Nottingham F	L 1-2	Storrie	32,776	1	2	3	4	5	6			8	10	11											
11		30 (h) Fulham	D 2-2	Storrie 2	31,260	1	2	3	4	5	6		8	9	10	11			7								
12	Oct	10 (a) Stoke C	W 3-2	Storrie 2, Greenhoff	27,561	1	2	9	4	5	6			8	10	11			7			3					
13		17 (h) Tottenham H	W 3-1	Belfitt, Giles, Bell (pen)	41,464	1	2	3	4	5	6	7		8	10	11					9						
14		24 (a) Burnley	W 1-0	Bell	24,329	1	2	3	4		6	7		8	10	11					9	5					
15		31 (h) Sheffield U	W 4-1	Collins, Storrie, Johanneson, Belfitt	33,357	1	2	3	4	5	6	7		8	10	11					9						
16	Nov	7 (a) Everton	W 1-0	Bell	43,605	1	2	3	4	5	6	7		8	10	11					9						
17		11 (h) Arsenal	W 3-1	Charlton, Belfitt, Storrie	38,620	1	2	3	4	5	6	7		8	10	11					9						
18		14 (h) Birmingham C	W 4-1	Storrie, Charlton, Collins, Giles (pen)	32,030	1	2	3	4	5	6	7		8	10	11					9						
19		21 (a) West Ham U	L 1-3	Belfitt	28,150	1	2	3	4	5	6	7		8	10					11	9						
20		28 (h) West Brom A	W 1-0	Johnson	29,553		2	3	4	5	6	7		8	10			11					1	9			
21	Dec	5 (a) Manchester U	W 1-0	Collins	53,374	1	2	3	4	5	6	7		9	10			11						8			
22		12 (h) Aston Villa	W 1-0	Johanneson	27,339	1	2	3	4	5	6	7		8	10	11								9			
23		19 (a) Wolves	W 1-0	Johnson	17,126	1	2		4	5	6	7		8	10	11		3						9			
24		26 (h) Blackburn R	D 1-1	Storrie	45,341	1	2	3	4	5	6	7		8	10	11								9			
25		28 (a) Blackburn R	W 2-0	Storrie, Johanneson	24,511	1	2		4		6	7		8	10	11		3				5		9			
26	Jan	2 (h) Sunderland	W 2-1	Charlton, Hunter	43,808	1	2		4	5	6	7		8	10			11				3		9			
27		16 (a) Leicester C	D 2-2	Charlton, Johnson	23,230	1	2	3	4	5	6	7		8	10	11								9			
28		23 (h) Chelsea	D 2-2	Storrie, Giles	47,109	1	2	3	4	5	6	7		9	10	11			8								
29	Feb	6 (a) Nottingham F	D 0-0		36,596	1	2	3	4	5	6	7	8	9	10			11									
30		13 (a) Arsenal	W 2-1	Giles, Weston	32,132	1	2	3	4	5	6	7	8	9	10			11									
31		27 (a) Tottenham H	D 0-0		42,202	1	2	3	4	5	6	7		8	10	11									9		
32	Mar	13 (a) Fulham	D 2-2	Peacock, Collins	24,704	1	2	3	4	5	6	7	8		10			11							9		
33		15 (h) Burnley	W 5-1	Collins 2, Charlton 2, Johanneson	38,506	1	2	3	4	5	6	7		8	10	11									9		
34		20 (h) Everton	W 4-1	Johanneson 2, Bremner, Peacock	29,701	1		2	4		6	7		8	10	11		3				5			9		
35	Apr	3 (h) West Ham U	W 2-1	Peacock, Bremner	41,918	1	2	3	4	5	6	7		8	10			11							9		
36		5 (h) Stoke C	W 3-1	Weston 2, Greenhoff	38,133	1	2	3	4	5		11	8		10				6					7	9		
37		12 (a) West Brom A	W 2-1	Peacock 2	20,007	1	2	3		5	6	7	8		10			11	4						9		
38		17 (h) Manchester U	L 0-1		52,368	1	2	3		5	6	7	8		10			11	4						9		
39		19 (a) Sheffield W	L 0-3		39,054	1	2	3	8	5	6	11	10	9					7			4					
40		20 (h) Sheffield W	W 2-0	Storrie, Giles (pen)	45,065	1	2	3	4	5	6	7	10	9		11										8	
41		24 (a) Sheffield U	W 3-0	Storrie, Bremner, Peacock	32,928	1	2	3	4	5	6	7		8	10	11									9		
42		26 (a) Birmingham C	D 3-3	Giles (pen), Reaney, Charlton	16,644	1	2		4	5	6	7	8		10	11		3							9		
FINAL LEAGUE POSITION: 2nd in Division One					Appearances	41	41	35	40	39	41	39	15	37	39	30	3	16	9	2	8	6	1	9	10	1	
					Goals		1	4	6	9	2	7	4	16	9	9			2		4			3	6		

1 own-goal

FA Cup

		Match	Result	Scorers	Att	Sprake	Reaney	Bell	Bremner	Charlton	Hunter	Giles	Weston	Storrie	Collins	Johanneson	Lawson	Cooper	Greenhoff	Henderson	Belfitt	Madeley	Williamson	Johnson	Peacock	Lorimer	Wright
3	Jan	9 (h) Southport	W 3-0	Greenhoff, Johanneson, Johnson	31,297	1	2		4	5	6			8	10	11		3	7					9			
4		30 (h) Everton	D 1-1	Storrie	50,051	1	2	3	4	5	6	7	8	9	10	11											
R	Feb	2 (a) Everton	W 2-1	Charlton, Weston	65,940	1	2	3	4	5	6	7	8	9	10			11									
5		20 (h) Shrewsbury T	W 2-0	Giles (pen), Johanneson	47,740	1	2	3	4	5	6	7	8	9	10	11											
6	Mar	10 (a) Crystal P	W 3-0	Peacock 2, Storrie	45,384	1	2	3	4	5	6	7		8	10			11							9		
SF		27(n†)Manchester U	D 0-0		65,000	1	2	3	4	5	6	7		8	10	11									9		
R		31(n‡)Manchester U	W 1-0	Bremner	46,300	1	2	3	4	5	6	7		8	10			11							9		
F	May	1(n§)Liverpool	L 1-2*	Bremner	100,000	1	2	3	4	5	6	7		8	10	11									9		
†Played at Hillsborough, Sheffield. ‡Played at the City Ground, Nottingham.					Appearances	8	8	7	8	8	8	7	3	8	8	5		4	1					1	4		
§Played at Wembley Stadium. *After extra-time.					Goals				2	1		1	1	2		2			1					1	2		

League Cup

		Match	Result	Scorers	Att	Sprake	Reaney	Bell	Bremner	Charlton	Hunter	Giles	Weston	Storrie	Collins	Johanneson	Lawson	Cooper	Greenhoff	Henderson	Belfitt	Madeley	Williamson	Johnson	Peacock	Lorimer	Wright
2	Sep	23 (h) Huddersfield T	W 3-2	Hunter, Storrie, Belfitt	9,837			3	4	5	6			8				11		7	9		1	10			2
3	Oct	14 (h) Aston Villa	L 2-3	Johanneson, Collins	10,656			3		5	6				10	11			7	8	9	4	1				2
					Appearances			2	1	2	2			1	1	1		1	1	2	2	1	2	1			2
					Goals						1			1	1	1					1						

1965-66

Manager: Don Revie

No	Date	Venue / Opponents	Result	Scorers	Att	Sprake	Reaney	Bell	Bremner	Charlton	Hunter	Giles	Weston	Peacock	Collins	Cooper	Lorimer	Johanneson	Johnson	Madeley	Storrie	O'Grady	Greenhoff	Gray	Belfitt	Hibbitt	Harvey	Williamson	Davey	Bates	Wright	Hawkins
1	Aug 21	(h) Sunderland	W 1-0	Hunter	36,348	1	2	3	4	5	6	7	8	9	10	11																
2	23	(a) Aston Villa	W 2-0	Peacock, Cooper	33,836	1	2	3	4	5	6	7	8	9	10	11																
3	28	(a) West Ham U	L 1-2	Peacock	27,995	1	2	3	4	5	6	10	7	9		11	8															
4	Sep 1	(h) Aston Villa	W 2-0	Peacock 2	33,575	1	2	3	4	**5**	6	7		9	10		8	11	12													
5	4	(h) Nottingham F	W 2-1	Bell, Lorimer	35,427	1	2	**3**	4	5	6	7		9	10	12	8	11														
6	8	(a) Tottenham H	L 2-3	Lorimer, Clayton (og)	48,114	1	2		4	5	6	7		9	10	3	8	11														
7	11	(h) Sheffield U	D 2-2	Bremner, Hunter	33,249	1	2		4	5	6	7		9	10	3	8	**11**	12													
8	15	(h) Tottenham H	W 2-0	Bremner, Charlton	41,920	1	2		4	5	6	7		9	10	3	8	**11**		12												
9	18	(a) Leicester C	D 3-3	Peacock 2, Madeley	23,276	1	2		4	5	6	7		9	10	11	8			3												
10	25	(h) Blackburn R	W 3-0	Lorimer 2, Cooper	31,098	1	2		4	5	6	7		9	10	11	8			3												
11	Oct 9	(a) Sheffield W	D 0-0		35,105	1	2		4	5	6	7		9			8		10	3	11											
12	16	(h) Northampton T	W 6-1	Lorimer 2, Bremner, Charlton, Peacock, Storrie	33,748	1	2	3	4	5	6	10		9			8				7	11										
13	23	(a) Stoke C	W 2-1	Peacock, O'Grady	30,093	1	2	3	4	5	6	10		9			8				7	11										
14	30	(h) Burnley	D 1-1	Storrie	41,628	1	2	3	4	5	**6**	10		9			8			12	7	11										
15	Nov 6	(a) Chelsea	L 0-1		39,373	1	2	3	4	5	6	10		9			8		11		7											
16	13	(h) Arsenal	W 2-0	Bremner, Giles	36,383	1	2		4	5	6	10		**9**		12	8			3	7	11										
17	20	(a) Everton	D 0-0		36,291	1	2	9	4	5	6	10					8			3	7	11										
18	Dec 11	(h) West Brom A	W 4-0	Giles 2, Storrie, O'Grady	33,140	1	2	3	4	5	6	10		9			8				7	11										
19	27	(a) Liverpool	W 1-0	Lorimer	53,430	1	2	3	4	5	6	**10**		9			8			12	7	11										
20	28	(h) Liverpool	L 0-1		49,192	1	2	3	10	5	6			9			8			4	7	11										
21	Jan 1	(h) Sheffield W	W 3-0	Storrie, Peacock, Gray	34,841	1	2	3	4	5	6			9							8	11	7	10								
22	8	(a) West Brom A	W 2-1	Peacock, Giles (pen)	24,900	1	2	3	4	5	6	10		9							8	11	7									
23	12	(h) Manchester U	D 1-1	Storrie	49,762	1	2	3	4	5	6	10		9							8	11	7									
24	15	(h) Stoke C	D 2-2	O'Grady, Storrie	34,802	1	2	3	4	5	6	10		9				11			8	7										
25	29	(a) Sunderland	L 0-2		35,942	1	2	3	4		6	10		**9**			8	11	12	5		7										
26	Feb 5	(h) West Ham U	W 5-0	Hunter 2, Lorimer, Bremner, Storrie	33,312	1	**2**	3	4	5	6	10					8			12	7	11			9							
27	19	(a) Nottingham F	W 4-0	Lorimer 2, Hibbitt, Giles (pen)	26,283	1	2	3	4	5	6	10					8			**9**	7	11				12						
28	26	(a) Sheffield U	D 1-1	Bell	35,682	1	2	3	4	5	6	10				11	9				7	8										
29	Mar 5	(a) Northampton T	L 1-2	O'Grady	21,548	1	2	3	4	5	6	10				11	8				9	7										
30	12	(h) Leicester C	W 3-2	Charlton 2, Hunter	35,957	1	2		4	5	6	10				3	8				9	11	7									
31	19	(a) Blackburn R	W 3-2	Bremner, Lorimer, Storrie	25,398	1	2		4	5	6	10				3	8				9	11	7									
32	26	(h) Blackpool	L 1-2	Charlton	30,727	1	2	3		5	6	10				11	8				9	7		4								
33	28	(a) Blackpool	L 0-1		19,017	1	2	3	4	5	6	10									8	11		7	9							
34	Apr 4	(h) Chelsea	W 2-0	Bremner, Hinton (og)	37,784	1	2	3	4	5	6	10					8	11		**9**		7	12									
35	8	(a) Fulham	W 3-1	Bremner, Johanneson, Storrie	38,960	1	2	3	4	5	6	10					8	11			9	7										
36	12	(h) Fulham	L 0-1		33,968		2	3	4	5	6	10					8	11			9	**7**	12				1					
37	16	(h) Everton	W 4-1	Charlton, Lorimer, Storrie, Johanneson	25,200			2	8	5	6	**10**				3	7	11			9		4	12			1					
38	30	(h) Newcastle U	W 3-0	Lorimer, Storrie, McGrath (og)	29,531	1	2	3	4	5	6	10					8				9	11	7									
39	May 5	(a) Arsenal	W 3-0	Storrie 2, Greenhoff	4,554	1	2	3	4	5	6	10					8				9	11	7									
40	7	(a) Burnley	W 1-0	Elder (og)	32,238	1	2	3	4	5	6	10				12	8				9	11	**7**									
41	16	(a) Newcastle U	L 0-2		21,660	1	2	3	4	5	6	10				11	8				9	7										
42	19	(a) Manchester U	D 1-1	Reaney	35,008	1	2	5	4			8			10			11			7	6	3		9							
FINAL LEAGUE POSITION: 2nd in Division One					Appearances	40	41	33	41	40	41	40	3	24	10	15	34	12	2	9	30	29	10	3	3		2					
					Sub appearances											3			3	4			2	1		1						
					Goals		1	2	8	6	5	6		11		2	13	1		1	13	3	1	1		1						

4 own-goals

FA Cup

Rd	Date	Venue / Opponents	Result	Scorers	Att	Sprake	Reaney	Bell	Bremner	Charlton	Hunter	Giles	Weston	Peacock	Collins	Cooper	Lorimer	Johanneson	Johnson	Madeley	Storrie	O'Grady	Greenhoff	Gray	Belfitt	Hibbitt	Harvey	Williamson	Davey	Bates	Wright	Hawkins
3	Jan 22	(h) Bury	W 6-0	Lorimer 3 (1 pen), Reaney, Greenhoff, Giles	30,384		2	3	4	5	6	10		9			8	11					7					1				
4	Feb 12	(a) Chelsea	L 0-1		57,847	1	2	3	4	5	6	10					8			9	7	11										
					Appearances	1	2	2	2	2	2	2		1			2	1		1	1	1	1					1				
					Goals		1					1					3						1									

League Cup

Rd	Date	Venue / Opponents	Result	Scorers	Att	Sprake	Reaney	Bell	Bremner	Charlton	Hunter	Giles	Weston	Peacock	Collins	Cooper	Lorimer	Johanneson	Johnson	Madeley	Storrie	O'Grady	Greenhoff	Gray	Belfitt	Hibbitt	Harvey	Williamson	Davey	Bates	Wright	Hawkins
2	Sep 22	(h) Hartlepools U	W 4-2	Cooper, Johnson, Belfitt, Storrie	11,081	1	2			5	6	7				11			4	3	8				9					10		
3	Oct 13	(h) West Brom A	L 2-4	Madeley, Belfitt	13,455			3					7			11			10	5	4				8		1		2		6	9
					Appearances	1	1	1		1	1	1	1			2			2	2	2				2		1		1	1	1	1
					Goals											1			1	1	1				2							

Leeds United also played in the Inter-Cities Fairs Cup (See *Leeds in Europe*).

1966-67

Manager: Don Revie

	Date	Opponent	Result	Scorers	Att	Sprake	Reaney	Bell	Bremner	Madeley	Hunter	Lorimer	Collins	Belfitt	Giles	Greenhoff	Cooper	Johanneson	Gray	Charlton	Bates	Storrie	Peacock	O'Grady	Harvey	Sibbald	Hibbitt	Johnson	Lumsden	Hawkins
1	Aug 20	(a) Tottenham H	L 1-3	Giles	43,844	1	2	3	4	5	6	7	8	9	**10**	11	12													
2	24	(h) West Brom A	W 2-1	Bell, Giles	35,102	1	2	3	4	5	6	9	**8**		10	7	12	11												
3	27	(h) Manchester U	W 3-1	Reaney, Lorimer, Madeley	45,092	1	2	5	4	9	6	7			10		3	11	8											
4	31	(a) West Brom A	L 0-2		22,303	1	2	3	4	9	6	7			10	11			8	5										
5	Sep 3	(a) Burnley	D 1-1	Gray	30,757	1	2	5	4	9	6	7					3	11	10		8									
6	7	(h) Sunderland	W 2-1	Giles (pen), Johanneson	37,646	1	2	5	4	9	6	7			10	12	3	**11**	8											
7	10	(h) Nottingham F	D 1-1	Gray	35,634	1	2		4	9	6	7			10		3	11	**6**		8	12								
8	17	(a) Fulham	D 2-2	Lorimer, Johanneson	19,985	1	2	3	4	8	6	7		9	10			11		5										
9	24	(h) Everton	D 1-1	Giles (pen)	38,486	1	2	3	4	12	6	7			10			**11**	8	5			9							
10	Oct 1	(a) Stoke C	D 0-0		28,987	1	2	3	4	6					10			11	8	5		7	9							
11	8	(a) Aston Villa	L 0-3		19,188	1	2	3	4	8	**6**	12			10			11	9	5		7								
12	15	(h) Arsenal	W 3-1	Bell, Madeley, Giles	31,481	1	2	3	4	9	6				10	8		11		5				7						
13	29	(h) Southampton	L 0-1		32,232		2	3	4	9	6	12			7	8		**11**	10	5					1					
14	Nov 5	(a) Arsenal	W 1-0	Charlton	24,227		2	3	4	7	6			8	10	9				5				11	1					
15	12	(h) Leicester C	W 3-1	Giles 2, Greenhoff	33,803	1	2	3	4		6				10	9	11		8	5				7						
16	19	(a) Liverpool	L 0-5		50,764	1	2	3	4	8	6				10	9	11			5				7						
17	26	(h) West Ham U	W 2-1	Giles, Johanneson	37,382	1	2	3	4		6	8			**10**	9		11		5		12		7						
18	Dec 3	(a) Sheffield W	D 0-0		35,264	1	2	3	4		**6**	8	10			9		11		5		12		7						
19	10	(h) Blackpool	D 1-1	Greenhoff	28,466	1	2	3	4		6	7	10			9		11	8	5										
20	17	(h) Tottenham H	W 3-2	Greenhoff 2, Gray	29,853	1	2	3	4		6		10			9		11	8	5				7						
21	24	(a) Newcastle U	W 2-1	O'Grady, Johanneson	29,160	1	2	3	4		6		10			9		11	8	5				7						
22	26	(h) Newcastle U	W 5-0	Lorimer 2, Charlton, Storrie, Cooper	40,680	1	2	3	4		6	8					11		10	5		9		7						
23	31	(a) Manchester U	D 0-0		53,486	1	2	3	4		6	8				**9**	12	11	10	5				7						
24	Jan 7	(h) Burnley	W 3-1	Greenhoff, Johanneson 2	37,465	1	2	3	4		6	8				9		11	10	5				7						
25	14	(a) Nottingham F	L 0-1		43,899	1	2	3	4		6	8				9	12	**11**	10	5				7						
26	21	(h) Fulham	W 3-1	Giles, Greenhoff, Johanneson	32,015	1	2		4	5	6				8	9	3	11	10					7						
27	Feb 4	(a) Everton	L 0-2		48,738	1	2	3	4	7	6	9			8		**11**		10	5						12				
28	11	(h) Stoke C	W 3-0	Bell, Lorimer, Belfitt	37,370	1		3	4	2	6	8	7	9				**11**	10	5							12			
29	25	(h) Aston Villa	L 0-2		34,398	1	2	3		4	6	8		9	7	12			10	5							**11**			
30	Mar 4	(a) Southampton	W 2-0	Charlton, Giles	26,150	1	2	3	4	8	6	7		12	10	9			**11**	5										
31	18	(h) Manchester C	D 0-0		34,366	1	2	3		4	6	8				9				5	10						11	7		
32	25	(a) Blackpool	W 2-0	Bremner, Charlton	22,548	1	2	3	4	8	6				10		11			5	7		9							
33	27	(a) Sheffield U	W 4-1	Giles (pen), Peacock, Bremner, Matthewson (og)	25,701	1	2	3	4	8	6				10		11			5	7		9							
34	28	(h) Sheffield U	W 2-0	Charlton, Peacock	38,755	1	2	3	4	8	6				10	7	11			5			9							
35	Apr 1	(h) Chelsea	W 1-0	Lorimer	39,728	1	2	3	4	8	6	7			10	9	11			5										
36	10	(a) Leicester C	D 0-0		15,437	1	2	5	4	3	6			8	7	9	11		10											
37	22	(a) West Ham U	W 1-0	Lorimer	25,500	1	2		4	5	6	7		8		9	3	**11**	10		12									
38	May 3	(h) Liverpool	W 2-1	Giles (pen), Greenhoff	36,547	1	2	3	4		5	7			6	8	9		10		11									
39	6	(a) Chelsea	D 2-2	Lorimer, Belfitt	35,882	1	2	3			5	8		9	10	4	11		6		7									
40	8	(a) Manchester C	L 1-2	Belfitt	24,924	1	2	5			6	11		8	10	9	3		4									7		
41	13	(a) Sunderland	W 2-0	Gray, Lorimer	23,686	1	2	3		5	6	8		12	10	**9**	11		4					7						
42	15	(h) Sheffield W	W 1-0	Hibbitt	23,052		2		12					10			3		**6**		7		5		1		11	9	4	8
FINAL LEAGUE POSITION: 4th in Division One					Appearances	39	41	38	36	27	40	27	7	10	29	27	20	22	29	28	8	3	6	14	3		3	3	1	1
					Sub appearances				1	1		2		2		2	4				1	3				1	1			
					Goals		1	3	2	2		9		3	12	7	1	7	4	5		1	2	1			1			

1 own-goal

FA Cup

	Date	Opponent	Result	Scorers	Att	Sprake	Reaney	Bell	Bremner	Madeley	Hunter	Lorimer	Collins	Belfitt	Giles	Greenhoff	Cooper	Johanneson	Gray	Charlton	Bates	Storrie	Peacock	O'Grady	Harvey	Sibbald	Hibbitt	Johnson	Lumsden	Hawkins
3	Jan 28	(h) Crystal P	W 3-0	O'Grady, Bell, Johanneson	37,768	1	2	3	4	12	6				8	**9**		11	10	5				7						
4	Feb 18	(h) West Brom A	W 5-0	Lorimer 2, Madeley, Belfitt 2	41,329	1	2	3		4	6	8		9	7				10	5	12			**11**						
5	Mar 11	(a) Sunderland	D 1-1	Charlton	55,763	1	2	3	4	7	6	11		8	10	9				5										
R	15	(h) Sunderland	D 1-1*	Giles	57,892	1	2	3	4		6	7		8	10	9	12	**11**		5										
2R	20	(n†) Sunderland	W 2-1	Belfitt, Giles (pen)	40,546	1	2	3	4		6	7		8	10	9	11			5										
6	Apr 8	(h) Manchester C	W 1-0	Charlton	48,877	1	2	3	4	8	6	7			10	12			11	5			**9**							
SF	29	(n‡) Chelsea	L 0-1		62,378	1	2	3	6	5	6	12		**8**	7	9	11		10											
*After extra-time. †Played at Boothferry Park, Hull. ‡Played at Villa Park, Birmingham.					Appearances	7	7	7	6	4	7	5		5	7	5	2	2	4	6			1	2						
					Sub appearances					1		1				1	1				1									
					Goals			1		1		2		3	2			1		2				1						

League Cup

	Date	Opponent	Result	Scorers	Att	Sprake	Reaney	Bell	Bremner	Madeley	Hunter	Lorimer	Collins	Belfitt	Giles	Greenhoff	Cooper	Johanneson	Gray	Charlton	Bates	Storrie	Peacock	O'Grady	Harvey	Sibbald	Hibbitt	Johnson	Lumsden	Hawkins
2	Sep 13	(h) Newcastle U	W 1-0	Peacock	18,131		2	3	4	8	6	7			10			11		5			9							
3	Oct 4	(a) Preston NE	D 1-1	Storrie	15,049	1	2	3	4	6					10	11			8	5		7	9		1					
R	12	(h) Preston NE	W 3-0	Lorimer 2 (1 pen), Greenhoff	17,221	1	2	3	4	10	6	8				9		11		5				7	1					
4	Nov 7	(a) West Ham U	L 0-7		27,474		2	3	4	7	6			8	10	**9**				5	12			11						
					Appearances	2	4	4	4	4	3	2		1	3	3		2	1	4		1	2	2	2					
					Sub appearances																1									
					Goals							2				1						1	1							

Leeds United also played in the Inter-Cities Fairs Cup (See *Leeds United in Europe*) and in the Glasgow Charity Cup (See *Invitation Tournaments*).

1967-68

Manager: Don Revie

No.	Date		Opponents	Result	Scorers	Att	Sprake	Reaney	Bell	Bremner	Charlton	Hunter	O'Grady	Madeley	Greenhoff	Gray	Johanneson	Lorimer	Giles	Cooper	Belfitt	Bates	Hibbitt	Johnson	Jones	Harvey	Hawkins	Davey	Sibbald	Yorath	Lumsden
1	Aug	19 (h)	Sunderland	D 1-1	Greenhoff	36,252	1	2	3	4	5	6	7	8	9	10	11														
2		23 (a)	Manchester U	L 0-1		53,016	1	2		4	5	6	7	3		9		8	10	11											
3		26 (a)	Wolves	L 0-2		35,368	1	2		4	5	6	11		**8**	10		7		3	9	12									
4	Sep	2 (h)	Fulham	W 2-0	Belfitt 2	25,760	1	2		4	5	6	11		8	10		7		3	9										
5		9 (a)	Southampton	D 1-1	Lorimer	25,522	1	2	3	4	5	6			9	10		7		11	8										
6		16 (a)	Everton	W 1-0	Gray	53,159	1	2	3	4	5	6	11			8		7	9	10											
7		20 (h)	Burnley	W 2-1	Lorimer 2	32,944	1	2		4	5	6		8	**7**	10		8		3			11	12							
8		23 (h)	Leicester C	W 3-2	Lorimer 2 (1 pen), Greenhoff	37,084	1	12		4	5	6		2	7	**10**		8		3			11		9						
9		30 (a)	West Ham U	D 0-0		28,940	1	2		4	5	6		8	7	10		11		3					9						
10	Oct	7 (h)	Chelsea	W 7-0	Johanneson, Greenhoff, Charlton, Lorimer, Gray, Hinton(og), Bremner	40,460	1	2		4	5	6		3	7	10	11	8					12		**9**						
11		14 (a)	West Brom A	L 0-2		21,300	1	2			5	6		4	**7**	10	12	8	11	3					9						
12		25 (h)	Newcastle U	W 2-0	Lorimer, Johanneson	30,347	1	2			5	6		4	9	10	11	8		3		7									
13		28 (a)	Manchester C	L 0-1		39,713	1	2			5	6		4	7	10	11	8		3					9						
14	Nov	4 (h)	Arsenal	W 3-1	Lorimer (pen), Jones, Gray	31,632	1	2			5	6		4	7	10	11	8		3			12		**9**						
15		8 (h)	Manchester U	W 1-0	Greenhoff	43,999	1	2		4	5	6		9	7	10	11	8		3											
16		11 (a)	Sheffield U	L 0-1		24,715	1	2		4	**5**	6		9	7	10	11	8		3			12								
17		18 (h)	Coventry C	D 1-1	Lorimer	32,469	1	2		4		6		5	7			8		3	9	10	11								
18		25 (a)	Nottingham F	W 2-0	Greenhoff, Lorimer	29,750		2		4		6		5	7			12		3	8	10	11			1	**9**				
19	Dec	2 (h)	Stoke C	W 2-0	Lorimer, Madeley	29,988	1	2		4	5	6		9		10		7		3	8		11								
20		9 (a)	Liverpool	L 0-2		39,675	1	2		4	5	6		9	7	11		8		3	10										
21		16 (a)	Sunderland	D 2-2	Greenhoff, Gray	21,189	1	2		4	5	6		9	7	10		8		3			11								
22		23 (h)	Wolves	W 2-1	Jones, Charlton	28,376	1	2		4	5	6		12	7	10		**8**	11	3					9						
23		26 (a)	Sheffield W	W 1-0	Giles (pen)	51,055	1	2		4	5	6		8	7	11			10	3					9						
24		30 (h)	Sheffield W	W 3-2	Greenhoff, Gray, Hunter	36,409	1	2		4	5	6		8	7	11			10	3					9						
25	Jan	6 (a)	Fulham	W 5-0	Greenhoff 3, Jones 2	24,419	1	2		4	5	6			7	11		8	10	3					9						
26		13 (h)	Southampton	W 5-0	Madeley 2, Lorimer, Jones, Hibbitt	31,474	1	2				6		5	7			8	10	3		4	11		9						
27		20 (h)	Everton	W 2-0	Jones, Giles (pen)	44,119	1	2		4	5	6			7	11		8	10	3					9						
28	Feb	3 (a)	Leicester C	D 2-2	Madeley, Giles	30,081	1	2		4		6		5	7	11		8	10	3					9						
29		10 (h)	West Ham U	W 2-1	Lorimer 2	41,814	1	2		4		6		5	7	**11**		8	10	3	9		12								
30	Mar	13 (h)	Nottingham F	D 1-1	Bremner	32,508	1	2		4	5	6		12	7			8		3		**10**	11		9						
31		16 (a)	Newcastle U	D 1-1	Hunter	45,190	1	2		4	5	6	11	3	7				10		8				9						
32		20 (a)	Chelsea	D 0-0		47,470	1	2		4	5	6		11	7			8	10	3					9						
33		23 (h)	Manchester C	W 2-0	Charlton, Giles	51,818	1	2		4	5	6		12	7			8	10	3			**11**		9						
34	Apr	6 (h)	Sheffield U	W 3-0	Madeley, Giles 2 (2 pens)	31,059	1	2		4	5	6		11	7			8	10	3					9						
35		12 (a)	Tottenham H	L 1-2	Madeley	56,597		2		4	5	6		11	7			8	10	3					9	1					
36		13 (a)	Coventry C	W 1-0	Hibbitt	38,778		2		4	5	6		8				7	**10**	3	12		11		9	1					
37		17 (h)	Tottenham H	W 1-0	Lorimer (pen)	50,000	1	2		4	5	6		8	12	11		7	**10**	3					9						
38		20 (h)	West Brom A	W 3-1	Gray (pen), Madeley, Charlton	38,334	1	2		4	5	6		8	11	10		**7**		3	12				9						
39		23 (a)	Stoke C	L 2-3	Charlton, Greenhoff	23,999	1	2		4	5	6		10	7	11		8		3					9						
40	May	4 (h)	Liverpool	L 1-2	Jones	44,553		2		4		6		5	7	11		8	10	**3**	12				9	1					
41		7 (a)	Arsenal	L 3-4	Lorimer, Jones, Giles	25,043		3		4				5	12	6		7	10		**8**		11		9	1		2			
42		11 (a)	Burnley	L 0-3		13,247								5		6	11				9	8	10			1		3	2	4	7
FINAL LEAGUE POSITION: 4th in Division One						Appearances	36	40	3	36	34	40	6	33	35	32	8	36	20	37	11	6	12		25	6	1	2	1	1	1
						Sub appearances		1						3	2		1	1			3	1	4	1							
						Goals				2	5	2		7	11	6	2	16	7		2		2		8						

1 own-goal

FA Cup

Round	Date		Opponents	Result	Scorers	Att	Sprake	Reaney	Bell	Bremner	Charlton	Hunter	O'Grady	Madeley	Greenhoff	Gray	Johanneson	Lorimer	Giles	Cooper	Belfitt	Bates	Hibbitt	Johnson	Jones	Harvey	Hawkins	Davey	Sibbald	Yorath	Lumsden
3	Jan	27 (a)	Derby C	W 2-0	Charlton, Lorimer	39,753	1	2		4	**5**	6		12	7	11		8	10	3					9						
4	Feb	17 (h)	Nottingham F	W 2-1	Jones, Giles	51,739	1	2		4		6		5	7	11		8	10	3					9						
5	Mar	9 (h)	Bristol C	W 2-0	Jones, Lorimer	45,227	1	2		4	5	6		12	7			8	**10**	3			11		9						
6		30 (h)	Sheffield U	W 1-0	Madeley	48,322	1	2		4	5	6	11	8				7	10	3					9						
SF	Apr	27(n†)	Everton	L 0-1		63,000	1	2		4	5	6		8		11		7	10	3					9						
*Played at Old Trafford, Manchester.						Appearances	5	5		5	4	5	1	3	3	3		5	5	5			1		5						
						Sub appearances								2																	
						Goals					1			1				2	1						2						

League Cup

Round	Date		Opponents	Result	Scorers	Att	Sprake	Reaney	Bell	Bremner	Charlton	Hunter	O'Grady	Madeley	Greenhoff	Gray	Johanneson	Lorimer	Giles	Cooper	Belfitt	Bates	Hibbitt	Johnson	Jones	Harvey	Hawkins	Davey	Sibbald	Yorath	Lumsden
2	Sep	13 (h)	Luton T	W 3-1	Lorimer 3 (1 pen)	11,473	1	2	3	4	5	6			9	10		7		11	**8**			12							
3	Oct	11 (h)	Bury	W 3-0	Charlton, Johanneson, Greenhoff	20,927	1	2			5	6		3	7	4	11	8			9			10							
4	Nov	15 (a)	Sunderland	W 2-0	Greenhoff 2	29,536	1	2		4		6		5	7	10				3	8	12	11				**9**				
5	Dec	13 (h)	Stoke C	W 2-0	Bremner, Lorimer	31,904	1	2		4	5	6			9	**10**		7		3	8	12	11								
SF	Jan	17 (a)	Derby C	W 1-0	Giles (pen)	31,904	1	2		4	5	6		9	7	11		8	10	3											
	Feb	7 (h)	Derby C	W 3-2	Belfitt 2, Gray	29,367	1	2		4		6		5	7	**11**		8	10	3	9	12									
F	Mar	2(n‡)	Arsenal	W 1-0	Cooper	97,887	1	2		4	5	6		9	7	**11**		8	10	3	12										
‡Played at Wembley Stadium.						Appearances	7	7	1	6	5	7		5	7	7	1	6	3	6	5		2	1			1				
						Sub appearances															1	3		1							
						Goals				1	1				3	1	1	4	1	1	2										

Leeds United also played in the Inter-Cities Fairs Cup (See *Leeds United in Europe*).

1968-69

Manager: Don Revie

No	Date	Opponents	Result	Scorers	Att	Sprake	Reaney	Madeley	Bremner	Charlton	Hunter	Lorimer	Greenhoff	Jones	Giles	Gray	Hibbitt	Cooper	Johanneson	Belfitt	O'Grady	Bates
1	Aug 10 (a)	Southampton	W 3-1	Lorimer, Jones, Hibbitt	25,479	1	2	3	4	5	6	**7**	8	9	10	11	12					
2	14 (h)	Queen's Park R	W 4-1	Jones, Giles, Reaney, Hibbitt	31,612	1	2		4	5	6	7	8	9	10		11	3				
3	17 (h)	Stoke C	W 2-0	Jones, Johanneson	30,383	1	2		4	5	6		8	9		**10**	11	3	12	7		
4	20 (a)	Ipswich T	W 3-2	O'Grady, Belfitt, Hibbitt	30,382	1	2		4	5	6			9		10	11	3		8	7	
5	28 (h)	Sunderland	D 1-1	Belfitt	37,797	1	2		4	5	6			9		10	11	3		8	7	
6	31 (h)	Liverpool	W 1-0	Jones	38,929	1	2		4	5	6	8		9			11	3		**10**	7	12
7	Sep 7 (h)	Wolves	W 2-1	Cooper, Charlton	31,227	1	2	10	4	5	6	8		9			11	3			7	
8	14 (a)	Leicester C	D 1-1	Madeley	28,564	1	2	10	4	5	6	8		9			11	3			7	
9	21 (h)	Arsenal	W 2-0	Charlton, O'Grady	39,946	1	2	10	4	5	6	8		9			11	3			7	
10	28 (a)	Manchester C	L 1-3	O'Grady	45,006	1	**2**	10	4	5	6	8		9		12	11	3			7	
11	Oct 5 (a)	Newcastle U	W 1-0	Charlton	41,915	1	2	9	4	5	6	8			10	11		3			7	
12	9 (a)	Sunderland	W 1-0	Jones	33,853	1	2	10	4	5	6			9	8	11		3			7	
13	12 (h)	West Ham U	W 2-0	Giles (pen), Lorimer	40,786	1	2	10	4	5	6	11		9	8			3			7	
14	19 (a)	Burnley	L 1-5	Bremner	26,423	1	2	10	4	5	6	12		9	8	11		**3**			7	
15	26 (h)	West Brom A	D 0-0		33,926	1	2	3	4	5	6	7		9		8					11	10
16	Nov 2 (a)	Manchester U	D 0-0		53,839	1	2	3	4	5	6	7		9	10						11	8
17	9 (h)	Tottenham H	D 0-0		38,995	1	2	8	4	5	6			9	10	11		3			7	
18	16 (a)	Coventry C	W 1-0	Madeley	33,224	1	2	8	4	5	6			9	10	11		3			7	
19	23 (h)	Everton	W 2-1	Giles (pen), Gray	41,716	1	2	8	4	5	6			9	10	11		3			7	
20	30 (a)	Chelsea	D 1-1	O'Grady	43,286	1	2	8	4	5	6	7		9	10			3			11	
21	Dec 7 (h)	Sheffield W	W 2-0	Lorimer 2	32,718	1	2	3	4	5	6	8		9	10	11					7	
22	14 (a)	West Ham U	D 1-1	Gray	27,418	1	2	3	4	5	6	8		9	10	11					7	
23	21 (h)	Burnley	W 6-1	Lorimer 2, Bremner, Jones, Giles, Gray	31,409	1	2	3	4	5	6	8		9	10	11					7	
24	26 (h)	Newcastle U	W 2-1	Lorimer (pen), Madeley	42,000	1	2	3	4	5	6	8		9	**10**	11	12				7	
25	Jan 11 (h)	Manchester U	W 2-1	Jones, O'Grady	48,145	1	2	3	4	5	6	8		9	10	**11**		12			7	
26	18 (a)	Tottenham H	D 0-0		42,396	1	2	8	4	5	6			9	10	11		3			7	
27	24 (a)	Queen's Park R	W 1-0	Jones	26,163	1	2	8	4	5	6	7		9	**10**	11		3		12		
28	Feb 1 (h)	Coventry C	W 3-0	O'Grady, Bremner 2	32,314	1	2	**8**	4	5	6	7		9		10	12	3			11	
29	12 (h)	Ipswich T	W 2-0	Belfitt, Jones	24,229	1	2		4	5	6			9	10	11		3		8	7	
30	15 (h)	Chelsea	W 1-0	Lorimer	35,789	1	2		4	5	6	8		**9**	10	11		3		12	7	
31	25 (a)	Nottingham F	W 2-0	Lorimer, Jones	36,249	1	2		4	5	6	12		9	10	11		3		**8**	7	
32	Mar 1 (h)	Southampton	W 3-2	Giles (pen), Jones, Kirkup (og)	33,205	1	2		4	5	6	8		9	10	11		3			7	
33	8 (a)	Stoke C	W 5-1	Jones, Bremner 2, O'Grady 2	24,327	1	2	8	4	5	6			9	10	11		3			7	
34	29 (a)	Wolves	D 0-0		27,986	1	2	**8**	4	5	6	12		9	10	11		3			7	
35	Apr 1 (a)	Sheffield W	D 0-0		34,278	1	2		4	5	6	8		9	10	11		3			7	
36	5 (h)	Manchester C	W 1-0	Giles	43,176	1	2		4	5	6	8		9	10	11		3			7	
37	9 (a)	West Brom A	D 1-1	Gray	28,959	1	2	8	4	5	6			9	10	11		3			7	
38	12 (a)	Arsenal	W 2-1	Jones, Giles	43,715	1	2	5	4		6	12		9	10	11		3			**7**	8
39	19 (h)	Leicester C	W 2-0	Jones, Gray	38,391	1	2	8	4	5	6			9	10	11		3			7	
40	22 (a)	Everton	D 0-0		59,000	1	2	8	4	5	6	9			10	11		3			7	
41	28 (a)	Liverpool	D 0-0		53,750	1	2	8	4	5	6			9	10	11		3			7	
42	30 (h)	Nottingham F	W 1-0	Giles	46,508	1	2	8	4	5	6	7		9	10			3			11	
FINAL LEAGUE POSITION: 1st in Division One					Appearances	42	42	31	42	41	42	25	3	40	32	32	9	34		6	38	3
					Sub appearances							4				1	3	1	1	2		1
					Goals		1	3	6	3		9		14	8	5	3	1	1	3	8	

1 own-goal

FA Cup

Rd	Date	Opponents	Result	Scorers	Att	Sprake	Reaney	Madeley	Bremner	Charlton	Hunter	Lorimer	Greenhoff	Jones	Giles	Gray	Hibbitt	Cooper	Johanneson	Belfitt	O'Grady	Bates
3	Jan 4 (a)	Sheffield W	D 1-1	Lorimer (pen)	52,111	1	2	3	4	5	6	8		9		11					7	10
R	8 (h)	Sheffield W	L 1-3	Johanneson	48,234	1	2	3	**4**	5	6	8		9		7			11	12		10
					Appearances	2	2	2	2	2	2	2		2		2			1		1	2
					Sub appearances															1		
					Goals							1							1			

League Cup

Rd	Date	Opponents	Result	Scorers	Att	Sprake	Reaney	Madeley	Bremner	Charlton	Hunter	Lorimer	Greenhoff	Jones	Giles	Gray	Hibbitt	Cooper	Johanneson	Belfitt	O'Grady	Bates
2	Sep 4 (h)	Charlton A	W 1-0	Jones	18,860	1	2		4	5	6	7		9			10	3		**8**	11	12
3	25 (h)	Bristol C	W 2-1	Johanneson, Jones	16,359	1	2	5	4			8		9	10	6		3	11		7	
4	Oct 16 (a)	Crystal P	L 1-2	Madeley	26,217	1	2	10		5	6	11		9	8	4		3			7	
					Appearances	3	3	2	2	2	2	3		3	2	2	1	3	1	1	3	
					Sub appearances																	1
					Goals			1						2					1			

Leeds United also played in the Inter-Cities Fairs Cup (See *Leeds United in Europe*).

1969-70

Manager: Don Revie

	Date	Opponent	Result	Scorers	Att	Sprake	Reaney	Madeley	Bremner	Charlton	Hunter	O'Grady	Lorimer	Clarke	Giles	Gray	Cooper	Jones	Yorath	Bates	Hibbitt	Belfitt	Harvey	Davey	Lumsden	Peterson	Kennedy	Galvin	Johanneson	Faulkner
1	Aug 9 (h)	Tottenham H	W 3-1	Bremner, Clarke, Giles (pen)	35,804	1	2	3	4	5	6	7	8	9	10	11														
2	13 (h)	Arsenal	D 0-0		37,164	1	2	5	4		6	7	8	9	10	11	3													
3	16 (a)	Nottingham F	W 4-1	Clarke, Giles (pen), Gray, Lorimer	34,290	1	2	5	4		6		7	8	10	11	3	9												
4	19 (a)	Arsenal	D 1-1	Lorimer	45,160	1	2	5	4		6		7	8	10	11	3	9												
5	23 (h)	Newcastle U	D 1-1	Jones	40,403	1	2	5	4		6		7	8	10	11	3	9												
6	26 (a)	Burnley	D 1-1	Jones	28,000	1	2	7	4	5	6			8	10	11	3	9												
7	30 (a)	Everton	L 2-3	Bremner, Clarke	51,797	1	2	7	4	5	6		12	10	8	**11**	3	9												
8	Sep 6 (h)	Manchester U	D 2-2	Sadler (og), Bremner	44,271	1	2	7	4	5	6	12	8		10	**11**	3	9												
9	13 (a)	Sheffield W	W 2-1	Clarke, Gray	31,998	1	2	7	4	5	6			8	10	11	3	9												
10	20 (h)	Chelsea	W 2-0	Giles (pen), Lorimer	33,130	1	2	7	4	**5**	6	11	12	8	10		3	9												
11	27 (a)	Coventry C	W 2-1	Clarke, Gray	36,091	1	2	5	4		6		7	8	10	11	3	9												
12	Oct 4 (h)	Stoke C	W 2-1	Giles 2 (2 pens)	35,860	1	2	7	4	5	6		12	8	**10**	11	3	9												
13	11 (a)	West Brom A	D 1-1	Jones	33,688	1	2	8	4	5	6		7		10	11	**3**	9	12											
14	18 (a)	Crystal P	D 1-1	Lorimer	31,910	1	2	3	4	5	6		7		10	11		9	**8**	12										
15	25 (h)	Derby C	W 2-0	Clarke 2	44,183	1	2	3	4	5	6		7	8		**11**		9		10	12									
16	29 (h)	Nottingham F	W 6-1	Lorimer 3, Charlton, Bates, Hibbitt	29,636	1	2	3	4	5	6		7	**8**		11		9		10	12									
17	Nov 1 (a)	Sunderland	D 0-0		31,842	1	2	3	4	5	6		7			11		9		10		8								
18	8 (h)	Ipswich T	W 4-0	Giles, Jones, Hunter, Gray	26,497	1	2	3		5	6		7		10	4		9	12	8	**11**									
19	15 (a)	Southampton	D 1-1	Jones	23,963	1	2	3	4	5	6		7		10			9	12	8	**11**									
20	19 (h)	Sunderland	W 2-0	Jones, Lorimer	25,890	1	2	8	4	5	6		7			11	3	9	12	**10**										
21	22 (h)	Liverpool	D 1-1	Giles (pen)	43,293	1	2	8	4	5	6		7		10	11	3	9												
22	29 (a)	Manchester C	W 2-1	Gray, Jones	44,590	1	2	8	4	5	6		7		10	11	3	9												
23	Dec 6 (h)	Wolves	W 3-1	Holsgrove (og), Charlton, Clarke	33,090	1	2	11	4	5	6		7	8	10		3	9												
24	13 (h)	Sheffield W	W 2-0	Clarke 2	31,114	1	2	9	4	5	6		7	8	10		3				11									
25	17 (h)	West Ham U	W 4-1	Lorimer 2, Clarke, Giles	30,699	1	2	11	4	5	6		7	8	10		3	9												
26	26 (a)	Newcastle U	L 1-2	Giles	54,527	1	2	11	4	5	6		7	10	8		3	9												
27	27 (h)	Everton	W 2-1	Jones 2	46,770	1	2	11	4	5	6		7	8	10		3	9												
28	Jan 10 (a)	Chelsea	W 5-2	Clarke, Cooper, Giles (pen), Lorimer, Jones	57,221	1	2	11	4	5	6		7	**8**	10		3	9		12										
29	17 (h)	Coventry C	W 3-1	Clarke 2, Charlton	34,295	1	2	11	4	**5**	6		7	8	10		3	9		12										
30	26 (a)	Manchester U	D 2-2	Jones, Bremner	60,514		2	11	4	5	6		7	8	10		3	9					1							
31	31 (a)	Stoke C	D 1-1	Giles	35,908	1	2	11	4	5	6		7	8	10		3	9												
32	Feb 10 (h)	West Brom A	W 5-1	Gray, Jones, Giles 2, Lorimer	31,515	1	2	8	4	5	6		7		10	11	3	9												
33	14 (a)	Tottenham H	D 1-1	Lorimer	41,713	1	2	8	4	5	6		7		10	11	3	9												
34	28 (h)	Crystal P	W 2-0	Jones 2	37,138	1	2	3	4	5	6		7	**8**	10	11	12	9												
35	Mar 7 (a)	Liverpool	D 0-0		51,435	1	2	9	4	5	6		7	8	10	11	3													
36	21 (a)	Wolves	W 2-1	Jones, Clarke	35,057	1	2	4		**5**			7	8		11	3	9	6	10		12								
37	28 (h)	Southampton	L 1-3	Lorimer	38,370	1		3		5			7	8		6			4	10	11	9		**2**	12					
38	30 (a)	Derby C	L 1-4	Kennedy	41,011														6	8	10	9	1	2	4	3	5	7	11	
39	Apr 2 (a)	West Ham U	D 2-2	Clarke 2	26,140	1	2	5					7	8	11	6			4	10	12	**9**		3						
40	4 (h)	Burnley	W 2-1	Gray 2	24,691			4					7			6			2	8	11		1			3		10	9	5
41	18 (h)	Manchester C	L 1-3	Belfitt	22,932				4				7	8		6	3			10	11	9	1	2		12				**5**
42	21 (a)	Ipswich T	L 2-3	Hibbitt, Gray	16,875								8			6			4	10	11	9	1	2		3	5	7		
					Appearances	37	37	39	35	32	35	3	36	28	32	30	29	32	7	13	8	6	5	5	1	3	2	3	2	2
					Sub appearances							1	3				1		4	3	3	1			1	1				
					Goals				4	3	1		14	17	13	9	1	15		1	2	1					1			

FINAL LEAGUE POSITION: 2nd in Division One

2 own-goals

FA Cup

	Date	Opponent	Result	Scorers	Att	Sprake	Reaney	Madeley	Bremner	Charlton	Hunter	O'Grady	Lorimer	Clarke	Giles	Gray	Cooper	Jones	Yorath	Bates	Hibbitt	Belfitt	Harvey	Davey	Lumsden	Peterson	Kennedy	Galvin	Johanneson	Faulkner
3	Jan 3 (h)	Swansea T	W 2-1	Giles (pen), Jones	30,246	1	2	11	4	5	6		7	8	10		3	9												
4	24 (a)	Sutton U	W 6-0	Clarke 4, Lorimer 2	14,000		2	11	4	5	6		7	8	10		3	9					1							
5	Feb 7 (h)	Mansfield T	W 2-0	Giles, Clarke	48,093	1	2		4	5	6		7	8	10	11	3	9												
6	21 (a)	Swindon T	W 2-0	Clarke 2	27,500	1	2	7	4	5	6			8	10	11	3	9												
SF	Mar 14 (n†)	Manchester U	D 0-0		55,000	1	2	11	4	5	6		**7**	8	10	12	3	9												
R	23 (n‡)	Manchester U	D 0-0*		62,500	1	2	6	4	5			7	8	10	11	**3**	9		12										
2R	26 (n§)	Manchester U	W 1-0	Bremner	56,000	1	2	6	4	5			7	8	10	11	3	9												
F	Apr 11 (n#)	Chelsea	D 2-2*	Charlton, Jones	100,000	1		2	4	5	6		7	8	10	11	3	9												
R	29 (n+)	Chelsea	L 1-2*	Jones	62,078			2	4	5	6		7	8	10	11	3	9					1							
					Appearances	7	7	8	9	9	7		8	9	9	6	9	9					2							
					Sub appearances											1				1										
					Goals				1	1			2	7	2			3												

†Played at Hillsborough, Sheffield. *After extra-time. ‡Played at Villa Park, Birmingham.
§Played at Burnden Park, Bolton. #Played at Wembley Stadium.
+Played at Old Trafford, Manchester.

League Cup

	Date	Opponent	Result	Scorers	Att	Sprake	Reaney	Madeley	Bremner	Charlton	Hunter	O'Grady	Lorimer	Clarke	Giles	Gray	Cooper	Jones	Yorath	Bates	Hibbitt	Belfitt	Harvey	Davey	Lumsden	Peterson	Kennedy	Galvin	Johanneson	Faulkner
2	Sep 2 (a)	Fulham	W 1-0	Charlton	20,446		2	4		5			7			6	3	9		8	11	10	1							
3	24 (h)	Chelsea	D 1-1	Madeley	21,933	1	2	5	4		6		7		10		3	9		12	**11**	8								
R	Oct 6 (a)	Chelsea	L 0-2		38,485		2	10	4	5	6		7			11	3	9				8	1							
					Appearances	1	3	3	2	2	2		3		1	2	3	3		1	2	3	2							
					Sub appearances															1										
					Goals			1		1																				

Leeds United also played in the European Cup (See *Leeds United in Europe*) and in the FA Charity Shield (See *Invitation Tournaments*).

1970-71

Manager: Don Revie OBE

No	Month	Date	Opponents	Result	Scorers	Att	Sprake	Madeley	Cooper	Bremner	Charlton	Hunter	Lorimer	Clarke	Jones	Giles	Gray	Bates	Belfitt	Yorath	Hibbitt	Reaney	Harvey	Davey	Galvin
1	Aug	15 (a)	Manchester U	W 1-0	Jones	59,365	1	2	3	4	5	6	7	8	9	10	11								
2		19 (a)	Tottenham H	W 2-0	Giles, Gray	39,927	1	2	3	4	5	6	7	8	9	10	11								
3		22 (h)	Everton	W 3-2	Bremner 2, Giles	46,718	1	2	3	4	5	6	7	8	9	10	11								
4		26 (h)	West Ham U	W 3-0	Jones, Giles (pen), Belfitt	42,677	1	2	3		5	6	7	8	9	**10**	11	4	12						
5		29 (a)	Burnley	W 3-0	Clarke 2, Jones	26,006	1	2	3	4	5	6	7	8	9		11	10							
6	Sep	1 (a)	Arsenal	D 0-0		47,749	1	2	3	4	5	6	7	8	9		11	10							
7		5 (h)	Chelsea	W 1-0	Clarke	47,662	1	2	3	4	5	6	7	8	9		11	10							
8		12 (a)	Stoke C	L 0-3		22,592	1	2	3	4		6	7	8	9		11	10		5					
9		19 (h)	Southampton	W 1-0	Giles (pen)	32,713	1	2	3	4	5	6	7	8	9	10	11								
10		26 (a)	Nottingham F	D 0-0		31,537	1	2	3	4	5	6	7	8	9	10	11								
11	Oct	3 (h)	Huddersfield T	W 2-0	Lorimer 2 (1 pen)	36,498	1	2	3	4	5	6	7	8	9		**11**	10			12				
12		10 (a)	West Brom A	D 2-2	Clarke, Jones	37,255	1	11	3	4	5	6	7	8	9			10				2			
13		17 (h)	Manchester U	D 2-2	Belfitt, Charlton	50,190	1	11	3	4	5	6	7	8				**10**	9		12	2			
14		24 (a)	Derby C	W 2-0	Lorimer, Clarke	32,797	1	11	3	4	5	6	7	8	9				10					2	
15		31 (h)	Coventry C	W 2-0	Charlton, Giles	31,670	1	11	3	4	5	6	7	8	9	10								2	
16	Nov	7 (a)	Crystal P	D 1-1	Lorimer	37,963	1	11	3		5	6	7	8	9	10		4						2	
17		14 (h)	Blackpool	W 3-1	Madeley, Charlton, Giles	32,921	1	2	3		5	6	7	8	9	10	11	4							
18		18 (h)	Stoke C	W 4-1	Madeley, Clarke, Lorimer, Giles (pen)	30,549	1	11	3		5	6	7	8	**9**	10		4	12					2	
19		21 (a)	Wolves	W 3-2	Madeley, Clarke, Holsgrove (og)	41,048	1	4	3		5	6	7	8	**9**	10		11	12					2	
20		28 (h)	Manchester C	W 1-0	Clarke	43,511	1	2	3	4	5	6	7	8		10	11	9							
21	Dec	5 (a)	Liverpool	D 1-1	Madeley	51,357	1	2	3	4	5	6	7	8	9	10	**11**					12			
22		12 (h)	Ipswich T	D 0-0		29,675	1	11	3	4	5	6	7	8	9	10						2			
23		19 (a)	Everton	W 1-0	Charlton	47,393		11	3	4	5	6	7	**8**	9	10		12				2	1		
24		26 (h)	Newcastle U	W 3-0	Clarke, Giles 2 (2 pens)	46,758	1	11	3	4	5	6	7	8	9	10						2			
25	Jan	9 (h)	Tottenham H	L 1-2	Clarke	43,907	1	11	3	4	5	6	7	8	9	10						2			
26		16 (a)	West Ham U	W 3-2	Hunter, Giles, Belfitt	34,396	1	7	3		5	6		8	9	**10**		4	12	11		2			
27		30 (a)	Manchester C	W 2-0	Clarke, Charlton	43,517	1	7	3		**5**	6		8	9	10		4	12	11		2			
28	Feb	6 (h)	Liverpool	L 0-1		48,425		11	3		5	6	7	8	9	10		4				2	1		
29		20 (h)	Wolves	W 3-0	Madeley, Clarke, Giles (pen)	37,273		2	3	4	5	6	7	8	9	10		11					1		
30		23 (a)	Ipswich T	W 4-2	Lorimer, Clarke 2, Giles (pen)	27,264		2	3	**4**	5	6	7	8	9	10		11	12				1		
31		26 (a)	Coventry C	W 1-0	Lorimer	40,012		11	3		5	6	7	8	9	10		4			12	**2**	1		
32	Mar	6 (h)	Derby C	W 1-0	Lorimer	36,467		11			5	6	7		9	10		4	8			3	1	2	
33		13 (a)	Blackpool	D 1-1	Lorimer	27,401		11	3		5	6	7	8	9	10		4				2	1		
34		20 (h)	Crystal P	W 2-1	Giles, Lorimer	31,876		11	3		5	6	**7**	8	9	10		4	12			2	1		
35		27 (a)	Chelsea	L 1-3	Cooper	58,462	1	11	3		5	6	7	8	9	10		4				2			
36	Apr	3 (h)	Burnley	W 4-0	Clarke 4	31,192	1	11	3		5	6	7	8	**9**	10		4	12			2			
37		10 (a)	Newcastle U	D 1-1	Lorimer	49,640	1	11	3		5	6	7	8	9	10		**4**	12			2			
38		12 (a)	Huddersfield T	D 0-0		43,011	1	11	3		5	6	**7**	8	9	10		4	12			2			
39		17 (h)	West Brom A	L 1-2	Clarke	36,812	1		3	7	5	6		8	9	10	11	**4**				2		12	
40		24 (a)	Southampton	W 3-0	Hollywood (og), Jones 2	30,001	1	2	3	4	5	6		8	9	10	11	7							
41		26 (h)	Arsenal	W 1-0	Charlton	48,350	1	2	3	4	5	6		8	9	10	11	7							
42	May	1 (h)	Nottingham F	W 2-0	Bremner, Lorimer	43,083	1	2	3	4	5	6	7	8	9	10	11								
FINAL LEAGUE POSITION: 2nd in Division One						Appearances	34	41	41	26	41	42	37	41	40	34	18	29	3	3		18	8	6	
						Sub appearances												1	10		3	1		1	
						Goals		5	1	3	6	1	12	19	6	13	1		3						

2 own-goals

FA Cup

Round	Month	Date	Opponents	Result	Scorers	Att	Sprake	Madeley	Cooper	Bremner	Charlton	Hunter	Lorimer	Clarke	Jones	Giles	Gray	Bates	Belfitt	Yorath	Hibbitt	Reaney	Harvey	Davey	Galvin
3	Jan	11 (a)	Rotherham U	D 0-0		24,000	1	11	3	4	5	6	7	8	9	10						2			
R		18 (h)	Rotherham U	W 3-2	Lorimer 2, Giles	36,890	1	11	**3**	4	5	6	7	8		10		12	9			2			
4		23 (h)	Swindon T	W 4-0	Jones 3, Clarke	36,985	1	11			5	6	**7**	8	9	10		4				2		3	12
5	Feb	13 (a)	Colchester U	L 2-3	Hunter, Giles	16,000	1	11	3		5	6	7	8	9	10		4				2			
						Appearances	4	4	3	2	4	4	4	4	3	4		2	1			4		1	
						Sub appearances												1							1
						Goals						1	2	1	3	2									

League Cup

Round	Month	Date	Opponents	Result	Scorers	Att	Sprake	Madeley	Cooper	Bremner	Charlton	Hunter	Lorimer	Clarke	Jones	Giles	Gray	Bates	Belfitt	Yorath	Hibbitt	Reaney	Harvey	Davey	Galvin
2	Sep	8 (a)	Sheffield U	L 0-1		29,573	1	2	3	4	**5**	6	7	8	9		11	10	12						
						Appearances	1	1	1	1	1	1	1	1	1		1	1							
						Sub appearances													1						
						Goals																			

Leeds United also played in the Inter-Cities Fairs Cup (See *Leeds United in Europe*).

1971-72

Manager: Don Revie OBE

	Date	Opponent	Result	Scorers	Att	Sprake	Reaney	Cooper	Bremner	Charlton	Hunter	Lorimer	Clarke	Belfitt	Giles	Madeley	Bates	Jones	Yorath	Harvey	Jordan	Galvin	Edwards	Mann	Gray	Davey
1	Aug 14	(a) Manchester C	W 1-0	Lorimer	38,566	1	2	3	4	5	6	7	8	9	10	11										
2	17	(a) Sheffield U	L 0-3		40,725	1	2		4	5	6	7	8	9	10	3	11									
3	21	(h) Wolves	D 0-0		20,686	1	2	3	4	5	6	7	8		**10**	11	12	9								
4	25	(h) Tottenham H	D 1-1	Bremner	25,099	1	2	3	4	5	6	7	8			11	10	9								
5	28	(a) Ipswich T	W 2-0	Lorimer, Belfitt	26,689	1	2	3	4	5	6	7	8	**9**		11	10		12							
6	Sep 1	(h) Newcastle U	W 5-1	Charlton, Lorimer, Giles (pen), Yorath, Madeley	18,623	1	2	3	4	5	6	7	8	**9**	10	11			12							
7	4	(h) Crystal P	W 2-0	Madeley, Giles (pen)	18,715	1	2	3	4	5	6	7	8	9	10	11										
8	11	(a) Arsenal	L 0-2		51,196		2		4	5	6	7	8	**9**	10	11			3	1	12					
9	18	(h) Liverpool	W 1-0	Lorimer	41,381	1	2	3	4	5	6	7		**9**	10	11					12	8				
10	25	(a) Huddersfield T	L 1-2	Charlton	26,340	1	**2**	3	4	5	6	7		9	10	11						8	12			
11	Oct 2	(h) West Ham U	D 0-0		30,942	1	2	3		5	6	7		9	10	11			4			12		**8**		
12	9	(a) Coventry C	L 1-3	Parker (og)	32,183	1	2	3	4	5	6	7		9	10	11			**8**		12					
13	16	(h) Manchester C	W 3-0	Clarke, Jones, Lorimer	36,004		2	3	4	5	6	7	**8**		10	11		9		1	12					
14	23	(h) Everton	W 3-2	Cooper, Charlton, Lorimer	34,208	1	2	3	4	5	6	7	9		**10**	11					8				12	
15	30	(a) Manchester U	W 1-0	Lorimer	53,960	1	2	3	4	5	6	7		12	10	11					**9**				8	
16	Nov 6	(h) Leicester C	W 2-1	Bremner, Lorimer	39,877	1	2	3	4	5	6	7			10	11					9				8	
17	13	(a) Southampton	L 1-2	Giles	25,331	1	2	3	4	5	6	7			10	11					9				8	
18	20	(h) Stoke C	W 1-0	Lorimer	32,012	1		3	4	5	6	7	8		10	2		9							11	
19	27	(a) Nottingham F	W 2-0	Lorimer, Clarke	29,463	1		3	4	5	6	7	8		10	2		9							11	
20	Dec 4	(h) West Brom A	W 3-0	Giles 2, Lorimer	32,521	1	12	3	4	5	6	7	8		10	2		9							**11**	
21	11	(a) Chelsea	D 0-0		45,867	1		3	4	5	6	7	8		10	2		9							11	
22	18	(a) Crystal P	D 1-1	Lorimer	31,456	1		3	4	5	6	7	8		10	2		9							11	
23	27	(h) Derby C	W 3-0	Gray, Lorimer 2	44,214	1		3	4	5	6	7	8		10	2		9							11	
24	Jan 1	(a) Liverpool	W 2-0	Clarke, Jones	53,847	1	2	3	4		6	7	8		10	5	12	9							**11**	
25	8	(h) Ipswich T	D 2-2	Bremner, Clarke	32,194	1	12	3	4	**5**	6	7	8		10	2		9							11	
26	22	(h) Sheffield U	W 1-0	Clarke	41,038	1		3	4	5	6	7	8		10	2		9							11	
27	29	(a) Tottenham H	L 0-1		46,774	1		3	4	5	6	7	8		10	2		9							11	
28	Feb 12	(a) Everton	D 0-0		45,935	1	**2**	3	4	5	6	7	8		10	9					12				11	
29	19	(h) Manchester U	W 5-1	Jones 3, Clarke, Lorimer	45,399	1		3	4	5	6	7	8		10	2		9							11	
30	Mar 4	(h) Southampton	W 7-0	Clarke 2, Lorimer 3, Charlton, Jones	34,275	1	2		4	5	6	7	8		10	3		9							11	
31	11	(h) Coventry C	W 1-0	Charlton	43,154	1	2		4	5	6	7	8		10	3		9							11	
32	22	(a) Leicester C	D 0-0		32,152	1		3	4	5	6	7	8		10	2		9							11	
33	25	(h) Arsenal	W 3-0	Clarke, Jones, Lorimer	45,055	1	2	3	4	5	6	7	8		10	11		9								
34	27	(h) Nottingham F	W 6-1	Lorimer 2, Gray 2, Clarke 2	40,866	1	2	3	4	5	6	7	8			11		**9**	12						10	
35	31	(a) West Ham U	D 2-2	Gray 2	41,003	1	2	3	4	5	6	7	8			11	12				**9**				10	
36	Apr 1	(a) Derby C	L 0-2		39,450	1	2	3	4	5	6	7	8		10	9									11	
37	5	(h) Huddersfield T	W 3-1	Jones, Lorimer, Gray	46,148	1	12	3	4	5	6	7	**8**		10	2		9							11	
38	8	(a) Stoke C	W 3-0	Jones 2, Lorimer	35,123		12	3	4	5	6	7	**8**		10	2		9		1					11	
39	19	(a) Newcastle U	L 0-1		42,006		2		4	5	6	7	8		10	3		9		1					11	
40	22	(a) West Brom A	W 1-0	Giles (pen)	39,724		2		4	5	6	7	**8**		10	3	11	9		1	12					
41	May 1	(h) Chelsea	W 2-0	Bremner, Jones	46,565		2		4	5	6	7	**8**		10	3	11	9		1	12					
42	8	(a) Wolves	L 1-2	Bremner	53,379		2		4	5	6	7	**8**		10	3	9		12	1					11	
FINAL LEAGUE POSITION: 2nd in Division One					Appearances	35	29	34	41	41	42	42	35	10	38	42	6	24	3	7	5	2		1	25	
					Sub appearances		4							1			3		4		7	1	1		1	
					Goals			1	5	5		23	11	1	6	2		11	1						6	

1 own-goal

FA Cup

Rd	Date	Opponent	Result	Scorers	Att	Sprake	Reaney	Cooper	Bremner	Charlton	Hunter	Lorimer	Clarke	Belfitt	Giles	Madeley	Bates	Jones	Yorath	Harvey	Jordan	Galvin	Edwards	Mann	Gray	Davey
3	Jan 15	(h) Bristol R	W 4-1	Giles 2 (1 pen), Lorimer 2	33,565	1	2	3	4		6	7			10	5	8				**9**	12			11	
4	Feb 5	(a) Liverpool	D 0-0		56,300	1	2	3	4		6	7	8		10	5	11	9								
R	9	(h) Liverpool	W 2-0	Clarke 2	45,821	1	**2**	3	4	5	6	7	8		10	9					12				11	
5	26	(a) Cardiff C	W 2-0	Giles 2	50,000	1		3	4	5	6	7	8		10	2		9							11	
6	Mar 18	(h) Tottenham H	W 2-1	Clarke, Charlton	43,937	1	12	**3**	4	5	6	7	8		10	2		9							11	
SF	Apr 15	(n†) Birmingham C	W 3-0	Jones 2, Lorimer	55,000		2		4	5	6	7	8		10	3		9		1					11	
F	May 6	(n‡) Arsenal	W 1-0	Clarke	100,000		2		4	5	6	7	8		10	3		9		1					11	
†Played at Hillsborough, Sheffield. ‡Played at Wembley Stadium.					Appearances	5	5	5	7	5	7	7	6		7	7	12	5		2	1				6	
					Sub appearances		1														1	1				
					Goals					1		3	4		4			2								

League Cup

Rd	Date	Opponent	Result	Scorers	Att	Sprake	Reaney	Cooper	Bremner	Charlton	Hunter	Lorimer	Clarke	Belfitt	Giles	Madeley	Bates	Jones	Yorath	Harvey	Jordan	Galvin	Edwards	Mann	Gray	Davey
2	Sep 8	(a) Derby C	D 0-0		34,023		2		4	5	6	7	8	9	10	11			3	1						
R	27	(h) Derby C	W 2-0	Lorimer 2	28,132	1	2	3	**4**	5	6	7		9	10	11			8					12		
3	Oct 6	(a) West Ham U	D 0-0		35,890	1		3	4	5	6	7		9	10	11			8							2
R	20	(h) West Ham U	L 0-1*		26,504		2	3	4	5	6	7	8		10	11		**9**		1					12	
				*After extra-time	Appearances	2	3	3	4	4	4	4	2	3	4	4		1	3	2						1
					Sub appearances																			1	1	
					Goals							2														

Leeds United also played in the UEFA Cup and in the play-off for the Inter-Cities Fairs Cup (See *Leeds United in Europe*). Elland Road closed by FA Order for four games: Matches 3 & 7 were played at Leeds Road, Huddersfield; Match 4 at Boothferry Park, Hull; Match 6 at Hillsborough, Sheffield.

1972-73

Manager: Don Revie OBE

	Date	Opponent	Result	Scorers	Att	Harvey	Reaney	Cherry	Bremner	Ellam	Madeley	Lorimer	Bates	Jones	Giles	Gray E	Yorath	Charlton	Jordan	Hunter	Clarke	Gray FT	McQueen	Hampton	Sprake	Galvin	Liddell	Mann	McGinley
1	Aug 12	(a) Chelsea	L 0-4		51,102	1	2	3	4	5	6	7	8	**9**	10	11	12												
2	15	(a) Sheffield U	W 2-0	Colquhoun (og), Giles (pen)	40,159	1	2	3	4		6	7	8		10	11		5	9										
3	19	(h) West Brom A	W 2-0	Clarke, Giles (pen)	36,555	1	2		4		3	7	11		10			5	9	6	8								
4	23	(h) Ipswich T	D 3-3	Jordan 2, Giles (pen)	32,461	1	**2**	12	4		3	7			10	11		5	9	6	8								
5	26	(a) Tottenham H	D 0-0		41,191	1		3	4		2	7			10	11		5	9	6	8								
6	30	(h) Southampton	W 1-0	Bremner	31,401	1	**2**	3	4		11	7	8		10		12	5	9	6									
7	Sep 2	(h) Norwich C	W 2-0	Jordan, Charlton	34,261	1	2	3	4			7			10	11		5	9	6	8								
8	9	(a) Stoke C	D 2-2	Lorimer, Clarke	26,705	1		3	4		2	7			10	11		5	9	6	8								
9	16	(h) Leicester C	W 3-1	Clarke, Jones, Bates	33,930	1		3	4		2	7	11	**9**	10			5	12	6	8								
10	23	(a) Newcastle U	L 2-3	Clarke, Jones	38,962	1	2	3	4			7	11	9	10			5	12	6	**8**								
11	30	(h) Liverpool	L 1-2	Jones	46,468	1		3	4		2	7	11	9	10			5		6	8								
12	Oct 7	(h) Derby C	W 5-0	Giles 2, Clarke, Bremner, Lorimer	36,477	1		3	4		2	7	12	9	**10**	11		5		6	8								
13	14	(a) Everton	W 2-1	Jones, Jordan	47,821	1		3	4		2	7	10	9		11		5	8	6									
14	21	(h) Coventry C	D 1-1	Charlton	36,240	1		3	4		2	7		**9**	10	11		5	12	6	8								
15	28	(a) Wolves	W 2-0	E.Gray, Lorimer	33,731	1		3	4	5	2	7	10			11	9			6	8								
16	Nov 4	(a) Ipswich T	D 2-2	Charlton, Lorimer	27,566	1		3	4		2	7	10	9		11		5		6	8								
17	11	(h) Sheffield U	W 2-1	Clarke 2	31,600	1	2	3	4			7	12	9	10	**11**		5		6	8								
18	18	(a) Crystal P	D 2-2	Jones, Giles	30,107	1	2	3	4	5		7	**11**	9	10		12			6	8								
19	25	(h) Manchester C	W 3-0	Cherry, Lorimer, Clarke	39,879	1	2	3	4		5	7	10	9			11			6	8								
20	Dec 2	(a) Arsenal	L 1-2	Lorimer (pen)	39,108	1	2	3	4		5	7	10	**9**			11		12	6	8								
21	9	(h) West Ham U	W 1-0	Jones	30,270	1	2	3	4		5	7	10	9			11			6	8								
22	16	(h) Birmingham	W 4-0	Clarke 2, Lorimer, Jones	25,285	1	2	3	4		5	7	11	9	10		6				8								
23	23	(a) Manchester U	D 1-1	Clarke	46,382	1	2	3			6	7	11	9	10		4	5			8								
24	26	(h) Newcastle U	W 1-0	Jordan	45,486	1	2	3			5	7	**11**	9	10		4		12	6	8								
25	Jan 6	(h) Tottenham H	W 2-1	Jones, Lorimer (pen)	32,404	1	2	3	4		5	7	11	9	10		12			**6**	8								
26	20	(a) Norwich C	W 2-1	Jordan, Clarke	27,447	1	2	3	4		5	7	11		10				9	6	8								
27	27	(h) Stoke C	W 1-0	Clarke	33,487	1	2	3	4		5	7	11		10		12		**9**	6	8								
28	Feb 10	(a) Leicester C	L 0-2		35,976	1	2	3			5	7	**11**	9	10		4			6	8	12							
29	17	(h) Chelsea	D 1-1	Jones	41,781	1	2	3	4		5	**7**	11	9	10	12				6	8								
30	Mar 3	(a) Derby C	W 3-2	Lorimer 2 (2 pens), Clarke	38,100	1	**2**	3	4		5	7	12	9	10					6	8		11						
31	10	(h) Everton	W 2-1	Clarke, Lorimer	39,663	1		3	4		2	7			10	11			9	6	8		5						
32	24	(h) Wolves	D 0-0		39,078	1	2		4		3	7		9	10	11	12		8	**6**			5						
33	28	(a) West Brom A	D 1-1	Clarke	33,057	1	2	3	4		6	7		9	10	**11**			12		8		5						
34	31	(a) Manchester C	L 0-1		35,772	1	2	3	4		6	7		9	10		**11**		12		8		5						
35	Apr 2	(a) Coventry C	W 1-0	Reaney	24,383	1	2	3	4		6	7		9	10		11	5			8								
36	14	(a) West Ham U	D 1-1	Clarke	38,804	1	2	3	4			7	**11**	9	10		5		12	6	8								
37	18	(h) Manchester U	L 0-1		45,450	1	2	3	4			7	11	**9**	10		6		12		8		5						
38	21	(h) Crystal P	W 4-0	Bremner, Lorimer, F.T.Gray, Clarke	31,173	1		3	**4**	5	2	7		9	10		6		12		8	11							
39	23	(a) Liverpool	L 0-2		55,738	1	2	3	4	5	11	7					10		9	6	8								
40	28	(a) Southampton	L 1-3	Hunter	24,108	1		2	4	12			7			10		**5**	9	6	8	11		3					
41	30	(a) Birmingham C	L 1-2	Jordan	34,449					**5**		8	11				4		9			6		3	1	2	7	10	12
42	May 9	(h) Arsenal	W 6-1	Lorimer 3 (1 pen), Bremner, Jordan 2	25,088	1	2	3	4		11	7		12	10		5		9	6	**8**								
FINAL LEAGUE POSITION: 3rd in Division One					Appearances	41	29	38	38	6	34	41	26	27	33	16	16	18	16	32	36	3	6	2	1	1	1	1	
					Sub appearances			1		1			3	1		1	6		10			1							1
					Goals		1	1	4			15	1	9	6	1		3	9	1	18	1							

1 own-goal

FA Cup

	Date	Opponent	Result	Scorers	Att	Harvey	Reaney	Cherry	Bremner	Ellam	Madeley	Lorimer	Bates	Jones	Giles	Gray E	Yorath	Charlton	Jordan	Hunter	Clarke	Gray FT	McQueen	Hampton	Sprake	Galvin	Liddell	Mann	McGinley
3	Jan 13	(a) Norwich C	D 1-1	Lorimer	32,310	1	2	3	4		5	7	11	9	10					6	8								
R	17	(h) Norwich C	D 1-1*	Giles	36,087	1	2	3	4		5	7	11	9	10					6	8								
2R	29	(n†) Norwich C	W 5-0	Clarke 3, Jones, Lorimer	33,225	1	2	3	4		5	7	11	9	10		12			6	**8**								
4	Feb 3	(h) Plymouth A	W 2-1	Clarke, Bates	38,374	1	2	3			5	7	11	9	10		4			6	8								
5	24	(h) West Brom A	W 2-0	Clarke 2	39,229	1	2	3	4		5	7		9	10	11				6	8								
6	Mar 17	(a) Derby C	W 1-0	Lorimer	38,350	1	2	3	**4**		5	7	12	9	10	11				6	8								
SF	Apr 7	(n‡) Wolves	W 1-0	Bremner	52,505	1	2	3	4		11	7		9	10		6	**5**	12		8								
F	May 5	(n§) Sunderland	L 0-1		100,000	1	2	3	4		5	7		9	10	**11**	12			6	8								
*After extra-time. †Played at Villa Park, Birmingham. ‡Played at Maine Road, Manchester. §Played at Wembley Stadium.					Appearances	8	8	8	7		8	8	4	8	8	3	2	1		7	8								
					Sub appearances								1				2		1										
					Goals				1			3	1	1	1						6								

League Cup

	Date	Opponent	Result	Scorers	Att	Harvey	Reaney	Cherry	Bremner	Ellam	Madeley	Lorimer	Bates	Jones	Giles	Gray E	Yorath	Charlton	Jordan	Hunter	Clarke	Gray FT	McQueen	Hampton	Sprake	Galvin	Liddell	Mann	McGinley
2	Sep 6	(h) Burnley	W 4-0	Lorimer 2, Jones, Cherry	20,857	1	2	3	4			7	8	12		10		5	9	6							**11**		
3	Oct 4	(a) Aston Villa	D 1-1	Charlton	46,185	1		3	4		2	7	10	9			11	5		6	8								
R	11	(h) Aston Villa	W 2-0	Nicholl (og), Jones	28,894	1		3	4		2	7	10	9		11	12	**5**		6	8								
4	31	(a) Liverpool	D 2-2	Jones, Lorimer	44,609	1		3	4	5	2	7	10	9		11				6	8								
R	Nov 22	(h) Liverpool	L 0-1		34,856	1	2	3	4		11	7		9	**10**			5	12	6	8								
					Appearances	5	2	5	5	1	4	5	4	4	1	3	1	4	1	5	4						1		
					Sub appearances									1			1		1										
					Goals			1				3		3				1											

1 own-goal

Leeds United also played in the European Cup-winners' Cup (See *Leeds United in Europe*).

1973-74

Manager: Don Revie OBE

No	Date	Venue	Opponents	Result	Scorers	Att	Harvey	Reaney	Madeley	Bremner	McQueen	Hunter	Lorimer	Clarke	Jones	Giles	Gray E	Cherry	Jordan	Yorath	Bates	Gray FT	Ellam	Cooper	Stewart	Liddell	O'Neill
1	Aug 25	(h)	Everton	W 3-1	Bremner, Giles, Jones	39,325	1	2	3	4	5	6	7	8	9	10	11										
2	28	(a)	Arsenal	W 2-1	Lorimer, Madeley	47,429	1	2	3	4	5	6	7	8	9	10	11										
3	Sep 1	(a)	Tottenham H	W 3-0	Bremner 2, Clarke	42,801	1	2	3	4	5	6	7	**8**	9	10	11	12									
4	5	(h)	Wolves	W 4-1	Lorimer 2 (1 pen), Jones, Bremner	39,946	1	2	3	4	5	6	7	8	9	10	**11**		12								
5	8	(h)	Birmingham C	W 3-0	Lorimer 3 (1 pen)	39,736	1	2	3	4	5	6	**7**	8	9	10	11		12								
6	11	(a)	Wolves	W 2-0	Jones, Clarke	36,980	1		3	4	5	6		8	9	**10**		2	11	7	12						
7	15	(a)	Southampton	W 2-1	Clarke 2	27,770	1	2	10	4	5	6		8	9		11	3	7								
8	22	(h)	Manchester U	D 0-0		47,058	1		3	4	5	6		8	9	10	11	2	7								
9	29	(a)	Norwich C	W 1-0	Giles	31,993	1	2	11	4	5	6		8	9	10		3	7								
10	Oct 6	(h)	Stoke C	D 1-1	Jones	36,562	1	2	5	4		6	**7**	8	9	10		3		12	11						
11	13	(a)	Leicester C	D 2-2	Jones, Bremner	36,978	1		3	4	5	6	7	8	9	**10**		2	12		11						
12	20	(h)	Liverpool	W 1-0	Jones	44,911	1		2	4	5	6	7	8	9			3		11	10						
13	27	(a)	Manchester C	W 1-0	Bates	45,346	1		3	4	5	6	7	8	9	**10**		2	12		11						
14	Nov 3	(h)	West Ham U	W 4-1	Bates, Jones 2, Clarke	36,869	1	2	11	4	5	6	7	8	9			3			10						
15	10	(a)	Burnley	D 0-0		37,894	1	2	11	4	5	6	7	8	9			3	12		**10**						
16	17	(h)	Coventry C	W 3-0	Clarke, Jordan, Bremner	35,552	1	2	11	4	5	6	**7**	8				3	9	12	10						
17	24	(a)	Derby C	D 0-0		36,003	1	2		4	5	6	7	8				3	9	11	10						
18	Dec 1	(h)	Queen's Park R	D 2-2	Bremner, Jones	32,194	1	2		4	5	6	7	8	9			3	12	11	**10**						
19	8	(a)	Ipswich T	W 3-0	Yorath, Jones, Clarke	27,110	1	2	11	4	5	6	7	**8**	9			3	12	10							
20	15	(a)	Chelsea	W 2-1	Jordan, Jones	40,768	1	2	11	4	5	6	7		9			3	8	10							
21	22	(h)	Norwich C	W 1-0	Yorath	34,747	1	2	11	4	5	6	7		9			3	8	10							
22	26	(a)	Newcastle U	W 1-0	Madeley	54,474	1	2	11	4	5	6	7		9			3	8	10							
23	29	(a)	Birmingham C	D 1-1	Jordan	50,451	1	2	11	4	5	6	7		9			3	8	10							
24	Jan 1	(h)	Tottenham H	D 1-1	Jones	46,545	1	2	11	4	5	6	7	**8**	9			3	10	12							
25	12	(h)	Southampton	W 2-1	Jones, Jordan	35,000	1	2	5	4		6	7		9			3	8	10		11					
26	19	(a)	Everton	D 0-0		55,811	1	2	5	4		6	7		9			3	8	10		**11**	12				
27	Feb 2	(h)	Chelsea	D 1-1	Cherry	41,510	1	2	11	4	5	6	7	8				3	9	12				**10**			
28	5	(h)	Arsenal	W 3-1	Simpson (og), Jordan 2	26,778	1	2	11	4		6	7	8				3	9	10			5				
29	9	(a)	Manchester U	W 2-0	Jones, Jordan	60,025	1	**2**	11	4	5	6	7	8	9			3	12	10							
30	23	(a)	Stoke C	L 2-3	Bremner, Clarke	39,598	1		11	4		6	7	8		**10**		3	9	2			5	12			
31	26	(h)	Leicester C	D 1-1	Lorimer (pen)	30,489		2	11	4		6	7	8				3	9	**10**		12	5		1		
32	Mar 2	(h)	Newcastle U	D 1-1	Clarke	46,611		2		4	5	6	**7**	8				3	9	10		11			1	12	
33	9	(h)	Manchester C	W 1-0	Lorimer (pen)	36,578		2	11	4	5	6	7	8				3	9	10					1		
34	16	(a)	Liverpool	L 0-1		56,003	1	2	11	4	5	6	7	8	12			3	**9**	10							
35	23	(h)	Burnley	L 1-4	Clarke	39,335	1	2	11	4	5	6	**7**	8	12			3	9	10							
36	30	(a)	West Ham U	L 1-3	Clarke	37,480	1	2	11	4	5	6		8	12	7		3	**9**	10							
37	Apr 6	(h)	Derby C	W 2-0	Lorimer, Bremner	37,838	1	2	11	4	5	6	7			8		3	9	10							
38	13	(a)	Coventry C	D 0-0		35,182	1	2	11	4	5	6	7			10		3	9	8							
39	15	(h)	Sheffield U	D 0-0		41,140	1	2	11	4	5	6	7	8	9	**10**		3				12					
40	16	(a)	Sheffield U	W 2-0	Lorimer 2 (1 pen)	39,972	1	2	11	4	5	6	7	**8**	9			3		10		12					
41	20	(h)	Ipswich T	W 3-2	Lorimer, Bremner, Clarke	44,015	1	2	10	4	5	6	7	8	9		11	3									
42	27	(a)	Queen's Park R	W 1-0	Clarke	35,353	1	**2**	11	4	5	6	7	8		10		3	9	12							
FINAL LEAGUE POSITION: 1st in Division One						Appearances	39	36	39	42	36	42	37	34	28	17	8	37	25	23	9	3	3	1	3		
						Sub appearances									3			1	8	5	1	3	1	1		1	
						Goals			2	10			12	13	14	2		1	7	2	2						

1 own-goal

FA Cup

Round	Date	Venue	Opponents	Result	Scorers	Att	Harvey	Reaney	Madeley	Bremner	McQueen	Hunter	Lorimer	Clarke	Jones	Giles	Gray E	Cherry	Jordan	Yorath	Bates	Gray FT	Ellam	Cooper	Stewart	Liddell	O'Neill
3	Jan 5	(a)	Wolves	D 1-1	Lorimer (pen)	38,132	1	2	11	4	5	6	7		9			3	8	**10**		12					
R	9	(h)	Wolves	W 1-0	Jones	42,747		2	11	4	**5**	6	7	10	9			3	8	12					1		
4	26	(a)	Peterborough U	W 4-1	Lorimer, Jordan 2, Yorath	28,000	1	2	11	4		6	7					10	9	8			5	3			
5	Feb 16	(a)	Bristol C	D 1-1	Bremner	37,000	1		11	4	5	6	7	12	9	**10**		3	8	2							
R	19	(h)	Bristol C	L 0-1		47,128	1		11	4		6	7	8	9	**10**		2	12				5	3			
						Appearances	4	3	5	5	3	5	5	2	4	2		5	4	3			2	2	1		
						Sub appearances								1					1	1		1					
						Goals				1			2		1				2	1							

League Cup

Round	Date	Venue	Opponents	Result	Scorers	Att	Harvey	Reaney	Madeley	Bremner	McQueen	Hunter	Lorimer	Clarke	Jones	Giles	Gray E	Cherry	Jordan	Yorath	Bates	Gray FT	Ellam	Cooper	Stewart	Liddell	O'Neill
2	Oct 8	(a)	Ipswich T	L 0-2		26,385	1	**2**	10	4		6			9			3		8		11	5			7	12
						Appearances	1	1	1	1		1			1			1		1		1	1			1	
						Sub appearances																					1
						Goals																					

Leeds United also played in the UEFA Cup (See *Leeds United in Europe*).

1974-75

Manager: Brian Clough until September then Jimmy Armfield

No	Month	Date / Opponent	Result	Scorers	Attendance	Harvey	Reaney	Cooper	Bremner	McQueen	Cherry	Lorimer	Madeley	Jordan	Giles	McKenzie	Bates	McGovern	Hunter	Clarke	O'Hare	Yorath	Gray FT	Stewart	Gray E	Hampton	Stevenson	Liddell	Letheran	Harris	Thomas
1	Aug	17 (a) Stoke C	L 0-3		33,534	1	2	3	4	5	6	7	8	9	10	11															
2		21 (h) Queen's Park R	L 0-1		31,497	1	2	3		5	6	7	8	9	10	11	4														
3		24 (h) Birmingham C	W 1-0	Clarke	30,820	1	2			5	3	7	**11**	12	10			4	6	8	9										
4		27 (a) Queen's Park R	D 1-1	Yorath	24,965	1	2			5	3	7			10			4	6	8	9	11									
5		31 (a) Manchester C	L 1-2	Clarke	37,919	1	2			5	3	7		12	10			4	6	8	9	**11**									
6	Sep	7 (h) Luton T	D 1-1	Clarke	26,450	1	2			5	3	7	11		10			4	6	8	9										
7		14 (a) Burnley	L 1-2	Lorimer	25,122	1	2			5	3	7	11	9	10				6	8		4									
8		21 (h) Sheffield U	W 5-1	Clarke 2, McQueen, Lorimer (pen), Yorath	33,382	1	2			5	3	7	11	9	10				6	8		4									
9		28 (a) Everton	L 2-3	Clarke, Yorath	41,824	1	2				3	7	5	9			10		6	8		4	11								
10	Oct	5 (h) Arsenal	W 2-0	McKenzie 2	32,784	1	2	**3**		5		7	11	9	10	8	12		6			4									
11		12 (a) Ipswich T	D 0-0		29,815	1	2	11		5	3	7		9	10				6	8		4									
12		15 (a) Birmingham C	L 0-1		36,513	1	2	11		5	3	7		9	10				6	8		4									
13		19 (h) Wolves	W 2-0	Clarke, McKenzie	31,224	1	2	3		5		7	11	9	12	10			**6**	8		4									
14		26 (a) Liverpool	L 0-1		54,996	1	2	3		5		7	11	9	**10**	8			6	12		4									
15	Nov	2 (h) Derby C	L 0-1		33,551	1	2	3		5		**7**	11		10	12			6	8	9	4									
16		9 (a) Coventry C	W 3-1	O'Hare, Hindley (og), Bremner	25,414	1	2	11	4	5	3	7	10							8	9	6									
17		16 (h) Middlesbrough	D 2-2	McKenzie 2	45,488	1	2	3	4	5			11	9	10	7				8		6									
18		23 (a) Carlisle U	W 2-1	Jordan, McKenzie	19,975	1	2		4	5	3		6	9	10	7				8		11									
19		30 (h) Chelsea	W 2-0	Cherry, Clarke	30,441	1	2		4	5	3		6	9	10	7				8		11									
20	Dec	4 (h) Tottenham H	W 2-1	McKenzie, Lortimer (pen)	25,832		2		4	5	3	10	6	9		7				8		11		1							
21		7 (a) West Ham U	L 1-2	McKenzie	39,562	1	2		4	5	3	10	6	9		7				8		11									
22		14 (h) Stoke C	W 3-1	McQueen, Lorimer, Yorath	34,685	1	2		4	5	3	10	6	9	12	7				8		**11**									
23		21 (a) Newcastle U	L 0-3		32,535	1	2		4	5	3	10	6	9		7				8		11									
24		26 (h) Burnley	D 2-2	Jordan, Lorimer	34,724	1	2		4	5		10	6	**9**	12	7				8		11	3								
25		28 (a) Leicester C	W 2-0	F.T.Gray, McKenzie	29,699		2		4	5		9	6		10	7				8		11	3	1							
26	Jan	11 (h) West Ham U	W 2-1	Clarke, McKenzie	40,099	1	2		4	5		9	6		10	7				8			3		11						
27		18 (a) Chelsea	W 2-0	McKenzie, Yorath	34,733	1	2		4	5		9	6		10	7				**8**		12	3		11						
28	Feb	1 (h) Coventry C	D 0-0		33,901	1	2		4	5		7	6			9				8		10	3		11						
29		8 (a) Derby C	D 0-0		33,641	1	2		4	**5**	12	7	6			9				8		10	3		11						
30		22 (a) Middlesbrough	W 1-0	Clarke	39,500		2	11	4			7	5	9	10				6	8			3	1							
31		25 (h) Carlisle U	W 3-1	Lorimer, Clarke, E.Gray	32,346		2		4			7	6	9	10				5	8			3	1	11						
32	Mar	1 (h) Manchester C	D 2-2	Lorimer 2	47,489		**2**		4			7	5	12		9			6	8		10	3	1	11						
33		15 (h) Everton	D 0-0		50,084				4		2	7	5			9			6	8		10	3	1	11						
34		22 (a) Luton T	L 1-2	Jordan	23,048		2			**5**	12		4	9	10	7			6			8	3	1	11						
35		29 (h) Newcastle U	D 1-1	Clarke	40,994		2		4		**3**		5	9	10	7			6	8			11	1		12					
36		31 (h) Leicester C	D 2-2	Clarke, Giles	29,898		2		4				5	9	10	7			6	**8**		11	3	1		12					
37	Apr	1 (a) Sheffield U	D 1-1	Madeley	38,442				4			7	5			9			6			10	3	1	11		2	8			
38		5 (h) Liverpool	L 0-2		34,971				4	5	12	7	2	9		8			6			10	**3**	1	11						
39		12 (a) Arsenal	W 2-1	Clarke, Hunter	36,619		2		4	5	3	12	11	9	10	**7**			6	8				1							
40		19 (h) Ipswich T	W 2-1	Cherry, Harris	30,174		2		4	5	3	7	8		**10**				6			9			11				1	12	
41		26 (a) Wolves	D 1-1	F.T.Gray	34,875		2		4	5	3	7	6							**8**		10	11	1						9	12
42		28 (a) Tottenham H	L 2-4	Jordan, Lorimer	49,886		2		4		3	7	**5**	9					6			10	8	1	11					12	
					Appearances	27	39	11	27	33	24	35	38	26	26	26	2	4	25	33	6	32	18	14	12		1	1	1	1	
					Sub appearances						3	1		3	3	1	1			1		1				2				2	1
					Goals				1	2	2	9	1	4	1	11			1	14	1	5	2		1					1	

FINAL LEAGUE POSITION: 9th in Division One

1 own-goal

FA Cup

Round	Month	Date / Opponent	Result	Scorers	Attendance	Harvey	Reaney	Cooper	Bremner	McQueen	Cherry	Lorimer	Madeley	Jordan	Giles	McKenzie	Bates	McGovern	Hunter	Clarke	O'Hare	Yorath	Gray FT	Stewart	Gray E	Hampton	Stevenson	Liddell	Letheran	Harris	Thomas
3	Jan	4 (h) Cardiff C	W 4-1	E.Gray, Clarke 2, McKenzie	31,572	1	**2**		4	5	12	7	6		10	9				8			3		11						
4		25 (h) Wimbledon	D 0-0		46,230	1	2		4	5		9	6		10	7						8	3		11						
R	Feb	10(a†)Wimbledon	W 1-0	Bassett (og)	45,071	1	2		4				6	9	10	7				8		5	3		11						
5		18 (a) Derby C	W 1-0	Nish (og)	35,298		2		4	5			6	9		7				8		10	3	1	11						
6	Mar	8 (a) Ipswich T	D 0-0		38,010				4	5			2	9	10				6	8		7	3	1	11						
R		11 (h) Ipswich T	D 1-1*	McKenzie	50,074		**2**		4			7	5	9	10	12			6	8		11	3	1							
2R		25(n‡)Ipswich T	D 0-0*		35,195		2		4			**7**	5	9	10	12			6	8		11	3	1							
3R		27(n‡)Ipswich T	L 2-3	Clarke, Giles	19,510		2		4				5	9	10	12			6	8		**11**	3	1	7						
					Appearances	3	7		8	4		4	8	6	7	4			4	7		7	8	5	6						
					Sub appearances						1					3															
					Goals										1	2				3					1						

†Played at Selhurst Park, London. *After extra-time. ‡Played at Filbert Street, Leicester.

2 own-goals

League Cup

Round	Month	Date / Opponent	Result	Scorers	Attendance	Harvey	Reaney	Cooper	Bremner	McQueen	Cherry	Lorimer	Madeley	Jordan	Giles	McKenzie	Bates	McGovern	Hunter	Clarke	O'Hare	Yorath	Gray FT	Stewart	Gray E	Hampton	Stevenson	Liddell	Letheran	Harris	Thomas
2	Sep	10 (a) Huddersfield T	D 1-1	Lorimer	15,013	1	2			5	3	7	11	9	10		4		6	8											
R		24 (h) Huddersfield T	D 1-1*	Clarke	18,496	1	2				3	7	5	9	**10**	11	12		6	8		4									
2R	Oct	7 (h) Huddersfield T	W 2-1	Bates, Lorimer (pen)	14,599	1	2			5	3	7	11			8	**10**		6		9	4	12								
3		9 (a) Bury	W 2-1	Lorimer, Cherry	16,354		2	8	**4**	5	3	7	12	9		11			6			10		1							
4	Nov	13 (a) Chester	L 0-3		19,000	1	2	3	**10**	5	6	7	11	9			12			8		4									
					Appearances	4	5	2	2	4	5	5	4	4	2	3	2		4	3	1	4		1							
					Sub appearances								1				2						1								
					Goals						1	3					1			1											

*After extra-time

Leeds United also played in the European Cup (See *Leeds United in Europe*) and in the FA Charity Shield (See *Invitation Tournaments*).

1975-76

Manager: Jimmy Armfield

	Date	Opponent	Result	Scorers	Att	Harvey	Reaney	Gray FT	Bremner	McQueen	Cherry	Lorimer	Clarke	McKenzie	Yorath	Madeley	Hunter	Gray E	Harris	Stewart	Jordan	Stevenson	Parkinson	Bates	Hampton	McNiven
1	Aug 16	(a) Aston Villa	W 2-1	Lorimer 2 (1 pen)	46,026	1	2	3	4	5	6	7	8	9	10	11										
2	20	(a) Norwich C	D 1-1	Cherry	25,301	1	2	3	4	5	6	7	8	9	10	11										
3	23	(h) Ipswich T	W 1-0	Lorimer	30,912	1	2	3		5	6	7	8	9	10		4	11								
4	26	(h) Liverpool	L 0-3		36,186	1	2	3	4	5	6	7	8	9	10	11										
5	30	(a) Sheffield U	W 2-0	McKenzie, Clarke	29,996	1		3	4	5	2	7	8	9	10	11	6									
6	Sep 6	(h) Wolves	W 3-0	McQueen, Clarke, McKenzie	24,460	1		3	4	5	2	7	8	9	10	11	6									
7	13	(a) Stoke C	L 2-3	Lorimer 2 (1 pen)	23,139	1		3	4	5	2	7	8	**9**	10	11	6		12							
8	20	(h) Tottenham H	D 1-1	Lorimer	27,372	1		3	4	5	2	**7**	8	9	10	11	6	12								
9	27	(a) Burnley	W 1-0	Cherry	23,190	1	2	3	9		6	7	8		10	5	4	11								
10	Oct 4	(h) Queen's Park R	W 2-1	Clarke, Lorimer	30,943	1	12	3	4	**5**	2	7	8	9	10	11	6									
11	11	(h) Manchester U	L 1-2	Clarke	40,264		2	3	4		7		8	**9**	10	5	6	11	12	1						
12	18	(a) Birmingham C	D 2-2	Cherry, Hunter	33,775	1	2	3	4		7		8	9	10	5	6	11								
13	25	(h) Coventry C	W 2-0	Yorath, Clarke	25,946	1	2	3	4		11	7	8	9	10	5	6									
14	Nov 1	(a) Derby C	L 2-3	Cherry, McKenzie	33,107	1	2	3	4		5	7	8	9	10	11	6									
15	8	(h) Newcastle U	W 3-0	McKenzie 2, Yorath	39,304	1	2	3	4	**5**	8	7		9	10	6		11	12							
16	15	(a) Middlesbrough	D 0-0		33,000	1	2	3	4		6	7	8	9	10	5		11								
17	22	(h) Birmingham C	W 3-0	Bremner, McKenzie 2	26,640	1	2	3	4		6	7	8	9	10	5		11								
18	29	(h) Everton	W 5-2	Lorimer 2 (1 pen), Clarke 2, E.Gray	30,879	1	2	3	4		6	7	8	9	**10**	5		11			12					
19	Dec 6	(a) Arsenal	W 2-1	McKenzie 2	36,003	1	2	3	4		6	7	8	9	10	5		11								
20	13	(a) Ipswich T	L 1-2	McKenzie	26,858	1	2	3	4		6	7	8	9	10	5		11								
21	20	(h) Aston Villa	W 1-0	Clarke	29,118	1	2	3	4		6	7	8	9	10	5		11								
22	26	(a) Manchester C	W 1-0	Madeley	48,077	1	2	3	4		6	7	8	9	10	5		11								
23	27	(h) Leicester C	W 4-0	Clarke, McKenzie 2, Lorimer	45,139	1	**2**	3	4		10	7	8	9		5	6	11	12							
24	Jan 10	(h) Stoke C	W 2-0	McKenzie, Bremner	36,906	1	2	**3**	4		11	7	8	9	10	5	6		12							
25	17	(a) Wolves	D 1-1	McAlle (og)	34,925	1	2	3	4		11	7	8	9	10	5	6									
26	31	(h) Norwich C	L 0-3		27,254	1	2	3			4	**7**	8	9	10	5	6	11			12					
27	Feb 7	(a) Liverpool	L 0-2		54,525	1	**2**	3				4	8	7	10	5	6	11			9	12				
28	21	(h) Middlesbrough	L 0-2		32,994	1	2	3				**4**	8	7	10	5	6	11			9		12			
29	23	(a) West Ham U	D 1-1	McKenzie	28,025	1	2	3			8			7	10	5	6	11			9			4		
30	28	(a) Coventry C	W 1-0	F.T.Gray	25,563	1	2	3			8		12	7	10	5	6	**11**			9			4		
31	Mar 2	(h) Derby C	D 1-1	F.T.Gray (pen)	40,608	1	2	3			11		8	7	10	5	6				9			4		
32	9	(h) West Ham U	D 1-1	Jordan	28,453	1	**2**	3			11		8	7	10	5	6	12			9			4		
33	13	(a) Manchester U	L 2-3	Cherry, Bremner	59,429	1		3	4		2	10	8	7	5		6	11			9					
34	20	(a) Everton	W 3-1	Bremner, Jordan, Harris	28,566	1		3	4		2		8		10	5	6	11	7		9					
35	27	(h) Arsenal	W 3-0	Clarke 2, Bremner	26,657	1	2	3	4		10		8	12		5	6	11	7		**9**					
36	31	(a) Newcastle U	W 3-2	Oates (og), Cherry, Harris	32,685	1	2	3	4		10		8			5	6	11	7		9					
37	Apr 3	(h) Burnley	W 2-1	McKenzie, Hampton	25,384		2	3	4		10			8	**11**	5	6		7	1	9				12	
38	10	(a) Tottenham H	D 0-0		40,359	1		3	4		2		8	10			6	11	7		9		5			
39	14	(h) Sheffield U	L 0-1		22,799	1		3	4		2	12	8	9		10	6	11	**7**				5			
40	17	(h) Manchester C	W 2-1	McNiven, Harris	33,514	1		3	4		2			10		8	6	11	7		9		**5**			12
41	20	(a) Leicester C	L 1-2	McKenzie	24,240	1		3	4		2			10	8	5	6	**11**	7		9					12
42	24	(a) Queen's Park R	L 0-2		31,002	1	2	**3**	4		8	12		10		5	6	11	7		9					
FINAL LEAGUE POSITION: 5th in Division One					Appearances	40	31	42	34	10	40	27	35	38	35	39	31	27	9	2	15		3	4		
					Sub appearances		1					2	1	1				2	5		2	1	1		1	2
					Goals			2	5	1	6	10	11	16	2	1	1	1	3		2				1	1

2 own-goals

FA Cup

	Date	Opponent	Result	Scorers	Att	Harvey	Reaney	Gray FT	Bremner	McQueen	Cherry	Lorimer	Clarke	McKenzie	Yorath	Madeley	Hunter	Gray E	Harris	Stewart	Jordan	Stevenson	Parkinson	Bates	Hampton	McNiven
3	Jan 3	(a) Notts C	W 1-0	Clarke	31,129	1	2	3	4		6	7	8	9	11	5	10									
4	24	(h) Crystal P	L 0-1		43,116	1	2	3	**4**		6	7	8	9	10	5	12	11								
					Appearances	2	2	2	2		2	2	2	2	2	2	1	1								
					Sub appearances												1									
					Goals								1													

League Cup

	Date	Opponent	Result	Scorers	Att	Harvey	Reaney	Gray FT	Bremner	McQueen	Cherry	Lorimer	Clarke	McKenzie	Yorath	Madeley	Hunter	Gray E	Harris	Stewart	Jordan	Stevenson	Parkinson	Bates	Hampton	McNiven
2	Sep 9	(h) Ipswich T	W 3-2	McKenzie, Lorimer (pen), Clarke	15,318	1		3	4		2	7	8	9	10	5	6	11								
3	Oct 8	(h) Notts C	L 0-1		19,122	1	2	10	4		3	7		9		5	6	11	12							**8**
					Appearances	2	1	2	2		2	2	1	2	1	2	2	2								1
					Sub appearances														1							
					Goals							1	1	1												

1976-77

Manager: Jimmy Armfield

No	Date	Opponent	Result	Scorers	Att	Harvey	Reaney	Gray FT	Cherry	Madeley	Hunter	Lorimer	Clarke	McNiven	Currie	Gray E	Harris	Yorath	Bremner	Jordan	McQueen	Hampton	Hankin	Stevenson	Stewart	Thomas	McGhie	Whyte
1	Aug 21	(h) West Brom A	D 2-2	Harris, Clarke	40,248	1	2	3	4	5	6	**7**	8	9	10	11	12											
2	24	(a) Birmingham C	D 0-0		35,399	1	2	3	4	5	6		8	9	10	11		7										
3	28	(a) Coventry C	L 2-4	F.T.Gray, Currie	18,227	1	2	3	7	5	6		8		10	11			4	9								
4	Sep 4	(h) Derby C	W 2-0	E.Gray, Cherry	33,352	1	2	3	7	5	6		8	9	10	11			4									
5	11	(a) Tottenham H	L 0-1		35,525	1	2	3	7	5	6		8	9	10	11			4									
6	18	(h) Newcastle U	D 2-2	McNiven, Harris	35,089	1	2	3	7	5	6		8	9	**10**	11	12		4									
7	25	(a) Middlesbrough	L 0-1		25,000	1	2	3	7	8	6	4		9		**11**	10				5	12						
8	Oct 2	(h) Manchester U	L 0-2		44,512	1	2	3	7	4	**6**	12	8		10	11				9	5							
9	6	(a) West Ham U	W 3-1	E.Gray, Lorimer, Harris	21,909	1	2	10	7	4	6	8				**11**	12			9	5	3						
10	16	(a) Norwich C	W 2-1	F.T.Gray, E.Gray	25,217	1	2	6	7	4		8			10	11				9	5	3						
11	23	(h) Liverpool	D 1-1	McNiven	44,696	1	2	**10**	4	6		7		12	8	11				9	5	3						
12	30	(h) Arsenal	W 2-1	Cherry, Jordan	33,566	1	2	6	7	4		**8**		12	10	11				9	5	3						
13	Nov 6	(a) Everton	W 2-0	McQueen, Jordan	32,618	1	2	6	7	**4**					10	11	12			9	5	3	8					
14	10	(h) Stoke C	D 1-1	Lorimer	29,199	1	2	6	4			7			10	11				9	5	3	8					
15	20	(a) Ipswich T	D 1-1	McQueen	30,096	1	2	6	4			7			10	11				9	5	3	8					
16	27	(h) Leicester C	D 2-2	Lorimer, McNiven	29,713	1	2	6	4			7		12	**10**	11				9	5	3	8					
17	Dec 11	(h) Aston Villa	L 1-3	McNiven	31,232	1	2	6	4			7		8		11				9	5	3		10				
18	27	(h) Manchester C	L 0-2		48,708	1	2	10	4	6		7	8			11				9	5	3						
19	29	(a) Sunderland	W 1-0	Jordan	26,999	1		10	6	4		7	8			11				9	5	3		2				
20	Jan 3	(a) Arsenal	D 1-1	Clarke	44,090	1	2	7	**4**	6		12	8		10	11				9	5	3						
21	22	(a) West Brom A	W 2-1	E.Gray, McQueen	25,958	1	2	7	4	6			8		10	11				9	5	3						
22	Feb 2	(h) Birmingham C	W 1-0	McQueen	22,805	1	2	7	4	6			8		10	11				9	5	3						
23	5	(h) Coventry C	L 1-2	Jordan	26,058	1	2	7	4	6		10	8			11	12			9	5	**3**						
24	12	(a) Derby C	W 1-0	Jordan	28,350	1	2	7	4	6		11	8		10					9	5	3						
25	19	(h) Tottenham H	W 2-1	Jordan, Clarke	26,858	1	2	7	4	6			8		10	11				9	5	3						
26	Mar 2	(a) Newcastle U	L 0-3		31,995	1	2	7	4	6			8	12	**10**	11				9	5	3						
27	5	(h) Middlesbrough	W 2-1	McQueen 2	32,152		2	7	**4**	6		12	8		10	11				9	5	3			1			
28	8	(a) Queen's Park R	D 0-0		20,386		2	7	4	6		10	**8**			11				9	5			3	1	12		
29	12	(a) Manchester U	L 0-1		60,612		2	7	4	6		8		12	**10**	11				9	5	3			1			
30	23	(h) Norwich C	W 3-2	Reaney, Hampton, Jordan	18,700		2	7	4	6		12	8		10	**11**				9	5	3			1			
31	Apr 2	(a) Liverpool	L 1-3	McQueen	48,791			7	6	4		**8**			10	11				9	5	3		2	1	12		
32	8	(a) Manchester C	L 1-2	Jordan	47,727		2	7	4	6		8			10	11				9	5	3			1			
33	9	(h) Sunderland	D 1-1	Cherry	32,966		2	7	4	6		8			10	**11**	12			9	5	3			1			
34	12	(a) Stoke C	L 1-2	Jordan	17,960		2	7	4	6		8			10		11			9	5	3			1			
35	16	(h) Ipswich T	W 2-1	McGhie, Clarke (pen)	28,578		2	3	4	6		12	8		10		7			**9**	5				1		11	
36	26	(h) West Ham U	D 1-1	Jordan	16,891				4	6				8	10	11	7			9	5	3		2	1			
37	30	(h) Bristol C	W 2-0	Thomas, E.Gray	21,461			3	4	6					10	11	12			**9**	5			2	1	7	8	
38	May 4	(h) Everton	D 0-0		22,175			3	4	6				8	10	11	9				5			2	1	7		
39	7	(a) Aston Villa	L 1-2	McNiven	38,205			8	4	6				**9**	10		11				5	3		2	1	7		12
40	10	(a) Bristol C	L 0-1		23,587			9	4	6				8	10	11	12				5	3		2	1	**7**		
41	14	(h) Queen's Park R	L 0-1		22,226			9	4	6				8	10	11	12			**7**		3		2	1			5
42	16	(a) Leicester C	W 1-0	F.T.Gray	13,642		2	9	4	6		5		8	10		11					3			1	7		
FINAL LEAGUE POSITION: 10th in Division One					Appearances	26	34	41	42	38	9	21	20	13	35	37	7	1	4	32	34	30	4	10	16	5	2	1
					Sub appearances							5		5			9					1				2		1
					Goals		1	3	3			3	4	5	1	5	3			10	7	1				1	1	

FA Cup

Rd	Date	Opponent	Result	Scorers	Att	Harvey	Reaney	Gray FT	Cherry	Madeley	Hunter	Lorimer	Clarke	McNiven	Currie	Gray E	Harris	Yorath	Bremner	Jordan	McQueen	Hampton	Hankin	Stevenson	Stewart	Thomas	McGhie	Whyte
3	Jan 8	(h) Norwich C	W 5-2	Clarke, Reaney, Jordan, McQueen, Hampton	28,130	1	2	4		6		7	8		10	11				9	5	3						
4	29	(a) Birmingham C	W 2-1	Jordan, Clarke	38,000	1	2	7	4	6			8		10	11				9	5	3						
5	Feb 26	(h) Manchester C	W 1-0	Cherry	47,731	1	2	7	4	6			8		10	11				9	5	3						
6	Mar 19	(a) Wolves	W 1-0	E.Gray	50,000		2	7	4	6			8		10	11				9	5	3			1			
SF	Apr 23	(n†) Manchester U	L 1-2	Clarke (pen)	55,000		2	**7**	4	6		12	8		10	11				9	5	3			1			
†Played at Hillsborough, Sheffield.					Appearances	3	5	5	4	5		1	5		5	5				5	5	5			2			
					Sub appearances							1																
					Goals		1		1				3			1				2	1	1						

League Cup

Rd	Date	Opponent	Result	Scorers	Att	Harvey	Reaney	Gray FT	Cherry	Madeley	Hunter	Lorimer	Clarke	McNiven	Currie	Gray E	Harris	Yorath	Bremner	Jordan	McQueen	Hampton	Hankin	Stevenson	Stewart	Thomas	McGhie	Whyte
2	Sep 1	(a) Stoke C	L 1-2	Currie	22,559		2	3	7	5	6		8		10		11		4	9					1			
					Appearances		1	1	1	1	1		1		1		1		1	1					1			
					Sub appearances																							
					Goals										1													

1977-78

Manager: Jimmy Armfield

No	Date	Opponents	Result	Scorers	Att	Stewart	Reaney	Cherry	Lorimer	McQueen	Madeley	Gray E	McNiven	Hankin	Currie	Graham	Gray FT	Jordan	Harris	Stevenson	Thomas	Parkinson	Harvey	Flynn	Hampton	Clarke	Parker	Hart
1	Aug 20	(a) Newcastle U	L 2-3	Hankin, Lorimer (pen)	36,491	1	2	3	4	5	6	7	8	**9**	10	11	12											
2	24	(h) West Brom A	D 2-2	Jordan, McQueen	21,000	1	2	3	4	5	6	7	8		10	11		9										
3	27	(h) Birmingham C	W 1-0	Hankin	24,551	1	2	3	4	5	6			8	10	11	7	9										
4	Sep 3	(a) Coventry C	D 2-2	Hankin, McQueen	21,479	1	**2**	3	4	5	6			8	10	11	7	9	12									
5	10	(h) Ipswich T	W 2-1	Hankin 2	24,280	1		**2**	4	5	6	7		8	10	11	3	9		12								
6	17	(a) Derby C	D 2-2	Lorimer, Graham	24,274	1		2	4	5	6	7		8	10	11	3	9										
7	24	(h) Manchester U	D 1-1	Hankin	33,514	1		2	4	5	6	**7**		8	10	11	3	9		12								
8	Oct 1	(a) Chelsea	W 2-1	Lorimer, Hankin	35,427	1		2	4	5	6	7		8	10	11	3	9										
9	5	(h) Aston Villa	D 1-1	McQueen	27,797	1		2	4	5	6	7		8	10	11	3	9										
10	8	(a) Bristol C	L 2-3	Hankin 2	26,215	1		2	4	5	6	7		8	10	11	3	9										
11	15	(h) Liverpool	L 1-2	Thomas	45,500	1		6	4	5		7		8	10	**11**	3			2	9	12						
12	22	(a) Middlesbrough	L 1-2	Harris	27,516			7	4		6			8	10		3	9	11	2		5	1					
13	29	(a) Leicester C	D 0-0		20,128			2	4	5	6	10			8	7	3	9	11				1					
14	Nov 5	(h) Norwich C	D 2-2	Lorimer 2	24,345			2	4	5	6	**7**		8		11	3	9	12				1	10				
15	12	(a) Manchester C	W 3-2	Jordan, Graham, Hankin	42,651			2	4	5	6			8		11	3	9	7				1	10				
16	19	(h) Nottingham F	W 1-0	Hankin	42,925			2			5			8	10	11	3	9	7			6	1	4				
17	26	(a) West Ham U	W 1-0	Hankin	26,883			2			6			8	4	11	3	9	7			5	1	10				
18	Dec 3	(h) Queen's Park R	W 3-0	Needham (og), Flynn, Currie	26,597		2	8		5	6				4	11	3	9	7				1	10				
19	10	(a) Arsenal	D 1-1	McQueen	40,162		2	8		5	6	9			4	11	5		7				1	10				
20	17	(h) Manchester C	W 2-0	McQueen, Cherry	37,380		2	8		5	6	12		9	4	11	3		**7**				1	10				
21	26	(a) Wolves	L 1-3	Jordan	27,704		**2**	4	12	5	6			8		11	3	9	7				1	10				
22	27	(h) Everton	W 3-1	Hankin 2, Lorimer	45,560	1		2	4	5	6			8		11	3	9	7					10				
23	31	(a) West Brom A	L 0-1		24,249	1		2	4	5	6			8		11	3	9	7					10				
24	Jan 2	(h) Newcastle U	L 0-2		36,643	1		2	4	5	6	12			8	**11**	3	9	7					10				
25	14	(a) Birmingham C	W 3-2	Graham 3	23,703		2	6	4			7		9	8	11	3					5	1	10				
26	21	(h) Coventry C	W 2-0	Hankin, Harris	27,062		2	9	4		6	11		8	10		3		**7**			5	1	12				
27	Feb 4	(a) Ipswich T	W 1-0	E.Gray	24,023			2	4		5	6		8	9	11	3					5	1	10				
28	25	(h) Chelsea	W 2-0	F.T.Gray, Currie	25,263	1	2	5			6			8	9	11	7							4	3	10		
29	Mar 1	(a) Manchester U	W 1-0	Clarke	49,101		2	5			6			8	9	11	7						1	4	3	10		
30	4	(h) Bristol C	L 0-2		24,830		**2**	5			6				9	11	7				8	12	1	4	3	10		
31	11	(a) Liverpool	L 0-1		48,233			6						8	9	11	7			2			1	4	**3**	10	12	5
32	18	(h) Middlebrough	W 5-0	Hankin, Graham 2, Clarke 2	25,158			**6**	4		2			8	9	11	3		12				1	7		10		5
33	25	(a) Everton	L 0-2		45,020			6	7		2	8			9	11	3						1	4	12	**10**		5
34	27	(h) Wolves	W 2-1	Graham, Hankin	24,440			6	7		2	10		8	9	11	3						1	4				5
35	28	(h) Leicester C	W 5-1	Hankin, F.T.Gray, E.Gray 3	21,145			6	12		**2**	9		8		11	10		7				1	4	3			5
36	Apr 1	(a) Norwich C	L 0-3		19,615		2	6	9			8				11	10		7		12		1	**4**	3			5
37	8	(h) West Ham U	L 1-2	Graham	22,953		2		7		6	8			9	11	3		10				1	4				5
38	12	(h) Derby C	W 2-0	E.Gray, Hankin	16,531			6			2	8		9	10	11	7						1	4	3			5
39	15	(a) Nottingham F	D 1-1	F.T.Gray (pen)	38,662	1		6			2	8		9	10	11	7							4	3			5
40	22	(h) Arsenal	L 1-3	Currie	33,263	1		6			2	**9**		8	10	11	7							4	3	12		5
41	26	(a) Aston Villa	L 1-3	Hankin	30,524			6			2	12		8	9	11	7						1	4	**3**	9		5
42	29	(a) Queen's Park R	D 0-0		23,993			6			2	7		8	10	11	3						1	4		9		5
		FINAL LEAGUE POSITION: 9th in Division One			Appearances	17	15	41	26	21	38	24	2	33	35	40	40	20	16	3	2	6	25	28	10	8		12
					Sub appearances			2				3					1		3	2	1	2		1	1	1	1	
					Goals			1	6	5		5		20	3	9	3	3	2		1			1		3		

1 own-goal

FA Cup

Rd	Date	Opponents	Result	Scorers	Att	Stewart	Reaney	Cherry	Lorimer	McQueen	Madeley	Gray E	McNiven	Hankin	Currie	Graham	Gray FT	Jordan	Harris	Stevenson	Thomas	Parkinson	Harvey	Flynn	Hampton	Clarke	Parker	Hart
3	Jan 7	(h) Manchester C	L 1-2	F.T.Gray (pen)	38,517		**2**	4		5	6			8	9	11	3		7				1	10		12		
					Appearances		1	1		1	1			1	1	1	1		1				1	1				
					Sub appearances																					1		
					Goals												1											

League Cup

Rd	Date	Opponents	Result	Scorers	Att	Stewart	Reaney	Cherry	Lorimer	McQueen	Madeley	Gray E	McNiven	Hankin	Currie	Graham	Gray FT	Jordan	Harris	Stevenson	Thomas	Parkinson	Harvey	Flynn	Hampton	Clarke	Parker	Hart
2	Aug 31	(a) Rochdale	W 3-0	Jordan, Cherry, Harris	8,644	1	2	6	7	5	4			8	10	**11**	3	9	12									
3	Oct 26	(h) Colchester U	W 4-0	Jordan, Graham, Lorimer, Hankin	17,713			2	4		6	10		8		7	3	9	11			5	1					
4	Nov 30	(a) Bolton W	W 3-1	Graham, Jordan, F.T.Gray	33,766		2	10			6			**8**	4	11	3	9	7			5	1		12			
5	Jan 18	(h) Everton	W 4-1	Currie, Lorimer 2 (1 pen), E.Gray	35,020		2	7	4		6	10		8	9	11	3					5	1					
SF	Feb 8	(h) Nottingham F	L 1-3	E.Gray	43,222		2	7	**4**		6	10		8	9	11	3		12			5	1					
	22	(a) Nottingham F	L 2-4	F.T.Gray, Graham	38,131	1	2	4			6	7		8	10	11	5								3	10		
					Appearances	2	5	6	4	1	6	4		6	5	6	6	3	2			4	4		1	1		
					Sub appearances														2						1			
					Goals			1	3			2		1	1	3	2	3	1									

1978-79

Manager: Jock Stein CBE until October then Jimmy Adamson

No	Date	Opponents	Result	Scorers	Att	Harvey	Madeley	Gray FT	Flynn	Hart	Cherry	Harris	Gray E	Hawley	Currie	Graham	Stevenson	Hankin	Stewart	Hampton	Lorimer	Thomas	Parkinson	Hird
1	Aug 19	(a) Arsenal	D 2-2	Currie, Cherry	42,057	1	2	3	4	5	6	7	8	9	10	11								
2	23	(h) Manchester U	L 2-3	Hart, F.T.Gray (pen)	36,845	1	6	3	4	5		7	9		10	11	2	8						
3	26	(h) Wolves	W 3-0	Hankin, F.T.Gray (pen), Currie	26,267		6	3	4	5		**7**	8	12	10	11	2	9	1					
4	Sep 2	(a) Chelsea	W 3-0	Graham, Hawley 2	30,099		6	3	4	5				9	10	11	2	8	1	7				
5	9	(a) Manchester C	L 0-3		40,125		6	**3**	4	5	7	12		9		11	2	8	1	10				
6	16	(h) Tottenham H	L 1-2	Graham	36,062	1	6	3	4	5	10	7				11	2	8			9			
7	23	(a) Coventry C	D 0-0		27,365	1	6	3	4	5	10	7				11	2	8			9			
8	30	(h) Birmingham C	W 3-0	Flynn, F.T.Gray (pen), Hankin	23,331	1	6	10	4	5	3	7				11	2	8			**9**	12		
9	Oct 7	(a) Bolton W	L 1-3	Graham	27,751	1	6	10	4	5	3	7	9			11	2	8						
10	14	(h) West Brom A	L 1-3	Stevenson	25,931	1	6	9	4	5	3		7		10	11	2	8						
11	21	(a) Norwich C	D 2-2	F.T.Gray, Hawley	19,981	1	6	3	4	5	2		7	9	10	11		8						
12	28	(h) Derby C	W 4-0	Flynn, Hart, Hankin, Hawley	25,449	1	6	3	4	5	2		7	9	10	11		8						
13	Nov 4	(a) Liverpool	D 1-1	Hawley	51,857	1	6	3	4	5	2		7	9	10	11		8						
14	11	(h) Arsenal	L 0-1		33,961	1	6	3	4	5	2	7		9	10	11		8						
15	18	(a) Wolves	D 1-1	Currie	18,961	1	6	3	4	5	2		7	9	10	11		8						
16	22	(h) Chelsea	W 2-1	Graham, Hankin	24,088	1	6	3	4	5	2		7	9	10	11		8						
17	25	(h) Southampton	W 4-0	Graham, Currie, Golac (og), Madeley	23,592	1	6	3	4	5	2		7	9	10	11		8						
18	Dec 2	(a) Ipswich T	W 3-2	Hankin, Harris, Cherry	22,526	1	6	3	4	5	2	11	7	9	10			8						
19	9	(h) Bristol C	D 1-1	Flynn	22,529	1	6		4	5	2	11	7		10		3	8				9		
20	16	(a) Everton	D 1-1	Hawley	37,997	1	6	3	4	5	2	11	7	9	10			8						
21	23	(h) Middlesbrough	W 3-1	Hawley, E.Gray, Currie	27,146	1	6	3	4	5	2	7	8	9	10	11								
22	26	(a) Aston Villa	D 2-2	E.Gray 2	40,973	1	6	3	4	5	2	8	7	9	10	11								
23	30	(a) Queen's Park R	W 4-1	Hawley 2, Harris, E.Gray	17,435	1	6	**3**	4	5	2	11	7	9	10	8							12	
24	Jan 13	(h) Manchester C	D 1-1	Hawley	36,303	1	6	3	4	5	2	11	7	9	10	8								
25	20	(a) Tottenham H	W 2-1	Hart, Hankin	36,828	1		3	4	5		11		9	10	8	2	7					6	
26	Feb 3	(h) Coventry C	W 1-0	Currie	22,928	1	6	7	4		2	9			10	11	3	8					5	
27	10	(a) Birmingham C	W 1-0	F.T.Gray (pen)	17,620	1	6	7	4	5	2	**8**	12	9	10	11	3							
28	24	(a) West Brom A	W 2-1	Graham 2	26,426	1	6	11	4	5	2	**7**		9	10	8	3						12	
29	Mar 3	(h) Norwich C	D 2-2	Hawley 2	23,038	1	6	3	4		2	7		9	10	11							5	8
30	10	(a) Derby C	W 1-0	Hawley	22,800	1	**6**	3	4	5	2	7	12	9	10	11								8
31	24	(a) Manchester U	L 1-4	Hankin	51,191	1		**8**	4	5	3	7	6	9	10	11		12						2
32	31	(a) Southampton	D 2-2	Hawley 2	21,805	1		3	4	5	6		7	9	10	11		8						2
33	Apr 7	(h) Ipswich T	D 1-1	Cherry	24,153	1	6	3	4	5	2		7	9	**10**	11		8						12
34	10	(a) Middlesbrough	L 0-1		23,260	1	10	3	4	5	6		7	9		11	12	**8**						2
35	14	(h) Aston Villa	W 1-0	Hart	24,281	1	6	3	4	5	2	12	**7**	9		11		8						10
36	16	(a) Nottingham F	D 0-0		37,397	1	10	3	4	5	6	7		9		11				8				2
37	21	(h) Everton	W 1-0	Currie	29,125	1	9	3	4	5	6	7			10	11		8						2
38	25	(h) Bolton W	W 5-1	Cherry, F.T.Gray (pen), Hart, Harris, Hawley	20,218	1	6	3	4	5	8	7		12	10	11		**9**						2
39	28	(a) Bristol C	D 0-0		25,388	1	6	3		5	4	7	10			11		9		8				2
40	May 4	(h) Queen's Park R	W 4-3	Graham, Hankin 2, Cherry	20,121	1	6	3	4	5	8	7		12	10	**11**		9						2
41	15	(h) Nottingham F	L 1-2	Cherry	33,544	1	6	3	4	5	8	**7**	12	9	10	11								2
42	17	(h) Liverpool	L 0-3		41,324	1	6	3	4	5	8	7	10	9		11								2
FINAL LEAGUE POSITION: 5th in Division One					Appearances	39	39	41	41	40	38	29	25	29	32	39	14	29	3	4	3	1	3	13
					Sub appearances							2	3	3			1	1				1	2	1
					Goals		1	6	3	5	6	3	4	16	7	8	1	9						

1 own-goal

FA Cup

Round	Date	Opponents	Result	Scorers	Att	Harvey	Madeley	Gray FT	Flynn	Hart	Cherry	Harris	Gray E	Hawley	Currie	Graham	Stevenson	Hankin	Stewart	Hampton	Lorimer	Thomas	Parkinson	Hird
3	Jan 18	(a) Hartlepool U	W 6-2	Hart, Graham, E.Gray 2, Harris, F.T.Gray (pen)	16,000	1	6	3	4	5	2	11	7	9	10	8								
4	Feb 26	(n†)West Brom A	D 3-3	F.T.Gray, Graham, Harris	34,000	1	6	3	4	5	2	7		9	10	11	8							
R	Mar 1	(a) West Brom A	L 0-2*		31,101	1	6	3	4		2	7		9	10	11	**8**					12	5	
†Played at The Hawthorns, West Bromwich. *After extra-time.					Appearances	3	3	3	3	2	3	3	1	3	3	3	2						1	
					Sub appearances																	1		
					Goals			2		1		2	2			2								

League Cup

Round	Date	Opponents	Result	Scorers	Att	Harvey	Madeley	Gray FT	Flynn	Hart	Cherry	Harris	Gray E	Hawley	Currie	Graham	Stevenson	Hankin	Stewart	Hampton	Lorimer	Thomas	Parkinson	Hird
2	Aug 29	(a) West Brom A	D 0-0		25,064		2	3	4	5				9	10	11	6	8	1	7				
R	Sep 6	(h) West Brom A	D 0-0*		29,316		6	3	4	5	7		12	9	**10**	11	2	8	1					
2R	Oct 2	(n‡)West Brom A	W 1-0	Hart	8,164	1	6	10	4	5	3		9			11	2	8			12	**7**		
3	10	(a) Sheffield U	W 4-1	Currie, F.T.Gray, E.Gray 2	40,899	1		9	4	5	3		7		10	11	2	8		6				
4	Nov 7	(a) Queen's Park R	W 2-0	Hawley, Hankin	22,769	1	6	3	4	5	2		7	9	10	11		8						
5	Dec 3	(h) Luton T	W 4-1	Cherry, Currie, E.Gray, F.T.Gray	28,177	1	6	3	4	5	2	11	7	9	10			8						
SF	Jan 24	(h) Southampton	D 2-2	Currie, Hankin	33,415	1	6	3	4	5	2	12	7	9	10	**11**		8						
	30	(a) Southampton	L 0-1		23,645	1	6	3	4	5	2	12	7	**9**	10	11		8						
*After extra-time. ‡Played at Maine Road, Manchester.					Appearances	6	7	8	8	8	7	1	6	6	7	7	4	8	2	2		1		
					Sub appearances							2	1								1			
					Goals			2		1	1		3	1	3			2						

1979-80

Manager: Jimmy Adamson

No	Date	Opponent	Result	Scorers	Att	Harvey	Hird	Stevenson	Flynn	Parkinson	Hampton	Curtis	Cherry	Hankin	Harris	Graham	Hart	Greenhoff	Hawley	Madeley	Gray E	Chandler	Hamson	Lukic	Entwistle	Connor	Firm	Parlane	Dickinson	Thomas
1	Aug 18	(a) Bristol C	D 2-2	Curtis 2	22,845	1	2	3	4	5	6	7	8	9	10	11														
2	22	(h) Everton	W 2-0	Hird, Harris	30,000	1	2	6	4		3	10	8	9	7	11	5													
3	25	(a) Norwich C	L 1-2	Hart	18,444	1	2	6	4	12	**3**	10	8	9	7	11	5													
4	Sep 1	(h) Arsenal	D 1-1	Hart	23,245	1	2	3	4	6		10	8			11	5	7	9											
5	8	(a) Nottingham F	D 0-0		26,914	1	2		4		3	10	8	9		11	5			6	7									
6	15	(h) Liverpool	D 1-1	Curtis	39,779	1	2		4		3	10	8	9		11	5			6	7									
7	22	(a) Bolton W	D 1-1	Gray (pen)	21,724	1	2		4		3	10	8	9		11	5	12		6	**7**									
8	29	(h) Manchester C	L 1-2	Hankin	29,592	1	2				3	10	8	9	7	11	5	4		**6**		12								
9	Oct 6	(h) Ipswich T	W 2-1	Cherry, Hird (pen)	19,342	1	2		4	6	3	10	8	9		11		5					7							
10	13	(a) Brighton & HA	D 0-0		27,002		2	6	4	5	3	10	8	9		11							7	1						
11	20	(h) Tottenham H	L 1-2	Hankin	25,203		2		4		3	10	8	9				**5**		6	7	12		1	11					
12	27	(a) Southampton	W 2-1	Entwistle, Curtis	23,259			2		5	3	10	8	9						6	7	4		1	11					
13	Nov 3	(h) Bristol C	L 1-3	Gray	17,376			3			**4**	10	2	9	12		5			6	11	7		1	8					
14	10	(a) Coventry C	L 0-3		19,402		7	3	**4**			10	2	9			5	8		6	11			1	12					
15	13	(a) Everton	L 1-5	Hird	23,000		7	3				10	2				5	4		6	11		9	1	8					
16	17	(h) West Brom A	W 1-0	Connor	17,481		4	3				10	2		11		5			**6**	7		8	1	9	12				
17	24	(a) Aston Villa	D 0-0		29,736		7	3				10	2			8	5	6			11		4	1		9				
18	Dec 1	(h) Crystal P	W 1-0	Hird	21,330		8	3				10	2			11	5	6			7		4	1		9				
19	8	(a) Manchester U	D 1-1	Connor	57,478		8	3				10	2		12	11	5	6			7		**4**	1		9				
20	15	(h) Wolves	W 3-0	Connor, Graham, Hamson	21,227		8	3				10	2			11	5	6			7		4	1		9				
21	21	(a) Stoke C	W 2-0	Connor, Harris	16,878		8	3				10	2		**11**		5	6			7		4	1	12	9				
22	26	(a) Middlesbrough	L 1-3	Entwistle	23,259		8	3				10	2		11		5	**6**			7		4	1	12	9				
23	29	(h) Norwich C	D 2-2	Hird, Hankin	23,493		8	3					2	10	11		5			6	7		4	1		9				
24	Jan 1	(h) Derby C	W 1-0	Hird	24,271		8	3					2	10	11		5			6	7		4	1		9				
25	12	(a) Arsenal	W 1-0	Connor	32,799		8	3			11		2					5		6	7		4	1	10	9				
26	19	(h) Nottingham F	L 1-2	Connor	29,816		8	3			11		2			12		5		6	7		4	1	**10**	9				
27	Feb 9	(h) Bolton W	D 2-2	Hird (pen), Graham	16,428		8		4		3		2	7		11		5		6			10	1		9				
28	16	(a) Manchester C	D 1-1	Graham	34,392		8		4		3		2			11		5		6	7			1		9	10			
29	23	(h) Brighton & HA	D 1-1	Flynn	17,216		8	2	4		10		3			11		**6**			7		12	1		9	5			
30	Mar 1	(a) Tottenham H	L 1-2	Chandler	35,331			3	4				**2**			11	5				7	8	10	1	12	9	6			
31	8	(h) Southampton	W 2-0	Hart, Parlane	21,169		2		4	3						11	5			6	7	8		1		9		10		
32	14	(a) Ipswich T	L 0-1		23,140		8		4	3			2			11	5			6	**7**	12		1		9		10		
33	19	(a) Liverpool	L 0-3		37,008		8		4	3			2			**11**	5			6		12	10	1		9		7		
34	22	(h) Coventry C	D 0-0		16,967		2			3			8			11	5			6		4	7	1		9		10		
35	29	(a) West Brom A	L 1-2	Chandler	18,898		2		4	**3**			7			11	5	12		6	8	9		1				10		
36	Apr 2	(h) Middlesbrough	W 2-0	Cherry, Flynn	17,906		2		4				8			11	5	3			7	9		1				10	6	
37	5	(a) Derby C	L 0-2		22,745		2		4				3			**11**	5	6			7	9		1		12		10	8	
38	8	(h) Stoke C	W 3-0	Parlane, Harris 2	15,541		2		4				3		9		5			6	7	8		1				10	11	
39	12	(a) Crystal P	L 0-1		25,318		2	3							11		5			6	7	8		1		9			4	10
40	19	(h) Aston Villa	D 0-0		15,840		2	3							11		**5**	6			7	8		1		12		9	4	10
41	26	(a) Wolves	L 1-3	Flynn	22,746		2	12	4				8					3		6		7		1		10		9	**5**	11
42	May 3	(h) Manchester U	W 2-0	Parlane, Hird (pen)	39,625		2	10	4				3		7	11		5		6		8		1				9		
					Appearances	9	39	25	24	10	17	22	39	16	13	26	30	22	1	25	30	13	18	33	7	20	3	11	6	3
					Sub appearances			1		1					2	1		2				4	1		4	3				
					Goals		8		3			4	2	3	4	3	3				2	2	1		2	6		3		

FINAL LEAGUE POSITION: 11th in Division One

FA Cup

Rd	Date	Opponent	Result	Scorers	Att	Harvey	Hird	Stevenson	Flynn	Parkinson	Hampton	Curtis	Cherry	Hankin	Harris	Graham	Hart	Greenhoff	Hawley	Madeley	Gray E	Chandler	Hamson	Lukic	Entwistle	Connor	Firm	Parlane	Dickinson	Thomas
3	Jan 5	(h) Nottingham F	L 1-4	Lloyd (og)	35,945		8	3				**10**	2		11		5			6	7		4	1	12	9				
					Appearances		1	1				1	1		1		1			1	1		1	1		1				
					Sub appearances																				1					
					Goals																									

1 own-goal

League Cup

Rd	Date	Opponent	Result	Scorers	Att	Harvey	Hird	Stevenson	Flynn	Parkinson	Hampton	Curtis	Cherry	Hankin	Harris	Graham	Hart	Greenhoff	Hawley	Madeley	Gray E	Chandler	Hamson	Lukic	Entwistle	Connor	Firm	Parlane	Dickinson	Thomas
2	Aug 29	(h) Arsenal	D 1-1	Stevenson (pen)	23,421	1	2	6	4		3	10	8		7	11	5	9												
	Sep 4	(a) Arsenal	L 0-7		35,129	1	2	6	4		3	10	8	7	12	11	5	**9**												
					Appearances	2	2	2	2		2	2	2	1	1	2	2	2												
					Sub appearances										1															
					Goals			1																						

Leeds United also played in the UEFA Cup (See *Leeds United in Europe*).

1980-81

Manager: Jimmy Adamson until October then Allan Clarke

No	Date	Opponent	Result	Scorers	Att	Lukic	Cherry	Stevenson	Flynn	Hart	Greenhoff	Gray E	Harris	Curtis	Sabella	Graham	Parlane	Connor	Chandler	Madeley	Hamson	Thomas	Hird	Firm	Parkinson	Butterworth	Dickinson
1	Aug 16	(h) Aston Villa	L 1-2	Stevenson (pen)	23,401	1	2	3	4	5	6	**7**	8	9	10	11	12										
2	19	(a) Middlesbrough	L 0-3		19,470	1	2	3	4	5	6	7		9		11	12	**8**	10								
3	23	(a) Norwich C	W 3-2	Hart, Graham, Connor	17,890	1	2		4	5	3				10	11		9	7	6	**8**	12					
4	30	(h) Leicester C	L 1-2	Hart	18,530	1	2		4	5	3				10	11		9	7	6	8						
5	Sep 6	(a) Stoke C	L 0-3		12,729	1	2		4	5	3		12		10	11	7	9		**6**	8						
6	13	(h) Tottenham H	D 0-0		21,947	1	4	3		5					10	11	8	**9**	7		12		2	6			
7	20	(h) Manchester U	D 0-0		32,539	1	7	3	4	5		10				11	9	8					2	6			
8	27	(a) Sunderland	L 1-4	Parlane	29,619	1	7	3	4	5		10	12			11	9	8					2	**6**			
9	Oct 4	(a) Ipswich T	D 1-1	Sabella	24,087	1	6		4	5	2	3	7	8	10	11	9										
10	8	(h) Manchester C	W 1-0	Harris	19,134	1	6		4	5	2	3	7	8	10	11	**9**				12						
11	11	(h) Everton	W 1-0	Curtis	25,601	1	6		4	5	2	3	7	8	10	11					9						
12	18	(a) Wolves	L 1-2	Connor	20,699	1	6		4	5	2	**3**	7	8	10			11			9		12				
13	22	(a) Nottingham F	L 1-2	Harris	25,033	1	6		4	5	2	3	**7**		10			9	11			12	8				
14	25	(h) Crystal P	W 1-0	Connor	19,208	1	6		4	5	2	10	7			11		9		3			8				
15	Nov 1	(a) Coventry C	L 1-2	Connor	13,970	1	6		4	5	2	10	7			11		9		3			8				
16	8	(h) Arsenal	L 0-5		20,855	1	6		4	5	2	10	12			11	7	9		**3**			8				
17	12	(h) Middlesbrough	W 2-1	Hird 2 (1 pen)	17,382	1	6		4	5	2	3	7		10	11		9					8				
18	15	(a) Aston Villa	D 1-1	Sabella	29,106	1	6		4	5	2	3	7		10	11		**9**			12		8				
19	22	(a) Southampton	L 1-2	Graham	20,278	1	6		4	5	2	3	7		10	11					9		8				
20	29	(h) Brighton & HA	W 1-0	Harris	14,333	1	6		4	5	2	3	7		10	11		9					8				
21	Dec 6	(a) West Brom A	W 2-1	Harris, Graham	17,771	1	6		4	5	2	3	7		10	11		9					8				
22	13	(h) Nottingham F	W 1-0	Greenhoff	21,882	1	6		4	5	2	3	7		10	11	12	**9**					8				
23	20	(a) Manchester C	L 0-1		31,866	1	6		4	5	2	3	7		10	11		9					8				
24	26	(h) Birmingham C	D 0-0		19,214	1	6		4	5	2	3	7		10	**11**	12	9					8				
25	27	(a) Liverpool	D 0-0		44,086	1	6		4	5		3	7		10	11	8	**9**			12		2				
26	Jan 10	(h) Southampton	L 0-3		21,007	1	6		4	5		3	12		10	11	**7**		9		8		2				
27	17	(a) Leicester C	W 1-0	Hart	16,094	1	6		4	5	2	3	7		**10**	11		9	12				8				
28	31	(h) Norwich C	W 1-0	Harris	15,836	1	6		4	5	2	3	7		10	11		9					8				
29	Feb 7	(a) Tottenham H	D 1-1	Harris	32,372	1	6	12	4	5	2	3	7			11		9	**10**				8				
30	14	(h) Stoke C	L 1-3	Flynn	16,530	1	6		4	5	2	3	7		12	11	10	**9**					8				
31	21	(h) Sunderland	W 1-0	Harris	23,236	1	6	10	4	5	2	3	7			11	9						8				
32	28	(a) Manchester U	W 1-0	Flynn	45,733	1	6	10	4	5	2	3	7			11	9						8				
33	Mar 14	(a) Everton	W 2-1	Parlane, Harris	23,014	1	6	10	4		2	3	7			11	9						8		5		
34	21	(h) Wolves	L 1-3	Harris	19,252	1	6	10	4		2	3	7			11	9	12	**8**						5		
35	28	(a) Crystal P	W 1-0	Parlane	15,053	1	6	10	4	5		3	8			11	9						7		2		
36	31	(h) Ipswich T	W 3-0	Hird, Harris, Hart	26,462	1	6	10	4	5	2	3	7			11	9						8				
37	Apr 4	(h) Coventry C	W 3-0	Stevenson, Parlane, Flynn	15,882	1		10	4	5	2	3	7			11	**9**						8	6		12	
38	11	(a) Arsenal	D 0-0		29,339	1	6	10	4	5	2	3	7			11	9						8				
39	18	(h) Liverpool	D 0-0		39,206	1	6	10	4	5	2	3	7			11	9						8				
40	21	(a) Birmingham C	W 2-0	Parlane, Hird (pen)	14,505	1	6	10	4	**5**	2	3	7			11	9						8	12			
41	May 2	(a) Brighton & HA	L 0-2		27,577	1	6	10	4		2	3	**7**			11	9	12					8	5			12
42	6	(h) West Brom A	D 0-0		17,218	1	6	**10**	4		2	3	7			11	9	5					8				
FINAL LEAGUE POSITION: 9th in Division One					Appearances	42	41	17	41	38	36	38	33	6	22	40	22	25	8	6	7		32	5	3	1	1
					Sub appearances			1					4		1		4	2	1		4	2	1	1			
					Goals			2	3	4	1		10	1	2	3	5	4					4				

FA Cup

Rd	Date	Opponent	Result	Scorers	Att	Lukic	Cherry	Stevenson	Flynn	Hart	Greenhoff	Gray E	Harris	Curtis	Sabella	Graham	Parlane	Connor	Chandler	Madeley	Hamson	Thomas	Hird	Firm	Parkinson	Butterworth	Dickinson
3	Jan 3	(h) Coventry C	D 1-1	Hird (pen)	24,523	1	6		4	5	**2**	3			10	11	7	9			12		8				
R	6	(a) Coventry C	L 0-1		22,057	1	6		4	5		2			10	11	7		8		9		3				
					Appearances	2	2		2	2	1	2			2	2	2	1	1		1		2				
					Sub appearances																1						
					Goals																		1				

League Cup

Rd	Date	Opponent	Result	Scorers	Att	Lukic	Cherry	Stevenson	Flynn	Hart	Greenhoff	Gray E	Harris	Curtis	Sabella	Graham	Parlane	Connor	Chandler	Madeley	Hamson	Thomas	Hird	Firm	Parkinson	Butterworth	Dickinson
2	Aug 27	(a) Aston Villa	L 0-1		24,238	1	2		4	5	3				10	11		9	8	6		7					
	Sep 3	(h) Aston Villa	L 1-3	Graham	12,236	1	2		4	5	3		12		10	11	7	9		6	**8**						
					Appearances	2	2		2	2	2				2	2	1	2	1	2	1	1					
					Sub appearances								1														
					Goals											1											

1981-82

Manager: Allan Clarke

No	Date	Venue	Opponent	Result	Scorers	Att	Lukic	Hird	Gray FT	Flynn	Hart	Cherry	Harris	Graham	Parlane	Gray E	Barnes	Greenhoff	Stevenson	Firm	Connor	Hamson	Thomas	Arins	Balcombe	Burns	Butterworth	Aspin	Worthington
1	Aug 29	(a)	Swansea C	L 1-5	Parlane	23,489	1	2	3	4	5	6	7	8	9	10	11												
2	Sep 2	(h)	Everton	D 1-1	Graham	26,502	1			4	5	6	7	8	9	3	11	2	10										
3	5	(h)	Wolves	W 3-0	Graham 3	20,216	1	12		4		6	7	8	9	3	11	**2**	10	5									
4	12	(a)	Coventry C	L 0-4		13,065	1	12		4		6	**7**	8		3	11	2	10	5	9								
5	19	(h)	Arsenal	D 0-0		21,410	1		5	4		6	7	8		3	11	2	10		9								
6	23	(a)	Manchester C	L 0-4		35,077	1	8	5	4		6	7			**3**	11	2	10		9	12							
7	26	(a)	Ipswich T	L 1-2	Barnes	22,319	1	10	3	4		6	7	8			11	**2**	5				9	12					
8	30	(a)	Manchester U	L 0-1		47,019	1	2	3	**4**		6	7	8			11		5		12	10	9						
9	Oct 3	(h)	Aston Villa	D 1-1	Balcombe	21,065	1	4	3		5	6	7	8			11		2			10			9				
10	10	(a)	Liverpool	L 0-3		35,840	1	2	3		5	6	7	8		10	11		12			**4**	9						
11	17	(h)	West Brom A	W 3-1	Graham, Cherry, Connor	19,164	1	4	3		5	2	**7**	8			11	12			9	10				6			
12	24	(h)	Sunderland	W 1-0	E.Gray	25,220	1	4	3		5	2		8		7	11				9	10				6			
13	31	(a)	Nottingham F	L 1-2	Butterworth	25,272	1	4	3		5	2		8		7			11			10				6	9		
14	Nov 7	(h)	Notts C	W 1-0	Butterworth	19,552	1	2	3		5	6		8		7	11		4			10					9		
15	21	(a)	Southampton	L 0-4		21,127	1		3	4	5	2		8			11		7			10				6	9		
16	28	(h)	West Ham U	D 3-3	Graham, Hird (pen), Cherry	25,637	1	11	3		5	2	7	8					4			10				6	9		
17	Dec 5	(a)	Stoke C	W 2-1	Graham, Hamson	13,901	1	11	3		5	2	7	8					4			10				6	9		
18	12	(h)	Tottenham H	D 0-0		28,780	1	11	3		5	2	7	8					4		12	10				6	**9**		
19	Jan 16	(h)	Swansea C	W 2-0	Stevenson, Butterworth	18,700	1	11	3		5	2		**8**		7		12	4			10				6	9		
20	30	(a)	Arsenal	L 0-1		22,408	1	**11**	3		5	2	12	8		7			4			10				6	9		
21	Feb 6	(h)	Coventry C	D 0-0		16,385	1	11	3	4	5	2		8	9	7				6		10							
22	20	(h)	Ipswich T	L 0-2		20,287	1	2	3		5			8	9	10	11		4								7	6	
23	27	(h)	Liverpool	L 0-2		33,689	1	7	3		5	2		8		**10**	11		4		12					6	9		
24	Mar 2	(a)	Brighton & HA	L 0-1		12,857	1	11	3	12	**5**	2	7	8				4			10					6	9		
25	10	(h)	Manchester C	L 0-1		20,797	1	4				6				3	11	2			10		8			5	7		9
26	13	(a)	Sunderland	W 1-0	Worthington	20,285	1	4	11			5			7	3		2			10		8			6			9
27	16	(a)	Wolves	L 0-1		11,729	1	4	11			5	12		7	3		**2**			10		8			6			9
28	20	(h)	Nottingham F	D 1-1	Worthington (pen)	18,036	1	2	4			5		8	**7**	3	11				10		12			6			9
29	27	(a)	Notts C	L 1-2	Worthington	13,316	1	2	10		5	6		4		3	11				7		8						9
30	Apr 3	(h)	Manchester U	D 0-0		31,118	1	2	4		5	6		8		3	11				10		7						9
31	6	(a)	Middlesbrough	D 0-0		15,494	1	4	3		5	2		8	11						10		7			6			9
32	10	(a)	Birmingham C	W 1-0	Hart	14,497	1	2			5			8	7	3	11				10		4			6			9
33	13	(h)	Middlesbrough	D 1-1	Parlane	20,458	1	**2**	3		5			8	7		11				10		4			6	12		9
34	17	(h)	Southampton	L 1-3	Worthington	21,353	1	2			5		12	8	7	**3**	11				10	4				6			9
35	24	(a)	West Ham U	L 3-4	Connor, Graham, Flynn	24,748	1	2	3	4	5	6		8		7	11				12						**10**		9
36	28	(a)	Aston Villa	W 4-1	Graham, Worthington 2, Connor	20,566	1	2	3	4	5	6		8		7	11				10								9
37	May 1	(h)	Stoke C	D 0-0		17,775	1	**2**	3	4	5	6		8		7	11				10					12			9
38	4	(a)	Everton	L 0-1		17,137	1		3	4	5	2		8		7	11				10					6			9
39	8	(a)	Tottenham H	L 1-2	Worthington	35,020	1	12	3	4	5	2		8		7	11				10					**6**			9
40	12	(h)	Birmingham C	D 3-3	Worthington 2 (1 pen), Connor	18,583	1	2	3	**4**	5	6		8		7	11				10		12						9
41	15	(h)	Brighton & HA	W 2-1	Hamson, Hird	19,831	1	2			5	6		8		7	11				10	3	4						9
42	18	(a)	West Brom A	L 0-2		23,118	1	2			5	6		8		7	11				10	9	4			3			
FINAL LEAGUE POSITION: 20th in Division One						Appearances	42	35	34	16	32	38	15	38	12	31	31	10	18	3	23	17	13		1	22	13	1	17
						Sub appearances		3		1			3					2	1		4	1	2	1		1	1		
						Goals		2		1	1	2		9	2	1	1		1		4	2			1		3		9

FA Cup

Rd	Date	Venue	Opponent	Result	Scorers	Att	Lukic	Hird	Gray FT	Flynn	Hart	Cherry	Harris	Graham	Parlane	Gray E	Barnes	Greenhoff	Stevenson	Firm	Connor	Hamson	Thomas	Arins	Balcombe	Burns	Butterworth	Aspin	Worthington
3	Jan 2	(a)	Wolves	W 3-1	Hamson, Hird, E.Gray	20,923	1	11	3		5	2		8		7			4			10					6	9	
4	28	(a)	Tottenham H	L 0-1		46,126	1	11	3	12	5	2		8		7			**4**			10					6	9	
						Appearances	2	2	2		2	2		2		2			2			2					2	2	
						Sub appearances				1																			
						Goals		1								1						1							

League Cup

Rd	Date	Venue	Opponent	Result	Scorers	Att	Lukic	Hird	Gray FT	Flynn	Hart	Cherry	Harris	Graham	Parlane	Gray E	Barnes	Greenhoff	Stevenson	Firm	Connor	Hamson	Thomas	Arins	Balcombe	Burns	Butterworth	Aspin	Worthington
2	Oct 7	(h)	Ipswich T	L 0-1		16,994	1	4	3		5	6	7	8		10	11		2							9			
	27	(a)	Ipswich T	L 0-3		16,494	1	**4**	3		5		7	8		6	11	2	12		9	10							
						Appearances	2	2	2		2	1	2	2		2	2	1	1		1	1				1			
						Sub appearances													1										
						Goals																							

1982-83

Manager: Eddie Gray MBE

						Lukic	Hird	Gray E	Dickinson	Hart	Thomas	Connor	Butterworth	Worthington	Gray FT	Graham	Cherry	Parlane	Burns	Gavin	Flynn	Sheridan	Aspin	McNab	Donnelly	Harvey	Ritchie	Wright	Brown	Sellars	Hamson
1	Aug	28 (a) Grimsby T	D 1-1	Connor	16,137	1	2	3	4	5	6	7	8	9	10	11															
2	Sep	4 (h) Wolves	D 0-0		16,462	1	2	3	4	5	6	**7**	8	9	10	11	12														
3		8 (a) Leicester C	W 1-0	Butterworth	12,963	1	7	3	4	5	6		8	9	10	11	2														
4		11 (a) Sheffield W	W 3-2	Worthington 2, Butterworth	29,050	1	7	**3**	4	5	6	12	8	9	10	11	2														
5		18 (h) Derby C	W 2-1	F.T.Gray, Worthington	16,889	1	**7**	3	4	5	6		8	9	10	11	2	12													
6		25 (a) Fulham	L 2-3	Thomas, Graham	12,798	1	7	**3**	4	5	6		8	9	10	11	2		12												
7	Oct	2 (h) Cambridge U	W 2-1	Butterworth, Hird	14,910	1	7		**2**	5	6		8	9	10	11	3		4	12											
8		9 (a) Chelsea	D 0-0		25,358	1	7	3		5	6		8	9	10	11	2		4												
9		16 (h) Carlisle U	D 1-1	Hart	14,141	1	7	3		5	6	12	8	9	**10**	11	2				4										
10		20 (h) Burnley	W 3-1	Worthington, Butterworth, Hird	13,827	1	7	3		5	6		8	9	10	11	2		4												
11		23 (a) Blackburn R	D 0-0		12,040	1	7	3		5	6		8	9	10	11	2		4												
12		30 (h) Newcastle U	W 3-1	Worthington, Burns, Butterworth	26,570	1	**7**	3	5		6	12	8	9	10	11	2		4												
13	Nov	6 (h) Charlton A	L 1-2	Connor	15,148	1	7	3	5		6	12	8	9	10	11	**2**		4												
14		13 (a) Crystal P	D 1-1	Connor	11,673	1	7			5	10	8		9	3	11	2		6		4										
15		20 (h) Middlesbrough	D 0-0		18,482	1	7			5	10	8	12	**9**	3	11	2		6			4									
16		27 (a) Barnsley	L 1-2	Butterworth	21,530	1	7			5	10	8	9		3	11	2		6			4									
17	Dec	4 (h) Queen's Park R	L 0-1		11,528	1	12		2	5			9		3	11	10		6	**8**		4	7								
18		11 (a) Rotherham U	W 1-0	Gavin	13,034	1	7		2	5	10		9		3	11			6	8		4									
19		18 (h) Shrewsbury T	D 1-1	Hird	8,741	1	7		4	5	2		9		3				6	11		8		10							
20		26 (a) Oldham A	D 2-2	Burns, Sheridan	15,658	1	7		2	5	10		9		3	11			6			4		8							
21		28 (h) Bolton W	D 1-1	Graham	16,180	1	7		**2**	5	10		8		3	11			6	12		4	9								
22	Jan	1 (a) Middlesbrough	D 0-0		17,000	1				5	10	8	9		3	11			6			4	2	7							
23		3 (a) Wolves	L 0-3		22,567	1	12			5	10	8	9		**3**	11			6			4	2	7							
24		15 (h) Grimsby T	W 1-0	Butterworth	13,583	1	12	**3**		5		8	9		10	11			6			4	2	7							
25		22 (a) Derby C	D 3-3	Graham 2, Hart	17,005	1	12	3		5	**7**	8	9		10	11			6			4	2								
26	Feb	12 (a) Cambridge U	D 0-0		6,909	1	12	3	**6**	5	7	8	9		10	11						4	2								
27		19 (h) Chelsea	D 3-3	Butterworth, F.T.Gray (pen), Graham	19,365	1	12	3	6	5	**7**	8	9		10	11						4	2								
28		26 (a) Carlisle U	D 2-2	Connor, Butterworth	6,419	1	12	3	6	5	7	9	8		10	11						**4**	2								
29	Mar	5 (h) Blackburn R	W 2-1	F.T.Gray (pen), Hird	12,280	1	12		6	5	**7**	9	8		3	11						4	2		8						
30		12 (a) Newcastle U	L 1-2	Connor	24,580		7		6	5		9	8		3	11			10			4	**2**		12	1					
31		19 (a) Charlton A	W 1-0	Sheridan	8,229		7		6	5	2	8	9		3	11						4			10	1					
32		26 (h) Crystal P	W 2-1	Ritchie, F.T.Gray (pen)	13,973		7		6	5	2		8		3	11						4			10	1	9				
33	Apr	2 (a) Bolton W	W 2-1	Butterworth, Hart	10,784		7		6	5	2		9		3	11						4			10	1	8				
34		5 (h) Oldham A	D 0-0		18,442		7	12	6	5	2		**8**		3	11						4			10	1	9				
35		9 (a) Burnley	W 2-1	Ritchie, Scott (og)	12,149		7	8	6	5	2				3	11						4			10	1	9				
36		16 (h) Fulham	D 1-1	Wright	24,328		7	8	6	5	2				3	11						4	12		10	1		**9**			
37		23 (a) Queen's Park R	L 0-1		19,573		7	8	6	5	2				3	11				12		4			**10**	1	9				
38		27 (h) Sheffield W	L 1-2	Ritchie	16,591		7		6	5	**2**		8		3	11				12		4			10	1	9				
39		30 (h) Barnsley	D 0-0		15,344		7		6	5	2		8		3	11						4			10	1	9				
40	May	2 (h) Leicester C	D 2-2	O'Neill (og), F.T.Gray (pen)	14,442				6		7		8		3							4	2		10	1	9	11	5		
41		7 (a) Shrewsbury T	D 0-0		6,052				6	5	7		**8**		3							4	2		10	1	9	12		11	
42		14 (h) Rotherham U	D 2-2	Butterworth, Donnelly	14,958		12		6	5	7		8		3	**11**							2		10	1	9	4			
FINAL LEAGUE POSITION: 8th in Division Two					Appearances	29	30	20	31	39	39	15	37	15	42	39	15		19	3	2	27	14	5	13	13	10	3	1	1	
					Sub appearances		9	1				4	1				1	1	1	4			1		1			1			
					Goals		4			3	1	5	11	5	5	5			2	1		2			1		3	1			

2 own-goals

FA Cup

						Lukic	Hird	Gray E	Dickinson	Hart	Thomas	Connor	Butterworth	Worthington	Gray FT	Graham	Cherry	Parlane	Burns	Gavin	Flynn	Sheridan	Aspin	McNab	Donnelly	Harvey	Ritchie	Wright	Brown	Sellars	Hamson
3	Jan	8 (h) Preston NE	W 3-0	Sheridan, Connor, Graham	16,816	1	12	3		5	10	8	9			11			6			**4**	2	7							
4		29 (a) Arsenal	D 1-1	Nicholas (og)	33,930	1	12	3	6	5	4	8	9		10	11							2								**7**
R	Feb	2 (h) Arsenal	D 1-1*	Butterwroth	24,410	1	7	3	6	5	4	9	8		10	11							2								
2R		9 (a) Arsenal	L 1-2	Connor	26,802	1		3	6	5	7	9	8		10	11						4	2								
				*After extra-time	Appearances	4	1	4	3	4	4	4	4		3	4			1			2	4	1							1
					Sub appearances		2																								
					Goals							2	1			1						1									

1 own-goal

League Cup

						Lukic	Hird	Gray E	Dickinson	Hart	Thomas	Connor	Butterworth	Worthington	Gray FT	Graham	Cherry	Parlane	Burns	Gavin	Flynn	Sheridan	Aspin	McNab	Donnelly	Harvey	Ritchie	Wright	Brown	Sellars	Hamson
2	Oct	6 (h) Newcastle U	L 0-1		24,012	1	7	3		5	6	12	8	9	10	11	**2**		4												
		27 (a) Newcastle U	W4-1*	Saunders (og), Worthington, Butterworth, Connor	24,173	1	7	**3**		5	6	12	8	9	10	11	2		4												
3	Nov	10 (h) Huddersfield T	L 0-1		24,215	1	12	**3**		5	6	7	8	9	10	11	2		4												
				*After extra-time	Appearances	3	2	3		3	3	1	3	3	3	3	3		3												
					Sub appearances		1					2																			
					Goals							1	1	1																	

1 own-goal

1983-84

Manager: Eddie Gray MBE

No	Date	Opponents	Result	Scorers	Att	Harvey	Thomas	Gray FT	Sheridan	Brown	Dickinson	Watson	McCluskey	Ritchie	Donnelly	Barnes	Butterworth	Hamson	Aspin	Gavin	Hughes	Gray E	Burns	Wright	Hird	McGoldrick	Sellars	Lorimer	Irwin	Thompson
1	Aug 27	(h) Newcastle U	L 0-1		30,806	1	2	3	4	5	6	**7**	8	9	10	11	12													
2	29	(h) Brighton & HA	W 3-2	Watson, F.T.Gray, Sheridan	13,303	1	2	3	7	5	6	4	8	9		11	12	**10**												
3	Sep 3	(a) Middlesbrough	D 2-2	F.T.Gray (pen), McCluskey	12,793	1	10	3	7	5	6	4	8	9	12	**11**			2											
4	6	(a) Grimsby T	L 0-2		8,000	1	10	3	7	5	6	4	8		12		9		**2**	11										
5	10	(h) Cardiff C	W 1-0	McCluskey	12,336		2	3	10	5	6	4	8	**9**			12			11	1	7								
6	17	(a) Fulham	L 1-2	Ritchie	10,055		2	3	10	5	6	4	8	9			12			11	1	**7**								
7	24	(h) Manchester C	L 1-2	Ritchie	21,918	1	2	3	7	5	6		**8**	9	10					11			4	12						
8	Oct 1	(a) Shrewsbury T	L 1-5	Ritchie	6,289	1	2	3	7	**5**	6	12	8	9	10					11			4							
9	8	(a) Sheffield W	L 1-3	F.T.Gray (pen)	26,814	1	11	3	7		6	**4**	8	9	10	12							5		2					
10	14	(h) Cambridge U	W 3-1	Hird, Watson, Donnelly	9,923	1	11	3	7		6	4	8	9	10								5		2					
11	22	(a) Barnsley	W 2-0	Donnelly, Barnes	18,236	1	11	3	**7**		6	4	8	9	10	12							5		2					
12	29	(h) Portsmouth	W 2-1	Watson, Barnes	16,254	1	7	3		6		4	8	9	10	11			2				5							
13	Nov 5	(h) Crystal P	D 1-1	McCluskey	14,847	1	7	3			6	**4**	8	9	10	11	12		2				5							
14	12	(a) Blackburn R	D 1-1	Donnelly	9,556	1		3			6	4	8	9	10	11			2				5	7						
15	19	(a) Derby C	D 1-1	Ritchie	16,726	1	7	3			6	4	8	9	10	11							5			2				
16	26	(h) Chelsea	D 1-1	McCluskey	20,680	1	7	3			6	4	8	9	10	11							5			2				
17	Dec 3	(a) Carlisle U	L 0-1		6,845	1	**7**	3		6	2	4	8	9	10	11		12					5							
18	15	(a) Charlton A	L 0-2		6,285	1		3			6	**4**	8	9	10	11		12					5	7		2				
19	26	(h) Huddersfield T	L 1-2	Wright	23,791	1		3			6		8	9	**10**			4					5	7	12	2	11			
20	27	(a) Oldham A	L 2-3	Wright, F.T.Gray	8,393	1		3			6		**8**	9	10			4	5					7	12	2	11			
21	31	(h) Middlesbrough	W 4-1	Sellars, McCluskey 2, Wright	14,215	1		3			6		**8**	9	10			4	5					7		2	11	12		
22	Jan 2	(a) Manchester C	D 1-1	Bond (og)	34,441	1		3			6		**8**	9	10			4	5					7		2	11	12		
23	21	(h) Fulham	W 1-0	Watson	11,421	1						4		9		11		3	5					7	2		8	10	6	
24	Feb 4	(h) Shrewsbury T	W 3-0	Watson 2, Brown	10,628	1				5	6	4	12	9		11		3						7	2		**8**	10		
25	11	(a) Cardiff C	W 1-0	McCluskey	9,407	1				5	6	4	12	9		**11**		3						7	2		8	10		
26	15	(h) Swansea C	W 1-0	Lorimer	10,031	1				5	6	4	12	9		**11**		3						7	2		8	10		
27	18	(a) Portsmouth	W 3-2	Wright, Watson, Lorimer (pen)	13,911	1				5	6	4	12	**9**		11		3						7	2		8	10		
28	25	(h) Barnsley	L 1-2	Wright	19,138	1		6		5		4	**9**			11		3		12				7	2		8	10		
29	Mar 3	(a) Crystal P	D 0-0		8,077	1	12			5		4				11				9		**3**		7	2		8	10	6	
30	10	(h) Blackburn R	W 1-0	Butterworth	12,857	1					6	**4**		9		11	12	3	5					7	2		8	10		
31	17	(h) Grimsby T	W 2-1	Aspin, Sellars	14,412	1				5	6			9		11		3	4					7	2		8	10		
32	24	(a) Brighton & HA	L 0-3		12,605	1		**3**		5	6			9		11	12		4					7	2		8	10		
33	28	(a) Newcastle U	L 0-1		30,877	1					6			9		11	7	3	5						2		8	10	4	
34	31	(h) Sheffield W	D 1-1	Ritchie	25,343	1					6			9		11	7	3	5						2		8	10	4	
35	Apr 7	(a) Cambridge U	D 2-2	Barnes, Sellars	4,700	1				6				9		11	7	3	5					12	**2**		8	10	4	
36	14	(h) Derby C	D 0-0		12,549	1					6			9	**4**	11		3	5	12				7			8	10	2	
37	21	(a) Huddersfield T	D 2-2	Wright, Barnes	16,270	1					6	4	12	9	**10**	11		3	5					7				8	2	
38	24	(h) Oldham A	W 2-0	Ritchie, Lorimer (pen)	9,576	1					6	4		9	8			3	5	11				7				10	2	
39	28	(a) Chelsea	L 0-5		33,447	1					6	4	12	9				3	5	11				7			**8**	10	2	
40	May 5	(h) Carlisle U	W 3-0	Gavin, Ritchie, McCluskey	8,278	1				6		4	12	9	8			3	5	**11**				7				10	2	
41	7	(a) Swansea C	D 2-2	Wright, Lorimer	5,498	1				6		4	12	**9**	8			3		11				7				10	2	5
42	12	(h) Charlton A	W 1-0	Wright	13,254	1				6		4	9		8			3	5			11		7				10	2	
FINAL LEAGUE POSITION: 10th in Division Two					Appearances	40	16	24	11	22	34	30	24	38	23	25	4	23	21	10	2	4	13	23	16	7	19	20	12	1
					Sub appearances		1					1	8		2	2	7	2		2				2	2			2		
					Goals			4	1	1		7	8	7	3	4	1		1	1				8	1		3	4		

1 own-goal

FA Cup

Rd	Date	Opponents	Result	Scorers	Att	Harvey	Thomas	Gray FT	Sheridan	Brown	Dickinson	Watson	McCluskey	Ritchie	Donnelly	Barnes	Butterworth	Hamson	Aspin	Gavin	Hughes	Gray E	Burns	Wright	Hird	McGoldrick	Sellars	Lorimer	Irwin	Thompson
3	Jan 7	(h) Scunthorpe U	D 1-1	Wright	17,130	1		**3**			6		8	9	10	11		4	5					7		2	11	12		
R	10	(a) Scunthorpe U	D 1-1*	Wright	13,129	1					6	4	8	9				3	5					7		2	11	10		
2R	16	(a) Scunthorpe U	L 2-4	Wright, Ritchie	13,312	1		4					8	9				3	5					7		2		10	6	
				*After extra-time	Appearances	3		2			2	1	3	3	1	1		3	3					3		3	2	2	1	
					Sub appearances																							1		
					Goals									1										3						

League Cup

Rd	Date	Opponents	Result	Scorers	Att	Harvey	Thomas	Gray FT	Sheridan	Brown	Dickinson	Watson	McCluskey	Ritchie	Donnelly	Barnes	Butterworth	Hamson	Aspin	Gavin	Hughes	Gray E	Burns	Wright	Hird	McGoldrick	Sellars	Lorimer	Irwin	Thompson
2	Oct 5	(h) Chester C	L 0-1		8,106	1	10	3			6	4	12	9			8			**11**			5		7	2				
	26	(a) Chester C	W 4-1	Ritchie 2, Burns, Barnes	8,044	1	7	3			6	4	8	9	10	11			2				5							
3	Nov 9	(h) Oxford U	D 1-1	McCluskey	13,349	1	7	3			6	4	8	**9**	10	11			2	12			5							
R	23	(a) Oxford U	L 1-4	Burns	13,389	1	7	3			6	4	8	9	10	11							5	12		**2**				
					Appearances	4	4	4			4	4	3	4	3	3	1		2	1			4		1	2				
					Sub appearances								1							1				1						
					Goals								1	2		1							2							

1984-85

Manager: Eddie Gray MBE

No	Date	Opponent	Result	Scorers	Att	Harvey	Irwin	Hamson	Watson	Linighan	Aspin	Wright	Sheridan	McCluskey	Lorimer	Gray FT	Gavin	Sellars	Ritchie	Dickinson	Donnelly	Eli	Hughes	Day	Stiles	Baird	Brown	Simmonds
1	Aug 25	(a) Notts C	W 2-1	Wright 2	12,196	1	2	**3**	4	5	6	7	8	9	10	11	12											
2	27	(h) Fulham	W 2-0	McCluskey, Wright	14,207	1	2		4	5	6	7	8	9	10	3		11										
3	Sep 1	(h) Wolves	W 3-2	Wright 2, Lorimer	17,843	1	2		4	5	6	7	8	9	10	3		11										
4	8	(a) Grimsby T	W 2-0	McCluskey, Lorimer	13,290	1	2		4	5	6	7	8	9	10	3		11										
5	12	(a) Cardiff C	L 1-2	Sellars	6,893	1	2		**4**	5	6	7	8	9	10	3	12	11										
6	15	(h) Portsmouth	L 0-1		19,438	1	2		4	5	6	7	8	**9**	10	3		11	12									
7	22	(a) Crystal P	L 1-3	Sellars	19,460	1	2		4	5	6	7	**8**		10	3	12	11	9									
8	29	(h) Oldham A	W 6-0	Wright, Ritchie 3 (1 pen), Sheridan, Linighan	14,290	1	2			5		7	8		10	3	11	4	9	6								
9	Oct 6	(h) Sheffield U	D 1-1	Lorimer (pen)	25,547	1	2			5		7	8		10	3	11	4	9	6								
10	13	(a) Barnsley	L 0-1		16,199	1	2			5		7	8	12	10	3	**11**	4	9	6								
11	20	(a) Huddersfield T	L 0-1		15,257	1	2			5		7	**8**		10	3	11	4	9	6	12							
12	27	(h) Middlesbrough	W 2-0	Lorimer (pen), Ritchie	14,838	1	2			5		7	8		10	3	11	4	9	6								
13	Nov 3	(a) Charlton A	W 3-2	Sheridan, McCluskey, Gavin	6,950	1		3		5	2	7	8	9	10		11	4		6								
14	10	(h) Carlisle U	D 1-1	Dickinson	13,327	1	2	3		5		7	8	**9**	10		11	4	12	6								
15	17	(h) Brighton & HA	W 1-0	Ritchie	13,127	1	2	3		5		7	8		10	11		4	9	6								
16	24	(a) Oxford U	L 2-5	Wright, Lorimer	12,192	1	2	3		5		7	8		10	11	12	**4**	9	6								
17	Dec 1	(h) Wimbledon	W 5-2	Wright, Ritchie 3, Sellars	10,899	1	2	3		5	6	7	8		**10**	11		4	9			12						
18	8	(a) Shrewsbury T	W 3-2	Ritchie 2, Linighan	6,358	1	2	3		5	6	7	8			11		4	9	10								
19	15	(h) Birmingham C	L 0-1		15,854	1	2	3		5	6	7	8			11		4	9	10								
20	22	(a) Wolves	W 2-0	Gray, McCluskey	9,259		2	3		5	6	7	8	9	10	11		4					1					
21	26	(a) Blackburn R	L 1-2	McCluskey	20,149		2	3		5	6	7	8	9	10	11		4					1					
22	29	(h) Cardiff C	D 1-1	Lorimer (pen)	11,798	1	2	3		5	6	7	8	9	10	11		4										
23	Jan 1	(h) Manchester C	D 1-1	Ritchie	22,626		2	3		5	6	7	8	12	10	11		4	**9**				1					
24	19	(h) Notts C	W 5-0	Sheridan, Wright 3, Irwin	11,369		2	3		5	6	7	8	12	10	**11**		4	9				1					
25	Feb 2	(a) Oldham A	D 1-1	Lorimer (pen)	8,824		2	3		5	6	7	8		10	11		4	9					1				
26	9	(h) Grimsby T	D 0-0		12,517		2	3		5	6	7	8	12	10	11		**4**	9					1				
27	23	(h) Charlton A	W 1-0	Lorimer	10,644		2	3		5	6	7	8	12	10	11		**4**	9					1				
28	26	(a) Carlisle U	D 2-2	Wright, Aspin	5,484		2	3		5	6	7	8	4	10	11			9					1				
29	Mar 2	(a) Middlesbrough	D 0-0		8,781		2	3		5	6	7	8		10	11			9					1	4			
30	9	(h) Huddersfield T	D 0-0		18,607		2	3		5	6	7	8		10	11		4	9					1				
31	12	(a) Portsmouth	L 1-3	Sheridan	16,208		2	**3**		5		12	8		10	11		4	9					1		7	6	
32	16	(h) Barnsley	W 2-0	Lorimer, Sellars	13,091		2	3		5		7	8		10	11		4		6				1		9		
33	23	(a) Sheffield U	L 1-2	Ritchie	21,468		**2**	3		5	6	7	8		10	11		4	12					1		9		
34	30	(a) Fulham	W 2-0	Wright 2	7,901		2	3		5	6	7	8	12	10	**11**		4	9					1				
35	Apr 6	(h) Blackburn R	D 0-0		15,829		2	3		5	6	7	8	**11**	10			4	9					1				12
36	8	(a) Manchester C	W 2-1	Baird, Sellars	33,553		2	3		5	6	7	8		10	11		4						1		9		
37	13	(h) Crystal P	W 4-1	Baird, Sellars, Sheridan 2	12,286		2	3		5	6	7	8		10	11		4						1		9		
38	20	(a) Brighton & HA	D 1-1	Sellars	17,279		2	3		5	6	7	8		10	11		4						1		9		
39	27	(h) Oxford U	W 1-0	Baird	17,992		2	3		5	6	7	8		10	11		4						1		9		
40	May 4	(a) Wimbledon	D 2-2	Baird 2	6,638		2	3		5	6	7	8		**10**	11		4	12					1		9		
41	6	(h) Shrewsbury T	W 1-0	Baird	12,423		2	3		5	6	**7**	8		10	11		4	12					1		9		
42	11	(a) Birmingham C	L 0-1		24,847		2	3		5	**6**	7	8		10	11		4	12					1		9		
FINAL LEAGUE POSITION: 7th in Division Two					Appearances	20	41	31	7	42	32	41	42	13	40	39	7	39	22	12			4	18	1	10	1	
					Sub appearances							1		6			4		6		1	1						1
					Goals		1			2	1	14	6	5	9	1	1	7	12	1						6		

FA Cup

Rd	Date	Opponent	Result	Scorers	Att	Harvey	Irwin	Hamson	Watson	Linighan	Aspin	Wright	Sheridan	McCluskey	Lorimer	Gray FT	Gavin	Sellars	Ritchie	Dickinson	Donnelly	Eli	Hughes	Day	Stiles	Baird	Brown	Simmonds
3	Jan 4	(h) Everton	L 0-2		21,211		2	3		5	6	7	8	**9**	10	11	12	4					1					
					Appearances		1	1		1	1	1	1	1	1	1		1					1					
					Sub appearances												1											
					Goals																							

League Cup

Rd	Date	Opponent	Result	Scorers	Att	Harvey	Irwin	Hamson	Watson	Linighan	Aspin	Wright	Sheridan	McCluskey	Lorimer	Gray FT	Gavin	Sellars	Ritchie	Dickinson	Donnelly	Eli	Hughes	Day	Stiles	Baird	Brown	Simmonds
2	Sep 25	(a) Gillingham	W 2-1	Wright, Ritchie	8,881	1	2			5		7	8		10	3	11	4	9	6								
	Oct 10	(h) Gillingham	W 3-2	Gavin, Sellars, Lorimer	11,109	1	2			5		7	8		10	3	11	4	9	6								
3	31	(h) Watford	L 0-4		21,221	1	2			5		7	8	12	10	3	11	**4**	9	6								
					Appearances	3	3			3		3	3		3	3	3	3	3	3								
					Sub appearances									1														
					Goals							1			1		1	1	1									

1985-86

Manager: Eddie Gray MBE until October then Billy Bremner

No	Date	Opponents	Result	Scorers	Att	Day	Irwin	Hamson	Snodin I	Linighan	Aspin	McCluskey	Sheridan	Baird	Lorimer	Sellars	Wright	Dickinson	Phelan	Ritchie	Swinburne	McGregor	Simmonds	Caswell	Robinson	Stiles	Thompson	Eli	Swan	Harle	Rennie	Ormsby	Taylor
1	Aug 17	(a) Fulham	L 1-3	Lorimer	5,772	1	2	3	4	5	6	7	8	9	10	11																	
2	21	(h) Wimbledon	D 0-0		12,426	1	2	3	4	5	6	7	8	9	10	11																	
3	24	(h) Hull C	D 1-1	Baird	16,689	1	2	3	4	5	6	7	8	9	**10**	11	12																
4	26	(a) Stoke C	L 2-6	Aspin, Snodin	7,047	1	2	3	4	5	6	**7**	8	9	10	11	12																
5	31	(h) Charlton A	L 1-2	Lorimer (pen)	10,860	1	2	3	4	5	6	12	8	**9**	10	11	7																
6	Sep 4	(a) Brighton & HA	W 1-0	McCluskey	9,798	1	2	3	4	5	6	9	8		10		7	11															
7	7	(a) Shrewsbury T	W 3-1	Wright, McCluskey, Baird	4,168	1	2		4	5	6	9	8	12	10		7	**11**	3														
8	14	(h) Sunderland	D 1-1	Sheridan	19,693	1	2		4	5	6	11	8	9	10	12	**7**		3														
9	21	(h) Bradford C	W 2-1	Lorimer, Sellars	21,104	1	2		4	**5**	6	7	8	9	10	11	12		3														
10	28	(h) Sheffield U	D 1-1	Baird	15,622	1	2		4	5			8	9	10	11	7	6	3														
11	Oct 5	(a) Huddersfield T	L 1-3	Baird	9,983	1	2		4	5		12	8	9	10	11	7	**6**	3														
12	12	(h) Middlesbrough	W 1-0	Lorimer (pen)	14,117	1	2	4		5	6	7	8	9	10		12		3	**11**													
13	19	(h) Grimsby T	D 1-1	Baird	11,244		2	4		5	6	7		9	10			8	3	11	1												
14	27	(a) Barnsley	L 0-3		8,302	1		8	4	5	6	7		9	10			2	3	11													
15	Nov 2	(h) Portsmouth	W 2-1	Simmonds 2 (1 pen)	15,672	1	2	10		5	6		8	9					3	7		4	11										
16	9	(a) Millwall	L 1-3	Ritchie	9,158	1		11		5	6	10	8	9				2	3	7		4											
17	16	(h) Crystal P	L 1-3	McCluskey	10,378	1		10	4	**5**	6	9	8					12	3	7		2	11										
18	23	(a) Carlisle U	W 2-1	Linighan, Ritchie	3,504	1		10	4	5		9	8					11		7		6		2	3								
19	30	(h) Norwich C	L 0-2		11,480			10	4	6		9	8					11		7	1	5	12	2	**3**								
20	Dec 7	(a) Wimbledon	W 3-0	Snodin, Baird, Dickinson	3,492	1		10	4	6	5			9				11		7				2	3	8							
21	14	(h) Fulham	W 1-0	Sheridan	9,998	1	2	10	4	6	5		8	9				11		7					3								
22	22	(a) Hull C	L 1-2	Sheridan	11,852	1		10	4	5	6	**9**	8					11	12	7				2	3								
23	26	(a) Blackburn R	L 0-2		8,666	1		10	4	**6**	5	9	8			12		11	3	7				2									
24	28	(h) Brighton & HA	L 2-3	Baird, Snodin	13,110	1	2	10	4		5		8	9		12		11		7							3	**6**					
25	Jan 1	(h) Oldham A	W 3-1	Baird 2, Ritchie	10,830	1	2	10	4		5			**9**		3		11		7									6	8			
26	11	(a) Sunderland	L 2-4	Baird, Sheridan	15,139	1	2	3	4	5	6		10	9				11		7										8			
27	18	(a) Charlton A	L 0-4		4,333	1	2	11	4		6		10	9				5		7				3							8		
28	Feb 1	(h) Stoke C	W 4-0	Stiles, Baird, Swan 2	10,425	1		10	4		5			9						7				2	3	11			8		6		
29	8	(a) Grimsby T	L 0-1		6,382	1		10	4		5			9				12		7				**2**	3	11			8		6		
30	15	(h) Barnsley	L 0-2		11,765	1		10	4		5			9					12	7					3	2			8	**11**	6		
31	Mar 8	(h) Huddersfield T	W 2-0	Ormsby, Snodin	14,667	1			4		2		8	9									7		3	11			10		6	5	
32	15	(a) Middlesbrough	D 2-2	Simmonds, Rennie	6,889	1			4		2		8	9						12			7		**3**	11			10		6	5	
33	22	(h) Shrewsbury T	D 1-1	Rennie	9,641	1		3	4		2		8	9									7			11			10		6	5	
34	28	(a) Oldham A	L 1-3	Ritchie	4,937	1		3	4		2		8	9						11			7						10		6	5	
35	31	(h) Blackburn R	D 1-1	Ritchie	9,919	1		3	4		2	7	8	9						11									10		6	5	
36	Apr 5	(a) Portsmouth	W 3-2	Ritchie 2, Baird	14,430	1			4		2	7	8	9						11					3				10		6	5	
37	9	(a) Bradford C	W 1-0	Aspin	10,751	1			4		2	**7**	8	9						11					3	12			10		6	5	
38	12	(h) Millwall	W 3-1	Sellars, Swan, Ritchie	15,067	1			4		2					**7**				9			12		3	8			10		6	5	11
39	19	(a) Crystal P	L 0-3		6,285	1			4		2		8	9		12				11					3				10		6	5	**7**
40	22	(a) Sheffield U	L 2-3	Ritchie, Snodin	9,158	1			4		2			9		8				11					3	7			10		6	5	
41	26	(h) Carlisle U	W 2-0	Ritchie 2	13,868	1		3	**4**		2		12	9		8				7						11			10		6	5	
42	May 3	(a) Norwich C	L 0-4		17,942	1		3			2			9		8				7					4	11			10		6	5	
					Appearances	40	19	30	37	24	38	20	31	34	14	13	6	17	12	28	2	5	6	8	16	11	1	1	16	3	16	12	2
					Sub appearances							2	1	1		4	4	2	2	1			2			1							
					Goals				5	1	2	3	4	12	4	2	1	1		11			3			1			3		2	1	

FINAL LEAGUE POSITION: 14th in Division Two

FA Cup

Rd	Date	Opponents	Result	Scorers	Att	Day	Irwin	Hamson	Snodin I	Linighan	Aspin	McCluskey	Sheridan	Baird	Lorimer	Sellars	Wright	Dickinson	Phelan	Ritchie	Swinburne	McGregor	Simmonds	Caswell	Robinson	Stiles	Thompson	Eli	Swan	Harle	Rennie	Ormsby	Taylor
3	Jan 4	(a) Peterborough U	L 0-1		10,137	1	2	10	4	6	5		12	9		3		11		7									**8**				
					Appearances	1	1	1	1	1	1			1		1		1		1									1				
					Sub appearances								1																				
					Goals																												

League Cup

Rd	Date	Opponents	Result	Scorers	Att	Day	Irwin	Hamson	Snodin I	Linighan	Aspin	McCluskey	Sheridan	Baird	Lorimer	Sellars	Wright	Dickinson	Phelan	Ritchie	Swinburne	McGregor	Simmonds	Caswell	Robinson	Stiles	Thompson	Eli	Swan	Harle	Rennie	Ormsby	Taylor
2	Sep 25	(h) Walsall	D 0-0		8,869	1	2		4	5		**7**	8	9	10	11	12	6	3														
	Oct 8	(a) Walsall	W 3-0	Linighan, Snodin 2	7,085	1	2	11	4	5		12	8	9	10			**6**	3	7													
3	30	(h) Aston Villa	L 0-3		15,444	1	2	11	4	5	6	10	8	9				3		7													
					Appearances	3	3	2	3	3	1	2	3	3	2	1		3	2	2													
					Sub appearances							1					1																
					Goals				2	1																							

Leeds United also played in the Full Members' Cup (See *Invitation Tournaments*).

1986-87

Manager: Billy Bremner

	Date	Opponents	Result	Scorers	Attendance	Sinclair	Haddock	Caswell	Snodin I	Ormsby	Rennie	Ritchie	Stiles	Baird	Edwards	Ashurst	Swan	Aspin	Thompson	Sheridan	Buckley	Day	Robinson	Taylor	Doig	Adams	Pearson	McDonald	Aizlewood	Wright
1	Aug 23	(a) Blackburn R	L 1-2	Ritchie	8,346	1	2	3	4	**5**	6	7	8	9	10	11	12													
2	25	(h) Stoke C	W 2-1	Sheridan, Baird	13,334	1			4		6	11	7	9	10	5		2	3	8										
3	30	(h) Sheffield U	L 0-1		18,294	1	3		4		6	11	7	9	10	5		2		8										
4	Sep 2	(a) Barnsley	W 1-0	Baird	6,839	1	3		4		6	11	7	9	10	5		2		8										
5	6	(a) Huddersfield T	D 1-1	Sheridan	9,306	1	3				6	11	**7**	9	10	5	4	2		8	12									
6	13	(h) Reading	W 3-2	Edwards, Ritchie, Buckley	12,248	1	3				6	11	7	9	10	5	**4**	2		8	12									
7	20	(a) Bradford C	L 0-2		13,525	1	3		**4**		6	11	7		10	5	12	2		8	9									
8	27	(h) Hull C	W 3-0	Ritchie (pen), Baird, Ormsby	13,551		3			4	6	11	7	9	10	5		2		8		1								
9	Oct 4	(a) Plymouth A	D 1-1	Baird	11,923		3			4	6	11	7	9	10	5		2		8		1								
10	11	(h) Crystal P	W 3-0	Sheridan (pen), Ormsby, Edwards	14,316					4	6	11	7	9	10	5		2		8		1	3							
11	18	(h) Portsmouth	W 3-1	Sheridan (pen), Ritchie, Baird	21,361					4	6	11	7	9	10	5		2		8		1	3							
12	25	(a) Grimsby T	D 0-0		7,223					4	6	11	**7**	9	10	5		2	12	8		1	3							
13	Nov 1	(h) Shrewsbury T	W 1-0	Aspin	14,966	1	**7**			4	6	11		9	10	5		2		8	12		3							
14	8	(a) Millwall	L 0-1		6,869		12		4	6	**7**	11		9	10	5		2		8		1	3							
15	15	(h) Oldham A	L 0-2		21,052				4	6		11		9		5		2		8	7	1	3	10						
16	21	(a) Birmingham C	L 1-2	Sheridan	7,836				4	6				9	10	5		2	7	8		1	3	11						
17	29	(h) Derby C	W 2-0	Sheridan, Edwards	19,129				4	6		11	7	9	10	5		2		**8**		1	3		12					
18	Dec 6	(a) West Brom A	L 0-3		19,853				4	6	**11**	12	7	9	10	5		2		8		1	3							
19	13	(h) Brighton & HA	W 3-1	Sheridan, Snodin, Baird	12,014				4	6	11		12	9	10	5		2		8		1	3		**7**					
20	21	(a) Stoke C	L 2-7	Baird, Sheridan (pen)	12,358						11	12		9	10	5	6	2	4	8		1	**3**		7					
21	26	(h) Sunderland	D 1-1	Bennett (og)	21,286						3	11		9	10	5	6	2	4	8	7	1								
22	27	(a) Oldham A	W 1-0	Ritchie	8,477				4	6	11	10	3	9			5	2		8	7	1								
23	Jan 1	(a) Ipswich T	L 0-2		14,125				4	6	11	10	3	9	12	5		2		8	**7**	1								
24	3	(h) Huddersfield T	D 1-1	Baird	17,983				4	6	11	7	3	9	10	5		2		8		1								
25	24	(h) Blackburn R	D 0-0		14,452					6	8	7	4	10		5		2			**11**	1			12	3	9			
26	Feb 7	(a) Sheffield U	D 0-0		12,494					6			7	10		5		2		8		1				11	9	3	4	
27	14	(h) Barnsley	D 2-2	Baird, Sheridan	14,216					6			**7**	10	12	5		2		8		1				11	9	3	4	
28	28	(h) Bradford C	W 1-0	Edwards	21,802					6		7	**11**	10	12	5		2		8		1					9	3	4	
29	Mar 7	(h) Grimsby T	W 2-0	Ritchie, Sheridan (pen)	14,270						6	7			10	5		2		8		1				11	9	3	4	
30	10	(a) Portsmouth	D 1-1	Adams	13,745					6			7	10		5		2		8		1				11	9	3	4	
31	21	(a) Crystal P	L 0-1		8,781					6			7	10		5		2		8		1				11	9	3	4	
32	28	(h) Plymouth A	W 4-0	Sheridan (pen), Baird 3	18,618					6		7		10	12	5		2		**8**		1				11	9	3	4	
33	Apr 4	(h) Millwall	W 2-0	Baird, Ritchie	18,304					6		7		10		5		2		8		1				11	9	3	4	
34	8	(a) Hull C	D 0-0		9,531					6		7	12	10		5		2		8		1				11	9	3	**4**	
35	14	(a) Shrewsbury T	W 2-0	Sheridan, Pearson	4,186					6		7		10		5		2		8		1				11	9	3	4	
36	18	(h) Ipswich T	W 3-2	McDonald, Sheridan, Ormsby	24,839					6		7		10		5		2		8		1				11	9	3	4	
37	20	(a) Sunderland	D 1-1	Pearson	14,725					6		**7**	12	10		5		2		8		1				11	9	3	4	
38	22	(a) Reading	L 1-2	Pearson	7,415					6				10	7	5		2		8		1				11	9	3	4	
39	25	(h) Birmingham C	W 4-0	Sheridan, Baird 2, Edwards	19,100					6				10	7	5		2		8		1				11	9	3	4	
40	May 2	(a) Derby C	L 1-2	Ashurst	20,087					6	**4**		7	10	12	5		2		8		1				11	9	3		
41	4	(h) West Brom A	W 3-2	Sheridan (pen), Pearson, Ormsby	24,688					6			7	10		5		2		8		1				11	9	3	4	
42	9	(a) Brighton & HA	W 1-0	Edwards	8,139		4			6			7	10	12	5		2		8		1				11	**9**	3		
FINAL LEAGUE POSITION: 4th in Division Two					Appearances	8	10	1	14	33	24	29	26	40	24	41	5	41	4	40	6	34	11	2	2	17	18	17	15	
					Sub appearances		1					2	3		6		2		1		3				2					
					Goals				1	4		7		15	6	1		1		15	1					1	4	1		

1 own-goal

Play-offs

	Date	Opponents	Result	Scorers	Attendance	Sinclair	Haddock	Caswell	Snodin I	Ormsby	Rennie	Ritchie	Stiles	Baird	Edwards	Ashurst	Swan	Aspin	Thompson	Sheridan	Buckley	Day	Robinson	Taylor	Doig	Adams	Pearson	McDonald	Aizlewood	Wright
SF	May 14	(h) Oldham A	W 1-0	Edwards	29,472					6		**7**		10	12	5		2		8		1				11	9	3	4	
	17	(a) Oldham A	L 1-2†	Edwards	19,216					6			**7**	10	12	5		2		8		1				11	9	3	4	
F	23	(a) Charlton A	L 0-1		16,680					6		12		10	7	5		2		8		1				11	**9**	3	4	
	25	(h) Charlton A	W 1-0	Ormsby	31,395					6		**7**		10	12	5		2		8		1		9		11		3	4	
R	29	(n‡) Charlton A	L 1-2*	Sheridan	18,000					**6**			7	10	12	5		2		8		1				11	9	3	4	
†After extra-time, won on away-goals rule. *After extra-time.					Appearances					5		2	2	5	1	5		5		5		5		1		5	4	5	5	
‡Played at St Andrew's, Birmingham.					Sub appearances							1			4															
					Goals					1					2					1										

FA Cup

	Date	Opponents	Result	Scorers	Attendance	Sinclair	Haddock	Caswell	Snodin I	Ormsby	Rennie	Ritchie	Stiles	Baird	Edwards	Ashurst	Swan	Aspin	Thompson	Sheridan	Buckley	Day	Robinson	Taylor	Doig	Adams	Pearson	McDonald	Aizlewood	Wright
3	Jan 11	(n‡) Telford U	W 2-1	Baird 2	6,460					6	4	7	3	9	10	5		2		8		1			11					
4	Feb 3	(a) Swindon T	W 2-1	Quinn (og), Baird	14,031					6	11	7	**4**	10	12	5		2		8		1				3	9			
5	21	(h) Queen's Park R	W 2-1	Baird, Ormsby	31,324					6	**4**	11	7	10	14	5		2		8	12	1				3	9			
6	Mar 15	(a) Wigan A	W 2-0	Stiles, Adams	12,479						6	7	4		10	5	11	2		8		1				3	9			
SF	Apr 12	(n†) Coventry C	L 2-3*	Rennie, Edwards	51,372		12			6	11	7	**4**	10	14	5		2		8		1				3	**9**			
‡Played at The Hawthorns, West Bromwich. †Played at Hillsborough, Sheffield.					Appearances					4	5	5	5	4	2	5	1	5		5		5			1	4	4			
*After extra-time					Sub appearances		1								3						1									
					Goals					1	1		1	4	1											1				

1 own-goal

League Cup

	Date	Opponents	Result	Scorers	Attendance	Sinclair	Haddock	Caswell	Snodin I	Ormsby	Rennie	Ritchie	Stiles	Baird	Edwards	Ashurst	Swan	Aspin	Thompson	Sheridan	Buckley	Day	Robinson	Taylor	Doig	Adams	Pearson	McDonald	Aizlewood	Wright
2	Sep 23	(a) Oldham A	L 2-3	Aspin, Taylor	5,569	1					6	11	4		9	5	10	2	3	8				**7**						12
	Oct 8	(h) Oldham A	L 0-1		11,449					4	6	11	**7**	9	10	5		2	3	8		1		12						
					Appearances	1				1	2	2	2	1	2	2	1	2	2	2		1		1						
					Sub appearances																			1						1
					Goals													1						1						

Leeds United also played in the Full Members' Cup (See *Invitation Tournaments*).

1987-88

Manager: Billy Bremner

	Date	Opponents	Result	Scorers	Att	Day	Aspin	Adams	Aizlewood	Ashurst	Rennie	Williams G	Sheridan	Pearson	Taylor	Snodin G	Edwards	Haddock	Buckley	Doig	Stiles	Grayson	Mummy	De Mange	Melrose	Swan	McDonald	Batty	Davison	Baird	Brockie	Maguire	Noteman
1	Aug 16	(a) Barnsley	D 1-1	Taylor	9,778	1	2	3	4	5	6	7	8	9	**10**	11	12																
2	19	(h) Leicester C	W 1-0	Sheridan (pen)	21,034	1	2	3	4	5	6	7	8	9	**10**	**11**	12	14															
3	22	(h) Reading	D 0-0		19,286	1	2	3	4	5	6	7	8	**9**			10	11	12														
4	29	(a) Bradford C	D 0-0		11,428	1	2	3	4	5	6	7	8	9	10			11															
5	31	(h) West Brom A	W 1-0	Sheridan	19,847	1	2	3	4	5	6	**7**	8	14	10		**9**	11		12													
6	Sep 5	(a) Ipswich T	L 0-1		11,163	1	2	3	4	5	6	7	8	12	**10**		9	11															
7	12	(h) Hull C	L 0-2		18,205	1	2	3	**4**	5	6		8	9		11	10	12			7												
8	15	(a) Huddersfield T	D 0-0		9,085	1	2	3		5	6		8	9		**7**	12	11			14	**4**	10										
9	19	(a) Middlesbrough	L 0-2		12,051	1	2	3		5	6		8	9	**10**	11	12	**4**			14		7										
10	26	(h) Manchester C	W 2-0	De Mange, Snodin	25,358	1	2	3		5	**6**		8	14	10	11		4					12	7	**9**								
11	30	(h) Stoke C	D 0-0		17,208	1	2	3		5	6		8	12	10	11		4						7	**9**								
12	Oct 3	(a) Blackburn R	D 1-1	Taylor	7,675	1	2	3		5	6		8	10	12	11		4						7	**9**								
13	10	(h) Aston Villa	L 1-3	Taylor	20,741	1	14	3		5	6		8		**9**	11		2			**4**		10	7	12								
14	17	(a) Plymouth A	L 3-6	Taylor, Snodin 2	9,358	1	2	**3**		5		6	8	**10**	9	11		4			12			7		14							
15	20	(a) Oldham A	D 1-1	Swan	6.312	1	2	3		5		8		**10**	9	11		6			4			7		12							
16	24	(h) Bournemouth	W 3-2	Taylor, Swan, Rennie	15,253	1		3		5	6	4	8		9	11		2						7		10							
17	31	(a) Sheffield U	D 2-2	Snodin, Swan	12,095	1		3		5		2	8		9	11		6		7				4		10							
18	Nov 7	(h) Shrewsbury T	W 2-1	Stiles, Taylor	13,760	1				5	7	2			9	11		6			8			4		10	3						
19	14	(a) Millwall	L 1-3	McLeary (og)	8,014	1				5	3	2		7	9	11		6			8			4		10							
20	21	(h) Swindon T	W 4-2	Rennie, Davison, Taylor, Haddock	15,457	1		3		5	8	**2**			9	11		6			12			4				7	10				
21	28	(a) Crystal P	L 0-3		8,749	1		3		5	**8**	2			9	11		6						4		12		7	10				
22	Dec 5	(h) Birmingham C	W 4-1	Sheridan (pen), Davison, Swan, Taylor	15,977	1	2	3		5		4	8		9	11		6								12		7	**10**				
23	12	(a) Reading	W 1-0	Sheridan (pen)	6,505	1	2	3		5			8		9			6						4		11		7	10				
24	19	(h) Huddersfield T	W 3-0	Sheridan 2, Davison	20,111	1	2	3		5		4	8		9			6								11		7	10				
25	26	(a) Manchester C	W 2-1	Redmond (og), Batty	30,153	1	2	3		5		4	8			**11**		6			12					9		7	10				
26	28	(h) Middlesbrough	W 2-0	Davison, Swan	34,186	1	2	3		5		4	8			11		6								9		7	10				
27	Jan 1	(h) Bradford C	W 2-0	Williams, Snodin	36,004	1	2	3		5		4	8			11		6								9		7	10				
28	3	(a) Hull C	L 1-3	Swan	14,694	1	2	3		5		4	**8**		14	**11**		6			12					9		7	10				
29	16	(h) Barnsley	L 0-2		19,028	1	2	3		5		4	8		**9**			6					14	12		11		**7**	10				
30	30	(a) West Brom A	W 4-1	Sheridan, Williams, Pearson, Davison	9,008	1	2	3		5	**11**	4	8	9	12			6						7					10				
31	Feb 6	(h) Ipswich T	W 1-0	Pearson	19,564	1	2	3		5	7	4	8	9		11		6											10				
32	13	(a) Leicester C	L 2-3	Williams, Sheridan (pen)	11,937	1	2	3		5	7	4	8	9	12			**6**										11	10				
33	23	(a) Stoke C	L 1-2	Pearson	10,129	1		3	4	5		2	8	9		11		6										7	10				
34	27	(h) Blackburn R	D 2-2	Sheridan (pen), Snodin	23,843	1		3	4	5	12	2	8	9	10	11		**6**										7					
35	Mar 5	(h) Plymouth A	W 1-0	Baird	18,115	1		3	4	5	12	**2**	8	10		11										6		7		9			
36	12	(a) Aston Villa	W 2-1	Swan, Taylor	19,677	1			**4**	5	12	2		10	8	11		3								6		7		9			
37	19	(h) Sheffield U	W 5-0	Swan, Pearson 3, Sheridan	22,376	1			**4**	5		2	12	10	8	11		3								6		7		9			
38	26	(a) Bournemouth	D 0-0		9,147	1		3	4	5		2	12	10		**11**		**8**								6		7	14	9			
39	Apr 2	(a) Shrewsbury T	L 0-1		7,369	1		3	4	5		**2**	8	**10**	11	14		7								6		12		9			
40	6	(h) Millwall	L 1-2	Sheridan (pen)	24,241	1		3	4	5			8	12	**11**	14		2								6		7	**10**	9			
41	23	(h) Oldham A	D 1-1	Snodin	13,442	1		3	4	5	10		8		12	11		2								**6**		7		9			
42	30	(a) Swindon T	W 2-1	Baird 2	8,299	1		3			6		8	12	**10**	11		2			4					5		7		9			
43	May 2	(h) Crystal P	W 1-0	Sheridan (pen)	13,217	1		3	14		6		8	12		11					**4**					5		7		9	2	**10**	
44	6	(a) Birmingham C	D 0-0		6,024	1		**3**			6		8			11						4				5		7		9	2	10	12
FINAL LEAGUE POSITION: 7th in Division Two					Appearances	44	25	40	16	41	25	31	36	21	27	33	4	38		1	7	2	3	14	3	21	1	22	15	10	2	2	
					Sub appearances		1		1		3		2	7	5	2	4	2	1	1	6		2	1	1	4		1	1				1
					Goals						2	3	12	6	9	7		1			1			1		8		1	5	3			

2 own-goals

FA Cup

	Date	Opponents	Result	Scorers	Att	Day	Aspin	Adams	Aizlewood	Ashurst	Rennie	Williams G	Sheridan	Pearson	Taylor	Snodin G	Edwards	Haddock	Buckley	Doig	Stiles	Grayson	Mummy	De Mange	Melrose	Swan	McDonald	Batty	Davison	Baird	Brockie	Maguire	Noteman
3	Jan 9	(h) Aston Villa	L 1-2	Davison	29,002	1	2	3		5		4	8		9	**11**		6							12			7	10				
					Appearances	1	1	1		1		1	1		1	1		1										1	1				
					Sub appearances																				1								
					Goals																								1				

League Cup

	Date	Opponents	Result	Scorers	Att	Day	Aspin	Adams	Aizlewood	Ashurst	Rennie	Williams G	Sheridan	Pearson	Taylor	Snodin G	Edwards	Haddock	Buckley	Doig	Stiles	Grayson	Mummy	De Mange	Melrose	Swan	McDonald	Batty	Davison	Baird	Brockie	Maguire	Noteman
2	Sep 23	(h) York C	D 1-1	Snodin	11,527	1	2	3		5	6	**7**	8	**9**	10	11				14	4		12										
	Oct 6	(a) York C	W 4-0	Sheridan 2, Taylor, Mumby	5,996	1		3		5	6		8	**9**	10	**11**		4		14	2		12	7									
3	28	(h) Oldham A	D 2-2	Swan 2	15,600	1	**2**	3		5		4	8		9	11		6			12			7		10							
R	Nov 4	(a) Oldham A	L 2-4*	Snodin, Taylor	7,058	1				5		2	8		9	11		6		**7**	12			4	14	**10**	3						
					Appearances	4	2	3		4	2	3	4	2	4	4		3		1	2			3		2	1						
					Sub appearances															2	2		2		1								
					Goals								2		2	2							1			2							

* After extra-time. Leeds United also played in the Full Members' Cup (See *Invitation Tournaments*).

1988-89

Manager: Billy Bremner until September then Howard Wilkinson

No	Date	Opponent	Result	Scorers	Att	Day	Haddock	Adams	Aizlewood	Balke	Ashurst	Stiles	Hilaire	Baird	Pearsonm	Snodin G	Davison	Rennie	Taylor	Williams G	Batty	Sheridan	Aspin	Williams A	Whitlow	Andrews	Swan	Fairclough	Strachan	Shutt	Kerr	Speed	Mumby	Ormsby
1	Aug 27	(h) Oxford U	D 1-1	Snodin	22,038	1	2	3	4	5	6	7	8	9	10	11	12	14																
2	Sep 3	(a) Portsmouth	L 0-4		15,263	1	2	3	4	5	6	8	11	9	10		12		7															
3	10	(h) Manchester C	D 1-1	Blake	23,677	1		3	4	5	6		11	9	14		10			2	7	8	12											
4	17	(a) Bournemouth	D 0-0		7,922	1	12	3	4	5	6		11		14		10		9	2	7	8												
5	21	(h) Barnsley	W 2-0	Davison, Hilaire	17,370	1	12	3	4	5	6		11	9			10			2	7	8												
6	24	(h) Chelsea	L 0-2		26,080	1	4	3		5	6		11	9	14	12	10			2	7	8												
7	Oct 1	(a) Brighton & HA	L 1-2	Baird	7,109	1		3	4	5			11	9	10	8		6		2	7	12												
8	4	(a) Sunderland	L 1-2	Davison	12,671	1	2	3		5		4	11	9	14		10	6			7	8	12											
9	8	(h) Watford	L 0-1		15,657	1		3		5		4	11	9	14	12	10	6			7	8	2											
10	16	(a) Swindon T	D 0-0		9,234	1			4	5	12		11	9	14	3	10	6			7	8	2											
11	22	(h) Leicester C	D 1-1	Hilaire	17,263	1			4	5		12	11	9	14	3	10	6			7	8	2											
12	26	(a) Bradford C	D 1-1	Davison	13,048	1			4	5		12	11	9	14	3	10	6			7	8	2											
13	29	(h) Hull C	W 2-1	Sheridan, Baird	17,536	1			4	5		14	11	9	12	3	10	6			7	8	2											
14	Nov 5	(a) Ipswich T	W 1-0	Sheridan (pen)	11.750	1			4	5		14	11	9	12	3	10	6			7	8	2											
15	12	(h) West Brom A	W 2-1	Aizlewood, Baird	20,442	1			4	5			11	9	14	3	10	6			7	8	2	12										
16	19	(a) Oldham A	D 2-2	Davison 2	8,824	1			4	5			11	9	14	3	10	6			7	8	2	12										
17	22	(a) Birmingham C	D 0-0		6,168	1		12	4	5			11	9		3	10	6	14			8	2	7										
18	26	(h) Stoke C	W 4-0	Baird 2, Davison, Sheridan (pen)	19,933	1			4	5			11	9		3	10	6			12	8	2		7									
19	Dec 3	(a) Walsall	W 3-0	Davison 2, Whitlow	6,885	1			4	5			11	9		3	10	6				8	2	12	7									
20	10	(h) Shrewsbury T	L 2-3	Sheridan (pen), Davison	19,967	1			4	5			11	9		3	10	6	12			8	2		7									
21	17	(a) Crystal P	D 0-0		9,847				4	5			11	9		3	10	6	12			8	2	14	7	1								
22	26	(h) Blackburn R	W 2-0	Baird, Davison	31,622	1			4	5			11	9	12	3	10	6				8	2	14	7									
23	31	(h) Plymouth A	W 2-0	Baird, Snodin	24,043	1			4	5			11	9	12	3	10	6				8	2		7									
24	Jan 2	(a) Manchester C	D 0-0		33,034	1			4	5			11	9	14	3	10	6			12	8	2		7									
25	14	(h) Birmingham C	W 1-0	Hilaire	21,937	1			4	5			11	9	12	3	10	6					2	8	7									
26	21	(a) Oxford U	L 2-3	Blake, Hilaire	7,928	1			4	5			11	9	14	3	10	6				8	2	12	7									
27	Feb 4	(h) Sunderland	W 2-0	Davison, Sheridan (pen)	31,985	1		4		5			11	9		3	10	6			7	8	2											
28	11	(a) Watford	D 1-1	Pearson	13,439	1		4		5			11	9	14	3	10	6			7	8	2	12										
29	18	(a) Leicester C	W 2-1	Davison, Snodin	14,151	1		4	14	5			11	9	12	3	10	6			7	8	2											
30	25	(h) Swindon T	D 0-0		22,651	1		4	12	5			11	9	14	3	10	6			7	8	2											
31	Mar 1	(h) Bradford C	D 3-3	Blake, Hilaire, Baird	33,325	1		4	12	5			11	9		3	10	6			7	8	2											
32	5	(a) West Brom A	L 1-2	Adams	15,914	1		4	12	5			11	9	14	3	10	6		2	7	8												
33	11	(h) Ipswich T	L 2-4	Hilaire, Blake	19,639	1			4	5			11	9	14	3	10	6		2	7	8			12									
34	14	(a) Hull C	W 2-1	Baird, Davison	8,887	1			4				11	9	14	3	10			2	7	8	6		12		5							
35	19	(a) Barnsley	D 2-2	Aizlewood, Sheridan (pen)	11,578	1	2		4	5			11		9	3	10		12			8	6	14	7									
36	25	(h) Portsmouth	W 1-0	Baird	27,049	1			4	5			11	9	14	3	10					8	2	12				6	7					
37	27	(a) Blackburn R	L 0-2		11,533	1			4	5			11	9	10	3					12	8	2	14				6	7					
38	Apr 1	(h) Bournemouth	W 3-0	Shutt 3	21,095	1			4	5				9		3						8	2	12	11			6	7	10				
39	5	(h) Crystal P	L 1-2	Shutt	25,604	1			4				11	9	12	3		5				8	2					6	7	10				
40	9	(a) Plymouth A	L 0-1		9,365	1				5				9	12	3		14			8		2	4	11			6	7	10				
41	15	(h) Brighton & HA	W 1-0	A.Williams	14,915	1	2		3	5					9		10	12				8		4	11			6	7		14			
42	22	(a) Chelsea	L 0-1		30,337	1			4	5				9	14		10					12	2	8	11			6	7		3			
43	29	(a) Stoke C	W 3-2	Sheridan (pen), Davison, Strachan	9,051	1	14		4	5			11	9			10				12	8		2	3			6	7					
44	May 1	(h) Walsall	W 1-0	Aizlewood	13,280	1	14		4	5			11	9			10				12	8		2	3			6	7					
45	6	(h) Oldham A	D 0-0		14,459	1	2			5		14	11	9				4			8				3			6	7			10	12	
46	13	(a) Shrewsbury T	D 3-3	Strachan 2 (1 pen), Rennie	4,693	1	2			5		14	11	9				10			8				3			6	7		12			4
					Appearances	45	8	15	34	44	6	4	42	43	6	33	37	30	2	8	25	38	31	7	18	1	1	11	11	3	1	1		1
					Sub appearances		4	1	4		1	6			27	2	2	3	4		5	2	2	11	2						2		1	
					Goals			1	3	4			6	10	1	3	14	1				7		1	1				3	4				

FINAL LEAGUE POSITION: 10th in Division Two

FA Cup

Round	Date	Opponent	Result	Scorers	Att	Day	Haddock	Adams	Aizlewood	Balke	Ashurst	Stiles	Hilaire	Baird	Pearsonm	Snodin G	Davison	Rennie	Taylor	Williams G	Batty	Sheridan	Aspin	Williams A	Whitlow	Andrews	Swan	Fairclough	Strachan	Shutt	Kerr	Speed	Mumby	Ormsby
3	Jan 7	(a) Brighton & HA	W 2-1	Baird 2	10,900	1	14		4	5			11	9	12	3	10	6				8	2	7										
4	28	(a) Nottingham F	L 0-2		28,107	1		10		5			11	9		3	12	6		14	7	8	2				4							
					Appearances	2		1	1	2			2	2		2	1	2			1	2	2	1			1							
					Sub appearances		1								1		1			1														
					Goals									2																				

League Cup

Round	Date	Opponent	Result	Scorers	Att	Day	Haddock	Adams	Aizlewood	Balke	Ashurst	Stiles	Hilaire	Baird	Pearsonm	Snodin G	Davison	Rennie	Taylor	Williams G	Batty	Sheridan	Aspin	Williams A	Whitlow	Andrews	Swan	Fairclough	Strachan	Shutt	Kerr	Speed	Mumby	Ormsby
2	Sep 27	(a) Peterborough U	W 2-1	Snodin, Baird	4,979	1	12	3	4	5			11	9	10	8		6		2	7													
	Oct 12	(h) Peterborough U	W 3-1	Davison, Hilarie, Sheridan (pen)	8,894	1			4	5			11	9	12	3	10	6			7	8	2											
3	Nov 2	(h) Luton T	L 0-2		19,447	1			4	5			11	9		3	10	6			7	8	2											
					Appearances	3		1	3	3			3	3	1	3	2	3		1	3	2	2											
					Sub appearances		1								1																			
					Goals								1	1		1	1					1												

Leeds United also played in the Full Members' Cup (See *Invitation Tournaments*).

1989-90

Manager: Howard Wilkinson

No.	Date	Opponent	Result	Scorers	Att	Day	Sterland	Beglin	Thomas	McClelland	Haddock	Strachan	Batty	Baird	Davison	Hendrie	Whitlow	Shutt	Fairclough	Jons	Speed	Balke	Williams A	Turner	Pearson	Kerr	Snodin G	Chapman	Kamara	Varadi	O'Donnell	Hilaire
1	Aug 19 (a)	Newcastle U	L 2-5	Davison, Baird	24,482	1	2	3	**4**	5	6	7	8	9	**10**	11	12	14														
2	23 (h)	Middlesbrough	W 2-1	Davison, Parkinson (og)	25,004	1	2		**4**		6	7	8	**9**	10	11	3	12	5	14												
3	26 (h)	Blackburn R	D 1-1	Fairclough	25,045	1	2		**4**		6	7	8	9	**10**	11	3	14	5	12												
4	Sep 2 (a)	Stoke C	D 1-1	Strachan	10,915	1	2				6	7	8	9	**10**	11	3		5	4	12											
5	9 (h)	Ipswich T	D 1-1	Jones	22,972	1	2				6	7	8	9	10	**11**	3		5	4	12											
6	16 (a)	Hull C	W 1-0	Davison	11,620	1	2					7	8	9	10	11	**3**		6	4		5	12									
7	23 (h)	Swindon T	W 4-0	Strachan 3 (1 pen), Davison	21,694	1	2				6	7	8	9	10	**11**	3			4		5	12									
8	27 (h)	Oxford U	W 2-1	Davison, Sterland	24,097	1	2				6	7	8	9	10	11	3			**4**		5	12									
9	30 (a)	Port Vale	D 0-0		11,156	1	2				6	7	8	9	**10**		3	14		**4**	12	5	11									
10	Oct 7 (a)	West Ham U	W 1-0	Jones	23,539	1	2				6	7	8	9	**10**		3	12	5	4			11									
11	14 (h)	Sunderland	W 2-0	Davison, Fairclough	27,815	1	2				6	7	8	9	10		3		5	4			11									
12	17 (a)	Portsmouth	D 3-3	Davison, Whitlow, Sterland	10,260	1	2				6	7	8	9	10		3		5	4			11									
13	21 (h)	Wolves	W 1-0	Davison	28,204	1	2				6	**7**	8	9	10		3	14	5	4	12		**11**									
14	28 (a)	Bradford C	W 1-0	Davison	12,527	1	2				6	7	8	9	10		3	12	5	4			**11**									
15	Nov 1 (h)	Plymouth A	W 2-1	Strachan (pen), Davison	26,791	1	2				6	7	8	9	10		3		5	**4**	12		11									
16	4 (h)	Bournemouth	W 3-0	Baird, Strachan (pen), Fairclough	26,484	1	2				6	7	8	9	10		3		5	4	12		**11**									
17	11 (a)	Leicester C	L 3-4	Baird, A.Williams, Strachan (pen)	18,032	**1**	2				6	7	8	9	10		3	12	5	4			11									
18	18 (h)	Watford	W 2-1	Fairclough, A.Williams	26,921		2				6	7	8	9	**10**		3	12	5	4			11	1								
19	25 (a)	West Brom A	L 1-2	Fairclough	15,116		2				6	7	8	9	10		3	14	5	**4**	12		**11**	1								
20	Dec 2 (h)	Newcastle U	W 1-0	Baird	31,715	1	2					7	8	9	10		3	12	5	4		6	**11**									
21	9 (a)	Middlesbrough	W 2-0	Shutt, Fairclough	19,686	1	2					7	8				3	10	6	4		5	11		9							
22	16 (h)	Brighton & HA	W 3-0	Strachan, Hendrie, Jones	24,070	1	2				6	7	8	12		**11**	3	**10**	5	4	14				9							
23	26 (a)	Sheffield U	D 2-2	Sterland, Shutt	31,254	1	2					7	8	9		11	3	10	6	4		5										
24	30 (a)	Barnsley	L 0-1		14,485	1	2				6	7	8	9		**11**	**3**	10	5	4					14	12						
25	Jan 1 (h)	Oldham A	D 1-1	Hendrie	30,217	1	2				6	7	8	**9**		11		**10**	5	4					14	3	12					
26	13 (a)	Blackburn R	W 2-1	Chapman, Strachan	14,485	1	**2**	12			6	7	8		10	11	3		5	4								9				
27	20 (h)	Stoke C	W 2-0	Strachan (pen), Hendrie	29,318	1		2			6	7	8		**10**	11	3		5	4					12			9				
28	Feb 4 (a)	Swindon T	L 2-3	Strachan (pen), Hendrie	16,208	1		2			6	7	8			11	**3**		5	4	12				14	**10**		9				
29	10 (h)	Hull C	W 4-3	Hendrie, Jones, Varadi, Strachan	29,977	1		**3**			6	7	8			11			5	4								**9**	2	10	12	14
30	17 (a)	Ipswich T	D 2-2	Chapman 2	17,102	1		3			6	7	8			**11**			5	4								9	2	10		12
31	24 (h)	West Brom A	D 2-2	Kamara, Chapman	30,004	1	12	3			6	7	8			**11**			5	4								9	2	10		
32	Mar 3 (a)	Watford	L 0-1		13,468	1	2	3			6	7	8			14			5	4	12							9	**11**	**10**		
33	7 (h)	Port Vale	D 0-0		28,756	1	2	3			6	7	8			**11**			5	4	12							9		10		
34	10 (a)	Oxford U	W 4-2	Chapman 2, Varadi, Fairclough	8,397	1	2	**3**			6	7				12			5	4	**8**					14	11	9		10		
35	17 (h)	West Ham U	W 3-2	Chapman 2, Strachan	32,356	1	2				6	7				**11**		12	5	4	8					14	3	9		**10**		
36	20 (a)	Sunderland	W 1-0	Sterland	17,851	1	2				6	7	8		14	12			5	4	11						**3**	9		**10**		
37	24 (h)	Portsmouth	W 2-0	Jones, Chapman	27,600	1	2	3			6	**7**	8			12	14		5	4	11							9		**10**		
38	31 (a)	Wolves	L 0-1		22,419	1	2				6	7	8			12	3		5	4	**11**							9	14	**10**		
39	Apr 7 (h)	Bradford C	D 1-1	Speed	32,316	1	2	3			6	7	8		12	**10**			5	4	11							9				
40	10 (a)	Plymouth A	D 1-1	Chapman	11,382	1	2	3			6	7	8		12	**10**			5	4	11							9				
41	13 (a)	Oldham A	L 1-3	Davison	16,292	1	2	3			**6**	7	8		12				5	4	14							9	11	**10**		
42	16 (h)	Sheffield U	W 4-0	Strachan 2 (1 pen), Chapman, Speed	32,727	1	2	3		6		7			**10**			12	5	4	11							9	8			
43	21 (a)	Brighton & HA	D 2-2	Speed, I.Chapman (og)	11,359	1	2	3		6		7	14					12	5	4	11							9	**8**	**10**		
44	25 (h)	Barnsley	L 1-2	Fairclough	31,700	1	2	3			6	7						**10**	5	4	11				12			9	8			
45	28 (h)	Leicester C	W 2-1	Sterland, Strachan	32,597	1	2	3			6	7	14		**10**				5	**4**	11							9	8	12		
46	May 5 (a)	Bournemouth	W 1-0	Chapman	9,918	1	2	3			6	7	14		**10**			**12**	5	4	11							9	8			
FINAL LEAGUE POSITION: 1st in Division Two					Appearances	44	41	18	3	3	40	46	39	23	25	22	27	6	42	43	12	7	13	2	2	2	3	21	10	12		
					Sub appearances		1	1					3	1	4	5	2	15		2	12		3		5	3	1		1	1	1	2
					Goals		5					16		4	11	5	1	2	8	5	3		2					12	1	2		

2 own-goals

FA Cup

Rd	Date	Opponent	Result	Scorers	Att	Day	Sterland	Beglin	Thomas	McClelland	Haddock	Strachan	Batty	Baird	Davison	Hendrie	Whitlow	Shutt	Fairclough	Jons	Speed	Balke	Williams A	Turner	Pearson	Kerr	Snodin G	Chapman	Kamara	Varadi	O'Donnell	Hilaire
3	Jan 6 (h)	Ipswich T	L 0-1		26,766	1	2				6	7	8	**9**		11		**10**	5	4					12	3	14					
					Appearances	1	1				1	1	1	1		1		1	1	1						1						
					Sub appearances																				1		1					
					Goals																											

League Cup

Rd	Date	Opponent	Result	Scorers	Att	Day	Sterland	Beglin	Thomas	McClelland	Haddock	Strachan	Batty	Baird	Davison	Hendrie	Whitlow	Shutt	Fairclough	Jons	Speed	Balke	Williams A	Turner	Pearson	Kerr	Snodin G	Chapman	Kamara	Varadi	O'Donnell	Hilaire
2	Sep 19 (a)	Oldham A	L 1-2	Strachan	8,415	1	2				6	7	8	9	**10**	11	3		**5**	4		12	14									
	Oct 3 (h)	Oldham A	L 1-2	Fairclough	18,092	1	2				6	7	8	9	10		3		12	**4**	14	**5**	11									
					Appearances	2	2				2	2	2	2	2	1	2		1	2		1	1									
					Sub appearances														1		1	1	1									
					Goals							1							1													

Leeds United also played in the Full Members' Cup (See *Invitation Tournaments*).

1990-91

Manager: Howard Wilkinson

No	Date	Opponents	Result	Scorers	Att	Lukic	Sterland	Snodin	Batty	Fairclough	Whyte	Strachan	Varadi	Chapman	McAllister	Speed	Kamara	Haddock	Whitlow	Jones	Pearson	Shutt	Williams	Davison	McClelland	Day
1	Aug 25	(a) Everton	W 3-2	Fairclough, Speed, Varadi	34,412	1	2	3	4	5	6	7	**8**	9	10	**11**	12	14								
2	28	(h) Manchester U	D 0-0		29,172	1	2	12	4	5	6	7	8	9	10	**11**		3								
3	Sep 1	(h) Norwich C	W 3-0	Chapman 2, Varadi	25,684	1	2	**3**	4	5	6	7	8	9	**10**	11		14	12							
4	8	(a) Luton T	L 0-1		10,185	1	2	**3**	4		6	7	12	9	10	14		5	11	**8**						
5	15	(h) Tottenham H	L 0-2		31,342	1	2	12	4	5	6	7	8	9	10	**11**		14	**3**							
6	23	(a) Sheffield U	W 2-0	Pearson, Strachan	26,078	1	2		4	5	6	7	**8**	9	10	11		3			12					
7	29	(h) Arsenal	D 2-2	Chapman, Strachan (pen)	30,085	1	2	**11**	4	5	6	7		9	10	12		3			8					
8	Oct 6	(a) Crystal P	D 1-1	Speed	21,676	1	2		4	5	6	7		9	10	11		3			8					
9	20	(h) Queen's Park R	L 2-3	Whyte, Chapman	27,443	1	2	3	4	5	6	7		9	**10**	11	12				**8**	14				
10	27	(a) Aston Villa	D 0-0		24,219	1	2		4	5	6	7		9	10	11	3				8					
11	Nov 3	(h) Nottingham F	W 3-1	Chapman, Strachan (pen), McAllister	30,409	1	2	12	4	5	6	7		9	10	11	3					**8**				
12	11	(a) Manchester C	W 3-2	Chapman, Shutt, Strachan	27,782	1	2		4	5	6	7		9	10	11	3				12	**8**				
13	17	(h) Derby C	W 3-0	Chapman, Strachan, Speed	27,868	1	2		4	5	6	7		9	10	11	3					8				
14	24	(a) Coventry C	D 1-1	Chapman	16,183	1	2		4	6	5	7		9	10	11	**3**	14			12	**8**				
15	Dec 1	(h) Southampton	W 2-1	Fairclough, Shutt	29,341	1	2		4	5	6	7		**9**	**10**	11		3			12	8	14			
16	8	(a) Manchester U	D 1-1	Sterland	40,927	1	2		4	5	6	7		9	10	11		3				8				
17	16	(h) Everton	W 2-0	Strachan (pen), Shutt	27,775	1	2	12	4	5	6	7		9	10	**11**		3				8				
18	23	(a) Sunderland	W 1-0	Sterland	23,773	1	2	12	4	5	6	7		9	10	11		**3**				8				
19	26	(h) Chelsea	W 4-1	Sterland, Chapman 2, Whitlow	30,893	1	2	3	4	5	6	7		9	10	**11**			12			8				
20	29	(h) Wimbledon	W 3-0	Chapman, Speed, Sterland	29,292	1	2	**3**	4	5	6	7		9	10	11			12		14	**8**				
21	Jan 1	(a) Liverpool	L 0-3		36,975	1	2	**3**	4	5	6	7		9	10	11			12		14	**8**				
22	12	(a) Norwich C	L 0-2		17,786	1	2	3	4	5	6	7		9	10	12			**11**		14	**8**				
23	19	(h) Luton T	W 2-1	Strachan (pen), Fairclough	27,010	1	2	**3**	4	5	6	7		9	10	11		12				8				
24	Feb 2	(a) Tottenham H	D 0-0		32,253	1	2	14		5	6	7		**9**	10	11		3	4		**12**		8			
25	Mar 2	(a) Southampton	L 0-2		16,858	1	2		4	5	6			9	10	11			3			8	**7**	12		
26	9	(h) Coventry C	W 2-0	Davison, Whyte	28,880	1	2		4	5	6	7		9	10	11			3			12		**8**		
27	17	(a) Arsenal	L 0-2		26,218	1	2		4	5	6	7		9	10	11			3			12		**8**		
28	23	(h) Crystal P	L 1-2	Speed	28,556	1	2		4	5	6	7		9	**10**	11			3		14	**8**	12			
29	30	(a) Chelsea	W 2-1	Shutt, Fairclough	17,585	1	2		4	5	6	**7**		9	10	11			3			8	12			
30	Apr 2	(h) Sunderland	W 5-0	Chapman 2, Shutt, Speed 2	28,132	1	2		4		6	7		9	10	11			3			8			5	
31	6	(a) Wimbledon	W 1-0	Chapman	6,800	1	2		4		6	7		9	10	11			3			**8**	12		5	
32	10	(h) Manchester C	L 1-2	McAllister	28,757	1	2		4		6			9	10	11			3			8	**7**	12	5	
33	13	(h) Liverpool	L 4-5	Chapman 3, Shutt	31,460	1	2		4	5	6	7		9	10	11			3			8				
34	17	(a) Queen's Park R	L 0-2		10,998	1	2		4	5	6	7		9	10	11			**3**			8	12			
35	23	(a) Derby C	W 1-0	Shutt	12,666	1	2	**3**	4	5	6	7		9	10	11						8	12			
36	May 4	(h) Aston Villa	W 5-2	Price (og), Chapman 2, Whyte, Shutt	29,188	1	2	3	4	5	6			9	10	11						8	**7**	12		
37	8	(h) Sheffield U	W 2-1	Sterland, Shutt	28,978	1	2	3	4	5	6			9	10	11						8	7			
38	11	(a) Nottingham F	L 3-4	Chapman 2, Shutt	25,067	1	2	3	4	5	6	**7**		9	10	11						8	12			
FINAL LEAGUE POSITION: 4th in Division One					Appearances	38	38	14	37	34	38	34	5	38	38	35	5	10	14	1	4	25	5	2	3	
					Sub appearances			6					1			3	2	5	4		9	3	7	3		
					Goals		5			4	3	7	2	21	2	7			1		1	10		1		

1 own-goal

FA Cup

Rd	Date	Opponents	Result	Scorers	Att	Lukic	Sterland	Snodin	Batty	Fairclough	Whyte	Strachan	Varadi	Chapman	McAllister	Speed	Kamara	Haddock	Whitlow	Jones	Pearson	Shutt	Williams	Davison	McClelland	Day
3	Jan 6	(a) Barnsley	D 1-1	Sterland	22,424	1	2	3	4	5		7		9	10	**11**			14		12	**8**			6	
R	9	(h) Barnsley	W 4-0	Smith (og), Chapman, McAllister, Strachan (pen)	19,773	1	2	3	4	5		7		**9**	10	**11**			14		12	8			6	
4	27	(a) Arsenal	D 0-0		30,905	1	2		4	5	6	7		9	10	11		3			12	**8**				
R	30	(h) Arsenal	D 1-1*	Chapman	27,753	1	**2**	12	4	5	6	7		9	10	11		3			8					
2R	Feb 13	(a) Arsenal	D 0-0*		30,433	1	2		4	5	6	7		9	10	11		**3**	12			**8**		14		
3R	16	(h) Arsenal	L 1-2	Chapman	27,190	1	2		4	5	6	7		9	10	11		3				**8**		12		
				*After extra-time	Appearances	6	6	2	6	6	4	6		6	6	6		4			1	5			2	
					Sub appearances			1											3		3			2		
					Goals		1					1		3	1											

1 own-goal

League Cup

Rd	Date	Opponents	Result	Scorers	Att	Lukic	Sterland	Snodin	Batty	Fairclough	Whyte	Strachan	Varadi	Chapman	McAllister	Speed	Kamara	Haddock	Whitlow	Jones	Pearson	Shutt	Williams	Davison	McClelland	Day
2	Sep 26	(a) Leicester C	L 0-1		13,744	1	2		4	5	6	7	**8**	9	10	11			**3**		14		12			
	Oct 10	(h) Leicester C	W 3-0	Walsh (og), Speed, Strachan	19,090		2		4	5	6	7		**9**	10	11	14	3			**8**	12				1
3	31	(h) Oldham A	W 2-0	Chapman, Speed	26,327	1		3	4	5	6	7		9	10	11	2				8					
4	Nov 27	(a) Queen's Park R	W 3-0	McAllister, Fairclough, Chapman	15,832	1	2	12	4	5	6	**7**		9	10	11		3				8				
5	Jan 16	(h) Aston Villa	W 4-1	Chapman 2, McAllister, Speed	28,176	1	2	**3**	4	5	6	7		9	10	11		12			14	**8**				
SF	Feb 10	(a) Manchester U	L 1-2	Whyte	34,050	1	2			5	6	7		9	10	11		3	4				8			
	24	(h) Manchester U	L 0-1		32,014	1	2		4	5	6	**7**		9	10	11		**3**	13		12	8				
					Appearances	6	6	2	6	7	7	7	1	7	7	7	1	4	2		2	3	1			1
					Sub appearances			1									1	1	1		3	1	1			
					Goals					1	1	1		4	2	3										

Leeds United also played in the Full Members' Cup (See *Invitation Tournaments*).

1 own-goal

1991-92

Manager: Howard Wilkinson

No	Date	Opponent	Result	Scorers	Att	Lukic	McClelland	Dorigo	Batty	Fairclough	Whyte	Strachan	Wallace Rod	Chapman	McAllister	Speed	Hodge	Sterland	Wetherall	Shutt	Varadi	Whitlow	Kamara	Newsome	Kelly	Davison	Cantona	Agana	Williams
1	Aug 20	(h) Nottingham F	W 1-0	McAllister	29,457	1	2	3	4	5	6	7	8	9	10	11													
2	24	(h) Sheffield W	D 1-1	Hodge	30,260	1	2	3	4	5	6	7	8	9	10	11	12	14											
3	28	(a) Southampton	W 4-0	Speed 2, Strachan 2 (2 pens)	15,847	1	2	3	4	5	6	7	8	9	10	11	12	14											
4	31	(a) Manchester U	D 1-1	Chapman	43,778	1	5	3	4		6	7	8	9	10	11	12	2											
5	Sep 3	(h) Arsenal	D 2-2	Strachan (pen), Chapman	29,396	1	5	3	4		6	7	8	9	10	11	12	2	14										
6	7	(h) Manchester C	W 3-0	Dorigo, Batty, Strachan (pen)	29,986	1	5	3	4		6	7	8	9	10	11	12	2											
7	14	(a) Chelsea	W 1-0	Shutt	23,439	1	5	3	4		6	7		9	10	11	12	2		8									
8	18	(a) Coventry C	D 0-0		15,488	1	5	3	4		6	7		9	10	11	12	2		8									
9	21	(h) Liverpool	W 1-0	Hodge	32,917	1	5	3	4		6	7		9	10	11	8	2		12									
10	28	(a) Norwich C	D 2-2	Dorigo, Speed	15,828	1	5	3	4		6			9	10	11	8	2		12	7	14							
11	Oct 1	(a) Crystal P	L 0-1		18,298	1	5	3	4		6			9	10	11	8	2		12	7	14							
12	5	(h) Sheffield U	W 4-3	Hodge 2, Sterland 2 (1 pen)	28,362	1	5	3	4	12	6			9	10	11	7	2		8		14							
13	19	(a) Notts C	W 4-2	Chapman, Hodge, Whyte, McAllister	12,964	1		3	4	5	6	7		9	12	11	10	2		8			14						
14	26	(h) Oldham A	W 1-0	Kilcline (og)	28,199	1		3	4	5	6	7	8	9	10	11		2		12			14						
15	Nov 2	(a) Wimbledon	D 0-0		7,025	1		3		5	6	7	8	9	10	11		2		4				12					
16	16	(h) Queen's Park R	W 2-0	Sterland, Wallace	27,087	1		3	4	5	6	7	8	9	10	11		2			12								
17	24	(a) Aston Villa	W 4-1	Wallace, Sterland, Chapman 2	23,666	1	11	3	4	5	6	7	8	9	10			2											
18	30	(h) Everton	W 1-0	Wallace	30,043	1	14	3	4	5	6	7	8	9	10	11	12	2											
19	Dec 7	(a) Luton T	W 2-0	Wallace, Speed	11,550	1		3	4	5	6	7	8	9	10	11		2											
20	14	(h) Tottenham H	D 1-1	Speed	31,404	1	5	3	4		6	7	8	9	10	11		2											
21	22	(a) Nottingham F	D 0-0		27,170	1	5	3	4		6	7	8	9	10	11		2							12				
22	26	(h) Southampton	D 3-3	Hodge 2, Speed	29,053	1	5	3	4		6		8	9	10	11	7	2											
23	29	(h) Manchester U	D 1-1	Sterland (pen)	32,638	1		3	4	5	6	7	8	9	10	11	12	2											
24	Jan 1	(a) West Ham U	W 3-1	Chapman 2, McAllister	21,766	1		3	4	5	6	7	8	9	10	11		2											
25	12	(a) Sheffield W	W 6-1	Chapman 3, Dorigo, Whitlow, Wallace	32,228	1		3		5	6		8	9	10	11	4	2		7		12				14			
26	18	(h) Crystal P	D 1-1	Fairclough	27,717	1		3	4	5	6	7	8		10	11	9	2				12				14			
27	Feb 1	(h) Notts C	W 3-0	Sterland, Batty, Wallace	27,224	1		3	4	5	6	7	8		10	11	9	2				12			14				
28	8	(a) Oldham A	L 0-2		18,409	1		3	4	5	6	7	8		10	11	9	2				12					14		
29	23	(a) Everton	D 1-1	Keown (og)	19,248	1		3	4	5	6	7	8		10	11		2		12							9		
30	29	(h) Luton T	W 2-0	Cantona, Chapman	28,231	1		3	4	5	6	7	8	9	10	11		2									12	14	
31	Mar 3	(h) Aston Villa	D 0-0		28,896	1	14		4	5	6	7		9	10	11		2				3					12	8	
32	7	(a) Tottenham H	W 3-1	Wallace, Newsome, McAllister	27,622	1			4	5	6	7	8	9	10	11		2				3		14			12		
33	11	(a) Queen's Park R	L 1-4	Speed	14,641	1			4	5	6	7	8	9	10	11						3		2			12		
34	14	(h) Wimbledon	W 5-1	Chapman 3, Wallace, Cantona	26,760	1			4	5	6	7	8	9	10	11				12				2			3		
35	22	(a) Arsenal	D 1-1	Chapman	27,844	1		3	4	5	6	7	8	9	10	11											2		
36	28	(h) West Ham U	D 0-0		31,101	1		3	4	5		7	8	9	10	11	12							6			2		
37	Apr 4	(a) Manchester C	L 0-4		30,239	1		3	4	5	6	7	8	9	10	11											2		
38	11	(h) Chelsea	W 3-0	Wallace, Chapman, Cantona	31,363	1		3	4	5	6	7	8	9	10	11	2							14			12		
39	18	(a) Liverpool	D 0-0		37,186	1		3	4	5	6		8	9	10	11	7							2			12		
40	20	(h) Coventry C	W 2-0	Fairclough, McAllister (pen)	26,582	1		3	4	5	6	7	8	9	10	11				14				2			12		
41	26	(a) Sheffield U	W 3-2	Wallace, Newsome, Gayle (og)	32,000	1		3	4	5	6	7	8	9	10	11				14				2			12		
42	May 2	(h) Norwich C	W 1-0	Wallace	32,673	1		3	4	5	6	7	8	9	10	11	12							2			14		
					Appearances	42	16	38	40	30	41	35	34	38	41	41	12	29		6	2	3		7			6	1	
					Sub appearances		2			1		1			1		11	2	1	8	1	7	2	3	2	2	9	1	
					Goals			3	2	2	1	4	11	16	5	7	7	6		1		1		2			3		

FINAL LEAGUE POSITION: 1st in Division One

3 own-goals

FA Cup

Rd	Date	Opponent	Result	Scorers	Att	Lukic	McClelland	Dorigo	Batty	Fairclough	Whyte	Strachan	Wallace Rod	Chapman	McAllister	Speed	Hodge	Sterland	Wetherall	Shutt	Varadi	Whitlow	Kamara	Newsome	Kelly	Davison	Cantona	Agana	Williams
3	Jan 15	(h) Manchester U	L 0-1		31,819	1		3		5	6		8	9	10	11	4	2				14				12			7
					Appearances	1		1		1	1		1	1	1	1	1	1											1
					Sub appearances																	1				1			
					Goals																								

League Cup

Rd	Date	Opponent	Result	Scorers	Att	Lukic	McClelland	Dorigo	Batty	Fairclough	Whyte	Strachan	Wallace Rod	Chapman	McAllister	Speed	Hodge	Sterland	Wetherall	Shutt	Varadi	Whitlow	Kamara	Newsome	Kelly	Davison	Cantona	Agana	Williams
2	Sep 24	(a) Scunthorpe U	D 0-0		8,392	1	5	3	4		6	7		9	10	11	8	2		12									
	Oct 8	(h) Scunthorpe U	W 3-0	Sterland (pen), Chapman, Speed	14,558	1	5	3	4	14	6			9		11	7	2		8					12				10
3	29	(h) Tranmere R	W 3-1	Chapman 2, Shutt	18,266	1		3		5	6	7	11	9	10		4	2		8			12						14
4	Dec 4	(a) Everton	W 4-1	Speed, Chapman, Wallace 2	25,467	1		3	4	5	6	7	8	9	10	11	12	2											
5	Jan 8	(h) Manchester U	L 1-3	Speed	28,886	1	12	3	4	5	6	7	8	9	10	11	14	2											
					Appearances	5	2	5	4	3	5	4	3	5	4	4	3	5		2									1
					Sub appearances		1			1							2			1			1		1				1
					Goals								2	4		3		1		1									

Leeds United also played in the Full Members' Cup (See *Invitation Tournaments*).
In match 42 Strachan, although coming on as substitute, wore the number-7 shirt, Cantona wore the number-14 shirt and Hodge wore the number-12 shirt. Strachan replaced Cantona and Hodge replaced Chapman.

1992-93

Manager: Howard Wilkinson

No	Date	Opponent	Result	Scorers	Att	Lukic	Newsome	Dorigo	Batty	Fairclough	Whyte	Cantona	Wallace Rod	Chapman	McAllister	Speed	Strachan	Hodge	Sellars	Wetherall	Shutt	Rocastle	Day	Wallace Ray	Varadi	Sterland	Strandli	Bowman	Kerslake	Forrester	Kerr	Tinkler	Sharp	Whelan	Beeney
1	Aug 15	(h) Wimbledon	W 2-1	Chapman 2	25,795	1	**2**	3	**4**	5	6	7	8	9	10	11	12	14																	
2	19	(a) Aston Villa	D 1-1	Speed	29,151	1	2	3	**4**	5	6	**7**	8	9	10	11	12	14																	
3	22	(a) Middlesbrough	L 1-4	Cantona	18,649	1	**2**	3	**4**	5	6	7	8	9	10	11	12	14																	
4	25	(h) Tottenham H	W 5-0	Wallace, Cantona 3, Chapman	28,218	1	2	3	4	5	6	7	8	9	10	11																			
5	29	(h) Liverpool	D 2-2	McAllister, Chapman	29,597	1	2	3	**4**	**5**	6	7	8	9	10	11	12	14																	
6	Sep 1	(a) Oldham A	D 2-2	Cantona 2	13,848	1	2	3	4	5	6	**7**	8	9	10	11		12																	
7	6	(a) Manchester U	L 0-2		31,296	1	**2**	3	4	5	6	7	**8**	9	10	11	12	14																	
8	13	(h) Aston Villa	D 1-1	Hodge	27,817	1	**2**		4	5	6	7		9	10	11	8	12	3																
9	19	(a) Southampton	D 1-1	Speed	16,229	1		3	4	5	6			9	10	11	7	**8**	12	**2**	14														
10	26	(h) Everton	W 2-0	McAllister (pen), Chapman	27,915	1		3	4	5	6	8		9	10	11	7		**2**		12														
11	Oct 3	(a) Ipswich T	L 2-4	Stockwell (og), Speed	21,200	1		3	4	5	6	8		9	10	11	7		**2**			12													
12	17	(h) Sheffield U	W 3-1	Chapman, Speed, Whyte	29,706	1	2	3	4	5	6	**8**		9	10	11	7				12														
13	24	(a) Queen's Park R	L 1-2	Strachan	19,326	1	2	3	4	5	6		**8**	9	**10**	11	7				12	14													
14	31	(h) Coventry C	D 2-2	Chapman, Fairclough	28,018	1	2	3	**4**	5	6	12	**8**	9	10	11	7					14													
15	Nov 7	(a) Manchester C	L 0-4		27,255		2			5	6	8	9	12	10	11	7	**4**		3			1												
16	21	(h) Arsenal	W 3-0	Fairclough, Chapman, McAllister	30,516	1	2	3		5	6		**8**	9	10	11	7				12	4													
17	29	(a) Chelsea	L 0-1		24,345	1	2	3		5	6		8	9	10	11	7					4													
18	Dec 5	(h) Nottingham F	L 1-4	Speed	29,364	1	2	3		5			**8**	9	10	11	7	14			12	**4**		6											
19	12	(h) Sheffield W	W 3-1	Speed, Chapman, Varadi	29,770	1	2	3		5	6		**8**	9	10	11	7	14				**4**			12										
20	20	(a) Crystal P	L 0-1		14,462	1	2	3		5	**6**		**8**	9	10	11	7	14				4			12										
21	26	(a) Blackburn R	L 1-3	McAllister	19,910	1	12	3	4	5	6			9	10	11	7								8	**2**									
22	28	(h) Norwich C	D 0-0		30,282	1	12	3	4	5				9	10	11	7			**6**					8	2									
23	Jan 9	(h) Southampton	W 2-1	Chapman, Speed	26,071	1	12	3		5			4	9	10	11	**7**			6	8	14				**2**									
24	16	(a) Everton	L 0-2		21,031		**2**	3	4	14	6		12	9	10	11	**7**			5	8		1												
25	30	(h) Middlesbrough	W 3-0	Strandli, Batty, Fairclough	30,344	1		3	4	5	6		**9**		10	11	7			2	**8**	14					12								
26	Feb 6	(a) Wimbledon	L 0-1		6,704	1	5	3	4		6			9	10	11			2		12	**7**					**8**	14							
27	8	(h) Manchester U	D 0-0		34,166	1	5	3	4		6			9	10	11		14	**2**		**8**						12	7							
28	13	(h) Oldham A	W 2-0	McAllister (pen), Chapman	27,654	1	5	3	4		6		8	9	10	11		14	**2**		**12**							7							
29	20	(a) Tottenham H	L 0-4		32,040	1	5	3	4		6		**8**	**9**	10	11		7				14					12	2							
30	24	(a) Arsenal	D 0-0		21,061	1	14	3	4	2	6		8	12	**10**	11	**7**			5							9								
31	27	(h) Ipswich T	W 1-0	Dorigo (pen)	28,848	1	2	3	4	5			8	12		11	7			6				10			**9**								
32	Mar 13	(h) Manchester C	W 1-0	Rocastle	30,840	1	14	3	4	**5**			8	12		11		10		6		7					**9**		2						
33	21	(a) Nottingham F	D 1-1	Wallace	25,148	1	6	3	4				**8**	9		11		10		5		7							2	12					
34	24	(h) Chelsea	D 1-1	Wetherall	28,135	1	6	**3**	4				8	**9**		11	12	10		5		7					14		2						
35	Apr 6	(a) Sheffield U	L 1-2	Strandli	20,562	1					6				10	11	7	12		5							9		2	8	3	4			
36	10	(h) Blackburn R	W 5-2	Strachan 3 (2 pens), Wallace, Chapman	31,791	1	12			5	6		8	9		11	7												2	**10**	3	4			
37	14	(a) Norwich C	L 2-4	Chapman, Wallace	18,613	1	12			**5**	6		8	9		11	7	14											2	**10**	3	4			
38	17	(h) Crystal Palace	D 0-0		27,545	1	6						8	9	**10**	11	7			5									2	4		12	3		
39	21	(a) Liverpool	L 0-2		34,992	1	5				6		8	9		11	7				10	4		12					**2**				3		
40	May 1	(h) Queen's Park R	D 1-1	Hodge	31,408	1	5		4		6		8	9				10				**7**		2			12			**11**		14	3		
41	4	(a) Sheffield W	D 1-1	King (og)	26,855	1	5		4		6		8	9				10						2							12	11	**3**	7	
42	8	(a) Coventry C	D 3-3	Wallace 3	19,591		5	3	4		6		8	9				10			**7**	14		2							12	**11**			1
					Appearances	39	30	33	30	29	34	12	31	36	32	39	25	9	6	13	6	11	2	5	2	3	5	3	8	5	3	5	4	1	1
					Subs		7			1		1	1	4			6	14	1		8	7		1	2		5	1		1	2	2			
					Goals			1	1	3	1	6	7	13	5	7	4	2		1		1			1		2								

FINAL LEAGUE POSITION: 17th in The Premiership

2 own-goals

FA Cup

Rd	Date	Opponent	Result	Scorers	Att	Lukic	Newsome	Dorigo	Batty	Fairclough	Whyte	Cantona	Wallace Rod	Chapman	McAllister	Speed	Strachan	Hodge	Sellars	Wetherall	Shutt	Rocastle	Day	Wallace Ray	Varadi	Sterland	Strandli	Bowman	Kerslake	Forrester	Kerr	Tinkler	Sharp	Whelan	Beeney
3	Jan 2	(h) Charlton A	D 1-1	Speed	21,287	1	12	3	**4**	5			14	9	10	11	7			6	8					**2**									
R	13	(a) Charlton A	W 3-1	Speed, Garland (og), McAllister	8,337			3		12	6		**4**	9	10	11	7			5	8	14	1			**2**									
4	25	(a) Arsenal	D 2-2	Speed, Chapman	26,516	1		3	4	5	6		12	**9**	10	11	7			2	8	14													
R	Feb 3	(h) Arsenal	L 2-3	Shutt, McAllister	26,449	1		3	4	**2**	6		12	9	10	11	**7**			5	8	14													
					Appearances	3		4	3	3	3		1	4	4	4	4			4	4		1			2									
					Subs		1			1			3									3													
					Goals									1	2	3					1														

1 own-goal

League Cup

Rd	Date	Opponent	Result	Scorers	Att	Lukic	Newsome	Dorigo	Batty	Fairclough	Whyte	Cantona	Wallace Rod	Chapman	McAllister	Speed	Strachan	Hodge	Sellars	Wetherall	Shutt	Rocastle	Day	Wallace Ray	Varadi	Sterland	Strandli	Bowman	Kerslake	Forrester	Kerr	Tinkler	Sharp	Whelan	Beeney
2	Sep 22	(h) Scunthorpe U	W 4-1	Strachan, Chapman, Speed, Shutt	10,113	1		**3**	4		6			9	10	11	7	12	**5**	2	8	14									3				
	Oct 27	(a) Scunthorpe U	D 2-2	Wallace, Chapman	7,419	1	2		4	5	14		8	9	10	11	**7**		**12**	6											3				
3	Nov 10	(a) Watford	L 1-2	McAllister	18,035	1	**2**			5	6	8	4	9	10	11	7					12													
					Appearances	3	2	1	2	2	2	1	2	3	3	3	3		1	2	1										2				
					Subs						1							1	1			2													
					Goals								1	2	1	1	1				1														

Leeds United also played in the European Cup (see *Invitation Tournaments*)

1993-94

Manager: Howard Wilkinson

No.	Date	Opponent	Result	Scorers	Att.	Lukic	Kelly	Dorigo	Batty	Fairclough	O'Leary	Strachan	Whelan	Deane	McAllister	Speed	Wallace Rod	Newsome	Beeney	Wetherall	Strandli	Rocastle	Hodge	Pemberton	Forrester	Sharp	Wallace Ray	White	Tinkler	Ford
1	Aug 14	(a) Manchester C	D 1-1	Deane	32,366	1	2	3	4	5	6	**7**	8	9	10	11	12													
2	17	(h) West Ham U	W 1-0	Speed	34,588	1	2	3	4	5	6	**7**	**8**	9	10	11	12	14												
3	21	(h) Norwich C	L 0-4		32,008	1	2	3	4	5	**6**	7	8	9	10	11		12												
4	24	(a) Arsenal	L 1-2	Strachan	29,042	1	2	3	4	5		7	**8**	9	10	11	12	6												
5	28	(a) Liverpool	L 0-2		44,068	1	2	3	4	5		7	12	9	10	11	**8**	6												
6	30	(h) Oldham A	W 1-0	Strachan	28,717		2	3	4			7		9	10	11	8	6	1	5										
7	Sep 11	(a) Southampton	W 2-0	Deane, Speed	13,511		2	3	4			7		9	10	11	**8**	6	1	5	12									
8	18	(h) Sheffield U	W 2-1	McAllister, Strachan	33,879		2	3	4	5		7		9	10	11	**8**		1	6	12									
9	25	(a) Coventry C	W 2-0	Wallace 2	13,933		2	3		5		7		9	10	11	8	4	1	6										
10	Oct 2	(h) Wimbledon	W 4-0	Speed 2, McAllister 2	30,255		2	3		5		7		9	10	11	**8**	4	1	6	12									
11	17	(a) Ipswich T	D 0-0		17,532		2	3		5				9	10	11	8	4	1	6	12	**7**								
12	23	(h) Blackburn R	D 3-3	McAllister (pen), Newsome, Sherwood (og)	37,827		2	3	12	5			14	9	10	11	8	4	1	**6**		**7**								
13	30	(a) Sheffield W	D 3-3	Fairclough, Wallace, Speed	31,892		2	3		5				9	10	11	8	4	1	6		**7**	12							
14	Nov 6	(h) Chelsea	W 4-1	Deane, Wallace 2, Rocastle	35,050		2	3		5				9	10	11	8	4	1	6		7								
15	20	(a) Tottenham H	D 1-1	Deane	31,275		2	3		5			12	9	10	11	8		1	6		**7**		4						
16	23	(a) Everton	D 1-1	Wallace	17,102		2	3		5			12	9	10	11	8		1	6		**7**		4						
17	27	(h) Swindon T	W 3-0	Deane, Wallace, Speed	32,630		2	3		5		7		9	10	11	8		1	6				**4**	12					
18	Dec 4	(h) Manchester C	W 3-2	Wallace, Speed, Deane	33,820		2	3		5		7	12	9	10	11	8		1	6						**4**	14			
19	8	(a) West Ham U	W 1-0	Wallace	20,468		2	3		5		7		9	10	11	8		1	6				12		4				
20	13	(a) Norwich C	L 1-2	Wallace	16,586		2	3		5		7	12	9	10		8		1	6			11			**4**				
21	18	(h) Arsenal	W 2-1	McAllister, Adams (og)	37,289		2	3		5		**7**		9	10		8	4	1	6		12	11							
22	22	(a) Newcastle U	D 1-1	Fairclough	36,388		2	3		5			**7**	9	10		8	4	1				11	6		12				
23	29	(h) Queen's Park R	D 1-1	Hodge	39,124		2	3		5		7		9	10		**8**	4	1				11			12		6		
24	Jan 1	(a) Manchester U	D 0-0		44,724		2	3		5		7		9	10			4	1				**11**	6		12		8		
25	15	(h) Ipswich T	D 0-0		31,317		2	3		5		7		9	10	12		4	1	14			11		**8**			**6**		
26	23	(a) Blackburn R	L 1-2	Speed	17,475		2	3		5		7	12	9	10	11		4	1					14	**8**			**6**		
27	Feb 6	(a) Aston Villa	L 0-1		26,919		2	3		5		7	12	9	10	11		4	1				8					**6**		
28	19	(h) Liverpool	W 2-0	Wetherall, McAllister	40,029	1	2	3		5	**6**	7		9	10	11	**8**	14		4								12		
29	28	(a) Oldham A	D 1-1	McAllister	11,136	1	2	3		5		7		9	10	11	8	6		4										
30	Mar 5	(h) Southampton	D 0-0		30,829	1	2	3		5	6	7		**9**	10	11	8			4								12		
31	13	(a) Sheffield U	D 2-2	Speed, Deane	19,425	1	2	3		5	6	7		9	10	11	8			4										
32	16	(h) Aston Villa	W 2-0	Wallace, Deane	33,126	1	2	3		5	**6**	7		9	10	11	8	12		4										
33	19	(h) Coventry C	W 1-0	Wallace	30,023	1	2	3		5		7		9	10	11	8	6		4										
34	26	(a) Wimbledon	L 0-1		9,035	1	2	3		5		7		9	10	11	8	**6**		4								12		
35	Apr 1	(h) Newcastle U	D 1-1	Fairclough	40,005	1	2	3		5		7		9	10	11	8	6		**4**								12		
36	4	(a) Queen's Park R	W 4-0	Deane, Wallace, White 2	15,365	1	2	**3**		5				9	10	11	8	6		4								7	12	
37	17	(h) Tottenham H	W 2-0	Wallace 2	33,658	1	2			5				9	10	11	8	6		4						**3**		7		
38	23	(a) Chelsea	D 1-1	Speed	18,544	1	2			5		12		9	10	11	8	6		4						3		**7**		
39	27	(h) Manchester U	L 0-2		41,127	1	2	**3**		5		7	12	9	10	11	8	6		**4**				14						
40	30	(h) Everton	W 3-0	McAllister, Watson (og), White	35,487	1	2			5	6	7	**9**		10	11	**8**			4						3		12	14	
41	May 3	(h) Sheffield W	D 2-2	White, Wallace	33,575	1	2			5	6	7		9	10	**11**	8			4						**3**		12	14	
42	7	(a) Swindon T	W 5-0	Deane 2, Wallace, White, Fairclough	17,228	1	2			5	6	**7**	12	9	10		8			4				3				**11**		14
					Appearances	20	42	37	8	40	10	32	6	41	42	35	34	25	22	31		6	7	6	2	7		9		
					Subs				1			1	10			1	3	4		1	4	1	1	3	1	3	1	6	3	1
					Goals					4		3		11	8	10	17	1		1		1	1					5		

FINAL LEAGUE POSITION: 5th in The Premiership

3 own-goals

FA Cup

Round	Date	Opponent	Result	Scorers	Att.	Lukic	Kelly	Dorigo	Batty	Fairclough	O'Leary	Strachan	Whelan	Deane	McAllister	Speed	Wallace Rod	Newsome	Beeney	Wetherall	Strandli	Rocastle	Hodge	Pemberton	Forrester	Sharp	Wallace Ray	White	Tinkler	Ford
3	Jan 8	(h) Crewe A	W 3-1	Deane, Forrester 2	23,475		2	3		5		7		9	10			4	1				11		8			6		
4	29	(a) Oxford U	D 2-2	Speed, Wetherall	11,029		2	3		5		7		9	10	11	**8**	**4**	1	14			12					6		
R	Feb 9	(h) Oxford U	L 2-3*	Strachan, White	22,167		2	3		5		7		**9**	10	11		4	1	14	**8**				12			6		
				*After extra-time	Appearances		3	3		3		3		3	3	2	1	3	3		1		1		1			3		
					Subs															2			1		1					
					Goals							1		1		1				1					2			1		

League Cup

Round	Date	Opponent	Result	Scorers	Att.	Lukic	Kelly	Dorigo	Batty	Fairclough	O'Leary	Strachan	Whelan	Deane	McAllister	Speed	Wallace Rod	Newsome	Beeney	Wetherall	Strandli	Rocastle	Hodge	Pemberton	Forrester	Sharp	Wallace Ray	White	Tinkler	Ford
2	Sep 21	(a) Sunderland	L 1-2	Speed	17,101		2	3		5		7		9	10	11	8		1	6			4							
	Oct 6	(h) Sunderland	L 1-2	Whelan	22,165		2	3		5		**7**	8	9	10	11		4	1	**6**	14	12								
					Appearances		2	2		2		2	1	2	2	2	1	1	2	2			1							
					Subs																1	1								
					Goals								1			1														

1994-95

Manager: Howard Wilkinson

No	Date	Opponent	Result	Scorers	Att	Lukic	Kelly	Worthington	Palmer	Wetherall	White	Strachan	Wallace Rod	Deane	McAllister	Speed	Masinga	Whelan	Fairclough	Pemberton	Tinkler	Radebe	Dorigo	Yeboah	Couzens	Sharp
1	Aug 20	(a) West Ham U	D 0-0		18,610	1	2	3	4	5	6	7	**8**	9	10	11	12									
2	23	(h) Arsenal	W 1-0	Whelan	34,318	1	2	3	4	5	6	**7**	8		10	11	9	12								
3	27	(h) Chelsea	L 2-3	Masinga, Whelan	32,212	1	2	3	4	5	6		8		10	11	9	7								
4	30	(a) Crystal Palace	W 2-1	White, Whelan	14,453	1	2	3	4	5	6		8		10	11	**9**	7	12							
5	Sep 11	(h) Manchester U	W 2-1	Wetherall, Deane	39,120	1	2	3	4	5	**6**		8	12	10	11	**9**	7	14							
6	17	(a) Coventry C	L 1-2	Speed	15,383	1	2	3	4	**5**		7	8		10	11	**9**	6	12	14						
7	26	(a) Sheffield W	D 1-1	McAllister	23,227	1	2	3	4	5			8	9	10	11	**7**	12			**6**	14				
8	Oct 1	(h) Manchester C	W 2-0	Whelan 2	30,938	1	2	3	4	6			8	**9**	10	11		7	5	12						
9	8	(a) Norwich C	L 1-2	Wallace	17,390	1	2	**6**	4	5			8	9	10	11		7	12	14			3			
10	15	(h) Tottenham H	D 1-1	Deane	39,362	1	**2**	6	4	5			8	9	10	11		7		12			3			
11	24	(h) Leicester C	W 2-1	McAllister, Whelan	28,479	1	2	6	4	5			8	9	10	11		7					3			
12	29	(a) Southampton	W 3-1	Wallace 2, Maddison (og)	15,202	1	2	6	4	5			8	9	10	11		7				12	**3**			
13	Nov 1	(a) Ipswich T	L 0-2		15,534	1	2	3	4	5	**6**		8	9	10	11	12	7								
14	5	(h) Wimbledon	W 3-1	Wetherall, White, Speed	27,246	1	2	3	4	5	**6**		8	**9**	10	11	12	7				14				
15	19	(a) Queen's Park R	L 2-3	McDonald (og), Deane	17,416	1	2	3	4	5	12		8	9	10	11		7				**6**				
16	26	(h) Nottingham F	W 1-0	Whelan	37,709	1	2		4	5	6		**8**	9	10	11	12	7		14			3			
17	Dec 5	(a) Everton	L 0-3		25,906	1	2		4	5	6		8	9	10	11		7					3			
18	10	(h) West Ham U	D 2-2	Worthington, Deane	28,987	1	2	**11**	4	5	12	7		9	10			8			6		3			
19	17	(a) Arsenal	W 3-1	Masinga 2, Deane	38,100	1	2		4	5	12			9		11	10	**8**		7		6	3			
20	26	(h) Newcastle U	D 0-0		39,337	1	2	12	4	5	7	14			10	11	**9**	8		**6**			3			
21	31	(h) Liverpool	L 0-2		38,468	1	2	12		5	14	**7**			10	11	9	8		6		4	**3**			
22	Jan 2	(a) Aston Villa	D 0-0		35,038	1	2	3		5	7		12	9	10	11	**8**			6		4				
23	14	(h) Southampton	D 0-0		28,969	1	2	3	4	5	**7**		14	9	10	11	12			6		**8**				
24	24	(h) Queen's Park R	W 4-0	Masinga 2, White, Deane	28,750	1	2	3	4	5	7			9	10	11	**8**			6				12		
25	Feb 1	(a) Blackburn R	D 1-1	McAllister (pen)	28,561	1	2	12	4		7			9	10	11	**8**			6		**5**	3	14		
26	4	(a) Wimbledon	D 0-0		10,211	1	2	11	4		7			9	10		8			6		5	3			
27	22	(h) Everton	W 1-0	Yeboah	30,793	1	2	12		5	7				10	11	8			6		**4**	3	9		
28	25	(a) Manchester C	D 0-0		22,892	1	2	6	4	5	7			12	10	11	8						3	**9**		
29	Mar 4	(h) Sheffield W	L 0-1		33,774	1	2		4	5			**7**	9	10	11	12			6			3	8		
30	11	(a) Chelsea	W 3-0	Yeboah 2, McAllister	20,174	1	2		4	5			7	9	10	11				6			3	8		
31	15	(a) Leicester C	W 3-1	Yeboah 2, Palmer	20,068	1	2		4	5			7	9	10	11				6			3	8		
32	18	(h) Coventry C	W 3-1	Wallace, Yeboah, Gould (og)	29,231	1	2		4				7	9	10	11					6	**5**	3	8	12	
33	22	(a) Nottingham F	L 0-3		26,299	1	**2**		4		12		7	9	10	11				6			3	8	5	
34	Apr 2	(a) Manchester U	D 0-0		43,712	1	2	12	4	5			7	**9**	10			14		6			3	8	11	
35	5	(h) Ipswich T	W 4-0	Speed, Yeboah 3	28,565	1	**2**		4	5			7	9	10	11				6			3	8	12	
36	9	(a) Liverpool	W 1-0	Deane	37,454	1	2		4	5			7	9	10	11				6			3	8		
37	15	(h) Blackburn R	D 1-1	Deane	39,426	1	2		4	5			**7**	9	10	11		12		6			3	8		
38	17	(a) Newcastle U	W 2-1	Yeboah, McAllister (pen)	35,626	1	2	12	4	5	**7**			9	10	11	14			6			3	**8**		
39	29	(h) Aston Villa	W 1-0	Palmer	32,973	1	2		4	5			7	9	10	11				6			3	8		
40	May 6	(h) Norwich C	W 2-1	McAllister (pen), Palmer	31,981	1	2		4	5			**7**	9	10	11		12		6			3	**8**		14
41	9	(h) Crystal Palace	W 3-1	Yeboah 2, Wetherall	30,963	1	2		4	5			7	9	10	11				6			3	8		
42	14	(a) Tottenham H	D 1-1	Deane	33,040	1	2		4	5			**7**	9	10	11				6			3	8		12
		FINAL LEAGUE POSITION: 5th in The Premiership			Appearances	42	42	21	39	38	18	5	30	33	41	39	15	18	1	22	3	9	28	16	2	
					Subs			6			5	1	2	2			7	5	4	5		3		2	2	2
					Goals			1	3	3	3		4	9	6	3	5	7						12		

3 own-goals

FA CUP

Rd	Date	Opponent	Result	Scorers	Att	Lukic	Kelly	Worthington	Palmer	Wetherall	White	Strachan	Wallace Rod	Deane	McAllister	Speed	Masinga	Whelan	Fairclough	Pemberton	Tinkler	Radebe	Dorigo	Yeboah	Couzens	Sharp
3	Jan 7	(a) Walsall	D 1-1	Wetherall	8,691	1	2	3	4	5	**7**		14	9	10	11	12			6		**8**				
R	17	(h) Walsall	W5-2*	Deane, Wetherall, Masinga 3	17,881	1	2	3	**4**	5			**7**	9	10	11	14	8		6		12				
4	28	(h) Oldham A	W 3-2	White, Palmer, Masinga	25,010	1	2	3	4	5	7			9	10	11	**8**			6				12		
5	Feb 19	(a) Manchester U	L 1-3	Yeboah	42,744	1	2	14		5	7		**8**		10	11	**9**	4		6			3	12		
				*After extra-time	Appearances	4	4	3	3	4	3		2	3	4	4	2	2		4		1	1			
					Subs			1					1				2					1		2		
					Goals				1	2	1			1			4							1		

League Cup

Rd	Date	Opponent	Result	Scorers	Att	Lukic	Kelly	Worthington	Palmer	Wetherall	White	Strachan	Wallace Rod	Deane	McAllister	Speed	Masinga	Whelan	Fairclough	Pemberton	Tinkler	Radebe	Dorigo	Yeboah	Couzens	Sharp
2	Sep 21	(h) Mansfield T	L 0-1		7,844	1	2	3	4		**7**		8	12	10	11	**9**	6	5			14				
	Oct 4	(a) Mansfield T	D 0-0		7,227	1	2	3	4	6			**7**	9	10	11		8	**5**	14			12			
					Appearances	2	2	2	2	1	1		2	1	2	2	1	2	2							
					Subs									1						1		1	1			
					Goals																					

1995-96

Manager: Howard Wilkinson

No	Date	Opponents	Result	Goalscorers	Att	Lukic	Kelly	Dorigo	Palmer	Pemberton	Wetherall	Deane	Wallace	Yeboah	McAllister	Speed	Whelan	Beesley	Worthington	White	Masinga	Tinkler	Couzens	Jobson	Sharp	Ford	Brolin	Bowman	Beeney	Radebe	Chapman	Gray	Harte	Maybury	Kewell	Blunt	Jackson
1	Aug 19 (a)	West Ham U	W 2-1	Yeboah 2	22,901	1	2	3	**4**	5	6	7	**8**	9	10	11	12	14	15																		
2	21 (h)	Liverpool	W 1-0	Yeboah	35,852	1	2	3	4	5	6	7	**8**	9	10	11	12																				
3	26 (h)	Aston Villa	W 2-0	Speed, White	35,086	1	2	3	4	5	6	7	**8**	9	10	11				12																	
4	30 (a)	Southampton	D 1-1	Dorigo	15,212	1	2	3	4	5	6	7	**8**	**9**	10	11			14	12																	
5	Sep 9 (a)	Tottenham H	L 1-2	Yeboah	30,034	1	2	3	4	5	6	7		9	10	11	12			**8**																	
6	16 (h)	Queen's Park R	L 1-3	Wetherall	31,504	1	2		4	5	6	7		9	10	11	**8**	14	**3**	12																	
7	23 (a)	Wimbledon	W 4-2	Palmer, Yeboah 3	13,307	1	2		4	5	6	8		9	10	11		3			**7**	12															
8	30 (h)	Sheffield W	W 2-0	Yeboah, Speed	34,076	1	2		4		5	12		9	10	11		3			**7**	8	6														
9	Oct 14 (h)	Arsenal	L 0-3		38,552	1	2	3	4	5	6	7	12	9		11						**8**	10														
10	21 (a)	Manchester C	D 0-0		26,390	1	2		4	5	6	7	**8**	9	10		12		3				11														
11	28 (h)	Coventry C	W 3-1	McAllister 3 (1 pen)	30,161	1	3		4	2	6	**7**		9	10	11	**8**						12	5	14												
12	Nov 4 (a)	Middlesbrough	D 1-1	Deane	29,467	1	2		4	5	6	7		9	10		8		3					11													
13	18 (h)	Chelsea	W 1-0	Yeboah	36,209	1	2	3	4		6	7	12	9	10	11							**8**	5													
14	25 (a)	Newcastle U	L 1-2	Deane	36,572	1	2	**3**	4		6	8		9	10	11								5		**7**	12	14									
15	Dec 2 (h)	Manchester C	L 0-1		33,249	1	2	3	4	14	6	8		9	10		12							5		**11**	**7**										
16	9 (h)	Wimbledon	D 1-1	Jobson	27,984	1		3	4	2	6	**8**	12	9	10	11								5			7										
17	16 (a)	Sheffield W	L 2-6	Brolin, Wallace	24,573	1	**2**	3	4		6	14	12	**9**	10	11							8	5			7										
18	24 (h)	Manchester U	W 3-1	McAllister (pen), Yeboah, Deane	39,801		2	3	4		6	8	12	**9**	10	11								5			7		1								
19	27 (a)	Bolton W	W 2-0	Brolin, Wetherall	18,414		2	3			6	8		9	10	11								5		4	7		1	12							
20	30 (a)	Everton	L 0-2		40,009		2	**3**			6	8	14		10	11			12		**9**			5		4	7		1								
21	Jan 1 (h)	Blackburn R	D 0-0		31,285		2		4			8	12	9	10	11			3					5		6	**7**		1								
22	13 (h)	West Ham U	W 2-0	Brolin 2	30,658		2	**3**	4		5		**8**		10	11							15			6	**7**		1		9	12	14				
23	20 (a)	Liverpool	L 0-5		40,254		2		4		5	14	8		10	11			3				12			6	**7**		1		**9**						
24	31 (a)	Nottignham F	L 1-2	Palmer	35,982		2	3	4			9	8		10	11						14	**6**	5			**7**	15	1			12					
25	Feb 3 (a)	Aston Villa	L 0-3		24,465			3	4	**5**		9	8		10	11			12			14	7					6	1					**2**			
26	Mar 3 (h)	Bolton W	L 0-1		30,106	1			4		6	7	8	9	10			5	**3**				12				11			2							
27	6 (a)	Queen's Park R	W 2-1	Yeboah 2	13,991	1			4		6			9	10			5	3		12					8	7			2		11					
28	13 (a)	Blackburn R	L 0-1		23,358	1	2		4		6	9	8		10			**5**	3								12			7		11					
29	17 (h)	Everton	D 2-2	Deane 2	29,421	1	3		4	2		9	12								14	10	**6**			8	**7**			5		11					
30	29 (h)	Middlesbrough	L 0-1		31,778	**1**	3		4	**2**	6	9	14		10	11														5		7			8	12	15
31	Apr 3 (h)	Southampton	W 1-0	Deane	26,077	1	2		4		6	12	14		10	11											**9**			5		7			**3**	8	
32	6 (a)	Arsenal	L 1-2	Deane	37,619	1	2		4		6	9			10	11											8			5		7	3				
33	8 (h)	Nottingham F	L 1-3	Wetherall	29,220	1	3		4		5	9	14		10	11											8			**2**		7	12			**6**	
34	13 (a)	Chelsea	L 1-4	McAllister	22,131	1	2		4	**5**	6	9			10	11											8			12		7	3				
35	17 (a)	Manchester U	L 0-1		48,382		2		4		6	9			10	11		5	3		14	15				**8**			1	12		**7**					
36	29 (h)	Newcastle U	L 0-1		38,862		2				6	9	12		10	**11**		4	3		14					**8**			1	5		7					
37	May 2 (h)	Tottenham H	L 1-3	Wetherall	30,061	1	2		4		6				10			5	3		9	7	12			**8**						11					
38	5 (a)	Coventry C	D 0-0		22,769	1	2		4		6		8		10				3		9	7	12							5		**11**					
					Appearances	28	34	17	35	16	34	30	12	22	36	29	3	8	12	1	5	5	8	12		12	17	1	10	10	2	12	2	1	2	2	
					Subs					1		4	12				5	2	4	3	4	4	6		1		2	2		3		2	2			1	1
					Goals			1	2		4	7	1	12	5	2				1				1			4										

FINAL LEAGUE POSITION: 13th in The Premiership

FA Cup

Rd	Date	Opponents	Result	Goalscorers	Att	Lukic	Kelly	Dorigo	Palmer	Pemberton	Wetherall	Deane	Wallace	Yeboah	McAllister	Speed	Whelan	Beesley	Worthington	White	Masinga	Tinkler	Couzens	Jobson	Sharp	Ford	Brolin	Bowman	Beeney	Radebe	Chapman	Gray	Harte	Maybury	Kewell	Blunt	Jackson
3	Jan 7 (a)	Derby C	W 4-2	Speed, Deane, McAllister, Yeboah	16,155		2	3	4		**6**	9	12	8	10	11								5		7			1								
4	Feb 14 (a)	Bolton W	W 1-0	Wallace	16,694	1	2	3	4		6	12	**8**	**9**	10	11		5								7				14							
5	18 (h)	Port Vale	D 0-0		18,607	1	2	3	4		6	12	8	9	10	**11**		5								7											
R	27 (a)	Port Vale	W 2-1	McAllister 2	14,023	1			4		6	11	**8**	9	10			5	3		**7**						12			2		14					
6	Mar 10 (h)	Liverpool	D 0-0		24,632	1	2		4	12	6	14		9	10			5	3							**11**	**8**			7							
R	20 (a)	Liverpool	L 0-3		30,812	1	2		4	6		9		**8**	10	11			3							**7**				5		12					
					Appearances	5	5	3	6	1	5	3	3	6	6	4		4	3		1			1		5	1		1	3							
					Subs					1		3	1														1			1		2					
					Goals							1	1	1	3	1																					

League Cup

Rd	Date	Opponents	Result	Goalscorers	Att	Lukic	Kelly	Dorigo	Palmer	Pemberton	Wetherall	Deane	Wallace	Yeboah	McAllister	Speed	Whelan	Beesley	Worthington	White	Masinga	Tinkler	Couzens	Jobson	Sharp	Ford	Brolin	Bowman	Beeney	Radebe	Chapman	Gray	Harte	Maybury	Kewell	Blunt	Jackson
2	Sep 19 (h)	Notts C	D 0-0		12,384	1	2		4	5	6	8		9	10	11		12	3	7												14					
	Oct 3 (a)	Notts C	W 3-2	McAllister, Couzens, Speed	12,477	1	2		4		6	7	12	9	10	11		5	14			**8**	3														
3	25 (a)	Derby C	W 1-0	Speed	16,030	1	2		4	5	6	8		**9**	10	11	12	7	3																		
4	Nov 29 (h)	Blackburn R	W 2-1	Deane Yeboah	26,006	1	2	3	4		6	8		9	10	11	12									5	7	14									
5	Jan 10 (h)	Reading	W 2-1	Masinga, Speed	21,023		2	3	4		6		**8**		10	11					**9**		12			5	**7**		1				14				
SF	Feb 11 (a)	Birmingham C	W 2-1	Yeboah, Whyte (og)	24,781	1	2	3	4		6	12	**8**	9	10	11		5								**7**				14							
	25 (h)	Birmingham C	W 3-0	Masinga, Yeboah, Deane	35,435	1	2	**3**	4		6	11	8	9	10			5			7						14			12							
F	Mar 24(n*)	Aston Villa	L 0-3		77,056	1	2		4	5	6	12		9	10	11										**8**	14			3		7					
					Appearances	7	8	4	8	3	8	5	3	7	8	7		4	2	1	2	1	1			4	2		1	1		1					
					Subs							2	1				2	1	1				1				2	1		2		1	1				
					Goals							2		3	1	3					2		1														

* Played at Wembley

1 own-goal

Leeds United also played in the UEFA Cup (see *Invitation Tournaments*)

Leeds in Europe

European Cup

1969-70
Round 1 (1st leg)
Sep 17 v SK Lyn Olso (h) 10-0
O'Grady, Jones 3, Clarke 2, Giles 2, Bremner 2
Sprake; Reaney, Cooper, Bremner, Charlton, Hunter, Madeley, Clarke, Jones, Giles(Bates), O'Grady.
Att: 25,979
Round 1 (2nd leg)
Oct 1 v SK Lyn Oslo (a) 6-0 (agg 16-0)
Hibbitt 2, Belfitt 2, Jones, Lorimer
Sprake; Reaney, Cooper, Bremner, Madeley, E.Gray, Lorimer, Belfitt, Jones, Bates, Hibbitt.
Att: 7,595
Round 2 (1st leg)
Nov 12 v Ferencváros (h) 3-0
Giles, Jones 2
Sprake; Reaney, Madeley, Bremner, Charlton, Hunter, Lorimer, Bates, Jones, Giles, E.Gray.
Att: 37,291
Round 2 (2nd leg)
Nov 26 v Ferencváros (a) 3-0 (agg 6-0)
Jones 2, Lorimer
Sprake; Reaney, Cooper, Bremner, Charlton, Hunter, Lorimer, Madeley, Jones, Giles, E.Gray(Galvin).
Att: 5,400
Round 3 (1st leg)
Mar 4 v Standard Liége (a) 1-0
Lorimer
Sprake; Reaney, Cooper, Bremner, Charlton, Hunter, Lorimer, Clarke, Jones, Giles, Madeley.
Att: 38,000
Round 3 (2nd leg)
Mar 18 v Standard Liége (h) 1-0 (agg 2-0)
Giles (pen)
Sprake; Reaney, Cooper, Bremner, Charlton, Hunter, Lorimer, Clarke, Jones, Giles, Madeley.
Att: 48,775
Semi-final (1st leg)
Apr 1 v Celtic (h) 0-1
Sprake; Reaney, Cooper, Bremner(Bates), Charlton, Madeley, Lorimer, Clarke, Jones, Giles, E.Gray.
Att: 45,505
Semi-final (2nd leg)
Apr 15 v Celtic (Hampden Park) 1-2 (agg 1-3
Bremner
Sprake(Harvey); Madeley, Cooper, Bremner, Charlton, Hunter, Lorimer(Bates), Clarke, Jones, Giles, E.Gray.
Att: 136,505

1974-75
Round 1 (1st leg)
Sep 18 v FC Zürich (a) 1-2 (agg 5-3)
Clarke 2, Lorimer (pen), Jordan
Harvey; Reaney, Cooper, Yorath, McQueen, Hunter, Lorimer, Clarke, Jordan, Giles, Madeley.
Att: 20,012
Round 1 (2nd leg)
Oct 2 v FC Zürich (a) 1-2 (agg 5-3)
Clarke
Harvey; Reaney, Cherry, Yorath, Madeley, Hunter, Lorimer, Clarke, Jordan, Bates, F.T.Gray(Hampton).
Att: 16,500
Round 2 (1st leg)
Oct 23 v Újpesti Dózsa (a) 2-1
Lorimer, McQueen
Harvey; Reaney, Cooper, Yorath, McQueen, Hunter, Lorimer, McKenzie, Jordan, Giles, Madeley.
Att: 20,000
Round 2 (2nd leg)
Nov 6 v Újpesti Dózsa (h) 3-0 (agg 5-1)
McQueen, Bremner, Yorath
Harvey; Reaney, Cooper, Yorath, McQueen, Hunter(Cherry), Lorimer(Harris), Clarke, Bremner, Giles, Madeley.
Att: 28,091
Round 3 (1st leg)
Mar 5 v Anderlecht (h) 3-0
Jordan, McQueen, Lorimer
Stewart; Madeley, F.T.Gray, Bremner(Yorath), McQueen, Hunter, Lorimer, Clarke, Jordan, Giles, E.Gray.
Att: 43,195
Round 3 (2nd leg)
Mar 19 v Anderlecht (a) 1-0 (agg 4-0)
Bremner
Stewart; Reaney, F.T.Gray, Bremner, McQueen, Hunter, Lorimer, Clarke, Jordan, Yorath, Madeley.
Att: 37,000
Semi-final (1st leg)
Apr 9 v Barcelona (h) 2-1
Bremner, Clarke
Stewart; Reaney, F.T.Gray, Bremner, McQueen, Madeley, Yorath, Clarke, Jordan, Giles, E.Gray.
Att: 50,393
Semi-final (2nd leg)
Apr 23 v Barcelona (a) 1-1 (agg 3-2)
Lorimer
Stewart; Cherry, F.T.Gray, Bremner, McQueen, Hunter, Lorimer, Clarke, Jordan, Yorath, Madeley.
Att: 110,000
Final
May 28 v Bayern Munich (Paris) 0-2
Stewart; Reaney, F.T.Gray, Bremner, Madeley, Hunter, Lorimer, Clarke, Jordan, Giles, Yorath(E.Gray).
Att: 48,374

1992-93
Round 1 (1st leg)
Sep 16 v VfB Stuttgart (a) 0-3
Lukic; Rocastle(Hodge), Dorigo, Batty, Fairclough, Whyte, Cantona(Shutt), Strachan, Chapman, McAllister, Speed.
Att: 38,000
Round 1 (2nd leg)
Sep 30 v VfB Stuttgart (h) 4-1 (agg 4-4*)
Speed, McAllister (pen), Cantona, Chapman
Lukic; Sellars, Dorigo, Batty, Fairclough, Whyte, Strachan, Cantona, Chapman, McAllister, Speed.
Att: 20,457
*Stuttgart would have gone through on the away goals rule but they played one more than the permitted four foreign players at Elland Road. The decision of UEFA was to award the game 3-0 to Leeds and 3-3 therefore on aggregate. This resulted in a Play-off for the tie in Barcelona.
Round 1 Play-off
Oct 9 v VfB Stuttgart (n) 2-1
Strachan, Shutt
Lukic; Newsome, Dorigo, Batty, Fairclough, Whyte, Strachan, Cantona(Shutt), Chapman, McAllister, Speed.
Att: 10,000
Round 2 (1st leg)
Oct 21 v Rangers (a) 1-2
McAllister
Lukic; Newsome, Dorigo, Batty, Fairclough, Whyte, Strachan(Rocastle), Cantona(Rod Wallace), Chapman, McAllister, Speed.
Att: 43,251
Round 2
2nd leg
Nov 4 v Rangers (h) 1-2 (agg 2-4)
Cantona
Lukic; Newsome, Dorigo, Rocastle(Hodge), Fairclough(Rod Wallace), Whyte, Strachan, Cantona, Chapman, McAllister, Speed.
Att: 25,118

European Cup-winners' Cup

1972-73
Round 1 (1st leg)
Sep 13 v Ankaragücü (a) 1-1
Jordan
Harvey; Reaney, Cherry, Bremner, Ellam, Hunter, Lorimer, Galvin(Yorath), Jordan, Giles, Madeley.
Att: 20,000
Round 1 (2nd leg)
Sep 27 v Ankaragücü (h) 1-0 (agg 2-1)
Jones
Harvey; Reaney, Cherry, Bremner, Ellam, Hunter, Lorimer, Clarke, Jones, Giles, Bates.
Att: 22,411
Round 2 (1st leg)
Oct 25 v Carl Zeiss Jena (a) 0-0
Harvey; Madeley, Cherry, Bremner, Charlton, Hunter, Lorimer, Clarke, Jordan, Bates, E.Gray.
Att: 18,000
Round 2 (2nd leg)
Nov 8 v Carl Zeiss Jena (h) 2-0 (agg 2-0)
Cherry, Jones
Harvey; Reaney, Cherry, Bremner, Charlton, Hunter, Lorimer, Clarke, Jones, Bates(Giles), Yorath.
Att: 26,885
Round 3 (1st leg)
Mar 7 v Rapid Bucharest (h) 5-0
Giles, Clarke, Lorimer 2, Jordan
Harvey; Reaney, Cherry, Bremner, McQueen (Yorath), Hunter, Lorimer, Clarke, Jordan, Giles, Madeley.
Att: 25,702
Round 3 (2nd leg)
Mar 21 v Rapid Bucharest (a) 3-1 (agg 8-1)
Bates, Jones, Jordan
Harvey; Reaney, E.Gray, Madeley, McQueen, Hunter, Lorimer, Jordan, Jones, Giles(F.T.Gray), Bates(Yorath).
Att: 25,000
Semi-final (1st leg)
Apr 11 v Hajduk Split (h) 1-0
Clarke
Harvey; Reaney, Cherry, Bremner, Yorath, Hunter, Lorimer, Clarke, Jones, Giles, Bates(Jordan).
Att: 32,051
Semi-final (2nd leg)
Apr 25 v Hajduk Split (a) 0-0 (agg 1-0)
Harvey; Reaney, Cherry, Bremner, Yorath, Hunter, Lorimer, Jones, Jordan, Giles, Madeley.
Att: 30,000
Final
May 16 v AC Milan (Salonika) 0-1
Harvey; Reaney, Cherry, Bates, Yorath, Hunter, Lorimer, Jordan, Jones, F.T.Gray(McQueen), Madeley.
Att: 45,000

UEFA Cup

(Formerly the Inter-Cities Fairs Cup)

1965-66
Round 1 (1st leg)
Sep 29 v Torino (h) 2-1
Bremner, Peacock
Sprake; Reaney, Madeley, Bremner, Charlton, Hunter, Giles, Lorimer, Peacock, Collins, Cooper.
Att: 33,852
Round 1 (2nd leg)
Oct 6 v Torino (a) 0-0 (agg 2-1)
Sprake; Reaney, Madeley, Bremner, Charlton, Hunter, Giles, Lorimer, Peacock, Collins, Cooper.
Att: 26,000
Round 2 (1st leg)
Nov 24 v SC Leipzig (a) 2-1
Lorimer, Bremner
Sprake; Reaney, Charlton, Madeley, Bremner, Hunter, Storrie, Lorimer, Bell, Giles, O'Grady.
Att: 8,000
Round 2 (2nd leg)
Dec 1 v SC Leipzig (h) 0-0 (agg 2-1)
Sprake; Reaney, Bell, Bremner, Charlton, Hunter, Storrie, Lorimer, Peacock, Giles, O'Grady.
Att: 32,111
Round 3 (1st leg)
Feb 2 v Valencia (h) 1-1
Lorimer
Sprake; Reaney, Bell, Bremner, Charlton, Hunter, Storrie, Lorimer, Belfitt, Giles, O'Grady.
Att: 34,414
Round 3 (2nd leg)
Feb 16 v Valencia (a) 1-0 (agg 2-1)
O'Grady
Sprake; Reaney, Bell, Bremner, Charlton, Hunter, Storrie, Lorimer, Madeley, Giles, O'Grady.
Att: 45,000
Round 4 (1st leg)
Mar 2 v Újpesti Dózsa (h) 4-1
Cooper, Bell, Storrie, Bremner
Sprake; Reaney, Bell, Bremner, Charlton, Hunter, O'Grady, Lorimer, Storrie, Giles, Cooper.
Att: 40,462
Round 4 (2nd leg)
Mar 9 v Újpesti Dózsa (a) 1-1 (agg 5-2)
Lorimer
Sprake; Reaney, Bell, Bremner, Charlton, Hunter, O'Grady, Lorimer, Storrie, Giles, Cooper.
Att: 30,000
Semi-final (1st leg)
Apr 20 v Real Zaragoza (a) 0-1
Sprake; Reaney, Bell, Bremner, Charlton, Hunter, Greenhoff, E.Gray, Storrie, Giles, Johanneson.
Att: 35,000
Semi-final (2nd leg)
Apr 27 v Real Zaragoza (h) 2-1 (agg 2-2)
Johanneson, Charlton
Sprake; Reaney, Bell, Bremner, Charlton, Hunter, Greenhoff, E.Gray, Storrie, Giles, Johanneson.
Att: 45,008
Replay
May 11 v Real Zaragoza (h) 1-3
Charlton
Sprake; Reaney, Bell, Bremner, Charlton, Hunter, Greenhoff, Lorimer, Storrie, Giles, O'Grady.
Att: 43,046

1966-67
Round 2 (2nd leg)
Oct 18 v DWS Amsterdam (a) 3-1
Bremner, Johanneson, Greenhoff
Sprake; Reaney, Bell, Bremner, Charlton, Hunter, O'Grady, Greenhoff, Madeley, Giles, Johanneson.
Att: 7,000
Round 2 (2nd leg)
Oct 26 v DWS Amsterdam (h) 5-1 (agg 8-2)
Johanneson 3, Giles, Madeley
Sprake; Reaney, Bell, Bremner, Charlton, Hunter, Storrie, Madeley, Greenhoff, Giles, Johanneson.
Att: 27,096
Round 3 (1st leg)
Jan 18 v Valencia (h) 1-1
Greenhoff
Sprake; Reaney, Madeley, Bremner, Charlton, Hunter, Giles, E.Gray, Greenhoff, Collins, Cooper.
Att: 40,644
Round 3 (2nd leg)
Feb 8 v Valencia (a) 2-0 (agg 3-1)
Giles, Lorimer
Sprake; Madeley, Bell, Bremner, Charlton, Hunter, Giles, Lorimer, Belfitt, E.Gray, Hibbitt.
Att: 48,000
Round 4 (1st leg)
22 Mar v Bologna (a) 0-1
Sprake; Reaney, Bell, Bremner, Charlton, Hunter, Lorimer, Belfitt, Madeley, Giles, Cooper.
Att: 20,000
Round 4 (2nd leg)
Apr 19 v Bologna (h) 1-0 (agg 1-1)
Giles (pen)
Sprake; Reaney, Madeley, Bremner, Bell, Hunter, Giles, Belfitt, Greenhoff, E.Gray, Cooper.
Att: 42,148
Leeds won on the toss of a disc.
Semi-final (1st leg)
May 19 v Kilmarnock (h) 4-2
Belfitt 3, Giles (pen)
Sprake; Reaney, Bell, Bremner, Madeley, Hunter, O'Grady, Lorimer, Belfitt, Giles, E.Gray.
Att: 43,000
Semi-final (2nd leg)
May 24 v Kilmarnock (a) 0-0 (agg 4-2)
Sprake; Reaney, Bell, Bremner, Madeley, Hunter, Lorimer, E.Gray, Belfitt, Giles, Cooper.
Att: 28,000
Final (1st leg)
Aug 30 v Dinamo Zagreb (a) 0-2
Sprake; Reaney, Cooper, Bremner, Charlton, Hunter, Bates, Lorimer, Belfitt, E.Gray, O'Grady.
Att: 40,000
Final (2nd leg)
Sep 6 v Dinamo Zagreb (h) 0-0 (agg 0-2).
Sprake; Bell, Cooper, Bremner, Charlton, Hunter, Reaney, Belfitt, Greenhoff, Giles, O'Grady.
Att: 35,604

1967-68
Round 1 (1st leg)
Oct 3 v Spora Luxembourg (a) 9-0
Lorimer 4, Bremner, Greenhoff 2, Madeley, Jones
Harvey; Reaney, Madeley, Bremner, Charlton, Hunter, Greenhoff, Lorimer, Jones, E.Gray, Cooper.
Att: 2,500
Round 1 (2nd leg)
Oct 17 v Spora Luxembourg (h) 7-0 (agg 16-0)
Johanneson 3, Greenhoff 2, Cooper, Lorimer
Sprake; Reaney, Cooper, Madeley (Bates), Charlton, Hunter, Greenhoff, Lorimer, Belfitt, Hibbitt, Johanneson.
Att: 15,196
Round 2 (1st leg)
Nov 29 v Partizan Belgrade (a) 2-1
Lorimer, Belfitt
Harvey; Reaney, Cooper, Bremner, Charlton, Hunter, Greenhoff, Lorimer, Madeley, Belfitt, E.Gray(Bates).
Att: 10,000
Round (2nd leg)
Dec 6 v Partizan Belgrade (h) 1-1 (agg 3-2)
Lorimer
Sprake; Reaney, Cooper, Bremner, Charlton, Hunter, Greenhoff, Lorimer, Madeley, E.Gray, Hibbitt(Johanneson).
Att: 34,258
Round 3 (1st leg)
Dec 20 v Hibernian (h) 1-0
Gray
Sprake; Reaney(Madeley), Cooper, Bremner, Charlton, Hunter, Greenhoff, Lorimer, Jones, E.Gray, Giles.
Att: 31,522
Round 3 (2nd leg)
Jan 10 v Hibernian (a) 1-1 (agg 2-1)
Charlton
Sprake; Reaney, Cooper, Bremner, Charlton, Hunter, Greenhoff, Lorimer, Jones, Giles, E.Gray.
Att: 30,000
Round 4 (1st leg)
Mar 26 v Rangers (a) 0-0
Sprake; Reaney, Cooper, Bremner, Charlton, Hunter, Greenhoff(Belfitt), Lorimer, Jones, Giles, Madeley.
Att: 80,000
Round 4 (2nd leg)
Apr 9 v Rangers (h) 2-0 (agg 2-0)
Giles (pen), Lorimer
Harvey; Reaney, Cooper, Bremner, Charlton, Hunter, Greenhoff, Madeley, Jones, Giles, Lorimer.
Att: 50,498
Semi-final (1st leg)
May 1 v Dundee (a) 1-1
Madeley
Harvey; Reaney, Cooper, Bremner, Charlton, Hunter, Greenhoff, Lorimer, Madeley, Giles, E.Gray.
Att: 30,000
Semi-final (2nd leg)
May 15 v Dundee (h) 1-0 (agg 2-1)
Gray
Sprake; Reaney, Cooper, Bremner, Madeley, Hunter, Greenhoff, Lorimer, Jones, Giles, E.Gray.
Att: 23,830
Final (1st leg)
Aug 7 v Ferencváros (h) 1-0
Jones
Sprake; Reaney, Cooper, Bremner, Charlton, Hunter, Lorimer, Madeley, Jones(Belfitt), Giles(Greenhoff), E.Gray.
Att: 25,268
Final (2nd leg)
Sep 11 v Ferencváros (a) 0-0 (agg 1-0)
Sprake; Reaney, Cooper, Bremner, Charlton, Hunter, O'Grady, Lorimer, Jones, Madeley, Hibbitt(Bates).
Att: 76,000

1968-69
Round 1 (1st leg)
Sep 18 v Standard Liége (a) 0-0
Sprake; Reaney, Cooper, Bremner, Charlton, Hunter, O'Grady, Lorimer, Jones, Madeley, Hibbitt.
Att: 35,000
Round 1 (2nd leg)
Oct 23 v Standard Liége (h) 3-2 (agg 3-2)
Charlton, Lorimer, Bremner

Sprake; Reaney, Cooper(Bates), Bremner, Charlton, Hunter, O'Grady, Lorimer, Jones, Madeley, Hibbitt(E.Gray).
Att: 24,178
Round 2 (1st leg)
Nov 13 v Napoli (h) 2-0
Charlton 2
Sprake; Reaney, Madeley, Bremner, Charlton, Hunter, O'Grady, Jones, Belfitt, Giles, Lorimer.
Att: 26,967
Round 2 (2nd leg)
Nov 27 v Napoli (a) 0-2 (agg 2-2)
Sprake; Reaney, Cooper, Bremner, Charlton, Hunter, O'Grady, Madeley, Jones, Giles, E.Gray.
Att: 15,000
Leeds won on the toss of a disc.
Round 3 (1st leg)
Dec 18 v Hannover 96 (h) 5-1
O'Grady, Hunter, Lorimer 2, Charlton
Sprake; Reaney, Madeley, Bremner, Charlton, Hunter, O'Grady(Hibbitt), Lorimer, Jones, Giles, E.Gray.
Att: 25,162
Round 3 (2nd leg)
Feb 4 v Hannover 96 (a) 2-1 (agg 7-2)
Belfitt, Jones
Sprake; Reaney, Cooper, Bremner, Charlton, Hunter, O'Grady, Lorimer, Jones, Belfitt, E.Gray.
Att: 15,000
Round 4 (1st leg)
Mar 5 v Újpesti Dózsa (h) 0-1
Sprake; Reaney, Madeley, Bremner, Charlton, Hunter, O'Grady, Belfitt(Lorimer), Jones, Giles, E.Gray.
Att: 30,906
Round 4 (2nd leg)
Mar 19 v Újpesti Dózsa (a) 0-2 (agg 0-3)
Sprake; Bates, Cooper, Bremner, Madeley, Hunter, Lorimer(Yorath), Belfitt, Jones(Hibbitt), Giles, E.Gray.
Att: 40,000

1970-71
Round 1 (1st leg)
Sep 15 v Sarpsborg (a) 1-0
Lorimer
Sprake; Madeley, Cooper, Bremner, Kennedy, E.Gray, Lorimer, Belfitt, Jones, Bates, Hibbitt.
Att: 10,000
Round 1 (2nd leg)
Sep 29 v Sarpsborg (h) 5-0 (agg 6-0)
Charlton 2, Bremner 2, Lorimer
Sprake; Madeley, Cooper(Reaney), Bremner, Charlton, Hunter, Lorimer, Clarke, Belfitt, Bates, E.Gray.
Att: 19,283
Round 2 (1st leg)
Oct 21 v Dynamo Dresden (h) 1-0
Lorimer
Harvey; Davey, Cooper, Bremner, Charlton, Hunter, Lorimer, Clarke, Jones, Belfitt(Galvin), Madeley.
Att: 21,292
Round 2 (2nd leg)
Nov 4 v Dynamo Dresden (a) 1-2 (agg 2-2)
Jones
Sprake; Davey, Madeley, Bremner, Charlton, Hunter, Lorimer, Clarke, Jones, Giles, Bates.
Att: 35,000
Leeds won on away-goals rule.
Round 3 (1st leg)
Dec 2 v Sparta Prague (h) 6-0
Clarke, Bremner, Gray 2, Charlton, Chovanec (og)
Sprake; Madeley, Cooper, Bremner, Charlton, Hunter, Lorimer, Clarke, Belfitt(Reaney), Giles, E.Gray.
Att: 25,843
Round 3 (2nd leg)
Dec 9 v Sparta Prague (a) 3-2 (agg 9-2)
Gray, Clarke, Belfitt
Sprake(Harvey); Reaney, Cooper, Bremner, Madeley, Hunter(Yorath), Lorimer, Clarke, Belfitt, Bates, E.Gray.
Att: 30,000
Round 4 (1st leg)
Mar 10 v Vitória Setúbal (h) 2-1
Lorimer, Giles (pen)
Harvey; Davey(Yorath), Reaney, Bates, Charlton, Hunter, Lorimer, Belfitt, Jones(Jordan), Giles, Madeley.
Att: 27,143
Round 4 (2nd leg)
Mar 24 v Vitória Setúbal (a) 1-1 (agg 3-2)
Lorimer
Harvey(Sprake); Reaney, Cooper, Bates, Charlton, Hunter, Lorimer, Clarke, Jones, Giles, Madeley.
Att: 30,000
Semi-final (1st leg)
Apr 14 v Liverpool (a) 1-0
Bremner
Sprake; Reaney(Davey), Cooper, Bremner, Charlton, Hunter, Bates, Clarke, Jones, Giles, Madeley.
Att: 52,877
Semi-final (2nd leg)
Apr 28 v Liverpool (h) 0-0 (agg 1-0)
Sprake; Madeley, Cooper, Bremner, Charlton, Hunter, Bates, Clarke(Reaney), Jones(Jordan), Giles, E.Gray.
Att: 40,462
Final (1st leg)
May 28 v Juventus (a) 2-2
Madeley, Bates
Sprake; Reaney, Cooper, Bremner, Charlton, Hunter, Lorimer, Clarke, Jones(Bates), Giles, Madeley.
Att: 45,000
Final (2nd leg)
Jun 2 v Juventus (h) 1-1 (agg 3-3)
Clarke
Sprake; Reaney, Cooper, Bremner, Charlton, Hunter, Lorimer, Clarke, Jones, Giles, Madeley(Bates).
Att: 42,483
Leeds won on away-goals rule.

1971-72
Round 1 (1st leg)
Sep 15 v Lierse SK (a) 2-0
Galvin, Lorimer
Sprake; Reaney, Yorath, Bremner, Faulkner, Hunter, Lorimer, Galvin, Belfitt, Giles, Bates.
Att: 17,000
Round 1 (2nd leg)
Sep 29 v Lierse SK (h) 0-4 (agg 2-4)
Shaw(Sprake); Reaney, Cooper, Yorath, Faulkner, Madeley, Lorimer, Mann(Hunter), Belfitt, Bates, Galvin.
Att: 18,680
Play-off between first and last winners of the Inter-Cities Fairs Cup for retention of the trophy.
1971
Sep 22 v Barcelona (a) 1-2
Jordan
Sprake; Reaney, Davey, Bremner, Charlton, Hunter, Lorimer, Jordan, Belfitt, Giles, Galvin.
Att: 35,000

1973-74
Round 1 (1st leg)
Sep 19 v Strömgodset Drammen (a) 1-1
Clarke
Sprake; Madeley, Cherry, Yorath, McQueen, F.T.Gray, Liddell, Clarke, Jones, Bates, E.Gray.
Att: 16,276
Round 1 (2nd leg)
Oct 3 v Strömgodset Drammen (h) 6-1 (agg 7-2)
Clarke 2, Jones 2, Gray, Bates
Harvey; Reaney(O'Neill), Cherry, Bremner, Ellam, Yorath, Lorimer, Clarke(McGinley), Jones, Bates, F.T.Gray.
Att: 18, 711
Round 2 (1st leg)
Oct 24 v Hibernian (h) 0-0
Harvey; Cherry, Madeley, Bremner, Ellam, Yorath, Lorimer, Clarke, Jones(Jordan), Bates, F.T.Gray(O'Neill).
Att: 27,145
Round 2 (2nd leg)
Nov 7 v Hibernian (a) 0-0 aet (agg 0-0)
Shaw(Letheran); Reaney, Cherry, Bremner, Ellam, Yorath, Lorimer, Clarke, Jordan, Bates, F.T.Gray.
Att: 36,051
Leeds won 5-4 on penalties.
Round 3 (1st leg)
Nov 28 v Vitória Setúbal (h) 1-0
Cherry
Harvey; Reaney(Davey), Cherry, Bremner, McQueen, Hunter, Lorimer, Clarke, Jordan, Bates, Yorath(F.T.Gray).
Att: 14,196
Round 3 (2nd leg)
Dec 12 v Vitória Setúbal (a) 1-3 (agg 2-3)
Liddell
Harvey; Reaney, Cherry, Yorath, McQueen (Liddell), Ellam, Lorimer, Mann, Jordan, Hampton, F.T.Gray.
Att: 25,000

1979-80
Round 1 (1st leg)
Sep 19 v Valletta (a) 4-0
Graham 3, Hart
Harvey; Hird, Hampton, Flynn, Hart, Madeley, E.Gray, Cherry, Hankin, Curtis, Graham(Harris).
Att: 18,000
Round 1 (2nd leg)
Oct 3 v Valletta (h) 3-0 (agg 7-0)
Curtis, Hankin, Hart
Lukic; Hird, Hampton, Flynn, Hart, Parkinson, Hamson, Cherry, Hankin, Curtis, Graham.
Att: 13,682
Round 2 (1st leg)
Oct 24 v Universitatea Craiova (a) 0-2
Lukic; Hird, Stevenson, Flynn, Hart, Madeley, Harris(Hamson), Cherry, Hankin, Curtis, E.Gray.
Att: 40,000
Round 2 (2nd leg)
Nov 7 v Universitatea Craiova (h) 0-2 (agg 0-4)
Lukic; Cherry, Stevenson, Flynn, Hart, Madeley, E.Gray, Parkinson(Harris), Hankin, Curtis, Graham.
Att: 14,438

1995-96
Round 1 (1st leg)
Sep 12 v AS Monaco (a) 3-0
Yeboah 3
Lukic; Kelly, Dorigo(Beesley), Palmer, Wetherall, Pemberton, Deane, Whelan, Yeboah, McAllister, Speed.
Att: 14,000
Round 1 (2nd leg)
Sep 26 v AS Monaco (h) 0-1 (agg 3-1)
Lukic; Kelly, Beesley, Palmer, Wetherall, Pemberton(Couzens), White(Tinkler), Deane, Yeboah, McAllister, Speed.
Att: 24,501
Round 2 (1st leg)
Oct 17 v PSV Eindhoven (h) 3-5
Speed, Palmer, McAllister
Lukic; Kelly, Dorigo(Beesley), Palmer, Wetherall, Pemberton, Deane,

Whelan(Wallace), Yeboah, McAllister, Speed(Couzens).
Att: 24,846
Round 2 (2nd leg)
Oct 31 v PSV Eindhoven (a) 0-3 (agg 3-8)
Lukic; Kelly, Beesley(Ford), Palmer, Wetherall, Pemberton, Bowman, Whelan(White), Yeboah, McAllister, Speed(Sharp).
Att: 25,570

European Appearances & Scorers

European Cup
Appearances (22 games)
Madeley 17, Lorimer 15, Bremner 14, Hunter 14, Reaney 14, Clarke 13, Giles 13, Cooper 10, Yorath 8/1, Jones 8, Jordan 8, Sprake 8, E.Gray 7/1, Charlton 7, McQueen 7, F.T.Gray 6, Cantona 5, Chapman 5, Dorigo 5, Fairclough 5, Lukic 5, McAllister 5, Speed 5, Stewart 5, Strachan 5, Whyte 5, Harvey 4/1, Batty 4, Bates 3/3, Newsome 3, Cherry 2/1, Rocastle 2/1, Belfitt 1, Hibbitt 1, McKenzie 1, O'Grady 1, Sellars 1, Hodge 0/2, Shutt 0/2, Rod Wallace 0/2, Galvin 0/1, Hampton 0/1, Harris 0/1.
Goalscorers
Jones 8, Lorimer 7, Bremner 6, Clarke 6, Giles 4, McQueen 3, Belfitt 2, Cantona 2, Hibbitt 2, Jordan 2, McAllister 2, Chapman 1, O'Grady 1, Shutt 1, Speed 1, Strachan 1, Yorath 1, Total 50.

European Cup-Winners' Cup
Appearances (9 games)
Harvey 9, Hunter 9, Lorimer 9, Cherry 8, Bremner 8, Giles 6/1, Jordan 6/1, Bates 6, Jones 6, Madeley 6, Clarke 5, Yorath 4/3, McQueen 2/1, Charlton 2, Ellam 2, E.Gray 2, F.T.Gray 1/1, Galvin 1.
Goalscorers
Jones 3, Jordan 3, Clarke 2, Lorimer 2, Bates 1, Cherry 1, Giles 1, Total 13

UEFA Inter-Cities Fairs Cup
(Not inlcuding trophy play-off v Barcelona)
Appearances (69 games)
Bremner 55, Hunter 54/1, Reaney 51/3, Lorimer 49/1, Sprake 48/2, Madeley 47/1, Charlton 46, Giles 41, Cooper 38, E.Gray 30/1, Jones 28, Belfitt 22/2, O'Grady 19, Greenhoff 18/1, Bates 17/6, Bell 17, Clarke 15, Harvey 12/1, Cherry 10, Storrie 10, Yorath 8/3, Hibbitt 7/2, Lukic 7, F.T.Gray 5/1, Johanneson 5/1, Curtis 4, Ellam 4, Flynn 4, Hankin 4, Hart 4, Kelly 4, McAllister 4, Palmer 4, Pemberton 4, Speed 4, Wetherall 4, Yeboah 4, Jordan 3/3, Davey 3/2, Collins 3, Deane 3, Graham 3, Hampton 3, Hird 3, McQueen 3, Peacock 3, Whelan 3, Beesley 2/2, Galvin 2/1, Dorigo 2, Faulkner 2, Mann 2, Parkinson 2, Shaw 2, Stevenson 2, Harris 1/2, Hamson 1/1, Liddell 1/1, White 1/1, Bowman 1, Kennedy 1, Couzens 0/2, O'Neill 0/2, Ford 0/1, Letheran 0/1, McGinley 0/1, Sharp 0/1, Tinkler 0/1, Rod Wallace 0/1.
Goalscorers
Lorimer 21, Bremner 10, Charlton 10, Johanneson 8, Belfitt 6, Clarke 6, Giles 6, Greenhoff 6, Jones 6, E.Gray 5, Madeley 4, Graham 3, Yeboah 3, Bates 2, Cooper 2, Hart 2, O'Grady 2, Bell 1, Cherry 1, Curtis 1, Galvin 1, F.T.Gray 1, Hankin 1, Hunter 1, Liddell 1, McAllister 1, Palmer 1, Peacock 1, Speed 1, Storrie 1, Own-goal 1, Total 116.

Locally born, Paul Madeley played in every position for Leeds, except goalkeeper, during his long career. He made 70 appearances in Europe for Leeds United.

Leeds United in Other Competitions

FA Charity Shield

1969
Aug 2 v Manchester City (Elland Road) 2-1 (0-0)
Gray, Charlton
Sprake; Reaney, Cooper, Bremner, Charlton, Hunter, Madeley, Clarke, Jones(Lorimer), Giles, Gray.
Att: 39,835

1974
Aug 10 v Liverpool (Wembley) 1-1 (0-1)
Cherry
Harvey; Reaney, Cherry, Bremner, McQueen, Hunter, Lorimer, Clarke(McKenzie), Jordan, Giles, E.Gray.
Att: 67,000

1992-93
Aug 8 v Liverpool (Wembley) 4-3
Cantona 3, Dorigo
Lukic, Newsome(Strachan), Dorigo, Batty, Fairclough, Whyte, Cantona, Rod Wallace, Chapman(Hodge), McAllister, Speed.
Att: 61,291

Challenge Matches Against Representative Opposition

1975
May 19 v Scotland Under-23 (Hampden Park) 2-3
Lorimer 2
Harvey(Letheran); Reaney(Cherry), F.T.Gray, Bremner, Madeley, Hunter, Lorimer, Clarke, Jordan(McKenzie), Yorath, E.Gray.
Att: 9,978

1993
Jul 23 v League of Ireland (Tolka Park) 2-2
Shutt, Speed
Beeney; Kelly, Dorigo, Batty, Wetherall, Newsome, Strachan, Rod Wallace, Tobin(Shutt), McAllister, Speed.
Att: 7,000
NB: Steve Tobin did not play for the first team.

Full Members' Cup

(1987-88 to 1988-89 the Simod Cup, 1989-90 the Zenith Data Systems Cup)

1985-86
Group Match
Oct 14 v Manchester City (a) 1-6 (0-3)
Lorimer (pen)
Day; Irwin, Phelan, Hamson, Linighan(Swan), Aspin, McCluskey(Simmonds), Sheridan, Baird, Lorimer, Sellars.
Att: 4,029

Group Match
Oct 16 v Sheffield United (h) 1-1 (0-0)
Sellars
Day; Iwin(Swan), Phelan, Sellars, Linighan, Aspin(Stiles), Simmonds, Sheridan, Baird, Lorimer, Thompson.
Att: 2,274

1986-87
1st Round
Oct 1 v Bradford City (h) 0-1 (0-0) aet
Day; Aspin, Haddock, Orsmby(Thompson), Ashurst, Rennie, Stiles, Sheridan, Taylor, Edwards, Buckley(Wright).
Att: 3,960

1987-88
1st Round
Nov 25 v Sheffield United (h) 3-0 (0-0)
Rennie, Taylor, Noteman
Day; Grayson, Adams, De Mange, Ashurst, Haddock, Batty, Rennie, Taylor, Davison, Noteman.
Att: 4,425
2nd Round
Dec 8 v Millwall (a) 0-2 (0-1)
Day; Aspin, Swan, De Mange, Ashurst, Haddock(Stiles[Pearson]), Batty, Sheridan, Taylor, Davison, Snodin.
Att: 5,034
Note: Substitute John Stiles was himself replaced during the match – the first Leeds substitute to be substituted.

1988-89
1st Round
Nov 9 v Shrewbury Town (h) 3-1 (1-1)
Davison 2, Aizlewood
Day; Aspin, Whitlow, Aizlewood, Blake, Rennie, Batty, Sheridan, Baird(Taylor), Davison, Hailaire.
Att: 3,220
2nd Round
Nov 29 v Millwall (a) 0-2 (0-1)
Day; Aspin, Snodin, Aizlewood, Blake, Rennie, Whitlow(Haddock), Sheridan, Baird, Davison, Hilaire(Pearson).
Att: 4,242

1989-90
1st Round
Nov 8 v Blackburn Rovers (h) 1-0
Davison
Day; Sterland(Speed), Whitlow, Jones, Fairclough, Haddock, Strachan, Batty, Baird, Davison, A.Williams.
Att: 5,070
2nd Round
Nov 28 v Barnsley (a) 2-1
Strachan (pen), A.Williams
Edwards; Sterland, Whitlow, Jones, Fairclough, Haddock(Kerr), Strachan, Batty, Baird, Davison(Shutt), A.Williams.
Att: 6,136
3rd Round
Dec 19 v Stoke City (a) 2-2 (90 mins 1-1) aet Leeds won 5-4 on penalties.
Shutt 2
Day; Sterland, Whitlow(Kerr), Jones, Blake, Haddock, Strachan, Batty, Pearson(Shutt), Baird, Hendrie.
Att: 5,792

4th Round
Jan 17 v Aston Villa (a) 0-2
Day; Blake, Whitlow, Jones, Fairclough, Haddock, Strachan, Batty, Baird, Beglin(Kerr), Hendrie(Pearson).
Att: 17,543

1990-91
2nd Round
Dec 19 v Wolves (a) 2-1
Varadi, McAllister
Day; Sterland, Snodin, Beglin, Fairclough, Haddock, Strachan(A.Williams), Varadi(Kerr), Pearson, McAllister, Speed.
Att: 11,080
3rd Round
Jan 22 v Derby County (h) 2-1
Shutt, Chapman
Lukic; Sterland, Snodin, Batty, Haddock, Whyte, Strachan, Shutt(Varadi), Chapman, A.Williams, Speed.
Att: 6,334
Semi-final (Northern Area)
Feb 20 v Manchester City (h) 2-0 aet
A.Williams, Strachan
Lukic; Sterland, Whitlow, Batty, Fairclough, Whyte, Strachan, Shutt, Chapman, McAllister (A.Williams), Speed(Davison).
Att: 11,898
Final (Northern Area)
1st leg
Mar 19 v Everton (h) 3-3
Sterland, Chapman 2
Lukic; Sterland, Whitlow, Batty, Fairclough, Whyte, Strachan, Davison(Shutt), Chapman, McAllister, A.Williams(Speed).
Att: 13,387
Final (Northern Area)
2nd leg
Mar 21 v Everton (a) 1-3 aet (agg 4-6)
Sterland
Lukic; Sterland, Whitlow, Batty, Fairclough, Whyte, Strachan, Shutt(Davison), Chapman, McAllister(Speed), A.Williams.
Att: 12,603

1991-92
2nd Round
Oct 22 v Nottingham Forest (h) 1-3
Rod Wallace
Lukic: Sterland(Rod Wallace), Dorigo, Batty, Fairclough, Whyte, Newsome(Grayson), Shutt, Snodin, Kamara, Speed.
Att: 6,145

Glasgow Charity Cup

1966
Aug 10 v Glasgow Select XI (Hampden Park) 1-1 (0-0)
Giles
Sprake; Reaney, Bell, Bremner, Charlton (Madeley), Hunter, Storrie, Collins, Lorimer, Giles, Gray.
Att: 18,000

Festival of Britain Matches

1951
May 9 v Rapid Vienna (h) 2-2 (1-0)
Iggleden, Hughes

Searson; Dunn, Jim Milburn, McCabe, Kirk, Burden, Harrison, Iggleden, Charles, Hughes, Williams.
Att: 18,000
May 14 v FC Haarlem (h) 2-0 (1-0)
Miller, Harrison
Scott; Ross, Hair, Kerfoot, Charles, Burden, Harrison, Miller, Browning, Hughes, Williams.
Att: 9,362

League Jubilee Fund Matches

1938
Aug 20 v Huddersfield Town (h) 1-1 (0-1)
Milburn (pen)
Twomey; Jack Milburn, Gadsby, Edwards, Holley, Makinson, Armes, Ainsley, Hodgson, Stephenson, Buckley.
Att: 7,352

1939
Aug 19 v Huddersfield Town (a) 0-5 (0-2)
Twomey; Goldberg, Gadsby, Edwards, Holley, Copping, Cochrane, Ainsley, Dunderdale, Stephenson, Buckley.
Att: 4,630

West Riding Senior Cup

The first trophy ever to be taken back to Elland Road was the West Riding Challenge Cup, won by Leeds City Reserves in 1907 when two goals by Alf Harwood gave them victory over Kippax Parish Church, a team from the West Yorkshire League.

City also figured in the first West Riding Senior Cup Final, in 1910, but were well beaten by Bradford. The Senior Cup competition had replaced the Challenge Cup and both United and City have been regular finalists.

Leeds City in the Final
1910-11
Nov 1 v Bradford (Valley Parade) 1-5 (0-3)
McLeod
Bromage; Affleck, Creighton, Harkins, T.Morris, Cubberley, Roberts, McLeod, Gillespie, Enright, Croot.
Att: 3,000

1914-15
Nov 11 v Hull City (Elland Road) 1-0 (0-0)
Speirs
Hogg; Blackman, McQuillan, Law, J.Hampson, Foley, Bainbridge, Jackson, McLeod, Speirs, Sharpe.
Att: 1,000 (Hampson was sent off)

1918-19
May 17 v Huddersfield Town (Valley Parade) 0-0 (0-0)
Sutcliffe; Millership, W.Hampson, Lamph, J.Hampson, McLachlan, Hall, C.Stephenson, Peart, McLeod, Bainbridge.
Att: 10,000
Replay
May 24 v Huddersfield Town (Valley Parade) 2-0 (2-0)
C.Stephenson 2
Sutcliffe; Millership, W.Hampson, Lamph, J.Hampson, Hall, Stephenson, Peart, McLeod, Bainbridge.
Att: 10,000

Leeds United in the Final
1921-22
May 13 v Huddersfield Town (Valley Parade) 0-1 (0-0)
Whalley; J.W.Baker, Frew, Sherwin, Hart, Walton, Coates, Poyntz, Armitage, Swan, Clark.
Att: 8,500

1922-23
Oct 25 v Halifax Town (Elland Road) 1-0 (0-0)
Poyntz
Whalley; Duffield, J.Potts, Sherwin, Hart, L.H.Baker, Mason, Dark, Poyntz, Swan, Harris.
Att: 6,000

1923-24
May 10 v Bradford (Elland Road) 1-2 (0-0)
Richmond
Down; Duffield, Menzies, L.H.Baker, Hart, J.W.Baker, Coates, Whipp, Richmond, Swan, Harris.
Att: 12,000

1925-26
May 8 v Huddersfield Town (Park Avenue) 4-1 (0-1)
Jennings 3, Jackson
Att: 10,700
Local FA has no record of teams and because of the 1926 General Strike there were no newspapers.

1926-27
May 14 v Bradford (Park Avenue) 2-3 (2-1)
Jennings, Wainscoat
J.F.Potts; Roberts, Allan, Edwards, Townsley, Reed, Turnbull, White, Jennings, Wainscoat, Mitchell.
Att: 11,082

1927-28
May 12 v Bradford (Elland Road) 4-2 (3-2)
Mitchell, Hart, Turnbull, Keetley
J.F.Potts; Roberts, Menzies, Edwards, Hart, Reed, Turnbull, White, Keetley, Wainscoat, Mitchell.
Att: 10,000

1928-29
May 11 v Halifax Town (Valley Parade) 4-0 (2-0)
Duggan 2, Keetley 2
J.F.Potts; Roberts, Menzies, Underwood, Townsley, Reed, Duggan, Keetley, Jennings, Wainscoat, Mitchell.
Att: 3,500

1929-30
May 10 v Huddersfield Town (Elland Road) 0-1 (0-0)
J.F.Potts; Roberts, J.Milburn, Edwards, Hart, Stacey, Turnbull, Longden, Keetley, Wainscoat, Cochrane.
Att: 10,000

1930-31
May 9 v Huddersfield Town (Valley Parade) 0-1 (0-1)
J.F.Potts; G.W.Milburn, Menzies, Edwards, Danskin, Copping, Green, Hornby, Keetley, Furness, Cochrane.
Att: 5,900

1932-33
Apr 26 v Huddersfield Town (Valley Parade) 0-1 (0-1)
Moore; G.W.Milburn, J.Milburn, Edwards, Hart, Copping, Duggan, Firth, Fowler, Hydes, Mahon.
Att: 2,700 (Hart was sent off)

1936-37
May 3 v Bradford City (Elland Road) 4-2 aet (2-1; 90 min 2-2)
Kelly, Hargreaves 2, Trainer
United fielded a reserve team to mark winning the Central League. Amongst those who played were G.W.Milburn, Thompson, Furness, Kelly, Trainor, Turner, Hargreaves.
Att: 1,500

1949-50
May 6 v Bradford City (Valley Parade) 2-3 (1-3)
Dudley, Kerfoot
Searson; Dunn, J.Milburn, McCabe, Charles, Kerfoot, Cochrane, Iggleden, McMorran, Dudley, Williams.
Att: 14,372

1950-51
May 12 v Bradford (Elland Road) 0-4 (0-3)
Searson; Dunn, J.Milburn, McCabe, Kirk, Burden, P.Harrison, Iggleden, Charles, Stevenson, Williams.
Att: 15,000

1951-52
Oct 8 v Halifax Town (Elland Road) 2-1 (1-0)
Charles 2
Scott; Dunn, Hair, Kerfoot, McCabe, Burden, Meek, Tyrer, Charles, Iggleden, Williams.
Att: 3,500
Note: Final held over until following season.

1953-54
Mar 15 v Huddersfeld Town (Elland Road) 2-1 (1-1)
Nightingale, Charles
Scott; Dunn, Hair, Kerfoot, Marsden, Burden, McCall, Nightingale, Charles, Forrest, Williams.
Att: 23,000

1954-55
May 8 v Bradford (Elland Road) 2-1 (0-0)
Smith, Nightingale
Wood; Dawson, Dunn, Gibson, Charles, Kerfoot, Williams, Nightingale, Smith, Henderson, Meek.
Att: 4,000

1955-56
Nov 28 v Huddersfield Town (Elland Road) 5-2 (3-1)
Charles 4, Vickers
Wood; Dunn, Hair, Nightingale, Charlton, Kerfoot, Williams, Hutchinson, Charles, Vickers, Overfield.
Att: 12,500

1956-57
Nov 26 v Halifax Town (Elland Road) 3-1 (2-1)
Ripley 3
Wood; Dunn, Hair, Rich, Charlton, Gibson, Meek, Charles, Ripley, Crowe, Overfield.
Att: 3,500

1957-58
Nov 25 v Bradford City (Valley Parade) 2-2 (2-0)
Crowe, Baird
Wood; Stanley, Hair, Ripley, Charlton, Cush, Francis, Gibson, Baird, Crowe, Overfield.
Att: 8,858
Replay
May 1 v Bradford City (Elland Road) 4-0 (0-0)
Baird (pen), Overfield, Charlton, Crowe
Wood; Dunn, Hair, Gibson, Charlton, Cush, Meek, Crowe, Baird, Forrest, Overfield.
Att: 6,037

1959-60
May 9 v Bradford (Elland Road) 1-1 (0-0)
McCole
Humphreys; Ashall, Caldwell, Gibson, Charlton, Goodwin, Bremner, Francis, McCole, Hawksby, Meek.
Att: 5,500
Replay
May 12 v Bradford (Park Avenue) 3-1 (1-1)
McCole 2, Goodwin
Humphreys; Ashall, Caldwell, McConnell, Charlton, Goodwin, Bremner, Francis, McCole, Hawksby, Meek.
Att: 5,766

1960-61
May 9 v Bradford (Park Avenue) 4-2 (2-1)
Bremner 2, Peyton, Hawksby
Carling; Jones, Kilford, Smith, Charlton, Bell, Johanneson, McConnell, Bremner, Peyton, Hawksby.
Att: 10,023

1963-64
May 7 v Bradford City (Elland Road) 4-1 (3-1)
Collins 2, Cooper, Storrie
Sprake; Reaney, Bell, Bremner, Charlton, Hunter, Giles, Storrie, Peacock, Collins, Cooper.
Att: 11,084

1965-66
May 20 v Bradford (Park Avenue) 4-0 (4-0)
O'Grady 2, Johanneson, Thomas (og)
Sprake; Reaney, Cooper, Bremner, Bell, Greenhoff, O'Grady, Lorimer, Storrie, Collins, Johanneson.
Att: 9,013

1968-69
May 16 v Huddersfield Town (Park Avenue) 2-1 (1-0)
Lorimer, Hunter
Sprake; Reaney, Cooper, Giles, Yorath, Hunter, Bates, Lorimer, Jones, Belfitt, Hibbitt.
Att: 10,794

1971-72
May 12 v Halifax Town (Elland Road) 4-3 (2-2)
Lorimer 3, Jordan
Sprake; Reaney, O'Neill, Bremner, Saunders, Yorath, Lorimer, Mann, Jordan, Bates(Hampton), Galvin.
Att: 6,256

1972-73
Aug 21 v Halifax Town (Elland Road) 2-1 (1-1)
Lorimer (pen), Jones
Harvey; Reaney, Cherry, Bremner, McQueen, Hunter, Lorimer, Clarke, Jones, Giles, Bates.
Att: 4,650
Note: Final held over until following season.

1975-76
Nov 15 v Huddersfield Town (Elland Road) 2-0 (1-0)
Hankin 2
Harvey; Reaney, F.T.Gray, McGhie, Parkinson, Stevenson, Lorimer(Thomas), McNiven, Hankin, Currie, Liddell.
Att: 2,971
Note: Final held over until following season.

1976-77
Oct 10 v Bradford City (Valley Parade) 5-2 (3-0)
McNiven, Lorimer 2 (1 pen), Thomas 2
Harvey; Stevenson, F.T.Gray, Lorimer(Felix), Parkinson, Firm, Harris, Whyte, Thomas, Currie(Parker), McNiven.
Att: 4,695
Note: Final held over until following season.

1977-78
On 4 May 1978, United were due to play Huddersfield Town in the Final but refused to alter a continental tour programme. Leeds were fined £2,000 and Huddersfield awarded the game.

1979-80
May 6 v Bradford City (Valley Parade) 4-1 (0-0)
Harris, Graham 3
Smith; Hird, Stevenson, Flynn, Firm, Madeley, Harris, Chandler, Parlane(Connor), E.Gray, Graham.
Att: 3,255

1981-82
Aug 23 v Halifax Town (Elland Road) 3-2 aet (0-1; 90 mins 2-2)
Worthington (pen), Butterworth, Gray
Lukic; Hird, Cherry, Flynn, Hart, Burns(Aspin), Sheridan, Parlane(Butterworth), Worthington, F.T.Gray, Graham.
Att: 1,228
Note: Final held over from previous season.

No competition was held in 1982-83 and in 1983-84 the competition was played as a pre-season mini-league with a revolutionary points scoring system. Two points were awarded for the team who won the first half, two points to the team winning the second half and a further two points for winning the match. United won the competition in the first season of the new format, Bradford City winning it for the next four years.

1983
Aug 13 v Huddersfield Town (h) 2-1 (1-0)
Ritchie, Sheridan
Harvey; Hird, F.Gray, Watson(Sellars), Brown, Dickinson, Thomas(Donnelly), McCluskey, Ritchie, Sheridan, Barnes.
Att: 3,761
Aug 16 v Halifax Town (a) 0-2 (0-1)
Harvey; Hird, F.Gray, Sheridan(Aspin), Brown, Dickinson, Sellars(Gavin), McCluskey, Ritchie, Donnelly, Barnes.
Att: 1,402
Aug 20 v Bradford City (h) 2-0 (1-0)
Donnelly Ritchie
Harvey, Hird, Hamson, Watson, Brown, F.Gray, Thomas, McCluskey(Butterworth), Ritchie, Donnelly, Barnes.
Att: 3,108

1984
Aug 11 v Bradford City (a) 0-2 (0-0)
Harvey; Irwin, Gray, Watson, Linighan, Aspin, Wright, Sheridan, Ritchie, Lorimer, Sellars.
Att: 3,079
Aug 13 v Huddersfield Town (a) 1-0 (1-0)
McCluskey
Harvey; Irwin, Hamson, Watson, Linighan, Aspin, Wright, Sheridan, McCluskey, Lorimer, Sellars.
Att: 1,726
Aug 15 v Halifax Town (h) 3-1 (2-0)
Lorimer 3
Hughes; Irwin, Hamson, Watson, Linighan, Aspin, Wright, Sheridan, McCluskey, Lorimer, Sellars.
Att: 1,469

1985
Aug 5 v Huddersfield Town (h) 2-1 (0-0)
Baird, Lorimer (pen)
Swinburne; Irwin, Hamson, Snodin, Bentley, Aspin, McCluskey, Sheridan, Baird, Lorimer, Sellars.
Att: 2,134
NB: David Bentley didn't play for the Leeds first team
Aug 7 v Halifax Town (a) 6-0 (2-0)
McCluskey 2, Baird 2, Sellars 2
Day; Irwin, Hamson, I.Snodin, Linighan, Aspin, McCluskey, Sheridan, Baird, Lorimer, Sellars.
Att: 1,473
Aug 10 v Bradford City (h) 2-4 (1-2)
McCluskey Sheridan
Day; Irwin, Hamson, I.Snodin, Linighan, Aspin, McCluskey, Sheridan, Baird, Lorimer, Sellars.
Att: 4,692

1986
Aug 6 v Bradford City (at Odsal) 0-3 (0-1)
Day; Haddock(Stiles), Caswell(Robinson), I.Snodin, Aspin, Rennie, Doig, Sheridan, Ritchie, Ashurst, Swan.
Att: 2,276

Aug 9 v Halifax Town (a) 3-0 (2-0)
Edwards 2, Ritchie
Day(Sinclair); Aspin(Stiles), Caswell, I.Snodin, Hazell, Rennie, Buckley(Doig), Sheridan, Edwards, Ashurst, Ritchie.
Att: 2,308
Note: Bob Hazel (former Wolves, QPR and Leicester) was on trial, but didn't sign and went on to play for Reading and Port Vale.
Aug 12 v Huddersfield Town (a) 2-2 (1-1)
Buckley Ormsby
Sinclair; Aspin, Caswell, Snodin, Hazell(Ormsby), Rennie, Buckley(Doig), Sheridan, Edwards, Ashurst, Ritchie.
Att: 1,365

1987
Aug 1 v Halifax Town (h) 1-0 (1-0)
G.Willlams
Day; Aspin, Haddock, Aizlewood, Ashurst (Rennie), G.Williams(Grayson), Batty, Sheridan, Pearson(Edwards), Taylor(Ritchie), G.Snodin.
Att: 2,606
Aug 3 v Huddersfield Town (h) 3-2 (2-0)
G.Snodin 2, Sheridan
Day; Aspin, Haddock(Rennie), Aizlewood, Ashurst, Ritchie(Doig), Batty, Sheridan, Pearson, Edwards, G.Snodin(Speed).
Att: 3,101
Aug 7 v Bradford City (h) 2-2 (1-2)
Doig, G.Snodin (pen)
Day; Aspin, Adams, Rennie, Ashurst, Williams, Batty, Doig, Pearson, Edwards, G.Snodin.
Att: 4,566
NB: There was a break from the West Riding Senior Cup for three seasons as clubs in the County FA joined the pre-season Yorkshire and Humberside Cup. The West Riding Senior Cup competition was restored in 1991.

1991
Jul 31 v Bradford City (a) 1-0 (1-0)
Fairclough
Day; McClelland, G.Snodin, Wetherall, Fairclough, Speed, Strachan(Dorigo), Davison(Varadi), Chapman, McAllister, Rod Wallace.
Att: 3,630
NB: This game doubled as Maurice Lindley's Testimonial game.
Aug 7 v Halifax Town (h) 0-2 (0-2)
O'Dowd; Ray Wallace, Whitlow, Kerr, Wetherall, Curtis, Grayson(Sterland), Williams, Davison (Nicholson), Varadi, G.Snodin.

Att: 2,174
NB: Tony O'Dowd, Len Curtis and Steve Nicholson didn't play first-team football for Leeds.
Aug 10 v Huddersfield Town (h) 0-1 (0-1)
Day; Sterland, Whitlow, Kerr, Wetherall, Curtis, Ray Wallace(A.Williams) Grayson, Davison, Varadi, G.Snodin.
Att: 1,678
NB: The competition was won by Bradford City.

Yorkshire and Humberside Cup

The Yorkshire and Humberside Cup was first played for as a pre-season tournament in 1988. The competition was formed as a result of a partnership between the Sports Council and 12 of the region's top professional clubs, the relevant County Football Associations and the Sports Aid Foundation (Yorkshire and Humberside). In effect, the new competition replaced the West Riding Senior Cup, North Riding Senior Cup and Hallamshire Cup competitions. The 12 clubs in the Yorkshire and Humberside Cup were split into two groups of six. Each club played three matches with the winners of each group going through to the Final. United were in Group A in the competition's first season, along with Huddersfield Town, Scarborough, Barnsley, Scunthorpe United and York City. United were one of the favourites to win the competition, but did badly and failed to reach the Final. Scarborough won Group A but lost in the Final to Sheffield United, the Group B winners, 2-1 after extra-time at the McCain Stadium, Scarborough, on 13 September. The 64lb trophy was presented at the Final by Leeds director Maxwell Holmes, the chairman of the Yorkshire and Humberside Cup competition.

1988
Aug 13 v York City (h) 0-0 (0-0)
Day; Aspin(G.Williams), Adams, Aizlewood, Blake, Ormsby, Batty, Hilaire, Baird, Swan(Davison), G.Snodin.
Att: 2,908
Aug 16 v Huddersfield Town (a) 0-1 (0-1)
Day; G.Williams, Adams, Aizlewood, Blake, Ormsby, Stiles, Hilaire, Baird(Pearson), Davison, G.Snodin.
Att: 2,407
Aug 20 v Barnsley (h) 1-1 (0-0)
Rennie
Day; Aspin, Adams, Aizlewood, Blake, Ormsby(Ashurst), G.Williams, Rennie(Batty), Baird, Pearson, Hilaire.
Att: 2,657

1989
Aug 5 v Rotherham United (h) 1-1 (0-1)
Whitlow
Day; Sterland, Whitlow, Jones, McClelland, Fairclough, Strachan, Batty, Baird, G.Snodin (Speed), Hendrie.
Att: 4,735
Aug 8 v Doncaster Rovers (h) 2-0 (0-0)
Hendrie, Speed
Day; Sterland(G.Williams), Whitlow, Grayson, McClelland, Haddock, Strachan(Parsley), Batty, Speed, Davison, Hendrie.
Att: 3,562
NB: Neil Parsley didn't play a first-team game for Leeds.

Aug 11 v Halifax Town (a) 1-2 (1-1)
Hendrie
Edwards; Sterland, Whitlow(G.Williams), Speed, McClelland, Haddock, Strachan, Batty, Baird(Grayson), Davison, Hendrie.
Att: The match was played behind closed doors at The Shay because improvements were being done to the ground.
NB: The competition was won by Hull City, who beat Bradford City in the Final.

1990
Aug 11 v Hull City (a) 1-2 (1-2)
McAllister
Lukic; Sterland, G.Snodin, Haddock(Varadi), Fairclough, Whyte, Strachan, Batty(A.Williams), Chapman, McAllister, Speed.
Att: 3,111
Aug 13 v Scarborough (a) 2-0 (0-0)
Chapman, Whyte
Day; Sterland, G.Snodin, Jones, Fairclough(Haddock), Whyte, Strachan, Varadi, Chapman(Pearson), McAllister, Speed.
Att: 3,608
Aug 18 v Lincoln City (a) 4-1 (0-0)
Willlams, Sterland, Snodin, Varadi
Lukic; Sterland, G.Snodin, Kamara, Whyte, Haddock, Strachan, Batty(Jones), Pearson, Varadi, Speed(A.Williams).
Att: 4,661
NB: This was the last time United entered the West Riding Senior Cup which was retained in 1992 by Bradford City, who beat Huddersfield Town 1-0 in the final at Leeds Road, the goal being scored by former United player Peter Mumby, who was on loan from Huddersfield

Makita Trophy Tournament

United hosted the 1992 Makita Trophy Tournament, a high profile pre-season invitation competition which had been held at Wembley in previous years. There was an added edge to the competition as United, the English champions, had been drawn against one of the participants, VfB Stuttgart, in the European Cup and the teams were scheduled to meet in the semi-final of the Makita tournament. The other Makita entrants were Nottingham Forest and Italian side Sampdoria.

1992
Aug 1 v VfB Stuttgart (h) 2-1 (0-1)
Wallace, Rocastle
Lukic; Newsome, Dorigo, Hodge, Sellars(Batty), Whyte, Rocastle(Cantona), Rod Wallace, Chapman, McAllister, Speed.
Att: 12,500
NB: Sampdoria beat Nottingham Forest 2-0 in their semi-final match on the same day.

Aug 2 v Sampdoria (h) 0-1 (0-1)
Lukic; Newsome(Whyte), Dorigo, Batty, Fairclough, Hodge, Rocastle(Cantona), Rod Wallace, Chapman, McAllister, Speed.
Att: 15,000
NB: Stuttgart beat Forest 1-0 in the third/fourth play-off game.

Transpennine Express Trophy

United fielded a mixture of reserves and juniors in this pre-season invitation tournament in 1993 which also involved Liverpool, Tottenham Hotspur and Sheffield Wednesday. Tottenham, who beat Sheffield Wednesday 2-1 in their semi-final, won the competition. Liverpool took third place with a 4-3 win over Wednesday. Both United matches were played at Queensgate, Bridlington.

1993
Jul 27 v Liverpool (at Bridlington) 4-0 (3-0)
Shutt, Chapman 2, Ford
Beeney; Couzens, Oliver, Hodge, Wetherall, Whyte, Shutt, Ray Wallace, Chapman, Tobin, Ford.
Jul 29 v Tottenham Hotspur (at Bridlington) 0-2 (0-1)
Beeney; Couzens, Sharp, Hodge, Wetherall, Whyte, Shutt, Tinkler, Chapman, Forrester, Ford.
NB: Simon Oliver and Steve Tobin have not played a first-team game for Leeds.

Ryedale Trophy

This competition effectively succeeded the Transpennine Trophy with all the games being played at Ryedale Stadium, the home of York Rugby League Club. The format was unchanged and Tottenham retained the trophy. The following year, the tournament was won by Nottingham Forest, who beat Tottenham 2-0.

1994
Jul 30 v Sheffield Wednesday 2-2 (1-1)
Hodge 2, Forrester (pen)
Pettinger; Couzens, Sharp, Ford, Ray Wallace, Jackson, Wharton, Hodge, A.Brown(Gray), Forrester, Smithard.
Jul 31 v Tottenham Hotspur 0-2 aet (0-0; 90 mins 0-0)
Pettinger; Couzens, Sharp, Ford, Ray Wallace, Jackson(O'Shea), Wharton, Blunt, A.Brown(Shepherd), Forrester, Smithard.

1995
Aug 5 v Tottenham Hotspur 1-4 (0-1)
Ford
Pettinger; Marks, Fidler, Bowman, O'Shea, Smithard, Wharton, A.Brown(Masinga), Forrester, Sharp(Blunt).
Aug 6 v Sheffield Wednesday 0-0 (0-0)
Pettinger; Smithard, Fidler(Shepherd), Blunt, O'Shea, Jackson(Maybury), Wharton, Ford, Grant, Lowndes(A.Brown), Gray.
NB: Paul Pettinger, Jamie Marks, Paul Wharton, Andrew Brown, Matthew Smithard, Alan O'Shea, Paul Shepherd, Richard Fidler, Tony Grant and Nathan Lowndes haven't played a first-team game for Leeds.

Mercantile Credit Football Festival

To celebrate the centenary of the Football League in 1988 a variety of events were staged by the Football League, the centrepiece being the Mercantile Credit Football Festival. The final of the festival was played at Wembley on 17 April 1985 – exactly 100 years to the day that officials from 12 clubs met at the Royal Hotel, Manchester, to form the first competetion in the world.

The Football League came up with the concept that 16 clubs – eight from Division One, four from Division Two and two each from Divisions Three and Four should qualify for the finals.

Qualification was based on the number of points teams gained in their first League fixtures between the start of November and the end of February. Provision was made that in the case of clubs not fulfilling 15 League fixtures during the specified period, points were to be allocated on a pro-rata basis for any missing games, if neccessary, to establish qualification. Leeds picked up 30 points to qualify as the third team in Division Two behind Blackburn Rovers and Aston Villa.

League fixtures for 16 and 17 April were cancelled to allow the event to be staged at Wembley. Because of the number of matches to be played, matches were only 40 minutes long in rounds one and two, and an hour in the semi-finals and final.

Leeds were drawn against Nottingham Forest and lost 3-0. Forest went on to beat Sheffield Wednesday 3-2 on penalties in the final after neither side scored in normal time. Many critics were quick to point out that the contrived nature of the competition had failed to grip the imagination of the public with only 40,000 entering the stadium and 20,000 being the maximum attendance at any one time.

1988

Apr 16 v Nottingham Forest (at Wembley) 0-3 (0-2)

Day; G.Williams, Adams(G.Snodin), Aizlewood, Ashurst, Rennie, Batty, Sheridan, Baird, Taylor (Pearson), Grayson.
Subs (not used): Swan, Stiles, Sinclair.
NB: Leeds adpoted squad numbers, Adams wore 11, Snodin 13, Rennie 15, Taylor 12, Pearson 10, Grayson 14, Swan 6, Stiles 17 and Sinclair 18. The remainder were numbered as listed.

Lee Chapman tussles for the ball with Sampdoria's Pietro Vierchowod during the Makita Trophy Final at Elland Road in 1992.

Leeds in Other Leagues

West Yorkshire League

See Leeds City's First Season

Season	*P*	*W*	*D*	*L*	*F*	*A*	*Pts*	*Pos*
1904-05	24	7	7	10	34	49	21	11th

North Eastern League

LEEDS CITY became the founder members of the North Eastern League at a meeting in Newcastle United's boardroom on 5 May 1906. Together with major clubs from the North-East, City fielded an 'A' team or 3rd XI, but stayed only two seasons because of the high travelling costs.

Season	*P*	*W*	*D*	*L*	*F*	*A*	*Pts*	*Pos*
1906-07	18	9	4	5	33	20	22	4th
1907-08	24	13	3	8	64	46	29	4th

Midland League

LEEDS CITY entered a reserve side in the Midland League for the first time in 1905-06 and finished in a respectable mid-table position. In 1913-14, City Reserves finished bottom, but were re-elected and the following season were runners-up, one point behind champions Rotherham County. After City were disbanded by FA order in 1919, newly-formed Leeds United were invited to take over from City Reserves and were elected to the Midland League on 31 October. In 1920-21, United were elected to the Football League and their Reserves played in the Midland League for one more season before joining to the Central League.

Season	*P*	*W*	*D*	*L*	*F*	*A*	*Pts*	*Pos*
1905-06	34	10	8	16	60	81	28	12th
1906-07	38	16	10	12	67	64	42	8th
1907-08	38	14	9	15	61	72	37	11th
1908-09	38	12	4	22	56	90	28	18th
1909-10	42	18	6	18	60	75	42	10th
1910-11	38	13	9	16	66	68	35	12th
1911-12	36	18	6	12	57	49	42	5th
1912-13	38	18	7	13	68	52	43	5th
1913-14	34	8	4	22	45	75	20	18th
1914-15	38	24	5	9	99	42	53	2nd
1919-20	34	11	9	14	57	55	31	12th
1920-21	38	15	8	15	49	51	38	12th

Central League

UNITED entered the Central League for the first time in 1921-22 and put in some respectable performances throughout the 1920s, but their only championship came in 1936-37. The Reserves, led by the redoubtable George Milburn, went into their last game of the season against bottom-of-the-table Oldham at Elland Road on 28 April, needing one point to pip Preston for the title.

United's second string did it in style with goals from George Ainsley, Jack Hargreaves and John Thomson clinching an easy 3-0 win. To add to the club's joy, the United 'A' team won the Yorkshire League Cup on the same night. As a tribute to the Reserves' achievement, they represented United in the West Riding Cup Final the following week against Bradford City.

After the war, United Reserves had a dismal Central League record, finishing bottom five times in 13 years. Even during Revie's days, when United's second-teamers were reckoned to be the strongest in the land, they struggled to make an impact in the Central League. When it was split into two divisions in 1982-83, United were in the top flight but were relegated the following season before regaining their place 12 months later when three points for a win was introduced for the first time. Since 1990-91 the League has been sponsored by Pontins.

Season	*P*	*W*	*D*	*L*	*F*	*A*	*Pts*	*Pos*
1921-22	42	14	15	13	61	60	43	10th
1922-23	42	23	7	12	74	45	53	5th
1923-24	42	17	7	18	64	58	41	11th
1924-25	42	20	7	15	64	55	47	8th
1925-26	42	20	4	18	103	71	44	7th
1926-27	42	23	7	12	89	70	53	4th
1927-28	42	21	8	13	112	60	50	3rd
1928-29	42	14	14	14	89	77	42	9th
1929-30	42	23	7	12	108	60	53	5th
1930-31	42	23	5	14	118	78	51	5th
1931-32	42	20	8	14	92	69	48	8th
1932-33	42	19	9	14	77	63	47	8th
1933-34	42	20	6	16	72	63	46	10th
1934-35	42	19	12	11	77	71	50	4th
1935-36	42	18	7	17	91	82	43	12th
1936-37	42	29	4	9	95	52	62	1st
1937-38	42	15	12	15	58	59	42	9th
1938-39	42	13	10	19	71	84	36	16th
1945-46	40	12	11	17	59	80	35	15th
1946-47	42	12	8	22	71	118	32	19th
1947-48	42	12	6	22	48	86	32	22nd
1948-49	42	8	5	29	40	89	21	22nd
1949-50	42	11	7	24	43	84	29	20th
1950-51	42	12	13	17	43	56	37	17th
1951-52	42	16	12	14	65	58	44	6th
1952-53	42	12	15	15	55	59	39	15th
1953-54	42	10	3	29	48	106	23	22nd
1954-55	42	10	9	23	58	100	29	20th
1955-56	42	12	6	24	71	92	30	20th
1956-57	42	8	10	24	42	85	26	22nd
1957-58	42	14	4	24	70	95	32	21st
1958-59	42	12	10	20	64	82	34	17th
1959-60	42	6	9	27	49	113	21	22nd
1960-61	42	10	10	22	58	109	30	19th
1961-62	42	14	8	20	57	93	36	17th
1962-63	42	13	11	18	54	76	37	16th
1963-64	42	12	12	18	47	54	36	16th
1964-65	42	12	13	17	56	71	37	15th
1965-66	42	9	11	22	52	61	29	19th
1966-67	42	16	8	18	65	63	40	12th
1967-68	42	10	11	21	48	69	31	18th
1968-69	42	12	12	18	42	57	36	15th
1969-70	42	9	16	17	40	74	34	16th
1970-71	42	11	17	14	52	56	39	15th
1971-72	42	12	15	15	47	43	39	13th
1972-73	42	15	7	20	50	55	37	18th
1973-74	42	11	13	18	43	63	35	17th
1974-75	42	14	14	14	56	60	42	11th
1975-76	42	21	9	12	76	52	51	5th
1976-77	42	19	10	13	84	54	48	7th
1977-78	42	16	12	14	69	60	44	8th
1978-79	42	14	16	12	50	49	44	9th
1979-80	42	9	9	24	47	75	27	20th
1980-81	42	10	20	12	42	56	40	12th
1981-82	42	18	5	19	60	53	41	11th
			DIVISION ONE					
1982-83	30	6	11	13	30	49	23	11th
1983-84	30	7	7	16	37	51	28	14th
			DIVISION TWO					
1984-85	34	21	3	10	85	37	66	3rd
			DIVISION ONE					
1985-86	34	16	3	15	63	70	51	7th
1986-87	34	17	3	14	64	61	54	8th
1987-88	34	15	5	14	58	56	50	6th
1988-89	34	13	7	14	59	59	46	9th
1989-90	34	14	8	12	62	49	50	9th
1990-91	34	11	12	11	44	47	45	9th
1991-92	34	14	11	9	47	41	53	5th
1992-93	34	15	8	11	59	44	53	4th
1993-94	34	13	8	13	42	48	47	9th
1994-95	34	19	4	11	53	37	61	3rd
1995-96	34	17	8	9	40	32	59	4th

Yorkshire League

United entered an 'A' team in the Yorkshire League for the first time in 1929-30 and won the title the following year, although they lost the traditional championship match against York City Reserves 5-1.

United gained revenge over City on 2 May 1931 by winning the play-off in a subsidiary competition between the winners of Groups A and B, 5-4. For the next two seasons the League was divided into two competitions but no more honours came United's way until they beat Selby Town 2-1 in the Yorkshire League Cup Final at Goole on 28 April 1937, with goals from Jimmy Carr and Sammy Armes.

Two seasons later, United were in the Final, again at Goole, but this time went down 2-1 to Barnsley 'A', John Short scoring United's goal. There was consolation the following week when, as runners-up, United beat Sheffield Wednesday 'A' 1-0 in the championship match. United reached the Final in 1947 but were thrashed 4-0 by York and also had left-winger Arnold Knight sent-off. In 1949-50, the Yorkshire League was split into divisions with United going into Division One – a status they lost in 1953. After a few more 'yo-yo' seasons, United pulled out of the Yorkshire League until returning in 1961 for one last season in Division Three.

Season	*P*	*W*	*D*	*L*	*F*	*A*	*Pts*	*Pos*
1929-30	26	17	6	3	86	29	40	2nd
1930-31	22	19	1	2	103	29	39	1st
			First Competition					
1931-32	12	6	2	4	28	18	14	3rd
			Second Competition					
1931-32	12	4	4	4	33	20	12	4th
			First Competition					
1932-33	18	12	3	3	45	25	27	2nd
			Second Competition					
1932-33	12	6	2	4	32	25	14	3rd
			Back to one League					
1933-34	24	12	3	9	57	45	27	5th
1934-35	34	19	8	7	90	59	46	4th
1935-36	38	20	6	12	112	70	46	6th
1936-37	36	17	7	14	114	75	39	8th
1937-38	38	18	6	14	83	54	42	7th
1938-39	38	30	1	7	125	47	61	2nd
1946-47	38	15	4	19	83	99	34	15th
1947-48	38	12	8	18	78	93	32	16th
1948-49	38	17	5	16	85	93	39	9th
			Division One					
1949-50	34	11	7	16	62	67	29	14th
1950-51	34	12	2	20	68	104	26	14th
1951-52	34	14	6	14	77	77	34	8th
1952-53	34	12	5	17	65	80	29	15th
			Division Two					
1953-54	30	19	3	8	97	40	41	5th
1954-55	30	20	3	7	86	38	43	4th
			Division One					
1955-56	34	9	6	19	52	77	24	17th
			Division Two					
1956-57	32	16	5	11	86	49	37	7th
1957-58	26	8	5	13	42	60	21	10th
			Division Three					
1961-62	16	8	0	8	39	35	16	3rd
1961-62 Cup	16	9	2	5	51	36	20	3rd

Yorkshire League Cup Finals

28 Apr 1936-37	v Selby T	Goole	2-1	Carr, Armes
27 Apr 1938-39	vBarnsley A	Goole	1-2	Short
6 Jun 1946-47	v York City Res	York	0-4	

Northern Intermediate League

United were founder members of the Northern Intermediate League in 1949-50 when the juniors achieved the 'double'. For the first few years league games occupied the first part of the season with a Challenge Cup, also run on a league basis, operating in the latter part. The top four clubs in the Challenge Cup table qualified for the semi-finals with the winners meeting in the Final. As the league expanded in the mid-1950s, the Cup was run on a straight-forward knockout basis.

Season	*P*	*W*	*D*	*L*	*F*	*A*	*Pts*	*Pos*
1949-50								
1950-51								
The Northern Intermediate League have no records for the above seasons.								
Cup	10	2	1	7	16	24	5	10th
1951-52	20	10	6	4	60	35	26	3rd
Cup	10	5	1	4	26	18	11	4th
1952-53	20	9	3	8	43	41	21	4th
Cup	10	5	3	2	20	12	13	3rd
1953-54	20	11	5	4	44	30	27	1st
Cup	10	6	2	2	27	14	14	2nd
1954-55	24	18	3	3	66	25	39	1st
Cup	12	5	3	4	29	25	13	6th
1955-56	26	10	4	12	47	58	24	7th
Cup	13	4	4	5	24	19	12	9th
1956-57	28	14	6	8	59	51	34	5th
1957-58	28	7	4	17	48	61	18	12th
1958-59	28	12	5	11	53	46	29	8th
1959-60	30	12	6	12	56	49	30	9th
1960-61	30	12	2	16	54	67	26	10th
1961-62	32	18	5	9	66	31	41	5th
1962-63	24	12	3	9	44	38	27	6th
1963-64	32	16	4	12	68	47	36	7th
1964-65	32	21	2	9	68	45	44	4th
1965-66	32	25	3	4	92	25	53	1st
1966-67	28	10	9	9	52	41	29	7th
1967-68	32	5	10	17	28	51	20	13th
1968-69	34	14	11	9	70	48	39	7th
1969-70	34	26	4	4	89	19	56	2nd
1970-71	28	16	7	5	61	27	39	3rd
1971-72	30	11	8	11	44	41	30	9th
1972-73	30	19	3	8	65	25	41	4th
1973-74	32	15	7	10	54	39	37	6th
1974-75	32	19	8	5	69	30	46	3rd
1975-76	30	13	12	5	51	49	31	7th
1976-77	28	13	7	8	36	34	33	7th
1977-78	30	13	8	9	38	24	34	6th
1978-79	30	8	7	15	54	52	23	11th
1979-80	30	15	5	10	59	38	35	4th
1980-81	34	17	5	12	67	41	39	7th
1981-82	30	14	9	7	60	40	37	5th
1982-83	30	14	4	12	56	44	32	8th
1983-84	28	16	5	7	46	24	37	5th
1984-85	28	18	1	9	79	53	37	3rd
1985-86	34	12	8	14	77	56	32	10th
1986-87	34	21	5	8	68	38	68	3rd
1987-88	34	20	4	10	82	52	64	3rd
1988-89	34	20	7	7	85	40	67	3rd
1989-90	34	13	10	11	68	64	49	8th
1990-91	34	21	6	7	63	25	69	2nd
1991-92	34	19	8	7	75	39	65	2nd
1992-93	32	18	7	7	85	41	61	3rd
1993-94	30	16	4	10	50	43	52	3rd
1994-95	32	19	8	5	84	47	65	3rd
1995-96	30	21	4	5	100	34	62	2nd

United's Successes in the Northern Intermediate League Cup

Some fairly well-known names have played their part in bringing the Northern Intermediate Cup to Elland Road. United's successes in the Final have been:

6 May 1950	v Rotherham U	(h) 2-1	Webb 2 (1 pen)
3 May 1952	v Rotherham U	(h) 4-1	Webb 2, Smith, Vickers
13 Apr 1959	v Newcastle U 1st leg	(h) 4-1	Harvey 2, Hawksby, Howieson
20 Apr 1959	v Newcastle U 2nd leg	(a) 3-3 (agg 7-4)	Bremner, McCall, Howieson
27 Apr 1965	v Sheffield W 1st leg	(a) 2-2	Hawkins 2
29 Apr 1965	v Sheffield W 2nd leg	(h) 1-0 (agg 3-2)	Hibbitt
2 May 1966	v Sheffield U 1st leg	(a) 1-0	Bates
12 May 1966	v Sheffield U 2nd leg	(h) 3-1 (agg 4-1)	Hawkins 2, Sibbald (pen)
24 Apr 1975	v Sunderland 1st leg	(a) 0-0	
6 May 1975	v Sunderland 2nd leg	(h) 3-0 (agg 3-0)	McNiven 3
15 May 1984	v Newcastle U 1st leg	(h) 4-0	Sellars, Opp own-goal, Wright 2
18 May 1984	v Newcastle U 2nd leg	(a) 2-1 (agg 6-1)	Scales, Simmonds
10 May 1996	v Newcastle U	(n*)2-0	Elliott (og), Matthews

* The 1996 Final was played at Bootham Crescent, York, as a two-legged Final between Leeds and Newcastle was not possible because work was being done at Elland Road and St James' Park to prepare for the European Championships.

The Death of David 'Soldier' Wilson

A DARK shadow was cast over Elland Road in October 1906 when centre-forward David 'Soldier' Wilson died at the home game against Burnley. It was a tragic passing which left City staff and supporters numb with disbelief.

After about an hour of a hard, physical battle against the men from Turf Moor, 23-year-old Wilson left the field complaining of chest pains.

As play continued, Wilson was examined by Dr Taylor, of New Wortley, who strongly advised the player not to return to the fray. But as news filtered through that two Leeds men, Harry Singleton and John Lavery, were hobbling with injuries, Wilson demanded to go back on the field.

Despite objections from club officials, he trotted slowly on to the pitch but it was immediately clear that he would not finish the game and before the end he came off again. As Wilson made his way down the tunnel to the dressing room, he collapsed and was carried to the treatment room where efforts were made to revive him. It was a vain battle and the gallant Leeds man lost his brief fight for life.

Wilson, who lived in Catherine Grove, Beeston, had promised to provide goals. Leeds had bought him from Hull City in December 1905 for £120 and he was an immediate success, finishing top scorer in his first City campaign.

Wilson was born in Hebburn on 23 July 1883, of Scottish parents, and began his career with Dundee and Heart was after military service in the Boer War – hence his nickname of 'Soldier'. He joined Hull for £100 in May 1905 but it was not long before he was on the Leeds payroll, netting 13 goals in 15 games. Fate, however, ruled that his talent would never reach fruition.

The proceeds of an Elland Road friendly, against Hull City on 19 November, were donated to Wilson's widow. The 3-3 draw was watched by 3,000 spectators.

In a curious footnote to the sad affair, the Football League rapped City's knuckles. According to a League minute of 5 November 1906, 'The secretary was instructed to write to the Leeds City chairman and point out that the word "transferred" opposite D.Wilson's name in the result sheet, for the match in which Wilson played and was injured, and his death took place before the close of the game, was uncalled for and entirely out of place, as this was a national calamity.'

Willis Walker Remembers...

THAT sombre October afternoon in 1919 when the Leeds City team was sold off to the highest bidder was recalled by Willis Walker shortly before he died in 1991, in his 100th year.

He was City's first-choice goalkeeper in those days and was the only surviving player from that historic occasion.

"It was a sad day because we had a fairly good side. There was Billy McLeod – a great finisher – George Law, Jimmy Speirs, George Affleck, John Jackson, Arthur Price, Tommy Lamph and others. It was a great shame for the city of Leeds," he said.

The City players had little idea of what fate lay in store for them as the drama unfolded behind the scenes.

"We were told everything would be alright," recalled Mr Walker who lived in Bingley.

But as the situation became more serious, the news was broken to the players that City would have to be disbanded.

Mr Walker was lodging with a policeman in Beeston and he made his way down to the city centre and prepared for the auction.

"We went to the Metropole. It was during the day, I think the bids were put into sealed envelopes and we were sold to the highest bidder."

South Shields were the club who secured the services of Willis Walker and he continued to live in the Leeds area and travelled to home games by train – a long and tortuous journey via Newcastle. He would have to catch the 7.25am train to the North-East and often would not return home until midnight on match days.

"After Leeds United were formed I trained with them. Leeds were very good to me and I was happy there. United had the same trainer as City – Dick Murrell."

Mr Walker also had a soft spot for Herbert Chapman, the Leeds City manager who later achieved soccer immortality with Huddersfield and Arsenal. "He was a lovely man and a great manager for the players."

Willis Walker, who was a native of Gosforth, joined Leeds from Doncaster Rovers and at 5ft 10in tall, he proved a safe, athletic goalkeeper with a growing reputation.

"I got a regular place before the war and got back into the Leeds side when I came out of the Royal Navy."

In the summer, Willis Walker donned a pair of whites and started as a cricketer with Nottinghamshire, for whom he scored 1,000 runs in a season ten times, and later played in the Bradford League, with Keighley.

The Leeds City Story

SOCCER was a late starter in the city of Leeds, where the game of rugby was the dominant force in the late 19th century and early efforts to form a soccer base met with little success.

On Boxing Day 1877, administrators of the dribbling code from Sheffield, where soccer was extremely popular, took two teams, umpires and goal-posts to Holbeck Recreation Ground in an attempt to convert the people of Leeds to their game. The experiment although apparently well-received, had no lasting impact.

During the 1880s, a Leeds Association Football Club was formed and played for several seasons, including matches against Blackburn Rovers and Preston North End, but the club failed to loosen the tight grip which rugby had on the city's sporting public.

Although soccer was beginning to flourish in many parts of the country, Leeds in particular, and the West Yorkshire area in general, did not really take to the game on an organised basis until 1894. On 22 February that year, another club called Leeds AFC was formed at a meeting at the Cardigan Arms. Four days later, the West Yorkshire League was founded.

Leeds enjoyed a successful first season, winning the new league by eight points. They played at a ground in Harehills Lane, Roundhay, before moving to Headingley, next door to the famous cricket arena, where they shared the ground with Leeds Rugby Club.

A further move took Leeds AFC to the Meanwood Ground but they soon returned to Headingley – and were quickly in trouble. Directors of the Leeds Cricket, Football and Athletic Club, which owned the Headingley ground, decided to abandon soccer unless Leeds AFC bowed to an ultimatum.

The soccer club, now members of the Yorkshire League, had struggled to attract large attendances and were told to come up with a scheme which would enable them to meet their expenses from gate receipts. At the club's annual meeting on 22 June 1898, only three people turned up to discuss the problem and the soccer section effectively collapsed.

Rugby's popularity, especially the Northern Union – forerunner of today's Rugby League – looked unshakable in Leeds, yet across the other side of the city, one club more than any other was seen as soccer's standard bearer there – Hunslet FC.

Hunslet had been formed in October 1889, by men working in the city's steelworks. Nicknamed 'The Twinklers', Hunslet indeed shone brightly, winning the West Yorkshire Cup four times and reaching the FA Amateur Cup quarter-finals twice, including a famous victory over the all-powerful Old Etonians.

With the West Yorkshire League maintaining its progress, more local teams sprang up and Hunslet, although regarded as the city's premier club, had difficulty in finding a ground of their own.

In 1895, they left the Wellington Ground in Low Road to move to the Laburnum Ground, off Dewsbury Road, before switching to Parkside where they shared facilities with Hunslet Rugby Club. Hunslet FC were always under pressure to move again and eventually they went under, shortly after the turn of the century, to deliver another blow to the local soccer fraternity.

Undaunted, the Hunslet committee and supporters decided that the city of Leeds could support a League club and out of that conviction came the birth of Leeds City FC, who entered the West Yorkshire League for the 1904-05 season. Even then, the new club, like their predecessors, had no permanent playing base.

Experimental teams were fielded, the public response was generally good, and the problem of a new home was solved when Holbeck Rugby Club disbanded after losing a promotion play-off against St Helens which would have put them in the First Division of the Northern Union.

Holbeck had used a ground at Elland Road and in October 1904, Leeds City FC became its new tenants.

Leeds was the biggest city in England without a premier soccer club but the new City officials were confident that they would gain admission to the Football League, bearing in mind that League officials were anxious to extend their sphere of influence.

In April 1905, the first Leeds City limited company was floated with capital of 10,000 £1 shares. Three men held the majority of those shares: Local clothier Mr Norris Hepworth who became the club's first chairman; Mr Ralph Younger, landlord of the Old Peacock Hotel close to the Elland Road ground; and Mr A.W.Pullin, better known as 'Old Ebor', a *Yorkshire Evening Post* sports journalist. On 5 June, the club was officially formed into a limited liability company.

Gilbert Gillies, then manager of Chesterfield, was tempted to Elland Road as secretary-manager of Leeds City and when the Football League extended its Second Division to 20 clubs, the Leeds outfit polled most votes – 5 – to gain election along with Chelsea, Hull City, Clapton Orient and Stockport County. City kicked-off with a 1-0 defeat at Bradford City, whilst the reserves entertained Nottingham Forest Reserves in a Midland League fixture at Elland Road. City made a highly satisfactory entrance to League soccer, finishing sixth in Division Two without ever finding real consistency.

More significant was the effect the new League club was having on the attendances at Headingley where Leeds RL's average gate nosedived from 9,022 to 5,632 in Leeds City's first season. At last rugby's monopoly was broken as soccer attracted new supporters.

City slumped to tenth place in 1906-07, largely due to poor away form, although the season did mark the emergence of the club's most notable player, centre-forward Billy McLeod who signed from Lincoln City in November 1906. Despite McLeod's goals and the sign-

Leeds City in 1908-09. Back row (left to right): Mr W.Preston (director), Mr W.Robinson (director), Mr F.Scott Walford (secretary), R.Shotton, W.Child, H.Williams, H.Rickard, D.Murray, L.Burnett, C.Simpson, Mr A.Eagle (director). Middle row: T.Thrupp (director), J.White, M.Guy, W.McDonald, Gemmell, McKeown, H.Bromage, T.Naisby, J.Kennedy. Front row: D.Dougal, T.Rodger, J.Watson, A.Bowman, McAllister, J.Hamilton, R.Joynes, S.Cubberley, W.McLeod.

ing of several Irish stars, City made little impact in either Division Two or the FA Cup, although they still attracted good attendances.

By 1910, a club called Leeds United – no relation to today's club – had been formed and was based in Kirkstall. The club played in the Yorkshire Combination League but soon folded.

Running a Football League club meant severe financial strain on the Leeds City board and in September 1910 shareholders were asked to take up debentures worth £4,000 which, together with £8,000 guaranteed by some directors, would secure the club's liabilities and provide much-needed working capital. The shareholders formed a committee to liaise with the directors on financial matters.

During this time, Frank Scott-Walford had taken over as secretary-manager from Gillies. In 1912, Scott-Walford quit due to failing health and the pressures of trying to cope with the club's increasing cash problems. His resignation came after City were forced to apply for re-election following a terrible season.

Leeds City reached another low ebb when the bank announced that it was going to call in the club's £7,000 overdraft, a move which would effectively put City out of business. Hepworth poured in more cash and appointed Mr Tom Coombes as Receiver. Coombes was to run City's affairs for the next three years as the club lurched from one financial crisis to another.

The extent of Hepworth's generosity was revealed at a public meeting at the Grand Central Hotel in April 1912. The club's major benefactor had spent the then huge sum of £15,000 on trying to keep City afloat.

An extraordinary general meeting at the Salem Hall, called to try to sort out the whole miserable mess, revealed that total liabilities were £15,782, total losses since the club's formation were £11,321 and assets stood at £7,084. The meeting agreed that the company should be wound up and that Coombes should run the club.

At one stage, Leeds Cricket, Football and Athletic Club offered to take over Leeds City FC and use Headingley to stage soccer – quite ironic considering the demise of Leeds AFC – but the proposal came to nought. By this time, Headingley had already staged two FA Amateur Cup Finals.

Into this monetary minefield stepped City's new manager, Herbert Chapman, who had achieved much at his previous club, Northampton Town. Chapman campaigned vigorously to keep City in the League and on 4 June, they were re-elected with 33 votes. Lincoln City (27 votes) replaced Gainsborough Trinity, who managed only nine votes.

The 1912-13 season began with renewed optimism and Chapman's team made a useful start, but in October the club found themselves in hot water with the Football League. During his team-building that

Leeds City in 1909-10, when they finished twelfth in Division Two. Back row, (left to right): Chapman (trainer), Affleck, Hogg, Bromage, Naisby, Morris, Dougal, McGowan, Thrupp (assistant trainer). Middle row: Beren, McAllister, White, Mr F. Scott-Walford (manager), Watson, Gemmell, Croot. Front row: Hamilton, Burnett, Halligan, Roberts, Mulholland, Bridgett.

summer, Chapman had signed three newcomers – Billy Scott, George Law and Evelyn Lintott – agreeing to pay each of them the full year's wage of £208 to the end of the following April. But two months had already elapsed since the end of their previous contracts. In effect, the players were getting more than the permitted wage of £4 per week.

Aston Villa had fallen foul of the League for the same offence and when their case came to light, City realised they had unwittingly breached the rules and reported themselves.

The League were swift to act and City were fined £125 plus expenses and the players were ordered to return the excess payments.

Despite this brush with authority, Chapman proved an inspirational manager and City finished sixth in his first season, with McLeod netting 27 League goals out of a club record of 70 for the season. To cap a fine season, City reported a £400 profit.

The following season, Leeds City came within two points of promotion, thanks to quite brilliant form at Elland Road where they set up a club League record by thrashing Nottingham Forest 8-0. Large crowds rolled up to see Ivan Sharpe's wing-craft creating goals for the mercurial McLeod, whilst goalkeeper Tony Hogg proved an exciting discovery. Two goals in the final two minutes of the FA Cup match against powerful West Brom cost City a deserved replay.

The club looked in good shape and in August 1914, a syndicate of Leeds sportsmen, headed by Mr Joseph Connor, president of the West Riding FA, announced that they had offered to run the club. Their offer of £1,000 down and an annual rent of £250 for Elland Road was accepted by Coombes.

City were confident of promotion in 1914-15, but their optimism was not justified as they slipped to 15th place in the final season before the League closed down for the war.

When the League programme proper resumed in 1919, Chapman's men made a useful start to the season, with ten points from eight games, before Leeds City Football Club was suspended and eventually expelled after an astonishing scandal involving alleged illegal payments during the war.

Leeds City's First Season: 1904-05

LEEDS City spent the 1904-05 season in the West Yorkshire League before gaining Football League status.

Their first competitive game was at Scatcherd Lane, Morley, on 1 September when the newly-formed City team struggled to a 2-2 draw.

City's early home games were played at Hunslet, on the Wellington Ground in Low Road, before the club clinched the move to Elland Road in mid-October.

West Yorkshire League fixtures were treated with little respect after City decided to arrange a series of friendly games against Football League opponents midway through the season. Several West Yorkshire League game were called off as City entertained top sides like Sheffield United, Preston North End and Derby County. Sometimes the friendlies and the League fixtures were played on the same day with a weaker City 'reserve' team fulfilling the League games.

Because Elland Road was used to host many of the friendlies, City often waived ground advantage in the League and ended up playing more games away than at home.

Inevitably a backlog of League fixtures developed and in a frantic effort to catch up, City sometimes played two League games a day, but at the end of the season they had still failed to complete their 26-match programme. In fact, only five of the 14 competing clubs managed to finish all their fixtures, including Bradford City Reserves, who nevertheless finished champions with 43 points.

Many players were invited to Elland Road to play for City, but very few were kept on for the following campaign. Some famous names appeared for City in the bigger friendly games, including Tom Morren (Sheffield United) and Fred Spiksley (Sheffield Wednesday), both England internationals, but neither were retained.

West Yorkshire League 1904-05

1904

1 Sep	(a)	Morley	2-2
3 Sep	(h*)	Altofts	1-2
10 Sep	(a)	Elland Ramdonians	1-2
24 Sep	(a)	Huddersfield	3-1
8 Oct	(a)	Mirfield	2-1
22 Oct	(a)	Starbeck	1-1
5 Nov	(a)	Rothwell White Rose	1-4
19 Nov	(h)	Heckmondwike	0-3
26 Nov	(a)	Beeston Hill Parish Church	0-3
3 Dec	(h)	Oulton	2-2
10 Dec	(h)	Bradford C Res	1-5
17 Dec	(h)	Rothwell White Rose	1-0
24 Dec	(a)	Morley	0-4
31 Dec	(a)	Altofts	2-4
1905			
28 Jan	(a)	Dewsbury & Savile	0-0
11 Mar	(a)	Elland Ramdonians	0-4
18 Mar	(a)	Beeston Hill Parish Church	5-1
18 Mar	(h)	Heckmondwike	1-3
12 Apr	(h)	Upper Armley Christ Church	2-2
22 Apr	(a)	Bradford C Res	1-1
24 Apr	(h)	Mirfield	1-0
25 Apr	(h)	Huddersfield	1-0
25 Apr	(a)	Upper Armley Christ Church	4-1

**at Wellington Ground, Low Road, Hunslet.*

Record

P	W	D	L	F	A	Pts
24	7	7	10	33	47	21

The fixtures against Dewsbury (h) and Oulton (a) were not played. The Dewsbury game was cancelled because of an outbreak of smallpox in the Dewsbury area.

City played only 23 of their 26 West Yorkshire League fixtures but it is believed that their match against Starbeck in the Leeds Hospital Cup second round on 14 January doubled as a League fixture – something which was not uncommon at the turn of the century – in an effort to clear the fixture backlog. The City-Starbeck result was 1-1 after 90 minutes.

FA Cup

Qual rd	17 Sep	(a)	Rockingham Coll	1-3

West Yorkshire Cup

1st rd	7 Jan	(a)	Bradford C Res	2-3

Leeds Hospital Cup

1st rd	12 Nov	(h)	Altofts	3-1
2nd rd	14 Jan	(h)	Starbeck (a.e.t.)	2-1
3rd rd	11 Feb	(a)	Upper Armley C Church	1-2

Friendlies

5 Sep	(h*)	Bradford C	0-3
1 Oct	(a)	Morley	1-1
15 Oct	(h)	Hull C	0-2
29 Oct	(h)	Harrogate Cor	5-1
26 Nov	(h)	Burton U	7-2
10 Dec	(a)	Grimsby T	0-8
24 Dec	(a)	Hull C	2-3
21 Jan	(h)	Darlington	3-1
4 Feb	(h)	West Bromwich A	0-5
18 Feb	(h)	Sheffield U	2-2
25 Feb	(h)	Leicester F	1-5
4 Mar	(h)	Hull C	2-5
11 Mar	(h)	Lincoln C	1-3
25 Mar	(h)	Derby C	1-2
1 Apr	(h)	Preston NE	1-4
29 Apr	(h)	Barnsley	4-3

**at Wellington Ground, Low Road, Hunslet.*

The Leeds City Scandal

WORLD War One was finally over and Leeds City were preparing to restart League action when the club was rocked by sensational allegations concerning illegal payments to wartime guest players.

The charges were brought by a former City full-back, Charlie Copeland, after he fell out with the club over a pay rise.

The practice of paying wartime guests other than normal expenses was widespread, but once Copeland raised the issue with the soccer authorities in July 1919, neither the Football Association nor the Football League could turn a blind eye to it.

Yet Copeland was just one character in the intricate story of City's decline, and ultimate collapse, which was played out behind closed doors in a string of private meetings.

Copeland's allegations and all the backroom bickering were not made public until City were punished by the soccer overlords. Only then, thanks to a series of revealing interviews and letters in the *Yorkshire Evening Post* were the shocked Leeds public informed of what had been going on behind the scenes.

Frank and startling details of secret showdowns worthy of any blockbusting soap opera were released on the unsuspecting public in cold, hard print.

City's problems essentially began when secretary-manager Herbert Chapman went to the Barnbow munitions factory in East Leeds in a managerial capacity to help the war effort. He recommended his assistant at Elland Road, George Cripps, a schoolteacher, to take charge of City's secretarial work, leaving chairman Joseph Connor and director Mr J.C. Whiteman in charge of team selection.

It soon became apparent that there was a personality clash, as Connor did not feel Cripps was up to the job and accused him of incompetence. Matters came to a head when Connor, who was also president of the West Riding Football Association, threatened to resign unless something was done because, he claimed, the club's books were in a mess. So in 1917, City brought in an accountant's clerk to take care of the bookkeeping, while Cripps, whose own health was breaking down, was placed in charge of the team and correspondence.

The friction continued during the 1917-18 season and things reached such a critical stage, because of both the war and lack of money, that the directors seriously thought about closing the club down rather than risk the dwindling amount of cash they had left. Only the intervention of Football League chairman Mr John McKenna, who persuaded the Leeds board to press on, prevented City from grinding to a halt.

The atmosphere at Elland Road remained sour as Cripps proved as unpopular with the players as he did with some members of the board. Before one wartime trip to Nottingham, for a Midland Section game, City skipper John Hampson sent a letter to the directors stating that if Cripps travelled with the team then they would go on strike. Connor stepped in to persuade Hampson that striking would be suicidal for the club and the players abandoned the idea.

When Chapman returned to Elland Road in 1918, it seemed as though ailing City's troubles would finally end. But it was only the start of their problems.

Cripps was pushed aside to his old role of assistant. Disenchanted, he was quick to respond, claiming he would sue for wrongful dismissal and promptly contacted his solicitor, Mr James Bromley, a former City director.

According to Connor, Cripps made a claim for £400 and told his solicitor that the board had paid improper expenses to players during the war.

Bromley was quickly in touch with the board and in January 1919, a deal was thrashed out between Cripps and the board. The terms of the settlement included a clause that Cripps should hand over all documents relating to the club, including his private cheque book, pass book and letters to and from various players, to Connor and Whiteman in the city-centre office of the club solicitor, Alderman William Clarke, in South Parade.

Alderman Clarke, who became Sir William in 1927, sealed the papers and evidence – incriminating or otherwise – in a strongbox so they could be kept secure under lock and key.

Connor said that Cripps gave a written undertaking not to disclose any of the club's affairs and that Bromley gave his word of honour that he would not reveal his knowledge of the documents. The price of Cripps' silence was £55 – well short of the £400 he had originally sought.

Bromley's version, however, did not match the story given to the local newspapers by Connor.

According to Bromley, he handed over a parcel of documents given to him by Cripps to be held in trust by Alderman Clarke and not to be parted with without the consent of Connor and himself.

One of the conditions of the handing over of the parcel was that the City directors make a £50 donation to Leeds Infirmary. Bromley said that he later asked for a receipt for the donation but was told by Alderman Clarke that Connor declined to discuss the affairs of Leeds City with him.

At that point it seemed stalemate had been reached, but it was not long before City's dirty laundry was being hung out to dry.

As City began to assemble their playing staff ready for the 1919-20 season, the first post-war League campaign, the renewal of Charlie Copeland's contract was considered. Before the war, Copeland received £3 a week with a £1 weekly increase when he played in the first team. The board had now offered Copeland £3 1s (£3.50) for playing in the reserves, and considerably more if he played for the first team, or they would release him on a free transfer.

Disgruntled Copeland demanded £6 a week and rocked the club by stating that if he did not get the cash, then he would report City to the Football Association and the Football League for making illegal payments to players during the war. City's directors felt they were being blackmailed. At the risk of forcing Copeland's hand they ignored his demands and gave him a free transfer to Coventry.

Copeland, who had got hold of certain documents or at least knew of their contents, carried out his threat in July 1919 and told the authorities of the alleged irregularities.

He later denied passing on the information, but the City directors suspected that Bromley, who happened to be Copeland's solicitor, could have supplied the critical information which now exploded around their ears.

In Copeland's defence, Bromley said that the player served Leeds City throughout the war on the promise that his wages would be increased when regulations allowed. In 1918, the Football League allowed a 50 per cent increase in wages and accordingly, Copeland asked for his increase, but was only offered £3 10s for 39 weeks and no summer wages so, in effect, his wages were going down.

Copeland said that a request to meet the board and discuss the issue was refused, so he placed the matter in the hands of his solicitor, Bromley.

Armed with the information about the allegations, the Football Association and the Football League set up a joint inquiry which was to trigger off City's downfall.

The commission was chaired by FA Chairman J.C.Clegg, and City were summoned to Manchester on 26 September 1919, to answer the charges. City were represented by Alderman Clarke, who was asked to present the club books before the inquiry.

The commission, which included a dozen members of the Football Association and the Football League, as well as members of the international selection committee, were stunned when City replied that it was not in their power to do so. Immediately, the inquiry ordered City to produce the documents by 6 October or face the consequences.

Despite all the wranglings, City had made a solid start to their new campaign and not even the players could have guessed what was in store as they set off to play Wolverhampton two days before the deadline. Because of a rail strike the team went to Molineux by charabanc and won 4-2, with ace marksman Billy McLeod netting a hat-trick. On the way home, the City coach gave several stranded people a lift back to the North and among them was none other than Charlie Copeland.

The trip to Wolves was to be City's last game. The inquiry's deadline arrived, but still there was no sign of the City documents, so the following Saturday's fixture against South Shields was suspended and after a meeting of the inquiry team at the Russell Hotel in London, City were expelled from the Football League and disbanded.

League chairman John McKenna announced: "The authorities of the game intend to keep it absolutely clean. We will have no nonsense. The football stable must be cleansed and further breakages of the law regarding payments will be dealt with in such a severe manner that I now give warning that clubs and players must not expect the slightest leniency."

An FA order formally closed the club, leaving City supporters numb with disbelief, the unfortunate players out of a job and City officials to face further punishment.

Although there had been no concrete evidence of the alleged illegal payments, City's silence – whether to protect themselves or a misguided move to shield players – was akin to putting a noose around their necks.

Not even the personal intervention of the Lord Mayor of Leeds, Alderman Joseph Henry, who offered to take over the club from the directors, could persuade the inquiry to reconsider and League football came to a halt in Leeds after just eight games of the 1919-20 season.

Five City officials were banned for life – Connor, Whiteman, fellow directors Mr S.Glover and Mr G.Sykes, and, rather surprisingly, manager-secretary Herbert Chapman. The board promptly resigned, but Chapman earned a reprieve after evidence was later given that he was working at the munitions factory when the illegal payments were supposed to have been made.

Connor complained that City were not given a fair hearing by the inquiry and Alderman Henry also believed that Burslem Port Vale – the club who had replaced City in the Football League – had brought undue pressure to bear on the inquiry team, in an effort to get City thrown out, so they could take their place.

Port Vale inherited City's playing record of Played 8, Won 4, Drawn 2, Lost 2, Goals For 17, Goals Against 10, Points 10. They completed City's remaining fixtures and finished in 13th place.

Bob Hewison, a guest player with City during the war, was asked by the inquiry to act as secretary during the winding up of the club, a job he tackled while recovering from a broken leg sustained in 1918-19. Also helping to sort out the tattered remnants of the club were Alderman Henry and Leeds accountant W.H.Platts.

Hewison later became Bristol City manager, and became embroiled in another illegal payments scandal. On 15 October 1938, another joint Football Association and Football League inquiry into payments made to amateur players fined Bristol City 100 guineas and suspended Hewison until the end of the season.

Biggest victims of the Leeds closure were the players. The Football League promised to pay their wages until they could get fixed up with new clubs and the best way to find them new employers was considered to be by auction.

Arrangements were made for a unique auction of footballing flesh at the Metropole Hotel in Leeds on 17 October when representatives from 30 League clubs turned up to haggle over prices they should pay for their acquisitions.

It was a humiliating experience for the players as they were sold off along with the club's nets, goal-posts, boots, kit and physiotherapy equipment. The entire squad fetched less than £10,150, with fees fixed at between £1,250 and £100 after would-be purchasers complained that the original prices were set too high. The League, who organised the sale, said that no player should be made to join any club he did not want to but, with the players anxious to get back into the action as quickly as possible, the clubs clearly held the whip hand.

The following players went under the auctioneer's hammer: Billy McLeod (£1,250 to Notts County); George Affleck (£500 to Grimsby Town); William Ashurst (£500 to Lincoln City); Billy Kirton (£500 to Aston Villa); George Stephenson (£250 to Aston Villa); John Hampson (£1,000 to Aston Villa); Simpson Bainbridge (£1,000 to Preston North End); Arthur Wainwright (£200 to Grimsby Town); Herbert Lounds (£250 to Rotherham County); Harold Millership (£1,000 to Rotherham County); Frederick Linfoot (£250 to Lincoln City); Francis Chipperfield (£100 to Sheffield Wednesday); Willis Walker (£800 to South Shields); William Hopkins (£600 to South Shields); Arthur Price (£750 to Sheffield Wednesday); John Edmondson (£800 to Sheffield Wednesday); Ernest Goodwin (£250 to Manchester City); Thomas Lamph (to Manchester City); William Pease (to Northampton Town); Walter Cook (to Castleford); Robert Wilkes (to South Shields); William Crowther (to Lincoln City).

For Kirton, recently converted from full-back to the front line, it proved a memorable move as he finished the season by scoring Aston Villa's FA Cup Final winner against Huddersfield Town. Kirton, Ashurst, Pease and Stephenson all went on to play for England and Millership was capped by Wales.

Looking back on the entire shabby episode some years later, John McKenna revealed he had some sympathy with the plight in which Leeds City found themselves trapped.

"Perhaps others have escaped being found guilty of malpractices but if they are found out now we shall not stand on ceremony or sentiment," he said.

Although the last rites had been uttered over the corpse of Leeds City, moves were already being made to breathe new life into a new club with a new name – Leeds United.

United attracted a bad name because of its hooligan element in the 1980s, but trouble at Elland Road was nothing new. On 21 April 1906, referee Mr T.P.Campbell (Blackburn) was booed by City fans during the game against Manchester United at Elland Road because he made several controversial decisions. For some City supporters it was too much and, as Mr Campbell walked off at the end of the game, he was hit on the nose by a lump of concrete and a sod of earth. Ironically, the same referee was assaulted earlier in the same season, at Bradford City when Manchester United were also the visitors.

* * * * * * *

Brian Woodward has served Leeds United both as player and director. The son of the late United chairman Percy Woodward, young Brian joined United as a right winger when he left Cockburn High School, but never made the first team. He was transferred to Hereford in February 1950 before moving to York City and later becoming a director at Elland Road, until resigning over the decision to sack manager Eddie Gray.

* * * * * * *

Little Christmas spirit was in evidence when Leeds City and Fulham met over the festive period in 1913. On Christmas Day, City could not immediately pay Fulham their full share of the takings so the Londoners took swift retribution by withholding money from the return game at Craven Cottage on Boxing Day. At an FA inquiry the following February, City said that there had been a tram strike on Christmas Day so many supporters arrived late and there were no police to stop them rushing into the ground, so the club had to take admission money on account. The inquiry ordered Fulham to pay the £20 4s 5d owed to City from the Boxing Day gate, plus three guineas expenses. City got away with a verbal warning for not taking money on the gate.

1904-05

FA Cup

Rd	Date	Venue/Opponent	Result	Scorers	Att	Mallinson	Sheldon	Dixon	Morris R	Morris J	Tennant	Heffron	Page	Musgrave	Cummings	Simpson
P1	Sep 17	(a) Rockingham ColL	1-3	Musgrave	1,000	1	1	1	1	1	1	1	1	1	1	1
					Appearances	1	1	1	1	1	1	1	1	1	1	1
					Goals									1	1	

(NB: The R.Morris who appeared in this match is not R 'Dickie' Morris who played in 1905-06. J.Morris is the same player though.)

1905-06

Manager: Gilbert Gillies

No	Date	Venue/Opponent	Result	Scorers	Att	Bromage	McDonald	Ray	Morgan	Stringfellow	Henderson	Parnell	Watson	Hargraves	Morris R	Singleton	Drain	Walker	Murray	Howard	Wilson D	Morris J	Lavery	Swift	George	Whitley	Freeborough	Clay
1	Sep 2	(a) Bradford C	L 0-1		15,000	1	2	3	4	5	6	7	8	9	10	11												
2	9	(h) West Brom A	L 0-2		6,802	1	2	3	4	5	6	7	8		10	11	9											
3	11	(h) Lincoln C	D 2-2	Drain 2	3,000	1	2	3	4	5	6	7	8		10	11	9											
4	16	(a) Leicester F	W 1-0	Singleton	5,000	1	2	3	4	5	6	7	8	9	10	11												
5	23	(h) Hull C	W 3-1	R.Morris 2, Hargraves	13,654	1	2	3	4	5	6	7	8	9	10	11												
6	30	(a) Lincoln C	W 2-1	Parnell (pen), Hargraves	3,000	1	2	3	4		6	7	8	9	10	11		5										
7	Oct 14	(a) Port Vale	L 0-2		1,500	1	2	3	4		6	7	8	9	10	11		5										
8	21	(h) Barnsley	W 3-2	R.Morris, Hargraves, Stacey (og)	12,000	1	2	3	4	6		7	8	9	10	11		5										
9	Nov 11	(h) Grimsby T	W 3-0	Hargraves 2, Stringfellow	7,000	1	2	3	4	5	6	7	8	9	10	11												
10	13	(a) Burton U	D 1-1	Parnell	1,500	1	2	3	4	5	6	7	8	9	10	11												
11	25	(h) Chelsea	D 0-0		20,000	1	2	3	4	5	6	7	8	9	10	11												
12	Dec 2	(a) Gainsboro' T	L 1-4	Watson	2,000	1	2	3	4	5	6	7	8	9	10	11												
13	9	(h) Bristol C	D 1-1	Morgan	15,000	1		3	4	5	6	7	8	9	10	11			2									
14	23	(h) Glossop	W 1-0	Hargraves	9,000	1		3	4		6		7	9		11		5	2	8	10							
15	26	(a) Stockport C	L 1-2	Singleton	5,000	1	2		5		6	7	4	9	10	11			3		8							
16	30	(h) Bradford C	L 0-2		22,000	1		2	4	5	6	7	8	9	10	11			3									
17	Jan 1	(a) Blackpool	W 3-0	R.Morris, Wilson, Singleton	3,000	1	2		4		6	7			10	11	8		3		9	5						
18	6	(a) West Brom A	L 1-2	Wilson	2,553	1		2	4		6	7	8		10	11			3		9	5						
19	15	(h) Manchester U	W 3-0	Watson, Wilson, Singleton	6,000	1		3	4		6	7	8		10	11			2		9	5						
20	20	(h) Leicester F	W 4-1	Murray (pen), Drain, Watson, Hargraves	8,000	1		2	4		6	7	8	9		11	10		3			5						
21	27	(a) Hull C	D 0-0		10,000	1		2	4		6	7	8	10		11			3		9	5						
22	Feb 3	(h) Burnley	D 1-1	Watson	7,129	1		2	4		6	7	8		10	11			3		9	5						
23	10	(a) Chesterfield	W 2-0	R.Morris, Singleton	4,000	1	3	2	4		6	7	8		10	11					9	5						
24	17	(h) Port Vale	W 3-1	Wilson, Hargraves, Parnell	9,000	1	3	2	4		6	7		8	10	11					9	5						
25	24	(a) Barnsley	L 0-3		5,000	1	3	2	4		6	7	8	10		11					9	5						
26	27	(h) Chesterfield	W 3-0	Wilson 2, Murray (pen)	2,000	1	2		4		6	7	8	10		11		5	3		9							
27	Mar 3	(h) Clapton O	W 6-1	Wilson 4, Hargraves, Parnell	8,000	1	2		4		6	7	8	10		11		5	3		9							
28	10	(a) Burnley	L 3-4	Wilson 2, Singleton	5,000	1	2		4		6	7	8	10		11		5	3		9							
29	17	(h) Grimsby T	D 1-1	Murray	3,000	1		3	4		6	7		8	10	11		5	2		9							
30	24	(h) Burton U	W 2-1	Watson, Singleton	5,000	1		2	4		6	7	8	10		11	9	5	3									
31	29	(a) Clapton O	D 0-0		1,000	1		2	4		6	7		8		11	9	5	3				10					
32	31	(a) Chelsea	L 0-4		15,000	1		2		4	6	7				9	8	5	3				10	11				
33	Apr 7	(h) Gainsboro' T	W 1-0	Hargraves	12,000	1	2				6	7		9	8	11		4	3				10		5			
34	13	(h) Stockport C	D 1-1	Lavery	10,000		2		4		6	7		9	8	11			3				10		5	1		
35	14	(a) Bristol C	L 0-2		12,000	1	2				6	7		9	8	11		5	3				10		4			
36	16	(h) Blackpool	W 3-0	Hargraves 2, Watson	10,000		3		4		6	7	8	9			11		2				10		5	1		
37	21	(h) Manchester U	L 1-3	Lavery	10,000				4			7	8			11	9	2	3				10		5	1	6	
38	28	(a) Glossop	W 2-1	Parnell, Wilson	1,500	1	2		4			7	8			11		6	3		9		10				5	
					Appearances	35	25	27	35	13	35	37	30	28	25	37	9	15	23	1	15	9	8	1	5	3	2	
					Goals				1	1		5	6	12	5	7	3		3		13		2					

FINAL LEAGUE POSITION: 6th in Division Two

1 own-goal

FA Cup

Rd	Date	Venue/Opponent	Result	Scorers	Att	Bromage	McDonald	Ray	Morgan	Stringfellow	Henderson	Parnell	Watson	Hargraves	Morris R	Singleton	Drain	Walker	Murray	Howard	Wilson D	Morris J	Lavery	Swift	George	Whitley	Freeborough	Clay
P1	Oct 7	(h) Morley	W11-0	Hargraves 4, Watson 2, R.Morris 4, Parnell	3,000	1	2	3	4		6	7	8	9	10	11		5										
P2	28	(h) Mexborough	D 1-1	Hargraves	4,000	1	2	3	4			7	6	9	10	11	8	5										
R	Nov 2	(a) Mexborough	D 1-1*	Parnell	3,000	1	2	3	4		6	7	8	9	10	11		5										
2R	6	(h) Mexboroguh	W 3-1	Watson, R.Morris, Hargraves	5,000	1	2		4	5	6	7	8	9	10	11												3
P3	22	(a) Hull C	D 1-1	Hargraves	3,000	1	2	3	4	5	6	7	8	9	10	11												
R	29	(h) Hull C	L 1-2	Parnell	7,186	1	2	3	4	5	6	7	8	9	10	11												
					Appearances	6	6	5	6	3	5	6	6	6	6	6	1	3										1
					Goals							3	3	7	5													

* After extra-time

1906-07

Manager: Gilbert Gillies

No	Date	Opponent	Result	Scorers	Att	Bromage	Murray DB	Clark	Morris J	George	Kennedy	Parnell	Watson	Wilson D	Lavery	Singleton	Walker	Cubberley	Murray W	Whitley	Hargraves	Freeborough	Jefferson	Morgan	Ray	Henderson	Page	Johnson	McLeod	Wilson TC	Pickard	Kirk	Harwood
1	Sep 1	(h) Bradford C	D 1-1	Lavery	20,000	1	2	3	4	5	6	7	8	9	10	11																	
2	8	(a) West Brom A	L 0-5		15,504	1	2	3		4	6	7	8	9			5	10	11														
3	10	(h) Lincoln C	D 1-1	Cubberley	5,000		2	3			6	7	9		10	11		8		1	4	5											
4	15	(h) Leicester F	D 1-1	Jefferson	11,000	1	2	3			6	7	8		10	11					4	5	9										
5	22	(a) Nottingham F	L 0-3		5,000		2	3			6	7	8		10				11	1	4		9	5									
6	29	(a) Lincoln C	D 1-1	Jefferson	4,000	1	2	3			6	7	9				5		11		10		8	4									
7	Oct 6	(a) Burton U	W 2-0	Lavery, Watson	3,000	1	2	3			6	7	8	9	10	11	5				4												
8	13	(h) Grimsby T	W 4-3	Watson 2, D.Murray (pen), Lavery	10,000	1	2	3			6	7	8	9	10	11	5				4												
9	20	(a) Port Vale	W 2-1	Lavery, Parnell	4,000	1	2				6	7	8	9	10	11	5				4				3								
10	27	(h) Burnley	L 0-1		14,000	1	2	3				7	8	9	10	11	5				4					6							
11	Nov 3	(a) Chesterfield	L 0-1		3,000	1	2	3			6	7	8		11		5	10			4						9						
12	10	(a) Barnsley	L 0-3		4,000	1	2	3			6	7			10		5		11		8			4			9						
13	17	(h) Chelsea	L 0-1		8,000	1	2	3			6	7	8		10		5				4						9	11					
14	24	(a) Wolves	L 2-3	Lavery, D.Murray (pen)	4,500	1	2	3			6	7	8		10		5		11		4								9				
15	Dec 1	(h) Clapton O	W 3-2	Watson, Parnell, McLeod	10,000	1	2	3		4	6	7	8		10		5		11										9				
16	5	(a) Blackpool	L 0-1		2,000	1	3				5	7	8		10						4	2				6	11		9				
17	8	(a) Gainsboro' T	L 0-1		3,000	1	3				5	7	8		10				11		4	2				6			9				
18	15	(h) Stockport C	W 6-1	McLeod, Lavery 3, Watson 2	8,000	1					5	7	8		10						4	2			3				9	11	6		
19	22	(a) Hull C	L 1-2	Lavery	10,000	1					5	7	8		10							2			3				9	11	6	4	
20	29	(a) Bradford C	D 2-2	McLeod, T.C.Wilson	17,000	1					6				10			8			4	2	7		3				9	11		5	
21	Jan 1	(a) Glossop	L 0-2		1,000	1					5				10			8			4	2	7		3	6			9	11			
22	5	(h) West Brom A	W 3-2	McLeod 2, Jefferson	14,000	1									10	11		8			6	2	7	4	3				9			5	
23	19	(a) Leicester F	D 2-2	McLeod, Kirk	8,000	1	3				6				10			8			4		7		2				9	11		5	
24	26	(h) Nottingham F	L 1-4	McLeod	14,000	1	2				6				10			8					7	4	3				9	11		5	
25	Feb 2	(h) Blackpool	D 1-1	Jefferson	7,000			3				7	8					10		1	6		9	4	2					11		5	
26	9	(h) Burton U	W 3-1	McLeod 2, Parnell	7,000			3			6	7	8					10		1	4				2				9	11		5	
27	16	(a) Grimsby T	L 0-4		4,000	1		3			6	7	8		10						4				2				9	11		5	
28	23	(h) Port Vale	W 2-0	Parnell, Watson	7,000	1		3			5	7	8						10		4	2				6			9	11			
29	Mar 2	(a) Burnley	W 2-1	Harwood, T.C.Wilson	5,000	1		3			5	7	10					8			4	2				6				11			9
30	9	(h) Chesterfield	W 1-0	McLeod	10,500	1		3			5	7	10					8			4	2				6			9	11			
31	16	(h) Barnsley	W 2-1	McLeod, Watson	14,000	1		3			5	7	10					8			4	2				6			9	11			
32	23	(a) Chelsea	L 0-2		25,000	1		3			5	7	10					8			4	2				6			9	11			
33	30	(h) Wolves	W 2-0	Watson, Cubberley	15,000	1		3			5	7	10					8			4	2				6			9	11			
34	Apr 1	(h) Glossop	L 1-4	McEwan (og)	8,000	1		3			5	7	10					8			4	2				6			9	11			
35	6	(a) Clapton O	D 1-1	Lavery	6,000	1	3				5	7			10			8			4	2				6			9	11			
36	13	(h) Gainsboro' T	W 4-0	Cubberley, Lavery 2, McLeod	3,000	1	3				5	7			10			8			4	2				6			9	11			
37	20	(a) Stockport C	D 2-2	Kennedy, McLeod	3,000	1	3				5	7			10			8			4	2				6			9	11			
38	27	(h) Hull C	D 2-2	McLeod 2	7,000	1	3				5	7			10			8			4	2				6			9	11			
FINAL LEAGUE POSITION: 10th in Division Two					Appearances	34	23	24	1	3	35	33	28	6	27	8	11	20	8	4	33	20	9	6	11	15	4	1	23	20	2	8	1
					Goals		2				1	4	9		12			3					4						15	2		1	1

1 own-goal

FA Cup

No	Date	Opponent	Result	Scorers	Att	Bromage	Murray DB	Clark	Morris J	George	Kennedy	Parnell	Watson	Wilson D	Lavery	Singleton	Walker	Cubberley	Murray W	Whitley	Hargraves	Freeborough	Jefferson	Morgan	Ray	Henderson	Page	Johnson	McLeod	Wilson TC	Pickard	Kirk	Harwood
1	Jan 12	(a) Bristol C	L 1-4	McLeod	14,000	1	2				6		8		10						4		7		3				9	11		5	
					Appearances	1	1				1		1		1						1		1		1				1	1		1	
					Goals																								1				

1907-08

Manager: Gilbert Gillies

No	Date	Opponent	Result	Scorers	Att	Bromage	Kay	Murray DB	Tompkins	Hynds	Henderson	Parnell	Watson	McLeod	Lavery	Croot	Thorpe	Cubberley	Naisby	Kennedy	Pickard	Jefferson	Thomas	Hargraves	Gemmell	Freeborough	Bates
1	Sep 2	(h) Glossop	W 2-1	Lavery, Tustin (og)	4,000	1	2	3	4	5	6	7	8	9	10	11											
2	7	(a) Leicester F	D 2-2	Watson, McLeod	10,000	1	2	3	4	5	6	7	8	9	10	11											
3	9	(h) Clapton O	W 5-2	Watson 2, Croot, Lavery 2	6,000	1	2	3	4	5	6	7	8	9	10	11											
4	14	(a) Blackpool	W 3-2	Watson, Lavery, Parnell	6,000	1	2	3	4	5	6	7	8	9	10	11											
5	21	(a) Stoke	L 1-2	Parnell	10,000	1	2	3		5	6	7	8	9	10	11	4										
6	28	(h) West Brom A	W 1-0	McLeod	24,000	1	2	3	4	5		7	8	9	10	11	6										
7	Oct 5	(a) Bradford C	L 0-5		27,000	1	2	3	4	5		7	8	9	10	11	6										
8	12	(h) Hull C	W 3-2	McLeod 2, Watson	15,000	1	2	3	4	5		7	8	9		11	6	10									
9	19	(a) Derby C	L 1-6	Atkin (og)	10,000	1	2	3	4	5		7	8	9		11	6	10									
10	26	(h) Lincoln C	W 2-1	Parnell, McLeod	10,000		2	3	4	5	6	7	8	9		11		10	1								
11	Nov 2	(a) Fulham	L 0-2		20,000		2	3	4	5	6	7	8	9		11		10	1								
12	9	(h) Barnsley	D 1-1	McLeod	11,000			2		5		7	8	9	10	11	3		1	4	6						
13	16	(a) Chesterfield	L 3-4	Thomas 2, Parnell	4,000			2	4	5		8		9		11	3	6	1			7	10				
14	23	(h) Burnley	D 2-2	Croot, McLeod	7,000			3		5		8		9		11	2	6	1			7	10	4			
15	30	(a) Oldham A	L 2-4	McLeod, Gemmell	8,000			3		5		7		9		11	2	6	1				10	4	8		
16	Dec 14	(h) Grimsby T	W 4-1	McLeod, Croot 2, Murray (pen)	5,000		2	3		5		7		9		11		6	1		4		10		8		
17	21	(a) Wolves	L 0-2		5,000		2	3		5		7	4	9		11		6	1				10		8		
18	25	(a) Stockport C	L 1-2	McLeod	8,000		2			5	4	7		9	10	11		6	1						8	3	
19	28	(h) Gainsboro' T	D 0-0		8,000		2	3		5		7		9		11		6	1	4			10		8		
20	Jan 1	(a) Glossop	W 2-0	Croot, McLeod	2,000		2	3		5		7		9		11		6	1	4			10		8		
21	4	(h) Leicester F	D 0-0		10,000		2	3		5		7		9		11		6	1	4			10		8		
22	18	(h) Stoke	L 0-1		10,000		2	3			4	7		9		11		6	1	5			10		8		
23	25	(a) West Brom A	L 0-1		8,000		2	3		5	4	7	8	9		11		6	1						10		
24	Feb 1	(h) Bradford C	L 0-1		35,000		2	3		5	4		8	9		11		6	1			7			10		
25	8	(a) Hull C	L 1-4	McLeod	9,000		2	3		5	4	7	8	9	10	11		6	1								
26	15	(h) Derby C	W 5-1	Murray (pen), Croot, Lavery, McLeod 2	8,000		2	3		5	4	7	8	9	10	11		6	1								
27	22	(a) Lincoln C	L 0-5		1,000		2	3		5	4	7	8	9	10	11		6	1								
28	29	(h) Fulham	L 0-1		10,000		2	3		5	4	7	8	9	10	11		6	1								
29	Mar 7	(a) Barnsley	W 3-1	Jefferson, McLeod, Croot	5,000		2	3		5	4		8	9	10	11		6	1			7					
30	14	(h) Chesterfield	D 0-0		6,000		2	3		5	4		8	9	10	11		6	1			7					
31	21	(a) Burnley	L 0-1		7,000		2	3		5	4	8		9	10	11		6	1			7					
32	28	(h) Oldham A	L 1-2	Parnell	15,000		2	3		5	6	7	8	9	10	11		4	1								
33	Apr 4	(a) Clapton O	D 0-0		8,000		2	3		5	4	7		9		11		6	1			8			10		
34	11	(a) Grimsby T	L 0-2		6,000		2	3		5	4	7		9	10	11		6	1						8		
35	17	(h) Stockport C	W 3-0	Gemmell, McLeod (pen), Croot	12,000			3		5	4	7		9	10	11		6	1						8		2
36	18	(h) Wolves	W 3-1	Parnell, Gemmell, Watson	10,000					3	4	7	8		10	11		6	1	5					9		2
37	20	(h) Blackpool	D 1-1	Lavery	7,000	1	3			5	4		8		10	11				6		7			9		2
38	22	(a) Gainsboro' T	L 1-2	McLeod	3,500					3	4	7	8	9		11		6	1	5					10	2	
FINAL LEAGUE POSITION: 12th in Division Two					Appearances	10	31	34	11	37	25	34	25	36	21	38	9	29	28	8	2	8	9	2	16	2	3
					Goals			2				6	6	17	6	8						1	2		3		

2 own-goals

FA Cup

No	Date	Opponent	Result	Scorers	Att	Bromage	Kay	Murray DB	Tompkins	Hynds	Henderson	Parnell	Watson	McLeod	Lavery	Croot	Thorpe	Cubberley	Naisby	Kennedy	Pickard	Jefferson	Thomas	Hargraves	Gemmell	Freeborough	Bates
1	Jan 11	(a) Oldham A	L 1-2	Parnell	14,000		2	3		5		7		9		11		6	1	4			10		8		
					Appearances		1	1		1		1		1		1		1	1	1			1		1		
					Goals							1															

1908-09

Manager: Frank Scott-Walford

No	Month	Date	Opponent	Result	Scorers	Att	Naisby	Watson	White	McAllister	Hamilton	Cubberley	Joynes	Gemmell	Bowman	Rodger	Croot	Dougal	Guy	Kennedy	Burnett	McLeod	McDonald	Bates	Cunningham	Murray DB	Morris	Bromage
1	Sep	5	(h) Tottenham H	W 1-0	Rodger	20,000	1	2	3	4	5	6	7	8	9	10	11											
2		7	(h) Clapton O	D 0-0		8,000	1	2	3	4	5	6		8	9	10	11	7										
3		12	(h) Hull C	W 2-0	Rodger, Bowman	12,000	1	2	3	4	5	6		8	9	10	11		7									
4		14	(h) Barnsley	W 2-0	McLeod 2	8,000	1	2	3	4		6				10	11		7	5	8	9						
5		19	(h) Derby C	L 2-5	McLeod 2 (1 pen)	20,000	1	2	3	4	5	6				10	11		7		8	9						
6		26	(a) Blackpool	L 0-1		5,000	1	2	3	4		6	7		9	10	11					8	5					
7	Oct	3	(a) Chesterfield	L 0-2		7,000	1	2	3		4	6	7	8		10	11			5		9						
8		10	(a) Glossop	D 0-0		4,000	1	2			4	6	7	8	10		11			5		9		3				
9		17	(h) Stockport C	W 2-1	McLeod, Molyneux (og)	8,500	1	2	3		4	6		8	10	7	11			5		9						
10		24	(a) West Brom A	L 1-2	McLeod	13,554	1	2	3		4	6		8	10	7	11			5		9						
11		31	(h) Birmingham	W 2-0	McLeod, Rodger	15,000	1	2	3	4		6	7	10		8	11			5		9						
12	Nov	7	(a) Gainsboro' T	D 1-1	McLeod	4,000	1	2	3	4		6	7	10		8	11			5		9						
13		14	(h) Grimsby T	W 4-1	Gemmell 2, McLeod 2	8,000	1	2	3	4		6	7	10		8	11			5		9						
14		21	(a) Fulham	W 1-0	McLeod	18,000	1	2	3	4		6	7	10		8	11			5		9						
15		28	(h) Burnley	D 1-1	Bowman	14,000	1	2	3	4		6	8	10	9		11		7	5								
16	Dec	12	(h) Wolves	W 5-2	McLeod, Gemmell 3, Guy	14,000	1	2	3	4			8	10			11		7	5		9	6					
17		19	(a) Oldham A	L 0-6		8,000	1	2	3	4				10		8	11		7	5		9	6					
18		25	(a) Bolton W	L 0-2		19,400	1		3	4	5			10	9	8	11		7				6	2				
19		26	(h) Bolton W	L 1-2	Joynes	15,000	1	2	6	4			8	10			11		7	5		9		3				
20	Jan	1	(a) Barnsley	L 1-2	Guy	6,500	1		3	4			8			10	11		7	5		9	6	2				
21		2	(a) Tottenham H	L 0-3		16,000	1		3	4	5					10	11		7		8	9	6	2				
22		9	(a) Hull C	L 1-4	McLeod	7,000	1		3	4	5			10		8	11		7			9	6	2				
23		23	(a) Derby C	L 1-5	Bowman	7,000			2	4	5			8	9			11	7		10		6		1	3		
24		30	(h) Blackpool	W 1-0	Bowman	8,000	1	2	3	4	5			8	9		11	7			10		6					
25	Feb	13	(h) Glossop	W 3-1	Croot, Burnett, Gemmell	10,000	1	2	3	4		6		8	9		11	7			10		5					
26		20	(a) Stockport C	L 0-1		6,000	1	2	3	4		6		8	9		11	7			10		5					
27		27	(h) West Brom A	D 1-1	McLeod	12,000	1	2	3	4	5	6		8			11	7			10	9						
28	Mar	13	(h) Gainsboro' T	L 0-2		7,000	1	2	3	4		6		8			11		7		10	9					5	
29		20	(a) Grimsby T	W 1-0	Gemmell	5,500	1	2	3	4		6	10	8			11		7		9						5	
30		27	(h) Fulham	W 2-0	Bowman, Guy	10,000	1	2	3	4		6		8	9		11		7		10						5	
31	Apr	3	(a) Burnley	D 0-0		5,000	1			4	3	6		8		10	11		7		9			2			5	
32		9	(h) Chesterfield	W 3-0	Rodger, Gemmell, Bowman	10,000	1			4	2			8	9	10	11		7	5			6	3				
33		10	(h) Bradford	L 0-3		11,000	1			4	2	6		8			11		7		10	9		3			5	
34		12	(a) Birmingham	L 0-1		3,000					4	6	8			10	11	7			9			3		2	5	1
35		13	(a) Clapton O	D 0-0		3,000					4		8			10	11	7			9		6	2		3	5	1
36		17	(a) Wolves	L 1-2	McLeod	7,000	1	3		4	2	6				8	11				10	9		7			5	
37		24	(h) Oldham A	W 3-0	Burnett, Croot, Dougal	4,500		2	3	4		6				8	11	7			10	9					5	1
38		27	(a) Bradford	L 0-2		6,000		2	3	8	5	6				10	11	7			9		4					1
FINAL LEAGUE POSITION: 12th in Division Two						Appearances	33	28	31	32	21	27	15	28	15	25	37	10	18	15	18	22	14	12	1	3	9	4
						Goals							1	8	6	4	2	1	3		2	15						

1 own-goal

FA Cup

No	Month	Date	Opponent	Result	Scorers	Att	Naisby	Watson	White	McAllister	Hamilton	Cubberley	Joynes	Gemmell	Bowman	Rodger	Croot	Dougal	Guy	Kennedy	Burnett	McLeod	McDonald	Bates	Cunningham	Murray DB	Morris	Bromage
1	Jan	16	(a) Oldham A	D 1-1	McLeod	7,000	1	2	3	4	5	6		8			11		7		10	9						
R		20	(h) Oldham A	W 2-0	McLeod (pen), Guy	19,047	1	2	3	4	5	6		8			11		7		10	9						
2	Feb	6	(h) West Ham U	D 1-1	Burnett	31,471	1	2	3	4	5	6	9	8			11		7		10							
R		11	(a) West Ham U	L 1-2*	Bowman	13,000	1	2	3	4	5	6		8	9		11		7		10							
					*After extra-time	Appearances	4	4	4	4	4	4	1	4	1		4		4		4	2						
						Goals									1				1		1	2						

1909-10

Manager: Frank Scott-Walford

No	Month	Date	Opponent	Result	Scorers	Att	Bromage	Watson	White	McAllister	Morris	Cubberley	Stockton	Mulholland	Halligan	Gemmell	Croot	Price	McLeod	Dougal	Joynes	Burnett	Roberts	Hamilton	Beren	Affleck	Horsley	Naisby	Pickard	Tyldesley	Bridgett	Ackerley	Hogg	Astill
1	Sep	1	(h) Lincoln C	W 5-0	Gemmell 2, Halligan 2, Morris	6,000	1	2	3	4	5	6	7	8	9	10	11																	
2		4	(a) Hull C	L 1-3	Halligan	10,000	1	2	3	4	5	6	7	8	9	10	11																	
3		11	(h) Derby C	W 2-1	Croot, Halligan	12,000	1	2	3	4	5		7		8	10	11	6	9															
4		18	(a) Stockport C	D 0-0		7,000	1	2	3		5	6			9	10	11	4		7	8													
5		25	(h) Glossop	L 1-2	McLeod	12,000	1	2	3		5	6			8	10	11	4	9	7														
6	Oct	2	(a) Birmingham	W 2-1	Halligan 2	14,000	1	2	3	4		5			9		11	6		7	8	10												
7		9	(h) West Brom A	L 0-1		7,500	1	2	3	4	5	6			9	10	11				8		7											
8		16	(a) Oldham A	L 1-2	Halligan	10,000	1	2	3	4	5			8	9		11	6				10		7										
9		23	(h) Barnsley	L 0-7		8,000	1	2	3		5	6		8	9	10	11	4						7										
10		30	(a) Fulham	L 1-5	Halligan	14,000	1	2	3		5	6		8	9			11		7	10				4									
11	Nov	6	(h) Burnley	W 1-0	Halligan	7,000	1		2	4		6			10	8	11		9	7						3	5							
12		13	(h) Bradford	L 2-3	McLeod 2	10,000	1		2	4		6			10	8	11		9	7						3	5							
13		20	(a) Wolves	L 0-5		5,500	1		2		5	4			10			6	9	11	8			7		3								
14		27	(h) Gainsboro' T	D 0-0		3,000		2	3		5	6			10	8	11		9	7								1	4					
15	Dec	4	(a) Grimsby T	L 1-3	Halligan	3,000		2	3	4	5	6		8	9	10	11				7							1						
16		11	(h) Manchester C	L 1-3	McLeod	5,000	1		2		5	6		8	10		11		9				7			3			4					
17		18	(a) Leicester F	L 2-6	McLeod, Halligan	12,000	1	2			5	6		8	10		11		9				7		4	3								
18		25	(h) Clapton O	W 2-1	Roberts, McLeod	6,000	1	2		4		6			10	8	11		9				7				5			3				
19		27	(h) Blackpool	W 3-2	McLeod, Roberts 2	10,000	1	2		4				8		10	11		9				7			3	5		6					
20		28	(a) Lincoln C	D 0-0		8,000	1				5	6		8	9	10							7			3	4			2	11			
21	Jan	1	(a) Blackpool	L 1-3	Halligan	4,000	1	2		4	5	6			10	8	11		9				7			3								
22		8	(h) Hull C	D 1-1	Gemmell	10,000	1			4		6			10	8	11		9				7			3	5			2				
23		22	(a) Derby C	L 0-1		7,000	1	2		4		6			10	8			9	11			7			3	5							
24	Feb	5	(a) Glossop	L 1-2	Roberts	1,000	1			4		6			10	8	11		9				7			3	5			2				
25		12	(h) Birmingham	W 2-1	Roberts, Croot	10,000	1			4		6			10	8	11		9				7			3	5			2				
26		26	(h) Oldham A	L 3-5	McLeod, Mulholland, Croot (pen)	6,000	1		2	4		6		8		10	11		9				7			3	5							
27	Mar	5	(h) Stockport C	L 0-2		5,000	1			4		6				10	11		9		8		7			3	5			2				
28		7	(a) West Brom A	L 1-3	McLeod	6,800	1		2	4	5	6		8			11		9	10			7			3								
29		12	(h) Fulham	D 2-2	Croot 2 (1 pen)	4,000	1		2	4		6		8		10	11		9				7			3	5							
30		17	(a) Barnsley	D 1-1	McLeod	2,000	1		2	4	5	6		8			11		9				7			3						10		
31		19	(a) Burnley	L 0-3		4,000	1		2			6		8		10	11		9				7		4	3	5							
32		26	(a) Bradford	L 2-4	Croot (pen), McLeod	12,000			2			6		8			11		9				7			3	5		4				1	10
33		28	(a) Clapton O	W 2-0	McLeod 2	7,000	1		2		5	6		8			11		9	10			7			3	4							
34	Apr	2	(h) Wolves	W 1-0	McLeod	5,000	1		2		5	6		8			11		9	10			7			3	4							
35		9	(a) Gainsboro' T	L 0-2		3,000	1		2		5	6		8			11		9	10			7			3	4							
36		16	(h) Grimsby T	W 3-1	Croot 2 (1 pen), McLeod	5,000	1		2		5	6		8			11		9	10			7			3	4							
37		23	(a) Manchester C	L 0-3		15,000	1		2		5	6		9			11		8				7			3	4					10		
38		30	(h) Leicester F	D 1-1	Dougal	2,000	1		2		5	6		8			11		9	10			7			3	4							
FINAL LEAGUE POSITION: 17th in Division Two						Appearances	35	17	28	21	24	35	3	22	24	23	34	8	28	15	7	2	24	3	3	25	20	2	4	6	1	2	1	1
						Goals					1			1	12	3	7		15	1			6											

FA Cup

No	Month	Date	Opponent	Result	Scorers	Att	Bromage	Watson	White	McAllister	Morris	Cubberley	Stockton	Mulholland	Halligan	Gemmell	Croot	Price	McLeod	Dougal	Joynes	Burnett	Roberts	Hamilton	Beren	Affleck	Horsley	Naisby	Pickard	Tyldesley	Bridgett	Ackerley	Hogg	Astill
1	Jan	15	(a) Sunderland	L 0-1		18,000	1			4		6			10	8	11		9				7			3	5			2				
						Appearances	1			1		1			1	1	1		1				1			1	1			1				
						Goals																												

1910-11

Manager: Frank Scott-Walford

No	Date	Opponent	Result	Scorers	Att	Hogg	Affleck	Creighton	Harkins	Morris	Cubberley	Cunningham	Foley	Gillespie	Enright	Croot	Horsley	McLeod	Roberts	Mulholland	Bromage	White	Kelly	Bridgett
1	Sep 3	(h) Blackpool	L 1-2	Enright	12,000	1	2	3	4	5	6	7	8	9	10	11								
2	10	(a) Glossop	L 1-2	Enright	8,000	1	2	3	4	5		7	8		10	11	6	9						
3	17	(h) Lincoln C	L 0-1		8,000	1	2	3	4	5	6				10	11		9	7	8				
4	24	(a) Huddersfield T	L 2-3	Croot (pen), McLeod	7,500			3	4					9	10	11	6	8	7		1	2	5	
5	Oct 1	(h) Birmingham	D 1-1	Gillespie	8,000		2	3		5	6			9	10	11		8	7		1		4	
6	8	(a) West Brom A	L 0-2		10,000		2	3		5	6			9	10	11		8	7		1		4	
7	15	(h) Hull C	W 1-0	Gillespie	8,000		2	3	4	5	6			9	10	11		8	7		1			
8	22	(a) Fulham	L 1-2	Gillespie	11,000		2	3	4	5	6			9	10	11		8	7		1			
9	29	(h) Bradford	W 2-0	McLeod, Gillespie	13,000		2	3	4	5	6			9	10	11		8	7		1			
10	Nov 5	(a) Burnley	L 1-4	McLeod	8,000		2	3	4	5	6			9	10	11		8	7		1			
11	12	(h) Gainsboro' T	W 4-0	Enright, Gillespie 2, McLeod	5,000		2	3	4	5	6			9	10	11		8	7		1			
12	19	(a) Bolton W	L 0-3		10,000		2	3	4	5	6			9	10	11		8	7		1			
13	26	(a) Stockport C	W 4-0	Gillespie 2, McLeod, Bridgett	4,000		2	3	4	5	6			9	10			8	7		1			11
14	Dec 3	(h) Derby C	W 3-2	Morris, Roberts 2	10,000		2	3	4	5	6			9	10			8	7		1			11
15	10	(a) Barnsley	L 0-4		4,000		2	3	4	5	6			9	10			8	7		1			11
16	17	(h) Leicester F	L 2-3	Enright, Morris	5,000		2	3		5	6			9	10		4	8	7		1			11
17	24	(a) Wolves	L 1-3	Gillespie	6,000		2	3		5	6			9	10		4		7	8	1			11
18	26	(h) Chelsea	D 3-3	Roberts, Croot, McLeod	18,000		2	3		5	6			9	10	11	4	8	7		1			
19	27	(h) Clapton O	W 1-0	Mulholland	10,000	1	3	2		5	6				10	11	4	9	7	8				
20	31	(a) Blackpool	W 2-1	McLeod, Bridgett	1,000	1	2	3	6	5	10						4	9	7	8				11
21	Jan 7	(h) Glossop	L 0-2		10,000		2	3		5	6	7		9	10		4	8			1			11
22	21	(a) Lincoln C	D 1-1	Enright	5,000	1	2	3	4	5					10		6	9	7	8				11
23	28	(h) Huddersfield T	W 5-2	Croot 2 (1 pen), McLeod 2, Mulholland	10,000	1	2	3	4	5	6				10	11		9	7	8				
24	Feb 4	(a) Birmingham	L 1-2	McLeod	15,000	1	2	3	4	5	6				10	11		9	7	8				
25	11	(h) West Brom A	W 3-1	McLeod, Mulholland, Enright	10,700	1	2	3	4	5	6				10	11		9	7	8				
26	18	(a) Hull C	D 1-1	Enright	6,000		2	3	4	5	6				10	11		9	7	8	1			
27	25	(h) Fulham	W 3-1	Croot (pen), Enright, Mulholland	6,000		2	3	4	5	6				10	11		9	7	8	1			
28	Mar 4	(a) Bradford	W 2-0	Croot (pen), Mulholland	12,000		2	3	4	5	6				10	11		9	7	8	1			
29	18	(a) Gainsboro' T	W 2-1	Enright, Roberts	4,000		2	3	4	5	6				10	11		9	7	8	1			
30	25	(h) Bolton W	W 1-0	Mulholland	15,000		2	3	4	5	6				10	11		9	7	8	1			
31	27	(h) Burnley	D 0-0		5,500		2	3	4	5	6				10	11		9	7	8	1			
32	Apr 1	(h) Stockport C	W 4-0	McLeod 2, Mulholland 2	9,000		2	3	4	5	6				10	11		9	7	8	1			
33	8	(a) Derby C	D 2-2	Croot (pen), Mulholland	5,000		2	3	4	5	6				10	11		9	7	8	1			
34	14	(a) Chelsea	L 1-4	McLeod	50,000		2	3	4	5	6				10	11		9	7	8	1			
35	15	(h) Barnsley	D 0-0		10,000	1	2	3	4	5	6				10	11		9	7	8				
36	17	(a) Clapton O	L 0-1		6,000	1	2	3	4	5			6	9	10	11			7	8				
37	22	(a) Leicester F	L 1-2	Croot	5,000	1	2	3	4	5	6				10	11		9	7	8				
38	29	(h) Wolves	W 1-0	Enright	6,000	1	2	3	4		6		8		10	11		9	7	8				
FINAL LEAGUE POSITION: 11th in Division Two					Appearances	13	37	38	31	36	34	3	4	18	37	30	9	35	35	21	25	1	3	8
					Goals					2				9	10	8		14	4	9				2

FA Cup

No	Date	Opponent	Result	Scorers	Att	Hogg	Affleck	Creighton	Harkins	Morris	Cubberley	Cunningham	Foley	Gillespie	Enright	Croot	Horsley	McLeod	Roberts	Mulholland	Bromage	White	Kelly	Bridgett
1	Jan 14	(h) Brighton & HA	L 1-3	Roberts	18,270		2	3	4	5	6				10			9	7	8	1			11
					Appearances		1	1	1	1	1				1			1	1	1	1			1
					Goals														1					

1911-12

Manager: Frank Scott-Walford

No	Date	Opponents	Result	Scorers	Att	Murphy	Affleck	Creighton	Harkins	Morris	Cubberley	Roberts	Mulholland	McLeod	Gillespie	Croot	Johnson	Moran	Enright	Fortune	Hogg	Reinhardt	Heaney	Bridgett	Foley	Kelly	Clarkin	Campbell	McDaniel
1	Sep 2 (a)	Nottingham F	L 1-2	McLeod	10,000	1	2	3	4	5	6	7	8	9	10	11													
2	4 (a)	Burnley	L 2-4	McLeod, Enright	15,000	1	2	3		5		7		8	9	11	4	6	10										
3	9 (h)	Chelsea	D 0-0		15,000	1	2	3	4	5	6	7		8	9				10	11									
4	16 (a)	Clapton O	L 1-2	McLeod	13,000	1	2	3	4	5	6	7	8	9	10				11										
5	23 (h)	Bristol C	W 3-1	Croot, Enright, McLeod	10,000	1	2	3	4	5	6	7	8	9		11			10										
6	30 (a)	Birmingham	L 3-4	Enright, Roberts, Croot	10,000	1	2	3	4	5	6	7	8	9		11			10										
7	Oct 7 (h)	Huddersfield T	W 2-0	McLeod, Enright	12,000		2	3	4	5	6	7	8	9		11			10		1								
8	14 (a)	Blackpool	L 0-3		4,000		2	3	4	5	6	7	8	9		11			10		1								
9	21 (h)	Glossop	W 2-1	Mulholland, Croot	6,000	1	2	3	4	5	6	7	8	9		11			10										
10	28 (a)	Hull C	L 0-1		10,000	1	2	3		5	6	7	8	9		11	4		10										
11	Nov 4 (h)	Barnsley	W 3-2	McLeod, Mulholland 2	12,000	1	2	3	4	5	6	7	8	9		11			10										
12	11 (a)	Bradford	D 1-1	Croot (pen)	13,000	1	2	3		5	6	7	8	9		11	4		10										
13	18 (h)	Fulham	L 0-2		8,000	1	2	3		5	6	7	8	9		11		4	10										
14	25 (a)	Derby C	L 2-5	McLeod, Roberts	12,000	1	2	3	4	5	6	7	8	9		11			10										
15	Dec 4 (h)	Grimsby T	L 1-2	McLeod	3,000	1	2	3	4	5		7	8	9		11		6	10										
16	9 (h)	Burnley	L 1-5	Gillespie (pen)	10,000	1	2	3	4	5		7	8	9	10			6	11										
17	16 (a)	Wolves	I 0-5		8,000		3		4	5		7	8		9			6	10			1	2	11					
18	23 (h)	Leicester F	W 2-1	Enright 2	6,000		2	3		5		7		9		11	4	6	10			1			8				
19	25 (h)	Gainsboro' T	D 0-0		9,000		2	3				7	8	9		11	4	6	10			1				5			
20	26 (a)	Gainsboro' T	L 1-2	Mulholland	6,000		2	3	4	5		7	8	9		11		6				1					10		
21	30 (h)	Nottingham F	W 3-1	Mulholland 2, Enright	8,000	1	2		4	5		7	8	9		11		6	10									3	
22	Jan 6 (a)	Chelsea	L 2-4	McLeod, Foley	10,000	1	2	3	4	5		7	8	9		11		6							10				
23	20 (h)	Clapton O	L 0-2		5,000	1	2	3	4	5		7	8	9		11		6	10										
24	23 (a)	Grimsby T	W 2-1	Johnson, Enright	3,000	1	3		4	5		7	8			11	6		10						9				2
25	27 (a)	Bristol C	L 1-4	Croot (pen)	7,000		2		4	5		7	8	9		11	6	3	10			1							
26	Feb 10 (a)	Huddersfield T	W 2-1	Mulholland 2	8,000		2	3	4	5		7	8			11		6	10			1			9				
27	17 (h)	Blackpool	W 1-0	Enright	6,000		2	3	4	5		7	8			11		6	10			1			9				
28	24 (a)	Glossop	L 1-2	Mulholland	3,000		2	3	4	5		7	8			11		6	10			1			9				
29	Mar 2 (h)	Hull C	D 0-0		8,000		2	3	4	5		7	8			11		6	10			1			9				
30	16 (h)	Bradford	L 1-2	Foley	10,000		2	3	4	5	6	7	8	9		11						1			10				
31	23 (a)	Fulham	L 2-7	Enright, Mulholland	3,000		2	3	4	5		7	8	9		11		6	10			1							
32	30 (h)	Derby C	L 0-1		4,500			3	4	5		7	8			11		6	10			1	2		9				
33	Apr 5 (h)	Birmingham	D 0-0		5,000		2		4	5	6	7	8	9				3	10		1			11					
34	6 (h)	Stockport C	D 1-1	Enright	4,000		2		4	5	6	7	8	9				3	10		1			11					
35	11 (a)	Barnsley	W 4-3	McLeod 2, Croot 2 (2 pens)	3,000		2		4	5	6	7	8	9		11		3	10		1								
36	15 (a)	Stockport C	D 3-3	McLeod 2, Mulholland	3,000		2		4	5	6	7	8	9		11		3	10		1								
37	20 (h)	Wolves	D 1-1	McLeod	5,000		2		4	5	6	7	8	9		11		3	10		1								
38	27 (a)	Leicester F	L 1-2	Enright	10,000		2		4	5	6	7	8	9		11		3	10		1								
FINAL LEAGUE POSITION: 19th in Division Two					Appearances	18	37	28	32	37	20	38	35	31	6	32	7	24	34	1	8	12	2	3	9	1	1	1	1
					Goals							2	11	14	1	7	1		12						2				

FA Cup

No	Date	Opponents	Result	Scorers	Att	Murphy	Affleck	Creighton	Harkins	Morris	Cubberley	Roberts	Mulholland	McLeod	Gillespie	Croot	Johnson	Moran	Enright	Fortune	Hogg	Reinhardt	Heaney	Bridgett	Foley	Kelly	Clarkin	Campbell	McDaniel
1	Jan 13 (h)	Glossop	W 1-0	Roberts	21,000	1	2	3	4	5		7	8	9		11		6	10										
2	Feb 3 (h)	West Brom A	L 0-1		21,320		2	3	4	5		7	8			11		6	10			1			9				
					Appearances	1	2	2	2	2		2	2	1		2		2	2			1			1				
					Goals							1																	

1912-13

Manager: Herbert Chapman

No	Date	Opponents	Result	Scorers	Att	Scott	Law	Ferguson	Allan	Lintott	Cubberley	Roberts	Robertson	McLeod	Gibson	Croot	Foley	Enright	Copeland	Affleck	Bainbridge	Moran	Price	Speirs	Broughton	Hogg	Bridgett	Fenwick
1	Sep 7	(a) Fulham	L 0-4		20,000	1	2	3	4	5	6	7	8	9	10	11												
2	14	(h) Barnsley	W 2-0	Robertson, Croot (pen)	15,000	1	2	3	4	5	10	7	8	9		11	6											
3	21	(a) Bradford	W 1-0	Cubberley	18,000	1	2	3	4	5	10	7	8	9		11	6											
4	28	(h) Wolves	D 2-2	McLeod, Croot (pen)	20,000	1	2	3	4	5	10	7	8	9		11	6											
5	Oct 5	(a) Leicester F	D 1-1	Robertson	10,000	1	2	3	4	5	10	7	8	9		11	6											
6	12	(h) Stockport C	W 2-1	McLeod 2	15,000	1	2	3		5	4	7	8	9	10	11	6											
7	19	(a) Preston NE	L 2-3	McLeod, Enright	9,000	1	2	3		5	4		8	9	10	11	6	7										
8	26	(h) Burnley	W 4-1	Robertson 2, McLeod, Cubberley	10,000	1	2	3	4	5	10		8	9		11	6	7										
9	Nov 2	(a) Hull C	L 2-6	McLeod, Croot (pen)	10,000	1	2	3	4	5	10	7	8	9		11	6											
10	9	(h) Glossop	W 4-0	McLeod 3, Foley	12,000	1	3			5	4	7	8	9		11	6	10	2									
11	16	(a) Clapton O	L 0-2		10,000	1	3			5	4	7	8	9		11	6	10	2									
12	23	(h) Lincoln C	D 2-2	Robertson, Lintott	15,000	1			4	5	10	7	8	9		11	6		2	3								
13	30	(a) Nottingham F	W 2-1	Robertson, Roberts	8,000	1	2	3	4	5		7	8	9	10	11	6											
14	Dec 7	(h) Bristol C	D 1-1	Robertson	10,000	1	2	3	4	5			8	9	10	11	6				7							
15	14	(a) Birmingham	D 2-2	McLeod 2	20,000	1	2	3	4	5	10		8	9		11	6				7							
16	21	(h) Huddersfield T	L 0-3		15,000	1	2	3	4	5	10		8	9		11	6				7							
17	25	(h) Grimsby T	L 1-2	Cubberley	15,000	1	2	3	4	5	10		8	9		11					7	6						
18	26	(h) Blackpool	L 0-2		8,000	1	2	3	4	5			8	9		11	6	10			7							
19	28	(h) Fulham	L 2-3	Bainbridge, Price	10,000	1	4	3		5				9		11	6		2		7		8	10				
20	Jan 1	(a) Blackpool	W 3-0	Croot, Bainbridge, McLeod	5,000	1	2			5			8	9		11	6			3	7			10	4			
21	4	(a) Barnsley	L 0-2		5,000	1	2			5				9		11	6			3	7		8	10	4			
22	18	(h) Bradford	W 2-0	Foley, Speirs	10,000					5	4			9		11	6		2	3	7		8	10		1		
23	25	(a) Wolves	D 2-2	Bainbridge, McLeod	8,000		4			5			8	9			6		2	3	7			10		1	11	
24	Feb 8	(h) Leicester F	W 5-1	Price 2, Speirs, Fenwick, McLeod	10,000		4			5				9			6		2	3	7		8	10		1		11
25	15	(a) Stockport C	L 0-6		7,000		4			5				9			6		2	3	7		8	10		1		11
26	22	(h) Preston NE	W 5-1	Affleck (pen), Fenwick 2, Bainbridge, Foley	18,000	1	4			5			8	9			6		2	3	7			10				11
27	Mar 1	(a) Burnley	D 2-2	McLeod, Speirs	12,000	1	4			5			8	9			6		2	3	7			10				11
28	8	(h) Hull C	W 1-0	McLeod	20,000	1	4			5			8	9			6		2	3	7			10				11
29	15	(a) Glossop	L 1-2	McLeod	2,000		4	3		5			8	9		11	6			2	7			10		1		
30	21	(a) Grimsby T	L 2-3	McLeod 2	8,000		4			5				9		11	6		2	3	7		8	10		1		
31	22	(h) Clapton O	W 3-1	Speirs 2, McLeod	6,000		4			5			8	9		11	6		2	3	7			10		1		
32	24	(a) Bury	D 1-1	McLeod	10,000		4			5			8	9		11	6		2	3	7			10		1		
33	25	(h) Buy	W 4-2	McLeod 3, Speirs	17,000		4			5				9		11	6		2	3	7		8	10		1		
34	29	(a) Lincoln C	D 3-3	Speirs, McLeod, Croot	9,000		4			5				9		11	6		2	3	7		8	10		1		
35	Apr 5	(h) Nottingham F	W 1-0	McLeod	20,000		4			5			10	9		11	6		2	3	7		8			1		
36	12	(a) Bristol C	D 1-1	Speirs	15,000		4			5				9		11	6	7	2	3			8	10		1		
37	19	(h) Birmingham	W 4-0	Speirs 2, McLeod, Foley	8,000					5				9		11	6		2	3	7		8	10	4	1		
38	26	(a) Huddersfield T	L 0-1		8,000		3			5				9		11	6		2		7		8	10	4	1		
FINAL LEAGUE POSITION: 6th in Division Two					Appearances	24	35	17	14	38	16	11	27	38	5	32	36	6	20	19	24	1	12	19	4	14	1	5
					Goals					1	3	1	7	27		5	4	1		1	4		3	10				3

FA Cup

No	Date	Opponents	Result	Scorers	Att	Scott	Law	Ferguson	Allan	Lintott	Cubberley	Roberts	Robertson	McLeod	Gibson	Croot	Foley	Enright	Copeland	Affleck	Bainbridge	Moran	Price	Speirs	Broughton	Hogg	Bridgett	Fenwick
1	Jan 15	(h) Burnley	L 2-3	McLeod, Foley	13,109		2		4	5			8	9		11	6			3	9			10		1		
					Appearances		1		1	1			1	1		1	1			1	1			1		1		
					Goals									1			1											

1913-14

Manager: Herbert Chapman

No	Date	Opponents	Result	Scorers	Att	Hogg	Copeland	Affleck	Lintott	Hampson	Foley	Bainbridge	Price	McLeod	Speirs	Sharpe	Law	Turner	Croot	Johnson	Jackson	Blackman	Scott	Peart	Dougherty	Lamph
1	Sep 6	(h) Glossop	W 3-0	Speirs, McLeod 2	8,000	1	2	3	4	5	6	7	8	9	10	11										
2	13	(a) Stockport C	L 1-2	McLeod	10,000	1	2	3	4	5	6	7	8	9	10	11										
3	20	(h) Bradford	W 5-1	Speirs, Price, Bainbridge 2, McLeod	23,000	1	2	3		5	6	7	8	9	10	11	4									
4	27	(a) Notts C	L 0-4		12,000	1	2	3		5	6	7	8	9	10	11	4									
5	Oct 4	(h) Leicester F	W 2-1	Bainbridge, Price	18,000	1	2	3		5	6	7	8	9	10	11	4									
6	11	(a) Wolves	W 3-1	Speirs 2, Sharpe (pen)	10,000	1	2	3		5	6	7	8	9	10	11	4									
7	18	(h) Hull C	L 1-2	Speirs	20,000	1	2	3		5	6	7	8	9	10	11	4									
8	25	(a) Barnsley	W 4-1	Speirs 2, Price, McLeod	12,000	1	2	3		5	6	7	8	9	10	11	4									
9	Nov 1	(h) Bury	W 2-1	Price, Speirs	20,000	1	2	3		5	6	7	8	9	10	11	4									
10	8	(a) Huddersfield T	D 1-1	Turner	9,000	1		3	4	5	6		8	9	10		2	7	11							
11	15	(h) Lincoln C	W 1-0	McLeod	12,000	1	2	3		5	6		8	9	10	11	4	7								
12	22	(a) Blackpool	D 2-2	Hampson, Croot	5,000	1	2	3		5	6		8	9	10	7	4		11							
13	29	(h) Nottingham F	W 8-0	McLeod 4, Price 2, Hampson, Speirs	14,000	1	2	3		5	6	7	10	9	8	11	4									
14	Dec 6	(a) W Arsenal	L 0-1		18,000	1	2	3		5	6	7	8	9	10	11	4									
15	13	(h) Grimsby T	W 4-1	McLeod 2, Hampson, Price	10,000	1	2	3		5	6		8	9	10	11	4			7						
16	20	(a) Birmingham	W 2-0	McLeod, Sharpe	15,000	1	2	3	5		6		7	9	10	11	4				8					
17	25	(h) Fulham	W 2-1	McLeod, Hampson	30,000	1	2	3		5	6		7	9	10	11	4				8					
18	26	(a) Fulham	W 1-0	McLeod	25,000	1	2	3		5	6	7	8	9	10	11	4									
19	27	(a) Glossop	D 1-1	Bainbridge	2,000	1	2	3		5	6	7		9	10		4		11		8					
20	Jan 3	(h) Stockport C	W 5-1	Speirs, Jackson 2, McLeod, Sharpe	10,000	1	2	3	4	5	6	7		9	10	11					8					
21	17	(a) Bradford	L 1-3	McLeod	32,184	1	2	3		5	6		7	9	10	11	4				8					
22	24	(h) Notts C	L 2-4	Sharpe, Hampson	25,000	1	2	3		5	6	7		9	10	11	4				8					
23	Feb 7	(a) Leicester F	L 1-5	Speirs	4,000	1	2	3		5	6		8	9	10		4		11		7					
24	14	(h) Wolves	W 5-0	McLeod 3, Speirs, Sharpe	10,000	1	2	3		5	6		7	9	10	11	4				8					
25	21	(a) Hull C	L 0-1		18,000	1		3		5	6		7	9	10	11	4				8	2				
26	28	(h) Barnsley	W 3-0	McLeod, Sharpe 2 (1 pen)	20,000			3		5	6		7	9	10	11	4				8	2	1			
27	Mar 2	(a) Clapton O	L 1-3	Hampson	7,000			3		5	6		7	9	10	11	4				8	2	1			
28	7	(a) Bury	D 1-1	Jackson	12,000	1		3		5	6		10	9		7	4		11		8	2				
29	14	(h) Huddersfield T	W 5-1	Hampson, McLeod 3, Price	14,000	1		3		5	6		10	9		7	4		11		8	2				
30	21	(a) Lincoln C	L 0-1		8,000	1		3		5	6		10	9		7	4		11		8	2				
31	28	(h) Blackpool	W 2-1	McLeod, Hampson	12,000	1		3		5	6		10	9		7	4		11		8	2				
32	Apr 4	(a) Nottingham F	L 1-2	Law	6,000	1		3		5	6		10	9		7	4		11		8	2				
33	10	(a) Bristol C	D 1-1	McLeod	20,000	1		3		5	6		7	9	10	11	4				8	2				
34	11	(h) W Arsenal	D 0-0		25,000	1		3		5	6		10	9		7	4		11		8	2				
35	13	(h) Bristol C	W 1-0	Turner	12,000	1		3			6		10	9		11	4	7			8	2		5		
36	14	(h) Clapton O	D 0-0		12,000	1		3		5	6		10			11	4	7			8	2			9	
37	18	(a) Grimsby T	W 1-0	Price	9,000	1		3		5	10		7	9		11	4				8	2				6
38	25	(h) Birmingham	W 3-2	Price, Stuart (og), McLeod	10,000	1		3		5	6		7	9	10	11	4				8	2				
FINAL LEAGUE POSITION: 4th in Division Two					Appearances	36	23	38	5	36	38	15	35	37	29	35	35	4	10	1	22	14	2	1	1	1
					Goals					8		4	10	27	12	7	1	2	1		3					

1own-goal

FA Cup

No	Date	Opponents	Result	Scorers	Att	Hogg	Copeland	Affleck	Lintott	Hampson	Foley	Bainbridge	Price	McLeod	Speirs	Sharpe	Law	Turner	Croot	Johnson	Jackson	Blackman	Scott	Peart	Dougherty	Lamph
1	Jan 10	(a) Gainsboro' T	W 4-2	Jackson 2, Law, McLeod	14,000	1	2	3		5	6	7		9	10	11	4				8					
2	31	(h) West Brom A	L 0-2		29,733	1		3	4	5	6	7		9	10	11	2				8					
					Appearances	2	1	2	1	2	2	2		2	2	2	2				2					
					Goals									1			1				2					

1914-15

Manager: Herbert Chapman

No	Date	Opponent	Result	Scorers	Att	Hogg	Blackman	McQuillan	Law	Peart H	Foley	Bainbridge	Jackson	Speirs	Price	Sharpe	Lawrence	Rothwell	Cowen	Croot	Hampson	McLeod	Richardson	Goodwin	Wainwright W	Affleck	Copeland	Lamph	Walker	Edmondson	Green
1	Sep 2	(h) Fulham	L 0-1		8,000	1	2	3	4	5	6	7	8	9	10	11															
2	5	(a) Stockport C	L 1-3	Sharpe	5,000	1	2	3	4		6			10	9	11	5	7	8												
3	9	(a) Fulham	L 0-1		5,000	1	2	3	5		6	7	8	10	9		4			11											
4	12	(h) Hull C	L 2-3	Speirs, Jackson	8,000	1	2	3	4				8	10	7		6			11	5	9									
5	19	(h) Blackpool	W 2-0	McLeod, Goodwin (pen)	8,000	1	2	3			6		8	10			4				5	9	7	11							
6	26	(a) Clapton O	L 0-2		9,000	1	2	3			6		8	10			4				5	9	7	11							
7	Oct 3	(h) Arsenal	D 2-2	Goodwin (pen), Speirs	10,000	1	2	3					8	10		7	4				5	9		11	6						
8	10	(a) Derby C	W 2-1	Speirs, McLeod	5,000	1	2	3	4	5	6		8	10		7						9		11							
9	17	(h) Lincoln C	W 3-1	McLeod, Speirs 2	10,000	1	2	3	4	5	6		8	10		7						9		11							
10	24	(a) Birmingham	L 3-6	Sharpe 2, Speirs	8,000	1	2	3	4		6		8	10		7					5	9		11							
11	31	(h) Grimsby T	W 5-0	McLeod 2, Speirs, Bainbridge, Jackson	5,000	1	2	3	4		6	7	8	10							5	9		11							
12	Nov 7	(a) Huddersfield T	L 0-1		14,000	1	2	3	4		6	7	8	10		11					5	9									
13	14	(h) Bristol C	D 1-1	McLeod	8,000	1	2	3	4		6	7	8	10		11					5	9									
14	21	(a) Bury	D 0-0		6,000	1	2		4			7		10	8						5	9		11	6	3					
15	28	(h) Preston NE	D 0-0		7,000	1			4		6	7		10	8						5	9		11		3	2				
16	Dec 5	(a) Nottingham F	L 1-3	Speirs	3,000	1	2		4		6	7	8	10		11					5	9				3					
17	12	(h) Leicester F	W 7-2	Bainbridge 2, McLeod 2, Price 3	5,000	1	2		4		6	7	8		10	11					5	9				3					
18	19	(a) Barnsley	L 1-2	Sharpe	3,000	1	2		4		6	7	8		10	11					5	9				3					
19	25	(a) Glossop	W 3-0	Jackson 2, McLeod	1,000	1	2		4		6	7	8	10						11	5	9				3					
20	26	(h) Glossop	W 3-0	Bainbridge, Price, McLeod	6,000	1	2		4		6	7	8		10					11	5	9				3					
21	Jan 2	(h) Stockport C	L 1-3	Speirs	7,000	1	2		4		6	7	8	10		11					5	9				3					
22	16	(a) Hull C	W 6-2	McLeod 5, Sharpe	5,000	1	2		4		6	7	8	10		11						9				3		5			
23	23	(a) Blackpool	L 0-1		6,000	1	2		4		6	7	8	10		11						9				3		5			
24	Feb 3	(h) Clapton O	L 0-1		4,000	1	2		4		6	7		8	10	11					5	9				3					
25	6	(a) Arsenal	L 0-2		10,000			3	4		6		7	8	10	11					5					2			1	9	
26	13	(h) Derby C	L 3-5	Edmondson, Speirs, Sharpe	5,000		2		4	5	6			10	7	11						8				3			1	9	
27	20	(a) Lincoln C	W 1-0	Edmondson	4,000		2		4		6		8		10	11					5			7		3			1	9	
28	27	(h) Birmingham	W 2-0	Jackson, Price	7,000		2		4		6		8		10	11					5			7		3			1	9	
29	Mar 6	(a) Grimsby T	W 5-2	Edmondson, Jackson, Sharpe, Goodwin, Price	4,000		2		4		6		8		10	11					5			7		3			1	9	
30	13	(h) Huddersfield T	W 1-0	Sharpe	12,000		2		4		6		8		10	11					5	9		7		3			1		
31	20	(a) Bristol C	L 0-1		5,000			3	4		6		8		10	11					5	9		7		3			1		
32	27	(h) Bury	W 2-1	McLeod, Price	6,000			2	4		6		8		10	11					5	9		7		2			1		
33	Apr 3	(a) Preston NE	L 0-2		5,000			2	4		6		8		10	11					5	9		7		3			1		
34	5	(a) Wolves	L 1-5	McLeod	15,000		2		4		6	7	8	11	10						5	9				3			1		
35	6	(h) Wolves	L 2-3	McLeod, Price	5,000			2	4	5	6	7			10				8	11		9				3			1		
36	10	(h) Nottingham F	W 4-0	Price 3, Sharpe	4,000			2	4	5	6		8		10	11						9		7		3			1		
37	17	(a) Leicester F	L 1-5	Jackson	3,000			2	4		6		8		10	11					5	9		7		3			1		
38	24	(h) Barnsley	L 0-2		5,000		2		4		6		8	11	10						5	9		7					1		3
					Appearances	24	30	20	35	6	35	18	32	25	24	26	6	1	2	5	28	31	2	19	2	24	1	2	14	5	1
					Goals							4	7	10	11	9						18		3						3	

FINAL LEAGUE POSITION: 15th in Division Two

FA Cup

No	Date	Opponent	Result	Scorers	Att	Hogg	Blackman	McQuillan	Law	Peart H	Foley	Bainbridge	Jackson	Speirs	Price	Sharpe	Lawrence	Rothwell	Cowen	Croot	Hampson	McLeod	Richardson	Goodwin	Wainwright W	Affleck	Copeland	Lamph	Walker	Edmondson	Green
1	Jan 9	(a) Derby C	W 2-1	McLeod, Sharpe	9,417	1	2		4	5	6	7	8	10		11						9				3					
2	30	(a) Queen's Park R	L 0-1		10,000	1	2		4		6	7	8	10		11					5	9				3					
					Appearances	2	2		2	1	2	2	2	2		2					1	2				2					
					Goals											1						1									

1915-16

Manager: Herbert Chapman

No	Date	Opponent	Result	Scorers	Att	Bradley	Law	Affleck	Lamph	Hampson J	Foley	Walden	Bennett	Edmondson	Price	Croot	Wrigglesworth	Walker	Dowling	Wainwright AH	Cowen	Goodwin	Copeland	Booth	Bainbridge	Dunn	Malcolm	Peart JG	Hughes	Lavery	Stephenson C	Hewison	Sharpe	Robinson S	Jennings	Wilson W	Williamson
1	Sep 4	(a) Derby C	W 3-1	Edmondson, Bennett, Price	3,000	1	2	3	4	5	6	7	8	9	10	11																					
2	11	(h) Sheffield W	W 2-1	Price, Hampson	8,000	1	2	3	4	5	6	7	8	9	10	11																					
3	18	(a) Bradford	L 3-4	Bennett, Edmondson 2	10,000	1	2	3	4	5	6	7	8	9	10	11																					
4	25	(h) Lincoln C	W 2-1	Edmondson, Price	6,000	1	4	3		5	6	7	8	9	10	11	2																				
5	Oct 2	(h) Hull C	W 3-1	Law, Price, Edmondson	7,000		4	3			6	7	8	9	10	11		1	2	5																	
6	9	(a) Nottingham F	L 0-2		5,000	1	2	3		5	6	7	8	9	10	11				4																	
7	16	(h) Barnsley	W 7-1	Price 5, Edmondson, Bennett	7,000	1	2	3	4	5	6	7	8	9	10	11																					
8	23	(a) Leicester F	L 0-4		5,000	1	2	3	4	5	6	7	8	9	10	11																					
9	Nov 6	(a) Bradford C	L 0-3		5,000	1	2	3	4	5	6	7		9	10						8	11															
10	13	(h) Huddersfield T	D 0-0		3,000	1	4	3	5		6	7	8	9	10							11	2														
11	20	(a) Grimsby T	D 0-0		4,000	1	4	3	5		6	7	9		10	11							2	8													
12	27	(h) Notts C	L 0-4		3,000	1	4	3	5		6	7			10	11						9	2	8													
13	Dec 4	(h) Derby C	W 4-1	Edmondson 3, Walden	1,000		4	3		5	6	7		9	10	11		1					2	8													
14	11	(a) Sheffield W	D 0-0		3,000		4	3	8	5	6	7		9	10	11		1					2														
15	18	(h) Bradford	D 1-1	Price	4,000		4	3		5	6	7	8	9	10	11		1					2														
16	25	(a) Lincoln C	L 0-2		6,000		4	3		5	6	7	8	9				1					2	10	11												
17	27	(h) Sheffield U	L 2-3	Bennett, Bainbridge	6,000		5	3			6	7	8	9	4			1						10	11	2											
18	Jan 1	(a) Hull C	W 3-0	Foley, Edmondson, Price (pen)	3,000			3	4	5	6	7	8	9	10			1					2		11												
19	8	(h) Nottingham F	W 1-0	Bainbridge	5,000		4	3		5	6	7	8	9	10			1					2		11												
20	15	(a) Barnsley	L 1-2	Lamph	4,000		5	3	4		6	7	8	9	10			1					2		11												
21	22	(h) Leicester F	W 1-0	Bainbridge	4,000		4	3	5	8	6	7		9	10			1					2		11												
22	29	(a) Sheffield U	L 1-4	Goodwin (pen)	8,000		4	3	5		6	7	9		10			1				11	2				8										
23	Feb 5	(h) Bradford C	L 0-1		10,000		8	3	4	5	6	7	10					1					2					9	11								
24	12	(a) Huddersfield T	L 1-5	Stephenson	6,000			3	8	5	6	7						1						8				9	11	2	10						
25	19	(h) Grimsby T	W 3-1	Peart, Sharpe, Stephenson	3,000			3		5	6	7						1					2	8				9			10	4	11				
26	Apr 21	(a) Notts C	D 1-1	Price	3,000			3		5	6	7			9			1					2								10	4		8	11		
FINAL LEAGUE POSITION: 10th in Midland Section Principal Tournament					Appearances	11	22	26	16	19	26	26	18	19	22	13	1	15	1	2	1	4	15	7	6	1	1	3	2	1	3	2	1	1	1		
					Goals		1		1	1	1	1	4	10	12							1			3			1			2		1				

No	Date	Opponent	Result	Scorers	Att	Bradley	Law	Affleck	Lamph	Hampson J	Foley	Walden	Bennett	Edmondson	Price	Croot	Wrigglesworth	Walker	Dowling	Wainwright AH	Cowen	Goodwin	Copeland	Booth	Bainbridge	Dunn	Malcolm	Peart JG	Hughes	Lavery	Stephenson C	Hewison	Sharpe	Robinson S	Jennings	Wilson W	Williamson
27	Mar 4	(a) Rochdale	W 1-0	Wilson	4,000			3		5	6	7			4			1					2	8					11					10		9	
28	11	(h) Bradford	W 3-2	Stephenson 3	4,000			3		5	6	7			8			1					2					9			10	4				11	
29	18	(a) Huddersfield T	D 1-1	Price	5,000			3		5	6	7			8			1					2					9			10	4				11	
30	25	(h) Bradford C	L 0-1		3,000			3		5	6	7			8			1					2					9			10	4				11	
31	Apr 1	(a) Barnsley	W 6-4	Peart 4, Walden, Stephenson	3,000			3		5	6	7			8			1					2					9			10	4				11	
32	8	(h) Rochdale	W 3-1	Wilson 2, Peart	3,000			3		5	6	7			8			1					2					9			10	4				11	
33	15	(a) Bradford	W 1-0	Price	4,000			3		5	6	7			8			1					2					9			10	4				11	
34	22	(h) Huddersfield T	L 1-2	Stephenson	5,000			3			6	7			10			1					2								8	4	11				5
35	24	(h) Barnsley	W 1-0	Stephenson	5,000			3			6	7			5			1					2						11		8	4		10		9	
36	29	(a) Bradford C	W 4-2	Price, Wilson, Sherwin, Peart (pen)	8,000			3			6	7			10			1					2					9			8	4				11	
FINAL LEAGUE POSITION: 1st in Midland Section Subsidiary Tournament (Northern Division)					Appearances			10		7	10	10			10			10					10	1				7	2		9	9	1	2		9	1
					Goals							1			3													6			6					4	

Davison played number-9 in Match 34; Sherwin played number-5 in Match 36 and scored one goal.

1916-17

Manager: Herbert Chapman

No.	Month	Match	Result	Scorers	Att.	Walker	Copeland	Hudson	Hewison	Hampson J	Thorpe	McCreadie	Stephenson C	Peart	Price	Stephenson J	Sherwin	Mayson	Walden	Pattison	Toms	James	Clipstone	Kaye	Feathers	Hampson, Wm	Barnshaw	Trotter	Dawson	Moore	Robinson A	Robinson S	Hampson T	Rose	Cawley	Hudspeth
1	Sep	2 (h) Leicester F	D 2-2	Price 2	3,000	1	2	3	4	5	6	7	8	9	10	11																				
2		9 (a) Grimsby T	W 6-1	Peart 2, C.Stephenson, Thorpe, Mayson, Price	4,000	1		3	2	5	6		7	9	10	8	4	11																		
3		16 (h) Notts C	W 5-0	C.Stephenson 3, Mayson, Peart	3,000	1		3	2	5	4		8	9	10	7	6	11																		
4		23 (a) Rotherham C	W 5-0	Price 4, Peart	5,000	1	2	3	6	5			8	9	10	7	4	11																		
5		30 (h) Huddersfield T	W 1-0	Peart	8,000	1	2	3	6	5			8	9	10		4	11	7																	
6	Oct	7 (a) Lincoln C	W 5-2	Peart 3, Pattinson, C.Stephenson	4,000	1	2		3	5			8	9	6	7	4	10		11																
7		14 (h) Sheffield W	W 1-0	C.Stephenson	5,000	1		3	2	5	6		8	9		11	4	10	7																	
8		21 (a) Bradford	W 3-1	Price 2, Peart	8,000	1		3	2	5	6		8	9	10	7	4	11																		
9		28 (h) Birmingham	D 1-1	Peart	6,000	1		3	2	5	6		8	9	10	7	4	11																		
10	Nov	4 (a) Hull C	D 1-1	C.Stephenson	4,000	1	2	3	11	5	6		8		10	7	4				9															
11		11 (h) Nottingham F	W 3-1	Peart, Sherwin, C.Stephenson	5,000	1	2	3	6	5			8	9	10	7	4					11														
12		18 (a) Barnsley	L 1-4	Peart	2,000	1	2		4		6			9	8		5	11			10		3	7												
13		25 (a) Chesterfield	W 4-3	Peart 2, C.Stephenson 2	4,000	1	2	3	4		6		8	9	10	7	5	11																		
14	Dec	2 (h) Sheffield U	W 2-0	Price, C.Stephenson	5,000	1	2		3	5	6		8	9	10	7		11							4											
15		9 (a) Leicester F	W 4-1	Price 3, Thorpe	3,000	1	2		4		6		8	9	10	7	5	11								3										
16		16 (h) Grimsby T	W 1-0	Price	3,000	1	2		4		6		8	9	10	7	5	11								3										
17		23 (a) Notts C	L 0-1		500	1	2		4		6		8	9	10	7	5	11								3										
18		25 (h) Bradford C	W 1-0	Mayson (pen)	10,000	1	2		4				8	9		7	5	10								3	6	11								
19		26 (a) Bradford C	W 3-0	J.Stephenson, Peart, Price	11,000	1	2		4		6		8	9	10	7	5	11								3										
20		30 (h) Rotherham C	W 2-0	Mayson, Hewison	4,000	1	2		6	5			8	9	10	7	4	11								3										
21	Jan	6 (a) Huddersfield T	D 1-1	Trotter	7,000	1	2				4			9		7	5	11								3		10	6	8						
22		13 (h) Lincoln C	W 3-1	Peart, Price, Moore	2,000	1	2				4			9	10	7	5	11								3			6	8						
23		20 (a) Sheffield W	D 2-2	J.Stephenson, Peart	5,000		2				4		8	9		7	5	11								3			6	10	1					
24		27 (h) Bradford	D 0-0		6,000		2		4		6		8	9			5	11								3				10	1	7				
25	Feb	3 (a) Birmingham	D 1-1	Peart	15,000		2		4		6			9	10	7	5	11								3				8	1					
26		10 (h) Hull C	D 1-1	Peart	2,000		2				6			9	10	7	5	11								3		8	4		1					
27		17 (a) Nottingham F	D 3-3	Moore, Peart 2	3,000		2		4		6			9	10	7	5									3				8	1	11				
28		24 (h) Barnsley	W 3-0	Peart 2, C.Stephenson	6,000		2				6		8	9	4	7	5	11								3				10	1					
29	Mar	3 (h) Chesterfield	W 1-0	Peart	4,000		2		4		6		8	9	10	7	5	11								3							1			
30		10 (a) Sheffield U	D 2-2	Price, Peart	6,000				4	2	6		8	9	10	7	5	11								3							1			
FINAL LEAGUE POSITION: 1st in Midland Section Principal Tournament					Appearances	22	24	11	25	14	24	1	24	29	25	27	28	26	2	1	2	1	1	1	1	16	1	3	4	7	6	2	2			
					Goals				1		2		12	25	17	2	1	4		1								1		2						

No.	Month	Match	Result	Scorers	Att.	Walker	Copeland	Hudson	Hewison	Hampson J	Thorpe	McCreadie	Stephenson C	Peart	Price	Stephenson J	Sherwin	Mayson	Walden	Pattison	Toms	James	Clipstone	Kaye	Feathers	Hampson, Wm	Barnshaw	Trotter	Dawson	Moore	Robinson A	Robinson S	Hampson T	Rose	Cawley	Hudspeth
31	Mar	17 (a) Bradford	D 1-1	Peart	6,000				4		6		8	9		7	5						2			3				10		11	1			
32		24 (h) Huddersfield T	L 0-2		4,000				4		6		8	9	10	7	5	11					2			3							1			
33		31 (h) Bradford C	D 1-1	Price (pen)	4,000				4		6		8	9	10	7	5						2			3				11			1			
34	Apr	7 (h) Bradford	L 0-2		3,000				4				8		10	7	5	11								3				9			1	2	6	
35		9 (a) Huddersfield T	W 1-0	C.Stephenson	3,000				4				8		9	7	5	10								3				11			1		6	2
36		21 (a) Bradford C	W 5-1	Moore 3, Peart, C.Stephenson	3,000				2		6		8	9	4	7	5	11								3				10			1			
FINAL LEAGUE POSITION: 7th in Midland Section Subsidiary Tournament					Appearances				6		4		6	4	5	6	6	4					3			6				5		1	6	2	2	1
					Goals								2	2	1															3						

1917-18

Manager: Herbert Chapman

No.	Date	Opponent	Result	Scorers	Att.	Walker	Hewison	Hampson, Wm	Sherwin	Hampson J	Lamph	Barrett	Stephenson C	Peart JG	Cawley	Robinson S	Price	Robinson A	Baines	Hampson T	Arkle	Goodwin	Stephenson J	Moore	Grant	Kirton	Hampson E	Chard	Millership	Buchan	Spratt	Croot	Rutherford W	Hampson, Walker	Wilson A	Kettle	Hibbert
1	Sep 1	(a) Sheffield W	W 1-0	Peart	8,000	1	2	3	4	5	6	7	8	9	10	11																					
2	8	(h) Sheffield W	W 5-0	Price 2, C.Stephenson, Peart, Barrett	6,000	1	2	3	4	5	6	7	8	9		11	10																				
3	15	(a) Bradford C	L 2-3	Wm.Hampson, C.Stephenson	4,000		2	3	4	5	6	7	8	9		11	10	1																			
4	22	(h) Bradford C	W 4-0	Peart, Price 3	4,000		4	3	5		6	7	8	9		11	10	1	2																		
5	29	(a) Rotherham C	W 3-0	Peart, C.Stephenson, Sherwin	5,000		4	2	5		6	7	8	9		11	10		3	1																	
6	Oct 6	(h) Rotherham C	W 6-0	Price 2, Peart 2, Goodwin, Hewison	5,000		4	2	5		6		8	9			10		3	1	7	11															
7	13	(h) Lincoln C	W 3-0	Peart, C.Stephenson, S.Robinson	4,000		4	2	5		6		8	9		7	10		3	1		11															
8	20	(a) Lincoln C	W 4-0	Peart, Hewison, J.Stephenson, Moore	3,000		6	3	5		4		8	9			10		2	1			7	11													
9	27	(h) Grimsby T	D 2-2	Peart 2	3,000	1	4	2	5		6			9		11	10		3						7	8											
10	Nov 3	(a) Grimsby T	W 4-0	S.Robinson, Price 2, Sherwin	1,500		4	2	5		6			9	8	11	10		3	1							7										
11	10	(h) Birmingham	W 1-0	Peart	5,000		4	2	5	7	6		8	9			10		3	1		11															
12	17	(a) Birmingham	L 1-3	Cawley	26,000		4	2	5		6		8	9	7		10		3	1		11															
13	24	(h) Notts C	W 2-0	Grant, C.Stephenson	2,000		4	2	5		6		8	9	7		10		3	1					11												
14	Dec 1	(a) Notts C	W 4-2	Peart 2, Price, Sherwin	3,000		4	2	5	8	6			9	7		10		3	1								11									
15	8	(a) Barnsley	W 4-3	Peart 2, J.Hampson, Cawley	1,400		4	2	5	8	6			9	7		10		3	1							11										
16	15	(h) Barnsley	W 2-1	Peart, Hewison	3,500		4	2	5		6		8	9	7		10		3	1					11												
17	25	(h) Huddersfield T	W 3-0	Price, Sherwin (pen), Hewison	5,000		4	2	5	11	6		8	9	7		10			1									3								
18	26	(a) Huddersfield T	W 3-1	C.Stephenson, Peart, Price	4,000		4	2	5	3	6		8	9	7		10			1		11															
19	Jan 5	(a) Hull C	W 2-0	Price, C.Stephenson	3,000		4	2	5		6		8	9	7		10			1					11				3								
20	12	(h) Hull C	L 1-3	Price	2,000		4	3	5	11	6		8	9	7		10			1									2								
21	19	(a) Leicester F	W 4-2	Sherwin, C.Stephenson, Cawley 2	3,000		4	3	5	11	6		8	9	7		10			1									2								
22	26	(h) Leicester F	W 4-0	Price, Peart, Goodwin, C.Stephenson	5,000		4	3	5	6			8	9	7		10			1		11							2								
23	Feb 2	(h) Nottingham F	W 2-0	Wightman (og), Buchan	3,000		4	3	5	6			8	9			10			1		11							2	7							
24	9	(a) Nottingham F	W 1-0	Peart	3,000		4	3	5	11	6		8	9	7		10			1									2								
25	16	(h) Bradford	W 2-1	Cawley, C.Stephenson	7,500		4	3	5	11	6		8	9	7		10			1									2								
26	23	(a) Bradford	W 2-0	Sherwin (pen), Peart	7,500		4	3	5	11	6		8	9	7		10			1									2								
27	Mar 2	(a) Sheffield U	L 1-2	Hewison	18,000		4	3	5		6		8	9	7		10			1									2		11						
28	9	(h) Sheffield U	W 2-0	Cawley, C.Stephenson	15,000		4	3	5	11	6		8	9	7		10			1									2								
FINAL LEAGUE POSITION: 1st in Midland Section Principal Tournament					Appearances	3	28	28	28	16	26	5	24	28	18	8	27	2	13	23	1	7	1	1	4	1	2	1	11	1	1						
					Goals		5	1	6	1		1	11	20	6	2	15					2	1	1	1					1							

1 own-goal

No.	Date	Opponent	Result	Scorers	Att.	Walker	Hewison	Hampson, Wm	Sherwin	Hampson J	Lamph	Barrett	Stephenson C	Peart JG	Cawley	Robinson S	Price	Robinson A	Baines	Hampson T	Arkle	Goodwin	Stephenson J	Moore	Grant	Kirton	Hampson E	Chard	Millership	Buchan	Spratt	Croot	Rutherford W	Hampson, Walker	Wilson A	Kettle	Hibbert
29	Mar 16	(a) Huddersfield T	L 2-4	Price, C.Stephenson	6,500		4	3	5	9	6		8		7		10			1									2			11					
30	23	(h) Huddersfield T	W 1-0	Cawley	6,000		4	3	5	11	6		8		7		10			1									2				9				
31	30	(h) Bradford	W 3-1	Price 2, C.Stephenson	1,000		4	3	5	9	6		8		7		10			1							11		2								
32	Apr 6	(a) Bradford	W 2-1	Wilson 2	7,000		4	3	5		6		8		7		10			1														2	9	11	
33	13	(h) Bradford C	D 0-0		3,000		4	2	5		6	11	8		7		10			1														3	9		
34	20	(a) Bradford C	D 0-0		3,000		4	2	5		6	11	8	9	7		10			1														3			
FINAL LEAGUE POSITION: 5th in Midland Section Subsidiary Tournament					Appearances		6	6	6	3	6	2	6	1	6		6			6							1		3			1	1	3	2	1	
					Goals								2		1		3																		2		

No.	Date	Opponent	Result	Scorers	Att.	Walker	Hewison	Hampson, Wm	Sherwin	Hampson J	Lamph	Barrett	Stephenson C	Peart JG	Cawley	Robinson S	Price	Robinson A	Baines	Hampson T	Arkle	Goodwin	Stephenson J	Moore	Grant	Kirton	Hampson E	Chard	Millership	Buchan	Spratt	Croot	Rutherford W	Hampson, Walker	Wilson A	Kettle	Hibbert
35	May 4	(h) Stoke	W 2-0	Hibbert, Peart	15,000		4	3	5		6			9	8		10			1		7							2								11
36	11	(a) Stoke	D 0-1		15,000		4	3	5		6			9	8		10			1		7							2								11
LEAGUE CHAMPIONSHIP PLAY-OFF: Leeds City won 2-1 on aggregate					Appearances		2	2	2		2			2	2		2			2		2							2								2
					Goals									1																							1

1918-19

Manager: Herbert Chapman

No.	Date	Opponents	Result	Scorers	Att.	Walker	Millership	Hampson, Wm	McLachlan	Sherwin	Lamph	Hampson E	Hibbert	Peart JG	Hampson J	Cawley	Cook	Price	Robinson S	Hugall	Scott	Hewison	Copeland	Smelt	McLeod	Bavin	Stephenson C	Hall	Moore	Linfoot	Gough	Lounds	Cartwright	Rutherford A	Voysey	Currie	Bainbridge
1	Sep 7	(h) Notts C	W 4-1	Peart, Cawley 2, Hibbert	5,000	1	2	3	4	5	6	7	8	9	10	11																					
2	14	(a) Notts C	L 2-5	Price, Peart	7,000		2	3		5	4	11	8	9	6	7	1	10																			
3	21	(h) Birmingham	W 3-1	Hibbert, Cawley, E.Hampson	3,000		2	3		5	6	11	9		4	7	1	10	8																		
4	28	(a) Birmingham	L 2-4	Hibbert, Peart	14,000		2	3		5	6	11	8	9	4	7	1	10																			
5	Oct 5	(h) Rotherham C	W 2-1	Price, Hibbert (pen)	2,000		2	3		5	6		8	9	11	7	1	10				4															
6	12	(a) Rotherham C	W 3-0	Sherwin, McLeod, Peart	7,000			3		5				9	4	7	1	10	11				2	6	8												
7	19	(a) Lincoln C	L 0-1		4,000			3		5	6		8	9	2	7	1	10	11							4											
8	26	(h) Lincoln C	W 2-0	C.Stephenson 2	6,000	1		3		5	6		11	9	4	7		10					2				8										
9	Nov 2	(a) Grimsby T	W 2-0	C.Stephenson, Peart	2,000	1	2	3	6	5			11	9	4	7		10									8										
10	9	(h) Grimsby T	W 3-1	Hibbert (pen), Price, Peart	4,000	1	2	3		5	6		11	9	4	7		10									8										
11	16	(a) Bradford C	L 1-3	Peart	8,000		2	3	4	5	6		10	9	11	7	1								8												
12	23	(h) Bradford C	W 2-1	J.Hampson 2	7,500		2	3	4	5	6			9	11	7				1								8	10								
13	30	(a) Sheffield W	W 2-0	Hall, Peart	10,000	1	2	3	6	5	4		10	9	11										7			8									
14	Dec 7	(h) Sheffield W	D 1-1	Hall	9,000		2	3	4	5	6		10	9	11	7	1											8									
15	14	(h) Hull C	D 0-0		5,000		3		6	5			11	9	4		1	10					2					8		7							
16	21	(a) Hull C	L 1-2	Peart	4,500		2	3	6	5	4		11	9			1	10										8		7							
17	25	(h) Huddersfield T	D 1-1	Price (pen)	5,000		3	2	6	5	4			9	11			10							7			8			1						
18	26	(a) Huddersfield T	W 1-0	Price (pen)	10,000		3	2	6	5	4			9	11			10							7			8			1						
19	28	(h) Coventry C	L 0-1		6,000		2	3		5	4			9	6		1	10			11				7			8									
20	Jan 11	(h) Barnsley	W 4-0	Hall, Price, C.Stephenson 2	6,000	1	2	3	6	5	4			9	11			10									8	7									
21	18	(a) Barnsley	W 1-0	Hall	7,000	1	2	3	6		4			9	5	11		10									8	7									
22	25	(h) Leicester F	W 4-2	C.Stephenson, Price 2, Peart	3,000	1	2	3	6		4			9	5			10									8	7				11					
23	Feb 1	(a) Leicester F	D 0-0		4,000	1	2	3			4			9	5	10		6									8	7				11					
24	8	(a) Nottingham F	W 2-0	C.Stephenson, Peart	10,000	1	2	3	6		4			9	5			10									8	7					11				
25	15	(h) Nottingham F	L 0-4		11,000	1	2	3	4		6			9				10					5				8	7					11				
26	22	(a) Bradford	W 3-1	Peart, C.Stephenson, Hall	5,000	1	2	3	6		4			9				10									8	7					11	5			
27	Mar 1	(h) Bradford	L 2-5	Hall, C.Stephenson	10,000	1	2	3			4			9	5			10									8	7					11		6		
28	8	(h) Sheffield U	W 2-1	Peart, Hall	8,000	1	2	3			4			9	11			10									8	7						5		6	
29	15	(a) Sheffield U	L 0-1		22,000	1	2	3	6		4			9	11										10		8	7						5			
30	Apr 22	(a) Coventry C	W 3-1	Peart, McLeod, Hall (pen)	9,000	1	2		6		4			9	5										10			8				7					11
FINAL LEAGUE POSITION: 4th in Midland Section Principal Tournament					Appearances	16	27	28	18	20	27	4	14	29	27	15	11	23	3	1	1	1	4	1	8	1	13	19	1	2	2	3	4	3	1	1	1
					Goals					1		1	4	14	2	2		8							2		9	7									

Roberts played number-3 in Match 30.

No.	Date	Opponents	Result	Scorers	Att.	Walker	Millership	Hampson, Wm	McLachlan	Sherwin	Lamph	Hampson E	Hibbert	Peart JG	Hampson J	Cawley	Cook	Price	Robinson S	Hugall	Scott	Hewison	Copeland	Smelt	McLeod	Bavin	Stephenson C	Hall	Moore	Linfoot	Gough	Lounds	Cartwright	Rutherford A	Voysey	Currie	Bainbridge
31	Mar 22	(h) Huddersfield T	W 3-0	Peart 2, McLeod	9,000	1	2	3	6		4			9	11										10		8			5		7					
32	29	(a) Huddersfield T	L 0-1		8,000	1	2	3	6		4			9	11										10		8	7		5							
33	Apr 5	(a) Bradford	L 0-5		12,000		2	3	6		4			9	5												8	10									11
34	12	(h) Bradford	W 3-1	McLeod, J.Stephenson, Hall	6,000	1	2	3	6						5										9		8	10		4							11
35	19	(a) Bradford C	L 1-2	Bainbridge	16,000	1	2		6		4			9	3										10		8			5		7					11
36	26	(h) Bradford C	W 3-0	McLeod 2, Bainbridge	7,000		2	3	6		4				5										10		8					7					11
FINAL LEAGUE POSITION: 3rd in Midland Section Subsidiary Tournament					Appearances	4	6	5	6		5			4	6										5		6	3		4		3					4
					Goals									2											4			1									2

Sutcliffe played number-1 in Matches 33 & 36; J.Stephenson played number-7 in Matches 33 & 34 and scored one goal; Edmondson played number-9 in Match 36.

1919-20

Manager: Herbert Chapman

No.	Date	Opponents	Result	Scorers	Att.	Walker	Millership	Hampson	Lamph	Hopkins	Foley	Lounds	Price	Short	McLeod	Bainbridge	Edmondson	Affleck	Kirton	Goodwin
1	Aug 30	(a) Blackpool	L 2-4	McLeod 2	10,000	1	2	3	4	5	6	7	8	9	10	11				
2	Sep 3	(h) Coventry C	W 3-0	McLeod 2, Bainbridge	8,000	1	2	3	4	5	6	7	8	9	10	11				
3	6	(h) Blackpool	W 1-0	Edmondson	10,000	1	2	3	4	5	6	7		8	10	11	9			
4	11	(a) Coventry C	W 4-0	McLeod 2, Edmondson, Bainbridge	12,000	1	2	3	4	5		7	6	8	10	11	9			
5	13	(h) Hull C	L 1-2	Bainbridge	10,000	1	2	3	4	5		7	6	8	10	11	9			
6	20	(a) Hull C	D 1-1	Edmondson	8,000	1	2	3	4	5	6	7	8		10	11	9			
7	27	(h) Wolves	D 1-1	Price (pen)	12,000	1	2		4	5	6	7	8		10	11	9	3		
8	Oct 4	(a) Wolves	W 4-2	Lamph, McLeod 3	15,000	1	2	5	4			7	6		10		9	3	8	11
Remaining fixtures undertaken by Port Vale after Leeds City were expelled from the Football League.					Appearances	8	8	7	8	7	5	8	7	5	8	7	6	2	1	1
					Goals				1				1		9	3	3			

Leeds City

League Record Against Other Clubs 1905-06 to 1919-20

		HOME					*AWAY*					
	P	W	D	L	F	A	W	D	L	F	A	Pts
ARSENAL	4	0	2	0	2	2	0	0	2	0	3	2
BARNSLEY	20	6	2	2	16	15	3	1	6	14	22	21
BIRMINGHAM	14	5	2	0	14	4	2	1	4	13	16	17
BLACKPOOL	22	7	2	2	16	9	4	1	6	16	18	25
BOLTON WANDERERS	4	1	0	1	2	2	0	0	2	0	5	2
BRADFORD	12	3	0	3	12	9	2	1	3	7	10	11
BRADFORD CITY	6	0	1	2	1	4	0	1	2	2	8	2
BRISTOL CITY	10	2	3	0	7	4	0	2	3	3	9	9
BURNLEY	16	2	4	2	10	11	1	2	5	10	19	12
BURY	6	3	0	0	8	4	0	3	0	2	2	9
BURTON UNITED	4	2	0	0	5	2	1	1	0	3	1	7
CHELSEA	8	0	3	1	3	4	0	0	4	3	14	3
CHESTERFIELD	8	3	1	0	7	0	1	0	3	5	7	9
CLAPTON ORIENT	20	6	2	2	20	10	1	4	5	5	11	20
COVENTRY CITY	2	1	0	0	3	0	1	0	0	4	0	4
DERBY COUNTY	12	3	0	3	15	15	1	1	4	8	20	9
FULHAM	16	3	1	4	11	11	2	0	6	6	21	11
GAINSBOROUGH TRINITY	14	3	3	1	9	2	1	1	5	6	13	12
GLOSSOP	20	7	0	3	20	11	3	2	5	12	12	22
GRIMSBY TOWN	18	7	0	2	29	11	4	1	4	13	16	23
HUDDERSFIELD TOWN	10	4	0	1	13	6	1	1	3	5	7	11
HULL CITY	22	5	3	3	17	13	1	3	7	14	25	18
LEICESTER FOSSE	18	5	3	1	24	11	1	3	5	12	25	18
LINCOLN CITY	16	4	3	1	16	8	2	4	2	8	12	19
MANCHESTER CITY	2	0	0	1	1	3	0	0	1	0	3	0
MANCHESTER UNITED	2	0	0	1	1	3	1	0	0	3	0	2
NOTTINGHAM FOREST	10	4	0	1	17	5	1	0	4	5	11	10
NOTTS COUNTY	2	0	0	1	2	4	0	0	1	0	4	0
OLDHAM ATHLETIC	6	1	0	2	7	7	0	0	3	3	12	2
PORT VALE	4	2	0	0	5	1	1	0	1	2	3	6
PRESTON NORTH END	4	1	1	0	5	1	0	0	2	2	5	3
STOCKPORT COUNTY	20	6	2	2	25	11	1	3	6	13	21	19
STOKE	2	0	0	1	0	1	0	0	1	1	2	0
TOTTENHAM HOTSPUR	2	1	0	0	1	0	0	0	1	0	3	2
WEST BROMWICH ALBION	12	3	1	2	8	7	0	0	6	3	15	7
WOLVERHAMPTON WANDERERS	20	6	3	1	23	10	2	1	7	14	30	20
TOTALS	388	106	42	46	375	221	38	37	119	217	405	367

Leeds City Who's Who

This section contains biographies of every player who has made a first-team appearance for Leeds City in their days as a League club. Each entry shows (where known) the player's position, date and place of birth, debut game, height, weight and appearance record. The year immediately following height and weight details are when those details were recorded.

ACKERLEY, George *1910*

Inside-forward. Born: Liverpool.
Debut v Barnsley (a) Division Two, 17 March 1910, D 1-1.
Liverpool (amateur), Leeds City March 1910.
League: App 2, Gls 0.

AFFLECK, George *1909-1919*

Full-back. Born: Auchendinney, Midlothian, Scotland, 8 July 1888.
Debut v Burnley (h) Division Two, 6 November 1909, W 1-0.

5ft 9in, 11st 6lb (1909).
Pennicuik, Leeds City June 1909, Grimsby Town October 1919, Coach to club in Rotterdam, Holland, July 1925.
League: App 182, Gls 1; FA Cup: App 9, Gls 0.

ALLAN, John *1912-1914*

Wing-half. Born: Newcastle-upon-Tyne, 11 May 1890.
Debut v Fulham (a) Division Two, 7 September 1912, L 0-4.
5ft 7½in, 11st 2lb (1910).
Benwell St James, Bentwick Mission, Newcastle North End, Bedligton United, Carlisle United, Everton cs 1909, Leeds City July 1912, Rochdale cs 1913, Coventry City May 1914, Walsall 1920.
League: App 14, Gls 0; FA Cup: App 1, Gls 0.
Known as Jack.

ASTILL, Thomas *1908-1911*

Inside-left. Born: Sheffield.
Debut v Bradford (a) Division Two, 26 March 1910, L 2-4.
Sheffield Douglas, Leeds City December 1908, Doncaster Rovers cs 1911.
League: App 1, Gls 0.

BAINBRIDGE, Simpson *1912-1919*

Outside-right. Born: Silksworth, County Durham, 3 April 1895.
Died: November 1988.
Debut v Bristol City (h) Division Two, 7 December 1912, D 1-1.
5ft 9in, 10st 2lb (1913).
Seaton Delaval, Leeds City November 1912, Preston North End October 1919, South Shields 1920-21, Aberdeen 1921-22, Wheatley Hill Alliance, Shildon Athletic.
League: App 64, Gls 15; FA Cup: App 5, Gls 0.

BATES, William E. *1907-1909*

Right-back. Born: Kirkheaton, Yorkshire, 5 March 1884. Died: Belfast, 17 January 1957.
Debut v Stockport County (h) Division Two, 17 April 1908, W 3-0.
5ft 7½in, 11st 6lb (1907).
Bolton Wanderers, Leeds City July 1907, Yorkshire County Cricketer 1907-1913, Glamorgan 1921-31.
League: App 15, Gls 0.
Son of William Bates, the Yorkshire and England cricket all-rounder. Father of Ted Bates, the Southampton inside-forward and manager.

BEREN, Hugh G. *1909-1910*

Right-half. Born: Scotland, *c.*1891.
Debut v Fulham (a) Division Two, 30 October 1909, L 1-5.
5ft 8in, 12st 7lb (1909).
Musselburgh, Leeds City June 1909.
League: App 3, Gls 0.
Occasionally listed as Berens

BLACKMAN, Frederick E. *1914-1919*

Right-back. Born: Brixton, London, 1889.
Debut v Hull City (a) Division Two, 21 February 1914, L 0-1.
5ft 10in, 12st 7lb (1914).
Woolwich Arsenal, Hastings and St Leonards, Brighton and Hove Albion January 1910, Huddersfield Town May 1911, Leeds City February 1914 (£1,000), Queen's Park Rangers 1919. Retired 1922.
League: App 44, Gls 0; FA Cup: App 2, Gls 0.
Won a Southern League championship medal with Brighton in 1910 and figured in their shock 1-0 win over Football League champions Aston Villa in the FA Charity Shield in the same year. He also played in the Southern League's 3-2 win over the Football League at White Hart Lane on 14 November 1910.

BOWMAN, Adam *1908-1909*

Centre-forward. Born: Forfar, Angus.
Debut v Tottenham Hotspur (h) Division Two, 5 September 1908, W 1-0.
5ft 11in, 12st 6lb (1908).
St Johnstone, East Stirling, Everton December 1901, Blackburn Rovers March 1903, Brentford May 1907, Leeds City May 1908, Brentford cs 1909, Portsmouth November 1909, Leith Athletic, Accrington Stanley March 1912.
League: App 15, Gls 6; FA Cup: App 1, Gls 1.

BRIDGETT, Harold *1909-1913*

Outside-left. Born: Stoke-on-Trent, c.1879.
Debut v Lincoln City (a) Division Two, 28 December 1909, D 0-0.
5ft 7½in, 10st 10lb (1909).
Stoke, Leeds City May 1909.
League: App 13, Gls 2; FA Cup: App 1, Gls 0.

BROMAGE, Harry *1905-1911*

Goalkeeper. Born: Derby.
Debut v Bradford City (a) Division

Two, 2 September 1905, L 0-1.
5ft 10in, 12st 8lb (1905).
Derby Constitutional, Derby County October 1898, Burton United 1901, Leeds City August 1905, Doncaster Rovers 1911, Bentley Colliery cs 1913.
League: App 143, Gls 0; FA Cup: App 9, Gls 0.
He left Leeds for Doncaster where his brother, Billy, a former Sheffield United and Gainsborough Trinity winger, was captain.

BROUGHTON, Tom W. *1912-1913*

Right-half.
Debut v Blackpool (a) Division Two, 1 January 1912, W 3-0.
Grangetown, Leeds City October 1912.
League: App 4, Gls 0.

BURNETT, James *1908-1910*

Inside-forward. Born: Scotland.
Debut v Barnsley (h) Division Two, 14 September 1908, W 2-0.
5ft 10in, 12st (1904).
Portsmouth 1902, Dundee cs 1904, Grimsby Town cs 1905, Brighton and Hove Albion May 1907, Leeds City May 1908. Retired cs 1910.
League: App 20, Gls 2; FA Cup: App 4, Gls 1.

CAMPBELL, Alex *1911*

Full-back. Born: Inverness, c.1885.
Debut v Nottingham Forest (h) Division Two, 30 December 1911, W 3-1.
5ft 10in, 12st (1906).
Inverness Clachnacuddin, Middlesbrough August 1906, Leeds City December 1911.
League: App 1, Gls 0.

CLARK, Andy *1906-1907*

Left-back. Born: Leith, Midlothian, 1881.
Debut v Bradford City (h) Division Two, 1 September 1906, D 1-1.
5ft 7in, 13st (1903).
Hamilton Academical, Buckhaven United, Heart of Midlothian August 1899, Stoke May 1901, Plymouth Argyle 1903, Leeds City May 1906.
League: App 24, Gls 0.
He made his League debut for Hearts v Rangers on 2 September 1899. He lost his place in 1901 because of disciplinary problems and was sold to Stoke.

CLARKIN, John *1911-1912*

Inside-forward. Born: Ireland.
Debut v Gainsborough Trinity (a) Division Two, 26 December 1911, L 1-2.
5ft 7in, 10st 5lb (1911).
Shelbourne, Leeds City May 1911, Belfast Celtic cs 1912.
League: App 1, Gls 0.

CLAY, William *1911-1912*

Full-back. Born: Ireland, 1882.

Debut v Mexborough (h) FA Cup (second preliminary round) 6 November 1905, W 3-1.
5ft 7½in, 10st 3lb (1905).
Belfast Celtic, Sheffield United 1903-04, Belfast Celtic, Leeds City May 1911, Belfast Celtic cs 1912.
FA Cup: App 1, Gls 0.
Represented the Irish Leaguev Football League in his first spell with Belfast Celtic, playing in the 3-2 defeat in Belfast on 11 October 1902. He was reserve to future Sheffield United teammate Peter Boyle for the full internationals against Scotland and Wales in 1902-03.

COPELAND, Charles W. *1912-1919*

Right-back. Born: Grangetown, near Middlesbrough.
Debut v Glossop (h) Division Two, 9 November 1912, W 4-0.
5ft 8½in, 12st 1lb (1913).
South Bank, Leeds City August 1912, Coventry City September 1919, Merthyr Town 1920.
League: App 44, Gls 0-; FA Cup: App 1, Gls 0.
See *Leeds City Scandal* section

COWEN, Robert W. *1914-1915*

Inside-right. Born: Milkwell, Newcastle-upon-Tyne.
Debut v Stockport County (a) Division Two, 5 September 1914, L 1-3.
5ft 10½in, 11st 9lb (1914).
Spen Black and White, Leeds City April 1914, Spen Black and White cs 1918.
League: App 2, Gls 0.

CREIGHTON, Alec *1910-1912*

Left-back. Born: Scotland.
Debut v Blackpool (a) Division Two, 3 September 1910, L 1-2.
5ft 7½in, 11st 6lb (1910).
Distillery, Leeds City August 1910, Glenavon cs 1912.
League: App 66, Gls 0; FA Cup: App 3, Gls 0.

CROOT, Fred R. *1907-1919*

Outside-left. Born: Rushden, Northamptonshire, Spring 1886.
Died: Rushden, 5 July 1958.
Debut v Glossop (h) Division Two, 2 September 1907, W 2-1.
5ft 7in, 12st 2lb (1907).
Wellingborough, Sheffield United 1905, Leeds City May 1907, Clydebank 1919.
League: App 218, Gls 38; FA Cup: App 9, Gls 0.

CUBBERLEY, Stan *1906-1913*

Wing-half. Born: London.
Debut v West Bromwich Albion (a) Division Two, 8 September 1906, L 0-5.
5ft 8in, 11st 3lb (1906).
Cheshunt, Leeds City May 1906, Swansea Town 1913Swindon Town 1914, Manchester United May 1914.
League: App 181, Gls 6; FA Cup: App 7, Gls 0.
His brother, Archie, played for Tottenham Hotspur in the Southern League.

CUNNINGHAM, George P. *1910-1913*

Outside-right. Born: Belfast.
Debut v Blackpool (a) Division Two, 3 September 1910, L 1-2.
5ft 7½in, 11st (1910).
Shelbourne, Leeds City May 1910, Crewe Alexandra 1913.
League: App 3, Gls 0.
He earned rave reviews as a youngster with Shelbourne, representing the Irish League against the Football League and Scottish League.

CUNNINGHAM, Thomas *1908-1909*

Goalkeeper. Born: Sunderland.
Debut v Derby County (a) Division Two, 23 January 1909, L 1-5.
Sunderland Juniors, Leeds City August 1908.
League: App 1, Gls 0.
A reserve called in for his only League appearance at the last minute.

DOUGAL, David *1908-1910*

Outside-right. Born: Scotland, 1884.
Debut v Clapton Orient (h) Division Two, 7 September 1908, D 0-0.
5ft 8½in, (1908).
Dundee, Preston North End, Grimsby Town, Clapton Orient 1905, Reading 1907, Brighton & Hove Albion 1908, Leeds City June 1908.
League: App 25, Gls 2.

DOUGHERTY, Joseph *1914-1919*

Centre-forward. Born: Darlington.
Debut v Clapton Orient (h) Division Two, 14 April 1914, D 0-0.
5ft 10in, 11st 7lb (1914).
Darlington Forge, Leeds City February 1914, Oldham Athletic April 1919 £100, Hartlepools United March 1921.
League: App 1, Gls 0.

DRAIN, Thomas *1905-1907*

Centre-forward. Born: Pollokshaws, Glasgow, 1880.
Debut v West Bromwich Albion (h) Division Two, 9 September 1905.
5ft 9in, 11st 7lb (1907).
Drongan Juniors, Celtic, Ayr FC, Maybole, Bradford City October 1903, Leeds City July 1905, Kilmarnock 1907, Aberdeen 1907-08, Carlisle United 1908, Exeter City cs 1908-09, Woolwich Arsenal May 1909, Nithsdale Wanderers 1910-11, Galston 1911-12.
League: App 9, Gls 3; FA Cup: App 1, Gls 0.

EDMONDSON, John *1914-1919*

Centre-forward. Born: Carleton, Lancashire.
Debut v Arsenal (a) Division Two, 6 February 1915, L 0-2.
5ft 11in, 11st 8lb (1914).
Leyland, Leeds City April 1014, Sheffield Wednesday October 1919, Swansea Town May 1920, Exeter City September 1923.
League: App 11, Gls 6.

ENRIGHT, Joseph *1910-1913*

Inside-forward. Born: Belfast.
Debut v Blackpool (h) Division Two, 3 September 1910, L 1-2.
5ft 7in, 10st 4lb (1910).
Shelbourne, Leeds City cs 1910, Newport County October 1913, Coventry City cs 1914, Athlone Town during World War One whilst on leave. Ireland (1 cap).
League: App 77, Gls 23; FA Cup: App 3, Gls 0.
Capped once for Ireland against Scotland in 1912 when he played alongside Joe Moran. He also represented the Irish League twice in 1909 against the Football League and the Scottish League. Served with the Army in the RAOC until 1919 when he returned to live in Ireland.

FENWICK, George *1913*

Winger. Born: Durham, *c.*1892.
Debut v Leicester Fosse (h) Division Two, 8 February 1913, W 5-1.
Shildon, Leeds City January 1913.
League: App 5, Gls 3.

FERGUSON, John *1912*

Left-back. Born: Dundee.
Debut v Fulham (a) Division Two, 7 September 1912, L 0-4.
5ft 8in, 11st 9lb (1912).
Dundee, Leeds City June 1912.
League: App 17, Gls 0.

FOLEY, Mick *1910-1916*

Wing-half. Born: Dublin, 1892.
Debut v Blackpool (h) Division Two, 3 September 1910, L 1-2.
5ft 8in, 11st 10lb (1912).
Shelbourne, Leeds City May 1910, Shelbourne 1920. Ireland (1 cap).
League: App 127, Gls 6; FA Cup: App 6, Gls 1.
Nicknamed 'Boxer', Foley captained Ireland in their first-ever international match, a 3-0 defeat against Italy in Turin on 21 March 1926 alongside ex-Leeds men John Joe Flood and Bob Fullam. It was his only cap, but he also played several times for the League of Ireland, including their first representative match, a 3-3 draw with the Welsh League in Dublin in February 1924.

FORTUNE, Jimmy J. *1911-1912*

Outside-left. Born: Dublin, *c.*1890.
Debut v Chelsea (h) Division Two, 9 September 1911, D 0-0
Shelbourne Distillery cs 1910, Leeds City cs 1911, Shelbourne cs 1912, Barrow, Queen's Park Rangers cs 1913, Bristol Rovers, *c.*1914.
League: App 1, Gls 0.

FREEBOROUGH, Jimmy *1906-1908*

Right-back. Born: Stockport, 13 February 1879. Died: 1961.
Debut v Manchester United (a) Division Two, 21 April 1906, L 1-3.
6ft, 12st 7lb (1906).
Stockport County cs 1902, Tottenham Hotspur cs 1904, Leeds City April 1906, Bradford Park Avenue July 1908.
League: App 24, Gls 0.
He also turned out for Stockport in wartime football.

GEMMELL, Jimmy *1907-1910*

Inside-forward. Born: Glasgow, 17 November 1880.
Debut v Oldham Athletic (a) Division Two, 30 November 1907, L 2-4.
5ft 9in, 12st 7lb (1907).
Clyde 1900, Sunderland November 1900, Stoke May 1907, Leeds City November 1907, Sunderland May 1910, Third Lanark April 1912.
League: App 67, Gls 14; FA Cup: App 6, Gls 0.
Won a Division One championship medal with Sunderland in 1901-02.

GEORGE, John S. *1905*

Centre-half. Born: Irchester, 4 February 1884. Died: 29 October 1931.
Debut v Gainsborough Trinity (h) Division Two, 7 April 1906, W 1-0.
5ft 10½in, 12st.
Kettering cs 1903, Tottenham Hotspur April 1904, Leeds City April 1905, Croydon Common cs 1907, Hastings and St Leonards United cs 1908.
League: App 8, Gls 0.

GIBSON, Andy *1912*

Inside-forward. Born: Glasgow.
Debut v Fulham (a) Division Two, 7 September 1912, L 0-4.
5ft 8½in, 10st 10lb (1912).
Strathclyde, Southampton cs 1911, Leeds City September 1912.
League: App 5, Gls 0.
Signed for Southampton by George Swift, the former Leeds City trainer.

GILLESPIE, Billy *1910-1912*

Inside-forward. Born: Londonderry, 6 August 1891. Died: Bexley, Kent, 2 July 1981.
Debut v Blckpool (h) Division Two, 3 September 1910, L 1-2.
5ft 10in, 11st 6lb (1910).
Derry Celtic, Leeds City May 1910, Sheffield United December 1912. Ireland (25 caps). Derry City

manager June 1932-48.
League: App 24, Gls 10.
The son of a policeman, he was about to sign for Linfield when Leeds came along and persuaded him to turn professional. He spent 17 seasons at Sheffield United and made 25 appearances for Ireland, making him the Blades' most capped player. He also won an FA Cup winners medal with them in 1925.

GOODWIN, Ernest W. *1914-1919*

Outside-left. Born: Chester-le-Street.
Debut v Blackpool (h) Division Two, 19 September 1914, W 2-0.
5ft 7in, 10st 5lb (1914).
Spennymoor, Leeds City May 1914, Spennymoor cs 1918, Manchester City October 1919, Rochdale May 1921.
League: App 20, Gls 3.

GREEN, Joe *1915*

Left-back.
Debut v Barnsley (h) Division Two, 24 April 1915, L 0-2.
Leeds City April 1015.
League: App1, Gls 0.

GUY, Richard W. *1908-1909*

Outside-right. Born: *c.*1880.
Debut v Hull City (h) Division Two, 12 September 1908, W 2-0.
5ft 8in, 11st 6lb (1908).
Manchester City, Bradford City June 1903, Hastings, Leeds City May 1908, Portsmouth cs 1909, Hastings cs 1910 £25.
League: App 18, Gls 3; FA Cup: App 4, Gls 1.

HALLIGAN, Billy *1909-1910*

Centre-forward. Born: Athlone, Ireland, 1886. Died: 1950.
Debut v Lincoln City (h) Division Two, 1 September 1909, W 5-0.
5ft 10in, 12st (1909).
Distillery cs 1908, Leeds City May 1909, Derby County February 1910 (£400), Wolverhampton Wanderers June 1911 (£450), Hull City May 1913 (£600), Manchester United and Rochdale both during World War One, Preston North End July 1919, Oldham Athletic January 1920 (£750), Nelson August 1921, Boston United 1922, Wisbech Town 1924. Retired in 1925.
Ireland (2 caps), Victory International (2 caps), Irish League (1 appearance). Retired cs 1922.
League: App 24, Gls 12; FA Cup: App 1, Gls 0.
Scored over 100 League goals in his career and won two Irish caps, against Wales in January 1911 and England in February 1912. He also played in two Victory internationals against Scotland in 1919-20 and represented the Irish League against the Scottish League in 1909.

HAMILTON, Edward McDonald 'Ted' *1909*

Outside-right. Born: Glasgow.
Debut v Oldham Athletic (a) Division Two, 16 October 1909, L 1-2.
Petershill, Leeds City August 1909.
League: App 3, Gls 0.

HAMILTON, John 'Jock' *1908-1909*

Centre-half. Born: Edinburgh.
Debut v Tottenham Hotspur (h) Division Two, 5 September 1908, W 1-0.
5ft 11in, 12st 7lb (1907).
Leith Athletic 1906, Brentford cs 1907, Leeds City June 1908, Brentford cs 1909, Swansea Town 1912-13.
League: App 21, Gls 0; FA Cup: App 4, Gls 0.

HAMPSON, John *1913-1919*

Centre-half. Born: Oswestry, Shropshire, 28 December 1887.
Died: Burslem, December 1960.
Debut v Glossop (h) Division Two, 6 September 1913, W 3-0.
5ft 9½in, 11st 4lb (1910).
Oswestry Town, Northampton Town cs 1910, Leeds City August 1913, Aston Villa October 1919 (£1,000), Port Vale September 1921, Hanley SC.
League: App 71, Gls 8; FA Cup: App 3, Gls 0.
His brother, who played for Northampton Town, played with John as a City guest in World War One. John retired *c.*1930.

HARKINS, John *1910-1912*

Right-half. Born: Musselburgh, Midlothian.
Debut v Blackpool (h) Division Two, 3 September 1910, L 1-2.
5ft 9in, 11st 6lb (1910).
Middlesbrough September 1906, Bathgate, Leeds City August 1910, Darlington cs 1912.
League: App 63, Gls 0; FA Cup: App 3, Gls 0.

HARGRAVES, J.Fred *1905-1907*

Inside-forward/wing-half.
Debut v Bradford City (a) Division Two, 2 September 1905, L 0-1.
Burton United 1903-04, Leeds City August 1905 Stoke 1909.
League: App 63, Gls 12; FA Cup: App 7, Gls 7.
Listed in some sources as Hargreaves.

HARWOOD, Alf *1906-1907*

Centre-forward. Born: Bishop Auckland, 16 May 1881.
Debut v Burnley (a) Division Two, 2 March 1907, W 2-1.
5ft 8in, 11st 6lb (1907).
Crook Town 1900-01, Bishop Auckland 1901-03, Fulham cs 1903, Leeds City May 1906, West Ham United cs 1907.
League: App 1, Gls 1.
Won an FA Amateur Cup winner's medal when Crook Town beat Kings Lynn 3-0 in 1901 and was in the Bishop Auckland side which lost 5-1 to Old Malvernians in the 1902 final at Leeds. He represented the Northern League in 1901-02 and 1902-03. He lost his amateur status when the Football League ruled he was a professional as he was working as Fulham's assistant manager.

HEANEY, Frank *1911-1912*

Right-back. Born: Ireland.
Debut v Wolverhampton Wanderers (a) Division Two, 16 December 1911, L 0-5.
6ft, 13st (1911).
St James' Gate, Leeds City May 1911.
League: App 2, Gls 0.

HENDERSON, James T. *1905-1907*

Left-half. Born: Morpeth, Northumberland, 1882.
Debut v Bradford City (a) Division Two, 2 September 1905, L 0-1.
5ft 8in, 12st (1907).
Reading 1903-04, Bradford City May 1904, Leeds City July 1905, Preston North End 1907, Rochdale 1910-11.
League: App 75, Gls 0; FA Cup: App 5, Gls 0.
A top-class sprinter with Morpeth Harriers and in 1908 clocked 11 seconds for 100 yards.

HOGG, Tony *1909-1915*

Goalkeeper. Born: Newcastle-upon-Tyne, *c.*1890.
Debut v Blackpool (h) Division Two, 3 September 1910, L 1-2.
5ft 10in, 11st 3lb (1909).
Walton-upon-Tyne, Church Lads, Leeds City September 1909, Newcastle United.
League: App 96, Gls 0; FA Cup: App 5, Gls 0.

HOPKINS, William 'Pop' *1919*

Centre-half. Born: Esh Winning, County Durham, 1888. Died: Blackpool, 26 January 1938 (aged 49).
Debut v Blackpool (a) Division Two, 30 August 1919, L 2-4.
Stanley United, Sunderland May 1912, Leeds City July 1919 (£50), South Shields October 1919, Hartlepools United June 1921.
Durham City coach 1924, Sheffield United assistant trainer, Charlton Athletic trainer, Grimsby Town trainer, Port Vale trainer 1935, Barnsley trainer 1936.
League: App 7, Gls 0.

HORSLEY, James T. *1909-1910*

Centre-half. Born: *c.*1887.
Debut v Burnley (h) Division Two, 6 November 1909, W 1-0.
5ft 9in, 11st 6lb (1907).
Newark, Leeds City cs 1909.
League: App 29, Gls 0; FA Cup: App 1, Gls 0.

HOWARD, Gordon *1905*

Inside-forward.
Debut v Glossop (h) Division Two, 23 December 1905, W 1-0.
Hoyland Town, Leeds City June 1905.
League: App 1, Gls 0.

HYNDS, Tom *1907-1908*

Centre-half. Born: Hurlford, Ayrshire, *c.*1880.
Debut v Glossop (h) Division Two, 2 September 1907, W 2-1.
5ft 10in, 11st (1907).
Hurlford Thistle, Celtic February 1898, Bolton Wanderers (loan) March 1899, Clyde (loan) October 1899, Bolton Wanderers (loan) September 1900, Manchester City (loan) October 1901, Manchester City September 1902, Arsenal December 1906, Leeds City May 1907, Hearts May 1908, Ladysmith FC (British Columbia) 1910, Scottish football December 1912.
League: App 37, Gls 0; FA Cup: App 1, Gls 0.
Retired through sciatica but returned to Canada and the United States to coach, later coaching in Italy. Never a Celtic regular, he was loaned to several clubs, including Manchester City, whom he joined permanently in 1902, winning a Second Division championship medal the following year and an FA Cup winners medal after beating Bolton 1-0 in the 1904 Final. He also played for the Anglo-Scots against the Home Scots in an international trial match at Cathkin Park, Glasgow, in March 1905, the homesters winning 2-0. Hynds was suspended between June and December 1906 for his part in an illegal payments scandal at Manchester City and was still banned when he signed for Arsenal.

JACKSON, John B. *1913-1915*

Inside-forward. Born: Dalry, 21 June 1893.
Debut v Birmingham (a) Division Two, 20 December 1913, W 2-0.
5ft 6½in, 10st 2lb (1913).
Ardeer Thistle, Clyde August 1908, Celtic (loan) January 1909 and October 1912, Leeds City December 1912 (£1,000), Ayr United (loan) December 1915, Clyde (loan) July 1916, Rangers (loan) May 1917, Celtic (loan) September 1917, Royal Scots Fusiliers May 1918, Clydebank (loan) January 1919, Motherwell October 1919, Dundee December 1919, Stevenston United (loan) 1920.
League: App 54, Gls 10; FA Cup: App 4, Gls 2.
Well known north of the border where he played in the 1910 Scottish Cup Final for Clyde

against Dundee which took two replays before Dundee won 2-1. Jackson put so much into the first replay, a goalless draw, that he collapsed during extra-time. During the war he is reported to have run from Waverley Station in Edinburgh to Hibernian's ground in Easter Road to play in a game for Celtic because he could not catch a taxi.

JEFFERSON, Bob W. *1906-1908*

Winger. Born: Sunderland. 1883.
Debut v Leicester Fosse (h) Division Two, 15 September 1906, D 1-1.
5ft 6½in, 11st (1908).
Sunderland Royal Rovers, Bradford City November 1904, Leeds City May 1906, Swindon Town cs 1908, Bath City 1922. Southern League representative.
League: App 17, Gls 5; FA Cup: App 1, Gls 0.
After leaving school he joined the Navy, but didn't enjoy it, deserted and eventually bought his way out and became an apprentice moulder at a foundry. He starred in Swindon's Southern League team which reached the 1912 FA Cup semi-final which they lost 2-0 to Newcastle United. He represented the Southern League 10 times v Football League (4), Scottish League (4) and Irish League (2) and played in Swindon's first-ever Football League game, a 9-1 thrashing of Luton in 1920 when he scored one of the goals.

JOHNSON, Garnet J. *1906*

Winger.
Debut v Chelsea (h) Division Two, 17 November 1906, L 0-1.
Upper Armley Christ Church, Leeds City November 1906.
League: App 1, Gls 0.

JOHNSON, James T. *1910-1914*

Winger. Born: Walton-upon-Tyne.
Debut v Grimsby Town (h) Division Two, 13 December 1913, W 4-1.
5ft 6in, 10st 2lb (1913).
Bedlington, Leeds City October 1910, North Leeds Athletic cs 1914.
League: App 1, Gls 0.

JOHNSON, Sam *1911-1912*

Wing-half. Born: Colne 1885.
Debut v Burnley (a) Division Two, 4 September 1911, L 2-4.
5ft 7½in, 11st 4lb (1911).
Newton Heath Albion, Colne 1904, Blackpool cs 1905, Colne cs 1907, Exeter City cs 1908, Coventry City cs 1909, Leeds City 1911.
League: App 7, Gls 1.

JOYNES, Dickie A. *1908-1910*

Outside-right/inside-forward. Born: *c.*1880.
Debut v Tottenham Hotspur (h) Division Two, 5 September 1908, W 1-0.
5ft 10½in, 12st 6lb (1908).
Newark, Notts County 1901-02, Newark 1903, Brighton and Hove Albion cs 1905, Leeds City May 1908.
League: App 22, Gls 1; FA Cup: App 1, Gls 0.

KAY, Harry *1907-1908*

Right-back. Born: Ainsworth, Lancashire, *c.*1884.
Debut v Glossop (h) Division Two, 2 September 1907, W 2-1.
5ft 9in, 11st 6lb (1907).
Bolton Wanderers 1906-07, Leeds City May 1907, Swindon Town cs 1908.
League: App 31, Gls 0; FA Cup: App 1, Gls 0.
Better known for his exploits at Swindon where locals referred to him as the best right-back never capped by England.

KELLY, Chris *1910-1912*

Wing-half. Born: Staffordshire.
Debut v Huddersfield Town (a) Division Two, 24 September 1910, L 2-3.
5ft 11in, 12st 6lb (1910).
Denaby United, Leeds City cs 1910, Denaby United.
League: App 4, Gls 0.

KENNEDY, Jimmy J. *1906-1909*

Wing-half. Born: Dundee, 8 May 1883.
Debut v Bradford City (h) Division Two, 1 September 1906, D 1-1.
6ft, 12st 4lb (1906).
Celtic, Brighton & Hove Albion cs 1905, Leeds City June 1906, Stockport County August 1909, Tottenham Hotspur March March 1910, Swindon Town April 1912, Norwich City July 1913, Watford December 1913, Gillingham December 1919.
League: App 58, Gls 1; FA Cup: App 2, Gls 0.
Won a Southern League championship medal with Watford. Appointed Gillingham trainer in 1920.

KIRK, Gerald *1906-1907*

Centre-half. Born: Ingleton, 14 July 1883. Died: Poperinghe 14 April 1915.
Debut v Hull City (a) Division Two, 22 December 1906, L 1-2.
Pocklington School, Bradford City April 1905, Leeds City December 1906, Bradford City September 1907-cs 1908.
League: App 8, Gls 1; FA Cup: App 1, Gls 0.
He was an Army lieutenant at the time of his death.

KIRTON, Billy J. *1919*

Centre-forward. Born: Newcastle-upon-Tyne, 2 December 1896. Died: Sutton Coldfield, 27 September 1970.
Debut v Wolverhampton Wanderers (a) Division Two, 4 October 1919, D 1-1.
5ft 6½in, 11st 11lb (1919).
Todds Nook School (North Shields), Pandon Temperance 1917, Leeds City May 1919, Aston Villa October 1919 (£5,000), Coventry City September 1928 (£1,700), Kidderminster Harriers cs 1920, Leamington Town October 1930. Retired July 1931. England (1 cap).
League: App 1, Gls 0.
Kirton was capped by England v Ireland in October 1921, scoring in a 1-1 draw. He also scored the winning FA Cup Final goal in 1920 when Villa beat Huddersfield 1-0. Four years later he gained a runners-up medal after a 2-0 defeat by Newcastle. After hanging up his boots he ran a newsagents and tobbacconists in Birmingham. He was also a golfer of some distinction.

LAMPH, Tom *1914-1919*

Wing-half. Born: Gateshead, 1893. Died: 24 february 1926.
Debut v Grimsby Town (a) Division Two, 18 April 1914, W 1-0.
5ft 9½in, 11st 2lb (1913).
Pelaw United, Spennymoor United, Leeds City April 1914, Manchester City October 1919, Derby County March 1920, Leeds United February 1921. Retired 1922.
League: App 11, Gls 1.
See *Leeds United Who's Who*.

LAVERY, John *1906-1908*

Inside-left. Born: 1884.
Debut v Clapton Orient (a) Division Two, 29 March 1906, D 0-0.
5ft 5½in, 10st 6lb (1908).
Jarrow 1903-04, Barnsley 1903-04, Denaby United 1904-05, Leeds City March 1906, Swindon Town cs 1908, South Shields 1910.
League: App 56, Gls 20; FA Cup: App 1, Gls 0.
An apprentice mason in the North-East, he left Leeds for Swindon with Jefferson and Kay, playing alongside them in the 1912 FA Cup semi-final against Newcastle.

LAW, George *1912-1915*

Full-back/right-half. Born: Arbroath, Angus, 13 December 1885.
Debut v Fulham (a) Division Two, 7 September 1912, L 0-4.
5ft 8¾in, 12st 12lb (1912).
Arbroath, Rangers March 1907, Leeds City July 1912. Retired August 1919 but resumed with Arbroath 1921-22. Scotland (3 caps).
League: App 105, Gls 1; FA Cup: App 5, Gls 1.
Capped three times by Scotland as a Rangers player in 1910 v Wales, Ireland and England. The following year he won a Scottish League championship medal with Rangers.

LAWRENCE, Valentine *1914*

Wing-half. Born: Arbroath, Angus, 1890.
Debut v Stockport County (a) Division Two, 5 September 1914, L 1-3.
5ft 8in, 11st 8lb (1914).
Dundee Violet, Forfar Athletic 1910-11, Manchester City July 1911, Oldham Athletic May 1912 (£50), Leeds City May 1914, Southend United August 1921.
League: App 6, Gls 0.

LINTOTT, Evelyn H. *1912-1916*

Centre-half. Born: Godalming, Surrey, 1 November 1883. Died: 1 July 1916 at the Somme.
Debut v Fulham (a) Division Two, 7 September 1912, L 0-4.
5ft 9¼in, 12st 4lb (1912).
King Edward VI Grammar School (Guildford), St Luke's Training College, Exeter, Woking, Surrey County, Plymouth Argyle 1906-07, Queen's Park Rangers cs 1907, Bradford City November 1908, Leeds City June 1912.
England (7 caps), Amateur International.
League: App 43, Gls 1; FA Cup: App 2, Gls 0.
A schoolmaster-footballer, he was an amateur throughout his career, winning seven full England caps in 1908 and 1909 against Hungary (2), Scotland (2), Ireland (2) and Wales. Prior to that he won five amateur caps against Belgium, France, Germany, Holland and Wales and a Southern League championship medal with QPR in 1908. That latter success saw him in the QPR side which contested the FA Charity Shield against Football League champions Manchester United, who cruised to a 4-0 replay win after a 1-1 draw. Lintott also played for the Football League against the Irish League in 1909. He served with the Light Infantry in World War One, losing his life in the Battle of the Somme.

LOUNDS, Herbert *1909*

Outside-right. Born: Masborough, South Yorkshire.
Debut v Blackpool (a) Division Two, 30 August 1919, L 2-4.
Gainsborough Trinity 1911-12, Leeds City August 1919 (£50), Rotherham County October 1919, Halifax Town cs 1923.
League: App 8, Gls 0.

McALLISTER, Tom *1908-1910*

Right-half.
Debut v Tottenham Hotspur (h) Division Two, 5 September 1908, W 1-0.
5ft 9in, 12st (1906).
Castleford Town, Blackburn Rovers March 1904 Brentford cs 1906, Leeds City May 1908 to 1910, Halifax Town.
League: App 53, Gls 0; FA Cup: App 5, Gls 0.

McDANIEL, Edward *1911-1912*

Right-back. Born: Ireland.
Debut v Grimsby Town (a) Division Two, 23 January 1912, W 2-1.
6ft, 12st (1911).
Belfast Celtic, Leeds City May 1911.
League: App 1, Gls 0.

McDONALD, John *1905-1906*

Right-back. Born: Ayr, c.1882.
Debut v Bradford City (a) Division Two, 2 September 1905, L 0-1.
5ft 10in, 12st 6lb (1905).
Arden Villa, Ayr FC, Blackburn Rovers May 1903 (£90), Leeds City July 1905, Grimsby Town August 1906, Queen's Park Rangers cs 1907 to 1913.
League: App 25, Gls 0; FA Cup: App 6, Gls 0.
Won Southern League championship medals in 1908 and 1912 with QPR, appearing in their Charity Shield sides against Football League champions Manchester United, playing alongside Evelyn Lintott, and Blackburn, his old club in 1912.

McDONALD, William *1908-1909*

Wing-half. Born: Scotland, c.1883.
Debut v Blackpool (a) Division Two, 26 September 1908, L 0-1.
5ft 10in, 13st (1908).
Nithsdale Wanderers, Kilmarnock 1903-04, Lanermark (loan), Brighton & Hove Albion cs 1906, Leeds City July 1908, Nithsdale Wanderers 1909-10, Lanermark 1909-10.
League: App 14, Gls 0.

McLEOD, Billy *1906-1919*

Centre-forward. Born: Hebburn, Co Durham, June 1887.
Debut v Wolverhampton Wanderers (a) Division Two, 24 November 1906, L 2-3.
5ft 9in, 11st 7lb.
Hebburn Argyle, Peebles Rovers, Lincoln City June 1906 (£25), Leeds City November 1906 (£350 plus proceeds from a match), BrAdford City (loan during World War One), Notts County October 1919 (£1,250), Doncaster Rovers cs 1921.
League: App 289, Gls 171; FA Cup: App 12, Gls 6.
Played more games and scored more goals than any other Leeds City player. Top scorer in nine successive seasons, his five goals at Hull City in a 6-2 win on 16 January 1915 is an individual City scoring record. He also scored four in an 8-0 home win against Nottingham Forest on 29 November. Although of Scottish parents, he was born in England and went close to international honours, being a non-playing reserve for England's game against Wales in Cardiff in 1914 and suffered the same fate when the Football League played the Scottish League that year. McLeod played for Bradford City during World War One when he was working for an engineering firm in Bradford, but returned to Leeds on the resumption of peacetime football to continue scoring freely. He scored a hat-trick at Wolves in his final game before being auctioned off with the rest of the squad, fetching the highest price, bid by Notts County.

McQUILLAN, Jack *1914-1915*

Left-back. Born: Boldon, County Durham, 1888.
Debut v Fulham (h) Division Two, 2 September 1914, L 0-1.
5ft 8½in, 11st 8lb (1912).
Jarrow, Hull City October 1906, Leeds City July 1914 (£100).
Retired during World War One.
League: App 20, Gls 0.
Guested for Fulham and Hull City in World War One. Later scouted for Hull in Wales. His career ended when he was injured by an exploding grinding machine in a Hull factory where he worked during World War One.

MILLERSHIP, Harry *1919*

Right-back. Born: Chirk, Wales, 1889. Died: Blackpool, 1959.
Debut v Blackpool (a) Division Two, 30 August 1919, L 2-4.
Chirk, Blackpool 1912-13, Leeds City August 1919, Rotherham County October 1919 (£1,000), Barnsley September 1922, Castleford Town 1923-24. Wales (6 caps).

League: App 8, Gls 0.
Because of the Leeds City payments scandal, Millership was only at Elland Road for a few weeks. He starred for Rotherham County in their early Football League campaigns, winning six Welsh caps against England, Ireland and Scotland in 1920 and 1921.

MORAN, Joe *1911-1913*

Wing-half. Born: Dublin.
Debut v Burnley (a) Division Two, 4 September 1911, L 2-4.
5ft 9in, 12st (1911).
Shelbourne 1910-11, Leeds City May 1911. Ireland (1 cap).
League: App 25, Gls 0; FA Cup: App 2, Gls 0.
Won an Irish cap, alongside Joe Enright, as a City player, against Scotland in 1912. An Irish Cup winner with Shelbourne in 1911, he also represented the Irish League against the Scottish League the following year.

MORGAN, Charles *1905-1909*

Right-back. Born: Bootle, 1882.
Debut v Bradford City (a) Division Two, 2 Setpember 1905, L 0-1.
5ft 8in, 11st 3lb.
Everton, Tottenham Hotspur 1904-05, Leeds City July 1905, Bradford Park Avenue August 1909.
League: App 41, Gls 1; FA Cup: App 6, Gls 0.

MORRIS, Dickie *1905-1906*

Inside-forward. Born: Newtown, Montgomeryshire, 1883.
Debut v Bradford City (a) Division Two, 2 September 1905, L 0-1.
Newtown RWW, Druids (Ruabon) February 1902, Liverpool March 1902, Leeds City July 1905, Grimsby Town June 1906, Plymouth Argyle cs 1907, Reading, Huddersfield Town 1908-09. Wales (11 caps).
League: App 25, Gls 5; FA Cup: App 7, Gls 5.
Morris became City's first international when he was capped by Wales against Scotland in 1906, a distinction he also holds with Plymouth when he scored against Ireland to give Wales their first-ever Home Championship title. He won a total of 11 caps in a much-travelled career. He fought in the Boer War prior to his football career.

MORRIS, John *1905-1906*

Centre-half. Born: Leeds.
Debut v Blackpool (a) Division Two, 1 January 1906, W 3-0.
Leeds Schools, Leeds City October 1905.
League: App 10, Gls 0, FA Cup: App 1, Gls 0.

MORRIS, Tom H. *1909-1913*

Centre-half. Born: Grimsby, 1884.
Debut v Gainsborough Trinity (h) Division Two, 13 March 1909, L 0-2.
5ft 10in, 12st 10lb (1912).
Haycroft Rovers, Grimsby Rovers, Grimsby Town February 1906, Brighton & Hove Albion May 1907, Leeds City February 1909, Scunthorpe & Lindsay United 1913 as player-coach, Coventry City May 1914.
League: App 106, Gls 3; FA Cup: App 3, Gls 0.
Joined the Army in March 1915 and was killed in action.

MULHOLLAND, Tom S. *1909-1912*

Inside-right. Born: Ireland, c.1888.
Debut v Lincoln City (h) Division Two, 1 Setpember 1909, W 5-0.
5ft 8in, 11st (1909).
Distillery, Leeds City May 1909, Distillery 1912, Scunthorpe & Lindsay United 1913-14, Belfast Cetlic 1919-20, Hartlepools United 1920-21.
League: App 78, Gls 21; FA Cup: App 3, Gls 0.

MURPHY, Leslie *1911-1912*

Goalkeeper. Born: Ireland.
Debut v Nottingham Forest (h) Division Two, 2 September 1911, L 1-2.
5ft 10in, 12st (1911).
Belfast Celtic1910-11, Leeds City May 1911, Glentoran cs 1912.
League: App 18, Gls 0; FA Cup: App 1, Gls 0.
On his return to Glentoran he played twice for the Irish League – a 0-0 draw v the Football League in Belfast on 23 October 1912 and a 3-1 defeat against the Scottish League a fortnight later.

MURRAY, David B. *1905-1909*

Full-back. Born: Busby, near Glasgow, 1882. Died: France, 10 December 1915.
Debut v Bristol City (h) Division Two, 9 December 1905, D 1-1.
5ft 8½in, 11st 12lb (1905).
Rangers, Everton 1903, Liverpool May 1904, Leeds City December 1905 £150, Mexborough Town 1909, Burslem Port Vale.
League: App 83, Gls 7; FA Cup: App 2, Gls 0.
A Rangers reserve, he is one of the few players to play with both big Merseyside clubs, having just two games before joining Liverpool where he won a Division Two championship medal. He was killed in action serving with the Seaforth Highlanders.

MURRAY, Willie B. *1906-1907*

Outside-left. Born: Forres, Morayshire,1883.
Debut v West Bromwich Albion (a) Division Two, 8 September 1906, L 0-5.
5ft 6in, 11st 7lb.
Forres Mechanics, Inverness Thistle, Sunderland June 1901, Northampton Town cs 1903, Tottenham Hotspur May 1904, Leeds City May 1906.
League: App 8, Gls 0.
Played for the Anglo-Scots vHome Scots in an international trial in 1902 when a Sunderland player.

NAISBY, Tom H. *1907-1910*

Goalkeeper. Born: Sunderland, 1878.

Debut v Lincoln City (h) Division Two, 26 October 1907, W 2-1.
5ft 8in, 13st (1907).
Sunderland East End, Sunderland September 1889, Sunderland West End, Sunderland 1902-03, Reading May 1903, Sunderland May 1905, Leeds City October 1907, Luton Town cs 1910, South Shields March 1913, Darlington.
League: App 63, Gls 0; FA Cup: App 5, Gls 0.

PAGE, George 1906-1907

Centre-forward. Born: London.
Debut v Chesterfield (a) Division Two, 3 November 1906, L 0-1.
5ft 8in, 11st (1910).
Cheshunt, Tottenham Hotspur (loan) April 1906, Tottenham Hotspur September 1906, Leeds City May 1906, Redhill cs 1907.
League: App 4, Gls 0.
Played as an amateur at Tottenham.

PARNELL, G.Fred 1905-1908

Outside-right. Born: Sutton-in-Ashfield, *c*.1886.
Debut v Bradford City (a) Division Two, 2 September 1905, L 0-1.
5ft 8in, 11st (1908).
Skegby, Pinxton, Derby County 1903, Leeds City July 1905, Exeter cs 1908, Preston North End May 1909, Queen's Park Rangers May 1910, Exeter City 1910, Rochdale 1912, Sutton Junction (Derby) 1913.
League: App 104, Gls 15; FA Cup: App 7, Gls 4.
His first name was Gresham, but it was seldom used.

PEART, Harry 1913-1915

Centre-half. Born: Newcastle-upon-Tyne, 3 October 1889.
Debut v Bristol City (h) Division Two, 13 April 1913, W 1-0.
5ft 5¾in, 10st (1912).
Glasgow Strathclyde, Bradford City June 1909, Leeds City September 1913, Blyth Spartans 1915.
League: App 7, Gls 0; FA Cup: App 1, Gls 0.

PICKARD, Herbert 1905-1910

Half-back.
Debut v Stockport County (h) Division Two, 22 December 1905, W 6-1.
Upper Armley Christ Church, Leeds City June 1905.
League: App 8, Gls 0.

PRICE, Arthur 1912-1919

Inside-right. Born: Sheffield.
Debut v Fulham (h) Division Two, 28 December 1912, L 2-3.
5ft 9in, 11st 8lb (1913).
Worksop Town, Leeds City December 1912, Sheffield Wednesday October 1919, Southend United 1922, Scunthorpe United 1924-25, Scarborough trainer November 1927, Barrow trainer 1934-35.
League: App 78, Gls 25.
When at Scarborough he was the steward at Scarborough Conservative Club.

PRICE, Haydn 1909-1910

Half-back. Born: Maerdy, 1883.
Died: Portsmouth, 7 March 1964.
Debut v Derby County (a) Division Two, 11 Setpember 1909, W 2-1.
5ft 8in, 11st 6lb (1909).
Maerdy Corinthians, Aberdare 1902, Aston Villa December 1904, Burton United 1907, Wrexham 1908, Leeds City May 1909, Shrewsbury Town, Grimsby Town manager July to November 1920, Walsall secretary November 1920-21, Mid-Rhondda secretary-manager 1922. Wales (5 caps).
League: App 8, Gls 0.
Price won the first of his five Welsh caps against Scotland in 1907 when he was still in Villa's third team. A schoolteacher by profession, he won a Welsh Cup winner's medal with Wrexham before joining Leeds for a season. His four-month spell as manager at Grimsby ended in acrimony when he resigned publically in a letter to the *Grimsby Evening Telegraph* and returned to one of his previous jobs as secretary at Walsall. Price's other international appearances were with Burton (1) and Wrexham. His first name, rarely used, was Ioan.

RAY, Dick 1905-1907

Full-back. Born: Newcastle-under-Lyme, 4 January 1873. Died: 29 December 1952.
Debut v Bradford City (a) Division Two, 2 September 1905, L 0-1.
Macclesfield Town 1893, Burslem Port Vale 1894, Manchester City 1896, Macclesfield Town cs 1900, Stockport County cs 1903, Chesterfield Town cs 1904, Leeds City July 1905, Non-League football. Retired 1912. Leeds United manager October 1919-February 1920, Doncaster Rovers manager 1923-July 1927, Leeds United manager July 1927-March 1935, Bradford City manager April 1935-February 1938, Millwall chief scout 1938.
League: App 38, Gls 0; FA Cup: App 6, Gls 0.
See *Leeds United Managers* and *Leeds United Who's Who*.

REINHARDT, Dr Cecil G. 1910-1912

Goalkeeper. Born: Leeds, *c*.1888.
Debut v Wolverhampton Wanderers (a) Division Two, 16 December 1911, L 0-5.
6ft ½in, 12st 2lb (1912).
Leeds University, Leeds City Setpember 1910.
League: App 12, Gls 0; FA Cup: App 1, Gls 0.
A doctor of chemistry at Leeds University, he later changed his surname to Goodwin, his middle name.

RICHARDSON, Webb F. 1913-1914

Outside-right. Born: St Albans, Hertfordshire.
Debut v Blackpool (h) Division Two, 19 September 1914, W 2-0.
5ft 7in, 10st 11lb (1913).
Barnet and Alston, Leeds City June 1913.
League: App 2, Gls 0.

ROBERTS, Hugh P. 1909-1913

Outside-right. Born: Rhyl, North Wales, *c*.1887.
Debut v West Bromwich Albion (h) Division Two, 9 October 1909, L 0-1.
5ft 7in, 11st (1907).
Southport Central 1908-09, Leeds City May 1909, Scunthorpe & Lindsey United 1913, Luton Town June 1914.
League: App 108, Gls 13; FA Cup: App 4, Gls 2.
He was one of three Roberts, all believed to be brothers from Rhyl, who were on City's books in 1910-11.

ROBERTSON, Jimmy 1912-1913

Inside-right. Born: Glasgow 1880.
Debut v Fulham (a) Division Two, 7 September 1912, L 0-4.
5ft 8½in, 11st 4lb (1912).
Glasgow United, Crewe Alexandra 1901, Small Heath April 1903 (£25), Chelsea August 1905 (£50), Glossop North End cs 1907, Partick Thistle, Ayr United, Barrow 1912, Leeds City July 1912, Gateshead cs 1913. Retired 1915
League: App 27, Gls 7; FA Cup: App 7, Gls 1.
Played in Chelsea's first season in the Football League.

RODGER, Tom 1908-1909

Inside-forward. Born: Scotland, 1883.
Debut v Tottenham Hotspur (h) Division Two, 5 September 1908, W 1-0.
5ft 8in, 12st (1908).
Dundee, Preston North End 1904, Grimsby Town July 1906, Reading June 1907, Brighton & Hove Albion 1907-1908, Leeds City May 1908.
League: App 25, Gls 4.

ROTHWELL, Alf 1914

Outside-right.
Debut v Stockport County (a) Division Two, 5 September 1914, L 1-3.
Accrington Stanley, Leeds City May 1914.
League: App 1, Gls 0.

SCOTT, Billy 1912-1914

Goalkeeper. Born: Belfast.
Debut v Fulham (a) Division Two, 7 September 1912, L 0-4.
5ft 11½in, 12st 11lb (1912).
Cliftonville, Linfield, Everton cs 1904, Leeds City August 1912.
Ireland (25 caps).
League: App 26, Gls 0.
One of Ireland's greatest 'keepers, he won 25 caps between 1903 and 1913, three of them with Leeds City, six at Linfield and the rest at Everton where he was a League championship runner-up in 1904-05, 1908-09 and 1911-12. He also kept goal in the 1902 FA Cup Final when Everton beat Newcastle 1-0 and was between the sticks in the 1907 Final, a 2-1 defeat by Sheffield Wednesday. At Linfield he played three times for the Irish League v Scottish League 1903, v Football League 1903 and v Scottish League again in 1904. His younger brother, Elisha, won 31 Irish caps in 22 years with Liverpool.

SHARPE, Ivan G. 1913-1915

Outside-left. Born: St Albans, Hertfordshire, 15 June 1889. Died: Southport, 9 February 1968.
Debut v Glossop (h) Division Two, 6 September 1913, W 3-0.
5ft 8in, 11st 2lb (1913).
St Albans Abbey, Watford 1907, Glossop North End August 1908, Derby County October 1911, Leeds City June 1913, Glossop North End 1915, Leeds United November 1920. Retired cs 1923.
League: App 61, Gls 16; FA Cup: App 4, Gls 1.
An amateur, he also won a gold medal with the Great Britain team in the 1912 Stockholm Olympic Games. His other appearances were with English Wanderers, Brighton & Hove Albion, in the FA Cup, Nottingham Forest Reserves and Luton Town Reserves. See *Leeds United Who's Who*.

SHORT, William 'Billy' 1919

Inside-forward. Born: Gosforth, Northumberland.
Debut v Blackpool (a) Division Two, 30 August 1919, L 2-4.
5ft 11in, 11st 6lb (1919).
Panton Temperance, Leeds City May 1919, Hartlepools United October 1919.
League: App 5, Gls 0.
Played in Hartlepools United's first-ever League game, a 2-0 home win over Wrexham on 27 August 1921.

SINGLETON, Harry B. 1905-1907

Outside-left. Born: Prescot, Lancashire, 1877. Died: Macclesfield, 5 July 1947.
Debut v Bradford City (a) Division Two, 2 September 1905, L 0-1.
5ft 9in, 12st 3lb (1905).
Bury 1901, Everton 1901, Grimsby Town cs 1902, New Brompton May 1903, Queen's Park Rangers cs 1904, Leeds City June 1905.
Retired 1907.
League: App 45, Gls 7; FA Cup: App 6, Gls 0.

SPEIRS, James H. *1913-1915*

Inside-left. Born: Govan, 22 March 1886. Died: *c.*20 August 1917.
Debut v Glossop (h) Division Two, 6 September 1913, W 3-0
5ft 10½in, 12st 5lb (1913).
Glasgow Annandale, Maryhill, Rangers August 1905, Clyde 1908, Bradford City September 1909, Leeds City cs 1913(£1,400).
Scotland (1 cap).
League: App 73, Gls 32; FA Cup: App 5, Gls 0.
Skippered Bradford City to their 1911 FA Cup Final triumph when his header beat Newcastle 1-0 in a replay at Old Trafford. Evelyn Lintott was a teammate at Valley Parade. Spiers was capped once, at Rangers, against Wales in 1908. A holder of the Military Medal, he was a sergeant killed in action with the Cameron Highlanders.

STOCKTON, Colin M. *1909*

Outside-right. Born: *c.*1886.
Debut v Lincoln City (h) Division Two, 1 September 1909, W 5-0.
5ft 9½in, 11st 6lb (1909).
Chester (amateur), Leeds City May 1909.
League: App 3, Gls 0.

STRINGFELLOW, Harry *1905-1906*

Centre-half. Born: Burscough, Lancashire, 1877.
Debut v Bradford City (a) Division Two, 2 September 1905, L 0-1.
5ft 8in, 11st (1905).
Everton, Swindon Town cs 1904, Leeds City July 1905, Preston North End September 1906, Wigan.
League: App 13, Gls 1; FA Cup: App 3, Gls 0.

SWIFT, George *1906*

Full-back. Born: Oakengates, 3 February 1870.
Debut v Chelsea (a) Division Two, 31 March 1906, L 0-4.
5ft 9in, 13st (1906).
St George's C of E School (Oakengates), St George's Swifts, Wellington Town 1885, Stoke (trials) 1886, Wellington St George's, Crewe Alexandra 1888, Wolverhampton Wanderers August 1891, Loughborough cs 1894, Leicester FosseAugust 1896, Notts County June 1902, Leeds City trainer cs 1904, Chesterfield secretary 1907 to 1910. Southampton manager April 1911 to April 1912.
League: App 1, Gls 0.
Won an FA Cup winners' medal with Wolves when they beat Everton 1-0 1893. The only Loughborough player to win senior representative honours, playing for the Football League against the Irish in 1895. Captained Leicester Fosse where he took a benefit from a friendly against his old club, Wolves. Retired from playing at Notts County and was appointed trainer at Elland Road. His only appearance for Leeds came, aged 36, during an injury crisis at Chelsea in March 1906, City losing 4-0. His managerial career was unsuccessful, with Chesterfield forced to apply for re-election in two of his seasons in charge and spending just a year at the helm at Southampton before resigning.

THOMAS, William *1906-1908*

Inside-left. Born: Liverpool, *c.*1885.
Debut v Chesterfield (a) Division Two, 16 November 1907, L 3-4.
5ft 8½in, 11st (1906).
Newcastle Swifts, Burslem Port Vale 1904-05, Everton, Leeds City cs 1906, Barnsley May 1908 to 1909, Huddersfield Town 1909-10.
League: App 9, Gls 2; FA Cup: App 1, Gls 0.

THORPE, James *1907-1908*

Wing-half. Born: *c.*1885.
Debut v Stoke (a) Division Two, 21 September 1907, L 1-2.
5ft 8in, 11st (1907).
Bolton Wanderers 1907, Leeds City May 1907, Crystal Palace cs 1908.
League: App 9, Gls 0.

TOMPKINS, Tom *1907*

Right-half. Born: *c.*1884.
Debut v Glossop (h) Division Two, 2 September 1907, W 2-1.
5ft 6in, 10st 11lb (1907).
Denaby United, Leeds City May 1907, Mexborough cs 1908.
League: App 11, Gls 0.

TURNER, Neil M. *1913-1914*

Outside-right. Born: Scotland.
Debut v Huddersfield Town (a) Division Two, 8 November 1913, D 1-1.
Petershill, Leeds City September 1913, Raith Rovers cs 1914Sunderland 1919-20.
League: App 4, Gls 2.

TYLDESLEY, James *1909*

Full-back. Born: Halesowen, 1882. Died: Newcastle, January 1963.
Debut v Clapton Orient (h) Division Two, 25 December 1909, W 2-1.
Halesowen St John, Newcastle United February 1903, Middlesbrough September 1906 (£200), Leeds City December 1909, Luton Town.
League: App 6, Gls 0; FA Cup: App 1, Gls 0.
After his playing days he acted as a scout for Newcastle for many years, discovering, among others, Bob Roxburgh, Leeds United's trainer of the 1950s. Some sources give Tyldesley's surname as Tildesley.

WAINWRIGHT, Wilson H. *1914*

Left-half. Born: Morley, near Leeds.
Debut v Arsenal (h) Division Two, 3 October 1914, D 2-2.
5ft 9in, 11st 7lb (1914).
Morley, Leeds City October 1914.
League: App 2, Gls 0.

WALKER, Fred *1905-1906*

Centre-half.
Debut v Lincoln City (a) Division Two, 30 September 1905, W 2-1.
5ft 10½in, 11st 8lb (1905).
Barrow, Leeds City June 1905.
League: App 26, Gls 0; FA Cup: App 3, Gls 0.

WALKER, Willis *1914-1919*

Goalkeeper. Born: Gosforth, Northumberland, 24 November 1892. Died: Keighley, 3 December 1991.
Debut v Arsenal (a) Division Two, 6 February 1915, L 0-2.
5ft 10in, 11st 4lb (1914).
Sheffield United, Doncaster Rovers cs 1912, Leeds City May 1914, South Shields October 1919 (£800), Bradford Park Avenue 1925, Stockport County August 1926.

League: App 22, Gls 0.
A marvellous all-round sportsman, he served with the Royal Navy during World War One and established himself at Leeds until being part of the infamous auction at the Metropole Hotel. A top-class cricketer, he played for Sheffield United CC in the summer and Sheffield United in winter at Bramall Lane and later played in the Bradford League with Keighley after starring with Nottinghamshire where he scored 1,000 runs in a season ten times. At Doncaster he was understudy to Harry Bromage for a season. He ran a sports shop in Keighley for many years.

WATSON, John *1908-1910*

Right-back. Born: Newarthill, Lanarkshire.
Debut v Tottenham Hotspur (h) Division Two, 5 September 1908, W 1-0.
6ft, 14st (1908).
Clyde, Newcastle United November 1902 (£200), Brentford cs 1903, Leeds City June 1908, Clyde.
League: App 45, Gls 0; FA Cup: App 4, Gls 0.
Played for Glasgow City select team when a Clyde player before joining Newcastle.

WATSON, Bob *1905-1908*

Inside-forward. Born: Middlesbrough 1885.
Debut v Bradford City (a) Division One, 2 September 1905, L 0-1.
5ft 9in, 12st (1908).
South Bank, Middlesbrough September 1902, Woolwich Arsenal June 1903, Leeds City July 1905, Rochdale April 1908, Exeter City cs 1908, Stalybridge Celtic 1912.
League: App 83, Gls 21; FA Cup: App 7, Gls 3.
Scored seven goals in a friendly game for Arsenal against a Paris XI, which was effectively the full French national team, in a 26-1 slaughter at Plumstead on 5 December 1904. He was Exeter's first professional captain.

WHITE, John W. *1908-1910*

Full-back. Born: Manchester.
Debut v Tottenham Hotspur (h) Division Two, 5 September 1908, W 1-0.
5ft 10¼in, 12st 6lb (1908).
Ollenshaw United, Grays Anchor, Swanscombe, Grays United, Queen's Park Rangers cs 1901, Leeds City May 1908, Merthyr Tydfil 1911-12.
League: App 60, Gls 0; FA Cup: App 4, Gls 0.
Although christened Jabez, he always used the first name John or Jack.

WHITLEY, Jack *1906-1907*

Goalkeeper. Born: Seacombe, April 1880. Died: London, *c.*1915.
Debut v Stockport County (h) Division Two, 13 April 1906, D 1-1.
5ft 11in, 13st (1906).
Liskeard YMCA 1897, Darwen 1899, Aston Villa May 1900, Everton 1902, Stoke August 1905, Leeds City April 1906, Chelsea August 1907. Retired from playing May 1914, trainer May 1914 to May 1939.
League: App 7, Gls 0.
As a player he helped Chelsea win promotion to Division One in 1911-12. He played cricket for Leeds and was a keen billiards player.

WILSON, David *1905-1906*

Centre-forward. Born: Hebburn, near Newcastle-on-Tyne, 23 July 1883. Died: 27 October 1906.
Debut v Glossop (h) Division Two, 23 December 1905, W 1-0.
Dundee, Heart of Midlothian February 1905 £120, Hull City May 1905 £100, Leeds City December 1905.
League: App 21, Gls 13.

Leeds City in 1905-06. Back row (left to right): R.Younger (director), R.S.Kirk (director), Morgan, D.Whittaker (director), Dooley, Macdonald, Austin, Walker, Singleton, R.M.Singleton, R.M.Dow (director), G.Swift (trainer). Middle row: G.Gillies (secretary and manager), Parnell, Watson, Hargreaves, Ray, Morris, Clay, O.Tordoff (director). Front row: (the City dog), Stringfellow, Drain, Henderson.

See *The Death of David Soldier Wilson*.

WILSON, Thomas C. *1906-1908*

Outside-left. Born: Preston, Lancashire, 20 October 1877. Died: Blackpool, 30 August 1940.
Debut v Stockport County (h) Division Two, 15 December 1906, W 6-1.
5ft 6in, 11st 6lb (1906).
Fishwick Ramblers (Preston), Ashton-in-Makerfield, West Manchester, Ashto Town, Ashton North End, Oldham County cs 1896, Kensal Rise, Swindon Town May 1897, Blackburn Rovers May 1898, Swindon Town May 1899, Millwall Athletic May 1900, Aston Villa April 1901, London Caledonians January 1902, Queen's Park Rangers cs 1902, Old Fleet 1904, Bolton Wanderers May 1904, Leeds City December 1906, Manchester United February 1908, Queen's Park Rangers cs 1909. Retired 1910. Chorley manager cs 1912, Rochdale chairman October 1919, chairman-manager until February 1923.
League: App 20, Gls 2; FA Cup: App 1, Gls 0.
An amateur during most of his much-travelled career, Tommy figured in an England international trial in 1901, playing for the South v the North. Married to the daughter of an Oldham licensee, he also became a publican in Bolton.

Leeds City

World War One Appearances and Goalscorers

Player	Team	App	Goals
Affleck, George	Leeds City	36	
Arkle, N.	Juniors	1	
Bainbridge, Simpson	Leeds City	11	5
Barnshaw, Richard	Aberdare	1	
Barrett, P.J. (Cpl)	Army	7	1
Bavin		1	
Bennett, Tom	Newcastle United	18	4
Booth, Curtis	Newcastle United	8	
Bradley, Bill	Newcstle United	11	
Buchan, Charlie M.	Arsenal	1	1
Cartwright, James E.	Manchester City	4	
Cawley, Tom E.	Rotherham	43	9
Chard (Cpl)	Army	1	
Clipstone, Fred	Northampton Town	4	
Cook, Walter	Leeds City	11	
Copeland, Charlie W.	Leeds City	53	
Cowen, Robert W.	Leeds City	1	
Croot, Fred R.	Leeds City	14	
Currie, T.		1	
Davison J.	Newcastle United	1	
Dawson, G.	Preston North End	4	
Dunn, John	Leeds City	1	
Edmondson, John	Leeds City	20	10
Feathers, W.		1	
Foley, Mick	Leeds City	36	1
Goodwin, Ernie	Leeds City	13	3
Gough, Harold	Sheffield United	2	
Grant, W. (Cpl)	Army	4	1
Hall, Tom	Newcastle United	22	8
Hampson, E.	Northampton Town	7	1
Hampson, John	Leeds City	92	4
Hampson, Tommy	Accrington Stanley	39	
Hampson, Walker	Burnley	3	
Hampson Wm. 'Billy'	Newcastle United	91	1
Hewison, Bob	Sunderland	79	6
Hibbert, Billy	Newcastle United	16	5
Hudson, Ernie K.	Manchester United	11	
Hudspeth, Fred C.	Newcastle United	1	
Hugall Jim C.	Clapton Orient	1	
Hughes, Robert	Northampton Town	4	
James, F.	Portsmouth	1	
Jennings, William	Notts County	1	

Player	Team	App	Goals
Kay, A.	Barnsley	1	
Kettle	Juniors		
Kirton, Billy, J.	Leeds City	1	
Lamph, Tommy	Leeds City	82	1
Lavery, G.D.		1	
Law, George	Leeds City	22	1
Linfoot, Fred	Leeds City	6	
Lounds, Herbert	Leeds City	6	
McCreadie, W.		1	
McLachlan, Albert	Aberdeen	24	
McLeod, Billy	Leeds City	13	6
Malcolm, W.		1	
Mayson, Tommy	Grimsby Town	30	4
Millership, Harry	Leeds City	49	
Moore, Billy G.B.	Sunderland	14	6
Pattison, John M.	Hull City	1	1
Peart, Jack G.	Notts County	107	71
Price, Arthur	Leeds City	120	59
Roberts R.		1	
Robinson, Arthur	Blackburn Rovers	8	
Robinson, Stan	Bradford PA	1	
Rutherford, A.		3	
Rutherford, W.		1	
Scott, E.		1	
Sharpe, Ivan G.	Glossop	2	1
Sherwin, Harry	Sunderland	91	9
Smelt, J.	Rotherham	1	
Spratt A.	Sheffield United	1	
Stephenson, Clem	Aston Villa	91	44
Stephenson, Jim	Aston Villa	36	4
Sutcliffe, Charlie S.	Leeds City	2	
Toms W.		2	
Thorpe, Levi	Burnley	28	2
Trotter, Ally	Jarrow	3	1
Voysey, Clem R.	Arsenal	1	
Wainwright, Arthur H.	Leeds City	2	
Walden, Fred I. 'Fanny'	Tottenham	38	2
Walker, Willis	Leeds City	70	
Williamson, J.R.	Newcastle United	1	
Wilson, Andy W.	Middlesbrough	2	2
Wilson, Willie	Hearts	9	4
Wrigglesworth, A.		1	
Own-goal – Wightman	Nottingham Forest		1
Totals		**1584**	**281**

Leeds United

World War Two Appearances and Goalscorers

Player	Team	App	Goals
Adam, Colin	Leeds United	23	6
Ainsley, George E.	Leeds United	64	35
Alberry, Bill E.	Leeds United	1	
Anson, Sidney	Army	1	
Antonio, George R.	Stoke City	10	5
Argue, Jim	Chelsea	4	1
Asquith, Beaumont	Bamsley	2	1
Attwell, Reg	West Ham United	2	
Baird, Henry	Huddersfield Town	2	1
Baker, Harold	Bradford PA	1	
Barton E.		4	
Batey, N.Bob	Preston North End	8	
Bedford, Harold		1	
Bean, Alf	Lincoln City	1	
Binns, Cliff H.	Bamsley	2	
Birch, Walter	Rochdale	1	
Blair, Doug		1	
Bokas,Frank	Bamsley	5	
Booth, W.Sammy	Cardiff City	2	
Boyes, Walter E.	Everton	30	8
Bratley, George	Hull City	2	
Brown, John M.	Leeds United	15	4
Browne, Bobby J.	Leeds United	7	
Buckley, Arthur	Leeds United	2	
Burbanks, WEddie	Sunderland	14	2
Burditt, George L.	Doncaster Rovers	9	3
Burton, Stanley	Leeds United	1	
Bush, Tom W.	Liverpool	6	
Butterworth, Frank	Leeds United	108	
Byrom, Tom	Tranmere Rovers	4	
Calverley, Alf	Huddersfield Town	2	
Campbell, Rob son	Charlton Athletic	20	1
Challinor, Jack	Stoke City	14	
Cherry, D.		1	
Chew, Jackie	Bumley	6	1
Clarke, Reg L.	Aldershot	1	
Clutterbuck, Jack		1	
Cochrane, David	Leeds United	13	7
Collier, Austin	York City	2	
Copping, Wilf	Leeds United	28	
Corbett, Norman G.	West Ham	1	
Coyne, Cyril	Leeds United	53	9
Crookes, Geoffrey		4	
Curry, Robert	Sheffield Wednesday	1	2
Dainty, Albert	Preston North End	1	
Daniels, John F.	Tranmere Rovers	121	
D'arcy, Lawrence		1	
Davie, John	Brighton & HA	5	4
Davies, Cecil J.	Barrow	6	1
Dempsey, Alan		3	
Dewis, George	Leicester City	2	
Dorling, George	Tottenham Hotspur	4	1
Dowen, John S.	Hull City	1	
Downing, H.		1	
Duffy, Ropbert	Blackpool	15	

Player	Team	App	Goals
Dunderdale, W.Len	Leeds United	4	2
Dunn, William M.	Southampton	1	
Dutchman, John	Leeds United	5	2
Duthoit, Jack	Leeds United	21	
Eastham, Harry	Liverpool	6	
Edwards, Willis	Leeds United	24	2
Fallaize, Reg	Halifax Town	5	2
Farrage, Tom O.	Birmingham City	3	
Farrell, Arthur	Bradford PA	1	
Fearnley, Harrison	Leeds United	10	
Forde, Steve	West Ham United	2	
Fowler, H.Norman	Middlesbrough		
Gadsby, Ken J.	Leeds United	84	1
Galley, Tom	Wolverh amp ton W	4	
Glackin, Tom		1	
Gleave, Colin	Stockport County	2	
Glover, Arthur	Barnsley	2	
Goldberg, Les	Leeds United	33	
Goodburn, H.		1	
Goslin, Harry A.	Bolton Wanderers	3	
Grainger, Dennis	Leeds United	35	9
Haddow, Johnny B.		6	
Hardaker, N.G.		2	
Hargreaves, Jack	Leeds United	48	18
Harper, Bernard	Barnsley	3	
Harper, Ken	Walsall	1	
Harris, William	Watford	2	
Harston, John	Wolves	2	
Harvey, Peter	West Ham United	1	
Heaton, Billy H.	Leeds United	23	3
Henry, Gerry R.	Leeds United	186	94
Hick, Jack B.	Bristol City	1	
Hindle, Tom	Leeds United	96	39
Hirst, Hubert		1	
Hodson, Gordon	Leeds United	33	14
Hodgson, John	Leeds United	40	
Holley, Tom	Leeds United	104	2
Houldershaw, Harry	Leeds United	3	
Houldershaw, Rex	Leeds United	22	3
Howitt, Harry		4	
Howe, A.K.B.		2	
Hudson, George	Portsmouth		
Hulbert J.		1	
Iceton, O.Lloyd	Preston North End	2	
Jackett, Stan		1	
James, John	Bradford PA	1	
Jameson, Percy	Darlington	1	1
Jones, Bill	Barnsley	2	
Jones, Bill 'W.H.'	Liverpool	2	
Jones, Eric, N.	Brentford	1	
Jones, Syd	Arsenal	14	
Jordan, Clarrie	Doncaster Rovers	1	
Keeping, Alex E.M.	Fulham	2	
Kidd, William E.	Chesterfield	1	
Kinghorn, William J.D.	Liverpool	2	

Player	Team	App	Goals
Kirby, Dennis	Leeds United	9	
Kirton, John	Stoke City	6	
Knight, Arnold W.	Leeds United	82	12
Laidman, Fred	Sunderland	3	
Laking, George	Middlesbrough	1	
Lambert, Reg	Liverpool	3	
Lawn, Maurice	Leeds United	3	1
Lee, Alec	Leeds United	45	2
Lichfield, Eric	Newcastle United	15	1
Lindley, W.Maurice	Everton	1	
Livingstone, R.Archie	Bury	2	
McClure, Duncan	Hearts	3	
McGraw, James	Leeds United	88	8
McInnes, John S.	Liverpool	3	
McKellor, Walter	Huddersfield Town	1	
McTavish, Hugh	Watford	1	
Maddison, Ralph	Doncaster Rovers	1	
Mahon, Johnny	Huddersfield Town	33	10
Makinson, Jim	Leeds United	103	2
Marshall, Dennis		1	
Meens, Harold	Hull City	1	
Milburn, George W.	Chesterfield	3	
Milburn, Jack	Norwich City	64	6
Milburn, Jim	Leeds United	52	4
Morton, Norman	Sunderland	1	1
Moss, Amos	Aston Villa	8	
Moule, Jack	Leeds United	21	7
Murgartroyd, Arthur	Leeds United	6	
Normanton, Sidney	Barnsley	2	
O'Farrell,John		1	
O'Neill, Tom H.	Newcastle United	1	
Oliver, Harry	Hartlepools	1	
Padgett, Herbert	Sheffield Wednesday	1	
Parker, William	Wolverhampton W	2	
Paton, John	Celtic	4	
Paton, Tom G.	Bournemouth	1	
Patterson, George L.	Liverpool	3	
Pickering, Bill	Sheffield Wednesday	2	
Pogson, Donald	Leeds United	1	
Poland, George	Liverpool	10	
Pope, Alf	Halifax Town	1	
Powell, Aubrey	Leeds United	126	38
Poxon, John		4	
Price, Arthur	Leeds United	21	1
Pyke, RD.		1	
Ramsden, Bernard	Liverpool	8	
Ramsey, J.		2	
Rhodes, Arthur	Cardiff City	6	
Robbins, Horace		1	
Rodgers, William		2	
Rozier, Alf	Fulham	3	
Ruecroft, Jacob	Halifax Town	2	
Rutherford, Eddie	Rangers	20	6
Saxon A.		1	
Scaife, George	Leeds United	2	
Sellar, Raymond		1	
Shafto, Johnny	Liverpool	1	
Shanks, Robert	Crystal Palace	6	1
Sharp, Norman	Everton	1	
Sharples, Kenneth		1	
Short, John	Leeds United	58	36

Player	Team	App	Goals
Shotton, Bob	Barnsley	5	
Simpson, John	Huddersfield Town	2	
Skidmore, William	Wolverhampton W	2	
Smith, Gavin		2	1
Smith, Jack	Chelsea	11	
Spike, Septimus	Newcastle United	6	
Spink, Ken		1	
Stacey, Alec	ex-Leeds United	1	
Stanton, Reg		3	
Steel, Fred C.	Stoke City	2	2
Stephens, Alf	Leeds United	6	5
Stephens, J.Bill	Leeds United	16	2
Stephenson, J.Eric	Leeds United	39	7
Stevens, Tom		1	1
Stokes, E.		5	
Sturrock, W.		2	
Sutherland, Harry	Leeds United	5	3
Swindin, George	Arsenal	9	
Tatton, Billy	Leeds United	5	2
Taylor, Leslie		3	
Taylor, Phil H.	Liverpool	2	
Taylor, Walter	Grimsby Town	2	
Thompson, Leslie	Leeds United	32	1
Tindall, J.		1	
Townsend, Len	Brentford	12	14
Tremelling, Jack		2	4
Turner, John	Bristol City	2	1
Twomey, Jim E	Leeds United	5	
Vickers, Harry	Leeds United	6	
Wakerfield, Albert	Leeds United	22	10
Walker, Jack		3	
Warburton, George	Chester	2	
Ward, Tim, V.	Derby County	4	
Ward, Tom A.	Sheffield Wednesday	1	1
Warren, Ray	Bristol Rovers	7	
Watson, George		1	
Weaver, Sam	Chelsea	27	2
Wesley, John C.	Bradford PA	1	
Westlake, Frank	Sheffield Wednesday	1	
Wheeler, S.		1	
Whittle, Roger		1	
Wilcocks, George E.	Derby County	4	
Wildon, Norman		1	
Wilkinson, Ken	Huddersfield Town	1	
Williams, Billy		1	
Williams, Cyril E.	Bristol City	1	
Williams, Tom	Cardiff Ctiy	1	1
Wofinden, Richard	Barnsley	1	
Wright, Horace	Wolves	3	
Yeomanson, Jack	Leeds United	20	1
Own-goals			8
Briggs	Huddersfield Town		
Gregory	Bradford City		
Harper	Barnsley		
Harston	Barnsley		
Heppelwhite	Middlesbrough		
Stelling	Sunderland		
Whalley	Manchester United		
Young	Huddersfield Town		
Totals		**2,673**	**486**

Leeds Internationals

Appearances given here refer to caps won whilst with Leeds. The number of caps won is shown in brackets after each players name. The figures in brackets after results are goals scored by the player in that match. Before 1924 there was only one Ireland team, then the Republic of Ireland began separate matches. WCQ = World Cup Qualifier; WCF = World Cup Finals; ECQ = European Championship Qualifier; ECF = European Championship Finals; ACQ = African Cup Qualifier; ACF = African Cup Finals.

Leeds City

Full Internationals

Wales

Dickie Morris (1 cap)

Date	Opponent	Venue	Score	Attendance
3 Mar 1903	Scotland	Tynecastle, Edinburgh	2-0	25,000

Morris won a total of 11 caps: Druids 2, Newtown 1, Liverpool 5, Grimsby Town 1, Plymouth Argyle 1.

Ireland

Joe Enright (1 cap)

Date	Opponent	Venue	Score	Attendance
16 Mar 1912	Scotland	Belfast	1-4	12,000

Joe Moran (1 cap)

Date	Opponent	Venue	Score	Attendance
16 Mar 1912	Scotland	Belfast	1-4	12,000

Billy Scott (3 caps)

Date	Opponent	Venue	Score	Attendance
18 Jan 1913	Wales	Belfast	0-1	8,000
15 Feb 1913	England	Belfast	2-1	20,000
15 Mar 1913	Scotland	Dublin	1-2	12,000

Scott won a total of 25 caps: Linfield 6, Everton 16.

Amateur Internationals

England

Ivan Sharpe (5 caps, 4 goals)

Date	Opponent	Venue	Score
7 Feb 1914	Wales	Plymouth	9-1(1)
24 Feb 1914	Belgium	Brussels	8-1(2)
5 Jun 1914	Denmark	Copenhagen	0-8
10 Jun 1914	Sweden	Stockholm	5-1(1)
12 Jun 1914	Sweden	Stockholm	5-0

Representative Games

Amateurs

Ivan Sharpe

Date	Opponent	Venue	Score	Attendance
6 Oct 1913	Professionals	Millwall	2-7	20,000

Leeds United

Full Internationals

England

Peter Barnes (2 caps)

Date	Comp	Opponent	Venue	Score	Attendance
9 Sep 1981	WCQ	Norway (sub)	Oslo	1-2	22,000
25 May 1982		Holland (sub)	Wembley	2-0	69,000

Barnes won a total of 22 caps: Manchester City 14, West Bromwich Albion 6.

David Batty (14 caps)

Date	Comp	Opponent	Venue	Score	Attendance
21 May 1991		USSR (sub)	Wembley	3-1	23,798
25 May 1991		Argentina	Wembley	2-2	44,497
1 Jun 1991		Australia	Sydney	1-0	36,827
3 Jun 1991		New Zealand	Auckland	1-0	17,500
12 Jun 1991		Malaysia	Kuala Lumpur	4-2	41,248
11 Sep 1991		Germany	Wembley	0-1	59,493
16 Oct 1991	ECQ	Turkey	Wembley	1-0	50,896
12 May 1992		Hungary	Budapest	1-0	12,500
14 Jun 1992	ECF	France	Malmö	0-0	26,535
17 Jun 1992	ECF	Sweden	Solna	1-2	30,126
14 Oct 1992		Norway	Wembley	1-1	51,441
17 Feb 1993	WCQ	San Marino	Wembley	6-0	51,154
9 Jun 1993	WCQ	United States	Boston	0-2	37,652
13 Jun 1993		Brazil	Washington	1-1	54,118

Batty currently has a total of 17 caps: Blackburn Rovers 3.

Jack Charlton (35 caps, 6 goals)

Date	Comp	Opponent	Venue	Score	Attendance
10 Apr 1965		Scotland	Wembley	2-2	98,199
5 May 1965		Hungary	Wembley	1-0	52,000
9 May 1965		Yugoslavia	Belgrade	1-1	60,000
12 May 1965		West Germany	Nuremburg	1-0	67,000
16 May 1965		Sweden	Gothenburg	2-1	18,000
2 Oct 1965		Wales	Cardiff	0-0	30,000
20 Oct 1965		Austria	Wembley	2-3	65,000
10 Nov 1965		Northern Ireland	Wembley	2-1	71,000
8 Dec 1965		Spain	Madrid	2-0	25,000
5 Jan 1966		Poland	Goodison Park	1-1	47,750
23 Feb 1966		West Germany	Wembley	1-0	75,000
2 Apr 1966		Scotland	Hampden Park	4-3	133,000
4 May 1966		Yugoslavia	Wembley	2-0	54,000
26 Jun 1966		Finland	Helsinki	3-0(1)	10,500
3 Jul 1966		Denmark	Copenhagen	2-0(1)	32,000
5 Jul 1966		Poland	Chorzow	1-0	70,000
11 Jul 1966	WCF	Uruguay	Wembley	0-0	87,148
16 Jul 1966	WCF	Mexico	Wembley	2-0	92,570
20 Jul 1966	WCF	France	Wembley	2-0	98,270
23 Jul 1966	WCF	Argentina	Wembley	1-0	90,584
26 Jul 1966	WCF	Portugal	Wembley	2-1	94,493
30 Jul 1966	WCF	West Germany	Wembley	4-2 aet	96,924
22 Oct 1966		Northern Ireland	Belfast	2-0	45,000
2 Nov 1966		Czechoslovakia	Wembley	0-0	75,000
16 Nov 1966	ECQ	Wales	Wembley	5-1(1)	76,000
15 Apr 1967	ECQ	Scotland	Wembley	2-3(1)	99,063
21 Oct 1967	ECQ	Wales	Cardiff	3-0	45,000
3 Apr 1967	ECF	Spain	Wembley	1-0	100,000
15 Jan 1969		Romania	Wembley	1-1(1)	77,000
12 Mar 1969		France	Wembley	5-0	83,000
7 May 1969		Wales	Wembley	2-1	72,000
5 Nov 1969		Holland	Amsterdam	1-0	40,000
10 Dec 1969		Portugal	Wembley	1-0(1)	100,000
14 Jan 1970		Holland	Wembley	0-0	75,000
11 Jun 1970	WCF	Czechoslovakia	Guadalajara	1-0	49,000

Trevor Cherry (27 caps)

Date	Comp	Opponent	Venue	Score	Attendance
24 Mar 1976		Wales	Wrexham	2-1	21,000
15 May 1976		Scotland (sub)	Hampden Park	1-2	85,165
23 May 1976		Brazil	Los Angeles	1-0	32,495
13 Jun 1976	WCQ	Finland	Helsinki	4-1	24,500
8 Sep 1976		Republic of Ireland	Wembley	1-1	51,000
17 Nov 1976	WCQ	Italy	Rome	0-2	70,750
30 Mar 1977	WCQ	Luxembourg	Wembley	5-0	78,000
28 May 1977		Northern Ireland	Belfast	2-1	34,000
4 Jun 1977		Scotland (sub)	Wembley	1-2	100,000
8 Jun 1977		Brazil	Rio de Janeiro	0-0	77,000
12 Jun 1977		Argentina	Buenos Aires	1-1	60,000
15 Jun 1977		Uruguay	Montevideo	0-0	36,000
7 Sep 1977		Switzerland	Wembley	0-0	43,000
12 Oct 1977	WCQ	Luxembourg	Luxembourg	2-0	9,250
16 Nov 1977	WCQ	Italy	Wembley	2-0	92,000
19 Apr 1978		Brazil	Wembley	1-1	92,000
13 May 1978		Wales	Cardiff	3-1	17,750
29 Nov 1978		Czechoslovakia	Wembley	1-0	92,000
23 May 1979		Wales	Wembley	0-0	70,250
10 Jun 1979		Sweden	Solna	0-0	35,691
6 Feb 1980	ECQ	Republic of Ireland	Wembley	2-0	90,250
13 May 1980		Argentina (sub)	Wembley	3-1	90,000
17 May 1980		Wales	Wrexham	4-1	24,250
20 May 1980		Northern Ireland	Wembley	1-1	32,000
24 May 1980		Scotland	Hampden Park	2-0	85,000
31 May 1980		Australia	Sydney	2-1	26,750
18 Jun 1980	ECF	Spain (sub)	Naples	1-2	14,500

David Batty
England

Allan Clarke (19 caps, 10 goals)

Date		Opponent	Venue	Score	Att
11 Jun 1970	WCF	Czechoslovakia	Guadalajara	1-0(1pen)	49,000
12 Nov 1970		East Germany	Wembley	3-1(1)	93,000
12 May 1971	ECQ	Malta	Wembley	5-0(1pen)	36,000
15 May 1971		Northern Ireland	Belfast	1-0(1)	33,500
19 May 1971		Wales (sub)	Wembley	0-0	70,000
22 May 1971		Scotland (sub)	Wembley	3-1	91,469
14 Feb 1973		Scotland	Hampden Park	5-0(2)	48,470
15 May 1973		Wales	Wembley	3-0	39,000
19 May 1973		Scotland	Wembley	1-0	95,950
27 May 1973		Czechoslavakia	Prague	1-1(1)	25,000
6 Jun 1971	WCQ	Poland	Chorzow	0-2	118,000
10 Jun 1973		USSR	Moscow	2-1	85,000
14 Jun 1973		Italy	Turin	0-2	52,000
26 Sep 1973		Austria	Wembley	7-0(2)	48,000
17 Oct 1973	WCQ	Poland	Wembley	1-1(1pen)	100,000
14 Nov 1973		Italy	Wembley	0-2	95,000
20 Nov 1974	ECQ	Portugal	Wembley	0-0	70,750
30 Oct 1975	ECQ	Czechoslovakia	Bratislavia	1-2	45,000
19 Nov 1975	ECQ	Portugal (sub)	Lisbon	1-1	30,000

Terry Cooper (20 caps)

Date		Opponent	Venue	Score	Att
12 Mar 1969		France	Wembley	5-0	83,000
7 May 1979		Wales	Wembley	2-1	72,000
10 May 1979		Scotland	Wembley	4-1	89,902
1 Jun 1979		Mexico	Mexico City	0-0	105,000
14 Jan 1970		Holland	Wembley	0-0	75,000
25 Feb 1970		Belgium	Brussels	3-1	20,500
21 May 1970		Colombia	Bogata	4-0	28,000
24 May 1970		Ecuador	Quito	2-0	22,250
2 Jun 1970	WCF	Romania	Guadalajara	1-0	50,000
7 Jun 1970	WCF	Brazil	Guadalajara	0-1	66,750
11 Jun 1970	WCF	Czechoslovakia	Guadalajara	1-0	49,000
14 Jun 1970	WCF	West Germany	Leon	2-3 aet	23,250
25 Nov 1970		East Germany	Wembley	3-1	93,000
12 May 1971	ECQ	Malta	Wembley	5-0	36,500
15 May 1971		Northern Ireland	Belfast	1-0	33,500
19 May 1971		Wales	Wembley	0-0	70,000
22 May 1971		Scotland	Wembley	3-1	91,469
13 Oct 1971	ECQ	Switzerland	Basle	3-2	58,000
10 Nov 1971	ECQ	Switzerland	Wembley	1-1	98,000
20 Nov 1974	ECQ	Portugal	Wembley	0-0	70,750

Wilf Copping (7 caps)

Date		Opponent	Venue	Score	Att
13 May 1933		Italy	Rome	1-1	50,000
20 May 1933		Switzerland	Berne	4-0	28,000
14 Oct 1933		Ireland	Belfast	3-0	35,000
15 Nov 1933		Wales	Newcastle	1-2	12,000
6 Dec 1933		France	Tottenham	4-1	17,097
14 Apr 1934		Scotland	Wembley	3-0	92,963
24 May 1939		Romania	Bucharest	2-0	40,000

Copping won a total of 20 caps: Arsenal 13.

Tony Currie (10 caps, 2 goals)

Date		Opponent	Venue	Score	Att
19 Apr 1978		Brazil	Wembley	1-1	92,000
13 Apr 1978		Wales (sub)	Cardiff	3-1(1)	17,750
16 May 1978		Northern Ireland	Wembley	1-0	48,000
20 May 1978		Scotland	Hampden Park	0-1	90,000
24 May 1978		Hungary (sub)	Wembley	4-1(1)	74,000
29 Nov 1978		Czechoslovakia	Wembley	1-0	92,000
7 Feb 1979	ECQ	Northern Ireland	Wembley	4-0	92,000
19 May 1979		Northern Ireland	Belfast	2-0	34,000
23 May 1979		Wales	Wembley	0-0	70,250
10 Jun 1979		Sweden	Solna	0-0	35,691

Currie won a total of 17 caps: Sheffield United 7.

Tony Dorigo (9 caps)

Date		Opponent	Venue	Score	Att
11 Sep 1991		Germany	Wembley	0-1	59,493
25 Mar 1992		Czechoslovakia (sub)	Prague	2-2	12,320
12 May 1992		Hungary	Budapest	1-0	12,500
17 May 1992		Brazil	Wembley	1-1	53,428
17 Feb 1993	WCQ	San Marino	Wembley	6-0	51,154
29 May 1993	WCQ	Poland	Katowice	1-1	60,000
9 Jun 1993		USA	Boston	0-2	37,652
13 Jun 1993		Brazil	Washington	1-1	54,118
13 Oct 1993	WCQ	Holland	Rotterdam	0-2	48,000

Dorigo currently has a total of 15 caps: Chelsea 6.

Willis Edwards (16 caps)

Date		Opponent	Venue	Score	Att
1 Mar 1926		Wales	Crystal Palace	3-1	23,000
17 Apr 1926		Scotland	Old Trafford	0-1	49,429
20 Oct 1926		Ireland	Anfield	3-3	20,000
14 Feb 1927		Wales	Wrexham	3-3	16,910
2 Apr 1927		Scotland	Hampden Park	2-1	111,214
11 May 1927		Belgium	Brussels	9-1	30,000
21 May 1927		Luxembourg	Luxembourg	5-2	
26 May 1927		France	Paris	6-0	25,000
31 Mar 1928		Scotland	Wembley	1-5	80,868
17 May 1928		France	Paris	5-1	25,000
19 May 1928		Belgium	Antwerp	3-1	25,000
22 Oct 1928		Ireland	Goodison Park	2-1	34,000
17 Nov 1928		Wales	Swansea	3-2	14,000
13 Apr 1929		Scotland	Hampden Park	0-1	110,512
19 Oct 1929		Ireland	Belfast	3-0	37,000
20 Nov 1929		Wales	Stamford Bridge	6-0	32,945

Billy Furness (1 cap)

Date		Opponent	Venue	Score	Att
13 May 1933		Italy	Rome	1-1	50,000

Brian Greenhoff (1 cap)

Date		Opponent	Venue	Score	Att
31 May 1980		Australia (sub)	Sydney	2-1	26,750

Greenhoff won a total of 18 caps: Manchester United 17.

Ernie Hart (8 caps)

Date		Opponent	Venue	Score	Att
17 Nov 1928		Wales	Swansea	3-2	14,000
19 Oct 1929		Ireland	Belfast	3-0	37,000
20 Nov 1929		Wales	Stamford Bridge	6-0	32,945
7 Dec 1932		Austria	Stamford Bridge	4-3	42,000
1 Apr 1933		Scotland	Hampden Park	1-2	134,710
14 Apr 1933		Scotland	Wembley	3-0	92,363
10 May 1934		Hungary	Budapest	1-2	40,000
16 May 1934		Czechoslovakia	Prague	1-2	40,000

Norman Hunter (28 caps, 2 goals)

Date		Opponent	Venue	Score	Att
8 Dec 1965		Spain (sub)	Madrid	2-0	25,000
23 Feb 1966		West Germany	Wembley	1-0	75,000
4 May 1966		Yugoslavia	Wembley	2-0	54,000
26 Jun 1966		Finland	Helsinki	3-0	10,500
27 May 1967		Austria	Vienna	1-0	85,000
8 May 1968	ECF	Spain	Madrid	2-1(1)	120,000
22 May 1968		Sweden	Wembley	3-1	72,500
1 Jun 1968		West Germany	Hanover	0-1	79,250
5 Jun 1968	ECF	Yugoslavia	Florence	0-1	40,000
8 Jun 1968	ECF	USSR	Rome	2-0	80,000
15 Jan 1969		Romania	Wembley	1-1	77,000
7 May 1969		Wales	Wembley	2-1	72,000
14 Jan 1970		Holland	Wembley	0-0	75,000
14 Jun 1970	WCF	West Germany (sub)	Leon	2-2 aet	23,250
3 Feb 1971	ECQ	Malta	Ta'qali	1-0	20,000
29 Apr 1972	ECF	West Germany	Wembley	1-3	95,000
13 May 1972	ECF	West Germany	Berlin	0-0	75,000
20 May 1972		Wales	Cardiff	3-0	33,000
23 May 1972		Northern Ireland	Wembley	0-1	43,000
27 May 1972		Scotland	Hampden Park	1-0	119,235
15 Nov 1972	WCQ	Wales	Cardiff	1-0	39,000
24 Jan 1973	WCQ	Wales	Wembley	1-1(1)	73,000
10 Jun 1973		USSR (sub)	Moscow	2-1	85,000
26 Sep 1973		Austria	Wembley	7-0	48,000
17 Oct 1973	WCQ	Poland	Wembley	1-1	100,000
15 May 1974		Northern Ireland (sub)	Wembley	1-0	47,000
18 May 1974		Scotland	Hampden Park	0-2	94,487
30 Oct 1974	ECQ	Czechoslovakia	Wembley	3-0	85,000

Mick Jones (1 cap)

Date		Opponent	Venue	Score	Att
14 Jan 1970		Holland	Wembley	0-0	75,000

Jones won a total of 3 caps: Sheffield United 2.

Paul Madeley (24 caps)

Date		Opponent	Venue	Score	Att
15 May 1971		Northern Ireland	Belfast	1-0	33,500
13 Oct 1971	ECQ	Switzerland	Basle	3-2	58,000
10 Nov 1971	ECQ	Switzerland	Wembley	1-1	98,000
1 Dec 1971	ECQ	Greece	Pireus	2-0	42,000
29 Apr 1972	ECF	West Germany	Wembley	2-3	95,000
13 May 1972	ECF	West Germany	Berlin	0-0	75,000
20 May 1972		Wales	Cardiff	3-0	33,000
27 May 1972		Scotland	Hampden Park	1-0	119,325
14 Feb 1973		Scotland	Hampden Park	5-0	48,470
27 May 1973		Czechoslovakia	Prague	1-1	25,000
6 Jun 1973	WCQ	Poland	Chrozow	0-2	118,000
10 Jun 1973		USSR	Moscow	2-1	85,000
14 Jun 1973		Italy	Turin	0-2	52,000
26 Sep 1973		Austria	Wembley	7-0	48,000
17 Oct 1973	WCQ	Poland	Wembley	1-1	100,000
14 Nov 1973		Italy	Wembley	0-1	95,000
30 Oct 1974	ECQ	Czechoslovakia	Wembley	3-0	85,000
20 Nov 1974	ECQ	Portugal	Wembley	0-0	70,750
16 Apr 1975	ECQ	Cyprus	Wembley	5-0	65,000
30 Oct 1975	ECQ	Czechoslovakia	Bratislava	1-2	30,000
13 Jun 1976	ECQ	Finland	Helsinki	4-1	24,500
8 Sep 1976		Republic of Ireland	Wembley	1-1	51,000
9 Feb 1977		Holland	Wembley	0-2	90,000

Mike O'Grady (1 cap, 1 goal)

Date		Opponent	Venue	Score	Att
12 Mar 1969		France	Wembley	5-0(1)	83,000

O'Grady won a total of 2 caps: Huddersfield Town 1.

Alan Peacock (2 caps, 1 goal)

2 Oct 1965		Wales	Cardiff	0-0	30,000
10 Nov 1965		Northern Ireland	Wembley	2-1(1)	71,000

Peacock won a total of 6 caps: Middlesbrough 4.

Paul Reaney (3 caps)

11 Dec 1968		Bulgaria (sub)	Wembley	1-1	80,000
10 Dec 1969		Portugal	Wembley	1-0	100,000
3 Feb 1971	ECQ	Malta	Ta'quali	1-0	20,000

Bert Sproston (8 caps)

17 Oct 1936		Wales	Cardiff	1-2	40,000
23 Oct 1937		Ireland	Belfast	5-1	40,000
17 Nov 1937		Wales	Middlesbrough	2-1	30,608
1 Dec 1937		Czechoslovakia	Tottenham	5-4	35,000
9 Apr 1938		Scotland	Wembley	0-1	93,267
14 May 1938		Germany	Berlin	6-3	120,000
21 May 1938		Switzerland	Zurich	1-2	25,000
26 May 1938		France	Paris	4-2	55,000

Sproston won a total of 11 caps: Manchester City 3.

Eric Stephenson (2 caps)

9 Apr 1938		Scotland	Wembley	0-1	93,267
16 Nov 1938		Ireland	Old Trafford	7-0	40,386

Russell Wainscoat (1 cap)

13 Apr 1929		Scotland	Hampden Park	0-1	110,512

Scotland

Willie Bell (2 caps)

18 Jun 1966		Portugal	Hampden Park	0-1	24,000
25 Jun 1966		Brazil	Hampden Park	1-1	74,933

Billy Bremner (54 caps, 3 goals)

8 May 1965		Spain	Hampden Park	0-0	60,146
13 Oct 1965	WCQ	Poland	Hampden Park	1-2	107,580
9 Nov 1965	WCQ	Italy	Hampden Park	1-0	100,393
7 Dec 1965	WCQ	Italy	Naples	0-3	79,000
2 Apr 1966	ECQ	England	Hampden Park	3-4	134,000
18 Jun 1966		Portugal	Hampden Park	0-1	24,000
25 Jun 1966		Brazil	Hampden Park	1-1	74,933
22 Oct 1966		Wales	Cardiff	1-1	32,500
16 Nov 1966		Northern Ireland	Hampden Park	2-1	45,281
15 Apr 1967		England	Wembley	3-2	99,063
22 Nov 1967		Wales	Hampden Park	3-2	57,472
24 Feb 1968		England	Hampden Park	1-1	134,000
16 Oct 1968		Denmark	Copenhagen	1-0	12,000
6 Nov 1968	WCQ	Austria	Hampden Park	2-1(1)	80,856
11 Dec 1968	WCQ	Cyprus	Nicosia	5-0	10,000
16 Apr 1969	WCQ	West Germany	Hampden Park	1-1	115,000
3 May 1969		Wales	Wrexham	5-3(1)	18,765
6 May 1969		Northern Ireland	Hampden Park	1-1	7,483
10 May 1969		England	Wembley	1-4	89,902
17 May 1969	WCQ	Cyprus	Hampden Park	8-0	39,095
21 Sep 1969		Republic of Ireland	Dublin	1-1	30,000
22 Oct 1969	WCQ	West Germany	Hamburg	2-3	72,000
5 Nov 1970	WCQ	Austria	Vienna	0-2	11,000
15 May 1971		Wales	Cardiff	0-0	19,068
22 May 1971		England	Wembley	1-3	91,469
13 Oct 1971	ECQ	Portugal	Hampden Park	2-1	58,612
10 Nov 1971	ECQ	Belgium	Aberdeen	1-0	36,500
1 Dec 1971		Holland	Amsterdam	1-2	18,000
20 May 1972		Northern Ireland	Hampden Park	2-0	39,710
24 May 1972		Wales	Hampden Park	1-0	21,332
27 May 1972		England	Hampden Park	0-1	119,325
29 Jun 1972		Yugoslavia	Belo Horizonte	2-2	4,000
2 Jul 1972		Portugal	Porto Alegre	0-0	15,000
5 Jul 1972		Brazil	Rio de Janeiro	0-1	130,000
18 Oct 1972	WCQ	Denmark	Copenhagen	4-1	31,000
15 Nov 1972	WCQ	Denmark	Hampden Park	2-0	47,109
14 Feb 1973		England	Hampden Park	0-5	48,470
16 May 1973		Northern Ireland (sub)	Hampden Park	1-2	39,018
19 May 1973		England	Wembley	0-1	95,950
22 May 1973		Switzerland	Berne	0-1	10,000
30 Jun 1973		Brazil	Hampden Park	0-1	70,000
26 Sep 1973	WCQ	Czechoslovakia	Hampden Park	2-1	100,000
14 Nov 1973		West Germany	Hampden Park	1-1	58,235
11 May 1974		Northern Ireland	Hampden Park	0-1	53,775
6 Jun 1974		Norway	Oslo	2-1	18,432
14 Jun 1974	WCF	Zaire	Dortmund	2-0	30,000
18 Jun 1974	WCF	Brazil	Frankfurt	0-0	62,000
22 Jun 1974	WCF	Yugoslavia	Frankfurt	1-1	56,000
20 Nov 1974	ECQ	Spain	Hampden Park	1-2(1)	92,100
5 Feb 1975	ECQ	Spain	Valencia	1-1	60,000
3 Sep 1975	ECQ	Denmark	Copenhagen	1-0	40,300

Bobby Collins (3 caps)

10 Apr 1965		England	Wembley	2-2	98,199
8 May 1965		Spain	Hampden Park	0-0	60,146
23 May 1965	WCQ	Poland	Chorzow	1-1	95,000

Collins won a total of 31 caps: Glasgow Celtic 22, Everton 6.

Arthur Graham (10 caps, 2 goals)

7 Sep 1977		East Germany (sub)	Berlin	0-1	50,000
20 Sep 1978	ECQ	Austria (sub)	Vienna	2-3	71,500
25 Oct 1978	ECQ	Norway	Hampden Park	3-2	65,372
19 May 1979		Wales	Cardiff	0-3	20,371
22 May 1979		Northern Ireland	Hampden Park	1-0(1)	28,524
26 May 1979		England	Wembley	1-3	100,000
2 Jun 1979		Argentina	Hampden Park	1-3(1)	61,918
7 Jun 1979	ECQ	Norway	Oslo	4-0	17,269
17 Oct 1979	ECQ	Austria	Hampden Park	1-1	72,700
16 May 1981		Wales	Swansea	0-2	18,935

Eddie Gray (12 caps, 3 goals)

10 May 1969		England	Wembley	1-4	89,902
17 May 1969	WCQ	Cyprus	Hampden Park	8-0(1)	39,095
22 Oct 1969	WCQ	West Germany	Hamburg	2-3	72,000
5 Nov 1969	WCq	Austria	Vienna	0-2	11,000
15 May 1971		Wales	Cardiff	0-0	19,068
18 May 1971		Northern Ireland	Hampden Park	0-1	31,643
10 Nov 1971	ECQ	Belgium	Aberdeen	1-0	36,500
1 Dec 1971		Holland	Amsterdam	1-2	18,000
6 May 1976		Wales	Hampden Park	3-1(1)	25,000
15 May 1976		England	Hampden Park	2-1	85,165
8 Sep 1976		Finland	Hampden Park	6-0(1)	16,338
17 Nov 1976		Wales	Hampden Park	1-0	63,233

Frank Gray (25 caps, 1 goal)

7 Apr 1976		Switzerland	Hampden Park	1-0	15,531
25 Oct 1978	ECQ	Norway	Hampden Park	3-2	65,372
29 Nov 1978	ECQ	Portugal	Lisbon	0-1	70,000
19 May 1979		Wales	Cardiff	0-3	20,371
22 May 1979		Northern Ireland	Hampden Park	1-0	28,524
26 May 1979		England	Wembley	1-3	100,000
2 Jun 1979		Argentina (sub)	Hampden Park	1-3	61,918
19 May 1981		Northern Ireland	Hampden Park	2-0	22,448
23 May 1981		England	Wembley	1-0	90,000
9 Sep 1981		Sweden	Hampden Park	2-0	81,511
18 Nov 1981	WCQ	Portugal	Lisbon	1-2	25,000
24 Feb 1982		Spain	Valencia	0-3	30,000
23 Mar 1982		Holland	Hampden Park	2-1(1)	71,000
24 May 1982		Wales	Hampden Park	1-0	25,284
15 Jun 1982	WCF	New Zealand	Malaga	5-2	20,000
18 Jun 1982	WCF	Brazil	Seville	1-4	47,379
22 Jun 1982	WCF	USSR	Malaga	2-2	45,000
13 Oct 1982	ECQ	East Germany	Hampden Park	2-0	40,355
17 Nov 1982	ECQ	Switzerland	Berne	0-2	26,000
15 Dec 1982	ECQ	Belgium	Brussels	2-3	48,877
30 Mar 1983	ECQ	Switzerland	Hampden Park	2-2	36,923
28 May 1983		Wales	Cardiff	2-0	14,100
1 Jun 1983		England	Wembley	0-2	84,000
12 Jun 1983		Canada	Vancouver	2-0	15,000

Gray won a total of 32 caps: Nottingham Forest 7.

David Harvey (16 caps)

15 Nov 1972	WCQ	Denmark	Hampden Park	2-0	47,109
26 Sep 1972	WCQ	Czechoslovakia	Bratislava	0-1	15,500
14 Nov 1973		West Germany	Hampden Park	1-1	58,235
11 May 1974		Northern Ireland	Hampden Park	0-1	53,775
14 May 1974		Wales	Hampden Park	2-0	41,969
18 May 1974		England	Hampden Park	2-0	94,487
1 Jun 1974		Belgium	Bruges	1-2	12,000
14 Jun 1974	WCF	Zaire	Dortmund	2-0	30,000
18 Jun 1974	WCF	Brazil	Frankfurt	0-0	62,000
22 Jun 1974	WCF	Yugoslavia	Frankfurt	1-1	56,000
30 Oct 1974		East Germany	Hampden Park	3-0	39,445
20 Nov 1974	ECQ	Spain	Hampden Park	1-2	92,100
5 Feb 1975	ECQ	Spain	Valencia	1-1	60,000
3 Sep 1975	ECQ	Denmark	Copenhagen	1-0	40,300
29 Oct 1975	ECQ	Denmark	Hampden Park	3-1	48,021
8 Sep 1976		Finland	Hampden Park	6-0	16,338

Joe Jordan (27 caps, 5 goals)

9 May 1973		England	Wembley	0-1	95,950
22 May 1973		Switzerland	Berne	0-1	10,000
30 Jun 1973		Brazil	Hampden Park	0-1	70,000
26 Sep 1973	WCQ	Czechoslovakia (sub)	Hampden Park	2-1(1)	100,000
17 Oct 1973	WCQ	Czechoslovakia	Bratislava	0-1	15,000
14 Nov 1973		West Germany (sub)	Hampden Park	1-1	58,235
11 May 1974		Northern Ireland (sub)	Hampden Park	0-1	53,775
14 May 1974		Wales	Hampden Park	2-0	41,969
18 May 1974		England	Hampden Park	2-0(1)	94,487

Arthur Graham
Scotland

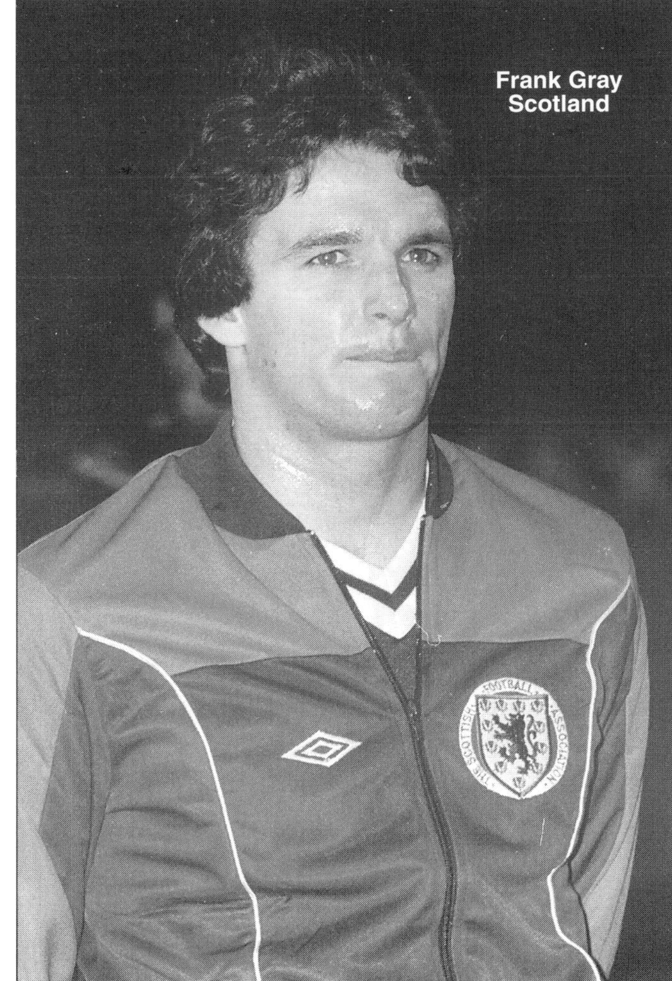
Frank Gray
Scotland

Peter Lorimer
Scotland

Joe Jordan
Scotland

Date	Comp	Opponent	Venue	Score	Att
1 Jun 1974		Belgium	Bruges	1-2	12,000
6 Jun 1974		Norway	Oslo	2-1	18,432
14 Jun 1974	WCF	Zaire	Dortmund	2-0(1)	30,000
18 Jun 1974	WCF	Brazil	Frankfurt	0-0	62,000
22 Jun 1974	WCF	Yugoslavia	Frankfurt	1-1(1)	56,000
30 Oct 1974		East Germany	Hampden Park	3-0	39,445
14 May 1974		Wales	Hampden Park	2-0	41,969
18 May 1974		England	Hampden Park	2-0	94,487
1 Jun 1974		Belgium	Bruges	1-2	12,000
20 Nov 1974	ECQ	Spain	Hampden Park	1-2	92,100
5 Feb 1975	ECQ	Spain	Valencia	1-1(1)	60,000
6 May 1976		Wales	Hampden Park	3-1	25,000
8 May 1976		Northern Ireland	Hampden Park	3-0	49,897
15 May 1976		England	Hampden Park	2-1	85,165
13 Oct 1976	WCQ	Czechoslovakia	Prague	0-2	38,000
17 Nov 1976	WCQ	Wales	Hampden Park	1-0	63,233
1 Jun 1977		Northern Ireland	Hampden Park	3-0	44,699
4 Jun 1977		England	Wembley	2-1	98,108
7 Sep 1977		East Germany	Berlin	0-1	50,000
21 Sep 1977	WCQ	Czechoslovakia	Hampden Park	3-1	85,000
12 Oct 1977	WCQ	Wales	Anfield, Liverpool	2-0	50,800

Jordan won a total of 52 caps: Manchester United 20, AC Milan 5.

Peter Lorimer (21 caps, 4 goals)

Date	Comp	Opponent	Venue	Score	Att
5 Nov 1969	WCQ	Austria (sub)	Vienna	0-2	11,000
15 May 1971		Wales	Cardiff	0-0	19,068
18 May 1971		Northern Ireland	Hampden Park	0-1	31,643
20 May 1972		Northern Ireland (sub)	Hampden Park	2-0(1)	39,710
24 May 1972		Wales	Hampden Park	1-0(1)	21,332
27 May 1972		England	Hampden Park	0-1	119,325
18 Oct 1972	WCQ	Denmark	Copenhagen	4-1	31,000
15 Nov 1972	WCQ	Denmark	Hampden Park	2-0(1)	47,109
14 Feb 1973		England	Hampden Park	0-5	48,470
19 May 1973		England	Wembley	0-1	95,950
14 Nov 1973		West Germany (sub)	Hampden Park	1-1	58,235
18 May 1974		England	Hampden Park	2-0	94,487
1 Jun 1974		Belgium	Bruges	1-2	12,000
6 Jun 1974		Norway	Oslo	2-1	18,432
14 Jun 1974	WCF	Zaire	Dortmund	2-0(1)	30,000
18 Jun 1974	WCF	Brazil	Frankfurt	0-0	62,000
22 Jun 1974	WCF	Yugoslavia	Frankfurt	1-1	56,000
20 Nov 1974	ECQ	Spain (sub)	Hampden Park	1-2	92,100
3 Sep 1975	ECQ	Denmark	Copenhagen	1-0	40,300
29 Oct 1975	ECQ	Denmark	Hampden Park	3-1	48,021
17 Dec 1975	ECQ	Romania	Hampden Park	1-1	11,375

Gary McAllister (41 caps, 4 goals)

Date	Comp	Opponent	Venue	Score	Att
12 Sep 1990	ECQ	Romania	Hampden Park	2-1	12,081
17 Oct 1990	ECQ	Switzerland	Hampden Park	2-1(1)	20,740
14 Nov 1990	ECQ	Bulgaria	Sofia	1-1	40,000
6 Feb 1991		USSR (sub)	Hampden Park	0-1	20,763
1 May 1991	ECQ	San Marino	Serravalle	2-0	3,412
11 Sep 1991	ECQ	Switzerland (sub)	Berne	2-2	48,000
13 Nov 1991	ECQ	San Marino	Hampden Park	4-0	35,170
19 Feb 1992		Northern Ireland	Hampden Park	1-0	13,650
25 Mar 1992		Finland (sub)	Hampden Park	1-1	9,275
17 May 1992		USA	Denver	1-0	24,157
21 May 1992		Canada	Toronto	3-1(2,1pen)	10,872
3 Jun 1992		Norway	Oslo	0-0	8,786
12 Jun 1992	ECF	Holland	Gothenburg	0-1	35,720
15 Jun 1992	ECF	Germany	Norrkoping	0-2	17,638
18 Jun 1992	ECF	CIS	Norrkopping	3-0(1pen)	14,660
9 Sep 1992	WCQ	Switzerland	Berne	1-3	10,000
14 Oct 1992	WCQ	Portugal	Ibrox Park	0-0	22,583
18 Nov 1992	WCQ	Italy	Ibrox Park	0-0	33,029
17 Feb 1993	WCQ	Malta	Ibrox Park	3-0	35,490
8 Sep 1993	WCQ	Switzerland	Aberdeen	1-1	24,000
13 Oct 1993	WCQ	Italy	Rome	1-3	61,78
17 Nov 1993	WCQ	Malta	Taq'uali	2-0	8.000
23 Mar 1994		Holland	Hampden Park	0-1	36,809
20 Apr 1994		Austria	Vienna	2-1	35,000
27 May 1994		Holland	Utrecht	1-3	17,500
7 Sep 1994	ECQ	Finland	Helsinki	2-0	12,845
16 Nov 1994	ECQ	Russia	Hampden Park	1-1	31,254
18 Dec 1994	ECQ	Greece	Athens	0-1	20,310
29 Mar 1995	ECQ	Russia	Moscow	0-0	25,000
26 Apr 1995	ECQ	San Marino	Serraville	2-0	2,738
16 Aug 1995	ECQ	Greece	Hampden Park	1-0	34,910
6 Sep 1995	ECQ	Finland	Hampden Park	1-0	35,505
11 Oct 1995	ECQ	Sweden	Stockholm	0-2	19,121
15 Nov 1995	ECQ	San Marino	Hampden Park	5-0	30,306
27 Mar 1996		Australia	Hampden Park	1-0	20,608
24 Apr 1996		Denmark	Copenhagen	0-2	23,031
26 May 1996		USA (sub)	New Britain	1-2	8,526
29 May 1996		Colombia	Miami	0-1	5,000
10 Jun 1996	ECF	Holland	Villa Park	0-0	34,363
15 Jun 1996	ECF	England	Wembley	0-2	76,864
18 Jun 1996	ECF	Switzerland	Villa Park	1-0	34,926

McAllister currently has a total of 44 caps: Leicester City 3.

Gordon McQueen (17 caps, 3 goals)

Date	Comp	Opponent	Venue	Score	Att
1 Jun 1974		Belgium	Bruges	1-2	12,000
20 Nov 1974	ECQ	Spain	Hampden Park	3-0	39,445
5 Feb 1975	ECQ	Spain	Valencia	1-1	60,000
13 May 1975		Portugal	Hampden Park	1-0	34,307
17 May 1975		Wales	Cardiff	2-2	23,509
20 May 1975		Northern Ireland	Hampden Park	3-0	64,696
24 May 1975		England	Wembley	1-5	98,241
1 Jun 1975	ECQ	Romania	Bucharest	1-1(1)	80,000
3 Sep 1975	ECQ	Denmark	Copenhagen	1-0	40,300
13 Oct 1976	WCQ	Czechoslovakia	Prague	0-2	38,000
17 Nov 1976		Wales	Hampden Park	1-0	62,233
28 May 1977		Wales	Wrexham	0-0	14,468
1 Jun 1977		Northern Ireland	Hampden Park	3-0(1)	44,699
4 Jun 1977		England	Wembley	2-1(1)	98,103
7 Sep 1977		East Germany	Berlin	0-1	50,000
21 Sep 1977	WCQ	Czechoslovakia	Hampden Park	3-1	85,000
12 Oct 1977	WCQ	Wales	Anfield, Liverpool	2-0	50,800

McQueen won a total of 30 caps: Manchester United 13.

David Stewart (1 cap)

Date	Comp	Opponent	Venue	Score	Att
7 Sep 1977		East Germany	Berlin	0-1	50,000

Gordon Strachan (8 caps, 1 goal)

Date	Comp	Opponent	Venue	Score	Att
11 Oct 1989	WCQ	France	Paris	0-3	25,000
6 Feb 1991		USSR	Hampden Park	0-1	20,763
27 Mar 1991	ECQ	Bulgaria	Hampden Park	1-1	33,119
1 May 1991	ECQ	San Marino	Serravalle	2-0(1pen)	3,512
11 Sep 1991	ECQ	Switzerland	Berne	2-2	48,000
16 Oct 1991	ECQ	Romania	Bucharest	0-1	30,000
19 Feb 1992		Northern Ireland	Hampden Park	1-0	13,650
25 Mar 1992		Finland	Hampden Park	1-1	9,275

Strachan won a total of 50 caps: Aberdeen 28, Manchester United 14.

Northern Ireland

Bobby Browne (6 caps)

Date	Comp	Opponent	Venue	Score	Att
19 Oct 1935		England	Belfast	1-3	40,000
11 Mar 1936		Wales	Belfast	3-2	20,000
23 Oct 1937		England	Belfast	1-5	40,000
16 Mar 1938		Wales	Belfast	1-0	15,000
8 Oct 1938		Scotland	Belfast	0-2	40,000
16 Nov 1938		England	Maine Rd, Manchester	0-7	40,386

David Cochrane (12 caps)

Date	Comp	Opponent	Venue	Score	Att
16 Nov 1938		England	Maine Rd, Manchester	0-7	40,386
15 Mar 1939		Wales	Wrexham	1-3	24,000
28 Sep 1946		England	Belfast	2-7	57,000
27 Nov 1946		Scotland	Hampden Park	0-0	98,776
16 Apr 1947		Wales	Belfast	2-1	43,000
4 Oct 1947		Scotland	Belfast	2-0	52,000
5 Nov 1947		England	Goodison Pk, Everton	2-2	68,000
10 Mar 1948		Wales	Wrexham	0-2	33,160
17 Nov 1948		Scotland	Hampden Park	2-3	100,000
9 Mar 1949		Wales	Belfast	0-2	22,800
1 Oct 1949		Scotland	Belfast	2-8	50,000
16 Nov 1949		England	Maine Rd, Manchester	2-9	70,000

Wilbur Cush (15 caps, 5 goals)

Date	Comp	Opponent	Venue	Score	Att
4 Dec 1957		Italy	Belfast	2-2(2)	50,000
15 Jan 1958	WCQ	Italy	Belfast	2-1(1)	60,000
16 Apr 1958		Wales	Cardiff	1-1	38,000
8 Jun 1958	WCF	Czechoslovakia	Halmstad	1-0(1)	10,647
11 Jun 1958	WCF	Argentina	Halmstad	1-3	14,174
15 Jun 1958	WCF	West Germany	Malmö	2-2	21,990
17 Jun 1958	WCF	Czechoslovakia	Malmö	2-1	6,196
19 Jun 1958	WCF	France	Norrkopping	0-4	11,800
4 Oct 1958		England	Belfast	3-3(1)	58,000
15 Oct 1958		Spain	Madrid	2-6	
5 Nov 1958		Scotland	Hampden Park	2-2	72,732
22 Apr 1959		Wales	Belfast	4-1	35,000
3 Oct 1959		Scotland	Belfast	0-4	56,000
18 Nov 1959		England	Wembley	1-2	60,000
6 Apr 1960		Wales	Wrexham	2-3	16,500

Cush won a total of 26 caps: Glenavon 8, Portadown 3.

Harry Duggan (8 caps)

Date	Comp	Opponent	Venue	Score	Att
19 Oct 1929		England	Belfast	0-3	37,000
20 Oct 1930		England	Bramall Ln, Sheffield	1-5	30,000
22 Apr 1931		Wales	Wrexham	2-3	11,693
17 Oct 1932		England	Blackpool	0-1	23,000
14 Oct 1933		England	Belfast	0-3	35,000
20 Oct 1934		Scotland	Belfast	2-1	39,752
27 Mar 1935		Wales	Wrexham	1-3	17,000
13 Nov 1935		Scotland	Tynecastle, Edinburgh	1-2	30,000

Billy McAdams (1 cap)

9 May 1962		Holland	Rotterdam	0-4	

McAdams won a total of 15 caps: Manchester City 5, Bolton Wanderers 9.

John McClelland (1 cap)

27 Mar 1990		Norway	Belfast	2-3	3,500

McClelland won a total of 53 caps: Mansfield Town 6, Glasgow Rangers 26, Watford 20.

Jim McCabe (6 caps)

17 Nov 1948		Scotland	Hampden Park	2-3	100,000
9 Mar 1949		Wales	Belfast	0-2	22,800
16 Nov 1949		England	Maine Rd, Manchester	2-9	70,000
7 Mar 1951		Wales	Belfast	1-2	12,000
15 Apr 1953		Wales	Belfast	2-3	45,000
3 Oct 1953		Scotland	Belfast	2-0	58,248

Con Martin (3 caps)

4 Oct 1947		Scotland	Belfast	2-0	52,000
5 Nov 1947		England	Goodison Pk, Liverpool	2-2	68,000
10 Mar 1948		Wales	Wrexham	0-2	33,160

Martin won a total of 6 caps: Glentoran 1, Aston Villa 2.

Jim Twomey (2 caps)

16 Mar 1938		Wales	Belfast	1-0	15,000
16 Nov 1938		England	Maine Rd, Manchester	0-7	40,386

Nigel Worthington (14 caps to date)

7 Sep 1994	ECQ	Portugal	Belfast	1-2	6,000
12 Oct 1994	ECQ	Austria	Vienna	2-1	26,000
16 Nov 1994	ECQ	Republic of Ireland	Belfast	0-4	10,336
29 Mar 1995	ECQ	Republic of Ireland	Dublin	1-1	32,200
26 Apr 1995	ECQ	Latvia	Riga	1-0	1,560
22 May 1995		Canada	Edmondton	0-0	12,112
26 May 1995		Chile	Edmondton	1-2	6,124
7 Jun 1995	ECQ	Latvia	Belfast	1-2	6,000
3 Sep 1995	ECQ	Portugal	Porto	1-1	50,000
11 Oct 1995	ECQ	Liechtenstein	Eschen	4-0	1,100
15 Nov 1995	ECQ	Austria	Belfast	5-2	8,000
27 Mar 1996		Norway	Belfast	0-2	41,600
24 Apr 1996		Sweden	Belfast	1-2	5,666
29 May 1996		Germany	Belfast	1-1	11,770

Worthington has currently won 64 caps: Sheffield Wednesday 50.

Wales

Mark Aizlewood (9 caps)

18 Feb 1987		USSR	Swansea	0-0	17,617
1 Apr 1987	ECQ	Finland (sub)	Wrexham	4-0	7,696
9 Sep 1987	ECQ	Denmark (sub)	Cardiff	1-0	20,535
27 Apr 1988		Sweden	Stockholm	1-4	11,656
1 Jun 1988		Malta	Valetta	3-2	7,000
4 Jun 1988		Italy	Brescia	1-0	21,000
14 Sep 1988		Holland	Amsterdam	0-1	58,000
31 May 1989	WCQ	West Germany	Cardiff	0-0	25,000

Aizlewood won a total of 39 caps: Charlton Athletic 5, Bradford City 4, Bristol City 21, Cardiff City 1.

John Charles (21 caps, 12 goals)

8 Mar 1950		Northern Ireland	Wrexam	0-0	33,000
16 May 1951		Switzerland	Wrexham	3-2	28,000
15 Apr 1953		Northern Ireland	Belfast	3-2(2)	45,000
14 May 1953		France	Paris	1-6	32,000
21 May 1953		Yugoslavia	Belgrade	2-5	40,000
10 Oct 1953		England	Cardiff	1-4	61,000
4 Nov 1953		Scotland	Hampden Park	3-3(2)	71,378
21 Mar 1954		Northern Ireland	Wrexham	1-2(1)	32,187
9 May 1954		Austria	Vienna	0-2	60,000
22 Sep 1954		Yugoslavia	Cardiff	1-3	48,000
16 Oct 1954		Scotland	Cardiff	0-1	60,000
10 Nov 1954		England	Wembley	2-3(2)	91,112
20 Apr 1955		Northern Ireland	Belfast	3-2(3)	30,000
22 Oct 1955		England	Cardiff	2-1	60,000
9 Nov 1955		Scotland	Hampden Park	0-2	53,887
23 Nov 1955		Austria	Wrexham	1-2	23,000
11 Apr 1956		Northern Ireland	Cardiff	1-1	45,000
20 Oct 1956		Scotland	Cardiff	2-2	60,000
14 Nov 1956		England	Wembley	1-3(1)	93,796
10 Apr 1957		Northern Ireland	Belfast	0-0	30,000
20 Oct 1962		Scotland	Cardiff	2-3(1)	50,000

Charles won a total of 38 caps: Juventus 7, Roma 4, Cardiff City 3.

Alan Curtis (6 caps, 2 goals)

23 May 1979		England	Wembley	0-0	70,250
25 May 1979		Wales	Belfast	1-1	6,500
2 Jun 1979	ECQ	Malta	Valetta	2-0	9,000
11 Sep 1979		Republic of Ireland	Swansea	2-1(1)	6,825
17 Oct 1979	ECQ	West Germany	Cologne	1-5(1)	60,000
21 Nov 1979	ECQ	Turkey	Izmir	0-1	50,000

Curtis won a total of 35 caps: Swansea City 23, Southampton 5, Cardiff City 1.

Brian Flynn (32 caps, 4 goals)

16 Nov 1977	WCQ	Czechoslovakia	Prague	0-1	20,000
14 Dec 1977		West Germany	Dortmund	1-1	53,000
18 Apr 1978		Iran (sub)	Teheran	1-0	45,000
13 May 1978		England	Cardiff	1-3	17,698
17 May 1978		Scotland	Hampden Park	1-1	70,241
19 May 1978		Northern Ireland	Wrexham	1-0	9,077
25 Oct 1978	ECQ	Malta	Wrexham	7-0(1)	11,475
29 Nov 1978	ECQ	Turkey	Wrexham	1-0	11,800
19 May 1979		Scotland	Cardiff	3-0	20,371
23 May 1979		England	Wembley	0-0	75,000
25 May 1979		Northern Ireland	Belfast	1-1	6,500
2 Jun 1979	ECQ	Malta	Valetta	2-0(1)	9,000
11 Sep 1979		Republic of Ireland	Swansea	2-1	6,825
17 Oct 1979	ECQ	West Germany	Cologne	1-5	60,000
17 May 1980		England	Wrexham	4-1	24,236
21 May 1980		Scotland	Hampden Park	0-1	24,236
23 May 1980		Northern Ireland	Cardiff	0-1	12,913
2 Jun 1980	WCQ	Iceland	Reykjavik	4-0(1pen)	10,254
15 Oct 1980	WCQ	Turkey	Cardiff	4-0(1)	11,770
19 Nov 1980	WCQ	Czechoslovakia	Cardiff	1-0	20,175
24 Feb 1980		Republic of Ireland	Cardiff	3-1	15,000
25 Mar 1981	WCQ	Turkey	Ankara	1-0	35,000
16 May 1981		Scotland	Swansea	2-0	18,985
20 May 1981		England	Wembley	0-0	34,250
30 May 1981	WCQ	USSR	Wrexham	0-0	29,366
9 Sep 1981	WCQ	Czechoslovakia	Prague	0-2	41,500
18 Nov 1981	WCQ	USSR	Tbilisi	0-3	80,000
27 Apr 1982		England	Cardiff	0-1	50,000
24 May 1982		Scotland	Hampden Park	0-1	25,284
27 May 1982		Northern Ireland	Wrexham	3-0	2,315
2 Jun 1982		France	Toulouse	1-0	35,000
22 Sep 1982	ECQ	Norway	Swansea	1-0	5,000

Flynn won a total of 66 caps: Burnley 34.

Carl Harris (24 caps, 1 goal)

24 Mar 1976		England	Wrexham	1-2	21,000
6 May 1976		Scotland	Hampden Park	1-3	35,000
14 Dec 1977		West Germany	Dortmund	1-1	53,000
18 Apr 1978		Iran (sub)	Teheran	1-0	45,000
13 May 1978		England	Cardiff	1-3	17,698
17 May 1978		Scotland	Hampden Park	1-1	70,241
19 May 1978		Northern Ireland	Wrexham	1-0	9,077
25 Oct 1978	ECQ	Malta	Wrexham	7-0	11,475
29 Nov 1978	ECQ	Turkey	Wrexham	1-0	11,800
2 May 1979	ECQ	West Germany	Wrexham	0-2	26,900
23 May 1979		England	Wembley	0-0	70,250
2 Jun 1979	ECQ	Malta	Valetta	2-0	9,000
23 May 1980		Northern Ireland (sub)	Cardiff	0-1	12,913
2 Jun 1980	WCQ	Iceland (sub)	Reykjavik	4-0	10,254
15 Oct 1980	WCQ	Turkey	Cardiff	4-0	11,770
19 Nov 1980	WCQ	Czechoslovakia (sub)	Cardiff	1-0	20,175
24 Feb 1980		Republic of Ireland	Cardiff	3-1	15,000
25 Mar 1981	WCQ	Turkey	Ankara	1-0(1)	35,000
16 May 1981		Scotland	Swansea	2-0	18,985
20 May 1981		England	Wembley	0-0	34,250
30 May 1981	WCQ	USSR	Wrexham	0-0	29,366
9 Sep 1981	WCQ	Czechoslovakia	Prague	0-2	41,500
7 Oct 1981	WCQ	Iceland	Swansea	2-2	20,000
27 Apr 1982		England	Cardiff	0-1	50,000

Aubrey Powell (5 caps)

19 Oct 1946		Scotland	Wrexham	3-1	29,568
13 Nov 1946		England	Maine Rd, Manchester	0-3	59,250
18 Oct 1947		England	Cardiff	0-3	55,000
12 Nov 1947		Scotland	Hampden Park	2-1	88,000
10 Mar 1948		Northern Ireland	Wrexham	2-0	33,160

Gary Speed (36 caps, 2 goals)

20 May 1990		Costa Rica (sub)	Cardiff	1-0	5,977
11 Sep 1990		Denmark	Copenhagen	0-1	8,700
14 Nov 1990	ECQ	Luxembourg (sub)	Luxembourg	1-0	6,800
6 Feb 1990		Republic of Ireland (sub)	Wrexham	0-3	9,168
1 May 1991		Iceland	Cardiff	1-0	3,656
5 Jun 1991	ECQ	Germany (sub)	Cardiff	1-0	38,000
11 Sep 1991		Brazil	Cardiff	1-0	20,000
16 Oct 1991	ECQ	Germany (sub)	Nuremburg	1-4	46,000
13 Nov 1991	ECQ	Luxembourg	Cardiff	1-0	20,000
19 Feb 1992		Republic of Ireland	Dublin	1-0	15,100
20 May 1992	WCQ	Romania	Bucharest	1-5	23,000
30 May 1992		Holland	Utrecht	0-4	20,000
3 Jun 1992		Argentina	Tokyo	0-1	31,000
7 Jun 1992		Japan	Matsuyama	1-0	30,000

9 Sep 1992	WCQ	Faeroes	Cardiff	6-0	6,000
14 Oct 1992	WCQ	Cyprus	Limassol	1-0	15,000
18 Nov 1992	WCQ	Belgium	Brussels	0-2	21,000
17 Feb 1993		Republic of Ireland	Dublin	1-2	9,500
31 Mar 1993	WCQ	Belgium	Cardiff	2-0	27,002
6 Jun 1993	WCQ	Faeroes (sub)	Toftir	3-0	4,209
8 Sep 1993	WCQ	RCS (sub)	Cardiff	2-2	37,558
13 Oct 1993	WCQ	Cyprus	Cardiff	2-0	10,000
17 Nov 1993	WCQ	Romania	Cardiff	1-2	40,000
9 Mar 1994		Norway	Cardiff	1-3	10,000
20 Mar 1994		Sweden	Wrexham	0-2	4,694
7 Sep 1994	ECQ	Albania	Cardiff	2-0	15,791
12 Oct 1994	ECQ	Moldova	Kishinev	2-3(1)	12,000
16 Nov 1994	ECQ	Georgia	Tblisi	0-5	45,000
14 Dec 1994	ECQ	Bulgaria	Cardiff	0-3	20,000
29 Mar 1995	ECQ	Bulgaria	Sofia	1-3	60,000
26 Apr 1995	ECQ	Germany	Dussledorf	1-1	45,000
6 Sep 1995	ECQ	Moldova	Cardiff	1-0(1)	5,000
1 Oct 1995	ECQ	Germany	Cardiff	1-2	25,000
15 Nov 1995	ECQ	Albania	Tirana	1-1	6,000
24 Jan 1996		Italy	Terni	0-3	20,000
24 Apr 1996		Switzerland (sub)	Lugano	0-2	8,000

Gary Sprake (32 caps)

20 Nov 1963		Scotland	Hampden Park	1-2	56,067
15 Apr 1064		Northern Ireland	Swansea	2-3	10,434
3 Oct 1964		Scotland	Cardiff	3-2	50,000
21 Oct 1964	WCQ	Denmark	Copenhagen	0-1	30,000
9 Dec 1964	WCQ	Greece	Athens	0-2	26,000
2 Oct 1965		England	Cardiff	0-0	30,000
27 Oct 1965	WCQ	USSR	Cardiff	2-1	34,521
30 Mar 1966		Northern Ireland	Cardiff	1-4	12,860
22 Oct 1966		Scotland	Cardiff	1-1	32,500
21 Oct 1967		England	Cardiff	0-3	45,000
22 Nov 1967		Scotland	Hampden Park	2-3	57,472
26 Mar 1969		West Germany	Frankfurt	1-1	40,000
3 May 1969		Scotland	Wrexham	3-5	18,765
7 May 1969		England	Wembley	1-2	70,000
10 May 1969		Northern Ireland	Belfast	0-0	12,500
28 Jul 1969		Rest of UK	Cardiff	0-1	14,000
22 Oct 1969	WCQ	East Germany	Cardiff	1-3	22,409
4 Nov 1969	WCQ	Italy	Rome	1-4	90,000
11 Nov 1969	ECQ	Romania	Cardiff	0-0	29,000
15 May 1971		Scotland	Cardiff	0-0	19,068
18 May 1971		England	Wembley	0-0	85,000
22 May 1971		Northern Ireland	Belfast	0-1	22,000
13 Oct 1971	ECQ	Finland	Swansea	3-0	10,301
20 May 1972		England	Cardiff	0-3	34,000
24 May 1972		Scotland	Hampden Park	0-1	21,332
27 May 1972		Northern Ireland	Wrexham	0-0	15,647
15 Nov 1972	WCQ	England	Cardiff	0-1	36,384
24 Jan 1973	WCQ	England	Wembley	1-1	62,000
28 Mar 1973	WCQ	Poland	Cardiff	2-0	12,000
12 May 1973		Scotland	Wrexham	0-2	17,765
19 May 1973		Northern Ireland	Anfield, Liverpool	0-1	4,946
26 Sep 1973	WCQ	Poland	Chorzow	0-3	120,000

Sprake won a total of 37 caps: Birmingham City 5.

Byron Stevenson (11 caps)

19 May 1978		Northern Ireland	Wrexham	1-0	9,077
25 Oct 1978	ECQ	Malta	Wrexham	7-0	11,475
29 Nov 1978	ECQ	Turkey	Wrexham	1-0	11,800
19 May 1979		Scotland	Cardiff	3-0	20,371
23 May 1979		England	Wembley	0-0	75,000
25 May 1979		Northern Ireland	Belfast	1-1	6,500
2 Jun 1979	ECQ	Malta	Valetta	2-0	9,000
17 Oct 1979	ECQ	West Germany	Cologne	1-5	60,000
21 Nov 1979	ECQ	Turkey	Izmir	0-1	50,000
2 Jun 1980	WCQ	Iceland (sub)	Reykjavik	4-0	10,254
9 Sep 1981	WCQ	Czechoslovakia	Prague	0-2	41,500

Stevenson won a total of 15 caps: Birmingham City 4.

Harold Williams (2 caps)

8 Mar 1950		Northern Ireland	Wrexham	0-0	33,000
21 Oct 1950		Scotland	Cardiff	1-3	60,000

Terry Yorath (28 caps, 1 goal)

4 Nov 1969	WCQ	Italy	Rome	1-4	90,000
15 May 1971		Scotland	Cardiff	0-0	19,068
18 May 1971		England	Wembley	0-0	85,000
22 May 1971		Northern Ireland	Belfast	0-1	22,000
27 Oct 1971	ECQ	Czechoslovakia	Prague	0-1	32,000
20 May 1972		England	Cardiff	0-3	34,000
24 May 1972		Scotland	Hampden Park	0-1	21,332
27 May 1972		Northern Ireland	Wrexham	0-0	15,647
24 Jan 1973	WCQ	England	Wembley	1-1	62,000
28 Mar 1973	WCQ	Poland	Cardiff	2-0	12,000
12 May 1973		Scotland	Wrexham	0-2	17,765
26 Sep 1973	WCQ	Poland	Chorzow	0-3	120,000
11 May 1974		England	Cardiff	0-2	26,000
14 May 1974		Scotland	Hampden Park	0-2	41,969
18 May 1974		Northern Ireland	Wrexham	1-0	9,311
13 Sep 1974	ECQ	Austria	Vienna	1-2	34,000
30 Oct 1974	ECQ	Hungary	Cardiff	2-0	8,445
20 Nov 1974	ECQ	Luxembourg	Swansea	5-0(1)	10,530
16 Apr 1975	ECQ	Hungary	Budapest	2-1	30,000
1 May 1975	ECQ	Luxembourg	Luxembourg	3-1	5,000
17 May 1975		Scotland	Cardiff	2-2	23,509
19 Nov 1975	ECQ	Austria	Wrexham	1-0	28,182
24 Mar 1976		England	Wrexham	1-2	20,987
24 Apr 1976	ECF	Yugoslavia	Zagreb	0-2	55,000
6 May 1976		Scotland	Hampden Park	1-3	25,000
8 May 1976		England	Cardiff	0-1	24,500
14 May 1976		Northern Ireland	Swansea	1-0	10,000
22 May 1976	ECF	Yugoslavia	Cardiff	1-1	30,000

Yorath won a total of 59 caps: Coventry City 20, Tottenham Hotspur 8, Vancouver Whitecaps 3.

Republic of Ireland

Jeff Chandler (2 caps)

26 Sep 1979		Czechoslavakia (sub)	Prague	1-4	12,000
29 Oct 1979		USA	Dublin	3-2	17,000

Harry Duggan (4 caps)

27 Apr 1927		Italy B	Dublin	1-2	20,000
11 May 1930		Belgium	Brussels	3-1	15,000
3 May 1936		Hungary	Budapest	3-3	20,000
9 May 1936		Luxembourg	Luxembourg	5-1	8,000

Duggan won a total of 5 caps: Newport County 1. He also won 8 caps for Northern Ireland.

Peter Fitzgerald (3 caps, 2 goals)

28 Sep 1960		Wales	Dublin	2-3	20,000
6 Nov 1960		Norway	Dublin	3-1(2)	26,000
7 May 1961	WCQ	Scotland	Dublin	0-3	36,000

Fitzgerald won a total of 5 caps: Chester 2.

Johnny Giles (32 caps, 2 goals)

23 Sep 1963	ECQ	Austria	Vienna	0-0	26,800
13 Oct 1963	ECQ	Austria	Dublin	3-2	40,000
11 Mar 1964	ECQ	Spain	Seville	1-5	27,200
8 Apr 1964	ECQ	Spain	Dublin	0-2	38,100
10 May 1964		Poland	Cracow	1-3	60,000
13 May 1964		Norway	Oslo	4-1(1)	14,354
24 May 1964		England	Dublin	1-3	40,000
5 May 1965	WCQ	Spain	Dublin	1-0	40,772
27 Oct 1965	WCQ	Spain	Seville	1-4	29,452
10 Nov 1965	WCQ	Spain	Paris	0-1	35,731
22 May 1966		Austria	Vienna	0-1	33,000
25 May 1966		Belgium	Liege	3-2	3,000
23 Oct 1966	ECQ	Spain	Dublin	0-0	37,000
16 Nov 1966	ECQ	Turkey	Dublin	2-1	20,000
22 Feb 1967	ECQ	Turkey	Ankara	1-2	35,000
10 Nov 1967		Austria	Dublin	2-2	18,000
4 Dec 1968	WCQ	Denmark*	Dublin	1-1(1)	23,000
4 May 1969	WCQ	Czechoslovakia	Dublin	1-2	32,002
21 Sep 1969		Scotland	Dublin	1-1	27,000
6 May 1970		Poland	Poznan	1-2	35,000
9 May 1970		West Germany	Berlin	1-2	60,000
10 May 1971	ECQ	Italy	Dublin	1-2	25,000
15 Nov 1972	WCQ	France	Dublin	2-1	30,000
13 May 1973	WCQ	USSR	Moscow	0-1	70,000
5 May 1974		Brazil	Rio de Janiero	1-2	74,696
8 May 1974		Uruguay	Montevideo	0-2	40,000
12 May 1974		Chile	Sanitago	2-1	
30 Oct 1974	WCQ	USSR	Dublin	3-0	35,000
20 Nov 1974	ECQ	Turkey	Izmir	1-1	67,000
10 May 1975	ECQ	Switzerland	Dublin	2-1	50,000
18 May 1975	ECQ	USSR	Kiev	1-2	100,000
21 May 1975	ECQ	Switzerland	Berne	0-1	20,000

*Abandoned after 50 minutes because of fog, caps were still awarded.

Giles won a total of 59 caps: Manchester United 11, West Bromwich Albion 7, Shamrock Rovers 9.

Gary Kelly (18 caps to date, 1 goal)

23 Mar 1994		Russia	Dublin	0-0	34,000
20 Apr 1994		Holland	Tilburg	1-0	30,000
24 May 1994		Bolivia (sub)	Dublin	1-0	32,500
29 May 1994		Germany (sub)	Hanover	2-0(1)	50,000
5 Jun 1994		Czech Republic	Dublin	1-3	43,465
28 Jun 1994	WCF	Norway	New York	0-0	76,332
4 Jul 1994	WCF	Holland	Orlando	0-2	61,355
7 Sep 1994	ECQ	Latvia	Riga	3-0	2,200
12 Oct 1994	ECQ	Liechtenstein	Dublin	4-0	32,980

Tony Dorigo
England

16 Nov 1994	ECQ	Northern Ireland	Belfast	4-0	10,336
29 Mar 1995	ECQ	Northern Ireland	Dublin	1-1	32,500
26 Apr 1995	ECQ	Portugal	Dublin	1-0	33,000
3 Jun 1995	ECQ	Liechtenstein	Eschen	0-0	4,500
11 Jun 1995	ECQ	Austria	Dublin	1-3	33,000
6 Sep 1995	ECQ	Austria	Vienna	1-3	24,000
11 Oct 1995	ECQ	Latvia	Dublin	2-1	33,000
15 Nov 1995	ECQ	Portugal	Lisbon	0-3	80,000
13 Dec 1995	ECQ	Holland	Anfield, Liverpool	0-2	40,000

Con Martin (3 caps)

2 Mar 1947		Spain	Dublin	3-2	42,102
23 May 1948		Portugal	Lisbon	0-2	50,000
30 May 1948		Spain	Barcelona	1-2	65,000

Martin won a total of 30 caps: Glentoran 3, Aston Villa 24.

Noel Peyton (5 caps)

11 May 1960		West Germany	Dusseldorf	1-0	51,000
18 May 1960		Sweden	Malmo	1-4	31,339
28 Sep 1960		Wales	Dublin	2-3	20,000
2 Sep 1962	ECQ	Iceland	Reykjavik	1-1	9,100
9 Jun 1963		Scotland	Dublin	1-0	26,000

Peyton won a total of 6 caps: Shamrock Rovers 1.

John Sheridan (5 caps, 1 goal)

23 Mar 1988		Romania	Dublin	2-0	15,000
27 Apr 1988		Yugoslavia	Dublin	2-0	12,000
22 May 1988		Poland	Dublin	3-1(1)	18,500
1 Jun 1988		Norway (sub)	Oslo	0-0	9,494
16 Nov 1988	WCQ	Spain	Seville	0-2	50,000

Sheridan has won a total of 33 caps: Sheffield Wednesday 28.

France

Eric Cantona (9 caps, 2 goals)

19 Feb 1992		England	Wembley	0-2	58,723
10 Jun 1992	ECF	Sweden	Stockholm	1-1	29,860
14 Jun 1992	ECF	England	Malmö	0-0	26,535
17 Jun 1992	ECF	Denmark	Malmö	1-2	25,763
14 Oct 1992	WCQ	Austria	Paris	2-0(1)	39,186
14 Nov 1992		Finland	Paris	2-1(1)	30,000
25 Mar 1992		Belgium	Paris	3-3	
27 May 1992		Switzerland	Lausanne	2-1	
5 Jun 1992		Holland	Lens	1-1	

Cantona currently has a total of 45 caps.

Ghana

Tony Yeboah (10 caps, 2 goals)

9 Apr 1995		Sierra Leone			
23 Apr 1995		Niger			
14 Dec 1995					
14 Jan 1996	ACF	Ivory Coast	Port Elizabeth	2-0(1)	8,000
19 Jan 1996	ACF	Tunisia	Port Elizabeth	2-1	1,000
25 Jan 1996	ACF	Mozambique	Bloemfontein	2-0	3,500
28 Jan 1996	ACF	Zaire	Port Elizabeth	1-0(1)	8,000
31 Jan 1996	ACF	South Africa	Johannesburg	0-3	80,000
4 Feb 1996	ACF	Zambia	Johnannesburg	0-1	80,000
27 Mar 1996		Brazil	Sep Jose Do Rio Preto	2-8(1)	

Yeboah currently has a total of 42 caps.

Norway

Frank Strandli (1 cap, 1 goal)

15 Jan 1994		USA	Phoenix	1-0(1)	20,000

Strandli has won a total of 7 caps: IK Start 6.

South Africa

Phil Masinga (10 caps, 4 goals)

Sep 1995	ACQ	Madagascar	Antananario	1-0((1))	-
15 Oct 1995	ACQ	Mauritius		1-0(1)	-
Nov 1995	ACQ	Zambia			
15 Dec 1995		Germany	Johnanesburg	0-0	27,500
13 Jan 1996	ACF	Cameroon	Johannesburg	3-0(1)	75,000
20 Jan 1996	ACF	Angola	Johannesburg	1-0	30,000
24 Jan 1996	ACF	Egypt	Johannesbrug	0-1	20,000
27 Jan 1996	ACF	Algeria	Johannesburg	2-1	30,000
4 Feb 1996	ACF	Tunisia	Johnanesburg	2-0	80,000
24 Apr 1996		Brazil	Johannesburg	2-3(1)	80,000

Masinga currently has a total of 23 caps.

Lucas Radebe (7 caps)

Sep 1995	ACQ	Madagascar	Antananario	1-0	
15 Oct 1995	ACQ	Mauritius		1-0	
Nov 1995	ACQ	Zambia			
24 Jan 1996	ACF	Egypt	Johannesbrug	0-1	40,000
31 Jan 1996	ACF	Ghana	Johannesburg	3-0	
4 Feb 1996	ACF	Tunisia	Johnanesburg	2-0	80,000
24 Apr 1996		Brazil	Johannesburg	2-3	80,000

Australia

Harry Kewell (1 cap)

23 Apr 1996	Chile	Antofagusta	0-3	15,000

'B' Internationals

England

David Batty (5 caps)

14 Nov 1989	Italy	Brighton	1-0	16,125
12 Dec 1989	Yugoslavia	Millwall	2-1	8,231
27 Mar 1990	Republic of Ireland	Cork	4-1	10,000
27 Apr 1991	Iceland	Watford	1-0	3,814
24 Mar 1992	Czechoslavakia	Budejovice	1-0	6,000

Lee Chapman (1 cap)

27 Apr 1991	Iceland	Watford	1-0	3,814

Jack Charlton (2 caps)

20 May 1970	Colombia	Bogata	1-0	28,000
24 May 1970	Liga Deportiva Universidad	Quito	4-1	22,250

Allan Clarke (2 caps)

20 May 1970	Colombia	Bogata	1-0	28,000
24 May 1970	Liga Deportiva Universidad	Quito	4-1	22,250

Tony Dorigo (2 caps)

18 Feb 1992	France	Loftus Rd, London	3-0	4,827
24 Mar 1992	Czechoslovakia	Budejovice	1-0	6,000

Norman Hunter (2 caps)

20 May 1970	Colombia	Bogata	1-0	28,000
24 May 1970	Liga Deportiva Universidad	Quito	4-1	22,250

John Lukic (1 cap)

11 Dec 1990	Algeria (sub)	Algiers	0-0	1,000

Mel Sterland (2 caps)

12 Dec 1989	Yugoslavia (sub)	Millwall	2-1	8,231
11 Dec 1990	Algeria	Algiers	0-0	1,000

Republic of Ireland

Jim Beglin (1 cap)

27 Mar 1990	England	Cork	1-4	10,000

Ian Harte (4 caps, 1 goal)

2 Jun 1996	Croatia (sub)	Dublin	2-2	29,100
4 Jun 1996	Holland	Rotterdam	1-3	-
12 Jun 1996	Mexico	New Jersey	2-2	21,322
15 Jun 1996	Bolivia	New Jersey	3-0(l)	14,624

John Sheridan (1 cap, 1 goal)

11 Apr 1989	Northern Ireland	Dublin	3-0(1pen)	3,200

Sheridan won a total of 3 caps: Sheffield Wednesday 2.

Under-23 Internationals

England

Chris Crowe (2 caps, 1 goal)

11 Nov 1959	France	Sunderland	2-0(1)	26,495
2 Mar 1960	Scotland	Hampden Park	4-4	25,000

Norman Hunter (3 caps)

4 Nov 1964	Wales	Wrexham	3-2	15,193
25 Nov 1964	Romania	Coventry	5-0	27,476
24 Feb 1965	Scotland	Aberdeen	0-0	25,000

Mike O'Grady (1 cap)

3 Nov 1965	France	Norwich	3-0	20,203

Paul Reaney (5 caps)

5 Feb 1965	Scotland	Newcastle	3-2	35,032
8 Apr 1965	France	Rouen	2-2	15,000

24 Feb 1965		Scotland	Aberdeen	0-0	25,000
25 May 1965		West Germany	Frieburg	0-1	15,000
29 May 1965		Czechoslovakia	Liberec	0-0	6,000

Scotland

Billy Bremner (3 caps, 1 goal)

24 May 1964		France	Nantes	2-0	1,000
2 Dec 1964		Wales	Kilmarnock	3-0(1)	6,000
24 Feb 1965		England	Aberdeen	0-0	25,000

Eddie Gray (2 caps, 2 goals)

30 Nov 1966		Wales	Wrexham	6-0(2)	5,341
1 Mar 1967		England	Newcastle	3-1	22,097

Frank Gray (5 caps)

13 Mar 1974		England	Newcastle	0-2	4,511
2 Sep 1975	ECQ	Denmark	Frederikshavn	1-0	6,000
28 Oct 1975	ECQ	Denmark	Easter Rd, Edinburgh	4-1	16,500
16 Dec 1975	ECQ	Romania	Falkirk	4-0	8,000
24 Mar 1975	ECQ	Holland	Easter Rd, Edinburgh	2-0*	32,593

*After extra-time. Holland won 4-3 on penalties. The first leg finished 2-0 to Holland in Breda.

Joe Jordan (1 cap)

24 Mar 1975	ECQ	Holland	Easter Rd, Edinburgh	2-0*	32,593

*After extra time. Holland won 4-3 on penalties. The first leg finished 2-0 to Holland in Breda.

Peter Lorimer (2 caps, 2 goals)

3 Dec 1969		France	Glasgow	4-0(2)	5,004
14 Jan 1970		Wales	Aberdeen	1-1	14,500

Wales

Carl Harris (1 cap)

4 Feb 1976		Scotland	Wrexham	2-3	2,222

Denis Hawkins (5 caps)

30 Nov 1966		Scotland	Wrexham	0-6	5,341
22 Feb 1967*		Northern Ireland	Belfast	1-2	8,000
1 Nov 1967		England	Swansea	1-2	14,928
20 Mar 1968		Northern Ireland	Cardiff	0-1	2,669
2 Oct 1968		England	Wrexham	1-3	11,084

*Abandoned after 73 minutes, ground waterlogged.

Glan Letheran (1 cap)

4 Feb 1976		Scotland	Wrexham	2-3	2,222

Gary Sprake (5 caps)

13 Nov 1963		England	Ashton Gate, Bristol	1-1	16,841
4 Dec 1963		Scotland	Wrexham	3-1	10,716
5 Feb 1964		Northern Ireland	Belfast	3-3	18,000
4 Nov 1964		England	Wrexham	3-2	15,193
10 Feb 1965		Northern Ireland	Cardiff	2-2	6,000

Terry Yorath (7 caps)

2 Oct 1968		England	Wrexham	1-3	11,084
1 Oct 1969		England	Ashton Gate, Bristol	0-2	22,286
14 Jan 1970		Scotland	Aberdeen	1-1	14,500
2 Dec 1970		England	Wrexham	0-0	16,367
5 Jan 1972		England	Swindon	0-2	18,028
26 Jan 1972		Scotland	Aberdeen	0-2	15,000
29 Nov 1972		England	Swansea	0-3	6,414

Under-21 Internationals

(1976 to date)

England

David Batty (7 caps, 1 goal)

28 May 1988		Switzerland (sub)	Lausanne	1-1	1,000
7 Feb 1989		Greece (sub)	Patras	0-1	2,000
5 Jun 1989		Bulgaria	Toulon	2-3	1,000
7 Jun 1989		Senegal	Toulon	6-1(1)	1,000
9 Jun 1989		Republic of Ireland	Toulon	0-0	1,000
11 Jun 1989		USA	Toulon	0-2	1,000
10 Oct 1989	ECQ	Poland	Jastrzbruj	3-1	5,000

Andy Couzens (3 caps)

8 Jun 1995		Malaysia (sub)	Toulon	2-0	700
10 Jun 1995		Angola	Toulon	1-0	250
12 Jun 1995		France (sub)	Toulon	0-2	650

John Lukic (7 caps)

9 Sep 1980		Norway	Southampton	3-0	6,973
14 Oct 1980	ECQ	Romania	Ploesti	0-4	10,000
25 Feb 1980		Republic of Ireland	Anfield, Liverpool	1-0	5,882
28 Apr 1981	ECQ	Romania	Swindon	3-0	8,739
31 May 1981	ECQ	Switzerland	Neuchatel	0-0	1,500
5 Jun 1981	ECQ	Hungary	Keszthely	2-1	8,000
17 Nov 1981	ECQ	Hungary	City Gd, Nottingham	2-0	8,734

Noel Whelan (2 caps, 1 goal)

11 Oct 1994		Austria (sub)	Kapfenburg	3-1	2,800
15 Nov 1994		Republic of Ireland	Newcastle	1-0(1)	25,863

Scotland

David McNiven (3 caps, 1 goal)

12 Oct 1976		Czechoslavakia	Pilsen	0-0	3,000
9 Feb 1977		Wales (sub)	Easter Rd, Edinburgh	3-2(1)	4,538
30 Mar 1978		Switzerland (sub)	Berne	0-2	500

Wales

Steve Balcombe (1 cap)

24 Feb 1982		Frances (sub)	Troyes	0-0	4,811

Glan Letheran (2 caps)

15 Dec 1976		England	Wolverhampton	0-0	4,389
9 Feb 1977		Scotland	Easter Rd, Edinburgh	2-3	4,538

Gary Speed (3 caps)

19 May 1990		Poland	Merthyr	2-0	1,785
5 Dec 1990		England	Tranmere	0-0	6,288
30 May 1991		Poland	Warsaw	2-0(2)	500

Byron Stevenson (3 caps)

15 Dec 1976		England	Wolverhampton	0-0	4,389
9 Feb 1977		Scotland	Easter Rd, Edinburgh	2-3	4,538
8 Feb 1978		Scotland	Chester	1-0	2,454

Gwyn Thomas (3 caps)

15 Dec 1976		England	Wolverhampton	0-0	4,389
6 Feb 1979		England	Swansea	0-1	5,642
20 Sep 1979	ECQ	Norway	Frederikstad	3-2	1,051

Republic of Ireland

Len Curtis (2 caps, 1 goal)

24 Mar 1992		Switzerland	Dublin	1-1	1,500
25 May 1992	ECQ	Albania	Dublin	3-1	1,200

Gary Kelly (5 caps)

17 Nov 1992	ECQ	Spain (sub)	Jerez	1-2	12,000
9 Mar 1993	ECQ	Germany	Dublin	0-1	
23 Mar 1993	ECQ	Germany	Baunatal	0-8	
26 May 1993	ECQ	Albania	Tirana	1-1	
12 Oct 1993	ECQ	Spain	Drogheda	0-2	5,000

Tony O'Dowd (3 caps)

30 May 1990		Malta (sub)	Valetta	1-1	
16 Oct 1990	ECQ	Turkey	Dublin	3-2	3,500
13 Nov 1990	ECQ	England	Cork	0-3	3,000

O'Dowd won a total of 4 caps: Shelbourne 1.

John Sheridan (2 caps)

25 Mar 1985		England	Portsmouth	2-3	5,489
17 Mar 1987	ECQ	Scotland	Easter Rd, Edinburgh	1-4	4,136

Curtis and O'Dowd have not played first-team football for Leeds United.

Unofficial Internationals

(Including Wartime and Victory games)

England

Jack Charlton

4 Jun 1969	Mexico XI	Guadalajara	4-0	45,000

This game was played as part of England's 1970 World Cup warm-up programme.

Trevor Cherry

31 May 1976	Team America	Philadelphia	3-1	16,231

This game was played as part of the United States bicentennial tournament.

Terry Cooper

17 May 1967	Young England	Highbury, Arsenal	1-4	20,077

Jack Charlton
England

Billy Bremner
Scotland

Wilf Copping
13 Apr 1939 Wales | Wembley | 0-1 | 40,000

Paul Reaney
17 May 1967 Young England | Highbury, Arsenal | 1-4 | 20,077

Scotland

Billy Bremner
24 Feb 1964 Scottish League | Ibrox Park, Glasgow | 3-1

Peter Lorimer
27 Jan 1971 Celtic/Rangers XI | Hampden Park | 2-1(1) | 81,405
This game was played to raise money for the Ibrox Park Disaster Fund.

Wales

Aubrey Powell

Date	Opponent	Venue	Score	Attendance
8 May 1943	England	Cardiff	1-1	25,000
25 Sep 1943	England	Wembley	3-8(1)	80,000
20 Oct 1945	England	West Bromwich A	1-0(1)	56,000
4 May 1946	Northern Ireland	Cardiff	0-1	45,000

All Ireland

Johnny Giles
4 Jul 1973 Brazil Dublin | 3-4 | 30,000
This match, at Landsdowne Road, was regarded as a full international by the Brazilian FA, but not the Irish.

Irish Free State

Harry Duggan
6 May 1936 Rhineland | Cologne | 1-4
The Irish international side were touring Germany and played a German international side which was chosen from players from the Rhineland only, so it has never been included by the Republic in official records.

Rest of United Kingdom

Billy Bremner, Jack Charlton and Terry Cooper all played for the Rest of the United Kingdom v Wales at Ninian Park on 28 July 1969 in a game to mark the investiture of Charles, the Prince of Wales. The Rest won 1-0 in front of 14,000 fans.

Great Britain

John Charles
13 Aug 1955 Rest of Europe | Belfast | 1-4 | 60,000

Young England

Norman Hunter
17 May 1967 England | Highbury, London | 4-1 | 20,077

Paul Reaney
13 May 1966 England | Stamford Bridge, London | 1-1 | 18,274

International Trials Matches

England

Matches involving Leeds players were England v The Rest, and Possibles v Probables

Wilf Copping

Date	Team	Venue	Score	Attendance
22 Mar 1933	England	Portsmouth	5-1	15,103
21 Mar 1934	The Rest	Sunderland	1-7	13,500

Willis Edwards

Date	Team	Venue	Score	Attendance
16 Feb 1926	The Rest	Newcastle	3-4	15,.000
17 Jan 1927	The Rest	Stamford Bridge, London	7-3	11,473
7 Feb 1927	The Rest	Bolton	2-3	14,000
23 Feb 1928	The Rest	West Bromwich	5-1	10,355
8 Feb 1928	The Rest	Middlesbrough	8-3	18,431
4 Feb 1929	The Rest	Hillsborough, Sheffield	4-3	17,400
11 Mar 1929	The Rest	Tottenham	1-2	16,000
12 Mar 1930	The Rest	Anfield, Liverpool	1-6	12,000

Billy Furness
21 Mar 1934 The Rest | Sunderland | 1-7 | 13,500

Ernie Hart

Date	Team	Venue	Score	Attendance
4 Feb 1929	The Rest	Hillsborough, Sheffield	4-3	17,400
11 Mar 1929	The Rest	Tottenham	1-2	16,000
21 Mar 1934	The Rest	Sunderland	1-7	13,500

Bert Sproston
13 Oct 1937 Possibles | Goodison Pk, Everton | 1-1 | 7,000

Russell Wainscoat
4 Feb 1929 The Rest | Hillsborough, Sheffield | 4-3 | 17,400

Scotland

Anglo Scots v Scots
Tom Jennings
13 Mar 1928 Scots Hampden Park | 1-1(1)

Football League Representatives

Jack Charlton (6 apps, 2 goals)

Date	Opponent	Venue	Score	Attendance
9 Oct 1957	League of Ireland	Goodison Pk, Liverpool	3-1	13,000
17 Mar 1965	Scottish League	Hampden Park	2-2(2)	38,409
27 Oct 1965	League of Ireland	Hull	5-0(1)	28,283
16 Mar 1965	Scottish League	Newcastle	1-3	32,900
21 Sep 1966	Irish League	Plymouth	12-0	35,458
27 Sep 1966	Belgian League	Brussels	2-2	35,000

Trevor Cherry (1 app, 1 goal)
17 Mar 1976 Scottish League | Hampden Park | 1-0(1) | 8,874

Wilf Copping (2 apps)

Date	Opponent	Venue	Score	Attendance
4 Oct 1933	Irish League	Preston	4-0	14,400
10 Feb 1934	Scottish League	Hampden Park	2-2	59,000

Willis Edwards (11 apps)

Date	Opponent	Venue	Score	Attendance
13 Mar 1926	Scottish League	Hampden Park	2-0	49,000
9 Oct 1926	Irish League	Belfast	6-1	14,000
19 Mar 1927	Scottish League	Leicester	2-2	26,000
21 Sep 1927	Irish League	Newcastle	9-1	1,122
10Mar 1928	Scottish League	Hampden Park	6-2	60,000
22 Sep 1928	Irish League	Belfast	5-0	15,000
7 Nov 1928	Scottish League	Villa Park, Birmingham	2-1	25,000
25 Sep 1929	Irish League	Goodison Park, Liverpool	7-2	18,000
2 Nov 1929	Scottish League	Hampden Park	1-2	40,000
23 Sep 1931	Irish League	Blackpool	3-0	15,233
7 Nov 1931	Scottish League	Hampden Park	3-4	51,000

Ernie Hart (3 apps)

Date	Opponent	Venue	Score	Attendance
7 Nov 1928	Scottish League	Villa Park, Birmingham	2-1	25,000
25 Sep 1929	Irish League	Goodison Park, Liverpool	7-2	18,000
2 Nov 1929	Scottish League	Hampden Park	1-2	40,000

Norman Hunter (6 apps)

Date	Opponent	Venue	Score	Attendance
28 Oct 1964	Irish League	Belfast	4-0	20,000
17Mar 1965	Scottish League	Hampden Park	2-2	38,409
27 Oct 1965	League of Ireland	Hull	5-0	28,283
16 Mar 1966	Scottish League	Newcastle	1-3	32,900
27 Sep 1967	Belgian League	Brussels	2-2	35,000
10 Sep 1969	League of Ireland	Barnsley	3-0	11,939

Paul Madeley (1 app)
10 Sep 1969 League of Ireland | Barnsley | 3-0 | 11,939

Paul Reaney (3 apps)

Date	Opponent	Venue	Score	Attendance
16 Mar 1966	Scottish League	Newcastle	1-3	32,900
10 Sep 1969	League of Ireland	Barnsley	3-0	11,939
17 Mar 1971	Scottish League	Hampden Park	1-0	17,657

Bert Sproston (2 apps)

Date	Opponent	Venue	Score	Attendance
22 Sep 1937	Scottish League	Hampden Park	1-0	40,000
6 Oct 1937	Irish League	Blackpool	3-0	14,700

FA Tours

George Ainsley: South Africa, 1939 (1 Test match). Ken Gadsby: South Africa, 1939 (1 Test match). Grenville Hair: West Indies, 1955; Ghana and Nigeria, 1958; New Zealand, 1960. Ernie Hart: South Africa, 1929 (3 Test matches). Norman Hunter: Canada, 1967. Paul Madeley: Canada, 1967. Bobby Turnbull: South Africa, 1929. Russell Wainscoat: Canada, 1926.

FA Charity Shield Representative

Ernie Hart played for the Professionals v Amateurs at Millwall on 7 October 1929. The Professionals won 3-0.

Trevor Cherry
England

Assorted Representative Matches

Yorkshire

Both Willis Edwards and Russell Wainscoat played for Yorkshire against Lancashire on 27 April 1925 at Turf Moor, Burnley, Yorkshire winning 4-3 in front of 6,000 fans. The match was a benefit game for the dependents of Jack Howarth, a Burnley player, and was used by the Football League to experiment with a new offside law.

FA XI

Jack Charlton
18 Oct 1961 British Army | Sunderland | 1-2

Willis Edwards
10 Oct 1928 Lancashire | Bolton | 5-6

Russell Wainscoat
10 Oct 1928 Lancashire (sub) | Bolton | 5-6

Irish National Lottery XI

Both Gordon Strachan and Gordon McAllister played for the Irish National Lottery XI against a Republic of Ireland XI at Dublin on 11 May 1994, the Republic winning 5-1 in front of 42,630 fans.

Common Market Celebration Match

Johnny Giles, Norman Hunter and Peter Lorimer all played for The Three against The Six in a match at Wembley to mark the entry of the United Kingdom, Republic of Ireland and Denmark (The Three) to the existing Common Market (The Six) comprising players from Belgium, France, Holland, Italy, Luxembourg and West Germany. The Three won 2-0 in front of 36,500 fans.

Wartime Representative Matches

Date	Team	Opponent	Venue	Score	Att
George Ainsley					
30 Mar 1940	RAF	v FA XI	Dulwich	3-2	11,745
Bobby Browne					
4 Nov 1939	All British XI	v Football League XI	Goodison Pk, L'pool	3-3	15,000
Arthur Buckley					
17 May 1945	Army XI	v The Army	Naples	0-2	
David Cochrane					
25 Mar 1940	Yorkshire XI	v FA XI	Bramall Ln, Sheffield	4-1(2)	14,814
12 Sep 1942	Irish FA	v The Army	Belfast	3-2	35,000
16 Sep 1942	Irish League	v The Army	Belfast	2-3	14,000
11 Sep 1943	Ireland	v The Army	Belfast	4-2(3)	30,000
9 Sep 1944	Ireland	v Combined Services	Belfast	4-8	49,875
11 Sep 1944	Irish League	v Combined Services	Belfast	0-4	
Wilf Copping					
18 Oct 1939	Aldershot & Army	v FA XI	Aldershot	0-1	10,000
20 Jan 1940	England XI	v The Army	Selhurst Park	4-3	10,057
15 Feb 1940	The Army	v French Army	Lille	1-0	13,000
9 Mar 1940	The Army	v Football League XI	Anfield, Liverpool	5-2	14,205
24 Apr 1940	The Army	v Scottish XI	Tynecastle, Edinburgh	1-4	
14 Feb 1942	The Army	v RAF	Aldershot	1-1	
14 Mar 1942	FA XI	v The Army	Aldershot	1-3	10,000
2 Jan 1943	The Army	v Metropolitan Police	Aldershot	5-5	
20 Jan 1943	Stan Cullis XI	v Metropolitan Police	Chichester	5-1(1)	
6 Mar 1943	Army XI	v Belgian Army	Aldershot	5-0	
27 Mar 1943	Army XI	v USA Army	Southampton	11-0	6,000
3 Apr 1943	Army XI	v Norwegian Forces	Southampton	11-0	6,000
Ken Gadsby					
24 Feb 1945	Northern Cmnd	v Western Cmnd	Wolverhampton	0-2	16,148
Les Goldberg					
30 Mar 1940	RAF	v FA XI	Leeds	2-2	13,000
Jack Hargreaves					
	FA XI	v Western Cmnd	Cardiff	0-2	6,000
21 Feb 1942	Northern Cmnd	v Scottish Cmnd	Leeds	1-1	8,500
Jim Milburn					
28 Mar 1942	AA Command	v Army XI	Derby	0-4	3,000
Aubrey Powell					
21 Feb 1942	Northern Cmnd	v Scottish Cmnd	Leeds	1-1	8,500
1 May 1943	Northern Cmnd	v Western Cmnd	Newcastle	4-3	
11 Sep 1943	The Army	v Ireland	Belfast	2-4(1)	30,000
9 Oct 1943	Northern Cmnd (England)	v Northern Cmnd (Scotland & Wales)	Chesterfield	6-3(1)	8,000
23 Oct 1943	Northern Cmnd	v Scottish Cmnd	Dundee	4-3(1)	
13 Nov 1943	Northern Cmnd	v Western Cmnd	Huddersfield	3-4	6,565
5 Feb 1944	The Army	v Civil Defence	Derby	4-3	16,000
18 Mar 1944	Northern Cmnd	v AA Command	Chesterfield	2-0	
25 Mar 1945	FA XI	v Belgium	Brussels	3-2	
Eric Stephenson					
18 Oct 1939	Aldershot & Army	v FA XI	Aldershot	0-1	10,000
15 Feb 1940	The Army	v French Army	Lille	1-0(1)	13,000
18 Feb 1940	The Army	v French Army	Rheims	2-1(1)	15,000
14 Dec 1940	FA XI	v Notts County	Meadow Ln, Nott'ham	1-2	
18 Jan 1941	Football League XI	v All British XI	Sheffield	5-3(1)	4,409
19Apr 1941	Football League XI	v All British XI	Anfield, Liverpool	9-7(1)	12,000
29 Nov 1941	The Army	v RAF	Aldershot	2-5	6,000

Internationals with other clubs

The following Leeds United and Leeds City players have all won full international honours only while with other clubs. The list does not include players who were on United's books as youngsters but failed to make the Leeds first team and went on to become internationals, for example, David Seaman, the Arsenal and England goalkeeper.

England

George Brown (Huddersfield Town 8, Aston Villa 1); Chris Crowe (Wolverhampton Wanderers 1); Brian Deane (Sheffield United 3); Colin Grainger (Sheffield United 6, Sunderland 1); Steve Hodge (Aston Villa 11, Tottenham Hotspur 4, Nottingham Forest 9); Gordon Hodgson (Liverpool 3); Billy Kirton (Aston Villa 1); Jim Langley (Fulham 3); Evelyn Lintott (Queens Park Rangers 3, Bradford City 4); Albert McInroy (Sunderland 1); Carlton Palmer (Sheffield Wed 18); Don Revie (Manchester City 6); David Rocastle (Arsenal 14); Mel Sterland (Sheffield Wednesday 1); David White (Manchester City 1); Ken Willingham (Huddersfield Town 12); Frank Worthington (Leicester City 8).

Scotland

Hugh Baird (Airdrie 1); Kenny Burns (Birmingham City 8, Nottingham Forest 12); George Law (Glasgow Rangers 3); John O'Hare (Derby County 13); Derek Parlane (Glasgow Rangers 12); Eric Smith (Glasgow Celtic 2); James Speirs (Glasgow Rangers 1); Tom Townsley (Falkirk 1); John White (Albion Rovers 1, Heart of Midlothian 1); Tommy Younger (Hibernian 8, Liverpool 16).

Northern Ireland

Tom Casey (Newcastle United 10, Portsmouth 2); Billy Gillespie (Sheffield United 25); Billy Halligan (Derby County 1, Wolverhampton Wanderers 1); Phil Hughes (Bury 3); Willie Humphries (Ards 1, Coventry City 10, Swansea Town 3); Eddie McMorran (Belfast Celtic 1, Barnsley 9, Doncaster Rovers 5).

Republic of Ireland

Jim Beglin (Liverpool 15); Ken De Mange (Liverpool 1, Hull City 1); Mick Foley (Shelbourne 1); Bob Fullam (Sharmock Rovers 2); Denis Irwin (Manchester United 36 to start of 1995-96); David O'Leary (Arsenal 68); Terry Phelan (Wimbledon 8, Manchester City 18 to start of 1995-96).

Wales

Vinnie Jones (Wimbledon 4 to start of 1995-96); Harry Millership (Rotherham County 6); Haydn Price (Aston Villa 1, Burton United 2, Wrexham 3); Mickey Thomas (Wrexham 11, Manchester United 13, Everton 1, Brighton and Hove Albion 5, Stoke City 10, Chelsea 9, West Bromwich Albion 2).

Argentina

Alex Sabella (Estudiantes 4).

Sweden

Tomas Brolin (Norrköping/Parma 48).

International Miscellany

- A TOTAL of 68 players have been capped by their country when at Leeds United and a further four won full honours with Leeds City.
- The breakdown of United players, country by country is: England 22, Scotland 13, Wales 11, Northern Ireland 10, Republic of Ireland 8, South Africa 2, France 1, Norway 1,

Ghana 1. That totals 69, but Harry Duggan represented both Northern Ireland and Republic of Ireland.

●United's first international was Willis Edwards, who played for England against Wales on 1 March 1926, the Welsh winning 3-1. That made him the 500th England international and he captained England in his last five internationals, thus becom ing the first United player to lead his country.

●When Ernie Hart made his debut alongside Edwards in the 3-2 win against Wales at Swansea on 17 November 1928 it was the first time two United players had played in the same England team.

●The first United player to score a goal for England was Alan Peacock, who netted in the 2-1 win against Northern Ireland on 10 November 1965.

●United's most capped England player is Jack Charlton with 35 appearances. He played in the 1966 and 1970 World Cups, playing in England's historic triumph in the 1966 Final against West Germany. He played alongside his brother, Bobby (Manchester United), in the Final. It was the third time that brothers had figured in a Final, following Juan and Mario Evaristo (Argentina) in 1930, and Fritz and Ottmar Walter in 1954. Since the Charltons played in 1966, Rene and Willy Van der Kerkof played in the Dutch side which lost to Argentina in the 1978 Final. Jack and Bobby played in the national side together 28 times.

●Charlton is among the oldest players to play for England, his last appearance coming against Portugal in 1970 when he was 35.

●Allan Clarke has scored more goals for England than any other Leeds player - 10. He scored on his debut from the penalty spot in the 1970 World Cup finals against Czechoslovakia to become the first player to score from the spot on his debut since Tommy Lawton netted against Wales in 1938. Three of Clarke's goals came from the penalty spot - v Malta in 1971 (when he also missed one) and Poland in 1973 were the others.

●Clarke scored in his first four appearances for England and is the only Leeds player to score twice in a match for England, a feat he achieved against Scotland and Austria in 1973.

●Mike O'Grady scored for England in his only appearance while a Leeds player, his goal coming in a 5-0 win over France. His only other appearance came six years 204 days earlier when he was a Huddersfield player, scoring twice in a 3-1 win over Northern Ireland.

●Trevor Cherry captained England against Australia in 1980 and was only the third England player to be sent off when he received his marching orders with Daniel Bertoni (Argentina) on England's 1977 tour of South America. Most observers reckon Cherry to be an innocent victim after losing several teeth during Bertoni's attack. The other England players to see red before Cherry were Alan Mullery against Yugoslavia and Alan Ball against Poland.

●Both Tony Currie's goals for England were scored after coming on as a substitute.

●Tony Dorigo is the only Australian-born player to be capped by England. His last international was also Graham Taylor's final match in charge.

●Paul Madeley's versatility at club level was also evident on the international stage, playing right-back, left-back, centre-half and in midfield in his 24 appearances. After Paul Reaney broke his leg and missed the 1970 World Cup, Madeley was invited to take his place, but turned down the chance to go with the squad to Mexico.

●Billy Bremner became the first Leeds United player to be capped by Scotland when he played in a goalless draw against Spain at Hampden Park on 8 May 1965. He went on to make 54 appearances, making him United's most capped player. He captained his country in 38 of those internationals including their matches in the 1974 World Cup Finals in Germany.

Gary Sprake
Wales

●Bobby Collins' international career began on 21 October 1950 against Wales when he was a Celtic player and his last cap came against Poland on 23 May 1965 - a career stretching almost 15 years and only beaten in terms of longetivity in Scottish history by Denis Law and Jimmy McMenemy.

●Leeds United lost to a Scottish Under-23 side 3-2 at Hampden Park on 19 May 1975. United had five current Scottish internationals in their ranks – David Harvey, Billy Bremner, Peter Lorimer, Joe Jordan, Eddie Gray and a future international, Frank Gray, in the side. Celtic's George McCluskey, later to join Leeds, was in the Scots' side.

●Frank and Eddie Gray never played in the Scottish team together. The pair were picked to play against Switzerland in April 1976, but Eddie pulled out through injury. Eddie Gray scored one of Scotland's goals in an 8-0 win over Cyprus on 17 May 1969, the Scots' biggest win since Ireland were thrashed 11-0 at Parkhead in 1901. Eddie's son, Stuart, is currently a Celtic and Scottish Under-21 player.

●Leeds-born goalkeeper David Harvey qualified to play for

Scotland because his father was born north of the border. He was widely regarded as the best goalkeeper in the 1974 World Cup.

●Goalkeeper David Stewart marked his only appearance for Scotland, a 1-0 defeat against East Germany with a 75th minute penalty save.

●Super-sub Joe Jordan headed Scotland's 75th minute winner just 11 minutes after coming on against Czechoslovakia to clinch a 2-1 victory to take Scotland to the World Cup finals the following year. Jordan played in three successive World Cups.

●Leeds players scored all Scotland's goals in the 1974 World Cup finals. Joe Jordan and Peter Lorimer netted in the 2-0 win over Zaire and after a goalless draw against Brazil, Jordan scored in the 1-1 draw against Yugoslavia. Despite being unbeaten, Scotland were eliminated on goal difference.

●Billy Bremner, Gordon McQueen, Gordon Strachan and Gary McAllister have all captained Scotland while at Leeds.

●Leeds international managers include: Don Revie (England and United Arab Emirates), Jack Charlton (Republic of Ireland), Terry Yorath (Wales and Lebanon), Jock Stein (Scotland), and Johnny Giles (Republic of Ireland). Stein was Scotland's team manager twice between June and December 1965 and October 1978 until his death in September 1985.

●John Charles and his brother, Mel, both played for Wales. His nephew, Jeremy, son of Mel, also won full Welsh caps. Alan Curtis was a nephew of Roy Paul, another multi-capped Welsh international.

●United have had four of the youngest-ever internationals on their books. John Charles was 18 years 71 days when he played his first game for Wales, Gary Sprake was 160 days older when he became, and remains, the youngest-ever Welsh goalkeeper and Johnny Giles, although a Manchester United player at the time, was 18 years 361 days old when first capped by the Republic of Ireland. Coventry's Jimmy Holmes is the youngest Eire player at 17 years 6 months 19 days. David Cochrane was 18 years 3 months old when he first played for Northern Ireland – a 7-0 defeat against England at Maine Road in 1938.

●John Charles was the first Welsh player to score a hat-trick (v Northern Ireland on 20 April 1955) since Trevor Ford in 1953. He also netted Wales's first goal in the World Cup finals, heading in a 27th minute equaliser in the 1-1 draw with one of the pre-tournament favourites, Hungary.

●Trevor Cherry is one of three Leeds internationals to be sent off. The others are Peter Lorimer v Denmark on 15 November 1972 and Byron Stevenson, who was ordered off in a 1-0 defeat in Turkey on 21 November 1979.

●John Charles and Brian Flynn have both captained Wales. Flynn was at one time the principality's third most-capped player.

●Carl Harris was able to establish himself in the Welsh side as a regular before being regarded as a first choice at Leeds in the mid 1970s. The same was also true of Terry Yorath who had only started four full games for Leeds by the time he collected his 11th Welsh cap. He went on to captain Wales 42 times.

●Gary Speed made his Welsh debut, as sub v Costa Rica, the day after playing for the Welsh Under-21 side against Poland in Merthyr. Speed needed just one more cap to join Gary Sprake and Brian Flynn on 32 caps, the most-capped Leeds Welshmen.

●Wilbur Cush scored Northern Ireland's first-ever goal in the finals of the World Cup, heading the only goal of the game against Czechoslovakia on 8 June 1954 in Halmstad. Northern Ireland, rank outsiders, reached the quarter-finals, losing 4-0 to France.

●Harry Duggan became the first Leeds United player to be capped by a country other than England when he won the first of his eight Irish caps against England on 19 October 1929.

●Former Leeds player Mick Foley (Shelbourne) is credited with captaining the Republic of Ireland in their first-ever international – a 3-0 defeat in Italy on 21 March 1926. It was his only cap.

●The Republic's first international goal was scored by another ex-Leeds man Bob Fullam (Shamrock Rovers) as the Irish went down 2-1 to Italy B in Dublin on 27 April 1927. That match saw Harry Duggan become United's first dual international – having previously played for Ireland. Con Martin also played for both Irish sides.

●Yet another ex-Leeds man, John Joe Flood, who failed to make the first team at Elland Road, scored the Republic's first-ever hat-trick in a 4-1 win over Belgium in Dublin on 20 April 1929.

●Con Martin and his son, Mick (Newcastle United) both played for the Republic of Ireland. Con Martin, who later played for Aston Villa, played as an outfield player and a goalkeeper for the Republic of Ireland.

●David O'Leary and his brother, Pierce, were also both capped by Eire. David won all his 68 caps when at Arsenal. Only Paddy Bonner (78), Paul McGrath (76), Liam Brady (72) and Frank Stapleton (71), have won more Irish caps.

●Johnny Giles captained the Republic of Ireland a record 30 times.

●Gary Kelly scored in the Republic's 2-0 win in Germany on 29 May 1994, but has yet to score for Leeds in over 130 appearances. He made his League debut at Manchester City on the opening day of the 1993-94 season and finished the season in the Republic of Ireland side which played in the World Cup.

●Lucas Radebe and Phil Masinga both played in South Africa's victorious 1995 African Nations Cup-winning side when their country hosted the tournament. They beat Ghana, including Tony Yeboah, 3-0 in the semi-final, although Masinga missed the match through suspension.

●Although still to play for Sweden since joining Leeds, Tomas Brolin has scored 27 times in 47 internationals, including the winner in the 2-1 victory which knocked England out of the 1992 European Championship finals. He scored twice on his debut as Sweden beat Wales 4-2 in 1990 and was prominent in their World Cup side that year and again in 1994 when Sweden finished third.

●On 15 May 1971, Leeds had eight players in action in the Home Internationals. Terry Cooper, Allan Clarke and Paul Madeley lined up for England against Northern Ireland while Peter Lorimer, Billy Bremner and Eddie Gray tackled a Welsh side containing Gary Sprake and Terry Yorath. In May 1973, Leeds had 15 internationals on their books – the eight aforementioned, plus Jack Charlton, Norman Hunter, Mick Jones and Paul Reaney (England), David Harvey and Joe Jordan (Scotland) and Johnny Giles (Republic of Ireland).

●In December 1995, United had a dozen internationals on their books: Tony Dorigo, Carlton Palmer, Brian Deane, David White (England); Gary Kelly (Republic of Ireland); Gary McAllister (Scotland); Gary Speed (Wales); Nigel Worthington (Northern Ireland); Tomas Brolin (Sweden); Tony Yeboah (Ghana); Phil Masinga and Lucas Radebe (South Africa).

●In 1978-79 Leeds goalkeepers were David Harvey, David Stewart, John Lukic and Henry Smith. Lukic won England 'B' and Under-21 honours, while all three Scots won full honours; Smith winning his three caps with Hearts over a decade later.

Gary Kelly
Eire

Top Appearances & Goalscorers

Top Twenty League Appearances

1. J.Charlton 629
2. W.J.Bremner 586/1
3. P.Reaney 549/8
4. N.Hunter 540
5. P.E.Madeley 528/8
6. P.P.Lorimer 503/22
7. E.Gray 441/13
8. E.A.Hart 447
9. K.G.A.Hair 443
10. J.Dunn 442
11. W.Edwards 417
12. T.J.Cherry 393/33
13. Jack Milburn 386
14. M.J.Giles 380/3
15. G.Sprake 380
16. J.Lukic 355
17. D.Harvey 350
18. E.Kerfoot 336
19. F.T.Gray 327/5
20. W.J.Charles 308

Overall Top Twenty Appearances

Including League FA Cup, League Cup, Europe, Fairs Cup play-off, FA Charity Shield & Full Members Cup.

1. J.Charlton 773
2. W.J.Bremner 772/1
3. P.Reaney 736/12
4. N.Hunter 724/2
5. P.E.Madeley 712/13
6. P.P.Lorimer 677/28
7. E.Gray 561/8
8. M.J.Giles 523/4
9. G.Sprake 505/2
10. T.J.Cherry 477/8
11. K.G.A.Hair 474
12. E.A.Hart 472
13. D.Harvey 445/2
14. W.Edwards 444
15. J.Dunn 443
16. J.Lukic 433
17. Jack Milburn 408
18. F.T.Gray 396/9
19. A.J.Clarke 361/5
20. E.Kerfoot 349

Top Ten League Goalscorers

1. P.P.Lorimer 168
2. W.J.Charles 153
3. T.H.O.Jennings 112
4. A.J.Clarke 110
5. C.F.Keetley 108
6. W.J.Bremner 90
7. M.J.Giles 88
8. W.R.Wainscoat 87
9. M.D.Jones 77
10. A.J.E.Hydes 74

Overall Top Ten Goalscorers

(*As for appearances*)

1. P.P.Lorimer 238
2. W.J.Charles 157
3. A.J.Clarke 151
4. T.H.O.Jennings 117
5. W.H.Bremner 115
6. M.J.Giles 115
7. M.D.Jones 111
8. C.F.Keetley 110
9. J.Charlton 96
10. W.R.Wainscoat 93

Player of the Year

1970-71 . . . . .Norman Hunter
1971-72 . . . . .Peter Lorimer
1972-73 . . . . .Allan Clarke
1973-74 . . . . .Mick Jones
1974-75 . . . . .Gordon McQueen
1975-76 . . . . .Paul Madeley
1976-77 . . . . .Gordon McQueen
1977-78 . . . . .Tony Currie
1978-79 . . . . .Brian Flynn
1979-80 . . . . .John Lukic
1980-81 . . . . .Trevor Cherry
1981-82 . . . . .Eddie Gray
1982-83 . . . . .Kenny Burns
1983-84 . . . . .Tommy Wright
1984-85 . . . . .Neil Aspin
1985-86 . . . . .Ian Snodin
1986-87 . . . . .John Sheridan
1987-88 . . . . .Peter Haddock
1988-89 .Ian Baird
1989-90 . . . . .Chris Fairclough
1990-91 . . . . .David Batty
1991-92 . . . . .Tony Dorigo
1992-93 . . . . .Gordon Strachan
1993-94 . . . . .Gary McAllister
1994-95 . . . . .Brian Deane
1995-96 . . . . .Tony Yeboah

Hat-Trick Heroes

Leeds United

Date	Goals	Player	Opponent	Venue	Competition
11 Sep 1920	3	Eugene O'Doherty	v Boothtown	(h)	FA Cup (Q1)
25 Sep 1920	3	Walter Butler	v Leeds Steelworks	(h)	FA Cup (Q2)
11 Dec 1920	3	Bob Thompson	v Notts County	(h)	Div 2
20 Feb 1922	3	Billy Poyntz	v Leicester City	(h)	Div 2
25 Mar 1922	3	Jack Swan	v Coventry City	(h)	Div 2
4 Nov 1922	3	Percy Whipp	v West Ham United	(h)	Div 2
29 Sep 1923	3	Joe Richmond	v Hull City	(h)	Div 2
25 Dec 1924	3	Percy Whipp	v Aston Villa	(h)	Div 1
6 Feb 1926	3	Tom Jennings	v Arsenal	(h)	Div 1
25 Sep 1926	3	Tom Jennings	v Arsenal	(h)	Div 1
2 Oct 1926	4	Tom Jennings	v Liverpool	(a)	Div 1
9 Oct 1926	4	Tom Jennings	v Blackburn Rovers	(h)	Div 1
20 Nov 1926	3	Tom Jennings	v Bury	(h)	Div 1
30 Apr 1927	4	Russell Wainscoat	v West Ham United	(h)	Div 1
10 Dec 1927	4	Tom Jennings	v Chelsea	(h)	Div 2
28 Jan 1928	3	Charlie Keetley	v Bristol City	(h)	Div 2
17 Mar 1928	3	Charlie Keetley	v Notts County	(h)	Div 2
14 Apr 1928	3	Charlie Keetley	v Clapton Orient	(h)	Div 2
25 Aug 1928	3	Charlie Keetley	v Aston Villa	(h)	Div 1
20 Oct 1928	3	Jock White	v Manchester City	(h)	Div 1
5 Jan 1929	3	Charlie Keetley	v Leicester City	(h)	Div 1
9 Mar 1929	3	Charlie Keetley	v Everton	(h)	Div 1
11 Jan 1930	3	Russell Wainscoat	v Crystal Palace	(h)	FA Cup
9 Apr 1930	3	Charlie Keetley	v Sheffield Wed	(h)	Div 1
8 Sep 1930	3	Charlie Keetley	v Manchester City	(h)	Div 1
20 Dec 1930	3	Bobby Turnbull	v Manchester United	(h)	Div 1
3 Oct 1931	3	Charlie Keetley	v Oldham Athletic	(h)	Div 2
14 Jan 1933	3	Arthur Hydes	v Newcastle United	(a)	FA Cup
11 Mar 1933	3	Charlie Keetley	v Wolverhampton W	(a)	Div 1

28 Aug 1933	4	Arthur Hydes	v Middlesbrough	(h)	Div 1
30 Dec 1933	3	Arthur Hydes	v Blackburn Rovers	(h)	Div 1
5 Jan 1935	3	Arthur Hydes	v Blackburn Rovers	(h)	Div 1
9 Nov 1935	3	Harry Duggan	v Sheffield Wed	(h)	Div 1
4 Dec 1937	3	Eric Stephenson	v Sunderland	(h)	Div 1
26 Feb 1938	4	Gordon Hodgson	v Everton	(h)	Div 1
23 Apr 1938	3	Gordon Hodgson	v Brentford	(h)	Div 1
1 Oct 1938	5	Gordon Hodgson	v Leicester City	(h)	Div 1
5 Oct 1946	3	George Ainsley	v Huddersfield Town	(h)	Div 1
10 Sep 1947	3	Aubrey Powell	v Plymouth Argyle	(h)	Div 2
1 May 1948	3	Albert Wakefield	v Bury	(h)	Div 2
11 Nov 1950	3	Frank Dudley	v Leicester City	(a)	Div 2
13 Jan 1951	3	Len Browning	v Southampton	(h)	Div 2
1 Nov 1952	3	John Charles	v Hull City	(h)	Div 2
29 Nov 1952	3	John Charles	v Brentford	(h)	Div 2
17 Jan 1953	3	John Charles	v Rotherham United	(h)	Div 2
19 Aug 1953	4	John Charles	v Notts County	(h)	Div 2
22 Aug 1953	3	John Charles	v Rotherham United	(h)	Div 2
10 Oct 1953	3	Bobby Forrest	v Bristol Rovers	(h)	Div 2
7 Nov 1953	3	Albert Nightingale	v Doncaster Rovers	(h)	Div 2
14 Nov 1953	3	John Charles	v Bury	(a)	Div 2
19 Dec 1953	3	John Charles	v Rotherham United	(a)	Div 2
2 Jan 1954	3	Ray Iggleden	v Leicester City	(h)	Div 2
13 Feb 1954	3	John Charles	v Lincoln City	(h)	Div 2
11 Sep 1954	3	Albert Nightingale	v Swansea Town	(h)	Div 2
24 Sep 1955	3	Keith Ripley	v Rotherham United	(h)	Div 2
2 Apr 1956	3	John Charles	v Fulham	(h)	Div 2
18 Aug 1956	3	Harold Brook	v Everton	(h)	Div 1
10 Nov 1956	3	John Charles	v Sheffield Wed	(h)	Div 1
26 Dec 1956	3	Harold Brook	v Blackpool	(h)	Div 1
26 Mar 1957	3	John Charles	v Sheffield Wed	(a)	Div 1
22 Nov 1958	3	Alan Shackleton	v Blackburn Rovers	(a)	Div 1
22 Apr 1959	3	Alan Shackleton	v Nottingham Forest	(a)	Div 1
13 Sep 1961	4	John McCole	v Brentford	(h)	League Cup
17 Nov 1962	3	Jim Storrie	v Plymouth Argyle	(h)	Div 2
15 Dec 1962	3	Don Weston	v Stoke City	(h)	Div 2
27 Apr 1963	3	Jim Storrie	v Cardiff City	(h)	Div 2
22 Jan 1966	3	Peter Lorimer	v Bury	(h)	FA Cup
26 Oct 1966	3	Albert Johanneson	v DWS Amsterdam	(h)	UEFA Cup
24 May 1967	3	Rod Belfitt	v Kilmarnock	(h)	UEFA CUP
13 Sep 1967	3	Peter Lorimer	v Luton Town	(h)	League Cup
3 Oct 1967	4	Peter Lorimer	v Spora Luxembourg	(a)	UEFA Cup
17 Oct 1967	3	Albert Johnanneson	v Spora Luxembourg	(h)	UEFA Cup
6 Jan 1968	3	Jimmy Greenhoff	v Fulham	(a)	Div 1
17 Sep 1969	3	Mick Jones	v SK Lyn Oslo	(h)	European Cup
29 Oct 1969	3	Peter Lorimer	v Nottingham Forest	(h)	Div 1
24 Jan 1970	4	Allan Clarke	v Sutton United	(a)	FA Cup
23 Jan 1971	3	Mick Jones	v Swindon Town	(h)	FA Cup
3 Apr 1971	4	Allan Clarke	v Burnley	(h)	Div 1
19 Feb 1972	3	Mick Jones	v Manchester United	(h)	Div 1
4 Mar 1972	3	Peter Lorimer	v Southampton	(h)	Div 1
29 Jan 1973	3	Allan Clarke	v Norwich City	(n)	FA Cup
9 May 1973	3	Peter Lorimer	v Arsenal	(h)	Div 1
8 Sep 1973	3	Peter Lorimer	v Birmingham City	(h)	Div 1
14 Jan 1978	3	Arthur Graham	v Birmingham City	(h)	Div 1
28 Mar 1978	3	Eddie Gray	v Leicester City	(h)	Div 1
19 Sep 1979	3	Arthur Graham	v Valletta	(a)	UEFA Cup
5 Sep 1981	3	Arthur Graham	v Wolverhampton W	(h)	Div 1
29 Sep 1984	3	Andy Ritchie	v Oldham Athletic	(h)	Div 2
1 Dec 1984	3	Andy Ritchie	v Wimbledon	(h)	Div 2
19 Jan 1985	3	Tommy Wright	v Notts County	(h)	Div 2
28 Mar 1987	3	Ian Baird	v Plymouth Argyle	(h)	Div 2
19 Mar 1988	3	John Pearson	v Sheffield United	(h)	Div 2
1 Apr 1989	3	Carl Shutt	v Bournemouth	(h)	Div 2
23 Sep 1989	3	Gordon Strachan	v Swindon Town	(h)	Div 2
13 Apr 1991	3	Lee Chapman	v Liverpool	(h)	Div 1
12 Jan 1992	3	Lee Chapman	v Sheffield Wed	(a)	Div 1
14 Mar 1992	3	Lee Chapman	v Wimbledon	(h)	Div 1
8 Aug 1992	3	Eric Cantona	v Liverpool	(n)	Charity Shield
25 Aug 1992	3	Eric Cantona	v Tottenham Hotspur	(h)	Prem
10 Apr 1993	3	Gordon Strachan	v Coventry City	(h)	Prem
8 May 1993	3	Rod Wallace	v Coventry City	(a)	Prem
17 Jan 1995	3	Phil Masinga	v Walsall	(h)	FA Cup
5 Apr 1995	3	Tony Yeboah	v Ipswich Town	(h)	Prem
12 Sep 1995	3	Tony Yeboah	v AS Monaco	(a)	UEFA CUP
23 Sep 1995	3	Tony Yeboah	v Wimbledon	(a)	Prem
28 Oct 1995	3	Gary McAllister	v Coventry City	(h)	Prem

Leeds City

7 Oct 1905	4	Fred Hargreaves	v Morley	(h)	FA Cup (Pre)
7 Oct 1905	4	Dickie Morris	v Morley	(h)	FA Cup (Pre)
3 Mar 1906	4	David Wilson	v Clapton Orient	(h)	Div 2
15 Dec 1906	3	John Lavery	v Stockport County	(h)	Div 2
12 Dec 1908	3	Jimmy Gemmell	v Wolverhampton W	(h)	Div 2
9 Nov 1912	3	Billy McLeod	v Glossop North End	(h)	Div 2
25 Mar 1913	3	Billy McLeod	v Bury	(h)	Div 2
29 Nov 1913	4	Billy McLeod	v Nottingham Forest	(h)	Div 2
14 Feb 1914	3	Billy McLeod	v Wolverhampton W	(h)	Div 2
14 Mar 1914	3	Billy McLeod	v Huddersfield Town	(h)	Div 2
12 Dec 1914	3	Arthur Price	v Leicester Fosse	(h)	Div 2
16 Jan 1915	5	Billy McLeod	v Hull City	(a)	Div 2
10 Apr 1915	3	Arthur Price	v Nottingham Forest	(h)	Div 2
4 Oct 1919	3	Billy McLeod	v Wolverhampton W	(a)	Div 2

●United have scored 96 trebles against 50 different League sides. They have netted 7 hat-tricks against 6 European teams and 3 against non-League opposition. City scored 12 trebles against 9 League sides and two players each scored four times against non-League Morley in 1905.

●Club's suffering most from Leeds sharpshooters over the years have been:

Leicester City	7	
Sheffield Wednesday	5	
Wolverhampton W	5	(including 3 by City)
Blackburn Rovers	4	
Bury	4	
Nottingham Forest	4	(including 2 by City)
Notts County	4	
Rotherham United	4	

●Top hat-tricks aces have been:

John Charles	11
Charlie Keetley	10
Peter Lorimer	7
Billy McLeod (City)	7
Tom Jennings	6

●Highest number of goals in one game were recorded by:

Gordon Hodgson	5	v Leicester City	(h)	1.10.1938
Billy McLeod (City)	5	v Hull City	(a)	16.1.1915

●Hat-tricks were scored in three consecutive games by Tom Jennings in 1926-27: 3 on 25 September v Arsenal, 4 on 2 October v Liverpool and another 4 goals on 9 October v Blackburn Rovers.

●The hat-trick scored by Billy Poyntz on 20 February 1922 was recorded on the afternoon of his wedding day!

●The hat-trick scored by Phil Masinga on 17 January 1995 was unique in that it was the first by a substitute and all three came in extra-time.

●There have been four instances of United scoring hat-tricks at home and away against the same opposition in the same season:

1953-54	Rotherham United	both netted by John Charles
1956-57	Sheffield Wednesday	both netted by John Charles
1967-68	Spora Luxembourg	the home hat-trick came from Albert Johanneson with Peter Lorimer scoring four times in the away tie.
1992-93	Coventry City	Gordon Strachan scored the home treble with Rod Wallace the away one.

●United's 106 hat-tricks to date have been netted in the following competitions (City's hat-tricks are in brackets):

	Home	Away	Neutral	Total
Premier Division	4	2		6
Division One	35	8		43
Division Two	35(10)	3(2)		38(12)
FA Cup	6(2)	2	1	9(2)
League Cup	2	0		2
Charity Cup	0	0	1	1
European Cup	1	0		1
UEFA Cup	3	3		6
Totals	**86(12)**	**18(2)**	**2**	**106(14)**

Best & Worst League Seasons

Victories

Most home wins	18	1968-69
Most away wins	12	1963-64, 1973-74
Most wins	27	1968-69, 1970-71
Fewest home wins	6	1946-47
Fewest away wins	0	1946-47, 1992-93
Fewest wins	6	1946-47
Successive home wins	12	1968-69
Successive away wins	5	1931-32, 1973-74
Successive wins	9	1931-32

Draws

Most home draws	11	1981-82, 1982-83
Most away draws	11	1952-53, 1969-70
Most draws	21	1982-83
Fewest home draws	2	1927-28, 1929-30, 1962-63, 1970-71
Fewest away draws	1	1926-27, 1936-37, 1946-47, 1981-82
Fewest draws	4	1936-37
Successive home draws	4	1926-27, 1958-59, 1974-75
Successive away draws	4	1952-53, 1961-62, 1969-70
Successive draws	5	1961-62

Defeats

Most home defeats	10	1946-47
Most away defeats	20	1946-47
Most defeats	30	1946-47
Fewest home defeats	0	1963-64, 1968-69, 1971-72
Fewest away defeats	2	1968-69, 1970-71
Fewest defeats	2	1968-69
Successive home defeats	3	1935-36, 1937-38, 1954-55, 1958-59, 1959-60, 1981-82, 1995-96
Successive away defeats	12	1946-47
Successive defeats	6	1946-47, 1995-96

Goals Scored

Most home goals scored	63	1927-28
Most away goals scored	42	1931-32
Most goals scored	98	1927-28
Fewest home goals scored	19	1980-81
Fewest away goals scored	10	1920-21
Fewest goals scored	39	1980-81, 1981-82

Goals Conceded

Most home goals conceded	46	1959-60
Most away goals conceded	60	1936-37, 1946-47
Most goals conceded	92	1934-35, 1959-60
Fewest home goals conceded	9	1968-69
Fewest away goals conceded	13	1973-74
Fewest goals conceded	26	1968-69

Clean Sheets

Most at home	14	1923-24, 1980-81
Most away	13	1973-74
Most	24	1968-69, 1970-71
Fewest at home	3	1926-27, 1928-29, 1934-35, 1946-47, 1953-54, 1959-60
Fewest away	0	1926-27, 1946-47
Fewest	3	1926-27, 1946-47
Successive	9	1927-28

Failed to score

Most at home	8	1921-22
Most away	13	1920-21
Most	19	1981-82
Fewest at home	0	1955-56, 1967-68
Fewest away	1	1927-28
Fewest	3	1927-28, 1962-63, 1963-64, 1969-70
Successive	6	1981-82

Points

Most at home (3 for a win)	54	1989-90
Most at home (2 for a win)	39	1968-69
Most away (3 for a win)	35	1991-92
Most away (2 for a win)	30	1963-64, 1970-71
Most points (3 for a win)	85	1989-90
Most points (2 for a win)	67	1968-69
Fewest at home (3 for a win)	25	1982-83, 1985-86
Fewest at home (2 for a win)	17	1946-47
Fewest away (3 for a win)	7	1992-93
Fewest away (2 for a win)	1	1946-47
Fewest points (3 for a win)	51	1992-93
Fewest points (2 for a win)	18	1946-47

League doubles in a season

Most home and away wins	8	1927-28, 1963-64, 1964-65, 1968-69
Most home and away defeats	9	1946-48

Best and Worst Sequences

(Dates from first to last in sequence)

League

Without a defeat

Most at home	39	14/8/68 to 28/2/70
Most away	17	2/11/68 to 26/8/69
Most	34	26/10/68 to 26/8/69
Most from start of season	29	1973-74

Without a victory

Most at home	10	6/2/82 to 12/5/82
Most away	26	1/4/39 to 27/8/47 (Not inc 2 games in 1939-40)
Most	17	1/2/47 to 26/5/47
Most from start of season	6	1935-36, 1951-52

Without a draw

Most at home	23	19/11/77 to 25/11/78
Most away	24	6/9/26 to 1/10/27
Most	19	2/1//29 to 8/3/30 and 17/12/77 to 12/4/78
Most from start of season	11	1947-48

FA Cup

Without a defeat

Most at home	15	6/1/62 to 30/3/68
Most away	14	5/2/72 to 18/1/79
Most	14	15/1/72 to 7/4/73

Without a victory

Most at home	7	23/2/52 to 6/1/62
Most away	14	7/1/22 to 9/1/32
Most	16	23/2/52 to 10/1/62

Without a draw

Most at home	13	16/1/29 to 21/1/39 and 8/4/67 to 18/3/72
Most away	14	10/1/53 to 12/2/66
Most	10	27/3/75 to 18/1/79

League Cup

Without a defeat

Most at home	10	13/9/66 to 27/9/71
Most away	4	8/9/71 to 31/10/72
Most	9	13/9/67 to 25/9/68

Without a victory

Most at home	8	24/1/79 to 9/11/83
Most away	8	6/10/69 to 10/9/74
Most	9	24/1/79 to 27/10/82

Without a draw

Most at home	18	13/9/61 to 25/9/68
Most away	21	10/10/78 to 24/9/91
Most	13	12/10/66 to 3/9/69 and 4/11/87 to 24/9/91

Europe

(not including ICFC Play-off)

Without a defeat

Most at home	14	26/10/66 to 18/12/68
Most away	11	9/12/70 to 7/11/73
Most	16	6/9/67 to 13/11/68

Without a victory

Most at home	3	28/4/71 to 29/9/71 and 4/11/92 to 17/10/95
Most away	6	10/1/68 to 27/11/68
Most	3	24/5/67 to 6/9/67 and 28/4/71 to 3/6/71 and 25/4/73 to 19/9/73

Without a draw

Most at home	16	20/12/67 to 10/3/71
Most away	10	27/11/68 to 9/12/70
Most	22	23/10/68 to 14/4/71

Attendances

Most at home

League	56,796	v Arsenal	27 Dec 1932
FA Cup	57,892	v Sunderland	15 Mar 1967
League Cup	43,222	v Nottingham F	8 Feb 1978
FM Cup	13,387	v Everton	19 Mar 1991
Europe	50,498	v Rangers	9 Apr 1968

Most away

League	60,612	v Manchester U	12 Mar 1977
FA Cup	68,287	v Sheffield U	15 Feb 1936
League Cup	46,185	v Aston Villa	4 Oct 1972
FM Cup	17,543	v Aston Villa	17 Jan 1990
Europe	136,505	v Celtic (Hampden Pk)	15 Apr 1970

Fewest at home

League	3,950	v Sheffield W	9 Apr 1930
FA Cup	10,144	v Bournemouth	17 Jan 1939
League Cup	4,517	v Brentford	13 Sep 1961
FM Cup	2,274	v Sheffield U	16 Oct 1985
Europe	13,682	v Valletta	3 Oct 1979

Fewest away

League	3,492	v Wimbledon	7 Dec 1985
FA Cup	10,137	v Peterborough	4 Jan 1986
League Cup	2,021	v Chesterfield	23 Nov 1960
FM Cup	4,029	v Manchester C	14 Oct 1985
Europe	2,500	v Spora Luxembourg	3 Oct 1967

(not including Preliminary Rounds of FA Cup in 1920-21)

Leeds City

Leeds United beat all the records established by Leeds City with the following exceptions:

Fewest home draws	2	1913-14	
Fewest away draws	1	1914-15	
Fewest draws	4	1914-15	
Successive home defeats	4	1912-13	
Successive defeats	7	1908-09	
Fewest home goals scored	16	1913-14	
Fewest away goals scored	8	1908-09	
Fewest away clean sheets	0	1911-12	
Most games without a League draw	23	1914-15	
Most games without an FA Cup draw	10	11/2/09 to 30/1/15	
Fewest home Legaue attendance	2,000	v Chesterfield	27/2/06
	2,000	v Leciester Fosse	30/4/10
Fewest away League attendance	1,000	on six occasions (3 v Glossop)	
Fewest home FA Cup attendance	7,000	v Oldham Athletic	11/1/08
Fewest away FA Cup attendance	9,417	v Derby County	9/1/15

(not including FA Cup Preliminary Rounds)

Transfer Records

To Leeds United

£53,000	Aug 1962	John Charles	from	Juventus
£53,000	Feb 1964	Alan Peacock	from	Middlesbrough
£100,000	Oct 1967	Mick Jones	from	Sheffield United
£165,000	July 1969	Allan Clarke	from	Leicester City
£250,000	Aug 1974	Duncan McKenzie	from	Nottingham Forest
£300,000	Mar 1978	Paul Hart	from	Blackpool
£357,000	Feb 1979	Kevin Hird	from	Blackburn Rovers
£370,000	May 1979	Alan Curtis	from	Swansea City
£930,000	Aug 1981	Peter Barnes	from	Manchester City
£1,700,000	July 1991	Rodney & Raymond Wallace	from	Southampton
£2,000,000	July 1992	David Rocastle	from	Arsenal
£2,700,000	July 1993	Brian Deane	from	Sheffield United
£3,400,000	Jan 1995	Anthony Yeboah	from	Eintracht Frankfurt
£4,200,000	Nov 1995	Tomas Brolin	from	Parma

(Raymond Wallace was valued at £100,000)

From Leeds United

£65,000	May 1957	John Charles	to	Juventus
£80,000	Sep 1969	Mike O'Grady	to	Wolves
£100,000	Sep 1973	Gary Sprake	to	Birmingham City
£200,000	Jun 1976	Duncan McKenzie	to	Anderlecht
£350,000	Jan 1978	Joe Jordan	to	Manchester United
£495,000	Feb 1978	Gordon McQueen	to	Manchester United
£500,000	July 1979	Frank Gray	to	Nottingham Forest
£825,000	Jan 1987	Ian Snodin	to	Everton
£1,200,000	Nov 1992	Eric Cantona	to	Manchester United
£2,700,000	Oct 1993	David Batty	to	Blackburn Rovers
£3,400,000	Jun 1996	Gary Speed	to	Everton

Abandoned Matches

Leeds City

Football League
4 Nov 1905 v Burnley (h) 1-1 (1-1) *(53 mins: fog)*
Morris
Bromage; McDonald, Ray, Morgan, Stringfellow, Henderson, Parnell, Watson, Hargreaves, R.Morris, Singleton.
Att: 6,000

FA Cup
18 Nov 1905 v Hull C 0-0 *(50 mins: fog)*
Bromage; McDonald, Ray, Morgan, Stringfellow, Henderson, Parnell, Watson, Hargreaves, R.Morris, Singleton.
Att: 3,000

Football League
16 Dec 1905 v Manchester U 0-1 (0-1)
(73 mins: fog)
Bromage; D.B.Murray, Ray, Morgan, Walker, Henderson, Howard, Watson, Hargreaves, R.Morris, Singleton.
Att: 16,000

FA Cup
11 Jan 1913 v Burnley (h) 2-4 (2-4) *(50 mins: snow)*
McLeod, Foley
Scott; Law, Affleck, Allan, Lintott, Foley, Bainbridge, Robertson, McLeod, Speirs, Croot.
Att: 12,000

Leeds United

Football League
16 Jan 1926 v Aston Villa (a) 0-1 (0-0)
(82 mins: fog)
Johnson; Allan, Menzies, Edwards, Townsley, Atkinson, Turnbull, Armand, Jennings, Chadwick, Jackson.
Att: 12,930

Football League
16 Feb 1935 v Portsmouth (h) 1-0 (1-0)
(53 mins: waterlogged pitch)
Kelly
Moore; G.W.Milburn, J.Milburn, Edwards, Hart, Hornby, Duggan, J.Kelly, Hydes, Cochrane, Mahon.
Att: 6,635

FA Cup
25 Jan 1936 v Bury (h) 2-1 (1-1)
(76 mins: fog)
Furness, Kelly
McInroy; Sproston, J.Milburn, Edwards, McDougall, Browne, Duggan, Brown, J.Kelly, Furness, Cochrane.
Att: 30,000

Football League
12 Dec 1936 v Wolves (h) 0-1 (0-1)
(83 mins: fog)
McInroy; Sproston, J.Milburn, Edwards, McDougall, Mills, Armes, J.Kelly, Hydes, Stephenson, Buckley.
Att: 11,987

Football League
25 Jan 1939 v Huddersfield T (h) 0-1 (0-1)
(63 mins: snow)
Twomey; Goldberg, Gadsby, Edwards, Holley, Mills, Armes, Powell, Hodgson, Stephenson, Hargreaves.
Att: 3,896
Although the above was a local derby, few people bothered to attend because it had been snowing all day and they assumed the match would not kick off.

Football League
15 Nov 1952 v Nottingham F (h) 0-0
(10 mins: fog)
Scott; Dunn, Hair, Kerfoot, McCabe, Burden, Meek, Nightingale, Charles, Iggleden, Williams.
Att: 15,729

Football League
24 Aug 1968 v Nottingham F (a) 1-1 (1-1)
(45 mins: stand fire)
Belfitt
Sprake; Reaney, Cooper, Bremner, Charlton, Hunter, O'Grady, Belfitt, Jones, Gray, Hibbitt.
Att: 31,126

European Fairs Cup
26 May 1971 v Juventus (a) 0-0
(51 mins: waterlogged pitch)
Sprake; Reaney, Cooper, Bremner, Charlton, Hunter, Lorimer, Clarke, Jones, Giles, Madeley.
Att: 65,000

Football League
4 Dec 1976 v Bristol City (a) 0-0
(45 mins; fog)
Harvey, Reaney, Hampton, Cherry, McQueen, F.Gray, Lorimer, Hankin, Jordan, Stevenson, E.Gray.
Att 31,400

FA Youth Cup

1952-53
Rd 1 v Manchester United (a) 0-4

1953-54
Rd 1 v Blackburn Rovers (h) 1-0
Rd 2 v Blackpool (h) 6-0
Rd 3 v Bury (a) 3-1
Rd 4 v Manchester City (h) 3-1
Rd 5 v West Brom Albion (a) 1-3 aet

1954-55
Rd 1 v Penrith (h) 7-1
Rd 2 v Bradford City (a) 4-3
Rd 3 v Newcastle United (a) 1-3

1955-56
Rd 1 v Huddersfield Town (a) 0-0
Replay v Huddersfield Town (h) 1-0
Rd 2 v Liverpool (h) 0-1

1956-57
Rd 1 v Bradford City (h) 1-0
Rd 2 v Blackpool (a) 3-4

1957-58
Rd 1 v Manchester City (h) 2-0
Rd 2 v Morecambe (a) 8-0
Rd 3 v Manchester United (h) 1-4

1958-59
Rd 1 v Everton (a) 0-3

1959-60
Qual v Burnley (a) 3-2
Rd 1 v Blackpool (h) 1-1 aet
Replay v Blackpool (a) 2-3

1960-61
Qual v Hyde United (a) 3-4

1961-62
Qual v Manchester City (a) 1-3

1962-63
Rd 1 v Bradford (h) 3-0
Rd 2 v Burnley (a) 0-2

1963-64
Rd 1 v Billingham Synthonia (a) 10-0
Rd 2 v Barnsley (a) 5-0
Rd 3 v Sheffield Wednesday (a) 1-0
Rd 4 v Everton (a) 2-1
Rd 5 v Manchester City (h) 3-4

1964-65
Rd 1 Bye
Rd 2 v Bradford City (a) 1-0
Rd 3 v Bolton Wanderers (a) 2-0
Rd 4 v Sunderland (a) 1-3

1965-66
Rd 1 Bye
Rd 2 v Mansfield Town (h) 8-1
Rd 3 v Scunthorpe United (a) 0-0
Replay v Scunthorpe United (h) 2-0
Rd 4 v Burnley (a) 1-1
Replay v Burnley (h) 4-0
Rd 5 v Sunderland (a) 0-3

1966-67
Rd 1 Bye
Rd 2 v Bradford City (a) 8-0
Rd 3 v Blackburn Rovers (h) 3-1
Rd 4 v Scunthorpe United (a) 0-1

1967-68
Rd 1 Bye
Rd 2 v Bury (a) 1-2

1968-69
Rd 1 v Darlington (a) 5-0
Rd 2 v Sheffield United (a) 1-1
Replay v Sheffield United (h) 2-1
Rd 3 v Rotherham United (a) 2-1
Rd 4 v Sunderland (a) 0-0
Replay v Sunderland (h) 0-1

1969-70
Rd 1 Bye
Rd 2 v Sheffield Wednesday (h) 2-1
Rd 3 v Liverpool (a) 0-0
Replay v Liverpool (h) 3-2
Rd 4 v Sunderland (a) 2-0
Rd 5 v Bristol City (a) 1-2

1970-71
Rd 1 Bye
Rd 2 v Middlesbrough (a) 1-2

1971-72
Rd 1 Bye
Rd 2 v North Kenton Juniors (h) 8-0
Rd 3 v Oldham Athletic (a) 3-1
Rd 4 v Bolton Wanderers (a) 0-1

1972-73
Rd 1 Bye
Rd 2 v Newcastle United (h) 0-1

1973-74
Rd 1 Bye
Rd 2 v Newcastle United (h) 1-0
Rd 3 v Middlesbrough (h) 1-1
Replay v Middlesbrough (a) 1-2

1974-75
Rd 1 Bye
Rd 2 v Sheffield United (h) 2-0
Rd 3 v Sunderland (a) 2-0
Rd 4 v Huddersfield Town (h) 1-2

1975-76
Rd 1 Bye
Rd 2 v Hull City (a) 1-0
Rd 3 v Sunderland (h) 1-1
Replay v Sunderland (a) 0-1

1976-77
Rd 1 Bye
Rd 2 v York City (a) 3-3
Replay v York City (h) 2-0
Rd 3 v Sunderland (h) 1-2

1977-78
Rd 1 Bye
Rd 2 v Huddersfield Town (a) 3-0
Rd 3 v Sunderland (h) 1-0
Rd 4 v Crystal Palace (a) 0-0
Replay v Crystal Palace (h) 0-1

1978-79
Rd 1 Bye
Rd 2 v Yorkshire Amateurs (h) 2-0
Rd 3 v Bolton Wanderers (a) 1-1
Replay v Bolton Wanderers (h) 3-1
Rd 4 v Charlton Athletic (h) 1-3

1979-80
Rd 1 Bye
Rd 2 v Sunderland (a) 2-3

1980-81
Rd 1 Bye
Rd 2 v Blackpool (a) 3-0
Rd 3 v Sunderland (h) 1-0
Rd 4 v Shrewsbury Town (a) 3-0
Rd 5 v Tottenham Hotspur (h) 1-3

1981-82
Rd 1 Bye
Rd 2 v Bolton Wanderers (a) 1-1
Replay v Bolton Wanderers (h) 2-0
Rd 3 v Newcastle United (a) 2-2
Replay v Newcastle United (h) 3-2
Rd 4 v Manchester United (h) 0-0
Replay v Manchester United (a) 0-1

1982-83
Rd 1 Bye
Rd 2 v Manchester City (h) 3-2
Rd 3 v Tranmere Rovers (a) 1-0
Rd 4 v Barnsley (a) 0-2

1983-84
Rd 1 Bye
Rd 2 v Wigan Athletic (h) 4-1
Rd 3 v Newcastle United (a) 0-1

1984-85
Rd 1 Bye
Rd 2 v Manchester United (a) 3-2
Rd 3 v Newcastle United (a) 0-1

1985-86
Rd 1 Bye
Rd 2 v Chester City (h) 0-5

1986-87
Rd 1 Bye
Rd 2 v Chester City (a) 2-0
Rd 3 v Birmingham City (h) 2-0
Rd 4 v Mansfield Town (a) 1-0
Rd 5 v Manchester City (a) 0-3

1987-88
Rd 1 Bye
Rd 2 v Wigan Athletic (a) 1-2

1988-89
Rd 1 Bye
Rd 2 v Burnley (a) 2-1
Rd 3 v Birmingham City (h) 0-0
Replay v Birmingham City (a) 1-1
2nd Replay v Birmingham City 2-4

1989-90
Rd 1 Bye
Rd 2 v Carlisle United (h) 4-1
Rd 3 v Wolverhampton Wanderers (a) 2-3

1990-91
Rd 1 Bye
Rd 2 v Blackburn Rovers (a) 1-1
Replay v Blackburn Rovers (h) 3-1
Rd 3 v Doncaster Rovers (a) 3-0
Rd 4 v Hull City (h) 1-2

1991-92
Rd 1 Bye
Rd 2 v Oldham Athletic (h) 3-3
Replay v Oldham Athletic (a) 2-3

1992-93
Rd 1 Bye
Rd 2 v Sheffield Wednesday (a) 2-1
Rd 3 v Stoke City (a) 6-2
Rd 4 v Queen's Park Rangers (h) 5-1
Rd 5 v Sheffield United (a) 2-2
Replay v Sheffield United (h) 2-1
Semi-final 1st leg v Norwich City (a) 4-1
Semi-final 2nd leg v Norwich City (h) 0-2
Final 1st leg v Manchester United (a) 2-0
Final 2nd leg v Manchester United (h) 2-1

1993-94
Rd 1 Bye
Rd 2 v Burnley (a) 0-3

1994-95
Rd 1 Bye
Rd 2 v Aston Villa (a) 0-1

1995-96
Rd 1 Bye
Rd 2 v Barnsley (h) 3-1
Rd 3 v Middlesbrough (h) 0-1

FA Youth Cup Winners

United's youngsters lifted the FA Youth Cup for the first time in the club's history by beating Manchester United 4-1 on aggregate in the two-legged Final played out in front of over 60,000 fans in 1993.

The boys from Manchester were hailed by their boss Alex Ferguson as the best batch of youngsters he had ever worked with, but they were eclipsed by the boys from Leeds.

Jamie Forrester caught the eye for Leeds in the early rounds, scoring hat-tricks against Stoke City and Queen's Park Rangers.

Leeds virtually booked a place in

the Final with a 4-1 win at Norwich in the semi-final first leg, going through despite losing the home leg 2-0.

In the Final, 'Fergie's Fledglings' started as favourites but were stunned by a rampant Leeds in front of 30,562 at Old Trafford. Leeds got their noses in front when Rob Bowman flicked on a Matthew Smithard corner which Forrester knocked in from close range. On the hour Noel Whelan made it 2-0 with a shot from the edge of the box.

Anticipating silverware success, 31,037 fans flocked to Elland Road to see if the Leeds youngsters could finish the job.

It didn't take Leeds long to extend their aggregate lead with a stunning overhead kick from Forrester. Paul Scholes levelled on the night with a penalty, but within a minute Leeds made the aggregate score 4-1 with a Smithard goal.

There were no more goals in the second half, so skipper Mark Ford hoisted the FA Youth Cup and led his jubilant players on a lap of honour. It was a great triumph for former United star Paul Hart, who was in his first season as Director of Youth Coaching at Elland Road.

Five of the Leeds players, Forrester, Whelan, Bowman, Kevin Sharp and Mark Tinkler, were all in the England Under-18 squad which won the European Championship. These five, plus Ford and Couzens, have since played for Leeds' senior side.

Of the Manchester United players, brothers Gary and Phil Neville (England), and Keith Gillespie (Northern Ireland) have been capped at full level.

First leg (10 April 1993)
Manchester United 0
Leeds United 2 *(Forrester, Whelan)*
Manchester United: Whitmarsh; O'Kane, Riley, Casper, G.Neville, Gillespie, Butt, Beckham (Savage), Irving(Murdoch), Scholes, Thornley.
Leeds United: Pettinger; Couzens, Sharp, Tinkler, Daly, Bowman, Smithard, Ford, Whelan, Oliver, Forrester.
Ref: Paul Durkin (Portland)
Att: 30,562

Second leg 13 May 1993
Leeds United 2 (Forrester, Smithard)
Manchester United 1 (Scholes pen)
Leeds United: Pettinger; Couzens, Sharp, Tinkler, Daly, Bowman (Tobin), Smithard, Ford, Whelan, Oliver(Byrne), Forrester.
Manchester United: Whitmarsh; P.Neville, Riley, Casper, G.Neville, Gillespie, Scholes, Beckham, Irving(Murdoch), Savage, Thornley.
Ref: Paul Durkin (Portland)
Att: 31,037
Leeds won 4-1 on aggregate.